Magruder's AMERICAN GOVERNMENT

1987

Magruder's AMERICAN GOVERNMENT

Revised by

William A. McClenaghan

Department of Political Science
Oregon State University

Allyn and Bacon, Inc., NEWTON, MASSACHUSETTS

AMERICAN GOVERNMENT, first published in 1917, and revised annually, is an enduring symbol of the author's faith in American ideals and American institutions. The life of Frank Abbott Magruder (1882–1949) was an outstanding example of Americanism at its very best. His career as a teacher, author, and tireless worker in civic and religious undertakings remains an inspiring memory to all who knew him.

STAFF CREDIT

Senior Editor: Donald B. Armin
Contributing Editors: Mary K. Delaney/Cory Morrissey
Art Director: L. Christopher Valente
Design: George McLean
Design Production: Shay J. Mayer
Design Consultant: Carol H. Rose
Technical Art: Martucci Studio
Preparation Service Manager: Martha E. Ballentine
Buyer: Roger Powers
Cover Design: John Martucci/L. Christopher Valente
Photo Research: Rebecca Hirsch/ Rose Corbett Gordon

Library of Congress Catalog Card Number: 17-13472

Printed in the United States of America

ISBN 0-205-08827-9

2 3 4 5 6 7 8 9   91 90 89 88 87 86

REVIEWERS/CONSULTANTS

Alice Allison
Chairman, Social Studies Department
Oxford High School
Oxford, Alabama

Thomas Bass
Chairman, Political Science Department
University of St. Thomas
Houston, Texas

Paul Blanchard
Professor of Government
Eastern Kentucky University
Richmond, Kentucky

James Malone
Teacher, Department of Social Studies
Vista High School
Vista, California

Elizabeth S. Mefford
Social Studies Coordinator
Northwest Local School District
Cincinnati, Ohio

Michael E. Milakovich
Associate Professor
Department of Politics and Public Affairs
University of Miami
Coral Gables, Florida

Robert Morgan
Chairman, Social Studies Department
Druid Hills High School
Atlanta, Georgia

Caroline Penn
Coordinator of Staff Development
Harris County Department of Education
Houston, Texas

Sharon L. Pope
12th Grade Teacher of Government and Economics
Cypress-Fairbanks Independent School District
Houston, Texas

Gail Riley
Secondary Consultant for Social Studies and Business
Hurst-Euless-Bedford Independent School District
Bedford, Texas

Barbara N. Sexton
Teacher, Government and International Baccalaureate Studies
L. V. Berkner High School
Richardson, Texas

Rose Mary Sullivan
Honors Teacher, Department of Social Studies
De La Salle Institute
Chicago, Illinois

Preface

If a nation expects to be ignorant and free, . . .
it expects what never was and never will be.

THOMAS JEFFERSON

THIS IS A BOOK ABOUT GOVERNMENT—and, more particularly, about government in the United States. Over the course of its 26 chapters and more than 800 pages, we shall consider the ways in which government in this country is organized, the ways in which it is controlled by the people, the many things that it does, and the various ways in which it does them.

American Government, 1987, is the latest in a long line of editions of this book. The first one appeared in 1917, and this one is the 67th edition. Every edition of this book has had one basic purpose: to describe, analyze, and explain the American system of government.

All of the many changes within the book illustrate a very important point:

The American system of government is extraordinarily dynamic. Change—growth, adaptation, innovation—is a basic element of its character. While it is true that its fundamental principles and its basic structure have remained constant over time, many of its other characteristics have changed. They continue to do so—from year to year and, frequently, from one day to the next, and sometimes remarkably.

To underscore the critical importance of this fact of continuing change, dwell for a moment on the phrase "the American system of government." You will come across it again and again, for it is an apt description of government in the United States. As you will soon discover, that system is a very complex one.

It is complex because it is made up of many different parts, performing many different functions. It is a system because all of its many different parts are interrelated. The whole cannot be understood without a knowledge of its several interacting parts; and those parts cannot be understood without a knowledge of the whole. Given all of this, the vital effects of ongoing change in the system are obvious.

Every effort has been made to see that this book is as accurate, as up-to-date, as readable, and as interesting and usable as possible. The wealth of factual information it contains has been drawn from the most current and reliable of sources. This is not a book on current events, however. It does contain much data and draws many examples from the contemporary scene. But they are purposefully woven into the context of its primary objective: the description, analysis, and explanation of the American system of government. Another major objective is to provide a basis for understanding how other nations are governed through a careful examination of other political and economic systems.

Some criticize textbooks because, they say, they are "too large" and "too factual," and they sometimes argue that they should be more "interpretive." *This* textbook includes that material which we believe to be absolutely necessary to a basic knowledge and understanding of the American governmental system. If it is a "large" one, it is because its subject is a very large *and* a very *important* one.

Every book, no matter its subject, reflects, in at least some degree, the biases of its author. This book is no exception. We have made a very conscious effort to minimize their appearance and to present a fair and balanced view of government in the United States. But, inevitably, those biases are present. Whenever they appear, they should be subjected to critical examination by the reader, of course. One of them is outstandingly obvious: the conviction that the American system of government, although it contains some and sometimes glaring imperfections, is in fact and should be government of the people, by the people, and for the people.

One final comment here—from both the original author, the late Frank Abbott Magruder, and the present one: Over the years we have received much valuable help from the many teachers and students who have used this book in classrooms across the nation. Their comments, suggestions, criticisms, and questions have played a large part in the making of each new edition—and they continue to be more than welcome, of course.

WILLIAM A. MCCLENAGHAN

Department of Political Science
Oregon State University
Corvallis, Oregon

Contents

Maps, Graphs, Charts, Diagrams

Tables

Unit 1

The Foundations of the American Governmental System

ON A FRIDAY in late May in 1787 a group of men met in Philadelphia to design a new government for their new country. The government they produced, after nearly four months of discussion, argument, and compromise, was put into written form in the remarkable document that is the Constitution of the United States.

This book is about that government. It is a government that has continued and prospered, adapting itself to changes that its Framers could not possibly have imagined would take place over the course of now very nearly 200 years.

In Unit 1 of this book, we set the scene for our study. We consider the foundations of the American system of government. We look at its origins and development, the fundamental principles on which it is built, and the structure of the American federal system—that is, the division of powers between the National Government and the States.

This lithograph by E. Sachse was done in 1851. Although drawn "from nature," it projected many future plans for the city of Washington, D.C. Some of these, such as the columned base for the Washington Monument, were never built.

Government is a contrivance of human wisdom to provide for human wants.
–EDMUND BURKE

1 Modern Political and Economic Systems

CHAPTER OBJECTIVES

To help you to

Learn · Know · Understand

The basic nature of the modern state and theories of its origin.

The major forms of government in the world today.

The basic concepts of American democracy.

The basic features of the major economic systems in the world today.

THE CONSTITUTION'S OPENING words read: "We the People of the United States . . ." No other words in all of that remarkable document are more important or more meaningful. For here, in these seven words, the Constitution proclaims the very essence of the American system of government.

As Americans, we take great and justifiable pride in that system of government. It is self-government under law—government of the people, by the people, and for the people. It is a government in which "We the People" rule, and a government that exists only to do our bidding.

We take pride, too, in the fact that our system of government is, and has been for generations, the envy of peoples the world over. Many other nations have tried governmental systems much like ours. But none of them has lasted for so long, nor has any of them been developed on so large a scale.

As we take that pride, however, it seems wise to remember this: We have learned much from—and we owe much to—some of those other peoples and nations. Our debts to the ancient Greeks and to the not-so-ancient English are especially great.

Philadelphia's Independence Hall was the site of a centennial celebration in 1876 (left) and, again 100 years later, of a bicentennial commemoration in 1976. Each celebration honored the signing of the Declaration of Independence in 1776 and reflected a spirit of national pride in the durability of our democratic system of government.

It seems wise to remember another fact, too: Systems of self-government have been exceedingly rare over the course of human history. Authoritarian systems—whether known as tyrannies, despotisms, or dictatorships—have been much more durable and considerably more numerous.

"We the People" rule the world's largest, and the world's most powerful, **democracy.** Yet, nearly five billion other people and more than 160 other nations share our globe.

Viewed against such a backdrop, then, this also seems wise: That we begin our study of the American system of government with a brief look at the many forms of government to be found in the world today. Much of what exists, and many of the things that happen, in even the farthest corners of the globe, can have an immediate and an important effect upon our daily lives. They may even affect the very future of our existence as a nation.

1. The State and Its Origins

As You Read, Think About:

- What the four basic characteristics of a state are.
- What the basic theories of the origins of the state are.

Government is among the oldest of all human inventions. Its origins are lost in the mists of prehistoric time. More than 2,300 years ago, Aristotle wrote that "man is by nature a political animal."[1] Aristotle was * only recording what, even then, had been obvious for thousands of years.

[1]In historical political writings, the words *man* and *men* are used in the generic sense, that is, to refer to all of humankind. Throughout this text, this form has been retained in quoted excerpts from those writings as well as in reference to those historical ideas.

*ENRICHMENT Aristotle observed: "Man is by nature a political animal," and "Everyone thinks chiefly of his own, hardly ever of the public interest." Discuss how these observations reflect societies' need for some system of order.

Aristotle, philosopher and citizen of Athens—the birthplace of democracy—wrote that constitutional democracy may be the ideal form of government.

Government first appeared when human beings realized that they could not live without it. Government emerged when people realized that they could not survive without some form of authority, some power, that could regulate both their own and their neighbors' conduct.

The State

Over the long course of human history, the state has emerged as the dominant political unit in the world. The **state** may be defined in these terms: A body of people, living in a defined territory, organized politically, and having the power to make and enforce law without the consent of any higher authority.

There are more than 160 states in the world today. They vary greatly in size and military power, natural resources and economic importance, and many other factors. Each of them, however, has all four of the characteristics in our definition: population, territory, sovereignty, and government.[2]

Population

Clearly, there must be people. The size of the population is not essential to the existence of a state, however. The smallest of them all, in terms of population, is San Marino.[3] Nestled high in the Apennines and bounded on all sides by Italy, it has some 22,000 people. The People's Republic of China is the largest. Its population is now well over one billion. If the Chinese people were to line up in single file, they could encircle the globe more than 20 times.

Territory

Just as there must be people, so must there be land, territory with known and recognized boundaries. Here, too, San Marino ranks as the smallest state in the world. It has an area of only some 63 square kilometers (24 square miles). The largest state is the Soviet Union, with 22,403,000 square kilometers (8,650,000 square miles)—about one-sixth the land surface of the earth. The total area of the United States is 9,372,614 square kilometers (3,618,770 square miles).

Sovereignty

Every state has supreme and absolute power within its own territory. This is known as **sovereignty.** Each state may decide its own policies and courses of action, both foreign and domestic. It is neither subordinate nor responsible to any other authority.

---

[2]Note that what we have defined here—the *state*—is a *legal* entity. In popular usage, a state is often called a "nation" or a "country." In a strict sense, however, the word *nation* is an ethnic term, referring to races or other large groups of people. The word *country* is a geographic term, referring to a particular place, region, or area of land.

[3]The United States also recognizes (maintains diplomatic relations with, acknowledges the sovereignty of) the State of Vatican City. The Vatican has a permanent population of some 750 persons, occupies a roughly triangular area of approximately 44 hectares (109 acres), and is wholly surrounded by the City of Rome. American recognition of the Vatican, which had been withdrawn in 1867, was renewed in 1984.

Thus, as a sovereign state, the United States may determine its own form of government. It may frame its own economic system, may shape its own foreign policies, and may decide as it will on all other matters—and so, too, may all other states.[4]

The *location* of sovereignty within a state—who, in fact, holds that power—is of supreme importance. If the people are sovereign, then the government is democratic. If, on the other hand, the power is held by a single person or a small group, a dictatorship exists.

Government

Every state is politically organized. That is, every state has a **government.** Government is the institution through which the **public policies** of a state are made and enforced and all of its other affairs are conducted. To define the term another way, government is the agency through which the state exerts its will and works to accomplish its goals. It consists of the machinery and the personnel by which the state is ruled (governed).

Origins of the State

For centuries, historians, political scientists, philosophers, and others have pondered the question of the origin of the state. What factor or set of circumstances first brought it into being?

Over time, many different answers have been offered, but history provides no conclusive evidence to support any of them. The four most widely accepted theories and those that have had the greatest impact are the: *force theory, evolutionary theory, divine right theory,* and *social contract theory.*

[4]In this book, *state* printed with a small "s" denotes a state in the family of nations, such as France, the United States, and the Soviet Union. *State* printed with a capital "S" refers to a State in the American Union, such as California, Illinois, and North Carolina.

Note that sovereignty is *the* distinctive feature of a state—the particular characteristic that distinguishes it from all other (lesser) political units in the world. The States within the United States are not sovereign, and so they are not states in the international legal sense. (A superior force, the Constitution of the United States, stands above each of them.)

The Force Theory Many scholars have long believed that the state was born of force. They hold that it developed because one person, or perhaps a small group, claimed control over an area and forced all within it to submit to his or their rule. When that rule was established, all the basic elements of the state—population, territory, sovereignty, and government—were present.

The Evolutionary Theory Others claim that the state developed naturally and gradually out of the early family. They hold that the primitive family, of which the father was the head and thus the "government," was the first stage in human political development. Over countless years the original family became a network of closely related families—a clan. In time the clan became a tribe. When the tribe first turned to settled agriculture—when it gave up its nomadic ways and first tied itself to the land—the state was born.

The Divine Right Theory Some theorists have argued that the state arose as the result of the "divine right of kings." According to this theory, God gave those of royal birth the right to rule. As unsound as this idea may seem today, it was widely accepted in the 17th and 18th centuries. Much of the thought upon which present-day democratic government rests was first developed as an argument against the "divine right" theory.

The Social Contract Theory In terms of our political system, the most significant of the theories of the origin of the state is that of the "social contract." It was developed in the 17th and 18th centuries by such philosophers as John Locke, James Harrington, and Thomas Hobbes in England and Jean Jacques Rousseau in France.

Hobbes wrote that in his earliest history man lived in unbridled freedom, in a "state of nature." No government existed; no man was subject to any power superior to his own will. Each man could do as he pleased and in any manner he chose. That which he could

*ENRICHMENT Have the class discuss: What benefits do governments provide? What obligations does an individual have to the government? What contributions can the individual make?

take by force was his. But all men were similarly free. Thus, each man was only as safe as his own physical prowess and watchfulness could make him. His life in the state of nature, wrote Hobbes, was "nasty, brutish, and short."

Men overcame their unpleasant condition, says the theory, by agreeing with one another to create a state. By *contract,* men within a given area joined together, and each agreed to give up to the state as much power as was needed to promote the safety and well-being of all. In the contract (that is, through a constitution), the members of the state created a government to exercise the powers they had voluntarily granted to the state.

In short, the social contract theory argues that the state arose out of a voluntary act of free men. It holds that the state exists only to serve the will of the people, that they are the sole source of political power, and that they are free to give or to withhold that power as they choose. The theory seems farfetched to many of us today. But the great concepts it fostered—popular sovereignty, limited government, and individual rights—were, as we shall see, immensely important to the shaping of our own governmental system.[5]

FOR REVIEW

1. **Identify:** state, divine right, social contract.
2. What are the four main characteristics of a state?
3. What is the difference between a state and a government?
4. Why is the location of sovereignty within a state so important?
5. According to the social contract theory, why does the state exist? Why is this theory important to the development of the American political system?

[5]The Declaration of Independence (see text, pages 720–723) laid its justification for revolution on the social contract theory, arguing that the king and his ministers had violated the contract. Thomas Jefferson called the document "pure Locke."

2. Forms of Government

As You Read, Think About:

- What the characteristics of unitary, federal, and confederate governments are.
- How presidential and parliamentary governments differ.
- How a dictatorship and a democracy differ.

No two governments are, or ever have been, exactly alike. Clearly this must be so, for governments are the products of human needs and human experiences. Governments have been shaped by a number of other factors—by geography, climate, history, customs, resources, and the capacities of the people, among others. *

All governments can be classified (grouped) according to one or more of their basic features. Over time, political scientists have developed many different bases upon which to classify—and so to describe, compare, and analyze—governments. Three of those classifications are especially important and useful for our purposes. These are classifications according to: (1) the geo-

Reproduced by permission of Johnny Hart and Field Enterprises

*ENRICHMENT Have the class discuss: If governments are the products of human needs and experiences, what factors helped to shape the United States?

graphical distribution of governmental power within the state, (2) the nature of the relationship between the **legislative** (lawmaking) and the **executive** (law-executing) branches of the government, and (3) the number of persons who may take part in the governing process.[6]

Geographic Distribution of Power

In every system of government the power to govern is located in one or more places, geographically. From this standpoint, three basic forms of government exist: *unitary* governments, *federal* governments, and *confederate* governments.

Unitary Government A **unitary government** is often described as a centralized government. It is one in which all of the powers held by the government belong to a single central agency. Local units of government are created by and for the convenience of the central government. Whatever powers local governments may have come only from that central source.

Most governments in the world are unitary in form. Great Britain is a classic illustration of the type. All of the power that the British government has is held by one central organ, the Parliament. Local governments do exist but solely to relieve Parliament of burdens it could perform only with much difficulty and inconvenience. Though hardly likely, Parliament could do away with all agencies of local government in Great Britain at any time.

Be careful *not* to confuse the unitary form of government with a dictatorship. In the unitary form *all of the powers the government possesses* are concentrated in the central government. But that government might not have *all* power. In Great Britain, for example, the powers held by the government are strictly limited. British government is unitary and, at the same time, is democratic.

President Reagan addresses the nation's lawmakers at a joint session of Congress.

Federal Government A **federal government** is one in which the powers of government are divided between a central government and several local governments. This *division of powers* is made on a geographic basis by an authority superior to both the central and the local governments. It cannot be changed by either level acting alone.

In the United States, for example, the National Government has certain powers and the 50 States have others. This division of powers is set out in the Constitution of the United States. The Constitution stands above both levels of government and cannot be changed unless the people, acting through both the National Government and the States, agree to that change.

Australia, Canada, Mexico, Switzerland, West Germany, Yugoslavia, and some 20 other states also have federal forms of government today. (Note that the government of each of the 50 States in the American Union is unitary, not federal, in form.)

Confederate Government A **confederation** is an alliance of independent states. A central organ (the confederate government) has the power to handle only those matters that the member states have assigned to it.

[6]Note that these classifications are not mutually exclusive. That is, they are really different ways of looking at the same information. Thus, as we shall see, the government of the United States is federal, presidential, and democratic; British government is unitary, parliamentary, and democratic; and so on.

Typically, confederate governments have had limited powers and only in such fields as defense and foreign commerce.

There are no confederations in the world today. But, in our own history, the United States under the Articles of Confederation (1781–1789) and the Confederate States (1861–1865) are examples of the form.

Relationship Between Legislative and Executive Branches

Viewing governments from the standpoint of the relationship between their legislative (law-making) and executive (law-executing) agencies yields two basic forms of government: presidential and parliamentary.

Presidential Government The **presidential** form features a *separation of powers* between the executive and legislative branches of the government. The two branches are independent of and co-equal with one another. The chief executive (president) is chosen independently of the legislature, holds office for a fixed term, and has broad powers not subject to the direct control of the legislature.

Usually, as in the United States (and each of the 50 States), a written constitution provides for the separation of powers between the branches of government. Thus, the Constitution of the United States provides for the selection of the President, independently of the Congress, for a fixed four-year term. It also assigns to the President and to the Congress their separate fields of power.

Parliamentary Government In the **parliamentary** form, the executive is made up of the prime minister (or premier) and that official's cabinet. They themselves are members of the legislative branch (the parliament). The prime minister is the leader of the majority party—or of a coalition of two or more parties—in parliament and is chosen to office by that body. With its approval, the prime minister selects the members of the cabinet from among the members of parliament. The executive is thus chosen by the legislature, is a part of it, and is subject to its direct control.

The prime minister and the cabinet—often called "the government"—remain in office only as long as their policies and administration have the confidence and support of a majority in parliament. If they are defeated on an important matter (if they do not receive a "vote of confidence"), they must resign from office. Then a new "government" must be formed. Either parliament chooses a new prime minister or, as often happens, a general election is held in which all of the seats in parliament go before the voters. The British, most European, and a majority of all other governments in the world today are parliamentary in form.

Compare and contrast the two forms of government illustrated below. In which form of government is the chief executive also a member of the legislature?

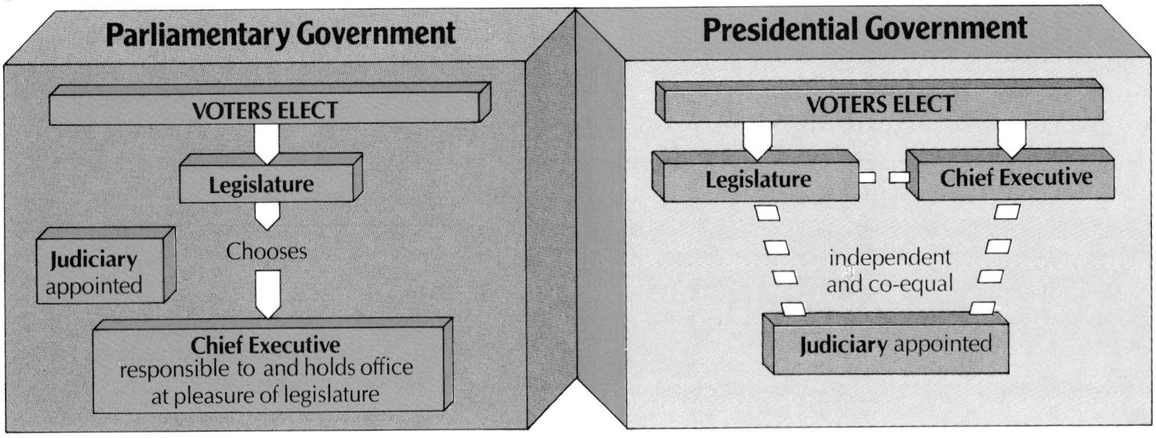

*REINFORCEMENT Ask the class to study the above charts, and to describe how the concept of "We the people . . ." is incorporated into a presidential government.

Margaret Thatcher is Great Britain's first woman Prime Minister. By what process does Britain's chief executive reach that office?

The Number Who May Participate

What is perhaps the most meaningful of classifications of government is that based upon the number of persons who may take part in the governing process. Here we have two basic forms to consider: *dictatorships and democracies.*

Dictatorship Where the power to govern is held by one person or held by a small group, a **dictatorship** exists. It is probably the oldest, and without a doubt the most common, form of government known to history.

All dictatorships are **authoritarian.** They are governmental systems in which those in power hold absolute and unchallengeable authority over the people.

Modern dictatorships have tended to be **totalitarian,** as well. That is, they exercise dictatorial (authoritarian) power over just about every aspect of human affairs. Their power embraces all (the totality of) matters of human concern.

The best examples of dictatorship in the 20th century are those that existed in Fascist Italy (from 1922 to 1943) and in Nazi Germany (from 1933 to 1945), and those that now exist in the Soviet Union (where the present dictatorial regime was established in 1917), and the People's Republic of China (where the dictatorship came to power in 1949).

One-man dictatorships have been and are rather uncommon. They are not unknown, however. Uganda's government of a few years ago is a classic example. Idi Amin Dada seized control of that East African state in 1971. Immediately, Amin proclaimed himself the country's "President-for-Life." For eight years he ruled with a harsh and autocratic (absolute, unlimited) hand. His government was finally overturned by the armies of Tanzania in 1979.

Dictatorships are much more often dominated by the will of a small, tight-knit group. The Soviet Union's leader, Mikhail Gorbachev, is a dictator, of course. But, in fact, he can act only with the approval of the other members of the Politburo—the executive council of the Central Committee of the Communist Party of the USSR.

The primary characteristic of any dictatorship is that *it is not responsible to the people and cannot be limited by them.* It is not accountable to any higher authority for its actions, nor for the manner in which it carries out those actions.

Dictatorships often present the outward appearance of control by the people. Popular elections are generally held. But elections are rigidly controlled and typically, the voter is offered the candidates of only one political party. There is often an elected legislative body but only to rubber-stamp the policies and programs of the dictatorship.

Public support is mobilized through massive propaganda programs and absolute control of the educational system. Opposition is put down, often ruthlessly, by a secret police. Only one political party, highly organized and rigidly disciplined, is allowed. Freedom of speech, thought, and association—so vital in a democracy—are not tolerated.

Typically, dictatorial regimes are militaristic in character. They usually gain power by force. Many of the major posts in the government are held by the military. After crushing all effective opposition at home,

FOCUS ON: STUDY

Roots of Political Thought

Our American system of government owes a great debt to the social contract theory of Thomas Hobbes, John Locke, and Jean Jacques Rousseau. The roots of American political ideas—popular sovereignty, limited government, and individual rights—may be found in the writings of these men. Does this mean that Hobbes, Locke, and Rousseau were the first to think in political terms? Where did Western political thought begin?

We can trace the roots of our political ideas back to 1700 B.C., and the Babylonian ruler, Hammurabi. Until this time, men lived according to unwritten rules, customs, and practices that evolved to protect their standing in their communities. (The concept of the state does not appear for another 1,200 years.) Among the things that were important to a man's standing were his rights and property. Often rules would be changed to fit new situations, but the concepts of rights and property were always protected.

Hammurabi was the first to record all of these unwritten rules, customs, and practices. The Code of Hammurabi became the first systematic code of law used to govern a society.

The idea of law was further defined and refined in ancient Greece. Athens under Pericles in the 5th century B.C. is considered the flowering of Greek democracy, although a limited democracy. Only men were allowed to vote; women and slaves were not considered citizens.

The Assembly of Citizens made laws for the city-state, declared war, approved treaties, and passed the city's budget. A Council of Five Hundred conducted the daily business of the city. The members of the Council were chosen from the various districts called *demes* in which the city was divided. The English word *democracy* is derived from the Greek *demes*.

The city-state was the forerunner of the modern democratic state. The government of Athens was set up to protect the rights of citizens and was governed by those citizens. Active participation by citizens in the political process made the government responsible to those it governed. The Greek philosopher and Athenian citizen, Aristotle, said it best when he stated that "man is by nature a political animal."

The Greek city-states eventually dissolved and were succeeded by a world under Roman domination. The principle that political authority comes from the people was carried over to the Roman Republic and the Roman Empire.

Although the Empire in the West declined and at last collapsed in 476, the Empire in the East continued for another thousand years. One of the greatest of its emperors was Justinian. His contribution to Western law and political thought lies in his codification of Roman law.

In 533 he published a single code of law for the Empire based on the laws from throughout the Empire. The resulting work, known as the Code of Justinian, is the foundation for most legal systems in the modern world. The Code reaffirmed the rights of the individual and the limitations on government. It also stressed the authority of the state in religious matters, a concept that is reflected in the social contract theory.

1. Trace the political ideas mentioned in this feature in the modern world. What aspects do you see reflected in American society today?

Adolf Hitler, leader of the Nazi Party, ruled as dictator of Germany from 1933 to 1945.

these regimes may turn to foreign aggression and other adventures to enhance the country's military power and prestige.

Benito Mussolini stated the basic philosophy of the modern-day totalitarian dictatorship when he proclaimed, "All is in the state and for the state, nothing outside the state, nothing against the state."

Democracy In a democracy, or democratic form of government, supreme political authority rests with the people. The people hold the sovereign power, and government is conducted only by and with their consent.[7]

Abraham Lincoln gave immortality to this definition of democracy in his Gettysburg Address in 1863: "government of the people, by the people, for the people." Nowhere is there a better, more concise statement of the American understanding of democracy.

A democracy may be either *direct* or *indirect* in form. A **direct** (or pure) **democracy** exists where the will of the people is translated into public policy (law) directly by the people themselves in mass meetings. Clearly, such a system can be made to work only in very small communities where it is possible for the citizens to meet in a given place and where the problems of government are few and simple. *

Direct democracy does not exist at the national level anywhere in the world today. But the old New England town meeting and the *Landsgemeinde* in a few of the smaller Swiss cantons are excellent examples of direct democracy in action.[8]

In the United States we are more familiar with the *indirect form*—that is, with representative democracy. In a **representative democracy** the popular will is expressed through a small group of persons chosen by the people to act as their representatives. These agents of the people are responsible for the day-to-day conduct of government. They are held accountable to the people for that conduct, especially at periodic elections. To put it another way, representative democracy is government by popular consent—government with the consent of the governed.

Some people insist that the United States is a *republic* rather than a democracy. They hold that in a **republic** the sovereign power is held by the electorate and is exercised by representatives chosen by and held responsible to the electorate. For them, democracy may be defined only in terms of direct democracy. To most Americans, however, the terms democracy, republic, representative democracy, and republican form of government generally mean the same thing.

Whatever the terms used, remember that in a democracy the people are sovereign.

[7]The word *democracy* is derived from the Greek words *demos* meaning "the people" and *kratia* meaning "rule" or "authority." The Greek word *demokratia* means, literally, "rule by the people."

[8]The *Landsgemeinde*, like the original New England town meeting, is an assembly open to all local citizens qualified to vote. In a more limited sense, law-making by initiative petition is also an example of direct democracy (see page 573).

*REINFORCEMENT Write the terms *republic* and *democracy* on the chalkboard and then have students read this column. Discuss with them the difference in meaning between the two terms.

They are the only source for any and all of the government's power. In other words, the people rule.

FOR REVIEW

1. What is the basic characteristic of a unitary government? A confederate government? A federal government? Which of these forms is the most common today?
2. What is the basic characteristic of a presidential government? A parliamentary government? Which of these forms is the most common today?
3. What is the basic characteristic of a dictatorial government? A democratic government? Which of these forms is the most common today?

3. Basic Concepts of Democracy

As You Read, Think About:

- What the basic concepts are on which American democracy is built.
- How the operation of American government illustrates these basic concepts of democracy.

Democracy does not exist in the United States simply because we regard it as the best of all possible political systems. Nor will it continue to exist for that reason.[9] Rather, democracy exists in this country because we believe in its basic concepts. It will continue to exist only for as long as we continue to subscribe to—and practice—those concepts.

[9]The late Sir Winston Churchill once argued for democracy in these terms: "No one pretends that democracy is perfect or all-wise. Indeed, it has been said that democracy is the worst form of government except all of those other forms which have been tried from time to time."

The basic concepts of democracy, as we understand and apply the term in the United States, are: *

1. A recognition of the fundamental worth and dignity of each and every person.
2. A respect for the equality of all persons.
3. A faith in majority rule and an insistence upon minority rights.
4. An acceptance of the necessity of compromise.
5. An insistence upon the widest possible area of individual freedom.

Of course, these ideas may be, and often are, worded in other ways. No matter what the wording, however, they form the very *minimum* that must be agreed to by anyone who professes to believe in democracy. Some people will argue that other concepts belong in such a listing—for example, the right of each person to a certain minimum level of economic security. But the point here is that, no matter what else *might* be included, at least these *must* be.

Fundamental Worth of the Individual

Democracy is firmly based upon a belief in the fundamental importance of the individual. Each and every individual, no matter what his or her station in life may be, is a separate and distinct being. Democracy insists that *each person's worth and dignity must be recognized and respected by all other individuals, and by all of society, at all times.*

This concept of the sanctity of the individual is of overriding importance in democratic thought. Anything and everything a democratic society does must and should be done within the limits of this great concept.

At various times, of course, the welfare of one or a few individuals is subordinated to the interests of the many in a democracy. People can be, and are, forced to do things, both large and small, whether they want to or not. The examples are many, and they range from paying taxes or registering for the draft to stopping at a stop sign.

When these or similar things are done, a democratic society is serving the interests of

*ENRICHMENT Have the class discuss: How can some representative democracies be more democratic than others?

the many. But it is *not* serving them simply as the interests of a mass of people who happen to outnumber the few. Rather, it is serving the many who, *as individuals,* together make up that society.

The distinction we are trying to make here between *an* individual and *all* individuals may be a very fine one. It is, however, critically important to a true understanding of the meaning of democracy.

Equality of All Persons

Hand-in-hand with the belief in the sanctity of the individual, democracy stresses the equality of all individuals. It holds, with Jefferson, that "all men are created equal."

Certainly, democracy does *not* insist on an equality of *condition* for all persons. Thus, it does not claim that all are born with the same mental or physical abilities. Nor does it argue that all persons have a right to an equal share of worldly goods.

Rather, the democratic concept of equality insists that all are entitled to (1) *equality of opportunity* and (2) *equality before the law.* That is, the democratic concept of equality holds that no person should be held back for any such artificial or arbitrary reasons as those based on race, color, religion, or sex. It holds that each person must be free to develop himself or herself as fully as he or she can (or cares to) and that each person should be treated as the equal of all other persons by the law.

We have come a great distance toward reaching the goal of equality for all in this country. But we are still a considerable distance from a genuine, universally recognized and respected equality for all.

Majority Rule and Minority Rights

In a democracy, public policy is to be made *not* by the dictate of a ruling few but in accord with the will of the people.

What is the "popular will," and how is it to be determined? How, that is, are public policy questions to be decided and public policies made? There must be some standard, some device, by which these crucial questions can be answered. The only satisfactory device democracy knows is that of *majority rule.*

Every person in our democratic society—regardless of race, color, religion, or sex—is entitled to live freely and equally, to fulfill his or her potential.

An ancient Arab proverb tells us that it is better to knock heads together than to count them. In effect, it suggests that we are more likely to find out what is inside those heads by breaking them open than we are by simply counting them. But, again, and most emphatically, democracy *does* believe in counting them.

Democracy is firmly committed to the proposition that a majority of the people will be right more often than they will be wrong. It also believes that the majority will be right more often than will one person or one small group.

Democracy may be quite usefully described as an experiment—a trial-and-error process—designed to find satisfactory ways to order human relations. Notice that it does *not* say that the majority will always be "right," that it will *always* arrive at the best of all possible decisions on public matters. In fact, the democratic process (the process of majority rule) does not intend to come up with "right" or "best" answers. Rather, it searches for *satisfactory* solutions.

Of course, democracy insists that the decisions that are made will more often be *more* rather than *less* satisfactory. It does admit the possibility of mistakes, however—the possibility that "wrong" or less satisfactory answers will sometimes be found. It also recognizes that seldom is any solution to a public problem so satisfactory that it cannot be improved. So, the process of experimentation, of seeking answers to public questions, is a continuous one.

Certainly, a democracy cannot work without the principle of majority rule. Unchecked, however, a majority could destroy its opposition and, in the process, destroy democracy as well. Thus, democracy insists upon majority rule *restrained by minority rights*. The majority must always recognize the right of any minority to become, if it can, by fair and lawful means, itself the majority. The majority must always be willing to listen to a minority's argument, to hear its objections, to bear its criticisms, and to welcome its suggestions. Anything less contradicts the very meaning of democracy.

Necessity of Compromise

In a democracy, public decision-making is (must be) very largely a matter of give-and-take. It is a matter of **compromise**—

The New England town meeting is an example of direct democracy in action. It is also an example of majority rule restrained by minority rights. How?

BUILDING GOVERNMENT SKILLS

Learning From What You Read: SQ3R

By now you have read, or at least have been exposed to, a number of textbooks—and you are now into Chapter 1 of this one. How much do you learn—really know, understand, and remember—when you read a textbook?

The SQ3R method—survey, question, read, recite, review—provides a guide for more effective study of this book and of other texts as well. Remember that being prepared is an important part of learning. Always read an assignment before that material is to be covered in class.

- **Survey:** Survey the assigned reading for an overview of its content. Read the chapter introduction and the Chapter Summary. Pay attention to the Chapter Objectives and the major headings throughout the chapter.
- **Question:** Read the "For Review" questions at the end of each section in the chapter. Also, rephrase the section headings into questions and write your questions on a piece of paper. In this chapter, for example, you might ask, "What is the social contract theory?"
- **Read:** Read the assigned material carefully. Take notes as you read. Note the answers to your questions, important points, and key passages. Unless the book belongs to you, do not mark the book by underlining key passages or making notes in the margins.
- **Recite:** Answer the "For Review" questions and your own questions after you have finished reading the chapter. Recite the answers aloud and then note the answers on your paper. By doing this, you will end with an outline of the assigned reading. If you cannot recite an answer, read that material again. (Now is a good time to find out what the Glossary is, and how to use it.)
- **Review:** Use your notes and answers to questions to review the assigned material. Refer to the assigned reading if you have further questions. Reviewing is a vital part of the learning process.

Your teacher can offer some additional helpful hints for improving your study habits, and so your learning. He or she will almost certainly emphasize such things as:

1. A regular study schedule—cramming sometimes helps just before a test, but it almost never results in real learning.
2. Seek help if you need it—that's what teachers are for.

the process of blending and adjusting, of reconciling competing views and interests, in order to find the position most acceptable to the largest number.

Compromise is an essential part of the democratic concept for two major reasons.* *First,* remember that democracy puts the *individual* first and, at the same time, insists that each individual is the *equal* of all others. How—in a society made up of many individuals and groups with many quite different opinions and interests—can public decisions be made except by compromise?

Second, few public questions have only "two sides." Most have many different sides and can be answered in several ways. As a case in point, take the apparently simple question of how a city should pay for the paving of a public street. Should it charge the costs to those who own property along

*ENRICHMENT Ask students for examples from their study of American history of compromises that shaped the nation's development.

the street? Or should all of the city's residents pay the costs from the city's general treasury? Or should the city and the adjacent property owners share the costs? What about those who will use the street but do not live in the city? Should they have to pay a toll or buy a license for that use?

Again, the point here is that *most* public policy questions can be answered in several different ways. Still, the fact remains that *some* answer must be found.

It would be impossible for the people in a democratic society to decide most public questions without the element of compromise. Remember: Compromise is a *process*, a way of achieving majority agreement. It is never an end in itself. Not all compromises are good, and not all are necessary. Some things—such as the equality of all persons—should never be the subject of any kind of compromise if democracy is to survive.

Individual Freedom

From all that has been said to this point, it should be clear that democracy can thrive only in an atmosphere of individual freedom. But democracy *does not* and *cannot* insist on complete freedom for the individual. Absolute freedom can exist only in a state of **anarchy**—in the total absence of government. Anarchy can only lead, inevitably and quickly, to rule by the strong and ruthless.

Democracy does insist, however, that each individual must be as free to do as he or she pleases as the freedom of all will allow. Justice Oliver Wendell Holmes once had this to say about the relative nature of each individual's rights: "The right to swing my fist ends where the other man's nose begins."

Drawing the line between the rights of one individual and those of another is a far from easy task. But the drawing of that line is a continuous and vitally important function of democratic government. It is because, as John F. Kennedy once said: "The rights of every man are diminished when the rights of one man are threatened."

Striking the proper balance between freedom for the individual and the rights of society as a whole is similarly difficult—and vital. Abraham Lincoln once stated democracy's problem in these words:

> Must a government of necessity be too *strong* for the liberties of its own people, or too *weak* to maintain its own existence?

The problem goes to the very heart of democracy. Human beings desire both liberty and authority. Democratic government must work constantly to strike the proper balance between the two. The authority of government must be adequate to the needs of society. But that authority must never be allowed to become so great that it restricts the individual beyond necessity.

Democracy looks upon all civil rights as vital, but it places its highest value on those guarantees necessary to the free exchange of ideas: on *freedom of expression* and *freedom of thought*. Several years ago, the President's Committee on Civil Rights made this point:

> In a free society there is faith in the ability of the people to make sound, rational judgments. But such judgments are possible only when the people have access to all relevant facts and to all prevailing interpretations of the facts. How can such judgments be formed on a sound basis if arguments, viewpoints, or opinions are arbitrarily suppressed? How can the concept of the marketplace of thought in which truth ultimately prevails retain its validity if the thought of certain individuals is denied the right of circulation?

We shall return to the whole subject of individual rights later, especially in Chapters 5 and 6. We shall also return to each of the other basic democratic concepts, again and again, throughout this book. *

FOR REVIEW

1. **Identify:** majority rule, minority rights.
2. What does the text suggest are the basic concepts of democracy?
3. Why is compromise an essential part of the democratic process?
4. Upon which individual freedoms does democracy place its highest values?

*REINFORCEMENT Ask the class to provide examples of each of the five concepts of democracy. Have them draw on their own experiences as citizens of the United States. List these on the board.

At the Chicago Commodities Exchange, brokers buy and sell for profit, but are subject to governmental regulation. Why are business activities regulated?

4. Capitalism, Socialism, Communism

As You Read, Think About:

- What the basic ideas are on which capitalism, socialism, and communism are founded.
- How these basic ideas have been put into practice.
- How history has confirmed or failed to confirm the theories of Karl Marx.

What are the functions a government, whatever its form, ought to undertake? What should it have the power to do? What should it not be allowed to do? Certainly, these questions may be asked of just about all areas of human activity, but they are raised most often, and most significantly, in the realm of economic affairs.

Questions of politics and of economics are, in fact, inseparable. Many of the most important and most difficult questions governments face are economic ones. What, for example, should be the relationship between management and labor in a nation's economy? On what basis should goods and services be distributed and exchanged within a nation? Should such basic industries as transportation, steel, and oil be privately or publicly owned and operated?

What provisions, if any, ought to be made for the welfare of the elderly? What of the poor, the physically or mentally handicapped, and those who are otherwise disadvantaged? Clearly, these are critical *economic* questions—and, just as clearly, they are critical *political* questions, as well.

Three major economic systems predominate in the world today: capitalism, socialism, and communism.

Capitalism

The American economic system—and that found in several other nations today—is known as **capitalism.** It is based upon private ownership, individual initiative, profit, and competition. Capitalism is often described, too, as the **free enterprise** or **private enterprise** system.

*REINFORCEMENT Use the above photograph to initiate a discussion of the fact that politics and economics are inseparable. How do government economic policies affect students' lives?

Basic Nature of the Capitalistic System
In the capitalistic system the means by which goods and services are produced are held, very largely, as private property. That is, the means of production, of distribution, and of exchange—factories, mines, stores, farms, railroads, airlines, banks—are privately owned and managed.

Those who own these means hire labor and *compete* with one another to produce goods and services at a *profit*. Competition is the lifeblood of the system, and in its purest form, involves providing the best possible product at the lowest possible price. Profit is what makes the system work. The profits of an enterprise are its earnings, that is, the returns realized by the owners over and above the costs of doing business. In short, profits are the rewards received for the risks taken and the initiative shown.

Generally speaking, any person or group may start an enterprise—try to produce or sell goods or offer services—and the risks and rewards are theirs. Most of the larger and many of the smaller businesses in the United States today are in fact owned by large numbers of persons—by stockholders who own shares in them.

Typically, part of the profits earned by an enterprise is paid out to shareholders as dividends and part is reinvested in the business. Thus, the investor receives a return on his or her investment, the business expands, more jobs are created, individual purchasing power increases, and a still higher standard of living results.

* ***Laissez-Faire Theory*** American capitalism, as we know it today, bears only a distant resemblance to classical capitalistic economics. The beginnings of capitalism are found in the concepts of *laissez-faire*, a doctrine developed in the late 18th and early 19th centuries.[10]

Under **laissez-faire** theory, government should play only a very limited—really a "hands off"—role in society. Its activities should be confined to three areas: (1) the conduct of foreign relations and national defense, (2) the maintenance of police and courts to protect private property and the health, safety, and morals of the people, and (3) the performance of certain necessary functions that cannot be provided by private enterprise at a profit.

The theory was given its classic expression by Adam Smith in *The Wealth of Nations*, first published in London in 1776. Its basic assumption was well summarized in Thomas Jefferson's remark: "That government is best which governs least." Its supporters insisted that government's place in economic affairs ought to be limited to those functions designed to protect and promote the free play of competition and the operation of the law of supply and demand.

The theory of laissez-faire economics never truly operated in this country, even in the earliest days of the Republic. Even so, it is clear that the concepts of laissez-faire had, and still have, a profound effect upon the nature of our economic system. Most business enterprises in the United States are owned by private persons, not by government. They are financed with private capital, not with public funds. Further, they are managed by private citizens, not by public officials.

A "Mixed Economy" Although the American economic system is essentially private in character, government has always played a considerable role in it. Indeed, our system may be properly described as a **mixed economy.** It is one in which private enterprise is combined with and supported by considerable government regulation and promotion. It is one in which there is a substantial amount of governmental activity and control intended to protect the public interest and to preserve private enterprise.

A vast amount of economic regulation and promotion takes place at all levels of government in the United States—National, State, and local. To give only a very few examples, economic activities are regulated by government in this country through antitrust laws, labor-management relations statutes, pure

[10]The term *laissez-faire* comes from a French idiom meaning "to let alone." Translated literally, it means "allow to act."

*REINFORCEMENT Have the class discuss: Although government regulates economic activities in the United States in many ways, a free enterprise system is still maintained. How do the concepts of laissez-faire theory contribute to such a system?

Left: Soviet shoppers wait to obtain goods in a government-run store. *Right:* An American consumer browses to make her selection in a privately owned market.

food and drug laws, the regulation of environmental pollution, the policing of investment practices, and city and county zoning ordinances and building codes.

Also, the nation's economic life is promoted in a great number of public ways; for example, by direct subsidies, public roads and highways, such services as the postal system and weather reports, public housing programs, research at State universities, loan programs for different purposes, and planting and marketing advice to farmers.

Our economy is also "mixed" in the sense that some enterprises and functions that might be carried on privately are, in fact, operated by government. Public education, the postal system, the monetary system, some forms of public transportation, and roadbuilding are examples of long standing.

How much should government participate, regulate and promote, police and serve? Many of our most heated political debates center on this question. In the search for answers, we tend to follow the general rule expressed by Abraham Lincoln:

> The legitimate object of government is to do for the community of people whatever they need to have done, but cannot do so well for themselves, in their separate and individual capacities.

Most Americans believe that a well-regulated capitalistic system—one of free choice, individual incentive, private enterprise—is the best guarantee of the better life for everyone.

Socialism

Socialism is a philosophy of *economic collectivism.* It advocates the collective—that is, the social, public—ownership of the instruments of production, distribution, and exchange. It holds that the means by which goods and services are produced should be *publicly* owned and managed. Socialism rejects the ideas of private ownership, competition, and profit, which lie at the heart of capitalist thought and practice.

The roots of socialism lie deep in history. Almost from the beginning there have been those who have dreamed and planned for a society built on socialist doctrine. Most of the earlier socialists foresaw a collective

British Airways is state–owned, state–managed, and state–operated. What principle of socialism is illustrated here?

economy arising out of and managed by voluntary private action. With few exceptions, they believed they could reach their goals without government action. For this reason, early socialist doctrine is often called "private socialism."

Socialism in its modern form—that is, *state socialism*—has emerged only over the course of the past 100 years or so. Only since the middle of the 1800s have most socialists argued that the reaching of their goal is too big a task for private action alone.

The most extreme form of socialism today is *communism*. Most socialists outside the Soviet and Chinese orbits are evolutionary socialists, or as they are often called, social democrats. They believe that socialism can best be brought about gradually and peaceably, by lawful means, and by working within the established framework of government. They believe that, even after they have won control of government, the new order should be introduced only in stages. The first stage, they believe, should be to **nationalize** (take over ownership) a few key enterprises, such as banking, transportation, and the steel industry.

Evolutionary socialists argue that political democracy, with its emphasis on popular participation in government, is incomplete. For them, true democracy can exist only when the people share in the management of their economic destinies. The British Labor Party and the major socialist parties of Western Europe and the Scandinavian countries are the major examples of evolutionary socialism in action today.[11]

Socialists insist that their philosophy is based on justice because it aims at a more nearly equal distribution of both wealth and opportunity among people. Opponents of

[11]Although socialism and communism are often identified with each other, the socialists of the noncommunist world (the evolutionary socialists) are generally bitter foes of the communists. They share many of the ideas supported by the Russian, Chinese, and other Marxists. But most evolutionary socialists do not accept the theory of the class struggle, the necessity of violent revolution, and the dictatorship of the proletariat—all fundamental to Marxian communism.

socialism condemn it because they believe that it kills individual initiative and denies to the capable and the industrious their just rewards. Many believe that the scope and reach of government, which socialism requires, can only lead to dictatorship.

The complexities of modern society have led to vast expansion of government functions in the United States and most other countries. Many of the activities undertaken by government in this country in the past 50 years or so have been attacked by opponents who insist that they are "socialistic" and thus ill-advised and a threat to the nation and its future.

Communism

As we know it today, **communism** was born in 1848 with the publication of *The Communist Manifesto*. A brief, inflammatory pamphlet, it was written by Karl Marx with the aid of his close colleague, Friedrich Engels. In *The Communist Manifesto* and his later and very extensive writings, Marx laid down the cardinal premises of scientific socialism, or communism.[12]

Since the death of Marx in 1883 and that of Engels in 1895, communism has been interpreted and expanded by his followers. The most important of these have been Vladimir Ilyich Lenin, and Josef Stalin, in the Soviet Union, and Mao Zedong in the People's Republic of China. The doctrines they have developed are very clearly both political and economic in nature.[13]

* ***Communist Theory*** Communist ideology rests upon four basic, and closely related, propositions: (1) its theory of history, (2) the labor theory of value, (3) its theory of the nature of the state, and (4) its concept of the dictatorship of the proletariat.

(1) The Communist Theory of History. According to Marx, all of human history has been a story of the "class struggle." The Communists say that there have always been two opposing classes in society—one an oppressor (dominating) class and the other an oppressed (dominated) class. Thus, in the Middle Ages those two classes were the nobility and their serfs. Today, say the Communists, the capitalists (the *bourgeoisie)* keep the workers (the *proletariat)* in bondage. Workers in capitalistic countries are described as "wage slaves," who are paid barely enough to allow them to eke out a starvation living as they toil for their masters.

The Communists hold that the class struggle has become so bitter and the divisions between the classes so sharp that a revolt of the masses and the downfall of the bourgeoisie are inevitable. They see their function as that of speeding up the "natural" course of history, by violence if need be.

(2) The Labor Theory of Value. Communist ideology also holds that the value of any good or service is determined by the amount of human labor needed to produce it. In other words, a suit of clothes is worth so much because it takes so much labor to produce it. Because the laborer produced the suit and thus created its value, the Communists claim that the laborer should receive that value in full. They are bitterly opposed to the free enterprise profit system and condemn profits as "surplus value" that should go to the worker.

(3) The Nature of the State. To the Communists, the state is the instrument of the dominating class—a tool with which the bourgeoisie keeps the proletariat in bondage. Because the bourgeoisie has so firm a hold on the state and its power, said Lenin, it is only through a "violent and bloody revolution" that the situation can be changed.

Communists see a number of other institutions in this same light. Thus, Marx described religion as the "opiate of the people." Religious beliefs, he wrote, are a drug fed to the people, a hoax through which they are led to tolerate their harsh lot in this life in the hope of gaining a "fictional afterlife."

[12] The term *scientific socialism* was used to separate Marxian thought from the older and less extreme forms of socialism. In later years, Marx and his followers came to prefer the term *communism.*

[13] Capitalism is also a political and an economic doctrine, but in a much more limited sense. To the capitalist, the proper role of government is that of stimulator, servant, and regulator or referee.

*REINFORCEMENT Have the class discuss: Communism is the most extreme form of socialism, yet many socialists do not consider themselves Communists. How can this be?

(4) The Dictatorship of The Proletariat. The Communists do not foresee a proletariat able to govern themselves after a revolution. Rather, the proletariat would need "guidance and education"—from the Communist Party, of course. Hence, the dogma calls for a *dictatorship of the proletariat.* That is, a totalitarian regime is to be set up to lead the people to the theoretical goal of communism: a "free classless society." As that goal is reached, it is claimed, the state will "wither away." The cardinal principle of the new society would be: "From each according to his ability, to each according to his need."

Evaluation of Communism. The USSR presents the outstanding example of communism in action. Strictly speaking, the Russians do not practice pure communism today, but an extreme form of socialism.[14]

Their present system stems from the October Revolution of 1917 when Lenin and his followers came to power.[15] Immediately, Lenin tried to set up a communist system. The attempt made the chaos of Russia's defeat and withdrawal from World War I even worse, and it failed. The inefficient and the lazy received as much as the efficient and the industrious. Workers and peasants rebelled. When the new government imposed severe reprisals, many thousands were executed. Finally, the Soviet leaders changed their approach, turning to their version of socialism. They now say they are working *toward* the goal of pure communism.

More than 135 years of Marxist theory and some 70 years of Soviet communism have exposed many of the fallacies of Communist doctrine. We shall note the major fallacies of this doctrine here.

Marx argued that the divisions between the bourgeoisie and the proletariat would become deeper and deeper, to the point at which capitalism would collapse under its own weight. The rich, said Marx, would become richer and the poor, poorer. The struggle between the bourgeoisie and the proletariat would grind the middle class down into the ranks of the proletariat.

In fact, the contrary has happened. The economic gap between workers and owners has narrowed almost to the point of extinction, especially in the United States. Marx and his followers failed to foresee the tremendous growth of the middle class. The poor have not become poorer. They have, in fact, become much, much richer.

Communist theory has little room for individual initiative and incentive, so vital in our own economic system. One of the basic differences between our system and that of the Communists is this: Where we try to

Drawing by Mahood; © 1959 The New Yorker Magazine, Inc.

"In a democracy, it would be nothing but choice, choice, choice all the time." *

[14]According to Marx, the guiding principle in a communist society should be "From each according to his ability, to each according to his need." But compare this with this provision (Article 13) of the Soviet Constitution of 1977: "The State shall control the measure of labor and consumption in accordance with the principle: 'From each according to his ability, to each according to his work.' . . . Socially useful work and its results shall determine a citizen's status in society."

[15]The revolution occurred on October 25, 1917, by the Julian calendar then in use in Russia. By the Western (Georgian) calendar, now also used in the Soviet Union, the date was November 7. The Communists did not, as is often supposed, revolt against the old czarist regime. Rather, they overthrew a fledgling democratic government headed by Alexander Kerensky. The Kerensky government had been created as a result of a revolution in March of 1917. It was this earlier, noncommunist revolt that deposed the czarist tyranny.

*ENRICHMENT Use the cartoon to initiate a discussion of the importance of choice in a society. What would the students' lives be like if they lived in a country where there was no freedom of choice?

promote *equality of opportunity,* the Communists argue for *equality of condition.*

Experience has forced the Communists to recognize the importance of incentive, however. The labor theory of value has been very largely ignored in Communist practice. Income in the Soviet Union today is based largely on the amount or the importance of the work one does. Thus, scientists, managers, administrators, teachers, and others in the professions receive larger incomes and many more privileges than do the masses in the working class.

The state has not been the tool of the dominant class in the non-Communist world. Rather, the state—acting through government controlled by, and responsive to, the people's will—has been a major agent in improving the welfare of the people.

Marx predicted that the emergence of communism would promote peace among the nations of the world. In fact, quite the opposite has occurred.

Marx, and then Lenin and later Soviet leaders, were confident that communism would appeal to workers throughout the world, regardless of nationality. Thus, the *Manifesto* closed with this cry: "Workingmen of all countries, unite!" But, in fact, the Communist dogma has not lessened *nationalistic* sentiments (pride in nationhood). That point has been demonstrated time and time again—in Poland and elsewhere in Eastern Europe, and by the swords-point relationships between the Soviet Union and the other major Communist power today, the People's Republic of China.

The state in the Soviet Union, in the People's Republic of China, and in other Communist countries shows no sign of "withering away." Indeed, under communism the power of the state has been sharply *increased.* The dictatorships established in these countries have become the most totalitarian the world has ever seen. All forms of opposition are ruthlessly put down. Basic freedoms are not permitted, lest the people examine and question the policies of the state. Fear is a weapon in the hands of the ruling group. The dictatorship easily perpetuates itself.

In the Soviet Union, ballots are cast only for candidates approved by the Communist Party.

FOR REVIEW

1. **Identify:** laissez-faire, *The Communist Manifesto.*
2. Upon what key factors is capitalism based?
3. According to laissez-faire theory, what is the proper role of government in society?
4. Why may the American economic system be described as a "mixed" one?
5. What is the basic tenet of the socialist philosophy?
6. Why can modern socialism be called "state socialism"?
7. Who founded present-day communism? When?
8. What are the four central propositions upon which Communist theory is built?
9. What fallacies in Communist theory and practice are noted in the text?

SUMMARY

The *state* is the dominant unit in the political structure of the world. All of the more than 160 states in the world today have four essential characteristics: (1) population, (2) territory, (3) sovereignty, and (4) government.

The different forms of government can be classified in several ways. On the basis of geographic distribution of power, governments are *unitary, confederate,* or *federal. Presidential* or *parliamentary* governments are based on the relationship between the executive and the legislative branches. *Democratic* or *dictatorial* governments are based on the number of people who may participate.

Especially in the American context, *democracy* rests upon five basic concepts: (1) the fundamental worth and dignity of every person; (2) the equality of all persons; (3) majority rule limited by minority rights; (4) the necessity of compromise; and (5) the widest possible area of individual freedom.

Capitalism is an economic doctrine based upon private ownership of the means by which goods and services are produced and upon individual initiative, competition, and profit.

Socialism is a philosophy of economic collectivism, advocating public ownership of at least the major instruments of production, distribution, and exchange. Evolutionary socialists are different from revolutionary socialists. Most of the latter are Communists.

Communism is an extreme form of socialism. It is built on four central concepts: (1) its theory of history; (2) the labor theory of value; (3) its theory of the nature of the state; and (4) the dictatorship of the proletariat.

CHAPTER REVIEW

Key Terms/Concepts*

democracy (3)
state (4)
sovereignty (4)
government (5)
public policies (5)
legislative branch (7)
executive branch (7)
unitary government (7)
federal government (7)
confederation (7)
presidential government (8)
parliamentary government (8)
dictatorship (9)
authoritarian (9)
totalitarian (9)
direct democracy (11)
representative democracy (11)
republic (11)
compromise (14)
anarchy (16)
capitalism (17)
free enterprise (17)
private enterprise (17)
laissez-faire (18)
mixed economy (18)
socialism (19)
nationalize (20)
communism (21)

*These terms are included in the Glossary.

Keynote Questions

•• 1. What is sovereignty? Why is it the one characteristic of a state that sets it apart from all other political units?

• 2. What is the difference between a state and a government?

• 3. List and explain each of the four principal theories of the origin of the state.

• 4. What ideas did the social contract theory contribute to the shaping of the American governmental system?

• 5. Identify and explain the forms of government classified according to: (a) geographic distribution of power; (b) the relationship between the legislative and executive branches; (c) the number who may participate.

• 6. Which forms of government best describe government in the United States?

• 7. What are the basic concepts of American democracy?

•• 8. Why are both the terms *free enterprise* and

The dots represent skill levels required to answer each question or complete each activity:
• requires recall and comprehension •• requires application and analysis ••• requires synthesis and evaluation

mixed economy used to describe the American economic system?

• **9.** What are the essential features of the three major economic systems in the world today? How do they differ regarding ownership of: (a) property? (b) the means of production, distribution, and exchange?

• **10.** How does the labor theory of value differ from the free enterprise profit system?

• **11.** State three ways in which Communist theory has differed from Communist practice.

Skill Application

Identifying the Main Idea and Supporting Details: The main idea is the key point of an article, a chapter, chapter section, or paragraph. By identifying the main idea of what you read, you can better understand and remember information.

Sometimes the main idea is stated directly; other times it is implied. Think of it as a headline —it describes who or what the reading passage is about and what is happening. Main ideas are supported by details that further describe or explain the key point.

1. Read the text section on Capitalism, pages 17-19. Then decide which of the following statements is the main idea of the section. The rest of the statements are supporting details.
   a. Under laissez-faire theory, government plays a very limited role in society.
   b. The profits of a business are its earnings, which are often distributed to stockholders and reinvested in the business.
   c. Capitalism, the American economic system, is based on private ownership, individual initiative, profit, and competition.
   d. Even though the American economic system is essentially private in character, government has always played a considerable role in it.

2. Now read the section on Socialism, pages 19-21. After reading, answer the following questions:
   a. What is the main idea of the section (in your own words)?
   b. List three details that support this main idea.

For Thought and Discussion

••• **1.** What characteristics of a democracy would prompt Lord Bryce to observe that "No government demands so much from the citizens as democracy and none gives back so much," and John F. Kennedy to say, "Ask not what your country can do for you; ask what you can do for your country"? Do you agree or disagree with these statements? Why?

••• **2.** In 1733, Alexander Pope penned these lines in his "Essay on Man": "For forms of government let fools contest; Whate'er is best administer'd is best." Restate Pope's view of forms of government in your own words. Do you agree or disagree with his view?

••• **3.** What are the advantages and disadvantages of direct democracy? Of representative democracy? Why does direct democracy not exist at the national level anywhere in the world today?

••• **4.** When the social contract theory was first discussed, it was widely condemned as revolutionary. What elements of the social contract theory would have seemed "dangerous" to divine right advocates? Why?

•• **5.** Karl Marx predicted that successful Communist revolutions would take place first in highly industrialized nations—Germany, England, and the United States. However, Communist revolutions have taken place in predominantly agricultural countries. Why?

Suggested Activities

•• **1.** Prepare a series of posters to illustrate the basic concepts of democracy listed in the text.

•• **2.** Draw up a list of as many examples as you can of (a) the ways in which economic activities in your community are regulated by government (Federal, State, and local); (b) the ways in which all three levels of government aid the economy of your area; and (c) publicly operated enterprises in your community.

••• **3.** Stage a debate or class forum on one of the following topics: (a) *Resolved,* That the United States is a republic, not a democracy; (b) *Resolved,* That government should strive to promote equality of opportunity for all, but not equality of condition.

We hold these truths to be self-evident, that all men are created equal, that they are endowed by their Creator with certain unalienable Rights, that among these are Life, Liberty, and the pursuit of Happiness.
–THE DECLARATION OF INDEPENDENCE

2 To Form a More Perfect Union

CHAPTER OBJECTIVES

To help you to

Learn · Know · Understand

The historical and theoretical origins of the American governmental system.

The development of that system through the colonial period to the coming of Independence.

The Critical Period and the governmental arrangements set up by the Articles of Confederation.

The events and the processes involved in the creation of the Constitution of the United States.

The events and processes involved in the adoption of the Constitution.

GOVERNMENT DID NOT suddenly come to the United States with the Declaration of Independence in 1776. Nor was it created by the Framers of the Constitution in 1787. Instead, the roots of the American governmental system reach deep into the past. Indeed, its origins may be traced to the very beginnings of western civilization.

Those who built the American system of government worked with what they knew. They built with a knowledge of ideas and of **institutions** (established customs, laws, practices) gained in their own lives. They worked, too, with a knowledge that had come to them from centuries of experience, tradition, thought, and deed.

In this chapter, we focus on the origins of the American governmental system. We shall review its historical development through the creation of the Constitution in the late 1780s. As we do so, keep this point in mind: The job of building government in the United States did not end some 200 years ago. Nor has it been completed since. Rather, as we shall see, it is a continuing and a never-ending process.

At the time the Declaration of Independence was signed in 1776 (left), the colonies were largely rural made up mostly of scattered farms and small settlements. How might this have influenced their views on the proper role of government?

1. Our English Heritage

As You Read, Think About:

- What basic ideas about government the English colonists brought with them.
- What kinds of colonial government developed in the thirteen colonies.

The colonial period of American history lasted for more than 160 years. During that period, peoples from many lands came to explore and settle in different parts of what was to become the United States.

The English, French, Dutch, Spanish, Swedes, and others all played a part in colonizing America. It was the English, however, who came in the largest numbers. They soon controlled the 13 colonies that stretched for some 1,300 miles (1,780 kilometers) along the Atlantic seaboard.[1]

The earliest English settlers were pioneers who braved the sea to come to America. Once here, they had to clear the wilderness and build homes and farms. They had to carve out their economic futures. But these settlers brought with them the knowledge of a political system that had been developing in England for centuries. Thus, they carried much of their political future with them.

The Basic Concepts

Most importantly, those early settlers brought with them three ideas that were to loom large in the shaping of government in the United States.

[1]England first began to claim territory in North America with the voyages of John Cabot in 1496 and 1498. By 1664, when it seized Holland's colonial holdings (New Netherlands), England held all of the Atlantic coast from the Gulf of Saint Lawrence south to Florida. With the end of the French and Indian War, in 1763, it had eliminated all French claims in North America; and in 1763 it also acquired Florida from Spain.

*ENRICHMENT Have the class discuss: Why did many of the early English Settlers leave their homeland for the Americas? Be sure students include religious and personal freedom, economic motives, and adventure.

Ordered Government They saw the need for an orderly regulation of their relationships with one another—that is, for government. They created local governments, based on those they had known in England.

Many of the offices and units of government the early settlers established can still be found at the local level around the country: the offices of sheriff, coroner, assessor, and justice of the peace, the grand jury, counties, townships, and several others.

Limited Government Those first colonists also brought with them the idea that government is *not* all-powerful. That is, government is *limited* in what it may do, and each person has certain rights that government cannot injure or take away.

The concept of **limited government** was deeply rooted in English belief and practice by the time the first English ships reached the Americas. It had been planted there with the signing of the Magna Carta in 1215—and it had been developing there for nearly 400 years before Jamestown was settled in 1607.[2]

Representative Government The early English settlers also carried another very important concept to America: **representative government.** The idea that government should serve the people had also been developing in England for centuries. With it had come a growing insistence that the people should have a voice in deciding what government should and should not do. As with the concept of limited government, this notion of "government of, by, and for the people" found fertile soil in America, and it flourished quickly.

We have built on, changed, and added to those ideas and institutions that came to us from England. Still, much in the American government of today bears the English stamp. Surely, this should not be surprising. The colonial period of American history lasted for over a century and a half, from 1607 to 1775. An independent United States has not existed for very much longer.

[2]For details on the Magna Carta, see feature on next page.

Government in the Colonies

England's colonies in North America have been described as "13 schools of government." The colonies were the settings in which Americans first began to learn the difficult art of government.

The 13 colonies were established separately, over a span of 125 years. Over that long period, outlying trading posts and isolated farm settlements developed into organized communities. The first colony, Virginia, was founded with the first permanent English settlement in North America at Jamestown in 1607. The Pilgrims began the second colony, Massachusetts, when they landed at Plymouth in 1620. The other colonies came into being during the next several decades. Georgia was the last to be formed, with the settlement of Savannah in 1733.

Each of the colonies was born out of a particular set of circumstances, and so each had its own character. Virginia was originally organized as a commercial venture. Its first colonists were employees of the Virginia Company, a private trading corporation.[3] Massachusetts was first settled by people who came to America in search of greater personal and religious freedom. Georgia was founded largely as a haven for debtors, victims of England's harsh poor laws.

But the differences between and among the colonies are really of little importance. Of much greater importance is the fact that all of them were shaped by their English origins. The many similarities among all 13 far outweighed the differences.

[3]In 1606, King James I had given the company the exclusive right to trade and colonize along the Atlantic coast from New England to the Carolinas. Under its original charter, the company was divided into two parts. The Virginia Company of London was to operate in Virginia and the Carolinas and The Virginia Company of Plymouth, in New England.

The Virginia Company was patterned after the highly profitable East India Company, set up in 1600 to trade with India. There were large differences between India and North America, however. Most importantly, India was densely populated, whereas the North American continent was largely uninhabited. Neither branch of the Virginia Company prospered, so England's major interest in the area soon turned from trade to settlement.

BUILDING GOVERNMENT SKILLS

Investigating Historical Documents

The history of many of the basic rights held by the people of the United States can be traced to several landmark documents from England. Together, these documents laid the foundations for such concepts as limited government, representative government, popular sovereignty, and civil liberties.

* **Magna Carta** (1215): A group of determined barons forced King John to sign the Magna Carta (Great Charter) at Runnymede in 1215. Weary of John's military campaigns and heavy taxes, the barons were seeking protection against arbitrary acts by the king.

The Magna Carta included such fundamental rights as trial by jury and due process of law (protection against the arbitrary taking of life, liberty, or property). The charter proclaimed:

> No freeman shall be taken, imprisoned, dispossessed, outlawed, banished, or in any way destroyed, nor will we proceed against or prosecute him, except by the judgment of his peers or by the law of the land.

These protections against the absolute power of the king were originally intended only for the privileged classes. Over time, they became the rights of all English people and were incorporated into other documents. The Magna Carta is important for the precedent it established —the power of the monarchy was not absolute.

Petition of Right (1628): The Magna Carta was respected by some monarchs and ignored by others for 400 years. During this time, Parliament slowly grew in influence. In 1628, when Charles I asked Parliament for more money in taxes, Parliament refused until he signed the Petition of Right.

The Petition of Right limited the king's power by demanding that the king not imprison political critics without trial by jury, declare martial law during peacetime, or require people to shelter troops without the homeowner's consent. In addition, the document stated that no man should be:

> compelled to make or yield any gift, loan, benevolence, tax, or such like charge, without common consent by act of parliament.

This document challenged the idea of the divine right of kings by stating that even a monarch was to obey the law of the land.

Bill of Rights (1689): In 1688, after years of revolt and turmoil, Parliament offered the crown to William and Mary of Orange. To prevent abuse of power by them, and by future monarchs, Parliament in 1689 drew up the Bill of Rights to which William and Mary had to agree.

The Bill of Rights stated that the monarchs could not maintain an army during peacetime without the consent of Parliament and that elections for Parliament should be free. Also included were the following rights:

- That the pretended power of suspending of laws, or the execution of laws, by regal authority, without consent of Parliament is illegal. . . .
- That levying money for or to the use of the crown . . . without grant of Parliament . . . is illegal. . . .
- That it is the right of the subjects to petition the king . . . and prosecutions for such petitioning are illegal. . . .

1. Compare the 5th Amendment of the Constitution with the excerpts discussed above. How did each document contribute to the idea that government must act fairly in enforcing the law?
2. What other provisions of the Constitution developed from the ideas presented in these documents?

*REINFORCEMENT Using the documents above, discuss how the concepts of ordered, limited, and representative government are reflected in these documents

Three Types of Colonies Each of the colonies was established on the basis of a **charter,** a written grant of authority from the king.[4] Over time, these instruments of government produced three kinds of colonies, and so three kinds of colonial government: royal, proprietary, and charter.

ROYAL COLONIES. The royal colonies were subject to the direct control of the Crown. On the eve of the Revolution in 1775, there were eight: New Hampshire, Massachusetts, New York, New Jersey, Virginia, North Carolina, South Carolina, and Georgia.

The Virginia colony was not the quick success its sponsors had promised. So, in 1624, the king revoked the London Company's charter and Virginia became the first royal colony. Later, as the original charters of other colonies were canceled or withdrawn, they, too, became royal colonies. Georgia was the last to join their list, in 1752.

[4]Except for Georgia. Its charter was granted by Parliament in 1732.

Gradually, a pattern of government emerged for each of the royal colonies. The king named a governor. The governor was the colony's chief executive and usually its most influential resident. A council, also named by the king, served as an advisory body to the royal governor. In time, the governor's council became the upper house of the colonial legislature. It also became the highest court in the colony. The lower house of the legislature was elected by those property owners qualified to vote.[5] It owed much of its influence to the fact that it shared with the governor and his council the "power of

[5]In 1619 the London Company allowed the creation of a legislature in Virginia. It held its first meeting in the church at Jamestown on July 30, 1619, and was the first representative body to meet in the English colonies. It was made up of burgesses elected from each settlement in the colony. The term *burgesses* was used because the local settlements were expected to grow into boroughs (towns), as in England. After 1634 the burgesses represented counties, and in 1776 their title was changed to *assemblymen.* Virginia called the lower house of its colonial legislature the House of Burgesses; South Carolina, the House of Commons; Massachusetts, the House of Representatives.

Patrick Henry addresses the Virginia House of Burgesses, the first elected legislature in America. Representative government was common in the colonies.

the purse"—that is, the power to tax and the power to spend. The governor, advised by the council, appointed the judges for the colony's courts.

The laws passed by the legislature had to be approved by the governor and the Crown. Royal governors often ruled with a stern hand, following instructions from London. Much of the resentment that flared into revolution was fanned by their actions.

THE PROPRIETARY COLONIES. At the time of the Revolution, there were three proprietary colonies: Maryland, Pennsylvania, and Delaware. The name came from the term *proprietor*—a person to whom the king had made a grant of land in America. By charter, that land could be settled and governed much as the proprietor, or owner, chose.

In 1634 the king had granted Maryland to Lord Baltimore and in 1681 Pennsylvania to William Penn. In 1682 Penn also acquired Delaware, which had first been settled by the Dutch in 1631 and by the Swedes in 1638.[6]

The governments of these three colonies were much like those in the royal colonies. The governor, however, was appointed by the proprietor. In effect, the proprietor, or the landlord, stood between his colony and the king. In Maryland and in Delaware, the legislature was **bicameral** (made up of two houses). The members of the upper house, who were also the members of the governor's council, were chosen by the proprietor. The members of the lower house were elected by the freemen, or property owners, of the colony. In Pennsylvania, the legislature was a **unicameral** (one-house) body. The governor's council had no legislative authority; it merely advised the governor. As in the royal colonies, appeals from the decisions of the courts could be carried to the king and his Privy Council in London.

The *Frame of Government*, a written constitution that William Penn first drew for Pennsylvania in 1682, was, for its time, exceedingly democratic.

[6]New York (New Netherlands before its capture from the Dutch in 1664), New Jersey, North Carolina, South Carolina, and Georgia also began as proprietary colonies. Each of them later became a royal colony.

THE CHARTER COLONIES. Connecticut and Rhode Island were charter colonies. They were based on charters granted in 1662 and 1663, respectively, to the colonists themselves, as a group. Thus, they were largely self-governing. Power over colonial affairs was held by the colonists rather than by a trading company, a proprietor, or the Crown.[7]

The governors of Connecticut and Rhode Island were elected each year by the freemen of the colony. Although the king's approval was required, it was not often asked. The members of both houses of the legislature were not subject to the governor's veto nor was the Crown's approval needed. Colonial judges were appointed by the legislature, but appeals could be taken from their courts to the King in Council.

The Connecticut and the Rhode Island charters were so liberal for their time that, with independence, they were kept with minor changes as State constitutions—until 1818 and 1843, respectively. In fact, many historians say that had Britain allowed the other colonies so much freedom and self-government, the Revolution might never have occurred.*

FOR REVIEW

1. **Identify:** Magna Carta, royal colonies, proprietary colonies, proprietor, charter colonies.
2. What were the major political concepts brought by the early English settlers?
3. Identify and describe the three types of colonial government in pre-Revolutionary America.

[7]The Massachusetts Bay Colony was established as the first charter colony in 1629. In that year the king issued a charter to a corporation known as the Governor and Company of Massachusetts Bay in New England. That document gave the corporation land for a colony and gave its stockholders (freemen) the authority to govern that territory. Its charter was later revoked and Massachusetts became a royal colony in 1691. Religious dissidents from Massachusetts founded Connecticut in 1633 and Rhode Island in 1636.

*ENRICHMENT Ask the class to cite examples of ordered, limited, and representative government in the three kinds of colonial governments that developed.

2. The Colonies and England[8]

As You Read, Think About:

- What the relationship was between the American colonies and Great Britain in the 18th century.
- Why the Stamp Act Congress was important to the relations between Great Britain and the colonies.

The 13 colonies, which had been separately established, were separately controlled under the king, largely through the Privy Council and the Board of Trade in London. Parliament took little part in the management of the colonies. Although it did become more and more interested in matters of trade, it left matters of colonial administration almost entirely to the Crown.[9]

Royal Control

Over the century and a half that followed the first settlement at Jamestown, the colonies developed within that framework of royal control. In *theory,* they were governed in all important matters from London. But London was 3,000 miles (4,800 kilometers) away; and it took nearly two months to sail that distance, across a peril-filled Atlantic. So, in *practice,* the colonists became used to a large measure of self-government.

In time, each colonial legislature assumed broad law-making powers. Many found the power of the purse to be very effective. They often bent a governor to their will by not voting the money for his salary until he met their demands.

By the mid-1700s, the relationship between Britain and the colonies had become —in fact, if not in form—*federal.* The central government in London was responsible for colonial defense and for foreign affairs. It also provided a uniform system of money and credit and a common market for colonial trade. Beyond that, the colonies were allowed a fairly wide measure of self-rule. Little was taken from them in direct taxes to pay for the central government. Further, the few regulations set by Parliament, mostly about trade, were largely ignored.

This all changed, dramatically, in the early 1760s. Shortly after George III came to the throne in 1760, Britain began to deal more firmly with the colonies. Restrictive trading acts were expanded and enforced. New taxes were imposed, mostly to support British troops in North America.

Many colonists took strong exception to these moves. Having enjoyed a large measure of self-government for over 100 years, they objected to taxes they had had no part in levying. This, they claimed, amounted to "taxation without representation." They saw little need for British troops since their biggest threat, the French, had been defeated and their power broken in the French and Indian War (1754–1763). The colonists considered themselves loyal British subjects. They flatly refused, however, to accept Parliament's claim that it had a right to control what the colonists believed to be their own local affairs.

The king's ministers were poorly informed and stubborn. They pushed ahead with their policies, despite the resentments they stirred in America. Within a few years, the colonists were to be forced to a fateful choice: to submit or to revolt.

The Colonies Unite

Long before the fateful 1770s, several attempts were made among the colonies to bring about union.

Early Attempts In 1643 the Massachusetts Bay, Plymouth, New Haven, and Connecticut settlements formed the New

[8]England became Great Britain by the Act of Union with Scotland in 1707.

[9]Parliament is the central and dominant organ in present-day British government, as noted in Chapter 1. Much of earlier English political history can be told in terms of the centuries-long struggle for supremacy between king and Parliament, however. That conflict was largely settled by England's Glorious Revolution of 1688, but it did continue on through the American colonial period and into the 19th century. But note this important point in American political history: Despite its growing power in British government, Parliament paid little attention to the colonies until late in the colonial period.

*ENRICHMENT Have the class discuss: what were the short-term and long-term ramifications of the "Federal" relationship between Britain and the colonies?

Steps to a More Perfect Union

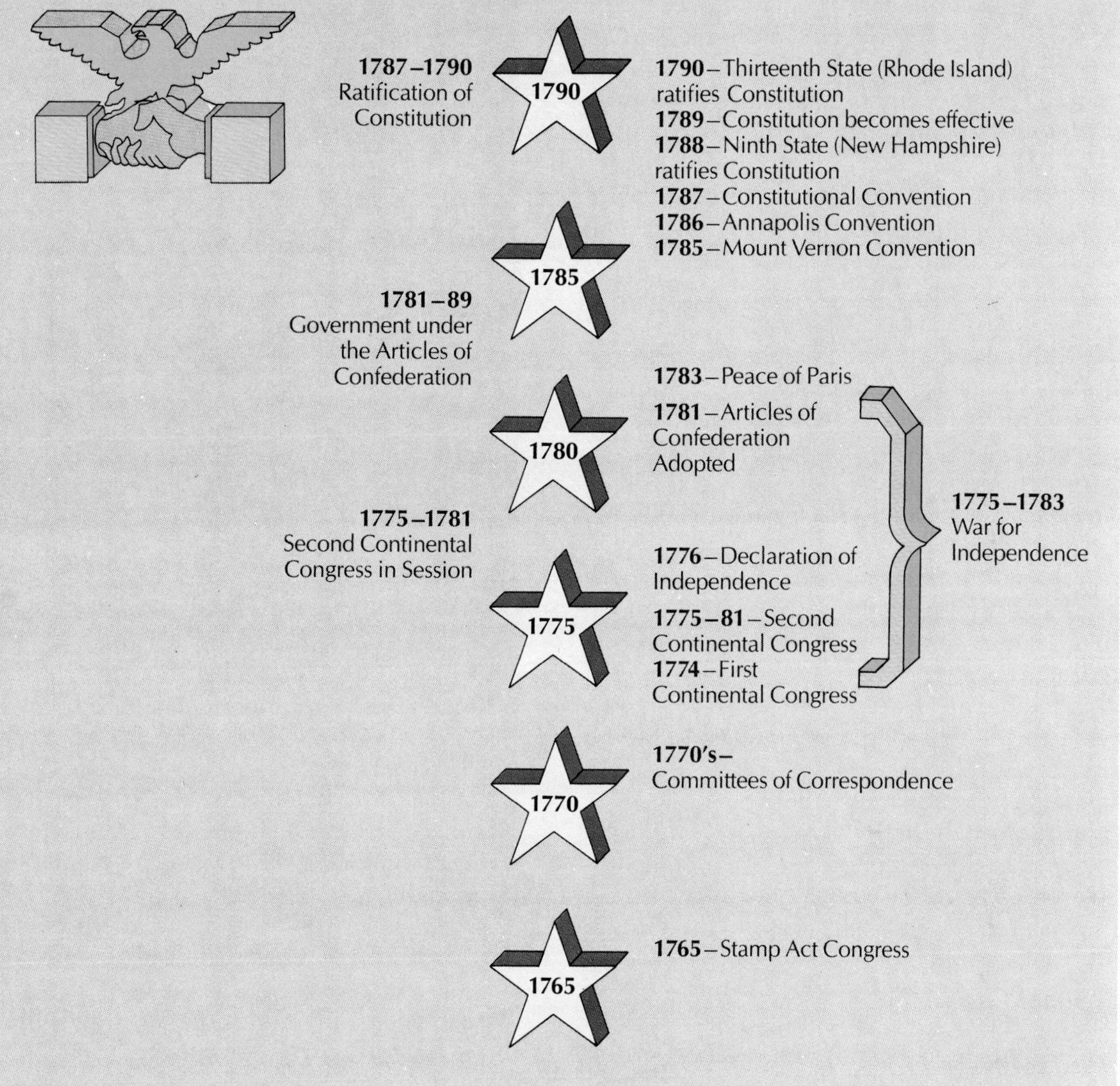

England Confederation, a "league of friendship" for defense against the Indians. As the Indian danger passed and frictions grew between the settlements, the confederation lost importance and finally died in 1684. In 1697 William Penn offered an elaborate plan for intercolonial cooperation, largely in trade, defense, and criminal matters. It was given little attention, and was soon forgotten.

The Albany Plan, 1754 In 1754 the British Board of Trade called a meeting of seven of the northern colonies[10] at Albany. The

[10]Connecticut, Maryland, Massachusetts, New Hampshire, New York, Pennsylvania, and Rhode Island.

main purpose of the meeting was to discuss the problems of colonial trade and the danger of French and Indian attacks. Here, Benjamin Franklin offered what came to be known as the Albany Plan of Union.

Franklin proposed the formation of an annual congress, an assembly or conference, of delegates from each of the 13 colonies. That body would have power to raise military and naval forces, make war and peace with the Indians, regulate trade with them, levy taxes, and collect customs duties.

Franklin's plan was ahead of its time. It was agreed to by the Albany meeting, but it was turned down by the colonies and by the Crown. Franklin's plan was to be remembered later, however, when independence came.

The Stamp Act Congress, 1765 The harsh tax and trade policies of the 1760s fanned resentment in the colonies. A number of new laws had been passed by Parliament, among them the Stamp Act of 1765. That law required the use of tax stamps on all legal documents, on certain business agreements, and on all newspapers circulating in the colonies.

The new taxes were widely denounced, in part because the rates were severe, but largely because they amountd to "taxation without representation." In October 1765 nine of the colonies[11] sent delegates to the Stamp Act Congress in New York. They prepared a strong protest, called the Declaration of Rights and Grievances, against the new British policies and sent it to the king. Their actions marked the first time a significant number of colonies had joined to oppose the home government.

Parliament repealed the Stamp Act, but frictions mounted. New laws were passed and new policies were made to tie the colonies more closely to London. Resentment and anger were expressed in wholesale evasion of the laws. Mob violence erupted at several ports, and many colonists **boycotted**—refused to buy or sell—English goods. On March 3, 1770, British troops in Boston fired on a jeering crowd, killing five, in what came to be known as the Boston Massacre.

Widespread popular protest marked the duration of the Stamp Act, 1765-1766. What were some results of this outcry?

Organized resistance grew and was carried on through Committees of Correspondence, which had grown out of a group formed by Samuel Adams in Boston in 1772. Within a year these committees were to be found throughout the colonies, providing a network for cooperation and the exchange of information among the patriots.

Protests multiplied. The famous Boston Tea Party came on December 16, 1773. A group of men, dressed as Indians and protesting a new monopoly on tea, boarded three ships in Boston harbor and dumped their offending cargoes of tea into the sea.

The First Continental Congress, 1774 In the spring of 1774, Parliament passed yet another set of laws, this time to punish the colonists for the troubles in Boston and else-

[11] All except Georgia, New Hampshire, North Carolina, and Virginia.

*REINFORCEMENT The Stamp Act of 1765 was one of many actions that led to the First Continental Congress. Have students organize a debate on whether to repeal or accept the Stamp Act.

where. These new laws, denounced in America as the Intolerable Acts, caused the Massachusetts and the Virginia assemblies to call a meeting of all the colonies.

Fifty-five delegates, from every colony except Georgia, met in Philadelphia on September 5, 1774. Many of the ablest men of the day were there: Samuel and John Adams from Massachusetts; Roger Sherman from Connecticut; Stephen Hopkins from Rhode Island; John Dickinson and Joseph Galloway from Pennsylvania; John Jay and Philip Livingston from New York; George Washington, Richard Henry Lee, and Patrick Henry from Virginia; and John Rutledge from South Carolina.

For nearly two months, the members of this First Continental Congress discussed the worsening situation and debated plans for action. A Declaration of Rights, protesting Britain's colonial policies, was addressed to George III. The delegates urged each of the colonies to refuse all trade with England until the hated taxes and trade regulations were repealed. The delegates also called for the creation of local committees to enforce that boycott.

The meeting adjourned on October 26, with a call for a second congress to assemble the following May. Over the next several months, all of the colonial legislatures, including Georgia's, gave their support to the actions taken by the First Continental Congress.

FOR REVIEW

1. **Identify:** Albany Plan, Stamp Act Congress, First Continental Congress.
2. What kind of governmental relationship had developed in fact, if not in form, between Britain and the colonies by the mid-1700s? Why?
3. How did the relationship change in the 1760s?
4. How was the Stamp Act Congress significant in the changing relationship between Britain and the colonies?

3. Independence

As You Read, Think About:

- Why the Second Continental Congress was of crucial importance.
- Why the Declaration of Independence is considered revolutionary.
- What the characteristics of the first State governments were.

During the fall and winter of 1774–75, the British government continued to refuse to compromise, let alone reverse, its colonial policies. It reacted to the Declaration of Rights as it had to other expressions of colonial discontent—with even stricter and more repressive measures.

The Second Continental Congress

The Second Continental Congress met in Philadelphia on May 10, 1775. By then, the Revolution had begun. The "shot heard 'round the world" had been fired. The battles of Lexington and Concord had been fought three weeks earlier, on April 19.

Each of the 13 colonies—soon to be States—was represented at the Congress. Most of those who had attended the First Continental Congress were again present. The most notable of the newcomers were Benjamin Franklin of Pennsylvania and John Hancock of Massachusetts.

Hancock was chosen president of the Congress.[12] Almost at once, a "continental army" was organized, and George Washington was appointed its commander in chief. Thomas Jefferson then took Washington's place in the Virginia delegation.

The Second Continental Congress became, by force of circumstance, our first national government. It rested on no constitutional base. It was condemned by the British

[12]Peyton Randolph, who had also served as president of the First Continental Congress, was originally chosen to the office. He resigned on May 24, however, because the Virginia House of Delegates, of which he was the speaker, had been called into session. Hancock was then elected to succeed him.

Colonial discontent with Britain's repressive measures erupted into armed rebellion when British troops marched on Lexington and Concord in April, 1775.

as "an unlawful assembly" and "a den of traitors." But it was supported by the force of public opinion and by practical necessity.

The Second Continental Congress served as the first government of the United States for five fateful years, from the signing of the Declaration of Independence in July 1776 until the Articles of Confederation went into effect on March 1, 1781. During that time, it prosecuted a war, raised armies and a navy, borrowed money, bought supplies, created a monetary system, made treaties with foreign powers, and did those other things that any government does.

The unicameral Congress exercised both legislative and executive powers. In legislative matters, each colony—later State—had one vote. Executive functions were handled by the delegates through committees.

The Declaration of Independence

* On June 7, 1776, Richard Henry Lee of Virginia proposed to the Second Continental Congress:

> *Resolved,* That these United Colonies are, and of right ought to be, free and independent States, that they are absolved from all allegiance to the British Crown, and that all political connection between them and the State of Great Britain is, and ought to be, totally dissolved.

A committee of five in the Congress —Benjamin Franklin, John Adams, Roger Sherman, Robert Livingston, and Thomas Jefferson—was named to prepare a proclamation of independence. Their momentous product, the Declaration of Independence,[13] was almost wholly the work of Jefferson.

On July 2, the final break came. The delegates unanimously agreed to Lee's resolution. Two days later, July 4, 1776, the Declaration of Independence was adopted and announced to the world.

Much of the Declaration speaks of "the repeated injuries and usurpations" that led the colonists to revolt. It proclaims the independence of the United States. At its heart, the Declaration declares:

> We hold these truths to be self-evident, that all men are created equal, that they are endowed

[13]The full text of the Declaration appears on pages 720–723.

*REINFORCEMENT Discuss the principal arguments for independence set out in the Declaration of Independence (see Appendix).

by their Creator with certain unalienable Rights, that among these are Life, Liberty and the pursuit of Happiness. That to secure these rights, Governments are instituted among Men, deriving their just powers from the consent of the governed; That whenever any Form of Government becomes destructive of these ends it is the Right of the People to alter or to abolish it, and to institute new Government, laying its foundations on such principles and organizing its power in such form, as to them shall seem most likely to effect their Safety and Happiness.

With these brave words, the United States of America was born. The 13 colonies became free and independent States. The 56 men who signed the Declaration sealed it with this final sentence:

And for the support of this Declaration, with a firm reliance on the protection of Divine Providence, we mutually pledge to each other, our lives, our Fortunes, and our sacred Honor.

The Second Continental Congress approved the Declaration of Independence on July 4, 1776, formally announcing the colonies' new nationhood.

The First State Governments

In January 1776, New Hampshire adopted a constitution to replace its royal charter. Less than three months later, South Carolina followed suit. Then, on May 10, nearly two months before the Declaration of Independence, Congress urged each of the colonies to adopt

such governments as shall, in the opinion of the representatives of the people, best conduce to the happiness and safety of their constituents.

Most of the States adopted written constitutions in 1776 and 1777. With minor changes, Connecticut and Rhode Island transformed their charters into new fundamental laws. Assemblies or conventions were commonly used to draft and then adopt these new documents. Massachusetts set a lasting precedent in the constitution-making process. There, a convention submitted its work to the voters for ratification. The Massachusetts constitution of 1780 is the oldest of the present-day State constitutions. In fact, it is the oldest written constitution in force anywhere in the world today.[14]

Common Features

The first State constitutions differed, sometimes widely, in detail. Yet, they shared many common features.

Popular Sovereignty Each of the new constitutions was based on the principle of **popular sovereignty.** Each constitution insisted that government could exist and function *only* with the consent of the governed.

Limited Government The twin concept of limited government was a major feature of each document. The powers delegated

[14]From independence until that constitution became effective in 1780, Massachusetts relied on its colonial charter, in force prior to 1691, as its fundamental law. We shall return to the subject of State constitutions in Chapter 19. For now, note this important point: The earliest of those documents were, within a very few years, to have a marked effect upon the drafting of the Constitution of the United States.

to government were granted sparingly and hedged by many restrictions.

Civil Liberties Seven of the new documents[15] contained a bill of rights, setting out the "unalienable rights" held by the people. In every State it was made clear that the sovereign people held certain **civil rights** that government must at all times respect.

Separation of Powers and Checks and Balances The powers granted to the new State governments were purposely divided among three distinct branches: executive, legislative, and judicial. Each branch was given powers with which to check, or restrain, each of the other branches of the government.

The new State constitutions were rather brief documents. For the most part, they were declarations of principle and statements of prohibition and limitation on governmental power. Memories of the royal governors were fresh, and the new State governors were given little real power. Most of the authority that was granted to State government was placed in the legislature. Elective terms of office were made purposely short—seldom more than one or two years. The right to vote was limited to those adult males who could meet property ownership and other rigid qualifications.

FOR REVIEW

1. **Identify:** Second Continental Congress, Declaration of Independence.
2. How and why did the Second Continental Congress become our first national government?
3. Who wrote the Declaration of Independence? Why are the opening lines of its second paragraph so important?
4. List the common features of the first State constitutions.

[15]Delaware, Maryland, Massachusetts, New Hampshire, North Carolina, Pennsylvania, and Virginia.

4. The Confederation and the Critical Period

As You Read, Think About:

- What the basic provisions and weaknesses of the Articles of Confederation were.
- What national problems resulted from the weaknesses of the Articles.
- How the States attempted to solve these problems.

The First and Second Continental Congresses rested on no legal base. They were called in haste, to meet an emergency, and they were intended to be temporary. Something more regular and lasting was needed.

Our First National Constitution

Richard Henry Lee's resolution that had led to the Declaration of Independence also called on the Second Continental Congress to propose "a plan of confederation." Off and on, for 17 months, that body considered the problem of uniting the former colonies. Finally, on November 15, 1777, the Articles of Confederation were approved.

The Articles did not go into effect immediately, however. The **ratifications,** or formal approval, of all 13 States had to be secured first. Eleven States agreed to the document within a year. Delaware added its approval in mid-1779. But Maryland did not ratify until February 27, 1781. The Second Continental Congress then set March 1, 1781, as the date when the Articles were finally to become effective.

The Articles established "a firm league of friendship" among the States. Each State kept "its sovereignty, freedom, and independence, and every power, jurisdiction, and right . . . not . . . expressly delegated to the United States, in Congress assembled." The States came together "for their common defense, the security of their liberties, and their mutual and general welfare."

Governmental Structure The government set up by the Articles was simple indeed. A Congress was the sole organ created. It was a single-chambered body, made up of delegates chosen yearly by the States in whatever way their legislatures might direct. Each State had one vote in the Congress, whatever its population or wealth.

There was neither an executive nor a judicial branch. These functions were to be handled by committees of the Congress. Each year the Congress would choose one of its members as its president. That person was its presiding officer, but not the president of the United States. Civil officers, for example, postmasters, were to be appointed by the Congress.

Powers of Congress Several important powers were given to the Congress. It could: make war and peace; send and receive ambassadors; enter into treaties; borrow money; set up a monetary system; build a navy; raise an army by asking the States for troops; fix uniform standards of weights and measures; and settle disputes among the States.

*****State Obligations*** By agreeing to the Articles, the States had pledged themselves to several things. They agreed to obey the Articles and acts of the Congress; provide the funds and troops requested by Congress; treat citizens of other States fairly and equally with their own; give full faith and credit to the public acts, records, and judicial proceedings of every other State; surrender fugitives from justice to each other; submit their disputes to Congress for settlement; and allow open travel and trade between and among the States.

In short, the Congress possessed only those powers "expressly delegated" to it by the Articles. The States retained those powers not given to the Congress. They, not the Congress, were primarily responsible for protecting life and property and for promoting the general welfare of the people.

Weaknesses The powers of the Congress appear, at first glance, to have been considerable. Several important ones were not given to it, however. The lack of them, together with other weaknesses, soon proved the Articles could not meet the needs of the time.

The Congress was not given the power to tax. It could raise money only by borrowing and by asking the States for funds. Borrowing was, at best, a poor source. The Second Continental Congress had borrowed heavily to support the Revolution, and many of those debts had not been repaid. While the Articles were in force, not one State came close to meeting the financial requests made by the Congress.

Nor did Congress have the power to regulate trade between and among the States. This lack of a central mechanism to regulate commerce was one of the major factors that led to the adoption of the Constitution, as we shall see.

The Congress had no power to make the States obey the Articles of Confederation or

What specific problems resulted from these weaknesses? What were the Articles' strengths?

Weaknesses in the Articles of Confederation

- One vote for each State, regardless of size.
- Congress powerless to lay and collect taxes or duties.
- Congress powerless to regulate foreign and interstate commerce.
- No executive to enforce acts of Congress.
- No national court system.
- Amendment only with consent of all of the States.
- A 9/13 majority required to pass laws.
- Articles only a "firm league of friendship."

*REINFORCEMENT Have the class discuss: How did the States endorse a "United States" as well as their own rights during the time between approval and ratification of the Articles of Confederation?

the laws it made. It could exercise the powers it did have only with the consent of 9 of the 13 State delegations. Finally, the Articles themselves could be changed only with the consent of all 13 State legislatures.[16]

The Critical Period, the 1780s

The long Revolutionary War finally ended on October 18, 1781. America's victory was confirmed by the Treaty of Paris in 1783. With peace, however, the new nation's economic and political problems came into sharp focus. The weaknesses of the Articles soon surfaced.

With a central government unable to act, the States bickered among themselves and grew increasingly jealous and suspicious of one another. They refused to support the new central government, financially and in almost every other way. Several of them made agreements with foreign governments, even though that was forbidden by the Articles. Most even organized their own military forces.

George Washington complained: "We are one nation today and 13 tomorrow. Who will treat with us on such terms?"

The States taxed each other's goods and even banned some trade. They printed their own money, often with little backing. Economic chaos spread as prices soared and sound credit vanished. Debts, public and private, went unpaid.

The historian John Fiske tells us:

> *The city of New York, with its population of 30,000 souls, had long been supplied with firewood from Connecticut, and with butter and cheese, chickens and garden vegetables from the thrifty farms of New Jersey. This trade, it was observed, carried thousands of dollars out of the city and into the pockets of the detested Yankees and despised Jerseymen. "It was ruinous to domestic industry," said the men of New York. "It must be stopped by . . . a navigation act and a protective tariff." Acts were accordingly passed, obliging every Yankee sloop which came down through Hell Gate, and every Jersey market boat which was rowed across from Paulus Hook to Cortlandt Street, to pay entrance fees and obtain clearances at the custom house, just as was done by ships from London and Hamburg; and not a cartload of Connecticut firewood could be delivered at the back door of a country house in Beekman Street until it should have paid a heavy duty. Great and just was the wrath of the farmers and lumbermen. The New Jersey legislature made up its mind to retaliate. The city of New York had lately bought a small patch of ground on Sandy Hook, and had built a lighthouse there. This lighthouse was the one weak spot in the heel of Achilles where a hostile arrow could strike, and New Jersey gave vent to her indignation by laying a tax of $1800 a year on it. Connecticut was equally prompt. At a great meeting of businessmen, held at New London, it was unanimously agreed to suspend all commercial intercourse with New York. Every merchant signed an agreement, under a penalty of $250 for the first offence, not to send any goods whatever into the hated State for a period of twelve months.[17]

Violence broke out in a number of places. Shays' Rebellion in western Massachusetts in 1786 was only the most spectacular of several incidents.

The Articles had not created a government able to deal with the nation's troubles. Inevitably, demands were made for a stronger, more effective national government. Those who were most threatened by economic and political instability—large property owners, merchants, traders, and other creditors—soon took the lead in efforts to that end. The movement for change began to take concrete form in 1785.

The Meetings at Mount Vernon and Annapolis

Maryland and Virginia, plagued by trade disputes, took the first step in this movement for change. Ignoring the Congress, the two

[16]No amendments were added to the Articles. To get all 13 of the jealous, increasingly unfriendly States to agree on anything seemed hopeless to many. In 1785 the Congress, in a final attempt to solve its money problems, proposed an amendment to permit it to levy import duties. Only New York, reaping income from its own tax on imports, refused to ratify the proposal.

[17]*The Critical Period of American History* (Boston: Houghton Mifflin, 1888), p. 146.

*ENRICHMENT Have the class discuss John Fiske's account of the States at odds with one another. What issues are at stake? What were the causes of tension?

In Shays' Rebellion, angry farmers seized several courthouses in Massachusetts in 1786 to prevent the loss of their farms to tax collectors and creditors.

States agreed to a conference on those problems. Their representatives met at Alexandria, Virginia, in March 1785. At George Washington's invitation, they moved their sessions to his home at Mount Vernon. Their negotiations proved so successful that, on January 21, 1786, the Virginia Assembly called for "a joint meeting of [all of] the States to recommend a federal plan for regulating commerce."

That "joint meeting" opened at Annapolis, Maryland, on September 11, 1786. Only 5 of the 13 States attended.[18] Disappointed, but still hopeful, the Annapolis Convention called for yet another meeting of the States

> at Philadelphia on the second Monday in May next, to take into consideration the situation of the United States, to devise such further provisions as shall appear to them necessary to render the constitution of the Federal Government adequate to the exigencies of the Union.

By mid-February of 1787, seven of the States had named delegates to the Philadelphia meeting.[19] Then, on February 21, the Congress, which had been hesitating, also called upon the States to send delegates to Philadelphia

> for the sole and express purpose of revising the Articles of Confederation and reporting to Congress and the several legislatures such alterations and provisions therein as shall when agreed to in Congress and confirmed by the States render the [Articles] adequate to the exigencies of Government and the preservation of the Union.

That Philadelphia meeting became the Constitutional Convention.

FOR REVIEW

1. **Identify:** Articles of Confederation, Critical Period.
2. When and by whom were the Articles of Confederation prepared?
3. Describe the government set up by the Articles. What powers were given to Congress?
4. What were the major weaknesses of the Articles?
5. Why is the period during which the Articles were in force called the "Critical Period" in American History?

[18]New York, New Jersey, Pennsylvania, Delaware, and Virginia. Although four other States (New Hampshire, Massachusetts, Rhode Island, and North Carolina) had appointed delegates, none of them attended the Annapolis meeting.

[19]Delaware, Georgia, New Hampshire, New Jersey, North Carolina, Pennsylvania, and Virginia.

5. The Constitutional Convention

As You Read, Think About:

- How the Constitution was written.
- Why compromises were necessary.
- What major compromises were involved.

The Philadelphia meeting began on Friday, May 25, 1787.[20] In all, 12 of the States were represented. Rhode Island did not take part in the convention.[21]

The Framers

In all, 74 delegates were chosen by the several State legislatures. For a number of reasons, however, only 55 of them actually attended the convention.

Of that 55, surely this much can be said: Never, before or since, has so remarkable a group been brought together in this country. Thomas Jefferson, who was not among them, later called the delegates "an assembly of demi-gods."

They included these outstanding personalities: George Washington, James Madison, Edmund Randolph, and George Mason from Virginia; Benjamin Franklin, Gouverneur Morris, Robert Morris, and James Wilson from Pennsylvania; Alexander Hamilton from New York; William Paterson from New Jersey; Elbridge Gerry and Rufus King from Massachusetts; Luther Martin from Maryland; Oliver Ellsworth and Roger Sherman from Connecticut; John Dickinson from Delaware; and John Rutledge and Charles Pinckney from South Carolina.

These were men of wide knowledge and public experience, and of wealth and prestige. Many of them had fought in the Revolution; 39 had been members of the Continental Congress or the Congress of the Confederation, or both. Eight had served in constitutional conventions in their own States, and seven had been State governors. Eight had signed the Declaration of Independence. Thirty-one of the delegates had attended college, in a day when there were only a few colleges in the land; their number included two college presidents and three professors. Two were to become President of the United States, and one a Vice President. Seventeen were later to serve in the Senate and 11 in the House of Representatives.

Is it any wonder that the product of such a gathering was described by the English statesman William E. Gladstone, nearly a century later, as "the most wonderful work ever struck off at a given time by the brain and purpose of man"?

Remarkably, the average age of the Framers was only 42, and nearly half were only in their 30s. Indeed, most of the real leaders were in that age group—Madison was 36, Gouverneur Morris 35, Randolph 34, and Hamilton 32. At 81, Franklin was the oldest. He was failing, however, and not able to attend many of the meetings. George Washington, at 55, was one of the few older members who played a key part in the making of the Constitution.

By and large, the Framers of the Constitution were of a new generation in American politics. Several of the better known leaders of the Revolutionary period were not in Philadelphia. Patrick Henry said he "smelt a rat" and refused to attend. Samuel Adams, John Hancock, and Richard Henry Lee were not selected as delegates by their States. Thomas Paine was in Paris. So, too, was Thomas Jefferson, as American minister to France. John Adams was our envoy to England and Holland at the time.

Organization and Procedure

The Framers met in Independence Hall, probably in the same room in which the Declaration of Independence had been signed 11 years earlier.

[20]Not enough of the States were represented on the date originally set, Monday, May 14. Those delegates who were present met and adjourned each day until May 25, when a quorum (majority) of the States were on hand.

[21]The Rhode Island legislature was controlled by the "soft-money" forces there—mostly debtors and small farmers who were helped by inflation and so were against a stronger central government. The New Hampshire delegation, delayed mostly by lack of funds, did not reach Philadelphia until late July.

Have the class discuss: How were the Framers of the Constitution representative of a new generation of American politics?

The Constitutional Convention, meeting in Independence Hall, Philadelphia, was noted for its disputes. However, what basic views did the Framers agree on?

They organized immediately, on May 25.[22] George Washington was unanimously elected president of the convention. Then, and at the second session on Monday, May 28, several rules of procedure were adopted. A majority of the States—seven—would be a quorum to conduct business. Each State delegation was to have one vote on all questions. A majority of the votes cast would carry any proposal.

The delegates also decided to keep their sessions secret. The convention had drawn much public attention—and speculation. So, to protect themselves from outside pressures, the delegates adopted a rule of secrecy. On the whole, the rule was well kept.

[22]Twenty-eight delegates from seven States were present on that first day. The full number of 55 was not reached until August 6, when John Francis Mercer of Maryland arrived and was seated. In the meantime, some delegates had departed, and others were absent from time to time. Some 40 members attended most of the daily sessions of the convention.

A secretary, William Jackson, and other minor, nonmember officers were appointed. Jackson kept the convention's *Journal.* That official record, however, was quite sketchy. It was mostly a listing of members present, motions put, and votes taken, and it was not always an accurate record, at that.

Fortunately, several delegates kept their own accounts of the proceedings—most notably, James Madison. Most of what is known of the work of the convention comes from Madison's careful and voluminous *Notes.* His brilliance and depth of knowledge led his colleagues to hold him in great respect. Quickly, he became the convention's floor leader. Madison contributed more to the Constitution than did any of the others, and still, he was able to keep a close record of its work. Certainly, he deserves the title "Father of the Constitution."

The Framers met on 89 of the 116 days from May 25 through their final meeting on September 17. They did most of their work on the floor of the convention. Some matters were handled by committees, but all questions were ultimately settled by the full body.

The Decision to Write a New Constitution

*The Philadelphia Convention was called to *recommend revisions* in the Articles of Confederation. However, almost at once the delegates agreed that they were, in fact, meeting to create a *new* government for the United States. On May 30 they adopted this proposal, which was put forth by Edmund Randolph of Virginia:

> *Resolved,* . . . that a *national* Government ought to be established consisting of a *supreme* Legislative, Executive and Judiciary.

With this momentous decision, the Framers redefined the purpose of the convention. From that point on, they set about the writing of a new constitution to *replace* the Articles of Confederation. Their debates were spirited, even bitter. At times the convention seemed near collapse. Once they had passed Governor Randolph's resolution, however, the goal of the majority of the convention never changed.

The Virginia Plan

No State had more to do with the calling of the convention than Virginia. It was not surprising, then, that its delegates should offer the first plan for a new constitution. On May 29 the Virginia Plan, largely the work of Madison, was presented by Randolph.

The Virginia Plan called for a new government with three separate branches: legislative, executive, and judicial. The legislature (Congress) would be bicameral—that is, it would have two houses. Representation in each house was to be based either upon each State's population or upon the amount of money it gave for the support of the central government. The members of the lower house, the House of Representatives, were to be popularly elected in each State. Those of the upper house, the Senate, were to be chosen by the lower house, from lists of persons nominated by the State legislatures.

Congress was to be given all of the powers it held under the Articles. In addition, it was to have the power to legislate "in all cases in which the separate States are incompetent" to act, to veto any State law in conflict with national law, and to use force if necessary to make a State obey national law.

A "National Executive" and a "National Judiciary" were to be chosen by Congress. Together, these two branches would form a "council of revision." They could veto acts of Congress, but a veto could be overridden by the two houses. The executive would have "a general authority to execute the national laws." The judiciary would "consist of one or more supreme tribunals, and of inferior tribunals."

The Virginia Plan also provided that all State officers should take an oath to support the Union, that each State be guaranteed a republican form of government, and that Congress have the power to admit new States to the Union.

The Virginia Plan called, then, for a thorough revision of the Articles. Its goal was the creation of a *national* government with greatly expanded powers and, more importantly, the power to enforce its decisions.

The Virginia Plan set the agenda for much of the convention's work. But some delegates —especially those from the smaller states of Delaware, Maryland, and New Jersey, and from New York[23]—found it too radical. Soon they developed their counterproposals. On June 15 William Paterson of New Jersey presented the position of the small States.

The New Jersey Plan

Paterson and his colleagues offered several amendments to the Articles, but not nearly so thorough a revision as proposed by the

[23]The Virginia Plan's major support came from the three largest States: Virginia, Pennsylvania, and Massachusetts. New York was then only the fifth largest. Alexander Hamilton, the convention's most outspoken champion of a stronger central government, was regularly outvoted by his fellow delegates from New York.

*REINFORCEMENT Although the Philadelphia Convention was called to recommend revisions to the Articles of Confederation, a decision was made to write a new constitution. Have the class discuss why this occurred.

By Burr Shafer, © 1960

"It is unthinkable that the citizens of Rhode Island should ever surrender their sovereignty to some central authority way off in Philadelphia."

Virginia Plan. The New Jersey Plan would have kept the unicameral Congress of the Confederation, with each of the States equally represented. To those powers Congress already had would be added closely limited powers to tax and to regulate interstate trade.

The New Jersey Plan also called for a "federal Executive" of more than one person. This plural executive would be chosen by the Congress and could be removed by it on the request of a majority of the States' governors. The "federal Judiciary" would be composed of a single "supreme Tribunal," appointed by the executive.

Among their several differences, the major point of disagreement between the two plans centered on this question: How should the States be represented in Congress? On the basis of their populations, or financial contributions, as in the Virginia Plan? Or on the basis of State equality, as in the Articles and the New Jersey Plan?

For weeks the delegates returned to this conflict, debating it again and again. The lines were sharply drawn. Several delegates, on both sides of the issue, threatened to withdraw. Finally, and fortunately, a compromise was reached. It proved to be one of the truly great compromises of the convention.

A "Bundle of Compromises"

The Constitution, as drafted at Philadelphia, has often been called a "bundle of compromises." The description is apt, *if* it is properly understood.

By no means did all, or even most, of what went into the document come from compromises. The Framers agreed on many of the basic issues they faced. Thus, nearly all the delegates were convinced that a *new* central government had to be created, a government empowered to deal with the nation's economic and social problems. The Framers were also dedicated to the concepts of popular sovereignty and of limited government. None questioned for a moment the wisdom of representative government. The principles of separation of powers and of checks and balances were accepted almost as a matter of course.

There were differences of opinion among the delegates, certainly, and often they were very important ones. How could matters have been otherwise? The delegates came from 12 different States, which were widely separated in both geographic and economic terms. It was only natural that the delegates often reflected the interests of their respective States.

Many disputes did occur, their resolution coming only after hours and days or even weeks of heated debate. The point here, however, is that the differences were *not* over the *most fundamental* of questions. Instead, they involved such vital, but lesser, points as these: the details of the structure of Congress, the method by which the President was to be chosen, and the particular limits that should be placed on the several new powers to be given to the new central government.

The Connecticut Compromise

The disagreement over representation in Congress was extremely critical. The large States expected to dominate the new government. The small States feared that they would not be able to protect their interests. Tempers flared, on both sides. The debate came so intense that Benjamin Franklin was moved to suggest that

> henceforth prayers imploring the assistance of Heaven . . . be offered in this Assembly every morning before we proceed to business.

The conflict was finally settled by a compromise first suggested by the Connecticut delegation. It was agreed that Congress should be composed of two houses, a Senate and a House of Representatives. In the smaller Senate, the States would be represented equally. In the House, the representation of each state would be based upon its current population.

*Thus, by combining basic features of the rival Virginia Plan and New Jersey Plan, the convention's most serious dispute was resolved. The Connecticut Compromise was so pivotal to the writing of the Constitution, and has had such a lasting impact on the shape of the Government of the United States, that it has often been called the Great Compromise.

The Three-Fifths Compromise

Once it had been agreed that the seats in the House would be based on each State's population, this question arose: Should slaves be counted in the populations of the southern States?

Again debate was fierce. Most delegates from the slave-holding States argued that slaves should be counted. Most of the northerners took the opposing view.

Finally, the Framers agreed that all "free persons" should be counted, and so, too, should "three-fifths of all other persons." For the "three-fifths," won by the southerners, the northerners exacted a price: That formula was also to be used in fixing the amount of money to be raised in each State by any direct tax levied by Congress. In short, the southerners could count their slaves, but they would also have to pay for them.

This odd compromise disappeared from the Constitution with the 13th Amendment, which abolished slavery, in 1865. For more than 120 years now, there have been no "all other persons" in this country.

The Commerce and Slave Trade Compromise

The convention agreed that Congress had to have the power to regulate foreign and interstate trade. To many southerners, that power carried a real danger. They worried that Congress, likely to be controlled by northern commercial interests, would act against the interests of the agricultural South.

They were particularly fearful on two counts. First, they feared that Congress would try to support the new government out of export duties—and southern tobacco was the major American export of the time. Second, they feared that Congress would interfere with the slave trade.

So, before they would agree to the commerce power, the southerners insisted on certain protections. Accordingly, Congress was forbidden the power to tax the export of goods from any State. It was also forbidden the power to act on the slave trade for a period of at least 20 years. It could not interfere "with the migration or importation of such persons as any State now existing shall think proper to admit"—except for a small head tax, at least until the year 1808.[24]

Other Compromises

These three compromises were the major ones in the making of the Constitution. But, again, there were many others. The convention spent much of its time, said Franklin, "sawing boards to make them fit."

Other sections of the Constitution—those dealing with the selection of the President, the treaty-making process, the structure of the national court system, and the amendment process—all took their final form as a product of give-and-take among the Framers. So did many of its other provisions, as we shall see in later chapters.

Sources of the Constitution

The Framers were well educated and widely read. They were familiar with the

---

[24] Article I, Section 9, Clause 1.

*REINFORCEMENT How did the Virginia Plan and the New Jersey Plan result in the "Connecticut Compromise"? Use this question to initiate discussion of the Constitution as a "Bundle of Compromises."

FOCUS ON:

Framers of the Constitution

When the Convention began, the members agreed not to publish their day-to-day deliberations. They wanted to be free to reach their decisions without the pressure of public opinion. Fortunately for us, James Madison kept a detailed record of the debates and the compromises that were reached as these men worked on the new Constitution.

In the selection below, from Madison's *Notes*, the delegates debate the question of State representation in Congress.

SATURDAY JUNE 30. 1787. IN CONVENTION

MR Brearly moved that the Presid^{t} write to the Executive of N. Hamshire, informing it that the business depending before the Convention was of such a nature as to require the immediate attendance of the deputies of that State. . . .[it was well understood that the object was to add N. Hamshire to the n^{o} of States opposed to the doctrine of proportional representation, which it was presumed from her relative size she must be adverse to].

MR Patterson seconded the motion. . . .

The motion of Mr Elseworth resumed for allowing each State an equal vote in ye 2^{d} branch. . . . The gentlemen from Connecticut in supposing that the preponderancy secured to the majority in the 1st branch had removed the objections to an equality of votes in the 2^{d} branch for the security of the minority, narrowed the case extremely. Such an equality will enable the minority to controul in all cases whatsoever, the sentiments and interests of the majority. Seven States will controul six: Seven States, according to the estimates that had been used, composed of the whole people. It would be in the power then of less than 1/3 to overrule 2/3 whenever a question should happen to divide the States in that manner. Can we forget for whom we are forming a Government? Is it for *men*, or for the imaginary beings called *States?* . . .

MR ELSEWORTH. The capital objection of Mr Wilson "that the minority will rule the majority" is not true. The power is given to the few to save them from being destroyed by the many. . . .

MR MADISON did justice to the able & close reasoning of Mr E. but must observe that it did not always accord with itself. On another occasion, the large States were described by him as the Aristocratic States, ready to oppress the small. Now the small are the House of Lords requiring a negative to defend them agst the more numerous commons. Mr E. had also erred in saying that no instance had existed in which confederated States had not retained to themselves a perfect equality of suffrage. . . . But notwithstanding this apparent defence, the majority of States might still injure the majority of people. 1. they could *obstruct* the wishes and interests of the majority. 2. they could *extort* measures repugnant to the wishes & interest of the Majority. 3. they could *impose* measures adverse thereto; as the 2^{d} branch will probly exercise some great powers, in which the 1st will not participate. He admitted that every peculiar interest whether in any class of citizens, or any description of States, ought to be secured as far as possible. . . .

1. What view did Madison support in this debate?
2. What was Ellsworth's position? Cite examples of both men's viewpoints.

governments of ancient Greece and Rome and those of contemporary England and Europe. They knew the political writings of their time, of such works as William Blackstone's *Commentaries on the Laws of England,* the Baron de Montesquieu's *The Spirit of the Laws,* Jean Jacques Rousseau's *Social Contract,* John Locke's *Two Treatises of Civil Government,* and many others.

More immediately, the Framers drew on their own experiences. Remember, they were familiar with the Second Continental Congress, the Articles of Confederation, and their own State governments. Much that went into the Constitution came directly, sometimes word for word, from the Articles. A number of provisions were drawn from the several State constitutions, as well.

The Convention Completes Its Work

For several weeks, through the hot Philadelphia summer, the members took up resolution after resolution. Finally, on September 8, a committee was named "to revise the stile of and arrange the articles which had been agreed to" by the convention. That group, headed by Gouverneur Morris, put the Constitution in its final, clear, concise form.

Then, on September 17, the convention approved its work and 39 names were placed on the finished document.[25] Perhaps none of the Framers was *completely* satisfied with their work. Wise old Benjamin Franklin put into words what many of the Framers must have thought on that final day, however:

> Sir, I agree with this Constitution with all its faults, if they are such; because I think a general Government necessary for us . . . I doubt . . . whether any Convention we can obtain, may be able to make a better Constitution. For when you assemble a number of men to have the advantage of their joint wisdom, you inevitably assemble with those men, all their prejudices, their passions, their errors of opinion, their local interests, and their selfish views. From such an assembly can a perfect production be expected? It therefore astonishes me, Sir, to find this system approaching so near to perfection as it does. . . .

On Franklin's motion, the Constitution was signed. Madison tells us that

> . . . Doct[r] Franklin, looking toward the President's chair, at the back of which a rising sun happened to be painted, observed to a few members near him, that Painters had found it difficult to distinguish in their art a rising from a setting sun. I have, said he, often and often in the course of the Session . . . looked at that behind the President without being able to tell whether it was rising or setting. But now at length I have the happiness to know that it is a rising and not a setting sun.

[25]Three of the 41 delegates present on that last day refused to sign the proposed Constitution: Edmund Randolph of Virginia, who later did support ratification and then served as Attorney General and then Secretary of State in the Washington administration; Elbridge Gerry of Massachusetts, who later became Vice President under Madison; and George Mason of Virginia, who continued to oppose the Constitution until his death in 1792. George Read of Delaware signed both for himself and for his absent colleague John Dickinson.

FOR REVIEW

1. **Identify:** Virginia Plan, New Jersey Plan, Connecticut Compromise, Three-Fifths Compromise, Commerce and Slave Trade Compromise.
2. When and where was the Constitution written?
3. Who is known as the "Father of the Constitution"? Why? Who were four other outstanding delegates to the Convention?
4. In what sense were the Framers "a new generation in American politics"?
5. What momentous decision did the Framers make at the beginning of the Convention?
6. What were the Virginia and the New Jersey Plans? What was the principal point of difference between them?
7. In what sense was the Constitution a "bundle of compromises"? What were the three major compromises reached by the Framers?
8. From what sources did the Framers draw in writing the Constitution?

George Washington served as presiding officer of the Philadelphia convention. Even though he rarely took part in the debates, the effect of his presence was a strong one.

6. Ratification and a New Government

As You Read, Think About:

- What the major objections were to the Constitution.
- How the Constitution was ratified.

With the proposed document approved by the Convention in Philadelphia, the next step was that of ratifications of the States.

Ratification

The new Constitution was intended to replace the Articles of Confederation. Remember, the Articles provided that changes could be made in them *only* if *all* of the State legislatures agreed. The Framers had seen how crippling that unanimity requirement could be. So, the new Constitution provided (in Article VII) that

> [T]he ratification of the conventions of nine States shall be sufficient for the establishment of this Constitution between the States so ratifying the same.

The Congress of the Confederation agreed to this irregular procedure. After a short debate, it sent the new document to the States on September 28, 1787.

Federalists and Anti-Federalists The proposed Constitution was printed, circulated, and debated vigorously. Two groups quickly emerged in each of the States: the **Federalists,** who favored ratification, and the **Anti-Federalists,** who opposed it.

The Federalists were led by many of those who had attended the Philadelphia Convention. Among them, the most active and the most effective were James Madison and Alexander Hamilton. Their opposition was headed by such well-known Revolutionary War figures as Patrick Henry, Richard Henry Lee, John Hancock, and Samuel Adams.

The Federalists stressed the weaknesses of the Articles. They argued that the many difficulties facing the Republic could be overcome only by a new government based on the proposed Constitution.

The Anti-Federalists attacked nearly every part of the new document. Many objected to the ratification process, to the absence of any mention of God, to the denial to the States of

REINFORCEMENT Divide the class into two teams representing the Federalists and Anti-Federalists. Have each team defend its constitutional position, using examples from the text.

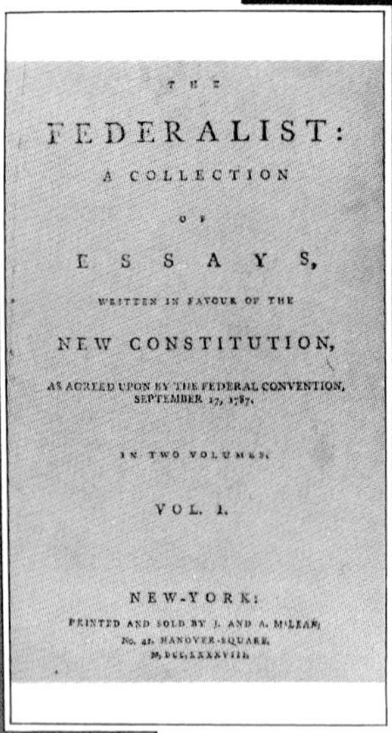
THE
FEDERALIST:
A COLLECTION
OF
ESSAYS,
WRITTEN IN FAVOUR OF THE
NEW CONSTITUTION,
AS AGREED UPON BY THE FEDERAL CONVENTION,
SEPTEMBER 17, 1787.
IN TWO VOLUMES.
VOL. I.
NEW-YORK:
PRINTED AND SOLD BY J. AND A. M'LEAN,
No. 41, HANOVER-SQUARE,
M,DCC,LXXXVIII.

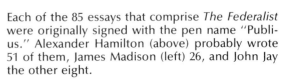

Each of the 85 essays that comprise *The Federalist* were originally signed with the pen name "Publius." Alexander Hamilton (above) probably wrote 51 of them, James Madison (left) 26, and John Jay the other eight.

a power to print money, and to many other provisions.

Two of the major features of the proposed Constitution drew the heaviest fire, however: (1) the much increased powers of the central government and (2) its lack of a bill of rights. The proposed document did not provide for such basic liberties as freedom of speech, press, and religion, nor for the rights of fair trial. Patrick Henry said of the proposed Constitution:

> I look upon that paper as the most fatal plan that could possibly be conceived to enslave a free people.

Success The contest for ratification was close in several States, but the Federalists finally won in all of them. The table on the next page lists the date and vote of each State's ratifying convention.

On June 21, 1788, New Hampshire brought the number of ratifying States to nine. Under Article VII, this ratification should have brought the Constitution into effect, but it did not. Neither Virginia nor New York had yet ratified, and without either of them the new government could not hope to succeed.

VIRGINIA. Virginia's ratification followed New Hampshires's by just four days. Intense and brilliant, the debates in its convention were followed closely throughout the State. The Federalists were led by Madison, the young John Marshall, and Governor Edmund Randolph (even though he had refused to sign the Constitution at Philadelphia).

Ratification of the Constitution

State	Date	Vote
Delaware	Dec. 7, 1787	30–0
Pennsylvania	Dec. 12, 1787	46–23
New Jersey	Dec. 19, 1787	38–0
Georgia	Jan. 2, 1788	26–0
Connecticut	Jan. 9, 1788	128–40
Massachusetts	Feb. 6, 1788	187–168
Maryland	Apr. 28, 1788	63–11
South Carolina	May 23, 1788	149–73
New Hampshire	June 21, 1788	57–46
Virginia	June 25, 1788	89–79
New York	July 26, 1788	30–27
North Carolina	Nov. 21, 1789*	184–77
Rhode Island	May 29, 1790	34–32

*Second vote; ratification was originally defeated on August 4, 1788, by a vote of 184–84.

Patrick Henry, leading the opposition, was joined by such outstanding Virginians as James Monroe, Richard Henry Lee, and George Mason (another of the nonsigners).

Although George Washington was not a delegate, his strong support for ratification proved vital. With Madison, he was able to move a reluctant Jefferson to agree. Had Jefferson fought as did other Anti-Federalists, Virginia might never have ratified the Constitution.

NEW YORK. A narrow vote in the New York convention brought the number of States to 11 on July 26, 1788. New York ratified only after a long battle. The Anti-Federalists were led by Governor George Clinton and by two of the State's three delegates to the Philadelphia Convention.[26]

The contest in New York gave rise to a remarkable campaign document: *The Federalist.* This was a collection of 85 essays written in support of the Constitution by Alexander Hamilton, James Madison, and John Jay. Those essays were first published as letters to the people in various newspapers of the State, and soon were collected in book form. Written in haste, they were purposely slanted in favor of ratification. Even so, they remain an excellent commentary on the Constitution.

Inauguration of the New Government

On September 13, 1788, with 11 of the 13 States "under the federal roof," the Congress of the Confederation paved the way for its successor. It chose New York as the temporary capital.[27] It set the first Wednesday in January as the date on which the States would choose presidential electors. The first Wednesday in February was set as the date on which those electors would vote. It set the first Wednesday in March as the date for the inauguration of the new government.

The new Congress convened on March 4, 1789. It met in Federal Hall, on Wall Street in New York City. Because it lacked a quorum, however, it could not count the electoral votes until April 6. Finally, on that day, it found that George Washington had been elected President by a unanimous vote and John Adams, Vice President, with a substantial majority. On April 30, after an historic trip from Mount Vernon to New York, Washington took the oath of office as the first President of the United States.

FOR REVIEW

1. **Identify:** *The Federalist.*
2. How was the Constitution ratified? What was "irregular" about that process?
3. The Anti-Federalists centered their opposition to the Constitution on what two points?
4. Why was George Washington important to the ratification of the Constitution?

[26] Robert Yates and John Lansing; both had quit Philadelphia in July, arguing that the convention had gone beyond its authority. Alexander Hamilton had been the State's other delegate. Like many other Anti-Federalist leaders, Governor Clinton later supported the Constitution. He was Vice President during Thomas Jefferson's second term and also in James Madison's first term in the Presidency.

[27] The District of Columbia did not become the nation's capital until 1800. Congress moved its sessions to Philadelphia in December, 1790. It held its first meeting in the new "federal city," Washington, D.C., on November 17, 1800.

*ENRICHMENT Distribute copies of *The Federalist* No. 1. Have students cite examples that show Hamilton's point of view (for ratification of the Constitution)

SUMMARY

Government in the United States is the product of centuries of development.

The English, who settled the 13 colonies, had much to do with the shaping of the American governmental system. Most importantly, they set the pattern of early government in America and brought with them the ideas of limited government and representative government.

Starting with Jamestown in Virginia in 1607, all 13 colonies were established by 1732. There were three types of colonies: royal, proprietary, and charter. The eight royal colonies were ruled by a royal governor appointed by and directly responsible to the king. The three proprietary colonies were governed under a proprietor who was, in turn, responsible to the king. The two charter colonies, the most democratic, were largely self-governing.

England tightened its control over the colonies in the 1760s. Colonial resistance to the policies of George III led, finally, to revolution in the mid-1770s. Several attempts had been made to head off the break, most notably and finally by the First Continental Congress in 1774.

By the time the Second Continental Congress assembled, on May 10, 1775, the American Revolution had in fact begun. By force of circumstance, that body became our first national government. It carried on the Revolution; proclaimed the Declaration of Independence on July 4, 1776; and wrote our first national constitution, the Articles of Confederation, which became effective on March 1, 1781.

The government created by the Articles proved too weak for the times. The political and economic chaos of the day led to the replacement of the Articles by the present Constitution.

The Constitution was drafted by a convention that met at Philadelphia from May 25 to September 17, 1787. It became effective with the formation of the new government in March and April, 1789.

CHAPTER REVIEW

Key Terms/Concepts*

institutions (26)
limited government (28)
representative government (28)
bicameral (31)
unicameral (31)
boycott (34)
popular sovereignty (37)
civil rights (38)
ratification (38)
Federalists (49)
Anti-Federalists (49)

*These terms are included in the Glossary.

Keynote Questions

•• 1. Why can the ideas of limited government and representative government be said to have contained the "seeds of revolution"?

•• 2. How might the British Government have forestalled, or even prevented, the coming of the American Revolution?

•• 3. Why did the colonists form the Stamp Act Congress and then the First Continental Congress? Why were these two assemblies significant to the "road to independence"?

• 4. What body became the first national government of the United States? When and for how long did it function in that capacity?

• 5. List the basic political ideas set forth in the second paragraph of the Declaration of Independence.

• 6. What document became the first constitution of the United States? When and for how long was it in force? What was the basic structure of the government it created?

• 7. In the 1780s, George Washington complained, "We are one nation today and 13 tomorrow. Who will treat with us on such terms?" What circumstances led him to make this comment?

The dots represent skill levels required to answer each question or complete each activity: •requires recall and comrehension ••requires application and analysis •••requires synthesis and evaluation

• **8.** What weaknesses in the Articles of Confederation were reflected in the States' actions of the 1780s?

•• **9.** What did Benjamin Franklin mean when he said the Philadelphia Convention spent much of its time "sawing boards to make them fit"? List three illustrations of his point.

•• **10.** Describe in a paragraph the differences between the positions of the Federalists and the Anti-Federalists on the ratification of the Constitution.

Skill Application

Using Primary and Secondary Sources: Information about government and politics comes from both primary and secondary sources. Primary sources are direct, firsthand accounts of an event. Primary sources include journals, official government documents, newsreels, and eyewitness accounts. Secondary sources are often based on primary sources. They are articles, text books, most magazine and newspaper articles, and other accounts written after an event has taken place, by a person who did not witness it.

Primary sources give insight into the attitudes, thoughts, and motivations of people who were directly involved in an event. Sometimes, however, the eyewitness may have seen or heard only part of the event. When reading primary sources, consider how the author's background and living conditions may have affected his or her impressions of the event.

Secondary sources summarize and interpret an event and can be more complete and balanced. However, information may be lost or distorted in summarizing. When reading secondary sources, be aware of the primary sources the author used in researching the event. Be aware, too, of any statements that cannot be proven.

1. Read the excerpt from John Fiske on p. 40. Is this a primary or secondary source? How do you know?

2. Read the feature on p. 47.

a. Which part of this feature is a primary source? Secondary source?

b. What is being discussed in the passage presented in the feature?

c. How did the delegates to the Constitutional Convention make decisions? Did they debate and vote or did one person make the decisions?

d. Why were the delegates concerned about arriving at a decision that was acceptable to all or most of the States?

e. Which position on representation in Congress did Madison support?

For Thought and Discussion

••• **1.** In what particular ways did the Constitution provide for "a more perfect Union" than did the Articles of Confederation?

••• **2.** How did the events leading to the Declaration of Independence and the Revolution demonstrate that "questions of politics and of economics are, in fact, inseparable"?

••• **3.** The Preamble to the Constitution states: "We the People of the United States . . . do ordain and establish this Constitution for the United States of America." Yet, the Constitution was put together by 55 men at Philadelphia and ratified by conventions in the 13 States. Is there a contradiction here? Why or why not? What processes made it legitimate for so few to "speak" for so many?

Suggested Activities

••• **1.** Write a short biographical sketch of one of these historic figures: George Washington, Benjamin Franklin, James Madison, Thomas Jefferson, Samuel Adams, Patrick Henry, John Hancock, Thomas Paine, Richard Henry Lee, Gouverneur Morris, Alexander Hamilton.

••• **2.** Look at a copy of *The Federalist* in your school library. Use some of the ideas found in these essays to write an editorial for or against one of the following statements: (a) The Framers of the Constitution should have provided for a unicameral Congress in which each of the States would be equally represented; (b) The 13 States should not have accepted the Constitution proposed by the Philadelphia Convention; (c) The Philadelphia Convention should have submitted the proposed Constitution to the people in each State, to accept or reject by popular vote.

••• **3.** Prepare a wall chart showing the major weaknesses of the Articles of Confederation and how those matters were treated in the Constitution.

The people made the Constitution and the people can unmake it. It is the creature of their own will, and lives only by their will.
–CHIEF JUSTICE JOHN MARSHALL
COHENS V. *VIRGINIA* (1821)

3 The Living Constitution

CHAPTER OBJECTIVES

To help you to

Learn · Know · Understand

The basic principles of the American constitutional system.

The essential meaning of those principles in both their historical and current settings.

The processes of constitutional change and development by formal amendment.

The processes of constitutional change and development by informal amendment.

THE **CONSTITUTION** OF the United States is this nation's fundamental law. It is, by its own terms, "the supreme law of the land"—the highest form of law in the United States.[1]

The Constitution sets out the basic principles on which the government of the United States was built and on which it is maintained. It lays out the basic framework and procedures by which, and the limits within which, that government must operate.

The Constitution is a fairly brief document. Its little more than 7,000 words can be read in a half hour. Read it now, and as you do, note this: It deals very largely with matters of basic principle. Unlike most other constitutions—those of the 50 States and of most other nations—it is not overweighted with unnecessarily detailed provisions.

In this chapter we look first at the basic principles of the American constitutional system. Then we turn to the subject of constitutional growth, to the various ways in which the Constitution has changed and been changed over the course of 200 years.

[1]In Article VI, Section 2. You will find the text of the Constitution, together with a two-page outline of its contents, on pages 724–753.

The Constitution of the United States, on display in the National Archives Building in Washington D.C. (above), is as vital to our governmental process today as it was 200 years ago when it was created in Philadelphia at Independence Hall (left), in 1787.

1. The Basic Principles

As You Read, Think About:

- What the basic principles are on which the Constitution of the United States is built.
- How the American system of checks and balances operates.
- What reasons prompted the adoption of a federal system.

*The Constitution is built on six basic principles: popular sovereignty, limited government, separation of powers, checks and balances, judicial review, and federalism.

Popular Sovereignty

In the United States, all political power belongs to the people. The people are sovereign. They are the *only* source of any and all governmental power. Government can govern only with the consent of the governed.

This principle of popular sovereignty is woven throughout the Constitution. In its very opening words, in the Preamble, it declares: "We the People of the United States . . . do ordain and establish this Constitution for the United States of America."

Acting through the Constitution, the sovereign people created the Government of the United States and have given to it certain powers. Through the Constitution and its own fundamental law, each State government received its powers from the people.

Limited Government

The principle of **limited government** holds that government is *not* all-powerful, that it may do only *certain* things—those things that the people have empowered it to do.

In effect, the principle of limited government is the other side of the coin of popular sovereignty. It is that principle stated the other way around: The people are the only source of any and all of government's authority; and government has only that authority the people have given to it.

*REINFORCEMENT Discuss the organization and content of the Constitution using the outline on p. 726. Point out how the above-mentioned six basic principles are reflected in its composition.

The highly important concept of limited government may be explained another way: Government must obey the law. Stated this way, the principle is often called **constitutionalism**—that is, that government must be conducted according to constitutional principles. The concept of limited government is also often described as the **rule of law**—that is, government and its officers in all that they do are always subject to, never above, the law.

In large part, the Constitution is a statement of limited government. Much of it is written as explicit prohibitions of power to government.[2] For example, notice the Constitution's guarantees of freedom of expression. Those great guarantees—of freedom of religion, of speech, of press, of assembly, and of petition—are absolutely indispensable to democratic government. They are set out in the 1st Amendment, which begins with the words: "Congress shall make no law. . . ."

Separation of Powers

Recall our short discussion of the parliamentary and the presidential forms of government, on page 8. In a parliamentary system the basic powers of a government—its legislative, executive, and judicial powers—are all gathered in the hands of a single agency. British government is a leading example. In a presidential system, these basic powers are separated among three distinct and independent branches of the government, as in the United States.

The Constitution distributes the powers of the National Government among the Congress (the legislative branch), the President (the executive branch), and the courts (the judicial branch). This **separation of powers** is clearly set forth in three Articles.

Article I, Section 1 declares:

> All legislative powers herein granted shall be vested in a Congress of the United States . . .

Thus, Congress is the lawmaking branch of the National Government.

[2]See, especially, Article I, Sections 9 and 10; the 1st through the 10th Amendments; and the 13th, 14th, 15th, 19th, 24th, and 26th Amendments.

Article II, Section 1 declares:

> The Executive power shall be vested in a President of the United States . . ."

Thus, the President is given the law-executing, law-enforcing, law-administering powers of the National Government.

Article III, Section 1 declares:

> The judicial power of the United States shall be vested in one Supreme Court, and in such inferior courts as the Congress may from time to time establish.

Thus, the federal courts, and most importantly the Supreme Court, *interpret and apply* the laws of the United States in cases brought before them. Remember, the Framers of the Constitution intended to create a stronger government for the United States. Recall, too, that they intended to limit the powers of that government. The doctrine of separation of powers was designed to that end.

Defending this arrangement, James Madison wrote in *The Federalist* No. 47:

> The accumulation of all powers, legislative, executive, and judiciary, in the same hands, whether one, a few, or many, . . . may justly be pronounced the very definition of tyranny.

Checks and Balances

The National Government is organized around three separate branches. As we have noted, the Constitution gives to each branch its own distinct field of governmental authority: **legislative, executive,** and **judicial.**

These three branches are not entirely separated nor completely independent of one another. Rather, they are tied together by a complex system of **checks and balances.** Each branch is subject to a number of constitutional checks, or restraints, by either or both of the others. In other words, each branch has certain powers with which it can check the operations of the other two.

The major features of the check-and-balance arrangement are set out in the chart on page 57. As you can see, the Congress has the power to make law, but the President may veto, or reject, any act of Congress. In its turn, Congress can override a veto by a

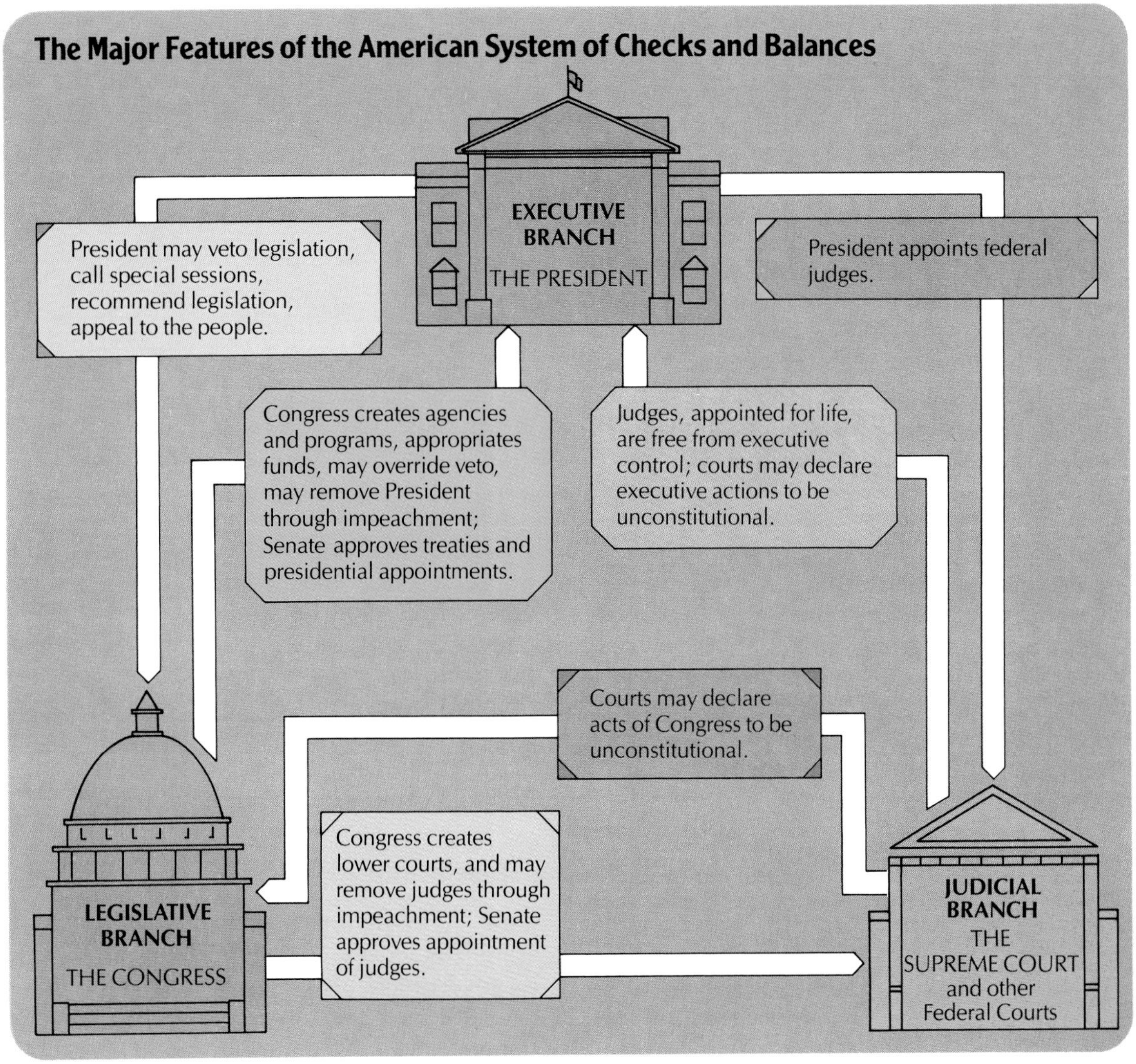
The Major Features of the American System of Checks and Balances
EXECUTIVE BRANCH
THE PRESIDENT
President may veto legislation, call special sessions, recommend legislation, appeal to the people.
President appoints federal judges.
Congress creates agencies and programs, appropriates funds, may override veto, may remove President through impeachment; Senate approves treaties and presidential appointments.
Judges, appointed for life, are free from executive control; courts may declare executive actions to be unconstitutional.
Courts may declare acts of Congress to be unconstitutional.
Congress creates lower courts, and may remove judges through impeachment; Senate approves appointment of judges.
LEGISLATIVE BRANCH
THE CONGRESS
JUDICIAL BRANCH
THE SUPREME COURT and other Federal Courts

Which branch of government appears to have the fewest restraints upon it? What control does this branch exert over the others?

two-thirds vote in each house. Congress can refuse to provide funds requested by the President, or the Senate may refuse to approve a treaty or an appointment made by the President. The President has the power to name all federal judges. Each appointment, however, must be approved by the Senate. The courts have the power to decide the constitutionality of acts of Congress and of presidential actions, and to strike down those found to be unconstitutional.

Head-on clashes between the branches do not often happen. The check-and-balance system operates all the time, however, and in almost routine fashion. The fact that each branch has its several checks, has an impact on much that happens in Washington. The point can be seen time and again.

For example, when the President picks someone to serve in some important office in the executive branch—as Secretary of State or as Director of the FBI or of the CIA—the President is quite aware that the Senate must confirm that appointment. So, quite purposely, the President picks someone who *will* be approved by the Senate. In a similar sense, when Congress makes law, it does so with a careful eye on both the President's

*REINFORCEMENT Use the chart above to illustrate how the principle of separation of powers is affected by the principle of checks and balances, and vice versa.

veto power and the power of the courts to review its actions.

Spectacular clashes—direct applications of the check-and-balance system—do sometimes occur, of course. Thus, the President does veto some acts of Congress. On rare occasion, Congress does override one of those vetoes. Even more rarely, the Senate does reject one of the President's appointees.

These and other direct confrontations are not common. Both Congress and the President, and even the courts, try to avoid them. The check-and-balance system makes compromise necessary. Recall, compromise is a vital part of democratic government.

Over time, the check-and-balance system has worked quite well. It has done what the Framers intended it to do. It has prevented "an unjust combination of the majority." At the same time, it has not very often stalled a close working relationship between the executive and the legislative branches.

A close working relationship has been especially true when the President and a majority in both houses of Congress have been of the same political party. When the other party controls one or both houses, partisan frictions play a larger than usual part in that relationship—as they have in recent years.

Judicial Review

*The judicial branch of government includes the nation's courts. Courts have the power of **judicial review**—the power to decide whether what government does is in accord with what the Constitution provides.

More exactly, judicial review may be defined in these terms: It is the power of a court to determine the constitutionality of a governmental action. In part, then, it is the power to declare **unconstitutional**—to declare illegal, null and void, of no force and effect—a governmental action found to violate some provision in the Constitution. The power of judicial review is held by all federal courts and by most State courts, as well.[3]

[3]Generally, the power is held by all courts of record. These are courts that keep a record of their proceedings and have the power to punish for contempt of court. Usually, only the lowest State courts—justice of the peace courts, for example—are not courts of record.

The Constitution does not provide for judicial review in so many words. Yet the Framers clearly meant that the federal courts, especially the Supreme Court, should have that power.

In practice, the Supreme Court established the power of judicial review in *Marbury* v. *Madison*, in 1803. We shall take a close look at that landmark case in Chapter 18. Since then, the High Court and other federal and State courts have used the power in thousands of cases. Mostly, the challenged governmental action has been upheld. That is, in most cases in which the power of judicial review is exercised, the actions of government are found to be constitutional.

The Supreme Court has not upheld all government actions, however. To date, the Supreme Court has decided more than 130 cases in which it has found an act or some part of an act of Congress to be unconstitutional. It has struck down several presidential and other executive branch actions, as well. It has also voided hundreds of actions of the States and their local governments, including more than 900 State laws.

Federalism

As we know, the American governmental system is federal in form. The powers held by government are distributed on a territorial basis. Some of those powers are held by the National Government and others belong to the 50 States.

The principle of **federalism** came to the Constitution out of both experience and necessity. At Philadelphia, the Framers faced any number of difficult problems, not the least of them: How to build a new, stronger, more effective national government while preserving the existing States and the concept of local self-government.

The colonists had rebelled against the harsh rule of a powerful and distant central government. They had fought for the right to manage their local affairs, without the meddling and dictation of the king and his ministers in far-off London. Surely, they would not now agree to another such government.

The Framers found their solution in federalism. In short, they constructed the federal

*ENRICHMENT Have the class discuss: Did the Framers of the Constitution intend the courts to have the power of judicial review? If not, why?

BUILDING GOVERNMENT SKILLS

Using General Government References

General reference books give you an overview of a topic. This overview can be a summary in written form or in the form of statistical or numerical information.

The books listed below are some of the general references that are useful in studying government. Most of these are available in school and/or local libraries. As you read the descriptions, think of ways that you could use the books for doing class projects or answering questions.

The *United States Government Manual,* published annually by the National Archives and Records Services, is a comprehensive guide to the Federal Government. The *Manual* contains information on all agencies in the legislative, executive, and judicial branches. It lists the address, telephone number, and key officials of each agency. A brief history and description of programs gives you background on the functions and duties with which each agency is charged.

The *Statistical Abstract of the United States,* published annually by the Department of Commerce, is a statistical summary of social, political, and economic facts about the United States. It contains charts, graphs, and tables of numerical information. Among the many subjects covered in the *Abstract* are population, immigration, health and nutrition, law enforcement, defense, and personal income.

The *World Almanac and Book of Facts* is published annually by the Newspaper Enterprise Association, Inc. It contains information about everything from spelling bees and movie stars to heads of foreign states and the Presidents of the United States. It consists of both written and statistical information.

The *Book of States,* published biennially by the Council of State Governments, is a summary of information about each of the 50 States. It includes information on State governments and constitutions, economies, taxes, transportation, elections, and many other topics. Most of the information is presented in tables, but essays introduce each section.

Two more specialized volumes deserve note here. The Congressional Quarterly's *Guide to Congress* and *Guide to the Supreme Court* are excellent sources of information on these two branches of government. Both volumes include a history, description of the structure and function, and summaries of major decisions made by that branch.

Listed below are ten questions. Read each question, then decide which source listed above would be the best to consult first. Write the name of the source on a separate sheet of paper.

1. What is the procedure for amending your State's constitution?
2. What role does the Office of Management and Budget play in the federal executive branch?
3. Who was President Lyndon B. Johnson's Vice President in 1965?
4. What was Babe Ruth's batting average in 1924?
5. Who is the President of France?
6. How many people work for the Department of Commerce?
7. Which Supreme Court decision declared Bible readings in public schools unconstitutional?
8. For how many days do you have to be a resident of your State in order to vote in a presidential election?
9. How many fish hatcheries are maintained by the United States Fish and Wildlife Service?
10. When was the Clean Water Act passed?

arrangement, with its division of powers, as a compromise. It was an alternative to the system of nearly independent States, loosely tied to one another in the weak Confederation, and a much feared, too powerful central government. We shall look at the federal system, at length, in the next chapter.

FOR REVIEW

1. **Identify:** unconstitutional.
2. What is the fundamental purpose of the Constitution of the United States?
3. Upon what six basic principles is the Constitution built?
4. How do each of these basic principles contribute to the Constitution as a "statement of limited government"?

2. Our Changing Constitution: Formal Amendments

As You Read, Think About:

- Why the Constitution has endured and been able to keep up with the change and growth of the American nation.
- How the Constitution may be amended formally.

The Constitution of the United States has now been in force for some 200 years —longer, by far, than the written constitution of any other nation in the world.[4]

In 1789 the young Republic was a small agricultural nation of fewer than four million people, scattered for some 2,100 kilometers (1,300 miles) along the eastern edge of the continent. The 13 States, joined together by horses and sailing ships, struggled to stay alive in a generally hostile world.

Today, the United States has more than 240 million people. Its 50 States stretch across the continent and beyond, and we have many far-flung dependencies and commitments. This country is the most powerful on earth. Our modern, highly industrialized and technological society has produced the highest standard of living any nation has ever known.

How has the Constitution, written in 1787, endured and kept up with that astounding change and growth? The answer lies in this highly important fact: The Constitution of today *is*, and at the same time, *is not* the document of 1787. Many of its words are the same, and much of their meaning remains the same. But some of its words have been changed, some have been eliminated, and some have been added. The meanings of many of its provisions have been modified, as well.

This process of constitutional change, of modification and growth, has come about in two basic ways: (1) by formal amendment and (2) by informal amendment.

Formal Amendment Process

The Framers knew that even the wisest of constitution-makers cannot build for all time. Thus, the Constitution provides for its own **amendment.**

Article V sets out two methods for the *proposal* and two methods for the *ratification* of constitutional amendments. So, there are four different methods of **formal amendments** as shown in the diagram on the next page.

First Method An amendment may be proposed by a two-thirds vote in each house of Congress and be ratified by three-fourths of the State legislatures. Today, 38 State legislatures must approve an amendment in order to make it a part of the Constitution. Twenty-five of the Constitution's present 26 amendments were adopted in this manner.

Second Method An amendment may be proposed by Congress and then ratified by conventions called for that purpose, in three-

[4]The British constitution dates from well before the Norman Conquest of 1066, but it is not a single, written document. Rather, it is an "unwritten constitution," a collection of principles, customs, traditions, and significant parliamentary acts that guide British government and practice.

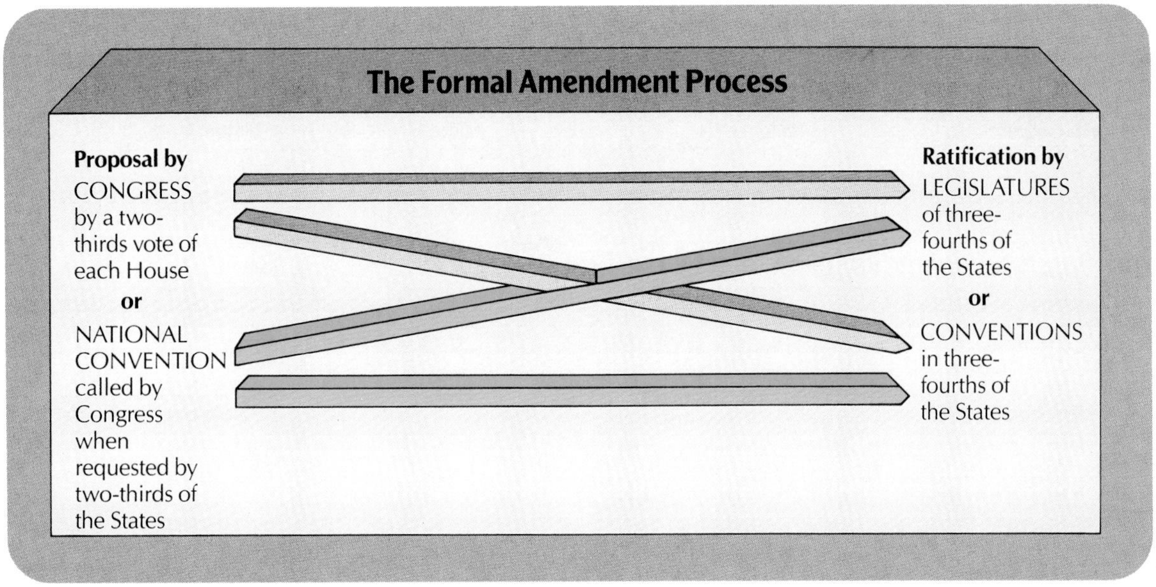

The diagram above illustrates the four different methods of formal amendment. In what way is the formal amendment process an example of federalism?

fourths of the States. Only the 21st Amendment, added in 1933, was adopted in this way.[5]

Third Method An amendment may be proposed by a national convention, called by Congress at the request of two-thirds of the State legislatures (today, 34), and ratified by three-fourths of the State legislatures. To date, Congress has not called such a convention.[6]

Fourth Method An amendment may be proposed by a national convention and ratified by conventions in three-fourths of the States. Remember that the Constitution itself was adopted in much this same way.

[5]The 21st Amendment repealed the 18th, which had established national prohibition. Conventions were used to ratify the amendment largely because Congress felt that their popularly elected delegates would be more likely to reflect public opinion on the question of repeal than would State legislators.

[6]The calling of a convention has been a near thing twice in recent years. Between 1963 and 1969, 33 State legislatures, one short of the necessary two-thirds, sought an amendment to erase the Supreme Court's "one-man, one-vote" decisions; see pages 301, 560. Also, between 1975 and 1987, 32 States asked for a convention to propose an amendment that would require that the federal budget be balanced each year, except in time of war or other national emergency.

The Constitution places only one restriction on the subjects with which a proposed amendment may deal. Article V declares that "no State, without its consent, shall be deprived of its equal suffrage in the Senate."

Note that the formal amendment process emphasizes the federal character of the governmental system. Proposal takes place at the national level and ratification is a State-by-State matter. Also, note that our political theory holds that adoption of an amendment represents the expression of the people's sovereign will.

When both houses of Congress pass a resolution proposing an amendment, it is not sent to the President to be signed or vetoed, though the Constitution would seem to call for it.[7] When Congress proposes an amendment, it is not making law (not legislating).

The practice of sending proposed amendments to the State legislatures rather than to ratifying conventions is sometimes criticized, especially because it permits a constitutional change without a clear-cut expression by the people. The critics lay

[7]See Article I, Section 7, Clause 3. This practice of not submitting proposed amendments to the President is an example of the many "informal amendments" to the Constitution, a matter we shall turn to shortly.

*ENRICHMENT Assign the following for a short report: Choose one of the 26 amendments, and use the diagram on this page to describe the method by which it was added to the Constitution.

Amendments to the Constitution

Amendments	Subject	Year Adopted	Time Required for Ratification
1st–10th	The Bill of Rights	1791	2 years, 2 months 20 days
11th	Immunity of States from certain suits	1795	11 months, 3 days
12th	Changes in Electoral College procedure	1804	6 months, 3 days
13th	Prohibition of slavery	1865	10 months, 3 days
14th	Citizenship, due process, and equal protection	1868	2 years, 26 days
15th	No denial of vote because of race, color, or previous condition of servitude	1870	11 months, 8 days
16th	Power of Congress to tax incomes	1913	3 years, 6 months 22 days
17th	Direct election of U.S. Senators	1913	10 months, 26 days
18th	National (liquor) prohibition	1919	1 year, 29 days
19th	Woman suffrage	1920	1 year, 2 months, 14 days
20th	Change of dates for congressional and presidential terms	1933	10 months, 21 days
21st	Repeal of the 18th Amendment	1933	9 months, 15 days
22nd	Limit on presidential tenure	1951	3 years, 11 months, 3 days
23rd	District of Columbia electoral vote	1961	9 months, 13 days
24th	Prohibition of tax payment as a qualification to vote in federal elections	1964	1 year, 4 months, 9 days
25th	Procedures for determining presidential disability, presidential succession, and for filling a vice presidential vacancy	1967	1 year, 7 months, 4 days
26th	Sets the minimum age for voting in all elections at 18	1971	3 months, 7 days

their arguments on these points: The State legislators, who do the ratifying, are elected to office for a mix of many reasons—party membership; name familiarity; incumbency; their stands on such matters as taxes, schools, welfare programs; and a host of other things. They are almost never chosen because of their stand on a proposed amendment to the Federal Constitution. In fact, many of them may have been elected even before the proposal was submitted to the States. On the other hand, critics claim, the delegates to a ratifying convention would be chosen by the people on the basis of one particular factor: a yes-or-no stand on the proposed amendment.

The Supreme Court has held that a State may not require that an amendment proposed by Congress be approved by a vote of the people of the State before it can be ratified by the State legislature. It made that ruling in a case from Ohio, *Hawke* v. *Smith*, in 1920. But a State legislature can call for an *advisory* vote by the people before it acts, as the Court most recently held in a case from Nevada, *Kimble* v. *Swackhamer*, 1978.

If a State rejects a proposed amendment, it is not forever bound by its vote. That is, it may later reconsider and ratify the proposal. But both the historical precedent and most constitutional scholars agree that the reverse is not true. Once a State has approved an amendment, that action is final and unchangeable.[8]

More than 9,000 joint resolutions calling for amendments to the Constitution have been proposed in Congress since 1789. Only

[8]The Supreme Court has never ruled on this point directly. However, its decisions in related cases indicate that it would hold that a rescision (a State's attempt to rescind, cancel a ratification) presents a "political question"—that is, one to be decided by Congress rather than the courts.

33 of them have been sent to the States. Of those, only 26 have been finally ratified.[9]

We shall take a brief look at each of those 26 Amendments in a moment. But, first, consider this very significant point about those formal additions to the Constitution: As important as they are, they have *not* in fact been especially responsible for the extraordinary vitality of the Constitution. That is, they have not been a major part of the process by which that document has kept pace with 200 years of far-reaching change.

The 26 Amendments

The first 10 amendments were all proposed by Congress in 1789 and ratified by the States in 1791. Each of them arose from the controversy surrounding the ratification of the Constitution itself. Many, including Thomas Jefferson, had agreed to support the Constitution only on the condition that a listing of the basic rights of the people be added to the document immediately.

*Collectively, the first 10 amendments are known as the **Bill of Rights.** They set out the great constitutional guarantees of freedom of expression and belief, of freedom and security of the person, and of fair and equal treatment before the law. We shall look at them, in detail, in Chapters 5 and 6. The 10th Amendment does not deal with civil rights, as such. Rather, it spells out the concept of reserved powers in the federal system.

After decades of bitter struggle, the 19th Amendment in 1920 secured women's right to vote.

The 11th Amendment was added in 1795. It declares that a State may not be sued in the federal courts by a citizen of another State or of a foreign state. The 12th Amendment (1804) made some slight changes in the presidential election process.

The 13th, 14th, and 15th Amendments are often called the Civil War Amendments. The 13th (1865) ended slavery and prohibits most other forms of "involuntary servitude." The 14th (1868) defined American citizenship and granted it to former slaves. It also contains the Due Process and Equal Protection Clauses, which protect basic civil rights from infringement by the States. The 15th Amendment (1870) forbids any restrictions on the right to vote based upon "race, color, or previous condition of servitude."

The 16th Amendment authorizes a federal income tax. The 17th Amendment provides for the popular election of United States Senators. Both were added in 1913. The 18th Amendment (1919) established prohibition.

The 19th Amendment (1920) provided for woman suffrage. The 20th set a new date for

---

[9] Two of the seven unratified amendments were offered in 1789, along with the 10 that became the Bill of Rights. One dealt with the distribution of seats in the House of Representatives, the other with congressional pay. A third, proposed in 1810, would have voided the citizenship of anyone accepting a foreign title or other honor. Another, in 1861, would have prohibited any amendment relating to slavery. A fifth, in 1924, would have given Congress the power to regulate child labor. A sixth one, proclaiming the equal rights of women (ERA), was proposed in 1972, but it fell three States short of ratification and died in 1982. A seventh, to give the District of Columbia seats in Congress, was proposed in 1978; only 16 States ratified it; it died in 1985.

Congress may place "a reasonable time limit" on the ratification process, *Dillon* v. *Gloss*, 1921. It first did so in 1917, when it proposed, and set a seven-year deadline for the approval of, what became the 18th Amendment. Congress wrote that deadline into the Amendment itself (Section 3); and it followed the same practice with the 20th, 21st, and 22nd Amendments. The later Amendments (the 23rd, 24th, 25th, and 26th) also carried seven-year deadlines.

*REINFORCEMENT Discuss with students, using the Bill of Rights on pp. 745–748: The Bill of Rights arose from the controversy surrounding the ratification of the Constitution.

FOCUS ON:

The 26th Amendment and the 18-Year-Old Vote

In 1971, the 26th Amendment extended the right to vote to nearly 11 million Americans between the ages of 18 and 20. Its proposal won nearly unanimous support in Congress, and the States ratified it in only three months and seven days. At the time, many claimed that the youth vote would soon have a major impact on the nation's politics. But, clearly, that has not been the case.

The Census Bureau reports that only half of all eligible voters between ages 18 and 24 said they had voted in the 1972 presidential election. In 1976 and 1980, only about 40 percent did so.

By permission of Johnny Hart and News America Syndicate.

Close to 174 million Americans were of voting age in 1984. Only about 92.6 million actually voted, however. The rate of turnout by age group in 1984 was:

Age Group	Percent Voting
18–20	35.9
21–24	43.8
25–44	58.4
45–64	69.8
65 and over	67.7

1. Why do you think the 26th Amendment was ratified so quickly, in fact, in record-breaking time?
2. Why is the rate of turnout among 18- to 24-year-olds lower than that of any other age group in the population?
3. Where could you find out how many 18- to 24-year-olds voted in the 1984 presidential election?

the beginning of each regular session of Congress and for the inauguration of the President. The 21st Amendment repealed the 18th. Both the 20th and the 21st Amendments were adopted in 1933.

The 22nd Amendment was ratified in 1951. It limits a President to two full terms or not more than 10 years in office. The 23rd Amendment (1961) provides for three presidential electors from the District of Columbia. The 24th Amendment (1964) bars the payment of any tax as a qualification for voting in any federal election.

The 25th Amendment (1967) deals with three matters: presidential succession, a vacancy in the Vice Presidency, and the determination of presidential disability.

The most recent amendment, the 26th, was ratified in 1971. It sets age 18 as the minimum age for voting in all elections in the United States.

FOR REVIEW

1. **Identify:** proposal, ratification.
2. By what two methods may amendments to the Constitution be proposed?
3. By what two methods may they be ratified?
4. How many amendments have been proposed? How many have been ratified?
5. What name is given to the first 10 amendments? Why were they given that name?
6. What were the Civil War Amendments? How did they change the Constitution?

3. Our Changing Constitution: Informal Amendment

As You Read, Think About:

- Why the informal amendment process is the real key to the changing Constitution.
- How the Constitution is amended informally.

For the most part, the Constitution deals with matters of principle and of basic organization and structure. Most of its sections are brief and undetailed, even skeletal in nature.

Because this is so, the real key to constitutional change and development in the United States lies in the process of **informal amendment.** That is, it lies in those many changes that have been made in the Constitution but that have not involved any changes in its written words.

No one can really understand the Constitution itself, let alone the processes of constitutional change, without understanding this important point: There is much—in fact, a great deal—in the Constitution that cannot be seen with the naked eye. Much has been put there, not by formal amendment, but rather by the day-to-day, year-to-year experiences of American government under the Constitution.

*This highly important process of informal amendment has taken place, and continues to occur, in five separate ways: through (1) the passage of basic legislation by Congress; (2) actions taken by the President; (3) decisions of the Supreme Court; (4) the activities of political parties; and (5) custom.

Basic Legislation

Congress has been a major agent of informal amendment in two different ways. First, it has passed many laws to spell out several of the Constitution's brief provisions. That is, Congress has added flesh to the bones of those sections the Framers left purposely skeletal—left for Congress to detail as circumstances required.

Take the structure of the federal court system as an example. In Article III, Section 1 the Constitution provides for "one Supreme Court, and . . . such inferior courts as the Congress may from time to time ordain and establish." Beginning with the Judiciary Act of 1789, then, all of the federal courts, except for the Supreme Court, have been set up by acts of Congress. Or, quite similarly, Article II creates only the offices of President and Vice President. All of the many departments, agencies, and offices in the huge executive branch have been created by acts of Congress.

Second, Congress has added to the Constitution by the way in which it has used many of its powers. For example, the Constitution gives to Congress the expressed power to regulate foreign and interstate commerce.[10] But what is "foreign commerce"? What is "interstate commerce"? What, exactly, does Congress have the power to regulate? The Constitution does not say. In passing thousands of statutes under the Commerce Clause, Congress, however, has done much to define its meaning. In doing so, it has informally amended, or added to, the Constitution.

Executive Action

The manner in which different Presidents have used their powers has also produced several informal amendments. For example, the Constitution states that only Congress may declare war.[11] But it also makes the President the Commander in Chief of the armed forces.[12] Acting under that authority, several Presidents have made war *without* a congressional declaration of war. They have used the armed forces abroad in combat without such a declaration, on no fewer than 150 separate occasions in our history.

Among many other examples that may be cited here is the use of **executive agreements** in the conduct of foreign affairs. An executive agreement is a pact made by the President directly with the head of a foreign state. The principal difference between these agreements and treaties is that they need not be

---

[10]Article I, Section 8, Clause 3.
[11]Article I, Section 8, Clause 11.
[12]Article II, Section 2, Clause 1.

*REINFORCEMENT Use the following question to initiate a class discussion on the process of informal amendment: How can the Constitution, written in 1787, apply to the United States of the 1980s?

PERSONALITY PROFILE

Susan B. Anthony: The 19th Amendment

> It may be delayed longer than we think; it may be here sooner than we expect; but the day will come when man will recognize woman as his peer, not only at the fireside but in the councils of the nation. Then, and not until then, will there be the perfect comradeship, the ideal union between the sexes that shall result in the highest development of the race. What this shall be we may not attempt to define, but this we know, that only good can come to the individual or to the nation through the rendering of exact justice.

Susan B. Anthony, American reformer, advocate of women's rights, abolitionist, and author, was born in Adams, Massachusetts, on February 15, 1820. Brought up by Quaker parents in western New York, she received an education based on Quaker principles. From this religious upbringing, she developed a sense of independence and moral zeal and a belief in the equality of men and women before God.

Anthony's early years were marked by her disappointment in discovering that the only female profession was teaching. Earning less than male teachers added to her dissatisfaction. She began to turn to the reform movements of the day, including temperance, antislavery, and women's rights.

Anthony first crusaded publicly in behalf of temperance. In 1848 she joined the Daughters of Temperance. In 1852, however, when male temperance workers refused to let her speak at a temperance rally, she and others formed the Woman's State Temperance Society of New York. A year later, at the World's Temperance Convention in New York City, women delegates, Anthony included, were refused recognition. Anthony became convinced that voteless and propertyless women could exert little influence in any reform movement.

At this point, Anthony joined the struggle for women's rights. Her decision was based in part on her frustrating experiences in earlier reform movements. Anthony quickly became the prime mover in a series of State and national women's rights conventions.

At the same time, Anthony was an ardent supporter of the abolitionist movement. She maintained close relationships with leading antislavery figures and became the New York representative for William Lloyd Garrison's American Antislavery Society. During the Civil War she also organized the Women's Loyal National League. *

When the 14th Amendment to the Constitution was first proposed, Anthony campaigned for extending the right to vote to all men and women. In its final form, the Amendment referred only to all "male inhabitants." Anthony tried to vote in Rochester, New York, and was arrested.

For the rest of her life, Anthony traveled, lecturing on women's rights. Anthony served as president of the National American Woman Suffrage Association between 1892 and 1900. Although many States began to give women some legal status, full equality was still years away.

Susan B. Anthony died on March 13, 1906. Her death came 14 years before her dream was realized in the "Anthony Amendment," the 19th Amendment providing for full women's suffrage:

> The right of Citizens of the United States to vote shall not be denied or abridged by the United States or by any State on account of sex.

1. What traits contributed to Anthony's success as a reformer?
2. What influence did Anthony's early life have on her convictions?

*ENRICHMENT Point out to students that among Anthony's colleagues were Frederick Douglass, William Lloyd Garrison, and Wendell Phillips. Ask students to identify these men from their study of American history. (2.2) approved by the Senate. They are as legally binding as treaties, however. Recent Presidents have often used them instead of the more cumbersome treaty-making process outlined in the Constitution.[13]

Court Decisions

The courts, most tellingly the Supreme Court, interpret and apply the Constitution in many cases they hear. We have already mentioned several of these instances of constitutional interpretation—that is, informal amendment—by the Court, for example, *Marbury* v. *Madison*, 1803. We shall encounter many more, for the Supreme Court is, as Woodrow Wilson once put it, "a constitutional convention in continuous session."

Party Practices

The nation's political parties have also been a major source of informal amendment.

The Constitution makes no mention of political parties. In fact, most of the Framers were opposed to their growth. In his Farewell Address in 1796, George Washington warned the people against what he called "the baneful effect of the spirit of party." Yet, even as he spoke, parties were developing in this country. They have played a major role in the shaping of government and its processes ever since. Illustrations of that point are almost without number.

Neither the Constitution nor any law provides for the nomination of candidates for the Presidency. From the 1830s on, however, the major parties have held national conventions to do just that. The parties have converted the Electoral College from what the Framers intended into a "rubber stamp" for the popular vote in presidential elections. Both houses of Congress are organized and conduct much of their business on the basis of party. The President makes appointments to office with an eye to party politics. In short, in many ways, government in the United States is government through party.

Custom

Unwritten customs may be as strong as written laws. Many customs have developed in our governmental system.

Again, there are many examples. By custom, not because the Constitution says so, the heads of the 13 executive departments make up the Cabinet, an advisory body to the President.

On each of the eight occasions when a President died in office, the Vice President succeeded to that office—most recently in 1963. Yet, the written words of the Constitution did not provide for this practice until the adoption of the 25th Amendment in 1967. Until then, the Constitution in fact said that the powers and duties of the Presidency—but *not* the office itself—should be transferred to the Vice President.[14]

Both the strength and the importance of unwritten customs can be seen in the reaction to the rare circumstances in which one of them has not been observed. For nearly 150 years, the "no-third-term tradition" was a closely followed rule in presidential politics. It was begun in 1796, when George Washington refused to seek another term as President. In 1940, and again in 1944, however, Franklin Roosevelt broke the custom. He sought and won a third, and then a fourth, term in the White House. As a direct result, the 22nd Amendment was added to the Constitution, in 1951. So, what had been an unwritten custom, an informal amendment, became a written part of the Constitution itself.

FOR REVIEW

1. What is meant by the informal amendment process? Why is this process important to understanding constitutional change?
2. What are the five processes by which the Constitution has been informally amended?

[13]Article II, Section 2, Clause 2.

[14]Read, carefully, Article II, Section 1, Clause 6 and then Section 1 of the 25th Amendment.

SUMMARY

The Constitution is this nation's fundamental law. It sets forth the six basic principles upon which the American system of government rests:

1. *Popular Sovereignty:* The people are sovereign; they are the *only* source for the authority of government.
2. *Limited Government:* Government is not all-powerful; it may do *only* those things the people have given it the power to do.
3. *Separation of Powers:* The basic powers of government (legislative, executive, and judicial) are divided, or separated, among three independent, co-equal branches.
4. *Checks and Balances:* The three separate branches of government are tied together through a complex system of checks, or restraints, each may use against the others.
5. *Judicial Review:* The courts (most importantly, the Supreme Court) have the power to decide the constitutionality of any act of government.
6. *Federalism:* The powers of government are distributed on a territorial basis, between the National Government and the several States.

The formal amendment process is set out in Article V. It provides for four methods. Only two have ever been used, however. To date, 26 amendments have been added.

Informal amendments have also changed the Constitution. Although these amendments have not changed the Constitution's written words, they have enabled it to keep up with the developments of 200 years. Informal amendments have been brought about by (1) basic legislation enacted by Congress, (2) precedent-setting actions by various Presidents, (3) important decisions of the Supreme Court, (4) practices of political parties, and (5) custom.

CHAPTER REVIEW

Key Terms/Concepts*

Constitution (54)
popular sovereignty (55)
limited government (55)
constitutionalism (56)
rule of law (56)
separation of powers (56)
legislative branch (56)
executive branch (56)
judicial branch (56)
checks and balances (56)
judicial review (58)
unconstitutional (58)
federalism (58)
amendment (60)
formal amendment (60)
Bill of Rights (63)
informal amendment (65)
executive agreement (65)

*These terms are included in the Glossary.

Keynote Questions

•• **1.** Identify the six basic principles of the Constitution and explain how each contributes to the establishment of a limited government.

• **2.** What is the difference between a formal and an informal amendment to the Constitution?

• **3.** How do the formal amendment processes reflect the federal character of government in the United States?

• **4.** Which formal amendments deal with: (a) suffrage? (b) civil rights? (c) the President's term of office?

• **5.** Which amendment process—the formal or the informal—has accounted for most constitutional changes? Why?

• **6.** Through what five ways, or processes, have changes occurred in our constitutional system, without changes in the wording of the Constitution itself? Give an example of each.

The dots represent skill levels required to answer each question or complete each activity:
•requires recall and comprehension • •requires application and analysis • • •requires synthesis and evaluation

•• **7.** Find evidence in the chapter to support the statement that "unwritten customs may be as strong as written laws."

Skill Application

Making Inferences: Sometimes an idea is not stated directly in what you are reading, but is implied. You may determine that implied meaning by inference. An inference is not a fact, but is based on fact. For example, in this chapter you read that "Thomas Jefferson had agreed to support the Constitution only if a listing of the basic rights of the people were added to the [Constitution] immediately." From this you can infer that Thomas Jefferson strongly supported the concept of limited government.

Read the 1st through the 5th Amendments to the Constitution. Then read the following statements. From which amendment can you infer each statement?

a. The Government of the United States cannot arrest a reporter for writing an editorial criticizing the government.
b. Property rights and privacy must be respected by the government.
c. To search a house for stolen goods, a police officer must have a warrant identifying the articles sought.
d. Government cannot require any person to attend religious services.
e. Citizens of the United States have a right to try to influence lawmaking.

For Thought and Discussion

••• **1.** How does the President's veto power reflect the principle of checks and balances? If the Constitution were rewritten, would you include this power in the new constitution? Why or why not?

• **2.** On what grounds can it be argued that the first 10 amendments may be viewed as a part of the original Constitution?

•• **3.** The Constitution of the United States has been in force longer than the written constitution of any other nation in the world. For 200 years, it has served as the basis for law and government in the United States. What characteristics of the Constitution, written in 1787, have enabled it to endure and keep up with the change and growth of the nation?

••• **4.** Select a provision of the Constitution that illustrates one of the basic principles of the constitutional system—for example, Congress's power to declare war (Article 1, Section 8, Clause 11), which illustrates the principle of separation of powers. Why was this provision included in the Constitution? If the Constitution were to be rewritten today, would you favor or oppose keeping that provision? Why?

•• **5.** Why do you think the author chose as the title for this chapter "The Living Constitution"?

••• **6.** In your view, is the Constitution too easily amended—either formally or informally?

••• **7.** In *The Federalist* No. 51 James Madison wrote:

> But what is government itself, but the greatest of all reflections on human nature? If men were angels, no government would be necessary.

Restate Madison's comment in your own words. Which provisions of the Constitution seem to be based upon Madison's comment?

Suggested Activities

••• **1.** Prepare a chart or poster to show: (a) the principles of separation of powers and checks and balances; (b) the formal amendment process; and/or (c) the informal amendment process.

••• **2.** Using current news sources, research one of the several current proposals to amend the Constitution—for example, the proposal to permit voluntary prayer in public schools. Why have its proponents offered that amendment? Present your findings to the class.

••• **3.** Locate a copy of your State's constitution and compare its guarantees of rights with the Constitution's Bill of Rights. Make a chart to illustrate the comparison.

••• **4.** Stage a debate or class forum on one of the following: (a) *Resolved,* That the Constitution be amended to permit the people to propose constitutional amendments by popular petition and to adopt or reject such amendments by popular vote; (b) *Resolved,* That the President be denied the power to veto acts of Congress; (c) *Resolved,* That the Supreme Court be deprived of its power of judicial review.

The Constitution, in all its provisions, looks to an indestructible Union, composed of indestructible States.
–CHIEF JUSTICE SALMON P. CHASE
TEXAS V. WHITE (1868)

4

The Nation and the States: Federalism

CHAPTER OBJECTIVES

To help you to

Learn · Know · Understand

The origins and meaning of federalism.

The division of powers in the American federal system, the delegated powers of the National Government, and the reserved powers of the States.

The Supremacy Clause and the Supreme Court in the federal system.

The Constitutional obligations placed on the National Government for the benefit of the States.

Federalism as a dual system.

Interstate relations.

The Statehood process.

RECALL THAT THE authors of the Constitution built their proposals for a new system of government for the United States on the concept of federalism. That is, they invented an arrangement in which the powers of government were to be divided geographically: Some of the powers were to be held by the new National Government and others by the already existing States.

The Framers had to deal with a number of both difficult and highly important problems at the Philadelphia Convention. Among the most prominent and complex of them was this: How could they design a strong, national government with the power to meet the nation's needs and, at the same time, preserve the existing States?

Few, if any, of the Framers favored a strong centralized government on the British pattern. They knew how the people had fought for the right of local self-government. Still, they knew that the government under the Articles (a confederation) was too weak to deal with the nation's difficulties.

Remember, too, that the authors of the Constitution were dedicated to the concept of limited government. They were convinced

Above: President Reagan meets with governors and State legislators to discuss programs which affect federal/State roles and relationships. *Facing page:* A New England town meeting in session, where town residents discuss and vote upon matters of local concern, as the school budget, property tax rates, or zoning ordinances.

that: (1) *any* governmental power is a threat to individual liberty, (2) the use of power must therefore be limited, and (3) to divide governmental power is to restrict it and thus prevent its abuse.

1. Federalism Defined

As You Read, Think About:

- What the major strength of federalism is.
- What the difference is between federalism and democracy.

* A federal system of government is one in which a written constitution divides the powers of government on a territorial basis. The division is made between a central, or national, government and several regional or local governments. Each level has its own area of powers. Neither level, acting alone, can change the basic division of powers the Constitution makes between them. Each level operates through its own agencies and acts directly on the people through its own officials and laws.

In effect, **federalism** produces a dual system of government. It provides for two basic levels of government, each with its own sphere of authority. Each operates over the same people and the same territory at one and the same time.

Federalism's major strength is that it allows *local* actions in matters of local concern while allowing *national* action in matters of wider concern. Local traditions, needs, and desires vary, sometimes widely, from one State to another, and federalism allows for States to make laws according to these differences. Illustrations of the point are nearly endless. To cite but a few: Most forms of gambling are legal in Nevada but are against the law in most other States. New Jersey buses private as well as public school students free of charge, but most States do not. Nebraska is the only State with a one-house,

*ENRICHMENT Using the outline on p. 724, discuss how the concept of federalism was incorporated into the Constitution.

unicameral, legislature. Only in North Carolina does the governor not have the power to veto acts of the legislature. A third of the States are directly involved in the liquor business today, operating it as a public monopoly, but in the other States liquor stores are owned and operated by private enterprise.

The chief advantage of federalism is that it allows and encourages local choice in many matters. It also provides for the strength that comes from union.

National defense and foreign affairs offer useful illustrations of the point. So, too, do domestic affairs. Take, for example, a natural disaster. When a flood, drought, winter storm, or other catastrophe hits some State, the resources of the National Government and all of the other States can be mobilized to aid the stricken area.

The terms *federalism* and *democracy* are not synonymous. Remember: Federalism involves a territorial division of the powers of government. Democracy involves the role of the people in the governing process. Still, it is all but impossible to imagine a democratic government operating over any large area in which a large degree of local self-government is not also present.

FOR REVIEW

1. Describe federalism. How does it differ from democracy?
2. Why did the Framers create a federal system for the United States?
3. How does federalism reinforce the concept of limited government?
4. What is the chief advantage of a federal system?

2. The Division of Powers

As You Read, Think About:

- What three kinds of power are held by the National Government.
- What powers are denied to the National Government.
- What powers are reserved to the States.
- What powers are denied to the States.
- What exclusive powers are held by the National Government.
- What concurrent powers are held by the National and State Governments.

This diagram displays how National and State governmental powers are divided and how they overlap. What powers are denied to both levels of government?

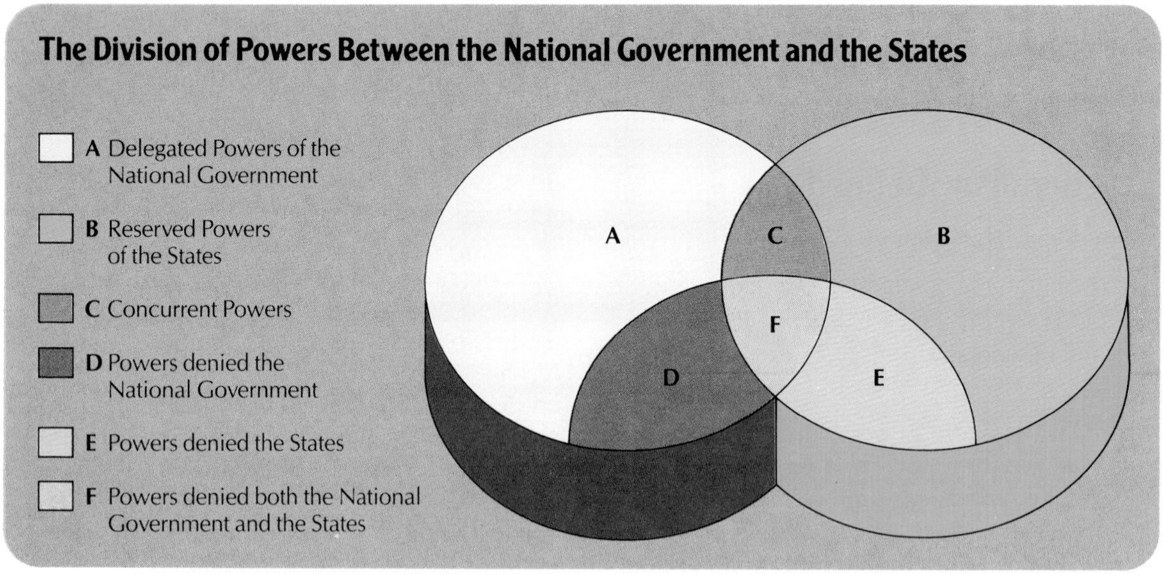

The Constitution sets out the basic design of the American federal system. At base, it provides for a **division of powers** between the National Government and the States. That division was intended (implied) in the original Constitution and then spelled out in the 10th Amendment:

> The powers not delegated to the United States by the Constitution, nor prohibited by it to the States, are reserved to the States respectively, or to the people.

The National Government — One of Delegated Powers

The National Government is a government of **delegated powers.** That is, it has only those powers delegated, or granted, to it in the Constitution. There are three distinct types of delegated powers: the expressed, the implied, and the inherent powers.

The Expressed Powers The **expressed powers** are those delegated to the National Government in so many words—spelled out, expressly—in the Constitution.

Most of them are to be found in Article I, Section 8. There, in 18 separate clauses, 27 different powers are expressly given to Congress. They include, among others, the power to lay and collect taxes, to coin money, to regulate foreign and interstate commerce, to raise and maintain armed forces, to declare war, to fix standards of weights and measures, to grant patents and copyrights, and to do many other things.

Note that several powers are set out elsewhere in the Constitution. Thus, Article II, Section 2 gives several of these powers to the President. They include the power to act as Commander in Chief of the armed forces, to grant reprieves and pardons, to make treaties, and to name major federal officeholders. Article III grants "the judicial power of the United States" to the Supreme Court and to the other courts in the federal judiciary. Several of the expressed powers are also found in various of the amendments to the Constitution; for example, the 16th Amendment gives Congress the power to levy an income tax.

The Implied Powers The **implied powers** are those that are not expressly stated in the Constitution but are *reasonably implied* by those powers that are.

The constitutional basis for the implied powers is to be found in one of the expressed powers. Article I, Section 8, Clause 18 gives to Congress the "necessary and proper" power. The Necessary and Proper Clause reads:

> Congress shall have power . . . to make all laws which shall be necessary and proper for carrying into execution the foregoing powers, and all other powers vested by this Constitution in the Government of the United States, or in any department or officer thereof.

Through congressional and court interpretation, the words "necessary and proper" have come to mean, in effect, "convenient and expedient." Indeed, the Necessary and Proper Clause is sometimes called the Elastic Clause. *

Here are but a few of the thousands of examples of the exercise of implied powers: Congress has provided for the regulation of labor-management relations, the building of hydroelectric power dams, and the building of a 67,200-kilometer (42,000-mile) interstate highway system. Congress has made federal crimes of such acts as moving stolen goods or kidnaped persons across State lines. It has prohibited racial discrimination in access to such places as restaurants, theaters, hotels, and motels. Congress has taken these actions, and many, many more, because the power to do so is reasonably implied by just *one* of the expressed powers. This is the power to regulate foreign and interstate commerce.[1]

The Inherent Powers The **inherent powers** are those that belong to the National Government because it is the national government of a sovereign state in the world community. Although the Constitution does not expressly provide for the inherent powers, the national government has historically

[1] Article I, Section 8, Clause 3. We shall return to the doctrine of implied powers in greater detail in Chapter 13, "The Powers of Congress."

*REINFORCEMENT Why is the Necessary and Proper Clause sometimes called the Elastic Clause? Use this question to initiate a discussion on the delegated powers (see examples on p. 71).

possessed them. It stands to reason that the Framers intended that these powers would be held by the National Government they created.

The inherent powers are few in number. The chief ones include the power to regulate immigration, to deport aliens, to acquire territory, to give diplomatic recognition to other states, and to protect the nation against rebellion or internal subversion.

One can argue that most of the inherent powers are *implied* by one or more of the expressed powers. Thus, the power to regulate immigration is rather clearly suggested by the expressed power to regulate foreign trade. The power to acquire territory can be drawn from the treaty-making power and the several war powers. But the doctrine of inherent powers holds that it is not necessary to go to those lengths to find these powers in the Constitution; these powers exist because the United States exists.

Powers Denied to the National Government

Although the Constitution delegates certain powers to the National Government, it also denies certain powers to it. It does so in three distinct ways.

First, some powers are denied to the National Government *in so many words*—expressly—in the Constitution.[2] Among them are the power to levy duties on exports; to deny freedom of religion, speech, press, or assembly; to conduct illegal searches or seizures; and to deny a speedy and public trial, or a trial by jury.

Second, several powers are denied to the National Government because of the *silence* of the Constitution. Recall, the National Government is a government of delegated powers; it has only those powers the Constitution gives to it.

Among the many powers not granted to the National Government are these: to create a public school system for the nation, to enact a uniform marriage and divorce law, and to set up units of local government. The Constitution says nothing about these matters. It does not give the National Government the power to do any of these things —expressly, implicitly, or inherently. That very silence denies such power to the National Government.

Third, some powers are denied to the National Government because of the nature of the federal system. That is, the National Government cannot be allowed to do those things that would threaten the existence of that system. For example, in the exercise of its power to tax, Congress cannot tax any of the States or their local units in the carrying out of their governmental functions. If it could, it would have the power to destroy, by taxing out of existence, one or more, or all, of the States.[3]

The States — Governments of Reserved Powers

The Constitution *reserves* power to each of the States. The **reserved powers** are the powers held by the States in the federal system. They are those powers not given to the National Government and yet, at the same time, are not denied to the States. Read again the words of the 10th Amendment. *

Thus, Texas, or any other State, may forbid persons under 18 to marry without parental consent or those under 21 to buy liquor. It may require that doctors, lawyers, hairdressers, or plumbers be licensed in order to practice in the State. It may set up public school systems and units of local government, set the conditions under which divorces may be granted, and permit certain forms of gambling and outlaw others.

The sphere of powers held by each of the States is, in a word, huge. They can do all of those things we have suggested and much,

[2]Most of the expressed denials of power are found in Article I, Section 9 and in the 1st through the 8th Amendments.

[3]But note that when a State, or one of its local units, performs a so-called "nongovernmental" function, for example, operating liquor stores, a bus system, a farmer's market, and so forth—it is liable to federal taxes; see page 655.

*REINFORCEMENT Have the class read the 10th Amendment and discuss the reserved powers. Have the class cite specific examples of these powers in use.

Many States have established lotteries to raise needed revenue, thus exercising a reserved power. Here, lottery customers in New York purchase tickets.

much more. They can because nothing in the Constitution forbids them to do so. The National Government can do none of those things because the Constitution does not give it the power to do so. The power to do those things is *reserved* to the States.

Powers Denied to the States

As the Constitution denies certain powers to the National Government, so too do the States face restrictions.

Some powers are denied to the States *in so many words* by the Constitution.[4] For example, no State may enter into any treaty, alliance, or confederation. Nor may a State print or coin money or deprive any person of life, liberty, or property without due process of law.

Some powers are also denied to the States because of the existence of the federal system. Thus, no State or local government may tax any of the agencies or functions of the National Government. Remember, too, that each State has its own constitution—and that document also denies many powers to the State.[5]

Local Government in the Federal System

Government in the United States is very often discussed in terms of three layers: national, State, and local. However convenient this view may be, it is at best misleading. Recall, there are *two* basic levels in the federal system: the National Government and the 50 States.

Of course, governments at the local level exist everywhere in the country. There are over 80,000 units of local government in the United States today. We shall take a close look at them later in this book. For now, keep in mind this important point: All of these

---

[4]Most of the expressed prohibitions of power to the States and, so, to their local governments are found in Article I, Section 10 and in the 13th, 14th, 15th, 19th, 24th, and 26th Amendments.

[5]Study your own State's constitution on this point and note the significance of the words "or to the people" in the 10th Amendment. We shall look at the States' constitutions in some detail in Chapter 19.

The Federal Government regulates many aspects of air travel through its Federal Aviation Agency (FAA). By what power does it have this right?

thousands of local governments are parts —subunits—of the various States.

Each of these local units is located within one of the 50 States. None has an existence apart from its parent State. In its constitution and in its laws, each of the States has created these units. To whatever extent local units can provide services, regulate activities, collect taxes, or do anything else, they do so only because the State has established them and given them the power to so act. In short, as local governments exercise the powers they possess, they are actually exercising State powers.

Another way of stating this is to remind you of a point we first made in Chapter 1: Each of the 50 States has a *unitary* form of government.

The Exclusive Powers

* The **exclusive powers** are those powers that in the federal system may be exercised *only* by the National Government. They include most of the delegated powers.

Some of the powers delegated to the National Government are also expressly denied to the States—for example, the powers to coin money, make treaties, and lay import duties. These powers are *exclusive powers* of the National Government.

Some of the powers given to the National Government but not *expressly* denied to the States are also among the exclusive powers because of the nature of the particular powers involved. For example, the States are not expressly denied the power to regulate interstate commerce. If they were to do so, however, there would be chaos.[6]

The Concurrent Powers

The **concurrent powers** are those that belong to and are exercised by *both* the National Government and the States. They include, for example, the power to lay and collect

[6]The States may not regulate interstate commerce as such. But in using their different powers, they do *affect* it. For example, in regulating highway speeds, the States regulate vehicles not only operating wholly within the State, that is, in intrastate commerce, but also those operating from State to State. Generally, the States may affect interstate commerce, but they may not impose an unreasonable burden on it.

*REINFORCEMENT Draw the diagram on p. 72 on the board large enough for examples of Reserved and Exclusive powers to be written in the spaces, or use the Transparency Master in the *Teacher's Resource Book*. Ask students for examples.

taxes, to define crimes and set punishments for them, and to condemn, or take, private property for public use.

The concurrent powers are not held and exercised *jointly* by the two basic levels of government, but, rather, *separately* and *simultaneously*. To rephrase the definition: The concurrent powers are those powers that the Constitution does not grant exclusively to the National Government and that, at the same time, it does not deny to the States.

FOR REVIEW

1. **Identify:** 10th Amendment, Necessary and Proper Clause.
2. What is meant by the phrase "division of powers"?
3. Why is the National Government properly described as a government of delegated powers?
4. What are the expressed powers? The implied powers? The inherent powers?
5. Why are the States properly described as governments of reserved powers?
6. On what three bases are powers denied to the National Government? To the States?
7. How do local governments fit into the federal system?
8. What are the exclusive powers? The concurrent powers?

3. The Supreme Law of the Land

As You Read, Think About:

- Why in a conflict between State law and national law, national law always takes precedence.
- What the role of the Supreme Court is as umpire in the federal system.

The division of powers in the American federal system is a very complicated matter, as we have seen. This division of powers produces a dual system of government. It is a system in which two basic levels of government operate over the same territory and the same people at the same time.

Such an arrangement is bound to result in conflicts between the two levels, conflicts between national law on the one hand and State law on the other. Realizing that this would be the case, the Framers wrote the Supremacy Clause into the Constitution. Article VI, Section 2 declares:

> This Constitution, and the laws of the United States which shall be made in pursuance thereof, and all treaties made, or which shall be made, under the authority of the United States, shall be the supreme law of the land; . . .

Significantly, Article VI goes on to add:

> . . . and the judges in every State shall be bound thereby, anything in the constitution or laws of any State to the contrary notwithstanding.

The Constitution and the acts and treaties of the United States are "the supreme law of the land." The Constitution stands above all other forms of law in the United States. Acts of Congress and treaties stand immediately beneath it.[7]

In other words, the Supremacy Clause forms a "ladder of laws" in the United States. The Constitution stands on the topmost rung. Then come the acts of Congress and treaties. Each State's constitution, supreme over all other forms of that State's law, stands beneath *all* forms of federal law. State statutes are on the next rung. At the base of the ladder are the different forms of local law: city and county charters and ordinances, and so forth.

The Supremacy Clause has been called the "linchpin of the Constitution," for it joins the National Government and the States into a single governmental unit, a federal state.

[7]Acts of Congress and treaties stand on equal planes with one another. Neither may conflict with any provision in the Constitution. In the rare case of conflict between the provisions of an act and those of a treaty, the more recently adopted takes precedence—as the latest expression of the sovereign people's will. The Supreme Court has regularly held to that position from the first case it decided on the point, *The Head Money Cases,* 1884.

The Supreme Court, the Umpire in the Federal System

The Supreme Court is the "umpire" in the federal system for one of its chief duties is to apply the Supremacy Clause to the conflicts which that dual system of government inevitably produces.

The Court was first called on to play this role—to settle a clash between a national and a State law—in 1819. The case, *McCulloch* v. *Maryland,* involved the controversial Second Bank of the United States. The Bank had been chartered (established) by Congress in 1816. In 1818 the Maryland legislature, hoping to cripple it, placed a tax on all notes issued by its Baltimore branch. James McCulloch, the branch cashier, refused to pay the tax, and he was convicted in the Maryland courts for that refusal.

The Supreme Court unanimously reversed the Maryland courts, however. Speaking for the Court, Chief Justice John Marshall based the decision squarely on the Supremacy Clause:

> If any one proposition could command the universal assent of mankind we might expect it to be this—that the government of the Union, though limited in its powers, is supreme within its sphere of action. . . . [T]he States have no power to retard, impede, burden, or in any manner control, the operation of the constitutional laws enacted by Congress.[8]

It is impossible to overstate the significance of the Court's function—past and present—as the umpire of the federal system. Had the Court not taken this role, it is likely the federal system, and probably the United States itself, could not have survived its early years. Justice Oliver Wendell Holmes made the point in these words:

> I do not think that the United States would come to an end if we [the Court] lost our power to declare an act of Congress void. I do think the Union would be imperiled if we could not make that declaration as to the laws of the several States.[9]

John Marshall, the fourth Chief Justice of the United States Supreme Court, established the principle of judicial review.

FOR REVIEW

1. **Identify:** Supremacy Clause, *McCulloch* v. *Maryland.*
2. Why does federalism necessarily produce a dual system of government?
3. What is the "supreme law in the land"?
4. If a State law conflicts with a national law, which must yield? Is this always true? Why?
5. Why was the Court's decision in *McCulloch* v. *Maryland* of such great importance to the federal system?

[8] The case is also critically important in the development of the constitutional system because, in deciding it, the Court for the first time upheld the doctrine of implied powers. It also held the National Government to be immune from any form of State taxation; see page 648. We shall return to this landmark case at some length in Chapter 13, "The Powers of Congress."

[9] *Collected Legal Papers* (New York: Harcourt, 1920), pp. 295–296. The Supreme Court first held a State law unconstitutional in a case from Georgia, *Fletcher* v. *Peck,* 1810. The Court found that a Georgia law of 1795, making a grant of land to John Peck, amounted to a contract between the State and Peck. It ruled that the legislature's later repeal of that law violated the Constitution's Contract Clause (Article I, Section 10, Clause 1): "No State shall . . . pass any . . . law impairing the obligations of contracts." Since then, the Court has found some 1,000 State laws unconstitutional and upheld the constitutionality of thousands of others.

*ENRICHMENT Have the class discuss: What was John Marshall's contribution to the concept of the "supreme law of the land"?

BUILDING GOVERNMENT SKILLS

Requesting Information from Government Sources

Do you know how to obtain a passport or how to go about starting your own business? Did you ever wonder about living in space? Information about these questions and much more is available in government publications. Federal, State, and local governments publish books, pamphlets, and fact sheets on a wide variety of topics. While some of these publications are available for a modest price, much of this information is free. In many cases, all you have to do is request it.

People request information from the government for many reasons. Some people are curious about a particular government program or agency, such as NASA. Others need to know if they are eligible for government programs, such as college loans. Still others may want information on a particular topic, such as nutrition. Many people depend on government data when conducting research.

Before writing a letter requesting information, pinpoint the nature of your request. The more clearly you state your request, the more likely you are to receive the information you need.

Two paragraphs are usually enough. Include a description of the information you need, and your purpose for asking, if you think it will help clarify your request.

Next, identify the level of government and the agency that would handle your request. Is it a matter for federal, State or local government? If it is federal, look through the index of the *United States Government Manual* to determine which agency would be appropriate. Use the *Manual,* too, to get the address of the agency. If your request is a State concern, use your State's *Manual* to identify the agency and its address. For local government, use your telephone directory. Most letters should be addressed to the Communications or Public Affairs Offices.

1. Look through the text and choose a topic. You may be interested, for example, in arms control, soil conservation, pollution, camping sites in Texas's National Parks, or boat safety regulations in New York Harbor. Determine which level of government and which agency would handle a request about that topic.
2. Write a letter of request to the appropriate agency.

The Government Printing Office

The Government Printing Office publishes thousands of books and pamphlets a year. They range in subject matter from agronomy to zoology.

Specific publications of the Federal Government are listed in *The Monthly Catalogue of the United States Government Printing Office* (GPO). You can order publications by writing to the Superintendent of Documents, Government Printing Office, Washington, D.C. 20402. When ordering a specific publication, be sure to include the publication number and the title.

Selected Titles Published by GPO:

Your Trip Abroad
Food News for Consumers
Current Wage Developments
Soil and Water Conservation Digest
Mariners' Weather Log
For Women: Managing Your Own Business
Medical Support of the U.S. Army in Vietnam
An Illustrated Guide to Electrical Safety
Japan, A Country Study
Vehicle Theft Prevention Strategies
Business Conditions Digest

4. The National Government's Obligations to the States

As You Read, Think About:

- What obligations the National Government has to the States under the Constitution.

The Constitution places several obligations on the National Government for the benefit of the States. Most of them are to be found in Article IV.

Guarantee of a Republican Form of Government

The National Government is required to "guarantee to every State in this Union a republican form of government."[10] The Constitution does not define "republican form of government," and the Supreme Court has regularly refused to do so. The term is generally understood to mean a "representative government," however.

The Supreme Court has held that the question of whether or not a State has a republican form of government is a political question. That is, it is one to be decided by the political branches of the government—the President and Congress—*not* by the courts, as a judicial question.

The leading case here is *Luther* v. *Borden,* 1849. It grew out of Dorr's Rebellion, a revolt led by Thomas W. Dorr against the State of Rhode Island in 1841–1842. Dorr and his followers had written and proclaimed a new constitution for the State.[11] When they tried to put the new document into operation, however, the governor in office under the original constitution declared martial—military—law. He also called on the Federal Government for help. President John Tyler then took steps to put down the revolt, and it quickly collapsed.

[10]Article IV, Section 4.

[11]Recall that Rhode Island had not written a new constitution at the time of independence in 1775; see page 31. Rhode Island's present constitution, which became effective in 1843, came as a direct result of Dorr's rebellion.

The question of which of the two competing governments was the legitimate one in the State at the time was a major issue in *Luther* v. *Borden.* But, again, the Supreme Court refused to decide the matter.

The only extensive use ever made of the republican-form guarantee came in the period after the Civil War. Congress declared that several southern States did not have governments of a republican form. It refused to admit Senators and Representatives from those States until the States had ratified the 13th, 14th, and 15th Amendments and broadened their laws to recognize the voting and other rights of blacks.

Protection Against Invasion and Domestic Violence

The National Government must also "protect each of them [States] against invasion; and on application of the legislature, or of the executive (when the legislature cannot be convened), against domestic violence."[12]

Foreign Invasion Today it is very clear that an invasion of any one of the 50 States would be met as an attack on the United States itself. Hence, this constitutional guarantee is now of little, if any, real significance.

However, that was not the case in the late 1780s. Then, it was not at all certain that all 13 States would stand together if one of them were attacked by a foreign power. So, before the 13 States agreed to give up their war-making powers, each of them demanded an ironclad pledge that an attack on any of them would be met as an attack on all.

Domestic Violence The federal system assumes that each of the 50 States will keep the peace within its own borders. Thus, the primary responsibility for curbing insurrection, riot, or other internal disorder rests with the individual States. However, the Constitution does accept the fact that a State may not be able to control some situations. So, it guarantees protection against domestic violence in each of them.

[12]Article IV, Section 4.

*REINFORCEMENT Divide the class into three groups, representing the above-mentioned obligations. Have each group present examples of how the National Government has met its obligations.

Historically, the use of federal force to restore order within a State has been a rare event. Several instances occurred in the 1960s. When racial unrest exploded into violence in Detroit during the "long, hot summer" of 1967, President Lyndon Johnson ordered units of the Regular Army into the city. He acted at the request of Michigan's Governor George Romney, and only after Detroit's police and firefighters, supported by State Police and National Guard units, found they could not control riots, arson, and looting in the city's ghetto areas. In 1968, again at the request of the governors involved, federal troops were sent into Chicago and Baltimore. State and local forces were aided in putting down the violence that had erupted in those two cities following the assassination of Dr. Martin Luther King, Jr.

Normally, a President has sent troops into a State only in answer to a request from its governor or legislature. But when national laws are being broken, national functions interfered with, or national property endangered, a President does not need to wait for such a plea.[13]

The ravages of nature—storms, floods, forest fires, and the like—can be far more destructive than human violence. Here, too, acting to protect the States against "domestic violence," the Federal Government stands ready to aid stricken areas.

The National Government stands ready to aid disaster victims, as in this California mud slide.

Respect for Territorial Integrity

The National Government is constitutionally bound to respect the territorial integrity of each of the States. That is, the National Government must recognize the legal existence and the physical boundaries of each State.

The whole scheme of the Constitution, its very existence, imposes this obligation. Several of its provisions do so, as well. For example, Congress must include, in both of its houses, members chosen in each one of the States.[14] Acting alone, Congress cannot create a new State from territory belonging to any one of the existing States. To do so, Congress first must have the consent of the legislature of the State involved.[15] Recall that Article V of the Constitution declares that no State can be deprived of its equal representation in the United States Senate without its own consent.

[13]President Grover Cleveland ordered federal troops to put an end to rioting in the Chicago railyard during the Pullman Strike in 1894. At the time, he acted despite the objections of Governor William Altgeld of Illinois. The Supreme Court upheld his actions in *In re Debs*, 1896. The Court found that rioters had threatened federal property and impeded the flow of the mails and interstate commerce. Thus, more than "domestic violence" was involved. Since then, several Presidents have acted without a request from the State involved. Most recently, President Dwight Eisenhower did so at Little Rock, Arkansas, in 1957, and President John Kennedy at the University of Mississippi in 1962 and at the University of Alabama in 1963. In each of those instances, the President acted to halt the unlawful obstruction of school integration orders that had been issued by federal courts.

[14]In the House, Article I, Section 2, Clause 1; in the Senate, Article I, Section 3, Clause 1 and the 17th Amendment.

[15]Article, IV, Section 3, Clause 1.

FOR REVIEW

1. **Identify:** republican form of government, political question.
2. Why has the Supreme Court never defined the term "a republican form of government"?
3. Why does the Constitution obligate the National Government to protect each of the States against foreign invasion?
4. When is the protection against domestic violence to be provided?
5. How (in what sense) does the Constitution require the National Government to respect the territorial integrity of each State?

5. Cooperative Federalism

As You Read, Think About:

- What kinds of aid are given to States by the National Government.
- What kinds of aid are given to the National Government by States.

At its very core, federalism involves a division of governmental powers on a territorial basis. That division is the primary and distinctive characteristic of any government that is federal in form, including our own. As we have seen over the last several pages, the division of powers in the American federal system is a very complicated matter.

Federalism produces a dual system of government in the United States. Two basic levels of government operate over the same territory and the same people—and both at the same time. Given this complex arrangement, it should come as no surprise that competition, tensions, and conflicts are a regular, ongoing part of American federalism. In short, our governmental system may be likened to a tug-of-war—a continuing power struggle between the National Government and the States.

Keep in mind the central importance of the concept of *divided* powers. Add to it this vital point: The American federal arrangement also involves a broad area of *shared* powers. That is, in addition to the two separate spheres of power held and exercised by the two basic levels of government, there are large and growing areas of cooperation between them.

Federal Grants-in-Aid

Perhaps the best-known examples of this intergovernmental cooperation are the many federal **grants-in-aid programs**—grants of federal money or, sometimes, other resources to the States and/or their cities, counties, and other local units. These grants provide those levels of government with the funds often needed to carry out many of their own functions.

The history of these programs can be traced back some 200 years, in fact, to the period before the Constitution. In the Northwest Ordinance of 1787, the Congress under the Articles provided for the government of the territory beyond the Ohio River. Looking forward to new States on that frontier, the Congress set aside sections of land for the support of public education in those future States. On through the 19th century, federal lands were given to the States for a number of purposes—schools and colleges, roads and canals, flood control work, and several others. Most of our major State universities were founded as "land-grant colleges"—schools built out of the sale of public lands given to the States by the Morrill Act of 1862.

Congress began to make grants of federal money quite early, too. In 1808 it gave the States $200,000 to support their militia. Cash grants did not come to play a large role until the Depression years of the 1930s, however. Much of the New Deal program of that era was built around cash grants.

Over the years since then, Congress has set up hundreds of grant programs. In fact, more than 500 of them are now in operation. Dozens of separate programs function in each of many different areas: in education, mass transit, highway construction, health care, on-the-job training, law enforcement, and many, many others.

Grants-in-aid are based on the taxing power. Article I, Section 8, Clause 1 in the Constitution gives Congress that power in order "to pay the debts, and provide for the common defense and general welfare of the United States."

Over time, most grants have been both categorical and conditional. That is, Congress has made them for certain closely defined purposes, and it has set certain conditions that the States must meet in order to receive them. Most often, the major "strings" attached to a grant have required a State to (1) use the federal funds only for the purpose specified, (2) make its own contribution, often of an equal amount, sometimes much less, (3) set up a suitable agency and procedures to manage the grant, and (4) obey the federal guidelines set for the program for which the aid is given.

In effect, the grants-in-aid process blurs the division-of-powers line in the federal system. It permits the Federal Government to operate in many areas in which it would otherwise have no constitutional authority, for example, public education, urban renewal projects, and local mental health programs.

Critics have long made that point in opposing grant programs. Many also object to the narrowly defined, or categorical, nature of most grants. They insist that those factors give Washington too much say in policy matters that they say should be set at the State and local levels.

* ***Block Grants*** To meet this latter objection, some categorical grants have been combined into larger programs. Congress has converted them into **block grants.** These are grants to State and local governments with more broadly defined purposes and fewer strings attached.

By 1982 federal grants-in-aid totaled nearly $95 billion. But the Reagan Administration pushed hard for two major changes: (1) a sharp cutback in overall spending, and (2) the conversion of most programs from a categorical to the block-grant format. As a result, total grant spending has declined over the past few years.

Mayors from U.S. cities meet at the Capitol to collaborate on methods to obtain federal aid.

Revenue Sharing A quite different form of federal money aid, the revenue sharing program, was in place from 1972 to 1987. Under that arrangement, Congress gave an annual share of the huge federal tax-take to the States and their principal local units (cities, counties, townships). Altogether, those "shared revenues" amounted to more than $83 billion over the years that the program was in force.

The revenue sharing program differed from the traditional grants-in-aid approach in a number of ways. Most importantly: (1) no State or local matching funds were involved in revenue sharing, and (2) the shared revenues were given with virtually no strings attached; the monies could be used very largely as the States or their local units chose to use them.

Needless to say, revenue sharing was quite popular with and strongly supported by many governors, mayors, and other State and local officials. It was opposed by the Reagan Administration, however, and it fell victim to the financial needs of the deficit-ridden Federal Government.

Other Forms of Federal Aid

The Federal Government aids the States in several other important ways. Some of the many illustrations are quite well known, for

* Block grants were developed in response to objections concerning categorical grants. Discuss the issue using examples from your State (for example, public education)

FOCUS ON:

Slicing the Federal Aid Pie

The Tax Foundation is a private research organization specializing in tax matters. Each year it compares each State's federal tax burden, that is, the total amount of all federal taxes paid in that State, with the total amount of all federal grants-in-aid received by that State and its local governments.

This map, drawn from the Foundation's most recent study, shows how much money the Federal Government collected in each State for every $1.00 of federal grant money that State received in 1985.

Some States "win" and others "lose" in this comparison of taxes paid to aid received. The amount each State gets back varies from year to year, of course, but only somewhat. The amount received also varies from State to State each year, and sometimes widely. For 1985, Texas was the big "loser." Its taxpayers contributed $1.59 to the federal treasury for every dollar it got back. South Dakota was the big "winner," paying out only 48¢ for each dollar of federal aid.

1. How did your State fare in the ratio of taxes paid to aid received in 1985?
2. Why do some States fare better, and some worse, than others in this ratio?

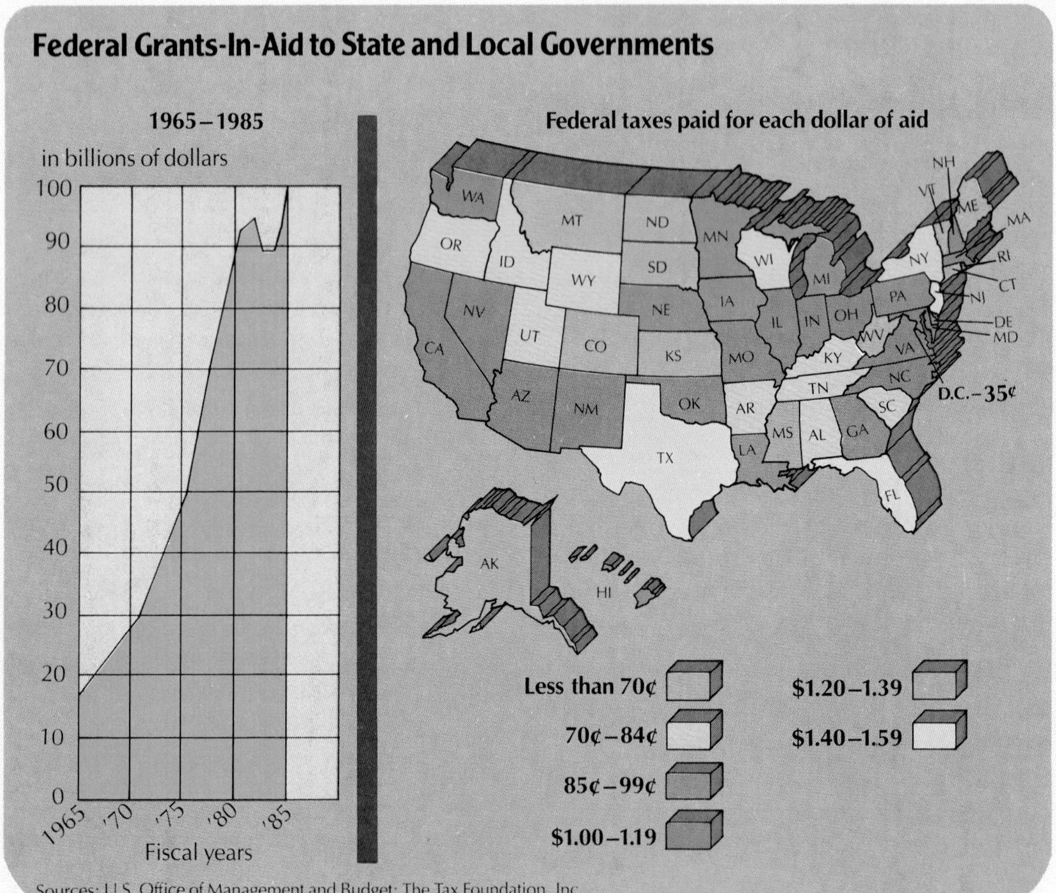

Sources: U.S. Office of Management and Budget; The Tax Foundation, Inc.

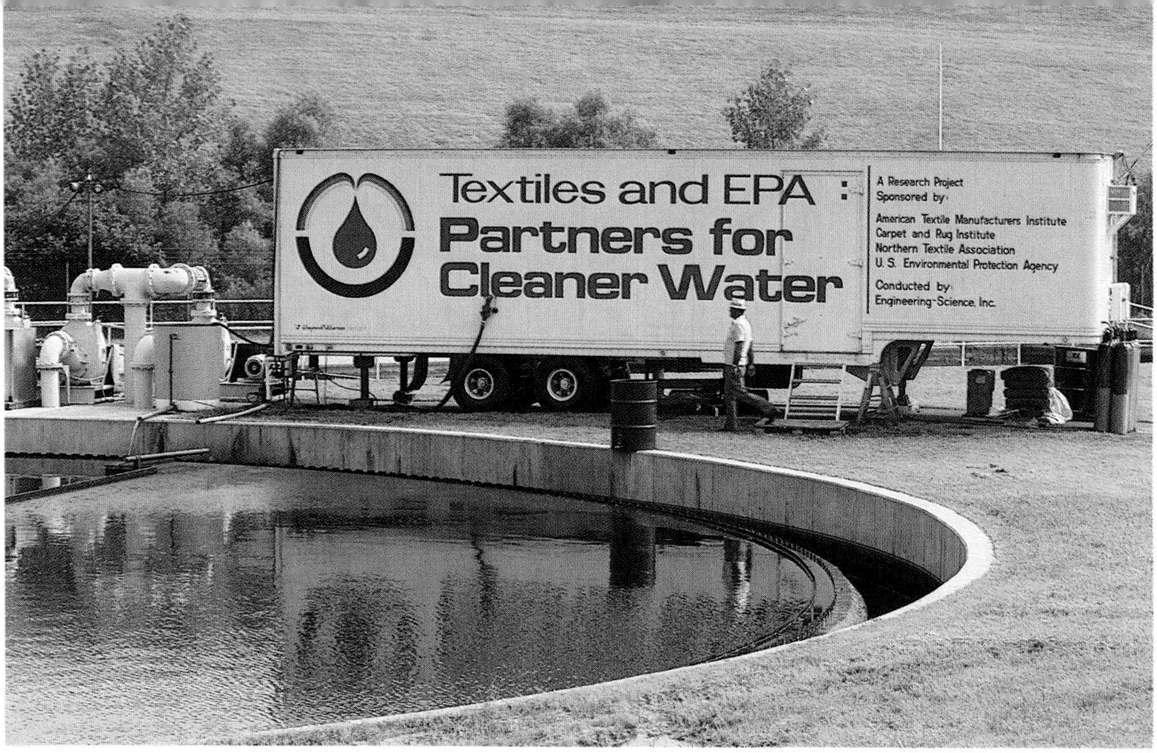

This cooperative venture between the Environmental Protection Agency and the textile industry seeks to overcome the industry's problem with waste water.

example, the FBI's extensive help to State and local police. But many forms of aid are not nearly so visible, for example, "lulu payments." These are federal monies that go to local governments in those areas in which there are large federal landholdings. These direct payments are made *in lieu of* (to take the place of) the property taxes that those local governments cannot collect.

Many other examples can be given. The Army and the Air Force equip and train each State's National Guard units. The Census Bureau's data are essential to State and local school, housing, and transportation officials as they plan for the future, and so on. . . .

State Aid to the National Government

Intergovernmental cooperation is a two-way street. That is, the States and their local units also aid the National Government in many ways. Thus, national elections are conducted in each State by State and local election officials. These elections are financed with State and local funds and are very largely regulated by State laws.

The legal process by which aliens can become citizens, called naturalization, takes place most often in State, not federal, courts. Fugitives from federal justice are often picked up by State or local police officers and then are held in local jails. And, again, on and on. . . . *

FOR REVIEW

1. **Identify:** cooperative federalism.
2. What are federal grants-in-aid? On what grounds do some oppose them? Support them?
3. What was the revenue sharing program? Why did it end?
4. In what ways do the States aid the National Government?

6. Interstate Relations

As You Read, Think About:

- How States cooperate for mutual benefit.
- What the meaning is of the Full Faith and Credit Clause in the Constitution.

Conflict among the States was a major reason for the adoption of the Constitution in 1789. The fact that the new document

*REINFORCEMENT Have the class discuss: What examples of intergovernmental cooperation can be seen in the relationship between their state and the National Government?

Today the New York Port Authority has jurisdiction over the railways, air transport, vehicular traffic, and waterfront facilities for the Port of New York.

strengthened the hand of the National Government, especially in the field of commerce, lessened many of those interstate frictions. So, too, did several of the Constitution's provisions that deal directly with the States' relationships with one another.

Interstate Compacts

* No State may enter into any treaty, alliance, or confederation. The States may, with the consent of Congress, enter into **interstate compacts,** that is, agreements, among themselves and with foreign states.[16]

The States made few compacts until this century—only 26 until 1920. Since then, however, and especially since the mid-1930s, they have been growing in number. New York and New Jersey led the way in 1921 with a compact creating the New York Port Authority to manage and develop the harbor facilities of that great metropolis.

[16]Article I, Section 10, Clause 3. The Supreme Court has held that congressional consent is not needed for compacts that do not "tend to increase the political power of the States," *Virginia* v. *Tennessee,* 1893. But it is often difficult to decide whether an agreement is "political" or "nonpolitical." So, most interstate agreements are submitted to Congress as a matter of course.

Some 200 compacts are now in force, and many involve several States. In fact, all 50 States have joined in two of them: the Compact for the Supervision of Parolees and Probationers and the Compact on Juveniles. Other agreements, many with multi-State membership, cover a widening range of subjects. They include, for example, the development and conservation of such resources as water, oil, wildlife, and fish; forest fire protection; stream and harbor pollution; tax collections; motor vehicle safety; the licensing of drivers; and the cooperative use of public universities.

Full Faith and Credit

The Constitution commands that:

> [f]ull faith and credit shall be given in each State to the public acts, records, and judicial proceedings of every other State.[17]

The words "public acts" refer to the laws of a State. "Records" refers to such documents as birth certificates, marriage licenses, deeds to property, car registrations, and the like. The words "judicial proceedings" relate to

[17]Article IV, Section 1.

*Discuss in class the ways in which the Constitution lessened interstate frictions. Have the students cite current examples.

the outcome of court actions: judgments for debt, criminal convictions, divorce decrees, and so forth.

Suppose that a man dies in Baltimore and leaves a will disposing of some property in Chicago. Illinois must give **full faith and credit**—respect the validity of—the probating, or proving, of that will as a judicial proceeding of the State of Maryland. One may prove age, marital status, title to property, or similar facts by securing the necessary documents from the State where the record was made.

Exceptions The Full Faith and Credit Clause is regularly observed and usually operates in a routine way between and among the States. Two exceptions to the rule must be noted, however. First, it applies only to *civil* matters. One State will not enforce another State's criminal law. Second, full faith and credit need not be given to certain divorces granted by one State to residents of another State.

On the second exception, the key question is always this: Was the person who got the divorce in fact a resident of the State that granted it? If so, the divorce will be accorded full faith and credit in other States. If not, then the State granting the divorce did not have the authority to do so and another State may refuse to recognize it.

The matter of interstate "quickie" divorces has been a troublesome one for years. It has been so especially since the Supreme Court's decision in a 1945 case, *Williams* v. *North Carolina*. In that case, a man and a woman had traveled to Nevada, where each wanted to obtain a divorce so they could marry one another. They lived in Las Vegas for six weeks, the minimum period of State residence required by Nevada's divorce law. They received their divorces, were married, and then immediately returned to North Carolina. But that State's authorities refused to recognize their Nevada divorces. They were brought to trial and each of them was convicted of the crime of bigamous cohabitation.

On appeal, the Supreme Court upheld North Carolina's denial of full faith and credit to the Nevada divorces. It ruled that the couple had not in fact established *bona fide*—good faith, valid—residence in Nevada. Rather, the Court held that through all of this the couple had remained legal residents of North Carolina. The Court thus found that Nevada did not have the authority to grant them divorces.

A divorce granted by a State court to a *bona fide* resident of that State must be given full faith and credit in all other States. To become a legal resident of a State, a person must intend to reside there permanently, or at least indefinitely. Clearly, the Williamses had not intended to do so.

The *Williams* case, and later ones, cast dark clouds of doubt over the validity of thousands of other interstate divorces. The later marriages of persons involved in them and/or the frequently tangled estate problems produced by their deaths suggest the confused and serious nature of the matter.

Extradition

According to the Constitution:

> A person charged in any State with treason, felony, or other crime, who shall flee from justice, and be found in another State, shall, on demand of the executive authority of the State from which he fled, be delivered up, to be removed to the State having jurisdiction of the crime.[18]

The practice of **extradition**—interstate rendition—is designed to prevent an accused or convicted person from escaping justice by leaving a State. The return of a fugitive is usually a routine matter. Sometimes, however, a governor does refuse to surrender someone, and there the matter ends. Ever since *Kentucky* v. *Dennison,* in 1861, the Supreme Court has held that a governor cannot be forced to act in an extradition case. So, the Constitution's word "shall" here must be read as "may."

---

[18]Article IV, Section 2, Clause 2. Extradition has been carried on between sovereign states for centuries. The word *extradition* is the term popularly used in the United States for what is technically known in the law as interstate rendition.

Instances of a governor's refusal to extradite are not common, but they do happen. In a fairly typical case, in 1978, Governor William Milliken of Michigan refused to return a woman to Alabama. She had been convicted of bank robbery there in 1942. Although her part in the crime had been a largely unknowing one, she was sentenced to 30 years in prison. She escaped in 1952, made her way to Detroit, and had lived there ever since. Governor Milliken refused to extradite her because, in his view, her 1942 punishment had been too severe. He felt, too, that she had long since paid for her crime.

Privileges and Immunities

The Constitution provides:

> The citizens of each State shall be entitled to all privileges and immunities of citizens of the several States.[19]

In short, this means that a resident of one State will not be discriminated against *unreasonably* by another State.

The courts have never given a full list of the privileges and immunities of "interstate citizenship." These are some of them: the right to pass through or reside in any other State for the purpose of trade, agriculture, professional pursuits, or otherwise; the right to use the courts; to make contracts; to buy, own, rent, and sell property; and to marry.

Of course, the provision does not mean that a resident of one State need not obey the laws of another State while in that State. Nor does it mean that a State may not make *reasonable* discrimination against residents of other States. Thus, any State can require that a person live in that State for a certain time before he or she can vote or hold any public office. A State may also require a period of residence within that State before it grants a person a license to practice law, medicine, dentistry, and so on.

The wild fish and game in a State are the common property of the people of that State. So, nonresidents can be asked to pay higher fees for fishing or hunting licenses than those paid by residents who pay taxes to provide fish hatcheries, enforce game laws, and so on. By the same token, a State university often charges higher tuition to students from other States than it does to residents.

[19]Article IV, Section 2, Clause 1; the provision is reinforced in the 14th Amendment.

FOR REVIEW

1. **Identify:** interstate compacts, Privileges and Immunities Clause.
2. What agreements does the Constitution prohibit the States from making?
3. What, in brief, does each of the following clauses provide for: (a) the Full Faith and Credit Clause? (b) the Extradition Clause?

7. The Admission of New States

As You Read, Think About:

- How new States are admitted to the Union.

Only Congress has the power to admit new States to the Union. The Constitution places only one restriction on that power. A new State may not be created by taking territory from one or more of the existing States without the consent of the legislature(s) of the State(s) involved.[20]

Congress has admitted 37 States since the original 13 formed the Union. Five States—Vermont, Kentucky, Tennessee, Maine, and West Virginia—were created from parts of already existing States. Texas was an independent republic before admission. California was admitted after being ceded to the United States by Mexico. Each of the other

[20]Article IV, Section 3, Clause 1. Some argue that this provision was violated with West Virginia's admission in 1863. That State was formed from the 40 western counties that had broken away from Virginia over the issue of secession from the Union. The consent required by the Constitution was given by a minority of the members of the Virginia legislature—those who represented the 40 western counties. Congress accepted their action, holding that they were the only group legally capable of acting as the Virginia legislature at the time.

30 States entered the Union only after a period of time, frequently more than 15 years, as an organized territory.

Admission Procedure

The process of admission is usually simple. The area desiring Statehood first petitions, or applies to, Congress for admission. If and when it is approved, Congress passes an **enabling act,** which directs the framing of a proposed State constitution. After the constitution has been prepared by a convention and approved by a popular vote, it is submitted to Congress. If Congress still agrees to statehood, it passes an **act of admission.**

The two newest States, Alaska and Hawaii, abbreviated the usual process. Each adopted a proposed constitution without waiting for an enabling act: Alaska in 1956 and Hawaii in 1950.

Conditions for Admission

Before finally admitting a new State, Congress has often set certain conditions. In 1896 Utah was admitted on the condition that its constitution outlaw polygamy. In the act admitting Alaska to the Union in 1959,

Locate the current territories of the United States on the map below. What is the process that would allow each to become a State?

Territorial Expansion of the United States and Acquisitions of Other Principal Areas

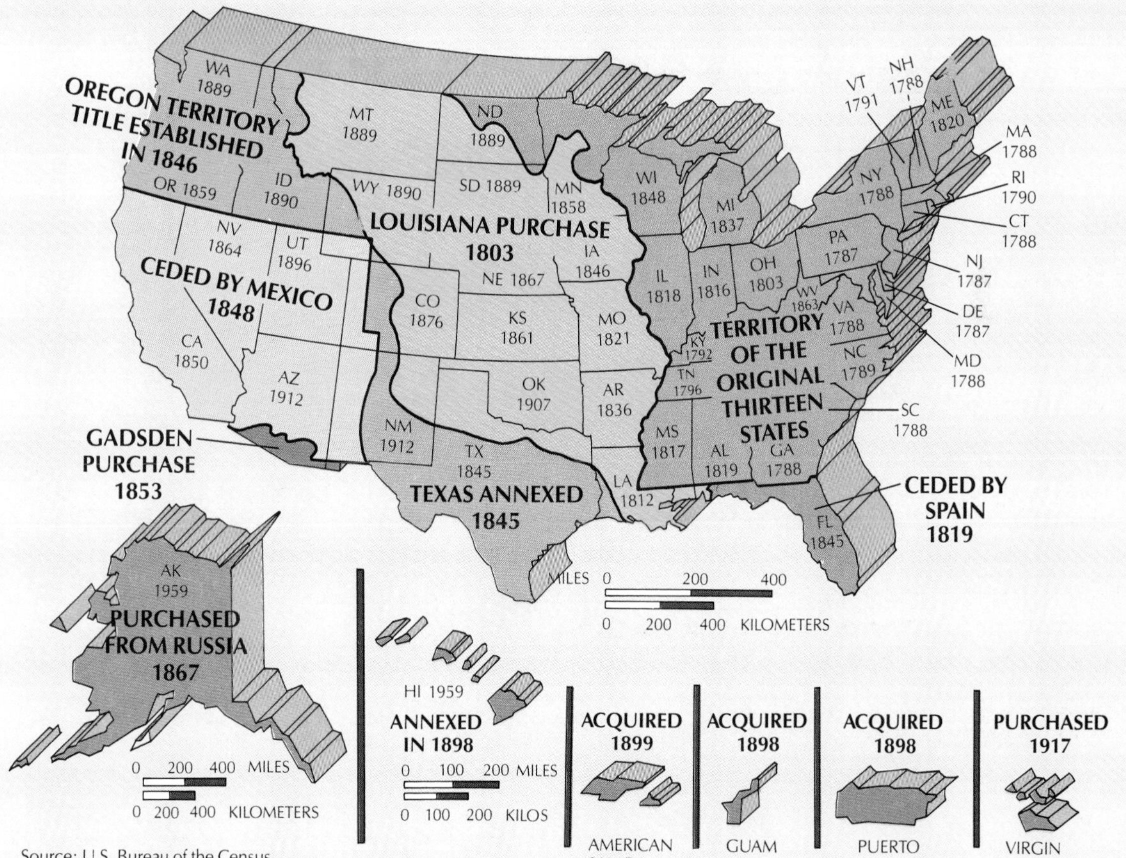

Source: U.S. Bureau of the Census

*REINFORCEMENT Trace the path that a territory follows to become a State, highlighting an enabling act, an act of admission, and the conditions imposed for admission.

ORIGIN AND ADMISSION OF THE 50 STATES

Order of Admission	Source of State Lands	Organized as Territory	Admitted as State
Delaware	Swedish Charter, 1638; English Charter, 1683	. . .	7 Dec. 1787*
Pennsylvania	English Grant, 1680	. . .	12 Dec. 1787*
New Jersey	Dutch Settlement, 1623; English Charter, 1664	. . .	18 Dec. 1787*
Georgia	English Charter, 1732	. . .	2 Jan. 1788*
Connecticut	English Charter, 1662	. . .	9 Jan. 1788*
Massachusetts	English Charter, 1629	. . .	6 Feb. 1788*
Maryland	English Charter, 1632	. . .	28 Apr. 1788*
South Carolina	English Charter, 1663	. . .	23 May 1788*
New Hampshire	English Charter, 1622 and 1629	. . .	21 June 1788*
Virginia	English Charter, 1609	. . .	25 June 1788*
New York	Dutch Settlement, 1623; English control, 1664	. . .	26 July 1788*
North Carolina	English Charter, 1663	. . .	21 Nov. 1789*
Rhode Island	English Charter, 1663	. . .	29 May 1790*
Vermont	Lands of New York and New Hampshire	**	4 Mar. 1791
Kentucky	Lands of Virginia	**	1 June 1792
Tennessee	Lands of North Carolina	**	1 June 1796
Ohio	Lands of Virginia; Northwest Territory, 1787	13 July 1787	1 Mar. 1803
Louisiana	Louisiana Purchase, 1803	24 Mar. 1804	30 Apr. 1812
Indiana	Lands of Virginia; Northwest Territory, 1787	7 May 1800	11 Dec. 1816
Mississippi	Lands of Georgia and South Carolina	17 Apr. 1798	10 Dec. 1817
Illinois	Lands of Virginia; Northwest Territory, 1787	3 Feb. 1809	3 Dec. 1818
Alabama	Lands of Georgia and South Carolina	3 Mar. 1817	14 Dec. 1819
Maine	Lands of Massachusetts	**	15 Mar. 1820
Missouri	Louisiana Purchase, 1803	4 June 1812	10 Aug. 1821
Arkansas	Louisiana Purchase, 1803	2 Mar. 1819	15 June 1836
Michigan	Lands from Virginia; Northwest Territory, 1787	11 Jan. 1805	26 Jan. 1837
Florida	Ceded by Spain, 1819	30 Mar. 1822	3 Mar. 1845
Texas	Republic of Texas, 1845	**	29 Dec. 1845
Iowa	Louisiana Purchase, 1803	12 June 1838	28 Dec. 1846
Wisconsin	Lands of Michigan; Northwest Territory, 1787	20 Apr. 1836	29 May 1848
California	Ceded by Mexico, 1848	**	9 Sept. 1850
Minnesota	Northwest Territory, 1787; and Louisiana Purchase, 1803	3 Mar. 1849	11 May 1858
Oregon	Louisiana Purchase, 1803; Treaty with Spain, 1819, and Treaty with Great Britain, 1846	14 Aug. 1848	14 Feb. 1859
Kansas	Louisiana Purchase, 1803; and lands from Texas	30 May 1854	29 Jan. 1861
West Virginia	Part of Virginia to 1863	**	20 June 1863
Nevada	Ceded by Mexico, 1848	2 Mar. 1861	31 Oct. 1864
Nebraska	Louisiana Purchase, 1803	30 May 1854	1 Mar. 1867
Colorado	Louisiana Purchase, 1803	28 Feb. 1861	1 Aug. 1876
South Dakota	Louisiana Purchase, 1803	2 Mar. 1861	2 Nov. 1889
North Dakota	Louisiana Purchase, 1803	2 Mar. 1861	2 Nov. 1889
Montana	Louisiana Purchase, 1803	26 May 1864	8 Nov. 1889
Washington	Louisiana Purchase, 1803; Treaty with Great Britain, 1846	2 Mar. 1853	11 Nov. 1889
Idaho	Louisiana Purchase, 1803; and Oregon Territory	3 Mar. 1863	3 July 1890
Wyoming	Louisiana Purchase, 1803	25 July 1868	10 July 1890
Utah	Ceded by Mexico, 1848	9 Sept. 1850	4 Jan. 1896
Oklahoma	Louisiana Purchase, 1803	2 May 1890	16 Nov. 1907
New Mexico	Ceded by Mexico, 1848	9 Sept. 1850	6 Jan. 1912
Arizona	Ceded by Mexico, 1848; Gadsden Purchase, 1853	24 Feb. 1863	14 Feb. 1912
Alaska	Territory, Purchased from Russia, 1867	24 Aug. 1912	3 Jan. 1959
Hawaii	Territory, Annexed 1898	14 June 1900	21 Aug. 1959

*Date of ratification of U.S. Constitution **No territorial status before admission to the Union

Hawaii's long struggle to become a State began in 1919 with the introduction of its first statehood bill. Hawaii was finally admitted into the Union in 1959.

the State was forever prohibited from claiming title to any lands legally held by an Indian, Eskimo, or Aleut.

Each State enters the Union on an equal footing with each of the other States. Thus, although Congress can set conditions like those just described, it *cannot* impose conditions of a political nature. For example, when Oklahoma was admitted in 1907, Congress said the State could not remove its capitol from Guthrie to any other place before 1913. In 1910, however, the legislature moved the capital to Oklahoma City. When this step was challenged, the Supreme Court in *Coyle* v. *Smith,* 1911, held that Congress may set conditions for admission. *But,* held the Court, the conditions cannot be *enforced* when they compromise the independence of a State to manage its own internal affairs.

Consider one more example here: President William Howard Taft vetoed a resolution to admit Arizona in 1911 because its proposed constitution provided that judges could be recalled (removed from office) by popular vote. This meant, said Taft, that a judge would have to keep but one eye on the law and the other on public opinion.

The recall section was then taken out of the document. In 1912 Congress passed, and the President signed, another act of admission for Arizona. Almost immediately, the new State amended its new constitution to provide for the recall of judges. That provision remains today. *

FOR REVIEW

1. Which branch of government has the exclusive power to admit new States to the Union?
2. Which States were created from already existing States? What State was an independent republic before its admission to the Union?

*REINFORCEMENT Have the class discuss: Did Arizona have the right to amend its constitution to provide for the recall of judges? Why or why not?

SUMMARY

The Constitution created a federal system —one based on a division of powers between the National Government and the States.

The National Government has only those powers delegated to it by the Constitution. Its delegated powers are of three kinds: (1) the expressed powers—those delegated in so many words by the Constitution; (2) the implied powers —those reasonably implied by the expressed powers; and (3) the inherent powers—those that belong to, or inhere in, the National Government because it is a sovereign state. The Constitution also denies certain powers to the National Government. It does so in three ways: (1) expressly; (2) by its silence; and (3) as a result of its creation of a federal system.

The States possess the reserved powers —those not delegated to the National Government and not denied to the States by the Constitution. The States are denied certain powers —expressly by the Constitution, by the existence of the federal system, and by their own constitutions. Local governments are created by their States and have no legal existence apart from them.

The exclusive powers are those that belong only to the National Government. Concurrent powers are those held by both the National Government and the States simultaneously.

The Constitution, acts of Congress in accord with it, and treaties made under its authority are the "supreme law of the land." No form of State law may validly conflict with that supreme law. The Supreme Court fills a crucial role as the umpire in the federal system.

The Constitution places certain obligations on the National Government with regard to the States. It must guarantee to each State a republican form of government, protect each of them against foreign invasion and domestic violence, and respect the territorial integrity of each of them.

The States and the National Government cooperate with one another in many ways, from grants-in-aid programs to election administration and law enforcement.

The Constitution imposes order on interstate relations through the Full Faith and Credit Clause, the Extradition Clause, and the Privileges and Immunities Clauses. The States may, with the consent of Congress, enter into compacts among themselves.

New States may be admitted to the Union only by Congress, as 37 have thus far.

CHAPTER REVIEW

Key Terms/Concepts*

federalism (72)
division of powers (73)
delegated powers (73)
expressed powers (73)
implied powers (73)
inherent powers (73)
reserved powers (74)
exclusive powers (76)
concurrent powers (76)
grants-in-aid programs (82)
block grant (83)
interstate compacts (86)
Full Faith and Credit Clause (87)
extradition (87)
enabling act (89)
act of admission (89)

*These terms are included in the Glossary.

Keynote Questions

• 1. Explain how federalism creates a dual system of government.

• 2. What is the difference between division of powers and separation of powers?

• 3. What powers does the Constitution assign to the States in the federal system? What does the 10th Amendment provide?

• 4. On what three bases does the Constitution deny powers to: (a) the National Government? (b) the States?

• 5. What is the Supremacy Clause and why is it important?

The dots represent skill levels required to answer each question or complete each activity: • requires recall and comprehension • • requires application and analysis • • • requires synthesis and evaluation

• **6.** Who or what is the "umpire" in the federal system? Why must that role be performed?
• **7.** What obligations does the Constitution impose upon the National Government with regard to the States?
• **8.** What are: (a) federal grants-in-aid? (b) categorical grants? (c) block grants?
• **9.** How does revenue sharing differ from the federal grants-in-aid programs?
• **10.** List four examples of concerns that have prompted the States to form interstate compacts.
• **11.** Explain why each of the following clauses is important to interstate relations: (a) the Full Faith and Credit Clause; (b) the Extradition Clause; and (c) the Privileges and Immunities Clause.
• **12.** Describe in a paragraph the conditions and admission procedures for a new State to enter the Union.

Skill Application

Classifying: Classifying is organizing data into categories by topics. Classifying helps you to remember information and to understand how it is related. For example, the Constitution grants some powers only to the National Government. Among these are the powers to make treaties, coin money, and tax imports. These powers are classified as exclusive powers. The powers held only by the States are classified as reserved powers. The powers shared by the National Government and the States are classified as concurrent powers. By classifying the powers, comparing and contrasting are easier.

Listed below are examples of several government activities. On a separate sheet of paper make a table with the following headings: *Federal, State/Local,* and *Both*. Classify each government activity by writing it in the appropriate column on your paper.

a. Issues driver's licenses.
b. Decides on length of school year.
c. Maintains a navy.
d. Cleans up water pollution in rivers and lakes.
e. Declares war.
f. Taxes individual and corporate income.
g. Sets up the process for administering public elections.

For Thought and Discussion

•• **1.** Why might a governor be reluctant to call for federal aid during a time when domestic violence broke out in a city in his or her State?
•• **2.** Why do the war powers and the foreign relations powers belong only to the National Government? The power to regulate interstate commerce? The power to coin money? The power to raise and maintain armed forces?
••• **3.** In the chapter opening, you read Chief Justice Salmon Chase's comment:

> The Constitution, in all its provisions, looks to an indestructible Union composed of indestructible States.

Why do you think Justice Chase used the term "indestructible"? What features of the Constitution provide for an "indestructible Union" and "indestructible States"?
•• **4.** The Constitution (Article I, Section 10, Clause 3) forbids the States to "engage in war." But there is a qualification to this prohibition. Why?
5. What do you think conditions might be like in what is now the United States if no federal system had been created and the 13 States had tried to continue under the Articles of Confederation?
•• **6.** Read again page 82 about federal grants-in-aid programs. How might guidelines imposed by grants-in-aid programs cause some friction between a State and the Federal Government?

Suggested Activities

•• **1.** Using current newspapers and periodicals, find examples of each of the types of power and denials of power shown in the diagram on page 72.
••• **2.** Write a letter to your State Budget Director's office. (See *State Blue Book* for address and title.) Request a copy of the current budget for your State. Find out how much money your State receives in federal grants. Which types of projects are most heavily funded: those for education, housing, or highways? What other types of programs receive federal grants? Share your findings with your class.
••• **3.** Prepare an illustrated report on the history of your State's admission to the Union.

Unit 2

The Unalienable Rights

IN UNIT 1 of this book, we considered the basic ideas, the concepts, on which democratic government in the United States is founded. Those basic concepts include a belief in the *fundamental worth and dignity of each and every individual* and in the *equality* of *all* persons. They include faith in the principle of *majority rule* and, at the same time, *respect for minority rights*. They also include recognition of the *necessity of compromise* in the making of public policy decisions. Finally, they include an insistence on the *widest possible area of freedom for the individual.*

To preach freedom is easy; to practice it with justice is much more difficult. Critics of American democracy are fond of telling us that we do not always practice what we preach.

The critics are right only to a point, however. We may not always succeed, but We, the People of the United States, have come closer to the realization of democracy in practice than have the people of any other nation.

Unit 2 illustrates this point. In its two chapters, we examine and discuss the rights guaranteed to all Americans by the Constitution. We also see how these guarantees have been applied and extended in practice, especially by court decisions and by laws passed by the Congress.

The Constitution stresses the unparalleled importance of freedom for the individual in this country. Unit 2 shows how that emphasis has been, and is still being, translated into fact.

Inscribed over the entrance to the Supreme Court Building is this motto: "Equal Justice Under Law."

The God who gave us life gave us liberty at the same time.
–THOMAS JEFFERSON

5 Civil Rights: Fundamental Freedoms

CHAPTER OBJECTIVES

To help you to

Learn · Know · Understand

The fundamental importance of the many constitutional guarantees of civil rights and their relationship to the concept of limited government.

The right to freedom of expression as the basis of a free society.

The 1st and 14th Amendments protect free speech and a free press.

The rights of the government to protect itself and the nation.

The essential meaning of the freedom of assembly and petition.

THE UNITED STATES was born out of a struggle for freedom. Those who founded this country loved liberty and prized it above all earthly possessions. For them, freedom for their country and freedom for the individual were the greatest of blessings that Providence could bestow. In proclaiming independence, they declared:

> We hold these truths to be self-evident, that all men are created equal, that they are endowed by their Creator with certain unalienable Rights, that among these are Life, Liberty and the pursuit of Happiness.

In the very next line of the Declaration of Independence, they added:

> That to secure these rights, Governments are instituted among Men . . .

Later, the Framers of the Constitution repeated this justification for the existence of government. The Preamble to the Constitution declares:

> We the People of the United States, in Order to . . . secure the Blessings of Liberty to ourselves and our Posterity, do ordain and establish this Constitution for the United States of America.

Under our democratic government, peaceable opposition to government policy is both protected and encouraged. *Above:* Demonstrators march past the White House. *Facing Page:* The Jefferson Memorial's statue of Thomas Jefferson, the great American statesman, drafter of the Declaration of Independence, and a renowned proponent of liberty.

1. Our System of Civil Rights

As You Read, Think About:

- Why guarantees of civil rights were included in the Constitution.
- How the courts function as guardians of the people's civil liberties.
- Why it is impossible to list all the rights that people have in the United States.
- Why the Due Process Clause of the 14th Amendment is so important.

In this chapter, and the one to follow, we *shall take a close look at each of the many civil rights held by the American people. Before we can do that, however, there are several things you must understand about the overall nature of those guarantees. Some of these matters are quite complicated, but they are also necessary to a real understanding of civil rights in the United States.

Civil Rights and the Principle of Limited Government

From its very beginnings, government in the United States has been firmly based on the concept of **limited government.** Limited government rests on the principle that government has *only* those powers the sovereign people have given to it.

This fact—that government can do only what the people have given it the authority to do—is nowhere better illustrated than in the field of civil rights. The Constitution is studded with guarantees of personal freedom—that is, with prohibitions and restrictions on the power of government to act.

All governments have and use authority over individuals. The all-important difference between a democratic government and a dictatorial one lies in the *extent* of that authority. In a dictatorship it is practically unlimited. In the Soviet Union, for example,

*REINFORCEMENT Ask the class to discuss the term "civil rights" and its effects on their daily lives.

opposition to the government is put down as a matter of course, and often harshly. Even such forms of expression as art, music, and literature must glorify the state. In the United States, on the other hand, governmental authority is closely limited. Peaceable opposition to government is not only allowed, it is encouraged. As Justice Robert H. Jackson once put that point:

> If there is any fixed star in our constitutional constellation, it is that no official, high or petty, can prescribe what shall be orthodox in politics, nationalism, religion, or any other matter of opinion or force citizens to confess by word or act their faith therein.[1]

Historical Background

As we noted in Chapter 2, our system of **civil rights** guarantees is one of the major elements of our English heritage. Over the centuries, the English people had waged a continuing struggle for individual liberties. The early colonists brought a dedication to that cause with them to America.

That commitment to freedom quickly took root and flourished. The Revolutionary War was fought to preserve and to expand the rights of the individual against government. The very first State constitutions contained long lists of the rights held by the people.

The National Constitution, as it was written at Philadelphia, contained a number of important civil rights guarantees—notably in Article I, Sections 9 and 10 and in Article III. Unlike many of the first State documents, however, it did not include a bill of rights, a general listing of the rights of the people.

The outcry that omission raised was so marked that several of the States ratified the original Constitution only with the understanding that such a listing be immediately added. The first session of Congress in 1789 met that demand with a series of proposed amendments. Ten of them, the **Bill of Rights,** were ratified by the States and became a part of the Constitution on December 15, 1791. Later amendments, especially the 13th and the 14th, have added to the Constitution's guarantees of personal freedom.

The Courts and Civil Rights

In the United States, the courts—and, especially, the Supreme Court of the United States—stand as the major guardian of individual liberties. *All* officers and agencies of government—executive and legislative, national and State and local—are also supposed to protect the people's rights. But it is the courts that must *interpret* and *apply* the constitutional guarantees whenever an individual claims that government has violated his or her liberty.

The fact that the courts do stand guard over our civil rights does *not* mean that we, the people, or any one of us, can sit back in assured safety. Nor does the fact that the National Constitution and each of the State constitutions set out long lists of basic rights mean that those rights have been so firmly established that they are ours forever. To preserve and protect those guarantees, each generation must learn and understand them

The right of free speech, whereby individuals are free to urge changes in public opinion or government policy, is a vital one in a democracy.

[1] In *West Virginia Board of Education* v. *Barnette*, 1943; see page 111.

anew, and be willing to fight for them, when necessary. The late Learned Hand, one of our great jurists, made the point this way:

> I often wonder whether we do not rest our hopes too much upon constitutions, upon laws and upon courts. These are false hopes; believe me, these are false hopes. Liberty lies in the hearts of men and women; when it dies there, no constitution, no law, no court can ever do much to help it. While it lies there it needs no constitution, no law, no court to save it.[2]

Civil Rights Relative, Not Absolute

Even though many basic rights are guaranteed to *everyone* in the United States, *no one* has the right to do as he or she pleases. Rather, individuals have the right to do as they please *as long as* they do not interfere with the rights of other individuals. That is, each person's rights are relative to—parallel, inseparably linked with—the rights of all other persons.

Thus, each person in the United States has the right of free speech. But no person enjoys *absolute* freedom of speech. One who uses obscene language can be punished by a court for committing a crime. So, too, can someone who uses words in a way that causes another person to commit a crime—for example, to riot, to destroy private property, or to desert from the armed forces. Or, a person who damages another by what he or she says can be sued for slander.

One of our greatest judges, Oliver Wendell Holmes, once put the relative nature of each person's rights in these oft-quoted words:

> The most stringent protection of free speech would not protect a man in falsely shouting fire in a theatre and causing a panic.[3]

Rights in Conflict

The relative nature of each person's rights can also be discussed in terms of *conflicting* rights.

Most of us usually think of the many different civil rights guarantees in ways that suggest that each of them, and so all of them, are to be observed all of the time. In fact, there are a great many situations in which different rights come into conflict, or compete, with one another.

We shall look at a number of cases involving such conflicts in this chapter and in the next one, too. For now, take this celebrated, but not really that uncommon, example of rights in conflict: free press vs. fair trial.

Dr. Samuel Sheppard of Cleveland, Ohio, had been convicted of murdering his wife. His lengthy trial was widely covered in the national news media. Many reporters wrote and broadcast many lurid details (some fact, much fiction) about his love life and other behavior. On appeal, he claimed that the highly sensational coverage had denied him a fair trial. The Supreme Court agreed. It rejected the free press argument, overturned his conviction, and subsequently ordered a new trial of the case, *Sheppard* v. *Maxwell*, 1966; see page 146.

Persons to Whom Rights Are Guaranteed

Most rights set out in the Constitution are extended to *all persons* in the United States. The Supreme Court has often held that the Constitution's word "persons" covers **aliens** —foreign-born residents, noncitizens—as well as citizens.

Not *all* rights are given to aliens, however. Thus, the right to travel freely throughout the country is one of the rights guaranteed to all citizens by the Constitution's two Privileges and Immunities Clauses.[4] But aliens may be, and especially in wartime are, restricted in this regard.

Early in World War II, all persons of Japanese descent living on the Pacific Coast were evacuated—forcibly moved—inland. Some 120,000 persons, two-thirds of them native-

---

[2] Irving Dillard (ed.), *The Spirit of Liberty: Papers and Addresses of Learned Hand.* (New York: Knopf, 2nd edition, 1953), pages 189–190.

[3] In *Schenck* v. *United States*, 1919; see page 121.

[4] Article IV, Section 2, Clause 1 and the 14th Amendment; see page 88. The guarantee does not extend to citizens under some form of legal restraint—in jail, on bail, committed to a mental institution, etc.

REINFORCEMENT Use the Bill of Rights on p. 743 to discuss the Constitutional guarantees that each citizen enjoys. Stress that these rights are relative, and intended for the good of all.

The forced relocation of Japanese Americans in World War II has disturbed Americans for many years.

born American citizens, were sent to "war relocation camps" set up and run by the Government. The relocation program caused severe economic and personal hardships for many. In 1944 the Supreme Court reluctantly upheld the forced evacuation as a reasonable wartime emergency measure.[5] The action has been strongly criticized ever since. Many Japanese Americans fought heroically in World War II, and not a single case of *Nisei* (American-born Japanese) disloyalty has ever been found.

We shall take a much longer look at the whole matter of citizenship and the place of aliens in our society in the next chapter.

Federalism and Civil Rights

Federalism produces this very complex pattern of civil rights guarantees:

1. Some of the rights guaranteed by the Constitution are guaranteed against the National Government *only*.
2. Some of those rights are guaranteed against the States and their local governments *only*.
3. Some, a great many of them, are guaranteed against *both* the National Government *and* the States and their local governments.
4. Some of the rights guaranteed against a State and its local governments arise from the National Constitution while others arise from that State's *own* constitution.

Clearly, the fact that we have a federal system of government in this country has large consequences in the field of civil rights—a topic we shall explore throughout this chapter and the next one.

Over time, the Supreme Court has modified, or lessened, some of the impact of federalism, most especially in a long series of decisions involving the 14th Amendment's Due Process Clause. Before we can turn to that particular matter, however, this very important point must be clearly understood: The provisions of the Bill of Rights apply against the National Government *only—not* the States.

The Scope of the Bill of Rights Remember, these first 10 amendments were added to the Constitution in 1791 to meet one of the major objections to its ratification. Those amendments were originally intended as restrictions on the new National Government, not as limits on the already existing States. That remains true today.[6] *

Take the 2nd Amendment to make the point here. It reads:

> A well-regulated militia being necessary to the security of a free state, the right of the people to keep and bear arms shall not be infringed.

As a provision in the Bill of Rights, this restriction applies *only* to the National Government. However, the States may, and very

[5] *Korematsu* v. *United States*, 1944; however, on the same day the Court held in *Ex parte Endo* that once the loyalty of any citizen internee had been established, no restriction could be placed on that person's freedom to travel that was not legally imposed on all other citizens.

Today, more than 40 years after the fact, the government appears ready to admit that the relocation program was both unnecessary and unjust. In 1980 Congress created a Commission on Wartime Relocation and Internment of Civilians. The commission, in its final report in 1983, urged that Congress make a "national apology" for the "grave injustice" done to those who were interned.

[6] In the first case in which that issue was raised, *Barron* v. *Baltimore*, in 1833, the Supreme Court held that the provisions of the Bill of Rights restrict the National Government only. They do not apply against the States. The Court has followed that holding ever since.

*ENRICHMENT Discuss: The provisions of the Bill of Rights apply against the National Government, not the States. Why? Use an amendment other than the 2nd to explain and support your response.

often do, limit the right to keep and bear arms. They may require the registration of all or of certain guns, forbid the carrying of concealed weapons, forbid the ownership of automatic or semi-automatic weapons, and so on. As a matter of fact, the 2nd Amendment does not really impose a very significant limit on the National Government, either—as we shall see in Chapter 6.

The Modifying Effect of the 14th Amendment Again, the provisions of the Bill of Rights apply against the National Government, not the States. This does *not* mean, however, that the States can deny basic civil rights to the people.

In part, the States cannot do so because each of their own constitutions contains a bill of rights. Also, and at least as importantly, they cannot do so because of the 14th Amendment's **Due Process Clause.** It says:

> No State shall . . . deprive any person of life, liberty, or property, without due process of law.

We shall take a close look at this very important civil rights guarantee in the next chapter. For now, however, we must understand its root meaning.

The Supreme Court has often held that this provision means, at base: No State may deny to any person any right that is "basic or essential to the American concept of ordered liberty."

But what rights are "basic or essential," and so are a part of the meaning of the 14th Amendment's Due Process Clause? The Court has answered that question in a long series of cases. In that process, it has ruled that most of the protections set out in the Bill of Rights and applicable against the National Government are also within the meaning of the 14th Amendment and so applicable against the States, as well.

This very complicated matter can be stated this way: The Supreme Court has "nationalized the Bill of Rights"—by holding that most of its protections apply against the States, as a part of the meaning of the 14th Amendment's Due Process Clause.

The Court began this historic process in *Gitlow* v. *New York,* in 1925. In that landmark case, Benjamin Gitlow, a Communist, had been convicted in the State courts of criminal anarchy. He had made speeches and published a pamphlet calling for the violent overthrow of government. On appeal, the Supreme Court upheld both his conviction and the State law under which he had been tried. In deciding the case, however, the Court made this crucial point: Freedom of speech and freedom of the press, which the 1st Amendment says cannot be denied by the National Government, are also "among the fundamental personal rights and liberties protected by the Due Process Clause of the 14th Amendment from impairment by the States."

Soon after *Gitlow,* the Court held each of the 1st Amendment's guarantees to be covered by the 14th Amendment. It struck down State laws involving speech (*Fiske* v. *Kansas,* 1927; *Stromberg* v. *California,* 1931), the press (*Near* v. *Minnesota,* 1931), assembly and petition (*De Jonge* v. *Oregon,* 1937), and religion (*Cantwell* v. *Connecticut,* 1940). In each of those cases, the Court declared a State law unconstitutional as a violation of the 14th Amendment's Due Process Clause.

The Court enlarged the scope of the 14th Amendment's Due Process Clause in several cases decided in the 1960s. The clause now covers nearly all of the rest of the provisions in the Bill of Rights. Thus, in *Mapp* v. *Ohio,* 1961, the Court held that the clause prohibits unreasonable searches and seizures by State and local authorities, and also forbids them the use of any evidence gained by such illegal actions—just as the 4th Amendment prohibits such actions by federal officers.

Since then, the Court has given the same 14th Amendment coverage to:

—the 8th Amendment's ban on cruel and unusual punishment, in *Robinson* v. *California,* 1962;

—the 6th Amendment's guarantee of the right to counsel, in *Gideon* v. *Wainwright,* 1963;

—the 5th Amendment's ban on self-incrimination, in *Malloy* v. *Hogan,* 1964;

—the 6th Amendment's right of persons accused of crime to confront the witnesses

*REINFORCEMENT Have the class discuss: How has the 14th amendment "nationalized" the basic guarantees of the Bill of Rights? What are the implications of this act?

against them, in *Pointer* v. *Texas*, 1965;

—the 6th Amendment's right of persons accused of crime to compel witnesses to testify in their behalf, in *Washington* v. *Texas*, 1967;

—the 6th Amendment's guarantee of trial by jury, at least in cases of serious crime, in *Duncan* v. *Louisiana*, 1968; and

—the 5th Amendment's prohibition of double jeopardy, in *Benton* v. *Maryland*, 1969.

We shall return to each of these guarantees shortly—the 1st Amendment rights in this chapter and the others in Chapter 6. For now, however, note the chief point here: The Supreme Court has "nationalized" each of these basic guarantees. By holding that they exist against the States in the 14th Amendment, it has made their basic content and meaning uniform throughout the nation. In the process, much of the effect that federalism has on our civil rights system has been sharply reduced.

No Complete Listing of Rights Possible

The Constitution contains many civil rights guarantees. Those protections can be found in Article I, Sections 9 and 10; in Article III, Sections 2 and 3; in the 1st through the 8th Amendments; and in the 13th and 14th Amendments. But nowhere in the Constitution—and, indeed, nowhere else—can one find a complete catalog of all of the rights held by the American people.

The too-little noted 9th Amendment declares that there are other rights beyond those set out in so many words in the Constitution:

> The enumeration in the Constitution of certain rights shall not be construed to deny or disparage others retained by the people.

Over the years, the Supreme Court has found that there are, in fact, a number of other rights "retained by the people." For example: The right of a person charged with a crime not to be tried on the basis of evidence gained by an unlawful search or seizure; see page 137.

FOR REVIEW

1. **Identify:** relative rights, 14th Amendment, nationalization of civil rights, 9th Amendment, 1st Amendment.
2. According to the Declaration of Independence, governments exist for what reason?
3. How do civil rights guarantees illustrate the principle of limited government?
4. Why do the courts stand as the principal guardians of individual liberties in this country?
5. Why does no person have an absolute right to do as he or she pleases?
6. In what sense has the Supreme Court "nationalized" most of the civil rights protections set out in the Bill of Rights?
7. Why is it impossible to list all of the civil rights guaranteed by the Constitution to the American people?

2. Freedom of Expression: Religion

As You Read, Think About:

- What the importance is of the guarantees of the 1st Amendment.
- What the impact has been of the guarantees of the 1st Amendment.
- What the extent is of the constitutional separation of church and State.

The right to freedom of expression is indispensable to the idea of democracy. Without it, there simply cannot be a free society.

That basic freedom is enshrined in the 1st Amendment, where freedom of religion, speech, press, assembly, and petition are all protected against the National Government.

> Congress shall make no law respecting an establishment of religion, or prohibiting the free exercise thereof; or abridging the freedom of speech, or of the press; or the right of the people peaceably to assemble, and to petition the government for a redress of grievances.

The 1st Amendment protects an individual's right to practice his or her chosen religion. Left: Catholics at worship. Right: A service in a Jewish synagogue.

As we have already noted, the 14th Amendment's Due Process Clause extends each of these rights against the States and their local governments.

The 1st and 14th Amendments set out two guarantees of religious freedom. They prohibit (1) an "establishment of religion" (the Establishment Clause) and (2) any arbitrary interference by government in "the free exercise" of religion (the Free Exercise Clause).[7]

Separation of Church and State

The Establishment Clause sets up, in Thomas Jefferson's words, "a wall of separation between church and state." That wall is not infinitely high, however, nor is it one that *cannot be penetrated. Church and government, while constitutionally separated in the United States, are neither enemies nor even strangers to one another. In fact, their relationship is a friendly one.

Government has done much to encourage churches and religion in this country. Thus, nearly all church-owned property and contributions to churches and religious sects are free from federal, State, and local taxation. Chaplains serve with each branch of the armed forces. Most public officials take an oath of office in the name of God. Sessions of Congress and of most State legislatures and city councils are opened with prayer. The nation's anthem and its coins and currency make reference to God.

The content of the Establishment Clause cannot be described in precise terms. The exact nature of the "wall of separation," how high it really is, remains a matter of continuing and often heated controversy.

Given that controversy, it is somewhat surprising that the Supreme Court did not decide its first Establishment Clause case until 1947. A few earlier cases had a bearing on the question, but none involved a direct consideration of the meaning of the "wall of separation."

[7]Also, Article VI, Section 3 provides that ". . . no religious test shall ever be required as a qualification to any office or public trust under the United States." In *Torcaso* v. *Watkins*, 1961, the Supreme Court held that the 14th Amendment puts the same restriction on the States. In that case the Court struck down a section of the Maryland constitution that required all public officeholders in that State to declare a belief in the existence of God.

*ENRICHMENT Have the class discuss: The concept of separation of church and State is one of the basic tenets on which our government rests. Why, then, is it continually challenged?

In *Pierce* v. *Society of Sisters,* 1925, for example, the Court held an Oregon compulsory school attendance law unconstitutional. That law required parents to send their children to *public* schools. It had been purposely designed to eliminate the private, and especially the parochial (church-related), schools in the State. In destroying the law, the Court did not reach the Establishment Clause question. Instead, it found the law to be an unreasonable interference with the liberty of parents to direct the upbringing of their children, and, so, in conflict with the Due Process Clause of the 14th Amendment.

Cochran v. *Louisiana,* 1930, was another of those earlier cases. There the Court upheld a State law allowing the use of public funds to supply "schoolbooks to the school children of the State." Under that law, textbooks were furnished to pupils in both public and private schools, including those in parochial schools. The law had not been attacked on Establishment Clause grounds, however. Rather, Cochran and others had charged that it violated the 14th Amendment's guarantee against the deprivation of property without due process, because it allowed the spending of public money for what they said was a private purpose. In turning down that argument, the Court found that "the school children and the State alone are the beneficiaries" of the law, not the schools they attend.

The first direct ruling on the Establishment Clause came in *Everson* v. *Board of Education,* a 1947 case often called the *New Jersey School Bus Case.* There the Court upheld a State law that provided for the public, and tax-supported, busing of students who attended parochial schools. The law was attacked as a support of religion, because, its critics said, it relieved parochial schools of the need to pay for busing and so freed their money for other, and religious, purposes. The Court disagreed, however. It found the law to be a safety measure intended to benefit school children, no matter what schools they might attend.

Since that decision, most of the Court's *Establishment Clause cases have involved, in one way or another, matters of religion and education.

Released Time Two of those cases involved "released time" programs in public schools. Such programs, now found in most States, allow students to be "released" from school time to attend religious classes.

In *McCollum* v. *Board of Education,* 1948, the Court struck down the program then used in Champaign, Illinois, because public school classrooms and other public facilities were being used for religious purposes.

In *Zorach* v. *Clauson,* 1952, however, New York City's program, much like the one in Illinois, was upheld, because New York's program states that the religious classes cannot be held on school grounds.

Prayers and the Bible Two later key, and still highly controversial, decisions dealt with the recitation of prayers and the reading of the Bible in public schools.

In *Engel* v. *Vitale,* 1962, the Court outlawed the use, even on a voluntary basis, of a nondenominational prayer written by the New York State Board of Regents. The "Regents' prayer" read:

> Almighty God, we acknowledge our dependence upon Thee, and we beg Thy blessings upon us, our parents, our teachers, and our country.

The Supreme Court held (8–1) that

> the constitutional prohibition against laws respecting an establishment of religion must at least mean that in this country it is no part of the business of government to compose official prayers for any group of the American people to recite as part of a religious program carried on by government.

That holding was extended twice in 1963. In *Abington School District* v. *Schempp,* the Court struck down a Pennsylvania law that required that each school day begin with readings from the Bible and a recitation of the Lord's Prayer. In *Murray* v. *Curlett,* the Court erased a similar rule in the city of Baltimore. In both cases the Court found (8–1) violations of

> the command of the 1st Amendment that the government maintain strict neutrality, neither aiding nor opposing religion.

*REINFORCEMENT Have the class discuss the above Establishment Clause cases and analyze the Court's decisions.

FOCUS ON:

"Equal Access"— "A Fourth 'R' in Our Schools"?

Is the wall of separation higher in the nation's public elementary and secondary schools than it is on the campuses of its public colleges and universities? In the Supreme Court's view: Yes.

As we have seen, the Court has held that the Establishment Clause forbids organized prayer, devotional reading of the Bible, recitation of the Lord's Prayer, the required posting of the Ten Commandments, and a required "moment of silence" (at least for prayer) in local public schools.

Also, the Supreme Court has refused to review, and so let stand, many lower court decisions that follow in that line. Among them are several to the effect that local public school facilities cannot be used by various groups for religious purposes.

The Court did just that in a recent Texas case, *Lubbock Independent School District* v. *Lubbock Civil Liberties Union,* in 1983. There, two lower federal courts had blocked the district's policy of allowing high school students to meet in the schools, before or after classes, for any "educational, moral, religious, or ethical purpose."

But the Court has made some very different—and to many, some very contradictory—decisions at the college and university level.

The leading higher education case is *Widmar* v. *Vincent,* 1981. The Court held that a State university may allow student groups to use its classrooms and other facilities for religious purposes. It struck down a University of Missouri regulation that made the university buildings and grounds generally available for student activities but specifically prohibited their use "for purposes of religious worship or religious teaching."

The Court rejected the university's argument that the Establishment Clause barred any religious uses of its publicly owned property. Instead, it found that the fact that the school banned religious activities but did allow other kinds of programs amounted to a violation of freedom of speech.

The Court said: "University students are, of course, young adults. They are less impressionable than younger students. . . ."

Congress has now stepped into this matter —with the Equal Access Law of 1984. At base, it requires that all public high schools that receive federal funds must allow student religious groups to meet in the school, before or after classes, on the same terms that other student groups may do so.

The measure was passed by a large majority in both houses. Its backers claim that the law strengthens the rights of those students who want to hold religious meetings at school. It gives them "equal access" to and puts them on the same footing as other students in the use of school facilities. "This is a constitutional issue, a question of free speech and free assembly," said Representative Marge Roukema (R., New Jersey).

The law's critics claim it violates the Establishment Clause and is really an attempt to skirt the ban on organized prayer. Representative Charles E. Schumer (D., New York) argued it "adds a fourth 'r' to our schools —reading, 'riting, 'rithmetic, and religion."

Clearly, the Supreme Court will soon hear a challenge to the law.

1. Do student religious groups now hold meetings in your school?
2. Do you agree with the Equal Access Law? Why or why not?

In *Stone* v. *Graham,* 1980, the Court struck down a Kentucky law requiring that copies of the Ten Commandments be posted in all public school classrooms.

Most recently, the Court found Alabama's "moment of silence" law unconstitutional, *Wallace* v. *Jaffree,* 1985. That law provided for a one-minute period of silence, for "meditation or voluntary prayer," at the beginning of each school day. The Court held (6–3) that the law's specific reference to "voluntary prayer" made it constitutionally unacceptable. The State's "endorsement . . . of prayer activities," it said, "is not consistent with the established principle that the government must pursue a course of complete neutrality toward religion." But, notice, the Court did not strike down *all* "moment of silence" laws here. Nearly half the States have passed such statutes in recent years, and most of them make no specific reference to "prayer." Their constitutionality remains an open question.

To sum up these rulings, the Supreme Court has held that the public schools, which are agencies of government, cannot sponsor religious exercises. But it has *not* held that individuals cannot pray, when and as they choose, in the schools, or in any other place. Nor has it held that the Bible cannot be studied, in a literary or historic frame, in the schools.

These rulings have stirred strong criticism, and in many places. Many, including President Reagan, have long proposed that the Constitution be amended to overturn them—that is, amended to allow "voluntary prayer" in the public schools. Despite those decisions, however, both organized prayers and Bible readings are to be found in many public classrooms today.

* ***Christmas Displays*** Many public bodies sponsor celebrations of the Christmas season, with street decorations, displays in public parks, programs in public schools, and the like. Can these publicly sponsored observances properly include expressions of Christian belief? Or, does the inclusion of a cross, the reenactment of the Nativity, or the use of some other symbol of Christianity violate the wall of separation?

The Court has decided only one case here, from Pawtucket, R.I., *Lynch* v. *Donnelly,* 1984. It held that a city may include a Nativity scene *as a part of* its seasonal display. But its 5–4 ruling left open this question: What about a public display that consisted *only* of a religious symbol of, for example, only a creche or a cross?

Chaplains in Congress and the State Legislatures Daily sessions of both houses of Congress and most of the State legislatures begin with prayer. In Congress, and in many State legislatures, the opening prayer is offered by a chaplain paid with public funds.

The Supreme Court has ruled that this practice, unlike prayers in the public schools, is constitutionally permissible. It made that decision in a case involving Nebraska's one-house legislature, in *Marsh* v. *Chambers,* 1983.

The Court rested its distinction between school prayers and legislative prayers on the point that prayers have been offered in the nation's legislative bodies throughout our history, "from colonial times through the founding of the Republic and ever since."

Evolution In *Epperson* v. *Arkansas,* 1968, the Court struck down a State law forbidding the teaching of the scientific theory of evolution in the public schools of that State. The Court held that the Establishment Clause

> forbids alike the preference of a religious doctrine or the prohibition of theory which is deemed antagonistic to a particular dogma. . . . The State has no legitimate interest in protecting any or all religions from views distasteful to them.

Tax Exemptions Every State exempts houses of worship, and other church-owned property used for religious purposes, from both State and local taxation. The Supreme Court has upheld this practice, *Walz* v. *New York City Tax Commission,* 1970.

Walz had challenged the exemption of churches from local property taxes. He argued that these exemptions made his and

*ENRICHMENT Have the class discuss the question of publicly sponsored Christmas observances and how it relates to the question of the separation of church and State.

others' property tax bills higher than they would otherwise be. Therefore, he claimed, the exemptions amounted to a public support of religion.

The Court turned down his plea. It found that those exemptions are evidence only of a State's "benevolent neutrality" toward religion, not support of it. Said the Court, the exemptions "create only a minimal and remote," and therefore permissible, "involvement between church and state."

But the Court has ruled that church-related schools that discriminate on the basis of race can be denied a tax-exempt status under federal law, *Bob Jones University* v. *United States* and *Goldsboro Christian Schools* v. *United States*, 1983. (Organizations with that status do not pay unemployment and social security taxes. Contributions to them may be claimed as federal income tax deductions.)

The schools involved in these 1983 cases argued that their racial policies reflect their sincerely held religious beliefs. The Supreme Court granted that point. It held, nevertheless, that the nation's interest in eradicating racial discrimination in education "substantially outweighs whatever burden denial of tax benefits places on [those schools in the] exercise of their religious beliefs."

Many parochial schools receive State aid which can be used only for non-religious purposes.

State Aid to Parochial Schools Most recent Establishment Clause cases have centered on this highly controversial question: What forms of State aid to parochial schools are constitutional?

Several States give help to private schools, including those that are church-related—for transportation, textbooks, laboratory equipment, standardized testing, and much else. Pressures to expand that aid have grown as school operating costs have soared.

Those who favor such aid regularly make several arguments for it. They note that parochial schools enroll large numbers of students who would otherwise have to be educated at public expense. They point to the fact that the Supreme Court has held that parents have a legal right to send their children to those schools (*Pierce* v. *Society of Sisters*). To give that right real meaning, they say, some aid must be given to parochial schools—to relieve parents of some of the double burden they carry because they must pay taxes to support the public schools their children do not attend.

Many advocates also insist that the church-run schools pose no real church-state problems, because, they say, those schools devote most of their time to secular (nonreligious) subjects rather than to sectarian, or religious, ones.

Opponents of aid to parochial schools base their arguments on a number of grounds, too. Most of them take the view that the public schools play an important democratizing role in bringing pupils of various religious backgrounds together. Many of them object to separating children in schools on the basis of religion, especially because religious differences are often tied to ethnic, social, and economic distinctions among people.

Many opponents argue, too, that those parents who choose to send children to parochial schools should accept the financial consequences of that choice and should not expect the rest of society to bear that load. Many of them also insist that it is impossible to draw clear lines between secular and sectarian courses in parochial schools. They say that church beliefs are bound to have an effect on the teaching of nonreligious subjects in church-run schools.

The Supreme Court has been picking its way through cases arising out of State aid programs for some 20 years now.[8] In the first of them, *Board of Education* v. *Allen,* 1968, it upheld a New York law providing secular textbooks for students in parochial schools. The Court applied what has come to be known as "the child-benefit theory": that the aid is directed to the student, not to the school.

In deciding *Allen,* the Court emphasized that a State may aid *only* secular education in church-related schools. Drawing the line between aid supporting only the nonreligious activities of a parochial school and aid promoting its religious purposes has proved to be a troublesome task.

Excessive Entanglement Since 1971, the Court has been developing and applying a three-pronged test for this purpose: the **excessive entanglement standard.** To be constitutional, a State's school aid law must meet these requirements: (1) the purpose of the aid must be clearly secular, not religious, (2) its primary effect must neither advance nor inhibit religion, and (3) it must avoid an "excessive entanglement of government with religion."

The Court first used the test in *Lemon* v. *Kurtzman,* 1971. The decision held that the Establishment Clause is designed to prevent three main evils: "sponsorship, financial support, and active involvement of the sovereign in religious activity."

In *Lemon,* the Court struck down a Pennsylvania law that provided for reimbursements, or money payments, to private schools to cover their costs for teachers' salaries, textbooks, and other teaching materials in nonreligious courses. At the same time, in *Earley* v. *DiCenso,* 1971, the Court also voided a Rhode Island law giving salary supplements to the teachers of secular courses in private elementary schools.

In both cases the Court held that the State programs were of direct benefit to the parochial schools, and so to the churches sponsoring them. It held that the programs required such close State supervision that they produced an excessive entanglement of government with religion.

The Court has been using its excessive entanglement standard for well over a decade now, upholding some programs and rejecting others. Thus, it recently struck down a Michigan law under which (1) public school teachers were paid to teach remedial courses to students in parochial schools during the regular school day and (2) parochial school teachers were paid to teach similar classes in their schools after regular school hours, *Grand Rapids School District* v. *Ball,* 1985.

In a Pennsylvania case, *Meek* v. *Pittinger,* 1975, the Court has allowed the use of public funds to lend textbooks to students in parochial schools. In that same case, however, the Court rejected the loan of such things as films, projectors, and recorders, and grants for counseling and speech therapy. Public payments for field trips by parochial school students were banned by the Court, in a case from Ohio, *Wolman* v. *Walter,* 1977.

Two New York cases may help you to better understand the standard shaped by the Court. In *Levitt* v. *Committee for Public Education,* 1973, the Court struck down a program in which the State repaid church-related schools for their costs in certain testing and reporting functions. That ruling focused on the point that many of the tests had been prepared by teachers in those schools, and so could be considered a part of their program of religious instruction.

In *Committee for Public Education* v. *Regan,* 1980, however, the Court allowed the State to pay church-related schools to administer, grade, and report the results of

[8]For about as long, Congress has been considering proposals to allow tuition tax credits—income tax exemptions for parents who pay private school tuitions. President Reagan is a staunch supporter of tuition tax credits. On this point, see the discussion of *Mueller* v. *Allen,* on the next page.

REINFORCEMENT Have the class discuss the basic arguments for and against State aid to parochial schools. Does the excessive entanglement standard satisfy the problems with this issue?

What are the parts of the three-pronged test applied by the Supreme Court in determining the constitutionality of aid to parochial schools?

standardized tests prepared by the State Department of Education.

One other and important case to note here is *Mueller* v. *Allen,* 1983, in which the Court upheld a Minnesota tax law. That law gives parents a State income tax deduction for the costs of tuition, textbooks, and transportation for their elementary and secondary schoolchildren. Parents may claim the tax break no matter what schools, public or private, their children attend. Most public school parents pay little or nothing for these items, for they are usually covered by public funds. Hence, the law is of particular benefit to parents with children in private, mostly parochial, schools.

The Court found that the law meets the three-pronged entanglement standard, and it also leaned on this point: The deduction is available to *all* parents with children in school, and they are free to decide which type of school their children attend.

The Court has taken a more generous view *in cases involving public aid to church-related colleges and universities. Thus, in *Tilton* v. *Richardson,* 1971, it upheld federal grants to such institutions for the construction of academic buildings to be used for nonreligious purposes. It could find no excessive entanglement in these "one-shot" grants.[9] Certainly, the Court's future holds many other "parochaid" cases.

The Free Exercise of Religion

The second part of the constitutional guarantee of religious freedom is set out in the Free Exercise Clause. That Clause guarantees to each person the right to *believe* whatever that person chooses to believe in matters of religion. No law, and no other action by government, may violate that *absolute* constitutional right. It is protected by both the 1st and the 14th Amendments.

No person has an absolute right to *act* as he or she chooses, however. The Free Exercise Clause does *not* give one the right to violate the criminal laws, offend public morals, or otherwise threaten the health, welfare, or safety of the community.

The Supreme Court laid down the basic shape of the Free Exercise Clause in the very first case it heard on the point, *Reynolds* v. *United States,* 1879. Reynolds, a Mormon living in Utah, had two wives. That circumstance, polygamy, was allowed by the teachings of his church, but it was prohibited by a federal law banning the practice in any of the territories of the United States.

Reynolds was tried and convicted under the law. On appeal, he argued that the law violated his constitutional right to the free exercise of his religious beliefs. The Supreme Court disagreed, however. It held that the 1st Amendment does not forbid Congress the power to punish those actions that are "violations of social duties or subversive of good order." To hold otherwise, said the Court

> would be to make the professed doctrines of religious belief superior to the law of the land, and in effect permit every citizen to become a law unto himself. Government would exist only in name under such circumstances.

[9]It has also sustained two similar State programs, one in South Carolina (*Hunt* v. *McNair,* 1973) and the other in Maryland (*Roemer* v. *Maryland Board of Public Works,* 1976). But in *Tilton* the Court held one section of the Higher Education Facilities Act of 1963 unconstitutional. That section limited to 20 years a college's obligation not to use a federally financed building for religious instruction or worship. The Court ruled that such buildings may *never* be used for those purposes.

*ENRICHMENT Discuss: Has the excessive entanglement standard been successful in drawing the line between aid that supports nonreligious purposes and aid that does not?

The Amish believe in a life apart from the world. The Supreme Court holds that Amish children cannot be forced to attend public schools after the 8th grade.

Over the years, the Court has approved many regulations of human conduct in the face of free exercise challenges. For example, it has upheld laws that require the vaccination of school children (*Jacobson* v. *Massachusetts,* 1905), that forbid the use of poisonous snakes in religious rites (*Bunn* v. *North Carolina,* 1949), and that require business to be closed on Sundays, or "blue laws" (*McGowan* v. *Maryland,* 1961).

Religious groups may be required to have a permit to hold a parade on the public streets (*Cox* v. *New Hampshire,* 1940); and laws regarding child labor must be obeyed if children are used to sell religious literature (*Prince* v. *Massachusetts,* 1944). Those who have religious objections to military service can nonetheless be drafted (*Welsh* v. *United States,* 1970).[10] The Hare Krishna can be required to limit their religious tracts and other fund raising at a State fair to a booth or to some other fixed location, even though such activities are a part of their ritual (*Heffron* v. *International Society of Krishna Consciousness,* 1981). And, the Air Force can forbid an Orthodox Jew the right to wear his *yarmulke* (skull cap) while on active duty (*Goldman* v. *Weinberger,* 1986).

But, over time, the Court has also found many actions by governments to be contrary to the free exercise guarantee. It did so for the first time in one of the landmark Due Process cases we cited earlier in this chapter, *Cantwell* v. *Connecticut,* 1940. There, it struck down a law requiring a license before any person could solicit money for a religious cause.

There are many other cases in that line. Thus, Amish children cannot be forced to attend school beyond the 8th grade, because that sect's centuries-old "self-sufficient agrarian lifestyle essential to their religious faith is threatened . . . by modern education" (*Wisconsin* v. *Yoder,* 1972). But the Amish, who take care of their own, must pay social security taxes, as all other employers do (*United States* v. *Lee,* 1982).

[10]The Court has made this ruling many times. *Welsh* is the leading case from the Vietnam War period. There, the Court held that the only persons who could not be drafted were those "whose consciences . . . would give them no rest if they allowed themselves to become part of an instrument of war."

*REINFORCEMENT The Constitution guarantees free exercise of religion. How can this interfere with the Supreme Court's duty to uphold the law of the land? Discuss, using the above cases.

A State cannot forbid ministers to hold elected public offices (*McDaniel* v. *Paty*, 1978). Nor can it deny unemployment compensation benefits to a worker who quit a job because it involved some conflict with his or her religious beliefs (*Sherbert* v. *Verner*, 1963; *Thomas* v. *Indiana*, 1981).[11]

Several important religious freedom cases have been carried to the Supreme Court by the Jehovah's Witnesses, a fundamentalist group that actively promotes its beliefs. Perhaps the stormiest of the many controversies that sect has stirred arose out of the Witnesses' refusal to obey compulsory requirements to salute the flag. That controversy and the two notable Court decisions it produced tell us much about the interpretation of the Free Exercise Clause. They also demonstrate how difficult many 1st Amendment questions can be for the courts to decide fairly.

The Witnesses refuse to salute the flag because they see such conduct as a violation of the Bible's commandment against idolatry.[12] In *Minersville School District* v. *Gobitis*, 1940, the Court upheld a Pennsylvania school board regulation requiring students to salute the flag at the beginning of each school day. Gobitis instructed his children not to do so, and they were expelled. He went to court, basing his case on the constitutional guarantee. He finally lost in the Supreme Court, however. It declared that the board's rule was not an infringement of religious liberty. Rather, the Court held that the rule was a lawful attempt to promote patriotism and national unity.

Three years later, in a remarkable turnabout, the Court reversed that decision. In *West Virginia Board of Education* v. *Barnette*, 1943, it held a compulsory flag-salute law unconstitutional. Justice Robert H. Jackson's quoted words on page 98 are from the Court's powerful opinion in that case. So are these:

> To believe that patriotism will not flourish if patriotic ceremonies are voluntary and spontaneous instead of a compulsory routine is to make an unflattering estimate of the appeal of our institutions to free minds.

FOR REVIEW

1. **Identify:** freedom of religion, separation of church and state, parochial schools, Equal Access Law, secular, sectarian, child-benefit theory.
2. What civil rights guarantees are set out in the 1st Amendment? Against whom do they apply?
3. What is the Establishment Clause? Does it provide for a complete separation of church and state?
4. Does the Constitution prohibit released time programs in public schools? Organized prayer or Bible readings? Tax exemptions for churches? All forms of "parochaid"?
5. What is the Free Exercise Clause? What is the basic shape of the right it guarantees?

3. Freedom of Expression: Speech and Press

As You Read, Think About:

- What limitations exist on the freedoms of speech and of the press.

The 1st and 14th Amendment's protections of free speech and a free press serve *two* fundamentally important purposes:

[11]Typically, State unemployment compensation laws bar such benefits to those who leave jobs voluntarily and "without good cause in connection with the work." In *Sherbert*, a Seventh Day Adventist lost her job in a South Carolina textile mill when she refused to work on Saturdays, her sabbath day. In *Thomas*, a Jehovah's Witness who worked for a machinery company quit after he was transferred from one section of the company that was being closed down to another where gun turrets for tanks were made. He left because, he said, his religious beliefs would not allow him to work on war materials.

[12]Specifically, these verses from Chapter 20 in the Book of Exodus:

"3. Thou shalt have no other gods before me.

"4. Thou shalt not make unto thee any graven image. . . .

"5. Thou shalt not bow down thyself to them, nor serve them. . . ."

1. To guarantee to *each person* a right of free expression—in the spoken and the written word, and by all other means of communication, as well; and
2. To ensure to *all persons* a full, wide-ranging discussion of public affairs.

These two Amendments give to each of us the right to have our say and to all of us the right to hear what others have to say. Most often, we think of these great freedoms in terms of that first purpose. The second one is just as important, however.

Our system of government depends on the ability of the people to make sound, reasoned judgments on matters of public concern. Clearly, such judgments can be made only when the people can know all of the facts in a given matter *and* can hear and weigh any and all interpretations and opinions of those facts.

Justice Oliver Wendell Holmes once underscored the importance of that second purpose:

> Persecution for the expression of opinions seems to me perfectly logical. If you have no doubt of your premises and want a certain result with all your heart, you naturally express your wishes in law and sweep away all opposition. . . . But when men have realized that time has upset many fighting faiths, they may come to believe even more than they believe the very foundations of their own conduct that the ultimate good desired is better reached by free trade in ideas—that the best test of truth is the power of the thought to get itself accepted in the competition of the market. . . . That at any rate is the theory of our Constitution.[13]

Before we can turn to the more exact meanings of the 1st and 14th Amendments here, you must understand two other important points:

First, the guarantees of free speech and press are intended, most of all, to protect the expression of *unpopular* views. The opinions of the majority need, after all, little or no constitutional protection. Again, in Justice Holmes's words:

The 1st and 14th Amendments protect freedom of expression for everyone, including groups with unpopular views, such as the American Nazi Party.

Demonstrators protest American Nazi Party policies. When is free expression *not* protected?

> . . . if there is any principle of the Constitution that more imperatively calls for attachment than any other it is the principle of free thought—not free thought for those who agree with us but freedom for the thought that we hate.[14]

Second, some forms of expression are *not* protected by the Constitution. No person has an unbridled right of free speech or free press. Many reasonable restrictions may be, and are, placed on those rights.

We shall look at a number of illustrations of this point over the next several pages. For now, recall Justice Holmes's comment about the right to shout "Fire!" in a crowded theater. Or, note this restriction: No person has the right to **libel** or **slander** another. Similarly, the use of obscene words, the printing

---

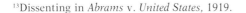

[13]Dissenting in *Abrams* v. *United States*, 1919.

[14]Dissenting in *United States* v. *Schwimmer*, 1929.

and distributing of obscene materials, and false advertising are prohibited by law.[15]

Obscenity

Obscenity is not protected by the 1st and 14th Amendments. Even so, no civil rights issue has given the Supreme Court more difficulty in recent years.

The Court has wrestled several times with these questions: What language, printed matter, films and other materials are, in fact, obscene? What restrictions can be properly placed on such materials?[16] The leading case is *Miller* v. *California,* 1973. There the Court laid down a three-part test to determine what material is obscene and what is not.

A book, film, or other piece of material is legally obscene if (1) "the average person applying contemporary [local] community standards," finds that the work, taken as a whole, "appeals to the prurient interest" —that is, tends to excite lust; (2) "the work depicts or describes, in a patently offensive way," a form of sexual conduct specifically dealt with in an antiobscenity law; and (3) "the work, taken as a whole, lacks serious literary, artistic, political, or scientific value." The very fact that the Court has developed so complex a test indicates how difficult the obscenity problem is.

That the problem is a very difficult one can be seen from several cases. In *Stanley* v. *Georgia,* 1969, the Court ruled that a State cannot make it a crime for a person to possess obscene materials for his or her own use in his or her own home.[17] Yet, in two 1971 cases it upheld laws that punish those who send obscene materials in interstate commerce or through the mails or import them from abroad (*United States* v. *Thirty-Seven Photographs; United States* v. *Reidel*). In short, the Court has upheld the right of a person to read whatever he or she wants in the privacy of the home. At the same time, however, it has upheld the laws that deny to that person the principal means of obtaining them.[18]

Prior Restraint

The Constitution allows government to punish *some* utterances, *after* they are made. With almost no exceptions, government cannot place any "prior restraint" on spoken or on written words. That is, except in the most extreme situations, it cannot curb ideas *before* they are expressed.

---

[15]Libel (the printed word) and slander (the spoken word) involve the use of words, *maliciously*—with vicious purpose—to injure a person's character or reputation or expose that person to public contempt, ridicule, or hatred. Truth is generally an absolute defense against a libel or slander claim. The law is less protective of public officials, however. In *New York Times* v. *Sullivan,* 1964, the Supreme Court held that public officials cannot recover damages for a published criticism, even if exaggerated or false, unless "the statement was made with actual malice—that is with knowledge that it was false or with reckless disregard of whether it was false or not." Several later decisions have extended that ruling to cover "public figures" and even private individuals who have become involved in newsworthy events.

[16]Congress passed the first of a series of laws to keep obscene matter from the mails in 1872. The current law was upheld by the Court in *Roth* v. *United States,* 1957. The law excludes "every obscene, lewd, lascivious, or filthy" piece of material. The Court found the law a proper exercise of the postal power (Article I, Section 8, Clause 7) and so not prohibited by the 1st Amendment. *Roth* marked the Court's first attempt to find an adequate definition of obscenity.

[17]Films were involved in the case. Said the Court: "If the 1st Amendment means anything, it means that the State has no business telling a man, sitting alone in his own home, what books he may read or what films he may watch." But, in *United States* v. *Orito,* 1973, it held that the "zone of privacy" protected by *Stanley* does not go beyond one's own home.

[18]Another chief source of such things is, of course, so-called "adult bookstores." Although most of the items they sell cannot be mailed, shipped across State lines, or legally imported, these "porno shops" are usually well supplied. The 1st Amendment does not forbid a city to regulate the location of "adult entertainment establishments" through its zoning ordinances (*Young* v. *American Mini Theatres,* 1976), and many cities now do so. The Court has recently upheld an ordinance that prohibits adult movie theaters within 1,000 feet of any residential zone or church, park or school, *City of Renton* v. *Playtime Theatres, Inc.,* 1986. A city cannot use its zoning laws to ban all live entertainment in commercial establishments, however, *Schad* v. *Borough of Mount Ephraim,* 1981 (nude dancing in an adult book store). Also, the 1st Amendment is not violated by a State law that prohibits nude dancing in all bars or nightclubs that serve liquor (*New York State Liquor Authority* v. *Bellanca,* 1981) or a city ordinance regulating "head shops," stores that sell items for use with illegal drugs (*Village of Hoffman Estates* v. *The Flipside,* 1982).

*REINFORCEMENT Discuss: Why are cases involving obscenity so difficult for the Supreme Court to decide? What issues must the Court address?

Near v. *Minnesota,* 1931, is a leading case on the point. There the Supreme Court struck down a State law that prohibited the publication of any "malicious, scandalous, and defamatory" periodical. Acting under that law, a local court had issued an order forbidding the continued publication of *The Saturday Press,* a weekly published in Minneapolis. The paper had printed several articles charging public corruption and attacking "grafters" and "Jewish gangsters" in that city. The Court held that the guarantee of a free press does not allow a "prior restraint" on publication, except in such extreme cases as wartime or when a publication is obscene or incites readers to violence. Even, in this case, "miscreant purveyers of scandal" and anti-Semitism have a constitutional protection against prior restraint.

The Court has purposely refused to say that all forms of prior censorship are unconstitutional. But it has said that "a prior restraint on expression comes to this Court with a 'heavy presumption' against its constitutionality," *Nebraska Press Association* v. *Stuart,* 1976.[19] It has used that general rule several times, for example, in the famous Pentagon Papers Case, *New York Times* v. *United States,* 1971.

The *Times* and several other newspapers had obtained copies of a set of classified documents. The documents, widely known as "The Pentagon Papers," were officially titled *History of U.S. Decision-Making Process on Viet Nam Policy.* They had been stolen from the Defense Department and then leaked to the press. The Government sought a court order to bar their publication. But the Court rejected that plea. It held that the Government had not shown that printing the documents would endanger the nation's security, and so had not overcome the "heavy presumption" against prior censorship.

On some few occasions, however, the Court has allowed prior restraints. Thus, it has upheld regulations that prohibit passing out political literature on military bases without the approval of military authorities, *Greer* v. *Spock,* 1976.

The most recent such case is *Snepp* v. *United States,* 1980. There the Court backed a prior censorship regulation of the Central Intelligence Agency. The CIA requires all of its agents to sign a contract in which they agree not to publish anything about the Agency or its activities without its approval. A former agent, Frank Snepp, wrote a book, *Decent Interval,* about the CIA's activities in South Vietnam. He did not submit his book to the Agency for screening before its publication, and the Government then sued him for breach of contract. Over his 1st Amendment objections, the Court upheld the Government's right to do so.

Confidentiality

Do news reporters have a constitutional right to withhold certain information from government? Or, may they be forced to testify before a grand jury, in court, or before a legislative committee, and there be required to name their sources and reveal other confidential information?

These questions are of immediate importance to those who gather and report the news. They also have a direct impact on the free flow of information and, therefore, on the public's right to know.

Many reporters and most news organizations insist that they must have the right to refuse to testify, the right to "protect their sources." They argue that without it they cannot assure confidentiality to their sources. That is, they cannot guarantee their sources that they will remain anonymous. Unless they can do that, reporters and news organizations say, many of their sources will not give them information they must have in order to keep the public informed.

Both State and federal courts have generally rejected the news media argument. In recent years several reporters have refused to obey court orders directing them to give information. As a consequence, a number of reporters have gone to jail, testifying to the importance of these issues.

[19]In this case a county judge had ordered the media not to report certain details of a sensational murder trial. The Court held the "gag order" to be unconstitutional.

*ENRICHMENT Ask the class to discuss: Many members of the press have been jailed for protecting their sources. What purposes do they hope to serve?

BUILDING GOVERNMENT SKILLS

Reading a Newspaper Article

Newspapers may be the best way to find out about what is happening in the world, from events in foreign countries to the scores of local high school games. Newspapers have more stories and more detailed information than that provided by television or radio news.

Newspaper articles usually follow a standard format. Understanding how newspaper articles are structured can help you read a paper more quickly and gain more information from it.

The Headline

The first thing you probably notice about a newspaper article is its headline. Headlines are printed in larger, bold type above the text of the story. They are written to catch your attention with just a few key words which capture the heart of the story and make you want to learn more.

Headlines can help you decide whether or not you want to read the story. A good headline will tell you the main idea of the story in just a few words. The size of the type used for the headline also tells you how important the story is. Most newspapers save their biggest type for really important stories. The *Washington Post,* for example, used its biggest type for the headline, "Nixon Resigns."

The Byline and the Dateline

Just below the headline are the byline and the dateline. The byline states who wrote the story, either an individual or often the name of a news service. The dateline includes the date and city where the story was filed, for example, "July 29—Cairo." Some papers do not include the date. Notice that in papers that give the date, many stories are written the day before they appear in the newspaper. This is especially true of morning newspapers.

The Lead

The most important sentence of any news article is the first sentence, called the lead. A good lead sentence summarizes the main idea of the story. It tells you the who did what, where, when and often why.

The Body

The why of the story is contained in the rest of the article, called the body of the story. This provides a more detailed account of the basic facts introduced in the lead. This is where you will find quotes and background facts.

News stories are built like inverted pyramids. As read through the story, you find less and less important details. News stories rarely have a conclusion, so that editors can cut them to fit the space available without losing important information and so that readers can stop reading the story before they actually reach the end.

1. Look at any daily newspaper and pick one of the major stories on the front page. Just from reading the headline, why do you think the editors put this story on the front page?
2. Now find the byline, dateline, and the lead. What are the basics of who, what, where, when, and how in the story?
3. Now read the rest of the story. Did the headline and the lead fit with the information in the rest of the article? Why or why not?
4. What details in the story made it more interesting to read? Why?

Television and radio are subject to more federal regulation than other media. Why doesn't the 1st Amendment prohibit these regulations?

In the leading case, *Branzburg* v. *Hayes,* 1972, the Supreme Court held that the 1st Amendment does not grant any special privileges to reporters. They, "like other citizens, [must] respond to relevant questions put to them in the course of a valid grand jury investigation or criminal trial." If any special exemptions are to be given to the news media, said the Court, they must come from Congress and the State legislatures.

To date, Congress has not acted on the Court's suggestion. However, some 30 States have passed so-called "**shield laws.**" These laws give reporters some degree of protection against having to disclose their sources or reveal other confidential information.

Motion Pictures

The Supreme Court took its first look at motion pictures and the Constitution very early in the history of the movie industry. In 1915, in *Mutual Film Corporation* v. *Ohio,* the Court upheld a State law that barred the showing of any film that was not of a "moral, educational, or harmless and amusing character." It declared that "the exhibition of moving pictures is a business, pure and simple," and "not . . . part of the press of the country." With that decision, nearly every State and thousands of local communities set up movie review, or movie censorship programs.

The Court reversed itself in 1952, however. In *Burstyn* v. *Wilson,* a New York censorship case, it found that "liberty of expression by means of motion pictures is guaranteed by the 1st and 14th Amendments."

Movie censorship is not necessarily unconstitutional, however. A State or local government can ban an obscene film, but only under a law that provides for a prompt judicial hearing. At that hearing that government must show that the picture in question is in fact obscene, *Teitel Film Corporation* v. *Cusack,* 1968.

Very few of the once common local movie review boards are still in operation. Most movie-goers now depend on newspaper movie critics and the film industry's own rating system.

Radio and Television

Both radio and television broadcasting are subject to extensive federal regulation.* Most of it is based on the often-amended Federal Communications Act of 1934, which is administered by the Federal Communications Commission; see page 454. As the Supreme Court has stated: "Of all forms of communication, it is broadcasting that has received the most limited 1st Amendment protection," *Red Lion Broadcasting Co.* v. *FCC,* 1969.

The Court has several times upheld this wide-ranging federal regulation as a proper exercise of the commerce power. Unlike newspapers and other print media, radio and television use the public's property—the public airwaves—to broadcast their materials. They have no such right without the public's permission—that is, without a proper license, *National Broadcasting Co.* v. *United States,* 1942.

The Court has regularly rejected the argument that the 1st Amendment prohibits such regulations. Instead, it has taken the view

*REINFORCEMENT Discuss: Censorship of movies, radio, and TV is used as a protective measure. From what are citizens being protected?

that that regulation *implements* the constitutional guarantee. It has stated: [There is no] "unabridgeable 1st Amendment right to broadcast comparable to the right of every individual to speak, write, or publish." However, "this is not to say that the 1st Amendment is irrelevant to broadcasting. But . . . it is the right of the viewers and the listeners, not the right of the broadcasters, which is paramount."[20]

Congress has forbidden the FCC to censor the content of programs before they are broadcast. But it may prohibit the use of indecent language, and it can take that matter into account when a station applies for the renewal of its operating license, *FCC* v. *Pacifica Foundation,* 1978. In some cases, the FCC has refused applications for renewal of licenses due to objectionable programs or practices. Congress itself cannot prohibit the broadcasting of editorials by public radio and television stations, *FCC* v. *League of Women Voters of California,* 1984.

Symbolic Speech

Ideas, views, and opinions are usually communicated in one of two ways. They can be presented *orally,* as in a conversation or a speech. Or, they can be in some *published* form, as in a newspaper, a book, a leaflet, a recording, or a film.

Importantly, a person's conduct—the way in which a person behaves or does a particular thing—can also be a means of expression. This way of saying something—expression by conduct—has come to be called **symbolic speech.**

Picketing in a labor dispute is a fairly common example. Picketing involves the patrolling of a business site by workers who are on strike. By their conduct, they attempt to inform the public of the controversy and to persuade customers and others not to deal with the firm involved. Picketing is, then, a form of expression. If peaceful, it is protected by the 1st and 14th Amendments.[21]

What conduct amounts to symbolic speech and is therefore protected by the Constitution? Clearly, the answer cannot be *all* conduct. If it were, murder, arson, robbery, or any other crime could be excused on grounds that the person who committed the crime meant to say something by doing so. Of course, drawing the line between protected speech and punishable conduct in real-life situations is not nearly so simple.

Generally, the Supreme Court has been sympathetic to the symbolic speech argument. But it has not given blanket 1st Amendment protection to that means of expression. As a quick sampling, consider the following cases.

United States v. *O'Brien,* 1968, involved four young men who had burned their draft cards as a protest against the war in Vietnam. They were then convicted of violating a federal law that makes it a crime to destroy or mutilate the cards. O'Brien defended his conduct by arguing that the 1st Amendment protects "all modes of communication of ideas by conduct." The Court upheld his conviction. Speaking for the majority, Chief Justice Earl Warren declared: "We cannot accept the view that an apparently limitless variety of conduct can be labeled 'speech' whenever the person engaging in the conduct intends thereby to express an idea."[22]

---

[20] *Red Lion Broadcasting Co.* v. *FCC,* 1969, in which the Court upheld the **fairness doctrine**—an FCC rule that says that radio and television broadcasters must present all sides of important public issues. The FCC also enforces the **equal time doctrine,** set out in the Communications Act of 1934. It provides that if a radio or television station or network makes air time available to one candidate for a public office, it must offer equal time to all other candidates for that office.

[21] The leading case on the point is *Thornhill* v. *Arizona,* 1940. There, the Court struck down a State law that made it a crime for one to loiter about or picket a place of business in order to influence others not to trade or work there. But picketing that is "set in a background of violence" may be prevented. Even peaceful picketing may be restricted if it is conducted for some illegal purpose, for example, to force someone to do something that is itself illegal, *Building Service Employees Union* v. *Gazzam,* 1950.

[22] The Court upheld the law under which O'Brien was punished. It found the cards to be a necessary part of the machinery of selective service. It ruled that acts of dissent by conduct can be punished if (1) the object of the protest—here, the war and the draft—is within the constitutional powers of the Government, (2) the incidental restriction on expression is no greater than necessary, and (3) the Government's real interest in the matter is not to squelch dissent.

Striking United Airline pilots picket to voice grievances with management. Picketing is protected by the 1st and 14th Amendments, as long as it is peaceful.

A police officer does not have a constitutional right to have long hair, even if he believes it to be a "a means of expressing his attitude and lifestyle," *Kelley* v. *Johnson*, 1976.

Giving money to a candidate for public office is a "symbolic expression of support" for that candidate. Nevertheless, the limits that Congress has placed on the amount that individuals may contribute to the campaigns of candidates for federal office do not violate the 1st Amendment, *Buckley* v. *Valeo*, 1976. The limits that Congress has put on the amounts that individuals may give to political action committees are also constitutional, *California Medical Association* v. *Federal Election Commission*, 1981.

Tinker v. *Des Moines School District*, 1969, on the other hand, is one of several cases in which the Court has come down on the side of symbolic speech.[23] A small group of students in the Des Moines public schools had worn black armbands to class. By that quiet behavior, they meant to publicize their opposition to the war in Vietnam. For it, they were suspended. The Court ruled that school officials had overstepped their authority and violated the Constitution. Said the Court: "It can hardly be argued that either students or teachers shed their constitutional rights to freedom of speech or expression at the schoolhouse gate."[24]

The Court reversed the Massachusetts

[23]The first such case was *Stromberg* v. *California*, 1931, which we cited on page 101. The Court held unconstitutional a State law making it a crime for any person to display a red flag "as a sign, symbol, or emblem of opposition to organized government."

conviction of a man sentenced to six months in jail for treating the American flag "contemptuously." He had worn a flag patch on the seat of his pants, *Smith* v. *Goguen,* 1974.

Remember, not all conduct can be justified as symbolic speech. Thus, in *Clark* v. *Community for Creative Non-Violence,* 1984, the Court upheld a rule that bans camping in certain national parks. Members of a protest group had been prevented from sleeping overnight in tents in Lafayette Park, across the street from the White House. They had claimed the right to do so, as a protest against the Reagan Administration's policies on the poor and homeless.

Billboards are regulated to combat "visual clutter," but those carrying political or non-commercial messages cannot be excluded.

Advertising

Until recently, it was generally thought that "commercial speech," or advertising, was not protected by the 1st and 14th Amendments. In *Bigelow* v. *Virginia,* 1975, however, the Court held unconstitutional a State law that prohibited the newspaper advertising of abortion services. In 1976 it struck down another Virginia law forbidding the advertising of prescription drug prices, *Virginia State Board of Pharmacy* v. *Virginia Citizens Consumer Council.*

It made similar rulings in two 1977 cases. In *Carey* v. *Population Services International,* it voided a New York law forbidding the advertisement of contraceptives. In *Bates* v. *Arizona Bar,* it invalidated rules that forbade attorneys to advertise services and fees.

The Court has also ruled that corporations ("artificial persons" in law) are entitled to freedom of speech. It first did so in a symbolic speech case, *First National Bank of Boston* v. *Bellotti,* 1978. The Court overturned a State law that prohibited corporations from spending money to influence votes in an issue election. More recently, the Court has held that a public utility cannot be prevented from inserting statements on controversial public issues in the monthly bills it sends to its customers, *Consolidated Edison* v. *Public Service Commission of New York,* 1980. However, a utility cannot be required to send political messages along with its customer billings, *Pacific Gas and Electric Co.* v. *Public Utilities Commission of California,* 1986. No group has a constitutional right to put political pamphlets or anything else in home mailboxes unless that material bears the correct amount of postage, *U.S. Postal Service* v. *Council of Greenburgh Civic Associations,* 1981.

Another recent case involved advertising, but with a different twist. In *Wooley* v. *Maynard,* 1977, the Court held that a State cannot force its citizens to act as "mobile billboards"—not, at least, when the words used conflict with their religious or moral beliefs. The Maynards, who were Jehovah's Witnesses, objected to the New Hampshire State motto on their automobile license plates. To them, the words "Live Free or Die" clashed with their belief in "everlasting life," and so they covered those words with tape. For this, Maynard was arrested three times, and on the third occasion he was jailed for 15 days. On appeal, the Supreme Court sided with the Maynards and ordered the State of New Hampshire to take no further action against them.

---

[24]The Court also said: "State-supported schools may not be enclaves of totalitarianism. School officials do not possess absolute authority over their students." Do not read too much into this, however, for the Court added, it "has repeatedly affirmed the comprehensive authority of the States and of school authorities, consistent with fundamental constitutional safeguards, to prescribe and control conduct in the schools." The fact that in *Tinker* the students' conduct did not produce any substantial disruption of normal school activities was an important factor in the Court's decision.

FOR REVIEW

1. **Identify:** freedom of speech, freedom of press, obscenity, prior restraint, "commercial speech"/advertising.
2. Why does the Constitution guarantee freedom of expression?
3. The rights of free speech and press are especially intended to protect the expression of what views?
4. May government impose a "prior restraint" on speech, writing, or other forms of expression?
5. Is obscenity entitled to constitutional protections? Are motion pictures? Radio and TV broadcasting?

4. Freedom of Expression: National Security

As You Read, Think About:

- What the limitations are that national security imposes on the freedom of expression.

What of those who seek to destroy this country and its form of government? Are they, too, protected by the constitutional guarantees of freedom of expression?

Remember, the guarantees of free speech and press are especially intended to protect *unpopular* opinions. Popular opinions do not need constitutional protection.

At the same time, however, recognize this point: Government has a right to protect itself and the nation against internal subversion—domestic threats to the nation's security. But how far can it go in doing so? How can government protect itself and at the same time preserve individual freedoms and democratic procedures?

*Clearly, government may punish espionage, sabotage, and treason. These are forms of action—conduct. **Espionage** is the practice of spying for a foreign power. **Sabotage** involves an act of destruction intended to hinder a nation's war or defense effort. **Treason** is specifically defined in the Constitution (Article III, Section 3). It can consist only in levying war against or adhering to the enemies of the nation; see page 155.

Sedition presents a much more delicate problem, for it involves the use of spoken or written words. **Sedition** is the incitement—the prompting, urging, fomenting—of resistance to lawful authority. It does not necessarily involve acts of violence or betrayal.

The Alien and Sedition Acts

Congress first acted to curb opposition to government in the Alien and Sedition Acts of 1798.[25] Those laws gave the President power to deport undesirable aliens and made "any false, scandalous, and malicious" criticism of the government a crime. The acts were intended to stifle the opponents of President John Adams and the Federalist Party.

The Alien and Sedition Acts were undoubtedly unconstitutional, but they were never tested in the courts. Some 25 persons were fined or jailed for violating them. The acts were a major issue in the elections of 1800, and a major reason for the defeat of the Federalists that year. In 1801 President Jefferson pardoned those sentenced under the acts; Congress soon repealed them.

Seditious Acts in Wartime

Congress passed another sedition law during World War I, as part of the Espionage Act of 1917. That law made it a crime to encour-

[25]This is the collective title given to a number of different laws passed by Congress at the time. They arose out of what President John Adams called this nation's "half war" with France. The French navy was seizing American merchant ships in the Atlantic to keep American goods from reaching England, with which France was then at war. The most important of these laws, the Sedition Act of 1798, made it a crime to write, utter, or publish "any false, scandalous, and malicious" statements "with intent to defame" the government or any of its officers or "to incite against them the hatred of the good people of the United States." Violations were punishable by a maximum fine of $2,000 and two years in prison. The first person convicted under the acts was Matthew Lyon, a member of Congress from Vermont. He had accused President Adams of "a continual grasp for power . . . an unbounded thirst for ridiculous pomp, foolish adulation and selfish avarice."

*REINFORCEMENT Ask for examples of internal subversion, specifically espionage, sabotage, and treason.

age disloyalty, interfere with the draft, obstruct recruiting, incite insubordination in the armed forces, or hinder the sale of government bonds. It also made it a crime to "willfully utter, print, write or publish any disloyal, profane, scurrilous, or abusive language about the form of government of the United States."

More than 2,000 persons were tried and convicted under its terms. The law was challenged and upheld several times. In the most important of those challenges, *Schenck* v. *United States,* 1919, the Supreme Court laid down the famous *clear and present danger rule.*

Schenck, the general secretary of the Socialist Party, and another party member had been convicted of trying to obstruct the war effort, in violation of the 1917 law. They had sent some 15,000 strongly worded leaflets to men who had been called to military service. These leaflets urged the men to resist the draft and not to cooperate in the conduct of the war.

The Supreme Court upheld both the law and the convictions. Speaking for the Court, Justice Holmes said:

> We admit that in many places and in ordinary times the defendants in saying all that was said in the circular would have been within their constitutional rights. But the character of every act depends upon the circumstances in which it is done. . . .

Senator Joseph McCarthy, during hearings he conducted in 1950s, branded many people as Communists. His smear tactics ruined thousands of reputations, based on little or no evidence.

Holmes continued:

> Words can be weapons. . . . The question in every case is whether the words used are used in such circumstances and are of such nature as to create a clear and present danger that they will bring about the substantive evils [that is, actions] that Congress has a right to prevent.

In short, the clear and present danger rule holds that words can be outlawed, and those who utter them can be punished when their use creates an immediate danger that criminal acts will follow.

But, and this is the vital point, *what* words used in *what* circumstances constitute a clear and present danger? That question can be answered only on the basis of the facts in each individual case to which the clear and present danger rule is applied.

Sedition in Peacetime

Congress had made the Espionage Act of 1917 effective only in time of war. In 1940, however, it passed a new sedition law, the Smith Act, and made it applicable in peacetime.[26] It later passed two other such statutes: the Internal Security (McCarran) Act of 1950 and the Communist Control Act of 1954.

The *Smith Act* makes it unlawful for any person to teach or advocate the violent overthrow of government in the United States or to organize or knowingly be a member of any group with such an aim. It also forbids conspiring with others to commit any of those acts. *

The Supreme Court first upheld the constitutionality of the Smith Act in *Dennis* v. *United States* in 1951. Eleven of the top leaders of the Communist Party had been convicted of teaching and advocating violent overthrow of the Government On appeal, they argued that the law violated the 1st Amendment's guarantees of freedom of speech and press.

[26]The Smith Act was passed as the United States moved closer to direct involvement in World War II.

*REINFORCEMENT Sedition poses a difficult problem for the Supreme Court because it involves the use of spoken or written words. Discuss the Smith Act as a response to this problem.

They also claimed that no act of theirs constituted a clear and present danger to this country.

The Court disagreed:

> An attempt to overthrow the government by force, even though doomed from the outset because of inadequate numbers or power of the revolutionists, is a sufficient evil for Congress to prevent. . . . We reject any principle of governmental helplessness in the face of preparation for revolution, which principle, carried to its logical conclusion, must lead to anarchy.

The Court has since modified that holding, however. In several later cases, it has sharply limited the use of the Smith Act. Thus, in *Yates* v. *United States,* 1957, it overturned the convictions of a number of lesser party leaders. Their convictions were reversed with this holding: Merely to urge someone to *believe* something, in contrast to urging someone to *do* something, cannot be made illegal. That is, the Smith Act can be applied only to those who teach or advocate *action* to bring about forcible overthrow.

The Court has upheld the "knowing membership" clause of the Smith Act, *Scales* v. *United States,* 1961. The Court also ruled that the Smith Act intends to punish only those who are active members of the Communist Party and those with a "specific intent" to overthrow the government, in *Noto* v. *United States,* 1961. The intent of the law is not to punish those who are passive or simply paper-affiliated members of the Communist Party.

The end result of the major Smith Act cases has been this: While the Court has upheld the constitutionality of the law, it has so construed its provisions as to make successful prosecutions under it very difficult.

The *McCarran Act* has proven to be an even less effective sedition law. Its major provisions require that all "Communist-action" and "Communist-front" organizations register with the Attorney General. They must report every year, naming their officers and all their members. The act also created the Subversive Activities Control Board to decide which groups are in fact subject to the law.

The Board first ordered the Communist Party to register in 1953, and the Supreme Court held that it could be forced to do so, *Communist Party* v. *SACB,* 1961. It never actually did, however, largely because any person who came forward to register the party, as required by the McCarran Act, could then be charged as a "knowing member" under the Smith Act. In 1965 the Court held that no person could be forced into this position. To do so would contradict the 5th Amendment's guarantee against self-incrimination, *Albertson* v. *SACB,* 1965.[27]

The Court further limited the effectiveness of the McCarran Act by holding other parts of it to be unconstitutional. Thus, for example, it struck down a provision denying members of Communist organizations the right to obtain or use passports. In *Aptheker* v. *Rusk,* 1964, it found that that section of the law was so broadly and loosely worded that it violated the 5th Amendment's Due Process Clause.

The net effect of court response to the McCarran Act has been to leave it a hollow shell. That result was far from unexpected. The several court decisions paralleled President Truman's veto that Congress overrode in passing the law in the first place.

The *Communist Control Act* declares the Communist Party in this country to be "a conspiracy to overthrow the Government of the United States." The act's goal was to outlaw the party and keep its candidates off the ballot in any election in this country. As a practical matter, the 1954 law failed. In 1984, as in every election since 1968, a Communist Party candidate for President appeared on the ballots of a number of States.

Two factors have made the matter of internal subversion less prominent today than it was only a few years ago. One is the overall ineffectiveness of the sedition laws. The other is that U.S.-Soviet relations, while still strained, are not as tense as they were in the Cold War period of the 1950s and 1960s.

---

[27]One practical effect of this decision was to leave the SACB with no real functions to perform. It finally passed out of existence when Congress stopped funding it in 1973.

FOR REVIEW

1. **Identify:** internal subversion.
2. What is sedition? Is it constitutionally protected? How does it differ from espionage, sabotage, or treason?
3. What were the Alien and Sedition Acts? Were they constitutional?
4. What is the "clear and present danger rule"?
5. What is the Smith Act? The McCarran Act? The Communist Control Act? What is the general effectiveness of each of those laws today?

5. Freedom of Expression: Assembly and Petition

As You Read, Think About:

- What limitations exist on the freedoms of assembly and of petition.

The 1st Amendment of the Constitution also guarantees

> the right of the people peacefully to assemble, and to petition government for a redress of grievances.

These rights are protected by the 14th Amendment's Due Process Clause, as well. As we noted on page 101, the Supreme Court first made that holding in *DeJonge* v. *Oregon*, 1937, and it has repeated it many times since.[28]

The Constitution protects the right of the people to assemble—to gather with one another—to express their views on public matters. It protects their right to organize, as in political parties and pressure groups, to influence public policy. It also protects their right to bring their views to the attention of public officials by such varied means as written petitions, letters, or advertisements, lobbying, or demonstrations.

Notice, however, that the right of *peaceable* assembly and petition is what is guaranteed. The Constitution does not give people the right to incite others to violence, to riot, to block a public street, to close a school, or otherwise to endanger life, property, or public order. In short, public assemblies must be carried out without disturbing the peace or causing any harm.

Time–Place–Manner Regulations

Government may make and enforce *reasonable* rules covering the time, place, and manner of assemblies. It must have that power in order to keep the public peace. Thus, the Supreme Court has upheld a city ordinance that prohibits making noise or causing any other diversion near a school if that action disturbs normal school activities,

LePelley in The Christian Science Monitor © 1984

"Step Carefully"

[28]DeJonge had been convicted of violating the State's law prohibiting acts of "criminal syndicalism," defined by the law as "the doctrine which advocates crime, physical violence, sabotage, or any unlawful acts" to bring about "industrial or political change or revolution." DeJonge had helped to conduct and had spoken at a public meeting sponsored by the Communist Party. For that behavior alone, he was sentenced to seven years in prison. The Court held that the 14th Amendment includes the rights of assembly and petition, declared the State law unconstitutional, and reversed DeJonge's conviction.

*REINFORCEMENT Discuss: The freedom of assembly and petition is yet another guarantee of the individual's rights. How can it be used to enhance the public's role in policymaking?

Grayend v. *City of Rockford,* 1972. It has also upheld a State law that forbids parades near a courthouse when they are intended to influence court proceedings, *Cox* v. *Louisiana,* 1965.

Rules for keeping the public peace must be more than reasonable. They must also be precisely drawn and fairly administered. In *Coates* v. *Cincinnati,* 1971, the Court struck down a city ordinance that made it a crime for three or more persons to assemble on a public sidewalk and there conduct themselves in a manner annoying to passersby. It found that law to be too vague and loosely worded. It also struck down an ordinance that banned all picketing around school buildings, except picketing involved in a labor dispute, *Police Department of Chicago* v. *Mosley,* 1972. Here the Court found that the ordinance went beyond time-and-place regulation and dealt with the *content* of an assembly.

The responsibility of public officials to control traffic or to keep a demonstration from growing into a riot can be, and sometimes is, used as an excuse to prevent speech. The line between crowd control and thought control can be very thin, and not always easy to recognize.

Demonstrations on Public Property

Over the past several years, most of the Court's freedom of assembly cases have involved organized demonstrations: mass meetings, parades, marches, sit-ins, picketing, and the like. Demonstrations are, of course, assemblies, or ways of communicating ideas and opinions.

Most demonstrations take place in *public* places—on streets and sidewalks, in parks or public buildings, and so on. They do because it is the *public* the demonstrators want to reach. They want to bring their message to those who may not be aware of it, and to reach those who may not agree with them.

Demonstrations almost always involve some degree of conflict. Mostly, they are held to protest something, and so a clash of ideas is present. Many times there is also a conflict with the normal use of streets or other public facilities. It is hardly surprising, then, that the heat generated by a demonstration can sometimes rise to a very serious level.

Given all this, the Supreme Court has often upheld State and local laws that require advance notice and permits for demonstrations in public places. In an early leading case, *Cox,* v. *New Hampshire,* 1941,[29] it unanimously approved such a law:

> The authority of a municipality to impose regulations in order to assure the safety and convenience of the people in the use of public highways has never been regarded as inconsistent with civil liberties but rather as one of the means of safeguarding the good order on which they ultimately depend. . . . The question in a particular case is whether the control is exercised so as to deny . . . the right of assembly and the opportunity for the communication of thought and the discussion of public questions.

"Right to demonstrate" cases raise many basic and thorny questions. How and to what extent can demonstrators and their demonstrations be regulated? Does the Constitution require that police officers allow an unpopular group to continue to demonstrate when its activities have excited others to violence? When, in the name of public peace and safety, can police properly order demonstrators to disband? *

Among these cases, *Gregory* v. *Chicago,* 1969, remains typical. Dick Gregory and several others had been arrested by Chicago police and charged with disorderly conduct. While under police protection, they had marched, singing, chanting, and carrying placards, from city hall to the mayor's home some five miles away. Marching in the streets around the mayor's house, they demanded the firing of the city's school superintendent and an end to de facto segregation in the city's schools.

A crowd of several hundred onlookers and residents of the all-white neighborhood

[29] This is one of the several Jehovah's Witness cases we referred to on page 111. Cox and several other Witnesses had violated a State law that required a license to hold a parade or procession on the public streets.

*REINFORCEMENT Have the class discuss the issues behind "Right to demonstrate" cases. Why does the Supreme Court have difficulty in deciding these types of civil rights cases?

quickly gathered. Soon, insults and threats, rocks, eggs, and other missiles were thrown at the marchers. The police tried to keep order, but after about an hour, they decided that serious violence was about to break out. At that point, they ordered the demonstrators to leave the area. When Gregory and the others failed to do so, they were arrested.

Their convictions were unanimously overturned by the High Court. It noted that the marchers had done no more than exercise their constitutional rights of assembly and petition. The disorders were caused by the neighborhood residents and others, not by the demonstrators. No matter how reasonable the police order, or how laudable the police motives, so long as the demonstrators acted peacefully, as they did, the Court ruled that they could not be punished.[30]

Right of Assembly and Private Property

What of demonstrations on private property, for example, at large shopping centers? So far, the Court has heard only a few cases raising this question. However, at least this much can be said at this point: The rights of assembly and petition do not give people a right to trespass on private property. People do not have a constitutional right to convert private property to their own uses, even if they wish to express political views.

Privately owned shopping centers are not public streets, sidewalks, parks, and other "places of public assembly." For that reason, no one has a constitutional right to do such things as hand out political leaflets or ask people to sign petitions in those places. Of course, private owners can allow peaceful political activities on their property.

These comments are based on the leading case here, *Lloyd Corporation* v. *Tanner*, 1972.

[30]At least they could not be punished under an ordinance making disorderly conduct a crime, for Gregory and the others had not acted in a disorderly way. The Court made it clear, however, that its decision might have been different if Chicago had acted under some specifically drawn time-place-manner ordinance, for example, one forbidding a demonstration in a residential neighborhood after a certain hour in the evening.

Store proprietors often permit the use of their property for such public purposes as gathering signatures for petitions or voter registration.

However, since that case the Court has held this: A State supreme court may interpret the provisions of that State's own constitution in such a way as to require the owners of shopping centers to allow the reasonable exercise of the right of petition on their private property. In that event, there is no violation of the property owners' rights under any provision in the federal Constitution, *Prune Yard Shopping Center* v. *Robbins*, 1980. In that case, several California high school students had set up a card table in the shopping center, passed out pamphlets, and asked passersby to sign petitions to be sent to the President and Congress.

FOR REVIEW

1. What does the constitutional guarantee of freedom of assembly and petition intend to protect?
2. May government ever regulate the rights of assembly and petition? If so, for what basic purpose?
3. Why do most demonstrations take place in public places? Why do they almost always involve some degree of conflict?
4. Does the Constitution guarantee a right to demonstrate on private property?

SUMMARY

The Constitution's many guarantees of civil rights are a major demonstration of the constitutional principle of limited government. Each of them is a prohibition or a restriction on the things that government may do.

Those guarantees are relative, however, not absolute. At times, different rights come into conflict with one another. With only minor exceptions, those rights belong to all persons, aliens as well as citizens.

Federalism produces a very complicated pattern of civil rights guarantees in this country. Much of that complication has been lessened over time, however, largely by the Supreme Court's interpretation and application of the 14th Amendment's Due Process Clause. The provisions of the Bill of Rights apply against the National Government *only*. In a now long series of cases, however, the Court has ruled that most of the protections set out in the Bill of Rights, which are applicable against the National Government, are also within the meaning of the 14th Amendment and so applicable against the States and their local governments, as well. The Court "nationalized" the Bill of Rights.

No all-inclusive listing of civil rights guarantees is possible. The seldom-noted 9th Amendment assures this. However, there are specific guarantees. The 1st Amendment protects freedom of expression. In broadest terms, it guarantees freedom of religion in both the Establishment Clause and the Free Exercise Clause, freedom of speech and press, and freedom of assembly and petition. All of these 1st Amendment protections of the right of expression are extended against the States by the 14th Amendment's Due Process Clause. All of the other constitutional guarantees of civil rights have to do with fair and equal treatment under the law, and are considered in the next chapter.

CHAPTER REVIEW

Key Terms/Concepts*

limited government (97)
Bill of Rights (98)
civil rights (98)
aliens (99)
Due Process Clause (101)
excessive entanglement standard (108)
libel (113)
slander (113)
shield laws (116)
picketing (117)
symbolic speech (117)
fairness doctrine (117)
equal time doctrine (117)
espionage (120)
sabotage (120)
treason (120)
sedition (120)

*These terms are included in the Glossary.

Keynote Questions

1. How is government authority in the United States limited? Give one example.
2. What is the difference between absolute rights and relative rights?
3. Do all of the rights guaranteed by the Constitution apply to all people in the United States? Explain.
4. What is the Bill of Rights? When and why was it added to the Constitution?
5. What effect has the Due Process Clause had on the Bill of Rights?
6. Why are the rights set out in the 1st Amendment called "fundamental freedoms"?
7. What is the excessive entanglement standard? Why is it important?
8. In what way is the free exercise of religion an absolute right? A relative right?

• **9.** What are the two fundamental purposes of the 1st and 14th Amendment's protections of free speech, free press, petition, and assembly?

•• **10.** List two examples of types of speech or expression that are not protected by the Constitution. Explain why these actions are not protected.

• **11.** What is prior restraint? Is it constitutional?

• **12.** What kinds of assembly are not protected by the Constitution? Why?

• **13.** Why has the Supreme Court often upheld State and local laws that require advance notice and permits for demonstrations in public places?

• **14.** What is the Smith Act? The McCarran Act? What has been the effect of Supreme Court decisions involving these laws?

Skill Application

Asking Effective Questions: In a courtroom, in business, and in everyday life, the ability to ask effective questions is an important skill. An effective question, when asked, will provide you with the information you need. Before you ask a question, think about the kind of information you are seeking as an answer. Most questions break down into several types.

1. Factual questions ask about a specific event, time, or process. For example: "In what year was the Constitution written?" or "What was the Supreme Court's decision in the *Tinker* case?"
2. Defining questions ask for an explanation of a word or term. For example: "What are relative rights?"
3. Opinion questions ask for the speaker's judgment without asking the speaker to support his or her opinion. For example: "What do you think of our current economic policies?"
4. Evaluation questions ask the speaker to discuss the pros and cons or the effects of a particular person or policy. For example: "How do you think *Sherbert* v. *Verner* affected business in the United States and why?"

When asking questions, think not only about the kind of information you need in the answer, but also about the speaker. What is the speaker's background? Is your question appropriate to this speaker?

The ability to ask effective questions—to ask exactly what you want to know—takes practice.

1. Read each of the questions below. Determine which type of question it is based on the categories above, and write the question-type on a separate piece of paper.
   a. What is confidentiality?
   b. Why have some States passed shield laws?
   c. Which Supreme Court case held that the 1st Amendment does not grant any special privileges to reporters?
   d. Do you think that reporters ought to have the right to protect their sources?
2. Read the section of this chapter on symbolic speech (page 117). Write four questions, one of each type, that you have about the concept of symbolic speech.

For Thought and Discussion

••• **1.** Do you agree that the law of libel and slander should be more tolerant of public officials than of private persons? Why or why not?

•• **2.** In what ways have some of the Supreme Court's decisions directly affected you?

Suggested Activities

•• **1.** Interview a member of your community who has been directly affected by a Supreme Court decision. Find out the person's attitude toward the decision and what the person thinks the consequences of the decision have been. Some examples of potential interviewees include: interviewing a reporter about *Branzburg* v. *Hayes;* a parochial school principal about *Lemon* v. *Kurtzman;* or a lawyer about *Bates* v. *Arizona Bar.*

••• **2.** Using current periodicals and newspapers, investigate four civil rights cases currently before the Supreme Court. What are the facts of each case? What constitutional issues are involved? How would you decide the case?

••• **3.** Stage a debate or class forum on this question: Resolved, That those who advocate the destruction of this country's free institutions are not entitled to the protections set out in the Constitution.

I have a dream that one day this nation will rise up and live out the true meaning of its creed: We hold these truths to be self-evident, that all men are created equal.
—MARTIN LUTHER KING, JR.

6 Civil Rights: Equal Justice Under Law

CHAPTER OBJECTIVES

To help you to

Learn · Know · Understand

The concept of due process of law and its pivotal place in the American system of civil rights.

The guaranteed rights to freedom and security of the person.

The guaranteed rights of persons accused of crime.

Safeguards of a fair trial for the accused in State and federal courts.

The guaranteed rights to equality under the law.

Civil rights laws of major importance passed by Congress in the last 30 years.

Qualifications for citizenship.

IN CHAPTER 5 we took a close look at the 1st Amendment freedoms—those constitutional guarantees of freedom of expression that lie at the heart of democratic belief and practice. Now we shall turn to those constitutional guarantees that are intended to ensure fair and equal treatment to all persons under the law.

Though it has had many successes, the American democratic system has not succeeded in extending the guarantees of fair and equal treatment to *all* persons in the United States, and most of all not to blacks or other ethnic minorities. At least it has not *yet* succeeded in doing so. None of our public problems is more compelling today.

1. Due Process of Law

As You Read, Think About:

- Why it is impossible to provide an exact definition of the due process guarantees.
- Why these guarantees are so important.
- What the difference is between procedural and substantive due process.

*ENRICHMENT Have the class discuss why some individuals in the United States do not enjoy the guarantees of fair and equal treatment. Are there any examples of this in their city? What can be done to change the situation?

The goal of the civil rights movement of the 1960s was to show the need for legislation making segregation and discrimination by race unlawful in public places, employment, housing, and voting. *Above:* Marchers walk (in 1965) to Montgomery, Alabama, to show their support for voting rights for blacks.

The Constitution contains two Due Process Clauses. The 5th Amendment declares that the Federal Government cannot deprive any person of "life, liberty, or property, without due process of law." The 14th Amendment also places the same restriction on each of the States and, very importantly, places these restrictions on all their local governments, as well.

Many people have said that these two provisions, and their meanings, are more difficult to understand than any other part of the Constitution. This may be true. But the fact remains that a thorough grasp of them is essential to an understanding of the American scheme of civil rights.

It is impossible to define the two due process guarantees in exact and complete terms. Over the years, the Supreme Court has consistently and purposely refused to give them an exact definition.[1] Fundamentally, however, they mean this: Government, in whatever it does, must act *fairly* and in accord with established *rules*. It may not act unfairly, arbitrarily, capriciously, or unreasonably.

Procedural and Substantive Due Process

As the two Due Process Clauses have been interpreted and applied by the Supreme Court, the meaning of due process has developed along two lines—one *procedural,* the other *substantive.*

Procedural Due Process The concept of due process began and developed in English and then in American law as a procedural

[1]Instead, it has relied on finding the meaning of due process on a case-by-case basis. The Court first described this approach more than a century ago, in *Davidson* v. *New Orleans,* 1878, as the "gradual process of judicial inclusion and exclusion, as the cases presented for decision shall require." It has followed this case-by-case approach ever since.

Handlesman, 1970, New Yorker Magazine, Inc.

"What's so great about due process? Due process got me ten years."

concept. That is, it developed as a requirement that government, in all that it does, must act fairly, use fair procedures.

Substantive Due Process Fair procedures are of little value, however, if they are used to administer unfair laws. The Supreme Court recognized this fact toward the end of the last century. It began to hold that due process requires that both the ways in which government acts *and* the laws under which it acts must be fair.

To the original notion of **due process** as a procedural requirement, then, the Court added the idea of substantive due process. In short, procedural due process has to do with the *how*, or the methods, of governmental action. Substantive due process involves the *what*, or the policies of governmental action.

Any number of cases can be used to illustrate these two elements of due process. For now, consider *Rochin* v. *California*, 1952, as an illustration of *procedural due process*.

Rochin was a suspected narcotics pusher. Acting on a tip, three Los Angeles County deputy sheriffs went to his rooming house. They found the door to the building open, entered, and then forced their way into Rochin's room. They found him sitting on a bed and spotted two capsules on a night stand beside it. When one of the deputies asked, "Whose stuff is this?" Rochin grabbed the capsules, popped them into his mouth, and although all three officers jumped him, managed to swallow the capsules.

Rochin was handcuffed and taken to a hospital, where his stomach was pumped. The capsules were recovered and found to contain morphine. Rochin was then prosecuted for violating the State's narcotics laws. The capsules proved to be the chief evidence against him and he was convicted and sentenced to 60 days in jail.

The Supreme Court overturned his conviction. It held that the deputies had violated the 14th Amendment's guarantee of procedural due process. Said the Court:

> This is conduct that shocks the conscience. Illegally breaking into the privacy of the petitioner, the struggle to open his mouth and remove what was there, the forcible extraction of his stomach's contents—this course of proceeding by agents of government to obtain evidence is bound to offend even hardened sensibilities. They are methods too close to the rack and the screw . . .

As an example of *substantive due process*, take a case we considered earlier, *Pierce* v. *Society of Sisters*, 1925. It involved an *initiative* measure.[2] In 1922 the voters of the State of Oregon had adopted a new compulsory school-attendance law. It required that all persons between the ages of 8 and 16 who had not completed the eighth grade had to attend *public* schools. The law's purpose was to destroy the private, especially the parochial, schools in the State.

A Roman Catholic order challenged the constitutionality of the law. It sued the governor to keep him from enforcing it. The Supreme Court ruled that the law violated the 14th Amendment's Due Process Clause.

The Court did not find that the State had enforced the law unfairly. In fact, the State's

[2]The **initiative** is a process by which a group may propose a law by gathering signatures on petitions. The process is available in 21 States; see page 573.

*REINFORCEMENT Ask the class to discuss the concept of due process of law. How does it apply to civil rights?

The Nationalization of the Bill of Rights

Year	Amend-ment	Provision Held to Be Within Meaning of 14th Amendment's Due Process Clause	Case
1925	1st	Freedom of speech	*Gitlow v. New York*
1931	1st	Freedom of press	*Near v. Minnesota*
1937	1st	Freedom of assembly, petition	*DeJonge v. Oregon*
1940	1st	Freedom of religion	*Cantwell v. Connecticut*
1947	1st	Establishment Clause	*Everson v. Board of Education*
1961	4th	Protection from unreasonable searches, seizures	*Mapp v. Ohio*
1962	8th	Prohibition of cruel and unusual punishment	*Robinson v. California*
1963	6th	Right to counsel in criminal cases	*Gideon v. Wainwright*
1964	5th	Protection from self-incrimination	*Mallory v. Hogan*
1965	6th	Right to confront witnesses	*Pointer v. Texas*
1967	6th	Right to speedy trial	*Klopfer v. North Carolina*
1967	6th	Right to obtain witnesses	*Washington v. Texas*
1968	6th	Right to trial by jury in criminal cases	*Duncan v. Louisiana*
1969	5th	Prohibition of double jeopardy	*Benton v. Maryland*

This table lists the landmark cases which protect individuals' basic rights against the States. What clause in the 14th Amendment makes nationalization possible?

courts had held the law unconstitutional, and it had never been put into effect. Rather, the Court said that the law itself, in its contents, "unreasonably interferes with the liberty of parents to direct the upbringing and education of children under their control." It also held that the law denied to private school teachers and administrators the liberty to "be engaged in an undertaking . . . long regarded as useful and meritorious."

The 14th Amendment and the Bill of Rights

On pages 101–102 we made the point that the Supreme Court has held that the 14th Amendment's Due Process Clause includes within its meaning many—most—of the provisions of the Bill of Rights. In a long series of decisions dating from 1925, the Court has *incorporated* those basic rights into the 14th Amendment and thus "nationalized" them. By holding that those rights are protected against the States through the 14th Amendment, as well as against the National Government in the Bill of Rights, the Court has made their meanings uniform throughout the country.

Does all this seem complicated? It is. But an understanding of this concept of nationalization of rights is crucial to an understanding of the meaning and importance of the 14th Amendment's Due Process Clause, and so to most of our civil rights law. The landmark cases in which the Supreme Court held that various of the Bill of Rights guarantees are within the meaning of the 14th Amendment are set out in the table on this page.[3]

Due Process and the Police Power

In the federal system, the reserved powers of the States include the very broad and very important **police power**—the power of each

[3]We looked at the key 1st Amendment cases in Chapter 5, and we shall look at those involving the 4th through the 8th Amendments over the next several pages in this chapter. As we shall see, the following provisions of the Bill of Rights have *not* been incorporated into the 14th Amendment's Due Process Clause: the 2nd and 3rd Amendments, the 5th Amendment's guarantee of grand jury, and the 7th Amendment's guarantee of jury trial in civil cases.

State to act to protect and promote the public health, public safety, public morals, and general welfare. It is, at base, the power of each State, and its local governments, to safeguard the well-being of its people.

The extent of the police power—a State's limits in exercising it—is decided by the courts when the use of that power conflicts with personal liberties.

Police power/civil rights cases are fairly common. As courts decide them, they face a very difficult task: Courts must strike a balance between the needs of society, on the one hand, and individual rights, on the other.

Any number of cases arising out of any number of situations can be used to illustrate the frequent conflict between the use of a State's police powers and the rights of individuals. Take, as an example, a matter often involved in drunk driving cases.[4]

Driving while under the influence of intoxicating liquor is a crime in every State. Every State's laws allow the use of one or more tests to determine whether a person arrested and charged with the offense was in fact drunk at the time of the incident. Some of those tests are fairly simple (at least for most sober people)—for example, those that require the accused to walk a straight line or touch the tip of his or her nose. Some are more sophisticated, however—notably the "breathalyzer test" or the drawing of a blood sample to measure the level of alcohol in a person's system. (In most States, a person who is suspected of drunk driving and refuses to submit to a breath or blood test faces the automatic suspension of his or her driver's license.)

Question: Does the requirement that a person submit to such a test violate his or her rights under the 14th Amendment? Does the test involve an unconstitutional search for and seizure of evidence? Does it amount to forcing a person to testify against himself or herself—unconstitutional compulsory self-incrimination? Or is the requirement a *proper* use of the police power?

Time after time, both the State and federal courts have come down on the side of police power. They have consistently upheld the right of society to protect itself against the drunk driver and rejected the individual rights' argument.

The leading case here is *Schmerber* v. *California,* 1966. The Supreme Court found no constitutional objection to a situation in which a police officer had directed a doctor to draw blood from a man the officer had arrested for drunk driving. The Court stressed these points: The blood sample was drawn in a hospital and in accord with accepted medical practice. The police officer had reasonable grounds to believe that the suspect was drunk. Further, had the officer taken time to secure a search warrant, the evidence could very well have disappeared from the suspect's system.

Again, any number of examples can be cited to show that legislators and judges have often found the public's health, safety, morals, and/or welfare to be of overriding importance. As a few more examples of the point, consider the following:

—*To promote health:* States and their local governments can forbid or limit the sale of intoxicants and dangerous drugs, forbid the practice of medicine or dentistry without a license, and require the compulsory vaccination of school children.

—*To promote safety:* States and their local governments can forbid concealed weapons; tall shrubs at intersections; and require adequate brakes, horns, lights, and shatter-proof glass on cars.

—*To promote morals:* States and their local governments can outlaw gambling,

[4]As another example, consider the highly controversial question of abortion. To what extent, if any, can a State limit a woman's right to an abortion? The leading case here is *Roe* v. *Wade,* 1973. A Texas law prohibited all abortions except those performed to save the life of the mother. The Supreme Court held that law unconstitutional. It ruled that: (1) during the first trimester of pregnancy (about three months) a State must recognize a woman's right to choose an abortion and cannot interfere with medical judgments in that matter; (2) during the second trimester a State, acting in the interests of women who undergo an abortion, may regulate but not prohibit that procedure; and (3) during the third trimester a State, acting to protect the unborn child, may regulate abortion and, if it chooses, even prohibit all abortions except those necessary to save the life of the mother.

*ENRICHMENT Have the class discuss: How does the police power of your State enter into your daily life? Do these limitations guard your civil rights?

The enforcement of regulations which protect the welfare of the public is the province of State and local police.

the sale of obscene materials, and prostitution, and forbid such establishments as taverns and adult theaters or bookstores in certain locations.

—*To promote welfare:* States and their local governments can enact minimum wage and maximum hours laws, limit profits of public utilities, and limit Sunday business operation.

Again, note the fact that though the States can regulate many activities through the police power, they cannot use that power in an unreasonable or unfair manner. Thus, a police officer may not use unnecessary force to make a person accused of drunk driving submit to a blood test. A city cannot forbid a street demonstration by some group just because the mayor opposes its political aims. Nor can a State ban the operation of private schools or the sale of all foreign-made cars.

FOR REVIEW

1. **Identify:** procedural due process, substantive due process, 14th Amendment.
2. Why does the Constitution contain two Due Process Clauses?
3. What does due process of law mean?
4. Briefly describe the difference between *procedural* and *substantive* due process.
5. What is the relationship between the Bill of Rights and the 14th Amendment's Due Process Clause?
6. What is a State's police power?

2. The Right to Freedom and Security of the Person

As You Read, Think About:

- What the constitutional ban on involuntary servitude is.
- What the ways are in which that ban has been extended.
- What constitutes unreasonable search and seizure.

Several constitutional guarantees are intended to protect the right of each and of all Americans to live as free persons.

Slavery and Involuntary Servitude: The 13th Amendment

The 13th Amendment was added to the Constitution in 1865. It ended over 200 years of black slavery in this country.

Section 1 of the Amendment states:

> Neither slavery nor involuntary servitude, except as a punishment for crime, whereof the party shall have been duly convicted, shall exist within the United States, or any place subject to their jurisdiction.

Importantly, Section 2 of this Amendment gives Congress the expressed power "to enforce this article by appropriate legislation."

Until 1865, each State could decide for itself whether or not to allow slavery within its borders. With the 13th Amendment, that power was denied to them, and to the National Government, as well.

Section 1 Section 1 of the Amendment is self-executing. That is, no action by Congress was needed to make it effective. Nonetheless, Congress has passed several laws to implement it. A violation of any of them can lead to a fine of up to $5,000 and/or as much as five years in prison.

As a widespread practice, slavery disappeared nearly 120 years ago. There are still occasional cases of it, however. As recently as 1984, in fact, a federal court in Michigan sentenced a farmer and his wife to prison for the crime. They had been convicted of holding two retarded men as slaves on their dairy farm for more than 11 years.

Most cases that have arisen under Section 1 have turned on the question of "involuntary servitude," or forced labor. The Antipeonage Act of 1867 makes it a federal crime for any person to hold another in peonage—a condition of servitude in which a person is bound to work for another in order to fulfill a contract or satisfy a debt. The act is still vigorously enforced.

Several times, the Supreme Court has struck down State laws making it a crime for any person to fail to work after having received money or other benefits by promising to do so. In destroying one of these State peonage laws, the Supreme Court said:

> The undoubted aim of the 13th Amendment as implemented by the Antipeonage Act was not merely to end slavery but to maintain a system of completely free and voluntary labor throughout the United States.[5]

The 13th Amendment does not forbid *all* forms of involuntary servitude, however.

[5]*Pollock* v. *Williams*, 1944. However, the fact that a person cannot be forced to work in order to satisfy a debt does *not* relieve that person of the legal obligation to pay the debt.

Civil Rights Guarantees in the Federal Constitution

Protections Against the National Government

- Writ of habeas corpus not to be suspended except during rebellion or invasion. *Article I, Section 9, Clause 2.*
- No bills of attainder. *Article I, Section 9, Clause 3.*
- No ex post facto laws. *Article I, Section 9, Clause 3.*
- Treason strictly defined and punishment limited. *Article III, Section 3.*
- No establishment of religion. *1st Amendment.*
- No interference with religious belief. *1st Amendment.*
- No abridgment of freedom of speech or press. *1st Amendment.*
- No interference with right of peaceable assembly or petition. *1st Amendment.*
- No infringement of the right of people to keep and bear arms. *2nd Amendment.*
- Soldiers not to be quartered in private homes in time of peace without owners' consent. *3rd Amendment.*
- No unreasonable searches, seizures; no warrants except on probable cause. *4th Amendment.*
- No criminal prosecution except grand jury action. *5th Amendment.*
- No double jeopardy. *5th Amendment.*
- No compulsory self-incrimination. *5th Amendment.*
- No person to be deprived of life, liberty, property without due process of law. *5th Amendment.*
- Trials to be speedy, public. *6th Amendment.*
- Trial of crimes by impartial jury. *Article III, Section 2; 6th Amendment.*
- Persons accused of crime must be informed of charges, confronted with witnesses, have power to call witnesses, have assistance of counsel. *6th Amendment.*
- Jury trial of civil suits involving more than $20. *7th Amendment.*
- No excessive bail or fines. *8th Amendment.*
- No cruel and unusual punishment. *8th Amendment.*
- No slavery or involuntary servitude. *13th Amendment.*

Protections Against States and Their Local Governments

- No bills of attainder. *Article I, Section 10, Clause 1.*
- No ex post facto laws. *Article I, Section 10, Clause 1.*
- No slavery or involuntary servitude. *13th Amendment.*
- No denial of privileges and immunities to citizens of other States. *Article IV, Section 2, Clause 1; 14th Amendment.*
- No person to be deprived of life, liberty, property without due process of law. *14th Amendment.*
- No person to be denied equal protection of the laws. *14th Amendment.*

REAL ESTATE

EQUAL HOUSING OPPORTUNITY

All real estate advertised herein is subject to the Federal Fair Housing Act of 1968 which makes it illegal to advertise "any preference, limitations, or discrimination based on race, color, religion, sex, or national origin, or an intention to make any such preferences, limitations, or discrimination based on race, color, religion, sex, or national origin, or an intention to make any such preferences, limitation, or discrimination."

We will not knowingly accept any advertising, for real estate which is in violation of the law. All persons are hereby informed that all dwellings advertised are available on an equal opportunity basis.

1080 Co-ops

It is illegal for newspapers to accept real estate ads that are discriminatory.

Thus, in 1918 the Court drew a distinction between "involuntary servitude" and "duty" in upholding the constitutionality of the selective service system (the draft).[6] Nor does imprisonment for crime violate the Amendment. Note that its guarantee, unlike any other in the Constitution, applies against *private* and public actions.

Section 2 Shortly after the Civil War, Congress passed several civil rights laws, based on the 13th Amendment and applicable to both public officials *and* private parties. But in several cases, especially the *Civil Rights Cases,* 1883, the Supreme Court sharply narrowed the scope of federal authority. In effect, the Court held that racial discrimination against blacks by private persons did not place the "badge of slavery" on blacks nor keep them in servitude.

Congress soon repealed most of those laws. Federal enforcement of the few that remained was, at best, unimpressive. For years it was generally believed that Congress did not have the power under the 13th, or the 14th, Amendment to deal directly with private parties who practice racial discrimination.

In *Jones* v. *Mayer,* 1968, however, the Supreme Court breathed new life into the 13th Amendment. The case centered on one of the post–Civil War acts Congress had not repealed. Passed in 1866, that almost forgotten law provided in part:

> All citizens of the United States shall have the same right in every State and Territory, as is enjoyed by white citizens thereof, to inherit, purchase, lease, sell, hold, and convey real and personal property.

Jones had sued because Mayer had refused to sell him a home in St. Louis County, Missouri, solely because he was black. Mayer contended that the 1866 law was unconstitutional, as it sought to prohibit *private* racial discrimination.

The Court decided, 7–2, for Jones. It upheld the law, declaring that the 13th Amendment abolished slavery *and* gives to Congress the power to abolish "the badges and the incidents of slavery." Said the Court:

> At the very least, the freedom that Congress is empowered to secure under the 13th Amendment includes the freedom to buy whatever a white man can buy, the right to live wherever a white man can live. If Congress cannot say that being a free man means at least this much, then the 13th Amendment made a promise the Nation cannot keep.

Since that decision the Court has reaffirmed it several times.[7] For example, it did so in *Runyan* v. *McCrary,* 1976. Two black students had been refused admittance to two private schools in Virginia. In doing so the schools had refused to enter into a contract of admission, which the schools advertised to the general public. The Court held that, by

[6]*Selective Draft Law Cases* (*Arver* v. *United States*), 1918. The Court held military conscription to be a proper exercise of the power of Congress "to raise and support armies," Article I, Section 8, Clause 12.

[7]While *Jones* v. *Mayer* was before the Court. Congress enacted the Civil Rights (Open Housing) Act of 1968; see page 163.

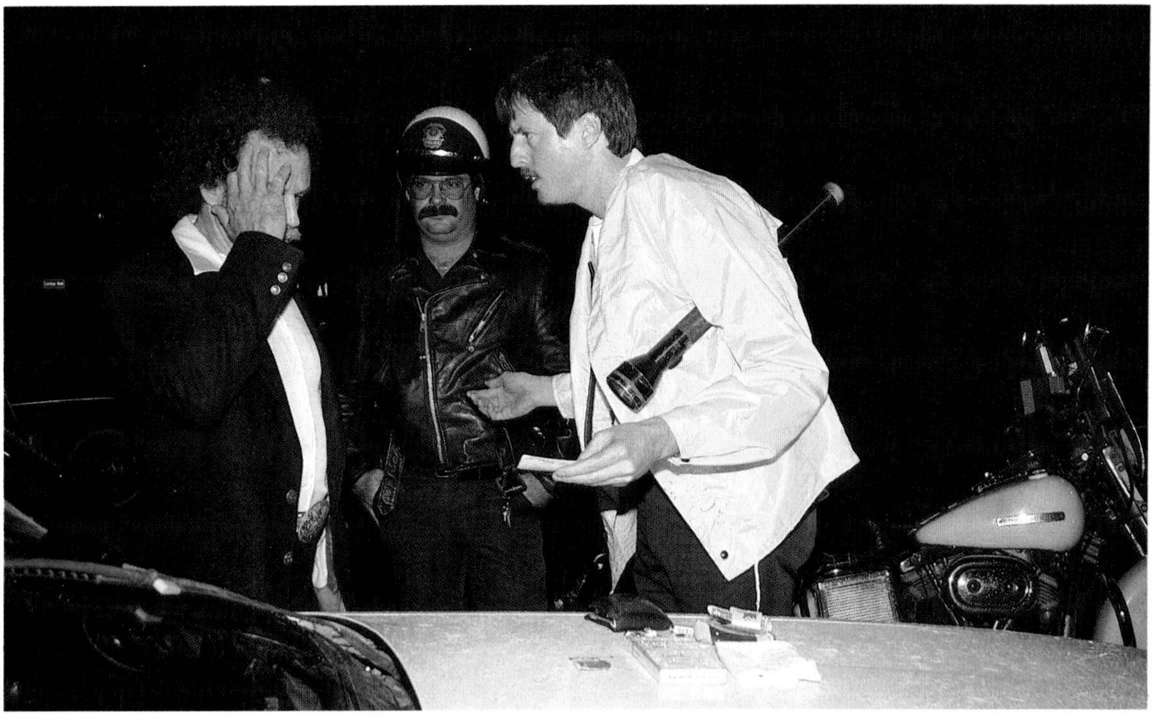

A motorist may be stopped if there is good reason to believe a law is being broken.

refusing to admit the black students solely because of their race, the schools had violated the century-old civil rights law. In its ruling the Court applied another provision of the 1866 law:

> All persons within the jurisdiction of the United States shall have the same right in every State and Territory to make and enforce contracts . . . as is enjoyed by white citizens . . .

In effect, the 13th Amendment, as it is now applied, gives Congress the power to enact whatever legislation is necessary and proper to overcome any of "the badges and the incidents of slavery," from whatever source.

"A Man's Home Is His Castle"

In several of its provisions, the Constitution enshrines the storied maxim that "a man's home is his castle."

The 3rd Amendment This Amendment forbids the quartering of soldiers in private homes in time of peace. It also prohibits the practice in time of war except "in a manner to be prescribed by law." The guarantee was added to the Constitution to prevent what had been British practice in colonial days. Recall that one of the grievances in the Declaration of Independence had been "Quartering large bodies of troops among us." The amendment has had almost no importance in our history.

The 4th Amendment This Amendment also grew out of colonial practice. It was designed to prevent the use of writs of assistance—blanket search warrants—with which customs officials had invaded private homes to search for smuggled goods.

The 4th Amendment has proved a highly important guarantee. It reads:

> The right of the people to be secure in their persons, houses, papers, and effects, against unreasonable searches and seizures, shall not be violated; and no warrants shall issue, but upon probable cause, supported by oath or affirmation, and particularly describing the place to be searched, and the persons or things to be seized.

Each of the 50 State constitutions has a similar provision. Recall, the guarantee also applies against the States through the 14th Amendment's Due Process Clause.

The general rule laid down by the 4th Amendment is this: Police officers have no *general* right to search for evidence or to seize either evidence or persons. Except in particular circumstances, they must have a proper **warrant,** or court order, obtained with **probable cause**—*i.e.* reasonable grounds.

* Note that the Constitution forbids only *unreasonable* searches and seizures. There are many situations in which a lawful search or seizure can be made *without* a warrant.

For example: No warrant is necessary when police are in "hot pursuit" of a suspect. In *United States* v. *Santana,* 1976, the Supreme Court upheld the arrest, the search that was made, and the later conviction of a woman whom police had first spotted standing outside her home. The officers, who were there to arrest her on a heroin charge, pursued and caught her just inside. There they arrested her. In searching her, they found both heroin and the marked bills with which an undercover agent had only minutes earlier made a buy. Because all of this had taken place without a warrant, she argued that her arrest and the search conducted in her home were prohibited by the 14th Amendment.

An arrest is the "seizure" of a person. When a lawful one is made, officers do not need a warrant to search "the arrestee's person and the area within his immediate control"—that is, "the area within which he might gain possession of a weapon or destructible evidence."[8]

In fact, most arrests take place without a warrant. Police may arrest a person in a *public place,* a street or park, for example, without one—*provided* they have probable cause to believe that that person has committed or is about to commit a crime. Nor do police need a warrant to search an automobile, a boat, an airplane, or other vehicle they have good reason to believe contains evidence of a crime or is being used to commit one—because such a "movable scene of crime" could disappear while the warrant was being sought.[9]

But, notice, police cannot stop a motorist "at random." They must *first* have good reason to believe that a law is being broken, *Delaware* v. *Prouse,* 1979. Once they do stop a car in connection with a crime, however, they may search any container in that car that they think might hold evidence of the crime involved, *United States* v. *Ross,* 1982.

Nor is a warrant needed to seize evidence "in plain view"—for example, ten amphetamine pills found during the routine inventory of the contents of a backpack, after its owner had been arrested for disturbing the peace, *Illinois* v. *Lafayette,* 1983.

The Court first held that police do not need a warrant to search open fields in *Hester* v. *United States,* 1924. It upheld that ruling in two 1984 cases, *Oliver* v. *United States* and *Maine* v. *Thornton.* In the recent cases, police had found marijuana growing in fields they had entered and searched, despite "no trespassing" signs, fences, and locked gates. As the Court noted, the 4th Amendment protects "persons, houses, papers, and effects"—and open fields are none of those things. Nor are warrants needed for the aerial surveillance of commercial properties (*Dow Chemical Company* v. *United States,* 1986) or the backyards of private homes (*California* v. *Ciraolo,* 1986).

Look at a 1978 case to illustrate the line between warrantless searches that are lawful and those that are not. In *Michigan* v. *Tyler,* 1978, the Court set aside the arson convictions of two furniture dealers. Much of the evidence against them had come from

---

[8]The Supreme Court has had much trouble with setting the limits to which a search incident to a lawful arrest can be carried. The present rule, quoted here, was first laid down in *Chimel* v. *California,* 1969.

[9]But in the leading case on the point, *Carroll* v. *United States,* 1925, the Court emphasized that "where the securing of a warrant is reasonably practicable it must be used . . . In cases where seizure is impossible except without a warrant, the seizing officer acts unlawfully and at his peril unless he can show the court probable cause." In *California* v. *Carney,* 1985, the Court ruled that a motor home that can be easily moved as a vehicle can be searched without a warrant. But, the Court noted, motor homes clearly being used as a fixed dwelling place—those elevated on blocks, connected to utilities, and otherwise not "readily mobile"—do not fall within the 4th Amendment's "automobile exception."

*ENRICHMENT Discuss in class: The need for a warrant has often prevented the police from following up on a good lead. Given this fact, do you feel that warrants should be required?

two separate sets of warrantless searches. One set had taken place as the fire department fought a blaze in their store and immediately thereafter. The other searches were made some weeks later.

The Court found that a burning building presents an emergency situation, one in which a warrantless entry is clearly reasonable. It held that the firefighters, once inside the store, could seize any evidence in plain view. The Court also held that the later searches, made *well after* the emergency, and also made without warrants, violated the 4th and 14th Amendments.

The Exclusionary Rule The real heart of the search and seizure guarantee lies in the answer to this question: *If* an unlawful search or seizure *does* occur, what use can be made of the evidence that is found? If that "tainted evidence" can be used in court, then the 4th Amendment offers no real protection to a person accused of crime.

To meet that problem, the Supreme Court adopted, and is still refining, the **exclusionary rule.** At base, the rule is this: Evidence gained as the result of an illegal act by police officers cannot be used against the person from whom it was seized.

The rule was first laid down more than 70 years ago. In *Weeks* v. *United States,* 1914, the Court held that evidence obtained by an illegal act by federal officers cannot be used in the federal courts.

For more than 40 years, however, the Court left the question of the use of such evidence in State courts for each State to decide for itself. But, in a historic decision in 1961, the Court extended the exclusionary rule against the States. In *Mapp* v. *Ohio* it held that the 14th Amendment forbids unreasonable searches and seizures by State and local officers, just as the 4th Amendment bars such actions by federal officers. The court also held that the fruits of an illegal search or seizure cannot be used in the State courts, just as they cannot be used in the federal courts.

In *Mapp,* Cleveland police had gone to Dollree Mapp's home to search for gambling materials. They entered her house forcibly, and without a warrant. Although they found no gambling evidence, their very thorough search did turn up some obscene books, the possession of which was prohibited by Ohio law. Mapp was later convicted of possession of the books and sentenced to jail. The Supreme Court overturned that conviction, because the evidence against her had been found and seized without a warrant.

The exclusionary rule has always been controversial. It was intended to put teeth into the 4th Amendment, and it has. It says to police: As you enforce the law, obey the law. To state the purpose of the exclusionary rule another way, it seeks to prevent, or at least deter, police misconduct.

Critics of the exclusionary rule note that the rule means that some persons who are clearly guilty nonetheless go free. Why, they often ask, should criminals be able "to beat the rap" on "a technicality"?

Of late, the High Court has been narrowing the scope of the rule.[10] It did so most particularly in two major cases in 1984. First, the Court found an "inevitable discovery" exception to it, in *Nix* v. *Williams.* It held that tainted evidence *can* be used *if* that evidence "ultimately or inevitably would have been discovered by lawful means." The case involved a murderer whom police had tricked into leading them to the corpse.

Then, in *United States* v. *Leon,* the Court found a "good faith" exception. There, police used what they thought was a proper warrant and seized large quantities of drugs. Their warrant was later shown to be faulty, however. Said the Court: "When an officer acting with objective good faith has obtained a search warrant . . . and acted within its scope . . . there is nothing to deter."

---

[10]For example, the Court has held that the rule does not apply to federal grand jury proceedings, *United States* v. *Calandra,* 1974. Thus, tainted evidence that cannot be used at a person's trial could nonetheless be presented to the grand jury—the body that indicted that person and so caused the trial. The Court has also held that evidence against a defendant that was gained by an illegal search of *another* person's property can be used in a criminal trial, *United States* v. *Payner,* 1980. Payner had been convicted of tax evasion. A private detective working for the IRS had stolen papers from a banker's briefcase. Those papers had led to the evidence of Payner's crime.

Wiretapping Wiretapping, electronic eavesdropping, videotaping, and other even more sophisticated means of "bugging" are now quite widely used. They present difficult search and seizure questions for the courts which the Framers of the 4th Amendment could not have begun to imagine.

In its first wiretapping case, in 1928, the Supreme Court held that intercepting telephone conversations without a warrant was not an unreasonable search or seizure. In 1967 it reversed that decision, however, holding that such communications are within the 4th Amendment's protection.

The earlier case, *Olmstead* v. *United States,* 1928, involved a large ring of bootleggers operating out of Seattle. Federal agents had tapped Olmstead's telephone calls over several months. That bugging produced a mass of evidence that was then used to convict him and others in the ring. The Supreme Court upheld their convictions. It ruled that even though the agents had had no warrants, they had not made any illegal searches or seizures. It found that there had been no "actual physical invasion" of Olmstead's home or office; the agents had tapped the lines *outside* those places.[11]

Congress reacted to the Court's decision in *Olmstead* in one part of the Federal Communications Act of 1934. Referring to radio, telegraph, and telephone communications, it forbade anyone to "intercept any communication and divulge or publish" its contents.

In several later cases, the Supreme Court held that that law effectively banned the use of wiretap evidence in the federal courts. Note that what the 1934 law prohibited was to intercept *and* divulge; thus wiretapping could, and did, go on. In the eyes of many, that practice amounted to a most serious and unjustifiable invasion of privacy. That view was supported by the widespread bugging activities of the FBI and the CIA in the 1960s and early 1970s.

[11]In a vigorous dissent, Justice Oliver Wendell Holmes was strongly critical of "such dirty business"—federal agents acting without a warrant. He wrote: "For my part I think it is a less evil that some criminals should escape than that the government should play such an ignoble part."

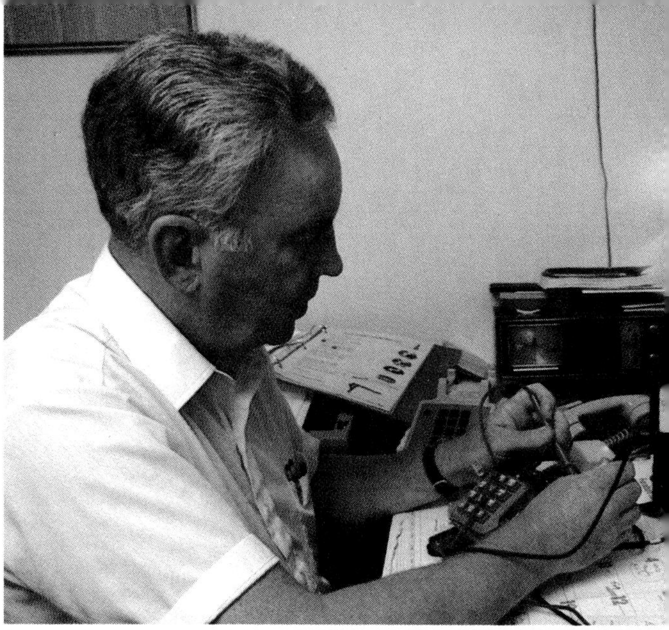
A telephone is tested for wiretapping.

The Supreme Court expressly overruled *Olmstead* in *Katz* v. *United States,* 1967. Katz had been found guilty of transmitting betting information across State lines, from a public phone booth in Los Angeles to his contacts in Boston and Miami. Much of the evidence against him had come from an electronic listening and recording device FBI agents had placed on the outside of the booth. The Court of Appeals, using the *Olmstead* rule, held that there had been no need for a warrant because there had been "no physical entrance into the area occupied" by the defendant.

The Supreme Court reversed the conviction and, in doing so, overruled *Olmstead.* It held, 7–1, that the 4th Amendment protects *persons* and not just places. Though Katz was in a public booth, he was entitled to make a *private* call. Said the Court:

> What a person knowingly exposes to the public, even in his own home or office, is not a subject of 4th Amendment protection. . . . But what he seeks to preserve as private, even in an area accessible to the public, may be constitutionally protected.

The Court went on to say, however, that the 4th Amendment could be satisfied in such situations if police officers have a proper warrant *before* they install a listening device.

Parts of the Omnibus Crime Control Act of 1968 show Congress's reaction to *Katz.* Those parts amended the Communications Act

*REINFORCEMENT Use the Watergate case to introduce a discussion of wiretapping. Remind the students that this case ultimately resulted in President Nixon's resignation.

of 1934. They make it illegal for any unauthorized person to tap telephone wires or use electronic bugging devices or sell those devices in interstate commerce.

The 1968 law does allow federal and State police agencies to search for and seize evidence by electronic means, however, under close court control. If officers can show probable cause, a federal or State judge may issue a warrant for a bugging operation.[12]

When it passed the 1968 law, Congress carefully avoided this knotty question: Does the President, acting under the inherent power to protect the nation against foreign attack and internal subversion, have the power to order the wiretapping or other bugging of suspected foreign agents or domestic subversives without a warrant? For many years, several Presidents had used the FBI, the CIA, and other federal police agencies in just that way.

The Supreme Court has since ruled that the President has no such power in cases of domestic subversion, *United States* v. *United States District Court,* 1972. In the Foreign Intelligence Surveillance Act of 1978, Congress, for the first time, required a warrant even for the wiretapping or other electronic bugging of foreign agents in this country.[13]

Right to Keep and Bear Arms

The 2nd Amendment reads this way:

> A well-regulated militia being necessary to the security of a free state, the right of the people to keep and bear arms shall not be infringed.

It was added to the Constitution to protect the right of each State to keep a militia. It was intended to preserve the concept of the citizen-soldier—the "minuteman"—as its text suggests. It does not guarantee the "right to keep and bear arms" free from government restriction.

The only important Supreme Court case dealing with the meaning of the 2nd Amendment was decided more than 40 years ago. In *United States* v. *Miller,* 1939, the Court upheld the constitutionality of a section of the National Firearms Act of 1934. That section of the law makes it a crime for any person to ship a sawed-off shotgun, a machine gun, or a silencer across State lines unless he or she has registered the weapon with the Treasury Department and paid a $200 tax on it. The Court said that it could find no reasonable relationship between the sawed-off shotgun involved in the case and "the preservation and efficiency of a well-regulated militia."

The Court has never found the 2nd Amendment to be within the meaning of the 14th Amendment's Due Process Clause. Thus, each of the States may limit the right to keep and bear arms, and all of them do, in various ways.

FOR REVIEW

1. **Identify:** peonage, 13th Amendment, 3rd Amendment, 4th Amendment, writs of assistance, wiretapping, 2nd Amendment.
2. Why does the 13th Amendment not forbid *all* forms of involuntary servitude? Why is Section 2 so important?
3. How has the Supreme Court "breathed new life" into the 13th Amendment?
4. Why is the 3rd Amendment of so little importance?
5. What does the 4th Amendment prohibit?
6. What is the exclusionary rule? How does it apply against the States?
7. Can evidence gained by wiretapping or other electronic bugging be used in court?
8. Why does the 2nd Amendment have much political but little legal significance today?

[12] In certain "emergency" situations, especially those involving national security or organized crime, the attorney general can authorize bugging operations by federal agents for up to 48 hours without a judge's approval—that is, without a warrant. A warrant must be sought during that period, however.

[13] The 1978 law set up a special federal court, the Foreign Intelligence Surveillance Court, with the power to issue such warrants. It is made up of seven U.S. district court judges appointed by the Chief Justice, and its proceedings are secret.

The law allows only one exception to its warrant requirement: The National Security Agency, the Defense Department's top-secret code-making and code-breaking agency, does not need a warrant to eavesdrop on the electronic communications of foreign governments.

*ENRICHMENT A warrant for a bugging operation may be issued if officers can show probable cause. Ask the students to discuss the meaning of the term probable cause.

FOCUS ON:

Gun Control: Yes or No?

The mere mention of gun control laws—of measures to restrict or prohibit the ownership of firearms—sparks intense debate nearly everywhere today.

Suppose that you are a member of your city's council and now, at today's council meeting, you must vote on a gun control ordinance. Your six colleagues on the council are evenly divided on the question. Three are for the measure and the other three oppose it. Your vote will decide the matter.

The proposed ordinance has been carefully drawn. It would apply only to handguns. At base, it would outlaw the private possession, use, or sale of nearly all such weapons within the city. The only exceptions to the ban would be those handguns kept in gun collections or used only for target-shooting purposes.

You have been bombarded by arguments, pro and con, at several long, crowded, and often stormy council sessions, in the newspapers, on television, and in many other places.

Most who support the ordinance have argued that its adoption would help to reduce violent crime in your city. They have built much of their case on the FBI's crime reports. The statistics in those reports show that handguns are now used to commit some 10,000 murders, 140,000 aggravated assaults, and 180,000 robberies in this country every year. Those who support the ordinance also point to the numerous accidental deaths and injuries each year because of careless handling of firearms.

Many who want to see the ordinance passed have said that they are most deeply concerned about "Saturday-night specials"—those small, cheaply made, and easily concealed pistols, which, they say, are the weapons most often used by criminals.

Most supporters of the proposal are deeply troubled by *all* handguns. They claim (again, with FBI support) that well over 50 million handguns are now in circulation in the United States. That mindboggling number, they say—the sheer, all-too-ready availability of those weapons—is itself a major cause of violent crime. As one of them put it at the last council meeting: "If you pass this ordinance, it will be much more difficult for the bad guys to get hold of guns. It's a heckuva lot harder to rob a bank with a knife or a baseball bat than it is to do that job with a pistol."

The opponents of the measure have made a strong case, too. Nearly all of them have cited the 2nd Amendment and what they insist is the Constitution's guarantee of their right to keep and bear arms. Most of them have also developed a number of other points.

They have said that the antigun people are aiming at the wrong target. *Guns* don't kill people, *people* kill people. They have also argued that criminals will always find guns somewhere, even if they are outlawed. Further, they have said that the only thing this law would do is make it more difficult for decent people to defend themselves against the criminals in your city.

One of the measure's opponents took the FBI's statistics and turned them back on its proponents: "If you look closely at the FBI's data," he said, "you will see that the average American citizen can expect to live for at least 23,000 years before he or she is murdered."

Other points were made, on both sides. But these were the major ones, and now the debate is over. Now you must cast your vote. How will you vote? What arguments most influenced your choice?

3. Rights of Persons Accused of Crime

As You Read, Think About:

- What the constitutional protections are that are extended to persons accused of crime.

The federal Constitution and each of the State constitutions set out several guarantees of fair treatment for those persons accused of crime. As we look at these protections, keep these fundamentally important points in mind.

Crimes are legal wrongs, wrongs against the public. They are acts that the law prohibits, and for which the law provides punishment. Those persons who commit them harm *not only* their immediate victims, they do harm to *all* persons—to the people as a whole. Criminals deserve to be punished, and society *must* punish them in order to preserve itself.

The law intends to protect *all* persons in criminal matters, *including* those persons who are suspected or accused of crime. Each of the protections to which we now turn is rooted in this historic concept: Any person who is suspected or accused of a crime must be presumed to be *innocent*—unless and until that person is *proved* guilty, by fair and lawful means.

Habeas Corpus

The **writ of habeas corpus**, sometimes called the "writ of liberty," is intended to prevent unjust arrests and imprisonments.[14] It is a court order directed to an officer holding a prisoner. It commands that the prisoner be brought before the court and that the officer show cause—explain, with good reason—why the prisoner should not be released. If that cause cannot be shown, the court will free the prisoner.

[14]The phrase *habeas corpus* comes from the Latin, meaning "you should have the body," and those are the opening words of the writ. The writ is almost always directed to a public official, a sheriff, a jailer, or other such public officer. It may also be used in disputes between private parties, however.

The right to seek a writ of *habeas corpus* is protected against the National Government in Article I, Section 9 of the Constitution. That right is guaranteed against the States in each of their own constitutions.

The right to the writ cannot be suspended, says the Constitution, "unless when in cases of rebellion or invasion the public safety may require it." But the Constitution does not make clear whether the right may be suspended throughout the country or, instead, only in those areas that are the actual scenes of rebellion or invasion.[15]

The single suspension of the writ since the Civil War, in Hawaii during World War II, was later decided to be illegal by the Supreme Court.[16]

Bills of Attainder

A **bill of attainder** is a legislative act that inflicts punishment without a court trial. Neither Congress nor the States can pass such measures.[17]

The ban on bills of attainder is both a protection of individual freedom *and* a part

[15]President Lincoln suspended the writ in 1861, early in the Civil War. His order covered various parts of the country, including several areas in which war was not then being waged. He issued the order on the basis of his military powers as Commander in Chief. Chief Justice Roger B. Taney, sitting as a circuit judge, held Lincoln's action unconstitutional. Taney ruled that the Constitution gives the power to suspend the writ only to Congress, *Ex parte Merryman,* 1861. Congress then passed the Habeas Corpus Act of 1863, giving the President the power to suspend the writ when and where, in his judgment, that action was necessary.

Whether the writ may be suspended where there is no actual fighting, or not likely to be any, was considered by the Supreme Court in *Ex parte Milligan* in 1866. The full Court agreed that the President could not do so, and a majority of five justices also held that even Congress does not have that power.

[16]The Hawaiian Islands were put under martial law by the territorial governor immediately after the Japanese attack on Pearl Harbor, December 7, 1941. His order was issued with the approval of President Roosevelt. It suspended the writ of *habeas corpus* and also replaced all civilian courts with military tribunals.

In *Duncan* v. *Kohanamoku,* 1946, the Supreme Court held that the governor's order had been too sweeping. The Court's decision was not based on the constitutional provision, however. Instead, it found that in the Hawaiian Organic Act of 1900, under which the governor had acted, Congress had not intended to allow so great a subordination of civil to military authority.

[17]Article I, Sections 9 and 10.

of the system of separation of powers. A legislative body may decide what conduct is criminal. That is, it may pass laws that define crime and set the penalties that may be imposed on those who violate those laws. But it *cannot* exercise the *judicial* function. A legislative body cannot decide that a person is guilty of a crime and then impose a punishment on that person.

The Supreme Court has held that the prohibition is aimed at all legislative acts that apply "to named individuals or to easily ascertainable members of a group in such a way as to inflict punishment on them without a judicial trial," *United States* v. *Lovett,* 1946.

The Framers put the ban on bills of attainder in the Constitution because both Parliament and the colonial legislatures had passed many of them. They have been rare in our history, however.

United States v. *Brown,* 1965, is one of the few cases, and the latest, in which the Court has struck down a law as a bill of attainder. There it overturned the part of the Landrum-Griffin Act of 1959 that made it a federal crime for a member of the Communist Party to serve as an officer of a labor union.

Ex Post Facto Laws

An **ex post facto law** has three features. It is (1) a *criminal* law, one defining a crime or providing for its punishment; (2) a law that is applied *retroactively*—that is, to an act committed *before* its passage; and (3) a law that works to the *disadvantage* of the accused. Neither Congress nor the State legislatures may pass such laws.[18]

For example, a law making it a crime to sell marijuana cannot be applied to one who sold it *before* that law was passed. A person who sold it after the law was passed could be punished under it. Or, a law that changed the penalty for murder from life in prison to death could not be applied to a person who committed a murder before the punishment

Constitutional Protections for Persons Accused of Crime

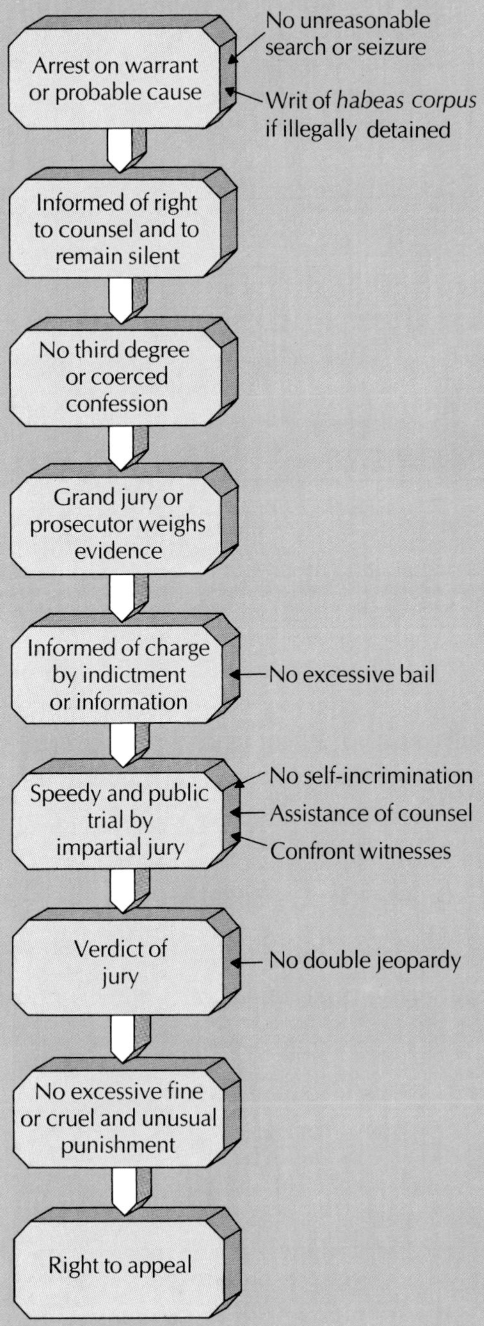

This chart displays the rights of accused persons. Why must trials be both speedy and public?

[18]Article I, Sections 9 and 10. The phrase *ex post facto* is from the Latin, meaning "after the fact."

REINFORCEMENT Use the above chart to discuss the right to a fair trial. Ask the class where the trial process begins and how it continues to the final declaration of innocence or guilt.

was changed. That person has to be sentenced under the old law.

Occasional ex post facto cases occur. The Supreme Court hears one every other year or so. In 1981, in *Weaver* v. *Graham,* it held that Florida ran afoul of the constitutional ban. The State had changed its rules for figuring the time off for good behavior to be subtracted from penitentiary terms and had then applied the new rules to prisoners doing time for crimes committed before the law was changed.

Retroactive civil laws are *not* forbidden. For example, a law raising income tax rates could be passed in November and made to apply to income earned through the whole year.

FOR REVIEW

1. **Identify:** show cause.
2. What is a crime? Why must society punish criminals?
3. What is a writ of *habeas corpus?* When may the right to the writ be suspended?
4. What is a bill of attainder? An *ex post facto* law? Who cannot make such laws?

4. A Major Guarantee: The Right to a Fair Trial

As You Read, Think About:

- What constitutes a fair trial.
- What rights a person arrested for a crime has.

The Bill of Rights contains several guarantees relating to fair trial in the federal courts.[19] Fair trial is guaranteed in the State courts by a State's constitution and by the 14th Amendment's Due Process Clause.

[19]See the 5th, 6th, 7th, and 8th Amendments and also Article III, Section 2, Clause 3. The practice of excluding evidence obtained in violation of the 4th Amendment is also intended to guarantee a fair trial.

The right to be represented by a lawyer is a fundamental part of the right to a fair trial. Which amendment deals with this right?

Double Jeopardy

The 5th Amendment says, in part, that no person shall be "twice put in jeopardy of life or limb." The taking of a life or the cutting off of an arm, leg, ear, or some other "limb" was a common punishment in ancient times. The old English phrase "life or limb" was carried into our Constitution.

Today, the provision means, in plain language, that once a person has been tried for a crime, he or she may not be tried again for that same crime. This needs some elaboration, however.

A person may violate both a federal *and* a State law in a single act—for example, by selling narcotics. That person can then be tried for the federal crime in a federal court and then for the State crime in a State court.

A single act may also result in the commission of several different crimes. One who breaks into a store at night, steals liquor, and later sells it, can be tried on at least three separate counts: for illegal entry, theft, and selling liquor without a license.

In a trial in which a jury cannot agree on a verdict, there is no "jeopardy." It is as though no trial had been held, and the accused may be tried again. Nor is **double jeopardy** involved when a case is appealed to

ENRICHMENT Discuss in class: If laws are put into effect to protect our freedom, how can an ex post facto law, which works to the disadvantage of the accused, be constitutional?

a higher court.[20] Recall that the Supreme Court has held that the 5th Amendment's ban on double jeopardy applies against the States through the 14th Amendment, *Benton* v. *Maryland,* 1969.

Grand Jury

The 5th Amendment also provides that:

> No person shall be held to answer for a capital, or otherwise infamous, crime, unless on a presentment or indictment of a grand jury. . . .

The **grand jury** is, then, the formal device by which a person may be accused of a serious federal crime. It is a body of from 16 to 23 persons drawn from the area of the federal District Court that it serves. The votes of at least 12 of the grand jurors are needed to return an indictment or to make a presentment.[21] An **indictment** is a formal complaint laid before a grand jury by the prosecutor, the United States Attorney. It charges the accused with one or more federal crimes. If the grand jury finds that there is enough evidence for a trial, it returns a "true bill of indictment." The accused is then held for prosecution. If the grand jury does not make such a finding, the charge is dropped.

A **presentment** is a formal accusation brought by the grand jury on its own motion, rather than at the insistence of the United States Attorney. It is little used in federal courts.

A grand jury's proceedings are not a trial, and since unfair harm could come if they were held in public, its sessions are secret. They are also one-sided, that is, only the prosecution, not the defense, is present.

The 5th Amendment's grand jury provision is the only part of the Bill of Rights relating to criminal prosecution that the Supreme Court has not brought within the coverage of the 14th Amendment's Due Process Clause. In fact, the Court specifically rejected that notion in *Hurtado* v. *California,* in 1887. The States may use any fair method of accusation they choose.

The right to grand jury is intended as a protection against overzealous prosecutors. Its use has long been the subject of criticism, however. Its critics say that it is too time-consuming, too expensive, and too likely to follow the dictates of the prosecutor. It has been abolished in England, where it began. In most of the States today, most criminal charges are not brought by grand juries, but rather by an information—an affidavit in which the prosecutor swears that there is enough evidence to justify a trial; see page 607.

Speedy and Public Trial

The 6th Amendment commands:

> In all criminal prosecutions, the accused shall enjoy the right to a speedy and public trial. . . .

The guarantee of a speedy trial is meant to ensure that a person accused of crime will be tried in a reasonable time, without undue delay. It seeks to prevent the accused from being forced to languish in jail while awaiting trial. It is also intended to prevent delays that could hinder the ability to put together an adequate defense.

The 6th Amendment's guarantee is of a prompt trial in *federal* cases. The Supreme Court first declared that this right applied against the States through the 14th Amendment in *Klopfer* v. *North Carolina,* 1967.

A trial must take place promptly, without undue delay. But how long a delay is too long? The Supreme Court has long recognized that there can be no pat answer to that question. No two cases are the same, and each must be looked at on its own merits. In *Barker* v. *Wingo,* 1972, the Court listed four considerations that must be taken into

---

[20]The Organized Crime Control Act of 1970 allows federal prosecutors to appeal sentences they believe to be too lenient. They may seek stiffer punishments in the Court of Appeals. The Supreme Court has held that such appeals do not violate the double jeopardy guarantee, *United States* v. *Di Francesco,* 1980. The case involved a "hardened habitual criminal" who had been sentenced to a total of only 10 years for the crimes of arson-for-hire, fraud, and bombing a federal building.

[21]Congress has provided that one may *waive,* or put aside, the right to grand jury if he or she chooses. When, as increasingly, this happens, the trial goes forward on the basis of an information accusation filed by the United States Attorney.

account: length of the delay, reasons for it, whether the delay did in fact harm the defendant, and whether or not the defendant asked for a prompt trial. Notice that a delay can work in *favor* of a defendant. For example, witnesses for the prosecution might die or for some other reason become unavailable, or their memories might fade or become faulty.

Federal law, namely the Speedy Trial Act of 1974, sets a deadline for the start of a federal criminal trial. Since 1980, the time span between a person's arrest and the beginning of his or her trial cannot be more than 100 days. If that deadline is not met, the judge is to dismiss the case. The law does allow for some exceptions, however—in a case where the defendant must undergo extensive mental tests, for example, or when the defendant or a key witness is ill.

The 6th Amendment says that a "speedy" trial must also be a "public" trial. The right to be tried in public, not in secret, is also an essential part of the 14th Amendment's guarantee of procedural due process. "The guarantee has always been recognized as a safeguard against any attempts to employ our courts as instruments of persecution," *In re Oliver,* 1948.

A trial must not be *too* speedy or *too* public, however. The Supreme Court threw out an Arkansas murder conviction in 1923 on just those grounds. In *Moore* v. *Dempsey,* five black men had been sentenced to death for the killing of a white man. Their trial had taken only 45 minutes, and it had been held in a courtroom packed by an angry and threatening mob.

Within reason, a judge may limit both the number and the kinds of spectators who may be present at a trial. The unruly, and especially those who seek to disrupt a courtroom, may be barred from it. A courtroom may be cleared when the testimony to be given may be embarrassing to a witness or to someone else not a party to the case.

Many of the hard questions about how public a trial should be involve the news media. As we noted in Chapter 5, the guarantees of fair trial and of free press often come into conflict in the courts. When they do, judges face the very difficult task of finding a proper balance between them.

On the one hand: "A trial courtroom is a public place where the people generally—and representatives of the media—have a right to be present," *Richmond Newspapers, Inc.* v. *Virginia,* 1980. On the other hand: "Trial judges must take strong measures to ensure that the balance is never weighted against the accused," *Sheppard* v. *Maxwell,* 1966; see page 99.

Champions of the public's "right to know" hold that the broadest possible press coverage of court proceedings should be allowed, especially of sensational criminal trials. The Supreme Court has often held, however, that newspaper, radio, and television reporters have only the *same* right as the general public to be present in a courtroom. That is, the press has no greater or special right to be there. The right to a public trial belongs to the defendant, not to the news media.

What of televised trials? Television cameras are barred from all federal courtrooms.* Until the mid-1970s the States generally followed the same rule.[22] More than half the States now allow some form of in-court television, however. Does the televising of a criminal trial violate a defendant's 6th and 14th Amendment rights?

In an early major case on the point, the Supreme Court reversed the conviction of a man who had been accused of swindling on a multibillion dollar scale, *Estes* v. *Texas,* 1965. It held that the radio and television reporting of his case, which had been allowed from within the courtroom and over his objections, had been so circus-like and disruptive that it denied Estes his constitutional rights to a fair trial.

The Court confined its ruling in *Estes* to that one case. It did not say that the Constitution bars any and all in-court televising of a criminal case.

Most recently, the Court held in *Chandler* v. *Florida,* 1981, that there is nothing in the Constitution to prevent a State from allowing the televising of a criminal trial. How-

[22]The exception is Colorado, which has allowed television in its courtrooms since 1956.

*ENRICHMENT Have the class discuss the arguments for and against televised trials. What viewpoint do the students support? In what cases might they make exceptions?

ever, steps must be taken to protect the defendant's rights. In that case, two Miami police officers had been convicted of burglary. Over their objections, their trial had been reported live on radio and television. On appeal, they claimed that that coverage had violated their rights to due process.

Their plea was rejected. The Court could find no evidence of the kinds of in-court distractions that would support their claim. However, the Court was careful to make this point: *Chandler* does not amount to a blanket endorsement of televised trials. Too much publicity, by television or otherwise, can threaten the fairness of a trial and so be constitutionally improper.

Trial by Jury

The 6th Amendment also says that a person accused of a federal crime must be tried "by an impartial jury."[23] This guarantee reinforces an earlier one set out in the Constitution, in Article III, Section 2. The right to trial by jury is also binding on the States through the 14th Amendment's Due Process Clause, *Duncan* v. *Louisiana,* 1968.[24]

The trial jury is often called the "petit jury"—*petit,* from the French, "small." The term is used to distinguish it from the grand jury. We shall return to the role of the trial jury in Chapter 22. For now, however, these points.

[23]The Amendment adds that the members of the jury must be drawn from "the State and district wherein the crime shall have been committed, which district shall have been previously ascertained by law." This clause gives the defendant any benefit there may be in having a court and jury familiar with the people and problems of the area. It was also aimed at preventing what had been British colonial practice: Many colonists were forced to stand trial in England for crimes they were accused of having committed in America; see the Declaration of Independence, page 720.

A defendant may ask to be tried in another place —seek a "change of venue"—on grounds that the people of the locality are so prejudiced in the case that an impartial jury cannot be drawn. The judge hearing the case must decide whether or not a change of venue is justified.

[24]The 7th Amendment also preserves the right to jury trial in civil cases "where the value in controversy shall exceed twenty dollars." This guarantee has not been incorporated into the 14th Amendment's Due Process Clause.

More than half the States today permit some form of in-court television. Here, a criminal trial is televised in a Florida courtroom.

A defendant may *waive,* or relinquish, the right to a jury trial. But that can be done only if the judge is satisfied that the defendant is fully aware of his or her rights and understands what that action means. In fact, a judge may order a jury trial even when a defendant does not want one, because there is no constitutional right *not* to be tried by a jury, *One Lot Emerald Cut Stones and One Ring* v. *United States,* 1972. If the right is waived, a "bench trial" is held. That is, the case is heard by the judge alone. Of course, a defendant can plead guilty to a charge. If a guilty plea is entered, the defendant avoids a trial of any kind. *

In federal practice a jury is made up of 12 persons, as it is in most States. Several States now provide for smaller juries, however, often with six members. A federal jury may convict only by unanimous vote: All 12

*REINFORCEMENT Why would a defendant waive his or her right to a jury trial? Discuss in class, pointing out that the defendant may feel that public opinion prevents an unbiased jury.

In most States, names of prospective jurors are drawn from poll books or tax assessor's rolls. When jurors are needed, names are picked—oftentimes, in lottery fashion—from these lists.

jurors must agree to a guilty verdict. Most of the States follow the same rule.[25]

In a long series of cases, dating from *Strauder* v. *West Virginia*, 1880, the Supreme Court has held that a jury must be "drawn from a fair cross section of the community." A person is denied the right to an impartial jury if he or she is tried by a jury from which members of any groups "playing major roles in the community" have been excluded, *Taylor* v. *Louisiana*, 1975.

In short, no person may be kept off a jury on such grounds as race, color, religion, national origin, or sex. Interestingly, the Court did not forbid the States to exclude women from jury service until as recently as 1975, in the Louisiana case just cited.

Right to an Adequate Defense

Every person accused of crime has the right to offer the best possible defense that circumstances will allow. To that end, the 6th Amendment says that a defendant has the right (1) "to be informed of the nature and cause of the accusation," (2) "to be confronted with the witnesses against him" and question them in open court, (3) "to have compulsory process for obtaining witnesses in his favor," and (4) "to have the assistance of counsel for his defence."

As parts of the Bill of Rights, these key safeguards apply in the federal courts. Still, if a State fails to honor any of them in its own courts, a conviction may be appealed on grounds that the 14th Amendment's Due Process Clause has been violated. Recall, the Supreme Court protected the right to counsel in *Gideon* v. *Wainwright*, 1963;[26] the right of confrontation in *Pointer* v. *Texas*, 1965; and the right to call witnesses in *Washington* v. *Texas*, 1967.

These guarantees are intended to prevent the cards in the court contest from being stacked in favor of the prosecution. A well-known right-to-counsel case, *Escobedo* v. *Illinois*, 1964, illustrates this point.

Danny Escobedo was picked up by Chicago police for questioning in the death of his brother-in-law. On the way to the police station, and then while he was being questioned there, he asked several times to see his lawyer. These requests were refused—even

[25]The 14th Amendment does not say that there cannot be juries of fewer than 12 persons, *Williams* v. *Florida*, 1970, but it does not allow juries of less than six members, *Ballew* v. *Georgia*, 1978. Nor does it prevent a State from providing for a conviction on a less than unanimous jury vote, *Apadaca* v. *Oregon*, 1972. But if a jury has only six members, it may convict only by a unanimous vote, *Burch* v. *Louisiana*, 1979.

[26]In *Gideon* the Court ruled that the States must provide lawyers for indigent defendants—those who cannot afford to hire their own attorneys. The Court broadened that holding in *Ake* v. *Oklahoma*, 1985. There it held that indigent defendants who plead guilty by reason of insanity must also be given the assistance of a psychiatrist to help support that defense. In fact, indigent defendants have had such help in the federal and in most State courts for several years.

*REINFORCEMENT Have the class discuss the provisions of the 6th Amendment and review the above mentioned cases.

though his lawyer was in the police station and was trying to see him, and the police knew that he was there. Through a long night of questioning by the police, and without the help of his lawyer, Escobedo made several damaging statements. Those statements were used later in court and were a major part of the evidence that led to his conviction for murder.

The Supreme Court ordered Escobedo freed from prison four years later. It held that he had been improperly denied his right to counsel since he had not had the advice of his lawyer at the time of the arrest. In other words, his right to an adequate defense had been denied.

Self-Incrimination

The 5th Amendment says that no person can be

> compelled, in any criminal case, to be a witness against himself.

GG. Wallmeyer in Independent Press-Telgram Long Beach, CA.

A cartoonist comments on the right of suspects to have a lawyer present when questioned by police.

This protection must be honored in both the federal and State courts, *Malloy* v. *Hogan,* 1964.

In a criminal case, the burden of proof is always on the prosecution. The defendant does not have to prove his or her innocence. Rather, the prosecution must show, if it can, that the criminal charge it has brought is true. The ban on self-incrimination prevents the prosecution from shifting the burden of proof to the defendant. As the Court stated in *Malloy* v. *Hogan,* the prosecution cannot force the accused to "prove the charge against" him "out of his own mouth."

The language of the 5th Amendment suggests that the guarantee applies only to criminal cases. In fact, it covers *any* governmental proceeding in which a person is legally compelled to answer any question that could lead to a criminal charge. Thus, a person may claim the right—"take the Fifth"—in any number of situations, such as in a divorce proceeding, which is a *civil* case, before a legislative committee, or in a disciplinary hearing before a local school board.

The courts, not the individuals who claim it, decide when the right may be properly invoked. If the plea of self-incrimination is pushed too far, a person may be held in *contempt.* That is, he or she may be punished by a court for the crime of obstructing the lawful processes of government.

The privilege against self-incrimination is a personal right. One can claim it only for himself or herself.[27] It cannot be invoked in someone else's behalf; a person *can* be forced to testify against another. Nor can it be used to protect such "artificial persons" as a corporation or a partnership.

The privilege covers only evidence given in compelled testimony, that is, in answers a person gives to lawful questions he or she must answer. It does not protect a person from being fingerprinted or photographed,

[27]With this large exception: A husband may refuse to testify against his wife, or a wife against her husband; either one can testify against the other voluntarily, but neither can be compelled to do so, *Trammel* v. *United States,* 1980.

Before asking you any questions, it is my duty to advise you of your rights:
1. You have the right to remain silent;
2. If you choose to speak, anything you say may be used against you in a court of law or other proceeding;
3. You have the right to consult with a lawyer before answering any questions and you may have him present with you during questioning;
4. If you cannot afford a lawyer and you want one, a lawyer will be provided for you by the Commonwealth without cost to you;
5. Do you understand what I have told you;
6. You may also waive the right to counsel and your right to remain silent and you may answer any question or make any statement you wish. If you decide to answer questions you may stop at any time to consult with a lawyer;

All over the United States, law enforcement officers are required to inform suspects of their rights when they are making an arrest as part of the Miranda rule. What is the nature of the controversy surrounding the Miranda Rule today?

submitting a handwriting sample, or appearing in a police lineup—or taking a blood test, as we saw earlier in *Schmerber* v. *California.*

A person cannot be forced to confess to a crime under duress—that is, as a result of torture or other physical or psychological force, or the threat of it. The Supreme Court has voided a number of State prosecutions based on such "third-degree" methods.

In *Ashcraft* v. *Tennessee,* 1944, for example, it threw out the conviction of a man accused of hiring another to murder his wife. The confession on which his conviction rested had been secured only after some 36 hours of continuous, abusive, and threatening interrogation. That questioning took place in a jail room under high-powered lights. It was conducted by police officers who worked in shifts because, they said, they became so tired they had to rest.

The gulf between what the Constitution says and what in fact goes on in some police stations can be wide, indeed. For that reason, for the last several years, the Supreme Court has come down hard in cases involving the protection against self-incrimination, and the closely related right to counsel. In many cases, it has said that police must obey the commands of the Constitution. Recall the Court's decision in *Escobedo* v. *Illinois.* There it held that a confession cannot be used against a defendant if it was obtained by police who refused to allow him to see his attorney and did not advise him of the right to refuse to answer their questions.

In a truly historic decision two years later, *Miranda* v. *Arizona,* 1966, the Court refined that holding. A mentally retarded man, Ernesto Miranda, had been convicted of kidnaping and rape. Ten days after the crime, the victim picked him out of a police lineup. After two hours of questioning, during which the police did not tell him of his rights, he confessed. The Supreme Court struck down his conviction. More importantly, the Court said that from that point on, it would not uphold convictions in any cases in which, before police questioning, suspects had not been told of their constitutional rights. It thus laid down what has since come to be called the **Miranda Rule.***

Today, under this rule, before police may question suspects, those persons must be:

1. Told of their right to remain silent;
2. Warned that anything they say can be used against them in court;
3. Informed of their right to have an attorney present during questioning;
4. Told that if they cannot afford to hire an attorney, one will be provided;
5. Told that they may bring any police questioning to an end at any time.

The Miranda Rule has been in force for more than 20 years now, and the Supreme Court is still refining it, case by case. Most often, the rule has been strictly enforced—several times by the Supreme Court and several hundreds of times by lower courts, both federal and State. It has been relaxed in some cases, however. Thus, in *Oregon* v. *Elstad,* 1985, the Supreme Court upheld the conviction of a man who had twice confessed to a burglary. The Court held that his first confession, which had been made without a Miranda warning, could not be used in court. But it also held that, because that first statement had been wholly voluntary, his second confession made after he had been properly warned could be used.[28]

Many police officials, and others, criticize the Miranda Rule. They see it as a serious obstacle to effective law enforcement. Many of them say that it "puts criminals back on the streets." Others applaud it, however. They hold that criminal law enforcement is most effective when it depends on independently secured evidence, rather than on confessions secured by questionable means and in the absence of counsel.

FOR REVIEW

1. **Identify:** 5th Amendment, information, 6th Amendment, adequate defense, self-incrimination.
2. What does the protection against double jeopardy mean?
3. What is the basic function of a grand jury?
4. Why does the Constitution guarantee a speedy trial? A public trial?
5. Can federal criminal trials be televised? State trials?
6. Must all criminal cases be tried by an impartial jury?
7. What are the 6th Amendment guarantees of the right to an adequate defense?
8. Why is compulsory self-incrimination forbidden?
9. What is the Miranda Rule?

[28]The Court has recently extended the Miranda Rule to cover many minor (misdemeanor) criminal situations. In *Berkemer* v. *McCarty,* 1984, the Court set aside McCarty's drunk driving conviction in Ohio, and with it his 90-day jail term and $300 fine. The Court held that the rule does not apply to routine traffic stops, where, even though a motorist might expect to receive a citation, "he most likely will be allowed to continue on his way." But once a person is placed "in custody," that is, arrested or otherwise put in a situation in which he or she is not free to leave, the rule must be observed "regardless of the nature or severity of the offense" involved.

*REINFORCEMENT Have the class discuss the Miranda Rule and its implications. Does it overprotect the "criminal"?

5. Additional Safeguards for Accused Persons

As You Read, Think About:

- What the additional rights are of a person accused of a crime.
- How the Constitution limits the punishment that may be given to a person found guilty of a crime.

In addition to the safeguards involved with accusation and trial, persons accused of crime have other guarantees of their rights. Among these are the rights to fair bail and fines.

Excessive Bail, Fines

The 8th Amendment says, in part:

> Excessive bail shall not be required, nor excessive fines imposed . . .

Each of the State constitutions sets out similar restrictions. The general rule here is that the bail or fine in a case must bear a reasonable relationship to the seriousness of the crime involved.

Bail is a sum of money that the accused may be required to post, or deposit with the court, as a guarantee that he or she will appear in court at the proper time. Its use is justified on two grounds: (1) A person is innocent until proved guilty and therefore should not be jailed unless and until guilt is established; and (2) a defendant is better able to prepare for trial *outside* of a jail.[29]

Bail is usually set on the basis of the nature of the charge and the reputation and resources of the defendant. Because the poor often have trouble raising bail, the federal courts and those of most States now release many defendants "on their own recognizance"—that is, on their honor.

The leading case on bail in the federal courts is *Stack* v. *Boyle,* 1951. It involved the prosecution of a Communist under the Smith Act; see pages 121–122. There the Court ruled that "bail set at a figure higher than the amount reasonably calculated" to insure a defendant's appearance at a trial "is 'excessive' under the 8th Amendment."

Cruel and Unusual Punishment

The 8th Amendment also forbids "cruel and unusual punishment." The 14th Amendment extends that prohibition against the States, *Robinson* v. *California,* 1962. Each of the State constitutions contains a similar provision.

The Supreme Court decided its first cruel and unusual case over 100 years ago. In *Wilkerson* v. *Utah,* 1879, a territorial court had sentenced a convicted murderer to death by a firing squad. The Court held that that punishment was not forbidden by the Constitution. The kinds of penalties the Constitution intended to prevent, said the Court, were such barbaric tortures as burning at the stake, crucifixion, drawing and quartering, "and all others in the same line of unnecessary cruelty."

Since then, the Court has heard only a small number of cruel and unusual cases—except for those relating to capital punishment, as we shall see in a moment. More often than not, the Court has come down on the side of the punishment. That is, it has usually rejected the cruel and unusual punishment claim.[30]

Louisiana v. *Resweber,* 1947, is typical. There the Court found that it was not unconstitutional to subject a convicted murderer to a second electrocution after the chair had failed to work properly on the first occasion.

The Court also sided with punishment in *Rummel* v. *Estelle,* 1980. There a Texas court *

[29] Bail is almost never allowed in capital cases—those involving crimes punishable by death. A defendant may appeal the denial of release on bail or the amount of the bail. If a person out on bail does not show up, the court may order the bail forfeited. "Jumping bail" is itself a punishable crime. In *Schall* v. *Martin,* 1984, the Court upheld a New York law that allows the "preventive detention" of a juvenile charged with the crime of delinquency when there is a serious risk that the juvenile will commit another crime before trial.

[30] The prohibition of cruel and unusual punishment is limited to criminal matters. It does not forbid paddling or similar punishments in the public schools, *Ingraham* v. *Wright,* 1977.

*REINFORCEMENT Use *Rummel* v. *Estelle* to introduce a discussion on cruel and unusual punishment. Ask the class if they feel that the defendant deserved the sentence he received. Why?

BUILDING GOVERNMENT SKILLS

Finding the Supreme Court's Decisions

As you can tell by now, Chapters 5 and 6 are filled with references to cases decided by the United States Supreme Court. In fact, over 200 cases are cited in these two chapters, and many more cases are discussed throughout this book. This reflects the critical role of the Supreme Court in every aspect of government in this country.

While knowing *what* the Supreme Court has decided is certainly more important than being able to recite the names of cases, some of these cases are so important that no person can hope to be a well-informed citizen without knowing them. Consider the *Miranda* case, for example. The Miranda Rule can be heard on almost any television show or movie when people are arrested: "You have the right to remain silent. If you choose to speak, anything you say may be used against you in a court of law or other proceeding. . . ." These words have become very familiar. Do you know what circumstances led to this decision?

Many cases are published in secondary sources—casebooks and other commentaries. You can find these volumes in law libraries or in the law section of a local library. Many of these books, however, have a narrow and specialized scholarly/legal focus. Some books are directed at a more general audience. Three of these more general volumes include:

Paul Bartholomew and Joseph Menez, *Summaries of Leading Cases on the Constitution* (Littlefield, Adams, 12th ed., 1983).

J.W. Peltason, *Understanding the Constitution* (Holt, Rinehart and Winston, 9th ed., 1982).

Congressional Quarterly's Guide to the Supreme Court (Congressional Quarterly Press).

Each of these books provides summaries of landmark Supreme Court cases. You can usually find these books in the reference or law section of a local library.

The text of the Court's decisions are published yearly in several different publications. The Government Printing Office publishes *United States Reports*. Two privately published volumes of the Supreme Court's decisions—*The Supreme Court Reporter* (West Publishing Company) and the *Lawyer's Edition, United States Supreme Court Reports* (Lawyer's Cooperative Publishing Company)—are usually more readily available and more useful than the *Reports*.

A privately published periodical, *The United States Law Week*, can also be useful in locating information about Supreme Court decisions. Some periodicals that are not specifically concerned with the Supreme Court often carry information on the Court's decisions. Among these, Congressional Quarterly's *Weekly Report* and the *National Journal* offer summaries of the Court's decisions and frequently feature articles on major cases.

In most of these publications, the cases are arranged according to the Constitutional provision concerned, for example, 1st Amendment—Freedom of religion or 5th Amendment—Due Process.

1. Select one of the cases discussed in this chapter, and read the Court's decision in one of the references cited above.
2. What additional information did you learn about the case? Write a brief summary of the circumstances of the case, the issues involved, the arguments, and the decision and rationale.

An arrestee is booked at a police station, where an administrative record is made of an arrest. Release on bail is often available at this point.

had imposed a mandatory life sentence on a "three-time loser"—even though the three crimes of which he had been convicted were all petty and nonviolent, and had altogether involved less than $230.

However, the Court has held some punishments to be cruel and unusual. Thus, in *Solem* v. *Helm,* 1983, it struck down the sentence a South Dakota court had given to a habitual criminal: life in prison, without the possibility of parole. Helm had been convicted of nonviolent crimes on seven separate occasions. His most recent offense: passing a bad check for $100. The Court drew a distinction between this case and *Rummel* v. *Estelle* by noting that Rummel's life sentence carried with it the possibility of a parole after 10 or 12 years.

In *Robinson* v. *California,* 1962, the Supreme Court held that a State law that defined narcotics addiction as a crime to be punished, rather than an illness to be treated, violated the 8th and 14th Amendments. In *Estelle* v. *Gamble,* 1976, it ruled that a Texas prison inmate could not properly be denied needed medical care.

Remember, most cases have gone the other way. In *Rhodes* v. *Chapman,* 1981, the Court held that "double-celling"—putting two prisoners in a cell built for one—is not cruel and unusual punishment. In that Ohio case, the Court said that the Constitution "does not mandate comfortable prisons."

Capital Punishment

Is the death penalty cruel and unusual and so forbidden by the Constitution? For years the Court was reluctant to face that highly charged issue. In fact, it did not give a direct answer to that question until 1976.[31]

The Court did meet the issue more or less directly in *Furman* v. *Georgia,* 1972. There it struck down all of the then existing State laws allowing the death penalty, but *not* because that penalty as *such* was cruel and unusual. Rather, those laws were voided because they gave too much discretion to judges or juries in deciding whether to impose the death penalty. The Court noted that of all those convicted of capital crimes, only "a random few," most of them black or poor or both, were "capriciously selected" for execution. The death penalty was "cruel and unusual in the same way that being struck by lightning is cruel and unusual."

Following that decision, 35 States passed new capital punishment laws. Generally they took one of two forms: Several States removed *all* discretion from the sentencing process. They made the death penalty *mandatory* for certain crimes, such as the killing of a police officer or murder done while committing rape, kidnap, or arson.

Other States provided for a two-stage process in capital cases: a trial first to settle

---

[31]The Court avoided a direct ruling on the constitutionality of capital punishment laws in several earlier cases. It did hold that neither death by firing squad (*Wilkerson* v. *Utah*) nor by a second electrocution (*Louisiana* v. *Resweber*) is unconstitutional, as we have seen. But in neither of those cases did it deal with the question of the death penalty *as such.* It also purposely avoided the basic question in several other cases. For example, in *Witherspoon* v. *Illinois,* 1968, it held that the death penalty had been unconstitutionally imposed on the defendant, but not because that punishment was cruel and unusual. Rather, because all persons opposed to capital punishment had been excluded from the jury that tried him, the Court held that Witherspoon had been denied his right to a trial by an *impartial* jury.

the issue of guilt or innocence; then a second, separate hearing to decide whether the circumstances justify a sentence of death.

Up to the present, the Supreme Court has considered scores of challenges to those newer laws, with these major results. The mandatory death penalty laws were found to be unconstitutional. They were "unduly harsh and rigidly unworkable," and simply attempts to "paper over" the decision in *Furman*, said the Court in *Woodson* v. *North Carolina*, 1976. Capital punishment laws "must allow for whatever mitigating circumstances" may be present in a case, *Roberts* v. *Louisiana*, 1977.

But the two-stage approach to capital punishment is constitutional. In *Gregg* v. *Georgia*, 1976, the Court held, for the first time, that the "punishment of death does not invariably violate the Constitution." It also ruled that well-drawn two-stage laws can practically eliminate "the risk that [the death penalty] will be inflicted in an arbitrary or capricious manner."*

Treason

Treason against the United States is the only crime that is defined in the Constitution. The Framers provided a specific definition of the crime because they knew that the charge of treason is a favorite weapon in the hands of tyrants. Examples of its use to do away with political opponents in more recent times are not hard to find. It was a common practice in Nazi Germany, and it still is used in several Latin American dictatorships and in the Communist nations of Eastern Europe and Asia.

Treason, says Article III, Section 3, can consist of only two things: either (1) levying war against the United States or (2) "adhering to their enemies, giving them aid and comfort." The Constitution adds that no person may be convicted of the crime "unless on the testimony of two witnesses to the same overt act, or on confession in open court." The penalty for treason can be imposed only on the traitors, not on their families.

The law of treason covers all American citizens, at home or abroad, and all permanent resident aliens. The maximum penalty for treason against the United States is death, but no person has ever been executed for the crime.

Note that treason may be committed only in wartime. But Congress has also made it a crime, in either peace or wartime, to commit espionage or sabotage, to attempt to overthrow the government by force, or to conspire to do any of these things; see pages 120–122.

Most of the State constitutions also provide for treason. John Brown was hanged as a traitor to Virginia after his raid on Harpers Ferry in 1859. He is believed to be the only person ever to be executed for treason against a State.

FOR REVIEW

1. **Identify:** 8th Amendment, capital cases, treason, cruel and unusual punishment, capital punishment.
2. What is bail? What bail or fine is "excessive"?
3. What punishments do the 8th and 14th Amendments prohibit? Does the Constitution outlaw capital punishment?
4. Why is treason so specifically defined by the Constitution?

6. Equality Before the Law

As You Read, Think About:

- What the meaning is of the Equal Protection Clause of the 14th Amendment.
- How the Clause has been interpreted and applied.
- What the difference is between de jure and de facto segregation.
- What the term *affirmative action* means.

Nothing, not even a constitutional command, can make all people equal in the literal sense. People differ in strength, intelligence, height, weight, health, and countless

*REINFORCEMENT Organize a class debate: Should the death penalty be abolished, even though the two-stage approach has been declared constitutional?

other ways. But the democratic ideal demands that, insofar as government is concerned, all persons must be treated alike.

The equality of all persons—so boldly set out in the Declaration of Independence—is not proclaimed in so many words in the Constitution. Still, that concept runs through all of the document.

The Equal Protection Clause

The closest approach to a literal statement of equality is to be found in the 14th Amendment's Equal Protection Clause. It declares:

> No State shall . . . deny to any person within its jurisdiction the equal protection of the laws.

The Clause was originally intended to benefit the newly freed slaves. Over time, it has acquired a much broader meaning, however. Today, it forbids States, and their local governments, to draw *unreasonable* distinctions between different classes of persons. The Supreme Court has often held that the 5th Amendment's Due Process Clause puts the same restriction on the Federal Government.

Reasonable Classification Government must have the power to draw distinctions between persons and groups. Otherwise, it could not possibly regulate any aspect of human behavior. That is, the States may and do discriminate. Thus, those who rob banks fall into a special class and are subject to a special treatment by the law. This sort of discrimination is clearly reasonable. Or, the State may legally prohibit marriage by those under a certain age, or by those who are married to other persons. Again, these are reasonable discriminations, or classifications.

The States may not discriminate unreasonably, however. Every State now levies a sales tax on cigarettes—and so taxes smokers, but not nonsmokers. But no State can lay a tax only on *blonde* smokers or only on *male* smokers. Nor for example, may a State make *women* eligible for alimony in divorce actions but provide that *men* are not—as the Court ruled in a case from Alabama, *Orr* v. *Orr*, in 1979.

Over time, the Supreme Court has rejected many Equal Protection challenges to the actions of State and local governments. That is, far more often than not, it has found that what those governments have done is, in fact, constitutional.[32] This has been especially true when a State has been able to show a *rational basis* for the classification that has been made—that is, that the classification is reasonably related to achieving some proper governmental purpose.

A recent California case, *Michael M.* v. *Superior Court*, 1981, illustrates the usual outcome. California law says that a man who has sexual relations with a girl under 18 to whom he is not married can be prosecuted for statutory rape, but the girl cannot be charged with that crime, even if she is a willing partner. The Court found the law to be an appropriate means to a proper public end: preventing teenage pregnancies. Justice Rehnquist wrote for the majority: "Because virtually all of the significantly harmful and inescapably identifiable consequences of teenage pregnancy fall on the young female, a legislature acts well within its authority when it elects to punish only the participant who, by nature, suffers few of the consequences of his conduct."

However, the Court does not always uphold the judgment a State legislature makes when it draws distinctions between persons or groups. This is especially true when a law deals with either of these matters: (1) such "fundamental rights" as the right to vote, the right to travel between the States, or the rights guaranteed in the 1st Amendment; or (2) such "suspect classifications" as those based on race, sex, or national origins.

In these instances, the Court has said many times in recent years that the *rational basis test* is not enough. Rather, such a law

[32]The Court has voided a number of those actions, however, as violations of the Equal Protection Clause. We shall consider a number of those cases in a moment, and we discuss several others elsewhere, for example, too lengthy residence requirements for voting purposes, page 208, and the malapportionment of State legislatures, pages 559-560.

must meet a higher standard, the strict scrutiny test. For a law to pass that stiffer check, to be upheld, the State must be able to show that some "compelling public interest" justifies the distinctions it has drawn in that law.

The alimony case we cited, *Orr* v. *Orr,* involved the use of the stricter test. The Alabama law was held unconstitutional, as a denial of equal protection. The Court found that need, not sex, is the factor on which the award of alimony must hinge.

The Separate-but-Equal Doctrine Beginning in the late 1800s, nearly half of the States passed racial segregation laws. Most of these "Jim Crow" laws were aimed at blacks. Some of them were drawn to affect other groups, as well—Mexican Americans, people of Asian descent, and American Indians. For the most part, these laws required segregation by race in the use of both public and private facilities: street cars, schools, parks and playgrounds, hotels, restaurants, even public drinking fountains.

In 1896, the Supreme Court provided a constitutional basis for these segregation laws: the **separate-but-equal doctrine.** In *Plessy* v. *Ferguson* it upheld a Louisiana law requiring the segregation of whites and blacks in rail coaches. It held that the law did not violate the Equal Protection Clause because the *separate* facilities for blacks were *equal* to those for whites.

The separate-but-equal doctrine soon became the constitutional justification for racial segregation in several other fields. It stood for nearly 60 years. Indeed, until the late 1930s, little real effort was made—by the courts or by any other arm of government—even to see that the separate accommodations for blacks were, in fact, equal to those reserved to whites. More often than not, they were not.

Brown* v. *Topeka Board of Education, 1954 The Supreme Court began to chip away at the separate-but-equal doctrine in several cases in the late 1930s and the 1940s. It did

"Jim Crow" laws required racial segregation in public places, including hotels.

*ENRICHMENT Discuss the role that the separate-but-equal doctrine had in the desegregation of schools, and how it consequently has had an effect on your students' lives. (2.1, 2.3; 1.B, 1.C, 2.I, 4.G)

so for the first time in *Missouri ex rel. Gaines* v. *Canada* in 1938. Lloyd Gaines had applied for admission to the law school at the all-white State university. He was wholly qualified for admission, except that he was black. The State did not have a law school for blacks. However, it did offer to pay his tuition at a public law school in any of four neighboring States, where blacks were admitted on equal terms with whites. But Gaines continued to hold to his position and insisted on a legal education in his own home State.

The Supreme Court held that the separate-but-equal doctrine left the State of Missouri with two choices. It could either (1) admit Gaines to the State's law school or (2) establish a separate-but-equal one for him. Needless to say, the State admitted Gaines to its law school.

Over the next several years the Supreme Court took an increasingly sterner attitude toward the doctrine's requirement of equal facilities for blacks. Finally, in an historic decision in 1954, the Court reversed *Plessy* v. *Ferguson.* In *Brown* v. *Topeka Board of Education,* it struck down the laws of four States requiring or allowing separate public schools for white and black students.[33]

Unanimously, the Supreme Court held that **segregation** by race in public education is unconstitutional:

> Does segregation of children in public schools solely on the basis of race, even though the physical facilities and other "tangible" factors may be equal, deprive the children of the minority group of equal educational opportunities? We believe that it does.
>
> . . . To separate them from others of similar age and qualifications solely because of their race generates a feeling of inferiority as to their status in the community that may affect their hearts and minds in a way unlikely ever to be undone. . . . We conclude that in the field of public education the doctrine of "separate but equal" has no place. Separate educational facilities are inherently unequal.

How was its decision to be carried out? The Court recognized that the question presented "a problem of considerable complexity." That observation proved to be a monumental understatement.

The Court held extensive hearings and, in 1955, directed the States to make "a prompt and reasonable start" and to end school segregation "with all deliberate speed." Federal District Courts were ordered to supervise the desegregation process.

A "reasonable start" was made in several places: Baltimore, Louisville, St. Louis, Washington, D.C., and elsewhere. In most of the Deep South, however, what came to be known as "massive resistance" soon developed. State legislatures passed a number of laws to block integration. Most of these laws were clearly unconstitutional, and the process of attacking them in the federal courts was both costly and slow. Many school boards, urged on by the white community, worked to bar progress. Until the 1960s, neither Congress nor the President gave either support or leadership to integration efforts.

The pace of desegregation quickened after Congress passed the Civil Rights Act of 1964. That act forbids the use of federal funds to aid any State or local activity in which racial segregation is practiced. It also directed the Justice Department to file court suits to prompt desegregation actions.

The Supreme Court itself pushed that pace along in 1969. In a case from Mississippi, *Alexander* v. *Holmes County Board of Education,* it ruled that, after 15 years, the time for "all deliberate speed" had finally run out. Said a unanimous Court: "The continued operation of segregated schools under a standard allowing for 'all deliberate speed' . . . is no longer constitutionally permissible."

De Jure and De Facto Segregation By fall 1970, school systems with **de jure segregation**—by law, with legal sanction—had been abolished. That is not to say that desegregation had been fully accomplished—far from it. But nowhere in the country was a public school *legally* identified as one reserved either for whites or for blacks. The

[33]Kansas, Delaware, South Carolina, and Virginia. The Court also struck down racially segregated schools in the District of Columbia, under the 5th Amendment's Due Process Clause, *Bolling* v. *Sharpe,* 1954.

*REINFORCEMENT Have the class discuss the issues and results of the landmark case of *Brown* v. *Topeka Board of Education.*

PERSONALITY PROFILE

Martin Luther King, Jr. and Civil Rights

Martin Luther King, Jr. was born in Atlanta, Georgia, on January 15, 1929, into a heritage of deep religious faith and activism. Like his father and maternal grandfather, King became a Baptist minister.

King's education was marked by an enthusiasm to learn and to achieve. He took a liberal arts degree from Morehouse College in 1948, a degree from the Crozer Theological Seminary in 1951, and a Ph.D. in theology from Boston University in 1955. During this period, King was married and, in 1954, became the pastor of the Dexter Avenue Baptist Church in Montgomery, Alabama.

King rose to national prominence in 1955 when he organized the boycott to break the "Jim Crow" bus laws of Alabama. A year of economic pressure, during which King's house was bombed, resulted in a 1956 Supreme Court ruling that declared the "separate but equal" law to be unconstitutional.

It is at this early point in King's career that his philosophy for improving race relations and the situation of blacks developed. Borrowing from his religious upbringing and from the beliefs of Thoreau and Gandhi, and his own assessment of the political climate of the country, King came to believe that progress for equality could only be made through direct, nonviolent action by the masses.

The minister's political career accelerated as he formed the Southern Christian Leadership Conference in Atlanta in 1957 and became co-pastor, with his father, of the Ebenezer Baptist Church in Atlanta. King lectured throughout the South and encouraged individuals to break segregation laws. In 1963 King was jailed in Birmingham, Alabama, for launching a major campaign against segregation in that city. His 1963 march on Washington and his antidiscrimination and voter registration drives in the ensuing years were rewarded by the passage of the Civil Rights Acts of 1964 and the Voting Rights Act of 1965. In 1964 King received the Nobel peace prize, the youngest man in history to do so, for his philosophy of nonviolent resistance in the struggle for racial equality.

After 1965 King extended his civil rights activities to the North. At the encouragement of his wife, Coretta Scott King, King began to criticize the Vietnam War on moral and financial grounds.

While on a trip to Memphis, Tennessee, on April 4, 1968, to aid the civil rights cause of black sanitation workers, King was assassinated at the age of 39.

King's courage and vision stand as a lasting testament to the pursuit of freedom in America. As his "I have a dream" speech attests, King looked to the time when racial equality would finally be realized.

> I have a dream that one day on the red hills of Georgia the sons of former slaves and the sons of former slaveowners will be able to sit down together at the table of brotherhood.
>
> I have a dream today.
>
> I have a dream that one day every valley shall be exalted, every hill and mountain shall be made low, the rough places will be made plains, and the crooked places will be made straight, and the glory of the Lord shall be revealed, and all flesh shall see it together . . .
>
> And if America is to be a great nation this must become true.

1. What are the major accomplishments of King's struggle for civil rights?
2. What was King's "dream", and to what extent has it been realized today?

process of achieving a complete integration of the country's schools still continues, some 30 years after the decision in *Brown*.[34]

For many years, segregation was seen by most as a problem of the South. Events of the recent past have shown, however, that the problem is, and long has been, one of *nation-wide* dimensions. Many of the more recent integration controversies have come in places where the schools have never been segregated by law. They are in communities in which de facto segregation has long been present, and continues.

De facto segregation exists where, although no law requires it, circumstances have in fact produced segregation. Housing patterns have most often been its major cause. The concentration of black populations in one or some sections of several cities inevitably led to local school systems in which some schools are largely black and others largely white. That condition is clearly apparent in many *northern* as well as southern communities.

Efforts to desegregate those school systems have taken several forms. School district lines have been redrawn, pupil assignment programs have been put in place, *and the busing of students out of racially segregated neighborhoods has been tried. These efforts have often brought strong protests in many places and violence in some.

The Supreme Court first sanctioned busing in a North Carolina case, *Swann* v. *Charlotte-Mecklenburg Board of Education,* 1971. There it held that "desegregation plans cannot be limited to walk-in schools." Since then, busing has been used to try to increase the racial mix in many school districts across the country—in some by court order, in others voluntarily.

The whole matter of school integration is packed with legal questions. It is just as clearly loaded with highly charged political and emotional issues. That point is sharply underlined by the ongoing national dispute over busing.

Segregation in Other Fields A complete integration of the public schools has not yet been achieved. Legally enforced racial segregation has been very largely eliminated in other areas of life, however. Many State laws and local ordinances have been repealed or struck down by the courts. The Supreme Court has found racial segregation in all other areas to be as unconstitutional as it is in education, for example, in public recreational facilities, *Dawson* v. *Baltimore,* 1955; in local transportation, *Gayle* v. *Browder,* 1956; in State prisons and local jails, *Lee* v. *Washington,* 1968. In *Loving* v. *Virginia,* 1967, it struck down all *miscegenation* laws, or laws that bar interracial marriages.

Classification by Sex In its many civil rights provisions, the Constitution speaks of "the people," "persons," and "citizens." Nowhere does it make its guarantees only to "men" or separately to "women."[35]

Sex has long been used as a basis of classification in the law, however. By and large, that practice reflected society's historic view of the "proper" role of women. Most often, those laws that treated men and women differently were seen as necessary to the protection of "the weaker sex." Over the years, the Supreme Court read that view into the 14th Amendment. It did not find *any* sex-based classification to be unconstitutional until as recently as 1971.

In the first case in which sex discrimination was challenged, *Bradwell* v. *Illinois,* 1873, the Court upheld a State law barring women from the practice of law. In that case, Justice Joseph P. Bradley wrote:

> The civil law, as well as nature itself, has always recognized a wide difference in the respective spheres and destinies of man and

[34]Most of the legal and political controversies surrounding desegregation have involved *public* schools. Some States, several school districts, and many parents and private groups have sought to block integration or avoid integrated schools through established or, often, newly created *private* schools. See the Court's rulings in two 1983 cases, *Bob Jones University* v. *United States* and *Goldsboro Christian Schools* v. *United States* (page 107) and *Runyan* v. *McCrary,* 1976 (page 135).

[35]The only reference to sex is in the 19th Amendment, which forbids the denial of the right to vote "on account of sex."

*ENRICHMENT Have the class discuss: Busing is being used to desegregate schools. Do you agree with this method? Why or why not?

Martin Luther King, Jr. gave his "I have a dream" speech in 1963 to thousands demonstrating in Washington for stronger civil rights laws.

woman. Man is, or should be, woman's protector and defender. The natural and proper timidity and delicacy of the female sex evidently unfits it for many of the occupations of civil life.

Even in 1961, in *Hoyt* v. *Florida,* the Court found no constitutional fault with a law that required men to serve on juries but gave women the choice of serving or not.

Matters are far different today. The Court now takes a very close look at cases involving claims of sex discrimination. In 1971, in *Reed* v. *Reed,* it struck down an Idaho law that gave fathers preference over mothers in the administration of their children's estates.

Since then, the Supreme Court has found a number of sex-based distinctions to be unconstitutional. We have already noted some of them, for example, *Taylor* v. *Louisiana,* 1975, holding that the Equal Protection Clause forbids the States to exclude women from jury service. Other unconstitutional findings include:

—A Utah law that made sons eligible for child support from their fathers until age 21, but daughters only to age 18, *Stanton* v. *Stanton,* 1975.

—An Oklahoma law that prohibited the sale of beer to males under 21 and to females under 18, *Craig* v. *Boren,* 1976.

—A provision in the social security law giving widows higher benefits than widowers, *Califano* v. *Goldfarb,* 1977; and another giving benefits to families with unemployed fathers but not to those with unemployed mothers, *Califano* v. *Westcott,* 1979.

—A New York law that allowed an unwed mother, but not an unwed father, to block the adoption of her infant children, *Caban* v. *Mohammed,* 1979.

—An Arizona rule permitting public employee retirement plans providing for smaller pensions for women than for men who paid the same premiums during their working years, *Arizona Governing Committee* v. *Norris,* 1983.

The court's present attitude was stated by Justice William Brennan in *Frontiero* v. *Richardson,* 1973:

> There can be no doubt that our nation has had a long and unfortunate history of sex discrimination. Traditionally, such discrimination was rationalized by an attitude of "romantic paternalism" which, in practical effect, put women, not on a pedestal, but in a cage.[36]

But not all sex-based distinctions are unconstitutional. The Court has upheld some of them in recent cases. We saw one example of this in *Michael M.* v. *Superior Court,* 1981, on page 156. In the following three cases, the Supreme Court has held that there was no denial of equal protection:

—A Florida law that gives an extra property tax exemption to widows, but not to widowers, *Kahn* v. *Shevin,* 1974.

—An Alabama law that does not allow women to serve as prison guards in all-male penitentiaries, *Dothard* v. *Rawlinson,* 1977.

—The federal selective service law that requires men but not women to register for the draft, and also its provisions that exclude women from any future draft, *Rostker* v. *Goldberg,* 1981.

*In effect, these recent cases say this: Classification by sex is not unconstitutional. However, laws that treat men and women differently will not be upheld *unless* (1) they are intended to serve an "important governmental objective" and (2) they are "substantially related" to achieving that goal.

[36]In this case the Court for the first time struck down a federal law providing for sex-based discrimination, as a violation of the 5th Amendment's Due Process Clause. That law gave various housing, medical, and other allowances to a serviceman for his wife and other dependents, but it made those same allowances available to a servicewoman only if her husband was dependent on her for more than half of his support.

Gradually, hiring practices that discriminate against the handicapped are being eroded.

Thus, in upholding the all-male draft, the Court found that Congress did have such an objective: to raise and support armies and, if necessary, to do so by "a draft of combat troops." "Since women are excluded from combat," said the Court, they may properly be excluded from the draft.

FOR REVIEW

1. **Identify:** Equal Protection Clause, strict scrutiny test.
2. The Equal Protection Clause expressly forbids what kinds of discrimination by the States?
3. What is the Court's rational basis test?
4. What was the separate-but-equal doctrine? What did the Court hold in *Brown* v. *Topeka Board of Education?*
5. What is the difference between de jure and de facto segregation?
6. Does the Constitution forbid laws that treat men and women differently?

*ENRICHMENT Recent court cases have said that classification by sex is not unconstitutional. Ask the class what the constitutional basis is for this decision.

7. Federal Civil Rights Laws

As You Read, Think About:

- What the importance is of the civil rights laws passed after 1957.
- What the reasons are behind the Federal Government adopting the policy of affirmative action.
- What the arguments are for and against affirmative action programs.

From the 1870s to the late 1950s, Congress did not pass a single piece of meaningful civil rights legislation. We shall look at several reasons for that sorry fact later, especially in Chapter 8, when we consider the right to vote, and in Chapter 12, when we look at Congress in action.

That historic logjam was broken in 1957, however. Over the past 30 years Congress has passed a number of civil rights laws—most notably, the Civil Rights Acts of 1957, 1960, 1964, and 1968 and the Voting Rights Acts of 1965, 1970, 1975, and 1982. Each of those statutes is designed to carry out the Constitution's insistence on the equality of all before the law.

The 1957 and 1960 laws set up modest safeguards for the right to vote.[37] Together with related provisions in the 1964 law and the much stronger Voting Rights Acts, we shall consider them in Chapter 8.

The Civil Rights Act of 1968 is often called the Open Housing Act. With minor exceptions, it forbids anyone to refuse to sell or to rent a dwelling to any person on grounds of race, color, religion, or national origin. The law has few teeth, however.

The Civil Rights Act of 1964 is a much broader statute with plenty of teeth. Beyond its voting rights provisions, it outlaws discrimination in a number of areas. With its several later amendments, its major sections now

(1) Provide that no person may be denied access to, or refused service in, various "public accommodations" on grounds of race, color, religion, or national origin (Title II).[38]
(2) Prohibit discrimination against any person on grounds of race, color, religion, national origin, sex, or physical handicap in any program which receives any federal funds (Title VI).
(3) Forbid employers and labor unions to discriminate against any person on grounds of race, color, religion, sex, physical handicap, or age (40 to 65) in hiring and all other job-related matters (Title VII).[39]

Affirmative Action

The several recent statutes and court decisions we have just reviewed all come down to this: Those discriminatory practices based on such factors as race, color, national origin, or sex are illegal.

But, notice, that very important point raises this equally important question: What about the *present* and *continuing* effects of *past* discriminations? The fact that the law *now* prohibits discrimination does almost nothing to overcome the consequences of the discriminatory practices of the past.

As only one of many illustrations of the point, consider the black man who, for no

[37]The 1957 law created the Civil Rights Commission. Its six members keep watch over the enforcement of the various civil rights laws, investigate cases of alleged discrimination, and report their findings and recommendations to the President, Congress, and the public.

[38]Congress based this section of the law on the commerce power; see page 346. It covers those places in which lodgings are offered to transient guests and those in which a significant portion of the things sold or the entertainment offered has moved in interstate commerce. These "public accommodations" include, for example, most restaurants, cafeterias, lunch counters, and other eating places; movie theatres, concert halls, and other auditoriums; gasoline stations; sports arenas and stadiums; and hotels, motels, and rooming houses, except owner-occupied units with less than six rooms for rent.

The Court upheld Title II and the use of the Commerce Clause as the basis for civil rights legislation in *Heart of Atlanta Motel, Inc.* v. *United States*, 1964. The Court found "overwhelming evidence of the disruptive effect [of] racial discrimination . . . on commercial intercouse."

[39]The 1964 law also created the Equal Employment Opportunities Commission. The six-member EEOC's major charge is the enforcement of Title VII. The Commission works to promote voluntary compliance with the law, but it can bring federal court suits to halt discriminatory practices and assure equal employment opportunities.

reason of his own making, did not get a decent education and so today cannot get a decent job. Of what real help to him are all of those laws and court decisions that make illegal *today* what was done to him years ago?

So far, the Federal Government's chief answer to this troubling question has been a * policy of **affirmative action.** That policy requires that most employers, both public and private, take positive steps, or affirmative action, to remedy the effects of past discriminations against women and blacks and the members of various other minority groups.

All public and private employers who receive any federal funds are required to adopt and implement affirmative action programs. Thus, the policy applies to all the agencies of the Federal Government, to all the States and their local governments, and to all other employers who hold government contracts of any kind.

This includes then, both business and industrial firms and all public and most private colleges and universities. In short, the policy covers nearly all the nation's major employers and many of its smaller ones.[40]

To illustrate the policy, take the case of a company that does business with the Federal Government. That private business must adopt an affirmative action plan designed to make its work force reflect the general make-up of the population in its locale. It must employ so many women, so many blacks, so many Hispanics, and so on. Its program must also include steps to correct or prevent inequalities in such job-related matters as pay, promotions, and fringe benefits. For many employers this has meant that they must hire and/or promote more workers with minority backgrounds and, often, more females, as well. It has also meant that many employers have had to comply even when better qualified white males are available.

Affirmative action programs necessarily involve race- and/or sex-based classifications. Is this wise public policy? Are such programs constitutional?

Those who support affirmative action argue that some form of preferential treatment is necessary to break down long-standing patterns of discrimination against women and minorities. They insist that such special considerations are especially important in the job market and in education. Critics of the policy say that, however good its intentions, affirmative action amounts to *reverse discrimination.* It demands that preference be given to females and/or nonwhites, solely on the basis of sex or race, and without regard to individual merit.

The Supreme Court has now decided several affirmative action cases. The first major case was *Regents of the University of California* v. *Bakke,* 1978. Allan Bakke, a white male, had twice been denied admission to the University's medical school at Davis. He sued, charging the school with **reverse discrimination,** because it had set aside 16 seats in each year's entering class for nonwhite students, and had then filled that quota with several nonwhites less qualified than Bakke.

The State Supreme Court agreed. It found that Bakke had been denied his 14th Amendment right to equal protection. It ordered the University not to use race as a factor in admissions.

On appeal, the Supreme Court was sharply divided. By one 5–4 majority, it agreed with the California court that Bakke had been denied equal protection and so should be admitted to the medical school.

However, a differently composed 5–4 majority made the really important ruling in the case. That majority of the Court held this: Although the Constitution does not allow race to be used as the *only* factor in the making of affirmative action decisions, both

[40]The Federal Government began to demand the adoption of affirmative action programs in 1965. There are now thousands of those programs in place throughout the country. Some are simply plans that call for the wide advertisement of job openings to attract applicants from many different groups. Most are much more sophisticated and detailed, however. They establish guidelines and timetables to overcome past discriminations. Some set quotas to ensure that a certain number of positions, that is, jobs or admissions to a university, will go to women and/or minority applicants.

Affirmative action was more vigorously enforced by the Federal Government from the mid-1960s to 1981 than is the case today. Critics of the Reagan Administration charge that it has backed away from a tough enforcement of that policy.

*ENRICHMENT The Reagan Administration is very selective in taking affirmative action cases to court because of reverse discrimination. Ask the class if they agree with this policy. Why or why not?

the Constitution and the 1964 Civil Rights Act do allow its use as *one among several* factors in such situations.*

The Court has upheld quotas in some later cases, however. Thus, it has said that a private company can set up an affirmative action plan in which black employees are given preference in on-the-job training programs, *United Steel Workers of America* v. *Weber,* 1979.

The Kaiser Aluminum Company had set up the training programs, especially to increase the number of skilled blacks in its work force. The USWA had agreed to them, provided that each training group include an equal number of blacks and whites. The trainees were picked from each racial group, one-for-one, and by seniority (length of employment by the company). Brian Weber, a white worker, was rejected for training three times. Each time, several blacks with less seniority were selected, however.

Weber went to court, claiming that the company and the union had engaged in reverse discrimination, and so had violated Title VII of the 1964 law. (Note the contrast with *Bakke,* which had to do with Title VI and, because a State was involved, the 14th Amendment. *Weber* did not involve any public agency and called for the interpretation of a statute, not the Constitution.)

On appeal, the Court ruled, 5–2, for the company and the union. It held that the training programs, although involving quotas giving special preference to blacks, did not violate the 1964 law. A literal reading of that law might suggest otherwise, said the Court, but that reading would contradict the purpose of "a law triggered by a nation's concern over centuries of racial injustice."

The Court has decided only five other affirmative action cases since *Weber*—one in 1980, another in 1984, and three in 1986.

The Court did not hold that any and all job plans that give special preferences to blacks or other minorities are legal. Yet many plans very much like Kaiser's are in force today, and they are conducted by hundreds of companies employing several million workers.

Fullilove v. *Klutznick,* 1980, centered on a law Congress had passed to combat unemployment in the construction industry. It provided for $4 billion in grants to State and local governments for public works projects.

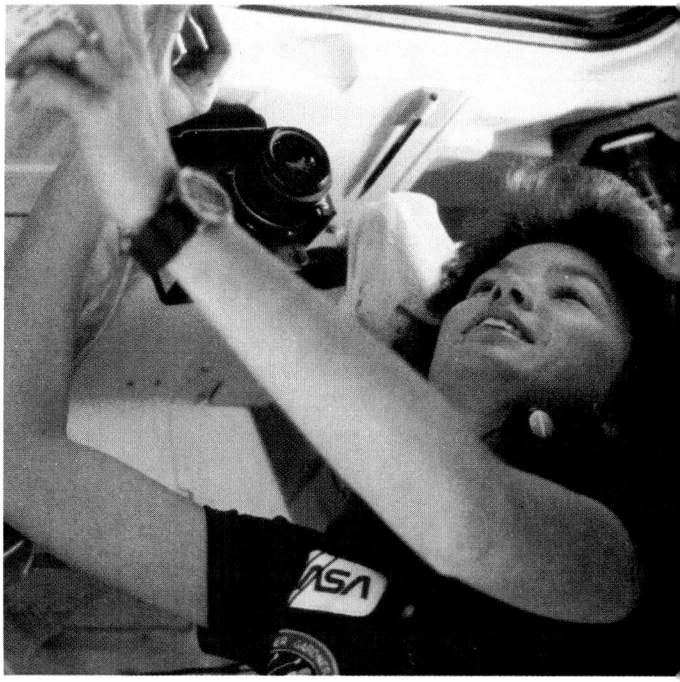

Women today work in fields formerly viewed as the sole province of the male. Shown here is astronaut Anna Lee Fisher, a crew member of space shuttle *Discovery.*

At issue in the case was the law's "minority set-aside" provision. It said that at least 10 percent of the grants had to be set aside for minority businesses.

A white contractor challenged the set-asides. He said that they were quotas and therefore unconstitutional because they did not give to white contractors an equal chance to compete with black contractors for all available funds.

He lost in the lower federal courts and then in the Supreme Court. It found, 6–3, that Congress had properly exercised its constitutional powers to spend and to regulate interstate commerce. In short, it held that the law was a permissible attempt to overcome the effects of long-standing discrimination in the construction industry.

In *Firefighters Local* v. *Stotts,* 1984. The Court held that a seniority rule, in a valid

*ENRICHMENT Assign the class a report on the Bakke case, highlighting the effect it has had on affirmative action and reverse discrimination.

labor contract that does not discriminate against blacks, cannot be ignored when workers must be laid off.

The case involved the Memphis, Tennessee, fire department. Budget problems had forced the layoff of a number of firefighters. To preserve racial balance, the department fired some white officers with more seniority than some blacks whose jobs were saved. In such situations, said the Court, the 1964 law allows the traditional "last hired, first fired" seniority rule to stand.

Wygant v. *Jackson Board of Education,* 1986, involved a teacher layoff plan adopted by the school board in Jackson, Michigan. The plan called for the layoff of a number of white teachers in order to preserve the jobs of an equal number of black teachers, even though the blacks had less seniority in the local schools. The plan, said the Court, denied the white teachers their 14th Amendment right to equal protection.

The other 1986 cases involve the application of Title VII of the 1964 Civil Rights law and in both the Court upheld affirmative action plans designed to remedy past discrimination. In *Sheet Metal Workers' International* v. *Equal Employment Opportunity Commission,* the Court upheld a lower federal court order directing a union that had persistently refused to admit blacks to raise its non-white membership to a specific level (29.23%) by a given date (August, 1987). And, in *International Association of Firefighters* v. Cleveland, the Court said that a city can agree that, for a limited time, it would promote one black firefighter for every white who received a promotion in its fire department.

In 1983, 6.5% of the nation's 6 million construction workers were black and 5.8% were Hispanic.

FOR REVIEW

1. What is the basic purpose of the civil rights laws passed by Congress in the past?
2. What are the major provisions of the Civil Rights Act of 1964?
3. What are affirmative action programs? What is meant by the phrase "reverse discrimination"?

8. American Citizenship

As You Read, Think About:

- How a person may acquire American citizenship.
- What the nation's policy has been toward immigration over time.
- What the problems are that are associated with illegal aliens today.

As it was originally written, the Constitution mentioned both "citizens of the United States" and "citizens of the States." It did not define either of those phrases, however. Through much of our early history it was generally agreed that national citizenship followed that of the States. That is, any person who was recognized as a citizen of one of the States was also regarded as a citizen of the United States.

The coming of the Civil War and the adoption of the 13th Amendment in 1865 raised the need for a constitutional definition, however.[41] That need was finally met by the 14th Amendment in 1868. The Amendment begins with these words:

> All persons born or naturalized in the United States, and subject to the jurisdiction thereof, are citizens of the United States and of the State wherein they reside.

Thus, the 14th Amendment declares that a person may become an American citizen either by birth or by naturalization.

Citizenship by Birth

More than 220 million Americans—more than 90 percent of all of us—are American citizens because we were born in the United States. Another several million are also citizens by birth, even though they were born abroad. **Citizenship** by birth is determined by either (1) ***jus soli*—**the law of the soil, *where* born, or (2) ***jus sanguinis*—**the law of the blood, to *whom* born.

Jus Soli The 14th Amendment confers citizenship according to the *location* of a person's birth: "All persons born . . . in the United States. . . ." By law, Congress has defined the United States to include, for purposes of citizenship, the 50 States, the District of Columbia, Puerto Rico, Guam, the Virgin Islands, and the Northern Mariana Islands. It includes, as well, all American embassies and all American public vessels anywhere in the world.[42]

[41]In the *Dred Scott Case (Scott* v. *Sanford)* in 1857, the Supreme Court had ruled that neither the States nor the National Government had the power to confer citizenship on blacks—slave or free. The dispute over that issue was one of the several causes of the Civil War.

[42]Under the international law doctrine of extraterritoriality, United States embassies are, in effect, parts of the United States. A public vessel is any ship or aircraft operated by any agency of the Government.

Some few persons are born physically in the United States but not "subject to the jurisdiction thereof" and so do not become citizens of the United States at birth. The very small number involved includes mostly the children born to foreign diplomats.

Until 1924, Indians born to tribal members living on reservations were not considered citizens. They were instead *wards,* persons under the legal guardianship, of the Government. In that year, however, Congress granted citizenship to all American Indians.

Just how broad the 14th Amendment's statement of *jus soli* is can be seen from one of the early leading cases in the law of citizenship, *United States* v. *Wong Kim Ark,* 1898. Wong Kim Ark was born in San Francisco in 1873 to parents who were both citizens of China. Wong made a brief trip to China in 1895. When he returned, immigration officials at San Francisco refused to admit him to the United States. In their view, he was an alien. They insisted that the 14th Amendment should not be read so literally as to mean that he was a citizen. They ruled that, as an alien, he was prohibited entry by the Chinese Exclusion Act of 1882. The Supreme Court rejected that view. The Court held that, under the clear words of the 14th Amendment, Wong was indeed a native-born citizen and that the Chinese Exclusion Act could not be considered applicable in his case.

Jus Sanguinis A child born abroad can become an American citizen at birth under certain circumstances. The child must be born to parents at least one of whom is a citizen who has at some time lived in the United States.[43]

The 14th Amendment does not provide for *jus sanguinis,* but Congress has included it as a part of American citizenship law since 1790. The constitutionality of the rule has never been challenged. But if it were, it would almost certainly be upheld—if for no other reason than because of its long-standing history.

Citizenship by Naturalization

Naturalization is the legal process by which a person becomes a citizen of another country at some time after birth. Congress has the exclusive power to provide for naturalization. No State may do so.[44] The naturalization process may be either an individual or a collective one.

[43]When a child is born in another country to American parents, the birth is usually registered at the nearest American consulate.

[44]Article I, Section 8, Clause 4.

*REINFORCEMENT Have the class discuss the two ways to become an American citizen as defined by the 14th Amendment.

Individual Naturalization The process is most often an individual one, conducted by a court. Some 200,000 aliens now become naturalized American citizens each year.

As a general rule, any person who has come to the United States as an *immigrant,* that is, an alien legally admitted as a permanent resident, can be naturalized. More specifically, current law provides that a person who wants to become a naturalized citizen must:

—Have entered the United States legally, lived here for at least five years and in some State for at least six months, and be at least 18 years old.[45]

—File a petition for naturalization with the clerk of a federal District Court or of a State Court of Record.

—Be literate in the English language.

—Be "of good moral character," "attached to the principles of the Constitution," and "well disposed to the good order and happiness of the United States."

—Have "a knowledge and understanding of the fundamentals of the history, and the principles and form of government, of the United States."

—Not, within the past 10 years, have believed in or advocated opposition to organized government, the overthrow of government by force or violence, the doctrines of world communism or of any other form of totalitarianism, or belonged to any organization with any of those aims.

—Take an oath or affirmation in which he or she absolutely renounces any allegiance to any foreign power and promises to "support and defend the Constitution and laws of the United States against all enemies, foreign and domestic."[46]

The Immigration and Naturalization Service in the Department of Justice investigates each applicant. An INS examiner then reports to the judge of the court in which the petition for naturalization was filed. If the judge is satisfied, the oath or affirmation is administered in open court, and the new citizen receives a certificate of naturalization.

Collective Naturalization At various times in our history an entire group of persons has been naturalized en masse. This has most often happened when the United States has acquired new territory. As the table on page 169 indicates, those living in the areas involved were naturalized by a treaty or by an act or a joint resolution passed by Congress. The largest single instance of collective naturalization came with the ratification of the 14th Amendment, however. The most recent instance occurred in 1977, when Congress gave citizenship to the more than 16,000 native-born residents of the Northern Mariana Islands.

Loss of Citizenship

Although it rarely happens, every American citizen, whether native-born or naturalized, has the right to renounce—voluntarily abandon—his or her citizenship. **Expatriation** is the legal process by which a loss of citizenship occurs.

The Supreme Court has several times held that the Constitution prohibits automatic

---

[45]The residence requirements are eased somewhat for the alien husbands, wives, and children of citizens and for present and former members of the armed forces. Also, the naturalization of both parents—one parent, if the other is dead or divorced—automatically naturalizes their children under 16 years of age if the children are living permanently in the United States.

[46]In an oath a person swears to something and binds that pledge with the words "so help me God." Those whose religious beliefs will not allow them to invoke a Supreme Being in that way and those who do not believe in one may instead make an affirmation (a legally binding pledge that does not refer to a Supreme Being.)

In the oath or affirmation the citizen-to-be also promises to "bear arms in behalf of the United States" if required to do so by law. However, those whose religious beliefs will not allow them to do so may promise to serve as noncombatants in the armed forces or perform some work of national importance under civilian direction.

*REINFORCEMENT Have the class discuss the various paths to citizenship and the qualifications that must be met. Does the system seem flexible? Too rigid?

How Citizenship is Acquired

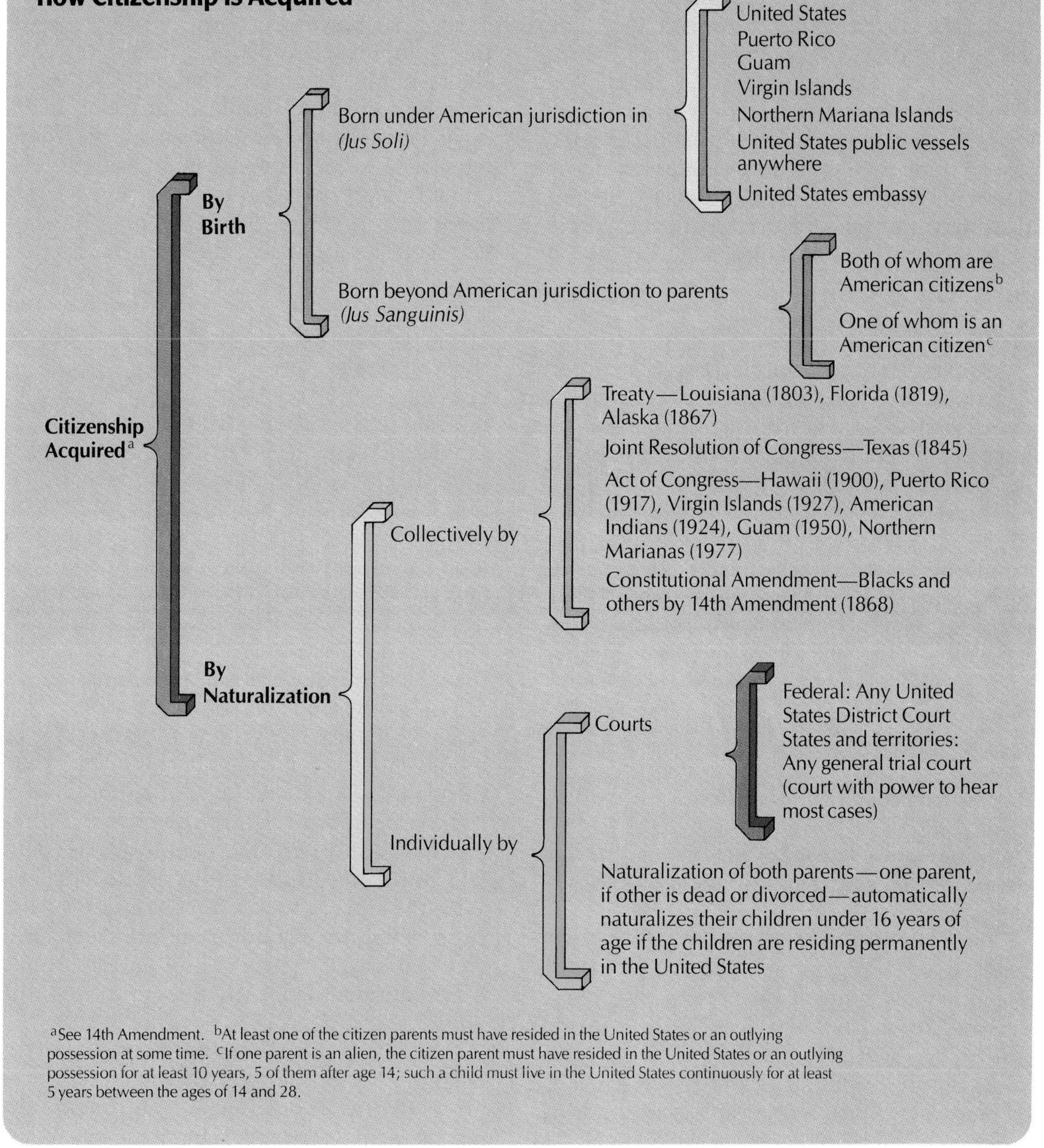

[a]See 14th Amendment. [b]At least one of the citizen parents must have resided in the United States or an outlying possession at some time. [c]If one parent is an alien, the citizen parent must have resided in the United States or an outlying possession for at least 10 years, 5 of them after age 14; such a child must live in the United States continuously for at least 5 years between the ages of 14 and 28.

expatriation. That is, Congress cannot provide for the involuntary loss of a person's citizenship for something he or she has done, for example, committing a crime, voting in a foreign election, or serving in the armed forces of another country.

In the leading case, *Afroyim* v. *Rusk*, 1967, the Court declared that every citizen has "a constitutional right to remain a citizen in a free country unless he voluntarily relinquishes that citizenship." In *Afroyim* the Court struck down a section of the Nationality Act of 1940 that provided for the automatic expatriation of any American citizen who voted in a foreign election. The Court has made similar rulings in several later cases.

A naturalized citizen may be stripped of citizenship–through **denaturalization,** or involuntarily expatriated, however. But that can occur only by court order, and only when it can be shown that the person became a citizen by fraud or deception.

American citizenship is neither gained nor lost by marriage. The only significant effect that marriage has on the matter is to shorten the time required for the naturalization of an alien who marries an American citizen.

A Nation of Immigrants

We are a nation of immigrants. Except for American Indians, and even they are the descendants of earlier immigrants, all of us have come here from abroad or are descended from those who did.

There were only some 2.5 million persons in the United States in 1776. Since then, our population has grown by nearly 100 times to more than 240 million people today. That extraordinary population growth has come from two sources: natural increase (births) and immigration. As the table on the next page shows, over 50 million immigrants have come here since 1776.

The Regulation of Immigration Congress has the exclusive power to regulate immigration, that is, to decide who may be admitted to the United States and under what conditions.[47]

The United States made no serious attempt to regulate immigration for more than a century after independence. In fact, Congress did not pass any law on the subject until 1819 when it first provided for the collection of immigration statistics. As long as land was plentiful and rapidly expanding industry demanded more and still more workers, immigration was encouraged.

By 1890, however, the open frontier was a thing of the past, and labor was no longer in short supply. Then, too, the major source of immigration had shifted. Until the 1880s most immigrants had come from the countries of Northern and Western Europe. The "new immigration" from the 1880s onward came mostly from Southern and Eastern Europe. The closing of the frontier, a more abundant labor supply, and the shift in the major source of newcomers all combined to bring changes in our traditional policy of encouraging immigration.

Congress placed the first major restrictions on immigration with the passage of the Chinese Exclusion Act in 1882. At the same time, it barred the entry of convicts, lunatics, paupers, and others likely to become public charges. Over the next several years a long list of "undesirables" was added to the law. Thus, contract laborers were excluded in 1885, immoral persons and anarchists in 1903, and illiterates in 1917. By 1920 more than 30 groups were denied admission on grounds of various personal traits.

The tide of newcomers continued to mount, however. In the 10 years from 1905 through 1914 an average of more than a million persons—most of them from Southern and Eastern Europe—came to this country. World War I slowed that tide to a trickle. With the end of the war it rose rapidly again. Ellis Island, the major immigration center in New York harbor, was swamped. Thousands of immigrants had to wait there for months while their admissability was checked.

Congress responded to the many pressures for tighter regulation by adding *quantitative* limits (numerical ceilings) to the *qualitative* restrictions (personal characteristics) already in place. The Immigration Acts of 1921 and 1924 and the National Origins Act of 1929 established a national origins quota system. Each country in Europe was assigned a quota, or a limit on the number of immigrants who could enter the United States from that country each year. Altogether, only some 150,000 quota immigrants could be admitted in any one year. The

[47]The power to control the nation's borders is an inherent power of the United States, and that power includes the control of immigration. On the inherent powers, see page 73. In an early leading case on the point, the Supreme Court upheld the constitutionality of the Chinese Exclusion Act of 1882. That law generally barred Chinese from entering this country. The Court ruled that the power of the United States to "exclude aliens from its territory . . . is not open to controversy," *Chae Chan Ping* v. *United States*, 1889. The States have no power in the field, *The Passenger Cases*, 1849.

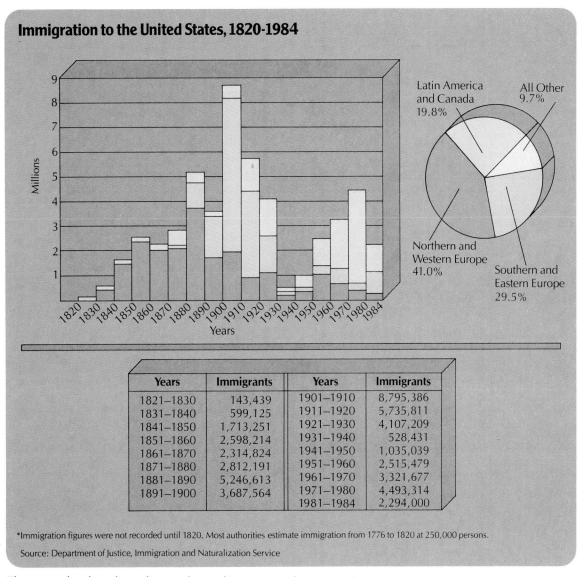

Immigration to the United States, 1820-1984

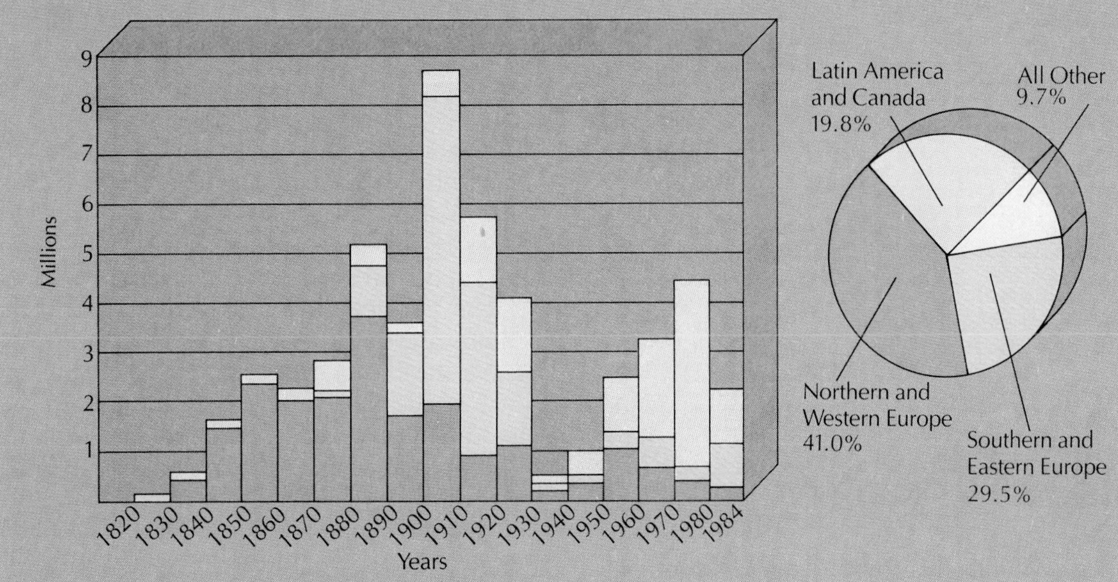

Years	Immigrants	Years	Immigrants
1821–1830	143,439	1901–1910	8,795,386
1831–1840	599,125	1911–1920	5,735,811
1841–1850	1,713,251	1921–1930	4,107,209
1851–1860	2,598,214	1931–1940	528,431
1861–1870	2,314,824	1941–1950	1,035,039
1871–1880	2,812,191	1951–1960	2,515,479
1881–1890	5,246,613	1961–1970	3,321,677
1891–1900	3,687,564	1971–1980	4,493,314
		1981–1984	2,294,000

*Immigration figures were not recorded until 1820. Most authorities estimate immigration from 1776 to 1820 at 250,000 persons.

Source: Department of Justice, Immigration and Naturalization Service

These graphs show how the numbers of immigrants have varied over the years. What attempts have been made in the past to restrict the influx of immigrants?

quotas were purposely drawn to favor Northern and Western Europe. Only a few thousand Southern and Eastern Europeans could be admitted annually. The quota system was not applied to the Western Hemisphere. Canadians and Latin Americans could continue to arrive in unrestricted numbers, but immigration from Asia, Africa, and elsewhere was generally prohibited.

In 1952 Congress passed yet another basic law, the Immigration and Nationality Act. That statute modified the restrictive legislation of the 1920s, but only slightly. The quota system was extended to cover every country outside the Western Hemisphere, but the annual ceiling on quota immigrants was raised to only some 165,000 persons. The Asian policy was eliminated, but China's quota was set at only 105 and Japan's at 100. *

Present Immigration Policy Today the Immigration Act of 1965 is the basic law governing the admission of aliens to the United States. That law was adopted only

*REINFORCEMENT Have the class discuss the quota system for immigration into the U.S. before the Immigration Act of 1965. Who did the quotas favor? Why?

These individuals in Miami, Florida, collectively take an oath to become naturalized citizens.

after years of intense debate, and it has now been amended several times.

The 1965 law eliminated the national origins, or country-by-country, quota system. Now, as many as 270,000 immigrants may be admitted each year without regard to race, nationality, or country of origin. Not more than 20,000 persons may come from any one country, however. The law purposely favors the admission of close relatives of American citizens and those other aliens who have special occupational talents.

Only those aliens who can qualify for naturalization can enter the United States as immigrants. The law's list of "excludable aliens"—those barred on grounds of some personal characteristic—now covers more than six pages in the *United States Code.*

The statute's ceiling on immigration of 270,000 a year is somewhat misleading because of the many exceptions. Thus, the Refugee Act of 1980 allows the admission of at least 50,000 political refugees outside that ceiling each year. The exact number is set by the President and Congress and now runs to as many as 100,000 a year. More than one million refugees have been admitted over the past 20 years, most of them from Cuba and Southeast Asia. Another approximately 150,000 *special immigrants,* mostly alien spouses and children of American citizens, are also admitted each year. Then, too, more than 11 million *nonimmigrants*—mostly tourists, students, and persons on business—come here annually for temporary stays.

Deportation As we noted on page 99, most of the civil rights set out in the Constitution are guaranteed to "persons." That term covers aliens as well as citizens. In one very large respect, however, the status of aliens is altogether unlike that of citizens: Aliens may be *deported,* or legally required to leave the United States.[48]

Congress has provided that an alien may be deported on any one of several grounds. The most common today is illegal entry. Hundreds of thousands of aliens who enter with false papers, sneak in by ship or plane, or slip across the border at night are caught each year—most of them by the Border Patrol, the police arm of the Immigration and Naturalization Service. Conviction of any serious crime, federal or State, usually leads to a deportation order by the INS. In recent years several thousand aliens have been expelled on the basis of their criminal records, especially narcotics violators.

Aliens may also be expelled for acts of disloyalty, for example, teaching or advocating the forcible overthrow of the government, or being a member of a Communist or some other totalitarian organization. In short, we have no place for those who would come here to enjoy our liberties while at the same time seeking to destroy them.

---

[48]The Supreme Court has long held that the United States has the same almost unlimited power to deport aliens as it has to exclude them. In an early major case, the Court ruled that (1) deportation is an inherent power, arising out of the sovereignty of the United States, and (2) deportation is not criminal punishment, and so does not require a criminal trial, *Fong Yue Ting* v. *United States,* 1893. Those major points remain basic to American law. Because deportation is a civil, not a criminal matter, several constitutional safeguards, for example, with regard to bail and *ex post facto* laws do not apply. In *Immigration and Naturalization Service* v. *Lopez-Mendoza,* 1984, the Court held that illegally seized evidence, which under the exclusionary rule cannot be used in a criminal trial, can be used at a deportation hearing.

Illegal Aliens

No one knows just how many illegal aliens there are in the United States today. The Census Bureau has put their number at somewhere between 3.5 and five million, and the INS at four to six million. Some authorities believe that the actual figure is at least twice those estimates.

However many there are, the number of illegal aliens is increasing, by at least half a million a year, according to the INS. Most of these "undocumented persons" enter the country by slipping across the Mexican or Canadian border, usually at night. Some come with forged papers. Many are aliens who entered legally, as nonimmigrants, but have now overstayed their legal welcomes.[49]

Once they are here, most illegal aliens find it fairly easy to become invisible, especially in our larger cities, and the understaffed INS finds it very difficult to locate them. Even so, immigration officials have found more than a million of them in each of the last several years. Nearly all are sent home. Most go voluntarily, but many leave only as the result of formal deportation proceedings. About a third of the illegal aliens the INS catches and deports are repeaters—aliens who have been previously deported, many of them several times and many of them several times in the same year.

The presence of so many "undocumented * persons" raises many difficult problems. Not the least of them are economic. It is not illegal to hire illegal aliens, and some authorities estimate that at least 3.5 million of them have jobs. However many are employed, the fact that they have jobs undoubtedly means that some citizens are deprived of work. Most jobs held by illegal aliens are unskilled and low-paying, for example, on farms, often as stoop laborers in the fields, or as dishwashers, and janitors. Some employers hire illegal aliens because often they work for substandard wages and under substandard conditions.

There is much disagreement over how the illegal alien problem should be solved. Many groups—labor, farm, business, religious, ethnic, civil rights, and others—are both troubled and divided by the matter. Congress itself has been wrestling with the problem for several years.

Some people call for the strengthening of the INS to stem the flow of illegal aliens and to expel those who are now here. They usually agree with those critics who think that stiff penalties should be imposed on those employers who hire, and exploit, illegal aliens. Many also propose that all workers, both citizens and legal resident aliens, carry a national identification card—a work permit that employers must verify.

Many people strongly oppose such steps, however. They challenge the wisdom of any policy that would force people back into the desperate economic situations that brought them here in the first place. Instead, they favor some form of amnesty for illegal aliens—a program under which those who have lived here for some time could become legal residents of the United States. (*Note:* For related details on the Immigration Reform and Control Act of 1986, see "Stop the Presses," page 712.)

[49]Well over half of all illegal aliens come from Mexico; most of the others come from other Latin American countries and from Asia. A majority of the Mexicans stay here only four to six months a year, working on farms or in other seasonal jobs. Most other illegal aliens hope to remain in the United States permanently.

FOR REVIEW

1. **Identify:** Citizenship, Chinese Exclusion Act, Immigration and Naturalization Service, Immigration Act of 1965, deportation, illegal aliens.
2. By what two ways can a person become an American citizen?
3. What is individual naturalization? Collective naturalization?
4. How are individuals naturalized?
5. How may a person lose citizenship?
6. Describe in a paragraph the history of United States immigration policy.
7. Why can a person be deported?
8. What problems are caused by the presence of so many illegal aliens?

*REINFORCEMENT Have the class discuss: What are the problems created by "undocumented persons" living and working in the United States?

SUMMARY

There are two Due Process Clauses in the Constitution. One, in the 5th Amendment, restricts the National Government. The other, in the 14th Amendment, restricts the States and their local governments. These guarantees require that government, in all that it does, must act fairly (procedural due process) and must act under fair laws (substantive due process).

The Supreme Court has used the 14th Amendment's Due Process Clause to extend most of the guarantees of the Bill of Rights against the States. Each State has, among its many reserved powers, the broad police power—the power to protect the public health, safety, morals, and welfare. A State law that can be justified as a valid use of the police powers does not violate the 14th Amendment's Due Process Clause.

All of the many constitutional guarantees to equal justice under law, set out in the Federal Constitution and in the State constitutions, may be grouped and described in these terms: (1) the rights to freedom and security of the person; (2) the rights of persons accused of crime; and (3) the rights to equality under the law.

The many guarantees in the Federal Constitution are summarized in the table on page 134. All of these individuals guarantees have been the subject of extensive interpretation and application by the United States Supreme Court in its many decisions.

We are a nation of immigrants. The 14th Amendment defines American citizenship, which can be acquired either by birth or by naturalization.

The power to regulate immigration is an inherent power of the United States. Congress exercises that power, in both qualitative and quantitative terms.

CHAPTER REVIEW

Key Terms/Concepts*

due process (130)
police power (131)
warrant (137)
probable cause (137)
exclusionary rule (138)
writ of habeas corpus (142)
bill of attainder (142)
ex post facto law (143)
double jeopardy (144)
grand jury (145)
indictment (145)
presentment (145)
Miranda Rule (151)
bail (152)
separate-but-equal doctrine (157)
segregation (158)
de jure segregation (158)
de facto segregation (160)
affirmative action (164)
reverse discrimination (164)
jus soli (167)
jus sanguinis (167)
naturalization (167)
citizenship (167)
expatriation (168)
denaturalization (170)

*These terms are included in the Glossary.

Keynote Questions

• **1.** What is the essential meaning of "due process of law"?

• **2.** What is the difference between procedural due process and substantive due process?

• **3.** Why are court cases involving the police power of the States and the civil rights of individuals difficult to decide?

• **4.** In what way does the 13th Amendment, unlike any other in the Constitution, apply against private as well as public action?

• **5.** Why do police officers usually have to have a warrant to search a house? What are the exceptions to this rule?

• **6.** Why is the exclusionary rule important? What exceptions are there to this rule?

• **7.** What is probable cause?

• **8.** To what extent does the 2nd Amendment guarantee the right to keep and bear arms?

The dots represent skill levels required to answer each question or complete each activity: • requires recall and comprehension • • requires application and analysis • • • requires synthesis and evaluation

- • **9.** Why did the Framers of the Constitution ban bills of attainder and ex post facto laws?
- • **10.** How do the protection against double jeopardy and the rights to a grand jury and to a speedy and public trial help to ensure a fair trial?
- • **11.** Under what circumstances can a person waive the right to a jury trial?
- • **12.** What is self-incrimination? The Miranda Rule?
- • **13.** Why did the Supreme Court in 1972 strike down all existing State laws allowing the death penalty? What has happened since then?
- • **14.** What is the Equal Protection Clause?
- • **15.** How does the rational basis test differ from the strict scrutiny test?
- • **16.** What was the Court's decision in *Brown* v. *Topeka Board of Education?* Why?
- • **17.** Are affirmative action programs constitutional? Why or why not?
- • **18.** Explain the two major ways by which a person can become a citizen of the United States.
- • **19.** How did the Immigration Act of 1965 change the immigration policy of the United States?

Skill Application

Recognizing Unstated Assumptions: Sometimes the way that a person makes a statement or phrases a question gives you an idea about what the person thinks about an issue or a problem. For example, in the statement, "Every citizen has the right to own a gun," the unstated assumption may be that the 2nd Amendment guarantees that right. The speaker assumes this, but does not come right out and say it. It is important to be able to recognize unstated assumptions because you will get a better idea of the speaker's beliefs and biases. Not all unstated assumptions are valid.

Read each of the sentences below and write one possible unstated assumption that may be behind each.

1. If the death penalty is eliminated, then the crime rate will go up.
2. Both women and men should be drafted.
3. Gun control would help to reduce violent crime in cities.
4. Even with gun control, criminals will be able to find guns.
5. The "good faith" exception to the exclusionary rule allows the police too much power.

For Thought and Discussion

- ••• **1.** On page 160, we noted the Supreme Court's recent change of attitude toward those laws that treat men and women differently. What factors do you think led the Court to its present position on those laws?
- ••• **2.** Some people believe that the Supreme Court over the last 25 years has granted too many protections for people accused of crimes. Do you agree or disagree with this viewpoint? Why?
- ••• **3.** Why do so many people choose to leave their native countries and enter this one illegally? What do you think should be done about the illegal aliens in this country? Why?
- ••• **4.** Would it be possible to guarantee due process of law if due process did not mean both procedural and substantive due process? Why or why not? Use an example to support your opinion.

Suggested Activities

- • **1.** Interview a local police officer about the Miranda Rule. Find out under what circumstances and at which point during an arrest the warning must be read to the arrested person.
- •• **2.** Select one of the cases discussed in this chapter and find out more about it. (Use the sources suggested on page 153.) Pay particular attention to the arguments of both sides, and the opinion of the Court delivered with the decision. Prepare a report that covers each of the following topics: facts of the case, constitutional issues involved; arguments by the plaintiff; arguments by the defendant; the Supreme Court's decision; the Supreme Court's rationale (reasons for the decision).
- ••• **3.** Stage a debate or class forum on one or more of the following topics: (a) Resolved, That the death penalty be (made legal/eliminated) in this State; (b) Resolved, That the laws of this State be amended to (allow/forbid) the live televising of criminal trials.

Happy Democrats Are We
Re-Elect
Carter
Mondale
HARRISON & REFORM
TRIUMFA CON
KENNEDY
A CLEAN SWEEP
HUGHES
ALLIANCE
ALL THE WAY WITH LBJ
Anderson Lucey
RICHMOND
TEDDY
FORD & DOLE
WALLACE IN '68
UNION AND LIBERTY
STATES RIGHTS
THURMOND WRIGHT
DEMOCRAT
OUR PRESIDENT
STUDENTS FOR KENNEDY
KEEP HOOVER
ADLAI LIKES ME
I LIKE IKE
GO 4TH TO WIN THE WAR
FOR PRESIDENT, FOR VICE-PRES.
LEVI P. MORTON
JIMMY CARTER
FOR PRESIDENT
UNION
LANDON
REAGAN IN 1980
PROGRESSIVE
TAFT
For President,
ABRAM LINCOLN
A FULL DINNER BUCKET
SOUND MONEY-GOOD MARKET
UNITE THE PARTY
REAGAN BUSH
1980
TRUMAN BARKLEY
LA FOLLETTE WHEELER
TRUMAN
FOR PRESIDENT
DEWEY
18 AND VOTIN NIXON
ABRAHAM LINCOLN
HOOVER
FOR PRESIDENT
WILSON
McGOVERN SHRIVER
MEMBER OF CONGRESS
FIRST DISTRICT
C. MC RUER
OF
SAN FRANCISCO
HAP - PY DEM - O - CRATS ARE WE!
His - to - ry.
lead us
great - est
© Copyright 1964 by Forward Music Publishing co.
Columbia Advertising Co., 133-17, 101st Ave., Richmond Hill 19, N.Y.

Unit 3

The Politics of American Democracy

PERHAPS THE MOST important idea underlying the American governmental system is that of government by the people. The design of the system makes the people the *only* source of governmental authority in this country. The system exists to turn the people's beliefs and desires into public policy and to carry out that policy.

The term *politics* describes the conduct of public affairs. It includes all parts of the governing process: the making of public policy, the carrying out of that policy, and the selection of the people who make and carry out policy.

Politics can also be described as "the pursuit and exercise of power." That is, it can be viewed in terms of the ability of some persons and groups to gain and use the power to make policies and to set up rules that others must follow.

In Unit Three we explore what Elihu Root, American statesman and Nobel Peace Prize winner, meant when he said that "Politics is the practical exercise of the art of self-government, and somebody must attend to it if we are to have self-government." We begin the unit by examining political parties. Then we consider the right to vote, the ways in which voters behave, and nominations and elections. Finally, we discuss the roles of public opinion and pressure groups.

A selection of political Americana—campaign buttons/emblems dating from the 1840s.

No America without democracy, no democracy without politics, no politics without parties, no parties without compromise and moderation. . . .
–Clinton Rossiter

7

Government by the People: Political Parties

CHAPTER OBJECTIVES

To help you to

Learn · Know · Understand

The nature of political parties and the essential functions parties perform in American politics.

The American two-party system, its history, and the reasons for its existence and retention.

The changes that have led to the present-day Democratic and Republican parties.

The nature and role of minor parties in American politics.

The organizational structure and composition of the two major parties.

The future of the two-party system.

Recall the derivation of the word *democracy.* As we noted in Chapter 1, it comes to us from two Greek words: *demos,* meaning "people", and *kratia,* meaning "rule" or "authority".

In a democracy the people rule. The people are sovereign. The people are the one and only source of any and all political authority. In a democracy, then, government must be "government by the people"—government by and with "the consent of the governed." To put it another way, a democratic government is one in which the people can and do participate.

In this chapter, and in the three to follow, we shall take a close look at that hallmark of democracy: popular participation. We shall study the ways in which people can and do take part in politics in this country—the ways in which they influence the actions of government and the means by which they give their consent for those actions. In short, we shall deal with the point that government in the United States is, in fact, "government by the people."

First, we shall look at political parties. They are one of the major vehicles of popular participation in our political system.

The democratic ideal of popular participation in politics is vividly portrayed in George Caleb Bingham's "On the Stump," painted in 1852. *Facing page:* Modern technology helps to reinterpret the idea of popular participation in the 1980s, as this televised coverage of the 1984 presidential election demonstrates.

1. Nature and Functions of Parties

As You Read, Think About:

- What a political party is.
- What political parties do.

Since political parties play such a vital role in our democratic system of government, it is important to examine the meaning of the term *political party* and to look at the major functions the parties perform.

What Is a Party?

A **political party** may be defined as a group of persons who seek to control government through the winning of elections and the holding of public office. This definition of party is a broad one. It fits *any* political party, including the two **major parties** in American politics.

Another, more specific, definition may be used to describe *most* political parties, both here and abroad: a group of persons, joined together on the basis of certain common principles, who seek to control government in order to bring about the adoption of certain public policies and programs.

But this definition, with its emphasis on principles and public policy positions, will not fit the two major parties in the United States. The Republican and the Democratic parties are *not* primarily principle- or issue-oriented groups. Rather, they are *election* oriented. The reasons are many.*

For now, our point can be stated this way: Neither the Republicans nor the Democrats may be properly described as a group of like-minded persons. Compare the public policy positions taken by various leading Republicans or, for that matter, by various leading Democrats. Senators Phil Gramm of Texas and Mark Hatfield of Oregon are both Republicans. Yet they often take opposing

*ENRICHMENT Have the class compare the Democratic and Republican platforms, p. 187. How does this comparison show that these parties are not primarily principle-oriented groups?

A tiny sampling of the kinds of devices that have been used by political parties and their candidates in conveying their "message" to the American voter.

sides. So do such other prominent Republicans as Jesse Helms of North Carolina and Lowell Weicker of Connecticut, and Orrin Hatch of Utah and John Danforth of Missouri. Much the same can be said of many Democrats—for example, Senators Edward Kennedy of Massachusetts and John Stennis of Mississippi, or Daniel Moynihan of New York and Sam Nunn of Georgia.

Again, neither of the two major parties is a group of like-minded persons. Instead, as we shall see, each is composed of a great many persons who, broadly speaking, share more or less similar views on many public questions.

What Do Parties Do?

We know from our own history, and from that of other peoples, as well, that political parties are essential to democratic government. They are a vital link between the people and their government—between the governed and those who govern. Many argue that they are *the* principal means by which the will of the people is made known to government and by which government is held accountable to the people.

Parties serve the democratic ideal in another highly important way. They work to blunt conflict. Or, as it is often said, they are "power brokers." They bring conflicting groups together. They modify and compromise the contending views of different interests and groups, and so help to unify rather than divide the people. They soften the impact of extremists at both ends of the political spectrum.

For all these reasons, political parties are indispensable to American government. This fact is underscored by a look at the major functions they perform.

The Nominating Function The major function of a political party is to nominate (name) candidates for public office. That is, the parties select candidates and then present them to the voters.

There must be some way to find—to recruit and choose—those candidates. There must also be some way to concentrate support (votes) for them. Parties are the best device we have yet found to do these jobs.

The nominating function is almost exclusively a party function in this country.[1] It is the one particular activity that most clearly sets political parties apart from all of the other groups operating in our politics.[2]

The Informer-Stimulator Function A party helps to inform the people and to stimulate their interest and participation in public affairs. It does so in many ways—most of all by campaigning for its candidates, taking stands on issues, and criticizing the candidates and stands of the opposition.

Of course, each party tries to inform the people as it thinks they should be informed—to the party's advantage. It conducts its "educational" process through pamphlets, signs, buttons, and stickers; with advertisements in newspapers and magazines and on radio and television; in speeches, rallies, and conventions; and by just about every other means available to it.

By taking at least *some* kind of stand on public issues, parties and their candidates offer the voters competing choices. But the major parties usually do not take *too* firm a stand on controversial questions. Remember, each party's chief aim is to win elections. It attempts to do this by attracting as many voters as possible while, at the same time, offending as few as possible.

The Bonding Agent Function A party serves, in a sense, as a "bonding agent" to ensure the good performance of its candidates and officeholders. In choosing its candidates, the party tries to see that they are men and women who are both qualified and of good character—or, at least, that they are not unqualified and that they have no serious blemishes on their records. The party also prompts its successful candidates to perform well in office. The very nature of the democratic process imposes this bonding agent function on a party, whether it really wants to perform it or not. If it fails to do so, both the party and its candidates may suffer the consequences in future elections, especially in areas with vigorous party competition .

The Governmental Function From several different points of view, government in the United States may be quite correctly described as government by party. Thus, public officeholders—those who govern—are regularly chosen on the basis of party. Congress and the State legislatures are organized and conduct much of their business on a partisan basis. Most appointments to executive offices, both federal and State, are also made on that basis.

In yet another sense, parties provide a basis for the conduct of government. Under our system of separation of powers, the party is usually the major agent through which the executive and legislative branches cooperate with one another.

In this connection, remember our discussion of constitutional change by informal amendment (on pages 65–67). Political parties have played a large part in that process. As a leading illustration of that fact, the Constitution's cumbersome electoral college system works principally because political parties reshaped it in its early years and have made it work ever since.

The Watchdog Function Parties act as a "watchdog" over the conduct of the public's business. This is particularly the function of the party out of power. It plays this role as it criticizes the policies and behavior of the party in power.[3] In effect, it attempts to *

[1]The exceptions are in nonpartisan elections and in those rare instances in which an independent candidate enters a partisan contest. Nominations are covered at length in Chapter 9.

[2]Including, most especially, the many kinds of pressure groups (special interest organizations) which are described in Chapter 10.

[3]In American politics the "party in power" is the party that controls the executive branch—*i.e.*, the Presidency at the national level, or the governorship at the State level. The label is regularly applied to that party even when it does not also control the legislative branch. Thus, the Republican Party is the "party in power" at the national level today.

*REINFORCEMENT List the five major functions of a political party on the board. Ask students for examples to illustrate each category.

convince the voters that they should "throw the rascals out"—that the "outs" should become the "ins," and the "ins" the "outs." Its attacks tend to make the "ins" more careful of their public charge and more responsive to the wishes of the people. In short, the party out of power serves as "the loyal opposition."

FOR REVIEW

1. **Identify:** informer-stimulator function, bonding agent function, governmental function, watchdog function, party in power, party out of power.
2. What pivotal role do parties play in democratic government?
3. What are the most important functions performed by parties in American politics?

2. The Two-Party System

As You Read, Think About:

- Why the United States has a two-party system.
- What factors are involved in multi-party and one-party systems.
- What the nature of party membership is.

Two major parties dominate American politics. That is, we have a **two-party system** in this country. In the typical election, only the candidates of the Republican and/or the Democratic parties have a reasonable chance of winning public office.

In some States, and in many communities, one of these two major parties may be overwhelmingly dominant, and for a long period of time. For example, the Democrats dominated southern politics for decades. But, on the whole, and through most of our history, we have been a two-party nation.

There have been and are other parties—**minor** or **third parties**—in American politics, of course. We shall look at them shortly. But only seldom does one of them make a serious bid for power, and then usually only at a local level.

Why a Two-Party System?

A number of factors help to explain why we have, and continue to have, a two-party system in this country. No one reason, taken alone, offers a wholly satisfactory explanation for the phenomenon. But, taken together, they provide a very persuasive answer.

The Historical Basis The two-party system is rooted in the beginnings of the nation itself. The Framers of the Constitution were opposed to political parties. As we saw in Chapter 2, their hope was a futile one.[4] The battle over the ratification of the Constitution saw the birth of our first two parties: the Federalists, led by Alexander Hamilton, and the Anti-Federalists, who followed Thomas Jefferson. In short, the party system began as a two-party system.

The Force of Tradition Once established, human institutions are likely to become self-perpetuating—and so it has been with our two-party system. The very fact that we began with a two-party system has been a leading reason for its retention and has become over time a more important, and self-reinforcing reason.

Most Americans accept the idea of a two-party system because we've always had one. This inbred support for the arrangement is a principal reason why challenges to it—minor or third party efforts—have made so little headway in our politics.

[4]The Framers hoped to create a unified country; they sought to bring order out of the chaos of the Critical Period of the 1780s. To most of them, parties were "factions," agents of divisiveness and disunity. George Washington reflected this view when, in his Farewell Address in 1796, he warned the new nation against "the baneful effect of the spirit of party." In this light, it is hardly surprising that the Constitution made no provision for political parties. The Framers could not foresee the ways in which the governmental system they set up would develop. Thus, they could not possibly know that two major parties would emerge as prime instruments of government in the United States. Nor could they know that those two major parties would tend to be moderate, to choose middle-of-the-road positions, and so help to unify rather than divide the nation.

Father of the Federalist Party, Alexander Hamilton served a principal role in the successful effort to gain New York State's ratification of the Constitution and was honored with this float, part of a huge celebration in New York City, 1788.

The Electoral System The basic shape and many of the details of the election process also work to promote the existence of a two-party system in American politics.

Among the most prominent of these features is the **single-member district** arrangement. A single-member district is one in which only one candidate is chosen by the voters to each office. The winning candidate is the one who receives a **plurality**—the largest number—of the votes cast for the office he or she is seeking.[5] Nearly all elections in the United States are conducted on this basis.

The single-member district pattern works to discourage third parties. Because only one winner can come out of each contest, voters usually face only two real choices: They can vote for the candidate of the party holding the office, or they can vote for the candidate of the party with the best chance of replacing the incumbent. In short, most voters think of a vote for a third-party candidate as a "wasted" one.

Another important aspect of the electoral system works to the same end. Much of American election law is purposely written to discourage third parties and third-party candidates. It is designed to protect the two-party system. For example, in most States it is more difficult for minor parties to nominate their candidates—get them listed on the ballot—than it is for the major parties to do so.[6]

[5]A candidate who wins a *plurality* of the votes wins more votes than does any of his or her opponents. A candidate who wins a **majority** wins more than half of all of the votes cast in the election. Thus, a majority is always a plurality, but a plurality is not necessarily a majority.

[6]Nearly all election law in this country is State, not federal, law, a point we shall discuss at length in the next two chapters. However, nearly all of the close to 7,500 State legislators–nearly all of those persons who make State law—are either Democrats or Republicans. Only a handful of minor party members or independents now sit, or have ever sat, in State legislatures.

*ENRICHMENT Have the class discuss: How does the American electoral system promote a two-party system? Be sure students emphasize single-member district elections and the concept of plurality.

The 1980 presidential election offers a striking illustration of the point. Both of the major party candidates, Ronald Reagan and Jimmy Carter, were on the ballots of all 50 States and the District of Columbia. But only two of the ten or more other, and serious, presidential hopefuls were also listed everywhere: only the Libertarian Party nominee, Ed Clark, and independent candidate John Anderson.

Because of the laws in most States, both Clark and Anderson were forced to spend critical amounts of time, effort, and money in order to accomplish what was nearly automatic for the two major party nominees. By gaining the ballot everywhere, Clark and Anderson became the first two nonmajor party contenders to do so in more than 60 years—since the Socialist Party's candidate, Allan L. Benson, appeared on the ballots of all the then 48 States in 1916.

In 1984 the minor parties suffered their usual frustrations. The best any of them could do was David Bergland, the Libertarians' nominee for President. He was listed on the ballots of 38 States and the District of Columbia. (Most of the minor-party candidates for President failed to make it to the ballots of even half of the States in 1984.)

The American Ideological Consensus

Another reason for the two-party system lies in this important fact: We Americans are, on the whole, an *ideologically homogeneous* people. That is, over time, we have shared much the same ideals, the same basic principles, and the same patterns of belief. There is a broad consensus—a general agreement among us—in fundamental matters.

This is not to say that Americans have always agreed with one another, and in all matters. Far from it. We have been deeply divided at some times in our history, and over various questions: during the Civil War and in the years of the Great Depression, for example; and over such critical issues as racial discrimination and the war in Southeast Asia.

However, we have not been regularly plagued by sharp cleavages in our politics. We have not seen long-standing, bitter disputes based on such factors as economic class, social status, religious beliefs, or national origins.

Those conditions that could produce several strong rival parties simply do not exist in this country, unlike the situation in most other democracies. The realities of American politics simply will not permit more than *two* major parties.

This fact of American life—the ideological consensus—has had another very important impact on our parties. It has given us two major parties that look very much alike. Both tend to be moderate. Both are built on compromise and regularly try to occupy "the middle of the road."

Both parties seek the same prize: the support (the votes) of a majority of the electorate. To do so, they must woo essentially the same voters. Inevitably, each party takes policy stands very much like those taken by the other. Often, and for very good reason, the competition between them becomes a struggle between competing political personalities.

The Multiparty Alternative

There are some who argue that the American two-party system should be scrapped. They would replace it with a **multiparty** arrangement, a system in which several major and many lesser parties exist. That arrangement exists in most European democracies today.

In the typical multiparty system, the various parties are each based on some particular and distinctive interest, such as economic class, religious belief, sectional attachment, or political ideology. Those who favor such an arrangement here say that it would be more representative and more responsive to the will of the people. They insist that a multiparty system would give voters a real choice among candidates and policy alternatives.

The practical effect of two of the factors we have just noted—single-member districts and the American ideological consensus—seem to make such an arrangement impossible, however. Beyond that, a multiparty system tends to produce instability in government. One party is often unable to win the support of a majority of the voters. The power to govern must, therefore, be shared among a number of parties, known as a coalition. Several of the multiparty nations of Western Europe have long been plagued by governmental crises and by frequent shifts in party control. Italy furnishes an almost nightmarish example: It has had a new government on the average of once every nine months ever since the end of World War II.

One-Party Systems

In most dictatorships, as in the Soviet Union and the People's Republic of China, only one political party—the party of the ruling group—is allowed. For all practical purposes, it is quite accurate to say that in those circumstances the **one-party system** is really a "no-party" system.

* In quite another sense, several States and many local areas in this country were, and many can still be, described in "one-party" terms. Thus, until the late 1950s, the Democrats almost completely dominated the politics of the South. The Republican Party was almost always the winner in New England and in the upper Middle West.

But effective two-party competition has spread fairly rapidly in the past 20 years or so. Democrats have won many offices in every northern State. Republican candidates have become more and more successful throughout the once-solidly Democratic South.[7]

Party Membership

Who are Republicans, and who are Democrats? Who are independents in American politics? We shall take a long look at answers to those questions in the next chapter. But, for now, this point: The answers to them can tell us much about both our parties and the party system.

Membership in either major party is purely voluntary. A person is a Republican or a Democrat—or belongs to a minor party or is an independent—simply because that's what he or she chooses to be.[8]

Remember, the two major parties are very broadly based. That is, they are multiclass in nature. They purposefully try to attract as much support from as many individuals and as many groups as they possibly can. Each party has always been composed, in greater or lesser degree, of a cross-section of the nation's population. Each is made up of Protestants, Catholics, and Jews; whites, blacks, Hispanics, and other minorities; professionals, farmers, employers, and union members. Each numbers the young, the

---

[7]Nevertheless, about a third of the States can still be said to have a "modified one-party system." That is, one or the other of the two major parties regularly wins elections in those States. Also, while most States may have vigorous two-party competition at the Statewide level, within them are many locales overwhelmingly dominated by one party.

[8]In most States a person must declare a preference for a particular party in order to vote in that party's primary election. That declaration is usually made as a part of the voter registration process, and it is often said to make one "a registered Republican (or Democrat)." See Chapter 9.

*REINFORCEMENT American politics is based on a two-party system, yet many States are dominated by one party or the other. Ask students to explain this phenomenon.

Political parties perform equally essential roles at the State and local levels as at the National level. These State Republican and Democratic headquarters illustrate the parties' role in promoting candidates.

middle-aged, and the elderly; city-dwellers, suburbanites, and small-town and rural residents among its members. These and all of the other groupings that make up American society are to be found in both parties.

It is true that the members of certain segments of the electorate tend to align themselves more solidly with one or the other of the major parties, at least for a time. Thus, in recent decades, blacks, Catholics and Jews, and labor union members have voted far more often for Democrats than for Republicans. In the same way, white males, Protestants, and those from the business community have been inclined to back the GOP. Yet, never have all members of any group tied themselves permanently, or indivisibly, to either party.

Individuals identify themselves with a party for many reasons. Family is almost certainly the most important among them. Studies of voter behavior show that nearly two out of every three Americans follow the party allegiance of their parents. That is, most of us inherit our party preferences.

Major events can also have a decided influence on party choice. Of these, the Civil War and the Depression of the 1930s have been the most significant in American political history, as we shall see in a moment.

Economic status also influences party choice, although generalizations are quite risky. Clearly, though, those in higher income groups are likely to think of themselves as Republicans, while those with lower incomes tend to be Democrats.

Several other factors also feed into the mix of both party choice and voting behavior, including, age, level of education, and the work environment. Some of those factors may conflict with one another in the case of any individual.

We shall return to this whole matter of partisan preference and voting behavior in Chapter 8.

FOR REVIEW

1. **Identify:** major party, party membership.
2. What four factors help to explain why we have a two-party system in the United States?
3. Define: (a) single-member districts, (b) the American ideological consensus.
4. What is a multiparty system? A one-party system?

*ENRICHMENT Have students find out if their families have traditionally been Democrats or Republicans, and for what reasons.

BUILDING GOVERNMENT SKILLS

Comparing and Contrasting Party Platforms

In the excerpts below, selected specific policy positions from the 1984 Republican and Democratic platforms are presented. As you read, look for similarities and differences in the statements. Also look for evidence of the American ideological consensus. (See text p. 184.)

Republican Platform

Taxes

The Republican Party pledges to continue efforts to lower tax rates, change and modernize the tax system, and eliminate the incentive-destroying effects of graduated tax rates.

Civil Rights and Affirmative Action

Just as we must guarantee opportunity, we oppose any attempts to dictate results. We will resist efforts to replace equal rights with discriminatory quota systems and preferential treatment. . . . We must always remember that, in a free society, different individual goals will yield different results.

Defense

We affirm the principle that the national security policy of the United States should be based upon a strategy of peace through strength, a goal of the 1980 Republican Platform. . . .

President Reagan has launched a bold new Strategic Defense Initiative to defend against nuclear attack. We enthusiastically support President Reagan's Strategic Defense Initiative. We enthusiastically support the development of non-nuclear, space-based defensive systems to protect the United States by destroying incoming missiles.

Equal Rights

For all Americans, we demand equal pay for equal work. With equal emphasis, we oppose the concept of "comparable worth."

Democrat Platform

Taxes

America needs a tax system that encourages growth and produces adequate revenues in a fair, progressive fashion. The Democratic Party is committed to a tax policy that embodies these basic values.

Civil Rights and Affirmative Action

The Party reaffirms its longstanding commitment to the eradication of discrimination in all aspects of American life through the use of affirmative action, goals, timetables, and other verifiable measurements to overturn historic patterns of discrimination. . . .

Defense

The Democratic Party seeks prudent defense based on sound planning and a realistic assessment of threats. . . . With this strength, we will restore the confidence of our fellow citizens and our allies; we will be able to mount an effective conventional defense; and we will present our adversaries with a credible capability to deter war. . . .

[Reagan's] Star Wars proposal would create a vulnerable and provocative "shield" that would lull our nation into a false sense of security. . . .

Equal Rights

The Democratic Party defines nondiscrimination to encompass both equal pay for equal work and equal pay for work of comparable worth. . . .

1. Do the parties tend to agree or disagree on basic principles? On specific policy positions?
2. Does this support or refute the concept of an American ideological consensus? Explain.

3. The Evolution of the Two-Party System

As You Read, Think About:

- How the two-party system began in the United States.
- How different eras have been dominated by different parties.

Today is the product of yesterday—with political parties as with all else. As we have seen, the beginnings of the American two-party system can be traced to the battle over the ratification of the Constitution. The conflicts of the time, centering on the proper form and role of government in the United States, were not stilled by the adoption of the work of the Philadelphia Convention. Rather, they were carried over into the early years of the Republic, and they led directly to the formation of the nation's first full-blown parties.

The Nation's First Parties

The Federalist Party was the first to appear. It formed around Alexander Hamilton, who had become Secretary of the Treasury in the new government organized by George Washington. The Federalists were, by and large, the party of "the rich and the well-born." Most of them had supported the Constitution. Now, led by Hamilton, they worked to make a stronger national government a reality. They favored vigorous executive leadership and a set of policies designed to correct the nation's economic ills. Their program was particularly beneficial to financial, manufacturing, and commercial interests. To reach their goals, they urged a liberal interpretation of the Constitution.

Thomas Jefferson, while serving as Secretary of State, led the opposition to Hamilton and his Federalists.[9] Jefferson and his followers were more sympathetic to the "common man." They favored a limited role for the new government. In their view, Congress should dominate that government, and its policies should help the nation's small shopkeepers, laborers, farmers, and planters. Jeffersonians insisted on a strict construction of the provisions of the Constitution.*

Jefferson resigned from Washington's Cabinet in 1793 to give his time to the organization of his party. Originally, the new party took the name Anti-Federalist. Then it was known as the Jeffersonian Republicans or the Democratic-Republicans, and finally (by 1828) as the Democratic Party.

These first two parties clashed in the elections of 1796. John Adams, the Federalists' candidate to succeed Washington as President, defeated Jefferson by just three votes in the electoral college. Over the next four years, Jefferson and James Madison worked tirelessly to build the Democratic-Republicans. Their efforts paid large dividends in the elections of 1800. Jefferson defeated the incumbent President Adams and his party also won control of Congress. The Federalists never returned to power.

The Eras of One-Party Domination

The history of the American party system since 1800 may be fairly neatly divided into three major periods. During each of them, one or the other of two major parties has regularly held the Presidency and, with it, usually both houses of Congress, as well.

In the first of these periods, from 1800 to 1860, the Democrats won 13 of 15 presidential elections. They lost the office only in the elections of 1840 and 1848. In the second era, from 1860 to 1932, the Republicans were in control. They won 14 of 18 elections, losing only in 1884, 1892, 1912, and 1916.

The third period came with Franklin Roosevelt's first election as President in 1932. Since then, the Republicans have been able to win the White House with but three of their candidates: Dwight Eisenhower in 1952 and 1956; Richard Nixon in 1968 and 1972; and Ronald Reagan in 1980 and 1984.

[9]Given his opposition to the rise of parties, President Washington named arch foes Hamilton and Jefferson to his new Cabinet to get them to work together in an (unsuccessful) attempt to avoid the creation of formally organized and opposing groups.

*ENRICHMENT The debate over the role of government can be traced to the positions of the Federalists and Anti-Federalists of the late 1700s. Discuss how this debate can be seen today in the positions of the Republican and Democratic parties.

There are many who insist that the 1980 elections marked the beginning of yet another era in American politics. At the very least, we must wait and see.

The Era of the Democrats, 1800–1860

Jefferson's election in 1800 marked the beginning of a period of Democratic domination that was to last until the Civil War. The Federalists, shattered in 1800, had disappeared altogether by 1816.

For a time, through the Era of Good Feeling, the Democratic-Republicans were unopposed in national politics. They had split into factions by the mid-1820s, however. By Andrew Jackson's administration (1829–1837), a potent National Republican (Whig) Party had arisen to challenge the Democrats. The major issues of the day—conflicts over public lands, the Second Bank of the United States, high tariffs, and slavery—all had made new party alignments inevitable.

The Democrats, led by Jackson, were a coalition of small farmers, debtors, frontiersmen, and slaveholders. Their main strength lay in the South and West. The years of Jacksonian democracy saw the coming of universal white male suffrage, a large increase in the number of elective offices around the country, and the spread of the spoils system.

The Whig Party was led by the widely popular Henry Clay and the great orator, Daniel Webster. A loose coalition of eastern bankers, merchants and industrialists, and southern planters, it was opposed to the tenets of Jacksonian democracy and dedicated to the high tariff. The Whigs' victories were few. As the other major party from the mid-1830s to the 1850s, they were able to elect only two Presidents, both of them war heroes: William Henry Harrison in 1840 and Zachary Taylor in 1848.

By the 1850s the growing crisis over slavery split both major parties. Left leaderless by the deaths of Clay and Webster, the Whig coalition fell apart. The Democrats split into two sharply divided camps, North and South. Through the decade the nation drifted toward civil war.

Of the several groupings that arose to compete for supporters, the Republican Party was the most successful. Born in 1854, it drew many Whigs and antislavery Democrats. The Republicans nominated their first presidential candidate, John C. Fremont, in 1856 and elected their first President, Abraham Lincoln, in 1860. The Republican Party

Political artifacts have often shown candidates as war heroes. The pitcher on the left displays the likeness of Democrat, Andrew Jackson. The plaque on the right shows Whig, Zachary Taylor.

thus became the only party in the history of our politics to make the jump from third-party to major-party status.

The Era of the Republicans, 1860–1932. The Civil War signaled the beginning of the second era. For nearly 75 years, the Republicans—supported by business and financial interests, and by farmers, laborers, and newly freed blacks—were to dominate the national scene.

The Democrats, crippled by the war, were able to survive mainly through their hold on the Solid South. For the balance of the century, they slowly rebuilt their electoral base. In all that time, they were able to place only one candidate in the White House: Grover Cleveland in 1884 and again in 1892. Those elections marked only short breaks in Republican supremacy, however. Riding the crest of both popular acceptance and unprecedented prosperity, the GOP remained the dominant party well into this century.

The election of 1896 was especially critical in the development of the party system. It climaxed years of protest by small businessmen, farmers, and the emerging labor unions against big business and financial monopolies and the railroads. The Republicans regained the Presidency with William McKinley. In doing so, they were able to gather new support from several segments of the electorate—new strength that allowed them to keep their majority role in national politics for another three decades. Although the Democratic nominee, William Jennings Bryan, lost, he championed the "little man"—and so helped to push the nation's party politics back toward the economic arena, and away from the divisions of sectionalism.

The Republicans suffered their worst setback of the era in 1912, when they renominated incumbent President William Howard Taft. Former President Theodore Roosevelt, denied the nomination, left the party to become the candidate of his "Bull Moose" Progressive Party. With Republican support divided between Taft and Roosevelt, the Democratic nominee, Woodrow Wilson, took the Presidency. He kept the office by a narrow margin four years later.

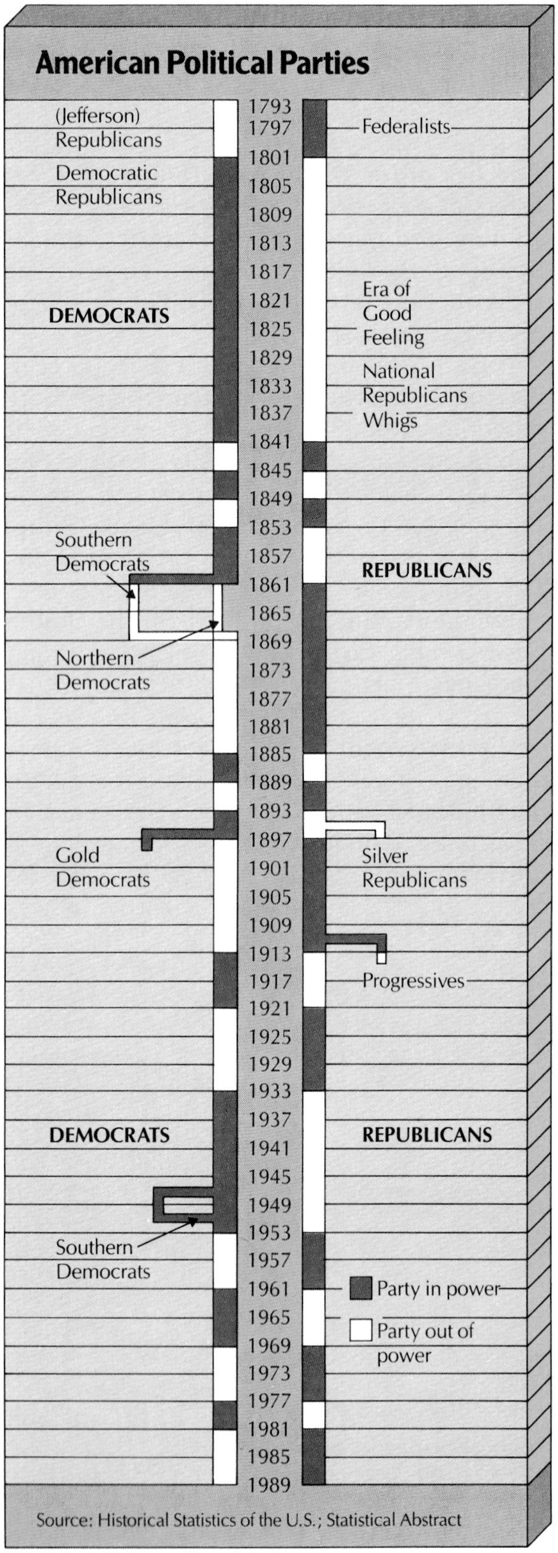

What factors account for shifts in leadership from one party to another as shown here?

*REINFORCEMENT Use the time line to illustrate the three periods of party domination. Point out how the presidential elections serve to reinforce the party system.

The ticket above admitted the bearer to the Franklin Field ceremonies which were part of the 1936 Democratic National Convention prior to Franklin Roosevelt's election to his second term.

But, again, the Democratic successes of 1912 and 1916 proved only an interlude. The GOP won each of the next three presidential elections—with Warren Harding in 1920, with Calvin Coolidge in 1924, and with Herbert Hoover in 1928.

The Return of the Democrats, 1932 to ??? The Great Depression, which began in 1929, had a massive impact on nearly all aspects of American life and politics. The landmark election of 1932 brought Franklin Roosevelt to the Presidency and the Democrats back to power at the national level. Also, and of fundamental importance, that election marked a basic shift in the public's attitude toward the proper place of government in the nation's social and economic life.

Over the years since then, the Democrats have generally been the dominant party in national politics. True, the Republicans have won 6 of the last 14 presidential elections and do hold the White House today. Through all of that period, however, the Democrats have regularly outpolled them in both the congressional elections and at the Statewide level in most parts of the country.

Franklin Roosevelt and the Democrats engineered their victory in 1932 with a new coalition of electoral support. It was built largely of southerners, small farmers, organized labor, and big-city political organizations. The economic and social welfare programs, which formed the heart of the New Deal of the 1930s, strengthened that coalition; and it soon brought increasing support from blacks and other minorities.

President Roosevelt won overwhelming reelection in 1936. He secured an unprecedented third term in 1940 and yet another term in 1944, both times by heavy majorities. Harry S Truman completed the fourth term following FDR's death in 1945. Truman was elected to a full term of his own in 1948, when he turned back the GOP challenge led by Governor Thomas E. Dewey.

The Republicans regained the White House in 1952 and kept it in 1956. They were led to victory both times by World War II hero Dwight Eisenhower, who both times defeated the Democrats' nominee, Adlai Stevenson.

The Republican return to power was short-lived, however. In 1960 John F. Kennedy recaptured the Presidency with a razor-thin plurality over the Republicans' nominee, then Vice President Richard M. Nixon. Lyndon Johnson then took office following

President Kennedy's assassination in 1963. In 1964, Johnson won by an overwhelming margin over his Republican opponent, Senator Barry Goldwater.

Richard Nixon staged a dramatic comeback in 1968. He defeated Vice President Hubert Humphrey, the candidate of a Democratic Party torn by conflicts over the war in Vietnam, civil rights, and social welfare issues. The Republican victory came with only a bare plurality over Humphrey and the strong third-party effort of the American Independent Party nominee, Governor George Wallace. Nixon remained in power by routing the choice of the still-divided Democrats, Senator George McGovern, in 1972.

But, once again, the GOP hold did not last. President Nixon's role in the Watergate scandal forced him from office in 1974. Gerald Ford filled out the balance of the presidential term. Beset by problems in the economy, by the continuing effects of Watergate, and by his pardon of former President Nixon, Ford lost the Presidency to Jimmy Carter and the resurgent Democrats in 1976.

A steadily worsening economy and his own inability to establish himself as an effective President spelled defeat for Mr. Carter in 1980, however. Led by Ronald Reagan, the Republicans scored an impressive victory that year and repeated their triumph in the most recent presidential election.

President Reagan's first election triggered wide-ranging efforts to alter the basic shape of many of the nation's domestic and foreign policies. Also, his reelection gave strong support to the argument that a majority of the voters now favor his more conservative stands on public policy.

Did the elections of 1980 and 1984 signal the start of yet another era in our politics, an era to be dominated by the Republican Party? As of now, at least, we must wait and see.

FOR REVIEW

1. Out of what circumstances did the nation's first two parties arise? Identify the two parties and describe how they differed.
2. Since 1800 the history of the American party system can be divided into what three major eras?
3. Why do many suggest that we are now in a new, fourth era in the history of the two-party system?

4. The Minor Parties

As You Read, Think About:

- Why different types of minor parties exist.
- What the importance of minor parties is.

The large fact of two major parties too often blinds us to the vital role that several minor parties have played in American politics. Many of them have come and gone over the years. Only a few have lasted for very long—the Prohibition Party, for example, founded in 1869. But all of them have had a considerable impact on the political system.

Types of Minor Parties

Their number and variety make minor parties, third parties, difficult to describe and classify. Some have limited their efforts to a particular locale, others to a single State, and some to one region of the country. Still others have tried to woo the entire nation. Most have been short-lived, but, as we've noted, a few have existed for decades. Whereas most have lived mothlike around the flame of a single idea, some have had a broader, more practical base.

Still, four quite distinct types of minor parties can be seen:

(1) The ideological parties—those based on a particular set of beliefs; some comprehensive view of social, economic, and political matters. Most of these minor parties have been built on some shade of Marxist thought —for example, the Socialist, Socialist Labor, Socialist Worker, and Communist parties. Some have had a quite different color, however, especially the Libertarian Party of today, which emphasizes individualism and

*REINFORCEMENT Ask the class: What type of minor party does each of the parties listed on p. 195 belong to? Refer them to the explanations in the text.

calls for doing away with most of government's present functions and programs.

The ideological parties have not often been able to win many votes. But, as a rule, they have been long-lived.

(2) The **single-issue parties—**those concentrating on a single public policy matter. Their names have usually indicated their primary concern—for example, the Free Soil Party, opposed to the spread of slavery in the 1840s and 1850s; the American Party (the "Know Nothings"), opposed to Irish Catholic immigration in the 1850s; and the Right to Life Party, opposed to abortion today.

Most of the single-issue parties have faded into history as events have passed them by, or as their theme has not brought voters flocking to the polls, or as one or both of the major parties have taken their key issue as their own.

(3) The economic protest parties—those rooted in periods of economic discontent. Unlike the socialist parties, these groups have not had any clear-cut ideological base. Rather, they have proclaimed their disgust with the major parties, demanded "better times," and focused their anger on such real or imagined enemies as the monetary system, "Wall Street bankers," the railroads, or foreign imports. Most often, they have been sectional parties, drawing their strength from the agricultural South and West. Thus, the Greenback Party tried to organize agrarian discontent from 1876 through 1884. It called for the free coinage of silver, federal regulation of the railroads, an income tax, and labor legislation. Its descendant, the Populist Party of the 1890s, also demanded public ownership of railroad, telephone and telegraph companies, lower tariffs, and the adoption of the initiative and referendum.

Each of these economic protest parties has disappeared as the nation has climbed out of the difficult economic period in which that party was born.

(4) The splinter parties—those which have split away from one of the major parties. Most of the more important minor parties in our politics have been of this kind. Among the leading groups that have split away from the Republicans are Theodore

This cologne bottle from the Presidential campaign of 1896 bears the image of the "Great Commoner," William Jennings Bryan.

Roosevelt's "Bull Moose" Progressive Party of 1912, and Robert La Follette's Progressive Party of 1924. From the Democrats have come Henry Wallace's Progressive Party and the States' Rights (Dixiecrat) Party, both of 1948, and George Wallace's American Independent Party of 1968.

Most splinter parties have formed around some strong personality—most often one who has failed to win his major party's presidential nomination. They have faded or collapsed when that leader has stepped aside. Thus, the Bull Moose Party passed away when TR returned to the Republican fold after the elections of 1912. And the American Independent Party lost nearly all of its brief strength when Governor Wallace rejoined the Democrats following the 1968 election.

A few of the minor parties have been successful at the State or local level. Some have elected a few members of Congress and occasionally won some electoral votes; but none has ever won the Presidency.

FOCUS ON:

The Winless Wonders

Well over a hundred minor parties have appeared over the course of our political history—and most of them have soon disappeared. Measured in terms of winning public office, these parties have been notably unsuccessful. Still, a number of them have had a substantial impact on the political system, as discussed on nearby pages.

Occasionally in the past, minor parties have played a significant role in some of the States. A few do so today. In New York, for example, both the Liberal Party and the Conservative Party sometimes hold the balance of power in elections in that State.

Some of these minor parties have been unusual, to say the least. The Poor Man's Party was certainly one of them. Formed in 1952, it was as often as not called the Pig Party—after its presidential candidate, Henry Krajewski, who raised pigs at his home in New Jersey. Among other things, its platform advocated the annexation of Canada and a mandatory year of farm work for every teenager in this country. Krajewski was listed on the ballot only in New Jersey. In 1952 he won 4,203 votes and in 1956 he picked up only 1,829 for President.

There have been others, like the Vegetarian Party. It wanted to outlaw the eating of meat in the United States. John Maxwell, one of its founders and a New York restaurant owner, ran as its presidential candidate in 1948, 1952, and 1956. He did not make the ballot in any of the States.

1. Why can it be said that the American electoral system may keep minor parties from winning but it does not prevent them from forming?
2. Why is it curious *not* that we have had so many minor parties but, rather, that we have not had *more* of them?

Importance of Minor Parties

Minor parties have had an impact on our politics and on the major parties. Thus, it was a minor party, the Anti-Masons in 1831, that first used a national convention to nominate a presidential candidate. The Democrats and then the Whigs followed suit for the election of 1832. Ever since, the national convention has been the means by which the major parties have picked their presidential tickets.

A strong third-party candidacy can play a decisive role—often a "spoiler role"—in an election. This can be true at any level—in national, State, or local politics, and especially where the two major parties compete on roughly equal terms. The point was dramatically illustrated in the presidential election of 1912. A split in the Republican Party and the resulting third-party candidacy of Theodore Roosevelt that year produced the results shown below. Almost certainly had

The 1912 Presidential Election

Party and Candidate	Popular Vote	%	Electoral Vote
Democrat—Woodrow Wilson	6,293,152	41.8	435
Progressive—Theodore Roosevelt	4,119,207	27.4	88
Republican—William H. Taft	3,486,333	23.2	8
Socialist—Eugene V. Debs	900,369	6.0	—
Prohibition—Eugene Chafin	207,972	1.4	—

Theodore Rooselvelt not quit the Republican Party, Woodrow Wilson would not have become President.

Historically, the most important roles of the minor parties have been those of critic and innovator. Unlike the major parties, they have been ready, willing, and able to take quite clear-cut stands on the controversial issues of their day. These actions have often drawn attention to some issue that the major parties have preferred to ignore or straddle. Over the years, many of the more important issues of American politics were first brought to the public's attention by a minor party—for example, the progressive income tax, woman suffrage, railroad and banking regulation, and old-age pensions.

But this very important function of the minor parties has also been a major source of their frustration. When their proposals have gained any real degree of popular support, one and then shortly both of the major parties have taken them over and presented them as their own. The late Norman Thomas, six times the Socialist Party's candidate for President, complained that "the major parties are stealing from my platform."

The presidential candidates of at least 16 minor parties appeared on the ballots of different States in 1984—and there will be at least that many in 1988. For 1984, the more (or at least somewhat) visible campaigns were those of the Citizens, Communist, Independent, Libertarian, Populist, Prohibition, Socialist Workers, and Workers World parties. More than 1,000 minor party candidates also sought seats in Congress or ran for various State and local offices, as well.

Significant Minor Parties in Presidential Elections, 1880–1984*

Year	Party and Candidate	Percent of Popular Vote	Electoral Votes
1880	Greenback		
	James B. Weaver	3.72	—
1888	Prohibition		
	Clinton B. Fisk	2.19	—
1892	Populist		
	James B. Weaver	8.50	22
	Prohibition		
	John Bidwell	2.25	—
1904	Socialist		
	Eugene V. Debs	2.98	—
1908	Socialist		
	Eugene V. Debs	2.82	—
1912	Progressive (Bull Moose)		
	Theodore Roosevelt	27.39	88
	Socialist		
	Eugene V. Debs	5.99	—
1916	Socialist		
	Allan L. Benson	3.18	—
1920	Socialist		
	Eugene V. Debs	3.42	—
1924	Progressive		
	Robert M. La Follette	16.56	13
1932	Socialist		
	Norman M. Thomas	2.22	—
1948	States' Rights (Dixiecrat)		
	Strom Thurmond	2.40	39
	Progressive		
	Henry A. Wallace	2.38	—
1968	American Independent		
	George C. Wallace	13.53	46

*Includes all minor parties that polled at least 2% of the popular vote. No minor party did so in the years not shown, including 1972, 1976, 1980, and 1984.

In 1976 independent (nonparty) candidate Eugene J. McCarthy won 0.8% of the popular vote, and in 1980 independent John B. Anderson won 6.61%; neither McCarthy nor Anderson received any electoral votes.

FOR REVIEW

1. **Identify:** ideological parties, economic protest parties, splinter parties.
2. What are the major characteristics of the typical minor party in American politics?
3. Why have minor parties been important in politics in the United States?

5. Party Organization

As You Read, Think About:

- Why the nature of the major political parties is decentralized.
- How party machinery works.
- What the basic elements of a party are.

We often speak of the two major parties in terms that suggest that they are highly organized, close-knit, well-disciplined groups.

*ENRICHMENT Have the class discuss the statement: The more successful a minor party is, the less its chance for survival. Point out that a party's popular proposals are often taken over by a major party.

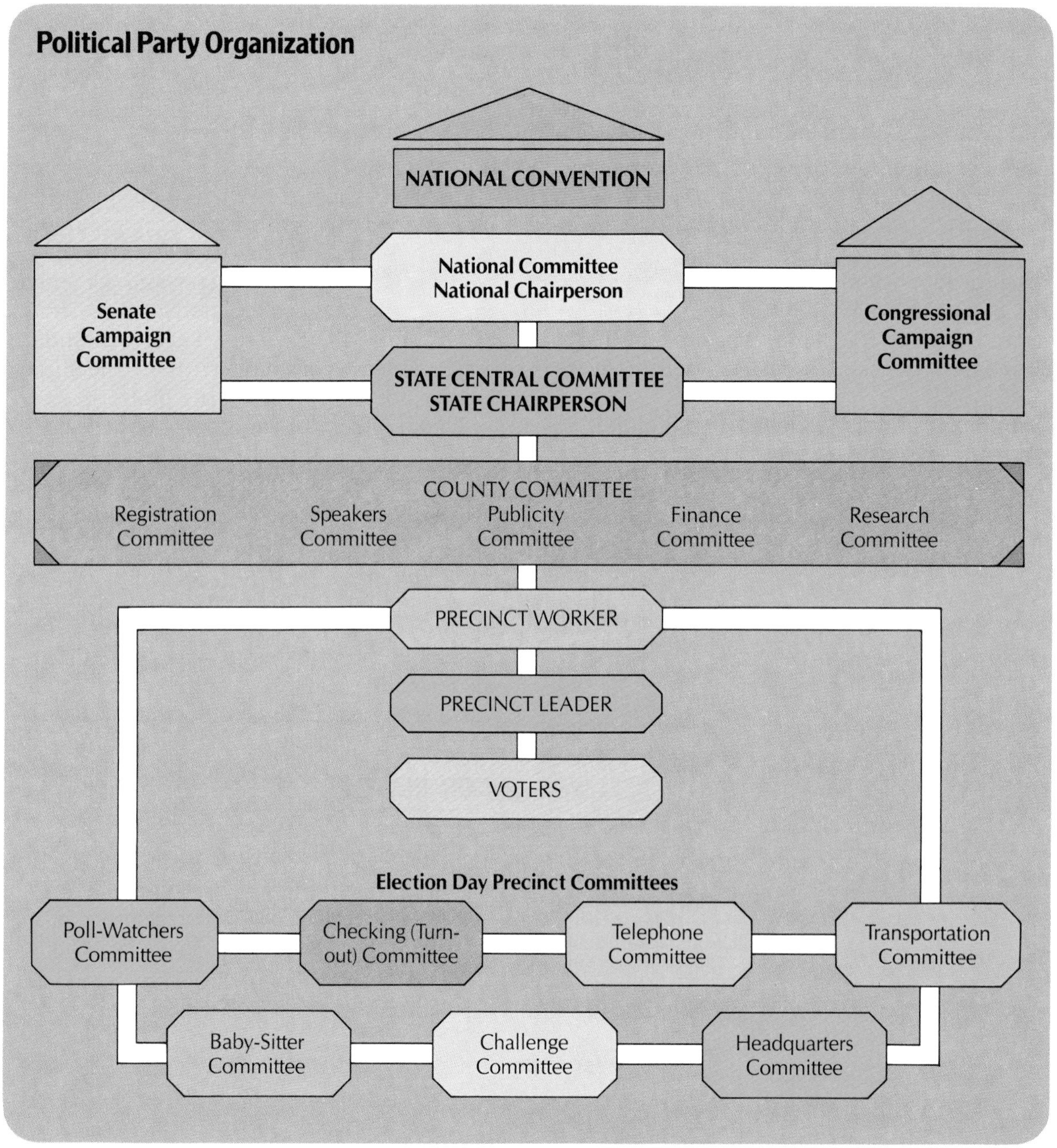

This table shows the complexity of party organization at the national, local, and State levels. What segments have the most power and influence at the national and State levels? What factors limit their power?

Even though they may look that way on paper, neither party is anything of the kind. Rather, both are highly decentralized—fragmented, and often torn by internal strife.

In neither of them is there a "chain of command" running from the national through the State to the local level. Each of the State party organizations is only loosely tied to the party's national structure. Local party organizations are often quite independent of their parent State organizations. These various party units usually, but not always, cooperate with one another.

The President's party is usually more solidly united and more cohesively organized than is the opposition. The President is automatically the party leader. That leadership can be asserted by a number of weapons. Among these are the President's access to the media, his popularity, and his power to make appointments to federal office and to * dispense other favors.

The other party, the party out of power, has no one in an even faintly comparable position. Indeed, in our party system, there is almost never any one personality in the opposition party who can be called, in fact, its leader. Rather, a number of personalities, frequently at odds with one another, form a more or less loosely identifiable leadership.[10]

Decentralization: Federalism

Federalism is a major reason for the decentralized nature of the two major political parties. Remember, the basic goal of the major parties is to gain control of government, and they try to do this by winning elective offices. In the American federal system, those offices are widely distributed at the national, the State, and the local levels. In short, because the governmental system is decentralized, so, too, are the major parties that serve it.

Decentralization: Nomination

The nominating process is also a major cause of party decentralization. As you recall from page 180, the nominating process has a central role in the life of political parties. We shall discuss the selection of candidates in Chapter 9, but, for now, look at two related aspects of this process.

First, candidate selection is an *intraparty* process. That is, nominations are made within the party. Second, that process can be, and often is, a *divisive* one. Where there is a fight over a nomination, it pits members of the same party against one another. Republicans compete with Republicans; Democrats do battle with Democrats. The prime function of the major parties—the making of nominations—is a prime cause of their highly fragmented character.

National Party Machinery

There are four major elements in the structure of both major parties at the national level. They are: the national convention, the national committee, the national chairperson, and the two Congressional Campaign Committees.

The National Convention The national convention is often described as the party's national voice. It meets only every presidential election year, in the summer.[11] The convention nominates the party's presidential and vice-presidential candidates. It performs some other functions, including the adoption of the party's rules and the writing of its platform. Beyond that, it has little authority. It has no control over the selection of the party's candidates for other offices nor over the policy stands those nominees take. We shall take a longer look at national conventions in Chapter 14, where we consider the presidential election process.

Darling in The Christian Science Monitor © 1984

[10]The exception is the party's presidential candidate from the time of nomination through the campaign period. A defeated presidential candidate is often called the titular leader—the party's leader in title, by custom, but not in fact.

[11]First in 1974 and again in 1978 and 1982, the Democrats held a midterm convention, a miniconvention between presidential elections to discuss issues and consider changes in party rules. They have since abandoned the practice. The GOP has never held an interim convention.

*ENRICHMENT Have the students discuss what advantages an incumbent President has in a presidential race. Also, discuss possible disadvantages of being the incumbent.

At every level of party organization, the work of many individuals is needed to prepare for an election. Left: Republican National Headquarters in Washington, D.C. Right: A Mondale-Ferraro campaign headquarters.

The National Committee Between conventions, the party's affairs are handled, at least in theory, by the national committee and by the national chairperson.

For years, each party's national committee was composed of a committeeman and a committeewoman chosen by the party organization in each State and several of the territories. Both parties have expanded the committee's membership in recent years, however.

Today, the Republican National Committee (RNC) also seats several of the party's State chairpersons—party leaders from those States that were carried by the party's presidential candidate or that elected a Republican to the Senate, a majority of Republicans to the House, or a GOP governor in the preceding election.

The Democratic National Committee (DNC) is an even larger body. In addition to the committeeman and -woman from each State, it now includes each State party's chair- and vice-chairperson, several additional members from the party organizations of the larger States, and 25 at-large members chosen by the DNC itself. Several members of Congress, governors, mayors, and Young Democrats also have seats.

On paper, the national committee appears to be a powerful organ. In fact, it does not have a great deal of clout. Most of its work centers on staging the party's national conventions.

The National Chairperson In each party the national chairperson heads up the national committee. In form, he or she is chosen to a four-year term by the national committee, at a meeting right after the national convention. In fact, the choice is made by the just-nominated presidential candidate and is then ratified by the committee.

To this point (1987), each party has picked only one woman for its top post. Jean Westwood of Utah chaired the DNC from the 1972 convention until early 1973, and Mary Louise Smith of Iowa headed the RNC from 1974 to early 1977. Each was replaced soon after her party lost a presidential election. Each woman suffered the usual fate of the national chairperson in the losing party.

The chairperson directs the work of the party's headquarters and its small staff in Washington. In presidential election years, the committee's attention is focused on the national convention and then the campaign. In between, the chairperson and the committee work to strengthen the party and its fortunes—promoting party unity, raising money, recruiting new voters, and otherwise preparing for the next presidential season.

The Congressional Campaign Committees Each party also has a campaign committee in each house of Congress; a Congressional Campaign Committee and a Senatorial Campaign Committee.* Each group works to re-elect incumbents and to save the seats being given up by retiring party members. The committees also take a hand in some campaigns to unseat incumbents in the other party, at least in those races where the prospects look favorable for the out-of-power party.

In both parties, and in both houses, the members of these campaign committees are chosen by their colleagues. They serve for two years, that is, for a term of Congress.

State and Local Party Machinery

National party organization is largely the product of custom and the rules adopted by successive national conventions. At the State and local levels, however, party structure is very largely set by State law.

The State Organization At the State level, party machinery is built around a State central committee, headed by a State chairperson. The members of the central committee who must often come from the party's county organizations, usually pick the chairperson.

The chairperson may be an important figure in his or her own right. More often than not, however, the chairperson fronts

A staff member of the National Republican Congressional Committee conducts a training session for campaign organizers.

*REINFORCEMENT Have the class discuss: Which, if any, of the four major elements of party organization is most important in making decisions about party policy?

for the governor, a U.S. Senator, or some other powerful leader or group in the politics of the State.

Together, the chairperson and the central committee are expected to further the party's interests in the State. Most of the time they do so, with more or less success, by building an effective organization and party unity, finding candidates and campaign funds, and so on. Remember, however, both major parties are highly decentralized and fragmented organizations that are sometimes torn by struggles for power within their own ranks.

Local Organization Local party structures vary so widely that they nearly defy a brief description. Generally, they follow the electoral map of the State, with a party unit for each constituency, or each district, in which elective offices are to be filled: congressional and legislative districts, counties, cities and towns, wards, and precincts. In most larger cities a party's organization is further broken down by residential blocks and sometimes even apartment buildings.

* In some places, local party organizations are active year-round, but most often they are lifeless except for those few hectic months before an election.

The Three Basic Elements of the Party

Look at the structure of the two major parties from another angle: the roles of their members, rather than their tables of organization. From this vantage point, they are made up of three basic elements:

(1) The Party Organization: the leaders, the activists, and the hangers-on who control and run the party machinery—"all those who give their time, money, and skills to the party, whether as leaders or followers."[12]

(2) The Party in the Electorate: the party's voters, its loyalists who vote the straight party ticket and those other voters who call themselves party members and usually vote for its candidates.

(3) The Party in Government: the party's officeholders, those who hold elective and appointive offices in the executive, legislative, and judicial branches of the Federal, State, and local governments.

We have taken a quick look at the party organization here. We shall consider the party in the electorate in the next chapter, and the party in government in several later chapters.

FOR REVIEW

1. **Identify:** national convention, national committee, party organization, party in the electorate, party in government.
2. How do federalism and the nominating process affect the structure of the two major parties?
3. What are the main elements of organization of the major parties at the national level?
4. What is the basic structure of party organization at the State level? At the local level?
5. What are the three elements of the major parties when viewed from the roles of their members, rather than from their tables of organization?

6. Parties and the Future

As You Read, Think About:

- What the current status of political parties in the United States is.
- What factors are responsible for that status.
- How political parties may change in the future.

Over time, most Americans have had very mixed feelings about political parties. Most of us have accepted them as quite necessary institutions. At the same time, we have felt that they should be closely watched and sternly controlled. To many they have seemed little better than necessary evils.

[12]Frank J. Sorauf, *Party Politics in America, 5th ed.* (Boston: Little, Brown, 1984,) p. 8.

*ENRICHMENT Have the students find out if any local party organizations exist, and what these organizatons do during an election.

Copyright 1985 by Herblock in The Washington Post.

There has always been a strong antiparty feeling in this country.[13]

Political parties are not very popular institutions today. In fact, they have been in a period of decline since at least the late 1960s. Their decline has even led some analysts to this very disturbing conclusion: Not only are the parties in serious trouble, the party system itself may be on the point of collapse.

The present, weakened state of the parties can be traced. The evidences of it are not hard to find. They include:

(1) A sharp drop in the number of voters willing to identify themselves as Republicans or Democrats, and a growing number who regard themselves as independents.

(2) A big increase in **split-ticket voting** (voting for candidates of *both* parties for the different offices at the same election).

(3) Various structural changes and "reforms"—from the introduction of the direct primary early in the 1900s to the more recent and far-reaching changes in campaign finance laws—that have made the parties more "open" but have also led to greater internal conflict and disorganization.

(4) More and more changes in the technology of campaigning for office—especially the heavy use of television and of such other devices as professional campaign managers and direct-mail advertising—that have made candidates less dependent on party organizations for promotion or "bonding."

(5) The growth, in both numbers and impact, of single-issue organizations in our politics, groups that take sides for or against candidates based on their own closely defined views in some specific area of public policy, such as nuclear power development, rather than on the candidates' stands on the whole slate of public policy questions.

We shall look at these and at several other matters affecting the condition of the parties over the course of the next three chapters. As we do so, bear in mind much of what we have said in this chapter. In particular, remember these points: Political parties are indispensable to democratic government —and so, then, to American government. Our present-day major parties have existed for longer than have any other parties anywhere in the world. As we have seen, they perform a number of necessary functions. In short, the reports of their passing may not only be premature; they may in fact be quite farfetched.

FOR REVIEW

1. Over time, how have most Americans viewed political parties?
2. What is the present state of the major parties?

[13]Recall that in 1796 George Washington warned the new nation of "the baneful effect of the spirit of party." That sentiment has been echoed often and by many prominent figures ever since. Thus, in 1844 Ralph Waldo Emerson wrote: "Our parties are parties of circumstance, and not of principle . . . ;[Both] are perpetually corrupted by personality . . . [and] the only safe rule is always to believe that the worst will be done."

ENRICHMENT Have the students organize a panel discussion on the following question: Does the growth of single-issue organizations serve to weaken political parties?

SUMMARY

Political parties are indispensable to democratic government. They are a necessary link between the people and their government and work to blunt conflict.

Based on our two major parties, we may define a political party as a group of persons who seek to control government through the winning of elections and the holding of public office. The major parties: (1) nominate candidates; (2) inform voters and stimulate their interest in public affairs; (3) act as bonding agents to insure the good performance of their candidates and officeholders; (4) provide a basis for the conduct of government; and (5) act as watchdogs over the conduct of the public's business.

Our two-party system is mostly the result of historical factors, the continuing force of tradition, several features of the electoral process, and the American ideological consensus. Membership in the two major parties is purely voluntary and multi-class in nature.

From its beginnings with the Federalists and the Anti-Federalists, the history of American political parties may be traced through three broad periods: The era of the Democrats, 1800–1860; the era of the Republicans, 1860–1932; and the return of the Democrats, 1932 to ???

Minor (or third) parties have played an important part in American politics. They may be classified as: (1) ideological, (2) single-issue, (3) economic protest, and (4) splinter parties.

Each of the major parties is highly decentralized and fragmented largely as the result of federalism and the potentially divisive nature of the nominating process. At the national level, both parties are organized around four principal elements: the national convention, the national committee, the national chairperson, and the congressional campaign committees. State and local party organization is generally built along geographic-electoral lines. Each of the major parties may also be viewed as a three-part structure: the party as an organization, the party in the electorate, and the party in government.

Political parties have not been held in high regard in the United States. However, they are a very necessary part of the American governmental system.

CHAPTER REVIEW

Key Terms/Concepts

political party (179)
major parties (179)
two-party system (182)
minor/third party (182)
single-member district (183)
plurality (183)
majority (183)
multiparty system (185)
one-party system (185)
single-issue parties (193)
nomination (197)
split-ticket voting (201)

*These terms are included in the Glossary.

Keynote Questions

• • 1. In what significant way do the two major parties in the United States differ from political parties in other democratic nations?

• 2. How do the major functions of political parties make them indispensable to government in the United States?

• 3. How have single-member districts and the American ideological consensus contributed to the existence of the two-party system in the United States?

• 4. Why did the Framers of the Constitution make no provision for political parties?

• 5. What are the three major eras of one-party domination in the United States?

*The dots represent skill levels required to answer each question or complete each activity: •requires recall and comprehension • •requires application and analysis • • •requires synthesis and evaluation

•• **6.** What is the difference between the following types of minor parties: (a) ideological and single-issue? (b) economic protest and splinter?

• **7.** Over the years, in what ways have the minor parties influenced the two major parties?

• **8.** Why are both federalism and the nominating process significant causes for the decentralized and fragmented character of our two major parties?

• **9.** What are the major elements of party organization at the national level? At the State and local level?

• **10.** State three reasons for the decline in the influence of political parties in recent years.

Skill Application

Identifying Facts: Making informed judgments about political parties, current events, and government policy requires an ability to identify facts and to distinguish fact from opinion. Facts are statements that can be proven or verified. By counting, observing, or checking other sources, you can determine whether a statement is factual or not factual. The statement, "Ronald Reagan and Walter Mondale were on the ballots of all 50 States and the District of Columbia in 1984," is a fact. You can verify it by checking with election officials in each of the 50 States or by consulting other authoritative sources.

You may agree or disagree with a statement, but if it cannot be verified, then the statement is not a fact. Take, for example, this statement: "If the United States had a multiparty system, political parties would be more responsive to the people." This is not a factual statement because no data or sources exist that could be used to verify this statement conclusively.

Read each statement below. If the statement is factual, write an "F" and indicate a possible source for verifying it. If the statement is not a fact, write "NF." Use a separate piece of paper.

1. In most contests for public office in the United States, only Republicans and/or Democrats have a reasonable chance of winning an election.

2. If the United States eliminated single-member districts, elections would be more democratic.

3. Political parties in the United States nominate candidates for public office.

4. The Congressional Campaign Committees of both major parties work to reelect incumbents.

5. In recent years, Republicans have been more successful in winning elections in the South.

6. Under a one-party system, government runs more efficiently.

For Thought and Discussion

••• **1.** If you were an adviser to the National Chairperson of one of the major parties in the United States, what advice would you offer to increase citizen participation in the party?

•• **2.** How do political parties in the United States serve as a "vital link between the people and the government"? Give specific examples.

••• **3.** Examine the various photographs of campaign devices throughout this chapter. What political symbols are used by the various candidates? What do the symbols represent? Why was a particular symbol chosen by the party (or the candidate)? How does the symbol influence your perception of the candidate?

••• **4.** Do you think that election laws should be changed to make it easier for candidates of minor parties to get on the ballots of the States? Why or Why not?

Suggested Activities

••• **1.** Investigate your State's party system by looking up election results from presidential, congressional, and State legislative races. You can find this information in your *State Manual,* or the *Blue Book*. Based on the election results, would you classify your State as one-party, modified one-party, or two-party? Why?

••• **2.** From your local newspaper, collect political cartoons about political parties, candidates, and/or elections. Use the observations in the feature on cartoons on page 419 to analyze each cartoon. Write a brief analysis on an index card and attach it to each cartoon. Combine your collection with other students' and display the cartoons on a bulletin board.

••• **3.** Draw your own political cartoon about political parties. Use newspaper stories and magazine articles for ideas.

I often think it's comical—
Fal, lal, la!
How Nature does contrive—
Fal, lal, la!
That every boy and every gal
That's born into the world alive
Is either a little Liberal
Or else a little Conservative!
—GILBERT AND SULLIVAN, *IOLANTHE*

8

Government by the People: Voters and Voter Behavior

CHAPTER OBJECTIVES

To help you to

Learn · Know · Understand

The historical development of the right to vote in the United States.

The present-day shape of the right to vote, and the several recent federal voting rights statutes.

Voter turnout and nonvoting in American elections.

The complex of factors affecting the behavior of the American voter.

WE HAVE NOTED several times that democratic government is, for us, representative government. It is "government by the people"—self-government conducted through the use of elected representatives. Those representatives are the agents of the people. They are chosen by the people to act for the people.

Those representatives are held accountable to the people at periodic elections. It is by voting at those elections that the typical citizen can most directly take part in the governing process in this country. **Suffrage**[1]—the right to vote—lies at the very heart of the democratic process.

The use of the word *right* in the phrase *right to vote* should be clearly understood. No one has the right to vote in quite the same sense as he or she has the right to free speech, to a fair trial, or to any of the other civil rights guaranteed by the Constitution.* The right to vote is not a civil right, one belonging to all persons. Rather, it is a

[1]The word comes from the Latin *suffragium*—literally, a vote. The word **franchise**, from the French, *franchir*, has the same meaning—the right to vote.

*REINFORCEMENT Have the class discuss: Although the right to vote is not a civil right, it too is protected by the Constitution. Illustrate by using the Amendments concerning suffrage.

When Americans vote, they directly participate in our democratic form of government. Here, voters in rural Iowa wait to cast their ballots. *Facing Page:* Citizens enter their polling place in the Chinatown section of San Francisco.

political right, one belonging to all those who can meet certain requirements set by law.

In this chapter we first take up the matter of suffrage qualifications, *who* has the right to vote in elections in the United States. Then we turn to nonvoting—to the fact that, and the reasons why, millions of potential voters do not go to the polls. Finally, we look at the *how* and the *why* of voter behavior.

1. Suffrage and the Constitution

As You Read Think About:

- Why the restrictive requirements for voting have been gradually eliminated.
- Why a gradual transfer of authority on suffrage from the States to the National Government has occurred.
- What the five stages in the growth of the American electorate are.

The overall size of the American **electorate** —the potential voting population—is truly impressive. More than 178 million persons, nearly all citizens who are at least 18 years of age, can qualify to vote. That huge number is a direct result of the legal definition of the right to vote. That is, it is the product of those laws that determine who may and who may not vote. It is also the product of some 200 years of continuing, often contentious, and sometimes violent struggle.

Historical Development of the Suffrage

Largely because the Framers could not agree on specific requirements, the Constitution left the power to set suffrage qualifications to the separate States.[2]

[2]Originally, the Constitution had only two provisions relating to the right to vote. Article I, Section 2, Clause 1 requires each State to allow those persons qualified to vote for members of "the most numerous branch" of its own legislature to vote as well for members of the national House of Representatives. The "most numerous branch" provision was extended to voting for members of the United States Senate by the 17th Amendment, 1913. Article II, Section I, Clause 2 provides that presidential electors be chosen in each State "in such manner as the legislature thereof may direct."

When the Constitution became effective in 1789, probably not one man in 15 could vote in elections in the different States. The long history of the development of the suffrage since then has been marked by two long-term trends. The first was the elimination of a number of restrictive requirements based on such arbitrary factors as religious belief, property ownership, tax payment, race, and sex. The second was the transfer of more and more authority over the suffrage from the States to the Federal Government. We shall see several illustrations of both of these long-term trends throughout the course of this chapter.

*The Five Historical Stages** The growth of the American electorate—its historical development to its present size and shape—has come in five fairly distinct stages. The first stage of the struggle to extend voting rights came in the early part of the 1800s. Religious qualifications, born in the colonies, rather quickly disappeared. No State has had a religious test since 1810. Property ownership and tax payment qualifications then began to fall, one by one, among the States. By midcentury, universal white adult male suffrage was very largely fact.

The second major effort to broaden the electorate followed the Civil War. The 15th Amendment, ratified in 1870, was intended to protect any citizen from being denied the right to vote because of race or color. Despite that amendment, black Americans have, until quite recently, made up the largest single group of disfranchised citizens.

The ratification of the 19th Amendment in 1920 marked the third expansion of suffrage. That amendment prohibited the denial of the right to vote on account of sex. Wyoming, while still a territory, had allowed women the right to vote in 1869. By 1920 more than half of the States had followed that lead.

A fourth major extension took place during the 1960s, as federal legislation and court decisions centered on securing to blacks a full role in the electoral process in all States. With the passing and then the strong enforcement of several civil rights acts, especially the Voting Rights Act of 1965 and its several later extensions, racial equality finally became a fact in polling booths throughout the country.[3] The 23rd Amendment, added in 1961, included the voters of the District of Columbia in the presidential electorate. The 24th Amendment, ratified in 1964, eliminated all taxes as conditions for voting in federal elections.

The fifth and latest expansion of the electorate came with the adoption of the 26th Amendment in 1971. It set the minimum age for voting in all elections in the United States at 18.

Power to Establish Voting Qualifications

The Constitution does not give to the Federal Government the power to set suffrage qualifications. Rather, that matter is reserved to the States. *But* the Constitution does place five particular restrictions on the States in the use of that power:

1. Any person whom a State allows to vote for members of the "most numerous branch" of its own legislature must also be allowed to vote for Representatives and Senators in Congress.[4] This restriction is of little real meaning today. With only minor exceptions, each of the States allows the same voters to vote in all elections within the State.
2. No State may deprive any person of the right to vote "on account of race, color, or previous condition of servitude."[5]
3. No State may deprive any person of the right to vote on account of sex.[6]
4. No State may require the payment of any tax as condition for taking part in the

---

[3] See pages 212-215.

[4] Article I, Section 2, Clause 1; 17th Amendment.

[5] 15th Amendment. The phrase "previous condition of servitude" refers to slavery. Note that this amendment does *not* guarantee the right to vote to blacks, or to anyone else. Instead, it forbids the States to discriminate against any person on these grounds in the setting of suffrage qualifications.

[6] 19th Amendment. Note that this amendment does *not* guarantee the right to vote to women as such. Technically, it forbids States the power to discriminate against either males *or* females in setting suffrage qualifications.

*REINFORCEMENT Authority over the suffrage has gradually transferred from the States to the Federal Government. Ask the students for examples of this from each of the five historical stages.

nomination or election of any federal officeholder. That is, no State may set a tax in any process connected with selecting the President, Vice President, or members of Congress.[7]

5. No State may deprive any person who is at least 18 years of age the right to vote on account of age.[8]

No State may violate any of these five restrictions, each of which relates expressly to the right to vote.

Beyond that, remember that according to the Supremacy Clause, no State may violate any other provision in the Constitution in the setting of suffrage qualifications or in anything else that it does. A case decided by the Supreme Court in 1975, *Hill* v. *Stone,* illustrates the point. The Court struck down a section of the Texas constitution that declared that only those persons who owned taxable property could vote in city bond elections. The Court found the drawing of such a distinction for voting purposes—between those who do and those who do not own taxable property—to be an unreasonable classification, prohibited by the 14th Amendment's Equal Protection Clause.

FOR REVIEW

1. **Identify:** political right, Voting Rights Act of 1965.
2. What is the difference between a political right and a civil right?
3. How large is the American electorate?
4. What two long-term trends have marked the development of the right to vote in the United States?
5. What specific restrictions does the Constitution place upon the States in the setting of suffrage qualifications?

[7]24th Amendment.

[8]26th Amendment. Note that this amendment does not prevent any State from allowing persons *younger* than age 18 to vote. But it does prohibit a State from setting a *maximum* age for voting.

The amendment promoting women's suffrage encountered strong opposition in the early 1900s.

2. Voter Qualifications Among the States

As You Read Think About:

- What two major qualifications for voting have been set by the fifty States.
- What other qualifications have been set by certain States.

Within the limits set by the Constitution, a State may determine who may and who may not vote.

Citizenship and Residence

Today, each State requires all voters to meet qualifications based on two factors: citizenship and residence.

Citizenship No alien may vote legally in any public election held anywhere in the United States. Still, nothing in the Constitution says that aliens cannot vote, and any State could allow them to do so if it chose.[9]

[9]At one time about a fourth of the States permitted those aliens who had applied for naturalization to vote. Typically, the western States did so to help attract settlers. In most eastern States, and especially those with large concentrations of the foreign born, a different, anti-immigrant attitude was present. Arkansas, the last State in which aliens could vote, adopted a citizenship requirement in 1926.

*REINFORCEMENT Ask the class: Which has had more impact on expanding voting rights in the United States, the Federal Government or the States? Point out the five Constitutional restrictions on the States.

Only one State now draws any distinction between native-born and naturalized citizens with regard to the suffrage. The Minnesota constitution requires a person to have been an American citizen for at least three months before being allowed to vote.

In practice, a few aliens do vote—though in what number no one knows. They either wrongly believe that they are citizens or unlawfully pass themselves off as citizens.

Residence Each State requires that a person live within the State for at least some period of time in order to qualify to vote.

The residence requirement rests on two principal justifications, one historical and the other of continuing significance. Historically the residence requirement was meant to keep a political machine from importing (bribing) enough outsiders to affect the outcome of local elections. The adoption and enforcement of residence qualifications dried up that once common practice. The second justification: that every voter must have at least some time in which to learn something about the candidates and issues in an election.

The period of time that a voter must have lived in the State is now quite brief. The details vary, but only slightly, among the 50 States. Today, in 19 States voters must live within the State for at least 30 days before an election.[10] In three others the minimum period is slightly longer: 32 days in Colorado and 50 days in Arizona and Tennessee. Eight States have shorter periods: 29 days in California and Maryland; 20 days in Kansas, Minnesota, and Oregon; 10 days in New Hampshire and Wisconsin; one day in Alabama. The other 20 States[11] require no fixed period; they simply say that a voter must be a legal resident.

The fact that the residence requirement is a fairly uniform one today is a direct result of a 1972 decision by the Supreme Court. Until then, every State had required a much longer period: typically, a year in the State, 60 or 90 days in the county, and 30 days in the local ward or precinct.[12] But in the Voting Rights Act Amendments of 1970, Congress prohibited any requirement of longer than 30 days for voting in presidential elections.[13] In *Dunn* v. *Blumstein*, 1972, the Supreme Court found Tennessee's requirement —at the time, a year in the State and 90 days in the county—unconstitutional. It held such a lengthy requirement to be an unsupportable discrimination against new residents and so in conflict with the 14th Amendment's Equal Protection Clause. While the Court did not state just how lengthy an acceptable period might be, it did say that "30 days appears to be an ample period of time." Election law and practice among the 50 States quickly accepted that standard.

Nearly every State does prohibit transients—persons in the State only for a short time and for a specific purpose—from gaining a legal residence there. Thus, a traveling salesperson, a member of one of the armed services, or an out-of-State college student usually cannot vote in a State where he or she has only a temporary, physical residence. In several States, however, the courts have held that college students who claim the campus community as their legal residence must be allowed to vote there. This is regardless of where a student's parents live or where the "permanent" home is. *

Age The 26th Amendment sets 18 as the minimum age for voting in all elections. Prior to its adoption in 1971, 21 was the generally accepted standard.

In fact, up to 1970 only four States had put the voting age at less than 21. Georgia first allowed 18-year-olds to vote in 1943 and

---

[10] Alaska, Idaho, Illinois, Indiana, Kentucky, Michigan, Mississippi, Montana, Nevada, New Jersey, New York, North Carolina, North Dakota, Ohio, Pennsylvania, Rhode Island, West Virginia, Utah, Washington.

[11] Arkansas, Connecticut, Delaware, Florida, Georgia, Hawaii, Iowa, Louisiana, Massachusetts, Maine, Missouri, Nebraska, New Mexico, Oklahoma, South Carolina, South Dakota, Texas, Vermont, Virginia, Wyoming.

[12] The **precinct** is the basic, smallest unit of election administration; for each precinct there is a polling place. The precinct is also the basic unit of party organization; see page 200. The **ward** is a unit into which cities are often divided for the election of members of the city council.

[13] The Supreme Court upheld the provision in *Oregon* v. *Mitchell* in 1970.

*ENRICHMENT Have the class discuss: College students may be considered "transient"; should a student be allowed to vote in the town where the college campus is located? What is your State's residency requirement?

BUILDING GOVERNMENT SKILLS

Registering to Vote and Voting

Democracy's ceremonial, its feast, its great function, is the election.
H.G. Wells, *Democracy*

Registering to Vote

If you meet the residency requirements for your State and are at least 18 years old, you are eligible to vote. In some states, you can vote in your State primary election if you are 17 years old, but will turn 18 by the general election. (See text pp. 208, 210.)

All States except North Dakota require voters to register. The registration process varies from State to State. Usually, however, you must register to vote 30 days before the election. Depending on your State, you will register by mail or in person.

The registration form contains spaces to fill in your name, address, date of birth, place of birth, and date of registration.

In States that hold closed primaries, registration forms ask you to declare affiliation with a political party. You can choose to declare any political party or no party affiliation. However, in some of these States if you do not register as either a Republican or a Democrat, you will not be permitted to vote in primary elections. (See text p. 210.)

After you have registered, your name will be added to the list of registered voters. Be sure you determine your congressional district, ward, precinct, and polling place.

Voting

Voters sign in with poll workers who verify that the voter is registered by checking the voters' list. Depending on where you live, you vote using one of three voting devices: a voting machine, an electronic data processing (EDP) device, or paper ballots.

Using a voting machine involves pulling a large lever to close the booth curtains, then making voting choices by pulling small levers under your candidates' names. Opening the curtain with the large lever as you leave both locks in and counts your votes.

Using an EDP device involves marking your paper ballot by hand and placing it in a ballot box.

If you know you will not be in your voting area on election day, you can request an absentee ballot. Check with your State for specific regulations.

In many elections, voters have an opportunity to vote on referenda, initiatives, or other questions. (See text pp. 573-575.) Do not be surprised to see questions on the ballot in addition to candidates' names.

Every two years, citizens in the United States vote for candidates to fill federal, State, and local offices. State and/or local elections are held annually. Ballots can become very long. To prepare yourself to vote for all offices, contact the local party organizations for information on the candidates and the positions for which they are running.

Contact your town clerk or county board of elections and:

1. Find out the age and residency requirements for voting in your State.
2. Determine the process (for in-person registering or for registering by mail) and the deadline for registering to vote in your State.
3. Request a sample voter registration form.
4. Request a sample ballot.
5. Find out which voting device is used in your area.
6. Determine your State's procedure for requesting an absentee ballot.

then Kentucky did so in 1955. Alaska entered the Union in 1959 with the age set at 19, and Hawaii did so later that same year with the age floor at 20. Both Alaska and Hawaii set the age above 18 but below 21 to avoid any problems that might be caused by high school students voting in local school district elections. Whatever the fears on that score, they have not been borne out by the experience under the 26th Amendment.

Other Qualifications

A few other qualifications, notably registration, are found in several of the States.

Registration Forty-nine States—all except North Dakota—require that all voters, or at least most of them, be registered to vote. **Registration** is a procedure of voter identification, intended to prevent fraudulent voting.[14] It gives election officials a list of those persons who may legally vote in an election. In a few States, the voter registration process is known as enrollment.

Most States require all voters to register. But in a few—Wisconsin, for example—only those in urban areas must do so. Typically, a prospective voter must register his or her name, age, place of birth, present address, length of residence, and similar pertinent facts with a local registration officer.[15]

Every State, except North Dakota, now has some form of *permanent* registration. Typically, a voter remains registered unless or until he or she moves, dies, is convicted of a serious crime, is committed to a mental institution, or fails to vote for a certain number of years or elections.

The registration requirement has become somewhat controversial in recent years. In fact, some people argue that it should be done away with. They see it as a serious bar to voter turnout, especially among the poor and the less educated.

Others favor keeping registration but making it easier. Three States (Maine, Minnesota, and Wisconsin) now allow voters to register at any time, including election day. Elsewhere, one must register at some time before an election is to be held, usually at least 30 days. Nearly half of the States now permit voters to register by mail.

Literacy In the Voting Rights Act Amendments of 1970, Congress suspended for five years the use of any **literacy** requirement as a voting qualification anywhere in the United States. Congress made that ban a permanent one in 1975.

Until 1970 some form of a literacy requirement was found in 18 States. In some, the ability to read was required; in others, to read and write. In still others, the ability to read, write, and "understand" a piece of printed material—usually a passage from the State or federal Constitution—was required.

Literacy qualifications were first adopted in Connecticut in 1855 and then in Massachusetts in 1857. They were aimed at Irish Catholic immigrants. Mississippi adopted a literacy requirement in 1890, and shortly, most of the other southern States followed suit, usually with an "understanding clause."[16]

A number of States outside the South also adopted literacy qualifications of various

---

[14]Several States also use their voter registration to identify voters in terms of their party preference and, hence, their eligibility to take part in closed primaries; page 236. In most States one must be registered in order to vote in any election held within the State, but a few do not impose the requirement for *all* elections—for example, registration is not required for some school district elections in Minnesota.

[15]Most often the officer is the registrar of elections but sometimes it is the county clerk. In a few States party officials and even candidates are allowed to register new voters.

[16]A "grandfather clause" was added to the Louisiana constitution in 1895, and six other States (Alabama, Georgia, Maryland, North Carolina, Oklahoma, and Virginia) soon added them, as well. These clauses stated that any person, or his male descendants, who had voted in the State at some time before the adoption of the 15th Amendment (1870) could become a legal voter without regard to any literacy or taxpaying qualifications. Those qualifications were specifically aimed at disfranchising blacks, and the grandfather clauses were designed to enfranchise those whites who would otherwise be disqualified by failure to meet the literacy or taxpaying requirements. The Supreme Court found the Oklahoma provision, the last to be adopted (in 1910), in conflict with the 15th Amendment in *Guinn* v. *United States* in 1915.

Millions of Americans "cast their fates" each year on election day.

sorts. Wyoming did so in 1889, California in 1894, Washington in 1896, New Hampshire in 1902, Arizona in 1913, New York in 1921, Oregon in 1924, and Alaska in 1949.

* The literacy requirement could be, and in many places was, used to make sure that a qualified voter had at least some capacity to cast an informed ballot. But it could also be, and in many places was, used unfairly to prevent or discourage certain groups from voting. The device was used in just that way to keep blacks from voting for many years in many parts of the South.

Its unfair use finally led Congress to destroy literacy as a suffrage qualification. The Supreme Court upheld that ban in *Oregon* v. *Mitchell,* 1970:

> In enacting the literacy ban . . . Congress had before it a long history of discriminatory use of literacy tests to disfranchise voters on account of their race.

Tax Payment Property ownership, as proved by the payment of property taxes, was once a common suffrage requirement. It has now all but disappeared. In the few States where it is still found, it is a prerequisite to voting on some bond issues or special assessments. It is of very doubtful constitutionality today; see page 207.

The **poll tax,** once found throughout the South, has now disappeared altogether as a voting qualification. Beginning with Florida in 1889, each of the 11 southern States had adopted it as part of an effort to disfranchise blacks. The device proved to be of only limited effectiveness. That fact, together with opposition to its use from within the South as well as elsewhere, led most of those States to abandon it.[17]

The 24th Amendment, ratified in 1964, outlawed the poll tax, or any other tax, as a condition for voting in any federal election. But the Amendment does not apply to State and local elections.

The Supreme Court finally destroyed the poll tax as a qualification for voting in *all* elections in 1966. In *Harper* v. *Virginia State Board of Elections,* the Court held the Virginia poll tax to be in conflict with the 14th Amendment's Equal Protection Clause. The Court could find no reasonable relationship between the act of voting, on the one hand, and the payment of a tax on the other.

Suffrage Disqualifications

Every State bars certain groups from voting. Thus, no State allows the inmates of mental institutions, or any other persons who have been legally found to be mentally incompetent, to vote. Nearly all States also disqualify those who have been convicted of serious crimes (including election offenses). A few States also do not allow anyone dishonorably discharged from the armed forces to vote. In some a few odd groups like duelists, vagrants, or polygamists are also disqualified.

---

[17]By 1966, the final year of its life, the poll tax was still in use in four States: Alabama, Mississippi, Texas, and Virginia. It had been abolished in North Carolina (1924), Louisiana (1934), Florida (1937), Georgia (1945), South Carolina (1950), Tennessee (1951), and Arkansas (1964, shortly after the ratification of the 24th Amendment).

*ENRICHMENT Introduce a discussion on the literacy requirement. Should a person be denied the right to vote if he or she cannot read the ballot?

Protesting voter discrimination, Martin Luther King and civil rights demonstrators complete their 50-mile march from Selma to Montgomery, Alabama, in 1965.

FOR REVIEW

1. **Identify:** citizenship qualification; residence qualification; age qualification; literacy qualification; poll tax.
2. On what two bases does each State now set voter qualifications?
3. How was the residence requirement affected by the Voting Rights Act Amendments of 1970? By the Supreme Court's decision in *Dunn* v. *Blumstein,* 1972?
4. What is the essential purpose of voter registration? Why do some urge its elimination?
5. Why, and on what constitutional grounds has Congress said that literacy cannot be used as a voting qualification?
6. Why may no State now impose a poll tax as a voting qualification?

3. Civil Rights Laws and the Suffrage

As You Read Think About:

- Why civil rights laws were necessary to enforce suffrage.
- What the effects of civil rights laws have been on voting qualifications.

The 15th Amendment was ratified in 1870. It declares that the right to vote cannot be denied on grounds of race, color, or previous condition of servitude. The Amendment is not self-executing, however; to make it effective, Congress had to act. Yet for almost 90 years the Federal Government paid little attention to the problem of black voting. *

Over that period, blacks were generally and systematically kept from the polls in much of the South. The white supremacists employed a number of tactics to that end.

*ENRICHMENT Ask the students to find out the suffrage disqualifications for their State. A starting point may be the town or county clerk, or the local board of elections.

Violence and threats of violence were a major weapon. So were more subtle intimidations and social pressures—such as firing a black man who tried to register or vote, or not giving his family credit at local stores.

More formal—"legal"—devices were used, as well. The most effective were the literacy tests. They were regularly manipulated by white election officials to disfranchise black citizens.

As written, registration requirements applied to all potential voters, black or white. In practice, however, they were often administered to keep blacks from qualifying to vote. Poll taxes, gerrymandering, "white primaries," and several other devices were used to that end, too.[18]

Led by decisions of the Supreme Court, the lower federal courts began to strike down many of these practices in the 1940s and 1950s. But those courts could act only when suits were filed by those who claimed to be the victims of discrimination. That case-by-case method was extremely slow.

Finally, Congress was moved to act very largely in response to the civil rights movement led by Dr. Martin Luther King, Jr. Congress has passed several civil rights laws since the late 1950s. We noted in Chapter 6 that they contain a number of sections specifically intended to implement the 15th Amendment.

[18]**Gerrymandering** is the practice of drawing electoral district lines to the advantage of a particular party or faction; see page 299. The Supreme Court outlawed gerrymandering when used for purposes of racial discrimination in a case from Alabama, *Gomillion* v. *Lightfoot,* in 1960.

The *white primary* arose out of the near-complete and decades-long Democratic party domination of the politics of the South. Almost always, only the Democrats nominated candidates for office, and generally in primaries. In several southern States, political parties were defined by law as "private associations." As such, they could admit or exclude members as they chose, and the Democrats regularly refused to admit blacks. Because only party members could vote in the party's primary, blacks were then excluded from *the* critical step in the public election process. The Supreme Court finally outlawed the white primary in a case from Texas, *Smith* v. *Allwright,* 1944. There it held that because nominations are an integral part of the election process, when a political party holds a primary it is performing a *public* function and its operations are bound by the 15th Amendment.

Civil Rights Acts of 1957 and 1960

The first of them, the *Civil Rights Act of 1957,* set up the United States Civil Rights Commission. One of its major duties is to inquire into claims of voter discrimination. It reports its findings to Congress and the President and, through the media, to the public. The Act also gave to the Attorney General the power to seek federal court orders to prevent interference with any person's right to vote in federal elections.

The *Civil Rights Act of 1960* added another safeguard. It provided for the appointment of federal voting referees. These officers were to serve anywhere a federal court found that voter discrimination was present. They were given the power to help qualified persons to register and to vote in federal elections.

Civil Rights Act of 1964

The *Civil Rights Act of 1964* is a much broader measure than either of the two earlier ones. With regard to voting rights, its most important section forbids the use of any registration requirement in an unfair or discriminatory manner.

The 1964 law continued a pattern set in the earlier laws. In major part, it relied on judicial action to overcome racial barriers. It emphasized the use of federal court orders. These **injunctions** are backed by the power of the courts to punish for contempt any public official or any other person who refused to obey those orders.

Dramatic events in Selma, Alabama, soon pointed up the shortcomings of this approach, however. Dr. King had mounted a voter registration drive in that city in early 1965. He and his supporters hoped that they could center national attention on the issue of black voting rights. Their registration efforts were met with unbridled abuse and violence—by local whites, by city and county police, and then by State troopers. The nation saw much of the drama on television and was shocked. An outraged President Lyndon Johnson urged Congress to pass new and stronger legislation to ensure the voting rights of blacks. Congress acted quickly.

Voting Rights Act of 1965 and Its Amendments

The *Voting Rights Act of 1965* made the 15th Amendment, at long last, a truly effective part of the Constitution. Unlike its predecessors, it applies to *all* elections held anywhere in this country—State and local as well as federal. The law has now been extended three times,* in the Voting Rights Act Amendments of 1970, 1975, and 1982.

The 1965 law directed the Attorney General to attack the constitutionality of the remaining State poll tax laws. That provision led directly to *Harper* v. *Virginia State Board of Elections,* in 1966 (see page 211).

It also suspended the use of any literacy test or similar device in any State or county where less than half of the population of voting age had been registered or had voted in the 1964 elections. The Attorney General was authorized to appoint voting examiners to serve in any of those States or counties. These federal officers were given the power to register voters and otherwise oversee the conduct of elections in those areas. The 1965 law also declared that no new election laws can go into force in any of those States unless first approved—given "preclearance"—by the Department of Justice.

Any State or county subject to its voter-examiner and preclearance provisions can be removed from the law's coverage through the law's "bail-out" process. That relief can come if the State can show a three-judge panel of the United States District Court in the District of Columbia that it has not applied voting procedures in any discriminatory way for at least the past 10 years.

The voter-examiner and preclearance provisions of the 1965 Act applied to six entire States—Alabama, Georgia, Louisiana, Mississippi, South Carolina, and Virginia, and also to 40 North Carolina counties.

The constitutionality of the Voting Rights Act was upheld by the Supreme Court in 1966. In *South Carolina* v. *Katzenbach,* the Court ruled that Congress had chosen both "rational and appropriate" means to implement the 15th Amendment.

The 1970 Amendments extended the law for another five years. The 1968 elections were added to its triggering formula. So several counties in six more States—Alaska, Arizona, California, Idaho, New Mexico, and Oregon—were added to its coverage.

Black Americans march in support of extending the Voting Rights Act, first passed by Congress in 1965. The third and most recent extension was passed in 1982.

*REINFORCEMENT Have the class discuss: Do the charts on p. 215 indicate that the Civil Rights and Voting Rights Acts have had an impact on black voter turnout?

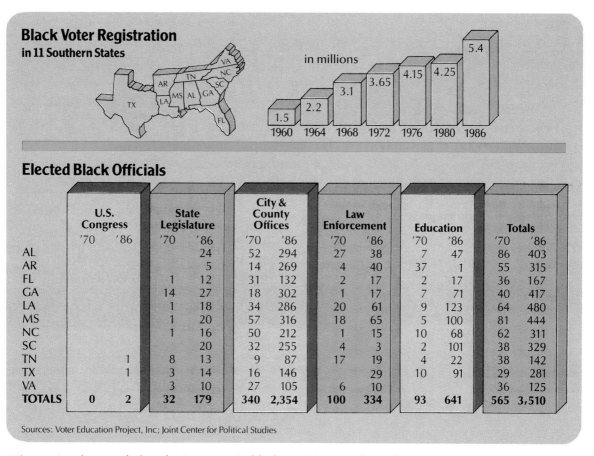

Black Voter Registration
in 11 Southern States

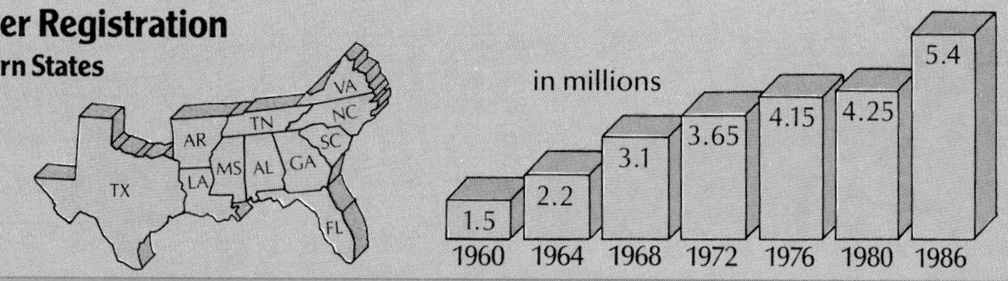

Elected Black Officials

	U.S. Congress		State Legislature		City & County Offices		Law Enforcement		Education		Totals	
	'70	'86	'70	'86	'70	'86	'70	'86	'70	'86	'70	'86
AL				24	52	294	27	38	7	47	86	403
AR				5	14	269	4	40	37	1	55	315
FL			1	12	31	132	2	17	2	17	36	167
GA			14	27	18	302	1	17	7	71	40	417
LA			1	18	34	286	20	61	9	123	64	480
MS			1	20	57	316	18	65	5	100	81	444
NC			1	16	50	212	1	15	10	68	62	311
SC				20	32	255	4	3	2	101	38	329
TN		1	8	13	9	87	17	19	4	22	38	142
TX		1	3	14	16	146		29	10	91	29	281
VA			3	10	27	105	6	10			36	125
TOTALS	**0**	**2**	**32**	**179**	**340**	**2,354**	**100**	**334**	**93**	**641**	**565**	**3,510**

Sources: Voter Education Project, Inc; Joint Center for Political Studies

What national events led to the increases in black participation shown here?

The 1970 law also provided that, for five years, no State could use literacy as the basis for any voting requirement. That temporary ban, and the law's residence provisions, were upheld by the Court in *Oregon* v. *Mitchell* in 1970 (see pages 208 and 211).

The law was extended again in 1975, this time for seven years. The five-year ban on literacy tests became a permanent one, and the law's voter-examiner and preclearance provisions were broadened. Since 1975 they have also covered any State or county where more than 5 percent of the voting-age population belongs to certain "language minorities." These groups are defined to include all persons of Spanish heritage, American Indians, Asian Americans, and Alaskan Natives. This addition spread the law's coverage to all of Alaska and Texas and to several counties in 24 other States, as well. In each of these areas, all ballots and official election materials must be printed both in English and in the language of the minority, or minorities, involved.

The 1982 Amendments extended the basic features of the Voting Rights Act for another 25 years, with this major exception: Its language-minority provisions are to remain in effect only until 1992.

FOR REVIEW

1. **Identify:** Civil Rights Acts of 1957, 1960, 1964; Voting Rights Act of 1965.
2. Identify the major civil rights laws enacted by Congress over the past 25 years. Outline their voting rights provisions.
3. Why did Congress pass these laws? Who played a leading part in this?

4. Nonvoting

As You Read, Think About:

- Who the large proportion of American voters are who do not vote.
- Why these people do not vote.
- Who "cannot voters" are.
- Why the so-called "cannot voters" do not vote.

We began this chapter by pointing out the critical relationship between voting and democratic government. Yet, despite the obvious importance of that relationship, there are millions of persons who, for one reason or another, do not participate in voting in this country.

Scope of the Problem

The table on page 218 lays out the major facts of the nonvoter problem in American elections. Notice that on election day in 1984 there were an estimated 173,936,000 persons of voting age in the United States. But only some 92.6 million persons—less than 56 percent—actually voted in the presidential election. That is, some 81 million did not vote.

In 1984 some 82.4 million votes, or 47.4 percent, were cast in the elections held across the country to fill the 435 seats in the House of Representatives. More than half of the potential electorate, therefore, did not vote in the congressional elections of 1984.

Little-Recognized Aspects of the Problem

The fact that we do have a nonvoter problem of considerable proportions is widely recognized. But several aspects of the problem are *not* widely known, even by many who are very much concerned about it. For example, there are millions of nonvoters *among those who vote.* Look again at the 1984 figures. More than 9 million persons who *did* vote in the presidential election did *not* vote, at that same election, for a candidate for a seat in the House of Representatives.

This "nonvoting voter" aspect of the problem is not confined to federal elections, of course. In fact, it is a much larger one at the State and local levels. As a general rule, the further down the ballot an office is, the fewer the number of votes that will be cast for it. This phenomenon is sometimes called "ballot fatigue." The expression suggests that many voters exhaust themselves (and/or their patience and/or their knowledge) as they work their way down the list of offices and candidates (and measures, as well).

Some quick illustrations of the point: More votes are regularly cast in the presidential election than in the gubernatorial election in every State. More votes are generally cast for the governorship than for such other Statewide offices as lieutenant governor and secretary of state. More voters in a county usually vote in the race for governor than vote in the more local contests for such county offices as sheriff or district attorney, and so on.

There are other little-recognized facets of the problem, too. Thus, the table on page 218 shows that turnout in congressional elections is consistently higher in presidential years than it is in "off-year elections."

That same pattern holds among the States in terms of the types of elections held; more people vote in general elections than in either primary or special elections.

Reasons for Nonvoting

Why do we have so many nonvoters? Why, even in a presidential election, do nearly half of all those who could vote stay away from the polls?

"Cannot-Voters" To begin with, look at another of those little-recognized aspects of the nonvoter problem: Several million persons who are regularly identified as "nonvoters" can be much more accurately described as "cannot-voters." That is, although it is true that they do not vote, the fact of the matter is that they *cannot* do so.

The 1984 data we have just looked at can be used to make the point. In that figure of some 81 million persons of voting age who did not vote in the last presidential election are some 5.5 million resident aliens—and,

*REINFORCEMENT Ask the class: Why is voter turnout higher in presidential years that in "off-years"? Use the graph on p. 217 to point out that presidential elections spark voter interest.

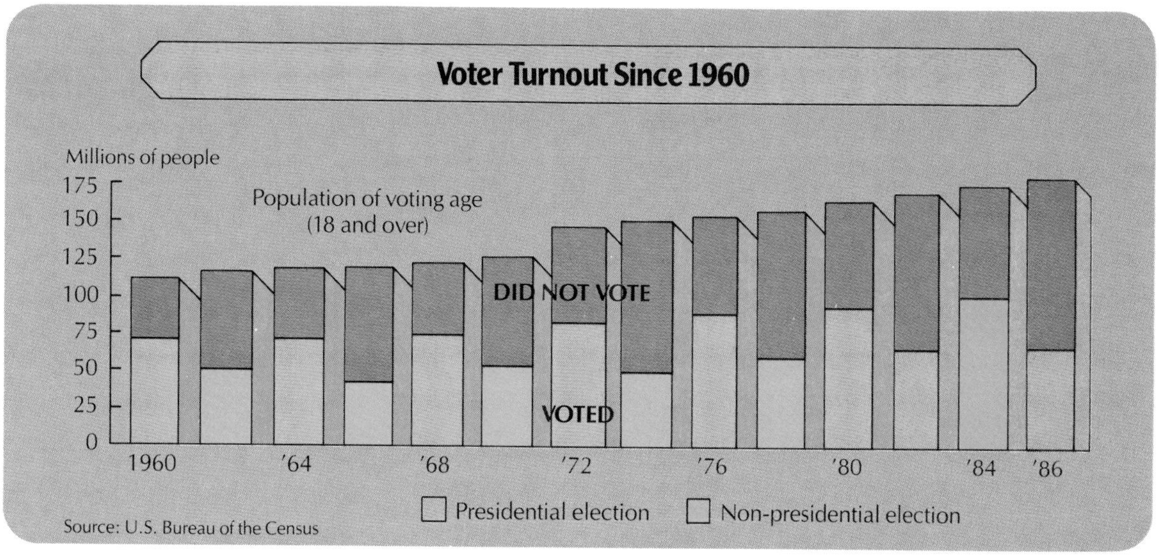

The graph above clearly shows the increase in nonvoters since the early 70s. What are the factors that influence a person not to vote? Are there more cannot-voters or more actual nonvoters in this country?

remember, they are barred from the polls in every State. Also there are 5 to 6 million citizens who were so ill or otherwise physically handicapped that they simply could not do such things as vote. There are another 2 or 3 million persons who were traveling, suddenly and unexpectedly, and so they were away from their home precincts on election day.

That figure counts several other groups of "cannot-voters," too. There are, for example: some 500,000 persons confined to mental care facilities or under some other form of legal restraint because of their mental condition; some 400,000 or so in jails and prisons; and perhaps as many as 100,000 who do not (cannot) vote because of their personal religious beliefs.

Racial, religious, and other discrimination still plays a part here, too. This is despite the many recent federal statutes, court decisions, and enforcement actions aimed at eliminating discrimination. An unknown number—but, certainly, more than a million persons—could not vote in 1984 because of (1) the purposeful administration of election laws to keep them from doing so, and/or (2) "informal" local pressures applied to that same end.

In short, that figure of about 81 million nonvoters in 1984 counts at least 16 million persons who, in fact, really should not be included in that number.[19]

Actual Nonvoters Even so, there are millions of *actual* nonvoters in the United States. Thus, in 1984 some 60 million Americans *could* have voted in the presidential election but did not.

There are any number of reasons for that behavior. As a leading example: Many do not go to the polls because they are convinced that it makes little real difference who wins a certain election.

Notice, though, that large group includes two quite different categories of nonvoters. On the one hand, there are those who approve of the way in which the public's business is currently being managed. They believe that, no matter who wins elections, things will continue to go well for themselves and for the country.

[19]This counting (or miscounting) problem arises out of the standard on which it is based. That standard is the Census Bureau's estimate of the population of voting age at the time a given election is held. Quite clearly, that estimate includes many persons who are *old enough* to vote but cannot do so for reasons *other than* age.

Voter Turnout, 1932–1986

Year	Population of Voting Age[a]	Votes Cast for President		Votes Cast for U.S. Representatives	
	(in millions)	(in millions)	(percent)	(in millions)	(percent)
1932	75.768	39.732	52.4	37.657	49.7
1934	77.997	—	—	32.256	41.4
1936	80.174	45.643	56.9	42.886	53.5
1938	82.354	—	—	36.236	44.0
1940	84.728	49.900	58.9	46.951	55.4
1942	86.465	—	—	28.074	32.5
1944	85.654	47.977	56.0	45.103	52.7
1946	92.659	—	—	34.398	37.1
1948	95.573	48.794	51.1	45.933	48.1
1950	98.134	—	—	40.342	41.1
1952	99.929	61.551	61.6	57.571	57.6
1954	102.075	—	—	42.580	41.7
1956	104.515	62.067	59.3	58.428	55.9
1958	106.447	—	—	45.818	43.0
1960	109.672	68.838	62.8	64.133	58.5
1962	112.952	—	—	51.261	45.4
1964	114.090	70.645	61.9	65.886	57.7
1966	116.638	—	—	52.900	45.4
1968	120.285	73.212	60.9	66.109	55.0
1970	124.498	—	—	54.173	43.5
1972	140.068	77.719	55.5	71.188	50.8
1974	145.035	—	—	52.397	36.1
1976	150.127	81.556	54.3	74.419	49.6
1978	155.712	—	—	55.332	35.5
1980	162.761	86.515	53.2	77.995	47.9
1982	169.342	—	—	64.514	38.1
1984	173.936	92.653	55.3	82.405	47.4
1986	178.335	—	—	66.240[b]	37.1

[a]As estimated by Census Bureau. Population 18 years of age and over since ratification of 26th Amendment in 1971; prior to 1971, 21 years and over in all States, except: 18 years and over in Georgia since 1943 and Kentucky since 1955, 19 years and over in Alaska and 20 and over in Hawaii since 1959.
[b]Preliminary estimate.
Sources: Census Bureau, *Statistical Abstract of the United States;* Clerk of the House of Representatives; Congressional Quarterly.

On the other hand, that group also includes many who feel alienated—many who deliberately refuse to vote because they don't trust political institutions and processes. They fear or scorn "the system." In their opinion, elections are meaningless, choiceless exercises.

Another large group of nonvoters is made up of those persons who have no sense of **political efficacy.** That is, they lack any feeling of influence or effectiveness in politics. They simply do not believe that they or their votes can have an impact on how government is run or what government does.

Cumbersome election procedures are another factor here—for example, inconvenient registration requirements, long ballots, and long lines at polling places. Other things such as bad weather also tend to discourage turnout.

But, of all the reasons that may be cited, the *chief* cause for nonvoting is, purely and simply, a *lack of interest.* Those who lack sufficient interest, who are indifferent and apathetic, who just can't be bothered, are usually uninformed. They often do not know even the simplest facts about an election.

The table on the next page sets out a number of factors that affect voter turnout.

As you can see, those persons most likely to vote display such characteristics as higher levels of income and education. Those per-

* To Vote or Not to Vote? Factors Affecting Turnout

Potential voters with these characteristics are:

More Likely to Vote	Less Likely to Vote
Higher level of income	Lower level of income
Higher level of education	Lower level of education
White	Nonwhite
35 years of age or older	Younger than age 35
Married	Not married
Catholic or Jew	Protestant
Occupation:	Occupation:
Business or profession	Unskilled
White-collar	Blue-collar
Union member	Nonunion member
Residence:	Residence:
Urban, suburban	Rural
Northeast, Middle West, West	South
Long-term in locale	Newcomer to locale
Homeowner	Renter
Member of civic groups	Isolated individual
Strong party identification in family	Weak or no party identification in family
Strong supporter of party	Weak partisan or independent
High sense of political efficacy	Little, no sense of political efficacy
High sense of civic duty	Little, no sense of civic duty
Much political interest in work group	Little, no political interest in work group
Perceives personal stake in election	Perceives no personal stake in election
Subject to few cross-pressures	Subject to many cross-pressures
Crisis political situation	Normal political situation
Absence of cumbersome registration, other election procedures	Restrictive, cumbersome election procedures
Vigorous two-party competition	One-party constituency
Lack of community pressures against participation	Community pressures work to discourage participation

Note this important point: The table reports *group* behavior. That is, it shows how those persons who belong to certain groups (for example have higher/lower incomes, live in urban/rural places) *tend* to behave.

sons are usually well integrated into community life. They tend to be long-time residents who are active in or at least comfortable with their surroundings. They are likely to have a strong sense of party identification, believe that voting is an important act, and are subject to few cross-pressures—contradictory, competing influences—that would discourage their participation. They also are likely to live in those States and locales where laws, customs, and interparty competition all work to promote turnout. The opposite characteristics give a profile of those United States citizens who are least likely to participate in voting.

A few of the factors in the table are so important that they influence turnout even when they are not supported by, or are in conflict with, other factors. Thus, those persons with a high sense of political efficacy are very likely to vote—no matter what their income, education, age, race, and so on, may be. The degree of two-party competition has much the same kind of general, across-the-board effect. It is a very influential factor in determining the volume of voter turnout. That is, the greater or lesser the degree of competition between candidates, the higher or lower the voter turnout will be, regardless of other factors.

*ENRICHMENT Use the above chart to discuss students' potential for becoming active voters. Stress that these factors are trends among groups of people, and do not necessarily apply to specific individuals.

Racial discrimination is one factor affecting the black nonvoter. Concerned NAACP members march to encourage nonvoters to register.

Despite the greater weight of some factors, however, notice this important point: It is the *combined* effect of several of them, rather than the force of one of them alone, that prompts the individual's decison to vote or not.

FOR REVIEW

1. **Identify:** ballot fatigue, "cannot-voters," voter turnout.
2. How many votes were cast in the last presidential election? Congressional elections of that year?
3. About how many potential voters did not vote in the last presidential election?
4. What does "nonvoting by voters" refer to?
5. Identify the causes for nonvoting. Who are the "cannot voters"?

5. Voting Behavior

As You Read, Think About:

- How sociological and psychological factors help determine how a person will vote.
- How important party identification is as a determinant of voter behavior.

Several million potential voters do not go to the polls, but many millions more do. How do those who do vote behave? Why do they vote as they do? What prompts many of them to vote most often for Republican candidates? What persuades other voters to support Democrats most often?

Clearly, these questions cannot be answered with absolute certainty. But voting has been studied more closely than any other form of political participation in the United States.[20] That research has produced a huge amount of information about why people *tend* to vote as they do.

Most of what we know about voter behavior comes from studies based on data from three sources:

1. The results of particular elections—As a quick illustration: The careful study of the returns from areas populated largely by blacks or by Catholics or by high-income families will indicate how those groups voted in a given election.

2. The field of survey research—the polling (questioning, interviewing) of scientifically drawn samples or cross sections of the population. It is the method by which public opinion is most often identified and measured. The Gallup Poll is perhaps the best known survey research organization today.

3. Studies of **political socialization**—the process by which people gain their political attitudes and opinions. That very complex process begins in early childhood and continues on through each person's life. Political

[20]Voting behavior has been so widely studied because of the importance of the topic and because of the almost unlimited amount of data available (innumerable elections in which millions of voters have cast billions of votes). Much of the most useful research on voter behavior is done by the Center for Political Studies at the University of Michigan.

socialization involves all of the experiences and relationships that lead each of us to see the political world, and to act in it, as we do.

Here we are especially concerned with voter behavior—with what those studies tell us about how and why people vote as they do. Later, in Chapter 10, we shall turn to the broader subject of public opinion. There, we shall take a closer look at both the techniques of survey research and the process of political socialization.

Factors Affecting Voter Behavior

There is still much to be learned about voter behavior, but it is quite clear that the ways in which people vote are heavily influenced by a number of *sociological* and *psychological factors*.

The sociological factors at work here are really the many pieces of a voter's social and economic life. Those pieces are of two broad kinds: (1) a voter's personal characteristics —age, race, income, occupation, education, religion, and so on, and (2) a voter's group affiliations—family, co-workers, and friends.

The psychological factors in the voting mix are a voter's perceptions of politics. That is, how the voter sees the parties, the candidates, and the issues in an election.

The differences between these two kinds of influences are not so great as they might seem. In fact, they are quite closely related and constantly interact with one another. How voters look at parties, candidates, or issues is very often shaped by their social and economic backgrounds.

The Sociological Factors From the table on page 222, it is possible to draw a composite picture of the American voter in terms of a number of sociological factors.

But a large word of caution here: Do not make too much of any one of these factors. The table reports how voters, grouped by a *single* characteristic, voted in each of nine successive presidential elections. Remember, *each* voter possesses *several* of the characteristics shown in the table.

Consider these examples: College graduates are more likely to vote Republican. So are persons over 50 years of age. Catholics are more likely to vote for Democrats. So are members of labor unions. What, then, of a 55-year-old college-educated Catholic who belongs to the AFL-CIO?

INCOME, OCCUPATION. Voters in the middle-to-upper income brackets are more likely to be Republicans. Voters with lower incomes tend to be Democrats. This pattern has held up over time, and it showed up even in the presidential election landslides of 1980 and 1984. Those with family incomes above $35,000 voted for Ronald Reagan, both times, by better than 2 to 1; a majority of those with incomes of less than $15,000 voted for Jimmy Carter in 1980 and Walter Mondale in 1984.

Most often, how much one earns and what one does for a living are closely related matters. Professional and business people, and others with higher incomes, tend to vote for Republican candidates. Manual workers, and others from lower income groups, are more likely to vote for Democrats. Thus, with the single exception of 1964, professional and business people voted heavily Republican in the nine presidential elections from 1952 through 1984.

EDUCATION. There is also a close relationship between the level of a voter's education and how he or she votes. A number of studies of voter behavior show that college graduates vote for Republicans in higher percentages than do high school graduates. Those studies also show that high school graduates vote more often Republican than do those who have only gone through grade school.

SEX, AGE. On the whole, sex does not appear to be a major factor in partisan voting behavior. That is, men are no more or less likely to favor one party and its candidates than are women. A number of studies, however, do suggest this: Men and women do vote in measurably different ways when issues related to war and national defense or human rights are prominent issues in an election.

Age is another matter, however. Younger voters have been more likely to be Democrats than Republicans. Older voters are likely to find the GOP and its candidates

*ENRICHMENT Ask the class: What questions would you include in a survey of voter behavior? Point out that behavior may be shaped by age, family, newspapers, television, etc.

Voting by Groups in Presidential Elections, 1952–1984 (By Percentage of Votes Reported Cast)

	1952		1956		1960		1964		1968			1972		1976			1980			1984	
	D	R	D	R	D	R	D	R	D	R	AIP	D	R	D	R	I	D	R	I	D	R
National	44.6	55.4	42.2	57.8	50.1	49.9	61.3	38.7	43.0	43.4	13.6	37.5	60.7	50	48	1	41	50.7	6.6	41	59
Sex																					
Men	47	53	45	55	52	48	60	40	41	43	16	37	63	53	45	1	38	53	7	36	64
Women	42	58	39	61	49	51	62	38	45	43	12	38	62	48	51	*	44	49	6	45	55
Race																					
White	43	57	41	59	49	51	59	41	38	47	15	32	68	46	52	1	36	56	7	34	66
Nonwhite	79	21	61	39	68	32	94	6	85	12	3	87	13	85	15	*	86	10	2	84	13
Education																					
College	34	66	31	69	39	61	52	48	37	54	9	37	63	42	55	2	35	53	10	39	61
High school	45	55	42	58	52	48	62	38	42	43	15	34	66	54	46	*	43	51	5	43	57
Grade school	52	48	50	50	55	45	66	34	52	33	15	49	51	58	41	1	54	42	3	51	49
Occupation																					
Professional and business	36	64	32	68	42	58	54	46	34	56	10	31	69	42	56	1	33	55	10	34	66
White-collar	40	60	37	63	48	52	57	43	41	47	12	36	64	50	48	2	40	51	9	47	53
Manual	55	45	50	50	60	40	71	29	50	35	15	43	57	58	41	1	48	46	5	46	54
Members of labor-union families	61	39	57	43	65	35	73	27	56	29	15	46	54	63	36	1	50	43	5	52	48
Age																					
Under 30 years	51	49	43	57	54	46	64	36	47	38	15	48	52	53	45	1	47	41	11	40	60
30–49 years	47	53	45	55	54	46	63	37	44	41	15	33	67	48	49	2	38	52	8	40	60
50 years and older	39	61	39	61	46	54	59	41	41	47	12	36	64	52	48	*	41	54	4	41	59
Religion																					
Protestants	37	63	37	63	38	62	55	45	35	49	16	30	70	46	53	*	39	54	6	39	61
Catholics	56	44	51	49	78	22	76	24	59	33	8	48	52	57	42	1	46	47	6	39	61
Politics																					
Republicans	8	92	4	96	5	95	20	80	9	86	5	5	95	9	91	*	8	86	5	4	96
Democrats	77	23	85	15	84	16	87	13	74	12	14	67	33	82	18	*	69	26	4	79	21
Independents	35	65	30	70	43	57	56	44	31	44	25	31	69	38	57	4	29	55	14	33	67
Region																					
East	45	55	40	60	53	47	68	32	50	43	7	42	58	51	47	1	43	47	9	46	54
Midwest	42	58	41	59	48	52	61	39	44	47	9	40	60	48	50	1	41	51	7	42	58
South	51	49	49	51	51	49	52	48	31	36	33	29	71	54	45	*	44	52	3	37	63
West	42	58	43	57	49	51	60	40	44	49	7	41	59	46	51	1	35	54	9	40	60

D = Democratic candidate; R = Republican candidate; AIP = American Independent Party candidate (George Wallace, 1968); I = Independent candidate (Eugene McCarthy, 1976; John B. Anderson, 1980). Figures do not add to 100% in some groups because of rounding and/or minor party votes. *Less than 1%.
Source: The Gallup Report, No. 230, November, 1984.

more attractive. Thus, in every presidential election from 1952 through 1980, the Democratic candidate received a larger percentage of the votes cast by the under-30 age group than of those cast by voters age 50 and over. But, notice, that long-standing pattern was broken by President Reagan's appeal to younger voters in 1984.

RELIGIOUS, ETHNIC BACKGROUND. A majority of northern Protestants prefer the GOP. Catholics and Jews are much more likely to be Democrats.

From the maps on the next page: what was unusual about the margin of victory for the Republican candidate in 1968? the Democratic candidate in 1976?

*ENRICHMENT Ask the class to discuss: How did your State vote in the above elections? Does this mean that all of the people in the State identify with that party?

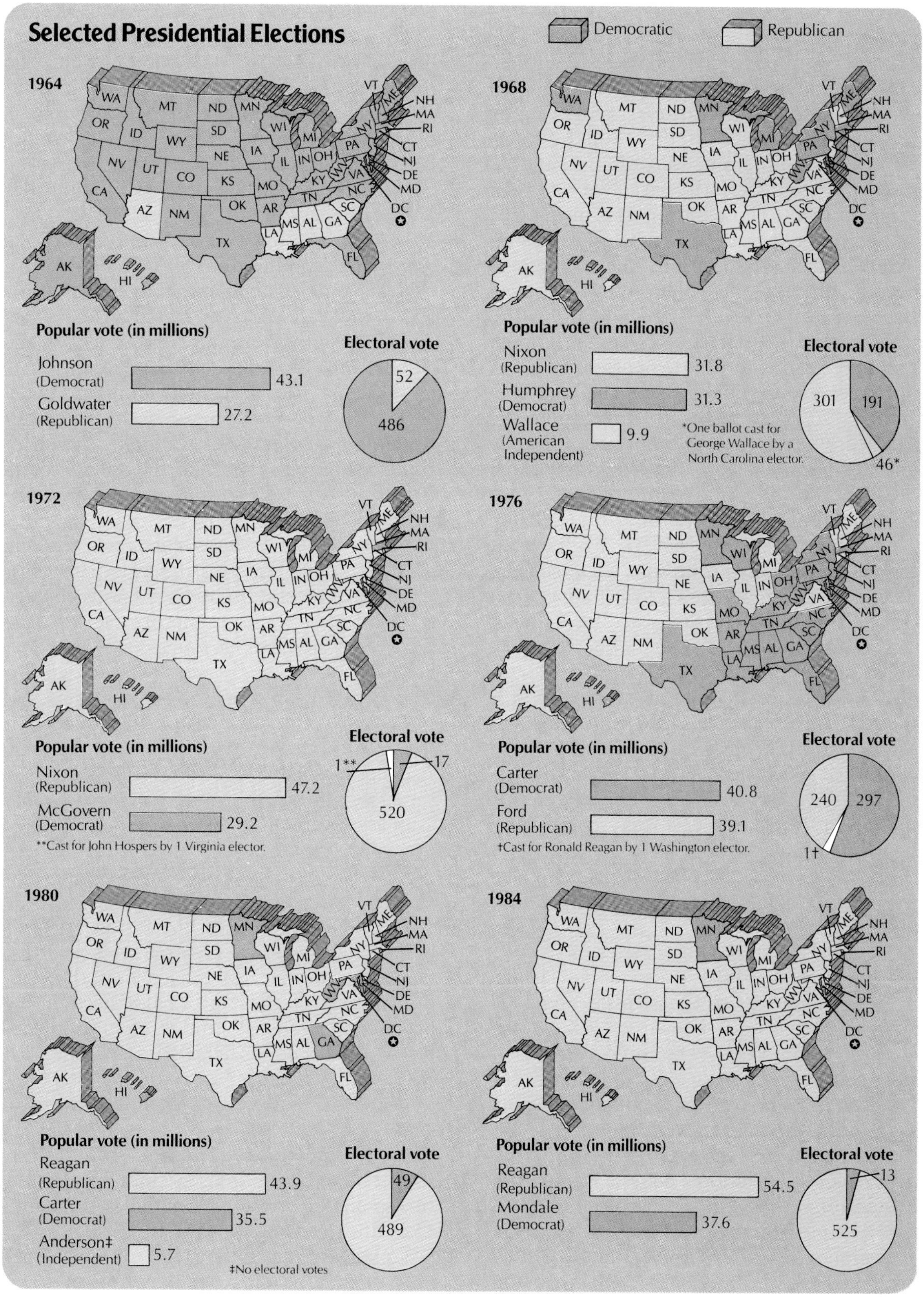

Selected Presidential Elections
Democratic
Republican
1964
Popular vote (in millions)
Johnson (Democrat) 43.1
Goldwater (Republican) 27.2
Electoral vote
52
486
1968
Popular vote (in millions)
Nixon (Republican) 31.8
Humphrey (Democrat) 31.3
Wallace (American Independent) 9.9
*One ballot cast for George Wallace by a North Carolina elector.
Electoral vote
301
191
46*
1972
Popular vote (in millions)
Nixon (Republican) 47.2
McGovern (Democrat) 29.2
**Cast for John Hospers by 1 Virginia elector.
Electoral vote
1**
17
520
1976
Popular vote (in millions)
Carter (Democrat) 40.8
Ford (Republican) 39.1
†Cast for Ronald Reagan by 1 Washington elector.
Electoral vote
240
297
1†
1980
Popular vote (in millions)
Reagan (Republican) 43.9
Carter (Democrat) 35.5
Anderson‡ (Independent) 5.7
‡No electoral votes
Electoral vote
49
489
1984
Popular vote (in millions)
Reagan (Republican) 54.5
Mondale (Democrat) 37.6
Electoral vote
13
525

Historical factors account for much of this pattern. Most of those who first settled this country were of English stock, and Protestant. The later tides of immigration, from southern and eastern Europe, brought many Catholics and Jews to the United States. Those later immigrants were often treated as minority groups by the largely Protestant establishment. Those immigrants most often settled in the larger cities, where local Democratic Party organizations helped them to become citizens and voters. From the New Deal period of the 1930s on, social welfare programs have strengthened the ties of most minority groups to the Democratic Party.

In 1960 John Kennedy became the first Roman Catholic President. His election was marked by a sharper split between Catholic and Protestant voters than in any of the others shown by the table on page 222.

Nonwhites support the Democratic Party —consistently and massively. Notice that they form the *only* group that has given the Democratic candidate a clear majority in *every* presidential election since 1952. Black Americans make up the single most important racial minority in the country. Northern blacks generally voted Republican until the 1930s. They moved away from the party of Abraham Lincoln with the coming of the New Deal, however. The civil rights movement of the 1960s led to greater black participation in the South—and there, too, blacks now vote overwhelmingly Democratic.

GEOGRAPHY. Geography—the locale in which a person lives—has an impact on voter behavior.

After the Civil War, the States of the old Confederacy voted so consistently Democratic that the entire Southeast quarter of the nation became known as the Solid South. For more than a hundred years now, most southerners, regardless of income, occupation, education, or any other factor, have been Democrats. Beginning in the 1960s, the Solid South disappeared in terms of presidential elections, but the Democrats still dominate most of southern politics.

Over time, the strongest and most consistent support for the Republicans by States can be found in Maine and Vermont in the Northeast and in Kansas, Nebraska, and the Dakotas in the Midwest. Lately, there has been much speculation about present and future voting patterns in the "Sunbelt" —that area stretching from the southeastern States westward to California. Some analysts see the region as a base for increased conservatism and new strength for the Republican Party in national politics.

Voters' attitudes also vary in terms of the size of the communities in which they live —larger cities, suburban areas, smaller cities, or rural areas. In general, the Democrats draw strength from the big cities of the North and East. Many white Democrats have moved from the central cities and taken their political preferences with them, but Republican voters still dominate much of suburban America. Outside the South, voters in the smaller cities and rural areas are likely to be Republicans.

FAMILY, OTHER GROUP AFFILIATIONS. To this point, we have sketched the American voter in terms of several broad social and economic characteristics. Our picture can also be drawn on the basis of much more personal groupings—especially such primary groups as family, co-workers, and friends.

Typically, the members of a family vote in strikingly similar ways. Nine out of ten married couples have the same partisan leanings; regularly, a husband and wife vote almost exactly alike. As many as two out of every three voters follow the political attachments of their parents. Co-workers and friends vote very much alike.

We shall come back to the effects that primary groups have on a person's political views in Chapter 10. Notice that the likemindedness of these groups is hardly surprising. People with similar social and economic backgrounds tend to associate with one another. Group associations often reinforce a voter's already held opinions. *

The Psychological Factors Again, it would be wrong to give too much weight to the sociological factors in the voting mix. They are clearly important, but they are also fairly static. That is, they tend to change only very gradually and over a period of time.

*REINFORCEMENT Write the sociological factors as headings on the board. Have the students discuss how they are affected by these factors, and write their responses under the appropriate heading.

FOCUS ON:

The Log Cabin Campaign

Before the coming of radio and then television, political candidates had to rely on other attention-getting devices to project their images. Just as candidates do today, they tried to create favorable images of themselves in the voters' minds.

However they went about it, most wanted to be seen as capable, hard-working, high-principled personalities dedicated to the public good. To that end, candidates have long used a variety of gimmicks, props, and other paraphernalia—from ribbons, flags, buttons, and bandannas to mugs, umbrellas, sunglasses, and peanuts—to grab the voter's attention.

The presidential contest of 1840 featured a classic example of campaign gimmickry. When the Whigs picked William Henry Harrison to run against President Martin Van Buren, a scornful Democrat said that all the 68-year-old hero of the War of 1812 really wanted to do was sit by his log cabin and swig hard cider.

Harrison's supporters quickly seized on that remark, trying to suggest that he had come from a humble, "man of the people" background. (He was, in fact, the son of a wealthy Virginia planter; and though he did own a log cabin, it had five rooms and by 1840 was a very large and attractive home.) From that point on, Harrison campaigned from a log cabin—which he'd had built on top of a wagon, with a seemingly bottomless barrel of cider attached to it. The crowds loved it, and Harrison won the election handily.

1. Why did Harrison use this slogan in 1840: "Tippecanoe and Tyler, too"?
2. What unusual, out-of-the-ordinary campaign devices have you seen?
3. If you were to run for office, how would you try to create a favorable public image?
4. Create an effective television campaign advertisement for yourself as a candidate for public office.

This hand-sewn silk banner promoted the candidacy of Whig Party nominee William Henry Harrison in 1840.

Party Identification in the American Electorate, 1940–1986

Year	Democrat	Republican	Independent
1986	39%	32%	29%
1984	40	31	29
1982	45	26	29
1980	46	24	30
1978	48	23	29
1976	47	23	30
1974	44	24	33
1972	43	28	29
1970	45	29	26
1968	46	27	27
1964	53	25	22
1960	47	30	23
1950	45	33	22
1940	42	38	20

Source: The Gallup Report, No. 250, July, 1986. (The question: "In politics, as of today, do you consider yourself a Republican, a Democrat, or an Independent?")

The percentage of Catholics or Jews or Protestants in the population remains fairly steady, for example. Yet, the electorate sometimes behaves very differently from one election to the next. Thus, Jimmy Carter won the Presidency with just over 50 percent of the popular vote in 1976, but he received only 41 percent of that vote and lost the office to Ronald Reagan in 1980.

So, in order to understand the voting process, we must look beyond such factors as occupation, level of education, ethnic background, and place of residence. We must also take into account a number of psychological factors. That is, we must look at the voters' *perceptions* of politics: how they see and how they react to the parties, the candidates, and the issues in an election.

PARTY IDENTIFICATION. Most Americans identify themselves with one or the other of the two major parties early in life. Many never change. They quite regularly support that party, election after election, and with little or no regard for either the candidates or the issues.

The hefty impact of **party identification**—party loyalty—on how people vote can be seen in the table above and on page 222. However it may have been acquired, party identification is the single most significant and lasting predictor of how a person will vote. A person who is a Democrat or a Republican will, for that reason, very likely vote for all or most of that party's candidates in an election.[21]

Party identification is, then, a key factor in American politics. Among many other things, it means that the major parties can regularly count on votes of millions of supporters in every election. The Democrats have enjoyed a substantial advantage over the Republicans in this matter.

Several signs suggest that, while it remains a major factor, party identification has lost some of its impact in recent years. One of those signs is the weakened condition of the parties themselves (see pages 200–201). Another is the marked increase in **split-ticket voting**—voting for candidates of *both* parties at the same election. That practice has increased remarkably since the 1960s.

[21] The practice of voting for the candidates of but one party in an election is known as **straight-ticket voting.** That behavior may or may not be an unthinking, irrational act. But a voter may have come to the conscious, thoughtful conclusion that that party best serves his or her own particular interests.

Another telling sign is the large number of voters who now call themselves **independents**. But "independent" is a very tricky term.[22] Many who claim to be independents actually support one or the other of the major parties quite regularly.

The loose nature of party membership makes it very difficult to determine just what proportion of the electorate is independent. The best estimate is between a fourth and a third of all voters today.

In the past, independents were generally less active in politics than those voters who identified themselves as Republicans or Democrats. A new breed appeared in the 1960s and 1970s, however. Largely because of the political events and personalities of that period, these "new" independents do not wish to join either major party. But they are like party identifiers in many ways, except that they are likely to be younger and above average in education, income, and job status.

CANDIDATES AND ISSUES. From much of what we have said about party identification, one might very well ask this question: How does the Republican Party ever win a presidential election? The answer consists of candidates and issues.

Party identification is a *long-term* factor. Most voters identify with one or the other of the major parties, and over time, they most often support its candidates. But they don't *always* vote that way. One or more *short-term* factors may cause them to switch sides in a particular election—or, at the least to vote a split ticket. For example, look again at the table on page 222—and notice that one out of every five voters who normally vote Democratic voted for Ronald Reagan in 1984.

[22]"Independent" is regularly used to identify those voters who have no partisan affiliation—voters who are independent of both the Republicans and the Democrats. But, notice, it is also sometimes *mistakenly* used in ways that suggest that independents form a more or less cohesive group in politics, and one that can be readily compared with Republicans and/or Democrats. Although the Gallup Poll tables on pages 222 and 226 do not intend such comparisons, they can be misread to that effect. In short, independents are not only independent of Republicans and Democrats; independents are also independent of all other independents.

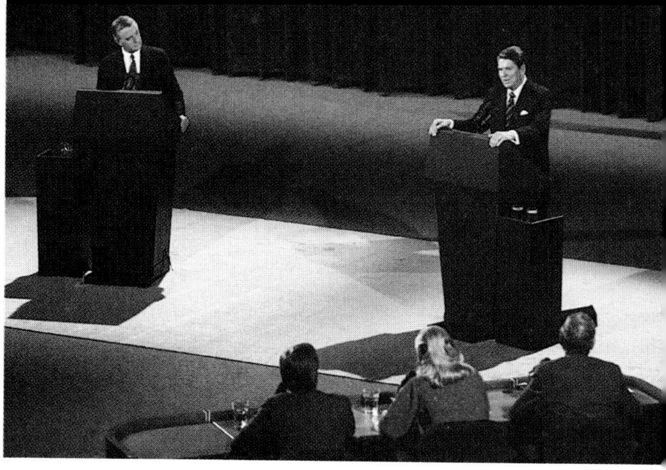

A televised debate reaches millions of voters.

The most important of these short-term factors are the candidates and the issues in an election. Clearly, the impressions a candidate makes on the voters can have an impact on how they vote. What "image" does a candidate project? How is he or she seen in terms of personality, character, style, appearance, past record, abilities, and so on?

Just as clearly, issues can also have a large impact on voter behavior. Their role varies from election to election, however, depending on such things as the emotional content of the issues themselves, the voters' awareness of them, and the ways in which they are presented to the electorate.

Issues now play a larger part in voter decisions than was true as recently as the early 1960s. The tumultuous nature of American politics over the past 20 years or so—highlighted by the civil rights movement, the Vietnam War, the Watergate scandal, and continuing economic problems—is likely responsible for renewed concern with issues.

FOR REVIEW

1. **Identify:** voter behavior, sociological factors, group affiliations.
2. List three of the sociological factors that affect voting behavior.
3. Why is it important not to give too much weight to any one of these factors?
4. List three of the psychological factors that affect voting behavior.
5. What is the most significant, lasting indicator of an individual's voting behavior?

*REINFORCEMENT Have the class discuss: Which is more important, party identification or the candidates and issues? Point out the short- and long-term factors involved with each of these.

SUMMARY

Some 178 million persons—just about every American citizen who is at least 18 years of age—can qualify to vote. The history of the right to vote in this country has been marked by two long-term trends: (1) the gradual elimination of such restrictive requirements as those based on property, race, and sex, and (2) more and more federal control over voting rights.

Voting qualifications are set by the States, subject to the limits set by the Constitution —most importantly the 15th, 19th, and 26th Amendments. All States now impose qualifications based upon citizenship and residence. The 26th Amendment sets 18 as the minimum voting age in all elections. Every State, except North Dakota, has a voter registration system intended to prevent fraudulent voting. The States commonly bar mentally impaired persons, felons, and some others from voting.

Congress has passed several laws in recent years to implement the 15th Amendment's guarantee: the Civil Rights Acts of 1957, 1960, and 1964, and the Voting Rights Act of 1965 and its substantial amendments in 1970, 1975, and 1982.

Millions of potential voters fail to vote for a number of reasons—but, chiefly, out of a lack of interest. About a fourth of the nonvoter population can be more accurately called "cannot-voters."

Extensive studies of voter behavior indicate that how people vote is heavily influenced by a number of (1) sociological factors—such characteristics as a voter's income, occupation, education, age, race, and so on, and his or her primary group affiliations—especially family, co-workers, and friends, and (2) psychological factors—how the voter sees the parties, candidates, and issues in an election. Of these factors, the single most important and lasting predictor of a person's voting behavior is his or her party identification.

CHAPTER REVIEW

Key Terms/Concepts*

suffrage (204)
franchise (204)
electorate (205)
precinct (208)
ward (208)
registration (210)
literacy (210)
poll tax (211)
gerrymandering (213)
injunction (213)
political efficacy (218)
political socialization (220)
party identification (226)
straight-ticket voting (226)
split-ticket voting (226)
independents (227)

*These terms are included in the Glossary.

Keynote Questions

• **1.** What are the five historical stages of the expansion of suffrage in the United States?

• **2.** Why is property ownership considered an unconstitutional restriction of suffrage?

• **3.** What two justifications are offered for the residence requirement?

• **4.** What is permanent voter registration?

• **5.** Why have Congress and the Supreme Court outlawed literacy tests and poll taxes as suffrage requirements?

• **6.** What event prompted enactment of the Voting Rights Act of 1965? What are its major provisions?

• **7.** What is the difference between a "cannot-voter" and an actual nonvoter?

• **8.** Explain two possible reasons for nonvoting.

• **9.** Most of the data on voter behavior comes from what three sources?

• **10.** What is the single most reliable indicator of the way in which the typical voter will cast his or her vote?

• **11.** How do independents differ from straight-ticket voters?

The dots represent skill levels required to answer each question or complete each activity: • requires recall and comprehension • • requires application and analysis • • • requires synthesis and evaluation

• **12.** What are two of the most important short-term factors affecting voter behavior?

Skill Application

Interpreting Tables: Tables consolidate numerical information so that the data is easier to study. By examining a table, you can compare information and detect trends over time.

For example, look at the "Occupation" category on the table on page 222. You will find that since 1952, most professionals and business people have voted for the Republican presidential candidate in every election except 1964. You can conclude that professionals and business people tend to vote for Republican presidential candidates.

Be aware, however, that the statistics in this table do not describe individuals. Rather, they describe group behavior or choices over time. You can conclude that within a large group of business people, most will probably vote for a Republican. You cannot conclude that because someone is a business person, he or she will vote Republican.

1. To analyze a table, you must first consider what data is presented and in what form it is presented. For the table on page 222, answer the following questions:
  - **a.** What is the title of the table?
  - **b.** What do the vertical headings represent?
  - **c.** What do the horizontal categories represent?
  - **d.** Is the numerical information presented in whole numbers or percentages?
  - **e.** If the data are percentages, of what are they a part?

2. Examine the table more closely. Answer the following questions with specific information from the table:
  - **a.** From 1952–1984, for which party's presidential candidate did people under age 30 tend to vote?
  - **b.** Did women or men support the Republican candidate more strongly in 1976? In 1984?
  - **c.** Since 1972, which regions of the country have most strongly supported the Republican candidate?
  - **d.** Which party's candidate usually finds the strongest support among labor union family members?

For Thought and Discussion

••• **1.** What are the pros and cons of a compulsory voting law? Would you be for or against such a law? Why?

••• **2.** Some criticize the election system in the United States for placing more emphasis on *quantity* of voter turnout rather than the *quality* of that participation. What is meant by quality of participation in voting? Do you think this is a valid criticism? Why or why not?

•• **3.** For what purposes might a political party use the table on page 222, "Voting by Groups in Presidential Elections, 1952–1984"? How might a candidate make use of this information?

•• **4.** What factors may contribute to a person's sense of alienation and, therefore, to nonvoting? What factors contribute to an individual's sense of political efficacy?

Suggested Activities

••• **1.** For an oral report to the class, find out the voting qualifications and voter registration process in your State. Check with the registrar, town or county clerk, or other local election officials. If possible, request sample registration materials.

••• **2.** Obtain information on election returns for the most recent general election in your State. These data are usually available in the State's *Manual* or *Blue Book* or from the secretary of state's office. Analyze the data based on voter turnout (see text pages 216-220) and/or voter behavior (see text pages 220-227). Are the trends in your State similar to or different from the national trends discussed in the text?

••• **3.** Using resources in your school or local library, research the voter turnout in the national elections of two other nations, for example, West Germany, New Zealand, France, Great Britain, Canada, and Australia. Make a table or a graph comparing voter turnout in these two nations with voter turnout in the United States.

As citizens of this democracy, you are the rulers and the ruled, the lawgivers and the law-abiding, the beginning and the end.
–Adlai Stevenson

9 Government by the People: The Electoral Process

CHAPTER OBJECTIVES

To help you to

Learn · Know · Understand

The critical place of the electoral process in democratic government.

The methods by which nominations are made in American politics.

The conduct of elections in the United States.

The place of money and its regulation in American politics.

In a representative democracy, there must be some means by which the people can choose those who govern—the officials who represent the people in the conduct of the people's business. There must also be some method by which those who govern with the consent of the people can be held accountable to the people.* Popular election is the only technique we know that meets both of these democratic needs.

In the United States, we elect far more public officeholders than most people realize —*more than 490,000* of them, in fact. We also hold far more elections than most people realize. Indeed, Sundays and holidays are about the only days in any year on which people do not go to the polls somewhere in this country.

In this chapter we deal with the two basic stages of the electoral process: (1) the nomination of candidates for public office and (2) the **general election**—the final selection of officeholders from among those who have been nominated. We shall also look at the very complex and troublesome matter of money in the electoral process.

*REINFORCEMENT Ask the class to discuss the relationship between periodic elections and the concept of representative government. Stress the factor of accountability.

Above: A tumultuous moment at the 1984 Republican National Convention. *Facing page:* A detail from "The Lost Bet," a painting by Joseph Klir, depicts Chicagoans celebrating Grover Cleveland's victory in the 1892 presidential election.

1. The Nominating Process: Several Methods

As You Read, Think About:

- What the procedures are for nominating candidates.
- Why the caucus system was replaced by the convention method for nominating candidates.

The nominating process is the process of candidate selection—the choosing or naming of those who will seek office. Candidates are nominated in a number of different ways in American politics.

But, whatever the method used, remember this crucial point: The making of nominations is a very significant matter, and from a number of standpoints. We have already seen two important illustrations of this. In Chapter 7, we discussed the making of nominations (1) as a prime function of political parties in the United States (page 180) and (2) as a leading reason for the decentralized character of the major parties in the American two-party system (page 197).

The nominating process has a very real impact on the exercise of the right to vote. In the typical election in this country, voters can make one of two choices for each office: They can vote for the Republican candidate or they can vote for the Democratic candidate.[1] As we have said before, this is another way of saying that we have a two-party system. It is also another way to say that the nominating process is critically important: Those who make nominations place real,

[1]The exception is nonpartisan elections; see page 237. Other choices are sometimes listed, of course—minor party or, once in a while, independent nominees. But these are not often meaningful alternatives; most voters choose not to "waste" their votes; see page 183. In 1980, for example, the very substantial campaign for independent candidate John B. Anderson produced only 6.6 percent (only one of every 16) of the votes cast in the presidential election.

practical limits on the choices that voters * can make in an election.

In one-party constituencies—those areas where one party regularly wins elections —the nominating stage is the only point at which there is usually any real contest for a public office. Once the dominant party has made its nominations, the general election is little more than a formality.

Dictatorial regimes underscore the importance of the nominating process. In the Soviet Union, for example, the way in which popular elections are held is much the same as it is in the United States. The comparison ends there, however. In Soviet elections, only candidates who are acceptable to the Communist Party can be nominated. Typically, the ballot lists only one candidate for each office. It is hardly surprising that the candidates who win office in the Soviet Union regularly win with majorities of 98 to 100 percent of all of the votes cast.

Methods used to nominate candidates in this country fall into five categories: (1) self-announcement, (2) caucus, (3) convention, (4) direct primary, and (5) petition.

Self-announcement

Self-announcement is the oldest form of the nominating process in American politics. First used in colonial times, it is still often found at the small-town and rural levels in many parts of the country.

The method is quite simple. A person who wishes to run for an office simply announces that fact. Modesty or local custom may dictate that someone else make the candidate's announcement, but even so the process amounts to the same thing.

The process is sometimes used by someone who tried for but failed to win a regular party nomination or by someone who is not happy with the party's choice. Note that whenever a "write-in" candidate appears in an election, the self-announcement process has been used.

Three prominent presidential contenders have made use of that process in recent years: George Wallace, the American Independent Party's nominee in 1968, and independent candidates Eugene McCarthy in 1976 and John Anderson in 1980.

The Caucus

As a nominating device,[2] a **caucus** is a group of like-minded persons who meet to select the candidates they will support in an upcoming election.

The first caucus nominations were made toward the end of the colonial period, probably in Boston in the mid-1720s. One of the earliest descriptions of the device can be found in John Adams's diary, in an entry he made in February 1763:

> This day learned that the Caucus club meets at certain times in the garret of Tom Dawes, the Adjutant of the Boston regiment. He has a large house, and he has a movable partition which he takes down, and the whole club meets in one room. There they smoke tobacco until you cannot see from one end of the garret to the other. There they drink flip, I suppose, and they choose a moderator who puts questions to the vote regularly; and selectmen, assessors, collectors, fire-wards, and representatives are regularly chosen before they are chosen in the town.[3]

Originally the caucus was a private meeting of a few influential figures in a locale. As political parties appeared, they soon took over the device and began to broaden the membership of the caucus.

The coming of independence brought the need to nominate candidates for governor, lieutenant governor, and other offices above the local level. That need was met rather

[2]Generally, the term *caucus* is used to describe any private meeting at which party members decide on some course of political action. Most often, it is used in connection with a legislative body today. The **legislative caucus** is now a meeting of a party's members in the legislature to decide on matters of legislative organization, committee assignments, the party's position on bills, and the like; see page 317.

[3]Charles Francis Adams (ed.), *The Works of John Adams* (Boston: Little, Brown, 1856), vol. II, p. 144. The origin of the term *caucus* is not clear. Most authorities suggest that it comes from the word *caulkers,* because the Boston Caucus Club met at times in a room formerly used as a meeting place by the caulkers in the Boston shipyards. (Caulkers made ships watertight by filling seams or cracks in the hulls of sailing vessels with tar or oakum.)

*REINFORCEMENT Ask the class: How does the nominating process limit the exercise of the right to vote? Emphasize the "sifting" character and range of choice consequences of nominations.

quickly in most of the new States. The legislative caucus, a meeting of a party's members in the State legislature, took on the job. By 1800 both the Federalists and the Democratic-Republicans in Congress were choosing their presidential and vice presidential candidates through the congressional caucus.

The legislative and congressional caucuses were quite practical in their day. Transportation and communication were difficult at best, and legislators regularly came together in a central place. The spread of democracy, especially in the newer States on the frontier, spurred opposition to caucuses, however. More and more, they were condemned for their closed and unrepresentative character.

Criticism of the caucus reached its peak in the early 1820s. The supporters of three of the leading contenders for the Presidency in 1824—Andrew Jackson, Henry Clay, and John Quincy Adams—boycotted the Democratic-Republicans' congressional caucus that year. In fact, Jackson and his people made "King Caucus" a leading campaign issue. The other major aspirant, William H. Crawford of Georgia, became the caucus nominee at a meeting attended by fewer than one-third of the party's members in Congress.

Crawford ran a poor third in the electoral college balloting in 1824, and the reign of "King Caucus" at the national level was ended. With its death in presidential politics, the caucus system soon withered at the State and local levels, as well.

The caucus is still used to make local nominations in some places, especially in New England. There a caucus is open to all members of a party, and it looks only faintly like the original device.

Tammany Hall in New York City, site of the 1868 Democratic National Convention, where 22 roll calls were needed to nominate Horatio Seymour for President.

The Convention

As the caucus method collapsed, its place was taken by the convention. The first national convention, to nominate a presidential candidate, was held by a minor party, the Anti-Masons, which met in Baltimore in 1831. Both the Democrats and then the newly formed Whigs picked up the practice in 1832. All major party presidential nominees have been chosen by conventions ever since. By the 1840s conventions had become the major means for making nominations at every level in American politics.

On paper, the convention process seems ideally suited to representative government. A party's members meet in a local caucus to pick candidates for local offices and, at the same time, to select delegates to represent them at a county convention.[4] At the county convention, the delegates nominate candidates for county offices and also select delegates to the next rung on the convention ladder, usually the State convention. There, the delegates from the county conventions pick the party's nominees for governor and other State-wide offices. State conventions also send delegates to the party's national convention, where its presidential and vice presidential candidates are chosen.

In the theory of the convention system, the will of the party's rank and file membership is passed on up through each of its representative levels. Practice soon pointed up the weaknesses of the theory, however, as party bosses found ways to manipulate the new process. By playing with the selection of delegates, mainly at the local levels, they soon dominated the entire system.

The caliber of most conventions, at all levels, declined, especially in the late 1800s. How low some of them fell can be seen in this description of a Cook County (Chicago) convention in 1896:

Campaign ribbons of Whig Party candidates nominated by conventions in the 1840s.

> Of [723] delegates, those who had been on trial for murder numbered 17; sentenced to the penitentiary for murder or manslaughter and served sentence, 7; served terms in the penitentiary for buglary, 36; served terms in the penitentiary for picking pockets, 2; served terms in the penitentiary for arson, 1; . . . jailbirds identified by detectives, 84; keepers of gambling houses, 7; keepers of houses of ill-fame, 2; convicted by mayhem, 3; ex-prize fighters, 11; poolroom operators, 2; saloon keepers, 265; . . . political employees, 148; . . . no occupation, 71; . . .[5]

Many had hailed the change from caucus to convention as a major reform. The abuses of the newer device soon dampened that view, however. The convention system was attacked as a source of evil in American politics. Gradually, and finally by the 1910s, it was replaced by the direct primary as the principal nominating method.

The direct primary is now used for all or at least most nominations in most States. The convention is still used in some States,

[4]The meetings at which delegates to local conventions are chosen are still often called *caucuses*. Earlier, they were also known as *primaries*—that is, first meetings. The use of that name gave rise to the term *direct primary*, to distinguish that newer nominating method from the convention process; see page 235.

[5]R.M. Easley, "The Sine-qua Non of Caucus Reform," *Review of Reviews*, September, 1897, p. 322.

however—in Connecticut, Michigan, Utah, and Virginia, for example, where it is closely regulated by State law. No adequate substitute for the convention has yet been found at the presidential level, as we shall see in Chapter 14.

FOR REVIEW

1. **Identify:** nomination, one-party constituency, self-announcement, convention.
2. What is the nominating process? Why is it an important part of the electoral process?
3. Which of the nominating methods now used is the oldest?
4. Why was the use of the caucus as a nominating device abandoned for the most part in the early 1800s?
5. Why does the convention method seem, in theory, well suited to representative government?

A portion of an 1864 campaign ticket. Sometimes, a ticket was, in fact, used as a ballot.

2. The Nominating Process: The Direct Primary; Petition

As You Read, Think About:

- What the different kinds of primary elections are.
- What the advantages and disadvantages are of the different kinds of primaries.
- How the petition is used as a nominating device.

The direct primary and petition are part of the nominating process. As you will read, there are various types of direct primary.

The Direct Primary

A **direct primary** is an *intra-party* nominating election. It is an election held *within* the party to pick its candidates for the general election.

Wisconsin adopted the first Statewide direct primary law in 1903, and several other States soon followed its lead. Every State now makes at least some provision for its use.

In most of them, State law requires that the major parties use the primary to choose their candidates for the United States Senate and House, for the governorship and all other State offices, and for most local offices, as well. In a few States, different combinations of convention and primary are used to pick candidates for the top offices. In Indiana and Michigan, the major parties must select their candidates for the U.S. Senate and House and for governor and lieutenant governor in primaries; nominees for other State offices are picked in conventions.[6]

Although the primaries are *party* nominating elections, they are now closely regulated in most States. The State usually sets the dates on which they are held and regularly conducts them. The State, not the parties,

[6] In most States minor parties are required to make their nominations by convention or petition—an important point, as we noted on page 183.

REINFORCEMENT Ask the class: Why can the evolution of the nominating process from caucus to convention to direct primary be described as the democratization of that process?

provides polling places and election officials, registration lists and ballots, and otherwise polices the process.

Two basic forms of the direct primary are used today: (1) the closed primary and (2) the open primary. The major difference between the two lies in the answer to this question: *Who* can vote in a party's primary —*only* those qualified voters who are *also* party members, or *any* qualified voter, without regard to party preference?

The Closed Primary Thirty-eight States[7] now use the **closed primary**—a party nominating election in which *only* declared party members may vote. It is *closed* to all others.

In most of the closed primary States, party membership is established by registration (see page 210). When voters appear at the polling places on primary election day, their names are checked against the poll books, which are the lists of registered voters for each precinct. Each voter is then handed the ballot of the party in which he or she is registered.

In the other closed primary States, voters simply declare their party preference at the polling place. In some States, that settles the matter; the person may vote in that party's primary. In other States, however, that person may be challenged by a party's poll watcher. If that happens, the voter is most often required to take an oath of party loyalty, swearing that he or she has supported that party and its candidates in the past and/or now does so.

The Open Primary Although it is the form the direct primary first took, the open primary is now found in only 12 States.[8] The **open primary** is a party nominating election in which *any* qualified voter may take part.

Volunteers play a critical part in any candidate's campaign. Here, Mondale volunteers are at work during the New Hampshire primary.

That is, it is *open* to any such person. No one has to declare a party choice at registration or at any other time.

When voters appear at the polling place, they are handed either the ballots of all of the parties holding primaries or one large ballot containing the separate ballots of the various parties. Voters then pick the particular party primary in which they wish to vote and mark that ballot.

A different version of the open primary is used in Alaska and Washington, where it is known as the "wide-open" primary or **blanket primary.** In each of those States, the voter receives a single large ballot listing each party's contenders for each nomination. The voter can vote in a single party's primary, as in the typical open primary. *Or* the voter can vote to nominate a Democrat for one office, a Republican for another, and so on.

Louisiana has yet another form of the open primary. Its unique "open election" law provides for what amounts to a combination primary and election. The names of *all* persons who seek nominations are listed, by office, on a single primary ballot.[9] A contender who wins a majority of the votes cast in the primary then runs unopposed for that office in the general election. This really means that he or she is elected at the primary. If there is no majority winner, the two candidates receiving the most votes in each

[7]All of the states except Alaska, Hawaii, Idaho, Louisiana, Michigan, Minnesota, Montana, North Dakota, Utah, Vermont, Washington, and Wisconsin; the District of Columbia uses the closed primary.

[8]Alaska, Hawaii, Idaho, Louisiana, Michigan, Minnesota, Montana, North Dakota, Utah, Vermont, Washington, Wisconsin. But see the text comments on Alaska, Louisiana, and Washington.

[9]Each aspirant's name is listed with or without a party label, as he or she chooses.

ENRICHMENT Ask the class to discuss: Given the fact that primaries are party nominating elections, should the State play the large part each does in the conduct of those elections?

primary race, regardless of party, run against one another in the general election.

Pro and Con: The Closed* v. *the Open Primary Those who favor the closed primary state three arguments for it. (1) It keeps the members of one party from "raiding" the other's primary, in the hope of nominating weaker candidates in the other party.[10] (2) The closed primary helps to make candidates more responsive and responsible to the party, its platform, and its members. (3) It helps to make voters more thoughtful, because they must choose between the parties in order to vote in the primaries.

The critics of the closed primary make two principal arguments against it. (1) It compromises the secrecy of the ballot, because it forces voters to make their party preferences known in public. (2) The closed primary tends to exclude independent voters from the partisan nomination process.

The major arguments most often made *for* the open primary are, in effect, those usually made against the closed form. That is, the open primary (1) protects the secrecy of the ballot and (2) allows the independent voter to vote in the primary of his or her choice.

The opponents of the open primary insist that it (1) permits primary raiding and (2) undercuts the concepts of party loyalty and party responsibility.

The Runoff Primary In most States, candidates need to win only a *plurality* of the votes in the primary to win their party's nomination.[11]

In 10 States,[12] however, an absolute majority is needed. If no one wins a majority in a race, a **runoff primary** is held a few weeks later. In the runoff, the two top contenders in the first race face one another, and the winner becomes the nominee.

The Nonpartisan Primary In most States all or nearly all of the elective school and municipal offices are filled in **nonpartisan elections**—elections in which candidates are not identified by party labels.[13] About half of all State judges are chosen on nonpartisan ballots, as well.

The nomination of candidates for these offices takes place on a nonpartisan basis, too—often in nonpartisan primaries. In these primaries, contenders are not identified by party labels.

Typically, a contender who wins a clear majority in a nonpartisan primary then runs unopposed in the general election—subject to write-in opposition. In many States, however, a candidate who wins a majority in the primary is declared elected at that point. If there is no majority winner, the names of the two top contenders are placed on the general election ballot.

The direct primary first appeared as a partisan nominating device, as we have seen. Many have long argued that it is really not very well suited for use in nonpartisan election situations. They favor, instead, the petition method, to which we shall turn in a moment.

---

[10] Raiding the opposition primary became so common in the early years of the direct primary that the closed form was developed to prevent it. The tactic is still found in some open primary States today.

[11] Recall, a plurality is a greater number of votes than the number received by any other candidate, whether a majority or not. Iowa and South Dakota require a candidate to win at least 35 percent of the votes cast in a primary contest. If no aspirant wins that many votes in a given race, the party must then nominate its candidate for that office by convention.

[12] Alabama, Arkansas, Florida, Georgia, Mississippi, North Carolina, Oklahoma, South Carolina, Texas—and Louisiana under its unique "open election" law.

[13] A small segment of the progressive reform movement of the early 1900s hoped to do away with public corruption by doing away with both parties and partisan elections in all of American politics. Many of those reformers focused their nonpartisan efforts at the local level, especially in the bigger cities. Nonpartisanship remains an article of faith for many who favor local governmental reforms in many parts of the country today.

Many opponents of nonpartisanship insist that the label *nonpartisan* is often more apparent than real. They argue that nonpartisan candidates and officeholders are frequently known by their partisan attachments, and eliminating party labels from the local election process cannot hide that fact.

The ongoing spread of nonpartisanship at the local level, especially in cities, has weakened the two major parties, at least to some extent, by severing some of their grass-roots strength. It is one of the several factors in their continuing decline in American politics; see pages 200–201.

*ENRICHMENT Ask the class to debate this proposition: This State should abandon the present (open/closed) primary arrangement and replace it with the (open/closed) primary.

FOCUS ON:

Voting Rights and 17-Year-Old Voters in the Primaries

If you read the 26th Amendment carefully, you will see this point: It does *not* say that a person who is less than 18 years of age cannot be allowed to vote. Rather, it says that no State can deny the vote to anyone who is at least 18 years old and is otherwise qualified.

In short, any State can permit those who are less than 18 to vote, if it chooses to do so.

Given that fact, consider this question: Should a person whose 18th birthday falls *after* the primaries but *before* the general elections are held in November be allowed to vote in the earlier primaries as well as in the November elections?

Students at San Rafael High School in California felt that the answer to that question should be a loud "Yes." So, with their teacher, Dr. Virginia Franklin, they set out to change the situation in their State in 1976.

They began by researching the history of voting rights and studying the ins and outs of the legislative process. They received lobbying tips from several groups, including the American Civil Liberties Union and the National Education Association. They wrote to public officials at both the State and federal levels and prepared information packets for the members of the State legislature.

Their efforts, and those of students who have come after them, have led to the introduction of several bills in both the California legislature and in Congress. These measures would allow anyone who will be old enough to vote in November to vote in the earlier primaries, as well.

To this point, none of their bills has been passed, either in Sacramento or in Washington. But the students are far from discouraged. They continue to hope that what they see as a real inequity in voting rights will be overcome. They agree with the late Representative Leo Ryan, who, when he sponsored one of their bills in the House in 1978, said that "voting is the ultimate field trip for students."

1. Do you think that 17-year-olds should be able to vote in the circumstances involved here? Why or why not?
2. A few States do in fact allow 17-year-olds to vote in these circumstances. Find out which States do permit 17-year-olds to vote in primary elections.

Students from San Rafael, California, meet with Representative Barbara Boxer (D. Calif.) to discuss their primary-vote project.

By Brickman, © King Features Syndicate

Evaluation of the Primary The direct primary, whether it is open or closed, is an *intraparty nominating election.* This intraparty nominating process came about as a direct reaction to the boss-dominated convention system. Most importantly, the direct primary was intended to take the nominating function away from the party organization and put it in the hands of the party's membership.

However, these basic facts about the primary have never been very well understood by most of the electorate. Thus, many voters resent having to declare their party choice in those States that have a closed primary. Where the typical open primary is used, many are upset because they cannot nominate in more than one party. Many voters are also annoyed by the "bed-sheet ballot," not understanding that the use of the primary almost automatically dictates a long ballot.

It is fairly clear, too, that a large part of the electorate does not see the critical importance of the nominating stage. Thus, the turnout in the primaries in most States is usually less than half of that in the general elections.

The fact that voter turnout is usually much lower in primary elections leads to this little-recognized point: There are often * two quite different electorates involved in the electoral process. One of the electorates, the smaller of the two, is that group of voters who vote in the primaries. Clearly, this group is made up mostly of those persons who are most likely to vote. The other electorate, and the larger one, is that group of voters who take part in the general election. To really grasp this point, look again at the table on page 219 of those factors that affect voter turnout.

When two or more candidates seek the same nomination, primary campaigns can be quite expensive. The fact that successful contenders for the nomination must mount—and find the money for—yet another campaign (for the general election) adds to the money problems. It is unfortunately true that the financial facts of political life mean that some well-qualified people will not be able to seek public office. See pages 246–255.

The nominating process, whatever its form, can have a very divisive effect on the unity of party. It takes place *within* the party. So, when there are conflicts, that is where they occur—among the members of the *same* party. The direct primary magnifies this aspect of the nominating process, because primaries are so *public* in nature. A bitter contest in the primaries can so wound and divide a party that it cannot be healed and united in time for the general election. Many a primary fight has cost a party an election.

*REINFORCEMENT Ask students to explain, expand on the point that there are two different electorates in the electoral process.

Because many voters are not very well informed, the primary places a premium on "name familiarity." That is, it often gives an edge to a contender who has a well-known name or a name that sounds much like that of a well-known person. Note that name familiarity may have little or nothing to do with a contender's qualifications.

Clearly, the primary is not without its problems—nor is any other nominating device. Still, it does give a party's members the opportunity to participate at the very core of the political process.

The Presidential Primary The presidential primary developed as an offshoot of the direct primary. It is *not* a nominating device, however. It is, rather, an *election* that is held as a part of the presidential nominating process.

The presidential primary is a very complex device. It is one or both of two things, depending on the State involved. It is a process in which a party's voters elect some or all of a State party organization's delegates to that party's national convention. *And/or* it is a preference election in which voters may choose—vote their preference—among various contenders for a party's presidential nomination.

Much of what happens in presidential politics in the early months of every fourth year centers on this very complicated process. We shall take a much closer look at it in Chapter 14, where we consider the whole matter of presidential selection.

Petition

One other nominating method is fairly widely used in American politics today—nomination by petition. Here, candidates are nominated by petitions signed by a certain number of qualified voters in the election district.[14]

[14]The petition device is also used in several other aspects of the electoral process. Thus, it and/or a filing fee is generally the method by which an aspirant's name is placed on the direct primary ballot. It is also an important part of the recall (page 581), initiative, and referendum processes (pages 573–575).

Nomination by petition is found most widely at the local level, chiefly for nonpartisan school posts and municipal offices in middle-sized and smaller communities. It is also the process usually required by State law for the nomination of minor party and independent candidates. As we noted on page 183, the States frequently make the process purposefully difficult for them. *

The details of the petition process vary widely from State to State, and even from one city to the next. As a general rule, however, the higher the office and/or the larger the constituency involved, the greater the number of signatures needed for nomination.

FOR REVIEW

1. **Identify:** presidential primary, petition.
2. What is a direct primary?
3. What is the difference between an open primary and a closed primary?
4. What are the pros and cons of a closed primary? An open primary?
5. What is a wide-open primary?
6. What is a runoff primary? A nonpartisan primary?

3. Elections

As You Read, Think About:

- How elections are administered and controlled.
- Where and when voting takes place.
- What the different kinds of ballots are that are used in elections.
- What the different kinds of machines are that are used in some elections.

Once candidates have been nominated, they must face their opponents, and the voters, in the general election—in what H. G. Wells once called democracy's "feast, its great function."

Most often and in most places, election outcomes are not certain. In some elections,

*REINFORCEMENT Ask the class to describe, analyze, evaluate the procedures now used in your school to select student council members and/or other student body and class officers.

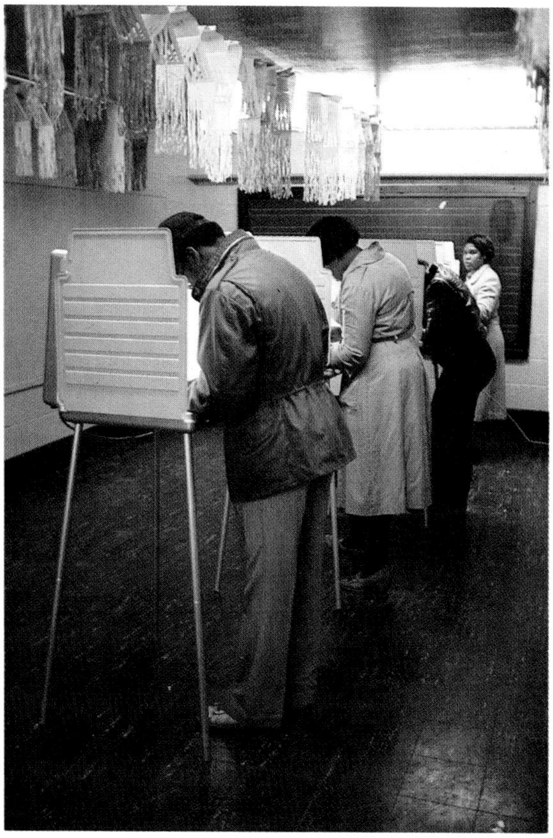

Voters exercise their right to vote at their precinct's polling place. What are the precinct board's responsibilities during elections?

however, the outcome is never in question. For example, this certainly is so in one-party constituencies. One of the parties is so dominant, so regularly and heavily supported by the voters that its candidates are just about certain of winning the election. In this case, as we noted on page 232, the nominating stage is far more important than the final election.

The Administration of Elections

Democratic government cannot succeed unless elections are free, honest, and accurate. Too many people look at the details of the election process as too complicated, too legalistic, too dry and boring, to worry about. But those who feel this way miss the vital part those details play in making democracy work.

How something *can* be done very often has a marked effect on what *is* done—and this is as true in politics as it is in other matters. The often lengthy and closely detailed provisions of election law are designed to protect the integrity of that process. Those provisions often have a telling significance on the outcome of elections, as well.

So far in our discussion of the election process, we have seen several demonstrations of that point—for example, when we looked at voter qualifications and at registration in the last chapter. We saw another only a few pages back, when we considered the details of the direct primary.

The Extent of Federal Control

Nearly all elections in this country are held to choose the more than 490,000 persons who hold public offices in the more than 80,000 units of government at the State and local levels. It is quite understandable, then, that the greatest bulk of election law in the United States is *State* law.

There is a body of federal election law, however. The Constitution gives to Congress the power to fix "the times, places, and manner of holding elections" of members of Congress.[15] Congress also has the power to set the time for choosing the presidential electors, to set the date for casting their electoral votes, and to regulate other aspects of the presidential election process.[16]

Congress has set the date for holding congressional elections as the first Tuesday following the first Monday in November of every even-numbered year. It has set the same date every fourth year for the presidential elections. Thus, the next (off-year) congressional elections will be held on November 6, 1990 and the next presidential election will be November 8, 1988.[17]

---

[15]Article I, Section 4, Clause 1; 17th Amendment; see pages 298–302.

[16]Article II, Section 1, Clause 4; 12th Amendment; see pages 391–393.

[17]Congress has made an exception for Alaska, which may, if it chooses, elect its congressional delegation and cast its presidential vote in October. Thus far, however, Alaska has used the November date.

Congress has required the use of secret ballots and allowed the use of voting machines in federal elections. It has passed several laws to protect the right to vote in all elections, as we saw on pages 212–215. It has also prohibited various corrupt practices and regulated the financing of campaigns for federal office, as we shall see on pages 246–255.

All other matters relating to national elections, and all of the details involved in choosing the many thousands of State and local officials, are dealt with in the laws of the individual States.

When Elections Are Held Most States hold their elections to fill State offices on the same date Congress has set for national elections—in November of every even-numbered year.[18]

Some States do fix other dates, however, for at least some offices. Thus, Louisiana, Mississippi, New Jersey, and Virginia elect the governor, other executive officers, and State legislators in November of the *odd*-numbered year. City, county, and other local election dates vary from State to State. Where those elections are not held in November, they generally take place in the spring.

The Coattail Effect Strong candidates running for top offices on the ballot can produce a **coattail effect.** Those candidates, with their broad appeal, can help to pull voters to other candidates on the party's ticket. In effect, the lesser known office-seekers "ride the coattails" of the more prestigious personalities. In 1980 and 1984, for example, Ronald Reagan's coattails helped many Republican candidates.

The coattail effect is usually most apparent in presidential elections. But a popular candidate for senator or governor can have the same kind of pulling power.

[18]The formula-like "Tuesday-after-the-first-Monday" is purposeful. It prevents election day from falling on Sundays, to maintain the principle of separation of church and state, and on the first day of the month, which is often payday and so peculiarly subject to campaign pressures.

There can be a *reverse* coattail effect, too. It comes when a candidate for high office is less than popular with many voters—for example, Barry Goldwater as the Republican presidential nominee in 1964, and George McGovern for the Democrats in 1972. Jimmy Carter had the same effect in 1980.

Some have long held that all State and local elections should take place on dates other than those set for federal elections. This, they say, would help make voters pay more attention to State and local candidates and issues making them less subject to the coattail effect.

Precincts and Polling Places

Precincts are voting districts. They are the basic and smallest geographic units for the conduct of elections. State law regularly restricts their size, generally to an area with no more than 500 or 1,000 or so qualified voters. A **polling place—**where the voters who live in a precinct may vote—is located somewhere in or near each precinct.

A precinct election board supervises the polling place and the voting process in each precinct. Typically, the county clerk or county board of elections draws precinct lines, fixes the polling place location, and picks the members of the precinct boards.

The precinct board opens and closes the polls at the times set by State law. In most States, the polls are open from 7 or 8 A.M. to 7 or 8 P.M.

The precinct board also has several other and important tasks. It must see that the ballots and the ballot boxes, or voting machines, are available. It must make certain that only qualified voters cast ballots in the precinct. The board must also count the votes and certify the results to the proper place, usually to the county clerk or board of elections.

Poll watchers, one from each party, are allowed at each polling place. They may challenge any person they have reason to believe is not qualified to vote, check to be sure that as many as possible of their own party's supporters do vote, and watch the

ENRICHMENT Ask the class: Did the fact that the Democrats nominated Geraldine Ferraro for the Vice Presidency have any kind of "coattail effect" in the 1984 presidential election? If so, what effect(s)? If not, why not?

Phil Gramm of Texas (at left), who won election to the U.S. Senate in 1984, on the Republican ticket, shared the speaker's platform for a moment with his party leader when President Reagan campaigned in Texas in 1984.

whole process, including the counting of the ballots, to ensure its fairness.

The Ballot

The ballot is the device by which a voter registers a choice in an election.[19] It can take a number of different forms. But, whatever its form, it is clearly an important and sensitive part of the electoral process.

Each of the States now provides for a secret ballot. That is, each requires that ballots be cast in such manner that others cannot know how a voter has voted—unless, of course, the voter wants to give out that information.

Voting was a public process through much of our earlier history. Paper ballots were used in some colonial elections, but voting was commonly by voice (*viva voce*). Voters simply stated their choices to election officials. With suffrage limited to the privileged few, oral voting was often defended as the only "manly" way in which to participate. Whatever the merits of that view, the expansion of the electorate brought with it a marked increase in intimidation, vote buying, and other corruptions of the voting process.

Paper ballots came into general use in the middle of the 19th century. The first ballots were unofficial—slips of paper that voters prepared themselves and dropped in the ballot box. Soon candidates and parties began to prepare ballots and hand them to voters to cast—sometimes paying them to do so. Those party ballots were often printed on colored paper, so that anyone watching could tell for what party voters were voting.

Political machines, strong in some areas and reaping their harvest from the unofficial ballots, fought all attempts to make voting a more dependably fair and honest process. The political corruption of the post–Civil

---

[19] The word comes from the Italian *balla*—"ball" or, more exactly, *ballota*—"little ball", and reflects the practice of dropping tokens (commonly black or white balls) into a box to indicate a choice. The term *blackball* comes from the same practice.

War years brought widespread demand for ballot reform, however.

The Australian Ballot A new voting arrangement was devised in Australia, where it was first used in an election in Victoria in 1856. It successes there led to its use in other countries. By 1900 nearly all of the States were using it, and it remains the basic form of the ballot in all of them today.

The Australian Ballot has four essential features: (1) it is printed at public expense; (2) it lists the names of all candidates in an election; (3) it is given out only at the polls, one to each qualified voter; and, (4) it is voted in secret.

Two basic varieties of the Australian ballot have developed over the years. In nearly half of the States the office-group version is used. The rest of the States use the party-column ballot.

* ***The Office-Group Ballot*** The office-group ballot is the original form of the Australian ballot. It is also sometimes called the Massachusetts ballot because of its early (1888) use there. On it, the candidates for each office are listed, or grouped, together. At first, the names of the candidates were listed in alphabetical order. In most States using the form, the names are now rotated, so that each candidate will have any psychological advantage there may be in having his or her name at the top of the list.

The Party-Column Ballot The party-column ballot is also known as the Indiana ballot, from its early (1889) use in that State. It lists each party's candidates in a column under the party's name. Often there is a square or circle at the top of each party's column, where with a single **X**, the voter can vote for all of that party's candidates.

Professional politicians tend to favor the party-column ballot. It encourages "straight-ticket" voting, especially if the party has a strong candidate at the head of the ticket. Most students of the political process favor the office-group form because it encourages voter judgment and "split-ticket" voting.

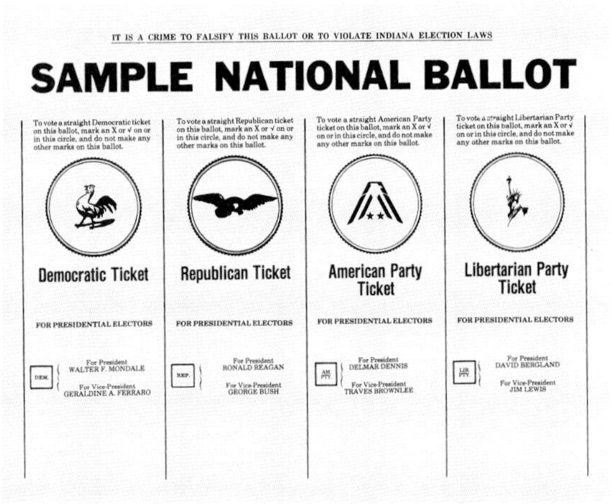

This party-column ballot from Indiana, 1984, lists the candidates by party name.

Sample Ballots Sample ballots, clearly marked as such, are available in most States. In some they are mailed to all voters before an election, and they appear in most newspapers. They cannot be cast, but they can help voters prepare for an election.[20]

The Long and the Short of It The ballot in a typical American election is a lengthy one, often and aptly called a "bed-sheet ballot." It often lists so many offices, so many candidates, and so many measures that even the most conscientious and well-informed voters have a difficult time marking it intelligently.

The long ballot came to American politics in the era of Jacksonian Democracy in the 1830s. Many held the view at the time that the greater the number of elective offices, the more democratic the governmental system. The idea remains widely accepted today.

Generally, the longest ballots are found at the local level, and especially among the nation's 3,000-odd counties. In most counties throughout the country, it is not at all unusual to find a large number of elected

[20]First in Oregon (1907), and now in several States, an official voter's pamphlet is mailed to all voters before an election. It lists all candidates and measures that will appear on the ballot. In Oregon each candidate is allowed space to present his or her qualifications and stands on the issues, and supporters and opponents of measures are allowed space to present their arguments, as well.

*ENRICHMENT Ask in class: Which of the ballots on this page, the office-group or the party-column, would you prefer if you were a candidate for public office? Ask each student to support the position he/she takes.

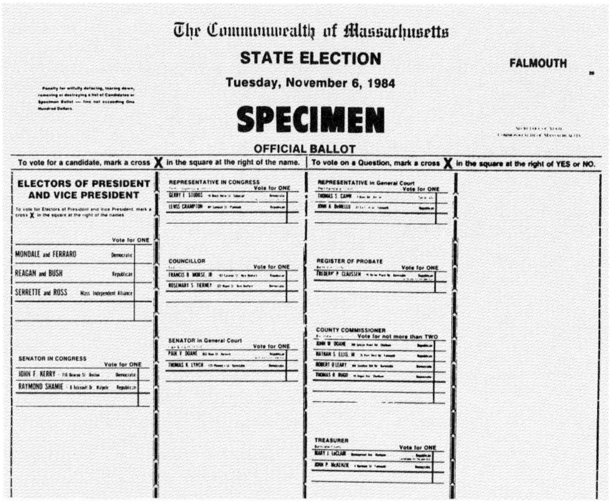
The Commonwealth of Massachusetts
STATE ELECTION
Tuesday, November 6, 1984
FALMOUTH
Penalty for wilfully defacing, tearing down, removing or destroying a list of Candidates or Specimen Ballot — fine not exceeding One Hundred Dollars.
SPECIMEN
OFFICIAL BALLOT
To vote for a candidate, mark a cross X in the square at the right of the name. | To vote on a Question, mark a cross X in the square at the right of YES or NO.

ELECTORS OF PRESIDENT AND VICE PRESIDENT
To vote for Electors of President and Vice President, mark a cross X in the square at the right of the names.
Vote for ONE
MONDALE and FERRARO — Democratic
REAGAN and BUSH — Republican
SERRETTE and ROSS — Mass. Independent Alliance

SENATOR IN CONGRESS — Vote for ONE
JOHN F. KERRY — Democratic
RAYMOND SHAMIE — Republican

REPRESENTATIVE IN CONGRESS — Vote for ONE
GERRY E. STUDDS
LEWIS CRAMPTON

COUNCILLOR — Vote for ONE
FRANCIS B. MORSE, JR.
ROSEMARY S. TIERNEY

SENATOR in General Court — Vote for ONE
PAUL V. DOANE
THOMAS K. LYNCH

REPRESENTATIVE in General Court — Vote for ONE
THOMAS S. CAPP
JOHN A. DeMELLO

REGISTER OF PROBATE — Vote for ONE

COUNTY COMMISSIONER — Vote for not more than TWO

TREASURER — Vote for ONE

This office-group ballot from Massachusetts, 1984, shows the candidates listed by office.

offices listed on ballots. The listing is likely to include several commissioners, a clerk, a sheriff, one or more judges, a prosecutor, a coroner, a treasurer, an assessor, a surveyor, a school superintendent, an engineer, a sanitarian, and in some places, even the proverbial dog-catcher.

Critics of the long ballot do not accept the argument that the more you elect the more democratic you are. They believe that quite the reverse is true: With a smaller number of elected offices to fill, the voter can better know the candidates and their qualifications. Critics also point to "ballot fatigue," the drop-off in voting that can run as high as 20 to 30 percent at or near the bottom of the ballot.

There seems little, if any, good reason to elect such local officials as clerks, coroners, surveyors, and engineers. Their jobs, and many others filled by the voters, do not carry basic policymaking responsibilities. Rather, they carry out policies made by others. For good government, the rule should be: *Elect* those who make public policies; *appoint* those who only administer them.

Voting Machines

Thomas Edison took out the first American patent for a voting machine. His invention was first used in an election in Lockport, New York, in 1892. The use of similar devices has long since spread to the election laws and polling places of every State.

Only a handful of States make the use of voting machines mandatory. Most often the machines are used only in some—usually the more populous—areas of a State. All told, however, more than half of all the votes in national elections today are cast on some form of voting machine.

The typical voting machine serves as its own booth. By pulling a lever, the voter encloses himself or herself within a three-sided curtain (the machine itself becomes the fourth side of the voting booth) and unlocks the machine. The ballot appears on the face of the machine, and the voter makes his or her choices by pulling down the small levers over the names of the candidates he or she favors. In most States using the party-column ballot, the voter may pull a master lever to vote a straight ticket.

The machine has space for measures, as well as candidates, with *yes* and *no* levers for each. The machine is programmed so that a voter can cast only one vote per contest. Once all levers are in their desired positions, the voter opens the curtain. That action records the votes and at the same time clears the machine for the next voter.

The use of voting machines does away with the need, and time, for manual vote counting, reduces the number of persons needed to administer elections, and speeds the voting process. It also increases the number of voters who can be handled per precinct, makes ballot mutilation impossible, and minimizes fraud and counting errors.

Electronic Vote Counting Electronic data processing (EDP) techniques have been applied to the voting process in recent years—first in California and Oregon and now, to at least some degree, in more than two-thirds of the States.

To date, EDP applications have followed two general lines. The most widely used adaptation involves punch-card ballots, which are counted by high-speed computers. The other involves paper ballots marked with sensitized ink and counted by optical scanners.

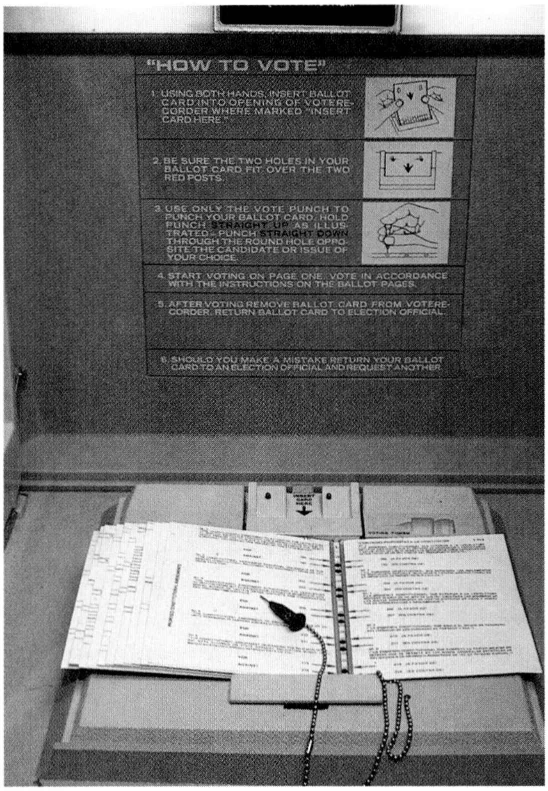

The punch card device is one of several voting machines in operation today. What advantages do these devices have over traditional ballots?

Vote-by-Mail Elections Some local elections are now conducted by mail—with mail-in ballots—in a handful of States around the country.

The first vote-by-mail election was held in Monterey County, California, in 1977. The first large-scale use of the process occurred in San Diego in 1981. Since then, mail-in ballots have been used in local elections in several other places, most notably in Kansas and Oregon.

Vote-by-mail elections have stirred a growing controversy. Critics fear that the process threatens the principle of the secret ballot and invites fraud. Its supporters say that it is, or can be made, as fraud-proof as any other method of voting. They also cite this fact: The process increases voter turnout in local elections and, at the same time, reduces the costs of conducting them.

The use of mail-in ballots has been confined to local issue elections—except in Oregon, where State law now allows their use in some local candidate elections.

FOR REVIEW

1. **Identify:** coattail effect, ballot.
2. Why are the details of the electoral process vital to the success of democratic government?
3. Why is most election law in this country State rather than federal law?
4. When are national elections held? When are most State general elections held? Why do some favor separate dates for national and for State and local elections?
5. What is the Australian ballot? How do the office-group and party-column forms of the ballot differ?
6. Why is the typical ballot used in American elections so lengthy? On what grounds are lengthy ballots criticized?

4. Money in Elections

As You Read, Think About:

- What the costs of elections are.
- Where money comes from to finance elections.
- What federal controls exist on election financing.

Political activities, especially campaigns for public office, cost money—and often a great deal of it. That fact gives rise to some of the most difficult of the many problems in American politics.

The threat is ever present that some candidates will try to buy their way into public office. Further, there is always the possibility that some special interest groups will try to buy favored treatment from those who are elected to office.

Our governmental system must be guarded against these dangers. But how? Parties and their candidates *must* have money. Without it, they cannot campaign. That is, they cannot take steps to inform the voters

*ENRICHMENT Some people advocate vote-by-mail elections as a way to increase voter turnout and reduce election costs. Have the class discuss the concept and the question of whether they would like to see such elections in their locale.

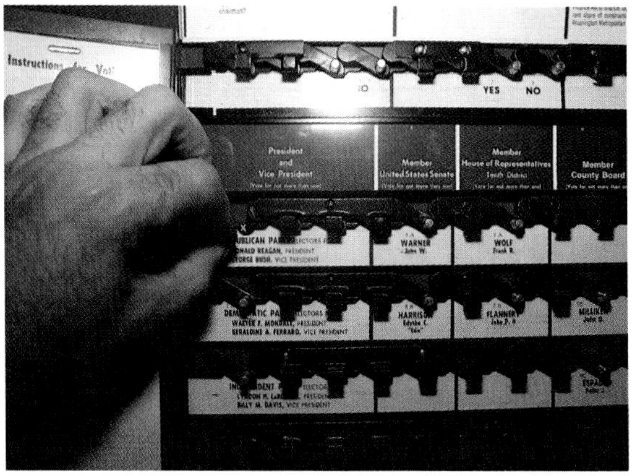

Ballots are cast by pulling a series of levers with this voting machine.

Total Campaign Spending, 1952-1984

	Estimated Spending	Vote Cast for President	Cost per Voter
1952	$140 million	61.6 million	$2.28
1956	155 million	62.0 million	2.50
1960	175 million	68.8 million	2.54
1964	200 million	70.6 million	2.83
1968	300 million	73.2 million	4.10
1972	425 million	77.7 million	5.47
1976	540 million	81.6 million	6.62
1980	1.2 billion	86.5 million	13.87
1984	1.8 billion	92.6 million	19.38

and attract their support, In short, dollars are an absolutely necessary campaign resource. Yet, the getting and the spending of campaign funds can corrupt the entire political process.

How Much?

No one really knows how much money is spent on elections in the United States. Reliable *estimates* of total campaign spending in *recent presidential election years—for all offices at all levels, including nominations and general elections—are shown in the table on this page.

The presidential election eats up by far the largest share of campaign dollars. For 1984, total spending—for all of the preconvention primaries, the national party conventions, the campaign itself, and for all minor party and independent efforts—was at least $325 million. The comparable figure for 1980 was $275 million (and $160 million in 1976).

The totals for all the U.S. Senate and House races in 1984 came to $374 million, up from $343 million in 1982. The totals for 1986 topped $400 million.[21]

Radio and especially television time, newspaper advertisements, pamphlets, buttons, posters and bumper strips, office rent, polls, data processing, mass mailings, travel —these and a host of other items make up the huge sums spent in campaigns. Television is by far the largest item in a typical campaign budget today. A single half hour of network TV time can run as much as $300,000, and a one-minute spot advertisement in prime time can cost $150,000. As Will Rogers said years ago: "You have to be loaded just to get beat."

The dollars spent on particular races vary, and widely. The amount spent depends on many factors: the office involved, the size of the constituency, the candidate (and whether he or she is the incumbent), the opposition, and, not least, the availability of campaign funds.

Drawing by Schoenbaum; © 1984 The New Yorker Magazine, Inc.
"According to our estimates, a campaign budget around six point two million is needed to successfully sing your praises."

[21]Principal sources for the data in this section are: Herbert E. Alexander, Citizens' Research Foundation; *Congressional Quarterly*; and the Federal Election Commission.

*ENRICHMENT Have the class discuss: Why is campaign spending a "necessary evil"? What are the reasons for and the problems that may be caused by expensive campaigns?

BUILDING GOVERNMENT SKILLS

Evaluating Political Commercials and Campaign Materials

Candidates spend much of their campaign treasuries on the political commercials and campaign materials. These commercials and campaign materials are intended not only to inform, but also to persuade. They are advertisements. Campaign strategies, like advertising strategies, are carefully developed to build an appealing image of the candidate and to demonstrate why you, the voter, should vote for that particular candidate.

By evaluating political commercials and campaign materials, you can make a more informed decision about which candidate to support.

Step 1: What Is the Main Message?

When reviewing campaign commercials or literature, first watch or read the entire ad. Determine what the candidate is trying to communicate. What does the candidate want you to think about him or her? Is the commercial or brochure aimed at influencing the broad audience or a specific part of that audience? In other words, to whom is the ad directed, and what is its main idea?

Step 2: How Is the Main Message Conveyed?

Next, analyze the commercial or brochure to determine how the main message is conveyed. Note the kinds of photos or film clips chosen, the tone of voice or the tone of the written narrative, the kind of music used, and the issues, if any, identified in the material. Is the opponent mentioned? Note, too, the use of political symbols.

Step 3: Use Criteria to Evaluate the Commercial or Other Material.

Now take an even closer look at the ad and use criteria, or standards, to judge it. Three criteria that are useful for examining political ads include:

Is the commercial fair?
Is it factual?
Is it appropriate to the office?

For example, you may ask yourself if the ad portrays the opponent fairly, or does it blame the opponent for conditions that may have been beyond his or her control? Does the commercial present any facts about the candidate or the issues, or is it an appeal to your emotions?

Step 4: Note Which Individual Or Group Paid for the Ad.

Every piece of political advertising must carry a line stating the group that paid for the ad. Listen for this line at the end of radio ads. The line is usually given at the end of a television commercial or printed in a brochure. What interest would this group have in getting the candidate elected?

Step 5: Synthesize What You Have Learned.

Finally, put together what you have learned. What do you know about the candidate's qualifications for office? What are his or her views on the issues that are important to you?

1. Use the 5-step approach to evaluate a current political commercial—in print or on television or radio.
2. Imagine that you are a candidate for mayor or the city council, or the United States Senate. Design a flyer or write a one-minute radio or television script to promote your candidacy.

Who Gives and Why?

In the broadest sense, parties and their candidates draw their money from two sources: private contributions and the public treasury. Recent campaign finance laws have had a major impact on both sources. Private contributions have been and still are the major source of campaign monies in American politics. Clearly, the democratic ideal would best be served if political campaigns were entirely supported by small contributions made by millions of Americans. But only about one in every 10 persons of voting age ever makes such gifts. Parties and their candidates have had to look to other places for much of their funding.

They have had to depend upon wealthier persons and families—the so-called "angels" or "fat-cats"; officeholders and office seekers; nonparty groups—the **political action committees (PACs**, political arms of special interests with a major stake in public policy); other groups, formed for the immediate purposes of a campaign, including fund-raising —for example, the Black Silent Majority Committee (pro–Reagan-Bush) or Women for Mondale-Ferraro in 1984; and special fund-raising events—including telethons, direct-mail campaigns, and such social-electioneering affairs as $25-, or $100-, or $1,000-a-plate dinners, picnics, concerts, receptions, cocktail parties, and rallies.

To these traditional sources, a newer one —public subsidies, funding from federal and/or State treasuries—has lately been added. To this point in time, subsidies have been most important at the presidential level, as we shall see.[22]

Campaign donations are a form of political participation. Those who make them do so for a number of reasons. Many small contributors give simply because they believe in a party or a candidate. But most of those who give want something in return for their donation. They want access to government, and they hope to get it by helping their "friends" win elections.[23]

Contributions, both large and small, are welcomed at a political rally.

Some big donors want appointments to public office, and others want to keep the ones they have. Some long for social recognition—for them dinner at the White House or knowing the governor on a first-name basis may be enough. Organized labor, business, professional, and various other groups have particular policy aims. They want certain laws passed, or changed, or repealed, or certain appropriations made, or certain administrative actions taken.[24]

Campaign Finance Regulation *

Congress first began to regulate the use of money in the federal election process in 1907. In that year it became unlawful for any corporation or national bank to make "a

[22]Public funds for presidential campaigns come from the federal treasury. Several States now also have some limited form of public financing for parties and/or candidates at the State and sometimes even at the local level.

[23]One of the better demonstrations of the point can be seen in the fact that some contributors give to *competing* candidates. They hedge their bets; heads they win and tails they still win.

[24]Among those "various other groups" is organized crime—which has an obvious stake in public policy and so in those who make public policy. Large-scale operations in narcotics, prostitution, gambling, loan-sharking, and other illegal activities cannot survive without close ties to at least some public officials. The profits of organized crime are huge, untold—and untaxed—billions. Campaign contributions to the "right" candidates can be a cheap form of insurance.

*ENRICHMENT Ask the class: What are the federal regulations concerning campaign contributions, and why are they important?

money contribution in any election" of candidates for federal office. Since then, Congress has passed several laws to regulate the use of money in presidential and congressional campaigns.

Today, these regulations are found in three very detailed laws: the Federal Election Campaign Act of 1971, the FECA Amendments of 1974, and the FECA Amendments of 1976.[25]

The Federal Election Commission All federal law dealing with campaign finance is administered by the Federal Election Commission. Set up by Congress in 1974, the FEC is an independent agency in the executive branch. Its six members are appointed by the President, with Senate confirmation.[26]

The laws that the Commission enforces cover four broad areas: They (1) require the timely disclosure of campaign finance data, (2) place limits on campaign contributions, (3) place limits on campaign expenditures, and (4) provide public funding for several parts of the presidential election process.

Disclosure Requirements Congress first required the reporting of certain campaign finance information in 1910. Today, the disclosure requirements are very detailed to spotlight the place of money in federal campaigns. In fact, the several reports that must be filed with the FEC are so comprehensive that nearly all candidates for federal office find that their campaign organizations must include at least one certified public accountant.

All contributions to a candidate for federal office must be made through a single campaign committee. Only that committee can spend that candidate's campaign money. Any and all of those contributions, and spendings, must be closely accounted for by that one committee. Any contribution, including any loan, of more than $200 must be identified by source and by date. So, too, must any spending over $200—by the name of the person or firm to whom payment was made, by date, and by purpose.

Any contribution of more than $5,000 must be reported to the FEC no later than 48 hours after it is received. So, too, must any sum of $1,000 or more received in the last 20 days of a campaign. A cash contribution of more than $100 cannot be accepted under any circumstances.

Any "independent committee" (or person) spending more than $250 for a candidate on its own—outside of that candidate's organization—must also file with the FEC. It must report the financial details of its operations and must swear, subject to perjury, that none of its activities was carried on in collusion with that candidate or his or her organization.

All reports must be filed with the FEC in timely fashion. Their due dates fall at the end of each calendar quarter. Reports must also be filed 12 days before an election and must be filed again not more than 30 days after an election.

Limits on Contributions Congress first began to regulate campaign contributions in

---

[25]The earlier federal laws were often called "more loophole than law"; they were loosely drawn, not often obeyed, and almost never enforced. The 1971 law, which became effective in 1972, replaced them. The 1974 law marked the major legislative response to the Watergate scandal; it tightened the provisions and broadened the coverage of the 1971 statute. The 1976 law was passed in direct response to the Supreme Court's decision in *Buckley* v. *Valeo,* 1976. A number of minor changes were made in these laws in 1980.

Note this important point: Congress does not have the power to regulate the use of money in State and local elections. That matter lies within the reserved powers of each of the States. Every State now regulates at least some aspects of campaign finance. Several do so quite extensively; but, unfortunately, in some States the regulations are either inadequate or are only haphazardly enforced, or both. A useful summary of current State campaign finance laws can be found in *The Book of the States,* a biennial publication of the Council of State Governments.

[26]The FEC was originally made up of two members appointed by the President, two by the Speaker of the House, and two by the President *pro tem* of the Senate, with the Clerk of the House and the Secretary of the Senate as *ex officio* (by virtue of office) members. However, the Supreme Court found this structure unconstitutional in *Buckley* v. *Valeo,* 1976. It held that, because the FEC is an *executive* agency, both the doctrine of separation of powers and Article II, Section 2 (giving the appointing power to the President) require that *all* of its members be appointed by the President. Congress restructured the FEC in 1976. The Clerk of the House and the Secretary of the Senate remain as *ex officio,* nonvoting members of the Commission.

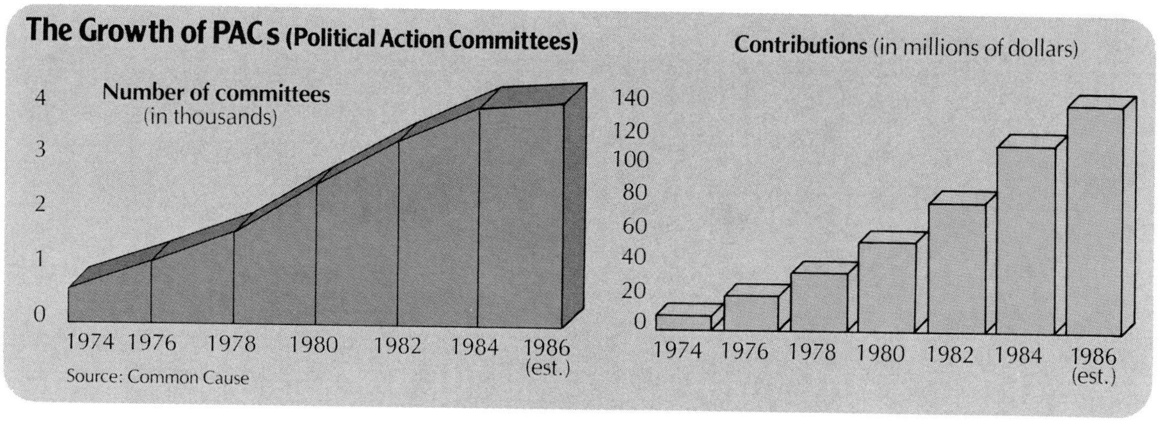

During the 1984 election campaigns for seats in the House of Representatives and the Senate, about 70 percent of PAC contributions were dispersed to incumbents—that is, to members of Congress running for re-election. Why do you think incumbents received such a large share of PAC donations?

1907, when, as we noted, it outlawed donations by corporations and national banks. A similar ban was first applied to labor unions in 1943. Individual contributions first became subject to regulation in 1939.

Today, no person may give more than $1,000 to any federal candidate in a primary election, and no more than $1,000 to any federal candidate's general election campaign. Also, no person may give more than $5,000 in any year to a political action committee, or $20,000 to a national party committee. The *total* of any person's contributions to federal candidates and committees must be limited to no more than $25,000 in any one year.

These limits have now been in place since 1976. They have finally curbed the longstanding and very substantial impact of the "fat-cats" in *federal* elections.[27] But, remember, the limits do *not* apply to campaigns of candidates who are running for State and local offices.

Neither corporations nor labor unions may themselves make campaign contributions. But their political action committees (PACs) can, and do. *

There were only some 600 PACs in 1974. Today they number more than 4,000, for example, BIPAC (Business-Industry Political Action Committee), COPE (the AFL-CIO's Committee on Political Education), and NCPAC (National Conservative Political Action Committee).

Mike Keefe, Denver Post Syndicate

[27]The limits may seem generous; in fact, they are very tight. Before 1976, many wealthy persons made contributions far larger than those amounts. In 1972, W. Clement Stone, a Chicago insurance executive, gave more than $2 million and Richard Mellon Scaife, heir to oil, aluminum, and banking fortunes, gave more than $1 million to President Nixon's reelection campaign. In that same year, Stewart Mott, heir to a General Motors fortune, contributed more than $820,000—most of it to Democratic candidates, including $400,000 to presidential nominee George McGovern. In all, the top ten individual contributors gave at least $7.4 million to federal candidates in 1972, most of it to the major party presidential nominees.

*ENRICHMENT Point out that large corporations and labor unions wield more power than smaller organizations because their PACs usually have more money to distribute.

The 1984 Democratic hopefuls, Walter Mondale and Geraldine Ferraro, wave to well-wishers while campaigning.

PACs fill their war chests with the voluntary contributions of their members—the executives, stockholders, and employees of a corporation; union members; doctors or dentists or teachers; those who favor or oppose gun control or abortion; and so on. The PACs pool all these comparatively small sums into a single, much larger fund. Then they distribute their monies to favored candidates. PACs put more than $112 million into the presidential and congressional campaigns of 1984—and untold millions more into various State and local races.

No PAC may give more than $5,000 to any one federal candidate. But there is no overall limit on PAC giving. Each may contribute up to the $5,000 ceiling to as many different candidates as it chooses.[28]

No contribution may be made by any person or group in the name of another. Cash gifts of more than $100 are absolutely prohibited. So, too, are contributions from any foreign source. All newspaper, radio, and television ads, circulars, and all other materials promoting a candidate for a federal office must carry the name of the persons or groups that sponsor them.

Limits on Expenditures Congress first began to limit campaign spending in 1925. Most of the spending limitations that are now in the law apply only to the presidential election process.[29]

---

[28]Note: An "independent PAC" (one operating on its own, without the approval of or any connection to a candidate) may spend—not contribute to, but spend on its own for a candidate—an unlimited amount. This point is particularly important in terms of presidential campaign finance, as we shall see.

[29]In *Buckley* v. *Valeo*, 1976, the Supreme Court struck down several restrictions that the 1974 law had placed on spending in federal campaigns. The Court held each of them to be contrary to the 1st Amendment's guarantees of freedom of expression. In effect, said the Court, in politics "money is speech." The voided provisions (1) placed strict limits on House and Senate campaign expenditures, (2) placed strict limits on how much of their own money candidates could put into their own campaigns, and (3) said no person or group (independent committees) could spend more than $1,000 on behalf of a candidate without his or her authorization. The Court also struck down limits on presidential campaign spending, *except* for candidates who accept FEC subsidies for their campaigns.

President Ronald Reagan and Vice President George Bush lock hands in a show of unity while on the campaign trail in 1984.

Those presidential contenders who accept federal campaign subsidies are subject to limits on their campaign spending. These limits apply in both the preconvention primaries and in the general election campaign.[30]

For 1984, no contender could spend more than $20.2 million in the preconvention period. After the conventions, the Mondale and Reagan campaigns could each spend up to $40.4 million (see table on page 254). Each of the major parties was allowed to spend only $8.08 million for the staging of its 1984 national convention.[31]

Public Funding of Presidential Campaigns Congress first began to provide for the public funding of presidential campaigns in the Revenue Act of 1971. It broadened sections of that law in 1974 and again in 1976.

The 1971 law set up the Presidential Election Campaign Fund. It also provided that each person who files a federal income tax return may "check off" $1 of the tax payment ($2 on a joint return) to go to the Fund.

As the law now stands, the monies in the Fund are to be used to pay for public subsidies for (1) the preconvention campaigns (presidential primaries and caucuses), (2) national conventions, and (3) presidential election campaigns.[32] The FEC administers the public subsidy process.

Preconvention Period The presidential primary and caucus campaigns are now

[30]The limits go along with the subsidies. Through 1984, only one major party aspirant has not accepted federal funds, former Governor John B. Connally of Texas. He raised and spent some $12 million in private funds in his unsuccessful bid for the Republican presidential nomination in 1980.

[31]The 1974 law set limits of $10 million, $20 million, and $2 million, respectively. However, the law took inflation into account and allows the FEC to adjust the amounts for each presidential year.

[32]The Revenue Act of 1971 also tried to stimulate and broaden the base of campaign giving. As amended in 1978, it allows an income-tax payer to take a *credit* (a subtraction from the total tax due) of up to $50, or $100 on a joint return, for political contributions. The tax laws of several States now include similar provisions. Reagan wants to eliminate the federal political contribution tax credit—and, in fact, federal subsidies altogether—in his tax reform proposals.

*ENRICHMENT Introduce a discussion of presidential campaign expenditures by asking if the current federal limitations are enough.

supported by the private contributions a candidate raises *plus* the public money he or she receives from the FEC.

To be eligible for the public funds, a presidential hopeful must first get past a rather complicated barrier. He or she must raise at least $100,000 from private sources. That amount must be gathered in $5,000 lots in each of at least 20 States, with each of those lots built from individual donations of not more than $250. This tangled requirement is meant to discourage both hopeless and frivolous candidates.

For each contender who passes that test, the FEC matches the first $250 of each of the additional private contributions he or she can raise, up to a total of half of the overall limit on primary spending. That is, in 1984, the FEC matched up to as much as $10.1 million per candidate because the ceiling was $20.2 million for each candidate.

These subsidies have had impacts on the nominating process, in both major parties. We come back to the point in Chapter 14, but, for now, remember this important effect: That public money is available now prompts more presidential hopefuls to enter the preconvention struggle than was the case before the subsidies were put in place.

The manager of the 1984 GOP National Convention takes a call from President Reagan at a sign painting party. Reagan welcomed the involvement of young people in the convention's activities.

In 1984, all presidential hopefuls, combined, spent some $140 million in the preconvention period—including the more than $36 million the FEC gave to the one GOP contender (Ronald Reagan) and altogether nine aspirants in the Democractic Party.

National Conventions If a major party applies for the money—and both of them did in 1976, 1980, and 1984—it automatically receives a grant to pay for its national convention. The Republicans and the Democrats each got $8.08 million from the FEC for that purpose in 1984.

Campaign Spending, Major Party Presidential Candidates, 1952–1984

(in millions of dollars)

1952	$ 6.61	Eisenhower*	$ 5.03	Stevenson
1956	7.78	Eisenhower*	5.11	Stevenson
1960	10.13	Nixon	9.80	Kennedy*
1964	16.03	Goldwater	8.76	Johnson*
1968	25.40	Nixon*	11.60	Humphrey
1972	61.40	Nixon*	30.00	McGovern
1976	21.79	Ford	21.80	Carter*
1980	29.19	Reagan*	29.35	Carter
1984	40.40	Reagan*	40.40	Mondale

*Indicates winner of presidential election.
Source: Adapted from Herbert E. Alexander, *Financing Politics: Money, Elections and Reform* (Washington, D.C.: Congressional Quarterly Press, 3rd ed., 1984), p. 7; 1984 data from Federal Election Commission.

Presidential Campaigns Every major party presidential nominee qualifies for a public subsidy to cover the costs of the general election campaign. For 1984, the Reagan and the Mondale campaigns each received $40.4 million from the FEC.

A party's candidate can refuse the public money, of course. Should that ever happen, the candidate would then be free to raise however much he or she could from private sources.

So far, the nominees of both major parties have taken the public money each time, in 1976, 1980, and most recently in 1984. Because they did so, each of them automatically (1) could spend no more than the amount of the subsidy for the presidential campaign and (2) could not accept campaign funds from any other source.[33]

A minor party candidate may also qualify for public funding, but not automatically. To * be eligible, the minor party must either (1) have won at least 5 percent of the popular vote in the last presidential election or (2) win at least that much of the vote in the current election.[34]

FOR REVIEW

1. **Identify:** campaign finance, public subsidy, public funding.
2. Why must campaign finances be regulated by law?
3. What are the major sources of campaign contributions in American politics?
4. For what reasons do people make campaign contributions?
5. What is the Federal Election Commission?
6. What four major areas of campaign finance are now covered by federal election laws?

Close-ups of delegates to the Democratic (top) and Republican (bottom) National Conventions.

[33]Recall, independent PACs can spend unlimited amounts in any federal campaign (see note 28). Congress tried to limit their spending to no more than $1,000 in the Federal Election Campaign Act of 1974. But the Supreme Court held that restriction unconstitutional, on 1st Amendment grounds, in *Buckley* v. *Valeo,* 1976 (see note 29). In *FEC* v. *National Conservative Political Action Committee,* 1985, the Court struck down another, closely related provision of the 1974 law. Independent PACs were limited to spending no more than $1,000 to support a presidential candidate who receives public subsidy money.

The number of independent PACs and their spending have increased substantially over the past three presidential elections. Those groups spent more than $17 million in the 1984 presidential campaign.

[34]In which case the public money would be received *after* the election and could not possibly help the candidate in that election. Again, as we noted on page 183, many provisions of election law are purposely drawn to discourage minor-party efforts. No minor-party candidate received 5 percent of the presidential vote in 1976 or in 1980. But independent candidate John Anderson won 6.6 percent in 1980. As a result, he received $4.2 million in post-election funds from the FEC.

To this point, only one other nonmajor party nominee has received any FEC money—Sonia Johnson, the Citizens Party's presidential candidate in 1984.

*ENRICHMENT Introduce a discussion of the relationship between the longevity of minor parties and the restrictions on FEC presidential campaign funds.

SUMMARY

Both the nomination and the election process are fundamental to democracy.

Five different methods have been and are used to make nominations in American politics. In order of their historical appearance, they are: (1) self-announcement, (2) the caucus, (3) the delegate convention, (4) the direct primary, and (5) petition. Presidential primaries, now found in just about half the States, are not nominating devices. They are elections held as a part of the presidential candidate selection process.

The direct primary, which developed at the turn of the century in reaction to the problems of the convention system, is the most widely used nominating method today. It is an intraparty nominating election. The direct primary now takes two forms among the States: (1) the closed primary, in which only party members may vote, and (2) the open primary, in which any qualified voter may take part. Runoff primaries are widely used in southern States, where a nominee must have a majority of the primary vote to win party nomination. Nonpartisan primaries are often used to nominate candidates for nonpartisan offices.

There is only a limited amount of federal control over the election process. It is very largely regulated by State law.

Presidential and congressional elections are held on the Tuesday following the first Monday in November in even-numbered years. Most States hold their general elections at the same time; local elections are generally held then, too, or in the spring. The elections take place in precincts, each of which has a polling place.

In all States today voters cast the Australian ballot, which is either of the office-group or the party-column type. Most ballots used in American elections are long. They often confuse and discourage voters, and cause "ballot-fatigue."

Money plays a key part in politics and presents serious problems for democratic government. The major sources of campaign funds are: (1) small individual contributors, (2) large individual donors, (3) officeholders and office seekers, (4) nonparty private organizations—special interest groups and their political action committees (PACs), (5) temporary party campaign committees, (6) party fund-raising events, and (7) public subsidies. Most who give political money want something in return.

The several recently enacted federal campaign finance laws are administered by the Federal Election Commission. They apply only to presidential and congressional elections, not to State and local contests.

CHAPTER REVIEW

Key Terms/Concepts*

general election (230)
caucus (232)
legislative caucus (232)
direct primary (235)
closed primary (236)
open primary (236)
blanket primary (236)
runoff primary (237)
nonpartisan elections (237)
coattail effect (242)
precinct (242)
polling place (242)
political action committees (PACs) (249)

*These terms are included in the Glossary.

Keynote Questions

• **1.** What is the purpose of the nominating process? How does it affect voter choices?

• **2.** Identify and describe in a sentence each of the five major methods used in the making of nominations in the United States.

• **3.** Why do most States now use the direct primary, rather than the convention system, as a nominating device?

• **4.** Who can vote in a closed primary? In an open primary?

The dots represent skill levels required to answer each question or complete each activity: • requires recall and comprehension • • requires application and analysis • • • requires synthesis and evaluation

5. Make a table that compares the pros and cons of the closed primary and the open primary.
6. What are two of the strengths of the primary as a nominating process? Two of its shortcomings?
7. What date has Congress set for holding congressional elections? Presidential elections?
8. List the four essential features of the Australian ballot.
9. How does an office-group ballot differ from a party-column ballot?
10. What are some of the consequences of the long ballots typically used in elections in the United States?
11. With what four broad areas do federal campaign finance laws now deal?
12. What are political action committees (PACs)? What role do they play in the electoral process?

Skill Application

Making Generalizations: Generalizations are conclusions based on specific data and facts. Making a generalization entails studying a set of facts or data and making one statement that expresses the common theme or trend among the facts. For example, the text states that, "Private contributions have been and still are the major source of campaign monies in American politics." This generalization is based on data from many different campaign finance records.

You can make generalizations based on many forms of data, for example, written reports, statistical tables, charts, and graphs.

1. Make a single generalization based on the following four statements.
   a. Candidates for federal office must file detailed financial reports with the Federal Election Commission.
   b. The total of any person's contributions to federal candidates and committees cannot be more than $25,000 in any one year.
   c. A campaign committee must report to the FEC within 48 hours any contribution of more than $5,000.
   d. A person may not give more than $1,000 to any federal candidate in a primary or a general election.
2. Read the excerpt on page 234 about the Cook County convention in 1896. Make a generalization about the delegates to that convention.
3. Look at the table on page 254, "Campaign Spending, Major Party Presidential Candidates, 1952–1984." What generalization can you make based on the data provided?
4. Examine the graphs on page 251, "The Growth of PACs." Make a generalization about PAC contributions since 1974.

For Thought and Discussion

1. Why are secret ballots vital to free elections? Do you agree that vote-by-mail elections threaten the principle of secret ballots? Why or why not?
2. Do you favor the closed primary or the open primary to nominate candidates? Why?
3. Some people argue that both presidential and congressional campaigns should be financed solely by public funds. What are some possible advantages of this idea? Disadvantages? Who might favor the plan? Oppose it?
4. Look at the graphs on page 251, "The Growth of PACs." What factors may have affected the tremendous growth in the number of PACs since 1974? What kinds of organizations form PACs? What do these organizations gain by forming PACs?

Suggested Activities

1. Prepare a bulletin board display of sample ballots and other materials such as voter pamphlets from recent elections in your State. On a notecard explain the various components of the ballots, for example, candidates for various offices and initiative questions.
2. Interview a recent candidate, either successful or unsuccessful, about his or her campaign experiences. If that person will permit it, tape the interview and replay it for your class.
4. Stage a debate or class forum on one of the following topics: (a) *Resolved,* That this State adopt the (open/closed) primary as its basic nominating device; (b) *Resolved,* That all campaigns for public office be financed entirely with public funds.

The common sense of the common people is the greatest and soundest force on earth.
—THOMAS JEFFERSON

10

Government by the People: Public Opinion and Pressure Groups

CHAPTER OBJECTIVES

To help you to

Learn · Know · Understand

Public opinion and its role in American politics.

The complex process out of which opinions are formed.

The means by which opinions are expressed and may be measured, including public opinion polls and the scientific polling process.

Pressure groups, their role in politics, and how they differ from political parties.

The bases upon which pressure groups are formed.

The varied tactics used by pressure groups to influence public opinion and public policy.

AMERICAN GOVERNMENT IS democratic government. It is, then, self-government—government by the people through their elected representatives. Above all else, its aim is to translate the public will into public policy. Somehow, says the American theory of democracy, the will of the people is supposed to become—to be translated into—law in the United States.

A very wise Englishman once said all this in several fewer words. Government in the United States, observed Lord James Bryce nearly 100 years ago, is "government by public opinion."[1]

So far, we have taken a close look at three of the major instruments of democratic government in this country: political parties, voting, and elections. In this chapter we shall look first at public opinion and its place in American politics and then at another of those vital instruments of democracy: pressure groups.

[1] James Bryce, *The American Commonwealth* (New York: Macmillan, 1888), 2:251.

The right to organize in order to influence public policy, as in pressure groups, is protected by the 1st and 14th Amendments. Also protected is a free press, which serves a basic purpose of giving to all persons an adequate and wide-ranging discussion of public affairs.

1. What Is Public Opinion?

As You Read, Think About:

- What public opinion is.

Few terms are more widely used, and less well understood, in American politics than *public opinion.* It appears regularly in newspapers and magazines and we hear it frequently on radio and television.

Quite often, the phrase is used in a way that suggests that all or at least most of the American people hold the same view on some public matter. Thus, time and again, politicians say that "the people" want such and such, television commentators tell us that "the public" favors this or opposes that, and so on.

In fact, however, there are very few matters in which all or nearly all of "the people" think alike. The "public" holds many different and often conflicting views on nearly every public question.

To understand what public opinion is, and what that phrase means, we must recognize this important point: Public opinion is a complex collection of the opinions of many different persons and groups. It is the sum total of all of their views. It is *not* the single and undivided view of some mass mind.

There are many publics in the United States—in fact, an uncountable number of them. Each public is a group made up of all those persons who hold the same view on some particular public question. Each group of people with a differing point of view is a separate public with regard to that matter. The view that its members share sets it apart from all the other publics, or groups with a differing viewpoint, in our politics.

To illustrate: All persons who think that public employees should not be allowed to strike belong to the public that holds that view. All who believe that the President is

*ENRICHMENT Introduce the discussion on public opinion by asking the students if they feel strongly about an issue, such as those pictured in this chapter. Do they belong to a "public"? Which public?

The struggle for ratification of the Equal Rights Amendment (ERA) was marked by strong support on both sides of the issue. The amendment was defeated in 1982 when it failed to be ratified by the required number of States.

doing an excellent job as Chief Executive, or that capital punishment should be abolished, or that prayers should not be permitted in the public schools are members of the separate publics with those particular opinions. Note this significant fact: Many persons belong to more than one of these publics; but almost certainly only a very few, and perhaps even none, belong to all four of them.[2]

This point is crucial, too: In its proper sense, public opinion includes *only* those opinions that are clearly *public*. It is made up only of those views that relate to matters of government—to politics, to public issues, and to the making of public policies. To be an opinion in the public sense, a view must involve something of general concern, something of interest to a significant portion of the people as a whole.

Of course, the people as a whole are interested in a great many things—in rock groups and symphony orchestras, the New York Yankees and the Dallas Cowboys, candy bars and green vegetables, and a great deal more. People have opinions on each of these things, views that are sometimes loosely called "public opinion." But, again, in its proper sense, public opinion involves only those views that people hold on such things as parties and candidates, taxes, unemployment, welfare programs, national defense, foreign policy, and so on.

Definition

Clearly, the thing that we call public opinion is so complex that it cannot be readily defined. But, with what we have said about it, **public opinion** may be described this way: *Those attitudes held by a significant number of persons on matters of government and politics.*

As we have suggested, the term can be better understood in the plural—that is, as public opinions, the opinions of publics. Or, to put it another way, public opinion is made up of expressed group attitudes.

A view must be expressed in order to be an opinion in the public sense. Unless an opinion is expressed in some way, it cannot be

[2]There are as many different publics on any given issue as there are sides to that question. For example, on the public employees strike question, one public holds the view that *no one* who works for government should be allowed to strike. Another thinks that *all* who do so should have that right. Yet another believes that all *except* those whose jobs have a direct bearing on the public's safety, police and fire, for example, should be able to strike, and so on. Students of public opinion often identify the several publics with differing views on the same issues as "subpublics."

known by others. If it cannot be known, it cannot be identified with any public.

FOR REVIEW

1. **Identify:** public opinion.
2. How is the term *public opinion* misused?
3. Views held on only what matters are properly part of public opinion?
4. Why is the meaning of public opinion best understood in terms of the opinions of publics?

2. The Formation of Public Opinion

As You Read, Think About:

- What factors influence the making of public opinion.

None of us is born with a set of attitudes about government and politics. Instead, we *learn* our political opinions, and we do so in a life-long "classroom" and from many different "teachers." In other words, public opinion is formed out of a very complex process, and the factors involved in it are almost without number.

Auth and Szep, 1983 The Washington Post Co.

We have already said much of this in Chapter 8, when we talked about voting behavior. In effect, that extensive look at why people vote as they do amounted to an extensive look at how public opinion is formed.

There, remember, we described the process by which each of us acquires our political opinions as the process of **political socialization.** As we said at the time, that very complex process begins in early childhood and continues on through a person's lifetime. It involves all of the means—all of the experiences and relationships—that lead each of us to see the political world and to act in it as we do.[3]

There are many different agents of political socialization at work in the opinion-shaping process. Again, we looked at these agents at some length in Chapter 8: age, race, income, occupation, residence, group affiliations, and many others. But two of them—the family and education—have such a vital impact that we must take another, and slightly different, look at them here.

The Family

Most parents do not think of themselves as agents of political socialization, nor do the other members of most families. They are, nonetheless, and very importantly so.

Children first see the political world from within the family and through the family's eyes. They begin to learn about politics much as they begin to learn about most other things—from what their parents have to say, from the stories that their older

[3]The concept of socialization comes from the fields of sociology and psychology. There it is used to describe all of the ways in which a society transforms individuals into social beings, making them members of that society. That is, socialization is the multisided, lifelong process in which people come to know, accept, and follow the beliefs and practices of their society. *Political* socialization is a part of that much broader process.

*ENRICHMENT Have the class discuss how political socialization starts at an early age. Invite them to cite examples from their own experiences.

brothers and sisters bring home from school, from watching the family's television set, and so on.

Most of what smaller children learn in the family setting cannot really be called political opinions. Clearly, they are not concerned with the wisdom of spending billions of dollars on an MX missile system or the pros and cons of the monetary policies of the Federal Reserve Board. They do pick up some basic attitudes, however, and with them, a basic slant toward such things as authority and rules of behavior, property, neighbors, people of other racial or religious groups, and the like. In short, children lay some very important foundations on which their political opinions will be built.

A large number of scholarly studies report what common sense also tells us. The strong influence the family has on the development of political opinions is very largely a result of the near monopoly the family has on the child in his or her earliest, formative, most impressionable years. They also show that:

> The orientations acquired in early childhood tend to be the most intensely and permanently held of all political views. They serve as the base on which all later political learning is built. . . . Adult political behavior is the logical extension of values, knowledge, and identification formed during childhood and youth.[4]

The Schools

The start of formal schooling marks the first break in the force of family influence. For the first time children become regularly involved in activities outside the home.

From the very first day, schools teach children the values of the American political system. They very purposely work to indoctrinate the young and train them to become "good citizens." Schoolchildren salute the flag, recite the pledge of allegiance, and sing patriotic songs. They learn about George Washington and Abraham Lincoln and other great figures of the American past. From the early grades on, they pick up growing amounts of more specific political knowledge and they begin to form their political opinions. As high school students, they are often required to take a course in American government and even to read books such as this one.[5]

Again, the family and education are not the only forces at work in the opinion-making process. Nor are preschoolers and students the only targets of political socialization. Rather, we have singled them out and re-emphasized them to underscore their importance.

A Mix of Factors

No one factor, by itself—family or school or any other—shapes any person's opinion on any matter. Some play a larger role than others, however. Thus, in addition to family and education, occupation and race are usually much more significant than, say, sex or place of residence.

But this is not *always* the case. On the question of public employee strikes, for example, the kind of job a person has—whether public or private, professional, white-collar or blue-collar, union or non-union, and so on—will almost certainly have a greater impact on that person's view than will his or her sex or where he or she happens to live. On the other hand, if the question involves something like equal pay for women or flood control projects in the Ohio River Valley, then sex or place or residence will almost certainly loom much larger in the opinion-making mix. In short, the relative weight of each of the many factors that influence public opinion depends a great deal on the nature of the particular issue involved.

---

[4]Richard Dawson, Kenneth Previtt, and Karen Dawson, *Political Socialization,* 2nd ed. (Boston: Little, Brown, 1977), 48.

[5]In fact, the schools may be even more significant than the family in political socialization. Much recent research on opinion formulation supports this finding: "The public schools appear to be the most important and effective instruments of political socialization in the United States." Robert Hess and Judith Torney, *The Development of Political Attitudes in Children* (Garden City, N.Y.: Doubleday, 1968), 120.

Opinion Leaders

The views expressed by certain people —opinion leaders—also bear heavily on public opinion. An opinion leader is any person who, for any reason, has a more than usual influence on the views of others.

These opinion shapers are a distinct minority in the total population, of course, but they are to be found everywhere. Many of them hold public office. Some write for newspapers or magazines or broadcast their opinions on radio or television. Others are prominent in business, labor, agriculture, civic organizations, and so on. Many are in professional occupations—doctors, lawyers, teachers, ministers, and the like—and have contact with fairly large numbers of people on a regular basis.

Whoever they may be—the President of the United States, a network television commentator, the governor, the head of some local citizens' committee, or even the neighborhood barber—these opinion leaders are persons to whom others listen and from whom others draw ideas and convictions. Whatever their political, economic, or social standing or outlook may be, opinion leaders play a very significant role in the formation of public opinion.

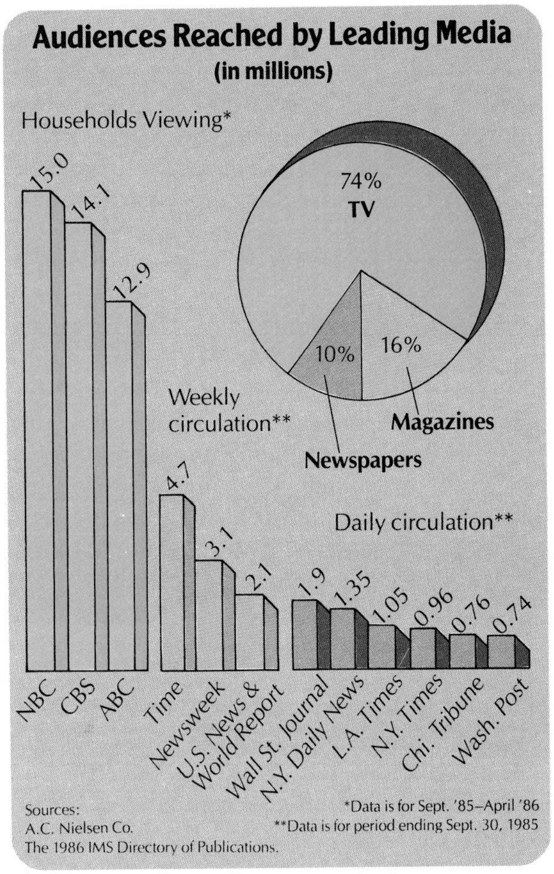

The mass media's influence on the lives of Americans is clearly shown here. Why do you think television reaches a larger audience than the printed media?

The Mass Media

Who really needs to be told that the **mass media**—newspapers, magazines, radio, and especially television—also have a large impact on public opinion in this country? Every day Americans buy more than 60 million daily newspapers. The three major news magazines (*Time, Newsweek,* and *U.S. News)* sell nearly 10 million copies every week. Some 60 million Americans watch the nightly news programs on CBS, ABC, and NBC, and tens of millions also hear reports and commentaries on radio.

Clearly, the media play a significant role in the shaping of public attitudes. But *how much* of a role is the subject of a long, still unsettled argument.

Whatever its weight, the media's influence can be seen in any number of situations. That influence is most often visible—most often has its greatest weight—in two particular areas: (1) in the level of the public's interest in certain issues at any given time and (2) in the voters' reactions to candidates in an election.

Interest in Issues Much of the media's impact on public attitudes stems from the fact that the media are a major source for the public's information about public affairs. Most of what most of us know about current events we learn from the media. Television, newspapers, radio, and magazines are, in that order, the leading sources of political information for most people.

Very largely, then, the media shape the public agenda. That is, as they report and

*ENRICHMENT Discuss the graph on this page by asking the students to which audience they most belong. You may want to find out the local affiliates for each of the major networks.

comment on the issues of the day, they have a considerable effect on the public's sense of the relative importance of the many items they cover. To put the point another way: The media do not tell people *what* to think but, rather, what to think *about.* A quick look at any issue of most daily newspapers or a quick review of the content of any television news program will demonstrate the point.

Reactions to Candidates As we've seen, how voters see a candidate—the impressions they have of that candidate's personality, character, abilities, and so on—is one of the major factors that influence voting behavior. The kind of "image" a candidate projects —often on television but also and very often in the other media—can have an enormous effect on the outcome of an election.

The inescapable presence of the mass media shapes the way Americans think and feel on every issue, from politics to entertainment, including all facets of American life.

Limits on Media Influence It is all too easy to overstate the media's role, however. There are a number of built-in factors that work to limit media impact.

For one thing, not very many people follow political events very closely, whether at the international level, in Washington or elsewhere in the country at large, or even in their own communities. Many studies of voting behavior show, for example, that in the typical election only about 10 percent of all of those who can vote and only about 15 percent of all of those who do vote can be said to be well informed on the candidates and issues. In short, only a very small part of the public takes in very much of what the media have to say about public affairs.

Moreover, most of those who do pay at least some attention to public affairs are likely to be selective about it. That is, they most often watch, listen to, and read those presentations that generally agree with their own viewpoints. They regularly ignore those that disagree. Thus, for example, many Democrats do not watch the televised speeches of Republican candidates, and many Republicans do not read the newspaper advertisements by Democrats.

Another important limit on the media's impact can be seen in the content of much of what they carry. This is especially true of radio and television. Most television programs, for example, have little or nothing to do with public affairs.[6] Advertisers, who pay the high costs of air time, want to reach the largest possible audience. So, because most people are far more interested in being entertained than they are in being informed, we find very few public affairs programs aired in prime time. There are a few exceptions —"60 Minutes" on CBS, ABC's "20/20," and NBC's occasional "White Papers," for example. But they are just that—exceptions.

Radio and television mostly "skim" the news. They report only what their news editors consider to be the most important events of the day. Even on the widely watched evening news programs, most stories are presented in 60- to 90-second time slots. In short, the broadcast media, or at least most of them, seldom give the kind of in-depth coverage that a good newspaper can supply.

[6]At least they do not directly. A number of popular programs do relate to public affairs indirectly, however. Thus, many of them are "crime shows"—and crime is certainly a matter of public concern. Many of them also carry a political message, telling us, for example, that police officers are hard-working public servants and that most of them are very decent human beings.

*REINFORCEMENT Assign the students to bring to class a newspaper article that they feel expresses a public opinion. Ask if it indicates the size of the group that holds the opinion. How can such articles be misleading?

BUILDING GOVERNMENT SKILLS

Expressing Your Opinion Effectively

Suppose that watching the news one evening, you learn that your school system's budget has to be trimmed. In an effort to cut spending, the school board is considering a plan to eliminate all after-school activities, including sports and clubs. You are opposed to the school board's proposal. How can you express your opinion so that it will receive serious consideration?

Decide What You Think and Why

Your opinion should be clearly thought out, and supported by evidence. This may involve doing some research. For example, you might want to find out what percentage of your school's budget is spent on after-school activities, and how the school board's plan would affect most students.

Choose a Form of Expression(s)

You can express your opinion in many ways. You have to decide which form would be most effective, and how much time you can commit to the issue. In this case, you might want to work with other students to present a group rather than an individual opinion. You could write letters to public officials, testify at a school board hearing, write letters to the editor of the local newspaper or prepare an editorial for local television or radio.

Important: Do not criticize individuals; rather, show sympathy for the school board's problem (not enough funding) and offer alternate proposals for trimming the budget. When you finally present your case, whether in written or spoken form, end with a summary of your position.

If you decide to organize a group, you could use more involved forms of expression. Some groups organize petition drives. Petitions are formal requests to a government official or agency to take, or not take, some action. They are signed by those persons who agree with the request. Groups are also sometimes organized to visit a public official to lobby him or her on the issue.

Determine Which Public Official(s) Can Do Something About the Issue

Contact or direct your editorial, petition, or other efforts to the appropriate public official. Your opinion on the school board plan, for example, would not concern your United States Senators, who are responsible for national issues and have no decision-making powers in local school matters. Be sure that you write letters or make phone calls to those officials who are directly responsible for dealing with the issue.

Although you might express your opinion effectively, democracy offers no guarantees that officials will take the action that you favor on a particular matter. However, remember, your vote counts. When you vote, you support one candidate over another.

1. Write your opinion on the school board's plan to eliminate after-school activities. Use one of the following forms of expression: a letter to a public official, a radio or television editorial, or testimony to be presented to the school board.
2. What step would you take if you were not satisfied with the response to your efforts? Why?

Newspapers are not so hampered in their ability to cover public affairs. Still, much of the content of most papers is nonpolitical. Most newspaper readers are more interested in the comics, the sports pages, or the social, advertising, travel, movies, or television sections of a paper than they are in its news and editorial pages.

All of this is not meant to say that in-depth coverage of public affairs is not available in the media. It is, to those who want it. There are a number of good newspapers around the country. In-depth coverage can also be found on a number of radio and television stations, including public broadcast outlets. Remember, though, there is nothing about democracy that guarantees an alert and informed public. Like voting and other forms of political participation, being an informed citizen requires some effort.

FOR REVIEW

1. **Identify:** opinion leader.
2. What factors shape public opinion?
3. What is political socialization?
4. Why are the family and schools especially important agents in that process?
5. What are the mass media? In what two matters do they usually have their greatest impact on public opinion? What three factors work to limit media impact?

3. The Measurement of Public Opinion

As You Read, Think About:

- How public opinion is measured.
- Why public opinion is measured.

If public policy is to be based on public opinion, it must be possible to find the answers to the following questions. What is the content of public opinion on a certain issue? How many persons share a given view on that matter? How firmly do they hold that view? That is to say, it must be possible to "measure" public opinion.

Means of Expression

The general content of public opinion on some matter—what different groups of people say they think about it—can be found in a very obvious way: By consulting the means by which opinions are usually expressed in our society. Those means are both many and varied. They include voting, lobbying, books, pamphlets, magazine and newspaper articles, editorial comments in the press and on radio and television, paid advertisements, letters to editors and public officials, and so on.

These and other means of expression are the devices through which the general shape of public opinion becomes known. But, usually, the *means* by which a view is expressed tell little, and often nothing reliable, about the *size* of the group that holds that opinion or how *strongly* it is held.

Measurement Through Elections

In a democracy the voice of the people is supposed to be heard through the ballot box. Election results are very often said to be indicators of public opinion. The votes cast for rival candidates are regularly taken as evidences of the people's approval or rejection of the stands taken by those candidates and their parties. A party and its victorious candidates regularly claim to have been given a **mandate** to carry out their campaign promises.[7] In American politics a mandate refers to the instructions or commands a constituency gives to its elected officials.

In fact, however, election results are seldom an *accurate* measure of public opinion. Voters make the choices they do in elections for any of several reasons, as we have seen. Very often, those choices have little or nothing to do with the candidates' stands on public questions. Then, too, candidates often disagree with some of the planks of their party's platform. As we have also seen, the stands taken by candidates, and by parties, are often put in broad, vague terms.

In short, much of what we have said about voting behavior, and about the nature of parties, adds up to this: Elections are, at best, only useful indicators of public opin-

[7]The term *mandate* comes from the Latin *mandare* —literally, "to place in one's hand or to commit to one's charge."

Techniques developed to measure the political preferences of the American people take many forms, including polling by telephone.

ion. To call the typical election a "mandate" for much of anything other than a general direction in public policy is to be on very shaky ground.[8]

Measurement Through Pressure Groups

We shall turn to pressure groups at some length in a moment. For now, remember that **pressure groups** are private organizations whose members share certain views and objectives and that actively work to influence the making and content of public policy.

As such, they serve as a chief means by which public opinion is made known. They present their view—exert their pressures—through their lobbyists, by letters, telephone calls, and wires, in political campaigns, and by a number of other methods. In dealing with them, public officials often find it very difficult to determine two things, however: Whatever its claims, how many people does a group really represent? Just how strongly do those people hold the views that an organization says they do?

Measurement Through the Media

A few moments ago we looked at some very impressive numbers that help to describe the place of the mass media in the opinion process. Here are some additional statistics:

More than 9,000 newspapers are published in the United States today, including some 1,700 dailies, 6,800 weeklies, and several hundred foreign-language newspapers. They have a combined circulation of more than 150 million copies per issue.

There are now more than 1,400 television stations, including about 1,100 commercial outlets and over 300 public broadcasters. Their programs can be seen on some 150 million television sets. No one knows how many hundreds of millions of radios there are, in homes, cars, offices, backpacks, and other places, but they can pick up more than 10,000 stations on the AM and FM dials.

There is at least one television set, according to the Census Bureau, in more than 98 percent of the nation's 88 million households. There are two or more sets in millions of homes and millions more in many other places. Most of them are turned on for at least seven hours every day, for a mind-boggling total of a billion hours a day.

All of these facts, and many more like them, tell us that the mass media are mass, indeed. They have also led many to describe the media as "mirrors" as well as "molders" of the public's attitudes. It is often said that the views expressed in newspaper editorials, syndicated columns, newsmagazines, television commentaries, and so on, are fairly good indicators of public opinion. *

The media are *not* very good mirrors, however. In fact, they cannot be because of a point we made very early in our discussion of the meaning of public opinion. Remember, as we noted on page 260, public opinion is made up of the many different opinions of many different publics.

[8]Initiative and referendum elections, at which voters approve or reject measures, *are* elections in which public opinion is registered much more directly on public policy questions; see pages 573–575. Still, their accuracy depends, in large part, on the rate of voter turnout.

*ENRICHMENT Discuss in class: The media is often accused of trying to shape public opinion rather than reporting it. Do students agree or disagree? Why?

Look at just one more illustration of that point: Most of the nation's daily newspapers almost always support the Republican Party's candidate for President. The large majority of them gave their editorial endorsements to the GOP candidate in all but one of the 14 presidential elections from 1932 through 1984. Yet, the Democrats won the Presidency in eight of those elections, and the Republicans took the office in only six of them.[9]

Measurement Through Personal Contacts

Most public officials have frequent and wide-ranging contacts in many different forms and in any number of situations with large numbers of people. In all of them, public officials try to read the public's mind. In fact, their jobs demand that they do so.

Members of Congress receive bags of mail, stacks of telegrams, and hundreds of phone calls. Many of them make frequent trips "to keep in touch with the folks back home." Cabinet officers and other top administration figures are often on the road, selling the President's programs and sensing the people's reactions. Even the President does some of this, with speaking trips and other visits to different parts of the country.

Governors, State legislators, mayors, and other officials also have any number of contacts with the public: in their offices, in public meetings, at social gatherings, at ball games, and so on.

Can public officials find "the voice of the people" in all of those contacts? Many can and do, and often with surprising accuracy. But some cannot. They fall into an ever-present trap: They find only what they *want* to find—only those views that support and agree with their own.

[9]We cite only the last 14 elections here because the magazine *Editor & Publisher,* which polls daily papers on this point every four years, first did so in 1932. The one exception in the last 14 elections is 1964, when 56 percent of the daily papers backed incumbent President Lyndon Johnson. In 1984, 58 percent of them supported the reelection of President Ronald Reagan, 9 percent backed Democrat Walter Mondale, and 33 percent made no endorsement in the last presidential election.

Measurement Through Public Opinion Polls

The public's opinions are best measured by public opinion polls. A **public opinion poll** attempts to collect information about public opinion by asking people questions. The more accurate polls are based on scientific polling techniques. *

Public opinion polls have been used in this country for far more than a century. Until the 1930s, however, they were far from scientific. Most earlier polling efforts were of the **straw vote** variety. That is, they were polls that sought to read the public's mind simply by asking the same question of a large number of people. Straw votes are still fairly common. Newspapers often run "clip-out and mail-in" ballots; radio talk shows ask listeners to respond to questions with phone calls; and so on.

The straw-vote technique is highly unreliable, however. It rests on the false assumption that a relatively large number of responses will give a fairly accurate picture of the public's views on a given question. But nothing in the process ensures that those who do respond, no matter how many, will in fact represent a reasonably accurate cross section, or sample, of the total population. The straw vote emphasizes the *quantity* rather than the *quality* of the sample to which its question is posed.

The most famous of all straw-polling snafus took place in 1936. The *Literary Digest* mailed postcard ballots to more than 10 million people and received answers from more than 2,376,000 of them. Based on that huge return, the magazine confidently predicted the outcome of the presidential election that year. It said that Governor Alfred Landon, the Republican nominee, would easily defeat incumbent Franklin Roosevelt. Instead, Roosevelt won in a landslide. He captured more than 60 percent of the popular vote and carried every State but two. Landon won only in Maine and Vermont.

The *Digest* had drawn its sample on an altogether faulty basis: from automobile registration lists and from telephone directories. But in the mid-Depression year of 1936,

*REINFORCEMENT Ask the class: How accurate are public opinion polls? What are the pros and cons behind conducting such surveys?

Reprinted by permission Tribune Media Services

"I used to be swayed by the media's analysis of every move but not any more. Now I wait for the polls!'

millions of people could not afford to own cars, and most private telephones were to be found in upper- and middle-class homes. In short, its poll failed to reach most of the poor and unemployed, millions of blue-collar workers, and most of the ethnic minorities.

Several million people responded to a straw poll conducted by the *Literary Digest* in 1936. Why were the results of this poll so misleading?

Those were the very segments of the population from which FDR and the Democrats drew their greatest support.[10]

Scientific Polling Serious efforts to take the public's pulse on a scientific basis date from the mid-1930s. They began with the work of such early pollsters as George Gallup and Elmo Roper. The techniques that they and others have developed since then have reached a highly sophisticated level.

There are now more than 1,000 national and regional polling organizations in this country. Many of them do mostly commercial work. They tap the public's preferences on everything from toothpastes and headache remedies to television shows and thousands of other things. At least 200 of them poll the political preferences of the American

[10]The magazine had predicted the winner of each of the three previous presidential elections, but its failure to do so in 1936 was so colossal that it ceased publication almost immediately thereafter.

The Gallup Poll's National Sample

The following table provides the approximate number of persons interviewed in each group for any single survey.

Sex		**Age**		**Occupation**	
Male	750	18–24 years	195	Professional & business	475
Female	750	25–29 years	165	Clerical & sales	115
Race		30–49 years	535	Manual workers	605
White	1,305	50 & older	605	Farmers	55
Nonwhite	195	**Income**		Non-labor force	250
Education		$40,000 & over	215	**Urbanization**	
College graduate	300	$30,000–$39,999	170	Center cities	481
Some college	340	$20,000–$29,999	295	Fringe	442
High school graduate	510	$10,000–$19,999	490	All others	577
Less	350	Under $10,000	330	**Labor Union**	
Region		**Politics**		Labor union families	280
East	405	Republican	405	Non-labor union families	1,220
Midwest	415	Democrat	650		
South	410	Independent	445		
West	270	**Religion**			
		Protestant	850		
		Catholic	420		
		Jewish	50		
		Other	180		

Design of the Sample

After stratifying the population geographically and by size of community in order to ensure conformity of the sample with the latest available estimates by the Census Bureau of the distribution of the adult population, over 350 different sampling locations or areas are selected on a mathematically random basis. . . . The interviewers have no choice whatsoever concerning the part of the city or county in which interviews are conducted.

Approximately five interviews are conducted in each such randomly selected sampling point. Interviewers are given maps of the area to which they are assigned, with a starting point indicated. They are required to follow a specified direction. At each occupied dwelling unit, interviewers are instructed to select respondents by following a prescribed systematic method and by a male-female assignment. This procedure is followed until the assigned number of interviews has been completed.

Since this sampling procedure is designed to produce a sample that approximates the adult civilian population (18 and older) living in private households in the United States (that is, excluding those in prisons and hospitals, hotels, religious and educational institutions, and on military reservations), the survey results can be applied to this population for the purpose of projecting percentages into number of people. The manner in which the sample is drawn also produces a sample that approximates the population of private households in the United States. Therefore, survey results can also be projected in terms of numbers of households when appropriate.

Source: The Gallup Report

What are the advantages of the Gallup Poll's system of scientific polling over the straw-polling technique?

people, however. Among the best known of the national pollsters today are the Gallup Organization (the Gallup Poll) and the organization of Louis Harris and Associates (the Harris Survey).

At best, we can only hope to outline the major features of scientific poll-taking. To that end, that complex process can be described in five basic steps. Pollsters must:

1. Define the universe to be surveyed. The universe is the whole population to be measured, the group whose opinions the poll will seek to discover. That universe can be all

voters in Chicago, or every high school student in North Carolina, or all Republicans in New England, or all Catholic women over age 35 in the United States, and so on.

2. Construct a sample. If a total universe is made up of the 35 members of a high school class, the best way to find out what they think about some issue would be to poll every one of them. In most cases, however, it is not possible to interview a complete universe. There are simply too many people to talk to. So, a **sample**—a representative slice of the total universe—must be selected.

Most professional pollsters now draw a **random sample,** also called a probability sample. In a random sample, a certain number of randomly selected people who live in a certain number of randomly selected places are picked to be interviewed. Here, the term *random* means that each member of the universe and each geographic area within it have a mathematically equal chance of being included within the sample.

Most major national polls interview just over 1,500 people to represent the nation's adult population of some 175 million people. The composition of the Gallup Poll's sample, and Dr. Gallup's description of its design, are described on the opposite page.

How can the views of so few people represent the opinions of so many? The answer to that question lies in something that most people, though they may have to be reminded of it, know quite well: the mathematical law of probability. Flip a coin 1,000 times. The law of probability says that, given an honest coin and an honest flip, heads will come up 500 times. The technique of relying on probability is used in a great many situations: by insurance companies to compute life expectancies, by a food processor to check the quality of a farmer's truckload of beans, and by others who "play the odds."

In short, if the sample is of sufficient size and is properly selected at random from the entire universe, the law of probability says that the result will be quite accurate, to within a very small margin of error. Mathematicians tell us that a properly drawn random sample of some 1,500 people will reflect the opinions of all the nation's population and will be accurate to within a margin of plus or minus (±) 3 percent.[11]

The validity of any poll depends on nonbiased wording of questions. But the appearance and manner of the interviewer is also important. A friendly manner will put people at their ease and make them more likely to answer honestly.

Some pollsters do use a less complicated, but less reliable, sampling method. They draw a **quota sample,** a sample deliberately constructed to reflect several of the major characteristics of the universe. For example, if 51.3 percent of that overall group is female, 17.5 percent of it is black, and so on, then the sample will be made up of 51.3 percent females, 17.5 percent blacks, and so on. Of course, most of the people in the sample will belong to more than one of the categories on which it is built.

3. Prepare valid questions. The way in which questions are worded is a very important matter. Wording can affect the reliabili-

[11]To bring the sampling error down from ± 3 percent to ± 1 percent, the size of the sample would have to be 9,500 people. The time and money needed to interview that big a sample make that a practical impossibility.

*REINFORCEMENT Have the class discuss: What are the problems with a quota sample? In what ways does it differ from a random sample.

FOCUS ON:

Discovering Your Political Roots

Recall, political socialization is the very complex process by which each of us acquires our political attitudes and opinions. It involves *all* of the experiences and *all* of the relationships that lead us to see the political world and to act in it as we do. See pages 220 and 261.

How have *you* been "socialized to politics"? Write an autobiographical comment —a brief one of two to three pages— focusing on that question. You might build that self-portrait around such questions as:

— What is the very first political event you can remember? Describe it in as much detail as you can. How did your parents feel about that event?

— Do you talk about public affairs—about politics and public policies—at home? With one or with both parents? Often?

— Are either or both of your parents politically active? To which of the major parties, if either of them, does each of your parents belong?

— What other persons have had some influence on your political views? Any groups, both formal and informal?

— What impact has school had on your views?

— What of television? Newspaper articles? Other media?

— Are any of your friends interested in politics? If so, do you discuss views with them? Do they influence your views?

Mulligan, 1981, the *New Yorker*

"My grandson, needless to say is also pro-Reagan"

— How would you describe, overall, your feelings about politics today? Are you a Republican or a Democrat or an independent or what? Why?

Explore your own political background and makeup as completely as you can. Do not limit the search for your political self to just those few questions we have suggested here. You may have been exposed, and very likely have, to a great many more socializing influences than you think.

ty of any poll. For example, most people will probably say "yes" to a question put this way: "Should local taxes be reduced?" But many of those same persons will also give the same answer to this question: "Should the city's police force be increased to fight the rising tide of crime in our community?" Yet, expanding the police force almost certainly will require more local tax dollars. Responsible pollsters phrase their questions

A victorious President Truman grins as he holds up a newspaper headline projecting his defeat in 1948. Pollsters and others had predicted a landslide victory for Thomas E. Dewey in that election.

very carefully. They purposely try not to use terms that are difficult to understand and "loaded" words, that is, words that will influence a person to give a particular answer.

4. Select and control the means by which the poll will be taken. In part, this point relates to how the pollsters communicate with the sample. Most polls are taken face-to-face. The interviewers question the respondents in person. Some surveys are conducted by telephone, however, and others by mail. Professional pollsters see both advantages and drawbacks in each of these approaches. They all agree, however, that the same technique must be employed in the questioning of all of the respondents in a sample.

The interview itself is a very sensitive point in the process. The poll-taker's appearance, dress, apparent attitude, or tone of voice in asking questions may influence the replies he or she receives. Some of those replies may be snap judgments or emotional reactions. Others may be of the sort that the person being interviewed thinks "ought" to be given, or they may be answers that the respondent thinks will please—or offend—the interviewer. Thus, polling organizations try to hire and train their interviewing staffs very carefully.

5. Report their findings. Polls, whether scientific or not, try to measure the attitudes of people. To be of any real value, however, poll results must be analyzed and reported. Scientific pollsters collect huge amounts of

*REINFORCEMENT Have the class discuss the pros and cons of scientific polls. How can they influence elections?

raw data today. In order to handle these data, computers and other electronic hardware have become routine parts of the processes by which pollsters tabulate and then interpret their data, draw their conclusions, and then publish their findings.

How good are the polls? On balance, the major national polls are fairly reliable. So, too, are most of the regional surveys around the country. Still, they are far from perfect. Fortunately, most pollsters themselves are quite aware of that fact. Many of them are involved in continuing efforts to refine every aspect of the polling process.

For example, pollsters know that they have difficulty measuring certain qualities of the opinions they report. These qualities are intensity, stability, and relevance. Intensity is the strength of feeling with which an opinion is held. Stablility or fluidity is the relative permanence or changeableness of an opinion. Relevance or salience is how important a given opinion is to the person who holds it.

Polls and pollsters are sometimes said to shape the opinions they are supposed to measure. Some critics of the polls say that in an election, for example, pollsters often create a "bandwagon effect." That is, some voters, wanting to be with the winner, jump on the bandwagon of the candidate who is ahead in the polls. The charge is most often leveled against those polls that appear as syndicated columns in many newspapers.

Even so, it is clear that scientific polls are the most useful tools we have in the difficult task of measuring public opinion. Though they may not be always or precisely accurate, they do offer reasonably reliable guides to public thought. Moreover, they help to focus attention on public questions and to stimulate discussion of them.

Reprinted with permission from the Minneapolis Star and Tribune.

Limits on the Force of Public Opinion

One last word here, before we turn to pressure groups. Government in the United States *is* "government by public opinion." That is true *only if* that description is understood to mean that public opinion is the *major,* but not the only, influence on public policy in this country. Its force is tempered by a number of other factors. We will look at some of them in a moment.

Most importantly, however, remember: Our system of constitutional government is *not* designed to give free and unrestricted play to public opinion—and especially not to *majority* opinion. In particular, the doctrines of separation of powers and of checks and balances and the constitutional guarantees of civil rights are intended to protect minority interests against the excesses of majority views and actions.

FOR REVIEW

1. **Identify:** poll, sample, probability sample.
2. Why must public opinion be measured?
3. How useful are elections as measurements of public opinion? Pressure groups? The mass media? Citizen contacts with public officials?
4. What device best measures public opinion?
5. What is scientific polling? A universe?
6. What is a random sample? On what mathematical principle is it based?
7. What is a quota sample?
8. Why is the wording of questions a critically important step in the polling process? The interview step?
9. Identify two shortcomings or criticisms of current scientific polling methods.

4. What Are Pressure Groups?

As You Read, Think About:

- What a pressure group is.
- What the relationship is between pressure groups and political parties.

One of the major ways in which Americans try to get government to respond to their individual opinions is by forming pressure groups. As you read earlier in the chapter, a pressure group is a private organization whose members are linked by a common opinion on some political question and who attempt to influence the making and content of public policy. For example, those who oppose nuclear power join with others who also oppose it. Those who favor prayer in public schools join with others who share that view, and so on. Each group works to persuade government to respond to the shared attitudes of its members. Such organizations are also called **interest groups** or **special-interest groups.**

Organized efforts to promote group interests are a fundamental part of the democratic process. The right to do so is protected by the Constitution. Remember, as we noted in Chapter 5, the 1st Amendment guarantees "the right of the people peaceably to assemble, and to petition the government for a redress of grievances."

Political Parties and Pressure Groups

Pressure groups are made up of people who join together for some political purpose. So, too, are political parties. These two types of political organizations overlap in a number of ways, as we shall see. However, they differ from one another in three very striking ways: in the making of nominations, in their primary interest, and in the scope (range) of their interest.

Nominations Parties nominate candidates for public office; pressure groups do not. Remember, the making of nominations is a major function of parties. If a pressure group were to nominate candidates, it would, in effect, become a political party.

Primary Interest Political parties are chiefly interested in winning elections and controlling government. Pressure groups are primarily concerned with controlling or influencing the policies of government. That is, political parties are mostly interested in the *who* and pressure groups in the *what* of government.

Scope of Interest Political parties are, and must be, concerned with the whole range of public affairs. Pressure groups are almost always interested only in those questions that directly affect the interests of their members.

Functions of Pressure Groups

Pressure groups perform several valuable functions in American politics. First, they help to stir up public interest in and discussion of public affairs. Most importantly, they do so by developing and pushing those policies they favor and, conversely, by opposing those policies they see as threats to their interests.

Second, these groups represent their members on the basis of shared attitudes rather than on the basis of geography—by what their members think as opposed to where they happen to live. Public officials are elected from districts drawn on maps. But many of the interests that unite people today have at least as much to do with *how* they make a living as with *where* they live. A labor union member who lives in Chicago, Illinois, may have much more in common with someone who does the same kind of work in Seattle, Washington, than he or she does with someone who owns a business in Chicago or runs a farm in another part of Illinois.

Third, organized interests often give useful, specialized, and detailed information to government. These data can be important to the making of public policy and often cannot be obtained from any other source. This

*ENRICHMENT Political parties and pressure groups share several characteristics since both are political organizations. Have the class identify these characteristics.

Citizens sometimes unite to inform government on their views on foreign affairs. Here, demonstrators show their opposition to the government of South Africa's policy of apartheid.

process is a two-way street, however; interest groups often get information from public agencies and pass it along to their members.

Fourth, these groups add another element to the check-and-balance features of the political process. When, for example, one pressure group makes an extreme and/or unreasonable demand on government, other groups are very likely to oppose it. Many pressure groups also keep fairly close track of public officials and help to make sure that those officials carry out their tasks in a responsible fashion.

Criticisms of Pressure Groups

Certainly, we do not mean to suggest that all pressure groups have no failings. They can be and have been criticized on several counts.

First, some groups have an influence on government far out of proportion to their size, or for that matter, to their importance or contribution to the public good. Thus, the struggle over "who gets what, when, and how" is not always a fair fight. The more highly organized and better financed groups often have a decided advantage in that struggle.

Second, it is sometimes very hard to tell just who or how many people a group really represents. Many groups have titles that suggest that they have thousands or even millions of dedicated members. Many do, but many others do not. Some groups that call themselves such things as "The American Citizens Committee for . . ." or "The People United Against . . ." are in fact only "fronts" for a very few persons with very narrow interests.

Third, many groups do not in fact represent the views of all the people for whom they claim to speak. Very often, both in and out of politics, an organization is dominated by its leaders, an active minority who conduct its affairs and make its policy decisions. To put this another way, many groups do not have to answer to anyone—except perhaps to their members, and not always to them.

Fourth, some groups use tactics that, if they were to become widespread, would undermine the whole political system. These practices—including bribery and other heavy-handed uses of money, crude threats of revenge, and so on—are not very common, but the danger is certainly there.

FOR REVIEW

1. What are pressure groups? By what other names are they known?
2. What are the basic differences between pressure groups and political parties?
3. What four functions do pressure groups perform?
4. List four major criticisms of pressure groups.

5. Types of Pressure Groups

As You Read, Think About:

- What types of pressure groups exist.
- What the aims are of the different types of pressure groups.

The United States has often been called "a nation of joiners." Wrote Alexis de Tocqueville in the 1830s:

> In no country in the world has the principle of association been more successfully used, or more unsparingly applied to a multitude of different objects, than in America.[12]

In a similar vein, he also observed that

> Americans of all ages, all conditions, and all descriptions constantly form associations . . . not only commercial and manufacturing . . . but . . . of a thousand different kinds—religious, moral, serious, futile, extensive or restricted, enormous or diminutive.[13]

Tocqueville's comments, accurate when they were made, have become even more true over time. No one really knows how many associations Americans belong to today. There are thousands upon thousands of them, however—and at every level in our society. Each and every one of them, remember, is a pressure group whenever it tries to influence the actions of government.

Pressure groups come in all shapes and sizes. They may have thousands or even millions of members, or only a handful. They may be well- or little-known, long-established or new and even temporary, highly structured or quite loose and informal, wealthy or with few resources, and so on. No matter what their characteristics, they are found in every field of human activity in this country.

The largest number of pressure groups have been founded on the basis of an economic (occupational) interest, especially on the bases of business, labor, agricultural, and professional interests. Some groups are grounded on a geographic area, like the South, the Columbia River Basin, or the State of Ohio. Others have been born out of a cause or an idea, such as prohibition, environmental protection, women's rights, or gun control. Still others exist to promote the welfare of certain groups of people—veterans, the aged, a racial minority, the handicapped, and so on.

Pressure groups often share members. Many people may belong to a number of

Groups of older Americans, such as the Gray Panthers, have organized to call attention to the special concerns and problems of the aged.

[12]Alexis de Tocqueville, *Democracy in America*, Henry Reeve, trans. (New York: Schocken Books, 1961), 1:216.
[13]*Ibid.*, 2:128.

*ENRICHMENT Ask students to identify at least several of the pressure groups that exist in your community. What is the particular (special) interest of each of the groups noted?

them. A car dealer, for example, may be a member of the local Chamber of Commerce, a car dealers' association, the American Legion, a local taxpayers' league, a garden club, a church, the PTA, the American Cancer Society, the National Wildlife Federation, and several other local, regional, or national groups. All of these are, to one degree or another, pressure groups, including the church and the garden club, even though the car dealer may never think of them in that light.[14]

Also, people may belong to groups that take conflicting stands on political issues. A program to improve the city's streets may be backed by the local Chamber and the car dealers' association but opposed by the taxpayers' league, and so on.

Groups Based on Economic Interests

Most pressure groups are formed on economic interests. That is, they are based on the manner in which people make their livings. Among them, the most active, and certainly the most effective, are those representing business, labor, agriculture, and at least certain professions.

Business Groups Business has long looked to government to promote and protect its interests. As we have seen, merchants, creditors, and property owners were most responsible for the calling of the Constitutional Convention in 1787. The idea of the protective tariff was fought for and won in the very early years of the Republic by business interests. Along with labor, they continue to work to maintain it.

Hundreds of business groups now operate in Washington, in the 50 State capitols, and at the local level across the country. The two best-known overall business organizations today are the National Association of Manufacturers (NAM) and the Chamber of Commerce of the United States. Formed in 1895, NAM now represents some 13,000 firms. It generally speaks for "big business" in public affairs. The Chamber of Commerce was founded in 1912. Over the years, it has become a major voice for the nation's thousands of smaller businesses. It has more than 4,000 local chambers and now counts over 200,000 business and professional firms and some 5 million individuals among its members. Another major group, the Business Roundtable, has also taken a large role in promoting and defending the business community in recent years. Begun in 1972, the Roundtable is composed of the chief executive officers of nearly 200 of the nation's largest, most prestigious corporations.

Most segments of the business community also have their own pressure groups, often called trade associations. They number in the hundreds—the American Trucking Associations, the Association of American Railroads, the American Bankers Association, the National Association of Retail Grocers, the National Association of Realtors, and many, many more.

Despite a common impression, business groups do not always present a solid front as they try to influence public policy. In fact, there are often strong differences, and sometimes fights, among them. The trucking industry, for example, does its best to get as much federal aid as possible for highway construction. But the railroads are less than happy with what they see as "special favors" for their competition. At the same time, the railroads see federal taxes on gasoline, oil, tires, and other "highway users fees" as legitimate and necessary sources of federal income. The truckers take quite another view, of course.

Labor Groups The interests of organized labor are also represented by a host of groups.* The largest, in both size and political power, is the AFL-CIO (the American Federation of Labor-Congress of Industrial Organi-

[14]Churches often take stands on such public issues as drinking, curfew ordinances, legalized gambling, and so on, and they often try to influence public policy in those matters. Garden clubs often try to persuade cities to do such things as improve public parks, beautify downtown areas, and the like. Not every group to which people belong can be properly called a pressure group, of course. But our point here is that many groups that are not often thought to be pressure groups are.

*ENRICHMENT Organized labor generally speaks with one voice, but sometimes sectional interests prevent this. Discuss this concept in class, pointing out local vs. national issues (or rural vs. urban.

Over the years, members of farm associations have traveled to the nation's capital to urge government action to help remedy economic problems.

zations).[15] It is now made up of some 105 separate unions, such as the Retail Clerks International Union, the International Association of Machinists and Aerospace Workers, the Postal Workers Union, and the American Federation of Musicians. With all its unions, the AFL-CIO has about 13 million members. Each union, like the AFL-CIO itself, is organized on a national, State, and local basis.

There are also a number of independent unions—that is, unions not affiliated with the AFL-CIO. The largest and most powerful of them include such groups as the International Brotherhood of Teamsters, the United Mine Workers, and the International Longshoremen's and Warehousemen's Union.

Organized labor generally speaks with one voice on such social welfare and job-related matters as social security programs, minimum wages, and the fight against unemployment. But labor sometimes opposes labor. White-collar and blue-collar workers, for example, do not always share the same economic interests. Then, too, such factors as sectional interests (East-West, North-South, urban-rural, and so on) and production interests (trucks versus railroads versus airplanes, for example) sometimes divide labor's forces.

Also, organized labor cannot possibly speak for all workers in the United States. The nation's labor force numbers some 120 million persons; fewer than a seventh of them, some 17 million, belong to labor unions.

Agricultural Groups Several powerful associations serve the interests of agriculture. They include a number of broad-based farm organizations and a larger number that represent farmers who raise commodities.

The most prominent farm groups are the National Grange, the American Farm Bureau Federation, and the National Farmers Union.

[15]The AFL was formed in 1886, as a federation of craft unions. A craft union is one made up only of those workers who have the same craft or skill—for example, a carpenters, plumbers, or electricians union. The growth of mass production created a large class of industrial workers not skilled in any particular craft, however. Many of them are organized in industrial unions—unions made up of workers, skilled or unskilled, in a single major industry, such as the Textile Workers Union and the United Steel Workers. The AFL found it hard to organize workers in the new mass production industries. Many of its craft unions were against having unions of unskilled workers in the AFL. After years of bitter fights over craft versus industrial unionism, a group led by John L. Lewis of the United Mine Workers was expelled from the AFL in 1935. They formed the CIO in 1938. The rivalries between these two major national unions cooled down to the point where merger, as the AFL-CIO, took place in 1955.

The Grange, established in 1867, is the oldest and generally the most conservative of them. Over the years, it has been as much a social as a political organization, concerned about the welfare of farm families. Some 450,000 farm families are now members, and much of its strength is centered in the Northeast and the Mid-Atlantic States.

The Farm Bureau is the largest and generally the most effective of the three. Formed in 1920, it soon developed a close working relationship with the Department of Agriculture. It has some 3.5 million farm-family members and is especially strong in the Midwest. The Farm Bureau generally supports federal programs to promote agriculture. However, it opposes most government regulation and favors the free market economy.

The smaller Farmers Union draws its strength from smaller and less prosperous farmers. It now has some 300,000 farm-family members, most of them in the upper Midwest and West. The Farmers Union often calls itself the champion of the dirt farmer and often disagrees with the other two major organizations. It generally favors high levels of federal price supports for crops and livestock and other programs to regulate the production and marketing of commodities.

Another group, the National Farmer's Organization, came to the fore in the 1970s. The NFO calls for efforts to withhold produce from the market in order to raise the prices paid to farmers. It has sponsored "tractorcades" to Washington and other cities to dramatize the farmers' high-costs/low-prices problems.

Many other groups speak for the producers of specific farm commodities—dairy products, grain, fruit, peanuts, livestock, cotton, wool, corn, soybeans, and so on. Dairy farmers, for example, are represented by three major organizations: the Associated Milk Producers, Inc., Mid-American Dairies, and Dairymen, Inc. Then, too, there are the National Association of Wheat Growers, the American Meat Institute, the American Cattlemen's Association, the National Wool Growers Association, the National Cotton Council, and many, many others.

Like business and labor groups, farm organizations sometimes find themselves at odds with one another. Thus, dairy, corn, soybean, and cotton groups compete as each of them tries to influence State laws regulating the production and sale of such products as margarine and yogurt. California and Florida citrus growers are sometimes pitted against one another, and so on.

Professional Groups The professions also have organizations that can be used for political purposes. Much of their effort is given over to such matters as the standards of the profession, the holding of professional meetings, and the publishing of scholarly journals. Still, each acts in some ways as a pressure group, intent on promoting the welfare of the profession and its members.

Most professional groups are not nearly so large, well-organized, well-financed, or effective as most business, labor, and farm groups. Three major groups are exceptions, however: the American Medical Association (AMA), the American Bar Association (ABA), and the National Education Association (NEA). Each has a very real impact on public policies—and at every level of government. There are dozens of less well-known, and less politically active, professional groups—the American Society of Civil Engineers, the American Library Association, the American Political Science Association, and a great many more.

The Maze of Other Groups

As we have said, most pressure groups are based on economic interests. But hundreds have been formed for other reasons, and many have a good deal of political clout.

Groups that Promote Causes A large number of these other groups exist to promote a *cause* or an *idea*. In fact, it would take several pages just to list them here, and so we can mention only a few of the more important ones. The Women's Christian Temperance Union (WCTU) has long sought prohibition. The American Civil Liberties

ENRICHMENT Have students contact local special-interest or pressure groups and find out how each presents its views to the public. Do students think those groups are effective in presenting their messages? Why or why not?

Union (ACLU) fights in and out of court to protect civil and political rights. Common Cause, discussed in the next section, works for major reforms in the political process and calls itself "the citizen's lobby." The League of Women Voters of the United States and its many local leagues are dedicated to stimulating participation in and greater knowledge about public affairs.

The list of cause groups goes on and on. Many women's rights groups—the National Organization for Women (NOW), the National Women's Political Caucus, and several others—carry that banner. Several, including the National Wildlife Federation, the Sierra Club, the Wilderness Society, and Friends of the Earth, are pledged to conservation and environmental protection. The National Right-to-Life Committee and other groups oppose abortion; they are countered by the National Abortion Rights Action League and its allies. The National Rifle Association fights gun control legislation; Handgun Control, Inc. works for it. The list is endless.

Organizations that Promote the Welfare of Certain Groups A number of groups seek to promote the *welfare* of certain segments of the population. Among the best-known and most powerful are the American Legion and the Veterans of Foreign Wars, which work to advance the interests of the country's veterans. Groups like Older American, Inc. and the American Association of Retired Persons are very active in such areas as old-age pensions and medical care for the aged. Several organizations—notably the National Association for the Advancement of Colored People (NAACP), the National Urban League, and People United to Save Humanity (PUSH)—are closely concerned with public policies of special interest to blacks. Again, the list goes on and on. . . .

Church-Related Organizations Many church-related organizations also try to influence public policy in several important areas. Thus, many individual Protestants and their local and national churches do so through the National Council of Churches.

A demonstration can be an effective method of influencing public opinion. What other modes of action do pressure groups use?

Public-interest groups exist to respond to the needs of all the people, not a select few. The League of Women Voters (left) works to inform the American electorate while Common Cause (above), "the citizens lobby," works to reform the political process.

Roman Catholics do so through the National Catholic Welfare Council; and Jewish communicants, through the American Jewish Congress and B'nai B'rith's Anti-Defamation League. Yet again, the list of these organizations is endless.

Public-Interest Groups

As we have said, pressure groups are *private* groups. Most of them represent some special interest—business, labor, agriculture, veterans, teachers, and so on. They seek public policies of special benefit to their members, and they work against policies that threaten their own interests.

There are some groups, often called public-interest groups, with a broader goal, however. They work for the "public good." That is, a **public-interest group** is a pressure group that seeks certain public policies of benefit to *all* the people of this country, whether they belong to or support that organization or not.[16]

Unlike most pressure groups, public-interest groups are based on roles that all Americans share. That is, they are set up to represent people as citizens, as consumers, as breathers of air, as drinkers of water, and

[16]Of course, nearly all pressure groups claim that they work for the "public good." Thus, the NAM says that lower taxes on business will stimulate the economy and so help everyone. The AFL-CIO says the same thing about spending more public dollars for more public works programs. The American Federation of Teachers insists that its opposition to public aid for private schools is in the best interests of the American people. The AMA says the same thing about its stand against a national health insurance program. But, as a general rule, most pressure groups support or oppose public policies on a much narrower basis: on what they see to be the best interests of their own members.

so on. They have become quite visible over the past 10 years or so. Among the best-known and most active of them today are Common Cause and the several organizations that make up Ralph Nader's Public Citizen, Inc. Some have been with us for a much longer time, however—for example, the League of Women Voters. The League, founded in 1920, has roots that reach deep into the long history of the women's suffrage movement.

FOR REVIEW

1. Most pressure groups are formed on the basis of what particular interest? List two examples.
2. Around what other interests are pressure groups formed?
3. What is a public-interest group? Name one of these groups.

6. Influencing Public Opinion and Public Policy

As You Read, Think About:

- What tactics pressure groups use.
- Why PACs are controversial.
- What kinds of activities lobbyists use to influence lawmakers.

Pressure groups exist to influence public policies, and they operate wherever those policies are made or can be influenced. That is, they operate at *all* levels of govenment in the United States. The fact that decisions are made in so many places in the American political system is a major reason why many of these groups are able to realize many of their goals. In short, we can still agree with Lord Bryce's somewhat indelicate comment: "Where the body is, there will the vultures be gathered."

Propaganda and Public Opinion

As hard as it may be to define, public opinion is the most significant long-term force in American politics. Over the long run, no public policy can be followed successfully without the support of a goodly portion of the population. Pressure groups know this and regularly court the public's opinions.

Pressure groups try to create the public attitudes they want with propaganda. **Propaganda** is a technique of persuasion, aimed at influencing individual or group views and actions. It is a vague and somewhat inexact term, much like public opinion. Its goal is to create a particular popular belief. That belief may be in something "good" or "bad," depending on who makes that judgment. It may be completely true or false, or it may lie somewhere between those extremes. As a *technique*, however, propaganda is neither moral nor immoral; it is amoral. It does not use objective logic; rather it begins with a conclusion and then brings together evidences to support it. Propaganda and objective analysis sometimes agree in their conclusions, but their methods are quite different. In short, propagandists are not teachers. Rather, propagandists are advertisers, persuaders, brainwashers.

Propaganda techniques have been brought to a high level in this country, first in the field of commercial advertising and more recently in politics. The major techniques propagandists use are outlined in the chart on the next page.

Talented propagandists almost never attack the logic of some policy they oppose. Instead, they often attack it with name-calling; that is, they paint such labels as "Communist," "Fascist," "ultraliberal," "ultraconservative," "pie-in-the-sky," or "greedy," and so on. Or they try to do the same thing by card-stacking—that is, presenting only material that will make something appear to be that which in fact it is not.

Policies they support are given labels that will produce favorable reactions, such glittering generalities as "American," "sound,"

*REINFORCEMENT Introduce a discussion on propaganda by using the chart on page 284. Ask for additional examples for each of the categories and a group that might use it.

Propaganda Techniques

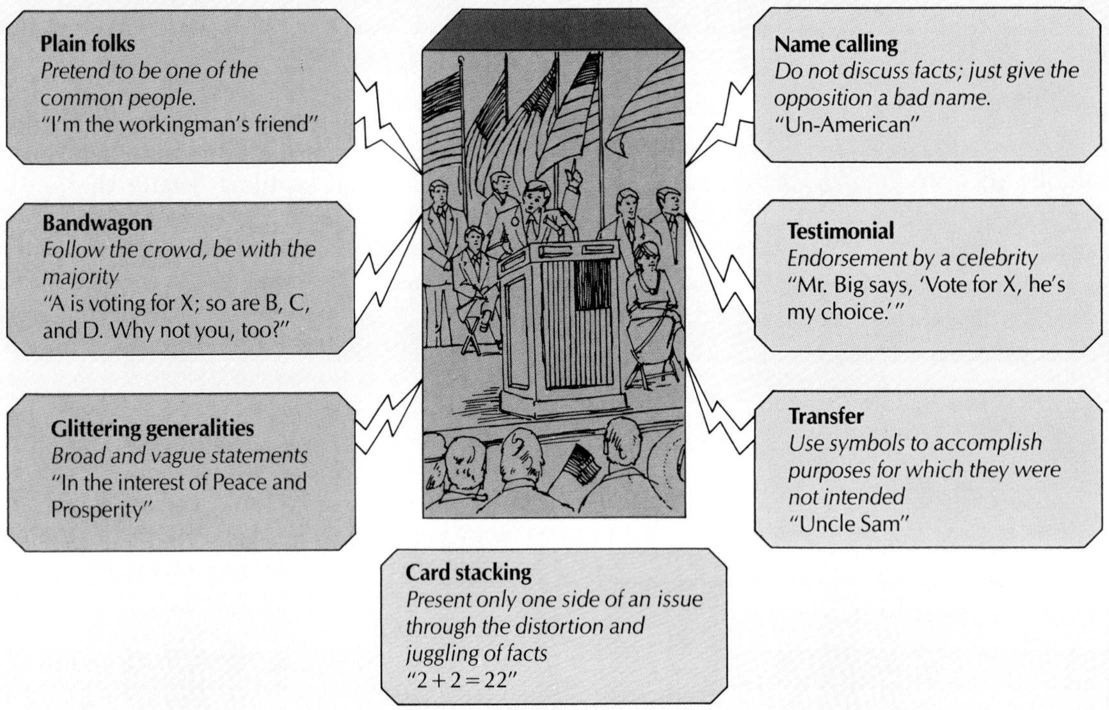

Plain folks
Pretend to be one of the common people.
"I'm the workingman's friend"
Bandwagon
Follow the crowd, be with the majority
"A is voting for X; so are B, C, and D. Why not you, too?"
Glittering generalities
Broad and vague statements
"In the interest of Peace and Prosperity"
Name calling
Do not discuss facts; just give the opposition a bad name.
"Un-American"
Testimonial
Endorsement by a celebrity
"Mr. Big says, 'Vote for X, he's my choice.'"
Transfer
Use symbols to accomplish purposes for which they were not intended
"Uncle Sam"
Card stacking
Present only one side of an issue through the distortion and juggling of facts
"2+2=22"

To become familiar with propaganda techniques, look for examples of each from such sources as: newspapers, magazines, television, billboards, and so on. Explain why each propaganda technique is effective and how each influences the public.

"fair," and "just." Symbols are often used to transfer those reactions, too: Uncle Sam and the flag are favorites. So, too, are testimonials—endorsements, or supporting statements, from well-known television stars, professional athletes, and the like. Both the bandwagon and the plain-folks approaches get heavy use, too.

Propaganda is spread through newspapers, radio, television, movies, billboards, books, magazines, pamphlets, posters, speeches—in fact, through every form of mass communication. The more controversial—or the less popular—a group's position may be, the more necessary the propaganda campaign becomes because competing groups will likely be conducting campaigns of their own.

Pressure Groups, Political Parties, and Elections

We know that pressure groups and political parties are very different. They exist in the same environment, however, and their paths cross often and in several places.

For their part, pressure groups know that political parties play a central role in selecting those people who make public policy decisions. They are quite aware, too, of the fact that much of government's policymaking machinery is organized by and through parties.[17] In short, many pressure groups are

[17]We have the two major parties in mind here. Many minor parties can be more readily compared with pressure groups than they can with the major parties; see page 192.

closely involved with efforts to elect their friends and defeat their enemies.

Pressure groups try to influence the behavior of political parties in a number of ways. Some keep close ties with one or the other of the major parties. Most hope to secure the support of both of them, however. Several urge their members to become active in party affairs and try to win posts in party organizations.

As we have seen, campaigns for public office cost money, and sometimes large amounts of it. Pressure groups also know this. They and their members are a major source of campaign contributions today. Much of their financial help now goes to parties and their candidates through political action committees (PACs), as we saw in Chapter 9.

The number of PACs has grown very rapidly in the past few years. One particular variety has grown most rapidly, however. These organizations are often called single-interest groups. They are PACs that concentrate their efforts on *one* issue—for example, abortion, gun control, nuclear power development, or women's rights. They work for or, more often, against a candidate *solely* on the basis of that candidate's stand on that *one* issue. For them, all other considerations —the candidate's record on other questions, his or her party identification or political experience, and so on—are not considered important.

A pressure group's election tactics often have to involve some very finely tuned decisions. If, for example, a group supports the Democratic candidate for a seat in the U.S. Senate, it may not want to help the campaign by attacking the Republican candidate for that post. The Republican might stand a good chance of winning, and then what? Or another Republican candidate who wins a seat in the House or wins some other office might be offended by attacks on a party colleague, even if he or she agrees with the group's policy aims. Most pressure groups try to remember that their *first* concern is with the making of public policy. Any part they play in the election process is only secondary to that objective. Single-interest groups do not follow this rule, however.

Lobbying

Lobbying is usually defined as those activities by which group pressures are brought to bear on legislators and the legislative process. Certainly, it is that, but it is also much more. Realistically, **lobbying** includes all of the means by which group pressures are brought to bear on *all* aspects of the public policymaking process. Lobbying takes place in legislative bodies, of course, and it often has important effects there. But it is also often directed at administrative agencies, and at times even at the courts.

What happens in a legislative body is often of deep concern to several different, and competing, interests. A bill to regulate the sale of firearms, for example, excites the interest of many persons and groups. Those companies that make guns, those that sell them, and those that produce or sell ammunition, targets, scopes, hunting jackets, sleeping bags, and a host of other things have a clear stake in that bill's contents and its fate. So, too, do law enforcement agencies, hunters, wildlife conservationists, such groups as the National Rifle Association and the American Civil Liberties Union, and many others.

But public policy is made by much more than the words in a statute. What happens *after* a law has been passed is often of real concern to organized interests, too. How is a law interpreted and how vigorously is it applied by the agency that enforces it? What attitude do the courts take if the law is challenged on some legal ground? These questions point up the fact that pressure groups often have to carry their lobbying efforts beyond the legislative arena—into one and sometimes several agencies in the executive branch and sometimes into the courts, as well.

Nearly all of the more important organized interests in the country—business groups, labor unions, farm organizations, the professions, veterans, the aged, churches, *

*ENRICHMENT Discuss in class: Lobbyists are hired to "get the message across." What qualifications would you look for if you were hiring someone to represent your interests?

and many more—maintain lobbyists in Washington.[18]

Lobbyists themselves often prefer to be known by some other title—"legislative counsel" or "public representative," for example. Whatever they call themselves, their major task is to work for those matters of benefit to their clients and against those that may harm them.

The competent lobbyist is thoroughly familiar with government and its ways, with the facts of current political life, and with the techniques of "polite" persuasion. Some have been members of Congress or the State legislature. They know the "legislative ropes" and have many close contacts among present-day members. Many others are lawyers, former journalists, or men and women who have come into lobbying from the closely related field of public relations.

Lobbyists at work use a number of techniques as they try to persuade legislators and other policymakers to their points of view. They see that articles, reports, and all sorts of other information reach those officeholders. Many testify before legislative committees. If the House Committee on the Judiciary is considering a gun control bill, for example, then representatives of all those groups we mentioned a moment ago are certain to be invited, or to ask for the opportunity, to present their views. The testimony that lobbyists give is usually "expert," but, of course, it is also couched in terms favorable to the interests they represent.

Most lobbyists also know how to bring "grass-roots" pressures to bear. The groups they speak for can mount campaigns by letter, phone, and wire from "the folks back home"—and often on short notice. Favorable news stories, magazine articles, advertisements, radio and television appeals, endorsements by noted personalities—these and the many other weapons of publicity are within the arsenal of the good lobbyist.

Armed with carefully researched information, lobbyists often try to meet personally with members of Congress to persuade them to support the views of the organization they represent. Here, a lobbyist meets with Representative Robert T. Matsui (D., California) in his office to discuss the Children's Defense Fund.

The typical lobbyist of today is a far cry from those of an earlier day—and from many of those still found on television and in novels and the movies. The once fairly common practice of bribery is almost unknown. Most present-day lobbyists work in the open, and their major techniques come under the headings of friendliness, persuasion, and helpfulness.

Lobbyists are ready to do such things as buy lunches and dinners, provide information, write speeches, and prepare bills in proper form. The food is good, the information usually quite accurate, the speeches forceful, and the bills well drawn. Most lobbyists know that if they behaved otherwise—give false information, for example—they

[18]Lobbyists are also stationed in the 50 State capitols, and their number grows whenever the State's legislature is in session. The "lobby" is actually an outer room or a main corridor or some other part of a capitol building to which the general public is admitted. The term *lobby-agent* was being used to identify favor-seekers at sessions of the New York State legislature in Albany by the late 1820s. By the 1830s it had been shortened to "lobbyist" and was in wide use in Washington and elsewhere.

would damage, if not destroy, their credibility and so their effectiveness.

Lobbyists work hard to influence committee action, floor debate, and the final vote in a legislative body. If they fail in one house they carry their fight to the other. If they lose there, too, they may turn to the executive branch[19] and, perhaps to the courts, as well.

Lobby Regulation Lobbying abuses do *occur now and then, of course. False or misleading testimony, bribery, and other unethical pressures are not at all common, but they are not unknown either. To try to keep lobbying within bounds, Congress passed the Federal Regulation of Lobbying Act in 1946. Each of the States now has a somewhat similar law.

The federal law requires lobbyists to register with the Clerk of the House and the Secretary of the Senate. More exactly, it requires individuals and groups to register if they collect or spend money or any other thing of value for the "principal purpose" of influencing legislation. The Supreme Court narrowed the scope of the law somewhat in 1954. In *United States* v. *Harris,* it upheld the law against 1st Amendment attacks on its constitutionality. But it also held that its registration provisions apply only to lobbying efforts aimed at Congress, not to those aimed at the public at large.

The law has proved to be quite inadequate over the past 40 years, and Congress has not seen fit to strengthen it. Its vague phrase "principal purpose" is a huge loophole through which many active groups avoid registration. They do so on grounds that lobbying is only "incidental" to their main objectives or that their monies are spent for "research" and "public information." Most estimates put the number of people who now earn at least part of their living by lobbying Congress at about 20,000. Yet only some 5,500 persons are registered under the law, and that number includes many multiple filings by persons who lobby for several different groups. The law does have penalties for its violation, but it has no enforcement provisions. Also, it does not apply to lobbying aimed at agencies in the executive branch nor does it cover testifying before congressional committees.

Robert Day, *New Yorker,* February 7, 1970

"So far, my mail is running three to one in favor of my position."

FOR REVIEW

1. **Identify:** single-interest group, political action committee, lobbyist.
2. At which level(s) of government do pressure groups try to influence public policy? Why?
3. What is propaganda?
4. What are the four major techniques of propagandists?
5. Why do pressure groups try to influence the outcomes of elections? How do they try to influence elections?
6. What is lobbying? What techniques are used by lobbyists?

---

[19]Notice that various government agencies often act much like pressure groups in their relations with Congress or with a State's legislature—for example, when they ask for funds or when they argue for or against some bill in committee.

*REINFORCEMENT Ask the class: Why is lobby regulation needed. Has it proved effective?

SUMMARY

Public opinion is both a much-used and a not-too-well-understood term. It is made up of all of the views and attitudes that people hold on matters of government and politics. Its meaning is best understood in the plural—that is, as the publics' opinions, the opinions of publics. Those opinions arise out of and are shaped by a wide range of factors.

Political socialization is the complex, life-long process by which each person acquires his or her political opinions. The family and formal education play leading roles in that process. So do many other agents—income, occupation, the mass media, peer groups, and several others.

The content of public opinion can be seen, and to some extent measured, in the varied means by which it is expressed, especially in elections, the competing claims of pressure groups, the mass media, and citizen contacts with public officials. Scientific polls are the most reliable device for the measurement of the public's attitudes, however.

Pressure groups, also known as special-interest groups, are private organizations that work to persuade government to respond to the shared attitudes of their members. They seek to influence both the making and the content of public policies.

Most pressure groups arise out of economic (occupational) interests. Many rest on other bases, however—sectional concerns, causes, the welfare of certain segments of the population, and a variety of others.

Those organized interests apply their pressures to government with all of the means available to them—especially through the several techniques of propaganda; through political parties, their candidates, and elections; and by lobbying.

CHAPTER REVIEW

Key Terms/Concepts*

public opinion (260)
political socialization (261)
mass media (263)
mandate (266)
pressure group (267)
public opinion poll (268)
straw vote (268)
sample (271)
random sample (271)
quota sample (271)
interest group (275)
special-interest group (275)
public-interest group (282)
propaganda (283)
political action committee (PAC) (285)
lobbying (285)

*These terms are included in the Glossary.

Keynote Questions

• 1. What is public opinion? Why can this term be better understood in the plural, that is, as the opinions of publics?

• 2. What is the process of political socialization? Why are the family and the school such key agents in this process?

• 3. How do the media influence the public's interest in issues and public reactions to candidates?

• 4. List five ways in which public opinion can be measured. Give an example of each.

• 5. Briefly describe each of the five basic steps involved in scientific polling.

• • • 6. Make a table that shows the differences between pressure groups and political parties in the following areas: nominations, primary interest, and scope of interest.

• 7. Explain in a sentence how pressure groups contribute to the political system in each of the following areas: public interest in public affairs, representation, information exchange, checks-and-balances.

• 8. What is the difference between a pressure group based on economic interests and a public-interest group?

• 9. For each of the following public policy concerns, name two pressure groups interested in that concern: business, labor, agriculture, professional, the environment, and retirees.

*The dots represent skill levels required to answer each question or complete each activity:
•requires recall and comprehension • •requires application and analysis • • •requires synthesis and evaluation

• **10.** What is the goal of propaganda? What techniques are used to achieve this goal?

• **11.** In what ways do pressure groups attempt to influence public policies?

• **12.** What role does lobbying play in the political process?

Skill Application

Recognizing Unsupported Generalizations Pressure groups and candidates try to influence public opinion through speeches, letters, brochures, articles, and other materials. Because candidates and pressure groups communicate much information to many people in a very short amount of time, these materials are often filled with generalizations. Being able to recognize unsupported generalizations enables you to understand better and make more informed decisions about issues and candidates.

Unsupported generalizations are conclusions that are not based on data or facts. They usually reflect the opinions, experiences, or observations of the writer or speaker.

Unsupported generalizations are too broad and too vague to be proven or disproven. For example, one candidate may declare, "Support our plan and you will be supporting democracy." No evidence exists to prove this statement; it is an unsupported generalization.

Read the paragraph below. Write down all the candidate's sentences that are unsupported generalizations. Next to each, write a question that might force the candidate to clarify the point.

My opponent's current plan to improve the economy would cause havoc. People would lose jobs and interest rates would go up. In the long run, you will have to pay higher taxes because of this plan. Support my economic plan and this community's economy will prosper. New businesses will be attracted to the area. You will end up having to spend less on taxes. A vote for me is a vote for the future welfare of this community!

For Thought and Discussion

•• **1.** In what specific ways can the average citizen become as fully informed as possible about public affairs?

••• **2.** Many candidates receive campaign contributions from pressure groups. Some people charge that this practice makes candidates "hostages to the special interests." Others claim that this practice makes candidates more accountable to the people on particular issues. Which side do you agree with? Why?

••• **3.** The structure of government in the United States contributes to the strength and importance of pressure groups, according to some analysts. Consider this comment by Fred R. Harris: "A fragmented system of power protects against a strong minority or a runaway majority. But it also results in a highly complicated system, which ordinary citizens may find confusing and difficult to influence. Hence, fragmentation of power is an important cause of the formation and influence of interest groups in America." Restate this comment in your own words. Do you agree with Harris? Why or why not?

••• **4.** Compare the advantages and disadvantages of the following as sources of information about public affairs: television news programs, newspapers, materials from pressure groups.

Suggested Activities

••• **1.** Select an important national, State, or local issue and list five pressure groups that might be involved in the issue. Your text and the following directories would be useful references: *Washington Information Directory*, and *Encyclopedia of Associations*. Write letters to two of the groups from your list. Ask for information on the issue. Compare the groups' positions on the issue, and look for any persuasive techniques.

••• **2.** Conduct a week-long analysis of a network television or radio news program, one which is devoted to national (not local) news. Watch or listen to the same program every day for seven days. Keep a log noting the following: the types of stories covered; the amount of time spent on each; a summary (two sentences) of the story, and any commercials that are aired during the news. At the end of the week, analyze your data. How much time was spent on "hard news"—national and international affairs? How much time was spent on other stories—sports, human interest, weather? Did you find any editorial biases in the presentations?

Unit 4

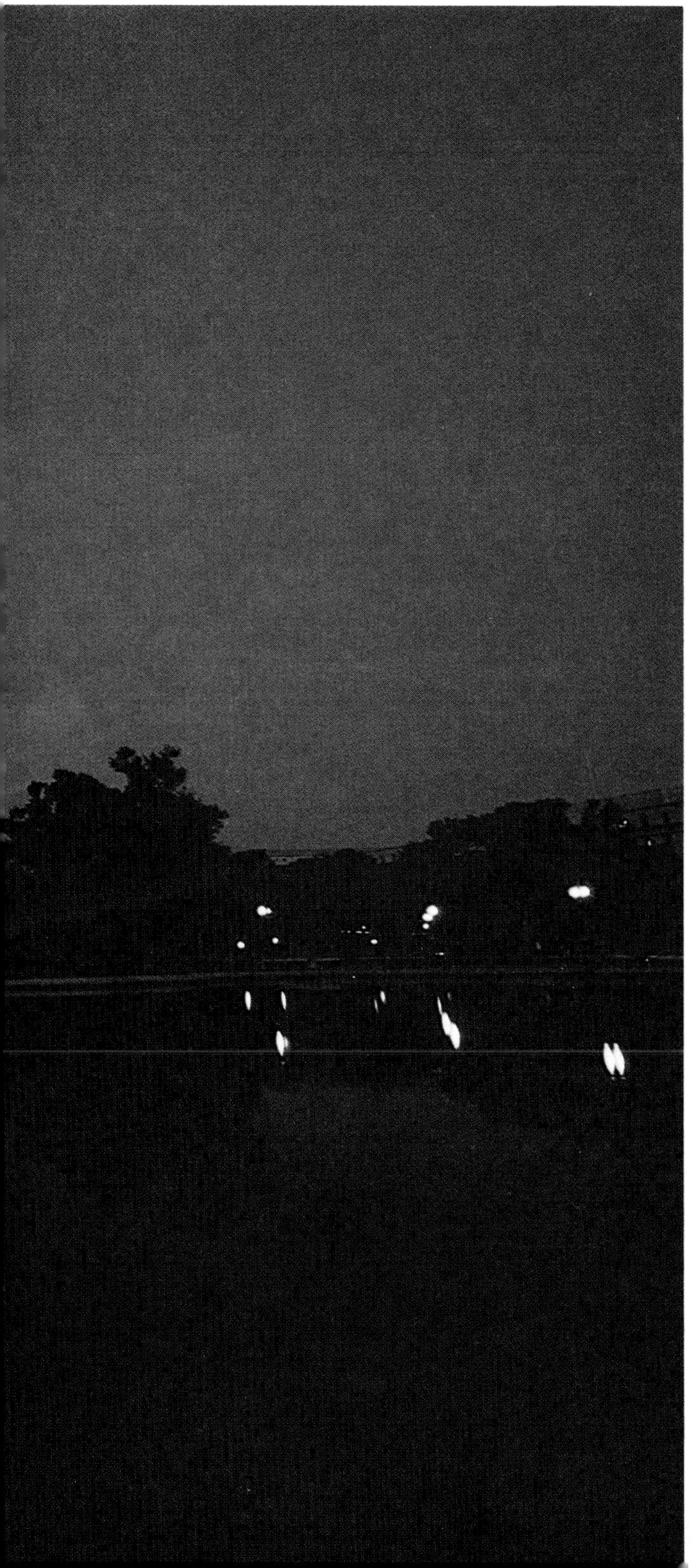

Congress: The First Branch

ONE DISTINCTIVE FEATURE of the American governmental system is its separation of the power of the Government into three distinct branches: legislative, executive, and judicial. In Unit 4 we examine the first of these branches at the national level, Congress—the legislative branch.

The legislative branch of the National Government consists of the two houses of Congress, the Senate and the House of Representatives. They are referred to here as "the first branch" both because the legislative is the branch of the National Government for which the Constitution first provides and because the Congress is the central institution of our representative democracy. It is the branch closest to the people and the one to which the Constitution gives the bulk of the powers held by the National Government.

In the next three chapters, we explore what Congress actually does and how it does it. We look first at its structure. Then we examine how the two houses operate and how a bill introduced in either house eventually becomes, or does not become, a law. Finally we consider the powers of the Congress, both those expressed in the Constitution, and those implied, that is, reasonably deduced from the expressed powers.

Congress "is too complex to be understood without an effort, without a careful and systematic process of analysis," President Wilson said. In Unit 4, we shall make that analysis.

A dramatic night view of the nation's Capitol in Washington, D.C.

Congress is neither as doltish as the cartoonists portray it nor as noble as it portrays itself. While it has its quota of knaves and fools it also has its fair share of knights. And sandwiched between these upper and nether crusts is a broad and representative slice of upper-middle class America.
–CABELL PHILLIPS

11
The Congress

CHAPTER OBJECTIVES

To help you to

Learn · Know · Understand

The place and the role of Congress, the structure of Congress: its bicameral character and its terms and sessions.

The structure of the House of Representatives: its size and composition, and the election, terms, and qualifications of its members.

The structure of the Senate: its size and composition, and the election, terms, and qualifications of its members.

The general characteristics of members of Congress.

A RESPONSIBLE, RESPONSIVE, and effective legislative body is absolutely indispensable to democratic government. Without such an agency, any "talk" about democratic government is only that.

Elected assemblies of some kind are found in nearly all governments in the world today. Many of these assemblies are shams, however. They are false fronts, masks for the real location and exercise of the public policymaking power. The Supreme Soviet in the USSR stands as a prime example. Its members are chosen by popular vote, but in elections in which there are no opposition candidates. It meets to be told and to agree, not to propose, debate, and decide.

1. Legislative Function

As You Read, Think About:

- What the term *bicameral* means.
- What the difference is between terms and sessions of Congress.

The painting above is Samuel F.B. Morse's *Congress Hall,* completed in 1822. It depicts the House in night session with the Supreme Court Justices in attendance. What contrasts can be found between Morse's painting and the photo of the modern chamber of the House of Representatives on the left?

In the American democratic system, Congress is the legislative branch of the National Government. Its major function is to make law. It, then, is charged with *the* basic governmental function in a democratic system: that of translating the public will into public policy in the form of law.

How profoundly important the Framers thought that function to be can be seen in the fact that the first, and the lengthiest, of the Articles of the Constitution is devoted to it. Article I, Section 1 reads:

> All legislative powers herein granted shall be vested in a Congress of the United States, which shall consist of a Senate and House of Representatives.

Bicameralism

Immediately, the Constitution establishes a **bicameral** legislature, that is, one made up of two houses. It does so for three major reasons:

Historically, the British Parliament, which the Framers and most other Americans knew quite well, had consisted of two houses since the 1300s. Most of the colonial assemblies, and all but two of the State legislatures in 1787, were also bicameral.[1]

Practically, a two-chambered body had to be created to settle the conflict between the Virginia and the New Jersey Plans at Philadelphia in 1787; see pages 44–46. Notice, bicameralism is also a reflection of federalism. Each State is equally represented in the Senate and by its population in the House.

[1]Only Georgia and Pennsylvania had had wide experience with unicameral colonial and then State legislatures. Georgia's legislature became bicameral in 1789 and Pennsylvania's in 1790. Among the 50 States today, only Nebraska (since 1937) has a unicameral legislature; see page 557.

ENRICHMENT Ask the class to discuss: Congress is charged with translating the public will into public policy in the form of law. Is this best served by a bicameral institution? Why?

Theoretically, the Framers favored a bicameral Congress in order that one house might act as a check on the other. A leading constitutional historian reports:

> Thomas Jefferson, who possessed great faith in "the voice of the people," was in France when the Constitution was framed. Upon his return, while taking breakfast with Washington, he opposed the two-body form of legislature, and was disposed to twit Washington about it. At this time Jefferson poured his coffee from his cup into his saucer. Washington asked him why he did so. "To cool it," he answered. "So," said Washington, "we will pour legislation into the Senatorial saucer to cool it."[2]

Some say that the equal representation of the States in the Senate should be scrapped as undemocratic.[3] Those critics often point to the two extremes to make their case. The State with the least population, Alaska, has only some 500,000 residents. The largest State, California, has more than 26 million. Yet each of these States has two Senators.

Those who argue against State equality in the Senate ignore a vital fact. The Senate was purposely created as a body in which the States would be represented as co-equal members and partners in the Federal Union. Remember, had the States not been equally represented in the upper house, there might never have been a Constitution.

Terms of Congress

Each **term** of Congress lasts for two years[4] and is numbered consecutively from the first term, which began on March 4, 1789.

The date for the start of each term was changed by the 20th Amendment in 1933. It is now "noon on the 3d day of January" of every odd-numbered year. Thus the term of the 100th Congress began at noon on January 3, 1987, and it will end at noon on January 3, 1989.

Sessions of Congress

There are two **sessions** to each term of Congress—one each year. Section 2 of the 20th Amendment states:

> The Congress shall assemble at least once in every year, and such meeting shall begin at noon on the 3d day of January . . .

Congress adjourns each regular session as it sees fit. Until World War II, a typical session lasted for perhaps four or five months. The many and pressing issues since then have forced Congress to remain in session through most of each year.

Neither house may adjourn *sine die*—that is, finally, ending session—without the consent of the other. Article I, Section 5, Clause 4 provides:

> Neither House . . . shall, without the consent of the other, adjourn for more than three days, nor to any other place than that in which the two Houses shall be sitting.[5]

Special Sessions

Only the President may call a **special session** of Congress.[6] Only 26 such sessions have ever been held. The last one was called by President Truman in 1948, to consider a number of anti-inflation and welfare measures. The fact that Congress now meets

[2]Max Farrand, *The Framing of the Constitution* (New Haven: Yale University Press, 1913), 74.

[3]The prospects for any such change are so slim as to be nonexistent. Article V of the Constitution provides, in part, that "no State, without its consent, shall be deprived of its equal suffrage in the Senate."

[4]Article I, Section 2, Clause 1 dictates a two-year term for Congress by providing that Representatives "shall be chosen . . . every second year."

[5]Article II, Section 3 gives the President power to adjourn *(prorogue)* a session, but only when the two houses cannot agree upon a date for adjournment. No President has ever had to use that power. The Legislative Reorganization Act of 1946 requires each regular session to adjourn no later than July 31, unless Congress should decide otherwise or a national emergency exists. But Congress has met this self-imposed deadline only twice, in 1952 and 1956. Both houses recess for several short periods during a session.

[6]Article II, Section 3 provides that the President may "convene both Houses, or either of them," in a special session. Only the Senate has been called into special session on 46 occasions, but not since 1933, to consider treaties and appointments.

Which party has more members in your State delegation to Congress?

*REINFORCEMENT Discuss in class: The composition of Congress reflects the intent of the Framers to ensure citizens' rights as well as maintain the federal nature of the government.

Composition of Congress

PARTY STRENGTH (at beginning of term)

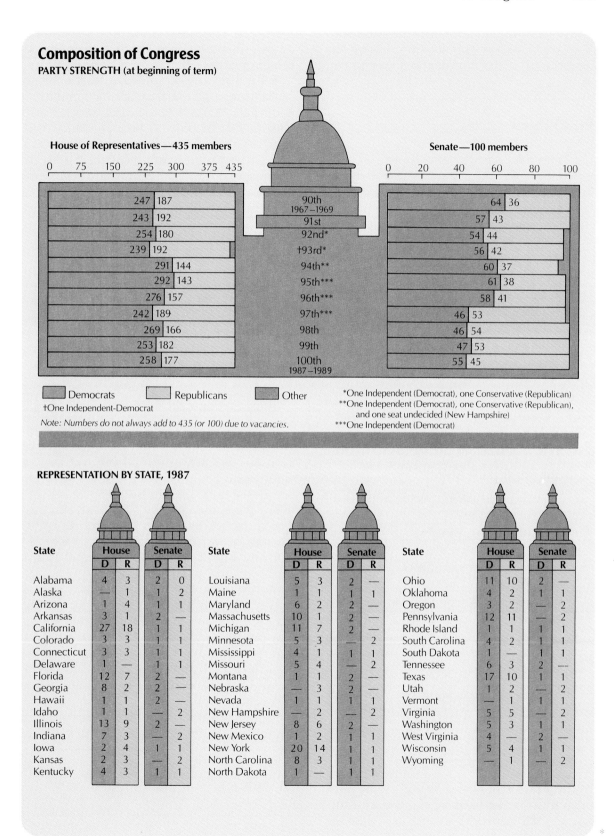

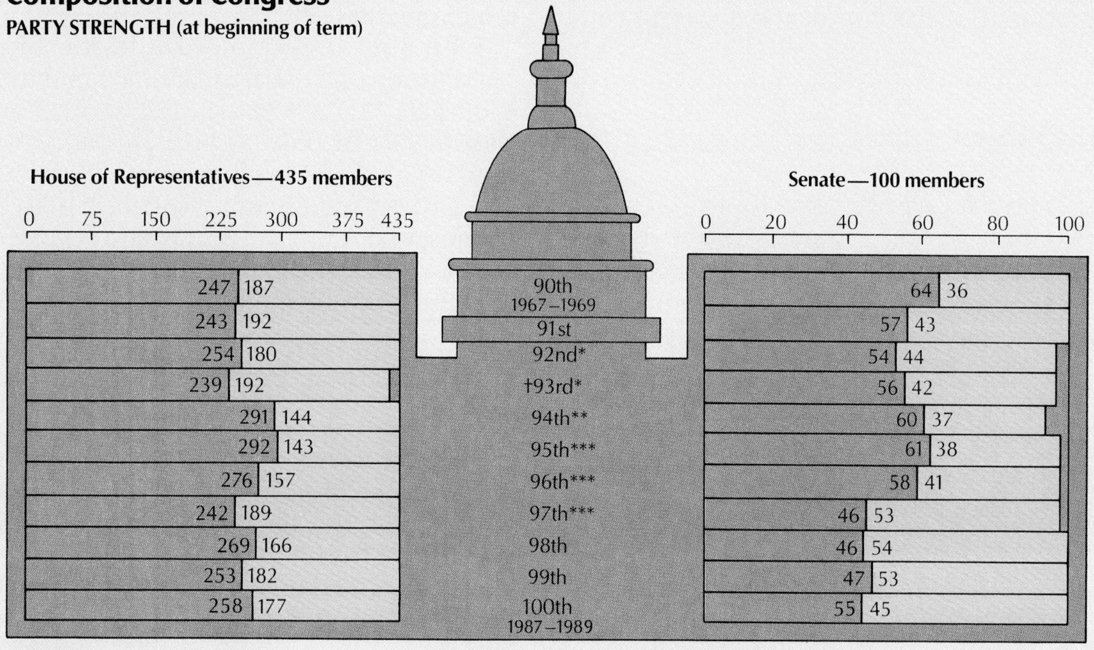

Democrats   Republicans   Other

†One Independent-Democrat

Note: Numbers do not always add to 435 (or 100) due to vacancies.

*One Independent (Democrat), one Conservative (Republican)
**One Independent (Democrat), one Conservative (Republican), and one seat undecided (New Hampshire)
***One Independent (Democrat)

REPRESENTATION BY STATE, 1987

State	House D	House R	Senate D	Senate R
Alabama	4	3	2	0
Alaska	—	1	1	2
Arizona	1	4	1	1
Arkansas	3	1	2	—
California	27	18	1	1
Colorado	3	3	1	1
Connecticut	3	3	1	1
Delaware	1	—	1	1
Florida	12	7	2	—
Georgia	8	2	2	—
Hawaii	1	1	2	—
Idaho	1	1	—	2
Illinois	13	9	2	—
Indiana	7	3	—	2
Iowa	2	4	1	1
Kansas	2	3	—	2
Kentucky	4	3	1	1

State	House D	House R	Senate D	Senate R
Louisiana	5	3	2	—
Maine	1	1	1	1
Maryland	6	2	2	—
Massachusetts	10	1	2	—
Michigan	11	7	2	—
Minnesota	5	3	—	2
Mississippi	4	1	1	1
Missouri	5	4	—	2
Montana	1	1	2	—
Nebraska	—	3	2	—
Nevada	1	1	1	1
New Hampshire	—	2	—	2
New Jersey	8	6	2	—
New Mexico	1	2	1	1
New York	20	14	1	1
North Carolina	8	3	1	1
North Dakota	1	—	1	1

State	House D	House R	Senate D	Senate R
Ohio	11	10	2	—
Oklahoma	4	2	1	1
Oregon	3	2	—	2
Pennsylvania	12	11	—	2
Rhode Island	1	1	1	1
South Carolina	4	2	1	1
South Dakota	1	—	1	1
Tennessee	6	3	2	—
Texas	17	10	1	1
Utah	1	2	—	2
Vermont	—	1	1	1
Virginia	5	5	—	2
Washington	5	3	1	1
West Virginia	4	—	2	—
Wisconsin	5	4	1	1
Wyoming	—	1	—	2

*REINFORCEMENT Ask students to study the above charts and discuss how legislation is affected by party strength. Point out that the President's party may not be in the majority in one or both houses.

nearly year-round cuts down the likelihood of special sessions. That fact also lessens the importance of the President's power to call one.

FOR REVIEW

1. **Identify:** Congress, term, session, adjournment.
2. With what basic governmental function is Congress charged?
3. Why did the Framers of the Constitution establish a bicameral Congress? What are the historical, practical, and theoretical reasons for bicameralism in our government?
4. What is the difference between a term and a session of Congress?
5. Who may call a special session of Congress?

2. The House of Representatives

As You Read, Think About:

- What the structure and size of the House of Representatives are.
- What the terms, election, and qualifications of its members are.
- How reapportionment affects the makeup of the House.
- What a congressional district is and how it is formed.
- What effect the "one-man, one-vote" rule has had on the House and on electoral politics in general.

The House of Representatives, the lower house, is the larger of the two chambers of Congress.

Size

The exact size of the House—today, 435 members—is not fixed by the Constitution. Rather, the Constitution provides that the total number of seats, however many that may be, shall be **apportioned,** or distributed, among the States on the basis of their respective populations.[7]

Each State is guaranteed at least one seat in the House, no matter what its population. Today, six States—Alaska, Delaware, North Dakota, South Dakota, Vermont, and Wyoming—have only one Representative apiece. The District of Columbia, Guam, the Virgin Islands, and American Samoa are represented by a Delegate, and Puerto Rico by a Resident Commissioner. However, they are not, in fact, *members* of the House.

Terms

The Constitution provides that "Representatives shall be . . . chosen every second year"[8]—that is, for two-year terms. This rather short term is intended to make the House more immediately responsive to popular pressures than the Senate.

Reapportionment

The Constitution directs Congress to **reapportion,** or redistribute, the seats in the House after each decennial census.[9] Until a first census could be taken, the Constitution set the size of the House at 65 seats, and there were that many in the 1st and 2nd Congresses (1789–1793). The Census of 1790 showed a national population of 3,929,214 persons, and in 1792 the number of House seats was increased by 41, to 106.

As the nation's population grew, and as the number of States increased, so did the size of the House. It went to 142 seats after the Census of 1800, to 186 seats 10 years later, and so on.[10] By 1912, following the Census of 1910 and the admissions of Arizona and New Mexico, the House had grown to 435 seats.

With the Census of 1920, Congress faced an extraordinary dilemma. The House had

[7] Article I, Section 2, Clause 3.
[8] Article I, Section 2, Clause 1.
[9] Article I, Section 2, Clause 3.
[10] Except following the Census of 1840, when, for the only time in its history, the size of the House was reduced—from 242 to 232 seats.

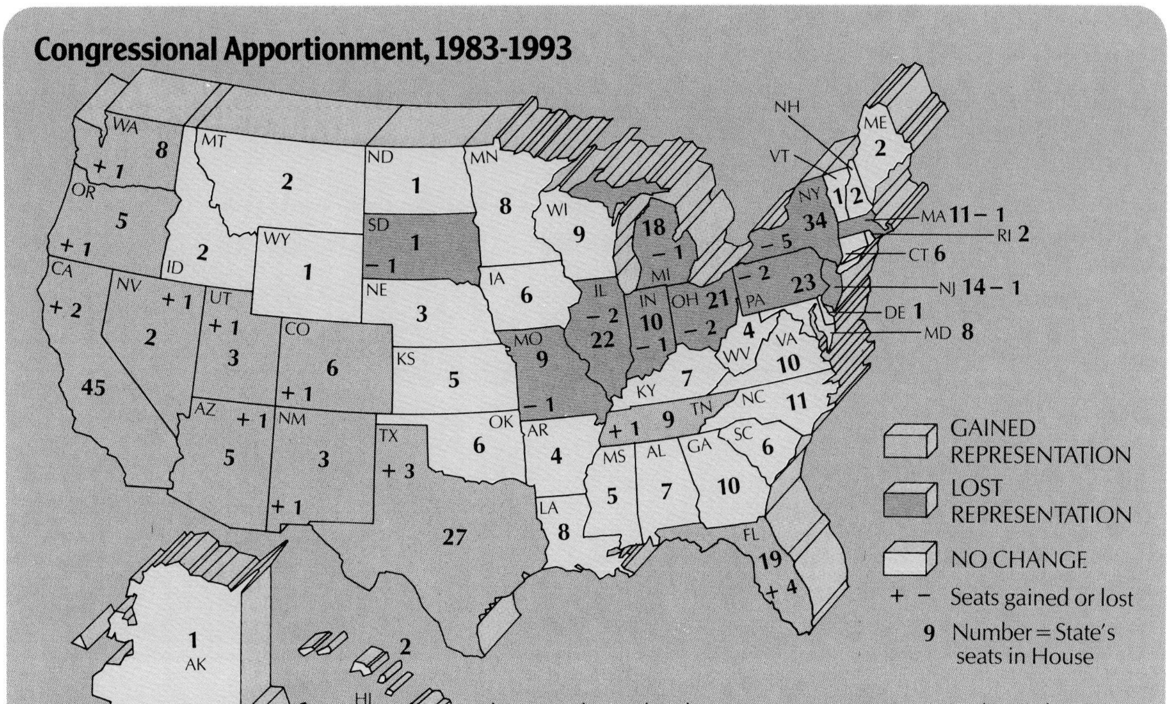

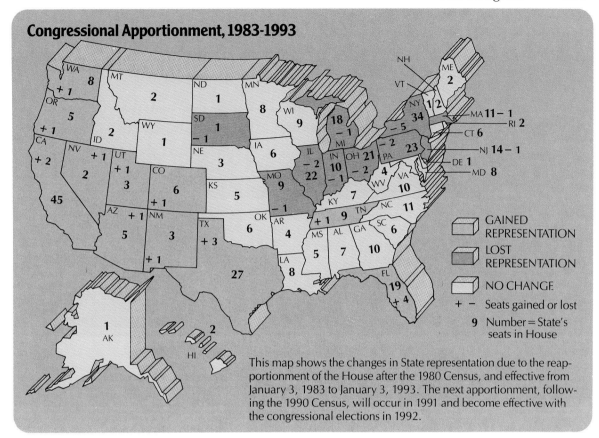

This map shows the changes in State representation due to the reapportionment of the House after the 1980 Census, and effective from January 3, 1983 to January 3, 1993. The next apportionment, following the 1990 Census, will occur in 1991 and become effective with the congressional elections in 1992.

Were there changes in your State's representation as a result of reapportionment of the House after the 1980 Census?

long since grown too large for effective floor action. But, to reapportion without adding more seats meant that some States would lose seats if every State was to be represented on the basis of its population.

Congress met the problem by doing nothing. So, despite the Constitution's command, no reapportionment on the basis of the 1920 Census was made.

The Reapportionment Act of 1929 Faced with the 1930 Census, Congress moved to avoid repeating its earlier lapse, with the Reapportionment Act of 1929. That law, still on the books, sets up what is often called an "automatic reapportionment." It provides for the following:

1. The "permanent" size of the House is 435 members. Of course, that figure is permanent only so long as Congress does not decide to change it.
2. Following each census, the Census Bureau is to determine the number of seats each State should have.
3. When the Bureau's plan is ready, the President must send it to Congress.
4. If, within 60 days of receiving it, neither house rejects the Census Bureau's plan, it becomes effective.

The scheme set out in the 1929 law has worked quite well through six reapportionments, most recently in 1981. The law leaves to Congress its constitutional responsibility to reapportion the House, but it gives to the Census Bureau the mechanical chores (and political heat) that go with that task. Today each seat in the House represents an average of 550,000 persons. *

*ENRICHMENT Have students find out whether your State was redistricted after the last census. If so, was a new Representative added or lost?

North Carolina's Congressional Districts

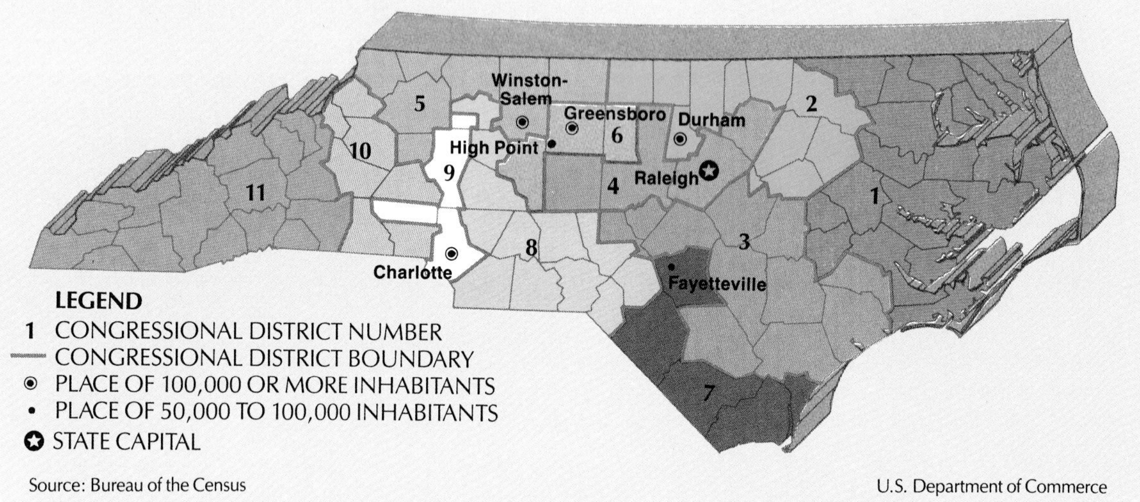

This map of North Carolina shows the eleven Congressional districts by number. The "thin" lines show county lines on this map.

Election

According to the Constitution, any person that a State allows to vote for members of "the most numerous branch" of its own legislature is qualified to vote in congressional elections.[11] The Constitution states

> The times, places, and manner of holding [congressional] elections . . . shall be prescribed in each State by the legislature thereof; but the Congress may at any time, by law, make or alter such regulations . . . [12]

Date Congressional elections are held on the same day in every State. Since 1872 Congress has required that those elections be held on the Tuesday following the first Monday in November of each even-numbered year.[13] In the same law, Congress directed that Representatives be chosen by written or printed ballots. The use of voting machines was sanctioned in 1899.

Districts The 435 members of the House are chosen by the voters in 435 separate congressional districts across the country. Recall, six States have only one seat in the House. There are, then, 429 districts *within* the other 44 States.[14]

The Constitution makes no mention of congressional districts. For more than half a century, Congress allowed each State to decide whether to elect its members by a general ticket system or on a **single-member district** basis.

Most States quickly set up single-member districts. Under this arrangement the voters in each district elected one of the State's

[11]Article I, Section 2, Clause 1.

[12]Article I, Section 4, Clause 1; see page 241.

[13]On the formula fixing the election date, see page 242. Congress has made an exception for Alaska, where the election may be held in October. To date, however, Alaskans have chosen their one Representative on the same day that congressional elections have been held in the other 49 States. Through 1958, Congress permitted Maine to hold its congressional (and its presidential) voting in September; but an amendment to Maine's constitution now provides that the State's congressional and other elections are to be held on the regular November date. Maine's early voting in congressional and presidential elections gave rise to an oft-repeated, but not always accurate, saying: "As Maine goes, so goes the nation."

[14]The Constitution allows only one method for filling a vacancy in the House—by a special election, which may be called only by the governor of the State involved. Article I, Section 2, Clause 4.

Representatives. Several States used the general ticket system, however. Under that arrangement, all of the State's seats were filled from the State **at-large**—that is, from the State as a whole. All the voters could vote for all of that State's Representatives.

At-large elections proved grossly unfair. A party with a plurality of the votes in a State, no matter how small, could win all of the State's seats in the House. Congress finally did away with the general ticket system in 1842. Thereafter, all of the seats in the House were to be filled from districts within each State.

The 1842 law made each State legislature responsible for the drawing of the congressional districts within its own State.[15] It also required that each district be made up of "contiguous territory." In 1872 Congress added the command that the districts within each State have "as nearly as practicable an equal number of inhabitants." In 1901 it further directed that all the districts be of "compact territory."

These requirements of contiguity, population equality, and compactness were often disregarded by State legislatures, and Congress made no real effort to enforce them. The requirements were left out of the Reapportionment Act of 1929, and in 1932 the Supreme Court held (in *Wood* v. *Broom*) that they had therefore been repealed. For decades, therefore, many districts were of odd geographic shape. In many States, districts also varied greatly in populations.

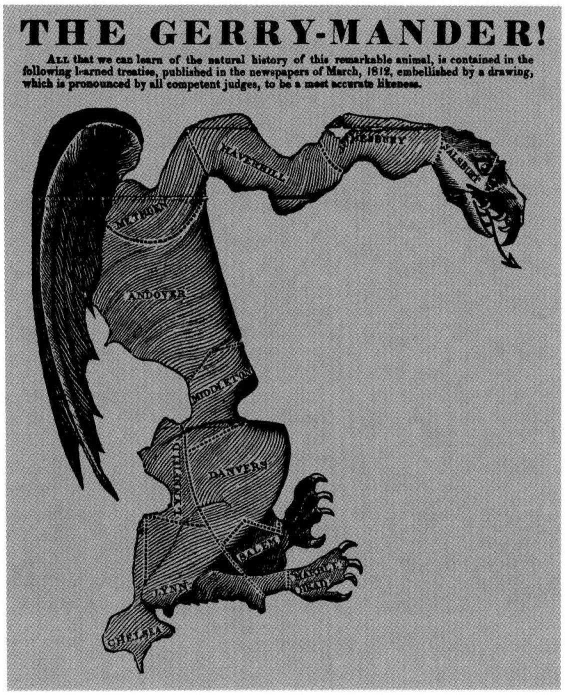
THE GERRY-MANDER!
ALL that we can learn of the natural history of this remarkable animal, is contained in the following learned treatise, published in the newspapers of March, 1812, embellished by a drawing, which is pronounced by all competent judges, to be a most accurate likeness.
HAVERHILL
ANDOVER
DANVERS

Gerrymandering takes its name from Elbridge Gerry (1744–1814). In 1812, while Gerry was governor of Massachusetts, his supporters in the legislature redrew the State's legislative districts to favor the Democratic-Republicans. It is said that the noted painter Gilbert Stuart added a head, wings, and claws to Essex County on a district map hanging over the desk of a Federalist newspaper editor. "That," he said, "will do for a salamander." "Better say Gerrymander," growled the editor.

Gerrymandering If you look at several maps of congressional districts, you will see some districts shaped like a shoestring, a dumbbell, the letter Y, or some other odd form. Such districts have usually been *** gerrymandered.** That is, they have been drawn to the advantage of the dominant party or faction in power in the legislature.

The practice of gerrymandering is both ancient and modern. It is also widespread. It can be found in most places where lines are drawn for the election of public officeholders—at the State and the local as well as at the congressional level. Most often gerrymandering takes one of two forms. Either the lines are drawn (1) to concentrate the opposition's voters in one or a few districts, thus leaving the other districts comfortably safe for the ruling party or (2) to spread the opposition as thinly as possible among several districts.

For decades, gerrymandering produced congressional districts of widely different populations. Clearly, the State legislatures were responsible for this situation. A number of them regularly drew the district lines on a strictly partisan basis—with the Republicans gouging the Democrats in some

[15]Except, of course, in States with only one Representative. In those States the one seat is filled at-large.

*ENRICHMENT The "Gerry-Mander" in the above cartoon has an evil connotation. Ask the class to discuss why gerrymandering has such a bad reputation and why it is still used today.

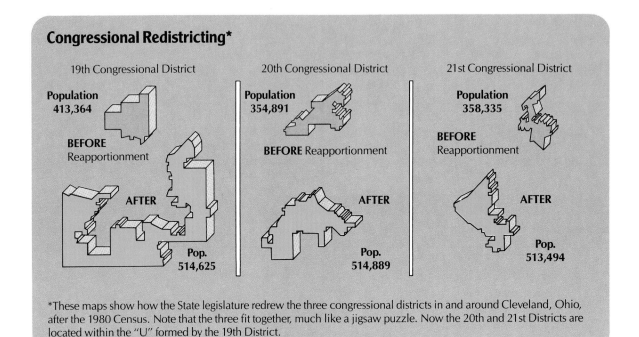

Congressional Redistricting*

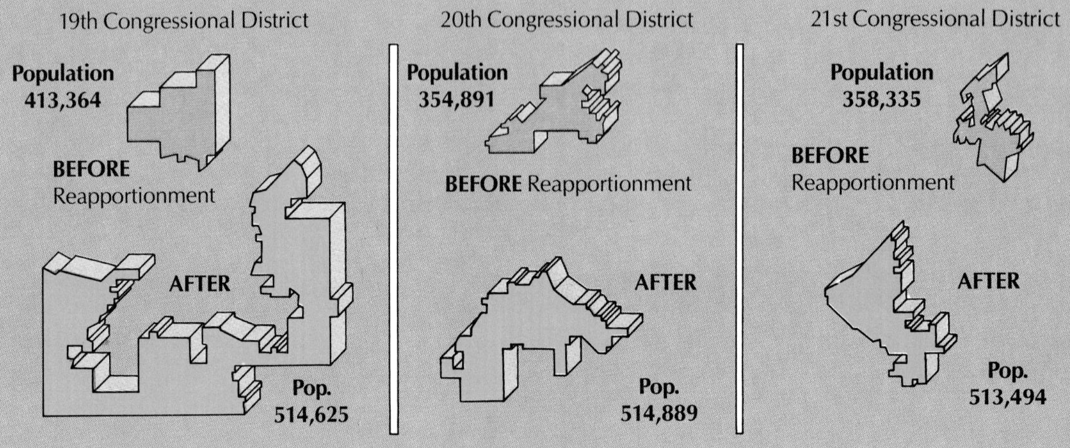

*These maps show how the State legislature redrew the three congressional districts in and around Cleveland, Ohio, after the 1980 Census. Note that the three fit together, much like a jigsaw puzzle. Now the 20th and 21st Districts are located within the "U" formed by the 19th District.

After the redistricting shown above, which of the three districts had the largest increase in population? Which district increased most in geographical area?

States and the Democrats only too willing to return the favor in others. Today, that is still the case in several States.

Most states were carved up on a rural versus urban basis. This occurred because until recently, the typical State legislature was dominated by the less-populated, overrepresented rural areas of the State.[16]

Wesberry v. *Sanders*, 1964. Suddenly, and quite dramatically, the longstanding patterns of wide population variation and of rural overrepresentation came to an end in the late 1960s. In State after State, congressional district lines were redrawn to produce districts of approximately equal populations.

These abrupt changes were the direct result of an historic decision by the Supreme Court in 1964. In *Wesberry* v. *Sanders,* the Court held that the population differences among Georgia's congressional districts were so great as to violate the Constitution.

In reaching its historic decision, the Court noted that Article I, Section 2 declares that Representatives shall be chosen "by the people of the several States" and shall be "apportioned among the several States . . . according to their respective numbers." These words, the Court held, especially when viewed in light of what the Framers intended, mean that

> . . . as nearly as practicable one man's vote in a congressional election is to be worth as much as another's.

The Court added:

> While it may not be possible to draw congressional districts with mathematical precision, that is no excuse for ignoring our Constitution's plain objective of making equal representation for equal numbers of people the fundamental goal of the House of Representatives. That is the high standard of justice and common sense which the Founders set for us.

[16]The longstanding pattern of rural overrepresentation and urban underrepresentation in the State legislatures has now all but disappeared as a direct consequence of the Supreme Court's several "one-man, one-vote" decisions of the 1960s and 1970s. In the leading case, *Reynolds* v. *Sims* (1964), the Court held that the seats in both houses of a State's legislature must be apportioned (districted) on the basis of population equality; see Chapter 20.

The importance of *Wesberry* and the Court's later "one-man, one-vote" decisions cannot be overstated. They have had an extraordinary impact on the makeup of the House, on the content of public policy, and on electoral politics in general. The nation's cities and suburbs now speak with a much larger voice in Congress than ever before.

However, it is still quite possible to draw congressional and other district lines in keeping with the "one-man, one vote" rule and also gerrymander those districts.[17]

Qualifications

According to the Constitution, a member of the House must be at least 25 years of age, must have been a citizen for at least seven years, and must be an inhabitant of the State from which he or she is chosen.[18]

Longstanding custom, not the Constitution, also requires that a Representative must live in the district he or she represents. The custom is based on the belief that the legislator should know thoroughly the locale he or she represents, its people, and its problems. Rarely, then, does a district choose an outsider to represent it.

The Constitution makes the House "the judge of the elections, returns, and qualifications of its own members."[19] Thus, when the right of a member-elect to be seated is challenged, the House has the power to decide the matter. Challenges are rarely successful.

The House may refuse to seat a member-elect by majority vote. It may also "punish its own members for disorderly behavior" by majority vote, and "with the concurrence of two-thirds, expel a member."[20]

[17]Except for gerrymandering based on race, a violation of the 14th Amendment's Equal Protection Clause, *Gomillion* v. *Lightfoot*, 1960; see page 213.

[18]Article I, Section 2, Clause 2. The Constitution also provides that neither a Representative nor a Senator "shall during the time for which he was elected, be appointed to any civil office under the authority of the United States, which shall have been created, or the emoluments whereof shall have been increased, during such time, and no person holding any office under the United States shall be a member of either House during his continuance in office" (Article I, Section 6, Clause 2).

[19]Article I, Section 5, Clause 1.

[20]Article I, Section 5, Clause 2.

The House has viewed its power to judge the qualifications of any member-elect as the power to impose additional, informal qualifications. In *Powell* v. *McCormack*, 1969, however, the Supreme Court held that the House could not exclude any member-elect who meets the Constitution's standards of age, citizenship, and residence.[21]

In nearly 200 years, the House has expelled only four members. Three were ousted in 1861 for their "support of rebellion." More recently, Michael Myers (D., Pennsylvania) was expelled in 1980 for corruption. Myers had been caught up in the Abscam probe, an undercover FBI investigation of corruption among public officials. Two FBI agents, pretending to represent an oil-rich Arab sheikh, had given him $50,000. In return, Myers had promised to introduce a bill to allow their supposed employer to enter the country as a permanent resident. For taking the money, Myers was convicted in court for bribery.[22]

The House has not often punished a member for "disorderly behavior," but such actions are not nearly so rare as expulsions. Three members were disciplined by their colleagues in the 98th Congress. In 1983 the House voted to **censure** (formally condemn) Daniel Crane (R., Ill.) and Gerry Studds (D.,

[21]Until then the House had excluded several members-elect on extra-constitutional grounds. Thus, in 1900 it refused to seat Brigham H. Roberts of Utah because he was a practicing polygamist. In 1919 and again in 1920 it excluded Victor L. Berger of Wisconsin, because he had been convicted of sedition during World War I. Berger's conviction was later overturned and, after being elected for the third time, he was finally seated in 1921. The late Representative Adam Clayton Powell of New York, reelected to a 12th term in 1966, was barred in 1967. A special committee had recommended that Powell be seated but then be censured for "gross misconduct." It found that he had misused public funds, defied the courts of his State, and been "contemptuous" in refusing to cooperate with its investigation of him. The House voted instead to exclude him. The Court held that, as Powell had been "duly elected by the voters of the 18th Congressional District of New York and was not ineligible to serve under any provision of the Constitution, the House was without power to exclude him from its membership." The House has not excluded a member-elect since the *Powell* case.

[22]A few other members have resigned their seats rather than face the possibility of expulsion. The most recent are John W. Jenrette (D., South Carolina) in 1980 and Raymond F. Lederer (D., Pennsylvania) in 1981. Both Jenrette and Lederer had also been convicted in Abscam bribery cases.

*ENRICHMENT Should House members have the power to discipline their colleagues? Discuss in class, pointing out that censured members have in some cases won reelection to Congress.

Mass.). Both had had sexual relations with congressional pages. The Committee on Standards of Official Conduct had recommended that both receive a "reprimand," the least severe penalty the House can impose. A floor vote brought the harsher action. In 1984 George Hansen (R., Idaho) was reprimanded after a court conviction for the crime of filing false financial disclosure forms. Both Crane and Hansen were ousted by their constituents in the 1984 elections, but Studds kept his seat.

FOR REVIEW

1. **Identify:** House of Representatives, decennial census, congressional district, "one man, one vote."
2. What is the present size of the House? How is that number fixed?
3. How long is the term of office for Representatives?
4. What is reapportionment? What are the major provisions of the Reapportionment Act of 1929?
5. Who draws congressional districts?
6. What did the Supreme Court decide in *Wesberry* v. *Sanders?*
7. For what term are members of the House elected? Qualifications?
8. What powers does the House have over the elections and qualifications of its members?

3. The Senate

As You Read, Think About:

- What the structure and size of the Senate are.
- What the terms, election, and qualifications of its members are.

Just as it does for the House of Representatives, the Constitution sets out the basic shape of the Senate.

The daughter of Alf Landon, Nancy Kassebaum (R., Kan.), first won election to the Senate in 1978.

Size

The Senate is a much smaller body than the House. The Constitution states that it "shall be composed of two Senators from each State."[23] Consequently, there are 100 Senators representing the 50 States.

Election

Until the adoption of the 17th Amendment in 1913, Senators were chosen by State legislatures. Since 1914, Senators have been chosen by the people at November elections.[24]

[23]Article I, Section 3, Clause 1; 17th Amendment.

[24]Only one Senator is elected from a State at any given election, except when the other seat has been vacated by death, resignation, or expulsion. The 17th Amendment gives each State a choice of methods for the filling of a vacancy in the Senate. A State may (1) fill the seat at a special election called by the governor, or (2) allow the governor to appoint someone to serve until the voters fill the vacancy at such a special election or at the next regular (November) election. Most States use the appointment-special election method.

*ENRICHMENT Ask the class to discuss: It is often said that the Senate is an "elite" club, while the House truly represents the people. Do students agree or disagree? Why?

FOCUS ON:

The Off-Year Elections

Congressional elections are held every two years, on the Tuesday after the first Monday in November of every even-numbered year. On each of those occasions, all 435 seats in the House and one-third of the seats in the Senate (33 or 34) are up for election.

Those congressional elections that occur in the nonpresidential years—that is, between presidential elections—are regularly called the **off-year elections.** The most recent ones were held in 1986, and the next ones will come in 1990.

Quite consistently, the party in power—the party that holds the Presidency—loses seats in the off-year elections. The accompanying table illustrates that point. It sets out the House and Senate seats gained (+) or lost (−) by the President's party in the 17 off-year elections over the 64 years from 1922 through 1986.

Year	Party in Power	House Seats	Senate Seats
1922	R	−75	−8
1926	R	−10	−6
1930	R	−49	−8
1934	D	+9	+10
1938	D	−71	−6
1942	D	−55	−9
1946	D	−55	−12
1950	D	−29	−6
1954	R	−18	−1
1958	R	−48	−13
1962	D	−4	+3
1966	D	−47	−4
1970	R	−12	+2
1974	R	−48	−5
1978	D	−15	−3
1982	R	−26	0
1986	R	−5	−10

1. Why do you think that the party in power usually loses seats in both houses in the off-year elections? Why might there be an exception to this rule?
2. In which of these 17 elections was the usual pattern *not* reflected by the results of both the House and the Senate contests? Why do you think that the elections that year proved to be an exception to the general rule?
3. Why do the results of off-year Senate elections differ more from the usual pattern than do House elections?
4. Many have suggested that the terms of members of the House be increased to four years. A constitutional amendment would be necessary to accomplish that. How would this change effect the historic pattern of off-year election results? Why have most members of the Senate regularly opposed such a change?
5. Over time, many have also proposed that the Constitution be amended to provide a single six-year term for the President. If that change were made, would it have any impact on the historic pattern of off-year election results?

Each Senator is elected from the State at-large. The 17th Amendment declares that all persons whom the State allows to vote for members of "the most numerous branch" of its legislature are qualified to vote for candidates for the United States Senate.

Terms

Senators are chosen for six-year terms, three times the length for which members of the lower house are chosen.[25] The terms are

[25] Article I, Section 3, Clause 1.

staggered. Only a third of them—33 or 34—expire every two years. The Senate is, then, a "continuous body." All its seats are never up for election at the same time.

The six-year term makes Senators less subject to the pressures of public opinion and to the pleas of special interests than their colleagues in the House. Also, the larger size and the geographic scope of their constituencies have much the same effect.

Qualifications

A Senator must meet a higher set of qualifications than those the Constitution sets for a Representative. A Senator must be at least 30 years of age, must have been a citizen for at least nine years, and must be an inhabitant of the State from which elected.[26]

The Senate, like the House, may judge the qualifications of its members and may exclude a member-elect by a majority vote.[27] It may also "punish its members for disorderly behavior" by majority vote and, "with the concurrence of two-thirds, expel a member."[28]

Fifteen members of the Senate have been expelled by that body, one in 1797 and 14 during the Civil War. Senator William Blount of Tennessee was expelled in 1797 for conspiring to lead two Indian peoples, supported by British warships, in attacks on Spanish Florida and Louisiana. The 14 Senators ousted in 1861 and 1862 were all from States of the Confederacy and were expelled for supporting secession. In 1982 Senator Harrison Williams (D., New Jersey) resigned to avoid expulsion by the Senate. He had been the only Senator caught up in the FBI's Abscam operation and was convicted of bribery in 1981. Following his trial, the Senate Ethics Committee had unanimously recommended that he be expelled.

Major Differences Between House and Senate

House	Senate
Larger body (435 members)	Smaller body (100 members)
Shorter term (2 years)	Longer term (6 years)
Smaller constituencies (elected from districts within States)	Larger constituencies (elected from entire State)
Younger membership	Older membership
Less prestige	More prestige
Lower visibility in news media	Higher visibility in news media
More rigid rules	More flexible rules
More committees	Fewer committees
Strict leadership control of floor proceedings	Less leadership control of floor proceedings

The punishing of a Senator for "disorderly behavior" has also been rare. The most recent case was in 1979. Then, the Senate voted to "denounce" one of its senior members, Herman Talmadge (D., Georgia). The Senate Ethics Committee found that Talmadge had mishandled thousands of dollars in Senate expense monies and campaign contributions. On the committee's recommendation, the Senate declared his conduct "reprehensible," tending "to bring the Senate into dishonor and disrepute." Senator Talmadge, first elected to the Senate in 1956, was defeated for reelection in 1980.

FOR REVIEW

1. **Identify:** Senate.
2. How many people serve in the United States Senate? How is that number fixed?
3. By whom are Senators chosen?
4. What is the term of office for Senators? Why is the Senate a "continuous body"?
5. What are the constitutional qualifications for serving in the Senate?
6. What powers does the Senate have over the election and qualifications of its members?

[26]Article I, Section 3, Clause 3. Under the inhabitant qualification, a Senator need not have lived in the State for any prescribed time. Most often, of course, Senators have been long-time residents of their States.

[27]Article I, Section 5, Clause 1. As has the House, the Senate has at times refused to seat a member-elect. Presumably, the Court's holding in *Powell* v. *McCormack* applies with equal force to the Senate.

[28]Article I, Section 5, Clause 2.

REINFORCEMENT Have the class discuss the table comparing the House and the Senate. What are the respective pros and cons of each of their differences?

4. The Members of Congress and Their Job

As You Read, Think About:

- Who the people are that make up the membership of Congress.
- What the many aspects are of the Congress member's job.
- How much compensation and what kinds of compensation a member of Congress receives.

Who are the members of Congress? What are their backgrounds? What is their job? Clearly, these are vital questions.

A Profile of Members

Whatever else they may be, the 535 members of Congress are *not* a representative cross section of the American people. Rather, the "average" member is a white male in his late 40s. The median age of the members of the House is just over 49 and of the Senate, 55. Only 25 women sit in Congress: 23 in the House and two—Nancy Landon Kassebaum (R., Kansas) and Barbara Mikulski (D., Maryland)—in the Senate. There are only 22 blacks and 10 Hispanics in Congress. All sit in the House of Representatives.

Nearly all members of Congress are married, a few are divorced, and they have, on the average, two children. Only a very few members say they have no church affiliation. Nearly two-thirds are Protestants, one-fourth are Roman Catholics, and about seven percent are Jewish.

Not quite half the members of the House and well over half the Senators are lawyers. Most others come from these major occupational backgrounds: business and banking, education, agriculture, journalism, and public service/politics. Nearly all went to college. More than four out of five have a college degree and a number have several.

Most Senators and Representatives were born in the States they represent. Only a handful were born outside the United States. Sprinkled among the members of Congress are several millionaires. A surprisingly large number, however, depend on their official salaries as their major source of income.

Most members of Congress have had considerable political experience. The average Senator is now serving a second term, and the average Representative has served four terms. Nearly a third of the Senate once sat in the House. Several Senators are former governors. A few Senators have held Cabinet or other high posts in the executive branch. The House has a large number of former State legislators and prosecuting attorneys among its members.

Again, Congress is not an accurate cross section of the nation's population. Rather, it is made up of upper-middle-class Americans who, on the whole, are quite able and hard-working people.

Their Job

The 535 members of Congress play several closely related and vital roles. Their major job, of course, is to make law. That is, they are (1) legislators. They also serve as: (2) committee members; (3) representatives of their **constituents,** the people of their State or district; (4) servants of their constituents; and (5) politicians. We have looked at some aspects of these roles in this and in earlier chapters, and we shall consider other facets of them in the next two chapters. For now consider this overview of the roles of a member of Congress.

As committee members, Representatives and Senators serve on those bodies to which proposed laws (bills) are referred in each House. They must screen those proposals and decide which of them will go on to floor consideration—that is, be considered, debated, and acted upon by the full membership of their respective chambers. As another and vital part of their committee work, Representatives and Senators also exercise the oversight function. They make sure that the laws passed by Congress are in keeping with their intended purposes and are being properly enforced by the executive branch.

Members of Congress are elected to represent their constituents. They are to reflect

BUILDING GOVERNMENT SKILLS

Developing Profiles of Your Members of Congress

You elect three people—a Representative and two Senators—to represent you in the United States Congress. How can you find out who these people are and if they are doing a good job representing your interests? One way is to begin to develop profiles of your representatives in Congress. A profile highlights the significant features and/or characteristics of a person or a place.

Sources

Three sources below are particularly helpful for gathering information on members of Congress and their constituencies:

The Congressional Directory; The Almanac of American Politics, by Michael Barone and Grant Ujifusa; and *Politics in America,* edited by Alan Ehrenhalt.

At least one of these books should be available in your school or local library.

Developing Profiles of Your Representatives

A profile of one of your representatives should include information on his or her personal background, political background, service in the Congress, and voting record.

Personal Background: Highlights of the member's education, professional experience, and military service, if any, should be included. If you perceive any other significant factors, such as religion, age, marital status, or place of birth, include these too. Were any of these personal factors an issue in the last election?

Political Background: A brief description of your representative's experience in local, State, and National Government should be included. Be sure to include the party to which he or she belongs and the number of years of service in Congress. From which parts of the constituency—rural, urban, or suburban—does he or she seem to draw the most support?

Service in Congress: In this part of your profile, note the committees to which the member belongs, any leadership positions he or she may hold, and length of service. If important, also include a description of any major bills the Representative or Senator authored or sponsored.

Voting Record: There are several ways to uncover a Representative's or Senator's voting record. Your local newspapers, Congressional Quarterly's *Weekly Report* and the *National Journal* report how Representatives and Senators voted on important bills. Since both houses conduct many votes during the year, you will find it next to impossible to keep up with every vote. Decide which issues are important to you, and then find out how your Senator or Representative voted on bills concerned with those issues.

In addition, you can learn about voting records in *The Almanac* and *Politics in America*. Both books carry two sections, "Key Votes" and "Group Ratings," that give you insight into the voting record of each member of Congress.

Your Senators' and Representative's voting records will provide useful insights into their political philosophies and their major legislative interests.

1. Choose one of your members of Congress and write a profile of the member.
2. Develop your own rating for your Senators and Representative. Select four bills that have been voted on by the current Congress. How would you have voted? How did your Representative and Senators vote?

Jeannette Rankin (R., Montana), the first woman to serve in Congress, was elected to the House in 1916 and again in 1940. Hiram Rhodes Revels (R., Mississippi), the first black to sit in the Senate, represented his State for a partial term, 1870–1871.

and to translate into action the interests and concerns of "the folks back home." They do so in light of their own beliefs and conscience, as they vote in committee and on the floor and otherwise act as a go-between in the relationship between citizens and their government.

Representatives and Senators also act as servants of their constituents. They do this particularly as they work to help them solve whatever problems they may have with the federal bureaucracy. Many constituents believe, and a large number of them act as though, members of Congress are in Washington especially to do favors for them.

The average member is swamped with constituent requests from the moment he or she takes office. The range of these requests is almost without limit—everything from help in securing a government contract or an appointment to West Point to asking for a free sight-seeing tour of Washington or even a personal loan. Consider this job description offered only half-jokingly by former Representative Luther Patrick of Alabama:

> A Congressman has become an expanded messenger boy, an employment agency, getter-outer of the Navy, Army, Marines, ward heeler, wound healer, trouble shooter, law explainer, bill finder, issue translator, resolution interpreter, controversy oil pourer, gladhand extender, business promoter, convention goer, civil ills skirmisher, veterans' affairs adjuster, ex-serviceman's champion, watchdog for the underdog, sympathizer with the upper dog, namer and kisser of babies, recoverer of lost luggage, soberer of delegates, adjuster for traffic violators, voters straying into Washington and into toils of the law, binder up of broken hearts, financial wet nurse, Good Samaritan, contributor to good causes—there are so many good causes—cornerstone layer, public building and bridge dedicator, ship christener—to be sure he does get in a little flag waving—and a little constitutional hoisting and spread-eagle work, but it is getting harder every day to find time to properly study legislation—the

ENRICHMENT Contact the district office of your local member of Congress to obtain an average day's schedule. Discuss in class, pointing out that the work of a member of Congress continues during recesses.

very business we are primarily here to discharge, and that must be done above all things.

Most members of Congress know that to refuse—or not to respond in some way to most requests—would mean to lose votes in the next election. All of the roles a member of Congress plays—legislator, committee member, constituent representative, constituent servant, and politician—are related, at least in part, to their reelection efforts.

Compensation

Congress sets its own pay and other compensation. The members of both houses are now paid an annual salary of $75,141.[29]

The Speaker of the House receives the same pay as the Vice President, $97,497 a year. The Senate's president *pro tem* and the majority and the minority floor leaders in each house make $81,167 a year.

Other Compensation and Financial Pressures Each member also receives a number of "fringe benefits," some of which are quite substantial. Each member is allowed a tax deduction to help keep up two residences, one at home and another in Washington. Liberal travel allowances cover the costs of several round trips between the home State and the capital each year.

Each member pays only small amounts for a $45,000 life insurance policy and for health insurance. A medical staff offers free care at the Capitol, and full care can be had, at very low rates, at any military hospital. Also, members contribute to a generous pension plan. The plan is based on years of service and can lead to a retirement income of as much as $50,000 a year. Until 1984, members of Congress were not covered by the social security system. They are now, however, and each now pays the maximum social security tax, some $3,000 a year.

[29]The Constitution gives that power to Congress. In Article I, Section 6, Clause 1 it provides: "The Senators and Representatives shall receive a compensation for their services, to be ascertained by law"—that is, fixed by an act of Congress. In fact, all salaries paid by the Federal Government are set by Congress.

Employees of the Congressional Research Service in the Library of Congress provide members of Congress with accurate, up-to-date information.

Each member also has offices in one of the Senate or House office buildings and allowances for offices in the home State or district. Each is allowed funds for hiring staff and for running the office. All of a member's official mail goes free under what is called the "franking privilege."

There is also free printing and distribution of speeches, newsletters, and other material. Radio and television tapes may also be produced and distributed at sharply reduced cost. Each member has free parking, plants for the office, the research help of the Library of Congress, and still more, for example, the use of several fine restaurants and two first-rate gymnasiums with swimming pools and saunas.

With the salary and the many allowances, the typical member's compensation amounts to well over $100,000 a year. Even so, to argue that members of Congress are overpaid does not seem reasonable. Their responsibilities are so great and the demands made on them so many and varied as to defeat any attempt to fix an "adequate" salary.

In fact, many Senators and Representatives insist that their usual "day-to-day expenses" are regularly more than their allowances. Senator Bob Packwood (R., Oregon) estimates that just two items—trips to his home State and newsletters to his constituents—push his expenses some $40,000 above his allowances each year. Add such items as the high cost of living in and around Washington, the need to maintain two homes, the many demands made by constituents, and coping with all the other "extras" imposed by the office, and it is easy to appreciate the argument that members of Congress are not overpaid.

There are only two real limits on the level of congressional pay. One limit is the President's veto power. The other, and the more potent limit, is the fear of voter backlash. That fear—in fact, the near certainty of election-day fallout—has always made most members reluctant to vote to raise their own salaries.

Most often, Congress has tried to skirt the pay question by providing for such fringe benefits as a special tax break, a liberal pension plan, more office and travel funds, and other "perks"—items that are much less apparent to "the folks back home." Higher salaries alone will not bring the most able men and women to Congress or to any other public offices. Certainly, higher salaries can make public service much more appealing.

Privileges of Members

The Constitution commands that Senators and Representatives

> shall, in all cases, except treason, felony, and breach of the peace, be privileged from arrest during their attendance at the session of their respective Houses, and in going to, and returning from, the same . . .[30]

The provision dates from English and colonial practice, when the king's officers often harassed legislators on petty grounds. The provision has been of little importance in our national history.[31]

Another much more important privilege is set out in the same place in the Constitution. The Speech and Debate Clause declares

> . . . and for any speech or debate in either House, they shall not be questioned in any other place.

The words "any other place" refer to the courts.

The privilege is intended to "throw a cloak of legislative immunity" about members of Congress. The clause protects them from suits for libel or slander arising out of their official conduct. The Supreme Court has held that the immunity applies "to things generally done in a session of the House [or Senate] by one of its members in relation to the business before it."[32] The protection goes, then, beyond floor debate, to include work in committees and all other things generally done by members of Congress in relation to congressional business. But a member is not free to defame another person in a public speech, an article, a conversation, or otherwise. The important and necessary goal of this provision of the Constitution is to protect freedom of legislative debate.

FOR REVIEW

1. **Identify:** franking privilege, legislative immunity.
2. Describe in a sentence the "average" member of Congress.
3. What are the five principal roles that a member of Congress plays?
4. Who sets the salary for members of Congress?
5. For what does the Speech and Debate Clause provide? Why?

[30] Article I, Section 6, Clause 1.

[31] The courts have regularly held that the words "breach of the peace" cover all criminal offenses, misdemeanors (minor crimes) as well as felonies. So the protection covers only arrest for civil (noncriminal) offenses while engaged in congressional business.

[32] The leading case is *Kilburn* v. *Thompson,* 1881. The holding has been affirmed many times since. In *Hutchinson* v. *Proxmire,* 1979, however, the Court held that members of Congress may be sued for libel for statements they make in news releases or in newsletters.

REINFORCEMENT Have the class discuss how the Speech and Debate Clause protects the freedom of legislative debate. How, then, can members of Congress be held accountable to their constituents?

SUMMARY

Congress is the legislative (lawmaking) branch of the National Government. It is made up of two houses—the House of Representatives and the Senate. Congress is bicameral for several reasons: because the Framers were familiar with two-chambered legislatures in British, colonial, and early State practice; the Connecticut Compromise; and the desire to have one house act as a check on the other.

A term of Congress lasts for two years. There are two regular sessions per term. Special sessions may be called by the President.

Members of the House serve a two-year term and are popularly elected. The Congress reapportions the seats in the House among the States based on their respective populations after each decennial census, but each State is entitled to at least one Representative. The House now has 435 members elected from districts drawn by the legislature in each State. The districts must contain about equal populations, but they can be, and often are, gerrymandered.

A Representative must be at least 25 years old, a citizen for seven years, and an inhabitant of the State from which chosen. Each house has the power to decide contests over the seating of its members-elect, and each has the power to refuse to seat a member-elect. Each house also has the power to discipline (censure or expel) any of its members.

Each State has two seats in the 100-member Senate. Senators serve six-year terms. One-third of those terms end every two years. Since 1913 (the 17th Amendment), Senators have been popularly elected. They must be at least 30 years old, a citizen for nine years, and an inhabitant of the State from which chosen.

Congress is not an accurate cross section of the American people. Rather, the "average" member is a white male in his late 40s.

As legislators, the members of Congress make law, serve as representatives and as servants of their constituents, as committee members, and as politicians. They fix their own salaries by law and provide themselves with a number of other compensations. They also enjoy freedom from petty (harassing) arrest during sessions and immunity in debate and other official conduct.

CHAPTER REVIEW

Key Terms/Concepts*

bicameral (293)
term (294)
session (294)
special session (294)
apportionment (296)
reapportionment (296)
single-member district (298)
at-large (299)
gerrymander (299)
censure (301)
off-year election (303)
constituent (305)

*These terms are included in the Glossary.

Keynote Questions

• **1.** What is the major function of Congress?
• **2.** Why is Congress bicameral?
• **3.** What is the difference between a term of Congress and a session of Congress?
• **4.** What is a special session of Congress?
• **5.** How many people serve in the House? The Senate?
• **6.** How is the total number of seats in the House determined? In the Senate?
• **7.** How are House seats distributed among the States? What is this process called?
• **8.** By whom are Representatives elected? Who draws congressional district lines?

The dots represent skill levels required to answer each question or complete each activity:
•requires recall and comprehension • •requires application and analysis • • •requires synthesis and evaluation

• **9.** Gerrymandering usually takes one of what two forms in practice?
• **10.** What is meant by the "one man, one vote" rule?
••• **11.** Make a table to compare and contrast the terms of office and constitutional qualifications for Representatives and Senators.
• **12.** How did the Framers of the Constitution ensure that the Senate would be a continuous body?
• **13.** List the five closely related roles of a member of Congress.
• **14.** What is the franking privilege?

Skill Application

Summarizing: In Congress, in business, and in conversations, people depend on summaries to understand in a short amount of time the major points of a book, speech, movie, study, or any large body of information. Being able to summarize enables you to communicate more effectively.

A summary includes the main idea and a few pertinent and/or interesting details. Less important and repeated information is not included in a summary.

••• **1.** Read the description of the "average" member of Congress on page 305. Then read the summaries below, and select the best.

a. The 535 members of Congress do not represent a cross section of the American population. Rather, the "average" member is a white male Protestant. Most members of Congress are lawyers who have had political experience.

b. The "average" member of Congress is a white male in his late 40s. There are 19 blacks and 11 Hispanics in Congress—all in the House of Representatives. Over two-thirds of the members are Protestant, one-fourth are Catholic, and seven percent are Jewish. Most Senators and Representatives were born in the State they represent.

c. Most Senators and Representatives are middle-aged white males who are lawyers.

••• **2.** The following excerpt is from *Central America and U.S. Foreign Assistance: Issues for Congress in 1984*. Read it and then write a summary of it.

U.S. assistance to Central America, a region of approximately 23 million people including approximately 4.5 million in El Salvador, began to expand rapidly in FY 80, when economic and military aid jumped from $30 million to nearly $200 million. This growth continued during the next few years, as aid levels climbed by at least 50% annually. Costa Rica, El Salvador, Guatemala, and Honduras each received a sizable portion of the President's $350 million [aid program] which [Congress] approved in 1982. The region gained another boost the following year largely due to a major reprogramming of military and economic funds announced in March 1983.

For Thought and Discussion

•• **1.** Why did James Madison speak of Congress as the "First Branch"? Do you think that Congress is still the "First Branch" today? Why or why not?

••• **2.** Sometimes members of the House of Representatives remark that they are elected to Congress and must start campaigning right away. They think the two-year term is too short. Why was the term of office for the House deliberately made brief? Do you think this reason still applies today?

••• **3.** The Constitution sets out three qualifications for serving in the House and the Senate. In deciding on which candidate to vote for, what other characteristics do you think are important? Do you think any of these characteristics should become requirements for office?

Suggested Activities

••• **1.** Find out if the congressional districts in your State are gerrymandered. Check newspaper reports from the last redistricting. If they are, to which party's benefit? Were there any court challenges to the redistricting? On what grounds?

••• **2.** Write a biographical sketch of your two Senators and Representative. The *Congressional Directory* and the *Almanac of American Politics* are good sources. Include the committee assignments and special legislative interests of the members, when each was elected and by how much.

For this reason the laws are made: That the strong shall not have the power to do all that they please.
–OVID

Essential Elements content: This chapter gives special attention to items: 2.A, 3.A, 3.B.

12 Congress in Action

CHAPTER OBJECTIVES

To help you to

Learn · Know · Understand

The procedures by which Congress convenes.

The formal and the party organizational structure in both houses of Congress.

The committee system in Congress and the types of committees to be found in both houses.

The steps of the legislative process in both houses of Congress.

The final stages in passing a bill, including the functions of conference committees and presidential action.

Social studies attitudes, values, and skills: In this chapter, students will have opportunities to develop and practice the following attitudes, values, and skills: 2.6, 4.A—4.M

WE HAVE JUST studied the overall structure of the Congress. We have looked at its bicameral character, the selection and terms of its members, and the shape of the different roles its members play. Now we turn to Congress at work, its internal organization, procedures, and practices. How, and how well, does Congress perform its lawmaking function? With what machinery and in what ways does it play its pivotal part in our governmental system?

The answers to these questions are of great importance because the lawmaking function is at the center of the democratic process. In this chapter, we shall see how power is distributed within Congress, in each of its houses. We shall see how bills are distributed to and considered in all the different types of House and Senate committees. We shall discuss who has and can exercise major influence and control over the making of law, and who then gets "what, when, and how."

Woodrow Wilson once said that "the making of law is a very practical matter." Lawmaking is also a very complicated matter, as we shall see.

*ENRICHMENT Congress plays an important role in the democratic process because of its lawmaking function. Ask the students if Ovid (above quote) would agree with this statement. (c 3.A, 3.B; avs 4.G, 4.J)

Members of the House meet for the opening day of the first session of the 99th Congress, 1985. *Facing Page:* Henry Clay offers the Senate his proposal leading to the Compromise of 1850.

c 3.A, 3.B; avs 4F

1. Congress Convenes

As You Read, Think About:

- What happens on the opening day of a new Congress.
- What the importance is of the President's State of the Union address.

As we know, a new Congress meets every two years. It convenes (begins a new term) on January 3 in every odd-numbered year, following the regular November elections.

Opening Day in the House

When the 435 men and women elected to the House come together at the Capitol on January 3 of every odd-numbered year, they are, in effect, just so many Representatives-elect. Because all 435 of its seats are filled by the voters every two years, the House has no sworn members, no rules, and no organization until its opening-day ceremonies are held.

The Clerk of the House in the preceding term presides at the beginning of the first day's session.[1] He calls the chamber to order and checks the roll of Representatives-elect. Those members-to-be then choose a Speaker as their permanent presiding officer.

The Speaker is always a senior member of the majority party, and election on the floor is only a formality. The majority party's **caucus**—conference of party members in the House—has settled the matter beforehand.

The Speaker then takes the oath of office. It is administered by the "Dean of the House," the member-elect with the longest record of service in the House of Representatives.[2] With that accomplished, the Speaker

[1]The Clerk is a nonmember officer, chosen by the House. He serves as that body's chief administrative officer. No woman has as yet held the post.

[2]Today, Representative Jamie L. Whitten (D., Miss.), who has been a member of the House since November 4, 1941.

At right is Thomas P. O'Neill (D., Mass.), Speaker of the House from 1977 to 1987, as he conferred with House Majority Leader James Wright, Jr. (D., Texas), the expected successor to the Speakership in 1987.

swears in the rest of the members, as a body. The Democrats take their seats to the right of the center aisle; the Republicans, to the left.

Next, the House elects its Clerk, Sergeant at Arms, Doorkeeper, Postmaster, and Chaplain. These choices are also a formality. The majority party's caucus has already decided who these nonmember officers will be.

Then, the House adopts the rules that will govern its proceedings through the term. The rules of the House have been developing for nearly 200 years, and they are contained in a volume of several hundred pages. They are readopted, most often with little or no change, at the beginning of each term.

Finally, the members of the 22 permanent committees of the House are appointed by a floor vote, and the House is organized.

Opening Day in the Senate

The Senate is a continuous body. It has been uninterruptedly organized since its first session in 1789. Recall, only one-third of the seats are up for election every two years. From one term to the next, then, two-thirds of the Senate's membership is carried over.

The Senate does not face the large organizational problems that the House does at the beginning of a new term. The Senate's first-day session is nearly always quite short and routine, even when the most recent elections have brought a change in party control. Newly elected and reelected members must be sworn in, vacancies in Senate organization and on committees must be filled, and a few other details attended to.

The President's State of the Union Message

When the Senate is notified that the House is organized, a joint committee of the two is appointed and instructed

> . . . to wait upon the President of the United States and inform him that a quorum of each House is assembled and that the Congress is ready to receive any communication he may be pleased to make.

Within a few days, the President delivers his annual State of the Union Message. From Woodrow Wilson's first one in 1913, each President has usually delivered his message in person. The members of both houses, together with the members of the Cabinet, the Supreme Court, the foreign diplomatic corps, and other dignitaries assemble in the House chamber to receive him. *

In his address, the Chief Executive reports on the state of the nation in all of its concerns, both foreign and domestic. His speech often includes a number of specific, and sometimes controversial, legislative recommendations, as well.

The message is followed very closely, both here and abroad. In it the President lays out the broad shape of the policies his administration will follow and the course he has charted for the nation.

With the conclusion of the President's speech, the joint session is adjourned and each house returns to the mass of legislative business before it.

FOR REVIEW

1. **Identify:** Clerk of the House, State of the Union Message.
2. Who is the "Dean of the House"?
3. Why is the first daily session of a term simpler and more routine in the Senate than in the House?
4. Why is the State of the Union Message so important?

*ENRICHMENT Ask the class: Does the President give an accurate description of the state of affairs when he delivers his State of the Union address? What might influence his description?

2. The Organization of Congress

As You Read, Think About:

- How the officers of each House are chosen and what their functions are.
- What the influence and importance are of the Speaker of the House.
- What the function is of floor leaders in the two Houses.
- How committee chairmen are chosen and what their powers are.

The national legislature is a far larger operation than most realize. Congress has appropriated some $1.6 billion to pay its bills in the current fiscal year. Of that huge sum, a little over $40 million—less than 3 percent—is spent to pay the salaries of the 535 members. Nearly $300 million now goes to hire staff assistants for members, and the yearly postage, or franking, bill runs to well over $140 million a year.

There are, all told, some 38,000 congressional employees. Congress employs hundreds of committee aides, legislative and administrative assistants, office clerks, secretaries, guards, maintenance personnel, and so on. Each employee is important to the workings of Congress.

The Presiding Officers

The Constitution provides for the presiding officers of each house. The **Speaker of the House** is by far the most important and influential member of the House of Representatives. The Speakership was created by the Constitution and, as that document commands, the post is filled by a vote of the House at the beginning of each of its two-year terms.[3] In practical fact, the Speaker is the leader of the majority party in the House and is chosen by the members of that party.

Although neither the Constitution nor its own rules require it, the House has always chosen the Speaker from among its own members. Usually, the Speaker is a long-time member who has risen in stature and influence through years of service.

The first Speaker, elected at the first session in 1789, was Frederick A. C. Muhlenburg, a Federalist from Pennsylvania. Sam Rayburn (D., Texas) held the office for a record 17 years, 62 days. Except for two terms in which the Republicans controlled the House (1947-48, 1953-54), "Mr. Sam" was the Speaker from September 16, 1940 until his death November 16, 1961.

At base, the immense power held by the Speaker arises from this fact: The Speaker is, at one and the same time, the elected presiding officer of the House *and* the acknowledged leader of its majority party. Speakers are expected to preside in a fair and judicial manner, and they regularly do so. They are also expected to aid the fortunes of their own party and their party's legislative goals, and they regularly do that, too.

Nearly all the Speaker's specific powers revolve about two duties: to preside and to keep order. The Speaker presides over all sessions of the House, or appoints a temporary presiding officer. No member may speak until "recognized" by the Speaker. The Speaker interprets and applies the rules, refers bills to the standing committees, rules on points of order (questions of procedure raised by members), puts questions to a vote, and determines the outcome of most of the votes taken.[4] The Speaker also names the members of all special committees and signs all bills and resolutions passed by the House.

As a member, the Speaker may debate and vote on any matter before the House. But to do so, a temporary presiding officer must be appointed and the chair vacated by the Speaker. The House rules *require* that the Speaker vote only to break a tie. Another House voting rule gives the Speaker additional power. According to this rule, a tie vote defeats the question. The Speaker can *choose* to vote and *cause* a tie. For example, if the vote was 200 for and 201 against, the

[3]Article I, Section 2, Clause 5.

[4]On most matters the House takes a voice vote. The Speaker puts the question, those members in favor respond, usually by shouting, "Aye." Those opposed respond "No." The Speaker then decides and declares the result; see page 331.

Discussing the 1987 budget are (at left) James Wright, Jr. (D., Texas), then serving as House Majority Leader, and William H. Gray, III (D., Penn.), Chairman of the House Budget Committee.

Speaker could choose to vote for the question, causing a tie which would defeat the question.

The Speaker of the House follows the Vice President in the line of succession to the Presidency. This is a considerable testimony to the power and importance of both the office and its occupant.

The **President of the Senate** is not a member of the Senate. The Constitution assigns that office to the Vice President of the United States.[5] Largely for this reason, the President of the Senate occupies a much less powerful chair than that of the Speaker of the House. In fact, the President of the Senate is sometimes not even a member of the party with a majority of seats in the upper house.

The President of the Senate does have the usual powers of a presiding officer—to recognize members, put questions to a vote, and so on. However, the Vice President cannot take the floor to speak or debate and may vote *only* to break a tie.

The influence a Vice President may have in the Senate is largely the result of personal abilities. Several of the more recent Vice Presidents came to that office from the Senate: Harry Truman, Alben Barkley, Richard Nixon, Lyndon Johnson, Hubert Humphrey, and Walter Mondale. Each of them was able to build some power into the position out of that earlier experience.

The Senate does have another presiding officer, the **President *pro tempore,*** who serves in the Vice President's absence. The President *pro tem* is elected by the Senate itself and is always a leading member of the majority party. Today, the Senate's President *pro tem* is Senator Strom Thurmond (R., South Carolina). First elected to the Senate in 1954, Thurmond became its President *pro tem* in 1981.

Other members of the Senate also preside over the chamber, on a temporary basis. Newly elected Senators are regularly given this "honor" early in their terms.

Floor Leaders and Other Party Officers

Congress is distinctly a *political* body. The two main reasons are: (1) because Congress is the nation's central *policy-making* organ and, (2) because of its *partisan* makeup. Reflecting its political complexion, both houses are organized along party lines.

The Floor Leaders Next to the Speaker, the most important officers in Congress are the **majority** and **minority floor leaders** in the House and Senate. They do not hold official positions in either chamber. Rather, they are party officers, picked for their posts by their partisan colleagues.

The floor leaders are legislative strategists. They try to carry out the decisions of the party's caucus and steer floor action to the party's benefit. All of that calls for political skills of a very high order.

The majority leader's post is the more powerful of the two in each house—for the obvious reason that the majority party has more seats (more votes) than the other party has. Together with the presiding officer and the minority leader, the majority leader plans the order of business on the floor.

The two floor leaders are assisted by party whips—a **majority whip** and a **minority**

[5]Article I, Section 3, Clause 4.

*REINFORCEMENT Discuss in class: Why is the Speaker of the House more powerful than the President of the Senate? Note that the Vice President may not even be a member of the majority party in the Senate.

whip—in both houses. They are, in effect, assistant floor leaders. Each of them is chosen by the party caucus, almost always on the floor leader's recommendation. There are a number of assistant whips in the House, and both floor leaders have a paid staff in both houses.

The whips check with party members and advise the floor leader of the number of votes that can be counted on in any particular matter. As part of their jobs, whips attempt to see that members are present when important votes are to be taken and that they vote with the party leadership. If a member must be absent for some reason, the whip sees that that member is "paired" with a member of the other party who is also absent or who agrees not to vote on certain measures. In this way, one nonvote cancels out another.

A congressional committee hearing helps members of Congress to gather the information they must have in order to vote on bills, both in committee and on the floor.

The Party Caucus The **party caucus** is a closed meeting of the members of each party in each house. It meets just before Congress convenes in January and occasionally during a session. In recent years the Republicans have called their caucus in each house the party conference, and the Democrats now use this term in the Senate, too.

The caucus deals mostly with matters of party organization, such as the selection of the party's floor leaders and questions of committee membership. It sometimes takes stands on particular bills, but neither party tries to force its members to follow its caucus decisions, nor can it.

The **policy committee,** composed of the party's top leadership, acts as an executive committee for the caucus.

In strict fact, that body is known as the policy committee in each party's structure in the Senate and in the Republicans' organization in the House. However, it is called the policy and steering committee by the Democrats in the lower chamber.

Committee Chairmen[6]

The large bulk of the work of Congress, especially in the House, is really done in committee. Thus, those members who head the standing committees in each chamber—the **committee chairmen**—also hold very strategic posts. The chairman of each of these permanent committees is chosen by the majority party caucus and is always a ranking member of that party.

Committee chairmen regularly decide when their committees will meet, which bills they will take up, whether public hearings are to be held, and what witnesses are to be called. When a committee's bill has been reported to the floor, the chairman usually

---

[6] We use the title *Chairman,* rather than *chairperson,* advisedly: first, because this is the form used in both houses of Congress, both officially and informally; and second, no woman now chairs a standing committee in either house. Only three women have ever done so; the most recent, Leonor K. Sullivan (D., Missouri), chaired the House Merchant Marine and Fisheries Committee from 1973 until her retirement from the House in 1977.

*ENRICHMENT Ask students to find out who the party officers and floor leaders are for the current Congress. Direct them to local party offices, newspapers, etc., for the information. (c 3.A, 4.B; avs 4.A)

FOCUS ON:

Seniority=Clout

The length of time a Representative or Senator serves in Congress—the member's seniority—has much to do with his or her place in the power structure of the House or Senate. With a few exceptions, the longer the record of service, the greater the clout.

Over time, Senators and Representatives develop a better understanding of the politics of Congress, of the rules governing debate and discussion, and of parliamentary tactics that can often be used to "make or break" a bill. They gain experience with a variety of issues and learn how to write legislation more effectively. They also get to know their colleagues better, and can call on some of these Senators or Representatives for help in supporting or opposing a bill. Longer service in Congress gives the members time to develop reputations as experts in a particular area. Some Senators or Representatives become known for their knowledge of particular issues, some for their skills as negotiators, and others for their ability to manipulate the rules of debate. Time in Congress allows a Representative or Senator to gain a deep understanding of the legislative process, and thus, to be a more effective legislator.

The leadership posts in both the House and the Senate are filled by vote in the parties. Caucuses, and those bodies almost always follow the seniority rule. The top positions regularly go to those members of Congress with the most seniority. Thus, in the 99th Congress (1985-1987), of the 10 most senior Republican Senators:

1 Senator served as both president *pro tempore* and a committee chairman;
1 Senator was the majority leader;
6 Senators were committee chairmen;
1 Senator was a subcommittee chairman.

Of the 10 most senior Democratic Senators:

1 Senator was the minority leader;
1 Senator was the minority whip;
6 Senators were ranking committee members;
1 Senator was the second ranking committee member;
1 Senator was the third ranking committee member.

As leaders of the Senate these members of Congress had more responsibility, and exercised more influence than most of their colleagues. Floor leaders, committee chairmen and subcommittee chairmen, and ranking minority members of a committee are all entitled to have additional staffs of professionals and administrative personnel to help them carry out their added duties.

With more experience, a better knowledge of the legislative process, more influence through leadership positions, and more staff to help, the senior members of Congress have more clout.

1. How would the added staff granted to committee chairmen, subcommittee chairmen, and ranking minority members contribute to the increased influence of these members of Congress?
2. In order to gain seniority, a Senator or Representative must be continually reelected. What are the advantages of being a constituent of a more senior member of Congress?
3. Does the "seniority=clout" formula apply to your Representative? Does it apply to your Senators?

manages the debate and tries to steer it to final passage.

An important aspect of the committee system is the **seniority rule.*** The seniority rule is, in fact, an *unwritten custom.* First practiced in the late 1800s, the rule is still closely followed in both houses today. The rule provides that the most important posts in both the formal and the party organization in each chamber will be held by the "ranking members." Those are party members with the longest records of service in Congress.

The rule is applied most strictly to the choice of committee chairman. The head of each committee is almost always that majority party member who has served for the longest period of time on that particular committee.

Critics of the rule are legion, and they do make a strong case. They insist that the seniority system ignores ability, puts a high value on mere length of service, and discourages younger members. Critics also note that the rule means that a committee head almost always comes from a "safe" constituency. That is a State or district in which, election after election, one party regularly wins. With no play of fresh and conflicting forces in those places, critics claim that the chairman of a committee is often out of touch with current public opinion.

Defenders of the rule argue that it means that a powerful and experienced member will head each committee, that the rule is easy to apply, and that it very nearly eliminates the possibility of intraparty fights.

Opponents of the rule have gained some ground in recent years. Thus, the House Republican conference (caucus) now picks several GOP members of House committees by secret ballot. House Democrats use secret ballots to choose a committee chairman whenever 20 percent of their caucus requests that procedure. The House Democrats did in fact oust three long-tenured committee chairmen in 1975, and another one in 1985.

Whatever the arguments against the rule, and despite its recent breaches, there is little chance that it will be eliminated. Those members with the real power to abolish the practice are the ones who reap the largest benefits from its operation.

FOR REVIEW

1. Who presides over the House? How is that officer chosen?
2. Who presides over the Senate? How is that officer chosen?
3. Who is the Senate's alternate presiding officer? Why does that post exist?
4. Who selects the floor leaders in each house? The whips? What are their functions?
5. How are committee chairmen chosen? What is the seniority rule?

3. The Committee System

As You Read, Think About:

- Why the committee system is necessary.
- What different kinds of committees exist in Congress.
- What the functions are of the various committees.
- What key role the House Rules Committee plays.
- Why the Congressional investigative power is important.

Both the House and the Senate are so large and the volume of their business is so great that each depends heavily on its committee system. Indeed, Representative Clem Miller (D., Calif.) once described Congress as "a collection of committees that comes together periodically to approve one another's actions."

Standing Committees

In 1789 the House and Senate each adopted the practice of naming a special committee to consider each bill as it is introduced.

*ENRICHMENT Discuss in class: Does the seniority rule reward members for their long service in Congress or unfairly increase the power of certain States?

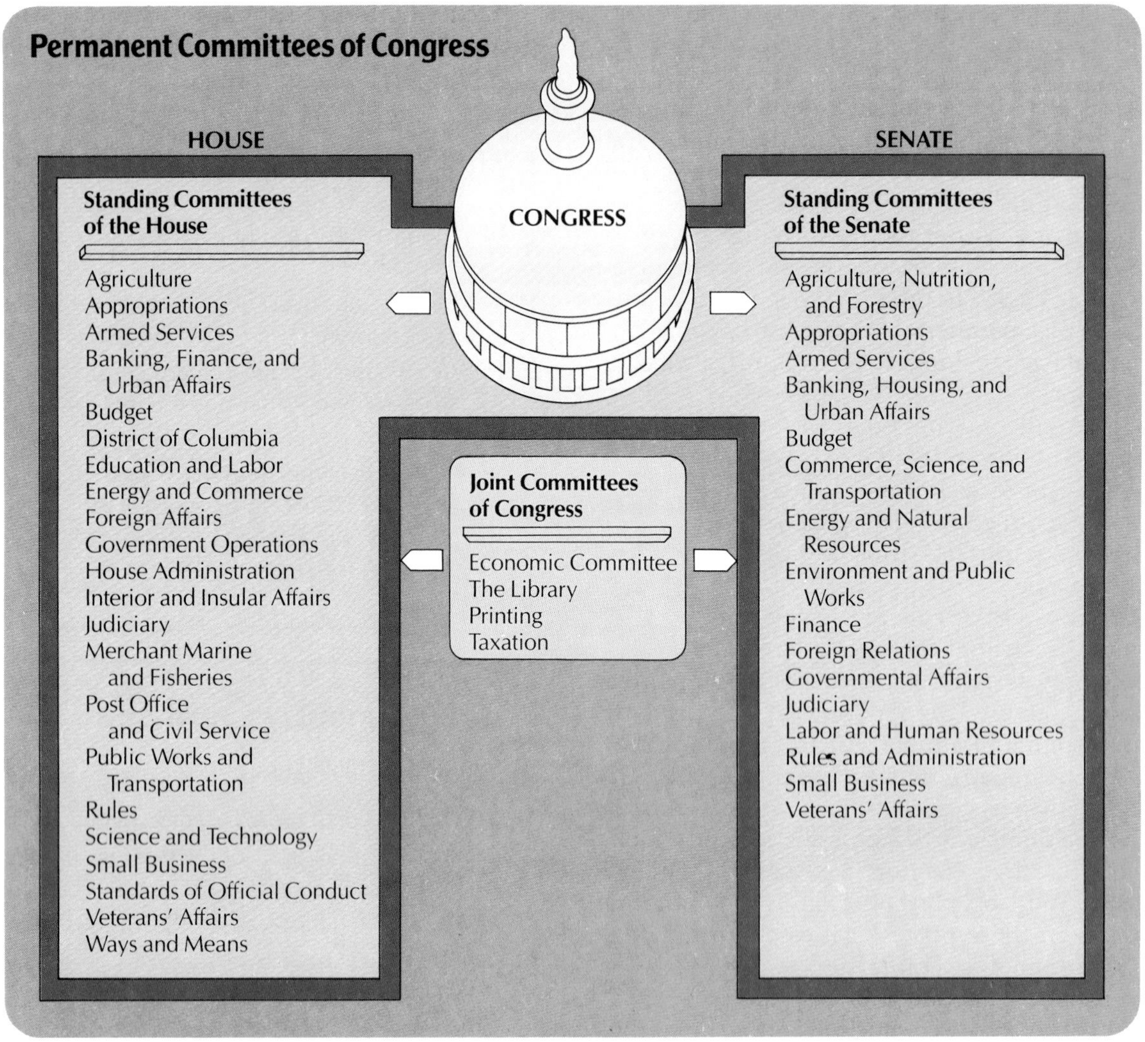

How do members of the House and Senate become members of committees? How is a bill assigned to a committee?

By 1794 there were more than 300 committees in each chamber. Each house then began to set up permanent groups, known as **standing committees,** to which all similar bills could be sent.

The number of these committees has varied over the years. Today there are 22 standing committees in the House and 16 in the Senate. Each committee has from 12 to as many as 57 members in the lower house and from 13 to 29 in the upper chamber. The rules of the House limit Representatives to service on one major committee, and the Senate allows its members to serve on two.

When a bill is introduced in either house, the Speaker or the President of the Senate refers the measure to the proper standing committee. For instance, the Speaker sends all tax measures to the House Ways and Means Committee, and in the Senate they go to the Finance Committee. A bill dealing with enlistments in the Army, Navy, Air Force, or Marines is sent to the Armed Services Committee in either chamber, and so on.

We have already seen how the chairman of each of the standing committees is chosen according to the seniority rule. That rule is

The Rules Committee, chaired by Claude Pepper (D., Florida) determines the future of most bills reported out by House committees.

also applied quite closely in each house when it elects the other members of each of its committees.[7]

The majority party controls each committee.[8] That is, it always holds a majority of the seats on each committee. The other party is always well represented, however. In fact, party membership on each committee is more or less in line with party strength in each house. Thus, if the Democrats hold 240 seats in the House and the Republicans 195, the party split on a 25-member committee will likely be 14 Democrats and 11 Republicans.

Except for the House Committee on Rules and the Senate Committee on Rules and Administration, each standing committee is a "subject-matter committee." Each deals with bills on certain subjects—for example, the House Committee on Veterans' Affairs or the Senate Committee on the Judiciary.

[7]In *form,* the members of each standing committee are elected by a floor vote at the beginning of each term of Congress. In *fact,* each party draws up its own committee roster, and those party decisions are then ratified on the floor.

[8]The only exception here is the House Committee on Standards of Official Conduct, with six Democrats and six Republicans. It investigates allegations of misconduct by House members and makes recommendations to the full chamber. In the Senate, a six-member bipartisan group, the Select Committee on Ethics, plays a similar role.

We shall look at the strategic role of these committees in the legislative process shortly. First, we must take special note of the House Rules Committee.

The House Rules Committee The House Committee on Rules is sometimes called the "traffic cop" in the legislative process in the lower house.

So many measures are introduced in the House each term—as many as 10,000 now—that some sort of screening is necessary. The standing committees carry out that chore. Most bills die in the committees to which they are referred. Still, several hundred bills are reported out every year. So, before most bills can reach the floor, they must also clear the Rules Committee.

This powerful 13-member committee usually, but not always, works in close cooperation with the House leadership. The committee manages the flow of bills for action by the full House. Normally, a bill cannot be brought to the floor unless it has been "granted a rule"—that is, scheduled for consideration—by the Rules Committee. That committee decides (1) whether or not and (2) under what conditions a bill will be taken up. In short, the Rules Committee can speed, delay, or even prevent House consideration of a measure.

In the smaller Senate, where the lawmaking process is not so strictly regulated, the Committee on Rules and Administration has much less power than its counterpart in the lower house.

Select Committees

At times, each house finds need for a **select committee.** That is a special group set up for some specific purpose and, most often, for a limited time. Most select committees are formed to investigate some particular and current matter. The members of these special committees are appointed by the Speaker or the President of the Senate, with the advice of majority and minority leaders.

The congressional power to investigate is an essential part of the lawmaking function.

*ENRICHMENT Use the chart on p. 322 to introduce a discussion on seniority. Ask the class if a committee chairmanship is a just reward for longevity. Have students support their views.

Congress must have the power to inform itself on matters before it. It must decide on the need for new laws, and the adequacy of laws it has already passed. It must also exercise its **oversight function.** That is, Congress must determine whether executive agencies are working effectively and in line with the policies Congress has set by law. Also, Congress sometimes conducts an investigation in order to focus public attention on some topic.

Most congressional investigations—the usual and routine, as well as the ones that *capture the headlines—are conducted by standing committees or their subcommittees. Select committees are also sometimes used for that work, however. Thus, over the past several years, both houses have created, and re-created, a Select Committee on Aging. Each of those bodies is concerned with the many different problems faced by the elderly in our society. These committees hold hearings in Washington and around the country, issue committee reports, and focus public and governmental attention on those problems.

At times, a select committee becomes a spectacularly important body. This happened, for example, to the Senate's Select Committee on Presidential Campaign Activi-

House Leadership, 1986

Position	Name	Age*	Year Entered House	State
Leadership				
Speaker	Thomas P. O'Neill, Jr.	74	1953	Massachusetts
Majority Leader	James C. Wright, Jr.	64	1955	Texas
Majority Whip	Thomas S. Foley	57	1965	Washington
Minority Leader	Robert H. Michel	63	1957	Illinois
Minority Whip	Trent Lott	45	1973	Mississippi
Committee Chairmen				
Agriculture	E (Kika) de la Garza	59	1965	Texas
Appropriations	Jamie L. Whitten	76	1941	Mississippi
Armed Services	Les Aspin	48	1971	Wisconsin
Banking, Finance and Urban Affairs	Fernand J. St. Germain	58	1961	Rhode Island
Budget	William H. Gray III	45	1979	Pennsylvania
District of Columbia	Ronald V. Dellums	51	1971	California
Education and Labor	Augustus F. Hawkins	64	1963	California
Energy and Commerce	John D. Dingell	74	1956	Michigan
Foreign Affairs	Dante Fascell	69	1955	Florida
Government Operations	Jack Brooks	79	1953	Texas
House Administration	Frank Annunzio	71	1965	Illinois
Interior and Insular Affairs	Morris K. Udall	60	1961	Arizona
Judiciary	Peter W. Rodino, Jr.	77	1949	New Jersey
Merchant Marine and Fisheries	Walter B. Jones	73	1966	North Carolina
Post Office and Civil Service	William D. Ford	59	1965	Michigan
Public Works and Transportation	James J. Howard	59	1965	New Jersey
Rules	Claude D. Pepper	85	1963	Florida
Science and Technology	Don Fuqua	53	1963	Florida
Small Business	Parren J. Mitchell	64	1971	Maryland
Standards of Official Conduct	Julian C. Dixon	52	1979	California
Veterans' Affairs	Gillespie V. Montgomery	65	1967	Mississippi
Ways and Means	Dan Rostenkowski	58	1959	Illinois

*As of birthdate in 1986.
Source: Congressional Directory, with additional data from the Clerk of the House.

*REINFORCEMENT Ask the class to report on the committee assignments of their Senators and Representative, and how these committees relate to their constituents. Refer to the chart above and on p. 324.

ties, popularly known as the Senate Watergate Committee. As the Watergate scandal began to unfold in 1973, the Senate created that committee. Chaired by Senator Sam Ervin (D., North Carolina), its job was to investigate "the extent, if any, to which illegal, improper, or unethical activities were engaged in by any persons . . . in the presidential election of 1972." Its lengthy, often televised, and frequently sensational hearings fascinated the nation for months. They were a major link in the chain that finally led to the resignation of President Nixon.

Most congressional investigations are not nearly so visible, nor are they very often so historic. Their more usual shape can be seen when, for example, the House Committee on Agriculture looks at some problem in the farm price support system, or a subcommittee of the Senate Armed Services Committee is interested in the need to upgrade the housing of military dependents abroad.

Senator Sam Ervin, the chairman of the Senate's Watergate Committee, administers the oath to H. R. Halderman, one of President Nixon's top White House aides.

Joint Committees

A **joint committee** is one that has members from both houses. Some are select committees set up to serve some temporary purpose. Most are permanent groups that serve on a regular basis.

Some joint committees are investigative in nature and issue periodic reports to the House and Senate, for example, the Joint Economic Committee. Most joint committees have housekeeping duties, however, for example, the Joint Committee on Printing and the Joint Committee on the Library of Congress.

Because the standing committees of the two houses often duplicate one another's work, many have long urged that Congress make a much greater use of the joint committee device.

Conference Committees

Before a bill may be sent to the President, it must be passed in *identical form* by each house. Sometimes, the two houses pass differing versions of a measure, and the first house will not agree to the changes the other has made. When this happens a **conference committee**—a temporary, joint body—is created to iron out the differences in the bill. Its job is to produce a compromise bill that both houses will accept. We shall come back to the strategic role of the conference committee later in this chapter.

FOR REVIEW

1. **Identify:** House Rules Committee.
2. What is a standing committee? Why are they called "subject-matter" committees?
3. How many standing committees are there in the House? In the Senate?
4. How are the members of the standing committees chosen?
5. What is the role of the House Rules Committee?
6. What is a select committee? A joint committee? A conference committee?
7. Why is the investigative power so important to Congress?

Senate Leadership, 1986

Position	Name	Age[a]	Year Entered Senate[b]	State
Leadership				
Majority Leader	Robert J. Dole	63	1969 (1961)	Kansas
Majority Whip	Alan K. Simpson	55	1979	Wyoming
Minority Leader	Robert C. Byrd	68	1959 (1953)	West Virginia
Minority Whip	Alan Cranston	72	1969	California
Committee Chairmen				
Agriculture, Nutrition, and Forestry	Jesse A. Helms	65	1973	North Carolina
Appropriations	Mark O. Hatfield	64	1967	Oregon
Armed Services	Barry Goldwater	77	1953	Arizona
Banking, Housing and Urban Affairs	Jake Garn	54	1975	Utah
Budget	Pete V. Domenici	54	1973	New Mexico
Commerce, Science, and Transportation	John C. Danforth	50	1977	Missouri
Energy and Natural Resources	James A. McClure	62	1973 (1967)	Idaho
Environment and Public Works	Robert T. Stafford	73	1971 (1961)	Vermont
Finance	Bob Packwood	54	1969	Oregon
Foreign Relations	Richard G. Lugar	54	1977	Indiana
Governmental Affairs	William V. Roth	70	1971 (1967)	Delaware
Judiciary	Strom Thurmond	84	1954	South Carolina
Labor and Human Resources	Orrin G. Hatch	52	1977	Utah
Rules and Administration	Charles McC. Mathias	64	1969 (1961)	Maryland
Small Business	Lowell Weicker, Jr.	55	1971 (1969)	Connecticut
Veterans' Affairs	Frank Murkowski	53	1981	Alaska

[a]As of birthdate in 1986.
[b]Date in parentheses indicates first year of prior service in House of Representatives.
Source: Congressional Directory, with additional data from the Secretary of the Senate.

c 2.A, 3.A; avs 2.G, 4.F

4. How a Bill Becomes a Law

As You Read, Think About:

- What the congressional steps are through which a bill must go in order to become a law.
- What kinds of bills go through these steps.
- What different ways of voting on bills exist in the House.

As many as 20,000 bills are now introduced in the House and Senate during a term of Congress. Fewer than 10 percent ever become law. Where do these measures come from? Why are so few of them passed? What steps are taken in the House and the Senate when Congress makes law?

To answer these questions, we shall first trace a bill through the House. Then, because the legislative process is quite similar in the upper chamber, we shall note the major differences to be found in the Senate.

Authorship and Introduction

Most bills introduced in either house do *not* originate with members of Congress themselves. Most of the more important measures, and the more routine ones, too, are born somewhere in the executive branch. Business, labor, agriculture, and other pressure groups often draft measures as well. Some bills, or at least the idea for them, come from private citizens who think "there ought to be a law . . ." Bills are also born in the standing committees of Congress.

The Constitution states that all bills for the raising of revenue must be first introduced in the House.[9] Measures dealing with

[9]Article I, Section 7, Clause 1.

*REINFORCEMENT Discuss in class why the Framers provided that all bills for the raising of revenue originate in the House. Include the concept of popular representation in the House. (c 2.A, 3.A; avs 4.G, 4.I)

any other matter may be introduced in either chamber. Once the lower house has passed a revenue bill, the Senate may amend it as it may any other measure.

Only members can introduce bills in the House. Puerto Rico's Resident Commissioner and the Delegates from Guam, the Virgin Islands, American Samoa, and the District of Columbia may also introduce bills. A bill is introduced by dropping it into the "hopper."[10]

Types of Bills and Resolutions

The thousands of measures—*bills* and *resolutions*—Congress considers at each session take several forms.

Bills are proposed laws, or drafts of laws, presented to the House or Senate for enactment. Each bill's enacting clause reads: "Be it enacted by the Senate and House of Representatives of the United States of America in Congress assembled, That . . ." and the content of the measure follows.

[10]The hopper is a large box hanging at the edge of the Clerk's desk. Only a Senator may introduce a measure in the upper house. He or she does so by addressing the chair.

Public bills are measures applying to the nation as a whole, for example, a tax measure, an amendment to the copyright laws, or an appropriation of funds for the armed forces.

Private bills are those measures that apply to certain persons or places rather than to the nation generally. For example, a few years ago Congress passed an act to pay a man in Wyoming $1,229.52. This was the amount he would have made on a government contract had a local post office handled his mail promptly.

Joint resolutions are little different from bills and when passed have the force of law. The wording of the enacting clause is "Resolved by the Senate and House of Representatives of the United States of America in Congress assembled, That . . ."

Joint resolutions most often deal with unusual or temporary matters. For example, they may be used to appropriate money for the presidential inauguration ceremonies or correct an error in a statute already passed. Recall that joint resolutions are used to propose constitutional amendments (page 60), and they have also been used for territorial annexations (page 418).

Only a very small number, less than 10 percent, of all of the bills "dropped into the hopper" (right) ever become law.

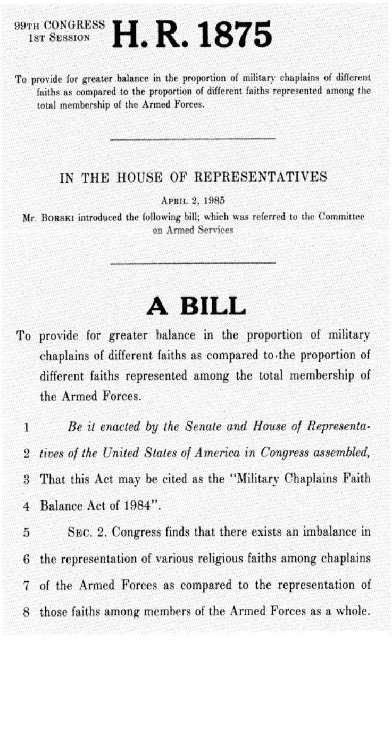

99TH CONGRESS
1ST SESSION **H. R. 1875**

To provide for greater balance in the proportion of military chaplains of different faiths as compared to the proportion of different faiths represented among the total membership of the Armed Forces.

IN THE HOUSE OF REPRESENTATIVES

APRIL 2, 1985

Mr. BORSKI introduced the following bill; which was referred to the Committee on Armed Services

A BILL

To provide for greater balance in the proportion of military chaplains of different faiths as compared to the proportion of different faiths represented among the total membership of the Armed Forces.

Be it enacted by the Senate and House of Representatives of the United States of America in Congress assembled, That this Act may be cited as the "Military Chaplains Faith Balance Act of 1984".

SEC. 2. Congress finds that there exists an imbalance in the representation of various religious faiths among chaplains of the Armed Forces as compared to the representation of those faiths among members of the Armed Forces as a whole.

Concurrent resolutions deal with matters in which the House and Senate must act jointly but for which a law is not needed. These resolutions usually begin in this form: "Resolved by the Senate, the House of Representatives concurring, That . . ." They are used most often by Congress to state a position, or an opinion, on some matter such as foreign affairs.

Resolutions deal with matters concerning either house alone and are taken up only by that house. They are regularly used for such things as the adoption of a new rule of procedure or the amendment of some existing rule. A simple resolution regularly begins: "Resolved by the Senate [or House], That . . ."

A bill or resolution usually deals with a single subject, but sometimes a rider dealing with an unrelated matter is included. A **rider** is a provision, not likely to pass on its own merit, attached to an important measure certain to pass. Its sponsors hope that it will "ride" through the legislative process on the strength of the other measure. Most riders are tacked on to appropriations measures. In fact, some money bills are hung with so many of them that they are called "Christmas trees." The opponents of those "decorations" and the President are forced to accept them if they want the bill's major provisions to become law.

Reference to Committee

The Clerk of the House numbers each bill as it is introduced. Thus, H.R. 3410 would be the 3,410th measure introduced in the House during the congressional term.[11] The Clerk also gives each bill a short title, a very brief summary of its principal contents.

Having received its number and short title, the bill is then entered in the House *Journal* and in the *Congressional Record* for the day.[12] The bill becomes part of the session's historical log.

With these actions the bill has received its first reading. Each bill that is finally passed in either house is given three "readings" along the legislative route. In the House, second reading comes during floor consideration if the measure gets that far. Third reading takes place just before the final vote on the measure.[13]

Each of these readings is usually by title only: "H.R. 3410, A bill to provide . . ." However, the more important or controversial bills are read in full and taken up line by line, section by section, at second reading.

After first reading, the Speaker refers the bill to the appropriate standing committee. This is the committee with jurisdiction over the bill's subject matter.

The Committee Stage

The standing committees have been described as "sieves," sifting out most bills and considering and reporting only those they judge to be the more important or worthwhile ones. As Woodrow Wilson once wrote, "Congress in its committee rooms is Congress at work."

Most bills die in committee. They are

[11]Bills originating in the Senate receive the prefix S.—as S. 210. Resolutions are similarly identified in each house in order of their introduction. Thus, H.J. Res. 12 would be the 12th joint resolution introduced in the House during the term, and, similarly in the Senate, S.J. Res. 19. Concurrent resolutions are identified as H. Con. Res. 16 or S. Con. Res. 4, and simple resolutions as H. Res. 198 or S. Res. 166.

[12]The *Journal* contains the minutes, or official record, of the daily proceedings in the House (Senate). The *Journal* for the preceding day is read at the beginning of each daily session, unless the chamber agrees to dispense with that reading, as almost always happens. The *Congressional Record* is a voluminous account of the daily proceedings (speeches, debates, other comments, votes, motions, etc.) in each house. The *Record* is not quite a word-for-word account, however. Members have five days in which to make changes in each temporary edition. They often insert lengthy speeches that were in fact never made on the floor, reconstruct "debates," and take out or revise thoughtless or inaccurate remarks. The *Record* is, nonetheless, extraordinarily valuable, both politically and historically.

[13]All bills introduced are immediately printed and distributed to the members. The three readings, an ancient parliamentary practice, are intended to ensure careful consideration of bills and prevent any of them from slipping by with little or no notice. The practice is not very significant today. In effect, the readings are now way stations along the legislative route. But they were quite important in the day when, quite literally, some members of Congress could not read.

*ENRICHMENT Copy a portion of a recent *Congressional Record* (school or local library) and distribute to the class. Ask students to identify proposed bills.

BUILDING GOVERNMENT SKILLS

How to Write to Your Lawmakers

Most members of Congress pay close attention to the mail that they receive from their constituents. Every day, they receive dozens to hundreds of letters from "the folks back home"—and all of the letters must, somehow, be answered. The volume of constituent mail has become so great that handling it now takes a large amount of staff time. Many congressional offices now use computers to churn out personalized form letters.

Many constituents write seeking information, and on every conceivable subject—on everything from how to obtain a passport or get a job with the Federal Government to the best ways to prune and fertilize roses. Many others ask for help—with everything from untangling a particular problem with the Social Security Administration or the Internal Revenue Service to a mother's plea that her soldier son be stationed somewhere closer to home.

Most members of Congress say that those letters that deal with public policy matters, and especially those in which constituents express their views on pending legislation, are the most welcome. Senator Phil Gramm (R., Texas) says that, after years in Congress, "I am more convinced than ever of the wisdom of the 'average' citizen and the value of his advice."

Congressman Morris Udall (D., Arizona) suggests these guidelines for writing an effective letter to a member of the House or the Senate:

- Address your letter properly. Send it to:

  Representative ____________________
  House Office Building
  Washington, D.C. 20515

  or to:
  Senator ____________________
  Senate Office Building
  Washington, D.C. 20510

- The letter should be timely. Don't wait until a bill is out of committee or has passed the House (or Senate).
- Identify the bill or issue that prompts your letter, preferably in the first paragraph. Be as specific as you can; give the bill number, or describe it by its popular title (Aid to the Contras, Balanced Budget Amendment, etc.).
- Be as brief as possible. It is not necessary that a letter be typed—only that it be legible.
- Give the reasons for the stand you take. Again, be brief, but be specific, and constructive, too.

Mr. Udall also offers these don't's:

- Don't make threats or promises.
- Don't berate your lawmaker.
- Don't pretend to wield vast political influence.
- Don't try to instruct your lawmaker on every issue. Don't be a pen pal.

1. Analyze each of Mr. Udall's do's and don't's. Why does he make each of those suggestions?
2. Where are your Representative's/Senators' local offices located? Why do those offices exist? How are they staffed? What work does the staff do?
3. Contact your Representative's/Senators' local office and find out about the mail your members of Congress receive. For example: How much comes in? How is it handled, and by whom?

Congressional Record

United States of America

PROCEEDINGS AND DEBATES OF THE 99th CONGRESS, FIRST SESSION

Vol. 131 | WASHINGTON, THURSDAY, JULY 11, 1985 | No. 92

House of Representatives

The House met at 10 a.m.

The Chaplain, Reverend James David Ford, D.D., offered the following prayer:

Gracious God, we pray that our words and deeds will be received as instruments of understanding and not to hurt or cause pain. May the spirit of forgiveness be our constant companion and may we remember that we are members of the human community, all created by Your grace. Help us to live together so that our words and deeds remind us of our common heritage and allow every person to live in peace. Amen.

THE JOURNAL

The SPEAKER. The Chair has examined the Journal of the last day's minute and to revise and extend his remarks.)

Mr. STRANG. Mr. Speaker, this week this House was offered the opportunity to examine what appeared to be a possible conflict between the rules of the House and the conduct of partisan activity on Federal premises. Our opportunity, Mr. Speaker, was to refer this matter to the Committee on Official Standards of Conduct. Nothing less, Mr. Speaker, should have been expected by the American people or indeed by us, the elected Members of this body.

To sweep this grave matter under the partisan carpet can serve only to reinforce the lurking suspicion that this body does not intend to abide by the rules or by law either here or in

The Clerk read as follows:

Mr. McCollum moves that the managers on the part of the House, at the conference on the disagreeing votes of the two Houses on the bill S. 1160, be instructed to insist on the House position on the McCollum amendment relating to the creation of a peacetime espionage offense with a death penalty in the Uniform Code of Military Justice.

The SPEAKER. The gentleman from Florida [Mr. McCollum] is recognized for 1 hour.

Mr. McCOLLUM. Mr. Speaker, the motion to instruct in this case is being offered for two primary reasons; one, it has been my feeling since we did not get a recorded vote on this issue on the floor when the amendment was adopted on the Department of De-

The *Congressional Record* is an account of the daily proceedings of both the House and the Senate.

"pigeonholed,"[14] and most deserve that fate. At times, however, a committee pigeonholes a measure that a majority of the House wishes to consider. When that happens, the bill can be "blasted out" of the committee with a **discharge petition.**[15] But this procedure is not often successful.

Those bills that a committee, or at least its chairman, does wish to consider are discussed and considered at times chosen by the chairman. Today, most committees do most of their work through their several **subcommittees.** There are some 140 of these "committees within committees" in the House, and more than 100 in the Senate. Where an important or controversial bill is involved, a committee, or more often one of its subcommittees, holds public hearings on the measure. Interested persons, special interest groups and their lobbyists, and government officials are invited to testify at these information gathering sessions.[16]

Occasionally, a subcommittee will make a "junket" (trip) to locations affected by a

[14]The term comes from the old-fashioned rolltop desks with pigeonholes into which papers were put and promptly forgotten. Most of the so-called "by-request" bills are routinely pigeonholed. These are measures that many members introduce, but only because some person or some pressure group has asked them to.

[15]After a bill has been in committee for at least 30 days (seven days in the Rules Committee), any member may file a *discharge motion.* If that motion, in effect a petition, is signed by a majority (218) of House members, the committee has seven days in which to report the bill. If it does not, any member who signed the petition may on the second and fourth Mondays of each month move that the committee be discharged—relieved of the bill. Debate on the motion to discharge is limited to 20 minutes. If the motion carries, the House turns to floor consideration of the discharged bill at once.

[16]If necessary, a committee may subpoena witnesses. A subpoena is an order compelling one to appear. Failure to obey a subpoena may lead the House or Senate to pass a resolution citing the offender for contempt of Congress. This is a federal crime punishable by imprisonment.

*ENRICHMENT Have the class read a newspaper and look for the report of a subcommittee. Have the students examine the topic of the report and discuss why the topic was investigated by a subcommittee instead of a full committee. (c 3.A, 3.B; avs 4.A, 4.H)

measure. Thus, some members of the National Parks and Recreation Subcommittee of the House Committee on Interior and Insular Affairs may take a firsthand look at a number of national parks. Or, the Water and Power Resources Subcommittee of the Senate Energy and Natural Resources Committee may visit the Pacific Northwest to gather information on a public power bill.

These junkets are made at public expense, and members of Congress are sometimes criticized for taking them. But an on-the-spot investigation often proves to be the best way a committee can inform itself.

When a subcommittee has completed its work on a bill it goes to the full committee. That body may do one of several things. It may:

1. Report the bill favorably, with a "do pass" recommendation. It is then the chairman's job to steer the bill through debate on the floor.
2. Refuse to report the bill, or pigeonhole it. Again, this is the fate suffered by most measures, and in both houses.
3. Report the bill in amended form. Many bills are changed in committee, and several bills on the same subject may be combined into a single measure before they are reported out.
4. Report the bill with an unfavorable recommendation. This does not often happen. But sometimes a committee feels that the full House should have a chance to consider a bill or does not want to take the responsibility for killing it.
5. Report a "committee bill." This is an entirely new bill that the committee has substituted for one or more referred to it.

The Rules Committee and the Calendars

Before it goes to the floor for consideration, a bill reported by a standing committee is placed on one of several calendars. A calendar is a schedule of the order in which bills will be taken up on the floor. There are five of these calendars in the House:

1. The Calendar of the Committee of the Whole House on the State of the Union, commonly known as the *Union Calendar,* for all bills having to do with revenues, appropriations, or government property.
2. The House Calendar for all other public bills.
3. The Calendar of the Committee of the Whole House, commonly called the *Private Calendar,* for all private bills.
4. The Consent Calendar for all bills from the Union or House Calendar that are taken up out of order by unanimous consent of the House of Representatives. These are most often minor bills to which there is no opposition.
5. The Discharge Calendar for petitions to discharge bills from committee.

The computerized voting system now used by the House saves a large amount of floor time in each session.

Under the rules of the House, bills are taken from each of these calendars on a regularly scheduled basis. Bills from the Consent Calendar are to be considered on the first and third Mondays of each month. Measures relating to the District of Columbia are to be taken up on the second and fourth Mondays, and private bills every Friday. On "Calendar Wednesdays" the various committee chairmen may call up any bills that have cleared their committees.

None of these arrangements is followed too closely, however. What often happens is quite complicated. First, remember, the Rules Committee plays a critical role. It must grant a rule before most bills can in fact reach the floor. That is, before a measure can be taken from a calendar, the Rules Committee must approve that step and set a time for its appearance on the floor.

By failing or refusing to grant a rule for a bill, the Rules Committee can effectively kill it. Or, when the rules Committee does grant a rule, that rule may be a special rule, one setting conditions under which the measure will be considered. A special rule regularly sets a time limit on floor debate. A special rule may even provide that amendments may not be offered to certain or even to any of the bill's provisions.

Then, too, certain bills are "privileged." They may be called up at almost any time, ahead of any other less privileged business before the House. The most highly privileged measures include general revenue (tax) and major appropriations (spending) bills, conference committee reports, and special rules from the Rules Committee.

On certain days, usually the first and third Mondays and Tuesdays, the House may suspend its rules. A motion to that effect must be approved by a two-thirds vote of the members present. When that happens, as it sometimes does, the House moves so far away from its established procedures that a measure can go through all the steps necessary to enactment in a single day.

All of this—the calendars, the role of the Rules Committee, and the other complex procedures—has developed over time and for several reasons. The two most important reasons are (1) the large size of the House and (2) the sheer number and variety of bills its members introduce. Another reason for the array of rules is because no one member could possibly know the contents, let alone the merits, of every bill on which he or she may have to vote.

Consideration on the Floor

When a bill does finally reach the floor, it receives its second reading.

Many bills the House passes are minor ones, with little or no opposition. Most minor bills are called from the Consent Calendar, get their second reading by title only, and are quickly disposed of.

Nearly all the more important measures are dealt with in a much different manner,

Bills can elicit a vast public response. Here, Sen. Bill Bradley (D., N.J.) and Rep. Richard Gephardt (D., Mo.) collect mail generated from their Surtax Bill.

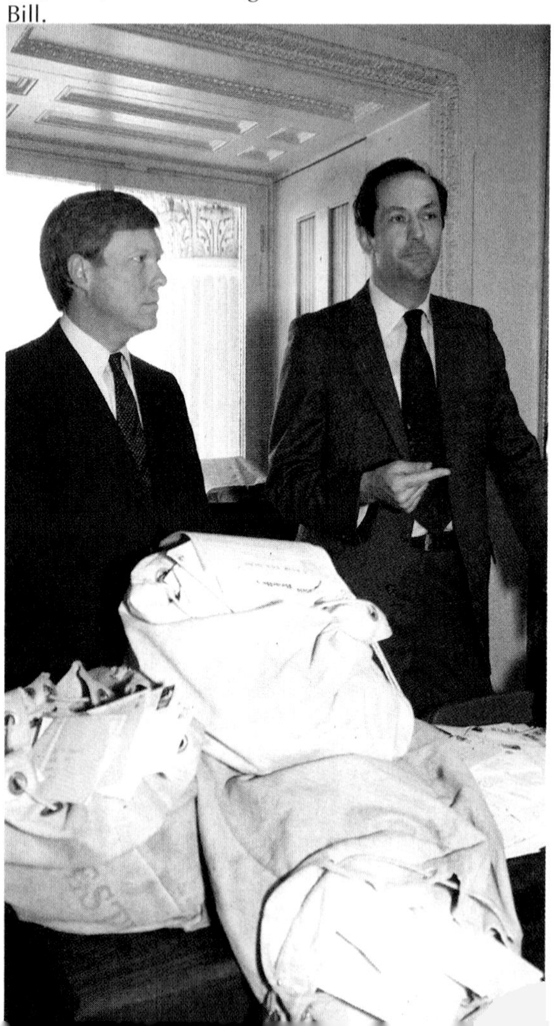

however. They are considered in Committee of the Whole, an old parliamentary device for speeding business on the floor.

The **Committee of the Whole** is the House sitting not as itself but as one large committee of itself. Its rules are much less strict and floor action moves along at a faster pace. A **quorum**—majority of the full membership, 218—must be present in order for the House to do business. However, only 100 members need be present in Committee of the Whole.

When the House resolves itself into Committee of the Whole, the Speaker steps down because the House is not legally in session. Another member presides.

General debate begins, and the bill receives its second reading, section by section. As each section is read, amendments may be offered. Under the "five-minute rule," supporters and opponents of each amendment have just that long to make their case. Votes are taken on each section and its amendment as the reading proceeds.

When the bill has been gone through —and many run to dozens of pages—the Committee of the Whole has completed its work. It then "rises," or dissolves itself. The House is now back in session, the Speaker resumes the chair, and the committee's work is formally adopted.

Debate Its large size has long since forced the House to impose severe limits on floor debate. A rule first adopted in 1841 forbids any member from holding the floor for more than one hour, unless he or she has unanimous consent to speak for a longer time. Since 1880 the Speaker has had the power to force any member who strays from the subject at hand to give up the floor.

The majority and minority floor leaders generally decide in advance how they will split the time to be spent on a bill. But, at any time, any member may "move the previous question." That is, any member may demand a vote on the issue before the House. If that motion passes, only 40 minutes of further debate is allowed before a vote is taken. This device is the only motion that can be used in the House to close, or end, debate, but it is a very effective one.

Voting A bill may be, and often is, the subject of several different votes on the floor. If amendments are offered, as they frequently are, each of them must be voted up or down. Then, too, a number of procedural motions may be presented, among them, one to table the bill (lay it aside), another for the previous question, and so on. These several other votes can be a better guide to a bill's friends and foes than is the final vote itself. Sometimes, a member votes for a bill that is now certain to pass, even though he or she supported amendments to it that, if adopted, would have defeated the measure. *

The House uses four different methods for the taking of floor votes:

1. Voice votes are the most common. The Speaker calls for the "ayes" and then the "noes," the members answer in chorus, and the Speaker announces the result.
2. If any member thinks the Speaker has erred in judging a voice vote, he or she may demand a standing vote, also known as a division of the House. All in favor, and then all opposed, stand and are counted by the Clerk.
3. A teller vote may be demanded by one-fifth of a quorum (44 members in the House or 20 in Committee of the Whole). When this procedure is used, the Speaker names two tellers, one from each party. The members pass between them and are counted, for and against. Teller votes are rare today. The practice has been replaced by electronic voting; see below.
4. A roll-call vote, also known as a record vote, may be demanded by one-fifth of the members present.[17]

In 1973, to replace the roll call by the Clerk, the House installed a computerized voting system for all quorum calls and record votes. Members now vote at any of 48 stations on the floor, by inserting a personalized plastic card in a box and then pushing

[17]The Constitution (Article I, Section 7, Clause 2) requires a record vote on the question of overriding a presidential veto. No record votes are taken in Committee of the Whole.

*REINFORCEMENT Unrelated amendments, riders, are often added to a bill because a member wishes to include an issue of interest to his or her constituents. How can this affect debate and vote on the bill?

one of three buttons—"Yea," "Nay," or "Present."[18]

A large master board, above the Speaker's chair, shows instantly how each member has voted. Smaller summary boards on the balcony ledges on either side of the chamber show the running vote totals and the time left for casting votes. The leadership tables on either side of the center aisle have consoles so the majority and minority floor leaders may follow voting patterns and the behavior of each member.

The House rules allow the members 15 minutes to answer quorum calls or cast record votes. Voting ends when the Speaker pushes a button to lock the electronic system. That also produces a permanent record of the vote. Under the former roll-call process, it took the Clerk up to 45 minutes to call each member's name and record his or her vote. Before 1973, roll calls took up about *three months* of floor time each session.

The computer also keeps track of every measure in both the House and Senate, reporting its legislative history and current status through an information storage and retrieval system.

Voting procedures are much the same in the Senate. The upper house uses voice, standing, and roll-call votes, but does not take teller votes or use an electronic voting process. Only six or seven minutes are needed for a roll-call vote in the upper chamber.

Final Steps in the House

Once a bill has been approved at second reading, it is engrossed—that is, printed in its final form. Then it is read a third time, by title, and a final vote is taken. If the bill is approved at third reading, it is signed by the Speaker. A page then carries it to the Senate and places it on the Vice President's (Senate President's) desk.

[18]The "Present" button is most often used for a quorum call—a check to make sure that a quorum of the members is in fact present. Otherwise, it is used when a member does not wish to vote on a question but still wants to be recorded as present. A "present" vote is not allowed on some questions, for example, overriding a veto.

FOR REVIEW

1. **Identify:** bill, *House* (Senate) *Journal, Congressional Record,* first, second, and third reading, pigeonhole, calendar, special rule, table, voice vote, standing vote, division of the house, teller vote, roll-call vote, record vote.
2. From what main sources do drafts of bills originate?
3. What kinds of bills must originate in the House? Why?
4. Who may introduce a bill in the House? In the Senate?
5. What are the different types of measures introduced in each house?
6. Who refers bills to committee in the House?
7. What is the purpose of public subcommittee hearings?
8. What options does a full committee have when acting on a bill?
9. What is the function of each of the calendars?
10. What is the Committee of the Whole? A quorum?

5. The Bill in the Senate

As You Read, Think About:

- How the Senate legislative process differs from that in the House.
- What filibuster and cloture are and how they are used.
- What the final steps are in the legislative process.

The steps in the lawmaking process are quite similar in both houses. So, we need not trace a bill through the Senate in the same detail with which we reviewed that process in the House. Rather, in this section, we shall look at the major differences in the legislative process to be found in the upper house.

How Bills Become Laws

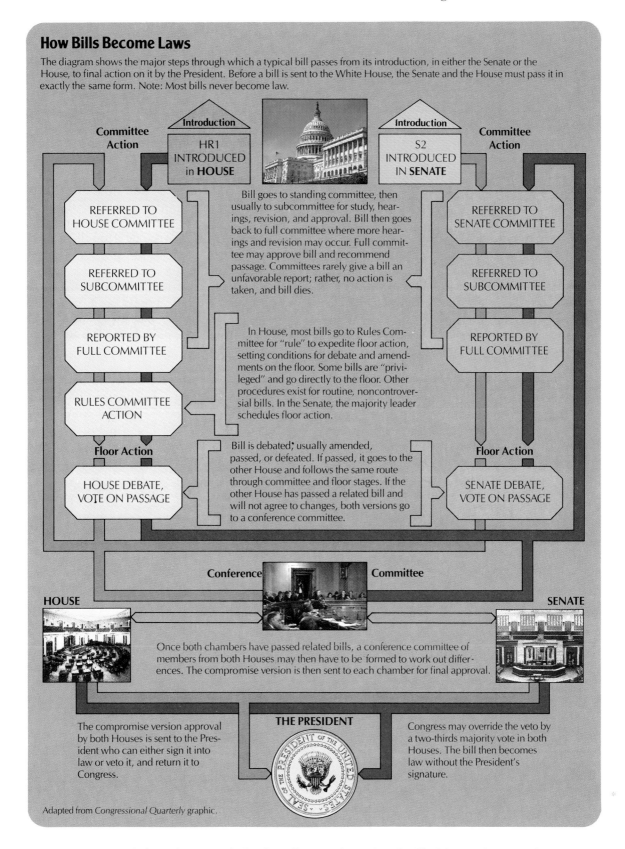

The diagram shows the major steps through which a typical bill passes from its introduction, in either the Senate or the House, to final action on it by the President. Before a bill is sent to the White House, the Senate and the House must pass it in exactly the same form. Note: Most bills never become law.

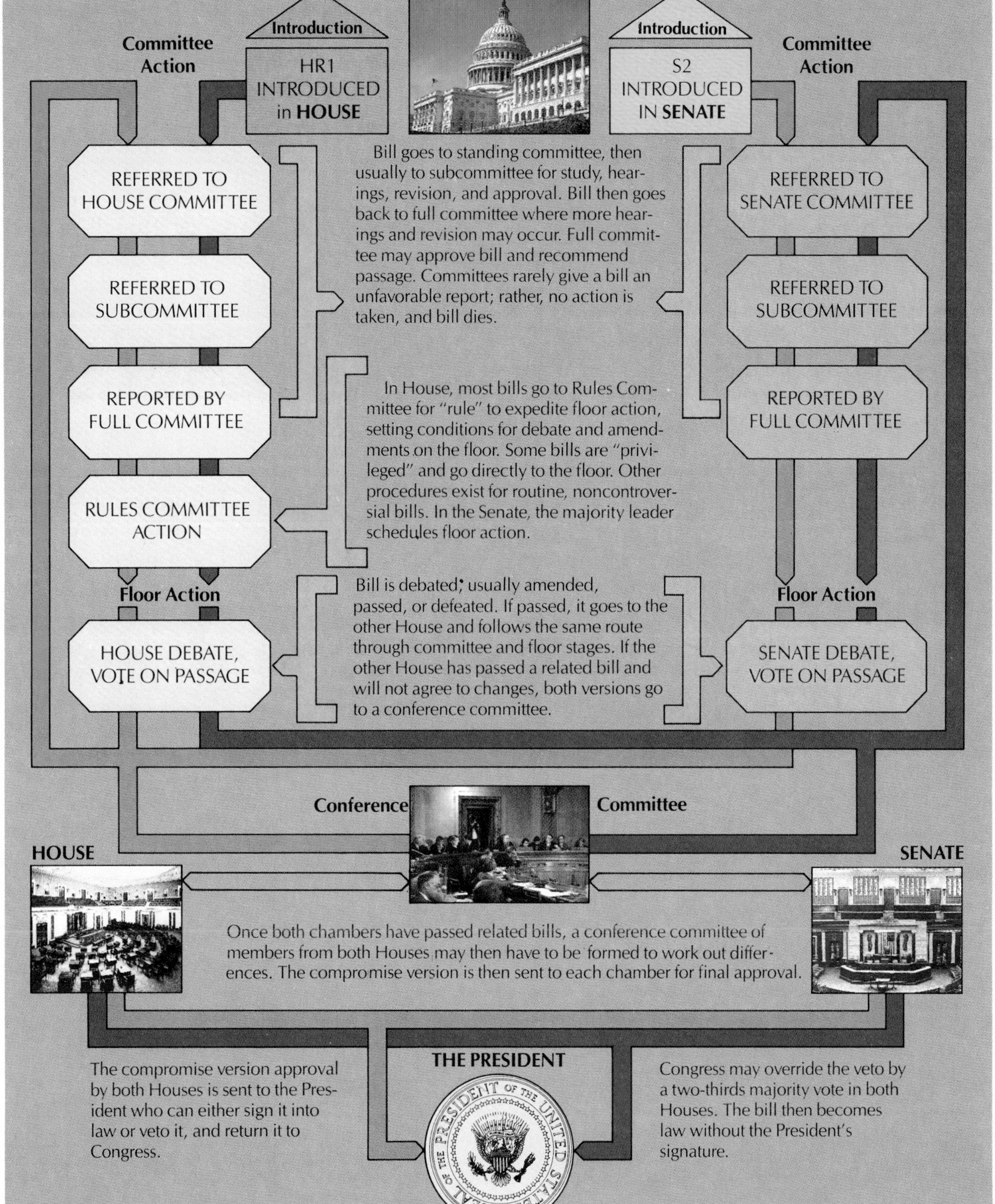
Committee Action
Introduction
HR1 INTRODUCED in HOUSE
Introduction
S2 INTRODUCED IN SENATE
Committee Action
REFERRED TO HOUSE COMMITTEE
Bill goes to standing committee, then usually to subcommittee for study, hearings, revision, and approval. Bill then goes back to full committee where more hearings and revision may occur. Full committee may approve bill and recommend passage. Committees rarely give a bill an unfavorable report; rather, no action is taken, and bill dies.
REFERRED TO SENATE COMMITTEE
REFERRED TO SUBCOMMITTEE
REFERRED TO SUBCOMMITTEE
REPORTED BY FULL COMMITTEE
In House, most bills go to Rules Committee for "rule" to expedite floor action, setting conditions for debate and amendments on the floor. Some bills are "privileged" and go directly to the floor. Other procedures exist for routine, noncontroversial bills. In the Senate, the majority leader schedules floor action.
REPORTED BY FULL COMMITTEE
RULES COMMITTEE ACTION
Floor Action
Floor Action
HOUSE DEBATE, VOTE ON PASSAGE
Bill is debated, usually amended, passed, or defeated. If passed, it goes to the other House and follows the same route through committee and floor stages. If the other House has passed a related bill and will not agree to changes, both versions go to a conference committee.
SENATE DEBATE, VOTE ON PASSAGE
Conference
Committee
HOUSE
SENATE
Once both chambers have passed related bills, a conference committee of members from both Houses may then have to be formed to work out differences. The compromise version is then sent to each chamber for final approval.
The compromise version approval by both Houses is sent to the President who can either sign it into law or veto it, and return it to Congress.
THE PRESIDENT
SEAL OF THE PRESIDENT OF THE UNITED STATES
Congress may override the veto by a two-thirds majority vote in both Houses. The bill then becomes law without the President's signature.

Adapted from *Congressional Quarterly* graphic.

*REINFORCEMENT Ask the students to study the above diagram. Discuss the role of both houses, from committee to conference, and the importance of compromise to this process. (c 3.A, 3.B; avs 2.G, 4.B, 4.G)

Drawing by Richter; © 1971 The New Yorker Magazine, Inc.

"My folks are in the gallery. If you can work it in, would you mind terribly calling me 'my esteemed colleague'?"

Bills are introduced by Senators who are formally recognized for that purpose. A measure is then given a number and short title, read twice, and then referred to committee, where bills are dealt with much as they are in the House.

All in all, the Senate's proceedings are less formal and its rules less strict than those of the much larger House. For example, the Senate has only one calendar for all bills reported out by its committees. Bills are called to the floor at the discretion of the majority floor leader.[19]

Debate

The major differences in House and Senate procedures are found in floor debates. Floor debates are strictly limited in the House but almost unrestrained in the Senate. Indeed, most Senators are intensely proud of belonging to what has often been called "the greatest deliberative body in the world."

As a general matter, Senators may speak on the floor for as long as they please. There is no rule that they speak only to the measure under consideration. They can speak to any topic they wish. Unlike the House, the Senate's rules do not allow the moving of the previous question.

The Senate's consideration of most bills is brought to a close by unanimous consent agreements. That is, discussion ends and a final vote is taken at a fixed time previously agreed to by the majority and minority leaders. But if any Senator objects—prevents unanimous consent—the device fails.[20]

The Senate's dedication to freedom of debate is almost unique among modern legislative bodies. That freedom is intended to encourage the fullest possible discussion of matters on the floor. The great latitude it allows, however, has been and is abused by the filibuster.

The Filibuster Essentially, a **filibuster** is an attempt to "talk a bill to death." It is a stalling tactic, a process in which a minority of Senators seeks to delay or prevent Senate action on a measure. The filibusterers try to so monopolize the Senate floor and its time that the Senate must either drop the bill or change it in some manner acceptable to the minority.

Talk is the filibusterers' major weapon—talking, holding the floor, on and on. But many time-killing motions, quorum calls, and other parliamentary maneuvers are also used. Indeed, anything to delay or obstruct is a tool for the minority as it attempts to block a bill that would probably pass if brought to a vote.

The history of the Senate is liberally dotted with filibusters, many prolonged and dramatic. Most filibusters have been team efforts, in which a small group of Senators

[19]The Senate does have another, nonlegislative calendar, the Executive Calendar, for treaties and appointments made by the President and awaiting Senate approval or, rarely, rejection. The majority leader controls that schedule, too.

[20]The Senate does have a "two-speech rule." Under it, no Senator may speak more than twice on a given question on the same legislative day. By recessing—temporarily interrupting—rather than adjourning a day's session, the Senate can prolong a "legislative day" indefinitely. Thus, the two-speech rule does have some limiting effect on the amount of time the Senate spends on some matters on its agenda.

speak in relay, passing the possession of the floor back and forth indefinitely.

Among the many better known filibusterers, Senator Huey Long (D., Louisiana) spoke for more than 15 hours in 1935. He stalled by reading from the Washington telephone directory and a mail-order catalogue and gave his colleagues his recipes for corn bread and turnip greens. In 1947, Glen Taylor (D., Idaho) used more than eight hours of floor time talking of his children, Wall Street, baptism, and fishing.

The current filibuster record was set some 30 years ago. Senator Strom Thurmond (R., South Carolina) held the floor for 24 hours and 18 minutes in an unsuccessful, one-man effort against what later became the Civil Rights Act of 1957.

No later efforts have come close to matching that one. Still, the practice is often used and to great effect in the Senate. Over the past century and more, well over 200 measures have been killed by filibusters. The *threat* alone of a filibuster has resulted in the Senate's failure to consider a number of bills and the amending of many more.

The Senate often tries to beat off a filibuster with lengthy, even day-and-night, sessions to wear down the participants. At times, some little-observed rules are quite strictly enforced. Among them are the requirement that Senators stand, not sit, lean on their desks, or walk about as they speak and that they not use "unparliamentory language." But these tactics seldom work.

The Cloture Rule The Senate's real check on the filibuster is its Cloture Rule, Rule XXII in the Standing Rules of the Senate. It was first adopted in 1917, after one of the most notable of all filibusters in Senate history.[21]

[21]That filibuster lasted for some three weeks, and took place less than two months before the United States entered World War I on April 6, 1917. In February, German submarines had renewed their attacks on shipping in the North Atlantic. Immediately, President Wilson asked Congress for legislation to permit the arming of American merchant vessels. The bill, widely supported in the country, was quickly passed by the House, by a vote of 403–12. The measure died in the Senate, however. It had strong support there, but 12 Senators filibustered it until the end of the congressional term on March 4th. The public was outraged. President Wilson declared: "A little group of willful men, representing no opinion but their own, has rendered the great Government of the United States helpless and contemptible." The Cloture Rule was passed by the Senate at its next session, later that same year.

Senators rest on cots set up in the old Supreme Court Chamber during a filibuster, one which attempted to prevent passage of the Civil Rights Act of 1960.

Rule XXII provides for **cloture** or limiting debate. While not in regular and continuing force, the rule can be brought into play only by a special procedure. A vote to invoke the rule must be taken two days after a petition calling for that action has been submitted by at least 16 members of the Senate. If at least 60 Senators—three-fifths of the full Senate—then vote for the motion, the rule becomes effective. Each member is then allowed no more than one hour of debate on the pending bill. Then the measure *must* be brought to a final vote.

Invoking the rule is no easy matter. Thus far, more than 200 attempts have been made to invoke the rule, and fewer than a third have succeeded.

Many Senators hesitate to support most cloture motions for two reasons: (1) their dedication to the Senate's tradition of free debate and (2) their practical worry that the frequent use of cloture will undercut the value of the filibuster as a minority weapon that they themselves may some day want to use.

FOR REVIEW

1. **Identify:** unanimous consent.
2. What is the major difference between floor debate in the House and in the Senate?
3. What is a filibuster?
4. What is the Senate's check on the filibuster? How is this procedure invoked?

6. The Final Stages

As You Read, Think About:

- What the function of conference committees is.
- What options are open to the President after a bill has been passed by both houses of Congress.

Any measure enacted by Congress *must* have been passed by both houses in *identical* form. Most often, a bill passed by one house and then approved by the other is not amended in the second chamber. When the House and Senate do pass different versions of the same bill, the first house usually "concurs" in the other's amendments—and, so, congressional action is completed.

The Conference Committee

There are times when the House or the Senate will not accept the other's version of a bill. When this happens, the measure is turned over to a conference committee—a temporary joint committee of the two houses. It seeks to "iron out" the differences and come up with a compromise bill.

The conferees, or "managers," are named by the respective presiding officers. Mostly, they are leading members of the standing committee that first handled the measure in each house.

Both the House and Senate rules restrict a conference committee to the consideration of those points in a bill on which the two houses disagree. The rules also forbid the committee's including any entirely new material in its compromise version. In practice, however, the conferees' product very often contains provisions that were not even considered in either house.

Once the conferees agree, their report—the compromise bill—is submitted to both houses. It must be accepted or rejected without amendment. Only rarely does either house turn down a conference committee's work. That a bill hammered out by a conference committee is seldom rejected by either house is not too surprising, for two major reasons: (1) the potent membership of the typical conference committee and (2) the fact that its report usually comes in the midst of the rush to adjournment at the end of a congressional session.

The conference committee stage is a most strategic step in the legislative process. A number of major legislative decisions are made at that point. Indeed, the late Senator George Norris (R., Nebraska) once quite aptly described conference committees as "the third house of Congress."

President Lyndon B. Johnson, having urged Congress to pass new and stronger civil rights legislation, celebrates the signing of the Civil Rights Act of 1964 with Martin Luther King and other black civil rights leaders.

The President's Action

The Constitution requires that

> Every bill which shall have passed the House of Representatives and the Senate [and] every order, resolution, or vote, to which the concurrence of the Senate and House of Representatives may be necessary (except on a question of adjournment) shall be submitted to the President. . . .[22]

* The Constitution presents the President with four options to shape the pending law at this point:

1. The President may sign the bill, and it then becomes law.

2. The President may **veto,** or refuse to sign, the bill. The measure must then be returned to the house in which it originated, together with the President's objections. These are called the veto message. Although it seldom does, Congress may then pass the bill over the President's veto, by a two-thirds vote in each house.

3. The President may allow the bill to become law without signing it—by not acting on it (neither signing nor vetoing it) within 10 days, not counting Sundays, of receiving it.

4. The fourth option is a variation of the third. If Congress adjourns its session within 10 days of submitting a bill to the President, and the President does not act, the measure dies. This is known as the **pocket veto.**

FOR REVIEW

1. When is a conference committee formed? What is its job?
2. Why is a conference committee's report seldom rejected by either house?
3. What four options does the President have on receiving a measure passed by Congress?

[22]Article I, Section 7, Clauses 2 and 3. We shall return to the President's veto power in Chapter 15.

*REINFORCEMENT The President's action on a bill is indicative of the separation of powers outlined in the Constitution. Discuss this concept in class, pointing out the importance of the presidential veto.

SUMMARY

Congress is somewhat similarly organized in both chambers. Major distinctions arise mainly because the larger House is completely reorganized every two years while the smaller Senate is a continuous body.

The Speaker of the House presides over the lower chamber. He is chosen by a floor vote and is a dominant force in the House. The Constitution makes the Vice President the President of the Senate. The upper house chooses an alternate presiding officer, the President *pro tem*.

In both houses, each party's organization is headed by a majority, or minority, floor leader, chosen by the party's caucus.

Congress does much of its work in its committees. Standing committees are the regular, permanent committees in both chambers. They are dominated by their chairmen chosen under the seniority rule. Select committees are special, often temporary bodies in both houses. Joint committees, made up of members of both houses, are usually permanent bodies. Conference committees are temporary, joint committees formed to "iron out" differences in House–Senate measures.

Bills introduced in either house are referred to the standing committees. Those reported out of committee reach the floor through the Rules Committee in the House and at the discretion of the majority leader in the Senate. The House, but not the Senate, considers most important bills in Committee of the Whole. Debate is severely limited in the House, but not the Senate where filibusters are not uncommon.

A bill must be passed in identical form by both houses before it may be sent to the President for his action. When the two chambers cannot agree on a measure, a conference committee attempts to produce a compromise version acceptable to both houses.

CHAPTER REVIEW

Key Terms/Concepts*

legislative caucus (313)
Speaker of the House (315)
President of the Senate (316)
President *pro tempore* (316)
majority/minority floor leader (316)
majority whip (316)
minority whip (316)
party caucus (317)
policy committee (317)
committee chairman (317)
seniority rule (319)
standing committee (320)
select committee (321)
oversight function (322)
joint committee (323)
conference committee (323)
bills (325)
public bill (325)
private bill (325)
joint resolution (325)
concurrent resolution (326)
resolution (326)
rider (326)
subcommittee (328)
discharge petition (328)
Committee of the Whole (331)
quorum (331)
filibuster (334)
cloture (336)
veto (337)
pocket veto (337)

*These are terms included in the Glossary.

Keynote Questions

• 1. What is the role of the Speaker of the House? The President *pro tem* of the Senate?

• 2. Why are the majority leader and the minority leader important to the legislative process?

• 3. What unwritten custom guides the selection of committee chairmen? Why are committee chairmen so powerful? What has happened to this custom in recent years?

••• 4. Make a table showing the four types of committees in Congress, their purposes, and an example of each type.

The dots represent skill levels required to answer each question or complete each activity:
•requires recall and comprehension • •requires application and analysis • • •requires synthesis and evaluation

5. Why is the House Rules Committee an especially powerful committee?
6. What is the difference between a public bill and a private bill? Between a joint resolution and a concurrent resolution?
7. Briefly outline the steps of how a bill becomes law. Start with the drafting of a bill.
8. What five options does a committee have when considering a bill?
9. In which chamber are filibusters possible? Why? How may a filibuster be stopped?
10. When a bill reaches the President, what two options does the President have if he wants the bill to become law?
11. What is the difference between the veto and the pocket veto?

Skill Application

Following a Flow Chart: A flow chart is a useful graphic device for showing the steps of a process or the ways to reach a desired goal. Pictures and/or geometric symbols are used with words to explain each step and arrows indicate direction. Flow charts can make the steps in a process easier to understand, for example: obtaining a driver's license, registering to vote, or understanding how a bill is passed in Congress.

When examining a flow chart, always note the title first. Then find the first arrow. Follow the arrows from one step to the next until you reach the conclusion of the process.

Follow the flow chart on page 333, and answer the following questions.

1. What is the title of this flow chart?
2. This flow chart is divided into two sides. What does each side represent?
3. What is the first step in this process?
4. Why does the flow chart show two sets of arrows, each set a different color? What does each color represent?
5. What House committee has no equivalent in the Senate?
6. If differences in House- and Senate-passed versions of a measure must be resolved, where does that bill go?
7. How does this process end?
8. Summarize in your own words in a brief paragraph the process illustrated by the flow chart.

For Thought and Discussion

1. The daily sessions of the House are now carried by many cable TV systems around the country. If these broadcasts are available in your area, you can learn much about the House, the legislative process, and much more by watching them, of course. Do you think that the sessions of the House and/or the Senate should be broadcast on TV? Why, or why not?
2. The *Congressional Record* reports the way in which each member responds to every roll-call vote in either house. Why might a Representative or a Senator not wish to vote on certain roll calls?
3. Many have long urged that the Senate do away with the filibuster and that both the House and the Senate give up the seniority rule. How do you feel about each of these practices? What other reforms in congressional organization or procedure do you think should be made?

Suggested Activities

1. Select a bill now before either house of Congress. Trace its origins and follow its progress through the lawmaking process. Newspapers, Congressional Quarterly's *Weekly Report,* the *National Journal,* and the *Congressional Record* are good sources for both selecting a bill and checking on its progress. Include some of the politics—which pressure groups supported the bill and which opposed it? Which Representatives or Senators supported the bill? Why? What tactics did supporters and opponents use to influence the outcome of the bill?
2. Use current newspaper articles to show examples of the following: introduction of a bill, committee hearings, committee reports, floor action, conference committee action, signing or veto by the President. Arrange your articles in a flow chart that illustrates the legislative process.
3. Stage a debate or class forum on one of the following: (a) *Resolved,* That the seniority rule be abolished in both houses of Congress; (b) *Resolved,* That filibusters be banned in the Senate.

All legislative powers herein granted shall be vested in a Congress of the United States. . . .
—ARTICLE I, SECTION 1,
CONSTITUTION OF THE UNITED STATES

13

The Powers of Congress

CHAPTER OBJECTIVES

To help you to

Learn · Know · Understand

The scope of the powers of Congress, in a governmental system both limited and federal in character.

The importance of the expressed monetary and commerce powers of Congress.

Other expressed powers of Congress relating to the postal service, copyrights and patents, weights and measures, territories and other areas.

The significance of the Necessary and Proper Clause to the powers of Congress and the broad field of implied powers.

The nonlegislative powers exercised by Congress.

AS THE OPENING words of Article I of the Constitution declare, the basic function of the Congress is to legislate, that is, to make law. It is the function of translating the public will into public policy in the form of law. As we have pointed out several times, that function is of pivotal importance to democratic government.

In this chapter we look at the two basic categories of power held and exercised by Congress. The first is its *legislative powers*—those constitutional powers that form the base on which Congress can and does make law. The second category is its *nonlegislative powers*—those constitutional powers through which Congress can and does carry out other functions closely related to its role as the lawmaking branch of the National Government.

1. Limited, Federal Government

As You Read, Think About:

- What impact the limited and federal nature of American government has had on the scope of Congress's powers.

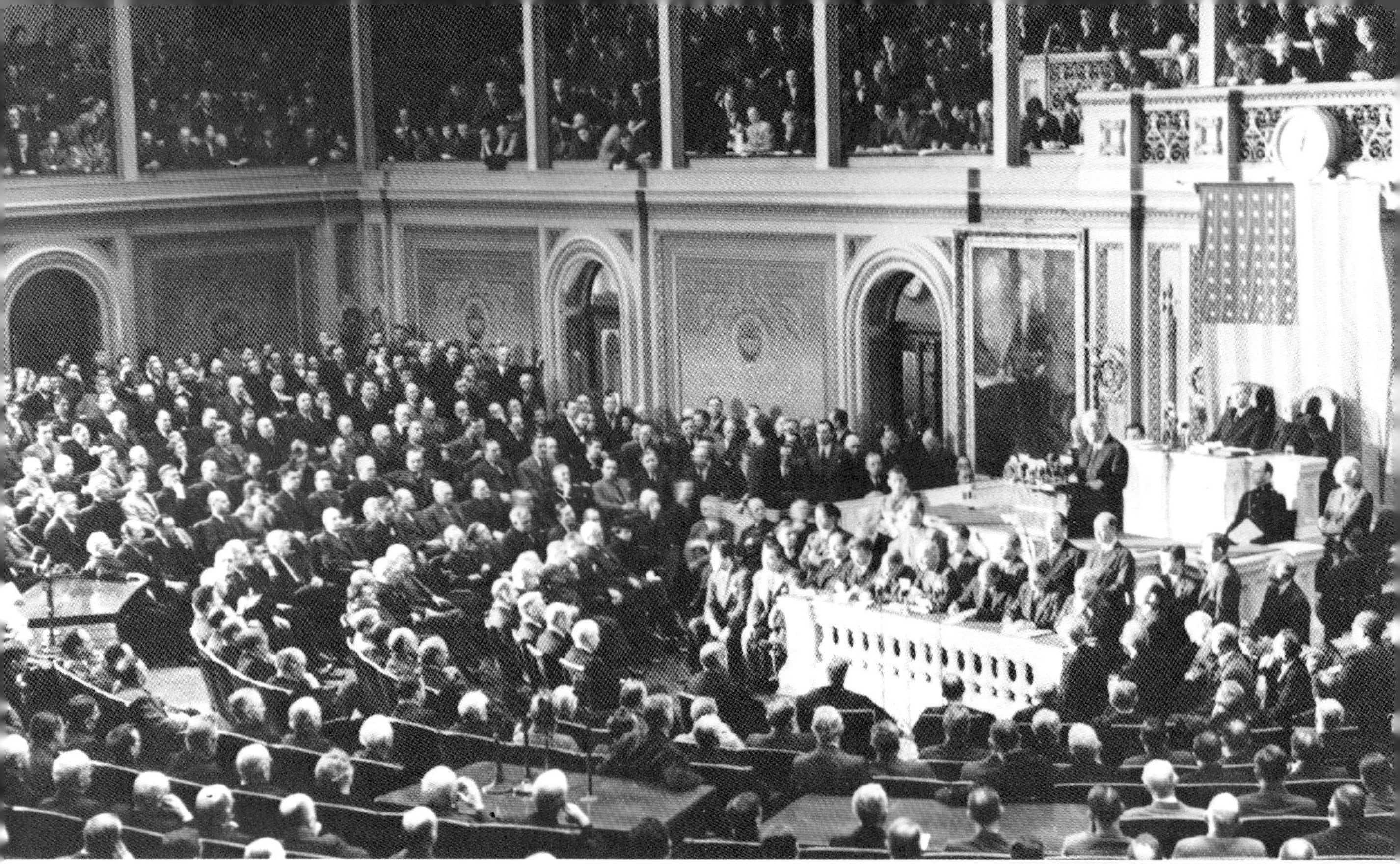

Congress alone has the power to declare war. It took such action in December of 1941 against Japan, Germany, and Italy. *Above:* President Franklin D. Roosevelt requests Congress to declare war following the attack on Pearl Harbor. *Left:* The Library of Congress

- How the controversy of strict versus liberal construction of the Constitution has affected American government.

At this point it would be well to recall two fundamentally important facts, for each has an impact on each and all of the powers held by Congress. First, government in the United States is *limited* government. Second, the American system of government is a federal system.

Scope of Congressional Power

The Constitution places a great many restrictions and prohibitions on Congress, as it does on the Federal Government as a whole. Large areas of power are denied to Congress. They are denied in so many words by the Constitution, because of its silence on many matters and because of the federal system itself.

In short, Congress has *only* those powers delegated to it by the Constitution. The power to do many things is not granted to Congress. Thus, it cannot create a national public school system, require that all eligible citizens vote on election day, or insist that all persons attend church. Among other things, Congress cannot pass a marriage and divorce law for the nation, set a minimum age for drivers' licenses, or prohibit trial by jury. Congress cannot do these and a great many other things because it has not been given the power to do them.

Recall, too, that Congress *does* have the power to do a great many things. The Constitution delegates specific powers to Congress in three different ways: (1) expressly, in so many words (the *expressed powers*); (2) by implication, that is, by reasonable deduction from the expressed powers (the *implied powers*); and (3) by creating a *national* government for the United States (the *inherent powers*). These three categories make up Congress's legislative powers.*

*REINFORCEMENT Review with the class the expressed, implied, and inherent powers granted to Congress by the Constitution. If necessary, use the outline of the Constitution on p. 724.

Strict Versus Liberal Construction

The Framers of the Constitution intended to create a stronger National Government. As we know, the ratification of their plan was strongly opposed by some. The Federalist–Anti-Federalist conflict continued into the early years of the Republic.

Through those early years, that conflict centered on the extent of the powers granted to Congress. How broad, in fact, were they?

The **strict constructionists,** led by Thomas Jefferson, continued to argue the Anti-Federalist position from the ratification period: That Congress should be able to exercise only (a) its expressed powers, those *spelled* * *out* in the Constitution and (b) those implied powers *necessary* to carry out those delegated powers. They wanted the States to keep as much power as possible. They agreed with Jefferson that "that government is best which governs least."

The **liberal constructionists,** led by Alexander Hamilton, had led the fight to adopt the Constitution. They favored a liberal interpretation of the Constitution, a broad construction of the powers given to Congress.

The liberal constructionists won that conflict, as we shall see. Their victory set a pattern that has been generally followed to the present day. It established a precedent from which, over the years, the powers wielded by the Federal Government have grown to a point that none of the Framers could possibly have imagined.

Several factors, working together with a liberal construction of the Constitution, have been responsible for that marked growth in national power. Wars, economic crises, and other national emergencies have been major factors. The spectacular advances we have made, especially in transportation and communication, have also had a real impact on the size of government. Equally important have been the demands of the people themselves for more and still more services from government.

Congress has been led by these and other factors to view its powers in broader and broader terms. Most Presidents have regarded and exercised their powers in similar fashion. The Supreme Court, in deciding cases involving the extent of the powers of the National Government, has generally taken a like position. Moreover, the American people have generally agreed with a liberal rather than a strict interpretation of the Constitution. This consensus has prevailed even though our political history has been marked, and still is, by controversies over the proper limits of national power.

FOR REVIEW

1. What two facts about the American system of government have a large impact upon the scope of the powers of Congress?
2. What was the position of the strict constructionists in the early years under the Constitution? Of the liberal constructionists? Which group's view prevailed?
3. What major factors have been largely responsible for the vast growth in the powers of the National Government since 1789?

2. The Expressed Powers: Money and Commerce

As You Read, Think About:

- Where the expressed powers are found in the Constitution.
- What the five major areas are into which these expressed powers of Congress fall.
- Why the Commerce Clause is of pivotal importance.

Most, but not all, of the expressed powers of Congress are found in Article I, Section 8 of the Constitution. There, in 18 separate clauses, some 27 different powers are explicitly given to Congress.[1]

[1]Several of the expressed powers of Congress are set out elsewhere in the Constitution. Thus, Article IV, Section 3 grants it the power to admit new States to the Union (Clause 1) and to manage and dispose of federal territory and other property (Clause 2). The 16th Amendment gives Congress the power to levy an income tax. The 13th, 14th, 15th, 19th, 24th, and 26th Amendments each vest in Congress the "power to enforce" their provisions "by appropriate legislation."

*ENRICHMENT Have the class discuss: What are the major differences between the strict-constructionists and the liberal-constructionists? What viewpoint do the students support?

PERSONALITY PROFILE

Alexander Hamilton

In the early morning of July 11, 1804, at Weehawkin on the banks of the Hudson River, Alexander Hamilton was fatally wounded in a duel with Aaron Burr, a man whose political career Hamilton had destroyed. In many respects Hamilton's death the next day seems hardly fitting for one of the most influential figures of the early years of the new nation. Hamilton's contributions to the United States span a wide range of achievements from fighting successfully for the ratification of the Constitution to the establishment of a federal banking system. Hamilton greatly enjoyed the political arena as an adviser to George Washington, a leader of New York State politics, and the leader of the Federalist Party. Although political intrigue was his final undoing, Hamilton is without doubt one of the country's greatest statesmen.

Hamilton was born in the East Indies in the late 1750s. In 1774 he entered King's College, now Columbia.

With characteristic enthusiasm, Hamilton threw himself into the conflict between Great Britain and the colonies. A speech attacking British policies in New York, a series of letters published in the *New-York Journal,* and two pamphlets written in 1774 and 1775 established Hamilton's reputation. His participation in several battles at the outset of the Revolutionary War were quickly rewarded when, on March 1, 1777, he was made an aide-de-camp to George Washington. He soon became Washington's close personal adviser.

During the closing years of the Revolution, Hamilton's views on the best form of government for the new nation took shape. He believed in a strong central government and distrusted the political capacity of the common man. He believed in the need for a system of federal taxation and a national bank. Above all, he sought to revise the Articles of Confederation, which he viewed as ineffectual.

As a delegate to the Constitutional Convention at Philadelphia in May, 1787, he argued for a strong executive and for greater federal control over the State legislatures. After the Convention, Hamilton led the fight for the adoption of the Constitution. With John Jay and James Madison, Hamilton authored a series of 85 essays supporting the proposed document. Those essays, the *Federalist Papers,* played a critical role in the ratification process, and Hamilton's contributions are clear, well-reasoned outlines of a strong federal system of government.

For Hamilton, the Confederation's lack of central authority ensured economic stagnation, discord, and vulnerability to foreign intrigue. Conflicting regulations among the States, he felt, impeded commerce and threatened the new nation's unity.

On September 11, 1789, Washington appointed Hamilton Secretary of the Treasury. He created the financial machinery that the new nation needed to overcome foreign debts and to establish a uniform system of money. It was during this same period that Hamilton had his most frequent clashes with his political opponent, Thomas Jefferson.

Hamilton's political career was marked by a sense of realism and, at times, by aristocratic political ideas. His chief weapon was his pen, and he used it unceasingly to achieve his aspirations for the new nation.

1. What governmental institutions exist today that Hamilton helped establish?
2. What are Hamilton's complaints with the relationships between the States?

These grants of power are quite brief. What they do, and do not, allow Congress to do often cannot be discovered merely by reading the few words involved. Rather, their content is to be found in the ways in which Congress has in fact exercised its several powers since 1789. One must also look to scores of Supreme Court cases arising out of actions taken by Congress.

As a case in point, take the Commerce Clause. Article I, Section 8, Clause 3 gives to Congress the following power:

> To regulate commerce with foreign nations, and among the several States, and with the Indian tribes.

Its wording is both brief and broad. Congress and the Court have had to answer hundreds of questions about its scope and content.

Here are a *few* examples: What does "commerce" include? Does it include persons entering or leaving the country or crossing State lines? Radio and television broadcasts? Air transportation? Business practices? Labor-management relationships? Does the Commerce Clause give Congress the power to do such things as fix a minimum wage, set maximum hours of work, and spell out other labor conditions? Does it allow Congress to prohibit the shipment of certain goods? To regulate banks and financial institutions? To prohibit discrimination? To provide for the construction of highways, airports, and multipurpose dams? What commerce is *foreign* and what is *interstate?* What commerce is *intrastate,* not subject to congressional regulation?

In answering these and hundreds of other questions on this *one* brief provision, Congress and the Court have spelled out, and are still spelling out, the meaning of the Commerce Clause. So it is with nearly all of the many other provisions of the Constitution that grant power to Congress.

Each of these powers has its historic significance. Most have a very substantial and

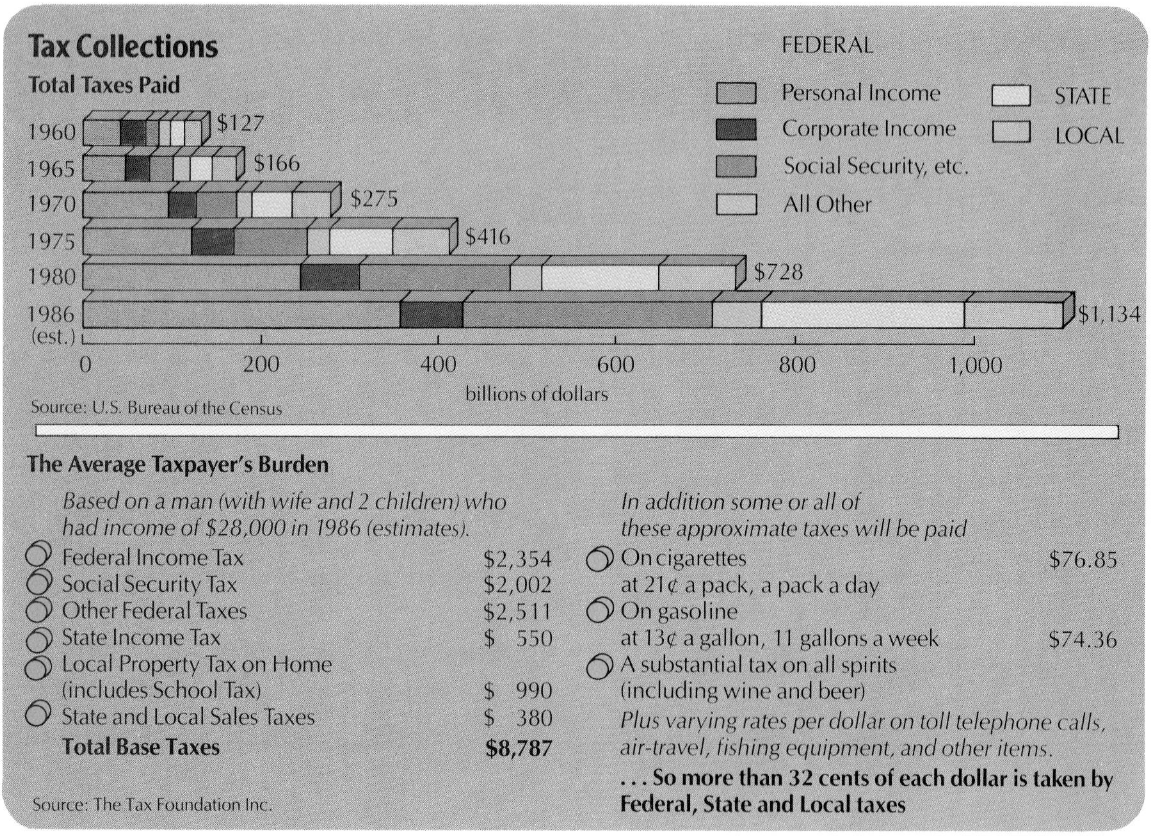

The Average Taxpayer's Burden

Based on a man (with wife and 2 children) who had income of $28,000 in 1986 (estimates).

Federal Income Tax	$2,354
Social Security Tax	$2,002
Other Federal Taxes	$2,511
State Income Tax	$ 550
Local Property Tax on Home (includes School Tax)	$ 990
State and Local Sales Taxes	$ 380
Total Base Taxes	**$8,787**

Source: The Tax Foundation Inc.

In addition some or all of these approximate taxes will be paid

On cigarettes at 21¢ a pack, a pack a day	$76.85
On gasoline at 13¢ a gallon, 11 gallons a week	$74.36
A substantial tax on all spirits (including wine and beer)	

Plus varying rates per dollar on toll telephone calls, air-travel, fishing equipment, and other items.

. . . So more than 32 cents of each dollar is taken by Federal, State and Local taxes

continuing present-day importance. Clearly, such powers as those to tax, to borrow, to declare war, and to regulate foreign and interstate commerce are of that order.

A few are of little moment, however. Thus, Congress has the power to grant letters of marque and reprisal; but it has not used that power in well over a hundred years.[2]

The Power to Tax

Article I, Section 8, Clause 1 gives Congress the power

> To lay and collect taxes, duties, imposts, and excises, to pay the debts, and provide for the common defense and general welfare of the United States . . . .

Recall, the Articles of Confederation had not given Congress the power to tax. Without it, the government was impotent; and the lack of that power was a leading cause for the coming of the Constitution.

We shall take a closer look at the field of federal finance in Chapter 16. But, for now, a number of important points:

The Federal Government will take in some $850 billion in fiscal year 1987, and an even larger sum in fiscal 1988. Most of that money —well over 90 percent of it—will come from the various taxes levied by Congress.

The basic purpose of the power to tax is to raise the money needed to finance the operations of government. Dictionaries tell us that a tax is "a charge laid by government on persons or property to meet the public needs." This usual dictionary definition, however, is not altogether complete.

Taxes are most often imposed in order to raise money—that is, "to meet the public needs." Taxes are imposed for other purposes, too. The protective tariff is perhaps the oldest example of the point. Although it does bring in some revenue, its real goal is to "protect" domestic industry against foreign competition. Taxes are also sometimes levied to protect the public health and safety. The Federal Government's regulation of the use of narcotics is a case in point. Most of that regulation is based on licensing. Only those who have a proper federal license may legally manufacture, sell, or deal in those drugs —and licensing is a form of taxation.

The power to tax is not unlimited. As with all other powers of the National Government, it must be used in accord with all other provisions of the Constitution. Thus, Congress cannot lay a tax on church services or the publication of a newspaper. Such taxes would be clear violations of the 1st Amendment.

More specifically, the Constitution places four explicit limitations on the taxing power.* First, Congress may tax only for *public purposes,* not for private benefit. Article I, Section 8, Clause 1 says that taxes may be levied only

> to pay the debts, and provide for the common defense and general welfare of the United States.

Second, Congress may not tax exports. Article I, Section 9, Clause 5 declares:

> No tax or duty shall be laid on articles exported from any State.

Thus, customs duties or tariffs, which are taxes, may be placed only on imports.

Third, direct taxes must be apportioned among the States, according to their populations. Article I, Section 9, Clause 4 declares:

> No capitation, or other direct tax, shall be laid, unless in proportion to the census or enumeration hereinbefore directed to be taken.

A **direct tax** is one that must be paid by the person on whom it is imposed—for example, a tax on the ownership of land or buildings, or a *capitation* (head or poll) tax. An income tax is a direct tax. But, notice, it may be laid without regard to population because of the 16th Amendment:

> The Congress shall have power to lay and collect taxes on incomes, from whatever source

[2] Article I, Section 8, Clause 11. The States cannot issue them, Article I, Section 10, Clause 1. Letters of marque and reprisal are relics of the past. They are commissions, written grants of power authorizing private persons to fit out vessels to capture and destroy the enemy in time of war. They are a form of legalized piracy. They are forbidden in international law by the Declaration of Paris, 1856, and the United States honors the rule in practice.

*REINFORCEMENT Four explicit limitations are placed on the taxing power of the Government. Ask the class for examples of the taxes they or their families pay, and the limitation applied to each type of tax.

derived, without apportionment among the several States, and without regard to any census or enumeration.

Finally, Article I, Section 8, Clause 1 provides that:

> . . . all duties, imposts, and excises, shall be uniform throughout the United States.

That is, all **indirect taxes** must be levied at the same rate in all parts of the country. As a general rule, an indirect tax is one that is actually paid by one person but is in fact passed on to another. That is, it is indirectly paid by that second person. Take, for example, the federal excise tax on each pack of cigarettes. It is paid to the Treasury by the tobacco company that makes the cigarettes. But that company then passes the tax on up the retail chain until it is in fact paid by the person who finally buys the cigarettes.

Congress and the Supreme Court decide whether a tax is direct or indirect.

The Commerce Power

The commerce power is as vital to the existence and the welfare of the nation as the taxing power. As we have seen, the commerce power also played a large role in the formation of the Union. The weak Congress created under the Articles had no power to regulate interstate trade and only very little authority over foreign commerce. The Critical Period of the 1780s was marked by intense commercial rivalries and bickerings among the States. High trade barriers and spiteful State laws created chaos and confusion in much of the country.

Consequently, the Framers wrote the Commerce Clause, Article I, Section 8, Clause 3. It gives Congress the power:

> To regulate commerce with foreign nations, and among the several states, and with the Indian tribes.

The Commerce Clause has been more responsible for building a strong Union of States out of a weak confederation than has any other provision in the Constitution. That clause has allowed the growth in the United States of the greatest open market in the world. Together with the taxing power, the commerce power has contributed most to the vast growth in the power and authority of the National Government.

The very first case to reach the Supreme Court involving the Commerce Clause was *Gibbons* v. *Ogden,* decided in 1824. That landmark case set the stage for the extensive development that the Commerce Clause has since undergone.

The case arose out of a clash over the regulation of steam vessels by the State of New York, on the one hand, and the Federal Government, on the other. In 1807 Robert Fulton's steamboat, the *Clermont,* had made its first successful run up the Hudson River, from New York City to Albany. The State legislature then gave Fulton an exclusive, long-term grant to navigate the waters of the State by steamboat. Aaron Ogden then secured a permit for navigation between New York City and New Jersey.

Thomas Gibbons, operating with a coasting license from the Federal Government, began to carry passengers on a competing line. Ogden sued him, and the New York courts held that Gibbons could not sail by steam in New York waters.

Gibbons appealed that ruling to the Supreme Court. He claimed that the New York grant conflicted with the congressional power to regulate commerce. The Court agreed. It rejected Ogden's argument that "commerce" should be defined narrowly, as simply "traffic" or the mere buying and selling of goods. Instead, it read the Commerce Clause in very broad terms. Wrote Chief Justice John Marshall:

> Commerce undoubtedly is traffic, but it is something more—it is intercourse. It describes the commercial intercourse between nations, and parts of nations, in all its branches, and is regulated by prescribing rules for carrying on that intercourse.

This broad view of the scope of the commerce power has led to the reach of federal authority into many areas of life far beyond any thoughts of the Framers of the Constitution. We cited a number of those areas a few pages earlier.

*REINFORCEMENT Have the class discuss: How does the case of *Gibbons v. Ogden* influence the distribution of goods and services?

FOCUS ON:

Right-to-Work Laws

The commerce power gives to Congress a broad authority to regulate many aspects of the nation's economic and social life, including the vitally important subject of labor-management relations. The Taft-Hartley Act (the Labor-Management Relations Act of 1947) is one of the key statutes in that field.

Among its provisions, the Taft-Hartley Act outlaws the **closed shop.** That is, it forbids any agreement between management and labor that makes membership in a labor union a qualification for employment. The law does allow the **union shop,** however. A union shop is one in which the labor contract requires that all newly hired workers must join a union soon after they are employed. Unlike the outlawed closed shop arrangement, a person need not belong to the union in order to get a job in a union shop. But that person must join the union within a specified time, usually 30 days.

But, in Section 14(b), the Taft-Hartley Act also permits any State to outlaw the union shop. That is, any State that chooses to do so many enact what is commonly known as a **right-to-work law.** This statute forbids the use of union membership as either a prerequisite to hiring or a condition of continued employment. Thus, a right-to-work law allows only the **open shop.** This is a place of employment in which a worker may join a union or not, as he or she chooses.

As you can see from the map, 21 States now have right-to-work laws, and there are ongoing campaigns for their enactment in several others. Only Indiana has passed and then repealed a right-to-work law.

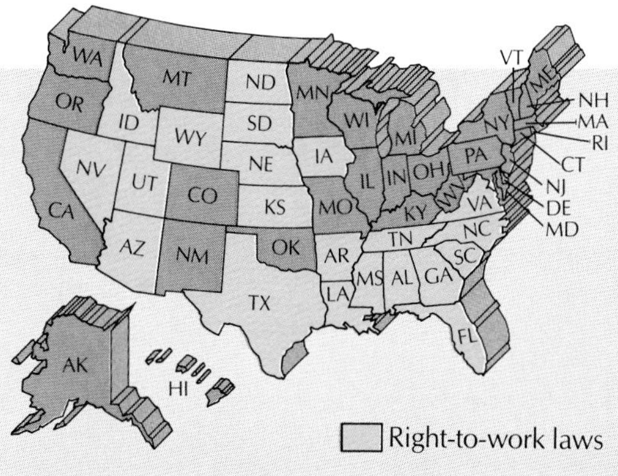

Most leaders of organized labor are opposed to these statutes, and they and others have long argued for the repeal of Section 14(b). They contend the laws are misnamed. They say that their real purpose is to destroy unions and with them the principle of collective bargaining. They also insist that nonunion workers in an open shop are "freeloaders." They receive the wages and other benefits gained by a union, but do not bear any of the burdens of the union's efforts.

The many supporters of right-to-work laws are led by the National Right to Work Committee. They deny the claim that those laws are aimed at the destruction of labor unions. Indeed, they point to the fact that some unions have gained membership in States where such laws are in force. They also say that both the closed shop and the union shop amount to "compulsory unionism." They force all employees in a given work situation to belong to a union, regardless of their individual preferences.

1. Does your State have a right-to-work law? If not, do you think that one should be passed?
2. What is collective bargaining?

As another of many examples of the point, note this: It is on the basis of the commerce power that the Civil Rights Act of 1964 prohibits discrimination in access to or service in hotels, motels, theaters, restaurants, and in other various public

The power of Congress to regulate all foreign commerce is absolutely vital to the nation's economic health.

accommodations on grounds of race, color, religion, or national origin.[3]

Based on the expressed powers to regulate commerce and to tax, Congress and the courts have built nearly all of the implied powers. Most of what the Federal Government does, day to day and year to year, it does as the result of legislation passed by Congress in the exercise of these two powers.

The **commerce power** is not an unlimited one. It, too, must be used in accord with all other provisions in the Constitution. Thus, Congress could not say that only those companies that employ only native-born citizens may carry on business in more than one State. Such an arbitrary and unreasonable regulation would violate the 5th Amendment's Due Process Clause.

More exactly, the Constitution places four explicit limitations on the use of the commerce power. First, as we have seen, Article I, Section 9, Clause 3 forbids Congress the power to lay any tax on exports. Second, Article I, Section 9, Clause 6 prevents Congress in the regulation of trade from favoring the ports of one State over those of any other. Third, the same provision forbids Congress to require that "vessels bound to, or from, one State, be obliged to enter, clear, or pay duties in another."

The fourth limitation is the curious "slave trade compromise" found in Article I, Section 9, Clause 1. Of course, that clause has been obsolete for more than 170 years (see page 46).

The Currency Power

The Constitution gives to Congress the power "to coin money [and] regulate the value thereof."[4] The States are forbidden that power.[5]

Until the Revolution, the English money system, built on the shilling and pound, was in general use in the colonies. With independence, that stable currency system collapsed, however. The Second Continental Congress and then the Congress under the Articles issued paper money. But without sound backing, and no taxing power behind it, the money was practically worthless. Each of the 13 States also issued its own currency. In several States, this amounted to little more than the State's printing its name on paper and calling it money. Compounding the confusion, English coins were still widely used, and Spanish money circulated freely in the southern States. It is easy to understand the need for a uniform system.

[3]The Supreme Court upheld this use of the commerce power in *Heart of Atlanta Motel, Inc.* v. *United States*, 1964. The unanimous Court noted that there was "overwhelming evidence of the disruptive effect of racial discrimination . . . on commercial intercourse." See page 163.

[4]Article I, Section 8, Clause 5.

[5]Article I, Section 10, Clause 1 forbids the States the power to coin money, issue bills of credit (paper money), or make anything but gold and silver legal tender. Legal tender is any kind of money a creditor must accept by law in payment of a monetary debt.

Nearly all the Framers agreed on the need for a single, national system of "hard" money. So the Constitution gave the currency power to Congress. From 1789 on, one vital task of the National Government has been to provide a uniform, stable monetary system.

From the beginning, the United States has issued coins—in gold (until 1933), silver, and other metals. Congress chartered the First Bank of the United States in 1791 and gave it the power to issue bank notes. But those notes, or paper money, were not made legal tender: No one had to accept them as payment of a debt. Congress did not create a national paper currency, and make it legal tender, until 1863.[6]

At first, the new national notes, known as greenbacks, could not be redeemed for gold or silver coin at the treasury. Their worth fell to less than half of their face value on the open market. Then, in 1870, the Supreme Court held their issuance to be unconstitutional. In *Hepburn* v. *Griswold,* it said "to coin" meant to stamp metal and, hence, the Constitution did not authorize paper money.

The Court soon changed its mind, however, in the *Legal Tender Cases* in 1871 and again in *Juliard* v. *Greenman* in 1884. In both cases it held the issuing of paper money as legal tender to be a proper use of the currency power and a power properly implied from the borrowing and the war powers.

The Borrowing Power

Congress has the power "to borrow money on the credit of the United States."[7] That power permits the Government to face both short-term and long-term problems with the funding needed to meet them. Thus, the borrowing power was much used in World War II, as it had been during the economic crisis of the 1930s. That power has also been heavily used to finance the high costs of war and defense over the years since then.

There is no constitutional limit on the amount that may be borrowed. Congress has placed a statutory ceiling on the public debt, however. But that limit is little more than a political gesture.* Congress adjusts the ceiling whenever fiscal realities seem to call for it. At the start of fiscal year 1987, the nation's public debt exceeded $2 trillion.

The Government most often borrows by selling bonds. They are much like the promissory notes, IOU's, given by individuals, promising to repay a certain sum of money at a certain time.

The Government's bonds are issued as both short-term and long-term obligations —for lengths of time as short as 30 days to as long as 10 years or more. Interest rates are competitive with those paid in the private market. The bonds are purchased as investments by individuals, businesses, and especially banks and other financial institutions.

The Government could likely borrow all its needs from banks. Or it could simply print enough money to satisfy its needs. But to do either of those things, and especially the latter, would have a highly inflationary effect on the nation's economy.

The fact that the Constitution gives Congress the power to borrow makes borrowing a national function. Thus, the interest the Government pays cannot be taxed by the States, which makes its bonds quite attractive to investors. The borrowing power also implies the power to create the Federal Reserve System and to regulate the nation's banking and other financial institutions.

Bankruptcy

Congress has power "to establish . . . uniform laws on the subject of bankruptcies, throughout the United States."[8] A bankrupt person is one whom a court has found to be

[6]Although they could not issue paper money themselves, the States chartered (licensed) private banks, whose notes circulated as money. When these private bank notes interfered with the new national currency, Congress levied a 10 percent tax on their issue in 1865, and they soon disappeared. The Supreme Court upheld the 1865 law as a proper exercise of the taxing power in *Veazie Bank* v. *Fenno,* 1869.

[7]Article I, Section 8, Clause 2.

[8]Article I, Section 8, Clause 4.

*ENRICHMENT Discuss in class: Congress has the ability to change the ceiling on the public debt on an as-needed basis. Is this acceptable, or should there be a permanent, unchangeable limit?

insolvent, that is, unable to pay his or her debts in full. **Bankruptcy** is the legal proceeding in which the bankrupt's assets are then distributed among those to whom a debt is owed. That proceeding frees the bankrupt from legal responsibility for debts acquired before bankruptcy.[9]

Both the States and the National Government have the power to regulate bankruptcy. It is, then, a concurrent power. Except for three short periods, Congress left the matter in the hands of the States for more than 100 years. In 1898, however, it passed a general bankruptcy law, and today that law is so broad that it all but excludes the States from the field. Most bankruptcy cases are heard in the federal district courts; only a very few are handled by State courts; see page 517.

FOR REVIEW

1. **Identify:** expressed powers, commerce power, currency power, *Gibbons* v. *Ogden,* borrowing power.
2. Where are the expressed powers of Congress set out in the Constitution?
3. What is the major purpose of the power to tax? Are taxes ever imposed for any other purpose?
4. What four specific limits does the Constitution place upon the taxing power?
5. What is a direct tax? An indirect tax?
6. What kind of trade does the Constitution give Congress the expressed power to regulate?
7. Why is *Gibbons* v. *Ogden* so important?
8. What four specific limits does the Constitution place upon the commerce power of Congress?
9. Why is the currency power not a concurrent power?
10. By what means does Government most often borrow? Is there a legal limit to the amount of the public debt?
11. How have bankruptcy laws changed since 1898?

[9]Article I, Section 8, Clause 4.

3. Other Expressed Powers

As You Read, Think About:

- What the other areas are in which Congress has expressed powers.
- How Congress may exercise these expressed powers.

To carry out its various legislative tasks, Congress is granted a number of other powers in the Constitution.

Naturalization

Naturalization, recall, is the process by which citizens of one country become citizens of another. Article I, Section 8, Clause 4 gives Congress the exclusive power "to establish a uniform rule of naturalization." We treated the details of the naturalization process in Chapter 6.

The Postal Power

Congress has the exclusive power "to establish post offices and post roads."[10] That power covers the authority to protect the mails and to ensure their quick and efficient distribution. Congress is also empowered to prevent the use of the mails for fraud or for the carrying of outlawed materials.

The United States Postal Service traces its history to the early colonial period. Benjamin Franklin is generally credited as the founder of the present-day postal system. It now operates on the basis of the Postal Reorganization Act of 1970; see page 434.

There are now some 30,000 post offices and more than 700,000 postal workers across the country. They do more than $25 billion in business and handle some 140 billion pieces of mail each year.

Congress has established a number of crimes based on the postal power. Thus, it is

[10]Article I, Section 8, Clause 7. Post roads are all postal routes, including railroads, airways, and waters within the United States, during the time that mail is being carried on them.

*REINFORCEMENT Ask students if they know any naturalized citizens, and by what means they became citizens. Have the class discuss the processes through which a recent immigrant can gain U.S. citizenship

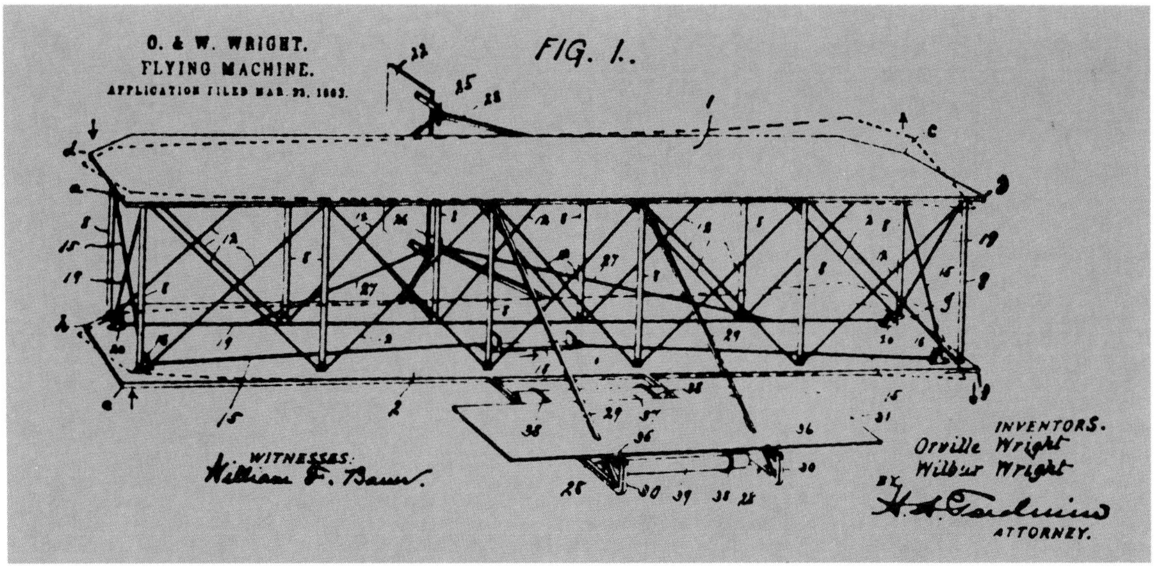

Orville and Wilbur Wright filed their application for a patent of invention for their flying machine with the Patent and Trademark Office in March of 1903, some three months after they successfully flew the first heavier-than-air machine.

a federal crime for any person to obstruct the mails, to use the mails to commit any fraud, or to use them as a part of any other criminal act.

The States cannot interfere with the mails unreasonably. Nor can they require a license for vehicles owned by the Postal Service or tax the gas they use. The States cannot tax the post offices or any other property of the United States Postal Service.

*Articles prohibited by a State's laws, such as firecrackers or switch-blade knives, cannot be sent into that State through the mails. A great many other items, including alcoholic beverages, lottery tickets, and obscene materials, are also barred from the mails.

Copyrights and Patents

Congress has the power:

> To promote the progress of science and useful arts, by securing, for limited times, to authors and inventors, the exclusive right to their respective writings and discoveries.[11]

[11]Article I, Section 8, Clause 8.

A **copyright** is the exclusive right of an author to reproduce, publish, and sell his or her literary, musical, artistic, or other creative work. That right may be assigned —transferred by contract—to another, as to a publishing firm by mutual agreement between the author and the other party.

Copyrights are registered by the Copyright Office in the Library of Congress. Under present law they are good for the life of the author plus 50 years. They cover a wide range of creative efforts: books, magazines, newspapers, musical compositions and lyrics, dramatic works, paintings, sculptures, cartoons, maps, photographs, motion pictures, sound recordings, and many other original works.

The Copyright Office does not enforce the protections of a copyright. If a copyright is infringed or violated, the owners of the right may sue for damages by taking their case to the federal courts.

The **patent** grants one the sole right to manufacture, use, or sell "any new and useful art, machine, manufacture, or composition of matter, or any new and useful improvement thereof." A patent is good for a

*REINFORCEMENT Have the class discuss: What are the pros and cons of having private mail services competing with the U.S. Postal Service?

varying number of years—today, 17 years on the patent of an invention. The term of a patent may be extended only by a special act of Congress. The patent laws are administered by the Patent and Trademark Office, in the Department of Commerce.

Weights and Measures

The Constitution gives Congress the power to "fix the standards of weights and measures" throughout the United States.[12] The power is an exclusive one and reflects the absolute need for accurate, uniform gauges of time, distance, area, weight, volume, and the like in practically every segment of the nation's daily life.

In 1838 Congress set the English system of pound, ounce, mile, foot, gallon, quart, and so on, as the legal standards of weights and measures in the United States. In 1866 Congress also legalized the use of the metric system gram, meter, kilometer, liter, and so on. There is increased usage of this system in our lives today. The original standards by which all other measures in the United States are tested and corrected are kept by the Bureau of Standards, in the Commerce Department.

Power Over Territories and Other Areas

Congress has power to acquire, manage, and dispose of various federal areas.[13] That power relates to the District of Columbia and to the several federal territories, including Puerto Rico, Guam, and the Virgin Islands. It covers much more, as well —hundreds of military and naval installations, arsenals, dockyards, post offices, prison facilities, park and forest preserves, and many other federal holdings throughout the country.

The Federal Government may acquire property by purchase or gift. It may do so, too, through the exercise of the power of **eminent domain**—the inherent power to take private property for public use.[14] Territory may also be acquired from a foreign

[12]Article I, Section 8, Clause 5.

[13]Article I, Section 8, Clause 17; Article IV, Section 3, Clause 2.

The U.S.S. *Constitution* ("Old Ironsides") is berthed on federal property at Boston's Naval Shipyard.

[14]The 5th Amendment restricts the Government's use of the power with these words: "nor shall private property be taken for public use, without just compensation." Each of the State constitutions has a similar provision. Private property may be taken by eminent domain only (1) for a public use, (2) with proper notice to the owner, and (3) for a fair price. What, in fact, amounts to a public use, proper notice, or a fair price often becomes a court matter.

*ENRICHMENT Have the class discuss: What arguments can be waged for and against the government's exercise of the power of eminent domain?

state based on the power to admit new States, the war powers, and the President's treaty-making power.[15] Under international law, any sovereign state may acquire unclaimed territory by discovery.

Judicial Powers

As an important part of the principle of checks and balances, Congress has several judicial powers. Thus, it has the expressed power to create all federal courts below the Supreme Court and to provide for the organization and composition of the federal judiciary.[16] We shall look at the federal courts in Chapter 18.

Congress has the power to define federal crimes and provide for their punishment.[17] It also has the power to impeach and remove any civil officer of the United States.[18]

Powers Over Foreign Relations

The National Government has greater powers in the field of foreign affairs than it has in any other. Congress shares power in this field with the President, who is primarily responsible for the conduct of our relations with other nations. Because the States in the Union are not sovereign, they have no standing in international law. The Constitution does not allow them to take part in foreign relations.[19]

Congressional authority in the field of foreign relations comes from two sources: (1) from several of its expressed powers—most of all from the war powers and the commerce power and (2) from the fact that the United States is a sovereign nation. As the nation's lawmaking body, Congress has the inherent power to act on matters affecting the security of the nation. We shall explore this whole matter at much greater length in Chapter 17.

The War Powers

Eight of the expressed powers given to Congress in Article I, Section 8 deal with war and national defense.[20] Here, too, Congress shares power with the Chief Executive. The Constitution makes the President the Commander in Chief of the nation's armed forces,[21] and, as such, the President dominates the field. The President always has the final authority over all military matters.

The congressional war powers, however, are both extensive and substantial. Congress, and only Congress, may declare war. It has the power to raise and support armies, to provide and maintain a navy, and to make rules pertaining to governing the land and naval forces.[22] It also has the power to provide for "calling forth the militia," and for the organizing, arming, and disciplining of it. Also, Congress has the power to grant letters of marque and reprisal and make rules concerning captures on land and water.[23]

With the passage of the War Powers Resolution of 1973, Congress was given the power to restrict the use of American forces in combat in areas where a state of war does not exist; see page 422.

---

[15]Article IV, Section 3, Clause 1; Article I, Section 8, Clauses 11–16; Article II, Section 2, Clauses 1 and 2.

[16]Article I, Section 8, Clause 9; Article III, Section 1.

[17]The Constitution mentions only four types of federal crimes: counterfeiting, piracies and felonies committed on the high seas, offenses against the law of nations (in Article 1, Section 8, Clauses 6 and 10), and treason (in Article III, Section 3). But Congress has the implied power to define many other offenses and provide for their punishment; see pages 73, 358.

[18]Article I, Section 2, Clause 5; Article I, Section 3, Clauses 6 and 7; Article II, Section 3, Clause 4. The impeachment power is one of the nonlegislative powers to which we shall turn shortly; see page 359.

[19]Article I, Section 10, Clauses 1 and 3; see pages 73–74.

[20]The war powers of Congress are set out in Clauses 11 through 16.

[21]Article II, Section 2, Clause 1; see pages 421–422.

[22]Congress cannot appropriate funds for "armies" for longer than a two-year period (Clause 12). The Constitution does not place that restriction on funding for the navy nor, under a 1948 Attorney General's opinion, on funding for the Air Force. The provision is intended to make certain that the Army will always remain under civilian authority.

[23]See note 2, page 345.

*REINFORCEMENT Have the class discuss why Congressional candidates generally campaign on local or national, rather than foreign policy, issues. How are constituents represented in matters of foreign policy?

Cadets here at the United States Military Academy at West Point, New York, will, upon completion of their training, become commissioned officers in the Army.

FOR REVIEW

1. **Identify:** naturalization, weights and measures, war powers.
2. What does the postal power grant Congress the authority to do?
3. Why did the Constitution give Congress the power to grant copyrights and patents?
4. Why does the Constitution give Congress the exclusive power to regulate standards of weights and measures?
5. What does the congressional power over territories and other areas include? How may the United States acquire territory?
6. What judicial powers does Congress have?
7. With whom does Congress share authority in the field of foreign relations? What specific powers does it have in that field?
8. With whom does Congress share authority in the field of war and national defense? What expressed powers does it have?

4. The Implied Powers

As You Read, Think About:

- Why the Necessary and Proper Clause is of pivotal importance.
- What the importance is of the Supreme Court decision in *McCulloch* v. *Maryland.*
- How the Necessary and Proper Clause is applied today.

Up to this point, we have looked at the expressed powers of Congress, most of which are to be found in Article I, Section 8, Clauses 1 through 17. In addition to these powers, which are spelled out word for word, Congress has powers that are *not* stated in so many words: These are defined as the **implied powers.**

The Necessary and Proper Clause

Clause 18 of Article I, Section 8 is the dramatically important Necessary and

Proper Clause. It is from this clause that the implied powers flow. The clause gives to Congress the power:

> To make all laws which shall be necessary and proper for carrying into execution the foregoing powers, and all other powers vested by this Constitution in the Government of the United States, or in any department or officer thereof.

Much of the vitality and adaptability of the Constitution can be traced directly to this provision—and, even more so, to the manner in which both Congress and the Supreme Court have interpreted and applied it over the years. For good reason, the Necessary and Proper Clause is often called the "Elastic Clause." As the name implies, it provides needed flexibility.

*Liberal Versus Strict Construction

The Constitution had barely come into force when the meaning of Clause 18 was called into question. In 1790 Alexander Hamilton, as Secretary of the Treasury, urged Congress to set up a national bank. That proposal touched off one of the most important disputes in the political history of our country.

The opponents of Hamilton's plan said that nowhere in the Constitution was Congress given the power to set up such a bank. These strict constructionists, led by Thomas Jefferson, argued that the new Government had no powers beyond those expressly granted to it by the Constitution.

Hamilton and other liberal constructionists looked to the Necessary and Proper Clause. They said that it gave to Congress the power to do anything that might be reasonably "implied" from any of the expressly delegated powers. As for the national bank, they argued that it was a necessary and proper way to carry out the taxing, borrowing, commerce, and currency powers.

The Jeffersonians countered this broad view of "implied powers" by insisting that such reasoning would give the new Government almost unlimited authority and would all but destroy the reserved powers of the States.[24]

Reason and practical necessity carried the day for Hamilton and his side. Congress established the Bank of the United States in 1791. Its charter was to expire in 1811. Over those 20 years, the constitutionality of both the Bank and the concept of implied powers went unchallenged in the courts.

McCulloch v. Maryland, 1819 In 1816 Congress created the Second Bank of the United States. Its charter came after another hard-fought battle over the extent of the powers of Congress.

Opponents of the new Bank carried their fight to the States. Having lost in Congress, they tried to persuade several State legislatures to cripple its operations. In 1818 Maryland placed a tax on all notes issued by any bank doing business in the State and not chartered by the State legislature. The tax was aimed directly at the Second Bank's branch in Baltimore. James McCulloch, the bank's cashier, purposely issued notes on which no tax had been paid. The State won a judgment against him in its own courts. Acting for McCulloch, the United States then appealed to the Supreme Court.

Maryland took the strict-construction position before the High Court. It argued that the creation of the Bank had been an unconstitutional act. In reply, the United States defended the concept of implied powers and held that no State could lawfully place a tax on any agency of the Federal Government.

Chief Justice John Marshall handed down one of the Supreme Court's most important

[24]In 1801 a bill was introduced in Congress to incorporate a company to mine copper. As Vice President, Jefferson ridiculed that measure with this comment: "Congress is authorized to defend the nation. Ships are necessary for defense; copper is necessary for ships; mines necessary for copper; a company necessary to work the mines; and who can doubt this reasoning who has ever played at 'This Is the House that Jack Built'?" While Jefferson himself was President (1801–1809), he and his party were many times forced to reverse their earlier stand. Thus, for example, it was only on the basis of the implied powers doctrine that the Louisiana Purchase in 1803 and the embargo on foreign trade in 1807 could be justified.

*REINFORCEMENT Organize a class debate on a liberal versus strict interpretation of the Constitution. Make sure that the students discuss the Necessary and Proper Clause.

BUILDING GOVERNMENT SKILLS

Decision Making

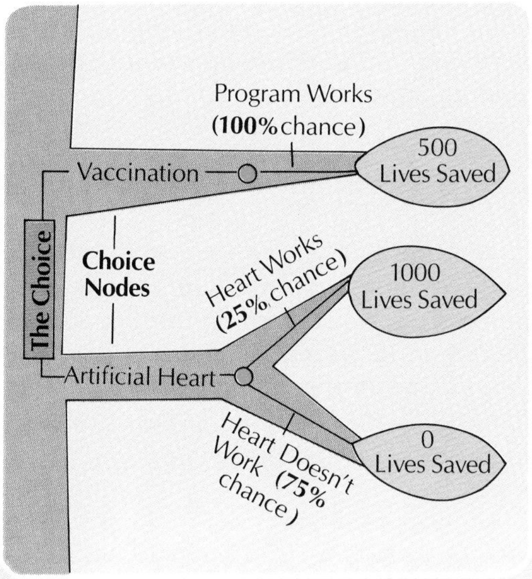

In many cases, drawing a decision tree can help a person make a good decision. A decision tree is a way of picturing the decision you face. It organizes the options open to you and shows all the possible outcomes as branches on a tree.

Suppose you are a Representative, forced to choose between funding two programs. One is a research program to develop an artificial heart, the other a program to vaccinate people against measles. The programs both cost the same amount of money. You know that the vaccine works and that it will save 500 lives a year if you fund it. The artificial heart, if it works, will save 1,000 lives per year, but there is a chance that the program will not produce a workable heart.

How would you decide which way to vote? One way is to draw a decision tree.

Step 1. Draw Branches for Your Choices The first step in drawing a decision tree is to draw a branch for every option you can choose to take. In our example, the Representative has only two options: vote for the heart research program or vote for the vaccination program.

***Step 2.* Draw Branches for All Possible Outcomes**
Sometimes, more than one outcome is possible as the result of a decision. In our example, the artificial heart research program has a chance of two outcomes: either it will work or it will not. Since we know that the vaccination program will work, we need only draw one outcome for it.

***Step 3.* Assign a Value to the Outcomes**
You now have the structure of your tree. The next step is to assign a value to each outcome, sometimes called assigning payoffs. All payoffs should be in the same units. For some decisions these payoffs will be in dollars. In our example, they are in terms of lives saved.

***Step 4.* Making a Decision**
The last step is to compare the value of choosing the vaccination program with the value of choosing the artificial heart program. The value of choosing the vaccination program is clear. It will save 500 lives. But what is the value of choosing the heart program? That depends on how likely the program is to succeed. Suppose you learn that there is a 25 percent chance that the program will succeed; conversely, there is a 75 percent chance that it will not. Now you can put the likelihood of all three outcomes on your tree.

1. Given this choice, between being sure of saving 500 lives and taking a 25 percent chance of saving 1,000, which outcome would you choose?
2. If recent advances in artificial heart technology increased the likelihood of success to 75 percent, which option would you choose?

Coast Guard cutters clear a channel through an ice–clogged waterway in the Great Lakes. Which of the expressed powers enables Congress to undertake this activity?

and far-reaching decisions in the case. For the first time, the Court was faced with the 30-year-old question of the constitutionality of the implied powers doctrine.

The Court unanimously reversed the Maryland courts. It found the creation of the Second Bank to be necessary and proper in order to carry out the taxing, borrowing, and currency powers. Far more importantly, the Court thereby upheld the doctrine of implied powers.

*The Court's decision in *McCulloch* v. *Maryland* is so significant that we quote these three key sentences from it:

> We admit, as all must admit, that the powers of the government are limited, and that its limits are not to be transcended. But we think the sound construction of the Constitution must allow to the national legislature that discretion, with respect to the means by which the powers it confers are to be carried into execution, which will enable that body to perform the high duties assigned to it, in the manner most beneficial to the people. Let the end be legitimate, let it be within the scope of the Constitution, and all means which are appropriate, which are not prohibited, but consist with the letter and spirit of the Constitution, are constitutional.

This broad interpretation of the powers granted to Congress has become firmly fixed in our constitutional system. Indeed, it is impossible to see how the nation could have developed as it has under the Constitution without it.[25]

The Doctrine in Practice As we have suggested several times, there are an almost uncountable number of examples of the application of the doctrine of implied powers. Both the way Congress has looked at and used its powers and the supporting decisions of the Supreme Court have made Article I, Section 8, Clause 18 truly the Elastic Clause. Today the words "necessary and proper" really read "convenient and useful." This is most especially true when applied to the power to regulate interstate commerce and the power to tax.

Yet, there is a real limit to how far the doctrine of implied powers may be pushed. Neither the Congress nor any other part of the Federal Government has the blanket authority to do anything that may *seem* desirable or that may *seem* to be for the "general welfare" or in the "public interest." The basis for *any* implied power must *always* be found among the expressed powers. The implied powers are those that may be *reasonably* drawn from the expressed powers.

[25]The Court also invalidated the Maryland tax. Because, said the Court, "the power to tax involves the power to destroy," no State may tax the United States or any of its agencies or functions; see page 648.

*REINFORCEMENT Have the class discuss the case of *McCulloch* v. *Maryland*. What issues were at stake? What was the lasting result?

The Powers Vested in Congress by Article I, Section 8 of the Constitution

Expressed Powers

Peace Powers

1. To lay taxes.
   a. Direct (not used since the War Between the States, except income tax).
   b. Indirect (customs [tariffs], excise for internal revenue).
2. To borrow money.
3. To regulate foreign and interstate commerce.
4. To establish naturalization and bankruptcy laws.
5. To coin money and regulate its value; to regulate weights and measures.
6. To punish counterfeiters of federal money and securities.
7. To establish post offices and post roads.
8. To grant patents and copyrights.
9. To create courts inferior to the Supreme Court.
10. To define and punish piracies and felonies on the high seas; to define and punish offenses against the law of nations.
17. To exercise exclusive jurisdiction over the District of Columbia; to exercise exclusive jurisdiction over forts, dockyards, national parks, federal buildings, and the like.

War Powers

11. To declare war; to grant letters of marque and reprisal; to make rules concerning captures on land and water.
12. To raise and support armies.
13. To provide and maintain a navy.
14. To make laws governing land and naval forces.
15. To provide for calling forth the militia to execute federal laws, suppress insurrections, and repel invasions.
16. To provide for organizing, arming, and disciplining the militia, and for its governing when in the service of the Union.

Implied Powers

18. To make all laws necessary and proper for carrying into execution the foregoing powers, for example:
    To define and provide punishment for federal crimes.
    To establish the Federal Reserve System.
    To improve rivers, canals, harbors, other waterways.
    To fix minimum wages, maximum hours of work.

FOR REVIEW

1. **Identify:** Necessary and Proper Clause, Elastic Clause, *McCulloch* v. *Maryland.*
2. Why is the Necessary and Proper Clause also called the Elastic Clause?
3. What is the doctrine of implied powers?
4. Why is *McCulloch* v. *Maryland* so important?
5. What is the fundamental limitation on the doctrine of implied powers?

5. The Nonlegislative Powers of Congress

As You Read, Think About:

- Why Congress has powers that are not concerned with legislation.
- What these nonlegislative powers are.

As we know, Congress is a legislative body. Its major function is to make law. But the Constitution gives it a number of *nonlegislative* powers and duties, as well.

Electoral

Congress on rare occasions has had to exercise its electoral duties. The House of Representatives may be called on to elect a President. If no candidate receives a majority of the electoral votes for President, the House, voting by States, must then choose one. It must choose by majority vote and from among the three top contenders in the electoral college. The Senate must choose a Vice President when no candidate wins a majority in the electoral college.[26]

The House has had to choose a President only twice: Thomas Jefferson in 1801 and John Quincy Adams in 1825. The Senate chose Richard M. Johnson as Vice President in 1837.

Remember, too, that the 25th Amendment provides for the filling of a vacancy in the Vice Presidency. When and if one occurs, the President nominates a successor, subject to a majority vote in both houses of Congress. That process has been used twice in recent years. Gerald Ford was confirmed as Vice President in 1973 and then Nelson Rockefeller in 1974. *

Constitutional Amendment

As we have seen, Congress may propose amendments to the Constitution by a two-thirds vote in each house. It may also call a national convention to propose an amendment if it is requested to do so by two-thirds of the State legislatures.[27]

Impeachment

The Constitution provides that the President, Vice President, and all civil officers of the United States may "be removed from office on **impeachment** for, and conviction of, treason, bribery, or other high crimes and

[26] 12th Amendment; see pages 391–393.

[27] Article V; see pages 60–63.

In accord with the 25th Amendment, Gerald Ford became Vice President on December 6, 1973. Chief Justice Warren Burger administered the oath of office, as President Richard Nixon, Mrs. Ford, and others looked on.

*ENRICHMENT Have the class discuss: What role did Congress play in the selection of Gerald Ford to replace Vice President Spiro Agnew? What congressional action led to Ford replacing Nixon as President?

misdemeanors.[28] The House has the sole power to impeach (bring charges) and the Senate the sole power to judge (sit as a court) in impeachment cases.[29]

The House may impeach by a majority vote. A two-thirds vote of the Senators present is needed for conviction. The Chief Justice must preside over the Senate when a President is tried. The penalty for conviction is removal from office. The Senate may add a prohibition against the person ever holding federal office again. In addition, a person who has been impeached and convicted can also be indicted, tried, convicted, and punished according to law in the regular courts.[30]

To date, there have been but 13 impeachments and only five convictions. Some officers have resigned under the threat of impeachment. The most notable was Richard Nixon, who resigned the Presidency in 1974. When the House impeached President Andrew Johnson in 1868, the Senate failed by a single vote to convict him.[31]

On July 30, 1974, the House Judiciary Committee voted three articles of impeachment against President Nixon. Ten days later, Nixon resigned.

Executive

The Constitution gives two "executive powers" to the Senate. One power has to do with appointments and the other with treaties made by the President.[32]

All major appointments made by the President must be confirmed by the Senate by majority vote. Each nomination by the President is referred to the appropriate standing committee of the Senate. When that committee's recommendation is brought to the floor, it may be, but seldom is, considered in executive, or secret, session.

The appointment of a Cabinet officer or of some other top member of the President's "official family" is very seldom turned down by the Senate.[33] But the unwritten rule of

[28]Article II, Section 4. Military officers are not "civil officers" and may be removed by court-martial. Nor are members of Congress. When the House impeached Senator William Blount of Tennessee in 1798, the Senate refused to try the case on grounds that it had the power to expel one of its own members if it chose to do so. Blount was expelled. The precedent then set has been followed ever since; see page 304.

[29]Article I, Section 2, Clause 5, Section 3, Clause 6.

[30]Article I, Section 3, Clauses 6 and 7.

[31]The five persons removed were federal judges. One other judge resigned after the House had impeached him and just before the Senate began his trial, and the case was dropped. Four other judges were acquitted by the Senate. On these judicial impeachments, see page 529. Aside from Senator Blount and President Johnson, W. W. Belknap, who was President Grant's Secretary of War, was impeached in 1876. He was acquitted by the Senate, however, on grounds that that body no longer had jurisdiction because he had resigned from office.

[32]Article II, Section 2, Clause 2.

[33]All told, only 11 of the now more than 600 Cabinet appointments have been rejected by the Senate. The first was Roger B. Taney, Andrew Jackson's choice for Secretary of the Treasury. Two years later President Jackson named Taney to succeed John Marshall as Chief Justice. The Senate confirmed him, and he served in that position until his death in 1863. The most recent rejection came in 1959 when the Senate refused to approve President Eisenhower's appointment of Lewis B. Strauss as Secretary of Commerce. On the other rejections, see page 407.

*ENRICHMENT Presidential appointments are not automatically confirmed by the Senate. Ask the class to discuss how party politics can play a role in this process.

"senatorial courtesy" comes into play with the appointment of federal officers who serve at the State level, for example, District Court judges, United States attorneys, and federal marshals. The Senate will turn down such an appointment if it is opposed by a Senator of the President's party from that State.[34] What this means is that some Senators practically dictate certain presidential appointments. We shall return to this in Chapter 15.

Treaties are made by the President "by and with the advice and consent of the Senate, . . . provided two-thirds of the Senators present concur."[35] For a time after the adoption of the Constitution, the advice of the Senate was asked when a treaty was being prepared. Now the President most often consults the members of the Senate Foreign Relations Committee and other influential Senators of both parties.

The Senate may accept or reject a treaty as it stands. It may, however, offer amendments, reservations, or understandings to it. Because the House has a hold on the public purse strings, influential members of that body also are often consulted in the treaty-making process. See page 418.

Representative James Wright (D., Texas) is photographed while on a fact-finding trip to strife-torn El Salvador in 1984.

Investigative

Congress, through its committees, has the power to investigate matters for three purposes: (1) to gather information useful to Congress in the making of law; (2) to review the present-day effectiveness of laws it has passed; and (3) to find out whether programs are in fact being administered and operated as Congress intended they should be. See pages 321–323.

FOR REVIEW

1. **Identify:** nonlegislative power, electoral power, executive power.
2. If the electoral college fails to elect a President, who then makes that choice? A Vice President?
3. How is a vacancy in the Vice Presidency now filled?
4. What roles does Congress play in the constitutional amendment process?
5. Which chamber of Congress has the power to impeach? The power to try those who are impeached?
6. What two "executive powers" are held by the Senate?
7. For what three purposes does Congress have investigative power?

---

[34]Those who criticize the practice often overlook the fact that a Senator is much more likely to be better informed about affairs in his own State than is the President.

[35]Article II, Section 2, Clause 2. It is often said that the Senate "ratifies" a treaty. It does not. The Senate may give or withhold its "advice and consent" to a treaty made by the President. Once the Senate has consented to a treaty, the President then ratifies it by exchanging the "instruments of ratification" with the other party or parties to the agreement.

SUMMARY

The scope of the many and important powers of Congress is fundamentally affected by the principles of limited government and of federalism. Its powers are those delegated to it by the Constitution: (1) those *expressly* granted to it by the Constitution, (2) those reasonably *implied* by the expressed powers, and (3) those *inherently* possessed because the Constitution creates a national government for the sovereign United States.

Most of the expressed powers of Congress are set out in Article I, Section 8, Clauses 1–18. Several of these powers are also found elsewhere in the Constitution.

Early in our history the question of strict or liberal interpretation of the powers given to Congress became a hard-fought issue. It was very largely settled by the Supreme Court in the landmark case of *McCulloch* v. *Maryland,* 1819. In this case, the Court gave a sweepingly broad interpretation to the Necessary and Proper Clause. In short, it upheld the doctrine of implied powers.

Congress performs several nonlegislative functions—in the electoral, constituent, impeachment, executive, and investigative fields.

CHAPTER REVIEW

Key Terms/Concepts*

strict constructionists (342)
liberal constructionists (342)
direct tax (345)
indirect tax (346)
commerce power (348)
bankruptcy (350)
copyright (351)
patent (351)
eminent domain (352)
implied powers (354)
impeachment (359)

*These terms appear in the Glossary.

Keynote Questions

• **1.** In what three ways does the Constitution delegate powers to Congress?

• **2.** How does a liberal constructionist's interpretation of the Constitution differ from a strict constructionist's?

• **3.** List three purposes of the power to tax and give an example for each.

• **4.** In what four ways does the Constitution limit the power of Congress to tax?

• **5.** Why is the 16th Amendment significant to the taxing power of Congress?

• **6.** What power does the Commerce Clause grant to Congress? What limits does the Constitution place on this power?

• **7.** Explain briefly the currency power and why the Framers agreed that Congress should have this power.

• **8.** Why does the Constitution give the borrowing power to Congress?

• **9.** What is a debt ceiling?

• • • **10.** Make a table showing each of the following powers of Congress, a description of the power, and the purpose of that power: bankruptcy power, postal power, power to establish copyrights and patents, power to set standard weights and measures.

• **11.** What powers does Congress have over federal territories?

• **12.** Why does the Constitution delegate some judicial and some executive powers to Congress?

• **13.** List the specific war powers held by Congress.

• **14.** What are the three purposes of Congress's power to conduct investigations through its committees?

The dots represent skill levels required to answer each question or complete each activity: •requires recall and comprehension • •requires application and analysis • • •requires synthesis and evaluation

Skill Application

Reading a Bar Graph: A bar graph is one way of presenting statistical information. It is composed of two axes—one vertical and one horizontal. Numerical information is plotted on the graph and represented by bars. Bar graphs make it easier to compare statistical information.

Look at the graph on page 344. Note the title. The vertical axis on this graph represents years, and the horizontal represents billions of dollars. Therefore, each bar on the graph represents total taxes paid (in billions of dollars) for one year. Examine a bar for one year. The bar is divided into six colors. The key for the graph shows that each color represents a level of government—federal, State, or local. Note, too, that the federal section of the bar is further divided to show the specific types of taxes.

Answer the following questions about this bar graph:

1. What kinds of federal taxes are shown?
2. In 1960, what was the total amount of taxes paid? Approximately how much of this was paid in federal taxes? State taxes? Local taxes?
3. In 1986, what was the total amount of taxes paid? Approximately how much of this was paid in federal taxes? State taxes? Local taxes?
4. In which year did the biggest increase in total Social Security taxes paid occur?
5. Have federal taxes or State and local taxes increased at a faster rate? How can you tell?
6. Based on this graph, would you expect taxes to increase or decrease in 1990?

For Thought and Discussion

1. How does the establishment of a national postal system, a monetary system, and a system of weights and measures contribute to "a more perfect Union"? What would happen if these were reserved powers rather than expressed powers?
2. How does each of the nonlegislative powers of Congress reflect the system of checks and balances?
3. In the Court's decision in *McCulloch* v. *Maryland,* Chief Justice Marshall wrote that "the power to tax involves the power to destroy." In what ways could the power to tax be used as the power to destroy? How do the constitutional limits on Congress's power to tax provide protections against its use as a power to destroy?
4. Throughout our history, Congress and the President have, at various times, disagreed about the course of United States foreign policy. How can Congress use its war powers, powers over foreign relations, and its executive powers to influence the President in matters of foreign policy?
5. Great Britain has no written constitution. Parliament may pass any law it believes to be necessary. Why does the Constitution limit Congress's lawmaking powers?

Suggested Activities

1. Investigate new tax proposals before the current Congress. Check such sources as newspapers and newsmagazines, Congressional Quarterly's *Weekly Report,* the House Ways and Means Committee, and the Senate Finance Committee. Prepare a brief summary of one proposal. Who proposed it, and why? What is the purpose of the new tax plan? Whom would it affect and how? Which pressure groups support it? Oppose it? Why? Present your findings to the class and lead a class discussion on the pros and cons of the new tax plan.
2. Using the sources cited above (as well as the House or Senate Judiciary Committee), investigate whether or not Congress is considering any bills regarding immigration or naturalization. Prepare a brief summary and outline the pros and cons of the bill. Based on your outline, write a letter to the editor of your local newspaper expressing your position on this bill.
3. Prepare a bulletin board display of the meaning, scope, and importance of one of the powers of Congress.
4. Stage a debate or class forum on one of the following: (a) *Resolved,* That Congress be allowed to exercise only those powers expressly delegated to it by the Constitution; (b) *Resolved,* That the federal monopoly over the postal system be ended; (c) *Resolved,* That Congress reassert its authority to grant letters of marque and reprisal.

Unit 5

The Executive Branch: The Presidency and the Bureaucracy

IN UNIT FIVE, we turn to the vast, complex, sprawling, and critically important executive branch of the National Government. Governments may operate without either legislatures or courts; but no government, whatever its form, can exist without some type of executive authority. Recall that a major weakness of the Articles of Confederation was the lack of such authority.

Our governmental system, like all others, demands an executive authority. And, it demands a strong one. Alexander Hamilton put the case for a strong executive in 1788:

> Energy in the Executive is a leading character in the definition of good government. . . . A feeble Executive implies a feeble execution of the government . . .

Chapters 14 and 15 of this unit deal with the Presidency. Chapter 16 addresses the bureaucracy—the vast number of offices and agencies, and their staffs, that make the government work, and the public dollars with which they do so. Chapter 17 closes the unit with a discussion of foreign affairs and the formation and administration of foreign policy.

Diplomatic honors are accorded to a head of state at the White House by President Reagan.

... the vital center of action in our whole scheme of government.
–JOHN F. KENNEDY

14

The Presidency

CHAPTER OBJECTIVES

To help you to

Learn · Know · Understand

The interrelated roles of the Presidency.

The constitutional shape of the office in terms of qualifications, tenure, and compensation.

The process of presidential succession in terms of both vacancy and disability.

The role of the Vice Presidency.

The early and present practices of presidential nomination and election.

The place of national conventions in the nominating process.

The presidential campaign and the role of the electoral college in the presidential election.

The principal defects in the electoral college system and the major proposals for change.

ON APRIL 30, 1789, George Washington placed his right hand on the Bible and his left hand on his heart and swore that he would "preserve, protect, and defend the Constitution of the United States." Thus, in the temporary capital at New York, he became the first President of the United States. Over the long course of 197 years, each of his successors has repeated that ceremony and spoken the words of the constitutional oath. Most Presidents have been sworn in in Washington, D.C., as was Thomas Jefferson for the first time in 1801. Most Presidents have repeated that oath on the steps of the Capitol, as James Monroe did for the first time in 1817.

Ronald Reagan repeated the solemn words of the Constitution, for a second time, at noon at the White House on Sunday, January 20, 1985, and so began his second term as the nation's 40th President.[1]

[1]President Reagan repeated the oath in a public ceremony at the Capitol the following day. That event marked the formal inauguration of his second term. The earlier (Sunday) ceremony was a private one, attended by a small group of invited guests. The 20th Amendment provides that each four-year presidential term shall begin, and end, on January 20th. When that date falls on a Sunday, the formal, public inaugural ceremonies are held on Monday.

*ENRICHMENT Ask the class to discuss why the Presidency is "the vital center of action" (Kennedy quote above). How can one person be so important?

As did George Washington in 1789 when he became the first President (facing page), Ronald Reagan recites the constitutional oath of office as he enters his second term in 1985.

As the nation's Chief Executive, Mr. Reagan holds the most important and the most powerful office known to history. His powers are vast, his responsibilities are immeasurable, and his functions are many.

In an earlier and a simpler day, Admiral George Dewey said that "the office of President is not such a very difficult one to fill, his duties being mainly to execute the laws of Congress." That view of the Presidency was wrong-headed at the time. As we shall see, it is an even more hugely mistaken one today.

1. The President's Many Roles

As You Read, Think About:

- What the many roles are that a President must play.

At any given time, of course, only one person is President of the United States. The office, with all of its powers and duties, belongs to that one, single individual. Whoever that person may be, he—and perhaps someday she[2]—must fill a number of different roles, and all of them at the same time.

The President is, to begin with, *Chief of State,* the ceremonial head of the government of the United States. He is, then, the symbol of all the people of the nation—in President William Howard Taft's words, "the personal embodiment and representative of their dignity and majesty."

In many countries, the chief of state reigns but does not rule. Among them are the Queens of England and of Denmark, the Emperor of Japan, the Kings of Norway and of Sweden, and the Presidents of Italy and of West Germany. It is most certainly *not* true of the President of the United States. He both reigns *and* rules.

The President is the nation's *Chief Executive,* vested by the Constitution with *"the* executive power of the United States." The President is also the *Chief Administrator* of

[2]To this point all of the Presidents have been men, but there is nothing in the Constitution to prevent the selection of a woman to that office.

President Reagan signs the Social Security Reform Act into law in 1983. What are the President's options after Congress has passed a bill?

the Federal Government, heading one of the largest governmental machines the world has known. Today, the President directs an administration with some three million civilian employees and that spends nearly $1 trillion a year.

The President is also the nation's *Chief Diplomat,* the chief architect of American foreign policy and the nation's chief spokesman to the rest of the world. "I make foreign policy," President Harry Truman once said —and he did. What the President says, and does, is carefully followed, not only in this country but everywhere abroad.

In connection with that role in foreign affairs, the Constitution also makes the President the *Commander in Chief* of the nation's armed forces. Two million men and women in uniform, and all of the incalculable power in the nation's military arsenal, are thus made subject to the President's direct and immediate control.

Importantly, the President is also the nation's *Chief Legislator,* the chief architect of its public policies. It is the President who sets the overall shape of the congressional agenda—initiating, suggesting, requesting, supporting, insisting, and demanding that Congress enact most of the major legislation that it does.

These six presidential roles all come directly from the Constitution. Yet they do not complete the list. The President must fill still other vital roles.

The President is *Chief of Party,* the acknowledged leader of the political party in control of the executive branch. A great deal of the real power and influence wielded by the Chief Executive depends on the manner in which this critical role is played.

The office also automatically makes of its occupant the nation's *Chief Citizen.* The President is expected to be "the representative of *all* the people," the one to work for and represent the *public* interest against the many different and competing private interests. "The Presidency," said Franklin Roosevelt, "is not merely an administrative office. That is the least of it. It is preeminently a place of moral leadership." *

Interrelated Nature of Presidential Roles

Again, the President performs each of these several roles; and listing them is a very useful way to describe the Presidency. But, remember, they are all played *simultaneously.*

Each of these roles is inseparable from, and closely interrelated with, each of the others. None of them is, or can be, performed in isolation. The manner in which the President plays any one role can have a very decided effect on the ability to play another or several or all of them.

As two illustrations, take the experiences of Presidents Lyndon Johnson and Richard Nixon. Each was a strong and a relatively effective President during his first years in office. But the agonizing and increasingly unpopular war in Vietnam persuaded Mr. Johnson not to run for reelection in 1968. In effect, the manner in which he acted as Commander in Chief seriously eroded his stature and effectiveness in the White House. The many-sided and sordid Watergate affair,

*ENRICHMENT Ask the class for examples of each of the President's six roles. For instance, as Chief of State, President Reagan welcomes foreign dignitaries to this country.

Each President has re-interpreted his role with the public. President Roosevelt's fireside chats gained public support for his New Deal program.

and the manner in which he filled the roles of party leader and chief citizen, so destroyed his Presidency that Mr. Nixon was forced to leave office in disgrace in 1974.

Surely, enough has been said to this point to confirm our description of the Presidency as "the most important and the most powerful office known to history." Enough has been said, too, to dismiss Admiral Dewey as, at best, a naive commentator.

We shall return to the several roles of the President shortly. But for now let us look at the constitutional structure of the office and then at the presidential election process.

FOR REVIEW

1. What several roles does (must) the President play?
2. How can the manner in which one role is played affect the ability of a President to play another or all of the other roles?

2. Qualifications, Term, Compensation

As You Read, Think About:

- What the formal qualifications are for the office of President.
- How long a person can serve as President.
- What the President is paid in salary and in fringe benefits.

Whatever else a President must be, the Constitution sets out three qualifications for the office.[3] The Constitution also sets the length of a presidential term and leaves to Congress the matter of the President's pay.

Formal Qualifications

The Constitution says the President must:

(1) Be "a natural-born citizen." Under the doctrine of *jus sanguinis* (page 167), it is apparently possible for a person born abroad to become President. Some dispute that view, however the real shape of this requirement cannot be known until someone born a citizen, but born abroad, does in fact become President.[4]

(2) Be at least 35 years of age. At 43, John F. Kennedy was the youngest person ever to be elected to the office. Theodore Roosevelt reached it by succession at age 42. Only five other Presidents entered office at less then 50 years of age: James K. Polk, Franklin Pierce, Ulysses Grant, James Garfield, and Grover Cleveland. Ronald Reagan, who was 69 when he was elected in 1980, is the oldest man ever elected and ever to hold the office. Before Mr. Reagan, William Henry Harrison was the oldest ever elected, at age 68, and Dwight D. Eisenhower, who left the White House at 70, had been the oldest man ever to serve in the office.

---

[3]Article II, Section 1, Clause 5.

[4]Martin Van Buren, who was born December 5, 1782, was the first President actually born in the United States. His seven predecessors and his immediate successor were each born before the Revolution. But notice that the Constitution anticipated that situation by stating, "or a citizen of the United States at the time of the adoption of this Constitution."

Presidents of the United States

Name	Party	State[a]	Born	Died	Entered Office	Age on Taking Office	Vice Presidents
George Washington	Federalist	Virginia	1732	1799	1789	57	John Adams
John Adams	Federalist	Massachusetts	1735	1826	1797	61	Thomas Jefferson
Thomas Jefferson	Dem.-Rep.[b]	Virginia	1743	1826	1801	57	Aaron Burr
							George Clinton
James Madison	Dem.-Rep.	Virginia	1751	1836	1809	57	George Clinton
							Elbridge Gerry
James Monroe	Dem.-Rep.	Virginia	1758	1831	1817	58	Daniel D. Tompkins
John Q. Adams	Dem.-Rep.	Massachusetts	1767	1848	1825	57	John C. Calhoun
Andrew Jackson	Democrat	Tenn.(S.C.)	1767	1845	1829	61	John C. Calhoun
							Martin Van Buren
Martin Van Buren	Democrat	New York	1782	1862	1837	54	Richard M. Johnson
William H. Harrison	Whig	Ohio (Va.)	1773	1841	1841	68	John Tyler
John Tyler	Democrat	Virginia	1790	1862	1841	51	. . . .
James K. Polk	Democrat	Tenn. (N.C.)	1795	1849	1845	49	George M. Dallas
Zachary Taylor	Whig	La. (Va.)	1784	1850	1849	64	Millard Fillmore
Millard Fillmore	Whig	New York	1800	1874	1850	50	. . . .
Franklin Pierce	Democrat	New Hampshire	1804	1869	1853	48	William R. King
James Buchanan	Democrat	Pennsylvania	1791	1868	1857	65	John C. Breckinridge
Abraham Lincoln	Republican	Illinois (Ky.)	1809	1865	1861	52	Hannibal Hamlin
							Andrew Johnson
Andrew Johnson	Democrat[c]	Tenn. (N.C.)	1808	1875	1865	56	. . . .
Ulysses S. Grant	Republican	Illinois (Ohio)	1822	1885	1869	46	Schuyler Colfax
							Henry Wilson
Rutherford B. Hayes	Republican	Ohio	1822	1893	1877	54	William A. Wheeler
James A. Garfield	Republican	Ohio	1831	1881	1881	49	Chester A. Arthur
Chester A. Arthur	Republican	N.Y. (Vt.)	1830	1886	1881	50	. . . .

[a]State of residence when elected; if born in another State that State in parentheses. [b]Democratic-Republican. [c]Johnson, a War Democrat, was elected Vice President, as Lincoln's running mate, on the coalition Union Party ticket. [d]Resigned October 10, 1973. [e]Nominated by Nixon, confirmed by Congress on December 6, 1973. [f]Nominated by Ford, confirmed by Congress on December 19, 1974.

(3) Have lived in the United States for at least 14 years.[5]

While these formal qualifications are clearly important, they are really not very difficult to meet. We shall look at the much more telling informal qualifications shortly.

[5]Given particularly Herbert Hoover's election in 1928 and Dwight Eisenhower's in 1952, the 14-year requirement means any 14 years in a person's life. Both Hoover and Eisenhower spent several years before election outside the United States.

Term

The Framers of the Constitution considered a number of different limits on the length of the presidential term. Most of their debate centered on a four-year term, with the President to be eligible for reelection, versus a single six-year or seven-year term. They finally settled on a four-year term.[6] They agreed, as Alexander Hamilton stated in *The Federalist*, that was long enough for a

[6]Article II, Section 1, Clause 1.

*ENRICHMENT Have the class discuss why some advocate a single, six-year presidential term. Point out that a President's own legislative calendar may require more than a four-year term.

Name	Party	State[a]	Born	Died	Entered Office	Age on Taking Office	Vice Presidents
Grover Cleveland	Democrat	N.Y. (N.J.)	1837	1908	1885	47	Thomas A. Hendricks
Benjamin Harrison	Republican	Indiana (Ohio)	1833	1901	1889	55	Levi P. Morton
Grover Cleveland	Democrat	N.Y. (N.J.)	1837	1908	1893	55	Adlai E. Stevenson
William McKinley	Republican	Ohio	1843	1901	1897	54	Garret A. Hobart
							Theodore Roosevelt
Theodore Roosevelt	Republican	New York	1858	1919	1901	42	. . . .
							Charles W. Fairbanks
William H. Taft	Republican	Ohio	1857	1930	1909	51	James S. Sherman
Woodrow Wilson	Democrat	N.J. (Va.)	1856	1924	1913	56	Thomas R. Marshall
Warren G. Harding	Republican	Ohio	1865	1923	1921	55	Calvin Coolidge
Calvin Coolidge	Republican	Mass. (Vt.)	1872	1933	1923	51	. . . .
							Charles G. Dawes
Herbert Hoover	Republican	Calif. (Iowa)	1874	1964	1929	54	Charles Curtis
Franklin D. Roosevelt	Democrat	New York	1882	1945	1933	51	John N. Garner
							Henry A. Wallace
							Harry S Truman
Harry S Truman	Democrat	Missouri	1884	1972	1945	60	. . . .
							Alben W. Barkley
Dwight D. Eisenhower	Republican	N.Y.-Pa. (Tex.)	1890	1969	1953	62	Richard M. Nixon
John F. Kennedy	Democrat	Massachusetts	1917	1963	1961	43	Lyndon B. Johnson
Lyndon B. Johnson	Democrat	Texas	1908	1973	1963	55	. . . .
							Hubert H. Humphrey
Richard M. Nixon	Republican	N.Y. (Calif.)	1913		1969	55	Spiro T. Agnew[d]
							Gerald R. Ford[e]
Gerald R. Ford	Republican	Michigan (Neb.)	1913		1974	61	Nelson A. Rockefeller[f]
James E. Carter	Democrat	Georgia	1924		1977	52	Walter F. Mondale
Ronald W. Reagan	Republican	Calif. (Ill.)	1911		1981	69	George H. W. Bush

President to gain experience, demonstrate abilities, and establish stable policies.

Until 1951, the Constitution placed no limit on the number of terms a President might serve. Several Presidents, beginning with George Washington, refused to seek more than two terms, however. Soon, the "no-third-term tradition" became an unwritten rule in presidential politics.

After Franklin D. Roosevelt broke the tradition by winning a third term in 1940, and then a fourth in 1944, the unwritten custom became a part of the written Constitution. The 22nd Amendment, adopted in 1951, reads in part:

> No person shall be elected to the office of the President more than twice, and no person who has held the office of President, or acted as President, for more than two years of a term to which some other person was elected President shall be elected to the office of the President more than once.

As a general rule, then, each President may now serve a maximum of two full terms, or eight years, in office. *But* a President who has *succeeded* in the office *beyond* the midpoint in a term to which another was originally elected may serve for more than eight years. He may finish out his predecessor's term and run for two terms of his own. However, a President may not serve more than 10 years.

Several Presidents, most recently Jimmy Carter, have urged a single, six-year term for the office. Significantly, they have each come to this view *after* having won the office.

Compensation

The President's salary is fixed by Congress, and it can neither be increased nor decreased during a term.[7]

The salary was first set at $25,000 a year in 1789. Congress put the figure at its present level—$200,000—in 1969. Since 1949 the President has also received a $50,000-a-year expense account. It is taxable as income and, is really a part of the President's pay.

The Constitution forbids the President "any other emolument from the United States, or any of them."[8] But this clause does not prevent the President from being provided with the White House, a magnificent 132-room mansion set on an 18.3-acre (7.8-hectare) estate in the heart of the nation's Capital; a sizable suite of offices and a large staff; a yacht, a fleet of automobiles, three lavishly fitted Boeing 707 jets, and several other planes and helicopters; Camp David, the resort hideaway in the Catoctin Mountains in Maryland; the finest medical, dental, and other health care available; generous travel and entertainment funds; and many other perquisites.

Many of these services and facilities cannot be measured in dollar terms. However, to have all the material benefits the Chief Executive receives, estimates are that a private citizen would need an after-taxes income of more than $15 million a year. That amount of "take-home pay" would require a gross income of about $30 million a year.

Since 1958 each former President has received a lifetime pension, now $86,200 a year, and each presidential widow is entitled to a pension of $20,000 a year.

[7]Article II, Section 1, Clause 7. At Philadelphia, Benjamin Franklin argued that, as money *and* power might corrupt a man, the President ought to receive nothing beyond his expenses; his suggestion was not put to a vote at the Convention, however. The present salary was set in the first measure passed by Congress in 1969. It was signed by President Johnson on January 17, three days before the new presidential term, President Nixon's first, began.

[8]Article II, Section 1, Clause 7.

FOR REVIEW

1. **Identify:** no-third-term tradition.
2. What are the formal qualifications for the Presidency?
3. For what term is a President elected?
4. To how many terms may a President be elected? What is the maximum length of time any person may serve as President?
5. Who fixes the President's pay? How much is it today?

3. The Vice Presidency

As You Read, Think About:

- What duties are assigned the Vice President by the Constitution.
- How a vacancy in the office of Vice President is filled.
- How recent Presidents have made use of their Vice Presidents.

"I am Vice President. In this I am nothing, but I may be everything." So said John Adams, the nation's first Vice President. Those words could have been repeated, very appropriately, by each of the 42 Vice Presidents who have followed him in that office.

The Constitution pays little attention to the office. It assigns the Vice President only two formal duties: (1) to preside over the Senate[9] and (2) to help decide the question of presidential disability.[10] Beyond them, the

[9]Article I, Section 3, Clause 4, see page 316.

[10]25th Amendment, Sections 3 and 4. The 12th Amendment states the Vice President must meet the same qualifications as those set out for the Presidency.

Vice President Calvin Coolidge was at his father's home in Vermont when he heard of President Harding's death in 1923. Coolidge's father, a justice of the peace, administered the oath of office by the light of a kerosene lamp.

Constitution makes the Vice President a "President-in-waiting" to become "everything" should the President die, resign, or be removed from office.

Through much of our history, the Vice Presidency has been slighted—treated as an office of little real consequence and, often, as the butt of jokes.

Several—in fact, nearly all—Vice Presidents themselves have had a hand in this. John Adams described his post as "the most insignificant office that ever the invention of man contrived or his imagination conceived." Thomas Jefferson, who followed him, found the office "honorable and easy" and "tranquil and unoffending."

Theodore Roosevelt, who had come to the White House from the Vice Presidency, was annoyed by the tinkling of the prisms of a chandelier in the presidential study. He ordered it removed, saying: "Take it to the office of the Vice President. He doesn't have anything to do. It will keep him awake." The fixture has been in the Vice President's office, just off the Senate floor, ever since.

Alben Barkley, who served during Harry Truman's second term, often told the story of a woman who had two sons. One of them, Barkley said, went away to sea and the other one became Vice President, "and neither of them was ever heard from again."

Importance of the Office

Despite these and a great many other such comments, the office is important. Its occupant is, literally, "only a heartbeat away from the Presidency." Remember, eight Presidents have died in office, and one, Richard M. Nixon, was forced to resign.

Much of the blame for the low state of the Vice Presidency belongs to the two major parties and the way in which they regularly nominate their candidates for the office. Traditionally, each convention names the hand-picked choice of its just-nominated presidential candidate. Invariably, the presidential candidate picks someone who will "balance the ticket." That is, the presidential candidate chooses a running mate who can

*REINFORCEMENT Presidential candidates try to choose running mates who will "balance the ticket." Ask the class what this phrase means. An example is Geraldine Ferraro's nomination.

Vice President George Bush reviews West German troops with Chancellor Helmut Köhl.

improve his electoral chances. In short, fate and the Vice Presidency do not have a very high priority in the vice presidential candidate selection process.

The Vice Presidency has been vacant 18 times thus far—nine times by succession to the Presidency, twice by resignation, and seven times by death.[11] Yet, not until the 25th Amendment did the Constitution deal with the matter. Section 2 provides:

> Whenever there is a vacancy in the office of the Vice President, the President shall nominate a Vice President who shall take office upon confirmation by a majority vote of both houses of Congress.

The provision was first implemented in 1973, when President Nixon selected and Congress confirmed Gerald Ford to succeed Spiro Agnew as Vice President. It came into play again in 1974, when President Ford named and Congress approved Nelson Rockefeller as Mr. Ford's successor.

Many have long urged that the Vice President be given a larger role in the executive branch. The more recent Presidents, from Eisenhower to Reagan, have in fact made greater use of their Vice Presidents. Today, Vice President Bush takes part in Cabinet meetings and is a member of the critically important National Security Council. Mr. Bush also carries out a number of social, political, diplomatic, and administrative chores for the President.

So far, however, no President has "upgraded" the Vice President to the role of a true "Assistant President." The major reason: Of all the President's official family, only the Vice President is not subject to the ultimate discipline of removal from office by the President. Remember, unlike Cabinet officers, for example, who are appointed by the President, the Vice President is elected.

[11]John C. Calhoun resigned to become a Senator from South Carolina in 1832. Spiro T. Agnew resigned in 1973, after a conviction for income tax evasion and in the face of charges of corruption dating from his service as a county executive and then governor of Maryland. The seven who died in office were: George Clinton (1812), Elbridge Gerry (1814), William R. King (1853), Henry Wilson (1875), Thomas H. Hendricks (1885), Garret A. Hobart (1899), and James S. Sherman (1912).

FOR REVIEW

1. What duties does the Constitution give to the Vice President?
2. How (on what basis) do the major parties select their vice presidential candidates?
3. How many Vice Presidents have succeeded to the Presidency? Who were they, and when and why did they succeed?
4. How is a vacancy in the Vice Presidency filled? Has this ever happened?
5. Why has no President yet made the Vice President a true "Assistant President"?

4. Presidential Succession

As You Read, Think About:

- What the constitutional provisions are for succession to the Presidency.
- How presidential disability is determined and dealt with.

Vice Presidents Who Succeeded to the Presidency

John Tyler—on the death (pneumonia) of William Henry Harrison, April 4, 1841.
Millard Fillmore—on the death (gastroenteritis) of Zachary Taylor, July 9, 1850.
Andrew Johnson—on the death (assassination) of Abraham Lincoln, April 13, 1865.
Chester A. Arthur—on the death (assassination) of James A. Garfield, September 19, 1881.
Theodore Roosevelt—on the death (assassination) of William McKinley, September 14, 1901.
Calvin Coolidge—on the death (undisclosed illness) of Warren G. Harding, August 2, 1923.
Harry S Truman—on the death (cerebral hemorrhage) of Franklin D. Roosevelt, April 12, 1945.
Lyndon B. Johnson—on the death (assassination) of John F. Kennedy, November 22, 1963.
Gerald R. Ford—on the resignation of Richard M. Nixon, August 9, 1974.

Section 1 of the 25th Amendment states:

> In case of the removal of the President from office or of his death or resignation, the Vice President shall become President.

In strictest terms, before the 25th Amendment was added in 1967, the Constitution did *not* say that in such situations the Vice President should become President. Rather, the Constitution declared that the *powers and duties* of the office, not the office itself, were to "devolve on the Vice President."[12]

However, in 1841 John Tyler had begun the practice that should the office become vacant, the Vice President succeeds to it. The only real effect of the addition of the 25th Amendment to the Constitution was to make what had been one of its informal amendments a part of the written document itself.

Congress fixes the order of succession following the Vice President.[13] The present law on the matter is the Presidential Succession Act of 1947. By its terms, the Speaker of the House and then the President *pro tem* of the Senate are next in line. They are followed, in turn, by the Secretary of State and then by each of the other 12 heads of the Cabinet departments, in order of precedence.[14] *

Presidential Disability

Before the 25th Amendment, there were serious gaps in the succession arrangement. Neither the Constitution nor Congress had made any provision for deciding *when* a President was disabled. Nor was there anything to indicate by *whom* such a decision was to be made.

For nearly 180 years, then, the nation played with fate. President Eisenhower suffered three serious but temporary illnesses while in office: a heart attack in 1955, ileitis in 1956, and a mild stroke in 1957. Two other Presidents were disabled for much longer periods of time. James Garfield lingered for 80 days before he died from an assassin's bullet in 1881. Woodrow Wilson suffered a paralytic stroke in 1919 and was an invalid for the rest of his second term. He was so ill that he could not meet with his Cabinet for seven months after his stroke.

Sections 3 and 4 of the 25th Amendment fill the disability gap, and in detail. The Vice President is to become Acting President (1) if the President informs Congress, in writing, "that he is unable to discharge the powers and duties of his office" or (2) if the Vice President and a majority of the members of the Cabinet inform Congress, in writing, that the President is so incapacitated.[15]

[12]Article II, Section 1, Clause 6. On removal of the President by impeachment, see Article I, Section 2, Clause 5; Article I, Section 3, Clauses 6 and 7; Article II, Section 4, and page 359.

[13]Article II, Section 1, Clause 6.

[14]That is, in the order in which their offices were created by Congress; see page 407. A Cabinet member is to serve only until a Speaker or President *pro tem* is available and qualified. But notice that Section 2 of the 25th Amendment provides for the filling of any vacancy in the Vice Presidency. In effect, that provision makes the Presidential Succession Act a law with little real significance—except in the quite unlikely event of simultaneous vacancies in the Presidency and Vice Presidency. The 25th Amendment almost certainly guarantees that the line of presidential succession will never pass below the Vice President.

[15]The 25th Amendment gives this authority to the Vice President and the Cabinet or to "such other body as Congress may by law provide." To 1987, no "such other body" has been established.

*ENRICHMENT Have students use the current Congress and administration to find out the names of those in line for presidential succession.

In either case, the President may resume the powers and duties of the office by informing Congress that no inability exists. However, the Vice President and a majority of the Cabinet may challenge the President on this score. If they do, Congress has 21 days in which to decide the matter.

To this point, those disability provisions have come into play only once and then only for a few hours. On July 13, 1985, a malignant tumor was removed from President Reagan's large intestine. Just before surgery, the President transferred the powers of the Presidency to Vice President Bush. He reclaimed those powers immediately after he awoke, seven hours and 54 minutes later. For that brief time, George Bush served as the Acting President of the United States.

FOR REVIEW

1. **Identify:** presidential succession, presidential disability.
2. Which amendment states that if the Presidency becomes vacant, the Vice President succeeds to that office?
3. Who follows the Vice President in the line of presidential succession?
4. Who serves as Acting President if the President becomes disabled?
5. How is presidential disability determined?

5. Presidential Nomination and Election: Early Practices

As You Read, Think About:

- How the presidential election system developed historically.

In strictly formal terms, the President is chosen according to the provisions of the Constitution.[16] In practice, however, the President is elected through an altogether extraordinary process, one that has developed over 50 presidential elections. That process is a composite of constitutional provisions, a few State and federal laws, and, in largest measure, a number of practices born of the nation's political parties.

No other election, here or abroad, can match its color, drama, or suspense. None can match the tremendous popular interest it attracts nor the huge amounts of time, effort, and money it consumes.

Original Constitutional Provisions

The Framers of the Constitution gave more time to the method for choosing the President than to any other matter. That method was, said James Wilson of Pennsylvania, "the most diffficult of all on which we have had to decide." It was difficult largely because most of the Framers were against selecting the President by the obvious ways: by Congress or by a direct vote of the people.*

Early in the Convention, most of the delegates favored selection by Congress. Later, nearly all delegates came to the view that congressional selection would, as Hamilton said, put the President "too much under the legislative thumb."

Only a few of the Framers favored choosing the President by popular vote. Nearly all agreed that that would lead "to tumult and disorder." Most delegates felt, too, that the people, scattered over so wide an area, could not possibly know enough about the available candidates to make wise, informed choices. George Mason of Virginia spoke for most of his colleagues at the Convention:

> The extent of the country renders it impossible that the people can have the requisite capacity to judge of the respective contentions of the candidates.

After weeks of debate, the Framers finally agreed on a plan first put forward by Hamilton. Under it, the President was to be chosen by a body of electors. They agreed:

1. Each State would have as many presidential electors as it has Senators and Representatives in Congress.

[16]The Constitution deals with the process of presidential selection in several places: Article II, Section 1, Clauses 2 and 4, and the 12th, 20th, and 23rd Amendments.

*REINFORCEMENT Have the class discuss: why the Framers of the Constitution were against selecting the President by a vote of Congress or by a direct vote of the people.

2. These electors would be chosen in each State in a manner the State legislature directed.
3. The electors, meeting in their own States, would each cast two votes—each for a different person.
4. The electoral votes from the several States would be opened and counted before a joint session of Congress.
5. The person receiving the largest number of electoral votes, provided that total was a majority of all the electors, would become President.
6. The person with the second highest number of electoral votes would become Vice President.
7. If a tie occurred, or if no one received the votes of a majority of the electors, the President would then be chosen by the House of Representatives, voting by States.
8. If a tie occurred for the second spot, the Vice President would then be chosen by the Senate.[17]

The Framers thought of the electors as "the most enlightened and respectable citizens" from each State. They were to be "free agents" who would "deliberate freely" in choosing the persons best qualified to fill the nation's two highest offices.

Impact of the Rise of Parties

The original version of the **electoral college** system worked as the Framers intended only for as long as George Washington was willing to seek and hold the Presidency. He was twice, and unanimously, elected President. That is, in 1789 and again in 1792, each elector cast one of his two ballots for the great Virginian.

Flaws began to appear in the system in 1796, however. By then, political parties had begun to form. John Adams, the Federalist candidate, was elected to the Presidency. Thomas Jefferson, an arch rival and Democratic-Republican who lost to Adams by just three votes in the electoral balloting, became his Vice President.

The system broke down in the election of 1800. By then there were two well-defined parties: the Federalists, led by Adams and Hamilton, and the Democratic-Republicans, headed by Jefferson. Each of these parties nominated presidential and vice presidential candidates. They also nominated elector-candidates in the several States. Those elector-candidates were picked with the clear understanding that, if elected, they would then vote for their party's presidential and vice presidential nominees.

Each of the 73 Democratic-Republicans who won posts as electors voted for their party's nominees: Jefferson and Aaron Burr. In doing so, they produced a tie for the Presidency. Remember that the Constitution

John Adams served as the nation's second President, from 1797 to 1801. With his defeat for reelection in the 1800 presidential election, the Federalists never again gained control of either the Presidency or Congress.

[17]Remember, these were the original provisions, in Article II, Sections 2 and 4; they were modified by the 12th Amendment, as we shall see. As curious as it may seem today, the electoral college system was one of the few major features of the proposed Constitution to escape widespread debate and criticism in the struggle over the ratification of that document.

gave each elector *two* votes, each to be cast for a *different* person but each to be cast for someone *as President.* Popular opinion clearly favored Jefferson for the Presidency, and the party had intended Burr for the Vice Presidency. Still, the House of Representatives had to take 36 separate ballots before it finally chose Jefferson.

The spectacular election of 1800 left a lasting imprint on the presidential election process. It marked the introduction of three new elements into the election process: (1) party nominations for the Presidency and Vice Presidency, (2) the nomination of candidates for **presidential electors** pledged to vote for their party's presidential ticket, and (3) the automatic casting of the electoral votes in line with those pledges. Gone forever was the notion that the electors were to be chosen as "free agents" who would "deliberate" in the selection of a President.

The 12th Amendment The election of 1800 produced another notable result. The 12th Amendment was added to the Constitution to make certain there would never be another such fiasco. The amendment is a lengthy one, but it made only one major change in the electoral college system. It *separated* the presidential and vice presidential elections: "The Electors . . . shall name in their ballots the person voted for as President, and in distinct ballots the person voted for as Vice President."[18]

With the appearance of parties, the elections of 1800, and then the 12th Amendment, the constitutional setting was laid for the presidential selection system as we know it today. What we now have is, indeed, a far cry from what was agreed on in 1787.

[18]Not only does the amendment mean there cannot be a repetition of the circumstances that led to the tie of 1800, it almost certainly guarantees that the President and Vice President will always be of the same party. With the adoption of the 12th Amendment, too, the character of the Vice Presidency underwent an unintended change. Ever since, the two major parties have regularly nominated their vice-presidential candidates with an eye to the electability of their presidential candidates, and with too little attention to their capacities for the Presidency, see pages 373, 389.

FOR REVIEW

1. Why were most of the Framers opposed to choosing the President by popular vote? To selection by Congress?
2. Outline the original provisions for the electoral college. How did the Framers expect electors to vote?
3. What three events combined to lay the constitutional setting for the present-day electoral college system?
4. What major change did the 12th Amendment make in the electoral college system?

6. Presidential Selection: The Nominating Process

As You Read, Think About:

- What function the national conventions of the major political parties serve.
- How the presidential primaries work.
- What the advantages and disadvantages are of primaries, caucuses, and conventions.

The Constitution makes no provision for the nomination of candidates for the Presidency. As the Framers set up the system, the electors would, out of their own knowledge, select the "wisest and best man" as President. As we have seen, the rise of parties altered that system drastically, and with the change came the need for nominations.

The Convention Process

The first method the parties developed to nominate presidential candidates was the congressional caucus. As we saw on page 233, that method was regularly used in the elections of 1800 to 1824. But, as we know, its closed character led to its downfall in the mid-1820s. For the election of 1832, both major parties turned to the national convention as their nominating device. It has continued to serve them ever since.

The Path to the Presidency

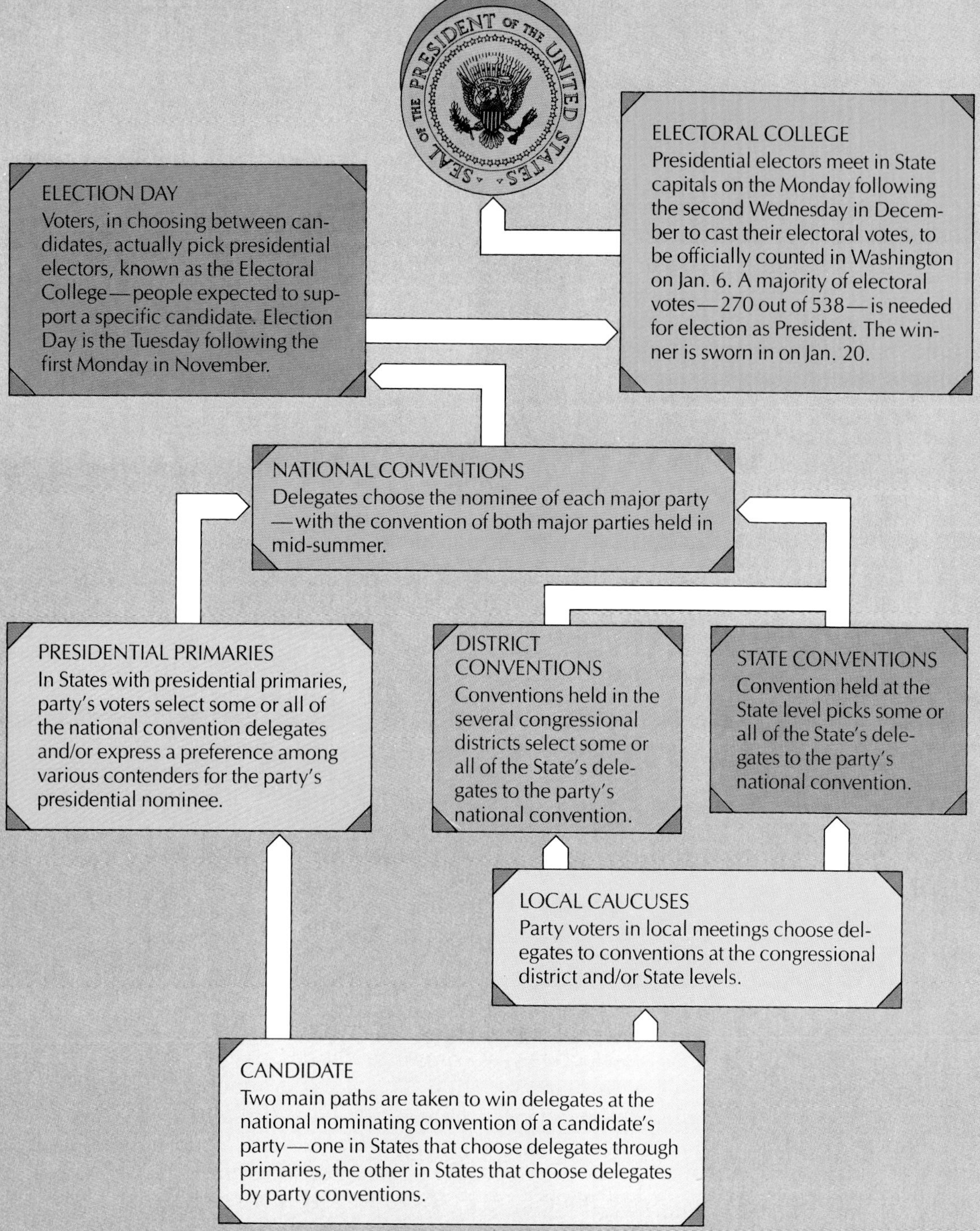
SEAL OF THE PRESIDENT OF THE UNITED STATES
ELECTION DAY
Voters, in choosing between candidates, actually pick presidential electors, known as the Electoral College—people expected to support a specific candidate. Election Day is the Tuesday following the first Monday in November.
ELECTORAL COLLEGE
Presidential electors meet in State capitals on the Monday following the second Wednesday in December to cast their electoral votes, to be officially counted in Washington on Jan. 6. A majority of electoral votes—270 out of 538—is needed for election as President. The winner is sworn in on Jan. 20.
NATIONAL CONVENTIONS
Delegates choose the nominee of each major party—with the convention of both major parties held in mid-summer.
PRESIDENTIAL PRIMARIES
In States with presidential primaries, party's voters select some or all of the national convention delegates and/or express a preference among various contenders for the party's presidential nominee.
DISTRICT CONVENTIONS
Conventions held in the several congressional districts select some or all of the State's delegates to the party's national convention.
STATE CONVENTIONS
Convention held at the State level picks some or all of the State's delegates to the party's national convention.
LOCAL CAUCUSES
Party voters in local meetings choose delegates to conventions at the congressional district and/or State levels.
CANDIDATE
Two main paths are taken to win delegates at the national nominating convention of a candidate's party—one in States that choose delegates through primaries, the other in States that choose delegates by party conventions.

Note: This outline indicates general procedures; many States vary them.

*ENRICHMENT Use the above chart to discuss: The electoral college has been called a "rubber stamp" for the elections. If this is so, why does it continue to exist?

Extent of Control by Law By the convention process, the final selection of the President is, for all practical purposes, narrowed to one of two persons: the Republican or the Democratic nominee. Yet, there is almost no legal control of that vital process.

We have already noted that the Constitution is silent on the subject of presidential nominations. There is, as well, almost no statutory law on the matter. The only provisions in federal law have to do with the financing of conventions; see page 254. Also, only a very small body of State law deals with a few aspects of convention organization and procedure. Among these are the choosing of delegates and the manner in which they may cast their votes; see pages 381–385. In short, the convention is very largely a creature and a responsibility of the political parties themselves.

Twin delegates take a break from a hectic schedule at the 1984 Democratic National Convention.

Convention Arrangements In both parties the national committee is charged with making the plans and arrangements for the national convention. As much as a year before it is held, the committee meets, usually in Washington, D.C, to set the time and place for the convention. July has been the favored month, but each party has met in convention as early as mid-June and also as late as the latter part of August.

Where the convention is held is a matter of prime importance. There must be an adequate convention hall, sufficient hotel accommodations, plentiful entertainment outlets, and convenient transportation facilities. Political considerations are also brought to bear. A city in a doubtful State —one likely to go either way in the election —is usually picked, in the hope of swaying the election outcome. Aspirants for the party's nomination often lobby for the selection of a city in a section of the country in which they have a strong base of popular support.

Many of the nation's larger cities bid for the "honor"—and the financial return to local business—of hosting a national convention. For 1984, the GOP chose Dallas, with their meeting slated for August. The Democrats picked San Francisco and July.

Both major parties have met in Chicago more often than in any other city, a fact that points to that city's central location and other physical attractions. Its selection points up, as well, the significance of Illinois as a doubtful or "pivotal" State.

The Democrats held each of their first six conventions, from 1832 through 1852, in Baltimore. Since 1856—when the Republicans held their first convention in Philadelphia, and the Democrats moved to Cincinnati —the two parties have met in the cities listed in the table to the right.[19]

The Apportionment of Delegates With the date and the location set, the national committee issues its "call" for the convention. That formal announcement names the time and place and also tells the party's organization in each State how many delegates it may send to the national meeting.

Traditionally, both parties give each State organization a number of convention votes based on that State's electoral votes. Over

[19]Notice that the two parties have met in the same city in the same year only six times: in Chicago four times, in 1884, 1932, 1944, and 1952; in Philadelphia in 1948; and in Miami Beach in 1972.

*REINFORCEMENT Have the class discuss the importance of the convention site. Where might the next Democratic and Republican conventions be held?

the past several conventions, however, both parties have developed complicated formulas that award bonus delegates to those States that have supported the party's candidates in recent elections.

For 1984, the Republican's apportionment formula produced a convention of 2,234 delegates, and the Democrat's more complicated plan, 3,944.[20] Given those numbers, it should be fairly clear that neither party's convention can really be called a "deliberative body."

Selection of Delegates There are really two campaigns for the Presidency in both major parties every four years. One campaign is the contest between the Republican and the Democratic nominees, of course. The other earlier and quite different one takes place *within* each of the parties: the struggle for convention delegates.

State laws and/or party rules fix the procedures by which the delegates are chosen in each State. The process is a reflection of federalism, of course, and it has produced a crazy-quilt pattern of presidential primaries, conventions, and caucuses among the States.[21]

National Convention Sites Since 1856

City	Republicans	Democrats
Atlantic City		1964
Baltimore	1864	1860, 1872, 1912
Chicago	1860, 1868, 1880, 1884, 1888, 1904, 1908, 1912, 1916, 1920, 1932, 1944, 1952, 1960	1864, 1884, 1892, 1896, 1932, 1940, 1944, 1952, 1956, 1968
Cincinnati	1876	1856, 1880
Cleveland	1924, 1936	
Dallas	1984	
Detroit	1980	
Denver		1908
Houston		1928
Kansas City, Mo.	1928, 1976	1900
Los Angeles		1960
Miami Beach	1968, 1972	1972
Minneapolis	1892	
New York		1868, 1924, 1976, 1980
Philadelphia	1856, 1872, 1900, 1940, 1948	1936, 1948
St. Louis	1896	1876, 1888, 1904, 1916
San Francisco	1956, 1964	1920, 1984

[20]The 3,944 Democratic delegates cast, altogether, 3,933 votes. The Democrats' rules allow for fractional voting; that is, a State party may select more delegates than its quota of convention votes, in which case some delegates cast a fraction of a vote at a convention. The GOP's rules do not provide for that practice. Each Republican delegate casts one full vote.

In addition to the delegates assigned to their State organizations, each party allots delegates to the District of Columbia, Guam, Puerto Rico, and the Virgin Islands. The Democratic convention also includes delegates representing American Samoa, Democrats Abroad (Europe), and Latin American Democrats.

For 1984, the Democrats added a varying number of "superdelegates" to each State's delegation—to give convention seats (and votes) to the top party officers in each State and also to Democrats who hold major public offices. All told, the Democrats provided for 568 of these "superdelegates": 377 party leaders and State and local officeholders (governors, mayors, legislators, and so on), chosen by their respective State party organizations, and 191 members of Congress (164 Representatives and 27 Senators), picked by the House and Senate Democratic caucuses.

In both parties, each State's delegation also includes a number of alternate delegates. The Republicans' rules have always provided for one alternate for each regular delegate. The Democrats, with their larger delegate body, have reduced the number of alternates in recent conventions. In 1984, the number was 1,313.

[21]To a very large extent, the GOP leaves the matter of selecting national convention delegates to its State party organizations and to State law.

The Democrats have added several rules in recent years that have in effect nationalized much of the delegate selection process. Their rules are a direct result of the divisive Democratic convention in Chicago in 1968 and of their loss of the presidential election later that year. Most of these rules are aimed at prompting broader involvement in the choosing of delegates (especially by the young, blacks, other minority groups, and women) and at making other aspects of convention organization and procedure more democratic. Those rules have been adopted by the Democratic National Committee and are enforced by it.

As an example, from 1980 on the DNC's rules require each State party organization to choose an equal number of men and women as convention delegates. (The RNC "requests" their State parties to do so.) Its rules also provide that *only* Democrats may take part in the party's delegate selection process. Thus, Democratic delegates cannot be chosen in an open primary (page 236) or by any other method in which Republicans, independents, or others may take part.

Presidential Primaries

Well over half of all the delegates to both national conventions now come from States where presidential primaries are held. Several of those primaries are major media events every fourth year. With their extensive television and other press coverage, they dominate much of the preconvention scene. Each of the serious contenders for either party's nomination has to make the best possible showing in at least most of them.

As we noted on page 240, a **presidential primary** is one or both of two things. Depending on the State, it is a process in which those who vote in a party's primary (1) elect some or all of a State party organization's delegates to the national convention, *and/or* (2) choose (express a preference) among various contenders for that party's presidential nomination.

The presidential primary first appeared in the early 1900s, as a part of the reform movement aimed at the boss-dominated convention system. Wisconsin passed the first presidential primary law in 1905, providing for the popular election of national convention delegates. Several States soon followed that lead, and Oregon added the preference feature in 1910.

By 1916 nearly half the States had adopted presidential primary laws. But many States later dropped the device. By 1968 it was found in only 16 States and the District of Columbia.

Efforts to reform the national convention process, especially in the Democratic Party, reversed that trend in the 1970s, however. Some form of the presidential primary was in place for 1984 in 28 States[22] and also in the District of Columbia and Puerto Rico.

Again, a presidential primary is either or both of two things: a delegate selection process and/or a preference election. Once that much has been said, the device becomes very hard to describe, except on a State-by-State basis. The difficulty comes largely from two sources: (1) the fact that the details of the process vary from State to State, and sometimes very considerably, and (2) the ongoing effects of reform efforts in both parties. In recent years, the parties, especially the Democratic Party at the national level, have written and rewritten rules to prompt more grass-roots participation in the delegate selection process. Those new rules have prompted many and frequent changes in State election laws.

Even a matter that seems so simple as the date for the primary shows the crazy-quilt pattern of State laws. By tradition, New Hampshire holds the first of the presidential primaries every four years, and it guards its first-in-the-nation distinction very jealously. For 1984, it slated its primary for March 6th. All other primaries were then scattered over the next three months. The last ones took place on June 5.

Presidential hopeful Gary Hart speaks to garment workers before New York's presidential primary.

[22]In Alabama, California, Connecticut, Florida, Georgia, Idaho, Illinois, Indiana, Louisiana, Maryland, Massachusetts, Montana, Nebraska, New Hampshire, New Jersey, New Mexico, New York, North Carolina, Ohio, Oregon, Pennsylvania, Rhode Island, South Dakota, Tennessee, Texas, Vermont, West Virginia, Wisconsin. In some of those States, the law permits but does not require a major party to hold a primary. Thus, in 1984, the Republicans held a presidential primary in Texas, but the Democrats did not. Also, these primaries sometimes occur under party rules in States without a presidential primary law. Arkansas has adopted a presidential primary law, to become effective in 1988.

From *The Herblock Gallery* (Simon & Schuster, 1968).

"You go first, sonny, then point me toward him"

Until fairly recently, most of these primaries were both delegate selection *and* preference exercises. Several primaries were also **"winner-take-all"** contests. That is, the presidential aspirant who won the preference vote automatically won the support of all delegates chosen at the primary.

* Winner-take-all primaries have all but disappeared, however, at least at the Statewide level.[23] For both 1976 and 1980, but not for 1984, the Democrats imposed a "proportional representation" rule. It required that no matter how Democratic delegates were chosen, they (and their convention votes) had to be apportioned among the contenders for the party's presidential nomination in line with the support each of them had within the party in that particular State. States with winner-take-all contests had to change their laws to accommodate the Democrats' rule. Most of those States did so by doing away with the winner-take-all feature.

The Democrat's proportional representation rule led several States—among them both Oregon and Wisconsin, the States that pioneered the presidential primary idea—to give up the popular selection of delegates.

More than half of the presidential primary States now hold *only* a preference primary, often called a "beauty contest." The delegates themselves are chosen later, at party conventions.[24]

Most of the preference contests are also "all-candidate" primaries: contests in which all generally recognized contenders for a party's presidential nomination are listed on that party's preference ballot.[25]

Evaluation of the Presidential Primary

No one who surveys the presidential primary system, as we have, needs to be told that it is very complicated, nor that it is filled with a number of confusing variations.

Nevertheless, these primaries play a vital role in the presidential nominating process. Overall, they are important for two major reasons. *First,* they tend to democratize the delegate selection process. *Second,* they usually force would-be nominees to test their candidacies in actual political combat.

Hard-fought contests seldom occur in the party in power. This tends to be true either because the President (1) is himself seeking reelection or (2) has groomed a successor. In either case the President is almost always able to get his way.

Both 1976 and 1980 were exceptions to that rule, but not altogether. In 1976 Ronald Reagan made a stiff run at President Ford in the Republican Party. Similarly, Senator Edward Kennedy gave President Carter a real fight in the Democratic Party in 1980. However, in the end the incumbent President *did* win his party's nomination.

For the party out of power, the primaries are often "knock-down, drag-out" battles.

---

[23]For 1984, the Democrats adopted a new rule that does allow for winner-take-all primaries, but only if they are held at the congressional district level. That is, the Democrats now permit winner-take-all primaries in those States where the presidential primary is held, separately, in each of the State's congressional districts.

[24]In most of these States, the delegates must be picked in line with the results of the preference primary—for example, for the Democrats in 1984, so many delegates for Walter Mondale, so many for Gary Hart, so many for Jesse Jackson, and so on.

[25]Until fairly recently, a contender could decide whether or not to enter a State's primary. Of course, most contenders picked and chose among the primaries, running in those States where they expected to win or at least do reasonably well, and avoiding the others. The "all-candidate" primary takes the enter-or-not decision out of the hands of the contenders. It gives the voters a full range of choice among the various contenders for a party's presidential nomination.

*ENRICHMENT Have students determine the type of presidential primary that is held in your State. Direct them to the county clerk's office, or the local board of elections for information.

A voter enters a New Hampshire polling place on the day of its primary elections in 1984.

Without the unifying force of the President as party leader, the several leaders and factions in the party vie with one another, vigorously, for the presidential nomination. Here one of the major functions of the presidential primaries can usually be seen: the screening out of lesser contenders to the point where only one or a few contenders are viable candidates for the nomination.

The recent "explosion" in the number of presidential primaries has had any number of consequences. Not the least centers on the candidates and their problems of time, effort, money, scheduling, and fatigue, to say nothing of the public's fatigue. Adlai Stevenson once said, in a day when there were only half as many primaries: "The hardest thing about any political campaign is how to win without proving that you are unworthy of winning."

Many critics think that each of the major parties should hold a single, *nationwide* presidential primary. Some critics would have both parties nominate their presidential candidates in those contests. They would do away with the conventions, except perhaps to pick vice presidential nominees or to write platforms. Indeed, President Wilson favored a constitutional amendment to that end back in 1913.

Other critics see a national primary as the best way for the parties either (1) to select all of their convention delegates or (2) to allow their voters to express their candidate preferences, which would then bind (instruct) the delegates from their States.

Still other critics favor a different plan. They would have a series of *regional* primaries, held at two- or three-week intervals in groups of States across the country.

Hope for any of these plans is dim at best. Each plan would require joint action by Congress, the States, and both major parties. Beyond that hurdle, recall this point from Chapter 9: The nominating process is an *intra*party process. However it is conducted, it can have a very *divisive* effect on a party; and the primary *magnifies* that ever-present possibility. In short, neither major party has ever been much interested in abandoning its national convention. Both parties see the convention as a device to promote compromise and, out of it, party unity.

Caucuses and Conventions In those States that do not hold presidential primaries, delegates are chosen in a system of caucuses and conventions.[26] Here, too, the details of the process are different from State to State. However, it works pretty much as we described it on pages 232-235.

The party's voters meet in local caucuses, generally at the precinct level. There they choose delegates to a local or district convention where delegates to the State convention are picked. At the State level, and sometimes in the district conventions, delegates to the national convention are chosen.

The caucus-convention process is the oldest method for picking national convention delegates. Notice, though, that less than half of all delegates to either party's convention

[26]More of the crazy-quilt point: Remember that in several of the presidential primary States, some and often all national delegates are actually picked in party conventions.

now come from those States that still use the caucus-convention process. The Iowa caucuses generally get the most attention every fourth year, largely because they are the first to be held in every presidential election season.

FOR REVIEW

1. **Identify:** national convention, delegate, caucus-convention.
2. To what extent does federal law deal with the national conventions? State law?
3. Which organization within the political parties plans and arranges for a party's national convention?
4. How are the delegates to each party's national convention apportioned?
5. What are the two possible purposes of a presidential primary?
6. Why are hard-fought presidential primaries fairly common in the party out of power and rather rare for the President's party?
7. Why have the two major parties shown little interest in abandoning the national convention in favor of a national primary?
8. By what other processes are convention delegates chosen?

7. The National Convention: Setting, Sessions, Outcomes

As You Read, Think About:

- How the national conventions operate.

Each party stages a national convention to do two major things: (1) to adopt a party platform and, most importantly, (2) to nominate its presidential and vice presidential candidates. A quick look at the setting in which these activities take place will reveal why the national conventions have been called "the greatest political show on earth." *

The Convention Setting

Each party's national convention meets in a huge auditorium lavishly hung with flags, bunting, and various party symbols. Portraits of great figures from the party's past adorn the hall. The front of it is dominated by a large platform and the speaker's rostrum from which the proceedings are managed. The floor itself is jammed with row upon row of hundreds of chairs. Standards and placards mark the seating reserved for each State delegation. Microphones and telephones are spotted at strategic points. There are extensive facilities for the army of press, radio, and television reporters, commentators, camera operators, technicians, and all their equipment. The galleries seat thousands who come from all over the country to see a spectacle H. L. Mencken once described this way:

> [T]here is something about a national convention that makes it as fascinating as a revival or a hanging. It is vulgar, it is ugly, it is stupid, it is tedious, it's hard upon both the cerebral centers and the *gluteus maximus*, and yet it is somehow charming. One sits through long sessions wishing heartily that all the delegates were dead and in hell—and then suddenly there comes a show so gaudy and hilarious, so melodramatic and obscene, so unimaginably exhilarating and preposterous that one lives a gorgeous year in an hour.

The Opening Session

Each party's convention generally runs four, sometimes five, days, and the order of business is much the same in both.

The opening session is called to order by the chairperson of the party's national committee. The "Star Spangled Banner" is sung, the official call is read, prayer is offered, and the temporary roll of delegates is called. Welcoming speeches are made by the national chairperson and party dignitaries.

The national chairperson then announces a slate of temporary officers—all named by the national committee—for the convention, one of whom is the temporary presiding officer. The delegates promptly elect them.

*REINFORCEMENT Have the class discuss: What purposes does a lavish convention serve? Does it affect public opinion?

Each party's national convention is both intensively and extensively covered by the news media, whose members record—and, report on—what has been called "the greatest political show on earth."

The temporary chairperson then takes the rostrum to give the first major speech. This speech and the *keynote address* that follows it run to a predictable pattern: the party is praised, the opposition is attacked, a plea for party harmony is made, and a smashing victory at the polls is forecast.

Following the keynoter's oratorical efforts, the delegates routinely elect the convention's standing committees. There are four major committees at every convention: rules and order of business, permanent organization, credentials, and platform and resolutions. Each State delegation now has two members, a man and a woman, on each of them. After these committees are selected, the first session generally ends.

The Second and Third Sessions

The next two or three, and sometimes four, sessions of the convention are given over to more speeches by leading party figures and to the receipt of committee reports. In the more recent conventions, both parties have slated these sessions for the late afternoon and/or early evening, hoping, of course, for prime time on network television.

Typically, the committee on rules and order of business reports first. It regularly recommends the adoption of the rules of the last convention, with, perhaps, a few changes. Its report, which also presents an agenda for the rest of the convention, is generally accepted with little or no dissent. Both parties have at times seen vigorous fights over their rules, however.

The credentials committee prepares the permanent roll of delegates entitled to seats and votes in the convention. Occasionally, there are contests over the seating of particular delegates and even whole delegations. When this happens, it generally involves a State in which the party is faction-ridden and delegates are chosen by the caucus-convention process. The credentials committee must decide those disputes. Its decisions may be appealed, but its report is almost always adopted, unchanged, on the floor.

The committee on permanent organization nominates a slate of permanent convention officers. Their selection, and especially the naming of the permanent chairperson, can be a major test of strength among the rivals for the presidential nomination. Those officers run the remaining sessions of the

*REINFORCEMENT The fight for the presidential nomination can be a "knock-down, drag-out" affair. Ask the class to discuss reasons why this may be so.

FOCUS ON:

Party Platforms . . . Like Jell-O?

Voters support presidential candidates for many different reasons. Recall, we looked at the whole complex of factors that affect voter behavior in Chapter 8. There we noted the role of issues in the voter-decision mix.

Much of what we said can be put this way: The promises a party and its candidates make—their stands on the issues of the day—have a major impact on the way the voters vote on election day.

Many of those promises/stands appear in the party's **platform,** of course, and the usual view of those documents is that they are designed for candidates to "run" on, not to "stand" on. The Republicans' presidential nominee in 1964, Barry Goldwater, has described them this way: "Platforms are written to be ignored and forgotten. . . . Like Jell-O shimmering on a dessert plate, there is usually little substance and nothing you can get your teeth into." Still, platforms do have their importance, as we suggest elsewhere.

Certainly, politicians, including Presidents, do sometimes break their promises. Ronald Reagan, like every President before him, is no exception to that rule. The Republican platform in 1980 promised to balance the federal budget. In fact, the budget's deficits soared to record heights after he took office. Among other examples, Mr. Reagan called for an end to peacetime draft registration; but, as President, he extended it.

Yet, we frequently forget how very often politicians do exactly what they say they will do. For every promise bent or broken, many more are kept. Thus, in 1980, Mr. Reagan and the GOP platform promised to raise defense spending, trim domestic social welfare programs, cut federal income taxes, and curb government regulatory activities. Each of these major pledges was, in fact, kept.

A Republican delegate reviews his party's platform.

In short, the notion that parties and politicians never produce policies out of promises does not hold up.

1. Obtain a copy of the Democratic and Republican party platforms. These are available from the National Committees in Washington, D.C. Make a table that compares and contrasts the two parties' positions on 10 major issues. Possible issues might include: tax reform, federal funding for education, defense policy, public housing, and federal aid to the States.
2. Summarize what you learned about each party's stand on each issue. Where do they agree and disagree? What can you say about each party's platform?

convention. The permanent chairperson takes the rostrum with another of those lengthy speeches glorifying the party, assailing the opposition, urging party unity, and foretelling a smashing victory in November.

The report of the committee on platform and resolutions, in the form of a proposed platform, usually reaches the floor by the third session.

Much of the party's platform emerges from a draft drawn up by party leaders or, for the party in power, by the President and his advisers. A struggle may, and often does, develop within the committee, and at times the fight spills over to the convention floor.

Platform-writing is a fine art. The document is supposed to be a basic statement of the party's principles and its stands on major policy matters. At the same time, it is a campaign statement intended to win as many votes as possible, while alienating none. So, both parties tend to produce somewhat generalized, less than specific, comments on many of the questions of the day.

Still, platforms do contain hard and fast policy positions. At the same time, platforms reflect the compromise nature of both our politics and each of the two major parties.*

Democratic nominees Walter Mondale and Geraldine Ferraro accept the cheers of delegates.

The Final Sessions

By its fourth, sometimes the fifth, session, the convention at last comes to its chief task: the nomination of the party's presidential candidate.

The names of any number of contenders may be offered to the delegates. For each contender, a nominating speech and then several seconding speeches are made. They are lavish hymns of praise, extolling the virtues of "The man who . . ." Although the "who" is well known before the nominator begins to speak, traditionally, that person's name is little more than hinted at until the very end of the speech. Its final announcement sets off a lengthy, wild, noisy demonstration on the floor. These "spontaneous" demonstrations—supposed to show widespread support for the aspirant, whether real or not—are carefully planned.[27]

After all the nominating speeches and their seconds have been made, the balloting begins. The secretary calls the States alphabetically, and each chairperson announces the vote of his or her delegation. Each complete roll call is known as a "ballot." In both parties, a majority vote is needed to select the presidential candidate. Balloting goes on until someone has the magic number.

Most often, the first ballot produces a choice. In the 22 conventions each party has held in the 1900–1984 period, the Republicans have made a first ballot nomination 18 times and the Democrats, 17 times.[28]

[27]Some candidates offered to a convention have no real chance of becoming the party's presidential nominee, but are put forward for some other reason. Thus, a "favorite son" may be offered because a State delegation wants to honor one of its own.

[28]From 1832 until 1936, the Democrats required a two-thirds vote for nomination. The Republicans have required a simple majority for nomination since their first convention in 1856. A convention can, and a few in both parties have, become deadlocked—that is, find itself unable to make a choice between the top two, or sometimes three, contenders for the nomination. In that event, a "dark horse" (someone who did not appear to be a likely choice before the convention) may finally be nominated. The most spectacular deadlock occurred at the Democratic convention in New York in 1924. The convention took 123 separate ballots, over a period of nine days, before John W. Davis became the party's candidate.

*ENRICHMENT Have the class discuss: How strictly should a presidential candidate be held to his platform? Does the American public expect the elected President to fulfill all campaign promises?

Once the presidential nomination has been decided, the choice of a running mate comes as an anticlimax. The vice presidential nominee is almost invariably the choice of the just-nominated presidential candidate; see page 373.

With candidates named, the convention comes to the last major item on its agenda: the presidential candidate's acceptance speech. As the acceptance speech ends, the delegates—all of them superpatriots of the party—nearly tear the convention hall apart.

In both 1980 and 1984, Ronald Reagan won his party's nomination on the first ballot.

Whom Does the Party Nominate?

If an incumbent President wants another term, the answer is almost always easy. The President is almost certain to get the nomination, and usually with no real opposition from within the party. Indeed, in this century, each time the incumbent has sought the nomination, he has received it. The President's advantages are immense: the majesty and publicity of the office and close control of the party's machinery.[29]

When the President is not in the field, from two or three to a dozen or so more or less serious contenders surface in the preconvention period. At least two or three candidates usually survive to contest the prize at the convention.

Who among them will win the nomination? The record argues this answer: the one who is, in the jargon of politics, the most *available*—the one who is the most nominatable and electable. Conventions want to pick candidates who can *win*, candidates with the broadest possible appeal within the party and to the electorate.

Most presidential candidates have come to their nominations with substantial and well-known records in public office. But those records have not been studded with controversies that could have antagonized important elements within the party or among the voting public. Generally, presidential candidates have served in *elective* office, where they have shown a considerable vote-getting ability. Seldom does a candidate step from the business world or from the military directly into the role of candidate, as did Wendell Willkie in 1940 or Dwight Eisenhower in 1952.

Historically, the governorships of larger States have produced the largest number of presidential candidacies. Eleven of the 20 men nominated by the two major parties between 1900 and 1956 were either then serving or had once served as a governor.

For a time, however, the Senate became the prime source. In the four elections from 1960 through 1972, each major party nominee had been a Senator. None had ever been a governor.

But the old pattern seems to have been restored. Jimmy Carter, the former governor of Georgia, was nominated by the Democrats in 1976 and 1980. Ronald Reagan, former governor of California, was the GOP choice in 1980 and again in 1984.

---

[29] In fact, only four sitting Presidents have ever been denied nomination: John Tyler, by the Whigs in 1844; Millard Fillmore, by the Whigs in 1852; Franklin Pierce, by the Democrats in 1856; and Chester Arthur, by the Republicans in 1884.

BUILDING GOVERNMENT SKILLS

Working on a Political Campaign

What can you contribute to a political campaign? The answer is plenty. Campaigns for every office—from school board to the Presidency—depend on volunteers. Volunteer campaign workers carry out the day-to-day tasks that keep a campaign going.

How Campaigns Are Organized

If you plan to work on a campaign, knowing how it is organized will be helpful. The candidate is "the boss." Although campaign organizations vary, the following members are likely to be part of any campaign.

The campaign manager helps the candidate develop strategy and is the adviser. He or she schedules the candidate for appearances or speaking engagements.

The press secretary writes press releases about the candidate's activities. A press release is a short article sent to the media to publicize the candidate. The press secretary makes sure that the press is kept well-informed about the candidate.

Fund-raisers are responsible for obtaining money to support the campaign—to pay for mailings, political advertising, and travel. The treasurer keeps track of campaign expenses and revenue. He or she has to ensure that federal and State campaign finance regulations are strictly followed.

Volunteer coordinators schedule and recruit volunteers to work for the campaign. Candidates for national, State, and local offices set up a campaign headquarters. To find a campaign office close to you, contact the local party organization.

What to Expect

Usually you will talk to the volunteer coordinator to establish a schedule for working on the campaign. Some kinds of work you may perform include:

Office work: Campaigns receive much mail and send much mail. Letters have to be written, typed, and sent. Phones ring constantly and have to be answered. You may also be asked to enter information into a computer. Many candidates keep lists of supporters on the computer.

Fund-raising: You could be asked to contact the candidate's supporters by phone to ask for contributions. Most campaigns provide fund-raisers with a script to follow.

Leafletting: Many campaigns choose busy days to hand out brochures and flyers.

Door-to-door canvassing: Campaign workers also try to enlist support for the candidate by talking to the people in their neighborhoods. Information useful for developing campaign strategies is sometimes collected by polling.

Organizing: The main purpose of campaigns is to organize support for the candidate. Toward this effort, some campaign workers hold informal meetings in their homes. Neighbors and friends may learn about the candidate or meet the candidate at these gatherings.

Poll work: On election day, campaign workers for the candidates gather outside of every polling place handing out flyers and saying to arriving voters, "We hope you will consider voting for Smith for school board."

1. What kind of activity could you organize in your area to gain support for a candidate?
2. For each activity described, who would be in charge of: (a) deciding in which States a presidential candidate should campaign for the longest periods; (b) contacting local television stations to let them know about the candidate's next appearance; (c) talking to local businesses to ask for financial support; (d) filling out campaign finance disclosure reports.

Despite the few exceptions, most notably Democrats Alfred E. Smith in 1928 and John F. Kennedy in 1960, most leading contenders for major party presidential nominations have been Protestants. Most have also come from the larger and doubtful States. Thus, candidates from such "pivotal" States as New York, Ohio, Illinois, and California are more available than those from smaller States. From this standpoint, the nominations of Senator Barry Goldwater of Arizona by the Republicans in 1964 and Senator George McGovern of South Dakota by the Democrats in 1972 were a little exceptional. So, too, was the Democratic nomination of Jimmy Carter from Georgia in 1976.

Neither party has, to this point, seriously considered a woman as its candidate for the Presidency—or, until 1984, for the Vice Presidency. Nor has either party seriously contemplated a black for either role.

The candidates usually have a pleasing and healthy appearance, seem to be happily married, and have a happy (and exploitable) family. Adlai Stevenson, the Democratic nominee in 1952 and 1956, and Ronald Reagan, the GOP candidate in 1980 and 1984, are the only major party nominees ever to have been divorced.

A well-developed speaking ability has always been a major factor of availability. Of course, being able to project well over television has become a *must* over the past 25 years or so.

FOR REVIEW

1. **Identify:** temporary chairperson, permanent chairperson, availability.
2. What is the general tone of a party platform? Why?
3. What is *the* major purpose of a national convention?
4. Why are incumbent Presidents almost certain to win their party's nomination to another term if they want it?
5. What does the term *availability* mean in presidential politics?

8. The Presidential Election: The Electoral College

As You Read, Think About:

- Why the electoral college was established.
- The way in which the electoral college system functions.

For a short period after the conventions, the opposing candidates rest and plan their campaigns. Then the presidential campaign,* the grinding effort to win votes, begins in earnest.

Candidates exert every means at their disposal to put their ideas before the voters and in the best possible light. Radio and television speeches; "whistle-stop" tours; press conferences and press releases; public rallies; party dinners; newspaper, radio, and television advertisements; campaign stickers and buttons; placards and pamphlets; billboards and matchcovers—all bombard the voters in behalf of each party's nominees. The candidates pose for hundreds of photographs, shake thousands of hands, and strive to convince the electorate that a victory for the other side would mean hard times for the country. Whether the campaign really changes an important number of votes is a debatable point. The massive efforts continue to election eve.

The Electoral College Today

The presidential campaign ends with election day. Millions of voters go to the polls in all 50 states and the District of Columbia.

Here we come to one of the least well understood parts of the American political process. As the people vote in the presidential election, they do *not* choose among the contenders for the Presidency. Instead, they vote to elect presidential electors.

Remember, the Constitution provides for the election of the President by the electoral college, in which each State has as many electors as it has members of Congress. The Framers expected that the electors would use their own judgment—be free agents—in selecting a President. However, for more

*REINFORCEMENT Potential presidential candidates often begin their campaigns as soon as the presidential election is over. Ask the class if this is currently the case.

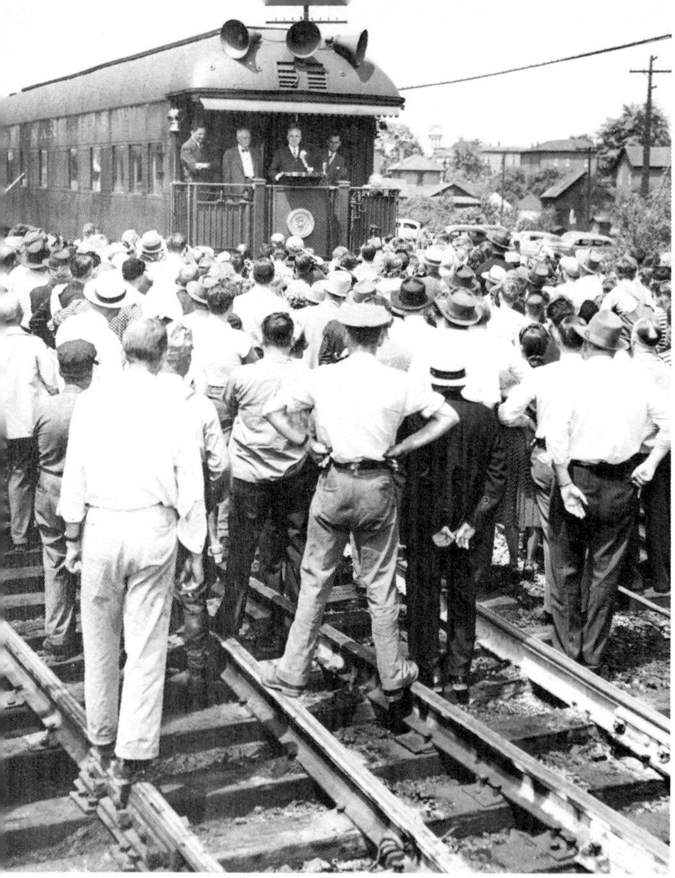

During his 1948 campaign, President Truman traveled 30,000 miles by train, making quick "whistle-stops" to speak to crowds of people.

than 180 years now, the parties have nominated slates of elector-candidates in each State. The electors, once chosen, are "rubber stamps." Despite the Framers' intent, the electors are expected to vote automatically for their party's candidates for President and Vice President.

In short, the electors go through the *form* set out in the Constitution, in order to meet the *letter* of the Constitution. However, their behavior is a far cry from the original *intent.*

The electors are chosen by popular vote in every State[30] and on the same day everywhere, the Tuesday after the first Monday in November every fourth year. In 1988 it will be held on November 8.

The electors are chosen at-large in every State except Maine.[31] They are chosen on a "winner-take-all" basis. The presidential candidate—technically, the slate of elector-candidates—receiving the largest popular vote in a State wins *all* of that State's electoral votes. Today, the names of the individual elector-candidates appear on the ballot in less than a fourth of the States. In most, only the names of the presidential and vice presidential candidates are listed. They stand as "shorthand" for the elector slates. *

The electors meet at their State capitol on the date set by Congress, now the Monday following the second Wednesday in the month of December.[32] There they each cast their electoral votes, one for President and one for Vice President. The ballots of the electors, signed and sealed, are sent by registered mail to the President of the Senate in Washington.[33]

Which party has won a majority of the electoral votes, and who then will be the next President of the United States, is usually known by midnight of election day, more than a month before the electors cast their ballots. But the *formal* election of the President and Vice President *finally* takes place on January 6.[34]

On that date, the President of the Senate opens the electoral votes from each State and counts them before a joint session of Congress. The candidate who receives a ma-

[30]The Constitution (Article II, Section 1, Clause 2) says that the electors are to be chosen in each State "in such manner as the legislature thereof may direct." In several States the legislatures themselves chose the electors in the first several elections. By 1832, however, every State except South Carolina had provided for popular election. The electors were picked by the legislature in South Carolina through the elections of 1860. Since then, all presidential electors have been chosen by popular vote in every State, with two exceptions. The State legislatures chose the electors in Florida in 1868 and in Colorado in 1876.

[31]Since the 1972 election, Maine has used the "district plan." Two of that State's four electors are chosen from the State at-large and the other two from each of the State's congressional districts. The district plan was used by several States in the first several presidential elections, but every State except South Carolina had provided for the choice of the electors from the State at-large by 1832. Since then, the district plan has been used only by Michigan in 1892 and by Maine in the last four elections.

[32]Article II, Section I, Clause 4 provides that the date Congress sets "shall be the same throughout the United States." The 12th Amendment provides that the electors "shall meet in their respective States."

[33]Two copies are also sent to the Archivist of the United States, two to the State's Secretary of State, and one to the local federal district court.

[34]Unless that day falls on a Sunday, as it did most recently in 1985. Then, the ballot-counting is held the following day.

*REINFORCEMENT Have the class discuss whether the "winner-take-all" aspect of choosing electors implies that some of the people of the State are not represented in the electoral college.

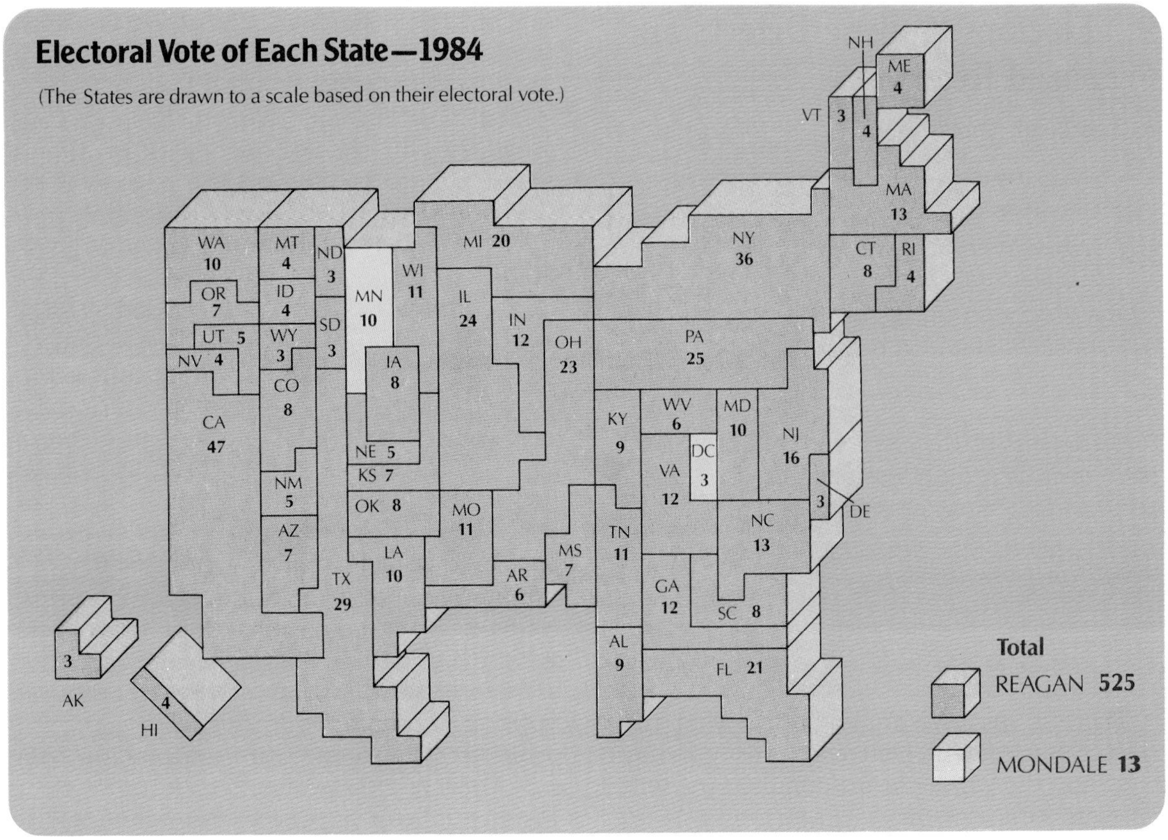

Why does the electoral vote usually fail to reflect the popular vote cast for each candidate in each State? (See map, page 223.)

jority of the electors' votes for President is declared elected, as is the candidate with a majority of the votes for Vice President.

If no one has a majority for President—at least 270 of the 538 electoral votes—the election is thrown into the House of Representatives. This happened in 1800, and again in 1824. The House chooses a President from among the top three candidates in the electoral college. Each State delegation has one vote, and it takes a majority of 26 to elect. If the House fails to choose a President by January 20, the 20th Amendment provides that the newly elected Vice President shall act as President until it does.[35]

If no person receives a majority for Vice President, the Senate decides between the top two candidates. It takes a majority of the whole Senate to elect. The Senate has had to choose a Vice President only once. It elected Richard M. Johnson in 1837.

FOR REVIEW

1. **Identify:** electoral votes.
2. How many electors does each State have? How are they chosen?
3. What is the total number of electors? How many electoral votes are needed to win the Presidency? The Vice Presidency?
4. If no candidate has at least that many votes, how is the President then chosen? The Vice President?

---

[35]The 20th Amendment further provides that "the Congress may by law provide for the case wherein neither a President-elect nor a Vice President-elect shall have qualified" by inauguration day. Congress has done so in the Succession Act of 1947; see page 375. The Speaker of the House would "act as President . . . until a President or Vice President shall have qualified."

1.4, 2.1, 2.2, 3.1; 4.B, 4.F

9. Electoral College Defects and Proposed Reforms

As You Read, Think About:

- What the major criticisms are of the electoral college.
- What proposals have been made to reform the electoral college.
- What the advantages and disadvantages are of each reform proposal.

Criticisms of the electoral college system have been heard almost from the beginning and so, too, have proposals for its reform. There are three major weaknesses in the present arrangement.

The First Major Defect

There is the ever-present threat that the electoral vote will contradict the popular vote, and the winner of the popular vote will *not* win the Presidency.

This continuing threat is largely the result of two factors. The most important is the "winner-take-all" feature. In each State the winning candidate customarily receives *all* that State's electoral votes. The other major party candidate's popular votes count for nothing in terms of the final outcome. In 1976, for example, Jimmy Carter carried Ohio by a paper-thin margin, by only 9,333 votes, less than three-tenths of 1 percent. Despite the fact that more than two million people in Ohio voted for Gerald Ford, Carter won all 25 of the State's electoral votes.

The other major problem is the way the electoral votes are distributed among the States. Remember that each State has two electors because of its Senate seats, regardless of its population. For this reason, the distribution of electoral votes cannot begin to match the facts of population and voter distribution.

Take the extreme case to illustrate this situation: California, the largest State, now has 47 electoral votes, or one for each 503,586 persons, based on its 1980 population of 23,668,562. Alaska has three electoral votes, or one for each 133,494 persons, with its 1980 population of 400,481.

The popular vote winner has, in fact, failed to win the Presidency three times: 1824, 1876, and 1888. In 1824, Andrew Jackson won the largest share (a plurality, but not a majority) of the popular votes: 151,174, or 40.3 percent of the total. Jackson's nearest rival, John Quincy Adams, received 113,122 votes, or 30.9 percent. Ninety-nine of the 261 electors then voted for Jackson, again a plurality but far short of the constitutionally required majority. The election thus went to the House, and early in 1825, it elected Adams to the Presidency.[36]

In the election of 1876, Republican candidate Rutherford B. Hayes received 4,034,311 popular votes and his Democratic opponent, Samuel J. Tilden, won 4,288,548. Tilden, with a popular plurality of 254,237, received 184 electoral votes. Hayes won 185 electoral votes and so became President.[37]

In 1888 President Grover Cleveland won 5,534,488 popular votes, 90,596 more than his Republican opponent, Benjamin Harrison. But Harrison received 233 electoral votes to Cleveland's 168, and so became the 23rd President.

The system has not "misfired" since 1888, but it *could* have happened on *several* occasions. In 1976 Jimmy Carter defeated his Republican opponent, Gerald Ford,

[36]Both Adams and Jackson were Democratic-Republicans; remember that the election of 1824 occurred during the one-party Era of Good Feeling; see page 189. Popular votes were cast in only 18 of the 24 States in 1824. The electors were chosen by the legislatures in Delaware, Georgia, Louisiana, New York, South Carolina, and Vermont. The popular vote figures given here are only approximately correct. Vote counts were neither well kept nor well recorded in 1824. These figures, as most of the popular vote results cited in this book, are drawn from the authoritative *Guide to U.S. Elections*, Congressional Quarterly, Inc., 2nd ed., 1985.

[37]The election of 1876 is often called "the Stolen Election." Two conflicting sets of electoral votes were received from Florida (4 votes), Louisiana (8 votes), and South Carolina (7 votes), and the validity of one vote from Oregon was disputed. Congress set up an Electoral Commission—with five Senators, five Representatives, and five Supreme Court Justices—to decide the matter. The Commissioners, eight Republicans and seven Democrats, voted on strict party lines, awarding all of the disputed votes, and so the Presidency, to Hayes.[20]

*REINFORCEMENT Have the class discuss weaknesses of the electoral system. Is it a valid system?

by 1,678,069 popular votes, but won only a bare majority of the popular vote.[38]

	Popular Vote	%	Electoral Vote	%
Carter	40,825,839	50.03	297	55.2
Ford	39,147,770	47.97	240	44.6
Others	1,629,737	2.00	1	0.2

If only a handful of voters in a few States had voted for Ford, instead of Carter, Ford would have had a majority of the electoral votes and so kept the Presidency. Different combinations of several States can be used to play this game, but the simplest one involves Ohio and Hawaii. If only 4,667 of the 2,009,959 Carter votes in Ohio (25 electoral votes) and only 3,687 of the 147,376 Carter votes in Hawaii (4 electoral votes) had gone to Ford instead, Ford would have received 270 electoral votes. Thus, Ford would have had a bare majority of the electoral votes and so won the election.

Several other presidential elections can be used to illustrate the point, as well. In 1960, John F. Kennedy won a popular plurality of

	Popular Vote	%	Electoral Vote	%
Kennedy	34,221,334	49.7	303	56.4
Nixon	34,106,671	49.6	219	40.8
Byrd	—	—	15	2.8
Others	500,945	0.7	—	—

[38]To this point, 13 Presidents have been elected although they did not win a majority of the popular vote: John Quincy Adams won in the House in 1824, Rutherford B. Hayes in 1876, and Benjamin Harrison in 1888. Each won the electoral vote count while losing the popular vote contest, as we have noted. The other 10 all were elected with a plurality, but not a majority, of the popular vote. These "minority Presidents": James K. Polk (1844), Zachary Taylor (1848), James Buchanan (1856), Abraham Lincoln (1860), James A. Garfield (1880), Grover Cleveland (1884 and 1892), Woodrow Wilson (1912 and 1916), Harry Truman (1948), John F. Kennedy (1960), Richard Nixon (1968).

114,673 votes—less than two-tenths of 1 percent of all the votes cast—over the Republican candidate, Richard M. Nixon. If only a comparatively few voters in a few States had voted for Nixon rather than Kennedy—for example, 4,430 in Illinois (27 electoral votes) and 23,122 in Texas (24 electoral votes) —Nixon would have won. Like Carter in 1976, Kennedy would still have been the popular vote winner.

In short, the "winner-take-all" factor produces an electoral vote result that is, at best, only a very distorted reflection of the popular vote. Even the lopsided results in the 1984 race demonstrate the point:

	Popular Vote	%	Electoral Vote	%
Reagan	54,455,074	58.8	525	97.6
Mondale	37,577,137	40.5	13	2.4
Others	620,582	0.7	—	—

The Second Major Defect

Nothing in the Constitution, nor in any federal statute, *requires* the electors to vote for the candidate favored by the popular vote in their States. Several States do have such laws, but they are of doubtful constitutionality, and none has ever been enforced.

The electors are expected to vote for the candidate who carries their State, and as loyal partisans, they almost always do. Thus far, electors have "broken their pledges" —voted for someone other than their party's presidential nominee—on only eight occasions: in 1796, 1820, 1948, 1956, 1960, 1968, 1972, and 1976. In the most recent case, one Republican elector from the State of Washington voted for Ronald Reagan instead of Gerald Ford, who had turned back Reagan's bid for the GOP nomination in 1976.

In no case has the vote of a "faithless elector" had a bearing on the outcome of a presidential election—but the potential is certainly there.

The Third Major Defect

In any presidential election, it is possible that the contest will be decided in the House of Representatives. This has happened only twice, as we know, and not since 1824. But in several other elections—especially in 1912, 1924, 1948, and most recently in 1968 (see table below) a strong third-party bid has threatened to win enough electoral votes to make it impossible for either majority party candidate to win in the electoral college.

	Popular Vote	%	Electoral Vote	%
Nixon	31,785,148	43.4	301	55.9
Humphrey	31,274,503	42.7	191	35.5
Wallace	9,901,151	13.5	46	8.6
Others	242,568		—	—

George Wallace, the American Independent Party's candidate, won five States and received 46 electoral votes, as the map on page 223 shows. If Democrat Hubert Humphrey had carried Alaska, Delaware, Missouri, Nevada, and Wisconsin—States where Richard Nixon's margin was thin and in which Wallace had a substantial vote—Nixon's electoral vote would have been 268 and Humphrey's 224. Neither would have had a majority. The House would then have had to choose among Humphrey, Nixon, and Wallace.[39]

Three serious objections can be raised to election by the House. First, the voting in such cases is by States, not by individual members. A small State, such as Alaska or Nevada, would have as much weight as even the most populous States, California and New York. Second, if the Representatives from a State were so divided that no candidate was favored by a majority of them, the State would lose its vote. Third, the Constitution requires a majority of the States for election in the House—today 26. If a strong third-party candidate were involved, a decision by inauguration day could prove to be almost impossible for the House.[40]

Proposed Reforms

The defects in the electoral college system have long been recognized. Constitutional amendments to change the process have been introduced in every term of Congress since 1789. Most of the reforms that have been offered can be grouped under three headings: the district plan, the proportional plan, and direct popular election.

The District Plan Under this plan, the electors would be chosen in each State as are members of Congress. That is, two electors would be chosen from the State at-large, and they would cast their electoral votes in line with the statewide popular vote result. The other electors would be elected, separately, in each of the State's congressional districts, and their votes would be cast in accord with a popular vote result in their district.[41]

[39]In 1968 Wallace received more popular votes than any other third-party presidential candidate, before or since. But Theodore Roosevelt in 1912 and Robert M. La Follette in 1924 each received a *larger share* of the popular vote, 27.4 percent and 16.6 percent, respectively; see page 195.

In 1948 the States Rights (Dixiecrat) candidate, Strom Thurmond of South Carolina, carried four southern States and received 39 electoral votes. Although Harry Truman won the election with 303 electoral votes to GOP candidate Thomas Dewey's 189, he won in several States by very slim margins. A switch of fewer than 21,000 votes in two large States—16,708 in Illinois and 3,554 in Ohio—would have given those States' electoral votes to Dewey, reduced Truman's total to 250, and thrown the election into the House.

[40]In such a case, Section 3 of the 20th Amendment states that "the Vice President-elect shall act as President until a President shall have qualified." If no Vice President-elect is available, the Presidential Succession Act (page 375) would come into play. Notice that it is even mathematically possible for the minority party in the House to have control of a majority of the individual State delegations. That party could then elect its candidate, even though he or she may have run second or even third in both the popular and the electoral vote contests.

[41]Maine now uses the district plan, as we noted on page 392. Any other State could do so, but it would take a constitutional amendment to make its use mandatory in all States.

*REINFORCEMENT Ask the students which of the proposed electoral college reform plans they would choose, and why they prefer it to the others.

The district plan would do away with the "winner-take-all" problem in the present system. Its supporters have argued that it would make the electoral vote a more accurate reflection of the popular returns.

The strongest argument against the plan is that it would *not* eliminate the possibility that the loser of the popular vote could still win the electoral vote. In fact, had it been in effect in 1960, Richard Nixon would have received 278 electoral votes, and he, not John Kennedy, would have won the Presidency.

Further, the results under the district plan would depend very much on how the congressional districts were drawn in each State. Its use would be yet another motive for gerrymandering.

The Proportional Plan Under this arrangement, each presidential candidate would receive the same share of a State's electoral vote as he or she received of that State's popular vote. If a candidate won 40 percent of the votes cast in a State with 20 electoral votes, he or she would get eight State electoral votes.

Clearly, this plan would cure the "winner-take-all" problem. The plan would also do away with the "faithless elector" possibility. Also, as its backers claim, it would produce an electoral vote more nearly in line with the popular vote, at least for *each State*.

The proportional plan would not, however, necessarily produce the same result *nationally*. Because each of the smaller States is overweighted by its two Senate-based electors, the proportional plan would still make it possible for the loser of the popular vote to win the Presidency in the electoral vote. In fact, this would have happened in 1896. William Jennings Bryan would have defeated William McKinley even though McKinley had a comfortable popular vote margin of 596,985 (5.1 percent).[42]

[42]In the closest of all the presidential elections, Winfield S. Hancock would have defeated James A. Garfield in 1880, even though Garfield had a popular plurality of only 1,898 votes, 0.0213 percent. On the other hand, there would have been no "Stolen Election" in 1876, and Cleveland would have defeated Harrison in 1888; see page 394.

Many critics of the proportional plan worry about its consequences for the two-party system and, therefore, for the whole fabric of the American political system. The adoption of the plan would almost certainly mean a substantial increase in both the number and the vigor of minor parties. Minor-party candidates would regularly receive at least some share of the electoral vote. The chance that one or more of them might be able to force a presidential election into the House would also be much greater.[43]

Direct Popular Election The proposal most often made, and most supported, is the most obvious one: Do away with the electoral college system altogether and provide for the direct popular election of the President.

The arguments for direct election seem overpowering. The strongest one is that it would support the democratic ideal: Each vote would count, and equally, in the national result. The winner would always be the majority or plurality choice. The dangers and confusions of the present system would be ended and replaced by a simple and easily understood process. Opinion polls have long shown that there is overwhelming public support for direct election.

Several "practical" obstacles stand in the way of this proposal, however. Because of them, there seems little real chance of its adoption any time soon.[44]

The constitutional amendment process itself is a major stumbling block. First, there are three built-in minority vetoes in the amendment process. Two vetoes are in Con-

[43]Most of the plan's backers agree than an inrease in minor party clout would mean that the popular vote winner would often fail to gain a clear majority of the electoral vote. In 1976, for example, Jimmy Carter would have received 261.148 electoral votes to Gerald Ford's 258.860. (The typical proportional plan would carry the arithmetic to three decimal points.) Hence, backers would reduce the majority requirements to that of a plurality of at least 40 percent. If no candidate won at least 40 percent of the electoral votes, a second election, with the two front-runners, would be held.

[44]The House of Representatives did approve a direct election amendment by the necessary two-thirds vote in 1969. The measure was killed by a Senate filibuster in 1970. President Carter championed a similar proposal, but it was rejected by a Senate floor vote in 1979.

gress, where one-third plus one of the members of *either* house can block the proposal of an amendment. Also, one-fourth plus one of the State legislatures or conventions can defeat an amendment once it is proposed.

Second, the smaller States are greatly overrepresented in the electoral college. They would lose that advantage in a direct election plan. Enough Representatives, or Senators, or small States would probably oppose a direct election amendment and so kill it.

In addition to those who take the small-State view here, many others oppose the reform. Some argue that it would weaken federalism, because the States, as *States*, would lose their role in the choice of a President.

Others believe that direct election would put too great a load on the election process. They say that because *every* vote cast in *each* State would count in the *national* result, the candidates would have to campaign strenuously in *every* State. The impact that would have on campaign time, effort, and finance would be huge and, opponents argue, probably unmanageable.[45]

Some insist that direct election would be an added spur to ballot-box stuffing and other forms of vote fraud. That result, they predict, would lead to lengthy, bitter, highly explosive post-election challenges. Such disputes could tear the nation apart.

In many States, a State-wide election often hangs on the behavior of some specific group in the electorate. The result depends on how those voters cast their ballots or, even more importantly, on how heavily they do or do not turn out to vote. Thus, for example, the black vote in Chicago is often decisive in the presidential election in Illinois. In a direct election, however, these groups would not hold the balance of power, the clout, they now have. As a result, many of these groups are also against the direct election plan.

All in all, given these objections, there seems little real chance for the adoption of the direct election proposal within the foreseeable future. Little real possibility, that is, *unless* the electoral college system malfunctions in another presidential election. Should that happen, a direct election amendment would very likely be adopted quickly.

The National Bonus Plan Another and very different plan for reform has recently surfaced. It is the "national bonus plan." At first glance, the plan seems quite complicated. In fact, it is not.

The national bonus plan would keep much of the present electoral college system, and especially its winner-take-all feature. It would weight that system very heavily in favor of the winner of the popular vote, however.

Under the plan, a national pool of 102 electoral votes would be awarded, automatically, to the winner of the popular vote contest. That is, that bloc of electoral votes would be added to the electoral votes that candidate won in the election. If all those votes added up to a majority of the electoral college—at least 321—that candidate would be declared the winner of the Presidency. In the unlikely event that they did not, a runoff election between the two front-runners in the popular vote would then be held.

The advocates of this plan see the electors themselves as unnecessary to it, and so would do away with them. They say that their plan meets all major objections to the present electoral college system and to all other proposals for its reform. They claim the national bonus plan would almost absolutely guarantee that the winner of the popular vote would also be the winner of the electoral vote.

[45]Under the present winner-take-all system, the candidates give most of their attention (1) to the doubtful States rather than those States that are fairly safe or those in which there is little real chance of winning and, especially (2) to the larger States, because of their large blocs of electoral votes. In fact, it is possible for a candidate to win the Presidency by carrying only the 12 largest States, because they have a total of 279 electoral votes, 9 more than the 270 needed to win. Those 12 States and their electoral votes are: California (47), New York (36), Texas (29), Pennsylvania (25), Illinois (24), Ohio (23), Florida (21), Michigan (20), New Jersey (16), North Carolina (13), Massachusetts (13), and Indiana (12). (Georgia and Virginia also have 12 electoral votes apiece, but are not among the largest States.)

REINFORCEMENT Have the class discuss: Does the national bonus plan seem worthwhile? Would it work? What are its advantages and disadvantages?

In the "Stolen Election" of 1876, Republican Rutherford Hayes won the Presidency by one electoral vote (185-184). Here, a commission's review of 20 disputed electoral votes is passed to the President *pro tem* in a joint session of Congress. (See page 395.)

To date, the national bonus plan has not attracted very much public attention—let alone understanding, interest, or support.

A Final Word Their case is not too often heard, but the present much-criticized electoral college system does have its defenders. They react to the several proposed reforms by raising various of the objections to them we have just noted. Beyond that, they argue that critics exaggerate the "dangers" in the system. Overall, they insist, it works. Only two elections have ever gone to the House of Representatives, and none in the last 160 years. True, the loser of the popular vote has three times won the Presidency, but that has not happened in nearly a century.

They also say that the arrangement, whatever its warts, has two major strengths:

(1) It is a *known* process. Each of the proposed, but untried, reforms may very well have defects that could not be known until either was tried.

(2) It identifies the winner of the presidential election, and it does so quickly and certainly. Even in a very close election, the nation does not have to wait for weeks or months to know the outcome.

FOR REVIEW

1. **Identify:** district plan, proportional plan, direct popular election, national bonus plan.
2. What are the three major weaknesses in the electoral college system? What is its winner-take-all feature?
3. Has the electoral college ever chosen a President who lost the popular vote contest? If so, when?
4. Briefly describe the three major plans for reform of the electoral college system.
5. Which plan is most widely supported?
6. What is the national bonus plan? What major points do the defenders of the electoral college system make?

SUMMARY

The scope, power, and importance of the Presidency are described by the several different roles the President must play. He is, simultaneously, all of these things: Chief of State, Chief Executive, Chief Administrator, Chief Diplomat, Commander in Chief, Chief Legislator, Party Chief, and Chief Citizen.

The Constitution sets formal qualifications for the office. But the informal qualifications set by practical politics are in fact the more telling ones. The President is chosen to serve a four-year term and may be elected only twice. He is paid $200,000 a year and receives many other compensations, as well.

The Vice President succeeds to the Presidency should the office become vacant. The Vice Presidency has become increasingly important in recent years, but it is in fact only as significant as the President chooses to make it.

In formal terms, the President and Vice President are selected in accord with the Constitution's provisions for the electoral college. In fact, they are picked through a largely extralegal process, which is the product of party practices. Technically, they are chosen by presidential electors elected by the voters in each State. But those electors have long since become rubber stamps for their parties, and their votes reflect the popular vote results in their States.

The electoral college system suffers many shortcomings. There are three major ones: First, a candidate may lose the popular vote contest yet win the Presidency in the electoral college balloting. Second, an elector may vote for someone other than the person selected by the voters. This is the faithless elector problem. Third, a strong third-party effort may throw the contest into the House of Representatives. Over time, many reforms have been proposed, but none will likely be approved in the foreseeable future.

CHAPTER REVIEW

Key Terms/Concepts*

electoral college (377)
presidential electors (378)
presidential primary (382)
winner-take-all primaries (383)
platform (387)

*These terms are included in the Glossary.

Keynote Questions

• **1.** List the several roles of the President and give an example for each.

• **2.** What are the constitutional qualifications for President?

• **3.** According to the 22nd Amendment, how many terms may a President serve?

• **4.** How does the 25th Amendment provide for: (a) Presidential succession? (c) Vice presidential vacancy? (b) Disability?

• **5.** What is the presidential succession order?

• **6.** What two formal duties does the Constitution assign to the Vice President? How have more recent Presidents made greater use of their Vice Presidents?

• **7.** How does the current process for electing the President and Vice President differ from the Constitution's original provisions for this process? Which Amendment changed the original provisions?

• **8.** How did the rise of political parties influence the constitutionally prescribed process for electing the President and Vice President?

• **9.** By what device do the two major parties nominate their presidential candidates?

The dots represent skill levels required to answer each question or complete each activity:
• requires recall and comprehension • • requires application and analysis • • • requires synthesis and evaluation

••• **10.** Make a chart to compare and contrast presidential primaries, caucuses, conventions. Include a description and the purpose of each.

• **11.** Why did the Framers establish the electoral college? How does it work?

• **12.** Which of the proposals to reform the electoral college system is most widely favored? Why?

Skill Application

Distinguishing Relevant from Irrelevant Information: Whether deciding whom to vote for or what economic policy would be most effective, Presidents and citizens in a democracy face an array of choices. For each choice to be made, many different viewpoints may surface. Being able to distinguish relevant from irrelevant information will enable you to make better judgments about different viewpoints and thus to make more informed choices.

Relevant information is directly related to the topic under consideration. It can clarify the topic or support it. Irrelevant information does not apply to the topic. The information itself may be factually correct, but it neither explains, supports, nor refutes the topic.

Read the two statements below. Then read the sentences following each. Decide which of the sentences are relevant and which are irrelevant to the topic. Write "R" on your paper if it is relevant; "IRR" if it is irrelevant.

1. As Chief Legislator, the President proposes and advocates many of the bills considered by Congress.
   a. In the State of the Union address, the President urged Congress to support an increase in defense spending.
   b. The President made several phone calls to key Senators urging their support for the foreign aid bill.
   c. Several world leaders traveled to Washington to discuss the international economy with the President.
   d. Members of the White House staff and the Treasury Department worked with Senate leaders to develop a new tax plan favored by the President.

2. Although the President is formally chosen by the electoral college, he is, in fact, chosen by an extralegal process which is chiefly the product of party practices.
   a. Several States have laws that require electors to vote for the candidate favored by the popular vote in their State.
   b. In 1800, the Federalists and the Democratic–Republicans became the first political parties in the United States to nominate candidates for the Presidency.
   c. In 1984, 28 States held presidential primaries.
   d. The keynote address at a party's national convention sets the tone for the convention.

For Thought and Discussion

••• **1.** Some political commentators have argued that the presidential primary process takes too long. By the time the general election takes place, some candidates have been campaigning for a year, and the American people have become weary of campaigns. Others argue that the primaries are good testing grounds for candidates, weeding out those who may not be able to sustain the stress of the Presidency. With which viewpoint do you agree? Why?

•• **2.** The inauguration of a new President can be described as a public pageant, a television spectacular, and a celebration of a political victory. It is also an important demonstration of this nation's continuing commitment to its basic principles of popular sovereignty and limited government. Why?

Suggested Activities

••• **1.** Find out how the Democrats and the Republicans in your State nominate their presidential elector candidates. When you have gathered this information, draw a flow chart to illustrate the process.

••• **2.** Write your own platform to run for election in your class. Make a list of the policies you would follow and the actions you would take if you were elected. Prepare a report on the promises that were reasonable and those that you knew were included only to attract votes. What have you learned about party platforms?

When I ran for the Presidency . . . I knew this country faced serious challenges, but I could not realize—nor could any man who does not bear the burdens of this office—how heavy and constant would be those burdens.
–John F. Kennedy

15 The Presidency in Action

CHAPTER OBJECTIVES

To help you to

Learn · Know · Understand

The Executive Office of the President, the several agencies within it, and their functions.

The Cabinet and its role in the executive branch.

The several factors that have worked to strengthen the role and powers of the Presidency.

The nature and the extent of "the executive power" of the President.

The President's several executive, diplomatic, military, legislative, and judicial powers.

Article II of the Constitution begins:

> The executive power shall be vested in a President of the United States. . . .

With those few words, the Framers established the Presidency. With them, they laid the basis for the vast power and influence the nation's chief executive has today.

The Constitution does set out several other, and somewhat more specific, grants of presidential power. Thus, the President is given the power to command the armed forces, to make treaties, to approve or veto acts of Congress, to send and receive diplomatic representatives, to grant pardons and reprieves, and "to take care that the laws be faithfully executed."[1]

Notice that the Constitution deals with the powers of the Presidency in only very sketchy fashion. Article II reads almost as an outline. It has been called "the most loosely drawn chapter" in the nation's fundamental

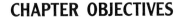

[1]Most of the specific grants of presidential power are found in Article II, Sections 2 and 3. A few are elsewhere in the Constitution, however, such as the veto power, in Article I, Section 7, Clause 2.

President Kennedy committed the United States to a program to make the nation foremost in space exploration. Here, he addresses NASA personnel in the space center in Houston, Texas, in 1962. *Facing page:* President Calvin Coolidge helps launch the 1925 baseball season.

law.[2] It does not define "the executive power," and the other grants of presidential authority are put in equally broad terms.

Much has been added to the constitutional outline of the Presidency over the past 190 years and more. Thus, the ways in which the stronger Presidents have used their powers have done much to shape both the office and the scope of its powers. The most notable of those Presidents have been Washington, Jefferson, Jackson, Lincoln, Wilson, the two Roosevelts, Truman, and the second Johnson. A large number of acts of Congress and court decisions have also helped to define and extend the powers of the Presidency. Very importantly, too, the way in which the public has viewed the presidential office has been a large factor in its development.

In this chapter we survey the whole field of presidential powers. First, we must take a look at the ways in which the Presidency is organized for the use of those powers. *

[2]Edward S. Corwin, *The President: Office and Powers* (New York: New York University Press, 1957) 4th ed. "To those who think that a constitution ought to settle everything beforehand it [Article II] should be a nightmare; by the same token, to those who think that constitution makers ought to leave considerable leeway for the future play of political forces, it should be a vision realized." This is *the* classic study of the Constitution's treatment of the Presidency.

1. The Executive Office of the President

As You Read, Think About:

- What function the White House Office serves.
- What the function and composition are of the National Security Council.
- Why the Office of Management and Budget is of pivotal importance.
- What the functions are of the other units in the Executive Office.

*ENRICHMENT Have the class discuss: In what ways has the public's view of the Presidency been a factor in its development?

Every officer, employee, and agency of the huge executive branch of the Federal Government is legally subordinate to the President. All of them exist to aid the Chief Executive in the exercise of the executive power.

The President's chief right arm, however, is the Executive Office of the President. It is an umbrella agency: a complex of several separate offices, staffed by most of the President's closest advisers and assistants. Created by Congress in 1939, the Executive Office has been reorganized in every administration since then, including President Reagan's.

The White House Office

The "nerve center" of the Executive Office —in fact, of the entire executive branch—is the White House Office. It houses the President's key personal and political staff, including a number of senior advisers and other top aides and several hundred professional and clerical people. Most of them have offices in the two wings on either side of the White House. They occupy most of the crowded West Wing, which is seldom seen by the public and where the fabled Oval Office and the Cabinet Room are located. Some of them work in the East Wing, where the public tours of the Executive Mansion begin.

The most influential of all these presidential aides today is Donald Regan, the Chief of Staff of the White House Office. In the Reagan White House, he is the President's closest adviser and he directs the operations of the whole presidential staff. A number of other top officials, Assistants and Special Assistants to the President, also aid him in such vital areas as foreign policy, defense, the economy, political affairs, congressional relations, and contacts with the news media and with the public at large.

The White House staff also includes such other major aides as the Counsel to the President, the Press Secretary, the President's Physician, and the Director of Staff for the First Lady. Altogether, the White House staff now numbers about 400 men and women who, in a very real sense, work for the President.

The National Security Council

Most of the President's major steps in foreign affairs are taken in close consultation with the National Security Council (NSC). It meets at the President's call, often on short notice, to advise him in all matters —domestic, foreign, and military—that bear on the nation's security.

The President chairs the Council. Its other members are the Vice President and the Secretaries of State and Defense. The Director of the Central Intelligence Agency (CIA) and the Chairman of the Joint Chiefs of Staff also attend all of its meetings.

The NSC has a small, highly competent staff of foreign and military policy experts. They work under the direction of the President's Assistant for National Security Affairs, another of his most influential advisers. The NSC also directs the operations of the supersecret CIA; see page 484.

The Office of Policy Development

Domestic affairs—matters of homefront policy—demand the President's constant attention, too. The Office of Policy Development gives him the staff necessary to stay on top of that whole, many-sided field. It is headed by another leading White House figure, the Assistant to the President for Policy Development.

The Office of Management and Budget

The Office of Management and Budget (OMB) is the largest and, after the White House Office, the most influential unit in the Executive Office. It directs the preparation of the federal **budget**, which the President must submit to Congress in January each year.

The budget-making function is far more than a routine bookkeeping chore. It is, in a very real sense, the preparation of an annual statement of the public policies of the United States put into dollar terms.

The federal budget is, at base, a financial

*REINFORCEMENT Have the class discuss why the Executive Office of the President is reorganized with every Administration. Consider such reasons as new agendas, party politics, etc.

The President interacts with many people and groups daily. Here he responds to reporters' questions at a press conference.

document. It is a very detailed estimate of receipts and expenditures, an anticipation of federal income and outgo, during the next fiscal year.[3] More than that, the federal budget is also a *plan*, a carefully drawn, closely detailed work plan for the conduct of government and the execution of public policy.

The budget-making process—the many steps by which each fiscal year's budget is built—is a lengthy one. In fact, the process begins more than a year before the start of the fiscal year for which it is intended. In its first stages, each federal agency prepares detailed estimates of its spending needs for that 12-month period. Those proposals are then reviewed by the OMB, generally in a series of budget hearings at which agency officials must defend their dollar requests. Following that agency-by-agency review, the revised, and usually lowered, spending estimates of all agencies are fitted into the President's overall program. They become a part of the budget document the Chief Executive presents to Congress.

The OMB is more than simply the President's budget-making arm. It also oversees the *execution* of the budget. It monitors the spending of the funds once they have been appropriated by Congress. The President's close control over both the preparation and the execution of the budget is a major tool with which the Chief Executive is able to manage the huge and sprawling executive branch.

Beyond its budget chores, the OMB is a sort of presidential "handyman" agency. It * makes continuing studies of the organization and management of the executive branch and keeps the President up to date on the work of all its agencies. The OMB checks and clears agency stands on all legislative matters to be certain that they agree with the President's own positions. It helps the President with executive orders and veto messages and does much else to live up to the word "management" in its title.

The Council of Economic Advisers

Three of the country's leading economists, chosen by the President with the consent of the Senate, make up the Council of Economic Advisers. They are the Chief Executive's major source of information and advice on the state of the nation's economy.

The Council, with the aid of a small professional staff, keeps a close watch on the economy and keeps the President informed of economic developments and problems. The Council also helps the President prepare his annual Economic Report to Congress. That report, together with a presidential message, goes to Capitol Hill in late January or early February each year.

Other Units in the Executive Office

There are other agencies within the Executive Office. Each houses key presidential assistants—men and women who give the President the information, advice,

[3] A *fiscal year* is the 12-month period used by a government for its record-keeping, budgeting, revenue-collecting, and other financial management purposes. The Federal Government's fiscal year now runs from October 1 through the following September 30.

*REINFORCEMENT Have the class discuss: Why is the OMB termed a "handy-man" agency? Is it appropriate? Why?

and other help he must have to carry out the executive function.

The *Council on Environmental Quality* aids the President in all environmental policy matters and in the writing of the annual "state of the environment" report to Congress. The Council's three members are named by the President, with the Senate's consent. They work closely with the Environmental Protection Agency and various agencies in the Departments of the Interior, Agriculture, and Energy.

The *Office of United States Trade Representative* advises the Chief Executive in all matters of foreign trade. The Trade Representative, appointed by the President and Senate, carries the rank of ambassador and represents the President in foreign trade negotiations.

The *Office of Science and Technology Policy* is the President's major adviser in all scientific, engineering, and other technological matters bearing on national policies and programs. Its Director, who is chosen by the President and Senate, is drawn from the nation's scientific community.

The *Office of Administration* is the general housekeeping agency for all the other units in the Executive Office. It provides them with all the many support services they must have in order to do their jobs. The list of those things is almost endless: clerical help, data processing, library services, transportation, and much more.

FOR REVIEW

1. **Identify:** executive power, Executive Office of the President, White House Office, budget, budget-making power.
2. To whom does the Constitution give *the* executive power?
3. From what sources have the President's power been filled out?
4. Name the agencies of the Executive Office of the President.
5. Why is the federal budget power a major administrative tool for a President?

2. The Cabinet

As You Read, Think About:

- What the Cabinet is and how its members are selected.
- How it has grown since its inception in 1789.
- What the Cabinet's role is.

The **Cabinet** is an informal advisory body brought together by the President to serve his needs. The Constitution makes no mention of it,[4] nor did Congress create it. Instead, the Cabinet is the product of custom and usage, developed over the years since George Washington's first term of office.

At its first session in 1789, Congress established four executive posts: Secretary of State, Secretary of the Treasury, Secretary of War, and Attorney General. By his second term, President Washington was regularly seeking the views and advice of the four outstanding men he had named to those offices: Thomas Jefferson in the Department of State, Alexander Hamilton at the Treasury, Henry Knox in the War Department, and Edmund Randolph, the Attorney General. So the Cabinet was born.

By long-established tradition, the heads of the executive departments form the Cabinet. It has 13 members today. Several other officials attend Cabinet meetings. Thus, every recent Vice President since Alben Barkley has been a regular participant. A number of the President's other topmost aides are usually there, as well—for example, the White House Chief of Staff and the Director of the OMB. *

Selection of Cabinet Members

The President appoints the head of each of the 13 executive departments. Each of these appointments is subject to confirmation by

[4]The closest approach to it is in Article II, Section 2, Clause 1, where the President is given the power to "require the opinion, in writing, of the principal officer in each of the executive departments, upon any subject relating to the duties of their respective offices." The Cabinet was first mentioned in an act of Congress in 1907, well over a century after its birth.

*ENRICHMENT Ask the class to find out the names of the members of the President's staff. (This information may be found in their school or local library.)

The first Cabinet (left to right): Henry Knox, Secretary of War; Thomas Jefferson, Secretary of State; Edmund Randolph (in background), Attorney General; Alexander Hamilton, Secretary of the Treasury; and President George Washington.

the Senate, but rejections have been exceedingly rare. Of the more than 600 appointments made to 1987, only 11 have been turned down by the Senate.[5]

Many factors influence these presidential choices. Party considerations are always important. Republican Presidents do not often pick Democrats, and vice versa. One or more

The President's Cabinet

Cabinet Post*	Year Created
Secretary of State	1789
Secretary of the Treasury	1789
Secretary of Defense[a]	1947
Attorney General[b]	1789
Secretary of the Interior	1849
Secretary of Agriculture	1889
Secretary of Commerce[c]	1903
Secretary of Labor[c]	1913
Secretary of Health and Human Services[d]	1953
Secretary of Housing and Urban Development	1965
Secretary of Transportation	1967
Secretary of Energy	1977
Secretary of Education	1979

*The Cabinet posts are listed in order of precedence—that is, the order in which each was established. This ranking is followed for formal and ceremonial purposes (protocol) and also is the order in which the Cabinet officers rank in the line of presidential succession; see page 375.

[a]Congress created the National Military Establishment, as an executive department headed by the Secretary of Defense, in 1947. It was renamed the Department of Defense in 1949. Since 1947 it has included the former Cabinet-level Departments of War (1789), and the Navy (1798), and the Department of the Air Force (1947). The Secretaries of Army, Navy and Air Force do not hold Cabinet rank.

[b]Although the post of Attorney General was created in 1789, the Department of Justice was not established until 1870.

[c]The Secretary of Commerce was originally the Secretary of Commerce and Labor. The Department of Commerce and Labor, created in 1903, was replaced by the separate Departments of Commerce and of Labor in 1913.

[d]The Secretary of Health and Human Services was originally the Secretary of Health, Education, and Welfare. The Department of Health, Education, and Welfare was created in 1953. HEW's education functions were transferred to a separate Department of Education in 1979 and HEW was renamed at that time.

Note: The Postmaster General, who headed the Cabinet-level Post Office Department, was a member of the Cabinet from Andrew Jackson's first year in the Presidency (1829) until Congress replaced the Department with an independent agency, the United States Postal Service, in 1971.

[5]The last rejection was in 1959, when the Senate refused to confirm President Eisenhower's selection of Lewis Strauss as Secretary of Commerce. The Senate also rejected Andrew Jackson's appointment of Roger B. Taney as Secretary of the Treasury in 1834; four of John Tyler's selections: Caleb Cushing as Secretary of the Treasury (three times on the same day) in 1843, James Green for the same post in 1844, David Henshaw as Secretary of the Navy in 1844, and James M. Porter as Secretary of War in 1844; Andrew Johnson's appointment of Henry Stanberry as Attorney General in 1868; and Calvin Coolidge's choice of Charles B. Warren (twice) as Attorney General in 1925.

*ENRICHMENT Discuss in class: Why are the President's Cabinet appointments rarely rejected by the Senate? Point out that he only appoints people who will promote his policies.

Burr Schafer/Saturday Review Associates

"Oh, Washington himself is all right. It's the men around him like Jefferson and Adams and . . ."

of a new President's appointees usually come from among those who had a large, quite influential hand in the recent presidential campaign.

Professional qualifications and practical experience are also taken into account, of course, particularly in selecting the Secretaries of State and Treasury and the Attorney General. Geography also plays a part. In broad terms, each President tries to give some sectional balance to the Cabinet. Thus, in more specific terms, the Secretary of the Interior almost always comes from the West, where most of the department's work is carried out.

A number of special-interest groups are especially interested in those who are appointed to head certain departments and have an influence on some of the choices. Thus, the Secretary of Agriculture is almost always a farmer or at least has a background closely related to agriculture. The Secretary of the Treasury usually comes from the financial community and the Secretary of Commerce from the ranks of business. The Secretary of Labor must be acceptable to labor, and the Secretary of Housing and Urban Development almost always has a "big-city" background.

Considerations of sex and race,[6] an appointee's stand on the "hot" issues of the day, management abilities and experience, and other personal characteristics—these and a host of other factors are a part of the decision mix in selecting Cabinet members. Indeed, those factors and the group pressures also at work here are so many and so different that they really cannot be catalogued.

The Cabinet's Role

The members of the Cabinet have *two* major jobs. *Individually,* each is the administrative head of one of the executive departments. *Together,* they are advisers to the President.

How, and how much, the President uses the Cabinet—how important it really is, then—is something for each President to decide. A number of Presidents have given great weight to the Cabinet and to its advice; others have given it only a secondary role. Cabinet meetings have a large place in the Reagan Administration. John Kennedy, on the other hand, thought that those sessions were "a waste of time."

William Howard Taft put the role of the Cabinet in its proper light years ago:

[6] To 1987, only eight women and four blacks have served in the Cabinet. Franklin Roosevelt appointed the first woman, Frances T. Perkins, who served as Secretary of Labor from 1933 to 1945. Olveta Culp Hobby, the first Secretary of Health, Education, and Welfare, served in the Eisenhower Cabinet from 1953 to 1955. Lyndon Johnson named the first black to the Cabinet, Robert C. Weaver as the first Secretary of Housing and Urban Development in 1966. Gerald Ford was the first President to select both a woman (Carla Hills, Secretary of HUD) and a black (William T. Coleman, Secretary of Transportation); both were named in 1975. Among Jimmy Carter's first selections were two women: Juanita M. Kreps as Secretary of Commerce and Patricia R. Harris, the first black woman to hold a Cabinet post, as Secretary of HUD and in 1979, as Secretary of Health and Human Services. He also picked Shirley Hufstedler to head the new Department of Education in 1979. Ronald Reagan's first Cabinet appointments (1981) included one black, Samuel R. Pierce, Secretary of HUD, and no women. He did appoint two women in 1983, however: Elizabeth H. Dole, Secretary of Transportation, and Margaret M. Heckler, Secretary of Health and Human Services.

President Reagan meets with his Cabinet early in his second term. The Reagan Cabinet usually meets twice a week.

> The Constitution . . . contains no suggestion of a meeting of all of the department heads in consultation over general governmental matters. The Cabinet is a mere creation of the President's will. It exists only by custom. If the President desired to dispense with it, he could do so.[7]

The Reagan Cabinet usually meets twice a week. Reports are made and discussed, and advice is offered to the Chief Executive. That advice need not be taken, of course. Abraham * Lincoln once laid a proposition he favored before his Cabinet. Each member opposed it, whereupon Lincoln declared: "Seven nays, one aye: the ayes have it."

Several Presidents have leaned on other, unofficial advisory groups, and sometimes more heavily than on the Cabinet. Andrew Jackson began the practice. Several of his close friends often met with him in the kitchen at the White House and, inevitably, came to be known as "the Kitchen Cabinet." Franklin Roosevelt's "Brain Trust" of the 1930s and Harry Truman's "Cronies" in the late 1940s were in the same mold.

At times, one or a few individuals have become close advisers, working with the President on a highly confidential and personal basis. These "President's Men" have had different titles with each administration. Some of them have held no public office, but they have each had a large hand in the shaping of White House decisions.

FOR REVIEW

1. How was the Cabinet created?
2. Who are the members of the Cabinet?
3. What two major jobs do Cabinet members have?

[7] *Our Chief Magistrate and His Powers* (New York: Columbia University Press, 1916), pages 29–30.

*ENRICHMENT President Reagan regularly meets with his Cabinet; President Kennedy did not. Ask the class to discuss how this reflects presidential style.

PERSONALITY PROFILE

George Washington and the Presidency

On April 30, 1789, on the balcony of the United States Building in New York City, George Washington of Virginia took the presidential oath of office of the fledgling United States.

Washington assumed the Presidency without any guidelines for conducting the affairs of state or any executive departments to help him. The Constitution states that there should be departments in the executive branch and that they should report to the President. However, the Constitution does not say what those departments should be or even how many there should be.

Washington recognized the importance of his position and acted cautiously. He realized that his actions and policies would set precedents that would be followed for years to come and he was anxious to set the nation on a true course.

Washington and Congress were faced with filling in the details of the Constitution. They established the first three executive departments, which within four years had become known as the President's Cabinet. Washington early established the precedent of the President's choosing and nominating executive officers and removing them if they failed in their duties.

Through the Judiciary Act of 1789, Washington and Congress set up the framework for the federal judiciary. This framework has remained the same, although the number of Supreme Court justices and of lower courts has grown as the nation has grown.

Faced with a huge debt to foreign nations and to American citizens following the Revolutionary War, Washington followed fiscal policies aimed at paying off the national debt and promoting economic growth.

In foreign affairs, Washington was against maintaining ties with other nations. He followed a policy of strict neutrality. To enhance the new nation's image abroad, Washington established official ceremonies such as the inaugural ceremony itself. In two terms in office, Washington created the machinery of the new government and established the framework in which it could work effectively.

Washington recognized the immense task confronting him that morning in 1789 when he accepted the leadership of the nation. His inaugural address, portions of which appear below, reflects both the apprehensions and visions of a man setting off in, as yet, uncharted territory.

> Fellow-Citizens of the Senate and House of Representatives:
>
> Besides the ordinary objects submitted to your care, it will remain with your judgment to decide, how far an exercise of the occasional power delegated by the fifth article of the Constitution is rendered expedient at the present juncture. . . . Instead of undertaking particular recommendations on this subject . . . I shall again give way to my entire confidence in your discernment and pursuit of the public good; for I assure myself, that . . . a reverence for the characteristic rights of freemen, and a regard for the public harmony, will sufficiently influence your deliberations on the question. . . .

1. How did Washington contribute to the role of the Presidency as we know it today?
2. How would you describe Washington's state of mind when he gave his first Inaugural address?

REINFORCEMENT Have the class discuss: In what ways has Congress contributed to the growth of presidential powers?

3. The Powers of the Presidency: An Historical View

As You Read, Think About:

- How presidential power has grown over time.
- Why presidential power has grown.

Again, the Constitution gives "the executive power" to the President of the United States. Article II, Section 1 of the Constitution vests the President with this power. But, as we have seen, the specific powers of the Presidency are set out in sparse, outline-like terms. In short, the Constitution does not spell out the content of "the executive power."

Much of the story of the development of the American system of government can be told in terms of the growth of the Presidency and of presidential power. A large part of our political history has revolved about a continuing struggle over the meaning of the constitutional phrase "executive power." That struggle has pitted those who have argued for a weaker Presidency, subordinate to Congress, on the one hand, against those who have pressed for a stronger, independent, and co-equal Chief Executive, on the other hand.

That never-ending contest and debate began at the Philadelphia Convention. The Framers were divided on the matter. Several of them agreed with Roger Sherman of Connecticut who, according to Madison's *Notes:*

> considered the executive magistracy as nothing more than an institution for carrying the will of the legislature into effect, and that the person or persons [occupying the Presidency] ought to be appointed by and accountable to the legislature only, which was the depository of the supreme will of the Society.

As we have seen, however, those who argued for a stronger executive—led by Alexander Hamilton, James Wilson, and James Madison—carried the day. They persuaded the Convention to establish a single executive, chosen independently of Congress and with its own distinct field of powers.

Reasons for Growth

The debate over the nature and extent of "the executive power" has gone on now for some 200 years. Over that period, and for a great many reasons, the champions of a stronger Presidency have almost always prevailed.

One of the leading reasons they have is the *unity* of the Presidency. The office and its powers are held by *one* person. The President is the *single,* commanding head of the executive branch. On the other hand, the Congress, though its powers are many and substantial, consists of *two* houses. Both of them must agree on a matter before the Congress can do anything. Moreover, one of those two houses is made up of 100 separately elected members and the other has 435.

Several other factors have worked to strengthen the role and the powers of the Presidency and so to enhance the scope of "the executive power." One highly important factor we have referred to a number of times: the influence the Presidents themselves, especially the stronger ones, have had on the office.

Yet another influence has been pressures from the increasingly complex nature of the nation's social and economic life. As the United States has become more and still more highly industrialized and technologically centered, the people have demanded that the Federal Government play a larger and still larger role in a long list of areas of public concern. Among those fields have been transportation, communications, labor-management relations, education, welfare, housing, civil rights, health, and environmental protection. The people have most often looked to the Presidency for leadership in these matters.

Congress itself has largely strengthened the role and powers of the Presidency. It has * passed thousands of pieces of legislation that have contributed to the growth of the scope of the Federal Government. Congress has neither the time nor the technical knowledge to do much more than set up the basic outlines of public policy in many new fields. Thus, Congress has been literally forced

*REINFORCEMENT Have the class discuss: In what ways has Congress contributed to the growth of presidential powers?

to delegate substantial authority to the President, a point we shall return to in a few pages.

Yet another of these closely related factors has been the frequent need for extraordinary and decisive action in times of national emergency and, most notably, in time of war. The ability of the President—the *single*, commanding Chief Executive—to act in such situations has done much to strengthen "the executive power."

A number of other factors have fed the growth of "the executive power." Among them have been the President's roles as Chief Legislator, Party Leader, and Chief Citizen, to which we referred in Chapter 14. Another is the huge amount of staff support a President has, also noted earlier. Yet another is the unique position from which the President can attract and hold the public's attention, and so gather support for policies and actions. Each of the most recent Presidents, from Franklin Roosevelt through Lyndon Johnson to Ronald Reagan, has very purposely used the press, radio, and television to that end.

Presidential Views of Presidential Power

Before we turn to the specific powers of the Presidency, ponder this vital point: What the Presidency is at any given time depends, in no small part, on the manner in which the President views the office and exercises its several powers.

Historically, two general and contrasting views of the Presidency have been held by the several Presidents. The stronger and the more effective have taken a broad view of their powers. Theodore Roosevelt defined their position in what he called the "stewardship theory":

> My view was that . . . every executive officer in high position, was a steward of the people bound actively and affirmatively to do all he could for the people, and not to content himself with the negative merit of keeping his talents undamaged in a napkin. I declined to adopt the view that what was imperatively necessary for the Nation could not be done by the President unless he could find some specific authorization to do it. My belief was that it was not only his right but his duty to do anything that the needs of the Nation demanded unless such action was forbidden by the Constitution or by the laws. . . . I did not usurp power, but I did greatly broaden the use of executive power. In other words, I acted for the public welfare, I acted for the common well-being of all our people, whenever and in whatever manner was necessary, unless prevented by direct constitutional or legislative prohibition.[8]

President Lincoln meets with Union officers during the Civil War, a period during which presidential powers were considerably broadened.

Ironically, the strongest presidential statement of the opposing view was made by Roosevelt's handpicked successor in the office, William Howard Taft. Looking back upon his Presidency, Taft had this to say about Roosevelt's view:

> My judgment is that the view of Mr. Roosevelt, ascribing an undefined residuum of power to the President, is an unsafe doctrine. . . . The true view of the executive function is, as I conceive it, that the President can exercise no power which cannot be fairly and reasonably traced to some specific grant of power or justly implied and included within such express

[8] *Theodore Roosevelt: An Autobiography*, (New York: Macmillan, 1913), page 389.

*REINFORCEMENT Have the class discuss the factors that have fed the growth of the executive power. List these factors on the board and ask the students to rank order them.

grant. . . . Such specific grant must be either in the Federal Constitution or in an act of Congress passed in pursuance thereof. There is no undefined residuum of power which he can exercise because it seems to be in the public interest.[9]

In the last chapter, we said that the Presidency and its powers may be viewed in terms of the many different roles the President must play. The President must be, at one and the same time, each and all of these vital things: Chief of State, Chief Executive, Chief Administrator, Chief Diplomat, Commander in Chief, Chief Legislator, Chief of Party, and Chief Citizen.

FOR REVIEW

1. **Identify:** unity of the Presidency.
2. Around what two competing views of "the executive power" can much of our political history be written?
3. What are at least three main reasons for the historical growth of presidential power?
4. What two contrasting views of the Presidency have been taken by those who have held the office?

4. The President's Executive Powers

As You Read, Think About:

- What powers constitute the President's executive powers.
- How the President exercises these powers.

As the nation's Chief Executive, the President has to execute—to enforce, put into effect, carry out—the provisions of federal law. The power to do so rests on two brief constitutional provisions. The first of them is the oath of office the President must take:

Theodore Roosevelt believed a President should act with boldness, energy, and optimism.

> I do solemnly swear (or affirm) that I will faithfully execute the office of President of the United States, and will, to the best of my ability, preserve, protect, and defend the Constitution of the United States.[10]

The other provision is the Constitution's command that "he shall take care that the laws be faithfully executed."[11]

The President's power to execute the law covers *all* federal laws. Their number, and the different subject matters they cover, nearly boggle the mind. The armed forces, social security, civil rights, housing, taxes, environmental pollution, collective bargaining, farm price supports, public health, and immigration—these 10 only begin the list; there are scores of others.

Just as do Congress and the courts, the President and the President's subordinates have much to say about the meaning of the

[9] *Our Chief Magistrate and His Powers* (New York: Columbia University Press, 1916), pages 139–40, 144.

[10] Article II, Section 1, Clause 8.

[11] Article II, Section 3; this provision gives to the President what is often called the "take care power."

FOCUS ON:

Ranking the Presidents

Who were the greatest, and who were the worst, of our Presidents?

A number of surveys of the Presidency by historians, political scientists, and other authorities show this:

Four Presidents were truly great: Abraham Lincoln, Franklin Roosevelt, George Washington, and Thomas Jefferson, and they are usually ranked in that order.

Six others are regularly classed as "near great" Presidents: Theodore Roosevelt, Woodrow Wilson, Andrew Jackson, Harry Truman, John Adams, and James K. Polk.

Most presidential scholars agree that two men clearly deserve to be called "failures" in the White House: Ulysses Grant and Warren Harding. Most also say that James Buchanan, Franklin Pierce, Andrew Johnson, and Richard Nixon stand very close to the bottom of the list.

Each of the other Presidents is most often placed somewhere in the "above-average" or "average" or "below-average" range.

Among the most recent Presidents, Lyndon Johnson, Dwight Eisenhower, and John Kennedy are regularly ranked toward the top of the "above-average" category. Gerald Ford and Jimmy Carter usually place in the lower middle of the scale.

Clearly, Ronald Reagan's standing cannot be measured until some time after he leaves office. Most students of the Presidency agree that neither William Henry Harrison nor James A. Garfield were in office long enough to be properly assessed.

1. By what factors would you judge a President's "greatness"? Choose a particular President and rank him on the basis of those factors.
2. Explain this comment: "Reading past history in the light of current politics may be good politics, but it is also very poor history."

law. In executing and enforcing law, the executive branch also *interprets* it.* The Constitution requires the President to execute *all* federal laws, no matter what the Chief Executive's own views of any of them may be. But the President may, and does, use some discretion as to how vigorously and in what particular way any given law will be applied in practice.

To look at the point more closely: Many laws that Congress passes are written in fairly broad terms. In them, Congress sets out the basic policies and standards to be followed. The specific details necessary to the actual, day-to-day administration of the law are usually left to be worked out in the executive branch.

To take an example, the immigration laws require that all immigrants seeking permanent admission to this country must be able to "read and understand some dialect or language." But what does this literacy requirement mean in everyday practice? How well must an alien be able to read and write? What words in some language must he or she know, and how many of them? What kind of test is to be given here? The law does not say. Rather, such answers come from within the executive branch—in this case, from the Immigration and Naturalization Service in the Department of Justice.

Direction of Administration

From what has just been said, it should be clear that the President deserves the title

*REINFORCEMENT Have a class discussion of the executive powers. The President, as Commander in Chief, has use of military transport; what are the implied powers?

Members of the President's Cabinet spend a considerable amount of time before committees of both the House and the Senate.

Chief Administrator as well as Chief Executive. The job of administering and applying most federal law is the day-to-day work of all of the many departments, bureaus, offices, boards, commissions, councils, and other agencies that make up the huge executive branch. All of the some three million men and women who staff those agencies are subordinate, or answerable, to the President. They are all subject to the President's control and direction.

The Ordinance Power The President has the power to issue **executive orders,** which have the effect of law. The power to do so, the ordinance power, arises from two sources: the Constitution and acts of Congress.

The Constitution does not mention the ordinance power in so many words, but it is clearly intended. In conferring certain powers to the President, the Constitution obviously anticipates their use. In order to exercise those powers, the President must have the power to issue the necessary orders—directives, rules, regulations—and as well, the power to implement them. The President must also have the power to authorize subordinates to issue such orders.[12]

As the number, the scope, and the complexity of governmental problems have grown, Congress has had to delegate more and still more discretion to the President and to presidential subordinates to spell out the policies and programs it has passed. Members of Congress are not, and cannot be expected to be, experts in all of the fields in which they must legislate.

When it does delegate authority to the executive branch, Congress cannot give away its constitutional power to make basic public policy. Rather, it sets out the broad standards within which the President and other executive officers and agencies must work. There are many, many examples. We have just noted one illustration involving the literacy of immigrants. For another, Congress has provided for the payment of subsidies to support the prices of certain farm products. It has named 12 commodities to be supported, and it has given the Secretary of Agriculture the power to add other commodities to that list. The additions are made by executive order.

Power of Appointment

A President cannot hope to succeed without loyal subordinates who support the administration's policies. No matter how able a President, no matter how wise those policies, no administration can work effectively without such loyalty and support.

The Constitution provides that the President

> by and with the advice and consent of the Senate . . . shall appoint ambassadors, other public ministers, and consuls, judges of the Supreme Court, and all other officers of the United States whose appointments are not otherwise herein provided for . . . but the Congress may by law vest the appointment of such inferior officers, as they think proper, in the

[12]All executive orders are published in the *Federal Register,* which appears five times a week. At least annually, all orders currently in force are published in the *Code of Federal Regulations.* Both of these publications are issued by the National Archives and Records Administration.

Elizabeth Dole, Secretary of Transportation, is sworn in following her confirmation by the Senate in 1983.

President alone, in the courts of law, or in the heads of departments.[13]

Acting alone, the President names only a handful of the some three million federal civilian employees. Many of that handful are members of the staff of the White House Office. With Senate consent, the President names most of the top-ranking officers of the Federal Government. Among them are ambassadors and other diplomats; Cabinet members and their top aides; the heads of such independent agencies as the Environmental Protection Agency and the Veterans Administration; all federal judges, attorneys and marshals; and all officers in the armed forces.

When the President makes one of these appointments, the "nomination" is sent to the Senate. The support of a majority of the Senators present and voting is needed for confirmation.

Recall, the unwritten rule of *senatorial courtesy* plays an important part in this process. That courtesy, as we noted on page 361, applies to the choice of those federal officers who serve within a State, such as a federal district judge or a federal marshal. The rule holds that the Senate will approve only those federal appointees acceptable to the Senator or Senators of the President's party from the State involved. The practical effect of this custom, which is closely followed in the Senate, is to place a meaningful part of the appointment power in the hands of particular Senators.

However, well over half of all the federal civilian workforce is selected on the basis of competitive civil service examinations. Today, the Office of Personnel Management examines applicants for some two million positions; see Chapter 16.

Removal Power

The power to remove is the other side of the appointment coin, and it is as critically important to presidential success. Except for the cumbersome and little-used impeachment process,[14] however, the Constitution is silent on the matter. It does not say how or by whom appointed officers may be dismissed, whether for incompetence, for opposition to presidential policies, or for any other cause. *

[13] Article II, Section 2, Clause 2. Those whose appointments are "otherwise provided for" are the Vice President, Senators, Representatives, and presidential electors.

[14] Article II, Section 4; see pages 359—360.

*ENRICHMENT Discuss: If the President has the power to appoint someone, should he not also have the power to remove that person? Stress the constitutional basis of these powers.

The question was hotly debated in the first session of Congress in 1789. Several members argued that for those offices for which Senate approval was required for appointment, Senate consent should also be required for removal. They insisted that this restriction on presidential authority was essential to congressional supervision, or oversight, of the executive branch. But others argued that the President could not "take care that the laws be faithfully executed" without a free hand to dismiss those who were incompetent or otherwise undesirable in the Chief Executive's administration.

The latter view prevailed. The 1st Congress gave to the President the power to remove any officer, except federal judges, whom he appointed. Over the years since then, Congress has sometimes tried, with little success, to restrict the President's freedom to dismiss.

One notable instance came in 1867. Locked with Andrew Johnson in the fight over Reconstruction, Congress passed the Tenure of Office Act. The law's plain purpose was to prevent President Johnson from removing several top officers in his administration, especially the Secretary of War, Edwin M. Stanton. The law provided that any person holding an office by presidential appointment with Senate consent should remain in that office until a successor had been confirmed by the Senate. The President vetoed the bill, charging that it was an unconstitutional invasion of executive authority. The veto, which was overridden, sparked the move for Johnson's impeachment. The law was ignored in practice and never challenged in the courts. It was finally repealed in 1887.

The question of the President's removal power did not reach the Supreme Court until *Myers* v. *United States,* 1926. In 1876 Congress had passed a law requiring Senate consent before the President could dismiss any first-, second-, or third-class postmaster.

In 1920, without consulting the Senate, President Woodrow Wilson removed Frank Myers as the postmaster at Portland, Oregon. Myers then sued for the salary for the rest of his four-year term. He based his claim on the point that he had been removed in violation of the 1876 law. The Court found the law unconstitutional, however. Its opinion was written by Chief Justice William Howard Taft, himself a former President. The Court held that the power of removal was an essential part of the executive power, clearly necessary to the faithful execution of the laws.

The Supreme Court did place some limit on the President's removal power in 1935, in *Humphrey's Executor* v. *United States.* President Herbert Hoover had appointed William Humphrey to a seven-year term on the Federal Trade Commission in 1931. When President Franklin D. Roosevelt entered office in 1933, he found Humphrey in sharp disagreement with many of his policies. He asked Humphrey to resign, saying that his administration would be better served with someone else on the FTC. When Humphrey refused, Roosevelt removed him. Humphrey challenged the legality of the action but died before a case could be brought. His heirs then filed a suit for back salary.

The Supreme Court upheld their claim. It based its decision on the act creating the FTC. That law provides that a member of the Commission may be removed only for "inefficiency, neglect of duty, or malfeasance in office."[15] The President had given none of these reasons. He had dismissed Humphrey because of political disagreements.

The Court further held that Congress does have the power to set the conditions under which a member of the FTC and other such agencies might be removed by the President. It did so because those agencies, the independent regulatory commissions, are not purely executive agencies. They are, instead, *quasi-legislative* and *quasi-judicial* in character.[16]

As a general rule, however, the President may remove those whom the President appoints.

---

[15]*Malfeasance* is wrongful conduct, especially by a public officeholder.

[16]Their duties are partly legislative and partly judicial; they *make rules* and *decide controversies.* The prefix *quasi* is from the Latin, meaning "in a certain sense, resembling, seemingly."

FOR REVIEW

1. **Identify:** Chief Executive, Chief Administrator, ordinance power, appointment/removal powers.
2. How does the executive branch have a lot to say about the meaning of the law?
3. Why is the President the Chief Administrator as well as the Chief Executive?
4. From what two sources does the ordinance power arise?
5. Why is a President's appointment power so critical to a President's success in office?
6. What officers does the President appoint? What is the Senate's role in the appointment process? What is senatorial courtesy?

5. The President's Diplomatic Powers

As You Read, Think About:

- What powers constitute the President's diplomatic powers.
- How the President exercises these powers.

The Constitution makes the President the nation's Chief Diplomat. It gives the President the power to make treaties with the consent of two-thirds of the Senate and to appoint ambassadors to other nations and other diplomatic officers subject to Senate confirmation. The Constitution also gives Presidents the power to receive foreign diplomatic representatives—that is, to *recognize* foreign governments.[17]

The Treaty Power

A **treaty** is a formal agreement between two or more sovereign states. The President, usually acting through the Secretary of State, negotiates these international agreements. The Senate must give its approval, by a two-thirds vote of the members present, before a treaty made by the President can become effective.[18]

The Framers considered the Senate—with, originally, only 26 members—a suitable council to advise the President in foreign affairs. Secrecy was thought to be necessary and was seen as an impossibility in a body as large as the House.

Turn the two-thirds rule around and it becomes a one-third-plus one-veto rule. That is, only one more than one-third of the Senators present and voting may defeat a treaty, no matter how important it might be to the nation's interests.

In 1919 the Senate rejected the Versailles Treaty, the general peace agreement to end World War I. The treaty included provisions for the League of Nations. Forty-nine Senators voted for the pact and 35 against, but the vote was 7 short of the necessary two-thirds. More than once a President has been forced to bow to the views of a few Senators in order to get a treaty passed, even when this meant making concessions opposed by the majority.

At times, a President has had to turn to roundabout methods. When a Senate minority defeated a treaty to annex Texas, President Tyler was able to bring about annexation in 1845 by a joint resolution—a move that needed only a majority vote in each house. In 1898 President McKinley used the same tactic to annex Hawaii, again after a treaty had failed in the Senate.

[17]Article II, Section 2, Clause 2; Section 3; see also Chapter 17.

[18]In spite of what many believe, the Senate does *not* "ratify" treaties. The Constitution requires Senate "advice and consent" to a treaty made by the President. *After* Senate approval, the President ratifies a treaty by the exchange of formal notifications with the other parties. Treaties have the same legal standing as do acts passed by Congress. Congress may repeal *(abrogate)* a treaty by passing a law contrary to its provisions, and an existing law may be repealed by the terms of a treaty. When a treaty and a statute conflict, the courts consider the latest enacted to be the law (*The Head Money Cases*, 1884). The terms of a treaty cannot conflict with the higher law of the Constitution (*Missouri* v. *Holland*, 1920), but the Supreme Court has never found a treaty provision to be unconstitutional. Money cannot be appropriated by a treaty. But in practice, whenever the Senate has approved a treaty that calls for an expenditure, the House has agreed to a bill providing the money.

*ENRICHMENT Have the class discuss: What (if any) are the problems with the process involved in the ratification of a treaty? Why is the process set up as it is?

BUILDING GOVERNMENT SKILLS

Interpreting Political Cartoons

The President, the most visible political leader of our nation, is often the subject of political cartoons. Political cartoons are pictures that express an opinion about a particular leader or current event using humor, sarcasm, and satire. Because cartoons can communicate an opinion quickly and because many people like to read and look at them, they can be an especially effective method of expressing an opinion.

Interpreting political cartoons requires some knowledge of current events. Also, cartoonists use certain techniques to portray their views of political events, organizations, and personalities.

To interpret a cartoon ask yourself the following questions:

- **How Are Caricature and Exaggeration Used in the Cartoon?**
  A caricature is a distorted drawing of a person that exaggerates certain characteristics. The person's nose, forehead, or hair may be enlarged in the drawing. The cartoonist may be trying to make the person look ridiculously angry, happy, evil, or just plain ridiculous. Note whether any particular subject of the cartoon is much larger than the others. Oversize is often used to illustrate power.
- **What Symbols Are in the Cartoon?**
  Often cartoonists use symbols to represent organizations or countries. For example, a donkey often represents the Democrats and an elephant represents the Republicans. "Uncle Sam" is the symbol for the United States.
- **What Are the Labels?**
  Sometimes unfamiliar symbols are used in a cartoon. When this happens, cartoonists use labels to let you know what the figure represents.

Chicago Historical Society

- **What Does the Caption Say?**
  The caption is the line, usually at the bottom of a cartoon, that tells you what the subject is thinking or saying; it is the punchline. The caption further explains the relationship or the action portrayed in the cartoon. Sometimes, instead of a caption, the cartoonist uses a bubble coming from the subject's mouth to show what the subject is saying.
- **What Is the Cartoonist's Opinion?**
  After you have examined all the pieces of the cartoon, you will have a good idea of the cartoonist's message.

1. Which of the techniques described here are employed in the above cartoon? What does President Truman seem to be requesting?
2. Compare several political cartoons showing President Reagan. How do different cartoonists portray him? Why?

Executive Agreements

More and more, international agreements, especially the routine ones, are made as **executive agreements.** These are pacts between the President and the heads of foreign states or their subordinates. Executive agreements do not require Senate consent.

Most executive agreements either flow out of legislation already passed by Congress or implement treaties the Senate has agreed to. The President, however, can make these agreements without any congressional action.[19]

Dozens of executive agreements are made each year, most of them of a fairly routine sort. At times, though, they are used for extraordinary purposes. For example, in the "Destroyer-Bases Deal" of 1940 the United States gave the hard-pressed British 50 "overage" destroyers early in World War II. In return, the United States received 99-year leases to several island bases extending from Newfoundland to the Caribbean.

Power of Recognition

When the President receives the diplomatic representatives sent to the United States by another sovereign state, the President exercises the power of **recognition.** That is, the President, acting for the United States, acknowledges the legal existence of that country and its government. By doing so, the President indicates that the United States accepts that country as an equal in the family of nations and is prepared to do business with it.[20]

Recognition does not mean that one government approves of the character and conduct of another. The United States recognizes several governments about which we have serious misgivings, most notably those of the USSR and the People's Republic of China. The facts of life in world politics make relations with these governments necessary.

Recognition is often used as a weapon in foreign relations, too. Prompt recognition of a new state or government may do much to guarantee its life. In the same way, the withholding of recognition may have a serious effect on its continued existence.

President Theodore Roosevelt's quick recognition of the Republic of Panama in 1903 is one of the classic examples of American use of the power as a diplomatic weapon. He recognized the new state less than three days after the Panamanians had begun a revolt against Colombia. His quick action guaranteed their success. In a very similar way, President Truman's recognition of Israel, within 24 hours of its creation in 1948, helped that new state to survive among its hostile Arab neighbors.

The President may show United States displeasure with the conduct of another country by asking for the recall of that nation's ambassador or other diplomatic representatives in this country. The official recalled is declared to be *persona non grata.* The same point can be made by the recalling of an American diplomat from a post in another country. The withdrawal of recognition is the sharpest diplomatic rebuke one government may give to another and has often been a step to war.

[19]The Supreme Court has held executive agreements to be as binding as treaties and a part of the supreme law of the land (*United States* v. *Belmont,* 1937; *Pink* v. *United States,* 1942).

[20]Sovereign states generally recognize one another through the exchange of diplomatic representatives. Recognition may be carried out in any of several other ways, however. For example, it may be accomplished by proposing to negotiate a treaty, since under international law only sovereign states can make such agreements.

FOR REVIEW

1. **Identify:** diplomatic powers, Chief Diplomat.
2. By whom are treaties made? Ratified?
3. What part does the Senate have in the treaty process?
4. What are executive agreements? Do they require the consent of the Senate?
5. What is the power of recognition? How does the President ordinarily exercise this power?

President Reagan, exercising his military powers, ordered Marines to serve in volatile Lebanon in 1982 as part of an international peace-keeping force. With what branch does the President share military powers?

6. The President's Military Powers

As You Read, Think About:

- What powers constitute the President's military powers.
- How the President exercises these powers.

The Constitution makes the President the Commander in Chief of the nation's armed forces.[21] Congress also has several important war powers. They include, especially, the power to declare war, to provide for the raising and maintaining of the armed forces, to make the rules by which they are governed, and to appropriate money for the nation's defense.[22]

The President's Dominant Position in Military Affairs

Even though Congress shares the war powers, the President's position in military affairs is as dominant as it is in the field of foreign affairs. In fact, it does not stretch the matter too far to say that the President's powers as Commander in Chief are almost without limit.

Take this illustration of the point: In 1907 Theodore Roosevelt sent the Great White Fleet around the world. He did so partly as a training exercise for the Navy, but even more to impress other nations with America's naval strength. Several members of Congress objected to the cost and threatened to block the necessary funds. To which TR replied: "Very well, the existing appropriation will carry the Navy halfway around the world and if Congress chooses to leave it on the other side, all right."

Presidents almost always delegate much of their command authority to military subordinates. They are not required to do so, however. George Washington actually took command of federal troops and led them into Pennsylvania in the Whiskey Rebellion of 1794. President Abraham Lincoln often visited the Army of the Potomac and instructed his generals in the field during the Civil War.

Most Presidents have not become so directly involved in military operations, however. Still, the President always has the final authority over and responsibility for any and all military matters. The most critical decisions are invariably made by the Commander in Chief. For example:

—President Truman's decisions to use the atomic bomb against Japan to end World War II and to send American troops to defend South Korea in 1950.
—President Johnson's decision to commit massive air and then ground forces in Vietnam in 1965.
—President Nixon's decisions to bomb targets in Cambodia (in secret) in 1969, to send American troops into that country in 1970, to resume bombing North Vietnam and mine its seaports in 1972, and to bomb Cambodian targets again in 1973.
—President Reagan's decision to use the Marines as part of an international peacekeeping force in war-torn Beirut in 1982.

[21]Article II, Section 2, Clause 1; see also Chapter 17.
[22]Article I, Section 8, Clauses 11-17; see also pages 73, 353.

*ENRICHMENT Congress may try to limit the President's power in military affairs through its power of the purse. Discuss how this can prove an effective means of limitation.

Several Presidents have used the armed forces abroad in combat without a declaration of war by Congress. In fact, most Presidents have, and on no fewer than 150 separate occasions in our history.

John Adams was the first to do so, in 1798. At his command, the Navy fought and won a number of battles with French warships harassing American merchantmen in the Atlantic and the Caribbean. Thomas Jefferson and then James Madison followed that precedent, in the war against the Barbary Coast pirates of North Africa in the early years of the 1800s. Many other similar foreign adventures occurred throughout the last century and into the present one. The long military conflicts in Korea and then in Vietnam were the largest of those "undeclared wars."

Ronald Reagan has used the armed forces in three combat situations: to repel attacks on the Marines in Lebanon in 1983 and 1984; in the lightning-quick invasion of Grenada in late 1983; and to bomb military targets in Libya in 1986. The latter action came in response to Libya's sponsorship of terrorist strikes against American citizens in Europe and the Middle East.

In today's world, no one can doubt that the President must be able to respond rapidly and effectively to threats to this nation's security. Still, many have long warned of the dangers inherent in the President's power to involve the nation in "undeclared wars." They insist that the Constitution never intended the President to have such power.

*The War Powers Resolution

The nation's frustrations and growing anguish over the war in Vietnam finally moved Congress to pass the War Powers Resolution of 1973. The act is designed to place close limits on the President's war-making powers. President Nixon vetoed the measure, calling it "both unconstitutional and dangerous to the best interest of our nation." Congress overrode the veto. The resolution's central provisions require that:

—Within 48 hours after committing American forces to combat abroad, the President must report to Congress, detailing the circumstances and the scope of his actions.

—That combat commitment must end within 60 days, unless Congress authorizes a longer period. That 60-day deadline may be extended for as much as 30 days, however, to allow for the safe withdrawal of the American forces involved.

—Congress may bring an end to the combat commitment at any time, by passing a concurrent resolution to that effect.

The constitutionality of the War Powers Resolution remains in dispute. A determination of the question must await a situation in which Congress demands that its provisions be obeyed but the President refuses to do so.

Wartime Powers

The President's military powers—his powers as Commander in Chief—are far greater during a war than they are in more normal times. In fact, his wartime authority goes far beyond the traditional military field. Thus, in World War II, for example, Congress gave the President the power to do such things as ration food and gasoline, control wages and prices, and seize and operate private industries vital to the nation's war effort.

The President may also use the armed forces to keep the domestic peace, as we saw in Chapter 4.[23] When necessary, he also has the power to call any State's militia, or all of them, into federal service.[24]

FOR REVIEW

1. **Identify:** Commander in Chief, military powers, War Powers Resolution.
2. What is the President's major military power?
3. How broad is that power?
4. For what purpose was the War Powers Resolution designed?

[23]See page 80 and Article IV, Section 4.

[24]Article I, Section 8, Clause 15; Article II, Section 2, Clause 1.

*REINFORCEMENT Discuss the separation of powers in light of the legislative powers given to the President by the Constitution. Make sure that the students understand Congress's "watchdog" role.

President Reagan meets with Republican Representatives from the House to explain—and, promote—his legislative program.

7. The President's Powers: Legislative and Judicial Powers

As You Read, Think About:

- What powers constitute the President's legislative and judicial powers.
- How the President exercises these specific powers.

As part of its system of checks and balances, the Constitution gives certain legislative and judicial powers to the President.

Legislative Powers

With his several legislative powers—and the skillful playing of his roles as Chief of Party and Chief Citizen—the President can (and often does) have a considerable influence on the actions of Congress. The President is in effect, then, the nation's Chief Legislator.

Power to Recommend Legislation The Constitution requires that the President

> shall, from time to time, give to the Congress information of the state of the Union, and recommend to their consideration such measures as he shall judge necessary and expedient.[25]

Soon after the beginning of each congressional session, the President delivers his State of the Union Message to Congress. This is quickly followed by the proposed budget and the annual Economic Report. At times, the President also submits special messages on certain subjects. In all of them the legislators are called on to enact those laws the President thinks are necessary.

The Veto Power The Constitution says that "every bill" and "every order, resolution, or vote to which the concurrence of the Senate and House of Representatives may be necessary (except on a question of adjournment) shall be presented to the President" for his action.[26]

As we noted in Chapter 12, the Constitution presents the President with four options

[25]Article II, Section 3; see also page 314.

[26]Article I, Section 7, Clauses 2 and 3. Notice, however, that practice has it that joint resolutions proposing constitutional amendments and concurrent resolutions, which do not have the force of law, are not sent to the President.

when the Congress sends a measure to the White House:

First, the President may sign the bill, thus making it law.

Second, the President may veto[27] the bill, and then must return it to the house in which it originated, together with a written statement of objections. Though it does not often do so, Congress may override a presidential veto by a two-thirds vote in each house.

Third, the President may allow the bill to become law without signature: by not acting on it, neither signing nor vetoing it, for 10 days (not counting Sundays). This rarely happens.

The *fourth* option, the "pocket veto," can be used only at the end of a congressional session. If Congress adjourns within 10 days of sending a bill to the President and the Chief Executive does not act on it, the measure dies. The pocket veto has been applied.

The **veto power** allows the President, who is the only representative of *all* the people, to act as a check on Congress. Often, just the *threat* of a veto is enough to defeat a bill or to

[27] *Veto,* from the Latin, literally, "I forbid."

Presidential Vetoes

President	Years	Vetoes Regular	Pocket	Total	Vetoes Overridden
Washington	1789-97	2	-	2	-
Madison	1809-17	5	2	7	-
Monroe	1817-25	1	-	1	-
Jackson	1829-37	5	7	12	-
Van Buren	1837-41	-	1	1	-
Tyler	1841-45	6	4	10	1
Polk	1845-49	2	1	3	-
Pierce	1853-57	9	-	9	5
Buchanan	1857-61	4	3	7	-
Lincoln	1861-65	2	5	7	-
Johnson	1865-69	21	8	29	15
Grant	1869-77	45	48	93	4
Hayes	1877-81	12	1	13	1
Arthur	1881-85	4	8	12	1
Cleveland	1885-89	304	110	414	2
Harrison	1889-93	19	25	44	1
Cleveland	1893-97	42	128	170	5
McKinley	1897-01	6	36	42	-
Roosevelt	1901-09	42	40	82	1
Taft	1909-13	30	9	39	1
Wilson	1913-21	33	11	44	6
Harding	1921-23	5	1	6	-
Coolidge	1923-29	20	30	50	4
Hoover	1929-33	21	16	37	3
Roosevelt	1933-45	372	263	635	9
Truman	1945-53	180	70	250	12
Eisenhower	1953-61	73	108	181	2
Kennedy	1961-63	12	9	21	-
Johnson	1963-69	16	14	30	-
Nixon	1969-74	26	17	43	7
Ford	1974-77	48	18	66	12
Carter	1977-81	13	18	31	2
Reagan	1981-85	18	21	39	4
		1,398	1,032	2,430	98

Source: Congressional Research Service, Library of Congress. Presidents not listed vetoed no measures.

bring about some changes in it before it is passed by Congress.

The historical record of presidential vetoes, and the fact that they are rarely overridden, can be seen in the table on page 424.

Bills must be vetoed in their entirety. The President has no "item veto," as do most State governors. With that power, needless or wasteful projects might be eliminated from an appropriations measure or an objectionable provision removed from a bill the President might otherwise wish to become law. On the other hand, the power could be used as a weapon to punish or pressure the President's opponents in Congress. Every President since Woodrow Wilson has favored a constitutional amendment to add the item veto to the President's legislative arsenal.

Other Legislative Powers Only the President may call special sessions of Congress, as we noted in Chapter 11. The President also has the power to adjourn *(prorogue)* Congress when the two houses cannot agree on an adjournment date (which has never happened).

Judicial Powers

The Constitution states that the President

> shall have the power to grant reprieves and pardons for offenses against the United States, except in cases of impeachment.[28]

A **reprieve** is the postponement of the carrying out of a sentence. A **pardon** is legal (though not moral) forgiveness of a crime.

The President's power to grant reprieves and pardons is absolute. In cases of impeachment, however, reprieves and pardons may never be granted. These powers of *clemency* (of mercy, leniency) may be used only in cases involving federal offenses. The President has no such authority with regard to those who violate State law.

*Presidential pardons are usually granted to persons accused of federal crimes *after* they have been convicted in court. The President may pardon a federal offender *before* that person is tried, however. In fact, a pardon may be issued even before that person has been formally charged.

Pardons in advance of a trial or charge have been rare. The most noteworthy pardon, by far, was granted in 1974. In that year, President Gerald Ford gave "a full, free and absolute pardon unto Richard Nixon for all offenses against the United States which he . . . has committed or may have committed or taken part in during the period from January 20, 1969, through August, 9, 1974."

To be effective, a pardon must be accepted by the person to whom it is granted. When one is granted before charge or conviction, as in Mr. Nixon's case, its acceptance is regularly seen as an admission of guilt by the person to whom it is given.

The pardoning power includes the power to grant *conditional* pardons if the conditions are reasonable. It also includes the power of **commutation**—that is, the power to commute or reduce, the length of a sentence and/or the fine to be paid.

It also includes the power of **amnesty**—in effect, a general pardon offered to a group of law violators. Thus, in 1889 President Benjamin Harrison issued a proclamation of amnesty forgiving all Mormons who had violated the antipolygamy laws in the federal territories.

FOR REVIEW

1. **Identify:** legislative powers, pocket veto.
2. Why does the Constitution give certain legislative powers to the President? What are they?
3. Outline the veto power. By what vote may Congress override a presidential veto? Why is the threat of a veto at times an important presidential tool?
4. Does the President have the item veto?
5. Under what circumstances may a President pardon someone? What must rank as the most noted of all presidential pardons?
6. What is a reprieve? A commutation?

[28] Article II, Section 2, Clause 1.

*ENRICHMENT Discuss in class: The Supreme Court declared the death penalty constitutional; should the President's power to pardon be allowed to supercede this decision?

SUMMARY

Every officer, employee, and agency of the executive branch is subordinate to the President and aids the President in carrying out the executive function. The President's chief right arm is the Executive Office of the President—a group of agencies staffed by key advisers and assistants. The Cabinet, made up of the heads of the 13 executive departments, is also a major source of advice to the President.

The President's powers arise from the Constitution, acts of Congress, and usage. The nature of the President's powers has been most tellingly shaped by the manner in which the stronger Presidents have used their powers. They include:

1. *Executive powers:* to execute and enforce the law, to direct administration, to issue executive orders, and to appoint and remove major officers.
2. *Diplomatic powers:* to make treaties, to make executive agreements, to send and receive diplomatic representatives, and otherwise conduct foreign relations.
3. *Military powers:* to act as Commander in Chief and to keep domestic peace.
4. *Legislative powers:* to recommend legislation, to approve or veto acts of Congress, to call special sessions of Congress, and to adjourn Congress when the two houses cannot agree on an adjournment date.
5. *Judicial powers:* to exercise executive clemency (pardons, reprieves, amnesties, commutations).

CHAPTER REVIEW

Key Terms/Concepts*

budget (404)
Cabinet (406)
executive orders (415)
treaty (418)
executive agreement (420)
recognition (420)
veto power (424)
reprieve (425)
pardon (425)
commutation (425)
amnesty (425)

*These terms are included in the Glossary.

Keynote Questions

• 1. What basic power does the Constitution assign to the President?

• 2. The Constitution deals with the Presidency in very broad, almost outline-like fashion. What factors other than the Constitution's provisions, have shaped both the office of the Presidency and the scope of its powers?

• 3. What is the main function of the Executive Office of the President?

• 4. What is OMB's role in making the federal budget? In managing the federal bureaucracy?

• 5. How are Cabinet members selected?

• 6. Who belongs to the Cabinet? What two major jobs do these Cabinet members perform?

• 7. How has the unity of the Presidency contributed to the growth and present-day scope of presidential power?

The dots represent skill levels required to answer each question or complete each activity: •requires recall and comprehension • •requires application and analysis • • •requires synthesis and evaluation

• **8.** Why, in executing and enforcing the law, does the executive branch also interpret the law?

• **9.** What are executive orders? What purpose do they serve?

• **10.** Why is the President's power to appoint so important to the President's ability to carry out the office?

• **11.** What limits have been set on the President's removal power?

• **12.** How does a treaty differ from an executive agreement?

• **13.** How are treaties ratified?

• **14.** Give one example of how a President has used the recognition power as a weapon in foreign relations.

• **15.** According to the Constitution, what is the President's role in military matters? How does the War Powers Resolution limit this power?

• **16.** List the legislative and judicial powers of the President. Why did the Constitution grant these powers to the President?

Skill Application

Predicting Alternative Futures: Whenever you answer a "what if" question, you are predicting alternative futures. When you do so, you look at some event or situation and then imagine the possible consequences of that event. For example, speculate on this question: "What if George Washington had accepted becoming President for life?" You might speculate that the Constitution would have been amended so that a President could hold office for life, that our political system would be very different today, or that our system of checks and balances would no longer be effective, and so on.

In this chapter you learned that two general and contrasting views of the Presidency have been held by several Presidents. Read the two excerpts on page 412 that represent these two views, then answer the following questions:

1. What if all Presidents had thought like Theodore Roosevelt? How would the Presidency be different from what it is today?

2. What if all Presidents had thought like William Howard Taft? How would the Presidency be different from what it is today?

For Thought and Discussion

•• **1.** Every President since Woodrow Wilson (including President Reagan) has favored a constitutional amendment giving the President the item veto power. Would you support such a constitutional amendment? Why or why not?

••• **2.** Some people argue that nuclear weapons and television have contributed significantly to the power of the President, shifting the balance of power between Congress and the President toward the President. Do you agree with this view? Why or why not?

•• **3.** How can the President use Cabinet members to promote policies which the President favors? Under what circumstances might a President prefer to ask a Cabinet member to promote a certain policy rather than do so himself?

••• **4.** How might the party composition of Congress (the proportionate number of Democrats and Republicans in the House and in the Senate) affect the President's ability to carry out his or her policies?

Suggested Activities

••• **1.** Make a chart of the President's present Cabinet. Include the department, name of the Secretary, date appointed, and some significant information on the Secretary's background, and a summary of why that person was selected and appointed to the Cabinet. Use news periodicals to find this information.

••• **2.** Using several cartoons from newspapers and newsmagazines (or your own cartoons), prepare a poster or booklet on "Cartoonists' Views on the President." Write a one paragraph summary of the issues highlighted by each cartoon. What was the political cartoonist trying to say?

••• **3.** Stage a debate or class forum on one of the following topics: (a) *Resolved,* That the Constitution be amended to forbid the President to use the armed forces in combat without a declaration of war by Congress; (b) *Resolved,* That the Constitution be amended to repeal the Senate's power to confirm or reject major presidential appointments.

The true test of good government is its aptitude and tendency to produce a good administration.
—ALEXANDER HAMILTON

16

Running the Federal Government: Bureaucracy/Dollars

CHAPTER OBJECTIVES

To help you to

Learn · Know · Understand

The need for and growth of the federal bureaucracy.

The overall shape of the organization of the executive branch and the nature of staff/line functions.

The organization/functions of the executive departments.

The organization/functions of the independent agencies.

The continuing need for reorganization in the executive branch.

The development and present shape of the federal civil service.

The Federal Government's finances.

AS WE HAVE said several times, and in several different ways, the basic function of government in the United States is to translate the public will into public policy. In short, what the people want is what government is supposed to do.

In its broadest sense, public policy may be defined as what government does. Government does *many* different things, of course. So, public policy is in fact made up of many different policies on many different matters. Clearly, those policies must first be made and then administered, put into effect. And, of course, they must be paid for.

To this point, we have been very largely concerned with the *making* of public policy in the United States. We have looked at the constitutional setting in which that happens; at the roles of public opinion, pressure groups, parties, and voters in that process; and at Congress and the Presidency. Now we turn to the other side of the whole matter of public policy—to its *administration,* to "policy in action."

In this chapter we look first at the overall shape of the federal administrative structure —at the federal bureaucracy, at the machin-

The data gathered by the Census Bureau are indispensable to both the making and administration of public policy. *Above:* Taking the census in 1940. *Facing page:* A census taker of 1980.

ery and the personnel through which the executive branch of the Federal Government operates. And then we shall look at the financing of the Federal Government—for, as we shall see, public money and public policy are really inseparable parts of the same whole.[1]

In Chapter 1 we said that there is nothing about democracy that guarantees that those who make public policy decisions will always find the "right" or the "best" answers to public problems. In fact, the democratic process is not even designed to find those kinds of answers. It looks, instead, for *satisfactory* solutions. Even if Congress and the President make the wisest of policies, their decisions still must be carried out. Without * an **administration**—without administrators and administrative agencies—the best of public policies amount to just so many words and phrases.

In other words, a **bureaucracy**—a large and complex administrative structure in the executive branch—is an altogether necessary feature of the Federal Government today. A number of factors have produced the need for it. Certainly, the many and extensive powers of the Presidency is a leading factor. No single person, alone and unaided, could possibly do the huge job that the Constitution assigns to the Chief Executive. Several other factors—the size of the nation's population, the sweep of its geography, and ongoing scientific, technological, and industrial developments—are also major contributors to that need. So, too, are government's concerns for economic growth, for social welfare and social justice, and for the nation's security at home and abroad, and for all other policy concerns of the Federal Government.

As we go on, come back to this thought: A large and extensive executive branch, often called "the administration" or "the bureaucracy," is a very common feature of modern

[1]We shall look at the institutions and process by which public policy is made, and financed, at the State and local levels of government in Chapters 19–24.

*ENRICHMENT We often hear the phrase "Reagan Administration," or "Carter Administration." Ask the class what the term *administration* means in this context.

governments both here and abroad. One central problem for democracy is to keep that structure responsive to the law and to the elected representatives of the people. The growth in the number, reach, and power of administrative agencies makes effective control of them absolutely necessary. Those agencies cannot be allowed to obstruct rather than promote the policies, interests, and wishes of "government by the people."

1. The Federal Bureaucracy

As You Read, Think About:

- Why the bureaucracy is necessary to the operation of the executive branch.
- What the various titles mean in the different offices of the bureaucracy.
- What the difference is between staff and line agencies.

As we know, the Constitution makes the President the *Chief Administrator* of the Federal Government. It does so quite directly. Article II, Section 3 declares that "he shall take care that the laws be faithfully executed."

The Constitution makes only the barest mention of the administrative machinery through which the President is to exercise that power, however. Article II does suggest the existence of several executive departments—by giving to the President the power to "require the opinion, in writing, of the principal officers in each of the executive departments."[2] Article II also suggests the existence of two departments, for military and for foreign affairs—by making the President the "Commander in Chief of the army and navy," and by giving him the power to make treaties and to appoint "ambassadors, other public ministers, and consuls."[3]

Beyond those few and quite general references, the Constitution is silent on the matter. Clearly, however, the Framers intended that administrative agencies be created—as, indeed, they have.

As the chart on page 431 shows, the executive branch is now made up of three major groups of administrative agencies: (1) the Executive Office of the President, (2) the 13 Cabinet Departments, and (3) a large number of independent agencies.[4]

We talked about the Executive Office, and its several agencies, in Chapter 15. We shall look at the other groups shortly. First a word on two matters: what is often called the "name game" and the difference between *staff* and *line* agencies and functions.

The Name Game

The titles given to the many units that make up the executive branch vary a great deal. The name *department* is reserved for agencies of Cabinet rank. Beyond that, however, there is little in the way of standardized use of titles, which can be confusing.

The term *agency* is often used to refer to any governmental body. "Agency" is sometimes used to identify a major unit headed by a single administrator of near-Cabinet status, such as the Environmental Protection Agency and the United States Arms Control and Disarmament Agency. But so, too, is the title *administration*—for example, the National Aeronautics and Space Administration, the General Services Administration, and the Veterans Administration.

The name *commission* is usually given to those agencies charged with the regulation of business activities, such as the Interstate Commerce Commission and the Securities and Exchange Commission. These units are seldom headed by a single administrator; they are composed of a varying number of top-ranking officers (commissioners). The

[2]In Section 2, Clause 1. There is also a reference to "heads of departments" in Clause 2, and to "any department or officer" of the government in Article I, Section 8, Clause 18, the Necessary and Proper Clause.

[3]In Section 2, Clauses 1 and 2.

[4]The chart is adapted from the current edition of the *United States Government Manual*, a yearly publication of the Office of the Federal Register in the General Services Administration. The *Manual* contains a brief description of the creation, authority, and functions of each of the agencies operating in each of the three branches of the Federal Government. The bulk (over 90 percent) of its now nearly 1,000 pages is devoted to the executive branch.

The Government of the United States

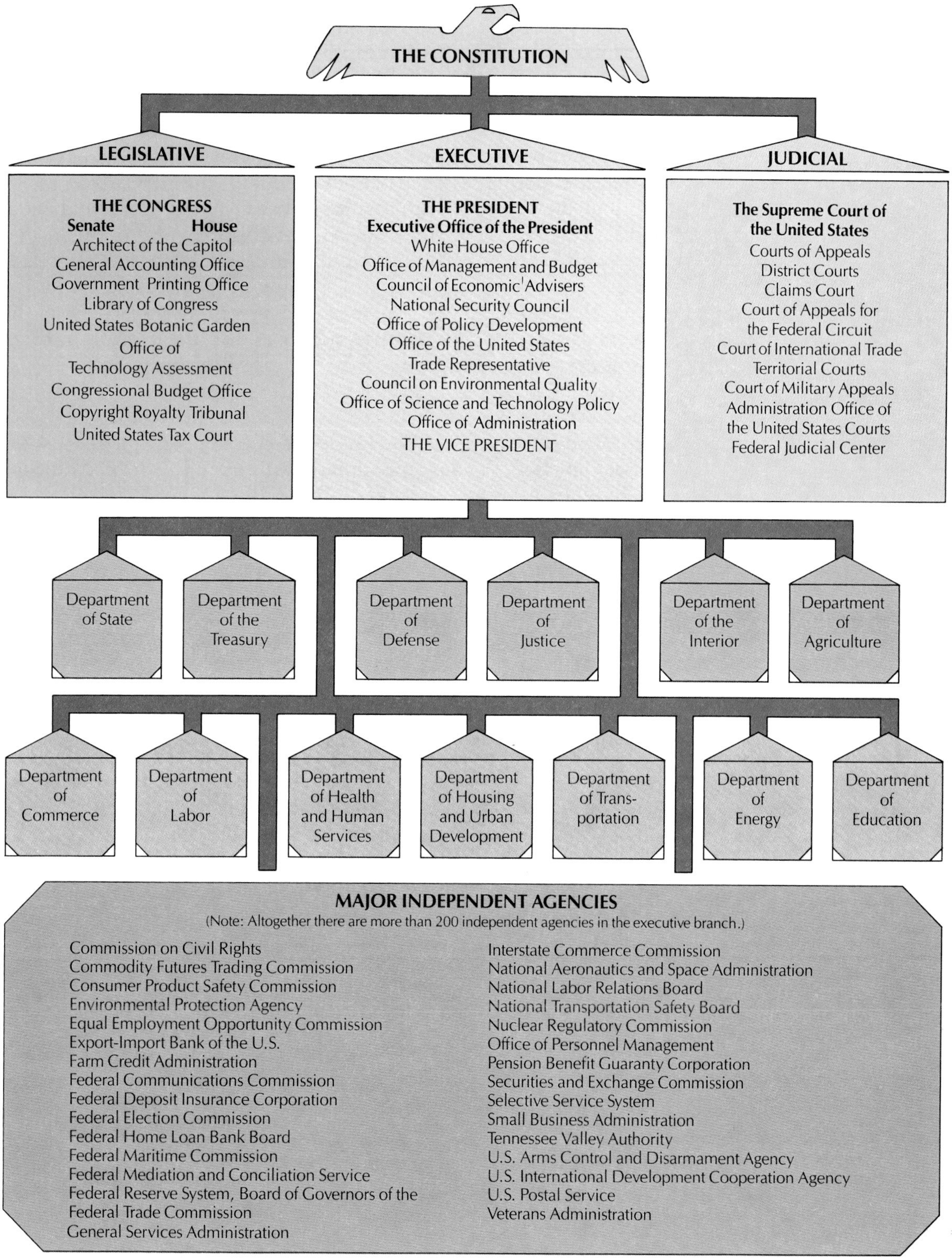

Under which major branch of the Federal Government is the Library of Congress?

*REINFORCEMENT Discuss in class: The chart above depicts the federal bureaucracy; in this form, the bureaucracy does not look as forbidding as many say it is. Do you feel each structure is necessary?

same title, however, is also given to some investigative, advisory, and other bodies, including the Civil Rights Commission and the Federal Election Commission.

Either *corporation* or *authority* is the title most often given to agencies headed by a board and a manager and that conduct businesslike activities, such as the Federal Deposit Insurance Corporation and the Tennessee Valley Authority.

Within each major agency, this same pattern—lack of uniformity and, so, confusion—is common. *Bureau* is the name often given to the major elements in a department, but *service, administration, office, branch,* and *division* are titles often used for the same purpose. Thus, the major units within the Treasury Department include the Internal Revenue Service, the Customs Service, the Bureau of the Mint, the Bureau of the Public Debt, and the Office of the Comptroller of the Currency.

Many federal agencies are very often referred to by their initials rather than by their full titles. EPA, IRS, VA, FBI, CIA, FCC, and TVA are but a few of dozens of familiar examples of the practice.[5] A few are also known by nicknames. The Federal National Mortgage Association is often called "Fannie Mae," and the National Railroad Passenger Corporation is better known as Amtrak.

Staff and Line

The several units that make up any administrative organization can be classified as either *staff* or *line* agencies. Staff agencies and their personnel serve in a support capacity. They aid the chief executive and other administrators by furnishing advice and other assistance in the management of the organization. Line agencies, on the other hand, are directly involved with, actually perform, the basic task for which the organization exists.

Take, as two quick illustrations of this distinction, the several agencies in the Executive Office of the President and, in contrast, the Environmental Protection Agency. The agencies making up the Executive Office —the White House Office, the National Security Council, the Office of Management and Budget, and so on—each exist as staff support to the President. Their primary mission is to assist the President in the exercise of the executive power and in the overall management of the executive branch. They are *not* operating agencies. That is, they do not operate (administer) public programs.

The Environmental Protection Agency has a quite different mission. It is responsible for the day-to-day enforcement of the several federal antipollution laws. It operates "on the line," where the action is.

This difference between staff and line can help us to understand the complexities of the federal bureaucracy. But, remember: the distinction can be oversimplified or pushed too far. For example, most line agencies do have staff units of their own, to aid them in their line operations. Thus, the EPA's Office of Congressional Liaison is the Administrator's right arm in the critical matter of relations with Congress, its several committees, and its individual members.

FOR REVIEW

1. **Identify:** Chief Administrator, Cabinet department, agency, staff/line agency.
2. Of what is public policy composed?
3. What is a bureaucracy?
4. Why is a bureaucracy an absolute necessity in the Federal Government today?
5. The federal bureaucracy is made up of what three major groups of agencies?
6. What terms are most often used in the titles of federal agencies?
7. What are staff agencies and functions? Line agencies and functions?

[5] The *Government Manual* carries a list of some 400 more or less well-known initial-designations (acronyms) for federal agencies. The use of acronyms can sometimes cause problems. When the old Bureau of the Budget was reorganized in 1970, it was also renamed. It is now the Office of Management and Budget (OMB). Until almost the very moment of its creation, however, it was slated to be known as the Bureau of Management and Budget (BOMB).

REINFORCEMENT Have the class discuss the general roles of staff agencies and line agencies. Which agency would they prefer to work for? Why?

2. The Executive Departments

As You Read, Think About:

- What the responsibilities are of each of the 13 executive departments.
- Why the departments have so many divisions.

Much of the Federal Government's work is done by the 13 executive departments. They are the traditional units of federal administration, and each is built around a broad field of activity.

The 1st Congress set up three of these departments in 1789: State, Treasury, and War. As the size and the workload of the Federal Government grew, new departments were added. Some of the later ones took over various duties originally assigned to older departments, and they gradually assumed new functions, as well. And a few departments have been created and later abolished by Congress.

The head of each department is known as the Secretary, except for the Attorney General, who directs the work of the Justice Department. Each department head is named by the President, subject to confirmation by the Senate.

The organizational chart of the Department of Labor, shown below, presents a fairly typical picture of the structure of the executive departments.

Together, the department secretaries serve as the members of the President's Cabinet, a matter we talked about in the last chapter. Their duties as the chief officers of their own agencies generally take most of their time, however. Each of them is the

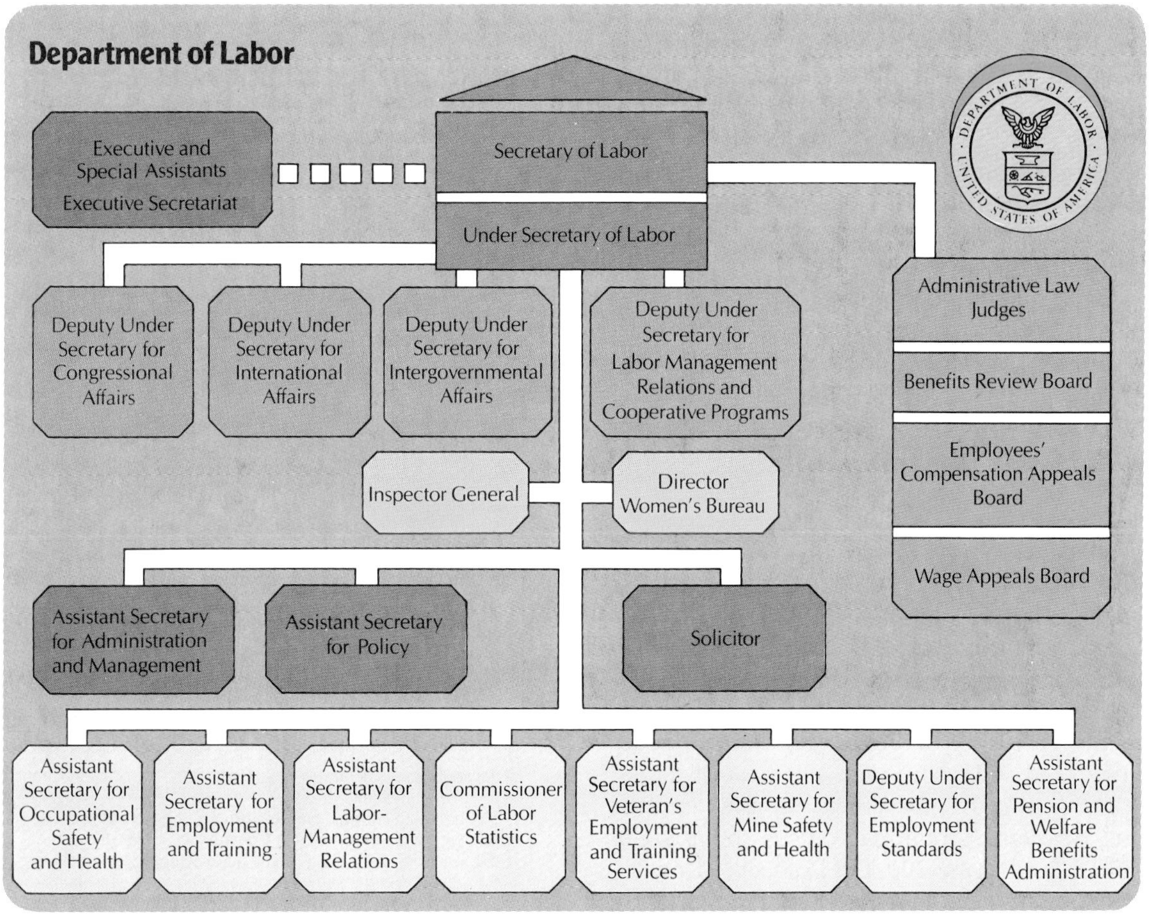

"Small Society" by Brickman. Washington Star Syndicate, Inc.

primary link between presidential policy and his or her own department. Just as importantly, each department head tries to promote and protect that department with the President, congressional committees, the rest of the bureaucracy, and the public.

The secretary is aided in that many-sided role by an under secretary or deputy secretary and several assistant secretaries. They, too, are named by the President and confirmed by the Senate. Staff help for the secretary comes from assistants and aides (with a wide range of titles) in such areas as personnel, planning, legal advice, budgeting, and public relations.

Each department is made up of a number of subunits, both staff and line. As we noted a moment ago, these agencies are known as bureaus, offices, services, divisions, and so on. Each agency is divided into smaller units. About 80 percent of the bureau and office chiefs, the "middle management" personnel, are career people.

The internal structure of most of the departments is also arranged on a geographic basis. That is, many of its activities are conducted through regional offices that direct the work of agency employees in the field. For example, the Treasury Department's Internal Revenue Service is headquartered in Washington. Yet most of its tax collection and enforcement work is carried out through 7 regional offices, 60 district offices, and some 200 local offices. Altogether, about 90 percent of all federal civilian employees work outside the nation's capital.

Over the next several pages, we summarize the work/functions of the principal agencies of 11 of the 13 executive departments. The Departments of State and Defense are discussed in Chapter 17.

The Executive Departments Today

Department	Created
State	1789
Treasury	1789
Defense[a]	1949
Justice[b]	1870
Interior	1849
Agriculture	1889
Commerce[c]	1903
Labor[c]	1913
Health and Human Services[d]	1953
Housing and Urban Development	1965
Transportation	1967
Energy	1977
Education[d]	1979

[a]Congress created National Military Establishment, as an executive department headed by Secretary of Defense, in 1947; renamed Department of Defense in 1949. Since 1947 has included former Cabinet-level Departments of War (1789) and Navy (1798) and Department of the Air Force (1947).

[b]Post of Attorney General established by Congress in 1789.

[c]Department of Commerce and Labor, established in 1903,

[d]Education functions transferred from Department of Health, Education, and Welfare to new Department of Education in 1979; HEW renamed in 1979.

Note: Another executive department, the Post Office Department, was abolished by Congress in 1971. Originally established in 1789, it was made an executive department in 1872. Congress transformed it into a government corporation, the United States Postal Service, in 1971.

ENRICHMENT Discuss in class: Departmental Secretaries change with each Administration, as do deputy and assistant secretaries. How might this affect the bureaucracies of the agencies?

THE EXECUTIVE DEPARTMENTS:

Principal Agencies and Functions*

Department of the Treasury

Established: 1789
Head: Secretary of the Treasury
Employees, 1987: 129,600 (est.)

The Treasury Department is the Government's leading financial agency. Its major functions include: the collection of tax revenue and customs duties; borrowing and the management of the public debt; criminal law enforcement (notably tax evasion, smuggling, counterfeiting); accounting for public monies; the manufacture of coins and currency; and the supervision of national banks.

Internal Revenue Service. Administers, enforces most federal tax laws; collects nearly all federal taxes (including, especially, personal and corporate income, social security, excise, estate, and gift taxes).

United States Customs Service. Administers, enforces customs laws; collects duties on imports; combats smuggling, other illegal practices in international trade.

Bureau of the Public Debt. Supervises most federal borrowing; manages the public debt.

Bureau of Alcohol, Tobacco and Firearms. Administers, enforces federal firearms, explosives laws, and those covering production, use, distribution of alcohol and tobacco products.

Financial Management Service. Government's central bookkeeper and principal financial reporting agency.

*The several agencies listed on these pages are the major units within Cabinet-level departments treated here. There are a number of other agencies within each of those departments; see the current edition of *The United States Government Manual.*

The use of computer technology has greatly speeded the processing of tax returns. According to the graph below, what tax has generated the most income since 1965?

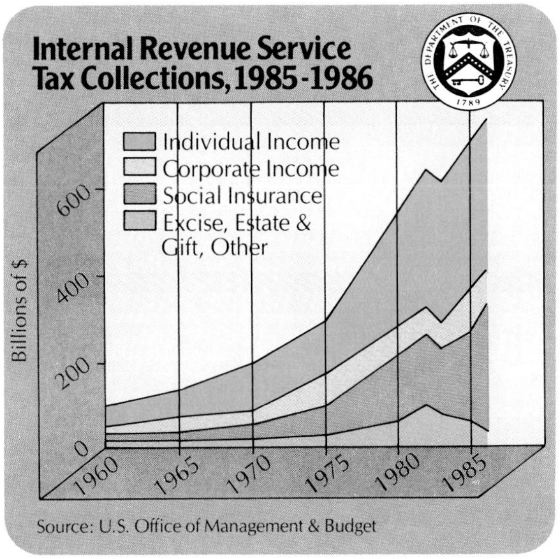

Public Debt of Federal Government, 1960-1986

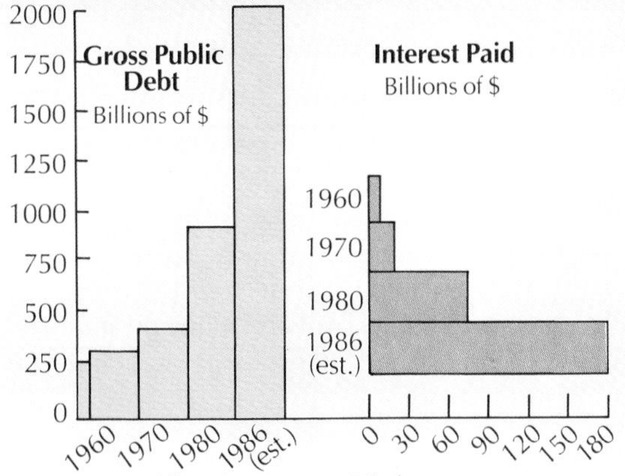

Source: U.S. Office of Management & Budget

Approximately how much has the interest payment on the U.S. public debt increased since 1980?

Bureau of Engraving and Printing. Designs, engraves, prints all currency (paper money), treasury bonds and notes, postage stamps, food coupons and similar financial items issued by the Government.

Bureau of the Mint. Manufactures all U.S. coins; holds stocks of gold, silver; operates Mints (Philadelphia, Denver), Assay Office (San Francisco), Gold Depository (Fort Knox, Kentucky), Silver Depository (West Point, N.Y.).

Office of the Comptroller of the Currency. Headed by the Comptroller of the Currency; administers federal banking laws and generally supervises the operations of 4,700 national banks; directs staff of 2,100 bank examiners to assure the soundness of the operations and financial condition of all national banks.

United States Secret Service. Protects the President and Vice President, the members of their immediate families, former Presidents and their wives or widows, presidential and vice presidential candidates, and visiting heads of foreign states; enforces laws against counterfeiting.

Department of Justice *

Established: 1870
Head: Attorney General
Employees, 1987: 65,800 (est.)

The Department of Justice is the nation's largest law firm. Among its major responsibilities, it: furnishes legal advice to the President and heads of the other Executive Departments; represents the United States in court; enforces most federal criminal laws; enforces federal civil rights, antitrust, public lands, immigration and naturalization laws, and supervises the federal penal system.

Solicitor General. Represents the United States in the Supreme Court; decides which lower court decisions Government should ask Supreme

The Bureau of Engraving and Printing prints all currency issued by the Government.

Justice Department officials unload confiscated marijuana at a dock in New York City.

* ENRICHMENT Have the class discuss the divisions of the Department of Justice. Which agency would they find the most exciting to work for?

Court to review and which position Government should take in cases heard by the High Court.

Antitrust Division. Handles court cases involving violations of antitrust laws, other federal statutes covering illegal business practices.

Land and Natural Resources Division. Handles most civil (noncriminal) cases involving the public lands and other real property owned by the United States; represents the Government's interests in civil cases involving Indians and Indian affairs; handles civil and criminal cases arising out of federal environmental protection laws.

Tax Division. Handles civil and criminal cases arising out of the tax laws; often acts as in-court attorney for the Internal Revenue Service.

Civil Rights Division. Handles both civil and criminal cases involving acts of discrimination prohibited by the various federal civil rights laws.

Civil Division. Handles most of the civil cases to which the United States is a party (all of those civil cases not handled by one of the other Divisions).

Criminal Division. Handles most court cases involving federal crimes (all criminal cases not handled by one of the other Divisions).

Immigration and Naturalization Service. Administers, enforces the immigration laws (involving aliens who seek to enter or remain in the United States) and the naturalization laws (relating to aliens who seek to become American citizens).

Federal Bureau of Investigation. Investigates most cases involving violations of federal criminal laws; pursues, arrests most persons suspected of or charged with federal crimes.

Drug Enforcement Administration. Administers, enforces federal laws relating to controlled substances (principally narcotics and dangerous drugs).

Bureau of Prisons. Operates the federal penal system (including five penitentiaries and several other correctional institutions).

Department of the Interior

Established: 1849
Head: Secretary of the Interior
Employees, 1987: 70,300 (est.)

The Interior Department is the Government's major conservation agency. Its principal work involves: the management of more than 500 million acres of public lands; conservation, development, and use of mineral, water, fish, and wildlife resources; reclamation of arid lands; operation of federal hydroelectric power facilities; administration of the national parks system; and responsibility for American Indian Reservations.

Which graph reflects Interior's role as the nation's major conservation agency?

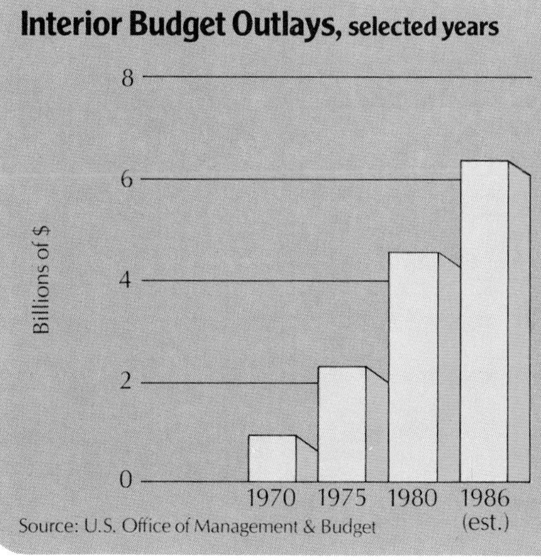

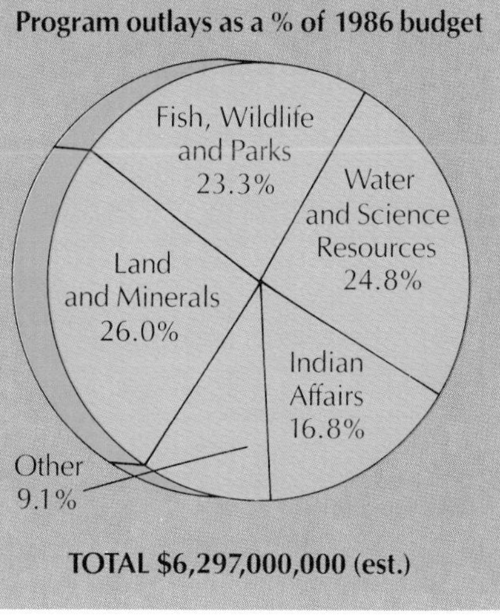

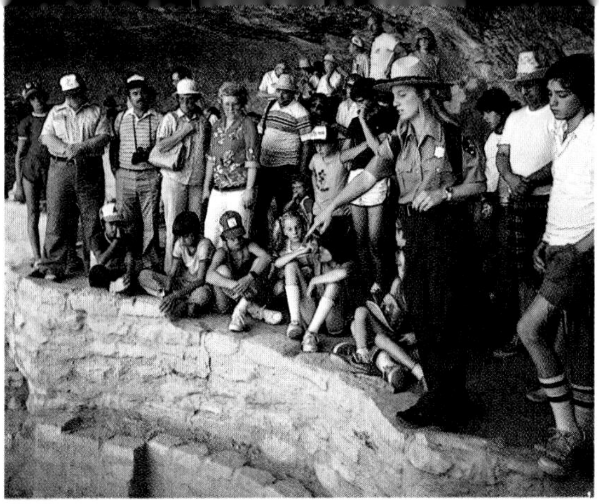

At Mesa Verde National Park, in Colorado, a guide discusses Indian ruins.

Bureau of Land Management. Controls, manages some 342 million acres of public lands (most of the land owned by the United States, located chiefly in the Far West and Alaska); manages timber, oil, gas, minerals, rangeland, recreation, and other resources of those lands; leases (and sometimes sells) public lands; leases Outer Continental Shelf lands for oil, gas, and other resource exploration and development.

Bureau of Reclamation. Builds, operates water projects to reclaim arid and semiarid lands in the western States; most BLM projects are multipurpose. That is, in addition to water conservation, storage, and irrigation, they serve such other purposes as hydroelectric power generation, flood control, municipal and industrial water supply, navigation, and outdoor recreation.

The U.S. Geological Survey employs cartographers to make detailed topographical maps.

National Park Service. Administers the more than 330 units of the National Park System (including national parks, national monuments of natural and scientific value, scenic rivers, lakeshores and seashores, recreation areas, and historic sites); plays host to more than 300 million tourist visits each year.

United States Fish and Wildlife Service. Responsible for protecting and increasing the nation's fish and wildlife resources; maintains more than 430 wildlife refuges, 73 fish hatcheries, a number of laboratories, and a nationwide network of wildlife law enforcement agents.

Geological Survey. Conducts surveys and other research to describe (map) the geography and geology of the United States and to locate the nation's oil, gas, mineral, water, power, and other natural resources; its very detailed topographic and geologic maps and other reports now cover more than half of the land area of the United States.

Office of Surface Mining Reclamation and Enforcement. Administers, enforces federal laws to protect people and the environment from the harmful effects of coal mining; regulates strip mining activities; works to reclaim abandoned mines and mined lands; aids the States in the development and enforcement of their own similar regulatory programs.

Voting in a tribal election are Navajo Indians who live on a reservation in Arizona.

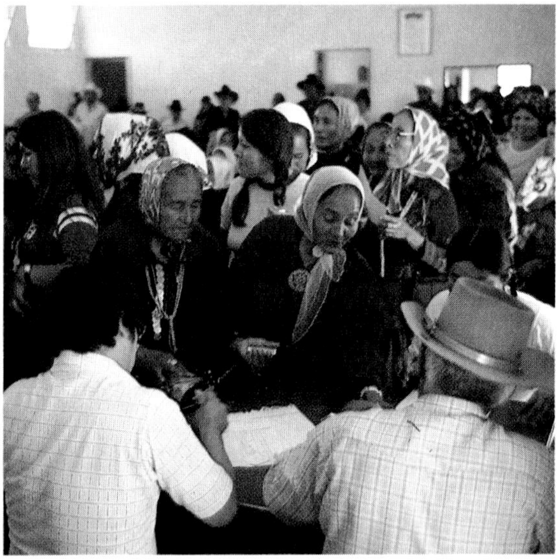

Bureau of Mines. Conducts research, issues factual reports on mining techniques, mine health and safety, environmental pollution, the recycling of solid wastes, and nearly all other phases of mining activity in this country.

Bureau of Indian Affairs. Administers educational, public health, and other social assistance programs for the nation's Indian population, especially the approximately 600,000 Indians who now live on or near some 260 reservations.

Office of Territorial and International Affairs. Works to promote the economic, social, and political development of the territories of the Virgin Islands, Guam, American Samoa, and the Trust Territory of the Pacific Islands.

A farmer harvests wheat in Palouse, Washington.

* Department of Agriculture

Established: 1889
Head: Secretary of Agriculture
Employees, 1987: 98,500 (est.)

The Department of Agriculture reflects this fundamentally important point: the nation's farms produce the food upon which all of us must depend and they also produce a goodly share of the raw materials essential to the nation's manufacturing industries. The USDA's several agencies have wide-ranging responsibilities in the areas of agricultural conservation and rural development, marketing, credit, crop stabilization, and research and education.

Farmers Home Administration. Makes several different types of low-interest, long-term loans to farmers and farm groups who are unable to get credit at reasonable terms from other (private) lenders; most FHA loans are made for the purchase, enlargement, improvement, or operation of family-sized farms.

Rural Electrification Administration. Makes low-interest, long-term loans to farm cooperatives and other rural-based nonprofit groups to provide electric power and/or telephone service to people in rural areas.

Outlays by the Food and Nutrition Service, which administers the food stamp program, represented nearly 34 percent of Agriculture's expenditures in 1986.

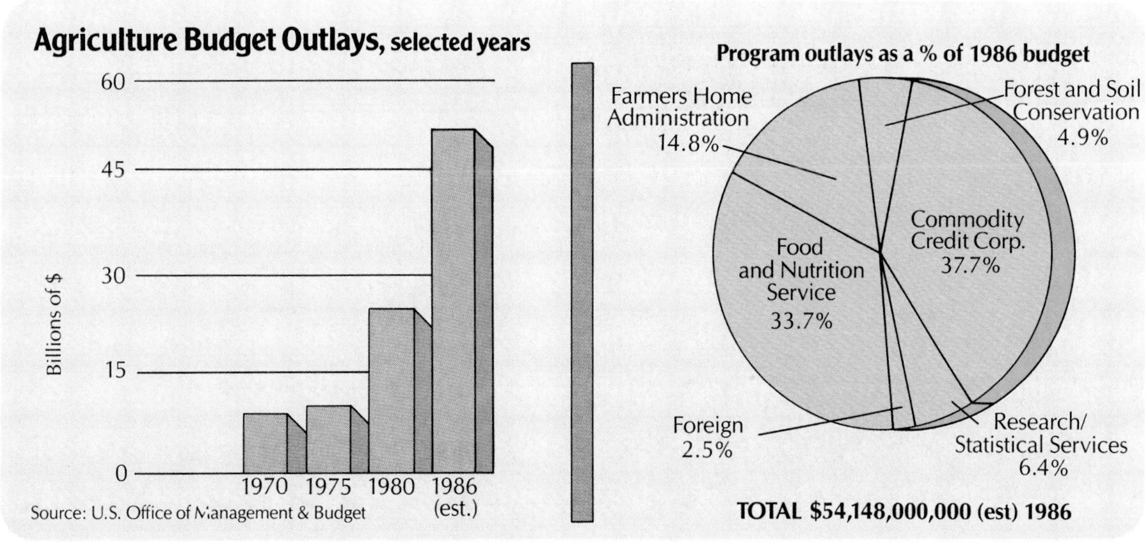

*REINFORCEMENT Ask the class if the Department of Agriculture has an effect on their lives. Start the discussion by mentioning food safety, meat inspection, subsidies, etc.

Agricultural Cooperative Service. Helps farmers to form and run cooperatives, especially to market their crops and to purchase farm supplies.

Agricultural Marketing Service. Aids farmers to market their products; issues daily reports on crop conditions, demands, prices, and other local and national agricultural market data, through press, radio, and television; enforces several laws that prohibit fraud and other deceptive market practices.

Animal and Plant Health Inspection Service. Conducts inspections to prevent, control, or eradicate animal and plant pests and diseases; may impose quarantines to prevent shipments in both interstate and foreign commerce; licenses, regulates the manufacture and sale of chemical and nonchemical products used in the prevention or the treatment of animal and plant pests and diseases.

Food and Nutrition Service. Administers the food stamp program (which provides coupons to low-income persons and families to increase their food purchasing power); provides grants and/or foodstuffs for several other food assistance programs (most notably, the National School Lunch Program).

Food Safety and Inspection Service. Inspects food and meat processing plants and grades their products under federal laws that require that those products are safe, of good quality, and properly labeled.

Agricultural Stabilization and Conservation Service. Administers several price support, commodity loan, and subsidy payment programs to "stabilize" (maintain, bolster) farm incomes and market prices for certain crops.

Commodity Credit Corporation. Holds (stores) crops purchased or accepted as payments of loans under the various programs administered by the ASCR; reduces surplus crop holdings (mostly by donations to federal, State, and private welfare agencies and programs).

Federal Crop Insurance Corporation. Offers (sells) insurance to producers of certain crops to protect them against unavoidable losses from such causes as weather, insects, and diseases.

Agricultural Research Service. Conducts a wide range of both basic and applied research programs, covering all phases of agriculture; makes grants to support research and other activities at State agricultural experiment stations and land-grant universities; provides financial support for the Cooperative Extension Service (which operates through land-grant universities and county extension agents, to promote "beyond-the-classroom" education and other farm-related activities, especially in rural areas); administers

Which agency in the Department of Agriculture administers the food stamp program?

When did farm prices paid equal farm prices received? What has been the trend in 1980s?

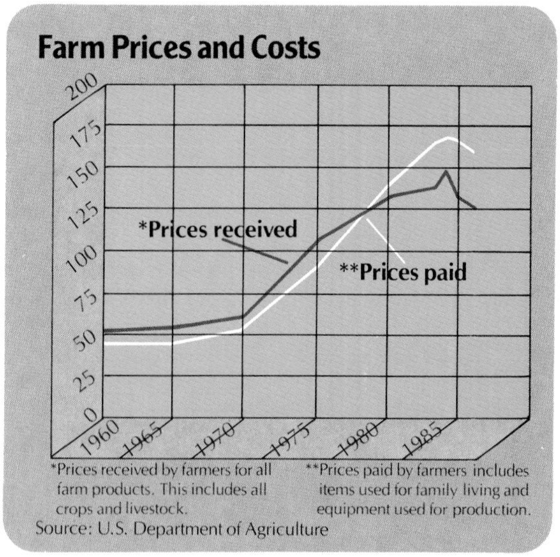

grants and other financial aid for higher education in food and agricultural sciences and veterinary medicine.

Forest Service. Manages the National Forest System (156 national forests and 19 national grasslands, totaling 191 million acres in 44 States, the Virgin Islands, and Puerto Rico); provides grants for research in forestry.

Soil Conservation Service. Directs and/or provides financial and other assistance for a broad range of soil conservation, watershed protection, and related programs; promotes the creation of and gives technical help to local soil conservation districts (which now number nearly 3,000 and cover more than 90 percent of the nation's farms and farmlands).

* Department of Commerce

Established: 1903
Head: Secretary of Commerce
Employees, 1987: 33,800 (est.)

Many of the Federal Government's programs to promote business and the overall well-being of the nation's economy are centered in the Commerce Department. Its several agencies are charged with this broad mission: to promote international trade, spur the nation's economic growth, and encourage technological advancement.

Strip farming, planting crops in alternating rows, is encouraged by the Soil Conservation Service.

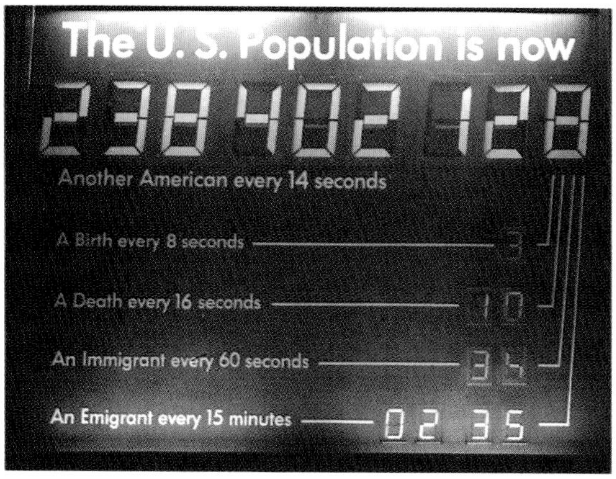

A Census Clock reading of the nation's estimated population during a day in August of 1985.

Bureau of the Census. Takes a census of the nation's population every 10 years (as required by the Constitution, particularly for the apportionment of seats in the House of Representatives); collects, analyzes and publishes a wide variety of other statistical data about the people and the economy of the nation.

National Bureau of Standards. Develops and maintains the uniform standards of all weights and measures that, by law, may be used in the U. S.; performs a wide range of advanced scientific and other experimental and testing functions; furnishes scientific and technological services to government and private industry.

National Weather Service officials record data to compile updated weather forecasts.

*REINFORCEMENT Have the class discuss: In what ways does the Department of Commerce affect your community and your own daily lives? The class should cite specific examples.

Patent and Trademark Office. Issues more than 75,000 patents each year (patents of invention, good for 17 years; patents of design, good for 14 years; and plant patents, good for 17 years); registers some 71,000 trademarks each year (good for 20 years, and renewable).

National Oceanic and Atmospheric Administration. Operates the National Weather Service, which forecasts and reports weather conditions throughout the country; makes satellite observations of weather and other features of the earth's environment; conducts oceanic, atmospheric, seismological, and other environmental research; publishes its findings in nautical and aeronautical maps, charts, and other reports; administers the Sea Grant program (which provides grants for marine research and education).

United States Travel and Tourism Administration. Works with the travel industry, here and abroad, to attract tourists and other foreign visitors to this country for study, business, vacation, other purposes.

National Technical Information Service. Central federal service for machine processable data files, computer software, in engineering, medical, and other scientific, technical fields.

Minority Business Development Agency. Promotes and coordinates federal and other public and private efforts to help organize and strengthen businesses owned and operated by members of minority groups; furnishes management and technical assistance to minority firms.

Bureau of Economic Analysis. Collects, analyzes, and publishes data to provide a reliable and detailed picture of the structure, condition, and prospects of the nation's economy; makes continuing reports on the gross national product (the GNP, the total national output of goods and services, measured in dollar terms).

International Trade Administration. Promotes American interests in foreign trade; maintains a network of Foreign Commercial Service offices to report on business conditions and investment opportunities abroad; conducts trade fairs and operates trade centers in other countries.

*Department of Labor

Established: 1913
Head: Secretary of Labor
Employees, 1987: 18,200 (est.)

For nearly 75 years now, the Labor Department's job has been the one Congress first assigned to it in 1913: "to foster, promote, and develop the welfare of the wage earners of the United States, to improve the working conditions, and to advance their opportunities for profitable employment."

"Alvin," a NOAA research submarine, is lowered into the water at Woods Hole, Massachusetts.

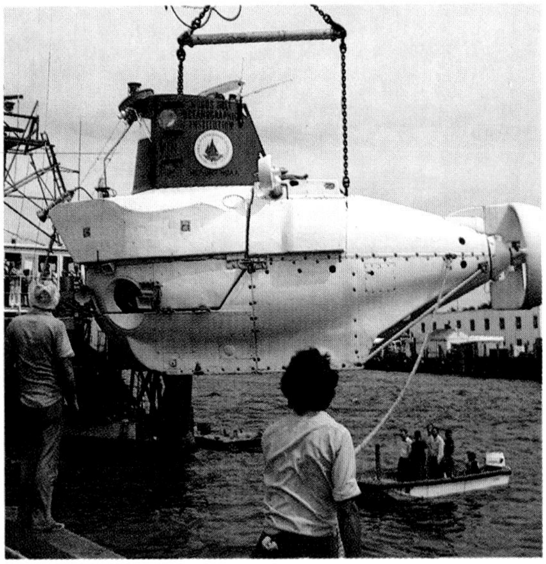

The GNP measures, in dollar terms, the total national output of goods and services.

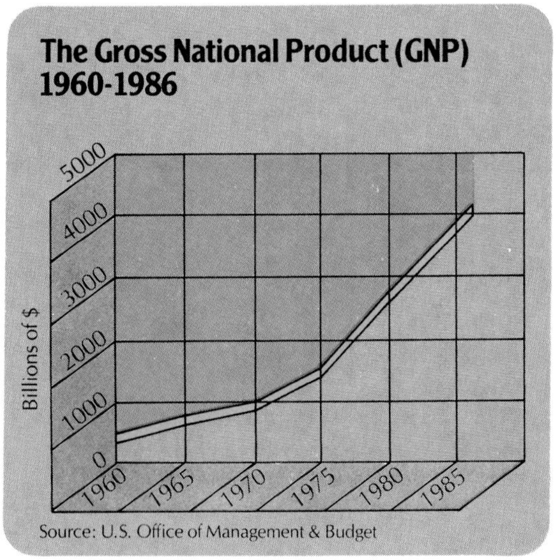

*REINFORCEMENT Have the class discuss: In what ways does the Department of Labor aid the American worker? How does the Department of Labor protect the workers?

Employment and Training Administration. An umbrella agency. Through the *United States Employment Service,* aids the States to operate a system of local employment offices; through the *Unemployment Insurance Service,* supervises the States' administration of their unemployment compensation programs (largely financed by a federal tax on employers); through the *Office of Employment and Training Programs,* makes grants for and administers job training, work experience, and public service employment programs; through the *Bureau of Apprenticeship and Training,* works to improve the standards of apprenticeship and training for skilled jobs.

Employment Standards Administration. An umbrella agency. Through the *Wage and Hour Division,* enforces federal minimum wage and maximum hours laws; through the *Office of Federal Contract Compliance Programs,* enforces laws prohibiting discrimination in employment on all federally supported construction projects; through the *Office of Workers' Compensation Programs,* administers laws providing injury and accident benefits for federal employees.

Labor-Management Services Administration. Administers laws guaranteeing the reemployment rights of veterans; enforces federal laws regulating the operations of private pension and welfare plans; acts as an advisory agency to help in the collective bargaining process.

Highly skilled workers are needed in the assembly of electronically controlled machinery.

Occupational Safety and Health Administration. Enforces federal laws setting minimum safety and health standards in most work situations.

Mine Safety and Health Administration. Enforces federal laws setting minimum safety and health standards for mining operations.

Bureau of Labor Statistics. Collects, analyzes, and publishes data on employment, unemployment, hours of work, wages, and prices.

The Consumer Price Index is based on average prices paid for day-to-day items as food, clothing, shelter, transportation, fuels, drugs, and other goods and services.

Trends in the Labor Force: 1960-1986

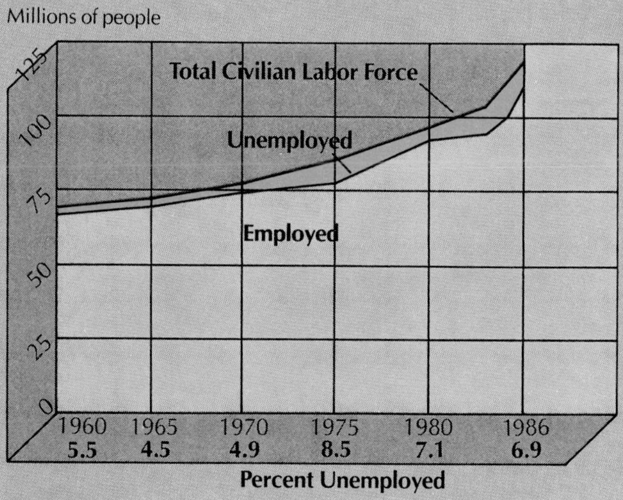

Source: U.S. Bureau of Labor Statistics

Consumer Price Index: 1960-1986

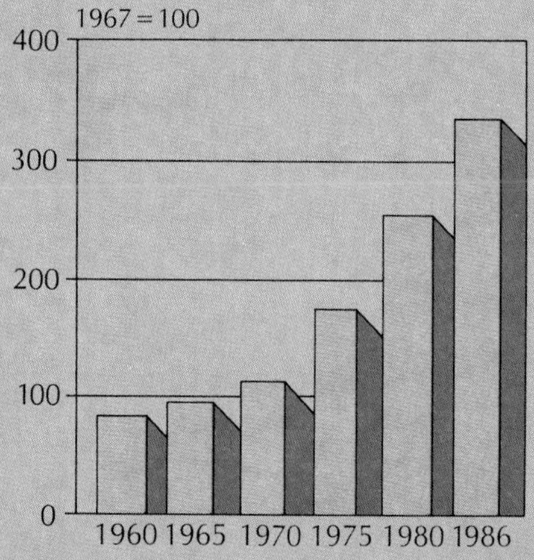

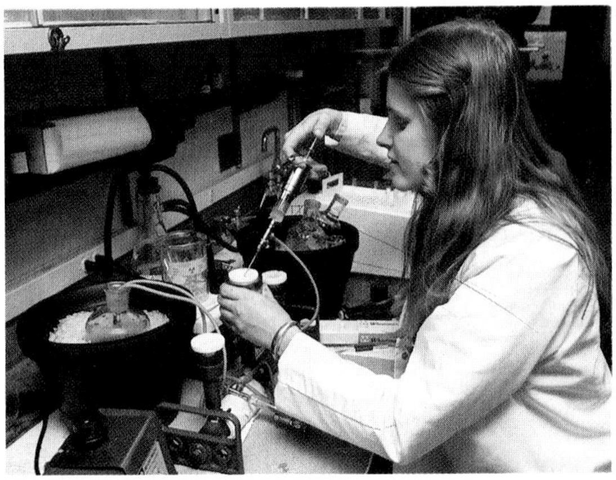

Products tested in FDA laboratories found to be harmful are banned from interstate shipment.

Department of Health and Human Services

Established: 1953
Head: Secretary of Health and Human Services
Employees, 1987: 123,600 (est.)

The Department of Health and Human Services administers several welfare, public assistance, and public health programs and also has a number of research, educational, and regulatory functions in those areas. HHS has described itself as "a department of people serving people, from newborn infants to our most elderly citizens."

Office of Human Development Services. An umbrella agency. Through the *Administration on Aging,* makes grants, gives other support to State and local programs to provide social services to older persons; through the *Administration for Native Americans,* makes grants, gives other support to social and economic development programs for American Indians, Alaskan Natives, and Native Hawaiians; through the *Administration on Developmental Disabilities,* makes grants, gives other support to rehabilitation and similar programs for handicapped persons.

Public Health Service. An umbrella agency. Through the *Centers for Disease Control* (based at Atlanta), conducts research and treatment programs for the prevention and control of communicable and other diseases; through the *Food and Drug Administration,* conducts research and administers federal laws that prohibit the manufacture, shipment, or sale of impure and unsafe foods, drugs, cosmetics, medical devices, and similar items; through the *Health Resources and Services Administration,* makes grants to strengthen State, local, and private nonprofit hospital and other health care facilities and programs; provides medical and other health care services to certain groups (e.g., Coast Guard personnel and their dependents, federal prisoners, American Indians); through the *National Institutes of Health,* makes grants to support

According to the bar graph below, by how many times has the average monthly payment to a single retiree increased from 1975 to 1986?

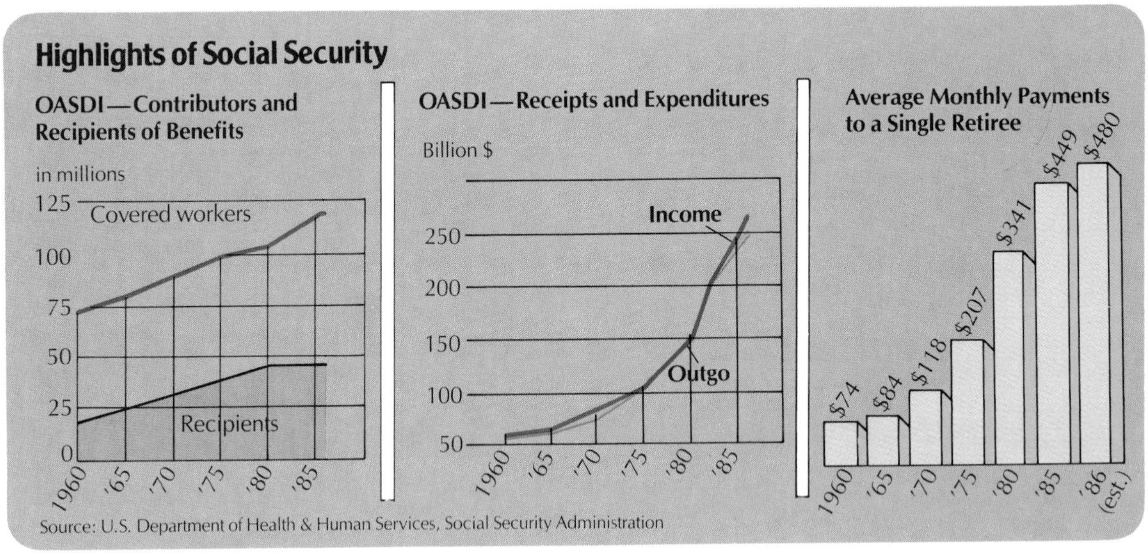

REINFORCEMENT Ask the class to discuss the contributions that the Department of Health and Human Services makes to their welfare. Have them give examples for each division named above.

medical research and operates several research institutes (e.g., the National Cancer Institute, the National Institute of Allergy and Infectious Diseases, and the National Institute of Environmental Health Services).

Social Security Administration. Administers several major elements of the social security programs, especially: (1) the Old-Age, Survivors, and Disability Insurance (OASDI) program —under which compulsory payroll taxes paid by employers, employees, and the self-employed finance payments (pensions, other benefits) to persons covered under the program when they retire or become permanently disabled and to their dependents or survivors; (2) the Supplemental Security Income (SSI) program—which gives direct federal assistance (payments) to needy aged, blind, and disabled persons; and (3) the Aid to Families with Dependent Children (AFDC) program—under which federal grants help the States to give financial assistance to children who lack adequate parental support.

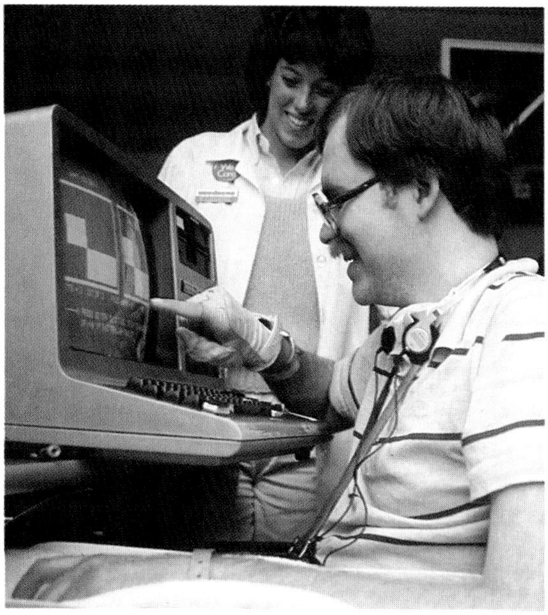

The Social Security Administration conducts several programs which provide aid to the disabled and handicapped.

Health Care Financing Administration. Administers two other major elements of the social security program: (1) *Medicare*—a health insurance program for most elderly persons (those over 65 who receive OASDI benefits), to help pay at least most of their hospital, medical, and other health care bills (financed by a combination of compulsory payroll taxes and optional monthly fees); and (2) *Medicaid*—a federal grant program, to help the States pay the hospital, medical, and other health care bills of the poor (principally, families who receive AFDC payments and the needy aged, blind, and disabled who receive SSI payments).

Expenditures for which program have increased the most since 1980, Medicare or Medicaid? Which program is funded through payroll taxes and monthly fees?

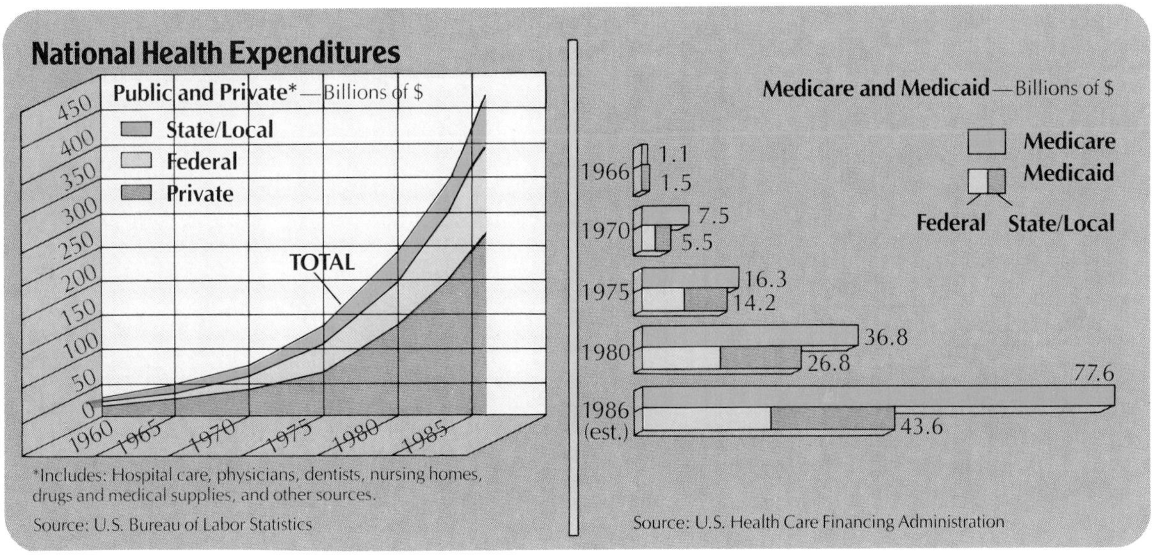

The FHA backs many home construction loans.

Department of Housing and Urban Development[a]

Established: 1965
Head: Secretary of Housing and Urban Development
Employees, 1987: 11,300 (est.)

The Department of Housing and Urban Development is the principal federal agency concerned with the nation's housing needs and with the development and rehabilitation of its urban communities. HUD conducts a number of insurance, rent subsidy, and grant programs in those fields.

Assistant Secretary for Community Planning and Development. Administers several grant programs to aid State and local government efforts to improve housing conditions in urban areas (e.g., water, sewer, slum clearance projects).

Assistant Secretary for Housing (Federal Housing Commissioner). Administers several programs, including: (1) mortgage insurance programs—in which the Government guarantees loans made by private lenders (mortgages) for the purchase of private housing (mostly single-family residences and such multifamily units as apartment houses and condominiums); (2) loan programs—to help both public and private borrowers finance housing projects for the elderly and the handicapped (e.g., nursing homes); (3) the Rent Supplement Program—in which HUD pays a portion of the monthly rents of low-income families.

Assistant Secretary for Public and Indian Housing. Administers several programs, including: (1) public housing programs—in which loans, subsidies, and other aid are given to local agencies to build, operate public housing projects (mostly for low-income families); and (2)

[a]HUD and two other departments (Energy and Education) are not organized in quite the same way as the other Cabinet departments. Most of their functions and programs are administered directly by a number of assistant secretaries (rather than by several bureaus, services, or similar line agencies).

For which type of FHA insured loan is the least activity shown? Which aspect of the housing industry is shown as most subject to "up and down" cycles?

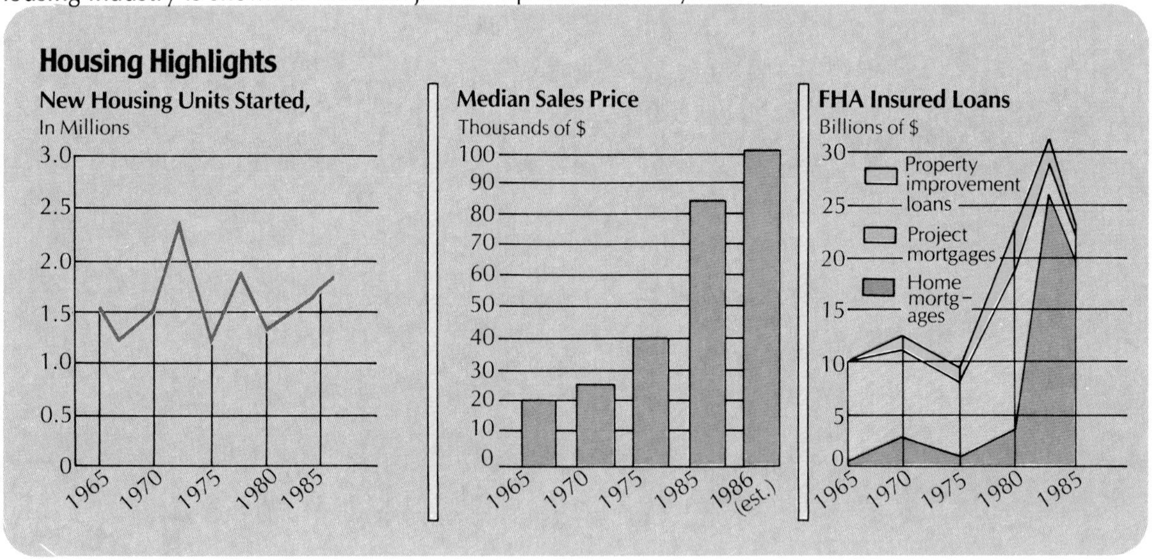

ENRICHMENT Discuss in class: The Department of Housing and Urban Development, as described here, seems geared toward urban, rather than rural, development. How does it aid those in rural areas?

Indian housing programs—to provide low-income public housing, promote private home ownership, on and near Indian reservations; also enforces laws to curb interstate land sale frauds.

Department of Transportation

Established: 1967
Head: Secretary of Transportation
Employees, 1987: 59,000 (est.)

Most of the Federal Government's activities relating to the movement of persons and goods by ground, water, or air are located in the Department of Transportation. DOT's several agencies conduct a number of promotional and regulatory programs covering matters varying from highway construction to offshore maritime safety to commercial air traffic.

United States Coast Guard. Enforces federal maritime laws (laws relating to the high seas and the navigable waters of the United States—e.g., smuggling, ship safety, port security, and spillage, pollution, and other marine environmental protection statutes); maintains ships and other vessels, aircraft, and communications facilities, especially for search and rescue operations; operates an extensive network of aids to navigation (e.g., lighthouses, buoys, icebreakers, radio and other electronic devices); operates the U.S. Coast Guard Academy (at New London, Ct.).

FAA investigators research the details of airplane disasters to prevent accidents in the future.

Federal Aviation Administration. Enforces federal laws regulating air commerce (including, for example, aircraft safety, pilot licensing, and air traffic); operates an extensive network of aids to

The United States Coast Guard is frequently involved in rescue operations at sea.

REINFORCEMENT Have the class discuss: How is the Department of Transportation both a national and a State agency? What are its specific duties in each?

air navigation (e.g., air traffic control towers and centers, radio and other electronic communications facilities); makes grants for the construction, improvement of public airports; conducts a wide range of aviation-related research projects.

Federal Highway Administration. Administers several grant programs to aid State and local construction, maintenance of highways and other roads (including the 42,500-mile interstate freeway system); makes grants for such other purposes as highway safety (e.g., traffic signs and signals, projects to eliminate traffic hazards) and beautification; enforces federal highway safety laws (e.g., laws regulating the movement of such dangerous cargoes as explosives, hazardous wastes); builds, maintains roads in such federal areas as national parks, national forests, Indian reservations; conducts research on a wide range of highway-related matters.

National Highway Traffic Safety Administration. Enforces federal motor vehicle safety laws; makes grants to support State and local motor vehicle safety and accident-prevention programs (including driver training); conducts research on matters relating to motor vehicle safety.

Federal Railroad Administration. Enforces federal rail safety laws; gives financial and other aid to certain railroads (especially those in financial difficulty); conducts research on most phases of rail transportation; operates the 482-mile Alaska Railroad.

Urban Mass Transportation Administration. Administers several grant and loan programs to help State and local governments develop and operate bus, rail, and other mass transit systems in urban areas; conducts research covering most phases of urban mass transportation and its operational efficiency.

Saint Lawrence Seaway Development Corporation. Operates that part of the Seaway within the United States (The American side of the stretch between Montreal and Lake Erie); sets and collects tolls and otherwise works in close cooperation with the St. Lawrence Seaway Authority of Canada.

Department of Energy

Established: 1977
Head: Secretary of Energy
Employees, 1987: 15,700 (est.)

The functions of the Department of Energy reflect the critical importance of the development, use, and conservation of the nation's energy resources. DOE's several agencies focus on such matters as high-technology research, nuclear weapons programs, the marketing of federal power, energy conservation, and much more.

Why do you think that federal outlays for highway construction are so much greater than for other categories shown on the graphs below?

Federal Outlays for Transportation: 1975- 1986 (est.)

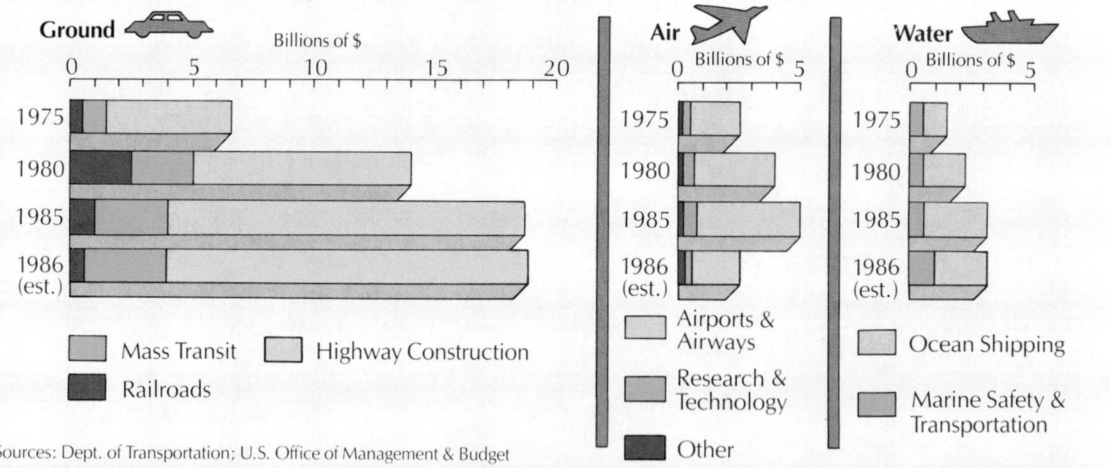

Sources: Dept. of Transportation; U.S. Office of Management & Budget

ENRICHMENT Discuss in class: The oil crisis of 1973 was a major factor in the creation of the Department of Energy. How can each of its divisions help to prevent yet another crisis?

Assistant Secretary, Fossil Energy. Directs research and development programs involving fossil fuels—coal, petroleum, and gas (e.g., study and demonstration projects relating to mining, drilling, other methods of fuel extraction); manages the Strategic Petroleum Reserve and other Petroleum storage projects.

Assistant Secretary, Nuclear Energy. Directs R & D programs involving fission energy (e.g., projects relating to the disposal of commercial nuclear reactor wastes).

Assistant Secretary, Defense Programs. Directs nuclear weapons research, development, testing, and production programs.

Assistant Secretary, Conservation and Renewable Energy. Directs R & D programs designed to promote more efficient uses (conservation) of energy and to increase the production and use of solar, wind, tidal, and other energy from renewable sources; makes grants to support State and local efforts in those areas (e.g., local projects to weatherize housing).

Energy Information Administration. Collects, analyzes, publishes a broad range of data relating to energy (e.g., information on energy resources, production, and consumption).

Civilian Radioactive Waste Management. Conducts research on, manages federal programs, for the storage, disposal of high-level radioactive waste and spent nuclear fuel.

Economic Regulatory Administration. Enforces laws regulating aspects of energy production, sale, and use (e.g., laws regulating drilling on leased federal lands, placing controls on fossil fuel exports, requiring increased industrial use of coal in place of oil and natural gas).

Bonneville Power Administration. Markets electric power generated by the vast network of federal multipurpose dams (constructed, operated by the Army's Corps of Engineers and Interior's Bureau of Reclamation) in the Pacific Northwest. (Smaller-scale operations are also conducted in four other regions.)

Department of Education

Established: 1979
Head: Secretary of Education
Employees, 1987: 4,500 (est.)

Nearly one-fourth of all of our people—more than 55 million Americans—attend school. The Department of Education administers a number of programs designed to aid the States and their local units in the field of public education.

Assistant Secretary for Special Education and Rehabilitative Services. Makes grants for research and to support teacher training and other

A solar energy project, where photovoltaic cells are used in harnessing energy from the sun.

Over the years, federal funds have been available to help improve laboratory facilities:

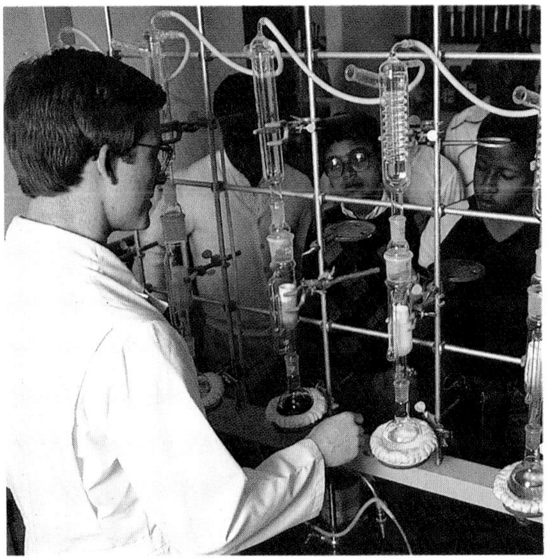

State and local programs for the education of handicapped children, and for rehabilitation programs for those children.

Assistant Secretary for Postsecondary Education. Administers several grant programs to support and expand instructional and other educational services and facilities in colleges, universities, and similar institutions; administers several different types of student grant and loan programs.

Assistant Secretary for Vocational and Adult Education. Administers grants and other programs to support and expand State and local efforts in vocational training and adult education.

Assistant Secretary for Elementary and Secondary Education. Administers grant programs to support a variety of State and local school efforts in preschool, elementary, and secondary education, including grants to local school districts for Indian and migrant education.

Assistant Secretary for Educational Research and Improvement. Directs research and administers grant programs to support State and local school efforts in a wide range of instructional service and resource areas (e.g., basic skills, alcohol and drug abuse, and health education; library, laboratory resources).

FOR REVIEW

Name the department and the agency in that department that: **(1)** collects nearly all federal taxes; **(2)** manages the public debt; **(3)** handles cases involving acts of discrimination prohibited by federal civil rights laws; **(4)** investigates most violations of federal criminal law, **(5)** administers the National Park System; **(6)** manages timber, oil, mineral resources on public lands; **(7)** administers the food stamp program; **(8)** administers price support and subsidy programs to help stabilize farm incomes; **(9)** enforces federal wage and hour laws; **(10)** publishes data on employment, wages, and prices; **(11)** operates the National Weather Service; **(12)** enforces laws that protect consumers from impure and unsafe food and drug products; **(13)** administers Medicare and Medicaid programs; **(14)** enforces maritime laws, provides navigation aids, and conducts rescue operations; **(15)** directs energy research programs; **(16)** administers grant programs to help support public education, as well as several types of student grant and loan programs.

While total school enrollment has remained fairly constant since 1970, expenditures for education have more than tripled since that year. Can you think of reasons for this? Which category of school enrollment has increased the most since 1960? Which category has shown a slight decrease in enrollment since 1960?

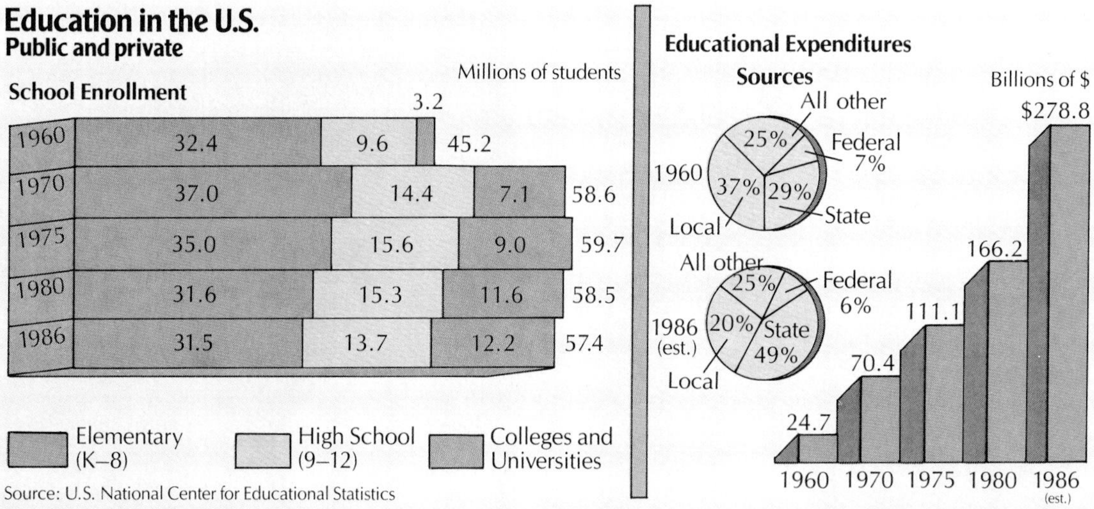

REINFORCEMENT Ask the class: What effect does the Department of Education have on the education you are receiving or hope to receive? Include discussion of research and grant programs.

FOCUS ON:

The Meaning of "Bureaucracy"

The word *bureaucracy* is both much used and much abused in politics.

The word is often used, in an objective and "unloaded" sense, to identify any large and complex administrative body. In dictionary terms, a bureaucracy is a formal organization (either public or private) with:

- a hierarchical (ranked, pyramidlike) structure,
- authority (the power to act) located in positions (offices, rather than in particular persons), and
- personnel who have specialized job assignments (defined duties and responsibilities).

The word is also used in quite another sense, however—as an epithet (as a critical and scornful term). It is most often used in that sense by those who see government ("the bureaucracy") and its officers ("bureaucrats") as too powerful, or always mired in red tape, or filled with an inflated sense of self-importance, or unresponsive, or overpaid and underworked, or all of those things.

But notice this: Many who do use the word that way do it selectively. The "bureaucracy" is responsible for those public policies they oppose; "bureaucrats" administer programs or take certain actions they dislike. Those policies and programs they happen to favor are often tagged in a much different way. They use such phrases as "a matter of top national priority" or "responsible actions to meet urgent public needs."

All of this is nothing new. "Big government" has never been popular in this country. To many Americans "big government" is another way of saying "bureaucracy." Recall, it was Thomas Jefferson who said that "that government is best which governs least."

This very important point must be made: Bureaucrats hold appointive public offices; they are unelected public policymakers. That is not to say that bureaucracies are necessarily undemocratic. But it is to say this: In a democracy much depends on how effectively the bureaucracy is controlled by those whom the people *do* elect.

James Madison made that point some 200 years ago, in *The Federalist,* No. 51:

> In framing a government, which is to be administered by men over men, the great difficulty lies in this: You must first enable the government to control the governed; and in the next place, oblige it to control itself.

1. Are there any safeguards—beliefs, institutions, processes—that work to forestall the growth of irresponsible bureaucracy? If so, what are some of them, and how effective are they?
2. What do you make of this remark, by the late Alben Barkley: "A bureaucrat is a Democrat who holds a job a Republican wants"? Who was Alben Barkley?

"Small Society" by Brickman. Washington Star Syndicate, Inc.

3. The Independent Agencies

As You Read, Think About:

- What the functions are of the various independent agencies.
- What the three types of agencies are.

Until the 1880s, nearly all of what the Federal Government did was done through the Cabinet departments. Over the years since then, however, Congress has created a large number of additional agencies—the *independent agencies*—located outside of any of the departments. Many have come, and some have gone. Today, they number close to 200. Their functions range from the fields of transportation and communications through labor-management relations and finance to veterans' affairs, nuclear energy, and natural resources. Most of the more important independent agencies are shown in the chart on page 431.

Several of these independent agencies administer programs that cannot be very easily distinguished from the major responsibilities of the Cabinet departments. Much of the work of the Veterans Administration, for example, is very much like that done by a number of agencies in the Department of Health and Human Services. The concerns of the VA are also not too far removed from those of the Defense Department, either.

Neither the budget size nor the number of employees provides a very good dividing line between many of these agencies and the executive departments. Thus, the VA's budget now runs to more than $26 billion a year, more than that of any of the departments except Defense, Health and Human Services, and Agriculture. And the VA now has some 240,000 employees, a total exceeded only by Defense.

The reasons for the separate existences of these agencies are nearly as many as the agencies themselves. A few major reasons stand out, however. Some agencies have been set up outside of the regular departmental structure because they do not fit well there. The General Services Administration (GSA) is a leading example. The GSA is the Federal Government's major housekeeping agency. Its main chores include the construction and operation of public buildings, purchase and distribution of supplies and equipment, management of real property, and a host of similar services to most other federal agencies. The Office of Personnel Management (OPM) is another example; the OPM is the hiring agency for nearly all other federal agencies, as we shall see in a few pages.

Congress has given some of these agencies an independent status to protect them from the play of both partisan and pressure politics. Again, the OPM provides an example. So, too, do the Civil Rights Commission and the Federal Election Commission. But the point can be turned on its head, too. Some agencies are located outside the Cabinet departments because that's where certain pressure groups wanted them. Thus, several veterans organizations were responsible for the separate identity of the VA, and they have fought for years to keep it that way.

Other federal agencies have been born as independents largely by accident. In short, no thought was given to the problems of administrative hodgepodge when they were created.

Finally, some agencies are independent because of the peculiar and sensitive nature of their functions. This is especially true of what are often called the "independent regulatory commissions"—a breed we shall look at in a moment.

The label "independent agency" is a catch-all. Most of them are independent only in the sense that they are not located within any of the 13 Cabinet departments. They are *not* independent of the President and the executive branch. Some of these agencies are independent in a much more concrete way, however. For most purposes, they *do* lie outside the executive branch and they *are* largely free of presidential control.

Perhaps the best way to get a good grasp on these agencies is to divide them into three main groups: (1) the independent executive agencies, (2) the independent regulatory commissions, and (3) the government corporations.

*ENRICHMENT Discuss: What are the reasons for the existence of independent agencies? Is their independence justified, or do they only add to an already overburdened bureaucracy?

An inspector from the Environmental Protection Agency (EPA) checks a shipment of pesticides.

The Independent Executive Agencies

This group includes most of the independent agencies. Some are large, with thousands of employees, multimillion-dollar or even billion-dollar budgets, and hugely important public tasks to perform. The VA, NASA, and the EPA are three leading examples of the larger independent executive agencies. They are organized much like the Cabinet departments—headed by a single administrator, with subunits operating on a regional basis, and so on. The most important difference between them and the 13 executive departments is simply this: They do not have Cabinet status.

Some of the agencies in this group are not administrative and policy giants. They do important work, however, and sometimes attract public notice. The Civil Rights Commission, the Farm Credit Administration, the Federal Election Commission, and the Small Business Administration all fall into this category.

Most independent executive agencies live far from the limelight, however. They have few employees, small to pocket-change budgets, and almost never attract any attention. The American Battle Monuments Commission, the Citizen's Stamp Advisory Committee, and the Migratory Bird Conservation Commission are rather typical of the dozens of these seldom seen or heard public bodies.

The Independent Regulatory Commissions

The independent regulatory commissions stand out among the independent agencies. They are largely beyond the reach of presidential direction and control.

There are 11 of these agencies today, each created to regulate, or police, important aspects of the nation's economy. Their vital statistics are set out in the chart on page 454.

Their large measure of independence from the White House comes mainly from the way in which Congress has structured them. Each is headed by a board or commission made up of from five to 11 members named by the President with Senate consent. However, those officials are chosen for terms of such length (five to 14 years) that it is quite unlikely that a President can gain control over any of these agencies through the appointment process, at least not in a single presidential term.

Several other features of the makeup of these boards and commissions also put them beyond the reach of effective presidential control. No more than a bare majority of the members of each board or commission can belong to the same political party. Thus, several of those officers must belong to the party out of power. Also, the appointed terms of all of them are staggered; the term of only one member on each board or commission expires in any one year. Finally, most of these officers can be removed from office by the President *only* for those causes Congress has specified.[6]

As with the other independent agencies, the regulatory commissions are executive bodies. That is, Congress has given them the power to administer the programs for which they were created. However, unlike those

[6]Recall, we discussed this point in Chapter 15, on page 417. The members of five of these bodies (the SEC, FCC, CPSC, NRC, and CFTFC) are exceptions here, however. Congress has provided that any of them may be removed at the President's discretion.

The Independent Regulatory Commissions

Agency, Date Established	Members Number/Term	Major Functions
Interstate Commerce Commission (ICC), 1887	11 7 years	Licenses, fixes rates, regulates other aspects of commercial transportation by railroad, highway, domestic waterway.
Board of Governors, Federal Reserve System (the Fed), 1913	7 14 years	Supervises banking system, practices; regulates money supply, use of credit in economy.
Federal Trade Commission (FTC), 1914	5 7 years	Enforces antitrust, other laws prohibiting unfair competition, price-fixing, false advertising, other unfair business practices.
Securities and Exhange Commission (SEC), 1934	5 5 years	Regulates securities, other financial markets, investment companies, brokers; enforces laws prohibiting fraud, other dishonest investment practices.
Federal Communications Commission (FCC), 1934	7 7 years	Licenses, regulates all radio and TV stations, operators, all satellite communications systems; regulates interstate telephone, telegraph rates, service.
National Labor Relations Board (NLRB), 1935	5 5 years	Administers federal labor-management relation laws; holds collective bargaining elections; prevents, remedies unfair labor practices.
Federal Maritime Commission (FMC), 1936	5 5 years	Regulates waterborne foreign, domestic off-shore commerce of the United States; supervises rates, services.
Consumer Product Safety Commission (CPSC), 1972	5 5 years	Sets, enforces safety standards for consumer products; directs recall of unsafe products; conducts safety research, information programs.
Nuclear Regulatory Commission (NRC), 1974	5 5 years	Licenses, regulates all civilian nuclear facilities, all civilian uses of nuclear materials.[a]
Commodity Futures Trading Commission (CFTC), 1974	5 5 years	Regulates commodity exchanges, brokers, futures trading in agricultural, metal, other commodities.
Federal Energy Regulatory Commission (FERC), 1977[b]	5 4 years	Regulates, fixes rates for transportation, sale of natural gas, transportation of oil by pipelines, interstate transmission, sale of electricity.[b]

[a]These functions performed by Atomic Energy Commission from 1946 to 1974 (when AEC was abolished); other AEC functions now performed by agencies in Energy Department.

[b]These functions performed by Federal Power Commission (created in 1930) until FPC was abolished in 1977. FERC is within Energy Department, but only for administrative purposes; otherwise is independent (except Energy Secretary may set reasonable deadlines for FERC action in any matter before it). Under terms of National Energy Act of 1978, FERC's authority to regulate natural gas prices ended in 1985.

other agencies, these commissions are also **quasi-legislative** and **quasi-judicial** bodies.[7] That is, Congress has also given them certain legislativelike and judicial-like powers.

These agencies exercise their quasi-legislative powers when they make rules and regulations. Those rules and regulations have the force of law. They implement (spell out the details of) the laws Congress has directed these regulatory bodies to enforce. For example, ever since it passed the Act to

[7]The prefix *quasi* is from the Latin, meaning "in a certain sense, resembling, seemingly."

*ENRICHMENT Use the chart above to introduce a discussion on the need for independent regulatory commissions. Point out that the areas they regulate are too time-demanding for Congress.

Regulate Commerce of 1887 (now known as the Interstate Commerce Act), Congress has said the railroads must offer "reasonable service" to the public and to charge "just and reasonable" rates for that service. The Interstate Commerce Commission implements those requirements—sets out how they are to be met by the railroads—by issuing detailed rules and regulations.

The regulatory commissions exercise their quasi-judicial powers when they decide disputes in those fields in which Congress has given them their policing authority. For example, if a railroad asks the ICC for permission to raise its rates for carrying goods between two points, that request is likely to be opposed by the companies that ship those goods. The ICC holds a hearing to determine the merits of the matter. It then makes a decision, much as a court would do. Appeals may be taken to the United States Courts of Appeals, as we shall see in Chapter 18.

In a sense, Congress has created these agencies to act for it, to act in its place. Congress *could* hold hearings and set freight rates, license radio and TV stations and nuclear reactors, check on business practices, and do the many other things it has directed these regulatory commissions to do. But these are complex and time-consuming matters, and they demand constant and expert attention. If Congress did all of those things, however, it would then have no time for its other and important legislative work.

As we've just seen, these regulatory bodies have all three of the basic governmental powers: executive, legislative, and judicial. They are, then, exceptions to the principle of separation of powers. Several authorities, and most recent Presidents, have urged that at least their administrative functions be given to Cabinet department agencies.

Even larger questions have been asked about these agencies and have prompted proposals to abolish or redesign them. The most troubling ones are these: Have some of them been captured by the special interests they are expected to regulate? Are all the many and detailed rules made by these agencies really needed? Do some of them have the effect of stifling legitimate competition in the free enterprise system? Do some of them add unreasonably to the costs of doing business and so the prices consumers must pay?[8]

The Interstate Commerce Commission regulates commercial traffic on the nation's waterways, as well as on its highways and railroads.

Back to our central point here: the location of these agencies in the federal bureaucracy. Notice that they really should not be grouped with the other independent agencies as they are in the chart on page 431. Instead, they should (somehow) be located somewhere between the executive and the legislative branches. At the same time, they should be placed somewhere between the executive and the judicial branches.

[8]Because Congress sets the basic shape of the policies of these regulatory bodies, it is mainly responsible for any answers to these questions. It has responded to some questions in the past few years. In particular, Congress has given transportation businesses much greater freedom to operate. Thus, in the Airlines Deregulation Act of 1978, it all but abolished the Civil Aeronautics Board's power to regulate the nation's commercial airlines. Instead, the CAB's mission became the promotion of competition in the air transport industry. That law also provided that the CAB itself was to be abolished on January 1, 1985, and it was. Congress has also done much the same thing with the ICC's authority over freight rates and other practices of railroads (in the Railroad Reorganization and Regulatory Reform Act of 1976) and truckers (in the Motor Carrier Act of 1980). The Reagan Administration has pushed for still more deregulation; one of its major targets is the FCC.

The Government Corporations

Several of the independent agencies are government corporations. Like most of the others, they are within the executive branch and subject to the President's direction and control. Unlike the others, however, they have been set up by Congress to carry out certain businesslike activities.

Congress established the first government corporation nearly 200 years ago, when it chartered the First Bank of the United States in 1791 (page 349). The device was little used until the First World War and then the Depression of the 1930s, however. In both periods Congress set up dozens of corporations to carry out "crash" programs. Most of those agencies have long since disappeared, though several are still with us. Among them, for example, are the Federal Deposit Insurance Corporation (FDIC), which insures bank deposits, and the Export-Import Bank (EXIM BANK), which makes loans to help the export and sale of American goods abroad.

There are at least 60 of these government corporations today. They have been formed to carry out a wide range of businesslike operations. Examples of these operations include: the generation and distribution of electric power (the Tennessee Valley Authority), intercity passenger trains (the National Railroad Passenger Corporation—Amtrak), mail service (the United States Postal Service), and the insurance of savings accounts (the FDIC and the Federal Savings and Loan Insurance Corporation).[9]

The typical government corporation is set up much like its counterpart in the private sector. It is run by a board of directors, with a general manager to direct its operations in line with the policies set by that board. Most government corporations produce income that is plowed back into the "business."

[9]State and local governments maintain many of their own government corporations, most often called "authorities"—to operate airports, turnpikes, seaports, power plants, liquor stores, housing developments, and for many other corporate (businesslike) activities. Of them all, the Port of New York Authority is probably the best known.

The United States Postal Service has been organized as a corporation since 1971.

There are several striking differences between government and private corporations, however. Among the major ones: Congress decides the purpose for which the public agencies exist and the function they may perform. Their officers are *public* officers; in fact, all who work for those corporations are *public* employees. Their top officers—board members and manager—are most often chosen by the President with Senate confirmation. The public agencies are financed (capitalized) by public monies appropriated by Congress, not by the funds of private investors, and the Government owns the stock.

The major advantage most often claimed for the use of the corporation is its flexibility. That is, it is said that the public agency—freed from the controls of the regular departmental organization—can carry on its businesslike activities with the incentive, efficiency, and ability to experiment that is often found in private concerns. Whether that claim is valid is at least open to question. At the very least, it raises this sticky point: How can a public corporation's need for flexibility in its operations be squared with democratic government's requirement that all public agencies be held responsible and accountable to the people?

The degree of independence and flexibility government corporations really have varies quite a bit. In fact, some of them are not independent at all. They are attached to some executive department, and so are subject to the control of the secretary of that department. The Commodity Credit Corporation, for example, is the Government's major crop-loan and farm-subsidy agency. It is located within the Department of Agriculture, and the Secretary of Agriculture chairs its seven-member board. Then, too, it carries out most of its functions through a line agency in the USDA, the Agricultural Stabilization and Conservation Service, which is also subject to the direct control of the Secretary.

Some of these corporations do have considerable independence, however. The Tennessee Valley Authority (TVA) is a case in point. It operates under a statute in which Congress has given it considerable discretion over its policies and programs. Although its budget is subject to review by the OMB and the President, and then by Congress, it has a large say in the uses of the income its several operations produce. It even has its own civil service system.[10]

FOR REVIEW

1. **Identify:** independent agency, independent executive agency, independent regulatory commission, government corporation.
2. What agencies are the traditional units of federal administration?
3. Why has Congress created many independent agencies in the executive branch? Of what three general types are they? In what sense is each type "independent"?
4. Why has Congress created a number of independent regulatory commissions? In what ways are they most strikingly different from other independent agencies?
5. What major advantage is claimed for the creation of some agencies as government corporations?

4. Reorganization of the Executive Branch

As You Read, Think About:

- Why the executive branch is frequently reorganized.
- What some of the important changes and improvements have been as a result of these reorganizations.
- Why the "legislative veto" was enacted.

We have just looked at the overall structure of the huge executive branch of the Federal Government. As we have seen, there are many good reasons for the shape of that bureaucracy. But, at the same time, some of it can be best described as confusingly complex or as a sprawling hodgepodge, a disjointed jumble, even a hopeless mess. *

Why? One very important reason is that the government of the United States is dynamic, not static. It is always changing, often growing here and sometimes shrinking

[10]Measured by any standard, TVA is one of the major illustrations of government in business. It was set up by Congress, after years of controversy, in the Tennessee Valley Authority Act of 1933. That law provided for the "orderly and proper physical, economic, and social development" of the Tennessee River Valley. It called for the coordinated development and use of the natural resources of a huge area that today includes large parts of seven States: Tennessee, Kentucky, Virginia, North Carolina, Georgia, Alabama, and Mississippi.

TVA is headed by a Board of Directors; its three members are appointed by the President and Senate for nine-year terms. Its operations are supervised by a general manager, chosen by and answering to the Board. Those operations include electric power development, flood control and navigation work, reforestation, soil conservation, fertilizer production, agricultural research, recreational facilities, and the promotion of industrial growth in the Tennessee River Valley. TVA's power program is self-supporting. Much of the support for its other activities comes from Congress. Still, it generates considerable revenues from sales of electricity and fertilizer and from its power to issue bonds.

TVA has had an extraordinary impact on the Valley and its now some four million residents. It has made the Tennessee River a navigable waterway from its mouth at Paducah, Kentucky, upstream some 650 miles to Knoxville, Tennessee. Nine huge dams span the main stem of the river, and several power and storage dams dot its tributaries and the nearby Cumberland. There has been no serious flooding in the Valley since the completion of the storage system, and flood pressures on the Ohio and Mississippi Rivers have been reduced. Per capita income rose dramatically with the introduction of scientific farming methods and plentiful electric power. Much new industry has been attracted to the region and sustained-yield forests now cover wide areas once denuded.

*ENRICHMENT The executive branch can be confusingly complex, as illustrated in the preceding pages. Ask the class to discuss ways in which they feel the bureaucracy could be better controlled.

there. The march of time, fresh circumstances, the adoption of new policies and programs, the expansion, deemphasis, or even abandonment of older ones all call for changes. They prompt the creation, reshuffling, and/or elimination of agencies. Wars, economic recessions, and other crises have a very hefty impact on the shape of government organization. So, too, do changes in party control of the White House and Congress. In short, the tale of the structure of the executive branch can be told in good part as a *continuing* story of organization and *reorganization.*

Basic responsibility for the structure of the executive branch rests with Congress. It has created nearly all of the complex of agencies under the President.[11] Over the years, however, Congress has been slow to react to the continuing need for change.

Because of this, every President, beginning with President Taft in 1911, has asked Congress for the authority to reorganize the executive branch. Since the Depression years of the 1930s, Congress has answered with several statutes. The earlier ones usually set up a commission to study the problems involved and to make recommendations for their solution. Among those bodies three were especially important: the President's Committee on Administrative Management, which made its report in 1937, and the two Commissions on Organization of the Executive Branch (the first and second Hoover Commissions), which reported in 1949 and in 1955.

The work of these groups did lead to several changes and improvements. The 1937 (Brownlow) Committee's report led to the creation of the highly important Executive Office of the President. The first Hoover Commission brought about a number of important steps, among them the creation of the Department of Health, Education, and Welfare. HEW brought dozens of agencies together under one more or less manageable roof. The first Hoover Commission's report also led to the Reorganization Act of 1949 and several later and similar laws.

[11]All of them except those it has given the President the specific authority to create and those set up, as we shall see in a moment, by presidential reorganization plans.

The Reorganization Acts

Several times since 1949, Congress has given the President a substantial authority to reshape executive branch agencies.

The latest of these reorganization acts was passed in 1977 and then extended for another year in 1980. When the extension ran out in 1981, Congress did not renew it. Nor has it done so since (to 1986, at least). So, President Reagan does not have the reorganization authority that Presidents Truman, Eisenhower, Kennedy, and Nixon each had.[12]

Under the 1977 law, the President could submit reorganization plans to Congress. If neither house turned down a plan within 60 days, the plan became effective. In effect, Congress provided an arrangement in which it could make law by doing nothing.

Over the time the 1977 and earlier laws were in force, there was always the chance of a "legislative veto." But of the 103 reorganization plans sent to Congress by six Presidents, 94 were accepted.

Several major federal agencies were created by this process. Among them are the Office of Management and Budget and the Environmental Protection Agency, by President Nixon in 1970, and the Office of Personnel Management, by President Carter in 1978. A number of lesser but important reorganizations were also put in place under the reorganization laws.

Beyond the "legislative veto," they were only three significant restrictions on the President's reorganization authority: (1) No plan could create, merge, or abolish an entire Cabinet department or any independent regulatory commission. (2) No plan could abolish any government function that Con-

[12]Nor did President Ford. The Reorganization Act of 1949 expired in 1953. It was then renewed several times (sometimes in slightly different form) to 1973. As the Watergate scandal grew that year, Congress refused to extend President Nixon's reorganization power. It did not pass a new version of the Reorganization Act until 1977, with the Carter Presidency.

gress had by law required the executive branch to perform. (3) No more than three reorganization plans could be before Congress at any one time.

FOR REVIEW

1. Why has every recent President asked Congress for power to reorganize the executive branch?
2. Outline the provisions of the Reorganization Act of 1977.

"First of all, you need to set up a Department of paperwork . . ."

5. The Civil Service

As You Read, Think About:

- How the civil service system began.
- What the spoils system was.
- How civil service operates today.

The Federal Government is the largest single employer in the United States. Some 3 million people now work in the federal bureaucracy.[13] Of that huge number, only about 2,500 are appointed by the President. The Chief Executive names the top-ranking men and women (and their immediate aides and assistants) who serve in the Executive Office, in the 13 Cabinet departments, in the many independent agencies, and in American embassies and other diplomatic posts.* Most of the other jobs in the Federal Government are now filled through the competitive civil service system.

Development of the Civil Service

The Constitution says very little about the staffing of the federal bureaucracy. In fact, its only direct reference is in Article II, Section 2, Clause 2. There the Constitution says that the President

> shall nominate, and by and with the consent of the Senate, shall appoint ambassadors, other public ministers, and consuls, judges of the Supreme Court, and all other officers of the United States whose appointments are not herein otherwise provided for, and which shall be established by law; but the Congress may by law vest the appointment of such inferior officers, as they think proper, in the President alone, in the courts of law, or in the heads of departments.

The Beginnings When he became President in 1789, George Washington knew that the success of the new government would depend in large part on those whom he appointed to office. Those to be chosen, he said, would be "such persons alone . . . as shall be the best qualified." Still, he favored members of his own party, the Federalists. So did those of his successor, John Adams.

In 1801 Thomas Jefferson found most federal posts filled by men both politically and personally opposed to him. He agreed with Washington's standard of "fitness for office," but he combined it with another: "political acceptability." Several hundred Federalists were dismissed; they were replaced by good Democratic-Republicans. Overall, not very many positions were involved. When the

[13]Another 2 million men and women serve in the armed forces; see Chapter 17. Altogether, there are now nearly 16 million civilian public employees in this country. Some 3.8 million work for the States, and another 9.7 million for local governments (including 5.5 million persons employed by school districts). About 2.5 million of all who work for State and local governments are employed on a part-time basis.

*ENRICHMENT Discuss in class: Presidents have the power to make a variety of appointments, such as department heads and ambassadors. Is this a modern "spoils system"? Why or why not?

An 1872 cartoon comments on the spoils system that prevailed in the administration of public affairs in the 1870s.

national capital was moved to the new city of Washington in late 1800, there were fewer than a thousand federal employees.

The Spoils System By the late 1820s, the number of federal employees had risen above 10,000. When Andrew Jackson became President in 1829, he dismissed more than 200 presidential appointees and nearly 2,000 other federal officeholders. They were replaced by loyal Jacksonian Democrats.

Ever since, Jackson has been called the father of the **spoils system**—the practice of giving offices and other favors of government to political supporters and friends.[14] This is not altogether fair. Jefferson had laid its foundations at the federal level in 1801, and the practice was in wide use at the State and local levels long before Jackson's Presidency. *

Jackson saw his appointing policy as "democratic." In his first message to Congress, he explained and defended it on four grounds: (1) Since the duties of public office are basically simple, any normally intelligent person can fill such office. (2) There should be a "rotation in office" so that a large number of people can have the privilege of serving in government. (3) Long service in office by any person can lead to both tyranny and inefficiency. (4) The people are entitled to have the party they have placed in power in control of all offices of government, top to bottom.

Whatever Jackson's view, many saw the spoils system as a way to build and hold power. For the next half-century, every change of administration brought a new round of rewards and punishments. As the

[14]The phrase comes from a statement made on the floor of the Senate in 1832. Senator William Learned Marcy of New York, defending Jackson's appointment of an ambassador, declared: "To the victor belongs the spoils of the enemy."

*REINFORCEMENT Have the class discuss Andrew Jackson's views on the spoils system. On what issues do the students agree or disagree?

Government's activities, agencies, and payrolls grew, so did the spoils. Many posts were filled by political hacks. Inefficiency and even corruption became the order of the day. Huge profits were made on public contracts at the people's expense, and much of the nation's natural wealth was plundered.

The Movement to Reform Able people, in and out of government, pressed for reforms. Congress did make some move in that direction in 1851 and again in 1853. Department heads were required to fill several thousand clerkships by examinations. But all of that came to nothing. Party loyalists passed those tests; others did not and could not. Congress tried again in 1871, when it set up the first Civil Service Commission and coupled it with the requirement of *competitive* examinations. That move soon faltered, too, mainly because of inadequate funding by Congress.

The cry for change went on. By 1880 civil service reform had become a major political cause and a leading issue in the presidential and congressional elections that year.

A tragedy at last brought fundamental changes in the hiring and other staffing practices of the Federal Government. President James Garfield was assassinated by a deranged and disappointed office-seeker in 1881. The nation was outraged. Congress, pushed hard by Garfield's successor, Chester Arthur, passed the Pendleton Act—the Civil Service Act of 1883.[15]

The Pendleton Act The 1883 law laid the foundation of the present federal civil service. The Act's main purpose was to take the civil service out of politics—to make merit the basis for hiring, promotion, and other personnel actions in the federal work force.

An independent agency, the United States Civil Service Commission, was formed to administer the law. That bipartisan body operated for 95 years. It was replaced, as we shall see, by two new agencies in 1979.

The Pendleton Act named two categories of employment in the executive branch: the *classified* and the *unclassified* service. The President was given the key power to decide into which of these categories most federal agencies (and so their personnel) were to be placed. All hiring for the classified service was to be based on merit, to be determined by "practical" examinations given by the Civil Service Commission.

Classified employees were forbidden to take any part in partisan politics. But the

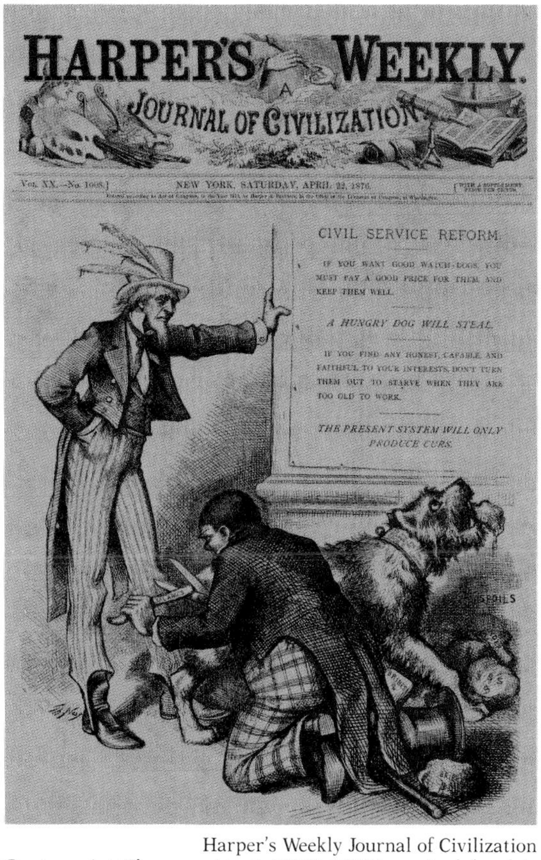

Harper's Weekly Journal of Civilization

Cartoonist Thomas Nast (1840-1902), noted for his cartoons aimed at corrupt public officials, points to the need for civil service reform.

[15]The 1880 Republican convention was sharply divided by the civil service question. Its nominee, Garfield, was a strong supporter of reform. To balance the ticket, it chose Arthur, a leader of the anti-reform faction, as his running mate. Garfield's assassination brought a complete change in Arthur's stand; as President he became the leading champion of reform.

President Garfield was shot by Charles J. Guiteau, at Washington's Union Station on July 2, 1881; he died 80 days later, on September 19; see page 375. Garfield had refused Guiteau's request that he be appointed American ambassador to Austria.

law's emphasis on merit was undercut, at least to a degree, by two of its other provisions. One, the requirement that hiring be geared to geography: The federal work force was to be made up of men and women from every State, and the number from each State had to bear a close relationship to that State's share of the total population. The other, veterans' preference: All veterans, and especially disabled veterans and veterans' widows, were given a preferred ranking in federal hiring.

The Pendleton Act itself put only about 10 percent of the Federal Government's then 130,000 employees into the classified service. The merit system grew by fits and starts, and fairly slowly, over the next 20 years. It began to grow rapidly when Theodore Roosevelt became President, however. When TR left office in 1909, the classified umbrella covered two-thirds of the federal work force, which by then had climbed to 365,000. Roosevelt's successors, and Congress, have generally followed his lead over the years since then. Today, nearly 90 percent of all the men and women who work for executive branch agencies are in the classified service.[16]

* Civil Service Today

The first goal of civil service reform—doing away with the spoils system—was largely reached in the early part of this century. Gradually, a newer goal emerged: recruiting and keeping the best available people in the federal work force.

On the whole, efforts to reach that goal have been generally successful. Sometimes they have stumbled over themselves, however. That is, they have most often stressed job *security* and too often neglected the equally important matters of job *performance* and *quality*. As critics have often said: Not enough attention has been paid to "merit" in the merit system.

President Carter put it this way in 1978:

> The Pendelton Act, . . . the Civil Service Commission and the merit system . . . have served our nation well in fostering the development of a federal work force which is basically honest, competent, and dedicated. . . .
>
> But the system has serious defects. It has become a bureaucratic maze which neglects merit, tolerates poor performance, and mires every personnel action in red tape, delay, and confusion.
>
> Most civil service employees perform with spirit and integrity. Nevertheless, the public suspects that there are too many government workers, that they are underworked, overpaid, and insulated from the consequences of incompetence.
>
> Such sweeping criticisms are unfair; but we must recognize that the only way to restore public confidence in the vast majority who work well is to deal effectively with the few who do not.

Reorganization Large changes in the civil service system were brought about both by the President, through a major reorgani-

What event explains the high figure for 1945?

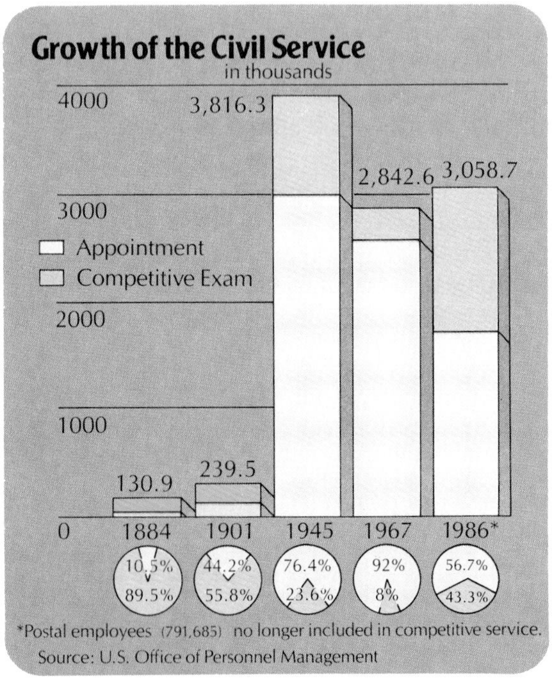

*Postal employees (791,685) no longer included in competitive service.
Source: U.S. Office of Personnel Management

[16]That is, 90 percent not counting the United States Postal Service and a few other federal agencies. The Postal Service, with about 735,000 employees, is the largest agency not covered by the civil service system. It is the only federal agency in which employment policies are set by collective bargaining and labor union contracts. The other major agencies not counted in fixing that 90 percent figure are the FBI, CIA, and TVA; each of those agencies has its own merit system.

*REINFORCEMENT Have the class discuss the need for civil service reform. The number of civil service positions peaked at the end of World War II, but is again on the rise. How did the Pendleton Act contribute to this?

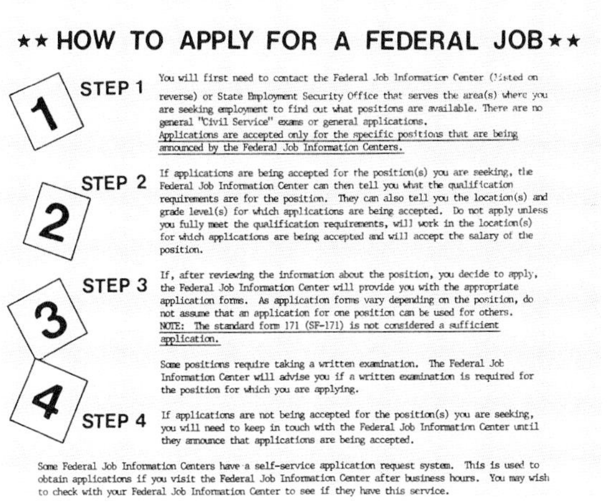

★★ HOW TO APPLY FOR A FEDERAL JOB ★★

STEP 1 You will first need to contact the Federal Job Information Center (listed on reverse) or State Employment Security Office that serves the area(s) where you are seeking employment to find out what positions are available. There are no general "Civil Service" exams or general applications.
Applications are accepted only for the specific positions that are being announced by the Federal Job Information Centers.

STEP 2 If applications are being accepted for the position(s) you are seeking, the Federal Job Information Center can then tell you what the qualification requirements are for the position. They can also tell you the location(s) and grade level(s) for which applications are being accepted. Do not apply unless you fully meet the qualification requirements, will work in the location(s) for which applications are being accepted and will accept the salary of the position.

STEP 3 If, after reviewing the information about the position, you decide to apply, the Federal Job Information Center will provide you with the appropriate application forms. As application forms vary depending on the position, do not assume that an application for one position can be used for others.
NOTE: The standard form 171 (SF-171) is not considered a sufficient application.

Some positions require taking a written examination. The Federal Job Information Center will advise you if a written examination is required for the position for which you are applying.

STEP 4 If applications are not being accepted for the position(s) you are seeking, you will need to keep in touch with the Federal Job Information Center until they announce that applications are being accepted.

Some Federal Job Information Centers have a self-service application request system. This is used to obtain applications if you visit the Federal Job Information Center after business hours. You may wish to check with your Federal Job Information Center to see if they have this service.

Left: A portion of an application for employment in the Federal Government. *Right:* Written civil service tests usually consist of short-answer questions.

zation plan, and by the Congress, when it passed the Civil Service Reform Act of 1978.

The Civil Service Commission was replaced by two new independent agencies: The *Office* of *Personnel Management* (OPM) is now the Government's central personnel agency. It is headed by a single director appointed by the President and Senate. OPM examines and recruits most new federal employees, carries on extensive training programs for career civil servants, sets position classifications, and manages the salary and other job benefits for some 2.1 million of the people who work for Uncle Sam.

The *Merit Systems Protection Board* handles the rest of the work once done by the Civil Service Commission. A bipartisan three-member panel picked by the President and Senate, it is *the* agency that polices and protects the merit principle in the federal bureaucracy.[17]

The Office of Personnel Management can best be described as the central clearinghouse in the federal recruiting, examining, and hiring process. It advertises for new employees, gives oral and written examinations, and keeps **registers,** or lists, of those persons who pass its tests.

OPM has registers for hundreds of different types of jobs. In fact, the Federal Government hires people for more than 2,000 separate occupational specialties. Included are clerks, typists, secretaries, telephone operators, janitors, doctors, nurses, lab technicians, chemists, botanists, psychologists, teachers, computer programmers, carpenters, plumbers, lawyers, truck drivers, pilots, and many, many more.

When there is a job opening in some agency, OPM usually sends it the names of the top three persons on its register for that type of position.[18] The agency then hires one of those three (and the other two names go back on the register). If the agency turns down all three, it asks OPM for another set, and the "rule of three" comes into play again. (Many jobs can also be filled by promotion from within an agency or by transfer from another. The OPM supervises those processes, too.)

[17]Another independent agency, the *Federal Labor Relations Authority,* now handles labor-management relationships in federal employment. It, too, is a bipartisan three-member body appointed by the President and Senate. The Director of the OPM is the Government's chief representative in its dealings with public employee unions.

[18]The place each applicant for a federal job has on a register is fixed by three factors: (1) time of application, (2) OPM test scores, and (3) veterans' preference points, if any. Nearly half of all federal jobs are now held by veterans, wives of disabled veterans, and unremarried widows of veterans. Some jobs, such as guards and messengers, are reserved especially for veterans.

All new federal employees must swear, or affirm, that they will support and defend the Constitution and laws of the United States. They must also sign a pledge not to strike against the government or any of its agencies. Such strikes are outlawed by the Labor-Management Relations (Taft-Hartley) Act of 1947. Within that framework, they may join any of several labor unions and other groups that promote the interests of government employees.

The merit system was put in place to protect federal workers from political pressures. Since 1883 the law has barred the firing or other disciplining of a classified employee who refuses to make a campaign contribution, and there are several similar protections in the law.

At the same time, several laws and many OPM rules place close restrictions on the partisan political activities of civil servants. The major law on the subject is the Hatch Act of 1939, and its formal title is quite telling: the Act to Prevent Pernicious Political Activities.

Federal employees *may* do a number of things in politics. They can vote, join a party and other political organizations, make voluntary campaign contributions, wear campaign buttons (off duty), and put bumper stickers on their own cars. They can voice their opinions on all political matters, attend and take part in (but not organize or lead) partisan rallies, take part in nonpartisan activities, run for and serve in nonpartisan local offices, and do many other such things. But they *cannot* take an active part in party politics or campaigns. That is, they cannot do such things as run for a partisan office, serve as an officer in a party organization or as a delegate to a party convention, or raise funds for a party or any of its candidates.

Many federal employees, and many others, object to these restrictions. They see them as both unnecessary and unjustifiable limits on their political and civil rights.[19] Supporters of them say that they prevent two main evils: the use of federal workers in presidential and congressional campaigns and the possibility that job security might come to depend on party loyalty.

Congress sets the pay and other job conditions for everyone who works for the Federal Government.[20] At the lower and middle levels, civil service pay compares quite well with salaries paid in the private sector. Government can never hope to compete dollar for dollar with private industry at the upper levels, however. How to attract and keep the better people for its higher positions is a major headache in the civil service system. On the whole, the fringe benefits in federal employment, such as vacations, sick leave, retirement, and group life, health, accident, and unemployment insurance are at least on par with those found most jobs outside of government.

FOR REVIEW

1. **Identify:** Reorganization Acts, Pendleton Act, merit system, civil service, classified employee, Office of Personnel Management, Merit Systems Protection Board.
2. What standard did George Washington set for federal employment?
3. What was the spoils system? How did Andrew Jackson defend his version of it? What conditions did it produce?
4. What event prompted the passage of the Pendleton Act? Outline its major features.
5. Over time, the primary goal of civil service efforts has shifted from what original aim to what major concern today?
6. What role does OPM have in the civil service system? The Merit Systems Protection Board?
7. What are OPM's registers? The "rule of three"?
8. Can federal workers strike? They may not take part in what kinds of political activity?

[19]The Supreme Court has upheld them, however, as reasonable restrictions on 1st Amendment rights. The leading case is *Civil Service Commission* v. *National Association of Letter Carriers, AFL-CIO*, 1973.

[20]Except postal workers; see page 462, note 16.

ENRICHMENT Organize a class debate: Should the political activities of civil servants be restricted, or should civil servants be allowed to participate in the political process as they wish?

6. Federal Finance

As You Read, Think About:

- What the Federal Government's sources of revenue are.
- How social security programs are funded.

For fiscal year 1987, the Federal Government expects to collect, from all sources, some $830 billion. It will spend much more —almost $1 trillion—in that same period.

Here, we take a brief look at many of the details of those huge numbers—at where all that money comes from and where it goes. As we do so, keep this very important point in mind: All of the dollar signs and all of the amounts we are dealing with here are a direct result of public policy decisions.

How much is collected? By what means, and from whom? How much is spent, and for what? These and a host of similar questions can be answered in dollar terms, of course. But these dollar-answers are also public-policy-answers. They tell us a great deal about both the content and the general direction of the nation's public policies. In short, in public finance public dollars = public policy decisions.

Sources of Revenue

Most of the Federal Government's revenue (the money it takes in each year) comes from taxes. However, a sizable portion of it also comes from several nontax sources, as we shall see.

Recall, we considered Congress' power to tax in Chapter 13, and we have just examined the process by which the Federal Government determines appropriations and revenue for each fiscal year. Now, we look at the several taxes it has imposed.

Income Taxes The 16th Amendment gave Congress the power to levy taxes on income; see pages 52, 325. Income taxes first became the major source of federal revenue during World War I, and (except for a few years during the Depression of the 1930s) they have remained so ever since.

Washington Star Syndicate, Inc.

Incomes of both individuals and corporations are taxed. The rates have always been progressive—that is, the higher the income the higher the tax rate applied to it.

The *individual income tax* regularly produces the larger amount. It is levied on a person's taxable income—one's total income in the previous year minus certain exemptions and deductions.

Each taxpayer has a personal exemption of $1080 plus another $1080 exemption is also allowed for each of his/her dependents; an additional $1080 exemption is also allowed for each person over age 65 or blind. Deductions are allowed for several things —mainly for medical and hospital care costs, most State and local taxes, interest payments, and charitable contributions.

By April 15 all persons with taxable income in the preceding year must file tax returns (declarations of that income) with the Internal Revenue Service. The rates applied to taxable income received in 1985 (and reported in 1986 returns) began at 11 percent in the lowest brackets $2390 to $3540 for single persons, $3540 to $5720 for married couples) and ranged on up to a maximum of 50 percent in the top brackets (above $85,130 for single persons, $169,020 for married couples.)[21]

The *corporation income tax* is applied to all of a corporation's net income—all of its earnings above its costs of doing business. (Nonprofit organizations—such as churches,

[21]The rates and other details of the various taxes dealt with here reflect federal tax laws as of late 1986. At President Reagan's urging, Congress made a number of changes in the personal and corporate income tax laws in late 1986—with many of the law's new provisions to become fully effective in 1988.

*REINFORCEMENT Have the class discuss the relationship between public finance and public policy decisions. How does this equation determine the course of the nation's public policies?

BUILDING GOVERNMENT SKILLS

Understanding Actual Number and Percent

From 1970 to 1985, the total amount of individual income tax paid to the Federal Government increased by $240.5 billion. Since 1970, individual income taxes as a percent of total Federal Government receipts have remained about the same.

How can both of these statements be true?

The answer lies in the definition of percent. Percent means "parts per one hundred." To figure out percent you divide the part by the whole and multiply by 100. In 1980, for example, individual income tax paid totaled (to the nearest billion) $244 billion. Total Federal Government receipts were $517. Therefore, individual income taxes accounted for 47 percent of total Government receipts: 244 ÷ 517 × 100 = 47.

You can find the actual number if you know the percent and the total number. Multiply the percent (using the decimal form) by the total number. In 1975, for example, individual income taxes accounted for 44 percent of total Government receipts. Total Government receipts were $279.1 billion. The actual number of dollars of individual income tax would be: .44 × 279.1 = $122.8 billion.

It is important to know both the actual number and the percent. Why are the statements in the first paragraph true? As the dollar amount of individual income taxes increased over the years, other Government receipts also increased. Therefore, income taxes as a percentage of total receipts stayed about the same.

1. What percent of total Federal Government receipts were individual income taxes in 1970, 1980, 1985 and 1986? Use the table below, "The Federal Government's Income by Major Source," for information.
2. Follow the same procedure for corporation income taxes.
3. Compare your findings. Why is it useful to know both percent and actual number?

The Federal Government's Income

(By Major Source for selected fiscal years, in billions of dollars)

	1970	1975	1980	1985	1986	1987 (est.)
Individual income taxes	$90.4	$122.4	$244.1	$334.6	$349.0	$381.7
Corporation income taxes	32.8	40.6	64.6	61.3	63.1	75.0
Social insurance taxes and contributions	45.3	84.5	157.8	265.2	283.9	304.6
Excise taxes	15.7	16.6	24.3	36.0	32.9	32.5
Estate and gift taxes	3.6	4.6	6.4	6.4	7.0	6.6
Customs duties	2.4	3.7	7.2	12.1	13.3	12.8
Miscellaneous receipts	3.4	6.7	12.7	18.5	19.9	18.1
Total receipts	**$193.7**	**$279.1**	**$517.1**	**$734.1**	**$769.1**	**$831.2**

Source: Office of Management and Budget

labor unions, charitable foundations, and cooperatives—are not subject to the tax.) This levy has been called the most complicated of federal taxes, largely because of the many deductions allowed in figuring a corporation's net (taxable) income.

The 1986 tax rates ran from 15 percent on the first $25,000 of taxable earnings on up to a top rate of 46 percent on that income above $100,000.

Social Insurance Taxes Three major social welfare programs are supported by "payroll taxes." (1) The Old-Age, Survivors, and Disability Insurance (OASDI) program—the basic social security program, established by the Social Security Act of 1935; (2) Medicare—health care for the elderly, added to the social security program in 1965; and (3) the unemployment compensation benefits to jobless workers, also established by the Social Security Act of 1935.

The payroll taxes for both OASDI and Medicare are collected from most employees and their employers, and from self-employed persons. Employees now (1987) pay a 7.15 percent tax on their salaries or wages (up to a ceiling of $43,800 of yearly pay—a maximum tax, then, of $3,131.70 for the year). Their employers are taxed an equal amount. The self-employed pay 14.3 percent on the first $43,800 of yearly income (a maximum of $6,263.40).

The unemployment insurance program is a joint federal-State operation, to make payments to workers who lose their jobs for reasons beyond their own control. It is financed by a 3.4 percent federal tax on the payrolls of nearly all businesses. The States administer the program, paying jobless benefits according to federal guidelines.

* ***Excise Taxes*** Taxes laid on the production, transportation, sale, or consumption of goods or services are **excise taxes.** Federal excise taxes are imposed on many items today, including: gasoline, oil, tires, cigarettes, pipe and chewing and smokeless tobacco, liquor, wine, beer, firearms, telephone service, and airline tickets. (Many of them are called "hidden taxes"—because they are collected from producers who figure them into the prices they charge to their retail customers.)

Estate and Gift Taxes The federal estate tax, levied since 1916, is a tax on the property of deceased persons. Congress added the gift tax in 1924, to plug a loophole in the estate tax (the giving of money or other property before death to avoid that tax).

The **estate tax** is applied to one's net estate—its full value minus certain exemptions and deductions. For 1987, the first $600,000 of an estate was exempt (so, in fact most estates are not taxed). Deductions are allowed for such things as State death taxes (see page 606) and bequests to religious and charitable groups. Anything a husband or

Reproduced here is a notice of payroll deduction rates applied to wages when the Social Security Act first took effect, in 1937. How do the 1937 deduction rates compare with those for 1987?

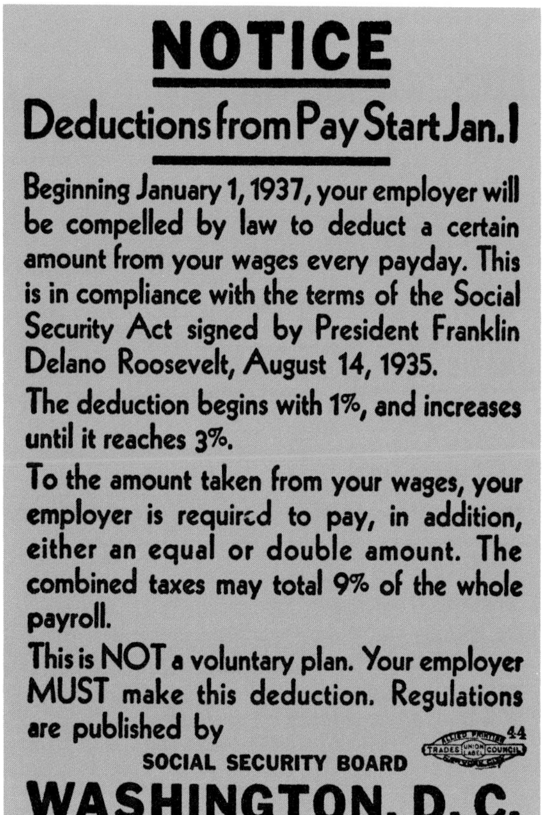
NOTICE

Deductions from Pay Start Jan. 1

Beginning January 1, 1937, your employer will be compelled by law to deduct a certain amount from your wages every payday. This is in compliance with the terms of the Social Security Act signed by President Franklin Delano Roosevelt, August 14, 1935.

The deduction begins with 1%, and increases until it reaches 3%.

To the amount taken from your wages, your employer is required to pay, in addition, either an equal or double amount. The combined taxes may total 9% of the whole payroll.

This is NOT a voluntary plan. Your employer MUST make this deduction. Regulations are published by

SOCIAL SECURITY BOARD

WASHINGTON, D. C.

*REINFORCEMENT Begin a class discussion on excise taxes by having the class cite specific items which are taxed in their community. How are these "hidden taxes" different from other tax forms?

Federal Spending, Fiscal Years 1982–1986

(By agency, in billions of dollars)

	Fiscal 1982	Fiscal 1983	Fiscal 1984	Fiscal 1985	Fiscal 1986
Legislative Branch	$1.4	$1.4	$1.6	$1.6	$1.7
Judicial Branch	.7	.8	.9	1.0	1.1
Executive Office of the President	.1	.1	.1	.1	.1
Funds appropriated to the President (Mostly for foreign economic/military aid)	6.1	5.4	8.5	12.0	11.4
Department of Agriculture	36.2	46.4	37.5	55.5	58.7
Department of Commerce	2.0	1.9	1.9	2.1	2.1
Department of Defense—Military	182.9	205.0	220.8	261.2	283.3
Department of Defense—Civil	3.0	2.9	3.0	3.0	2.8
Department of Education	14.1	14.6	15.5	16.7	17.7
Department of Energy	7.6	8.4	8.3	10.6	11.0
Department of Health and Human Services	251.3	276.5	292.3	325.5	333.9
Department of Housing and Urban Development	14.5	15.3	16.5	28.7	14.1
Department of the Interior	3.9	4.6	5.0	4.8	4.8
Department of Justice	2.6	2.8	3.2	3.6	3.8
Department of Labor	30.7	38.2	24.5	23.9	24.1
Department of State	2.2	2.3	2.4	2.6	2.9
Department of Transportation	19.9	20.6	24.0	25.0	27.4
Department of the Treasury	110.5	116.2	141.1	165.0	176.2
Interest on the Public Debt	(117.4)	(128.8)	(153.8)	(178.9)	(187.1)
Other	(11.6)	(13.7)	(13.0)	(13.1)	(14.2)
Offsetting receipts	(−18.5)	(−26.3)	(−25.7)	(−26.7)	(−25.0)
Environmental Protection Agency	5.0	4.3	4.1	4.5	4.9
National Aeronautics and Space Administration	6.0	6.7	7.0	7.3	7.4
Veterans Administration	23.9	24.8	25.6	26.3	26.5
Other independent agencies	33.1	32.3	34.1	34.0	36.2
Deductions (undistributed offsetting receipts)					
Contributions to federal employee retirement	−7.0	−8.1	−8.8	−27.4	−28.5
Interest received by various trust funds	−16.0	−17.0	−20.4	−26.1	−27.8
Rents, royalties on Outer Continental Shelf	−6.3	−10.5	−6.7	−5.5	−4.7
Total Outlays	**$728.4**	**$795.9**	**$841.8**	**$946.0**	**$989.8**
Deficit (Outlays greater than Receipts)	**−110.7**	**−195.4**	**−175.3**	**−212.0**	**−220.7**

Source: Financial Management Service, Department of the Treasury

The Public Debt

(At end of selected fiscal years, in billions of dollars)

1916 (pre-World War I)	$ 1.3	1950 (pre-Korean War)	$ 256.1
1919 (post-World War I)	25.5	1954 (post-Korean War)	271.3
1930 (start of Depression)	16.2	1964 (pre-Vietnam War)	308.1
1940 (decade of Depression)	43.0	1974 (post-Vietnam War)	474.2
1941 (pre-World War II)	48.9	1985 (preceding fiscal year)	1,823.1
1946 (post-World War II)	269.4	1986 (latest fiscal year)	2,125.3

Source: Bureau of the Public Dept, Department of the Treasury

*ENRICHMENT Have the class discuss trends in federal spending from 1982 to 1986. In what areas did spending increase and decrease? Why?

wife leaves to the other is taxed, if at all, only when the surviving spouse dies.

Any person may make up to $10,000 in tax-free gifts to any other person in any one year. Gifts husbands/wives make to one another are not taxed, regardless of value.

The estate and gift taxes are separate federal taxes, but both are taxes on the transfer of property (before or after death)—and so they are now levied at the same rates. For 1987, those rates range from a minimum of 18 percent on up to a maximum of 55 percent on a net estate or a gift worth more than $3.0 million.

Customs Duties **Customs duties** (tariffs) are taxes on goods brought into the United States. Congress decides which imports will be taxed (dutied) and at what rates. Most imports (some 30,000 different items) are dutied; but some are not—for example, Bibles, coffee, and up to $300 of an American tourist's purchases. Many duties are set purposefully high (the "protective tariff"), to protect industries and jobs in this country.

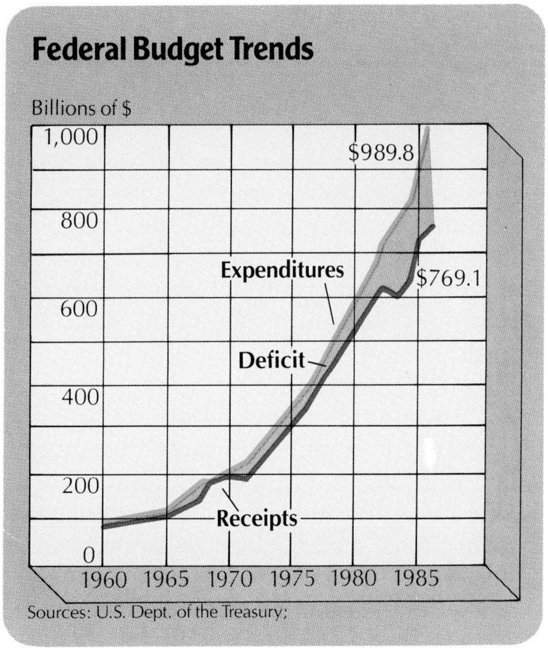

During what five-year period did receipts exceed expenditures by the Federal Government? Which five-year period shows the greatest increase in the federal deficit?

Salt and Pepper, The Wall Street Journal, by James Estes

"Income tax guides? Yes, sir—they're over in Section R, between our Greek manuscripts and our books on integral calculus."

Miscellaneous Receipts Huge sums come every year from a multitude of nontax sources, including interest payments on many types of loans, court fines, sales/leases of public lands, sales of surplus property, canal tolls, fees for passports, copyrights, trademarks, and patents, seignorage (the profit on minting coins), and many others.

FOR REVIEW

1. **Identify:** OASDI program, tariff.
2. About how much money does the Federal Government expect to collect in fiscal year 1987? To spend in that year?
3. Which of the various federal taxes produces the greatest amount of revenue each year?
4. What three major social welfare programs are supported by payroll taxes?

SUMMARY

As Chief Administrator, the President heads the federal bureaucracy—the large and complex administration structure within the executive branch of the Federal Government. The realities of the modern world make bureaucracy a standard feature of government, both here and abroad.

The Constitution says little about the federal bureaucracy. Nearly all of it has been created by Congress. It is now made up of three major groups of administrative agencies: (1) the Executive Office of the President (which we treated in Chapter 15), (2) the 13 Cabinet departments, and (3) the many independent agencies.

The several units of an administrative organization can be classed as either (1) staff agencies—those which serve in a support capacity, or (2) line agencies—those which carry out the tasks for which the organization exists.

The now 13 Cabinet departments are the traditional units of federal administration; each of them is built around a major field of governmental activity.

The many independent agencies are a part of the executive branch but outside of any of the Cabinet departments. They are independent of the regular departmental structure for a number of reasons, carry out a wide range of functions, and are of three main types. Most of them are (1) independent executive agencies; the others are either (2) independent regulatory commissions or (3) government corporations.

The Federal Government now employs some 3 million people. The present-day federal civil service system was begun with the passage of the Pendleton Act in 1883. That system, based upon merit, is now managed by two independent agencies: the Office of Personnel Management and the Merit Systems Protection Board.

In fiscal year 1987, the Federal Government expects to collect some $830 billion and spend even more in the same period. Income taxes on individuals and corporations produce more than half of the Federal Government's revenue; payroll taxes that support social security programs yield about one-third of the federal tax receipts.

CHAPTER REVIEW

Key Terms/Concepts*

administration (429)
bureaucracy (429)
quasi-legislative (454)
quasi-judicial (454)
spoils system (460)
registers (463)
excise taxes (467)
estate tax (467)
customs duties (469)

*These terms are included in the Glossary.

Keynote Questions

• **1.** What is public policy?
• **2.** What is the role of the federal bureaucracy in the Federal Government?
• **3.** How do staff agencies differ from line agencies?
• **4.** List the 13 executive departments.
• **5.** Identify two of the reasons why Congress set up independent agencies.
• **6.** What is the most important difference between independent executive agencies and executive departments?
• **7.** Why did Congress create the independent regulatory commissions?
• **8.** In what ways did Congress ensure that the independent regulatory agencies would be free from presidential control and direction?
• **9.** What are government corporations? How do government corporations differ from private corporations?
• **10.** What factors have influenced the organization of the federal bureaucracy?

The dots represent skill levels required to answer each question or complete each activity:
• requires recall and comprehension • • requires application and analysis • • • requires synthesis and evaluation

• **11.** How did the Pendleton Act change the original notion of the federal civil service?
• **12.** What is the main function of OPM? Of the Merit Systems Protection Board?
• **13.** From which source does most of the government's revenue come?
• **14.** What characterizes a tax rate that is "progressive"?
• **15.** What was the size of the public debt in fiscal year 1985?
• **16.** What basic social security program was established by the Social Security Act of 1935?
• **17.** What are excise taxes? Customs duties? Estate and gift taxes? Identify five significant nontax sources of federal revenue.

Skill Application

Using Graphs to Note Trends: Graphs present numerical information in an easily understood format. They can be useful in noting comparisons, relationships, or trends. Name, by its title, the graph in this chapter which supports these statements:

1. The gross public debt did not increase dramatically between 1960 and 1970, but it jumped sharply after 1970.
2. Federal outlays for highway construction exceeded outlays for mass transit and railroads in 1975, 1980, and 1986.
3. Petroleum imports have declined since 1978.
4. Since the late 1970s, farm costs have exceeded the prices received by farmers for their farm products.
5. The construction of new homes has undergone sharp "ups and downs," but the median sales price of housing has consistently risen since 1965.

For Thought and Discussion

•• **1.** Explain this statement: "public dollars = public policy decisions." Use the table on page 468 for examples to illustrate your explanation.
•• **2.** For most of our history, a civil service career was considered an honorable one. How might the Federal Government make a civil service career more attractive to young people today?
• **3.** One of the central problems for a democracy is to keep the bureaucracy responsive to the law and to the elected representatives of the people. What steps can be taken to keep the bureaucracy responsive?
•• **4.** Do you think that the legal restrictions on the political activities of federal employees should be abolished? Why or why not?
•• **5.** Should the independent regulatory commissions come under the control of the President? Why or why not?
••• **6.** Study the cartoon below. Do you think that many taxpayers feel this way? Give reasons for your view.

"The Small Society," by Brickman. Washington Star Syndicate, Inc.

Suggested Activities

•• **1.** Investigate one of the executive departments or independent regulatory agencies. What is the purpose of the agency? When was it established and why? What kinds of programs does it administer? What kinds of employees are required to run these programs? The *United States Government Manual* is a good source with which to start your research.
•• **2.** Interview a person from your area who works for a federal agency. What is the individual's position and primary responsibility? What are the advantages and disadvantages of working for the Federal Government? Do national politics affect the individual's work? How have different Presidents affected the agency?
•• **3.** Find out how the executive departments actually execute the law. Write to a department and ask for information on regulation writing and law enforcement.
••• **4.** Stage a debate or class forum on one of the following topics: (1) *Resolved,* That all federal employees be given the right to strike; (2) *Resolved,* That the independent regulatory commissions be abolished and their functions assigned to regular Cabinet departments.

We have no choice as to whether or not we shall play a great part in the world. That has been determined for us by fate. The only question is whether we will play that part well or badly.
* –THEODORE ROOSEVELT

17

Foreign Affairs and National Security: Providing for the Common Defense

CHAPTER OBJECTIVES

To help you to

Learn · Know · Understand

The one historic, continuing, and overriding goal of America's foreign and defense policies.

The important and inseparable linkage of the nation's foreign relations and its defense.

The institutions and process of foreign and defense policymaking.

The major features of American foreign policy, both historically and presently.

The role of the United Nations in world affairs.

THE IMPORTANCE OF our foreign relations and the manner in which they are conducted cannot be overstated. Today, as throughout our history, our foreign and defense policies are directed to one overriding end. That end is to safeguard the security of the United States. So, in a very real sense, our subject here can be accurately described as the national security policy of the United States.

1. Foreign and Defense Policies: An Overview

As You Read, Think About:

- Why a nation's foreign policy is really many policies.
- How our foreign policy is related to the foreign policies of other nations.

Through much of our history, American politics turned very largely on questions of domestic policy. For more than 150 years, we were chiefly concerned with what was happening at home. For most Americans, foreign

*ENRICHMENT Ask the students to read the above quote by Teddy Roosevelt. Why does he say that "We have no choice . . . "? Point out that isolationism was prevalent at that time.

Facing page: U.S. neutrality in World War II ended when President Roosevelt asked Congress to declare war on Japan after the Japanese attacked Pearl Harbor in December of 1941. *Above:* America emerged from W.W. II determined to be involved in world affairs. With this resolve, the United Nations was formed in 1945. Shown here is the UN's Security Council.

affairs were matters of little or no concern. Our relationships with other countries were largely shaped by a policy of **isolationism**—a refusal to become generally involved in the affairs of the rest of the world.

From Isolationism to Internationalism

The years since World War II have been marked by a profound change in the place of the United States in world affairs, however. That historic shift, from isolationism to internationalism, has brought major changes in our foreign and defense policies. World War II taught us that we cannot live in isolation. We have learned, whether we like it or not, that we live now in "one world."

That we do live in "one world" can be seen most clearly in terms of national security. The well-being of the American people and in fact the very survival of the United States are closely affected by much that happens elsewhere on the globe. The realities of ultra-rapid travel and of instantaneous communications in today's world make that point clear.

Wars and other political upheavals anywhere in the world have a decided impact on the interests of the United States—and on the daily lives of each and of all Americans. Four times in this century, we have become involved in wars thousands of miles from our shores. On several other occasions, our security has been threatened by events abroad. They include, among others, an outbreak in the Middle East, racial tensions in South Africa, acts by terrorists in Europe and Asia, and a revolution in Latin America.

Economic conditions elsewhere are also felt quite directly in this country. Japanese automobiles, European steel, Arab oil, Brazilian coffee, Italian shoes, Australian wheat, and all of the many other things we import make that fact obvious to all of us, every day.

In these and several other ways, then, we live in "one world." In some ways, however, we do not. The communist world, especially the Soviet Union, and the free world, led by the United States, confront one another on many issues and in many places. Most of the newer nations of Africa and Asia make up yet another grouping, a "nonaligned" Third World bloc of growing power in world politics. In this other, divided world of today, we have come to see that only through policies designed to promote and protect the security and well-being of all nations can the security and well-being of the United States ever be assured.

Athenians show their appreciation for Marshall Plan aid in 1949, aid that helped prevent a Soviet takeover of Greece during the Cold War years.

Foreign Policy: What It Is

Every nation's **foreign policy** is actually many different policies on many different topics. It is made up of all of the stands and actions which that nation takes in every aspect of its relationships with other countries—diplomatic, military, commercial, and and all others. Restated, a nation's foreign policy is made up of all of its many foreign policies. In short, it includes everything which that nation's government says and does in world affairs.

Thus, American foreign policy consists of all of the official statements made and all of the actions taken by the Government of the United States as it conducts this nation's foreign relations. It involves such matters as treaties and alliances, international trade, the defense budget, foreign economic and military aid, the United Nations, nuclear weapons testing, and disarmament negotiations. It also includes the American position on oil imports, grain exports, immigration, space exploration, fishing rights in the Atlantic and Pacific oceans, cultural exchange programs, economic sanctions, computer technology exports, and a great many other matters, as well.

Some of our foreign policies remain fixed, or largely unchanged, over time. For example, an insistence on freedom of the seas has been a basic part of American policy from the very earliest years of our history. Other policies are more flexible, subject to change as circumstances change. Thus, little more than a generation ago, opposition to the German and Japanese dictatorships was a major part of our foreign policy. Today, however, West Germany and Japan are among our closest and staunchest allies in the world community.

Sometimes the United States is able to take the lead in international relations. We are able to launch new policies that win support and heighten American power and prestige abroad. Take, as an example, the decision to rebuild the war-torn countries of Europe and restore their shattered economies after World War II (the Marshall Plan). It was a bold and effective step at that critical point in history, and it was a major signal of American postwar intentions.

Very often, American policy must be defensive in nature. It must be adjusted to meet the actions of some other country. Thus, "containment"—resisting the spread of Soviet influence in the world—became a basic part of our foreign policy nearly 40 years ago. It was begun with the Truman Doctrine

*ENRICHMENT Ask the students to list the ways in which foreign policy affects their lives. Point out that the shoes they are wearing most likely were made outside the U.S.

in 1947, in direct response to the Soviet Union's policy of aggressive expansion in the period immediately after World War II.

The President's Responsibilities in Foreign and Military Affairs

The President is both the nation's Chief Diplomat and the Commander in Chief of its armed forces. As we have seen, Congress also has significant powers in the fields of foreign and military affairs, especially with its power of the purse, its power to declare war, and in the Senate's role in the treaty-making and the appointment processes.[1] But, as we have also seen, it is the President who dominates those policy fields. Both constitutionally and by tradition, he bears the major responsibility for both the making and conduct of foreign policy.[2]

The President depends on a number of officials and agencies to meet his immense responsibilities as Chief Diplomat and Commander in Chief. Recall that we considered the National Security Council, in the Executive Office of the President, in Chapter 15 (page 404). We shall now look at other elements of what is often called "the foreign policy bureaucracy." We'll begin with the Departments of State and Defense, and then discuss several others.

FOR REVIEW

1. **Identify:** "one world," Chief Diplomat.
2. Why can the foreign and defense policies of the United States be properly called this country's national security policy?
3. In what ways do we live in "one world"? In what ways do we not?
4. Of what does a nation's foreign policy consist?
5. Who is the nation's Commander in Chief of the armed forces?

[1]See, especially, Chapter 13, page 353.

[2]See Chapter 15, pages 418–420. Recall, the Constitution forbids to the States any role in foreign relations, Article I, Section 10, Clauses 1 and 3.

2. Making Foreign Policy: The Department of State

As You Read, Think About:

- The history of the State Department and how it is organized.
- What the role of the State Department is in foreign policy.

The State Department, headed by the Secretary of State, is the President's right arm in both the formulation and execution of American foreign policy. The Secretary is appointed by the President, subject to Senate confirmation. Obviously, anyone being chosen for this vital post must be expert in diplomacy and foreign relations.

The Secretary of State ranks first among the members of the President's Cabinet. This is true in part because of the importance of the office, but also because the Department of State was the first of the now 13 executive departments which were created by Congress in 1789.

The Second Continental Congress handled the foreign relations of the new United States through the years of the Revolution. In 1775 it created a Committee of Secret Correspondence, chaired by Benjamin Franklin, for the "sole purpose of corresponding with our friends in Great Britain, Ireland, and other parts of the world." That body was replaced by a Committee for Foreign Affairs in 1777.

The new Congress under the Articles of Confederation established a separate Department of Foreign Affairs in 1781. Congress continued to make foreign policy, however. The Department had only a very limited role in its conduct, through fewer than 25 American diplomatic agents abroad.

The Department of Foreign Affairs was re-created by Congress in 1789, as the first major unit in the executive branch of the new government under the Constitution. Later that same year, its name was changed to the Department of State, and President Washington appointed Thomas Jefferson as the nation's first Secretary of State. For nearly 200 years now, 58 other men, many of

Secretary of State George Schultz (at left) is greeted by the Soviet Union's Foreign Minister Eduard Shevardnadze outside the Soviet Embassy in Washington, D.C.

them quite distinguished, have held that important post.[3]

The duties of the Secretary relate almost solely to foreign affairs today: to the making and conduct of policy and to managing the work of the Department, its many overseas posts, and its more than 26,000 employees.[4]

Some Presidents have relied very heavily on the Secretary of State; others have chosen to keep foreign policy more tightly in their own hands. In either case, the Secretary has been an important and influential officer in every administration.

Organization

The Department is organized along both geographic and functional lines. Some of its agencies, such as the Bureau of African Affairs and the Bureau of Near Eastern and South Asian Affairs, deal with matters involving certain countries or regions of the world. Other agencies have more broadly defined responsibilities, such as the Bureau of Economic and Business Affairs and the Bureau for Refugee Programs. Most of these bureaus are headed by an Assistant Secretary and include several "offices." Examples include the Office of Soviet Union Affairs in the Bureau of European Affairs, and the Passport Office and the Visa Office in the Bureau of Consular Affairs. This arrangement makes it possible for the Department to keep abreast of the many different and often fast-breaking events of world politics.

The Foreign Service

More than 3,400 men and women now represent the United States abroad as members of the Foreign Service. *

Under *international law*[5] every nation has the **right of legation**—the right to send and receive diplomatic representatives. An ancient practice, its roots can be traced back to the Egyptian civilization of 6,000 years ago.

The Second Continental Congress named this nation's first foreign service officer in 1778, when it chose Benjamin Franklin to be our minister to France.

Ambassadors

Today the United States is represented by an **ambassador** stationed at the capital of

[3]Six Presidents served as Secretary of State before reaching the White House: Jefferson (1789–1794); James Madison (1801–1809); James Monroe (1811–1817); John Quincy Adams (1817–1825); Martin Van Buren (1829–1831); and James Buchanan (1845–1849). But, note, the office has not been a steppingstone to the Presidency in more than 125 years now. In fact, the last major party presidential nominee to have previously served in the post was James G. Blaine (Secretary of State in 1881 and Republican presidential candidate in 1884).

[4]The Secretary does have some domestic responsibilities. Thus, when Richard Nixon resigned the Presidency on August 9, 1974, his formal, legal announcement of that fact had to be submitted to the Secretary of State (at the time, Henry Kissinger). Over the years, the Secretary and the Department have had (and been relieved of) various domestic functions—including, for example, publishing the nation's laws, issuing patents, and supervising the decennial census.

[5]International law consists of those rules and principles that guide sovereign states in their dealings with one another and their treatment of foreign nationals (private persons and groups). Its sources include treaties, decisions of international courts, and custom, with treaties the most important source today.

*ENRICHMENT Discuss: The Foreign Service represents the U.S. abroad. What do you think Foreign Service officers do? Point out that their duties are political, consular, economic, and administrative.

each state the United States *recognizes*.[6] American embassies are found in more than 140 countries around the world today.

Ambassadors are appointed by the President, with Senate consent, and serve at the President's pleasure. Some of their posts are much desired political plums, and many new appointments are made when a shift in party power occurs in Washington. Too often, amateurs have been picked, usually because of their record of service in the President's party. Fortunately, most of our ambassadors are now career Foreign Service officers.

President Truman named the first woman as an ambassador, to Denmark, in 1949. President Johnson appointed the first black (also a woman), as our ambassador to Luxembourg in 1965. Now, several women, blacks, and other minority persons hold high ranks in the Foreign Service.

Each American ambassador is the personal representative of the President of the United States, and he or she reports to the President through the Secretary of State. Each of them must keep the President fully informed of events in the host country, negotiate diplomatic agreements, protect the rights of American citizens abroad, and do whatever else is in the best interests of the United States.

To carry out these duties effectively, an ambassador must have the closest possible contacts with the leaders of the host country as well as with its people. A well-grounded knowledge of the language, history, customs, and culture of that country is an almost indispensable qualification for the job.

Every ambassador is assisted by one or more diplomatic secretaries. Every embassy's top staff also includes a *counselor,* a high-ranking Foreign Service officer who advises the ambassador on matters of international law and diplomatic practice. Trade, agricultural, and communications experts,

The American Embassy in the People's Republic of China, located in Beijing (Peking), was reestablished in 1973.

military attachés, clerks, interpreters, and a number of other people are stationed at each American embassy.[7]

Diplomatic Immunity

In international law, every sovereign state is supreme within its own boundaries, and all persons or things found within its territory are subject to its jurisdiction.

As a major exception to that rule, ambassadors are regularly granted **diplomatic immunity.** That is, they are not subject to the laws of the state to which they are accredited. They cannot be arrested, sued, or taxed. Their official residences (embassies) cannot be entered or searched without their consent, and their official communications, papers, and other properties are protected in

[6]See page 420. An ambassador's official title is *Ambassador Extraordinary and Plenipotentiary.* When the office is vacant or the ambassador is absent, the post is usually filled by a lesser-ranking Foreign Service officer. That officer, temporarily in charge of embassy affairs, is known as the *chargé d'affaires.*

[7]The United States also has some 130 consular offices abroad. There, Foreign Service officers promote American interests in a multitude of ways—*e.g.*, encouraging trade, gathering intelligence data, advising persons who seek to enter this country, and aiding American citizens who are abroad and in need of legal advice or other help.

the same way. This same immunity is normally given to all other embassy personnel and to their families, as well.

Sovereign states grant diplomatic immunity to the representatives of other nations in order to promote the ability of every nation to conduct its foreign relations. The practice assumes that diplomats will not abuse their * privileged status. If a host government finds a diplomat's conduct unacceptable, that official may be declared *persona non grata* and be expelled from the country. The mistreatment of diplomats can lead to a serious break in the relationships of the countries involved.

Diplomatic immunity is a generally accepted and widely honored practice. But there are occasional exceptions. The seizure of the American embassy in Iran in late 1979 and the subsequent holding of 52 Americans as hostages for more than a year is an outrageous illustration of that fact.

Special Diplomats

Those persons whom the President names to certain other top diplomatic posts also carry the rank of ambassador—for example, the United States Representative to the UN and the American member of the North Atlantic Treaty (NATO) Council. There are also times when the President gives the *personal* rank of ambassador to those who take on special assignments abroad, such as representing the United States at an international conference on arms limitations.

Passports

Passports are certificates issued by a government to its citizens who travel or live abroad. They entitle their holders to the privileges accorded to them by international custom and treaties. Few states will admit persons who do not hold valid passports. Legally, no American citizen may leave the United States without a passport, except for trips to Canada, Mexico, and few other nearby places.

The State Department's Passport Office now issues some five million passports to American citizens each year. (Passports are not the same as *visas*. A **visa** is a permit to enter another state and must be obtained from the country one wishes to enter. Most visas to enter this country are issued at American consulates abroad.)

FOR REVIEW

1. **Identify:** Department of State.
2. What is the Secretary of State's first responsibility?
3. Why is the State Department organized along both geographic and functional lines?
4. What is the Foreign Service?
5. What are the principal duties of an ambassador?
6. What does the term *diplomatic immunity* mean?
7. What is a passport? What is a visa? Is a passport needed for a trip to Canada or Mexico?

3. Making Foreign Policy: The Department of Defense

As You Read, Think About:

- How the Department of Defense is organized.
- What the role of the Defense Department is in foreign policy.

The Defense Department also plays a leading role in the foreign policy process. The Secretary of Defense is always among the President's closest advisers in all matters touching on national security.

The Department, headed by the Secretary, was established by Congress in the National Security Act of 1947. It is the present-day successor to two historic Cabinet-level agencies: the War Department,

*ENRICHMENT Have the class discuss: What are the reasons behind diplomatic immunity? How can this privilege be abused?

BUILDING GOVERNMENT SKILLS

Evaluating TV News

Every day, all over the world, thousands of events occur that can be classified as "news." An act of terrorism in the Middle East, another battle in Afghanistan, violence in South Africa, important bills making their way through Congress, a speech by the President, hundreds of disasters—small and large—from fires to plane crashes, and much more may all occur on any given day. Of course, we can only learn about a small fraction of all the daily world events.

Many Americans depend on television news to tell them about world events. Understanding how the news programs work can help you learn more from watching television news programs.

It is very easy to be a passive TV watcher. The news is well produced and easy to watch. But you will understand much more if you think critically about what you are watching. Here are three principles to remember as you watch the news.

- **Time Is Precious**—The nightly news programs on the three major national networks are each only 30 minutes long. Since commercials take some of the time, the actual time available for news is even less. There is very little time to report all the stories that happen in a day. As a result, news editors can select only a small number of stories that will actually be used in the news program.
- **News Is Business**—In part, editors select stories that they feel are most important, but they must also select them with an eye toward "entertainment." An editor may decide that a story about a fire, with a videotape of the blaze, makes a better story than a speech by the Vice President.
- **The Cameras Can Affect the News They Cover**—For stories like fires, the cameras may have no effect on what happens. Fires burn regardless of whether there are cameras around. On the other hand, politicians like to make speeches with cameras present. Press conferences, speeches, demonstrations, and many other events may be affected by the presence of TV news cameras.

Because news programs move so fast, it can be very helpful to take notes while you watch. One good way to do this is to make a viewing guide. Take a few sheets of paper and write headings on each of them.

In the first column, write the topic of the story. In the second column, record the approximate amount of time that the story received on the air. In the third column, make notes on what the story was about.

Use the information you record on the viewing guide to answer these questions.

1. What was the first (or lead) story? Why do you think it was chosen?
2. How many news stories were there in total? How many stories were there that were at least 30 seconds long? Would you have preferred more news stories or longer ones?
3. Which story do you think will have the biggest effect, directly or indirectly, on your life? Which did you find most interesting? Are they the same story?
4. What makes a good story?
5. How many of the stories did you believe were affected by the presence of the cameras? Which ones? Why?
6. Keep a viewing guide for a week for one network's news program. Do you find any trends? If so, what do they tell you about that network's choice of news stories to cover?

created by Congress in 1789, and the Navy Department, created in 1798.[8]

Civil Control of the Military

The authors of the Constitution understood, absolutely, the importance of the nation's defense. They emphasized that fact clearly in the Preamble, and they underscored it in the body of the Constitution by mentioning defense more frequently than any other governmental function.

The Framers also saw the dangers inherent in military power. They knew that its very existence can pose a threat to free government. For that reason, the Constitution is studded with provisions to keep the military always subject to the control of the nation's civilian authorities.

Thus, the Constitution makes the elected President the Commander in Chief of the armed forces. To the same end, it gives wide military powers to Congress, that is, to the elected representatives of the people. The Constitution reinforces the principle of civilian control by giving to Congress the tremendously important power of the purse. With that power, Congress decides such basic matters of military policy as the size of the armed forces and how much money will be available for military purposes, such as pay, training, and equipment.[9]

We have obeyed the principle of civilian control throughout our history. It has been a major factor in the making of defense policy, and in the creation and the staffing of the various agencies responsible for the execution of that policy. The point is clearly illustrated by this fact: The National Security Act of 1947 provides that the Secretary of Defense cannot have served on active duty in any of the armed forces for at least 10 years before being named to that post.

The Secretary of Defense

The Secretary, who serves at the President's pleasure, has two major responsibilities: (1) as the President's chief aide and adviser in making and carrying out defense policy and (2) as the operating head of the Defense Department, with more than two million men and women in uniform and more than one million civilian employees.

The Secretary's huge domain is often called "the Pentagon"—because of its massive five-sided headquarters building on the Virginia side of the Potomac River, across from the Capitol. Year in and year out, its operations take a large slice of the federal budget—today, in fact, approximately 30 percent of all federal spending. For fiscal year 1987, the total outlay for national defense will approach $300 billion.

Chief Civilian Aides

The Secretary's chief assistant, the Deputy Secretary, directs the day-to-day operations of the Department. There are a number of other civilians at the top levels of the

---

[8]Congress created the Defense Department in order to unify the nation's armed forces—that is, to bring the then separate Army (including the Air Force) and the Navy under the control of a single Cabinet department. The new Department was first called the National Military Establishment; Congress gave it its present name in 1949. The Secretary of Defense has been known by that title from 1947 on.

[9]Recall, too, that the Constitution makes defense a *national* function and practically excludes the States from that field. Article I, Section 10, Clause 3 provides: "No State shall, without the consent of Congress . . . keep troops or ships of war, . . . or engage in war, unless actually invaded, or in such imminent danger as will not admit of delay." Each State does have a *militia*, which it may use to keep the peace within its own borders. Each State's militia is legally separate from that of every other, but all are, collectively, "the militia of the United States." Congress has the power (Article I, Section 8, Clauses 15, 16) to "provide for calling forth the militia to execute the laws of the Union, suppress insurrections, and repel invasions," and to provide for organizing, arming, and disciplining it.

Congress first delegated to the President the power to call the militia into federal service in 1795, and the Commander in Chief has had that authority ever since. In the National Defense Act of 1916, Congress defined the militia of the United States to include all able-bodied males between 17 and 45 years of age. That same law declared the *organized* portion of the militia to be the *National Guard*, which is largely financed with federal funds. Today the governor of each State is the commander in chief of that State's units of the Army and the Air National Guard, except when the President has ordered any or all of those units into federal service; see page 586.

*REINFORCEMENT Discuss: The Constitution ensured civil control of the military because the Framers saw dangers inherent in military power. Use military dictatorships to illustrate this.

In the course of fulfilling his duties as Secretary of Defense, Caspar Weinberger is called upon to inspect military installations, equipment, and personnel—abroad, as well as at home. At left, he reviews Chinese troops during a visit to China in 1983.

Pentagon. The most important of them are the two Under Secretaries, one for Policy and the other for Research and Engineering; the several Assistant Secretaries of Defense, often referred to as ASDs; and the Secretaries of the Army, the Navy, and the Air Force. All of them are appointed by the President with Senate consent.

Chief Military Aides

The five members of the Joint Chiefs of Staff serve as the principal military advisers to the Secretary, and to the President and the National Security Council, as well. They are the highest ranking uniformed officers in the armed services: the Chairman of the Joint Chiefs, the Army Chief of Staff, the Chief of Naval Operations, the Commandant of the Marine Corps, and the Air Force Chief of Staff. Each is also named by the President, subject to Senate approval.

The *Armed Forces Policy Council* is the Department's major planning and decision-making body. Its meetings are chaired by the Secretary of Defense. Its other members are the Deputy Secretary; the two Under Secretaries; the Secretaries of the Army, the Navy, and the Air Force; and the members of the Joint Chiefs of Staff.

The Military Departments

The three military departments—the Departments of the Army, the Navy, and the Air Force—are major units (sub-Cabinet departments) within the Department of Defense. Each is headed by a civilian Secretary, named by the President and directly responsible to the Secretary of Defense. The nation's armed forces—the Army, the Navy, and the Air Force—operate within that unified structure.[10]

[10]The United States Marine Corps is a separate branch of the armed forces, but, for organizational purposes, it is located within the Navy Department.

The United States Coast Guard is also, and at all times, a branch of the armed forces. It is organized as a military service, with a present strength of some 38,000 commissioned officers and enlisted personnel. The Coast Guard was created as an arm of the Treasury Department in 1925. Its history dates back to 1790, however—to the Revenue Marine, a maritime law enforcement agency established by Congress that year. Since 1967, the Coast Guard has been located in the Department of Transportation; see page 447. In time of war, or at any other time at the President's direction, the Coast Guard becomes a part of the United States Navy.

The Department of the Army

The Army is the largest of the armed services. It is also the oldest of them. The American Continental Army, now the United States Army, was established by the Second Continental Congress on June 14, 1775. This occurred more than a year before the Declaration of Independence was announced to the world.

The Army is essentially a ground-based force, responsible for military operations on land. Its primary mission is twofold. The Army must be ready (1) to defeat any attack on the United States itself and (2) to take swift and forceful action to protect American interests in any other part of the world. It must organize, train, and equip its active duty forces (the Regular Army) and its reserve units (the Army National Guard and the Army Reserve) for those purposes. All of its forces are under the direct command of the Army's Chief of Staff.

The Regular Army is the nation's standing army, the heart of its land forces. It now has a strength of about 704,000 men and 77,000 women—officers and enlisted personnel, professional soldiers, and volunteers. The women on active duty today serve in nearly all of the Regular Army's units; they are excluded from all direct combat roles, however.

The Army's combat units are made up of soldiers trained and equipped to fight enemy forces. The infantry takes, holds, and defends land areas. The artillery supports the infantry, smashes enemy concentrations with its heavier guns, and gives antiaircraft cover. The armored cavalry also supports the infantry, using armored vehicles and helicopters to spearhead assaults and oppose enemy counteroffensives.

The other units of the Army provide the many services and supplies for the soldiers in those combat organizations. They could not fight without the help of those other troops: the soldiers of the engineer, quartermaster, signal, ordnance, transportation, chemical, military police, finance, and medical corps.

The Department of the Navy

The United States Navy was first formed as the Continental Navy, a fledgling naval force formed by the Second Continental Congress on October 13, 1775. From that day to this, its major responsibility has been sea warfare and defense.

The Chief of Naval Operations (CNO) is the Navy's highest ranking officer and is responsible for its preparations and readiness for war and for its use in combat. The CNO has direct command of all its seagoing forces and all of its shore units and land-based facilities. Some 550,000 officers and enlisted personnel, including more than 30,000 women, serve in the Navy today.

The United States Marine Corps was established by the Second Continental Congress on November 10, 1775. Today it operates as a separate armed service, within the Navy Department but not under the control of the Chief of Naval Operations. Its Commandant answers directly to the Secretary of the Navy for the efficiency, readiness, and performance of the Corps.

The Marines are essentially a combat-ready land force for the Navy. They have two major combat missions: (1) to seize or defend land bases from which the ships of the fleet

An aircraft carrier at sea, one of the more than 500 ships that make up the active fleet of the United States Navy.

and the Navy and Marine air arms can operate and (2) to carry out other land operations essential to a naval campaign. Today some 190,000 men and nearly 7,000 women serve in the USMC.

The Department of the Air Force

The Air Force is the youngest of the military services. Congress established the United States Air Force and made it a separate branch of the armed forces, in the National Security Act of 1947. However, its history dates back to 1907, when the Army assigned an officer and two enlisted men to a new unit, the Aeronautical Division of the Army's Signal Corps. They were ordered to take "charge of all matters pertaining to military ballooning, air machines and all kindred subjects." From that small beginning, and over the next 40 years, what was to become the United States Air Force developed as a part of the Army.

Today the USAF is the nation's first line of defense. It has primary responsibility for military air and aerospace operations. In time of war, its major duties are to defend the United States, attack and defeat enemy air, ground, and sea forces, strike military and other war-related targets in enemy territory, and provide transport and combat support for our land and naval operations.

The Air Force now has about 608,000 officers and enlisted personnel, including some 60,000 women. The Chief of Staff of the Air Force is commander of all personnel.

The striking power of the Air Force is truly awesome. Huge, eight-engined B-52s are the backbone of its strategic, long-range bomber fleet. Several hundred of those giant aircraft

Examine the "By Function" graph and determine the area of military spending that has increased the most since 1980. Can you think of reasons why this would be so?

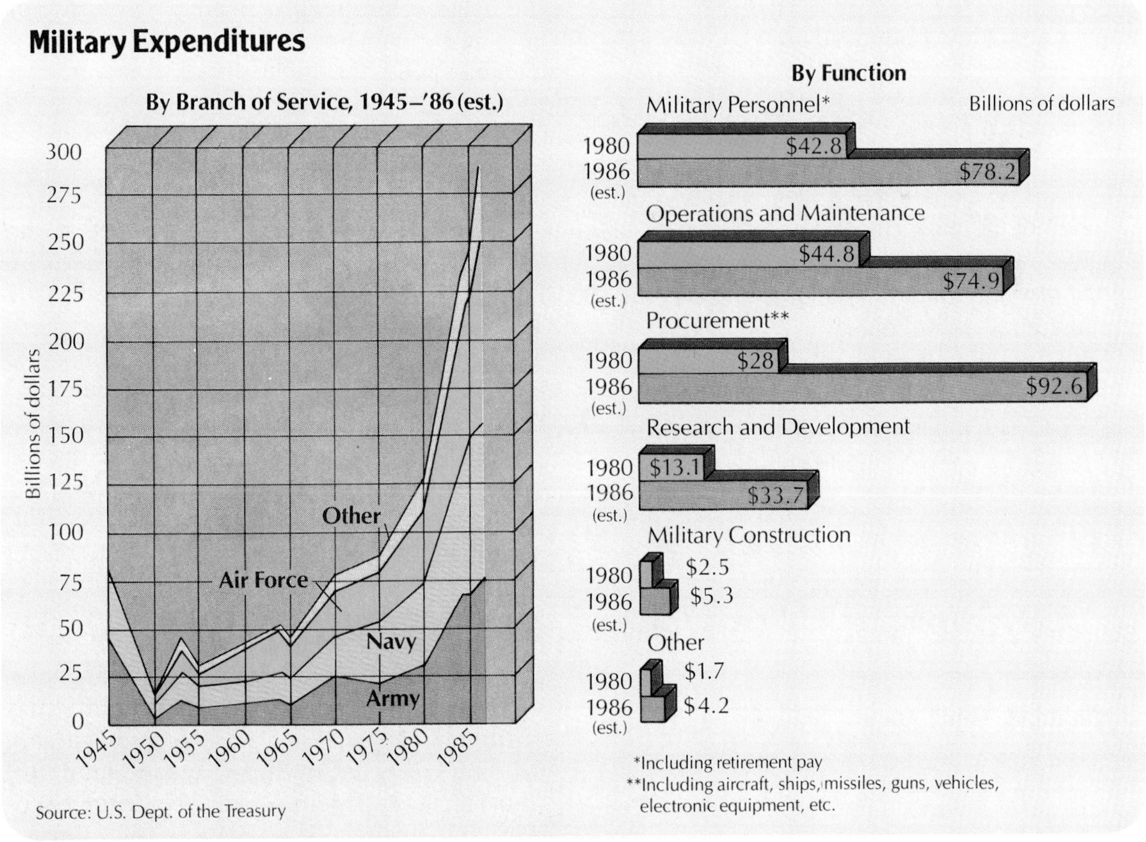

Source: U.S. Dept. of the Treasury

*ENRICHMENT Use the above charts to introduce a discussion of the Defense budget. Point out that it is the largest budget of any Department, and is often used as a political tool.

are kept in a state of constant combat readiness, at a number of bases here and abroad. Just *one* B-52 carries a nuclear bomb load with a destructive power greater than that of all the bombs dropped by both sides during all of World War II.

Today's B-52s are improved versions of planes that first flew in the 1950s. Plans now are to replace them with supersonic, missile-firing B-1s, sometime in the late 1980s.

All USAF tactical (short-range) aircraft —jet fighters and interceptors and attack bombers—are now armed with air-to-air missiles. Most tactical aircraft now carry air-to-ground missiles, as well. The Air Force also flies weather, reconnaissance, and hospital planes; transports; trainers; and several other types of aircraft. Like the other services, the Air Force is also armed with different surface-launched missile weapons—and, especially, the long-range intercontinental (ICBM) and intermediate-range (IBM) ballistic missiles. Many of the newest Air Force missiles can seek out and destroy fast-flying targets even hundreds of miles away.

FOR REVIEW

1. **Identify:** Department of Defense, civil control of the military.
2. Why does the Constitution provide for civilian control of the nation's military forces? How does it do so?
3. What is the primary role of the Secretary of Defense?
4. Describe briefly the basic features of the structure of the Department of Defense.

4. Other Foreign/Defense Policy Agencies

As You Read, Think About:

- What other agencies are involved in foreign policy.
- Agency functions in making and carrying out of foreign/defense policies.

We have already said that several federal agencies outside the Departments of State and Defense are involved in the field of foreign affairs. A few quick illustrations of the point follow.

The Immigration and Naturalization Service, in the Department of Justice, deals with those who come here from abroad. The Customs Service, in the Treasury Department, is concerned with goods imported from other nations and combats international smuggling operations. The Public Health Service, in the Department of Health and Human Services, works with a number of UN agencies and foreign governments to conquer disease and other health problems in many parts of the world. The Coast Guard, in the Department of Transportation, keeps an iceberg patrol in the North Atlantic to protect the shipping of all nations.

A listing of that sort could go on for several pages. In fact, nearly *all* federal agencies are in some way or another involved in the fields of foreign and defense policy. But here we turn to the several independent agencies with the most direct involvements in that field.

The Central Intelligence Agency

The CIA is a very important part of the foreign policy establishment. Created by Congress in 1947, the CIA works under the direction of the National Security Council. The "agency," as it is often called, is headed by a Director appointed by the President and confirmed by the Senate.

Clearly, the President and his chief advisers must have vast amounts of information—very reliable and timely intelligence—on which to base foreign policy and national security decisions. The CIA fills that need. On paper, it has three major tasks: (1) to coordinate the information-gathering activities of all state, defense, and other federal agencies involved in the areas of foreign affairs and national defense, (2) to analyze and evaluate all data collected by those agencies, and (3) to brief the President and the National Security Council—that is, keep them fully informed of all of that intelligence. *

*ENRICHMENT Have the class discuss: What sort of limits, if any, should be placed on the authority of the CIA? What are the advantages and disadvantages of the secrecy within which it operates?

The CIA is far more than a coordinating and reporting body, however. It also conducts its own worldwide intelligence operations. In fact, it is a major "cloak-and-dagger" agency. Much of the information it gathers comes from such more or less open, or overt, sources as foreign newspapers and other publications, radio broadcasts, travelers, satellite photos, and the like. But a large share of information comes from its own *clandestine,* or secret, covert, activities. Those operations cover the full range of espionage.

The nature of the CIA's work, its methods, the results it achieves, and its reports are regularly shrouded in deepest secrecy. Even Congress has generally shied away from more than a surface check on its activities; only a few key members are closely informed about them. Indeed, the agency's operating funds, which now run to several billions of dollars a year, are hidden in the federal budget each year.

The United States Information Agency

The United States Information Agency (USIA) is, at base, a propaganda unit. Its mission is to promote the image of the United States and to sell its policies and its way of life abroad. The agency describes its work as building "two-way bridges of understanding between the people of the United States and the other peoples of the world."

The USIA works to sell America in a number of ways: in radio and television broadcasts; by distribution of books, magazines, and other publications; with films and tapes; by sponsoring educational and cultural exchange programs; and through a number of other channels. It now operates more than 200 libraries, film centers, and other posts in some 130 foreign countries.

The USIA is best known for the Voice of America. The VOA's round-the-clock radio programs are beamed in English and some 40 other languages to audiences all over the world.

The National Aeronautics and Space Administration

From the days of the ancient Greeks more than 2,400 years ago, people have dreamed of the exploration and conquest of outer space. The modern space age is only some 30

The crew of space shuttle *Discovery* celebrates a successful mission in 1984. *Right:* The *Discovery* lifts off from Cape Canaveral, Florida.

Gene Bassett, United Feature Syndicate

years old, however. It began on October 4, 1957, when the Soviet Union put its first satellite, *Sputnik I*, in space. The first American satellite, *Explorer I*, was fired into orbit a few months later, on January 31, 1958. From that point on, a great number of space vehicles—of various types, manned and unmanned, and now "womanned," as well—have been thrust into the heavens by both of the superpowers.

NASA is an independent agency formed by Congress in 1958 to handle this nation's space programs. The military importance of those programs can hardly be exaggerated, but Congress has ordered the space agency to bend its efforts "to peaceful purposes for the benefit of all humankind," as well. NASA's work has opened new frontiers in several fields: in astronomy, physics, and the environmental sciences, in communications, medicine, and weather forecasting, and in many more.

The space agency conducts its various and many-sided operations at a number of flight centers, research laboratories, and other installations throughout the country. Among the best known: the Kennedy Space Center, at Cape Canaveral in Florida; the Johnson Space Center, near Houston; the Ames Research Center and the Jet Propulsion Laboratory, both in California; and the Goddard Space Flight Center, at Greenbelt, Maryland.

The United States Arms Control and Disarmament Agency

For more than a generation now, the world has lived under the shadow of nuclear war. The danger of a holocaust, begun by design or by accident, could destroy all forms of life on this planet. That awesome, terrifying fact has given new and compelling urgency to the ancient hope for the day when, in the words of Isaiah

> They shall beat their swords into plowshares, and their spears into pruning-hooks; nation shall not lift up sword against nation, neither shall they make war any more.

The USACDA is responsible for American participation in arms limitations and disarmament negotiations with the Soviet Un-

Max Kampelman (second from left), USACDA Director, met with Soviet diplomats in Switzerland in 1985 to hold preliminary arms control talks. Further arms control talks were scheduled to be held in Geneva in 1986.

ion and other countries. Its Director also serves as the principal adviser to the President, the National Security Council, and the Secretaries of State and Defense in all matters dealing with those policy areas.

Much of the agency's work to date has centered on nuclear test ban and arms limitation negotiations, which have been held, on and off, since 1958.

The Selective Service System

Through most of our history, as today, the armed forces have depended on voluntary enlistments to fill their ranks. But from 1940 to 1973, military conscription (compulsory service) was a major source of military manpower. At present, the **draft,** which is administered by the Selective Service System, exists only on a standby basis.

Conscription has a long history in this country. Several of the colonies and later nine States required all able-bodied males to serve in their militia. Proposals for a national draft, made by the first Secretary of War, Henry Knox, and endorsed by George Washington, were rejected by Congress in the 1790s, however.

Both the North and the South did use a limited conscription program in the Civil War. It was not until 1917, however, that a national draft was first used in this country, even in wartime. More than 2.8 million of the 4.7 million men who served in World War I were drafted under the terms of the Selective Service Act of 1917.

The nation's first peacetime draft came with the Selective Service and Training Act of 1940, as World War II raged in Europe. More than 10 million of the 16.3 million Americans in uniform in World War II entered the service under that law.

The World War II draft was ended in 1947. The crises of the postwar period, however, quickly moved Congress to revive the draft with the Selective Service Act of 1948. The present law is the Military Selective Service Act of 1971. From 1948 to 1973, nearly 5 million young men were drafted for the armed forces, most notably during the Korean War and, later, the war in Southeast Asia.

Mounting criticisms of compulsory mili-

*REINFORCEMENT Have the class discuss: What duties does the USACDA perform and why is it such an important agency?

tary service, fed by opposition to Vietnam policy, led many Americans to call for an end to the draft in the late 1960s. Fewer than 30,000 men were drafted in 1972, and selective service was suspended in 1973. The draft law is still on the books, however. So, compulsory military service could become a part of young men's lives once more, should Congress find that to be necessary.

The draft law places a military obligation on all males in the United States between ages 18½ and 26. Over the years in which the draft operated, it was largely conducted through hundreds of local selective service boards. All young men had to register for service at age 18. The local boards then "selected" those who were to enter the armed forces.

The registration requirement is now back in place. President Carter reactivated it in 1980, and his executive order is still in force. All young men, but not women, are required to sign up soon after they reach their 18th birthday.[11]

FOR REVIEW

1. **Identify:** Central Intelligence Agency, clandestine, selective service.
2. Why is it incorrect to view the making and execution of national security policy only in terms of the President and the State and Defense Departments?
3. What is the primary function of each of these agencies: the USIA? NASA? USACDA?
4. What is the status of the Selective Service System today?

[11]The President's power to order the induction of men into the armed forces expired on June 30, 1973. If the draft is ever to be reactivated, Congress must first renew that presidential authority. Recall that the Supreme Court first upheld the constitutionality of the draft in the *Selective Draft Law Cases* in 1918 and also ruled that its all-male features are constitutional in *Rotsker* v. *Goldberg* in 1981; see page 162.

5. American Foreign Policy: Past and Present

As You Read, Think About:

- Why the United States in the 19th century followed a policy of isolationism.
- What the events and forces were that ended the nation's isolationist policy.

The basic purpose of America's foreign policy has always been to protect the security of the United States. A complete presentation of our foreign relations history is impossible in these pages. We can review its major themes and highlights, however, because history is *not* "bunk," as Henry Ford once said it is. It is the raw material out of which today is made.

Isolationism

From its beginnings, and for 150 years, American foreign policy was very largely built on a policy of *isolationism*. Throughout that period, the United States refused to become generally and permanently involved in the affairs of the rest of the world. This policy reflected the fact that the Western Hemisphere was minding its own business.

Isolationism was born in the earliest years of our history. In his Farewell Address in 1796, George Washington declared "our true policy" to be "to steer clear of permanent alliances with any portion of the foreign world." Our "detached and distant situation," he said, made it desirable for us to have "as little political connection as possible" with other nations. In 1801 Thomas Jefferson added his own warning against "entangling alliances."

At the time, and for decades to come, isolationism seemed a wise policy to most Americans. The United States was a new and a relatively weak nation. We had a great many problems of our own, a huge continent to explore and settle, and two oceans to separate us from the rest of the world. That policy did not demand a complete separa-

*REINFORCEMENT Discuss: The Selective Service System administers the draft, which now exists on a standby basis. If the draft were reinstated, what would be the responsibilities of this system?

tion, however. From the first, the United States developed ties abroad—by exchanging diplomatic representatives with other nations, making treaties with many of them, building an extensive foreign commerce, and in other ways. In fact, isolationism was, over time, more a statement of our desire for noninvolvement *outside* the Western Hemisphere than within it.

The Monroe Doctrine

James Monroe gave the policy of isolationism a wider shape in 1823. In an historic message to Congress, he proclaimed what has been known ever since as the *Monroe Doctrine.*

A wave of revolutions had swept Latin America, destroying the old Spanish and Portuguese empires there. The prospect that other European powers would now help Spain and Portugal to take back their lost possessions was seen as a threat to our own security and a challenge to our economic interests.

In his message, President Monroe restated America's intentions to stay out of the affairs of Europe. At the same time, he warned the nations of Europe—including Russia, then in control of Alaska—to stay out of the affairs of the New World. He declared that the United States would look on

> any attempt on their part to extend their system to any portion of this hemisphere as dangerous to our peace and safety.

The Monroe Doctrine is not a law. Rather, it is a self-defense policy, a policy of "America for the Americans." It opposes any non-American encroachment on the independence of any country in the Western Hemisphere. It has been consistently supported by Congress and by every President for more than a century and a half.

At first, most Latin Americans took little notice of the Doctrine. They knew that it was the Royal Navy and British interest in their trade, not Monroe's paper pronouncement, that protected them from European domination. Later, as the United States became more powerful, many Latin Americans came to view the Doctrine as a selfish policy. They felt that we were more concerned with our own security and commercial fortune than with their independence. Matters have taken a somewhat brighter turn recently, as we shall see.

The cartoon above appeared in the January 26, 1889, issue of *Judge*, a widely read magazine of that time. The cartoon's caption read:
"Uncle Sam (Waking up) - Halt! I had no objection to its being constructed by private enterprise, but no European government shall take a hand in it!"

Continental Expansion

At the close of the Revolutionary War, the United States was a confederation of 13 States stretching for some 1,300 miles along the Atlantic seaboard. By the Treaty of Paris, which officially ended that war in 1783, the new nation also held title to all of the territory from the Great Lakes in the north to Spanish Florida in the south and westward to the Mississippi.

We began to fill out the continent almost at once. Taking advantage of France's conflict with England in the early 1800s, President Jefferson negotiated the Louisiana Purchase in 1803. At a single stroke, the nation's size was doubled, with territory reaching from the mouth of the Mississippi up to what is now Montana. With the Florida Purchase in 1819, we completed our expansion to the south.

Neither isolationism nor the Monroe Doctrine blocked further expansion to the west. Through the second quarter of the 19th century, we pursued what most Americans believed was this nation's "Manifest Destiny"*: the expansion of our boundaries to the Pacific Ocean. Texas was annexed in 1845. We obtained the Oregon Country (and British Columbia became a part of Canada) by treaty with Great Britain in 1846. Mexico ceded California and the land between after its defeat in the Mexican War of 1846–1848. The southwestern limits of the United States were rounded out by the Gadsden Purchase in 1853: By treaty, we bought from Mexico a strip of territory, in what is now the southern parts of Arizona and New Mexico, to provide the best rail route to the Pacific.

In 1867 we bought Alaska from Russia and so became a colonial power. The treaty of purchase was negotiated by President Andrew Johnson's Secretary of State, William H. Seward. At the time, many criticized the $7 million purchase as "Seward's Folly" and called Alaska "Seward's Icebox."

In that same year, 1867, the Monroe Doctrine got its first real test. While we were beset by the Civil War, France, under Napoleon III, had invaded Mexico and installed Prince Maximilian of Austria as its puppet emperor. We backed the Mexicans in forcing the French to withdraw, and the Maximilian regime fell.

The United States, a World Power

The United States emerged as a first-class power in world politics with the Spanish-American War in 1898. Spain's mistreatment of its few remaining possessions in the Caribbean had fanned wide resentment in this country. The war was triggered by the mysterious sinking of an American battleship, the U.S.S. *Maine,* in Havana Harbor on February 15, 1898. The fighting lasted only four months. With Spain's decisive defeat, we gained the Philippines and Guam in the Pacific and Puerto Rico in the Caribbean. Cuba became independent, under American protection. We also annexed Hawaii in 1898.

By 1900, the United States had become a colonial power with interests extending across the continent, to Alaska, to the tip of Latin America, and across the Pacific to the Philippines.

The Good Neighbor Policy

Our relations with Latin America have ebbed and flowed. The Monroe Doctrine has always served two purposes. It has (1) guaranteed the independence of Latin American countries, and (2) protected our position (our "backyard") in the New World.

The threat of European intervention, which gave rise to the Doctrine, declined in the last half of the 19th century. That threat was replaced by problems within the hemisphere. Political instability, revolutions, unpaid foreign debts, and injuries to citizens and property of neighboring countries plagued Central and South America.

Under what came to be known as the Roosevelt Corollary to the Monroe Doctrine, the United States began to police Latin America in the early 1900s. Several times, the Marines were used to put down domestic disorders in Nicaragua, Haiti, Cuba, and elsewhere. Political and financial conditions were stabilized, boundary disputes were settled, foreign lives and property were protected, and order was more or less generally maintained.

In 1903 Panama revolted and became independent of Colombia, with American blessings. In the same year, we gained the right to build a canal across the Isthmus, and the Panama Canal was opened in 1914. In 1917 we bought the Virgin Islands from Denmark to help guard the Canal. These and other steps were resented by many in Latin America. They complained of "the Colossus

*ENRICHMENT Have the class compare the way the United States viewed the ideas of "Manifest Destiny" and the Monroe Doctrine, with how a foreign country such as Spain may have viewed these two policies.

Construction of the Panama Canal lasted from 1903 to 1914, a mammoth project which greatly extended our influence in Latin America, especially in Central America.

of the North," of "Yankee imperialism," and of "dollar diplomacy" (and many still do).

Our Latin American policies took an important turn in the 1930s. Theodore Roosevelt's Corollary was replaced by Franklin Roosevelt's *Good Neighbor Policy,* a conscious attempt to win friends to the south. New life was breathed into the Pan American Union, first formed in 1890 and now known as the Organization of American States (OAS). For some 50 years now, we and most of our Latin American neighbors have worked to promote "hemispheric solidarity" and "inter-American cooperation."

The central provision of the Monroe Doctrine—the warning against foreign encroachments—is now set out in the Inter-American Treaty of Reciprocal Assistance (the Rio Pact) of 1947. The treaty is enforced by both the United States and the OAS. Still, the United States is, without question, *the* dominant power in the Western Hemisphere, and the Monroe Doctrine is still a vital part of American foreign policy.

Today, our most urgent problems in the region revolve about the existence of a communist government in Cuba, its close ties with the Soviet Union, and its efforts to promote revolutionary movements throughout Central and South America. Our support of the government of El Salvador and our opposition to the Sandinista regime in Nicaragua spotlight that difficult situation. So, too, did the lightning-quick invasion of Grenada in late 1983. That event also underscored the continuing importance of the Monroe Doctrine in American foreign policy.

The Open Door in China

Historically, American foreign policy interests have centered on Europe and on Latin America. Our involvements in the Far East reach back to the middle of the 1800s, however. Forty-five years before the United States acquired territory in the far Pacific, the Navy's Commodore Matthew Perry had opened Japan to American trade. The next several decades were marked by intense rivalries among a number of European powers to win territorial holdings and trade advantages in the Far East, especially China.

By the latter years of the 19th century, America's thriving trade in Asia was seriously threatened. The British, French, Germans, and Japanese were each ready to take slices of the Chinese coast as their own exclusive trading preserves. In 1899 Secretary of State John Hay announced this country's insistence on an *Open Door Policy.* That doctrine promoted equal trade access for all nations and a demand that China's independence and sovereignty over its own territory be preserved.

The other major powers came to accept the American position, however reluctantly. Our relations with Japan worsened from that point on until the climax at Pearl Harbor in 1941. Over the same period, through World War II, we built increasingly strong ties with China. They came to an end when the communists won control of the Chinese mainland in 1949. For nearly 30 years, the United States and the People's Republic of China refused to recognize one another.

The People's Republic took on a new role in world affairs when it replaced Nationalist China in the UN in 1971. President Nixon's historic visit to Peking in 1972 signaled the beginnings of a new era in American-Chinese affairs. Preliminary diplomatic contacts came with the exchange of "liaison officers" in 1973.

At last, the realities of world politics have led the two powers to a full-fledged relationship. The United States and the People's Republic formally recognized one another in 1979, and trade, cultural, and other contacts have grown fairly steadily since then.

World War I and the Return to Isolationism

Germany's submarine campaign against American shipping in the North Atlantic forced the United States out of its isolationist cocoon in 1917. We entered World War I "to make the world safe for democracy."

With the defeat of Germany and the Central Powers, however, we pulled back from the involvements brought on by the war. The United States refused to join the League of Nations, conceived by President Woodrow Wilson. Europe's problems and those of the rest of the world, so many Americans thought, were no concern of ours.

The rise of Mussolini in Italy, of Hitler in Germany, and of the militarists in Japan cast dark clouds on the world of the 1920s and the 1930s. Yet for more than 20 years after World War I, an isolationist United States wrapped itself with its two oceans.

World War II

Our historic commitment to isolationism was finally ended by World War II. That massive conflict, which began in Europe in 1939, spread to engulf much of the world and lasted for nearly six years. By the time it ended in 1945, the war had cost the lives of at least 45 million people. The war's other costs, in human suffering and in physical destruction, were at least as appalling.

The United States became directly involved in the war when the Japanese attacked Pearl Harbor on December 7, 1941.

This painting portrays U.S. forces in action several days after the Allied invasion of Normandy, June 6, 1944, which marked the beginning of the end for Hitler's Germany.

From that point on, together with the British, the Russians, the Chinese, and our other Allies, we waged an all-out effort to defeat the Axis Powers (Germany, Italy, and Japan). America became the "arsenal of democracy." Our resources and industrial capacity supplied most of the armaments and other materials we and our allies needed to win the war. Within a very short time, the United States was transformed into the world's mightiest military power. American land, naval, and air forces fought and defeated the enemy in the Pacific, in the Far East, in North Africa, and in Europe.

World War II ended, with the Allies victorious everywhere, in mid-1945. In Europe, Germany—devastated by the attacks of American and British forces from the west and by Russian troops from the east—surrendered unconditionally in May. The war in the Pacific came to a sudden end in August. Japan capitulated soon after the United States dropped two atomic bombs, which destroyed the Japanese cities of Hiroshima and Nagasaki.

FOR REVIEW

1. **Identify:** national security, Monroe Doctrine, Good Neighbor Policy, Open Door Policy.
2. What was the policy of isolationism? Why did it dominate our foreign policy for 150 years?
3. Was the Monroe Doctrine a departure from isolationism?
4. Trace the growth of the United States from the original 13 States to the acquisition of the lands that now make up the 50 States.
5. When did the United States take its place as a first-class power in world politics?
6. What has been the historic shape of this country's relations with Latin America?
7. What is the shape of our relations with China now?
8. Did World War I convince the U.S. to give up isolationism? Explain.

6. American Foreign Policy Today

As You Read, Think About:

- What the basic elements are of American foreign policy.
- How the United States has resisted Soviet aggression in the world.

World War II led to a fundamental change in the shape of American foreign policy: an historic shift from a position of isolationism to one of internationalism. In just a few years, the United States rose from its place as *one* of several major powers in the world to its present place as *the* leading power among the free nations of the world. From its isolationist past, the United States emerged from World War II as a permanent and global participant in international affairs.

Our foreign policy has been cast in that newer direction for some 40 years now. Even so, the overall objective of that policy remains what it has always been: the protection of the security of the United States. The major features of current American foreign policy, to which we now turn, are all reflections of that overriding goal.

Peace Through Collective Security

The United States, and most of the rest of a war-weary world, looked to the principle of **collective security** to keep international peace and order after World War II. That is, we hoped to forge a worldwide system of security—a world community, in which all or at least most nations would agree to act together against any nation that threatened or broke the peace.

We were determined not to repeat the error of 1919–1920, when the United States refused to join the League of Nations. To that end, we took the lead in creating the United Nations in 1945. Its Charter declared that the UN was formed to promote international cooperation and so "to save succeeding generations from the scourge of war . . . and to maintain international peace and security." See pages 504–507.

*REINFORCEMENT Have the class discuss the causes of the United States' return to the world stage following World War I. Remind them of Teddy Roosevelt's quote that opens the chapter.

The first hydrogen bomb was exploded in a test conducted in the South Pacific in 1952. What steps have the superpowers taken since then to avert nuclear war?

It soon became clear that the future of the world would not be shaped in the UN, however. Rather, international security would depend very largely on the nature of the relations between the world's two superpowers, the United States and the Soviet Union. Those relations, never very close, quickly deteriorated. Much of American foreign policy into the 1980s has been built around that fact.

Still, the principle of collective security remains a cornerstone of our foreign policy. We have consistently supported the United Nations and several other efforts to further international cooperation. Because the UN has not fulfilled the dreams on which it was founded, we have taken another path to collective security: We have built a system of defensive alliances (regional collective security treaties) with many of the other free nations of the world; see pages 500–502.

Deterrence

*The policy of deterrence is another major plank of current American foreign policy. It was begun under President Truman, as the antagonisms between the United States and the Soviet Union grew after World War II. It has been maintained by every President ever since. **Deterrence** is the policy of making ourselves and our allies so militarily strong that that very strength will deter, or prevent, any attack on us.

As President Reagan stated that policy:

> We are not a warlike people. Quite the opposite. We always seek to live in peace. We resort to force infrequently. . . . But neither are we naive or foolish. We know only too well that war comes not when the forces of freedom are strong, but when they are weak. It is then that tyrants are tempted.

Throughout his Presidency, Reagan has urged Congress to raise the level of defense spending each year. As he has done so, he has made much the same point, arguing that this spending is needed in order "to buy peace for the rest of this century." In a very real sense, the policy of deterrence comes down to this: This country's military might is most effective if, in fact, it does not have to be used.

Resisting Soviet Aggression

Much of the content of American foreign policy today is fixed, as it has been for more than a generation now, by one crucial factor: the state of our relations with the Soviet Union. Ever since the end of World War II,

*REINFORCEMENT Discuss: The policy of Mutually Assured Destruction (MAD) gave way to the policy of deterrence. In what ways can deterrence help to prevent the destruction of nations?

those relations have been at least tense and, more often than not, distinctly hostile.

We had planned to work with the Russians, particularly through the UN, to build international cooperation and keep the peace in the postwar world. Those plans were quickly dashed, however, by aggressive, expansionist policies of the Soviets.

At the Yalta Conference, in early 1945, Soviet Premier Josef Stalin had agreed (with President Franklin Roosevelt and British Prime Minister Winston Churchill) that "democratic governments" would be established by "free elections" in the liberated countries of Eastern Europe. Instead, the Russians imposed communist governments on those countries. Very quickly, the Soviet Union erected an empire of Soviet-dominated satellites along their western frontier. What Mr. Churchill promptly described as an "Iron Curtain" had dropped across Europe, dividing it between East and West. What soon became known as the **Cold War** had begun.

As they devoured Eastern Europe, the Russians tried to move in several other directions, as well. They attempted to take over the oil fields of Iran, to the south. At the same time, the Russians supported communist guerrillas in a civil war in Greece. Pursuing the historic Russian dream of a "window to the sea," they demanded military and naval bases in Turkey.

The Truman Doctrine and Containment The United States began to counter the Soviet Union's aggressive thrusts in the early months of 1947. The *Truman Doctrine* marked the first step in that now longstanding process. Both Greece and Turkey were in danger. Without immediate American help, they were certain to fall under Soviet control. At President Harry Truman's urgent request, Congress approved a massive program of economic and military aid, and both countries were saved. In his message to Congress, the President declared that it was now

> the policy of the United States to support free peoples who are resisting subjugation by armed minorities or outside pressures.

The Truman Doctrine soon became part of a broader American plan for dealing with the Soviet Union. Since mid-1947 we have generally followed the policy of **containment.** Over that period, the United States has taken many different actions in line with that overall strategy. A large number of political, economic, and military moves were made to contain (halt, check) the spread of communist power. The policy is based on the belief that if Soviet expansion can be stopped, then Soviet communism will collapse under the weight of its own internal problems.

The policy of containment dominated our relations with the Soviet Union during the Cold War—from the late 1940s on through the 1950s and the 1960s. First put in place under President Truman, the policy was followed by Presidents Dwight Eisenhower, John Kennedy, and Lyndon Johnson. Each applied the policy many times. The results were mixed.

The United States and the Soviet Union confronted one another often, and in many places, during the Cold War years. Two of those confrontations were of major, near-war proportions: in Berlin in 1948–1949 and in Cuba in 1962. During that same time, the United States fought two wars against communist forces in Asia.

The Berlin Blockade At the end of World War II, the city of Berlin, surrounded by Russian-occupied East Germany, was divided into four sectors. One sector, East Berlin, was controlled by the Soviet Union. The other three sectors, comprising West Berlin, were occupied by the United States, Britain, and France.

In 1948 the Soviets tried to force their three former allies to withdraw. The Soviets clamped a land blockade around the city, stopping the shipment of food and other supplies to the western sectors. The United States mounted an airlift that kept the city alive until the blockade was finally lifted, a year and a half after it had been imposed. *

The Cuban Missile Crisis The United States and the Soviet Union came perilously

*REINFORCEMENT Assign students a report on the Truman Doctrine: what it was, whom it served, and how it promoted the policy of containment.

Newly elected President Eisenhower inspects U.S. Army installations as part of his tour of the Korean front during the Korean War, 1952.

close to a nuclear shoot-out during the Cuban missile crisis in 1962.

Cuba had slippped into the Soviet orbit not long after Fidel Castro gained power there in 1959. Cuban-American relations quickly broke down, and the United States cut diplomatic ties with the Castro regime in early 1961. Cuba was pushed deeper into the Soviet camp when a band of CIA-trained Cuban exiles attempted to invade the island, at the Bay of Pigs in April 1961.

By mid-1962 huge quantities of Soviet arms and thousands of Russian "technicians" had been sent to Cuba. Both Cuba and the Soviet Union insisted that the military build-up was purely defensive, to protect Cuba from an American invasion. Suddenly, in October, the build-up became unmistakably offensive in character. Despite Moscow's repeated assurances to the contrary, aerial photographs revealed the presence of several Soviet missiles capable of nuclear strikes against this country and much of Latin America.

Immediately, President Kennedy declared that the United States would "not tolerate deliberate deception and offensive threats by any nation, large or small." He ordered a naval blockade of Cuba to prevent the delivery of any more missiles. Cuba and the Soviet Union were warned that the United States would attack Cuba unless the existing Soviet missiles were removed.

After several tension-filled days, the Soviets backed down. Rather than risk all, so far from home, they dismantled their missile installations and returned the weapons to the USSR. *

The Korean War During the years of the Cold War, the United States fought two hot wars against communist aggression in Asia. The first was fought in Korea and the other, in Vietnam.

The Korean War began on June 25, 1950. South Korea (the UN-sponsored Republic of Korea) was attacked by communist North Korea (the People's Democratic Republic of Korea). Immediately, the UN's Security Council called on all UN members to help South Korea repel the invasion. President Truman ordered U.S. forces into action at once.

The war lasted for more than three years. It pitted the United Nations Command, largely made up of American and South Korean forces, against Soviet-trained and Soviet-equipped North Korean and communist Chinese troops.[12] A cease-fire agreement was signed in July 1951, but sporadic fighting continued for another two years, until an armistice was finally signed on July 27, 1953. Final peace terms have never been agreed to, however. American and South Korean forces still stand guard against any further aggression from the north.

The long and bitter Korean conflict did not end in a clear-cut UN victory in the sense

[12]The UN Command also included combat and/or support units from 15 other UN members: Australia, Belgium, Canada, Colombia, Ethiopia, France, Great Britain, Greece, Luxembourg, the Netherlands, New Zealand, the Philippines, Thailand, Turkey, and South Africa.

*REINFORCEMENT Have the class discuss: What U.S. policies were tested by the Cuban missile crisis? What was the final result of the crisis?

that the enemy was beaten to its knees. The war cost the United States 157,530 casualties, including 33,629 combat dead, and more than $20 billion. South Korea's military and civilian casualties ran into the hundreds of thousands, and much of Korea, north and south, was laid to waste.

Still, much was accomplished. The invasion was turned back, and the Republic of Korea was saved. Perhaps more importantly, for the first time in history, armed forces fought under an international flag against aggression. In the hope of preventing World War III, the tide of communist aggression had to be stopped somewhere, and soon. There is no telling how far that tide might have carried had the United States not come to the aid of South Korea.

The War in Vietnam The United States became increasingly involved in Vietnam over a period of several years, beginning in the early 1950s. In very large part, that involvement grew out of the collapse of French colonial rule in Southeast Asia in 1954. It developed into the longest, most controversial, and most unpopular war in our history.

A Vietnamese nationalist movement, seeking independence from France and made up mostly of communist forces led by Ho Chi Minh, fought and defeated the French in a lengthy political and military conflict that had begun soon after World War II. Under truce agreements signed at Geneva in 1954, France withdrew from Southeast Asia entirely. What had been French Indochina was divided into two zones: a communist-dominated North Vietnam, with its capital in Hanoi, and an anti-communist South Vietnam, based in Saigon.

Almost at once, communist guerrillas (the Viet Cong), supported by the Ho Chi Minh government in Hanoi, began a civil war in South Vietnam. The Eisenhower administration responded with economic and then military aid to Saigon. This aid was increased by President Kennedy. By the end of 1963, more than 16,000 American military advisers were on duty in Vietnam, building and training the South Vietnamese Army and often leading it in combat. But, even with stepped-up U.S. support, the Viet Cong—and growing numbers of North Vietnamese troops, supplied with mostly Russian and some Chinese weapons—continued to make major gains.

America's involvement in South Vietnam ultimately failed in preventing a communist takeover of that nation. *Left:* Infantrymen wade through a Vietnamese swamp. *Right:* American G.I.'s evacuate Vietnamese villagers from their homes.

It was President Johnson who, in early 1965, committed the United States to full-scale war in Vietnam. Military operations were quickly stepped up and "Americanized" as the United States took over the major burdens of the fight against both the Viet Cong and North Vietnam. By 1968, more than 540,000 Americans were involved in a fierce ground and air conflict. By that time, however, the war had become a seemingly endless struggle and, in this country, increasingly unpopular.

In 1969, President Nixon began what he called the "Vietnamization" of the war. Over the next four years, American troops were pulled out of combat and responsibility for the fighting was turned over to the South Vietnamese. Finally, after lengthy negotiations which had begun in Paris in 1968, a cease-fire agreement was signed in early 1973. The United States, said President Nixon, had won "peace with honor" in South Vietnam, and the last American units were withdrawn. In spite of the cease-fire, the war between North and South Vietnam went on. By 1975, South Vietnam had been overrun and the two Vietnams became the Socialist Republic of Vietnam.

The ill-fated war in Vietnam cost the United States a staggering $200 billion and, irreplaceably, more than 56,000 American lives. The issue of our involvement in that conflict divided the American people for more than a decade, and more deeply than had any other issue since the Civil War. It caused many to lose faith in the workings of the American political system. For that reason alone, that war's costs will be with us for many years to come.

Détente and the Return to Containment As the United States withdrew from Vietnam, the Nixon Administration embarked on * a policy of *détente*[13] with the two major communist powers. A purposeful attempt was made to improve our relations with the Soviet Union and, separately, with the People's Republic of China.

Secretary of State Henry Kissinger was the chief architect of this new direction in American foreign policy: a move away from containment toward a thaw in Cold War tensions. The policy was built on a number of factors. Chief among them were: concerns over the rapidly rising costs and dangers of the nuclear arms race between this country and the Soviet Union; a belief that improved relations would lead to a marked increase in international trade; and a desire to exploit worsening relations between the USSR and China.

President Nixon flew to Peking in 1972 to begin a new era in American-Chinese relations. His visit paved the way to further contacts and led finally to formal diplomatic ties between the United States and the People's Republic.

Less than three months later, the President also journeyed to Moscow. There, he and Soviet Premier Leonid Brezhnev signed the first Strategic Arms Limitations Talks agreement, SALT. It was a five-year pact in which the two superpowers agreed to a measure of control over their nuclear weapons.

Our relations with mainland China have improved fairly steadily into the 1980s. Efforts at détente with the Soviet Union proved far less successful, however. Moscow continued to apply its expansionist pressures on a global scale and provided increasing economic and military support to revolutionary movements in the Middle East, Africa, Asia, and Latin America. The spread of Soviet influence was checked in some places. In Egypt, for example, Soviet troops and civilian technicians were expelled in 1972. The Soviets made substantial gains elsewhere, however, and often with the use of Cuban troops, as in Angola in 1975 and Ethiopia in 1977.

The short-lived period of détente was ended altogether by the Russians' invasion of Afghanistan in 1979. From that point, American foreign policy has placed renewed emphasis on containing Soviet power.

---

[13]The term is French, meaning "a relaxation of tensions," and has long been used in international politics to describe an easing of strained relations between two or more countries.

*ENRICHMENT Discuss: Détente was heralded as a sane way in which to deal with the threat of nuclear war, yet we currently see a move back to containment. Why?

FOR REVIEW

1. **Identify:** collective security, containment, Cold War.
2. What decisive impact did World War II have on the overall shape of American foreign policy?
3. When and why did collective security become a basic plank in our foreign policy? What role did we hope the United Nations would play in the postwar world?
4. What is the policy of deterrence?
5. Identify, describe: The Berlin Blockade. The Cuban Missile Crisis. The Korean War. The War in Vietnam. Détente.

A relief worker unloads food from the United States, food sent to ease the effects of a famine raging in Ethiopia.

7. American Policy on Foreign Aid and Defense Alliances Since World War II

As You Read, Think About:

- What the purposes are of American foreign aid.
- What alliances the United States has with other nations.

The dramatic shift from isolationism to full-scale involvement in world affairs since World War II is reflected in two features of present-day American foreign policy: foreign aid and regional security alliances.

Foreign Aid

Economic and military aid to other countries has been a basic feature of American *foreign policy for more than 40 years. It began with the Lend-Lease program of the early 1940s, in which we gave nearly $50 billion in food, munitions, and other supplies to our allies in World War II. Since then, we have given some $365 billion to more than 100 countries.

Foreign aid became a part of the containment policy with our aid to Greece and Turkey in 1947. Under the Marshall Plan, named for its author Secretary of State George C. Marshall, the United States poured some $17 billion into 16 nations in Western Europe between 1948 and 1952. That massive American help prompted Western Europe's remarkable postwar economic recovery.

Our aid policy has taken several directions over time. Immediately after World War II, most aid was economic in form; in the 1950s and 1960s, much of it was military. More recently, most aid has become economic once again. Until the mid-1950s, Europe received the lion's share of our help. Since

*ENRICHMENT Organize a class debate: Foreign aid is an expensive tool of foreign policy. With the economic problems existing in the U.S. today, can this expenditure be justified?

American Foreign Aid (U. S. Overseas Loans & Grants)

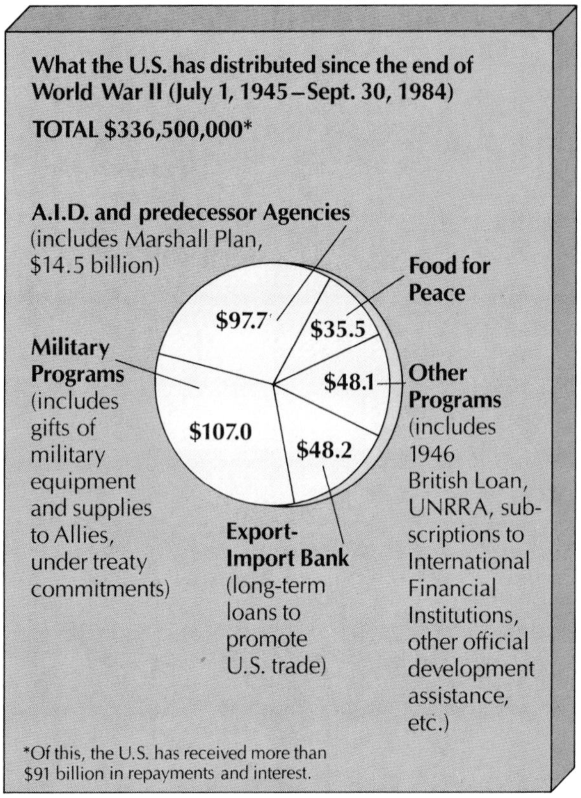

Where the U.S. distributed Aid (through Sept. 30, 1984)*

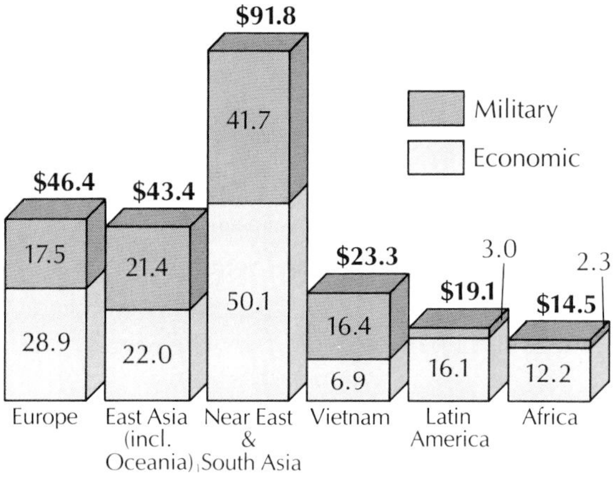

*excluding Inter-Regional and other aid of more than 74 billion dollars

Annual Foreign Aid since 1945*

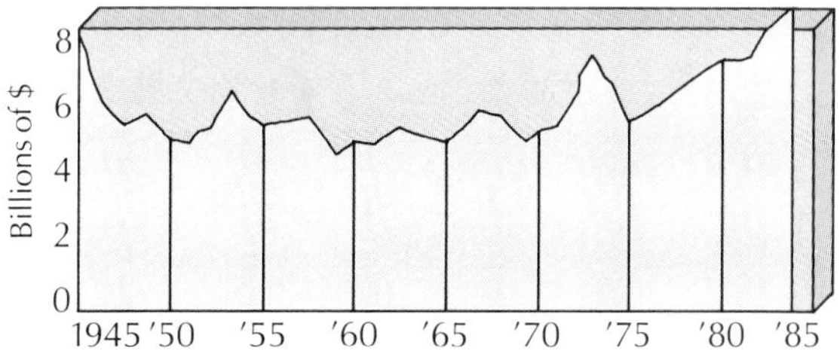

*excluding Military Aid July 1945–Dec. 1946

Sources: Department of State, International Development Cooperation Agency; Office of Management and Budget

According to the bar graphs above, which region(s) have received the largest share of foreign aid? Can you explain why?

then, the largest amounts have gone to nations in Asia and Latin America.

On balance, most of our aid has been sent to those countries regarded as the most critical to the realization of our foreign policy objectives. Over the past 25 years, South Vietnam, Israel, and Taiwan have been the major recipients of military aid. India has received the most in economic assistance.

Most of the foreign aid we provide must be used to buy American goods and services. So, most of the billions we spend for that aid amount to a substantial subsidy to both business and labor in this country. Most of our economic aid programs are administered by the independent Agency for International Development (AID), in close cooperation with the Departments of State and Agriculture. Military aid is channeled through the Defense Department.

Security Through Alliances

Present-day American foreign policy is also based on the concept of security through defensive alliances. Over the past 40 years, the United States has concluded mutual defense treaties with more than 50 countries. Through those pacts, we have set up a network of **regional security alliances.** In each of them, the United States and the other countries involved have agreed to take collective action to meet aggression in various parts of the world.

The *North Atlantic Treaty*, signed in 1949, established NATO, the 16-member North Atlantic Treaty Organization. The chief object of the NATO alliance is the collective defense of Western Europe, particularly against Soviet aggression. Each member has agreed that "an armed attack against one or more of them in Europe or in North America shall be considered an attack against them all."

NATO was originally composed of the United States and 11 other countries: Canada, Great Britain, France, Italy, Portugal, the Netherlands, Belgium, Luxembourg, Denmark, Norway, and Iceland. Greece and Turkey joined the alliance in 1952, West Germany in 1955, and Spain in 1982.

The NATO alliance has been the cornerstone of American foreign policy in Europe ever since its creation. The North Atlantic Treaty Council is made up of the foreign ministers of the 16 NATO countries. Through it, we and our allies in Western Europe have worked out political-military responses to actions of the Soviet Union.[14]

The *Rio Pact*, the Inter-American Treaty of Reciprocal Assistance, was signed in 1947. In it, the United States and now 30 Latin American countries have agreed "that an armed attack by any state against an American state shall be considered as an attack against all the American states." The treaty also pledges those countries to the mutual peaceful settlement of all disputes.

In effect, the Rio Pact is a restatement of * the Monroe Doctrine. Remember, when we made that point earlier, we also noted the fact that the United States continues to dominate the politics of the Western Hemisphere. When President Kennedy moved against the Soviet missile build-up in Cuba in 1962, he acted under the terms of the Rio Pact. The Organization of American States supported our actions.[15]

Economic problems and the growing political unrest in much of Latin America today point up the importance of the Rio Pact in American foreign policy. So, too, do Cuban-Soviet efforts to exploit those conditions —most recently in Central America and the Caribbean.

The *ANZUS Pact* of 1951 unites Australia, New Zealand, and the United States in another of these defensive alliances. It reflects how important the Pacific region is to this nation's security and also the fact that much of the Pacific Ocean has been, in effect, an American lake ever since the end of World War II.

The *Japanese Pact* also dates from 1951. After six years of American military occupation, we and our World War II allies (but not the Soviet Union) signed a peace treaty with Japan. At the same time, the United States and Japan signed a mutual defense treaty. In return for American protection, we are permitted to maintain land, sea, and air forces in and about Japan. We have added to our own security by making a close political friend of a former enemy.

The *Philippines Pact* was also signed in 1951. As we know, the United States acquired the Philippines as a result of the Spanish-American War in 1898 and gave the islands independence in 1946. The 1951 pact is a continuing American guarantee of that independence.

The *Korean Pact* of 1953 pledges this country to come to the aid of South Korea should it be attacked again. American military forces have been stationed there since the end of the Korean War.

The *Taiwan Pact* was in effect between the United States and Nationalist China from 1954 to 1980. It pledged American support should the People's Republic of China attempt to conquer the Nationalist-held island of Taiwan.

[14]In answer to NATO, the Soviets formed the Warsaw Treaty Organization (the Warsaw Pact) in 1955. With its headquarters in Moscow, it is a mutual defense alliance among Albania, Bulgaria, Czechoslovakia, East Germany, Hungary, Romania, and the USSR.

[15]Technically, Cuba, one of the original signers of the Rio Pact, is still a member of the OAS, but that body formally excluded Cuba from all OAS activities in 1962. That ban remains in effect today.

*REINFORCEMENT Have the class discuss: In what ways is the Rio Pact a restatement of the Monroe Doctrine? How is the Rio Pact important today?

The United States and the People's Republic established full diplomatic relations in 1979. At that time, the United States withdrew recognition of the Nationalist government; it also served the one-year notice required by the 1954 treaty to abrogate (end) that agreement.

We continue to maintain trade and other relations with "the people of Taiwan," however. Those ties are conducted through a unique agency, the American Institute in Taiwan. It is a "private, non-profit, tax-exempt corporation," created by Congress and financed by contracts with the State Department.

The United States and the Middle East Our network of regional alliances covers several areas of the globe, each critical to American security. That network does not cover all areas, however, most importantly today, not the Middle East.

The Middle East is both oil-rich and conflict-ridden. Its vast oil resources and its deeply rooted frictions make it the one region of the world in which there is the greatest danger that the United States and the Soviet Union could become involved (either directly or indirectly) in a shooting war. Our foreign policy interests in the region are often torn in two quite opposite directions: by our support of Israel and by our need for Arab oil.

Israel, the "historic homeland" of the Jewish people, was established as an independent state by the United Nations in 1948. Carved out of what had been Arab Palestine, Israel has been continuously embroiled and often at war with its Arab neighbors. During Israel's 39-year history, the United States has been its strongest and most steadfast ally, while the Soviet Union has regularly supported its Arab opposition. The more militant Arab nations, and the Palestine Liberation Organization (PLO), are committed to the destruction of Israel.

In spite of our support of Israel, we have gone to considerable lengths to promote friendly relations with most of the Arab states, especially because of our dependence on Arab oil. Today we import about 30 percent of all oil consumed in the United States, and a large portion of it comes from the Middle East.

With joy and relief, Egypt's President Sadat (left), President Carter (middle), and Israeli Prime Minister Begin (right) shake hands in reaching the Camp David Peace Agreement.

With the active involvement of President Carter, Israel and Egypt negotiated a peace treaty, which became effective in 1979. That agreement, the Camp David Accord, ended more than 30 years of hostilities between those two countries. But no other Arab state has joined the ongoing American-Israeli-Egyptian effort to build peace in the Middle East. So our precarious diplomatic balancing act there continues. *

FOR REVIEW

1. **Identify:** foreign aid.
2. Why has the United States provided massive amounts of foreign aid since the end of World War II?
3. Why have we built a network of regional alliances covering much of the globe? What is the nature of each alliance?
4. Our foreign policy interests in the Middle East are torn by what two often conflicting considerations?

*ENRICHMENT Discuss: Why is the United States so concerned with the conflict in the Middle East? Point out strategic location, oil reserves, historic support of Israel, etc.

FOCUS ON:

The Nuclear Freeze Debate

Millions of Americans, individually and in organized groups, come down on dramatically opposed sides of this question: "Should the United States and the Soviet Union conclude an immediate, mutually verifiable agreement to halt the development, production, and deployment of nuclear weapons?"

Those who support a nuclear freeze believe that the continuing nuclear arms build-up (by both superpowers) greatly increases the likelihood of a nuclear holocaust. They agree with Senator Allan Cranston (D., Calif.) that "without a freeze, sooner or later," by accident or otherwise, "a nuclear war will happen." The world is involved, says Senator Mark Hatfield (R., Ore.) in a "senseless race to oblivion."

The opponents of a freeze reject that view. They argue that nuclear weapons are an absolutely essential part of the policy of deterrence, and that it has been that policy which has prevented a nuclear war.

Most advocates of a freeze support deterrence, but they challenge the need for larger and still larger nuclear arsenals. They say that both the United States and the Soviet Union have long since acquired a capacity to destroy one another (and the world).

Critics counter that point, too. They claim that the Soviet Union has a larger nuclear arsenal and that a freeze would lock the United States into a dangerously unequal and vulnerable position. President Reagan has often agreed. He says that a freeze is "dangerous" and would "preserve today's high, unequal, and unstable levels of nuclear forces."

Many religious leaders, and many others, call for a freeze on moral grounds. Most particularly, they condemn the indiscriminate killing of untold thousands of innocent civilians that would inevitably occur if nuclear weapons were ever used.

"Herman," by Unger. © 1980 Universal Press Syndicate.

"Let's hope we never have to use it!"

For their part, the critics argue that the moral questions raised by the behavior of totalitarian communist regimes far outweigh those raised by the possession and potential use of nuclear arms. They believe that the fact that millions of persons behind the Iron Curtain are denied basic human rights should be the real focus of moral concerns.

Proponents of a freeze also claim that a halt to the nuclear build-up is a necessary first step to any meaningful arms control agreements with Moscow. There is, they say, no real hope for such agreements unless and until the nuclear arms race is stopped. But their critics insist that a freeze would have precisely the opposite effect. It would eliminate, they argue, a major source of pressure on the Soviets, a major incentive for them to negotiate the nuclear arms question.

1. What other arguments can you make for and against a nuclear freeze?
2. How do you stand on this question? Why?

8. The United Nations

As You Read, Think About:

- What the history, purposes, and membership are of the United Nations.
- How the United Nations is organized.
- What the importance is of the veto power in the Security Council.

The decisive change in American foreign policy that occurred during and immediately after World War II—the shift from isolationism to a full-scale involvement in global affairs—is strikingly illustrated by our participation in the United Nations.

The United Nations was formed at the UN Conference on International Organization, which met in San Francisco from April 25 to June 26, 1945. There, the representatives of 51 nations—the victorious allies of World War II—drafted the United Nations Charter. The Charter is a treaty, and it serves as its constitution.

The UN Building in New York City is the headquarters of the United Nations, formed in 1945.

The United States became the first nation to ratify the UN Charter. The Senate approved it by an overwhelming vote, 89–2, on July 24, 1945. The Charter was then ratified in quick order by Great Britain, France, China, the Soviet Union, and the other states that had taken part in the San Francisco Conference. The Charter went into force on October 24, 1945, and the UN held its first formal meeting, a session of the General Assembly, in London, on January 10, 1946.

The UN Charter

The Charter is a lengthy document. It consists of a preamble and 111 articles that set forth the purposes, structure, and powers of the United Nations.

The Charter opens with an eloquent preamble, which declares that the UN was created "to save succeeding generations from the scourge of war." The body of the document begins in Article I with a statement of the organization's purposes. They are: the maintenance of international peace and security, the development of friendly relations between and among all nations, and the promotion of justice and cooperation in the solution of international problems.

Membership Today the UN has 159 members: the 51 original members and the 108 states that have been admitted to the organization since its founding. Under the Charter, membership is open to those "peace-loving states" that accept the obligations of the Charter and are, in the UN's judgment, able and willing to carry out those obligations. New members may be admitted by a two-thirds vote of the General Assembly, upon recommendation by the Security Council.

Basic Organization The Charter sets forth the complicated structure of the UN, built around six "principal organs": the General Assembly, the Security Council, the Economic and Social Council, the Trusteeship Council, the International Court of Justice, and the Secretariat.

The General Assembly

The General Assembly has been called "the town meeting of the world." It is composed of representatives of each of the UN's now 159 member nations, each having one vote.

The General Assembly meets once a year, normally in September. Most of its sessions are held at the UN's permanent headquarters in New York. Special sessions may be called by the Secretary-General, either at the request of the Security Council or a majority of the UN members.

The Assembly may take up and debate any matter within the scope of the Charter,[16] and it may make whatever recommendation it chooses to the Security Council, the other UN organs, and any or all of the member-states. The recommendations it makes to UN members are not legally binding on them. Yet those recommendations do carry weight because they have been approved by a significant number of the governments of the world. On important questions, such as those on finances, decisions must be made by a two-thirds vote. On lesser matters, a simple majority vote is enough.

The Assembly elects the 10 nonpermanent members of the Security Council, the 54 members of the Economic and Social Council, and the elective members of the Trusteeship Council. With the Security Council, the Assembly also selects the Secretary-General and the 15 judges of the International Court of Justice. The Assembly also shares with the Security Council the power to admit, suspend, or expel members of the UN. It alone may propose amendments to the Charter.

The Assembly controls the UN's finances. It sets the annual budget and the share of it that each member must pay. The UN's regular budget for 1986 is close to $1 billion. The United States is required to pay about one-fourth of that total. The minimum payment for any member, paid by many of the smaller states, is now 1/100 of 1 percent of the budget—some $100,000 per year.

[16]Except those matters currently under consideration by the Security Council.

The Security Council

The Security Council is made up of 15 members. Five of them—the United States, Britain, France, the Soviet Union, and China—are permanent members of the Council. The 10 nonpermanent members[17] are chosen by the General Assembly for two-year terms; they cannot be immediately reelected. The Council meets in continuous session at the UN's headquarters.

The Security Council bears the UN's major responsibility for maintaining international peace. It may take up any matter involving a threat to or a breach of that peace. It may adopt measures ranging from calling on the parties to settle their differences peacefully to placing economic and/or military sanctions on an offending nation. The only time the Security Council has undertaken a military operation against an aggressor came in Korea in 1950. It has provided UN peace-keeping forces in several trouble spots, however—most notably in the Middle East. *

On *procedural* questions—routine matters—decisions of the Security Council can be made by the affirmative vote of any nine members. On the more important matters—*substantive* questions—at least nine affirmative votes are also needed. But a negative vote by any one of the permanent members is enough to kill any substantive resolution. Thus, each of the five permanent members holds the **veto power**—a power with which it can block any action by the Security Council in any important matter.[18]

Because of that veto power, the Security Council is effective only when and if the Big Five (the permanent members) cooperate. The Soviet Union has often used its veto to block UN actions; to date, it has cast more than 150 vetoes. Other permanent members

[17]The number of nonpermanent members on the Security Council was increased from 6 to 10 by a 1965 amendment to the Charter. In 1971 the People's Republic of China replaced the Nationalist Chinese regime on Taiwan as a permanent member of the Security Council and acquired China's membership in the UN in all other respects, as well.

[18]The veto does not come into play in a situation in which one more of the permanent members abstains (does not cast a vote).

*REINFORCEMENT Discuss: UN Peacekeeping Forces, composed of troops from member nations, are often sent to "hot spots" to preserve peace. What are other examples of the UN's expressed purposes?

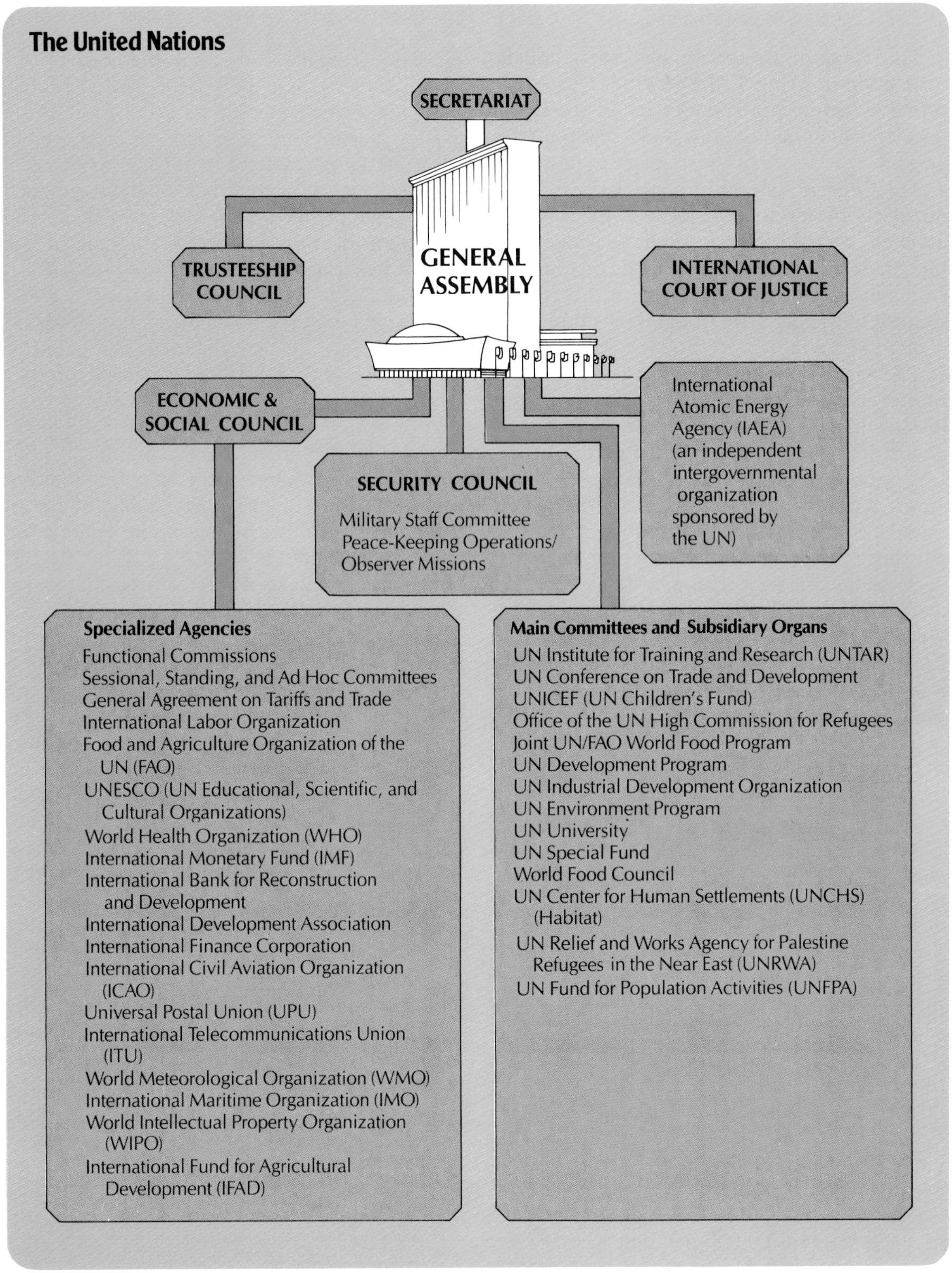

The chart above shows the principal organs and agencies of the United Nations. How does the Security Council work to maintain peace? What five nations are *permanent* members of the Security Council?

have used it much less often. The United States did not cast its first veto until 1970 and has done so only some 45 times since.[19]

The Economic and Social Council

The Economic and Social Council is made up of 54 members elected by the General Assembly to three-year terms. The Council is responsible to the Assembly for carrying out the UN's many economic, cultural, educational, health, and related activities. It also * coordinates the work of the UN's specialized agencies—see facing page.

The Trusteeship Council

The UN Charter requires each member to promote the interests and well-being of the peoples of all "non-self-governing territories" as a "sacred trust." The Trusteeship Council sets guidelines for the government of all dependent areas and makes rules for the administration of all UN trust territories.[20] The Council receives periodic reports from all member-states with non-self-governing possessions and seeks to encourage self-government for all dependent peoples.

The International Court of Justice

The International Court of Justice (ICJ) is the UN's judicial arm. It is dealt with only very briefly in the Charter, but is the subject of a lengthy and detailed Statute appended to that document.

All members of the UN are automatically parties to the ICJ Statute. Under certain conditions the services of the Court are also available to nonmember states. A UN member may agree to accept the Court's jurisdiction over cases in which it may be involved either unconditionally or with certain reservations (those reservations may not conflict with the ICJ Statute).

The ICJ is made up of 15 judges selected for nine-year terms by the General Assembly and the Security Council. It sits in permanent session at The Hague, in the Netherlands. It handles cases brought to it voluntarily by both members and nonmembers of the UN. The ICJ also advises the other UN organs on legal questions arising out of their activities. If any party to a dispute fails to obey a judgment of the Court, the other party may take that matter to the Security Council.

The Secretariat

The Secretariat is the civil service branch of the UN. It is headed by the Secretary-General, who is chosen to a five-year term by the General Assembly on the recommendation of the Security Council. The staff of the Secretariat now numbers some 18,000 men and women, drawn from most of the UN's member-states.

Javier Perez de Cuellar, a Peruvian diplomat, is now the Secretary-General. He became the UN's top administrative officer in 1982. In addition to his housekeeping chores, the Charter gives him a very important power. He may bring before the Security Council any matter he believes poses a threat to international peace and security.

FOR REVIEW

1. **Identify:** United Nations, Security Council.
2. When, where, and by whom was the UN Charter drafted? What, according to the Charter, are the UN's basic purposes?
3. The UN began with how many members? What is the UN's membership today?
4. What are the UN's six principal organs? Their major functions? How is the veto power used in the Security Council?

---

[19]When, on June 25, 1950, the Security Council called on all UN members to aid South Korea to repel the North Korean invasion, the Soviet delegate was boycotting sessions of the Security Council and so was not present to veto that action. The Soviets have not repeated their boycott tactic in more than 35 years now.

The United States has used the veto more frequently than has the Soviet Union in recent years.

[20]There were 11 of those territories originally—most of them former possessions of the defeated Axis Powers of World War II. Today there is but one: the Trust Territory of the Pacific Islands, administered by the United States.

*ENRICHMENT Have the class discuss: The United Nations was organized to benefit all nations. Given the tensions existing in the world today, can it be truly effective?

SUMMARY

America's foreign and defense policies have one major purpose. They are designed to protect the security of the United States.

American foreign policy consists of all of the official statements and actions of the Government of the United States that have a bearing on foreign relations. Although Congress has a number of important powers in the field, the President is the country's Chief Diplomat. The Secretary of State is the President's principal aide in both making and carrying out foreign policy. The State Department, headed by the Secretary, is set up on both a functional and a geographic basis. It includes the Foreign Service, made up of our diplomatic agents abroad.

The Constitution makes defense a national function and places control of the nation's military establishment in civilian hands. Congress has several important war powers and the President is the Commander in Chief of the armed forces. The Secretary of Defense is the President's chief aide in all defense matters. The Defense Department, headed by the Secretary includes the sub-Cabinet Departments of the Army, the Navy, and the Air Force.

Several other federal agencies also work in the fields of foreign affairs and defense—in particular, the Central Intelligence Agency, the United States Information Agency, the National Aeronautics and Space Administration, the United States Arms Control and Disarmament Agency, and the Selective Service System.

World War II brought about a major change in American foreign policy—from a historic pattern of isolationism to a full-scale involvement in world politics. That dramatic shift is reflected in these basic features of present-day American foreign policy: collective security, deterrence, containment, foreign aid, and regional security alliances.

CHAPTER REVIEW

Key Terms/Concepts*

isolationism (473)
foreign policy (474)
right of legation (476)
ambassador (476)
diplomatic immunity (477)
passport (478)
visa (478)
draft (487)
collective security (493)
deterrence (494)
containment (495)
regional security alliances (500)
veto power (505)

*These terms are included in the Glossary.

Keynote Questions

• **1.** What is, and always has been, the basic aim of this nation's foreign policies?

• **2.** What is foreign policy?

• **3.** Who bears the primary responsibility both for making and for carrying out this nation's foreign and defense policies? Why?

• **4.** What is the primary role of the Secretary of State? Of the Foreign Service?

• **5.** What are the duties of an ambassador?

• **6.** Why did the Framers of the Constitution provide for civilian control of the military?

• **7.** List the two major responsibilities of the Secretary of Defense.

• **8.** Briefly explain the role in foreign and/or defense policy of each of the following agencies: CIA, USIA, NASA, and ACDA.

• **9.** Who is required to register for the draft today?

• **10.** Why did the United States choose to pursue an isolationist foreign policy for most of the first 150 years of its history?

The dots represent skill levels required to answer each question or complete each activity: •requires recall and comprehension • •requires application and analysis • • •requires synthesis and evaluation

• **11.** What is the Monroe Doctrine? What two purposes has it served?

• **12.** Briefly describe in a paragraph the fundamental change in American foreign policy following World War II.

• **13.** Identify the five major features of American foreign policy today.

• **14.** According to the United Nations Charter, why was the UN created and what three major purposes does it serve?

• **15.** What are the six principal organs of the UN? State the function of each.

• **16.** How does the veto power of the UN's Security Council affect its ability to make policy?

Skill Application

Reading an Organization Chart: An organization chart is a drawn outline showing the structure of an international organization, a government agency, a company, or any other organization. Organization charts are most useful for understanding how the various component parts of an organization are related. By using an organization chart, you can learn what the various divisions and subdivisions of an organization are and to which principal organizations certain agencies must report.

Look at the chart of the United Nations on page 506. Lines indicate how decisions flow. The boxes represent the different parts of the United Nations. On this chart, the main organs of the UN are indicated by capital letters.

Examine the chart and then answer the following questions:

1. What is the main policy-making body of the United Nations?

2. Is the Secretariat directly responsible for making policy? How can you tell?

3. Which Council is responsible for overseeing the Specialized Agencies?

4. To which body do all the councils and the International Court of Justice report?

5. List two agencies that report directly to the General Assembly.

For Thought and Discussion

• **1.** Constitutionally, the President and Congress share power in the fields of foreign affairs and defense. What factors have contributed to presidential supremacy in both fields?

••• **2.** The only truly effective checks on the Government's power in foreign affairs are political, not legal, in character. Explain this statement. Do you agree or disagree with it? Use current events to support your answer.

••• **3.** Many people have observed that nations fall "from within," not "from without." What does this statement imply about the relationship between a nation's domestic policies and its national security? About national power?

•• **4.** The United States and the Soviet Union insisted on the veto power in the Security Council when the UN Charter was drafted. Why? The United States has never favored the abolition of the veto. Why?

•• **5.** What did President Eisenhower mean when he said, "Americans, indeed all free men, remember that in the final choice a soldier's pack is not so heavy a burden as a prisoner's chains."

Suggested Activities

•• **1.** Using current news periodicals, find a recent speech or announcement on foreign policy given by the President. Read the speech and identify the ways in which it relates to the five major features of American foreign policy discussed in this chapter.

••• **2.** Investigate a recent event or problem in international relations and United States foreign policy. For example, you might look into our policy toward the People's Republic, the PLO, Israel, one of the Central American countries, the American-Soviet arms race, or NATO. Write a brief summary of the situation, then analyze it. What is our present policy? Why is it important for the United States to be involved? Do you agree or disagree with present policy? Why?

••• **3.** Stage a debate or class forum on one of the following questions: (1) *Resolved,* That Congress provide for a universal system of military training; (b) *Resolved,* That the Constitution be amended to provide that the United States cannot make war in any circumstances until such action is approved by a vote of the people; (c) *Resolved,* That the United States withdraw from the United Nations.

Unit 6

The Federal Judiciary

IN THE AMERICAN system of separation of powers, it is the prime function of the legislative branch to make the law, of the executive branch to enforce and administer the law, and of the judicial branch to interpret and apply the law. As the great Chief Justice John Marshall declared in *Marbury* v. *Madison,* "It is emphatically the province and the duty of the judicial department to say what the law is." By "the judicial depar-ment" he meant the federal courts. As with the Congress and the Presidency, the federal "judicial department"—and particularly the Supreme Court of the United States—has played a major part in the building of the constitutional system.

The democratic ideal insists that there are areas of activity prohibited to government and into which government may not intrude. In America, it is upon the courts that major reliance is placed for the preservation of this concept of limited government.

One of the distinctive features of the American legal system is its two-fold organization. There are two separate and distinct judicial structures, one for the federal government, and one for the 50 States—actually 50 separate structures. Unit Six in this book deals with the federal courts.

We describe the structure, jurisidiction, and operations of the national court system. We also consider the judges and other court officers. Finally, we look at the Department of Justice.

The Supreme Court sat in this chamber in the basement of the Capitol from 1810 to 1860.

It is emphatically the province and the duty of the judicial department to say what the law is.
—CHIEF JUSTICE JOHN MARSHALL
MARBURY V. *MADISON* (1803)

18 The Federal Court System

CHAPTER OBJECTIVES

To help you to

Learn · Know · Understand

The basic role of the judiciary in the governmental process.

The structure and function of the constitutional courts.

The role of the Supreme Court as the nation's highest court, and judicial review and its extraordinary significance in the American governmental system.

The roles of special courts in the federal court system.

The process by which federal judges are selected.

The concept of justice in the American political system.

TO THIS POINT, we have often spoken of the Supreme Court and the other courts in the federal judiciary. We shall now take a systematic look at the judicial branch of the National Government.

Most of the authors of the Constitution pointed to the lack of a national judiciary as a major weakness in the government set up by the Articles of Confederation. They were convinced that an independent **judiciary**—a system of *national* courts—was needed if the new government they had put together at Philadelphia was to work.

1. The Creation of a National Judiciary

As you Read, Think About:

- How the national court system was established.
- What two types of cases the federal courts decide.

Over the time the Articles were in force (from 1781 to 1789), the laws of the United

Inscribed over the entrance to the United States Supreme Court Building is the motto "Equal Justice Under Law." *Facing page:* The Courtroom in the Supreme Court Building, the home of the Court since 1935.

States were interpreted and applied among the States as each of them chose, or chose not, to do. Disputes between States and between residents of different States were decided, if at all, by the courts of one of the States involved.[1] Often, decisions by the courts of one State were neither accepted nor enforced in the other States.

Alexander Hamilton spoke to the point in *The Federalist,* No. 78. He described "the want of a national judiciary" as a "circumstance which crowns the defects of the Confederation." He added:

> Laws are dead letters without courts to expound and define their true meaning and operation.

[1]The Articles of Confederation did provide (in Article IX) a complicated procedure for the settlement of disputes between States, but it was not often used.

To meet the need, the Framers wrote Article III into the Constitution. It created the national judiciary in a single sentence:

> The judicial power of the United States shall be vested in one Supreme Court, and in such inferior courts as the Congress may from time to time ordain and establish.

Congress is given the expressed power "to constitute tribunals inferior to the Supreme Court," in Article I, Section 8, Clause 9.

A Dual Court System

In this chapter we are especially concerned with the national court system: the Supreme Court, created by the Constitution, and the other federal courts, set up by act of Congress. But keep in mind that there are *two* separate court systems in the United States.[2] On one hand, there is the national *

[2]Notice that federalism does not require two separate court systems. Article III provides that Congress "may" establish lower federal courts; but it does not require that that be done. At its first session, in 1789, Congress decided to construct a complete set of federal courts to parallel those of the States.

*ENRICHMENT The establishment of a federal court system is another way in which the Framers ensured the separation of powers. Ask the class how this arrangement also promotes limited government.

judiciary, with its more than 100 courts across the country. On the other hand, each of the 50 States has its own system of courts. Their number runs well into the thousands, as we shall see in Chapter 22.

Types of Federal Courts

Beneath the Supreme Court, Congress has created two distinct types of federal courts: (1) constitutional courts and (2) special courts.

The *constitutional courts* are the federal courts that Congress has formed under Article III to exercise "the judicial power of the United States." Together with the Supreme Court, they now include the Courts of Appeals, the District Courts, and the Court of International Trade.

The *special courts* do not exercise the broad "judicial power of the United States." Rather, they have been created by Congress to hear cases arising out of certain of the expressed powers given to Congress in Article I. They hear a much narrower range of cases than those that may come before the constitutional courts.

These special courts are sometimes called the "legislative courts." Today, they include the Court of Military Appeals, the Claims Court, the Tax Court, the various territorial courts, and the courts of the District of Columbia.[3]

FOR REVIEW

1. **Identify:** national judiciary, dual court system, constitutional courts, special courts, legislative courts.
2. Why did the Framers provide for a national judiciary?
3. Why is there a dual system of courts in the United States?
4. What is the chief difference between the constitutional and the special courts?

[3]Recall the Foreign Intelligence Surveillance Court, a very "special" court, indeed; see page 140, especially footnote 13.

U.S. News and World Report, Inc., 1984

"I had a terrible nightmare last night. I dreamt everyone settled out of court."

2. The Constitutional Courts: The Inferior Courts

As You Read, Think About:

- What the jurisdiction is of the federal courts.
- What the roles are of the other constitutional courts.

As we have noted, the Constitution leaves to Congress the creation of the "inferior courts" . . . those beneath the Supreme Court. They are sometimes called the "regular courts."

Jurisdiction

The term **jurisdiction** may be defined as the authority of a court to hear (to *try* and to *decide)* a case. The term means, literally, the power "to say the law."

Under Article III the federal courts have jurisdiction over a case either because of (1) the subject matter or (2) the parties involved in the case. *

*REINFORCEMENT Use Article III of the Constitution (p. 738) to introduce a discussion of the federal courts' jurisdiction. How did the Framers promote federalism in assigning jurisdictions?

Subject Matter In terms of subject matter, the federal courts may hear a case if it deals with:

1. the interpretation and application of a provision in the Constitution or in any federal statute or treasury; or
2. a question of admiralty or a question of maritime law.[4]

Any case that falls into either of these categories can be brought in the proper federal court.

Parties A case comes within the jurisdiction of the federal courts if any of the parties, one of the *litigants,* in the case is:

1. the United States or one of its officers or agencies;
2. an ambassador, consul, or other official representative of a foreign government;
3. a State suing another State, or a citizen of another State, or a foreign government or one of its subjects;[5]
4. a citizen of one State suing a citizen of another State;
5. an American citizen suing a foreign government or one of it subjects;
6. a citizen of one State suing a citizen of that same State where both claim land under grants from different States.

Any case falling into any of these categories can be brought in the proper federal court.

All of this may seem quite complicated, and it is. But notice that it is a reflection of federalism and, so, of the dual system of courts in this country. To state the whole point of the jurisdiction of the federal courts in another way: All cases that are not heard by the federal courts are within the jurisdiction of the States' courts. As we shall see in Chapter 22, the State courts hear by far the larger number of court cases in this country. Still more must be said on the federal courts' power "to say the law."

Exclusive and Concurrent Jurisdiction In several categories of cases we have just listed, the federal courts have *exclusive jurisdiction.* That is, those cases can be heard only in the federal courts. For example, a case involving an ambassador or some other official of a foreign government cannot be heard in a State court. It must be tried in a federal court. Or, the trial of a person charged with a federal crime, or a suit involving the infringement of a patent or a copyright, or a case involving any other matter arising out of an act of Congress falls within the exclusive jurisdiction of the federal courts.

Many cases may be tried in *either* a federal court *or* a State court, however. That is, the federal courts and the State courts have *concurrent jurisdiction* over these cases. Cases involving citizens of different States are fairly common examples of the type. Such cases are known in the law as cases in *diverse citizenship.*[6]

Congress has provided that the federal District Courts may hear cases in diverse citizenship only if the amount of money involved in a case is over $10,000. In such cases the **plaintiff** may bring the suit in the proper State or federal court, as he or she chooses. If the case is brought before the

---

[4]Admiralty law relates to matters that arise on the high seas or the navigable waters of the United States—for example, crimes committed aboard ships, collisions, and the like. Maritime law relates to matters arising on land but directly related to the water—for example, a contract to deliver a ship's supplies at dockside. The Framers gave the federal courts exclusive jurisdiction in all admiralty and maritime cases to make certain of national supremacy in the regulation of all waterborne commerce.

[5]Note that the 11th Amendment says that a State may not be sued in the federal courts by a citizen of another State or of a foreign state. A State may be sued without its consent in the federal courts only by the United States, another State, or a foreign state. If a citizen of a State (or of another State or of a foreign state) wants to sue a State, he or she may do so only with that State's consent and only in that State's own courts.

[6]The major reason that cases in diverse citizenship may be heard in federal courts is to provide a neutral forum to settle the disputes involved. That reason reflects an early fear that State courts (and their juries) might be prejudiced against "foreigners," residents of other States. There seems little real likelihood of such bias today. Many judicial authorities have long urged Congress to eliminate federal jurisdiction in these cases—most particularly to eliminate the heavy burden they impose on federal courts.

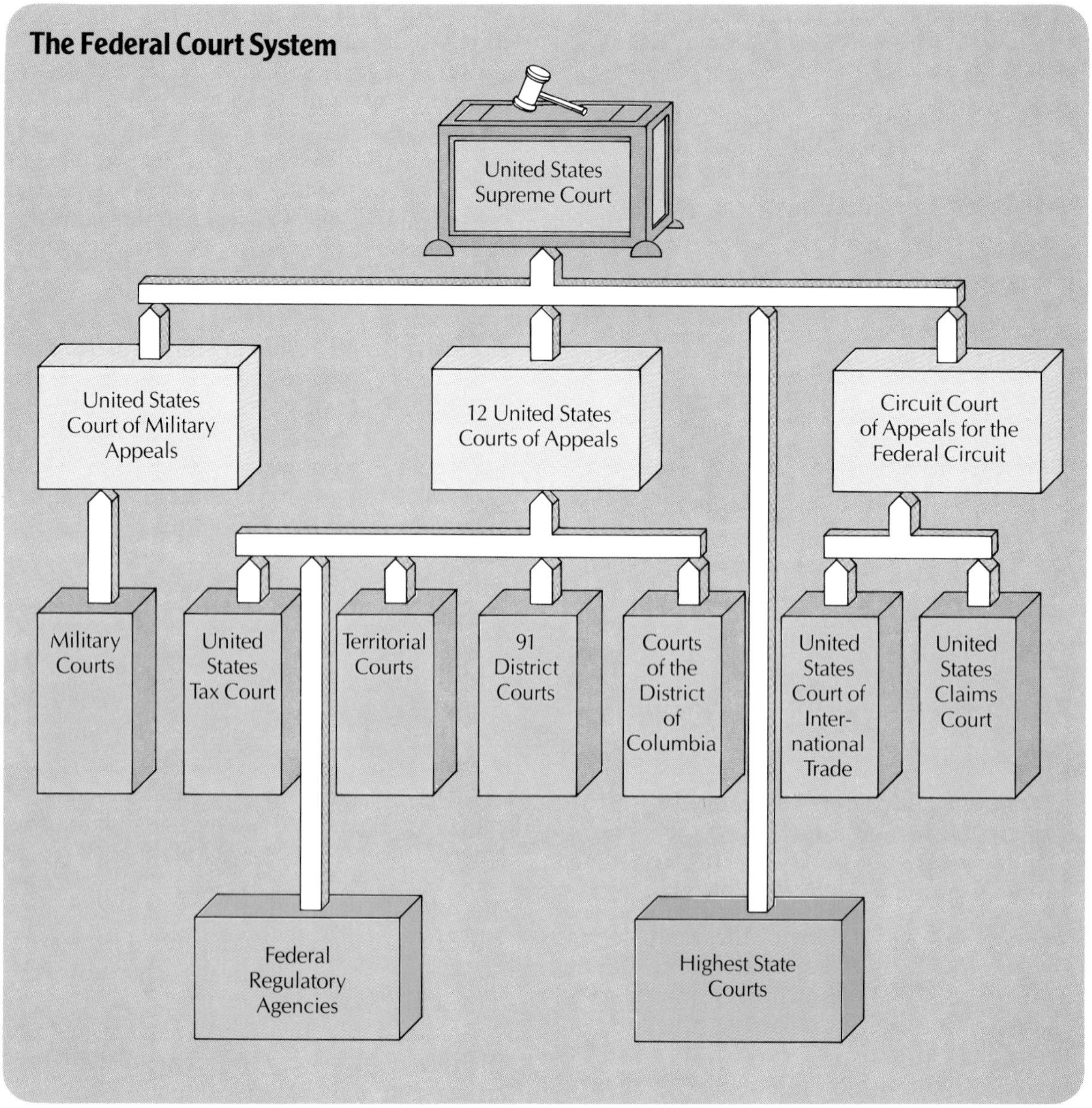

The arrows above indicate the passage of authority from the lowest to the highest courts. From which federal Appeals Courts may the Supreme Court hear cases?

State court, the **defendant** may have it moved to the federal District Court.[7]

Original and Appellate Jurisdiction A court in which a case is heard firsthand is said to have *original jurisdiction* over it. A court that hears a case on appeal from a lower court has *appellate jurisdiction.* (The term *appellate* is derived from the Latin word *appello* which means to move or bring to or towards a person or thing.)

In the federal court system, the District Courts have only original jurisdiction and the Courts of Appeals have only appellate jurisdiction. The Supreme Court has both jurisdictions.

[7]A **plaintiff** is one who brings a suit in law against another. A **defendant** is a party who must make answer, defend against a complaint, in a legal action.

REINFORCEMENT Have the class discuss the relationships between the Supreme Court, the federal District Courts, and the Courts of Appeals. How does the system work? Who hears what cases?

The nation's 94 federal District Courts hear cases that deal with transgressions against federal law.

The District Courts

The United States District Courts are the federal trial courts. Its 575 judges now handle over 200,000 cases a year, some 90 percent of all of the federal caseload.

The District Courts were created by Congress in the Judiciary Act of 1789. There are now 94 of them. The 50 States are divided into 89 judicial districts, with one court in each district. There is also a District Court in the District of Columbia and one each in Puerto Rico, the Virgin Islands, Guam, and the Northern Mariana Islands.

Each State forms at least one federal judicial district. The larger, more populous States are divided into two or more districts due to more judicial business there.

At least one judge is assigned to each district, but many have several. Thus, New York is divided into four judicial districts; and one, the United States Judicial District for Southern New York, now has 27 judges.

Cases tried in the District Courts are most often heard by a single judge; but certain cases may be heard by a three-judge panel.[8]

Jurisdiction The District Courts have original jurisdiction over most cases heard in the federal courts. That amounts to another way of saying that District Courts are the federal trial courts. They hear criminal cases ranging from bank robbery, kidnaping, and mail fraud to counterfeiting, tax evasion, and treason. They try civil cases arising under the bankruptcy, postal, tax, labor relations, public lands, civil rights, and other laws of the United States.[9] They are the only federal courts that regularly use *grand juries* (to indict) and *petit juries* (to try) defendants.

Most of the decisions made in the 91 federal District Courts are final. As we shall see, however, some cases are appealed to the Court of Appeals in that judicial circuit or, in a few instances, are taken directly to the Supreme Court.

The Courts of Appeals

The Courts of Appeals were created by Congress in 1891. They were established to relieve the Supreme Court of much of the burden of hearing appeals from the District Courts.[10] Those appeals had become so numerous that the High Court was then three years behind its docket.

There are now 12 Courts of Appeals. The United States is divided into 11 judicial circuits, with one Court of Appeals for each of those circuits, and also one in the District of Columbia.

---

[8]Congress has directed that three-judge panels hear certain cases. Chiefly, these are cases that involve congressional districting or State legislative apportionment questions, those arising under the Civil Rights Act of 1964 or the Voting Rights Acts of 1965, 1970, 1975, and 1982, and certain antitrust actions.

[9]In the federal courts, a criminal case is one in which a defendant has been charged with and is tried for committing a federal crime (some action that Congress has declared by law to be a crime, a wrong against the public). A federal civil case involves some noncriminal matter, such as a dispute over the terms of a contract or a claim of patent infringement. The United States is always a party to a federal criminal case, as prosecutor. Most civil cases involve private parties, but here, too, the Government may be one of the litigants, as either plaintiff or defendant.

[10]These tribunals were originally known as the Circuit Courts of Appeals. Before 1891, Supreme Court Justices "rode circuit" to hear appeals from the District Courts. Congress renamed these courts in 1948, but they still are often called the Circuit Courts.

There is yet another federal court with a quite similar title but a quite different role—the Court of Appeals for the Federal Circuit. It was created by Congress in 1982; see page 519.

Federal Judicial Circuits and Districts

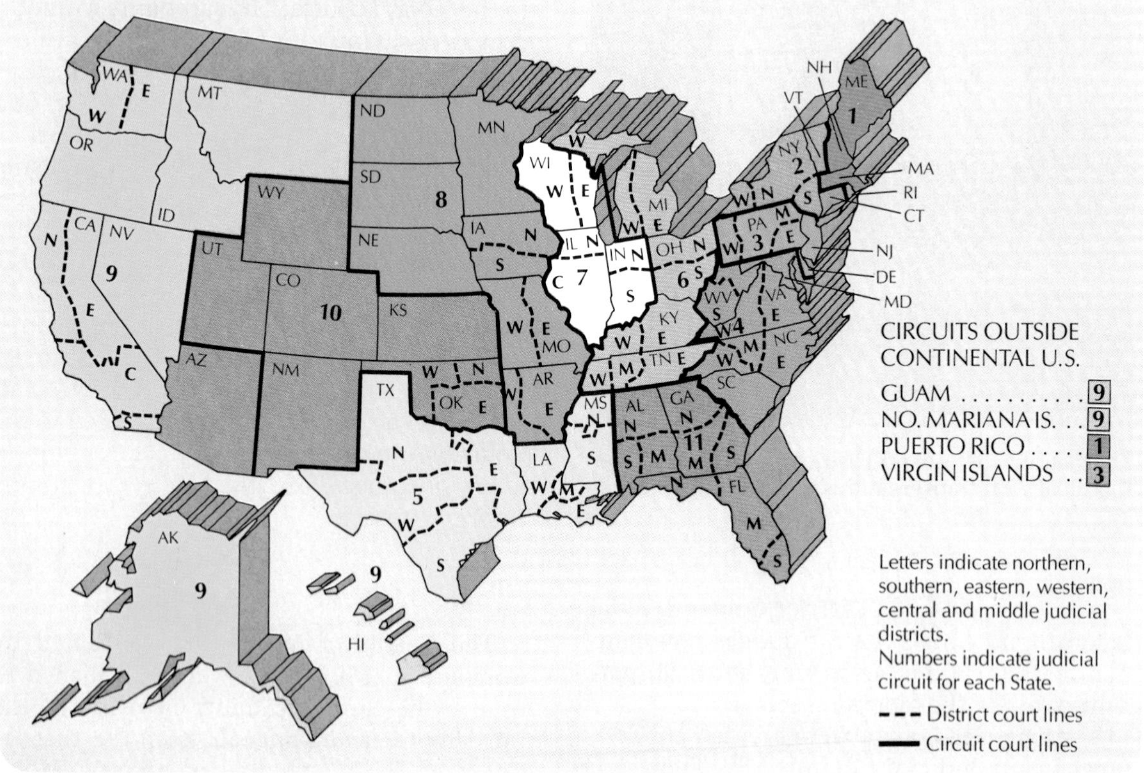

Examine the judicial circuits and districts on the map above. How do you think the size of judicial districts was determined?

Altogether, 168 circuit judges sit on these appellate courts. In addition, a Justice of the Supreme Court is assigned to each of them. Take the United States Court of Appeals for the Seventh Circuit, for example. The Seventh Circuit covers three States: Illinois, Indiana, and Wisconsin. The court has 11 circuit judges, and Supreme Court Justice John Paul Stevens is also assigned to the circuit. The court sits in Chicago. In contrast, the Fifth Circuit's jurisdiction includes three States: Louisiana, Mississippi, and Texas. Its Court of Appeals has 16 judges, plus Associate Justice Byron White. It holds its sessions in a number of different cities within the circuit.

Each of the Courts of Appeals usually sits in panels of three judges. But, occasionally, to hear an important case, a court will sit *en banc*—that is, with all of the circuit judges participating.

Jurisdiction The Courts of Appeals have only appellate jurisdiction. Most often, their cases come from the District Courts within their circuits. Appeals Courts hear cases appealed from the United States Tax Court and from the territorial courts, as well. They also hear appeals from the decisions of several federal regulatory agencies—from such quasi-judicial agencies as the Interstate Commerce Commission and the Federal Trade Commission, as noted on page 454.

The Courts of Appeals now handle about 25,000 cases a year. Their decisions are final, unless the Supreme Court chooses to hear appeals taken from them.

Two Other Constitutional Courts

Two other inferior courts exist today: the Court of International Trade and the Court of Appeals for the Federal Circuit.

The Court of International Trade The Trade Court was originally created as the Board of United States General Appraisers in 1890. That body became the Court of Customs in 1926 and was renamed by Congress in 1980.

The Trade Court now has nine judges, one of whom is its chief judge. It hears civil cases arising out of the tariff and other trade-related laws. Its judges sit in panels of three and often hold trials at such major ports of entry as New Orleans, San Francisco, Boston, and New York.

Appeals from decisions of the Trade Court are taken to the Court of Appeals for the Federal Circuit.

The Court of Appeals for the Federal Circuit Congress created the Court of Appeals for the Federal Circuit in 1982. It established the new tribunal to centralize, and so speed up, the handling of appeals in certain kinds of civil cases. This Court, unlike the 12 other federal Courts of Appeals, has a nationwide jurisdiction.

It hears appeals from several places. Many of its cases come from the Trade Court, and others from the Claims Court, one of the special courts we shall look at in a moment. It also hears appeals in certain cases—those involving patents, trademarks, or copyrights—decided by any of the 94 District Courts around the country. Then, too, it takes cases that arise out of the administrative rulings made by the International Trade Commission, the Patent and Trademark Office (in the Department of Commerce, page 442), and the Merit Systems Protection Board (page 463).

The Court of Appeals for the Federal Circuit has 12 judges. Appeals from their decisions may be carried to the Supreme Court.

FOR REVIEW

1. **Identify:** Exclusive jurisdiction, concurrent jurisdiction, original jurisdiction, appellate jurisdiction.
2. On what two general bases do the federal courts have jurisdiction over cases?
3. There are how many federal District Courts today? How many District Court judges?
4. Over what cases do the District Courts have jurisdiction?
5. Why were the Courts of Appeals created? How many are there today? How many circuit judges?
6. From where do cases reach the Court of Appeals?
7. Over what type of cases does the Court of International Trade have jurisdiction? The Court of Appeals for the Federal Circuit?

3. The Highest Constitutional Court: The Supreme Court

As You Read, Think About:

- Why judicial review is such an important power of the court system.
- How the Supreme Court functions and how cases are heard.

The Supreme Court of the United States is the only court specifically created in the Constitution.[11] It is made up of the Chief Justice of the United States, whose office is also established by the Constitution,[12] and eight Associate Justices.[13]

The significance of the role of the Supreme Court in both the development and the present-day operations of the American system of government cannot be overstated. The Framers quite purposely placed the Court on an equal plane with the President and Congress and designed it as the apex of the nation's judicial system. As the highest court in the land, the Supreme Court stands

[11]Article III, Section 1.

[12]Article I, Section 3, Clause 6.

[13]Congress sets the number of Associate Justices and thus the size of the Supreme Court. The Judiciary Act of 1789 created a Court of six Justices, including the Chief Justice. Its size was reduced to five members in 1801, but increased to seven in 1807, to nine in 1837, and to 10 in 1863. It was reduced to seven in 1866 and raised to its present size in 1869.

*ENRICHMENT Ask the class to discuss: Why trade-related cases dealt with in the Trade Court rather than the District Courts? What types of cases are heard?

Mirochi, *New Yorker Magazine*, Inc.

"Do you ever have one of those days when everything seems un-Constitutional?"

as the court of last resort in *all* questions of federal law. That is, it is the final authority in *any* case involving *any* question arising under the Constitution, an act of Congress, or a treaty of the United States.

The Supreme Court and Judicial Review

As we have noted, most courts in this country, federal and State, may exercise the critically important power of **judicial review.** They have the extraordinary power to decide the constitutionality of an act of government, whether executive, legislative, or judicial (see pages 56–58). The *ultimate* exercise of that power rests with the Supreme Court of the United States. That single fact makes the Supreme Court the final authority on the meaning of the Constitution.

The Constitution does not *in so many words* provide for the power of judicial review. Still, there is little room for doubt that the Framers intended that the federal courts —and, in particular, the Supreme Court should have the power.[14] In *The Federalist* No. 78 Alexander Hamilton wrote:

> The interpretation of the laws is the proper and peculiar province of the courts. A constitution is, in fact, and must be regarded by the judges, as a fundamental law. It therefore belongs to them to ascertain its meaning, as well as the meaning of any particular act proceeding from the legislative body. If there should happen to be an irreconcilable variance between the two, that which has the superior obligation and validity ought, of course, to be preferred; or, in other words, the Constitution ought to be preferred to the statute, the intention of the people to the intention of their agents.

The Court first asserted that it had the power of judicial review in the classic case of *Marbury* v. *Madison* in 1803.[15] The case arose after the stormy elections of 1800. Thomas Jefferson and his Anti-Federalists had won the Presidency and control of both houses of Congress.

The outgoing Federalists, stung by their defeat, then tried to pack the judiciary with loyal party members. Several new federal judgeships were created by Congress in the early weeks of 1801. President John Adams quickly filled those posts with Federalists.

William Marbury had been appointed a justice of the peace for the District of Columbia. The Senate had confirmed his appointment and, late the night of March 3, 1801, the President had signed his and a number of other new judges' commissions of office. The next day, Jefferson became President and found that Marbury's commission, and several others, had not been delivered.

Angered by the Federalists' court-packing, Jefferson at once told James Madison, the new Secretary of State, not to deliver those commissions to the "midnight justices." William Marbury then went to the Supreme Court, seeking a writ of mandamus[16] to compel delivery.

[14]To the point, see Article III, Section 2, setting out the Court's jurisdiction, and Article IV, Section 2, the Supremacy Clause.

[15]It is often said that the Court first *exercised* the power in this case, but, in fact, the Court did so at least as early as *Hylton* v. *United States* in 1796. In that case it *upheld* the constitutionality of a tax Congress had laid on carriages. The opponents of the tax had argued that it was a "direct tax" and so had to be apportioned among the States in accord with Article I, Section 2, Clause 3. But the court ruled that it was an "indirect tax" and so could be levied and collected as Congress had provided.

[16]A court order compelling an officer of government to perform an act which that officer has a clear legal duty to perform.

ENRICHMENT Discuss: What does it mean when a case "goes to the Supreme Court"? Point out that the Court's ultimate power of judicial review is being called upon to interpret the law.

PERSONALITY PROFILE

John Marshall and Judicial Review

Scholars of American history would find it difficult to underestimate the impact that John Marshall, fourth Chief Justice of the United States Supreme Court, has had on the American political system. Marshall's formulation of the principle of judicial review and his subsequent constitutional interpretations have played a major role in shaping this system.

Marshall was born on the Virginia frontier on September 24, 1755. He served with distinction in the Revolutionary War.

Marshall studied the law on his own after the war and attended lectures at William and Mary College. In 1781 he became a lawyer and soon after served in the Virginia legislature and became a member of the Federalist Party.

Marshall's advocacy of a strong central government in the 1780s drew the attention of Federalist leaders. He became Washington's adviser on Virginia affairs and in 1788 he served as a delegate to the State convention that approved the new Federal Constitution. He served as Minister to France in 1797 and was elected to the United States House of Representatives in 1799. President John Adams appointed Marshall Secretary of State in 1800.

In 1801 he became Chief Justice of the United States Supreme Court. The Chief Justice's decisions defined the relationships among the three branches of government, established a strong National Government with power over the States, created a powerful Supreme Court, and, most importantly, founded the doctrine of judicial review.

Note Marshall's persuasive style in the following passage from *Marbury* v. *Madison*. In his opinion, or written ruling, Marshall anticipates his critics' objections, and answers them convincingly. Many politicians, including President Jefferson, were outraged by his daring. But Marshall's theory of judicial review became an enduring part of our government of checks and balances.

> It is emphatically the province and duty of the judicial department to say what the law is. Those who apply the rule to particular cases, must of necessity expound and interpret that rule. If two laws conflict with each other, the courts must decide on the operation of each.
>
> So if a law be in opposition to the constitution; if both the law and the constitution apply to a particular case, so that the court must either decide that case conformably to the law, disregarding the constitution; or conformably to the constitution, disregarding the law; the court must determine which of these conflicting rules governs the case. This is of the very essence of judicial duty.
>
> If, then, the courts are to regard the constitution, and the constitution is superior to any ordinary act of the legislature, the constitution, and not such ordinary act, must govern the case to which they both apply . . .
>
> This doctrine would subvert the very foundation of all written constitutions. It would declare that an Act which, according to the principles and theory of our government, is entirely void, is yet, in practice, completely obligatory. It would declare that if the legislature shall do what is expressly forbidden, such Act, notwithstanding the express prohibition, is in reality effectual. It would be giving to the legislature a practical and real omnipotence, with the same breath which professes to restrict their powers within narrow limits.

1. What was Marshall's feeling about the strength of the National Government?
2. Summarize the meaning of the term *judicial review.*

The nine Justices of the Supreme Court today, from left to right: Associate Justices Sandra Day O'Connor, Lewis F. Powell, Jr., Thurgood Marshall, William J. Brennan, Jr., Chief Justice William H. Rehnquist, and Justices Byron R. White, Harry A. Blackmun, John Paul Stevens, and Antonin Scalia.

Marbury based his suit on a provision of the Judiciary Act of 1789, in which Congress had created the federal court system. That law gave the Supreme Court the right to hear such suits in its *original* jurisdiction (not on appeal from a lower court).

In a unanimous opinion written by Chief Justice John Marshall, the Court refused Marbury's request.[17] It did so because it found the pertinent section of the Judiciary Act in conflict with the Constitution and, therefore, void. More exactly, it found the statute in conflict with Article III, Section 2, Clause 2, which reads in part:

> In all cases affecting ambassadors, other public ministers and consuls, and those in which a State shall be a party, the Supreme Court shall have original jurisdiction. In all other cases before mentioned, the Supreme Court shall have appellate jurisdiction . . .

Marshall's powerful opinion was based on three propositions. First, the Constitution is, by its own terms, *the* supreme law of the land. Second, all legislative enactments, and all other actions of government, are subordinate to and cannot be allowed to conflict with the supreme law. Third, judges are sworn to enforce the provisions of the Constitution and therefore must refuse to enforce any governmental action they find to be in conflict with it.

As we have seen, the Court has used its power of judicial review in thousands of cases since 1803. Usually it has upheld, although sometimes denied, the constitutionality of federal and State actions.

The dramatic and often far-reaching effects of the Supreme Court's exercise of the power of judicial review tends to overshadow much of its other work. Each year it hears dozens of cases in which questions of constitutionality are *not* raised but in which federal law still is interpreted and applied. Thus, many of the more important statutes that Congress has passed have been brought to the Supreme Court time and again for decision. So, too, have many of the lesser ones. In interpreting those laws and applying them to specific situations, the Court has had a

[17]Marshall was appointed Chief Justice by President John Adams, and he took office on January 31, 1801. He served in the post for 34 years, until his death on July 6, 1835. He also served as Adams's Secretary of State, from May 13, 1800 to March 4, 1801. Thus he served as Secretary of State *and* as Chief Justice for more than a month at the end of the Adams Administration. What is more, he was the Secretary of State who had failed to deliver Marbury's commission in timely fashion.

real impact on their meaning and effect when carried out.

Remember, too, that the Court has a very large role as the "umpire" in the federal system, as we noted on page 78. It decides those legal disputes that arise between the National Government and the States and those that arise between or among the States.

*Jurisdiction

The Supreme Court has both original and appellate jurisdiction. Most of all, however, it is an appellate tribunal. Most cases it hears come to it on appeal from the lower federal courts and from the State supreme courts.

Article III, Section 2 spells out two classes of cases that may be heard by the High Court in its *original* jurisdiction: (1) those to which a State is a party and (2) those affecting ambassadors, other public ministers, and consuls.

Congress cannot enlarge on this constitutional grant of original jurisdiction. Recall, this is what the Court held in *Marbury* v. *Madison*. If Congress could do so, it would in effect be amending the Constitution. Congress can implement the constitutional provision, and it has. It has provided that the Court shall have original *and* exclusive jurisdiction over (1) all controversies between two or more States and (2) all cases *against* ambassadors or other public ministers, but not consuls. The Court may, if it chooses, take original jurisdiction over any other case covered by the broad wording in Article III, Section 2. But, almost always, those cases are tried in the lower courts.

How Cases Reach the Court

Some 3,500 to 4,000 cases are now appealed to the Supreme Court each year. Of these, only a few hundred are accepted for decision. In most cases, then, the petitions for review are denied, usually because at least most of the Justices agree with the decision of the lower court or believe that the case involves no significant point of law.

More than half the cases decided by the Court are disposed of in brief orders. For example, an order may *remand*, or return, a case to a lower court for reconsideration in the light of some other recent and related cases decided by the High Court. All told, the Court decides only 120 or so cases yearly.

Generally, cases come to the Supreme Court either by *certiorari* or on *appeal*. Most cases reach the Court by **writ of certiorari** (from the Latin, "to be made more certain"). This is an order by the Court directing a lower court to send up the record in a given case because one of the parties states an error was made in the lower court's handling of that case. An **appeal** is a petition by one of the parties to a case asking the Court to review the lower court's decision in the case. A few cases do reach the Court in a third way, by **certificate.** This process is used when a lower court is not clear about the procedure or the rule of law that should apply in a case. The lower court asks the Supreme Court to certify the answer to a specific question in the matter.

Most cases that reach the Court do so from the highest State courts and the federal Courts of Appeal. A few do come, however, from the federal District Courts and a very few come from the Court of Military Appeals.

The Supreme Court at Work

The Supreme Court sits for a term of about nine months each year, from the first Monday in October until some time the following June or July. As a rule, the Justices hear arguments in the cases before them for two weeks, then recess for two weeks. While arguments are being heard, the Court opens at 10 A.M., Monday through Thursday.

Monday is usually "decision day." The decisions ready for release are announced at the beginning of that day's session.[18]

The lawyers for each side in a case are normally allowed one hour to present their

[18]Since 1965, however, the Court has adopted the occasional practice of releasing decisions on other days, as well.

*REINFORCEMENT Have the class discuss: What two forms of jurisdiction does the Supreme Court have? How are they similar? How are they different?

FOCUS ON:

Judicial Review: Activism v. Self-Restraint

As we have said several times, the power of judicial review is a cardinal feature of the American system of government. It is the power of courts to determine the constitutionality of a governmental action—their power to decide whether what government has done agrees, or does not agree, with what the Constitution provides.

That extraordinary power is held by most courts in the United States—by all of the federal courts and by nearly all State and local courts, as well. With it, they have the power to determine the meaning of the Constitution—as they decide cases in which the constitutionality of actions taken by government are challenged.

Clearly, the most important uses of that power come when it is wielded by the Supreme Court of the United States. We have seen dozens of illustrations of that point in this book.

The High Court established its power of judicial review in *Marbury* v. *Madison* in 1803. There, as we have just noted, it struck down a provision of an act of Congress (Section 13 of the Judiciary Act of 1789). "[T]he Constitution," wrote Chief Justice John Marshall for a unanimous Court, "is superior to any ordinary act of the legislature"; and, he added, "a law repugnant to the Constitution is void."

The Court's power of judicial review has long since become a fundamentally important part of the governing process in this country. But, from *Marbury* on, this question has remained the subject of intense debate: *How* should the Court exercise its immense power?

For more than 180 years now, many have argued that the Court should be guided by a policy of *judicial self-restraint,* and many others have argued for a policy of *judicial activism.*

Those who urge the policy of restraint say that the Court should avoid ruling on constitutional questions whenever that is possible. In those cases where that cannot be done, the Court should strike down some challenged governmental action *only* when there has been a clear violation of some specific provision of the Constitution. Otherwise, it should accept (uphold) what government has done. It should defer to the legislative and executive branches, those organs of government politically responsible to the people.

Judicial activists, on the other hand, hold that the Court should *not* avoid constitutional issues. Rather, it should play an active, creative role in the shaping of public policies. It should act to protect the long-range interests of the people, even against the short-range wishes of the voters. The Court, they say, should apply the Constitution to the pressing problems of the nation's social and political life whenever it can.

1. Identify three cases in which, during its current term, the Supreme Court has exercised its power of judicial review.
2. What evidence can you find to support this observation: On the Court today, Chief Justice Warren Burger and Associate Justice William Rehnquist are the leading exponents of judicial self-restraint, and Associate Justices William Brennan and Thurgood Marshall are the leading advocates of judicial activism. Where do the other justices lie in terms of their judicial self-restraint or activism?
3. On which side of the judicial self-restraint/activism argument are you? Why?

oral arguments. The Justices often interrupt them with questions. The lawyers also prepare written **briefs,** detailed and systematic arguments that often run to hundreds of pages. As a rule, the Justices depend a great deal on those briefs in reaching their decisions and writing their opinions.

On Friday of most weeks of a term, the Justices confer. They discuss the cases they have heard and try to decide their disposition. These conferences are held in the closest secrecy, and no formal report of them is ever made. More than 50 years ago, Chief Justice Harlan Fiske Stone wrote one of the very few first-hand accounts that exist:

> At Conference each case is presented for discussion by the Chief Justice, usually a brief statement of the facts, the question of law involved, and with such suggestions for their disposition as he may think appropriate. No cases have been assigned to any particular judge in advance of the Conference. Each Justice is prepared to discuss the case at length and to give his views as to the proper solution of the questions presented. In Mr. Justice Holmes' pungent phrase, each must be able to "recite" on the case. Each Judge is requested by the Chief Justice, in the order of seniority, to give his views and the conclusions which he has reached. The discussion is of the freest character and at its end, after full opportunity for each member of the Court to be heard and for the asking and answering of questions, the vote is taken and recorded in the reverse order of the discussion, the youngest, in point of service, voting first.
>
> On the same evening, after the conclusion of the Conference, each member of the Court receives at his home a memorandum from the Chief Justice advising him of the assignment of cases for opinions. Opinions are written for the most part in recess, and as they are written, they are printed and circulated among the Justices, who make suggestions for their correction and revision. At the next succeeding Conference these suggestions are brought before the full Conference and accepted or rejected as the case may be. On the following Monday [usually] the opinion is announced by the writer as the opinion of the Court.[19]

[19]"Fifty Years of Work of the United States Supreme Court," Report of the American Bar Association, 1928.

Supreme Court Justice John Paul Stevens discusses the legal background of a case with his law clerks.

Six justices make up a quorum for the decision of a case, and at least four must agree before a case can be decided. If all nine Justices take part, as they mostly do, a case may be decided by a 9–0, 8–1, 7–2, 6–3, or 5–4 vote. Many cases are decided unanimously, but several find the Court "split" or divided.

The Court is sometimes criticized for its "split decisions." Notice, however, that many of its cases present difficult and often hotly disputed questions. Many cases also involve questions on which lower courts have disagreed. In short, most of the Court's cases are the "hard" ones; the "easy" cases seldom get that far in the judicial process.

As Chief Justice Stone indicated, a **majority opinion** regularly accompanies the decision of a case. A Justice who does not agree with the majority often writes a **dissenting opinion.** Indeed, two, three, or even four dissents may be presented. A Justice who agrees with the Court's decision, but not with the reasoning by which it was reached, often prepares a **concurring opinion.** One or more of these opinions are often presented.

The written opinions are really not necessary to the decision of a case. In fact, decisions are sometimes handed down without opinion.

ENRICHMENT Have the class discuss the caseload of the Supreme Court. What can be done to lessen the load of work and speed along the judicial process?

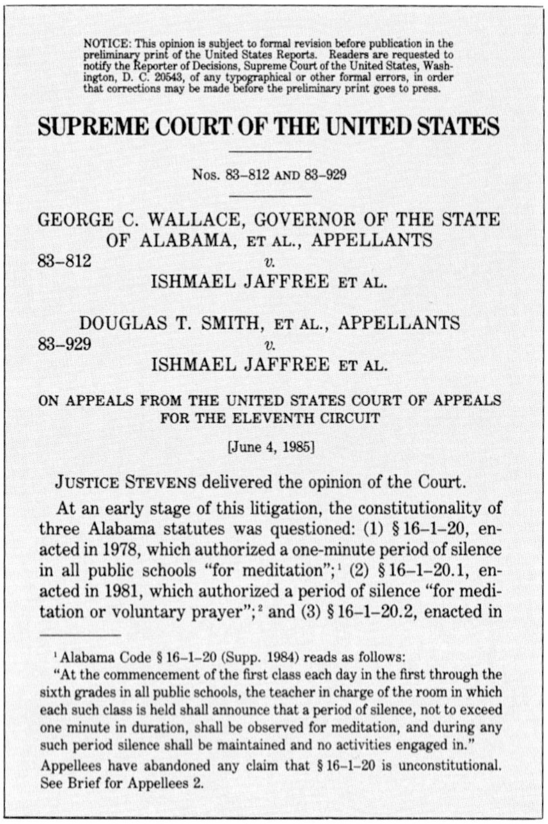

NOTICE: This opinion is subject to formal revision before publication in the preliminary print of the United States Reports. Readers are requested to notify the Reporter of Decisions, Supreme Court of the United States, Washington, D. C. 20543, of any typographical or other formal errors, in order that corrections may be made before the preliminary print goes to press.

SUPREME COURT OF THE UNITED STATES

Nos. 83–812 AND 83–929

GEORGE C. WALLACE, GOVERNOR OF THE STATE OF ALABAMA, ET AL., APPELLANTS
83–812 *v.*
ISHMAEL JAFFREE ET AL.

DOUGLAS T. SMITH, ET AL., APPELLANTS
83–929 *v.*
ISHMAEL JAFFREE ET AL.

ON APPEALS FROM THE UNITED STATES COURT OF APPEALS FOR THE ELEVENTH CIRCUIT

[June 4, 1985]

JUSTICE STEVENS delivered the opinion of the Court.

At an early stage of this litigation, the constitutionality of three Alabama statutes was questioned: (1) § 16–1–20, enacted in 1978, which authorized a one-minute period of silence in all public schools "for meditation";[1] (2) § 16–1–20.1, enacted in 1981, which authorized a period of silence "for meditation or voluntary prayer";[2] and (3) § 16–1–20.2, enacted in

[1] Alabama Code § 16–1–20 (Supp. 1984) reads as follows:
"At the commencement of the first class each day in the first through the sixth grades in all public schools, the teacher in charge of the room in which each such class is held shall announce that a period of silence, not to exceed one minute in duration, shall be observed for meditation, and during any such period silence shall be maintained and no activities engaged in."
Appellees have abandoned any claim that § 16–1–20 is unconstitutional. See Brief for Appellees 2.

This is a printed version of a Supreme Court decision on school prayer in the State of Alabama.

Still, the opinions are valuable. The majority opinions stand as precedents to be followed in similar cases as they arise in the lower courts or reach the Supreme Court. The concurring opinions may bring the Supreme Court to modify its present stand in future cases. Chief Justice Hughes once described dissenting opinions as "an appeal to the brooding spirit of the law, to the intelligence of a future day." On rare occasion, the Supreme Court does reverse itself; the minority opinion of today could become the Court's majority position in the future.

FOR REVIEW

1. **Identify:** writ of mandamus.
2. Which is the only federal court specifically created in the Constitution? The only judicial office?
3. How is the size of the Supreme Court set? What is it now?
4. What is the power of judicial review? Why is its use by the Supreme Court so vitally important?
5. Over what cases does the Supreme Court have original jurisdiction? Exclusive jurisdiction?
6. From what courts are cases appealed to the Supreme Court?
7. What is a majority opinion? A concurring opinion? A dissenting opinion?

4. The Special Courts

As You Read, Think About:

- What the functions and jurisdiction are of the special courts.

The special courts are often called the *legislative courts*. They are the federal courts Congress has created to exercise jurisdiction only in certain cases. Those cases deal with particular subjects that fall within the expressed powers of Congress. That is, these courts have *not* been set up under Article III, and they do not possess "the judicial power of the United States." Rather, they have been created to hear certain cases arising out of the exercise of specific congressional powers. *

The United States Claims Court

The United States cannot be sued, by anyone, in any court, for any reason, without its consent. It may be taken to court only in those cases in which Congress has declared that the Government is open to suit.[20]

[20] The government is shielded from suit by the doctrine of *sovereign immunity*. It comes down from an ancient principle of English public law summed up by the phrase: "The King can do no wrong." The rule is not intended to protect public officials from charges of corruption or any other wrongdoing. Congress has long since agreed to a long list of legitimate court actions against the Government.

*REINFORCEMENT Ask the class for examples of the types of cases that go before the Special Courts. For instance, someone may sue the Government because he or she was injured on federal property.

Originally, any person with a claim against the United States could secure *redress* (satisfaction of the claim, payment) only by an act of Congress. In 1955, however, Congress set up a special court, the Court of Claims, to hear these pleas. It did so acting under its expressed power to pay the debts of the United States.[21] Congress restructured the Court of Claims, as the United States Claims Court, in 1982.

The court now has 16 judges. They hold trials—hear claims for damages against the Government—throughout the country.[22] Those claims they uphold cannot in fact be paid until Congress appropriates the money, which it does almost as a matter of course.

Occasionally, those who lose in the Claims Court still manage to win some compensation. Some years ago, for example, a Puget Sound mink rancher lost a case in which he claimed that low-flying Navy planes had frightened his animals and caused several of the females to become sterile. He asked $100 per mink; but the Government was able to show that any one of several factors—including diet, weather, and fights and jealousies among the mink—could have caused the condition. Even so, his Congressman introduced a private bill that eventually paid him $10 for each animal. Appeals from the Court's decisions may be carried to the Court of Appeals for the Federal Circuit.

The Territorial Courts

Acting under its powers to "make all needful rules and regulations respecting the territory . . . belonging to the United States,"[23] Congress has created courts for the nation's territories. Today these territorial courts sit in the Virgin Islands, Guam, and the Northern Mariana Islands in the Pacific Trust Territory. These Courts have the same jurisdiction over cases arising from federal law as the District Courts; they also have jurisdiction in local cases.

The Courts of the District of Columbia

Acting under its power "to exercise exclusive legislation in all cases whatsoever, over such District . . . as may . . . become the seat of the Government of the United States,"[24] Congress has set up a judicial system for the nation's capital. Both the federal District Court and the Court of Appeals for the District of Columbia hear many local cases as well as those they try as constitutional courts. Congress has also established two *local* courts, much like the courts in the States: a Superior Court, which is the general trial court, and a Court of Appeals.

The Court of Military Appeals

Acting under its power "to make rules for the government and regulation of the land and naval forces,"[25] Congress created the Court of Military Appeals in 1950. The court has a chief judge and two associate judges, appointed by the President and Senate for 15-year terms. It has been called "the GI Supreme Court." It reviews the more serious court-martial convictions of members of the armed forces. Appeals from its decisions are almost never heard by the Supreme Court. The Court of Military Appeals is, then, the court of last resort in most cases involving offenses against military law.

The United States Tax Court

Acting under its power to tax, Congress established the Tax Court in 1969.[26] It has 19 judges, one of whom serves as chief judge.

---

[21]Article I, Section 8. Clause 1.

[22]Under the Federal Tort Claims Act of 1946, the District Courts also have jurisdiction over many claims cases, but only where the amount sought is not more than $10,000. The same statute also gives executive agencies the authority to settle claims under $1,000.

[23]Article IV, Section 3, Clause 2.

[24]Article I, Section 8, Clause 17.

[25]Article I, Section 8, Clause 14. This provision, and the 5th Amendment, allows Congress to regulate the conduct of members of the armed forces under a separate (noncivilian) code of military law. Today, the Uniform Code of Military Justice, passed by Congress in 1950, and the Military Justice Acts of 1968 and 1983 (which provide for the appeal process to the Supreme Court) are the major statutes designed to meet the special disciplinary needs of the armed forces.

[26]Article I, Section 8, Clause 1.

Lawyers meet outside the federal courthouse in Harrisburg, Pennsylvania. There are many types of federal courts, all with different functions.

Each of these judges is named by the President and Senate for a 12-year term.

The Tax Court hears civil, but not criminal, cases involving disputes over the application of the tax laws. Most of its cases, then, are generated by the Internal Revenue Service and other Treasury agencies. Its decisions are subject to review by (may be appealed to) the federal Courts of Appeals.

FOR REVIEW

1. Which are the special courts in the national judiciary?
2. Over what types of cases do the territorial courts have jurisdiction? The courts of the District of Columbia? The Court of Military Appeals? The Tax Court?

5. The Judges

As You Read, Think About:

- How federal judges are appointed, the length of their service, and how they are compensated.
- What the roles are of court officers.

The Constitution makes provisions for the procedure by which federal judges are se-

The National Judiciary

Court	Created	Number of Courts	Number of Judges	Term of Judges	Judges Appointed by[a]	Salary of Judges
District Court	1789	94	575	Life	President	$ 78,700
Court of Appeals	1891	12	156	Life	President	$ 83,200
Supreme Court	1789	1	9	Life	President	$104,100[b]
Trade Court	1926	1	9	Life	President	$ 78,700
Court of Appeals for the Federal Circuit	1982	1	12	Life	President	$ 83,200
Claims Court	1982	1	16	15 years	President	$ 78,700
Court of Military Appeals	1950	1	3	15 years	President	$ 83,200
Tax Court	1969	1	19	12 years	President	$ 78,700

[a]With Senate confirmation. [b]Chief Justice receives $108,400.

lected, their term in office, and leaves to Congress the matter of setting the salaries for all federal judges.

Appointment

The President appoints all federal judges, subject to confirmation by the Senate. The Constitution declares that the President "shall nominate, and, by and with the advice and consent of the Senate, shall appoint . . . judges of the Supreme Court."[27] Congress has provided the same procedure for the selection of all other federal judges. Hence, the President is free to name to the federal bench anyone the Senate will confirm. Recall the very real impact of the unwritten rule of senatorial courtesy; see page 416.

Most federal judges are drawn from the ranks of leading attorneys, legal scholars and law school professors, former members of Congress, and from the State courts. Judicial selections are shaped by the same sorts of considerations as other exercises of the Chief Executive's appointing power we considered on pages 415-416.

The President and his closest political and legal aides, especially the Attorney General, take leading parts, of course. But major roles are also played by influential Senators, most of all those from the nominee's home State; by the legal profession, especially the American Bar Association's Committee on the Federal Judiciary; and by various other personalities in the President's political party.

Term

Article III, Section 1 reads, in part:

> The judges, both the Supreme and inferior courts, shall hold their offices during good behavior . . .

This means, then, that all judges of the constitutional courts are appointed for life, until they resign, retire, or die in office. They may be removed only through the impeachment process. Only ten federal judges have ever been impeached. Of the ten impeached by the House, only five were found guilty by the Senate.[28]

The Constitution's grant of what amounts to life tenure for judges is intended, and works, to ensure the independence of the federal judiciary.

The judges of the territorial courts and those of the District of Columbia are appointed for terms varying from four to eight years. The judges of the Claims Court and the Court of Military Appeals serve 15-year terms and those of the Tax Court, 12 years.

Compensation

Article III, Section 1 also states that federal judges

> . . . shall, at stated times, receive for their services a compensation which shall not be diminished during their continuance in office.

Congress sets the salaries for all federal judges. For the salaries they receive, see page 528.

Congress has provided a fairly generous retirement arrangement for the judges of the constitutional courts. They may retire at age 70, and if they have served for at least 10 years, they receive their full salary for the rest of their lives. Or, they may retire at full salary at age 65, after at least 15 years of service on the federal bench. The Chief Justice may call any retired judge back into service in the lower federal courts at any time, however.

[27]Article II, Section 2, Clause 2.

[28]Judge John Pickering of the District Court in New Hampshire, for irregular judicial procedures, loose morals, and drunkenness, in 1803; Judge West H. Humphreys of the District Court in Tennessee, for disloyalty, in 1862; Judge Robert W. Archibald of the old Commerce Court, for improper relations with litigants in his court, in 1913; Judge Halstead L. Ritter of the District Court in Florida, for bringing his court into "scandal and disrepute," in 1936; and Judge Harry E. Clairborne of the District Court in Nevada, for filing false income tax returns, in 1986. Four other judges were impeached by the House but acquitted by the Senate: District Judge James H. Peck of Missouri in 1831; Charles Swayne of Florida, 1905; Howard Louderback of California, 1933; and Associate Justice Samuel Chase of the Supreme Court in 1804-1805. Justice Chase, a Federalist, had been impeached for extreme partisanship and overzealous conduct in sedition cases. One, Judge George W. English of the District Court in Illinois, was impeached by the House in 1926. A few other District Court judges have resigned to avoid impeachment. See pages 359–360.

*ENRICHMENT Ask the class to discuss: What are the advantages and disadvantages of federal judges being appointed for life?

One of the judges of the District of Columbia's federal District Court, Norma Johnson hears cases arising from violations of federal civil and criminal law.

Court Officers

Today, federal judges are little involved in the day-to-day administrative operations of the courts over which they preside. Their primary mission is to hear and decide cases. Other judicial personnel provide the support services necessary to permit federal judges to perform that basic task.

Each federal court appoints a clerk who has custody of the seal of the court and keeps a record of the court's proceedings. The clerk is helped by deputy clerks, stenographers, bailiffs, and others as needed.

Each of the 91 federal District Courts now appoints at least one United States Magistrate, a court officer who handles a number of legal matters once dealt with by the judges themselves. Magistrates issue warrants of arrest and often hear evidence to decide whether or not a person who has been arrested on a federal charge should be held for action by the grand jury. They also set bail in federal criminal cases, and even have the power to try those who are charged with certain minor offenses.

There is also at least one Bankruptcy Judge in each federal judicial district. These court officers handle bankruptcy cases, at the direction of the District Court to which they are assigned.[29] There are now, altogether, 232 of them; they are appointed, for 14-year terms, by the judges of each of the federal Courts of Appeals.

The President appoints, subject to Senate confirmation, a United States Attorney for each federal judicial district. Attorneys and their assistants are responsible for the prosecution of all persons charged with federal crimes and they represent the United States in all civil actions brought by or against the Government in their district.

The President and Senate also appoint a United States Marshal to serve each District Court. Each federal marshal and the marshal's deputies carry out duties much like those handled by a county sheriff and the sheriff's deputies. They make arrests in federal criminal cases, keep accused persons in custody, secure jurors, serve legal papers, keep order in the courtroom, and execute court orders and decisions.

United States Attorneys and Marshals are each appointed for four-year terms. Al-

[29]Recall, bankruptcy is a legal proceeding in which a debtor's assets are distributed among those to whom the bankrupt person, business firm, or other organization owes money. Although some bankruptcy cases are heard in State courts, nearly all of them fall within the jurisdiction of the federal District Courts; see page 517.

*ENRICHMENT Have the class research the identities of the United States Magistrate, United States Attorney, and United States Marshal of their federal judicial district. Have the class prepare reports on the activities of each of these officials.

though they are officers of the court, they serve under the direction of the Attorney General and are officials of the Department of Justice.

FOR REVIEW

1. **Identify:** United States Magistrate, United States Attorney, United States Marshal.
2. Who appoints federal judges? For what terms?
3. How may federal judges be removed from office?
4. What restriction does the Constitution place on Congress' power to set judicial salaries?
5. What are the major functions of the clerks of the federal courts?
6. What are the major duties of United States Magistrates? Bankruptcy judges? Attorneys? Marshals?

6. The Administration of Justice

As You Read, Think About:

- Why justice is a vital concept of the American political system.
- How the Department of Justice is organized.

No matter is, or can be, of greater importance to a democratic government than justice. To establish it, declares the Preamble to the Constitution, is one of the high purposes for which that great charter was written. To provide justice, said Thomas Jefferson, is "the most sacred of the duties of government."

What, precisely, is "justice"? The question is far from simple, for justice is a concept, an idea. It has no physical existence; it cannot be seen or touched or weighed or measured. Rather, like "truth", "liberty", "good", and all other concepts, justice is an invention of the human mind. Precisely because it is a product of human thought, it means what human beings make it mean.

As the concept has been developed over time in American thought and practice, justice has come to mean this: That the law, in both its content and its administration, must be reasonable, fair, and impartial.

As we have suggested before, those standards of justice have not always been met in practice in this country. We have not in fact attained our professed goal of "equal justice for all." On the other hand, we have also made this crucial point: Our history can be told very largely in terms of our efforts to reach that goal and very largely in terms of our ever-improving attempts to do so.

Clearly, the courts play a very special role in those efforts. In fact, courts are often described as "tribunals for the administration of justice according to law." As you know, we have just examined the federal court system, the judicial machinery by which the Federal Government seeks to do justice. Later, in Chapter 22, we shall consider the much larger network of State and local courts.

Recall, justice is a matter of vital concern to *all* of government in this country, not just to the courts alone. The concept is supposed to guide the behavior of all legislative and executive agencies, too.

The reality—the practical day-to-day fact —of a government's commitment to the concept of justice can be measured by a close look at its policies and its actions. In short, how does all that government says and all that it does square with that concept?

The Department of Justice

Of the many agencies in the executive branch of the Federal Government, one in particular is an especially telling indicator of that government's commitment to the concept of justice: the Department of Justice.

We identified the Department's major agencies and summarized their principal functions in Chapter 16. A review of that material will demonstrate its central role here. So, too, do these words, chiseled into the marble outside the office of the Attorney

BUILDING GOVERNMENT SKILLS

Analyzing Crime Statistics

The "crime clock" on this page is drawn from the FBI's *Uniform Crime Reports*. Each of these annual reports (the UCR) is an extensive statistical examination of *known* crime in the United States for a given year.

As you can see, the clock shows the frequency of occurrence of major crimes. Thus, on the average, 20 such offenses were committed during *every minute*. A violent crime occurred every 24 seconds, a murder every 28 minutes, a robbery every 63 seconds, and so on. Altogether, the FBI reported the commission of some 12 million serious crimes in 1985.

Among many other things, the UCR also shows that the incidence of crime is spread unevenly, both geographically and within population groups. Thus:

— The rate of crime is higher in larger cities than it is in middle-sized and smaller communities; and the crime rate is higher in cities than in their suburbs, and higher in urban areas than in rural areas.

— More crimes are committed by the poor, and against the poor, than other segments of the population.

— By age groups, the largest number of serious crimes (those shown in the clock) are committed by younger persons. Some 30 percent of all persons arrested for those crimes are under 18 years of age; about 45 percent are less than 21 years old; and some 60 percent are less than 25.

— By sex, males commit far more crimes than females do.

The costs of crime are difficult to calculate. In economic terms, most authorities put the annual loss to crime at least $150 billion, not counting the billions spent to fight it. The costs in social and human terms is beyond calculation.

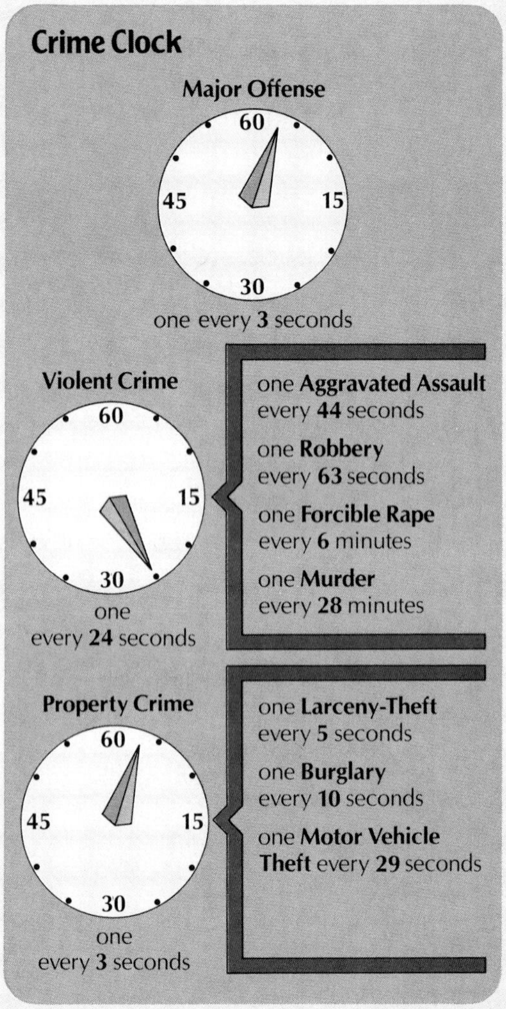

1. Locate a copy of the most recent UCR in your school or local library. Using the data in its appendices (and/or by contacting your State's agency listed there), construct a "crime clock" for your locale.
2. What reactions do you have, and what conclusions can you draw, from the data on the arrests for serious crimes of persons under 18 years of age?

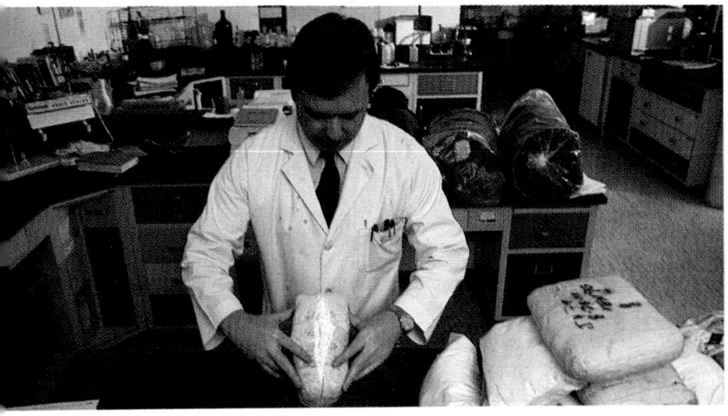

Top: Confiscated drugs are examined by an employee of the Drug Enforcement Agency. *Middle:* A Border Patrol agent on duty. *Bottom:* An automated FBI fingerprint identification unit.

General of the United States: "The United States wins its point whenever justice is done one of its citizens in the courts."

The Department, headed by the Attorney General, was created by Congress in 1870. The post of Attorney General was established much earlier, however, by the very first session of Congress in 1789. The nation's first Attorney General, Edmund Randolph, was a member of Washington's original Cabinet. Most of Randolph's now 74 successors have followed him in the role of intimate adviser to the Presidents they have served.

Until 1870, the Attorney General's only official duties were to provide legal advice to the President and his aides and to represent the United States in court. Over the years since then, those duties have multiplied considerably. Today, the Department describes itself as "the largest law firm in the nation."[30]

Through its thousands of lawyers, investigators, agents, and other employees—some 65,800 in all—the Justice Department: furnishes legal advice to the President and to the heads of the other executive departments; enforces most of the federal criminal laws; investigates violations of those statutes * and arrests those who commit federal offenses; supervises the work of the United States Attorneys and Marshals throughout the country; represents the United States in court; operates the federal prison system; and enforces the nation's immigration, naturalization, and narcotics laws.

FOR REVIEW

1. Why is "justice" a difficult term to define? What has it come to mean?
2. What are the principal duties of the Justice Department?

[30]Altogether, some 20,000 attorneys work for the Federal Government. They hold positions throughout the executive branch. The Treasury Department (especially the IRS) and the several independent regulatory commissions have large legal staffs. Yet, well over half of all federal attorneys are employed by the Justice Department.

*ENRICHMENT The FBI is a part of the Department of Justice. Ask the class to discuss how it helps to promote justice.

SUMMARY

Among its several weaknesses the Articles of Confederation did not provide for a national judiciary. The Framers corrected this in Article III of the Constitution. There, the Supreme Court is established, Congress is given the power to create lower federal courts, and the jurisdiction of the national judiciary is set out. The federal system gives rise to a dual system of courts in this country: national and State.

Congress has created two types of federal courts: (1) the constitutional (or regular) courts —today, the District Courts, the Courts of Appeals, the Supreme Court, and the Court of International Trade; and (2) the special (or legislative) courts—the territorial courts, those of the District of Columbia, the Claims Court, the Court of Military Appeals, and the United States Tax Court.

The constitutional courts exercise the broad judicial power of the United States. They have jurisdiction over a case either because of its subject matter or the parties involved. Some cases are within their exclusive jurisdiction; those heard on appeal are within their appellate jurisdiction.

The 94 District Courts hear most federal cases. The 12 Courts of Appeals hear cases appealed from the District Courts and the independent regulatory commissions.

The Supreme Court is the highest court in the land. The importance of its exercise of the power of judicial review cannot be overstated. The High Court generally chooses the cases it will hear on appeal from the lower federal courts and the highest State courts. It has original jurisdiction over cases against ambassadors and other public ministers and cases involving disputes between two or more States.

The Trade Court hears cases arising out of the tariff and other laws relating to international trade. Appeals from its decisions are taken to the Court of Appeals for the Federal Circuit—which also hears appeals from the Claims Court, certain decisions in the District Courts, and administrative rulings made by some executive agencies.

The special courts are not created under Article III. They do not hold the judicial power of the United States; rather, they handle cases arising out of the exercise of particular congressional powers.

The President appoints federal judges, subject to Senate confirmation. The judges of the constitutional courts serve for life (during good behavior); those of the special courts are appointed for various terms. Each of the federal courts is aided by a judicial staff. Magistrates and federal Bankruptcy Judges serve each of the District Courts, as do United States Attorneys and Marshals.

CHAPTER REVIEW

Key Terms/Concepts*

judiciary (512)
jurisdiction (514)
plaintiff (515)
defendant (516)
judicial review (520)
writ of certiorari (523)
appeal (523)
certificate (523)
brief (525)
majority opinion (525)
dissenting opinion (525)
concurring opinion (525)

*These terms are included in the Glossary.

Keynote Questions

• **1.** To which governmental body does the Constitution grant "the judicial power of the United States"? Why?

• **2.** What is the "dual court system" in the United States?

• **3.** How do the special courts differ from the constitutional courts?

• **4.** What is jurisdiction?

* The dots represent skill levels required to answer each question or complete each activity:
•requires recall and comprehension • •requires application and analysis • • •requires synthesis and evaluation

- **5.** As established by the Constitution, the federal courts have jurisdiction over a case if the case deals with what subject matter? If the case involves which parties?
- **6.** Which federal courts have original jurisdiction over most federal court cases?
- **7.** What is the major role of the Courts of Appeals in the federal court system?
- **8.** Why was the Court's decision in *Marbury* v. *Madison* one of the most important of all cases ever decided by the Supreme Court?
- **9.** Briefly describe in a paragraph how most cases reach the Supreme Court.
- **10.** Why are the written opinions prepared by Justices of the Supreme Court valuable?
- **11.** Why did Congress create the Court of Appeals for the Federal Circuit?
- **12.** What is a special court? List two examples and the jurisdiction of each.
- **13.** How are federal judges selected? For what terms do most federal judges serve?

Skill Application

Supporting Conclusions with Evidence: During a trial, the defense lawyer tries to present evidence that will show that the defendant is not guilty, while the prosecuting attorney tries to present evidence that will prove that the defendant is guilty. Good legal arguments and good political arguments consist of conclusions that are supported by evidence.

Evidence can be an eyewitness account, a statistic, or other factual information. Evidence should be relevant to the conclusion, and it should be unbiased. To express your opinion effectively, you must cite supporting evidence.

Each of the sentences below is a conclusion based on information presented in this chapter. Read each sentence; then find two factual statements in the chapter that support the conclusion. Write these statements on your paper.

1. The Supreme Court's decision in *Marbury* v. *Madison* established the Supreme Court as having the power to decide the constitutionality of an act of government.
2. Under the Articles of Confederation, a dual court system did not exist.
3. Most of the cases the Supreme Court hears come to it on appeal from the lower courts.

For Thought and Discussion

- **1.** Federal judges frequently interpret provisions of federal law and/or of the Constitution, and apply them to cases before their courts. When they do so, do they "make law"? Explain your answer.
- **2.** Why did Woodrow Wilson describe the Supreme Court as "a constitutional convention in continuous session"?
- •• **3.** What qualifications should a President consider in appointing federal judges? Would you favor or oppose the popular election of federal judges? Why?
- ••• **4.** Do you agree or disagree with this observation: The principles of popular sovereignty and of majority rule, on the one hand, and that of judicial review on the other, are contradictory and cannot exist logically in a governmental system. Why?
- ••• **5.** Sometimes the Supreme Court has been criticized for being "cloaked in secrecy" because little is known about its decision-making process. What purpose does secrecy serve for the Supreme Court? Do you think this practice should continue? Why or why not?

Suggested Activities

- ••• **1.** Write an essay or a speech on the following comment by Chief Justice Charles Evans Hughes. (You might want to compare it to Judge Learned Hand's comment, quoted on page 99.)

> Democracy will survive only as long as the quick whims of the majority are held in check by the courts in favor of a dominant and lasting sense of justice. If democratic institutions are long to survive, it will not be simply by maintaining majority rule and by the swift adaptation to the demands of the moment, but by the dominance of a sense of justice which will not long survive if judicial processes do not conserve it.

- •• **2.** Interview a federal judge or a lawyer who has experience with federal cases. What is his or her perception of the purpose of the law? Of the role of the courts? What does he or she think are the advantages of trying a case in federal court, as compared to a State court? The disadvantages?

Unit 7

State and Local Governments

ONE OF THE most distinctive features of the American governmental system is the division of powers between the National Government and the States. At the Constitutional Convention in 1787, many delegates feared that a strong National Government would mean the end of the States' powers.

In fact, the federal system set up by the Constitution gives the States vast powers. It reserves to them—or, to the people—all of those "powers not delegated to the United States by the Constitution nor prohibited by it to the States."

Most of the contacts that most citizens have with government in this country are with the States and their local governments, not the National Government. Operating under written constitutions, the States make and enforce laws, build and maintain schools, roads, and other facilities, and provide for public health and safety. The States also create local governments—counties, towns, townships, boroughs, cities, and other districts.

In Unit 7 we turn to the States and their thousands of units of local government. We shall look, first, at the 50 State constitutions and at the legislative, executive, and judicial branches of State government. We shall then consider the many different kinds of local government which exist across the country. Finally, we shall examine the various ways in which we pay for all of those governments and all that they do.

An interior view of the dome of the Capitol Building in Austin, Texas.

Constitutions govern governments.
–THOMAS R. DYE

19

State Constitutions

CHAPTER OBJECTIVES

To help you to

Learn · Know · Understand

The nature of the first State constitutions.

The nature of present-day State constitutions.

The processes of constitutional change and development among the States.

The general and urgent need for constitutional revision among the States today.

EACH OF THE 50 States has a *written* constitution. That fact, in itself, is very important. From the very beginning, government in this country has been based on written constitutions—a point we first made in Chapter 2. In fact, the United States has sometimes been described as "a land of constitutions."

Our experience with such documents dates from 1606, when King James granted a charter to the Virginia Company. That act led to the settlement at Jamestown in the following year and, with it, the first government in British North America. Later, each of the other English colonies was also established and governed on the basis of a written charter.

Since the first State constitutions were written in 1776, the States have drafted and approved nearly 150 of them. In a very real sense, each of the present-day State constitutions is a link in a chain of written documents that now stretches over nearly 400 years of American history.

In this chapter we take a close look at the various State constitutions. As we do, remember their place in the scheme of Ameri-

James Madison addresses the chair at the Virginia Constitutional Convention of 1829-1830. Other prominent delegates included James Monroe, John Marshall, and John Randolph. Facing page: The State House of Boston, Massachusetts, a State whose constitution dates from 1780.

can federalism. A State constitution is that State's supreme law. It sets out the way in which the government of that State is organized, and it distributes power among the various branches of the State government. It authorizes the exercise of power by government and, at the same time, it places limits on the exercise of governmental power. A State's constitution is superior to any and all other forms of State and local law within that State.

Recall, however, each State's constitution * is subordinate to the Constitution of the United States. Therefore, each State's constitution may not conflict with any form of federal law.[1]

[1]Reread Article VI, Section 2, the Supremacy Clause in the national Constitution, and page 77.

1. The First State Constitutions

As You Read, Think About:

- What the origins were of the first State constitutions.
- How the first State constitutions were adopted.
- What the general content was of these documents.
- Why age is a significant factor in the need for reform of State constitutions.

When the 13 colonies became independent, each faced the problem of establishing a new government. On May 15, 1776, the Second Continental Congress advised each of the new States to adopt

> such governments as shall, in the opinion of the representatives of the people, best conduce to the happiness and safety of their constituents in particular, and America in general.

Despite their several shortcomings, most of the colonial charters served as models for the first State constitutions. Indeed, in the

*REINFORCEMENT Discuss: What are the differences and similarities between the U.S. Constitution and State constitutions?

This historic document is entitled: "A Constitution or Form of Government for the Commonwealth of Massachusetts." Adopted in 1780, it is the oldest written constitution in force in the world today.

States of Connecticut and Rhode Island, the old charters seemed so well suited to the needs of the day that they were carried over as constitutions almost without change.[2]

The earliest State constitutions were adopted in a variety of ways. The people played no direct part in the process in any State. In Connecticut and in Rhode Island, the legislature made the small changes considered necessary in the charters, and no further action was taken in either State.

Six of the Revolutionary legislatures drew up new documents and proclaimed them in force in 1776. In none of those States—Maryland, New Jersey, North Carolina, Pennsylvania, South Carolina, and Virginia—was the new constitution offered to the people for judgment.

In Delaware and New Hampshire, in 1776, and in Georgia and New York, in 1777, new constitutions were prepared by conventions called by the legislature. In each case, the new document had to be approved by the legislature and then became effective; but in none was popular approval required.

In 1780 a popularly elected convention prepared a second constitution for Massachusetts, and it was then ratified by a vote of the people. Thus, Massachusetts set the pattern of popular participation in the constitution-making process, a pattern followed generally among the States since.[3]

All of the present State constitutions were drafted by assemblies representing the people, and most of them became effective

[2]Connecticut did not write a new document until 1818 and Rhode Island, not until 1842.

[3]As noted in Chapter 2, with independence Massachusetts relied on the colonial charter in force prior to 1691 as its first State constitution. New Hampshire adopted its second and present constitution in 1784. It followed the Massachusetts pattern of popular convention and popular ratification. The Massachusetts constitution of 1780 and New Hampshire's constitution of 1784, both still in force, are the oldest written constitutions in effect anywhere in the world today.

only after a popular vote. Only the present constitutions of Delaware (1897), Mississippi (1890), South Carolina (1895), and Vermont (1793) came into force without popular ratification.

Contents

The first State documents differed in many ways. As we saw in Chapter 2, however, they came out of the same revolutionary ferment and so shared many basic features.

Each of them proclaimed the twin principles of **popular sovereignty** and **limited government.** That is, in each of them the people were recognized as the sole source of authority for government, and the powers given to the new government were closely limited. Seven constitutions began with a lengthy bill of rights. All of them made it clear that the sovereign people held "certain unalienable rights" that government must respect.

The doctrines of **separation of powers** and of **checks and balances** were also built into each of the new charters. In practice, however, the memory of the hated royal governors was still fresh, and most of the authority that each State government had rested with the legislature.

Everywhere, except in Georgia until 1789 and Pennsylvania until 1790, the legislature was *bicameral.*[4] At first, only Massachusetts and South Carolina allowed the governor to veto acts of the legislature. The governor was generally limited to a one-year term and was chosen by the legislature in each of the States except Massachusetts and New York.

For their time, the early State constitutions were democratic documents. Each had, however, several provisions and some important omissions that, by today's standards, were quite undemocratic. Thus, no constitution provided for full religious freedom, each set rigid qualifications for voting and for officeholding, and all gave property owners a highly favored standing.

[4]Vermont, which became the 14th State in 1791, had a unicameral legislature until 1836. Only Nebraska has a one-house legislative body today and that only since 1937.

FOR REVIEW

1. **Identify:** written constitutions, colonial charters.
2. What is a State's constitution?
3. What is the relationship between each State's constitution and the national Constitution? Other forms of federal law? Other forms of State law?
4. What pattern of constitution-making was first set by Massachusetts? When?
5. Describe in a paragraph the general shape of the first State constitutions.

2. State Constitutions Today

As You Read, Think About:

- What the major provisions are of most present-day State constitutions.

The present-day State constitutions are the direct descendants of those earlier documents. Not surprisingly, they are somewhat like and, at the same time, very different from their predecessors. On the one hand, only 17 of the State constitutions were written in this century. On the other hand, most of them have been amended several dozens of times, as we shall see.

Each document sets up a framework of government much like that to be found in the other States. All of them rest on nearly uniform principles. Still, there are unique provisions in each of them, as well as several other variations among them.

A close look at your State's constitution will show that it can be fairly well described in terms of the following categories: basic principles; civil rights; governmental structure, powers and processes; and amendment provisions.[5] *

[5]A copy of your State's constitution can usually be obtained from the Secretary of State's office in the State capitol.

*ENRICHMENT Obtain copies of your State's constitution from the legislature. Have students compare it to the U.S. Constitution on p. 726.

The State Constitutions

State	Present Document Became Effective In[a]	State Entered Union In[b]	Number of Previous Documents	State	Present Document Became Effective In[a]	State Entered Union In[b]	Number of Previous Documents
Alabama	1901	1819	5	Montana	1973	1889	1
Alaska	1959	1959	0	Nebraska	1875	1867	1
Arizona	1912	1912	0	Nevada	1864	1864	0
Arkansas	1874	1836	4	New Hampshire	1784	1788	1
California	1879[c]	1850	1	New Jersey	1948	1787	2
Colorado	1876	1876	0	New Mexico	1912	1912	0
Connecticut	1965	1788	3	New York	1895	1788	3
Delaware	1897	1787	3	North Carolina	1971	1789	2
Florida	1969	1845	5	North Dakota	1889	1889	0
Georgia	1983	1788	9	Ohio	1851	1803	1
Hawaii	1959	1959	0[d]	Oklahoma	1907	1907	0
Idaho	1890	1890	0	Oregon	1859	1859	0
Illinois	1971	1818	3	Pennsylvania	1874	1787	3
Indiana	1851	1816	1	Rhode Island	1843	1790	1
Iowa	1857	1846	1	South Carolina	1896	1788	6
Kansas	1861	1861	0	South Dakota	1889	1889	0
Kentucky	1891	1792	3	Tennessee	1870	1796	2
Louisiana	1975	1812	10	Texas	1876	1845	4
Maine	1820	1820	0	Utah	1896	1896	0
Maryland	1867	1788	3	Vermont	1793	1791	2
Massachusetts	1780	1788	0	Virginia	1971	1788	5
Michigan	1964	1837	3	Washington	1889	1889	0
Minnesota	1858	1858	0	West Virginia	1872	1863	1
Mississippi	1890	1817	3	Wisconsin	1848	1848	0
Missouri	1945	1821	3	Wyoming	1890	1890	0

[a]Twenty-four of the present-day State constitutions were actually ratified in a year prior to the year in which they became effective: Alaska (1956), Arizona (1911), Florida (1968), Georgia (1982), Hawaii (1950), Idaho (1889), Illinois (1970), Kansas (1859), Louisiana (1974), Maine (1819), Michigan (1963), Minnesota (1857), Montana (1972), New Jersey (1947), New Mexico (1911), New York (1894), North Carolina (1970), Oregon (1857), Pennsylvania (1873), Rhode Island (1842), South Carolina (1895), Utah (1895), Virginia (1970), Wyoming (1889).
[b]For each of the original 13 States, the year in which the State ratified the national Constitution.
[c]California's constitution became effective July 4, 1879, for purposes of the election of officers, the beginning of their terms of office, and the meeting of the legislature; it became effective for all other purposes January 1, 1880.
[d]Prior to 1898, Hawaii (as a kingdom and then a republic) had five written constitutions.

Basic Principles

Every State's fundamental law is built on the principles of popular sovereignty and limited government. That is, each State constitution recognizes that government exists only with the consent of the people and that it must operate within certain, often closely defined, bounds.

In every State, the powers of government are divided among executive, legislative, and judicial branches: Each of those branches has powers with which it can restrain the actions of the other two. That is, each of the 50 documents proclaims the concepts of separation of powers and checks and balances. Each also provides, either expressly or by implication, for the power of **judicial review.**

Protections of Civil Rights

Each document has a **bill of rights,** a listing of the rights that individuals hold against the State and its officers and agencies. Most constitutions set out guarantees much like those found in the first 10 amendments to the national Constitution. Several documents have a number of other guaran-

From the *Rotarian*, June 1972. By permission of the publisher.

"Now you try to get a fire started while I draft a constitution."

tees, as well, such as the right to self-government, to be safe from imprisonment for debt, to migrate from the State, and to organize labor unions and bargain collectively.

Structure of Government

Any constitution is, in major part, a statement of governmental organization. Every State constitution deals with the structure of government at both the State and the local levels. Among them, the major variations come largely in terms of the detail with which that matter is treated. A few follow the national pattern, providing only a more or less broad outline. Most, however, cover the subject of governmental organization at length and often in specific detail.

Governmental Powers and Processes*

All State constitutions deal with the powers and processes of government at some length. The powers vested in the governor and other elements of the executive branch, the legislature, the courts, and units of local government are treated in detail.

The powers to tax, spend, borrow, and provide for education are very prominent. So, too, are such processes as elections, legislation, and intergovernmental (State-local) relations. In several States the initiative, referendum, and recall are also described.

Constitutional Change

Constitutions are the product of human effort. No constitution is perfect. Sooner or later, changes become necessary or at least desirable. Each of the State documents recognizes that fact. Each sets out the means by which it may be formally changed, that is, revised or amended.

As constitutions are *fundamental* laws, they cannot be changed by those methods employed to change ordinary law. Rather, they require more complex procedures, which are somewhat more difficult to bring about—as we shall see in a moment.

Miscellaneous Provisions

Every State constitution has several provisions of a miscellaneous or "other" character. Thus, most begin with a preamble, which has no legal force but does set out the purposes of those who drafted and adopted the document.

Most constitutions also have a schedule for putting a new document into effect and avoiding conflicts with its predecessor. All of them contain a number of "dead letter" provisions. These have no current force and effect but still remain, nonetheless, a part of the constitution.

FOR REVIEW

1. **Identify:** preamble, schedule.
2. What are the major features of the 50 State constitutions?
3. What are "dead letter" provisions in State constitutions?

*ENRICHMENT Discuss in class, using a copy of your State's constitution: The above categories are a part of every State's constitution. How are they included in our State's?

3. Constitutional Change

As You Read, Think About:

- Why there is a need for amendments to any constitution.
- Why the process of informal amendment is not important at the State level.
- What the various methods are by which State constitutions are amended.

Constitutions reflect the goals, the ideals, and the attitudes of those who framed and adopted them. Times change, however; circumstances and attitudes change. Inevitably, constitutions, or at least major portions of them, become outdated. A vital part of any constitution, then, is its provision for the means by which it may be altered. As you can see from the table on page 542, some State constitutions have proved to be more durable than others.

Like the national Constitution, the State documents have been altered over the years by both the *formal* and the *informal* **amendment** process. *But*—and this is a very important *but*—the informal process has not been nearly so important at the State as at the national level.

State constitutions are much less flexible than the national document. The structures, powers, and procedures of State government are treated at great length, so there is much less room for the play of informal change. The State courts have generally been strict in their role as constitution-interpreters. In short, the States have had to depend largely on formal amendments for constitutional change and development.

To understand the formal amendment process and the kind of changes that constitutions undergo, the meanings of two quite distinct sets of terms are crucial. They are: proposal/ratification and amendment/revision.

First, the process of formal change involves two basic steps: *proposal* and then *ratification*. Proposals for change may be made by a constitutional convention, by the legislature, or in several States by the voters

Delegates to New Hampshire's 17th Constitutional Convention, held in Concord in May of 1984, vote on a proposed amendment.

*REINFORCEMENT Why is the process of informal amendment less important at the State level? Discuss in class, stressing the distinction between proposal/ratification and amendment/revision.

FOCUS ON:

New Hampshire's Constitutional Convention

New Hampshire is one of four States in which the question of calling a constitutional convention must be submitted to the voters every 10 years. In 1982, the voters approved the convention call and, in 1984, New Hampshire held its 17th Constitutional Convention.

The convention was convened on May 9. The delegates proposed 175 changes to the constitution, and set up 17 committees to deal with them. Each change was assigned to one of the committees for study, possible hearings, and recommendations. Only 10 of the proposed 175 received the three-fifths majority vote required for placement on the ballot.

A mere 10 out of 175! The reason for so little change is one common to most State constitutional conventions. It can be best described by a phrase often heard at the New Hampshire convention: "If it ain't broke, don't fix it."

People have great respect for the traditions that have served our country and are reluctant to tamper with them. New Hampshire's constitution is the second oldest still in operation. Consequently, the delegates were hesitant to offer too many changes in the fear that the voters would defeat them all.

The proposed constitutional changes that did make it onto the ballot on November 6, 1984, were these ("N" indicates rejection by the voters.):

1. Make voter registration and all polling places accessible to elderly and handicapped.
2. Forbid insertion of other changes in law into budget bills.
3. Require state funding or local approval of state-mandated programs.
4. Reduce the size of the House of Representatives by 12 to 388 members and increase the Senate by 12 to 36 members. (N)
5. Provide for annual legislative sessions and payment of mileage for legislators for 45 legislative days.
6. Lower the minimum age for State Senator and executive councilor from 30 to 25 years. (N)
7. Lower the standard of proof in criminal insanity hearings.
8. Raise the monetary threshold for jury trials in civil cases to suits exceeding $5,000. (N)
9. Eliminate the power of the governor and the council to extend a legislative recess. (N)
10. Restrict the use of retirement system assets to the retirement system.

Although the Constitutional Convention proposed the 10 changes listed above, there were also 3 legislative proposals which are not listed.

1. Have New Hampshire voters, since their Constitution became effective, approved a convention every 10 years?
2. As you can see, New Hampshire's new constitutional amendments cover issues that are important to most States. Find out what other States have recently held constitutional conventions, and whether the proposed changes were similar to these.
3. Do you agree with all these changes? Choose one change and write a paragraph agreeing or disagreeing with it.

"Every voter who wishes to vote "Yes" will make a cross in the square near the word "Yes". Every voter who wishes to vote "No" will make a cross in the square near the word "No". If no cross is made in either square for any question, the ballot will not be counted on that question."

(Questions Relating to Constitutional Amendments Proposed by the Convention to Revise the Constitution.)

4. Are you in favor of amending the constitution to change the size of New Hampshire's legislative bodies without changing the total number of legislators by decreasing the current size of the House of Representatives by 12, to 388 members, and increasing the current size of the Senate by 12, to 36 members? (This question is submitted to the voters by the 1984 Constitutional Convention by a vote of 270 Yes, 76 No.) YES ☐ NO ☐

5. Are you in favor of amending the constitution to provide for annual sessions of the legislature; and to restrict mileage payments for actual attendance on legislative days to a maximum of 45 legislative days per session but not after the first day of July of each year? (This question is submitted to the voters by the 1984 Constitutional Convention by a vote of 278 Yes, 76 No.) YES ☐ NO ☐

6. Are you in favor of amending the constitution to reduce the age requirement for persons being elected to the office of state senator or executive councilor from 30 years of age to 25 years of age? (This question is submitted to the voters by the 1984 Constitutional Convention by a vote of 279 Yes, 66 No.) YES ☐ NO ☐

7. Are you in favor of amending the constitution to provide that, in order to commit a person in a criminal insanity proceeding, the state must establish that the person is potentially dangerous to himself or to others and suffers from a mental disorder by a standard of "clear and convincing evidence" only, rather than by the current, stricter standard of "proof beyond a reasonable doubt"? (This question is submitted to the voters by the 1984 Constitutional Convention by a vote of 297 Yes, 35 No.) YES ☐ NO ☐

In 1984, New Hampshire voted on proposed changes in the State constitution. A portion of this ballot is shown above. This vote concerned amendment, not revision.

themselves. Ratification is by popular vote in every State except Delaware.

As to the second set of terms, *amendment* usually refers to a limited change, dealing with only one or a few provisions in a constitution. The term *revision* is regularly used to describe changes of a broader scope, for example, an entire new document.

Constitutional Conventions

The convention is the usual device by which new constitutions have been written and older constitutions revised. To this point, at least 230 conventions have been held among the States.[6]

In every State the legislature has the power to call a convention, and that call is generally subject to voter approval.[7] In 14 States the question of calling a convention must be submitted to the voters at regular intervals.[8] The people commonly vote three times during the process of constitution-making by convention: (1) to authorize the calling of the convention, (2) to elect delegates, and (3) to ratify or reject the document framed by the convention.

[6]In several States, a *constitutional revision commission* may be used to propose extensive changes in the existing document or to frame a new one. Only the Florida constitution expressly provides for a revision commission; there it must assemble every twentieth year and may itself submit unlimited changes to the voters. In other States, a revision commission is generally set up by and reports to the legislature, which may modify and send some or all of its proposals on to the voters.

[7]In Alaska, Georgia, Louisiana, Maine, South Carolina, South Dakota, and Virginia, the legislature may call a convention without first submitting the question to the voters. In Florida, Montana, and South Dakota, a convention may be called by the initiative process.

In four States the legislature itself may propose a new constitution to the people—in California, Georgia, and Oregon by a two-thirds vote in each house, and in Florida by a three-fifths vote. In those States, then, the legislature may both call a convention and act as such a body itself.

[8]Every 20 years in Connecticut, Illinois, Maryland, Missouri, Montana, New York, Ohio, and Oklahoma; every 16 years in Michigan; every 10 years in Alaska, Iowa, New Hampshire, and Rhode Island; and every 9 years in Hawaii.

Amendment by Initiative Proposal

State	Number of Petition Signatures Required[a]	Distribution of Signatures	Popular Vote for Ratification
Arizona	15% of votes cast for governor	—	Majority on amendment
Arkansas	10% of votes cast for governor	Must be at least 5% in each of 15 counties	Majority on amendment
California	8% of votes cast for governor	—	Majority on amendment
Colorado	8% of votes cast for secretary of state	—	Majority on amendment
Florida	8% of votes cast for presidential electors	Must be 8% in each of one-half of congressional districts	Majority on amendment
Illinois[b]	8% of votes cast for governor	—	Majority at election, or three-fifths on amendment
Massachusetts[c]	3% of votes cast for governor	Not more than one-fourth from any one county	Majority on amendment[d]
Michigan	10% of votes cast for governor	—	Majority on amendment
Missouri	8% of votes cast for governor	Must be 8% in each of two-thirds of congressional districts	Majority on amendment
Montana	10% of votes cast for governor	Must be 10% in each of two-fifths of legislative districts	Majority on amendment
Nebraska	10% of votes cast for governor	Must be at least 5% in each of two-fifths of counties	Majority on amendment[e]
Nevada	10% of all voters who cast ballots	Must be 10% in each of three-fourths of counties	Majority on amendment in two consecutive general elections
North Dakota	4% of the population	—	Majority on amendment
Ohio	10% of votes cast for governor	Must be a least 5% in each of one-half of counties	Majority on amendment
Oklahoma	15% of highest vote cast	—	Majority on amendment
Oregon	8% of votes cast for governor	—	Majority on amendment
South Dakota	10% of votes cast for governor	—	Majority on amendment

[a]Based on number of votes cast in most recent general election, except in North Dakota.
[b]Initiative process may be applied only to Article IV, The Legislature.
[c]Initiated measure must first be approved by at least one-fourth of legislature, sitting in joint session, at two successive legislative sessions before submission to voters for ratification.
[d]Majority must equal at least 30% of all votes cast in election.
[e]Majority must equal at least 35% of all votes cast in election.

ENRICHMENT Assign to the class: Find out if our State allows proposal by initiative. If so, has it happened recently? Describe the proposed amendment, and how the people voted.

Proposal of Amendments

Most of the formal changes in State constitutions come as amendments—additions or modifications or deletions of particular provisions—rather than by revision. The latter involves large-scale changes in much of the document, or an entirely new one.

Convention Proposal The convention is most often used for the broader purpose of revision, but it can be and sometimes is used in several States to propose amendments. Because conventions are both costly and time consuming, they are not widely used for amendment purposes.

Legislative Proposal Most amendments added to State constitutions are proposed by the legislature. The process varies from State to State as you can see in the accompanying table on page 549.

The process is comparatively simple in some States, quite difficult in others. As a general rule, and as one might expect, the easier the process the more often are amendments proposed and adopted. The California constitution, which dates from 1879, has been amended some 450 times. Conversely, the Massachusetts document of 1780, in force for twice as long, has been changed only some 115 times.[9]

Only a few States limit the number of amendments that may be submitted to the voters at any one election. For example, in Kentucky no more than four amendments may be offered and in Kansas, five.

Proposal by Initiative The voters themselves can propose constitutional amendments in 17 States. They may do so by the **initiative,** a process in which a certain number of qualified voters must sign petitions in favor of the proposal. The proposal then goes directly to the ballot for approval or rejection by the people.

[9]The number of amendments that have been proposed and added to each State's constitution is the result of several other factors, too. Two factors figure most prominently: the *content* of the document (whether well drawn or not, flexible or rigid and detailed, and so on) and its *age.*

Voters in Oregon may propose amendments to their State constitution, but note the specific requirements that must be met before their signatures will be accepted as valid.

INSTRUCTIONS

FOR CIRCULATORS

— A petition circulator must be an elector of the state.
— Only electors may sign a petition.
— Do not use ditto marks.
— It is advisable to use a pen or indelible pencil for signing petitions.
— Only one circulator may collect signatures on any one sheet of a petition.
— All signers on any one sheet of a petition must be electors of the same county.
— The signature sheet affidavit must be completed for each sheet by the circulator of that sheet.
— It is unlawful for a person circulating a petition to knowingly make any false statement to any person who signs it or requests information about it.
— It is unlawful to circulate or file a petition knowing it to contain a false signature.

FOR SIGNERS

— Only electors may sign a petition.
— Do not use ditto marks.
— Sign your full name, as you did when you registered, and fill in the date on which you signed the petition, your residence address and your precinct in the spaces provided.
— If your signature is difficult to read, print your name clearly in the space provided.
— It is unlawful to sign any person's name other than your own. Do not sign another person's name under any circumstances.
— A woman should sign her own name, not her husband's or her husband's initials; for example, "Mary A. Jones", not "Mrs. John A. Jones."
— It is unlawful to sign a petition more than once.
— It is unlawful for a person to knowingly sign a petition when not qualified to sign it.

PROSPECTIVE PETITION

FOR STATEWIDE ☐ INITIATIVE ☐ REFERENDUM MEASURE

To the Secretary of State:

We, the undersigned, request that the Attorney General prepare a ballot title for the attached proposed measure to be submitted to the people of Oregon for their approval or rejection at the election to be held on ______________ 19___.

Amendment by Legislative Proposal

Legislative Vote Required	Popular Vote for Ratification	States
Majority vote, each house	Majority on amendment	Arizona, Arkansas, Missouri, New Mexico[a], North Dakota, Oklahoma, Oregon[b], Rhode Island, South Dakota
Majority vote, each house	Majority at election	Minnesota
Two-thirds vote, each house	Majority on amendment	Alaska, California[b], Colorado, Georgia[b], Idaho, Kansas, Louisiana, Maine, Michigan, Mississippi, Montana, South Carolina[e], Texas, Utah Washington, West Virginia
Two-thirds vote, each house	Majority at election	Wyoming, Hawaii[c]
Three-fourths vote, each house	Majority on amendment	Connecticut[c]
Three-fifths vote, each house	Majority on amendment	Alabama, Florida, Kentucky, Maryland, Nebraska[d], New Jersey[c], North Carolina, Ohio
Three-fifths vote, each house	Majority at election or three-fifths on amendment	Illinois
Three-fifths vote, each house	Two-thirds on amendment	New Hampshire
Majority vote, each house at two successive sessions	Majority on amendment	Connecticut[c], Hawaii[c], Indiana, Iowa, Nevada, New Jersey[c], New York, Pennsylvania[f], Virginia, Wisconsin
Majority vote in joint session, at two successive sessions	Majority on amendment	Massachusetts
Two-thirds vote, each house, two successive sessions	(No popular vote required)	Delaware
Majority vote, each house at one session; two-thirds vote each house at next session	Majority of votes cast for governor	Tennessee
Two-thirds vote of senate, majority vote of house at one session; majority vote of each house at next session	Majority on amendment	Vermont

[a]Amendments relating to voting qualifications or to the guarantee of equal treatment of Spanish-speaking students in public schools may be proposed only by a three-fourths vote of each house, and must be approved by three-fourths of all voting in the election, including at least two-thirds of those voting in each county.
[b]By a two-thirds vote in each house, the legislature may propose a revision of all or a part of the constitution.
[c]Either method may be used in Connecticut, Hawaii, New Jersey.
[d]Majority for ratification must equal at least 35 percent of the total vote cast in the election.
[e]Subsequent majority vote of each house required to complete ratification.
[f]An "emergency amendment" may be proposed by two-thirds vote of each house at a single session; such an amendment must be ratified by a majority of voters who vote in the election.

*ENRICHMENT Use the above chart to discuss constitutional change. Ask the class how your State amends its constitution. How would students amend their constitution?

Voter advice is given on a ballot question (left); hand-marked ballots are dropped into a ballot box in a town which does not have voting machines (right).

The process varies among these 17 States. As you can see in the table on page 547, Illinois and Massachusetts place great restrictions on its use.

Ratification of Amendments

In every State except Delaware, an amendment must be approved by vote of the people in order to become a part of the constitution.[10] As with the matter of proposal, the ratification process varies among the States, as shown in the tables on pages 547 and 549.

Typically, the approval of a majority of those voting on an amendment adds it to the State constitution. A greater margin, however, is needed in some States. On many occasions, constitutional amendments have been defeated in those States even though they received more *yes* than *no* votes. Most often, that has happened because, as we suggested on page 216, many voters fail to vote on ballot measures.

[10]In Delaware if an amendment is approved by a two-thirds vote in each house of the legislature at two successive sessions, it then becomes effective. In South Carolina, *final* ratification, after a favorable vote by the people, depends on a majority vote in both houses of the legislature. Both the Alabama and South Carolina constitutions provide that amendments only of local, as opposed to Statewide, application need be approved only by the voters in the affected locale.

FOR REVIEW

1. **Identify:** formal amendment, informal amendment, revision, Constitutional Convention.
2. Why must constitutions provide for formal change?
3. Why has the process of informal amendment been less significant at the State than at the national level?
4. What device is usually used for writing a new constitution or revising an existing one?
5. How are amendments to State constitutions usually proposed? Ratified? What is the initiative?

BUILDING GOVERNMENT SKILLS

Analyzing Your State's Constitution

Only a very few people ever read State constitutions. Perhaps not more than one in 100 people in your State has read the State's fundamental law. Despite this, State constitutions remain vital documents.

State constitutions are defined in detail in this chapter, but they can also be described as sets of rules about rule-making. Most, if not all, of the major problems facing a State government involve one or several provisions of the State's constitution. Public policy questions at the local level also involve the State constitution.

By studying your State's constitution and by analyzing it, you can learn much about how your State government works. You will also learn of the civil rights guaranteed to you by the constitution.

You can obtain a copy of your State's constitution in your school or local library or from the office of the Secretary of State.

1. Outline your State's constitution. Use the outline of the Federal Constitution on pages 724–725 as a model.
2. Analyze the constitution based on how State constitutions were described in the chapter: How is it organized? What basic principles are set out? Is it relatively brief or long? Does it seem difficult or easy to amend? How many times has it been amended? What amendments (if any) were added at the most recent election? Rejected? Does it contain any obsolete provisions? Any statutory material?
3. Use your outline and analysis to compare and contrast your State's constitution to the Federal Constitution. Can you make any generalizations about the similarities? About the differences?
4. If you could change one provision of your State's constitution, which one, if any, would you change? Why?

4. The Need for Reform: Some General Observations

As You Read, Think About:

- What problems are found in most State constitutions.
- Why most State constitutions are in need of reform.
- How the failure to separate fundamental law from statutory law affects most State constitutions.

Almost without exception, State constitutions are in urgent need of reform. The typical document is outdated. It is cluttered with unnecessarily detailed provisions, overly burdensome restrictions, and obsolete sections. It carries much repetitious, even contradictory, material and much clumsy and confusing language. Not least among its sins are those of omission: it fails to deal with many of the pressing problems that the States and their local governments face in the latter part of the 20th century.

Unfortunately, this indictment may be read against even the newest and most recently rewritten documents. They carry over much from earlier documents, with little or no change.

The need for reform can be pointed up in several ways. The odds are very good that, wherever you live, a close look at your State's constitution will reveal that need for reform.* Another way is to look at the 50 documents as a whole in terms of two points: length and age.

*REINFORCEMENT Have the class discuss: In what ways are State constitutions outdated? Does your State's constitution need to be reformed?

In shopping centers and on busy streets, registered voters may be approached to sign petitions to support or oppose some legislative action as in the top photo. Below, a polltaker gathers data on voter opinions.

The Problem of Length

The first State constitutions were quite short. They were meant to be statements of basic principle and organization. Purposely, they left to the legislature and to time and practice the task of filling in the details as they became necessary.

The longest of the original documents was the Massachusetts constitution of 1780, with some 12,000 words. The shortest, New Jersey's constitution of 1776, ran to only some 2,500 words.

Through the years State charters have become longer and still longer. Today, most State charters are between 15,000 and 30,000 words. The shortest are those of Vermont (1793) with fewer than 7,000 words, and Connecticut (1965), not quite 9,000 words long. At the other extreme, the Alabama document of 1901 now contains more than 170,000 words, more than can be found in most novels today.

Why are the documents so long? Why are most of them becoming even longer? The leading reason is popular distrust of government, a long-established fact of American political life. That distrust has often led to quite detailed provisions, specifically aimed at preventing the misuse of governmental power. Many restrictions on that power, which might be set out in ordinary law, have been purposely placed in the fundamental law, where they cannot be easily ignored or readily, and quietly, changed.

Special interest groups—veterans' organizations, private utilities, the liquor industry, and many others—long ago learned that public policies of benefit to them are much safer in the constitution than in a mere statute. These groups, which usually have a good deal of political clout, have managed to carve out their special preserves in the constitutions of most States.

Then, too, court decisions can be and often have been overridden by constitutional amendments. This is exactly what happened with capital punishment (page 154).

There has been a marked failure in nearly every State to separate *fundamental law*—that which is of basic and lasting import and

REINFORCEMENT Discuss: The States must separate fundamental law from statutory law, not only to keep the constitution to a reasonable length, but to protect the rights of all citizens.

ought to be in the constitution—from **statutory law.** The latter should be the subject of laws passed by the legislature.

There may be some gray areas in drawing the line between what is fundamental law and what is not. Nevertheless, we can pick a few from dozens of examples that are obviously not in the gray area: Who can seriously argue the fundamental character of the New York constitution's provision authorizing an exchange of 10 acres of State land for 30 acres owned by the village of Saranac Lake, in order to give the village a place for a dump? Or the California ban on taxing fruit and nut trees planted within the past four years?

Two other factors have had much to do with the ever-lengthening shape of State constitutions. First, the functions performed by the States, and by many of their local governments, have multiplied in the past few decades. That development has called forth many new constitutional provisions. Second, the "people," in fact, organized groups, have not been stingy in the use of the initiative where it is available.

The Problem of Age

If you look again at the table on page 542, you can see that most of the State constitutions are rather old. Though most of them have been amended dozens of times, those changes have, as often as not, added to the clutter of the documents.

The Oregon constitution offers a typical example. It was written by delegates, most of them farmers, to a territorial convention in 1857, and it became effective in 1859. It has now been amended more than 170 times, runs to some 30,000 words, and contains *two* Articles VII and *eleven* Articles XI!

Like most of the other State constitutions, it is overloaded with statutory material and in serious need of reform. For example, one of its Articles XI gives nearly 2,000 closely detailed words to the subject of veterans' farm and home loans. Another Article XI spends some 500 words to give the State and its local governments the right to issue bonds "for the purpose of planning, acquisition, construction, alteration or improvement of facilities for the collection, treatment, dilution, and disposal of all forms of waste in or upon the air, water, and lands of this State."

Like most of the other States' documents, the Oregon constitution includes many obsolete, outdated provisions. One of those provisions, for example, prohibits any person who engages in a duel from ever holding any public office in the State. Another provision forbids the legislature to tax, spend any money, or contract any debt for the construction of a capitol building before the year 1865. Still another requires that all voters in school district elections be at least 21 years of age.

From the table on page 542, you can see that the oldest of all the fundamental laws in force today are those of Massachusetts (1780), New Hampshire (1784), and Vermont (1793). In all, 19 States still have the constitutions with which they entered the Union. Twenty-two States have documents at least 100 years old, and 15 constitutions were written 50 to 100 years ago.

Several States have adopted revised constitutions in recent years: Michigan in 1963; Connecticut in 1965; Florida in 1968; Illinois, North Carolina, and Virginia in 1970; Montana in 1972; Louisiana in 1974; and, most recently, Georgia in 1982. Even counting them, the average age of the 50 State constitutions is nearly 90. Most of the more recent documents are subject to the same criticisms we have aimed at State constitutions over the past few pages.

FOR REVIEW

1. Why are most State constitutions in urgent need of reform?
2. Why has the typical State constitution become a longer and still longer document?
3. Which is the oldest of the present-day documents? The most recently revised? When was your State's present constitution adopted?

SUMMARY

Each State has a written constitution, the State's fundamental law. It sets out the structure of that State's government and divides its powers among its several branches. It both authorizes the exercise of power by the State and its local governments and restricts the use of governmental power. The constitution is the supreme form of State law; however, it may not conflict with any provision in the national Constitution nor with any other form of federal law.

With independence, 11 of the original States adopted new constitutions: in Connecticut and Rhode Island the colonial charters were adapted to that purpose. Generally, the people had little part in the constitution-making process until 1780. In that year, the Massachusetts constitution was written by a popularly elected convention and then ratified by a vote of the people. Since then, popular participation has been the rule in State constitution-making.

Despite their many variations, the first State constitutions were born out of the common revolutionary atmosphere and were similar documents. Each of them stated the principles of popular sovereignty, limited government, separation of powers, and checks and balances. In each State, the legislature was relatively strong, the governor weak, and the suffrage confined to the propertied class.

The present-day constitutions, direct descendants of those early documents, also vary in particulars. But all have major sections making similar provision for certain basic principles, civil rights guarantees, the structure of State and local government, the powers and process of government, and methods of constitutional change.

The details of the process of formal constitutional change differ among the States. The proposed revision or replacement of a constitution is generally the function of a convention. Amendments may be proposed by the legislature in every State, and in 17 of them by initiative petition. Ratification must be by popular vote in all but Delaware.

Nearly every one of the State constitutions is in urgent need of reform. Most are outdated, too lengthy and detailed, and overloaded with statutory material.

CHAPTER REVIEW

Key Terms/Concepts*

popular sovereignty (541)
limited government (541)
separation of powers (541)
checks and balances (541)
judicial review (542)
bill of rights (542)
amendment (544)
initiative (548)
statutory law (553)

*These terms are included in the Glossary.

Keynote Questions

• **1.** What is the purpose of a State's constitution? Why may it be said that "constitutions govern governments"?

• **2.** Why may each State's constitution not conflict with federal law?

• **3.** What provisions and omissions in the first State constitutions make these early documents seem undemocratic by today's standards?

• **4.** What basic principles are included in each State's constitution?

• **5.** What civil rights protections, not found in the federal Bill of Rights, are contained in several States' constitutions?

• **6.** What aspects of government structure, powers, and processes are covered by State constitutions?

• **7.** Why can State constitutions not be changed as ordinary law is changed?

• **8.** What is a preamble?

*The dots represent skill levels required to answer each question or complete each activity:
• requires recall and comprehension • • requires application and analysis • • • requires synthesis and evaluation

- **9.** Why are the provisions for formal change so important a part of each of the 50 State constitutions?
- **10.** What is the purpose of a constitutional convention?
- **11.** How does proposal by initiative differ from a legislative proposal?
- **12.** What factors have influenced the length of State constitutions?
- **13.** Why is the age of a State constitution a problem?

Skill Application

Formulating a Hypothesis: In order to better understand how government works or why, it is important to be able to formulate hypotheses. A hypothesis is an unproven generalization based on limited data. A hypothesis helps to explain how the data are related.

We often formulate hypotheses in everyday life. For example, suppose you found that the price of orange juice in the grocery store had risen by $.20. You remember that you heard on the news about a cold spell in the South. With these two pieces of data—increase in orange juice price and cold spell in the South—you hypothesize that the cold spell ruined some of the orange crop in Florida, and because of this, the price rose.

All hypotheses have to be tested to determine whether or not they are valid. However, the first step is to formulate a hypothesis.

Listed below are two sets of data about State constitutions. For each set of data, formulate a hypothesis that might explain the relationship of the data.

1. a. Seven of the original 13 State constitutions began with a lengthy bill of rights.
b. In many original State constitutions, most of the authority of the State was given to the legislature.
c. The governor, according to the first State constitutions, was limited to serving one term.

2. a. State constitutions describe the duties and powers of the State's governor, legislature, and courts.
b. Some State constitutions contain provisions concerning veterans, land sales, and public utilities.
c. The first State constitutions were short; through the years these documents have become longer and longer.

For Thought and Discussion

- ••• **1.** Can your State's constitution be amended through the initiative process? If not, do you think the process should be available in your State? If so, is the process used often? Do you think the initiative process undercuts the principle of representative government? Why or why not?
- ••• **2.** If each of the States abolished their constitutions, would government be more or less democratic? Why?
- • **3.** In *The Federalist*, No. 57, Alexander Hamilton set this standard for constitutions:

  > The aim of every political constitution is, or ought to be, first to obtain men who possess most wisdom to discern, and most virtue to pursue, the common good of the society; and in the next place, to take the most effectual precautions for keeping them virtuous whilst they continue to hold their public trust.

  How do the six categories used to describe State constitutions serve to meet this standard? In what ways do the problems of length and age keep States from meeting this standard?
- •• **4.** Why do you think that statutory provisions remain in State constitutions? How would you propose to eliminate these? What problems might you encounter?
- •• **5.** What are the advantages and disadvantages of a process by which a State constitution is easily amended? Of a process by which a State constitution can be amended only with difficulty?

Suggested Activities

- • **1.** Interview a State legislator (or staff member), or a State judge (or staff member), about your State's constitution, its contents, and changes he or she would recommend.
- ••• **2.** After examining your State's constitution, write a proposed amendment. Debate various proposals in class.

Representative government is in essence self-government through the medium of elected representatives of the people.
–CHIEF JUSTICE EARL WARREN
REYNOLDS v. SIMS, 1964

20 The State Legislatures

CHAPTER OBJECTIVES

To help you to:

Learn · Know · Understand

Why all but one of the 50 State legislatures are bicameral.

The critical issue of apportionment.

The powers held by State legislatures.

The structure and organization of the State legislatures.

The legislative process at the State level.

The process of direct legislation: the initiative and referendum.

THE SIZE OF the legislature, the details of its organization, the frequency and the length of its sessions, and its official name vary among States. But, in every State the legislature is the lawmaking branch of State government. It is charged with translating the public will into the public policy of the State.

The legislature has been described as "the powerhouse of State government." With its vast lawmaking powers, it creates the energy needed to operate the governmental machinery of the State and its local units.

What is generally called "the Legislature" is officially known by that title in 27 States. In 19 others it is the General Assembly.[1] In North Dakota and Oregon it is called the Legislative Assembly, and in Massachusetts and New Hampshire, the General Court.

Forty-nine of the 50 State legislatures have two chambers. The upper house is called the Senate.[2] The lower house in most is the House of Representatives. In Nevada,

[1]Arkansas, Colorado, Connecticut, Delaware, Georgia, Illinois, Indiana, Iowa, Kentucky, Maryland, Missouri, North Carolina, Ohio, Pennsylvania, Rhode Island, South Carolina, Tennessee, Vermont, Virginia.

[2]Nebraska applies that name to its single chamber.

*ENRICHMENT Have students discuss: If you were planning to run for public office, would you run for your State legislature or for Congress? Why?

Nebraska's unicameral legislature, referred to as "the Senate" in that State, has 49 members (called "Senators") elected on a nonpartisan ballot for four-year terms. *Facing page:* At their seats are two members of the Texas State Senate.

California, and New York, it is the Assembly, and in Maryland, Virginia, and West Virginia, the House of Delegates.

1. Bicameralism

As You Read, Think About:

- What the difference is between bicameralism and unicameralism.
- Why all but one State have bicameralism.
- What the major arguments are for and against bicameralism and unicameralism.

Except for Nebraska, all State legislatures are **bicameral** today.[3] Bicameralism has been the dominant pattern for two major reasons. The first is the influence of both English and colonial experience. The second is the tendency among the newer States to follow the lead of the original States and the National Government.

The first colonial legislatures were typically **unicameral.** The elected representatives commonly sat with the governor and his council in the making of colonial laws. In most of the colonies, as the popularly chosen legislators gained political power, the governor's council took on the role of a second, upper chamber. Thus, well before the Revolution, most of the colonies had bicameral bodies structured much like the British Parliament. After independence, those States that remained unicameral soon established two-chambered legislatures.

Unicameralism vs. Bicameralism

Unicameralism is often recommended as one of the major steps that could raise the quality of State legislatures, their procedures, and their product.

Those who support bicameralism have long argued that one house can act as a

[3]Nebraska's voters approved the creation of a unicameral legislature in 1934, and that body held its first session in 1937. Georgia until 1789, Pennsylvania until 1790, and Vermont until 1836 also had unicameral legislatures.

check on the other in a two-chambered body and so prevent unwise legislation. The critics of bicameralism point to the many examples where that theory has not worked well in practice. Indeed, very often the real check on "hasty and ill-considered legislation" comes from places outside the legislature. Those checks come from the governor's veto, from coverage in and comment by the news media, and from public opinion.

The fact that bicameralism has worked well in Congress is often used to support it at the State level. The bicameral Congress is a reflection of the *federal* character of the Union, however. The States are not federal; they are *unitary* in form. Remember, too, a bicameral Congress came out of the Connecticut Compromise. It was a practical solution to a very serious political dispute at the Philadelphia Convention in 1787.

Until fairly recently, many supported bicameralism because they favored a "little federal plan" for their own State's legislature. That is, despite the nonfederal character of the States, they favored a body with one house based on area and the other on population. Otherwise, they claimed, the more populous cities would so dominate the lawmaking process that small-town and rural interests would be practically unrepresented. As we shall see in a moment, the Supreme Court destroyed their position in 1964 when it ruled that the 14th Amendment's Equal Protection Clause requires that *both* houses of a State's legislature *must* be apportioned on the basis of population.

Critics of bicameralism argue that in the complicated structure and procedures of a two-house system, special interests have more opportunities to block popular legislation. As an example, they point to conference committees, which are unnecessary in a unicameral legislature; see page 323.

The advocates of unicameralism also point out that with two chambers involved in the lawmaking process, it is almost impossible to fix the responsibility for some legislative action or inaction. With only one house to watch, the people can more readily discover and understand what the legislature is doing. In a one-house system, the legislature itself, they add, can more easily watch lobbyists' activities for special-interest groups.

Although the Nebraska experience has not proved a cure-all, it appears to have worked well for some 50 years. Legislative costs have been cut, greater efficiency has been achieved, and lobbyists' influence has been reduced. A generally higher caliber of legislator has been chosen. Moreover, the typical legislator has been more responsive to his or her constituents than under the old two-house system.

All in all, the weight of the argument favors unicameralism. Nevertheless, proposals to adopt it elsewhere have made almost no headway since the Nebraska reform. Both tradition and inertia stand on the side of bicameralism. So, too, does a lack of knowledge and interest on the part of the general public.[4]

FOR REVIEW

1. What is the basic function of each State's legislature?
2. By what official name is the legislature, and each of its houses, known in your State?
3. Why are all of the State legislatures except one bicameral today?
4. What major arguments are usually made for bicameralism? For unicameralism?

2. Size and Apportionment

As You Read, Think About:

- How State legislatures vary in size.
- What the significance is of the "reapportionment revolution."

The size of the legislature varies among the 50 States. In each State, however, there are constitutional provisions for how seats in each house are to be distributed.

[4]Notice, however, that nearly all *local* legislative bodies—city, county, and special district—are composed of only one chamber; see Chapter 23.

*REINFORCEMENT Ask the class: Should the State legislature be unicameral or bicameral? Discuss in terms of legislative costs, monitoring lobbyists and special-interest groups, checks and balances, etc.

Size

There is no exact figure for the ideal size of a legislative body. Two basic considerations are important, however. First, a legislature, and each of its houses, should not be so *large* as to hamper the orderly conduct of the people's business. Second, it should not be so *small* that the many views and interests within the State cannot be adequately represented.

The *upper house* in most States has from 30 to 50 members. Alaska's senate has only 20 seats, however, and Minnesota now has the largest upper house with 67 members.

The *lower house* usually ranges between 100 and 150 members. However, only 40 representatives are elected to Alaska's lower chamber. On the other hand, Pennsylvania has 203 seats in the house and New Hampshire, an almost incredible 400.

Sanders in the Kansas City Star

"Great Scott! We've lost our vote!"

Apportionment

Each State's constitution makes some provision for the **apportionment** of legislative seats in the State. That is, it states how those seats will be allocated, or distributed, among districts in the State.

On what basis should the legislature be apportioned? Should the seats be distributed among districts of about equal populations? Or should the seats be apportioned on the basis of area, with district lines drawn according to area and/or economic factors? Or should one house be based on population and the other on area?

Clearly, these are vital questions. The answers largely identify the groups and regions within a State that control its legislative machinery and shape its public policies.

Most State constitutions have always provided for population as the only or at least the major basis for the distribution of legislative seats. As we shall see, population is now the only standard that may be used, no matter what the provisions of a State's constitution may be.

Reapportionment Most State constitutions direct the legislature to adjust periodically the distribution of its seats to account for increases, decreases, and shifts of population in the State. Usually, the constitution orders the legislature to reapportion itself every 10 years, in line with the most recent federal census.[5]

The "Reapportionment Revolution" Although the pattern has now changed, most State legislatures were long controlled by the rural, less populated sections of the State.

The general pattern of rural overrepresentation and urban underrepresentation lasted long after the United States became a

[5]In some States reapportionment is no longer a legislative function—a direct result of the "reapportionment revolution." In Ohio, for example, reapportionment is now done by a commission composed of the governor, secretary of state, auditor, and a representative from each of the major parties. A few States now provide that if the legislature fails to reapportion itself, or does so inadequately, it will be done otherwise—in Maine, for example, the Supreme Judicial Court and in Oregon the secretary of state.

nation of mostly city-dwellers. Two factors accounted for this imbalance: (1) The fact that many legislatures failed to reapportion themselves and (2) the frequent use of area as well as (or instead of) population as a basis for **reapportionment.**

Baker v. Carr, 1962 The long-standing fact of rural domination has now come to an end in nearly all States.

In *Baker* v. *Carr,* 1962, the Supreme Court held, for the first time, that federal courts could properly hear cases in which it is claimed that the way a State legislature is apportioned violates the 14th Amendment's Equal Protection Clause.[6]

In *Baker* the Court decided only a *jurisdictional* question. It did not face this critically important and controversial question: On what factor(s) can a reapportionment be based? But cases presenting the question were not long in coming.

Reynolds v. Sims, 1964 In a now lengthy series of cases, the Court has consistently applied the "one-man, one-vote" rule. That is, the Court has consistently held that population is the *only* constitutionally acceptable basis for the apportionment of seats in a legislative body. Said the Court in the leading case, *Reynolds* v. *Sims,* from Alabama in 1964:

> Legislators represent people, not trees or acres. Legislators are elected by voters, not farms or cities or economic interests . . . The Equal Protection Clause requires that the seats in both houses of a bicameral State legislature must be apportioned on a population basis.[7]

Since 1964, the Court has regularly rejected all other bases of apportionment.

The significance of the "reapportionment revolution," begun with *Baker* v. *Carr* in 1962, cannot be overstated. Within only a couple of years, some redistribution of legislative seats took place in each one of the 50 States. In a few States, only minor adjustments were needed to meet the "one-man, one-vote" standard. In many States, however, the redistricting was extensive. In most cases, changes came only after hard-fought court, legislative, and ballot battles.

Today there is very little malapportionment at the State legislative level. A majority of the seats in most State legislatures are now held by lawmakers from metropolitan areas—from cities and their suburbs. Only in the few largely rural States, where the economy is mostly agricultural, has the "reapportionment revolution" had little effect.

To grasp the vital importance and the practical meaning of the "reapportionment revolution," look at it in these terms. The *location* of political power, *where* that clout is based, has recently shifted in most States. In several of them, that shift has been quite dramatic. Most of the real muscle in State politics was moved from the once-dominant rural interests to the cities and suburbs. Remember this, too: the State legislatures draw congressional districts and so have a large impact on the election of the members of the national House of Representatives, as we noted on pages 298–301.

FOR REVIEW

1. **Identify:** "one-man, one-vote" rule.
2. How many members serve in each house of your State legislature?
3. What did the Supreme Court hold in *Baker* v. *Carr,* 1962? Why was that decision so important?
4. What did the Supreme Court hold in *Reynolds* v. *Sims*? Why was that decision so important?

[6]Before *Baker,* both federal and State courts regularly refused to hear cases involving the composition of legislative bodies. Such cases were held to involve "political questions," to be decided by legislatures or voters, not by the courts.

[7]In *Reynolds* the Court voided an Alabama apportionment that had been in place since 1921 and by 1964 had produced rural-urban splits of as much as 43 to 1 among senate districts and 16 to 1 among house districts. When it decided *Reynolds,* the Court also disposed of very similar cases from 14 other States. In each of them, as in *Reynolds,* the Court held that the State legislature was unconstitutionally apportioned because of substantial violations of the "one-man, one-vote" (population equality) standard.

*ENRICHMENT Have the class discuss: On what basis should State legislatures be apportioned? What formula would work best in your State?

3. Qualifications, Election, Terms, Compensation

As You Read, Think About:

- What informal qualifications are placed by the realities of politics on those who seek seats in State legislatures.
- How legislators are elected.
- How important the lack of adequate compensation is on the willingness of men and women to serve in State legislatures.

The qualifications that legislators must meet for membership in State legislatures differ from State to State. The length of sessions, terms of office, and the salaries paid to lawmakers also vary from State to State.

Qualifications

Every State's constitution sets out certain qualifications—of age, citizenship, and residence—for membership in the legislature. They do vary but, on the whole, they are easy to meet.

In most States, representatives must be at least 21, although in several States the minimum age for service in either house is now 18. Most States set a higher minimum age for senators, usually 25.

Regularly, a legislator must be a citizen of the United States, a legal resident of his or her State, and also live in the district he or she represents.

The realities of politics place still other* —*informal* and more meaningful—qualifications on those who seek seats in the legislature. These factors of *political availability* vary somewhat from State to State, and even from district to district within a State. They have to do with a candidate's vote-getting abilities and are based on such characteristics as occupation, name familiarity, party identification, race, national origin, and the like. The "right" combination of these factors will help a candidate to win nomination and then election to the legislature. One or more "wrong" ones can often spell defeat.

A Texas State senator waves to constituents.

Election

Legislators are chosen by popular vote in every State. Candidates for the legislature are nominated in party primaries, and opposing candidates face one another in a partisan general election. Legislative nominees are picked by party conventions in only a few States—Delaware, for example. In only one State, Nebraska, are the candidates nominated in nonpartisan primaries. There the opposing candidates are not identified by party in the general election, either.

In most States the lawmakers are elected in November of even-numbered years. This is not the case in four States, however. In Mississippi, New Jersey, and Virginia, legislative elections are held in November and in Louisiana, in December, of the *odd*-numbered years. This is done to separate State and local issues from national politics.

Terms

From the table on page 562, you can see that legislators serve either two-year or four-year terms. Senators are usually elected for longer terms than are their colleagues in the lower house. They serve for four years in 37 States and Nebraska and for two years in the other 12. Representatives are picked for two-year terms in all but four States: Alabama, Louisiana, Maryland, and Mississippi.

The rate of turnover in legislative seats —the number of new members in each session—is fairly high among the States. Typically, there are more new faces in the lower house than in the senate each term. This is mostly the result of the larger size of the house and the usually longer senate

*REINFORCEMENT Have the class discuss the formal and informal qualifications for membership in the State legislature. Which factors of "availability" count most heavily in your State?

The State Legislatures

State	Year Held	Regular Sessions: Limitations on Length*	Regular Sessions: Month Convenes	Upper House: No. of Members	Upper House: Term	Lower House: No. of Members	Lower House: Term	Salary of Members[d]
Alabama	annual	30 L days	Feb	35	4	105	4	$10,050 ann.
Alaska	annual	120 C days	Jan	20	4	40	2	$46,800 ann.
Arizona	annual	None	Jan	30	2	60	2	$15,000 ann.
Arkansas	odd[g]	60 C days	Jan	35	4	100	2	$7,500 ann.
California	[f]	None	Dec	40	4	80	2	$37,105 ann.
Colorado	annual	140 C days	Jan	35	4	65	2	$17,500 ann.
Connecticut	annual[b]	5 months[c]	Jan	36	2	151	2	$15,000 ann.
Delaware	annual	June 30	Jan	21	4	41	2	$20,000 ann.
Florida	annual	60 C days	Apr	40	4	120	2	$18,900 ann.
Georgia	annual	40 L days	Jan	56	2	180	2	$10,000 ann.
Hawaii	annual	60 L days	Jan	25	4	51	2	$15,600 ann.
Idaho	annual	None	Jan	42	2	84	2	$30 per day
Illinois	annual	None	Jan	59	4	118	2	$35,661 ann.
Indiana	annual	61 L days, 30 L days	Jan	50	4	100	2	$11,600 ann.
Iowa	annual	None	Jan	50	4	100	2	$14,600 ann.
Kansas	annual	None, 90 C days	Jan	40	4	125	2	$54 per day
Kentucky	even	60 L days	Jan	38	4	100	2	$100 per day
Louisiana	annual	60 L days	Apr	39	4	105	4	$16,800 ann.
Maine	annual[b]	100 L	Dec	35	2	151	2	$15,000 bien.
Maryland	annual	90 C days	Jan	47	4	141	4	$22,000 ann.
Massachusetts	annual	None	Jan	40	2	160	2	$30,000 ann.
Michigan	annual	None	Jan	38	4	110	2	$36,520 ann.
Minnesota	odd[g]	120 L days	Jan	67	4	134	2	$23,355 ann.
Mississippi	annual	90 C days[e]	Jan	52	4	122	4	$10,000 ann.
Missouri	annual	6 months[c]	Jan	34	4	163	2	$20,244 ann.
Montana	odd	90 L days	Jan	50	4	100	2	$4,694 session
Nebraska	annual	90 L days, 60 L days	Jan	49	4	—	—	$4,800 ann.
Nevada	odd	60 C days[a]	Jan	21	4	42	2	$104 per day
New Hampshire	annual	45 L days	Jan	24	2	400	2	$100 ann.
New Jersey	annual	None	Jan	40	4	80	2	$25,000 ann.
New Mexico	annual[b]	60 C days, 30 C days[b]	Jan	42	4	70	2	$75 per day
New York	annual	None	Jan	61	2	150	2	$43,000 ann.
North Carolina	odd[g]	None	Jan	50	2	120	2	$10,140 ann.
North Dakota	odd	80 L days	Jan	53	4	106	2	$90 per day
Ohio	annual	None	Jan	33	4	99	2	$33,243 ann.
Oklahoma	annual	90 L days	Jan	48	4	101	2	$20,000 ann.
Oregon	odd	None	Jan	30	4	60	2	$18,600 bien.
Pennsylvania	annual	None	Jan	50	4	203	2	$35,000 ann.
Rhode Island	annual	60 L days[a]	Jan	50	2	100	2	$5 per day
South Carolina	annual	5 months[c]	Jan	46	4	124	2	$10,000 ann.
South Dakota	annual	40 L days	Jan	35	2	70	2	$3,200 session
		35 L days	Jan					$2,800 session
Tennessee	odd[g]	90 L days[a]	Jan	33	4	99	2	$12,500 ann.
Texas	odd	140 C days	Jan	31	4	150	2	$7,200 ann.
Utah	annual	45 C days	Jan	29	4	75	2	$65 per day
Vermont	odd[g]	None	Jan	30	2	150	2	$320 per wk.
Virginia	annual	30 C days, 60 C days	Jan	40	4	100	2	$11,000 ann.
Washington	annual	105 C days, 60 C days	Jan	49	4	98	2	$14,500 ann.
West Virginia	annual	60 C days	Jan	34	4	100	2	$6,500 ann.
Wisconsin	annual	None	Jan	33	4	99	2	$29,992 ann.
Wyoming	annual[b]	40 L days	Jan	30	4	64	2	$75 per day
		20 L days[b]	Feb					

Note: See footnotes on facing page.

*ENRICHMENT As a project, assign the class to determine what the qualifications, election, terms, and compensation are for the members of your State legislature for the current year.

term. It also reflects the fact that members of the lower house often seek "promotion" to the upper chamber.

In any given year, more than one-fourth of all the 7,461 State legislators in the country are serving their first term in office. The major reasons for this high turnover seem to be two: low pay and partisan politics. The fact that legislators generally remain in office longer in those States where the pay is higher and where one party regularly wins most of the elections suggests just how important these reasons are.

Compensation

How much legislators are paid is a very important matter—and not only to legislators themselves. Some people feel that the honor and the supposed prestige of sitting in the State's lawmaking body are payment enough. Some people apparently think that legislators are not worth paying at all. But most people seem to be quite unaware of the matter.

However, the cold, hard facts are these: It costs money for legislators to live, and it costs them money to take time away from their normal occupations to serve the State. Far too often, capable men and women refuse to run for the legislature because of the financial sacrifices they would have to make.

From the table, you can see the salaries paid in each State. Most States also provide some sort of additional allowances. Oregon is a fairly typical example. The basic salary is now $775 a month or $18,600 for the *biennium*, a two-year period. In addition, each member receives an expense allowance: $50 for each day of the legislative session, which usually lasts for about 180 days, and for each day he or she attends interim committee meetings (between sessions). Each member also has a $400 per month expense allowance for each month in which the legislature is not in session. The total compensation per member, when both salary and allowances are combined, comes to about $17,500 a year.

Legislative pay is set by the constitution in a few States. In most States, the legislature decides the matter. Lawmakers often hesitate to vote for higher salaries for themselves, usually because of their worries about voter reactions. They fear that the action will be used against them in the next election. They often attain the same end by raising the expense allowances.

Legislative Sessions

As the table shows, 38 States hold their regular legislative sessions on an annual basis, and the California legislature meets in a continuous two-year session. The other 11 States hold regular sessions only every other year.

Most States have turned to annual sessions only in the past decade or so, as it has become more and more apparent that the legislative workload cannot be handled on an every-other-year-for-a-few-months basis.

In four of the annual-session States —Connecticut, Maine, New Mexico, and Wyoming—the second, that is, every other, session is a budget session. That meeting is limited either entirely or mainly to budget and related fiscal matters.

As a general rule, regular sessions, whether annual or biennial, are becoming longer.

*L = legislative (in-session) days; C = calendar days.
[a]Indirect limit; legislators' pay and/or expenses cease, but session may continue.
[b]Annual session every other year is budget session, held in even-numbered years.
[c]Approximate length. In Connecticut, session must adjourn by the Wednesday after first Monday in June (odd years) and May (even years); in Missouri, session must adjourn by June 30 in odd-numbered years and by May 15 in even-numbered years; in South Carolina, first Thursday in June.
[d]Most States also provide substantial expense allowances for legislators.
[e]Except 125 days every fourth year (the first year of a new gubernatorial term).
[f]Continuous two-year session.
[g]Session may be (and in practice is) divided, so often meets in even years also.
Sources: State constitutions and statutes, and information furnished by appropriate State officials and Council of State Governments.

Party Control of Governorships and State Legislatures, 1987*

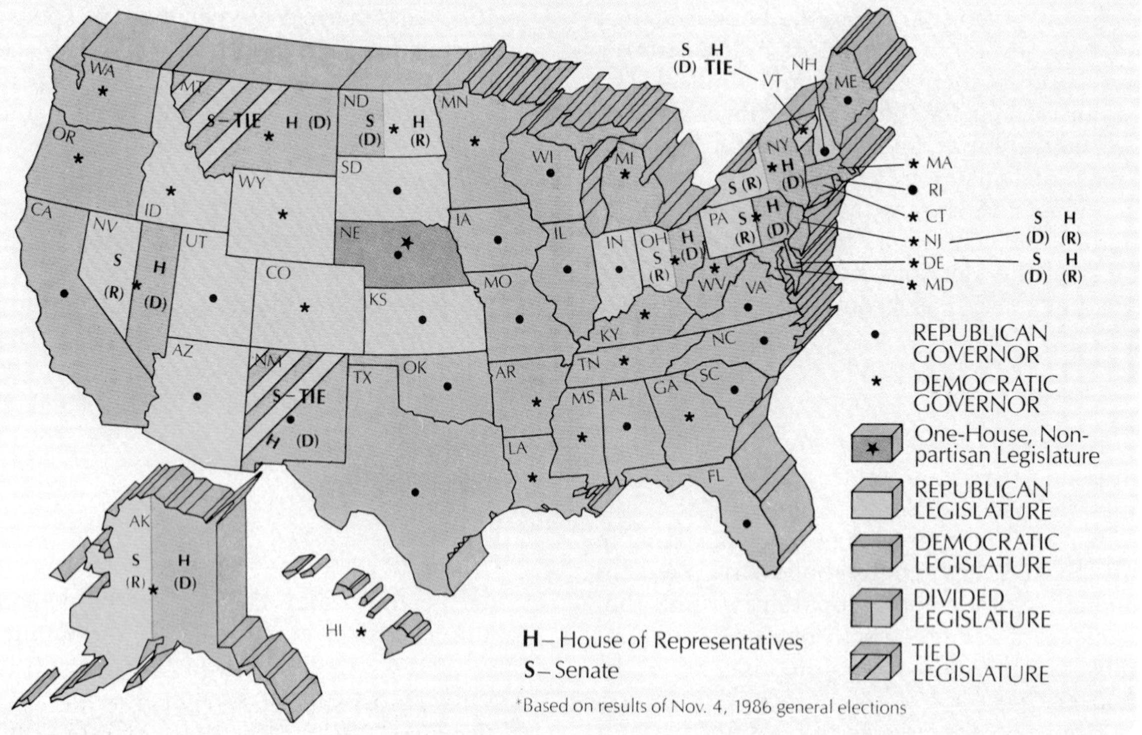

According to the map above, which party controls both houses of the legislatures in the majority of the States? The governorships?

As the table shows, some State constitutions put a time limit on sessions, but that is gradually disappearing.

Special Sessions

A special session of the legislature may be called by the governor in every State, and by the legislature itself in just over half of them.

As the term suggests, special sessions are held to allow the lawmaking body to take up urgent matters between its regularly scheduled meetings. These sessions are fairly common today, especially where regular sessions still meet only every other year.

Another kind of special session is the "veto session." A veto session now meets in eight States: Connecticut, Hawaii, Louisiana, Missouri, New Jersey, Washington, Utah, and Virginia. That session is held shortly after each regular session. The purpose of the veto session is to allow the legislature to reconsider bills vetoed by the governor in the days immediately following the adjournment of a regular session.[8]

FOR REVIEW

1. **Identify:** veto session, special session.
2. Why are the informal qualifications for membership in the legislature more meaningful than the formal ones?
3. For what terms are the members of each house chosen in your State? How much are they paid?
4. Why do most State legislatures now meet yearly?

[8] In those States where veto sessions are not held (most States), either the governor has the pocket-veto power or the legislature cannot react to post-session vetoes until it meets in its next session; see pages 587–589. Montana has recently taken a different approach. There the secretary of state conducts a mail poll of legislators on the question of overriding post-session vetoes.

*ENRICHMENT Use the map above to discuss the effects of party control in State governments. How might the domination of one party over another influence the course of legislation? What type of situation exists in your State?

4. Powers of the Legislature

As You Read, Think About:

- What legislative powers are possessed by State legislatures.
- What nonlegislative powers are possessed by these legislatures.

In the American federal system, governmental power is divided between the nation and the States. The National Government has only those powers *delegated* to it by the Constitution, and the States have those powers *reserved* to them by that document. As you recall, the 10th Amendment lays out the basic division of powers between the nation and the States:

> The powers not delegated to the United States by the Constitution, nor prohibited by it to the States, are reserved to the States, respectively, or to the people.

Most of the powers reserved to each State are in fact held by its legislature.

None of the 50 State constitutions sets out a complete list of all powers held by the legislature. Nor could it—for, in the complex arrangements of federalism and of separation of powers, all of those powers that are not given to some other agency of government in the United States belong to the State legislatures.

To put this rather complicated point another way: In each State the legislature has all of those powers (1) that the State constitution does not grant exclusively to the executive or judicial branches of the State's government or its local units, and (2) that neither the State nor the United States Constitution denies to the legislature.

Legislative Powers

Each State's legislature can pass any law that does not conflict with any federal law or with any part of that State's constitution. It is, therefore, impossible to catalog all of the powers held by a State's legislature. Even so, most of the State constitutions do list several of the legislature's more important powers. Those most often mentioned include the powers to tax, spend, borrow, establish courts, define crimes and provide for their punishment, regulate commercial activities, and maintain public schools.

*The powers of every legislature include the extremely important *police power*—the State's power to protect and promote the public health, safety, morals, and welfare, as we noted on pages 131–133. Although this broad power cannot be more exactly defined, it is the basis for thousands of State laws. Among them are laws that require vaccinations and authorize quarantines, restrict automobile exhaust emissions, forbid certain forms of gambling, regulate the sale and use of alcoholic beverages, prohibit the ownership of dangerous weapons, fix highway speed limits, impose safety requirements in industrial plants, limit campaign contributions and spending, set the minimum legal age for marriage, and provide for food

Translating the public will into public policy is the main function of State legislators.

*REINFORCEMENT Ask the class: What State laws affect your lives? Are these laws the result of the exercise of legislative or nonlegislative powers?

PERSONALITY PROFILE

Thomas Jefferson: Building State Governments

Thomas Jefferson's co-authorship of the Declaration of Independence and his two terms as President (1801–1809) reflect his influence on national politics. But Jefferson was also a leader of local politics in his native Virginia. His service to Virginia made him a staunch defender of States' rights as a limitation on federal power.

Jefferson's fervent belief in individual liberties led him to support States' rights as the best defense for those liberties. Excessive powers in the Federal Government, Jefferson believed, could lead to a revival of the tyranny that had caused the Revolutionary War. He thought many functions of government were best left to local officials, who he believed were more accountable to the citizens. Defense and foreign policy were the Federal Government's tasks according to Jefferson. Local matters should remain the State's exclusive concerns.

Jefferson did recognize the potential for even State governments to become tyrannical and took measures to ensure individual rights. If any one branch of government gained too much power, individual liberty, Jefferson feared, would be eroded. He believed strongly in the doctrine of separation of powers and helped build a system of checks and balances among the three branches of the Virginia government.

In the 1790s Jefferson's emphasis on States' rights made him a leader of a new national party, the Democratic-Republican Party. The Federalist Party, in contrast, led by Jefferson's opponent Alexander Hamilton, sought to centralize power in the Federal Government. These two opposing views of the appropriate role of the Federal Government came to a head when Congress enacted the Alien and Sedition Laws in 1798. The laws, supported by the Federalists, were aimed at freedom of speech and of the press and were born from a fear that the revolutionary sentiments released by the French Revolution might find fertile soil in the new nation.

Jefferson, responding to the obvious infringement of individual liberty inherent in the laws, saw the matter as a question of States' rights and drafted the Kentucky Resolutions. In the resolutions Jefferson claimed that the States had the right to nullify a federal law if the State believed the law to be unconstitutional. Jefferson's views were not accepted into law, but were widely popular at the time and helped turn public opinion against the Federalist Party.

In *Notes on Virginia* (1784), Jefferson described his view of the ideal State government.

> An elective despotism was not the government we fought for, but one which should not only be founded on free principles, but in which the powers of government should be so divided and balanced among several bodies of magistracy, as that no one could transcend their legal limits, without being effectually checked and restrained by the others. For this reason that convention which passed the ordinance of government, laid its foundation on this basis, that the legislative, executive, and judiciary departments should be separate and distinct, so that no person should exercise the powers of more than one of them at the same time.

1. Why did Jefferson fear excessive power in the Federal Government?
2. Contrast Jefferson's views with those of Hamilton and the Federalists.

inspections. The list could go on for several pages. In a word, the powers of the State legislatures are enormous.

Nonlegislative Powers

Each State legislature has certain nonlegislative powers as well. These powers are in addition to those it exercises in the making of law.

Executive Powers Some legislative powers are executive in nature. For example, the governor's power to appoint certain State officials is often subject to approval by the legislature, or at least its upper house. In some States the legislature itself appoints one or more executive officeholders. Thus, the secretary of state, elected by the voters in most States, is chosen by the legislature in Maine, New Hampshire, and Tennessee. The treasurer is also selected by the legislature in each of those States and in Maryland. The lawmakers also pick the attorney general in Maine.

Judicial Powers Each State legislature also has certain judicial powers. The chief illustration is the power of impeachment. In every State except Oregon, the legislature can remove any executive officer or judge through that process.

Each legislature also has judicial powers with regard to its own members. Thus, disputes about the election or the qualifications of a member-elect are usually decided by the house involved in the matter. Then, too, because legislators themselves are not subject to impeachment, each chamber has the power to discipline—and, in extreme cases, even expel—any of its members.

Constituent Powers As we saw in Chapter 19, each State legislature plays a significant role in both the constitution-making and the constitutional amendment processes. When the legislature calls a constitutional convention or proposes an amendment to the State constitution, it does not make law. Rather, the legislature exercises a nonlegislative power, the *constituent* power.

FOR REVIEW

1. **Identify** legislative powers, nonlegislative powers, constituent power, police power.
2. Why is the police power an extremely important legislative power?

5. Organization of the Legislature

As You Read, Think About:

- How State legislatures are organized and who their presiding officers are.
- How committees are used in the legislatures.
- What the principal function is of interim committees.

In general terms, each of the State legislatures is organized in much the same manner as Congress.

The Presiding Officers

Those who preside over the sessions of the nation's 99 State legislative chambers are almost always powerful political figures—in the legislature itself and elsewhere in State politics.

The lower house in each of the 49 bicameral legislatures elects its own presiding officer, known everywhere as the *speaker.*

The senate chooses its own presiding officer in only 22 States. In the other 28 States, the lieutenant governor serves as the *president of the senate.*[9] Where the lieutenant governor does preside, the senate selects a *president pro tempore* to serve when he or she is absent.[10]

---

[9]The office of lieutenant governor exists in 43 States today, see pages 580, 590. In 15 of them, the lieutenant governor does not double as the president of the senate, however. The Tennessee senate elects its presiding officer (known, uniquely, as the "speaker") and that officer is also, by statute, that State's lieutenant governor.

[10]The term *pro tempore* means "temporary." In practice this officer's title is generally shortened to *president pro tem.*

*REINFORCEMENT Have the class discuss the State's judicial power to impeach. Is this a legislative or nonlegislative power?

Women are becoming increasingly prominent in State government. Here, Minnesota's first woman majority leader, Representative Connie Levi, addresses fellow legislators.

Except for the lieutenant governors, each of these presiding officers is chosen by a vote of the full membership in his or her legislative chamber. In fact those who fill leadership posts are usually picked by the majority party's caucus in that body just before the legislature meets.

The chief duties of those presiding officers center on the conduct of the legislature's floor business—and are a major source of their power. They refer bills to committee, recognize members who seek the floor, and interpret and apply the rules of their body to its proceedings.

Unlike the Speaker of the House in Congress, the speaker in nearly every State appoints the chairperson and other members of each house committee. The senate's president or president pro tem has the same power in just over half the States. The presiding officers regularly use the power to name committees as they do their other powers: to reward their friends, punish their enemies, and otherwise use their influence on the legislature.

The Committee System *

The number of measures introduced at each session of a legislature varies among the States. The measures run from 500 or so in some of the smaller States to several thousand in many of the larger ones. This flood makes the committee system as necessary at the State level as it is in Congress. Also as in Congress, much of the work of the legislature is done in its committee rooms.

Committees make their most important contributions to the lawmaking process (1) as they sort out those bills that should reach the floor and (2) when they inform the full chamber on measures they have handled.

The **standing committees** in each house are generally set up by subject matter, such as committees on highways, local government, elections, the judiciary, education, and so on. It is to them that all bills are sent, and it is in them that most bills are given the closest attention they receive. A bill may be amended or even very largely rewritten in committee or, as often happens, ignored altogether. The question of whether a bill will ever reach the floor is usually decided by the committee to which it has been sent.[11]

The typical legislature has 15 to 20 standing committees in each house. As in most other matters, there is much variation among the States. Thus, Massachusetts now has only five standing committees in each house, whereas in some States the number runs to 30 or more in both chambers.

The number of members per committee also varies greatly. Ten to 12 is a fairly common size, but in some States some committees have as many as 40 or more members. Moreover, a legislator may serve on three or four committees. In short, in too many States too little attention is given

---

[11]The "pigeonholing" of bills is as well known in the States as it is in Congress; see page 328. In fact, in most States one of the standing committees in each house is regularly the "graveyard committee," a body to which bills are sent to be buried. The judiciary committee, to which bills may be referred "on grounds of doubtful constitutionality," often fills this role. A vivid illustration of a graveyard committee existed for several years in the lower house in landlocked Oklahoma: the Committee on Deep Sea Navigation.

*ENRICHMENT Ask the class to find out if their State legislator is a presiding officer, and on which committees he or she sits. How can these committee assignments aid their constituents?

The committee system is an integral part of the State legislative process.

to the obvious relationship between the number and the size of committees, on the one hand, and how well the legislature functions, on the other.

Joint committees—permanent groups made up of members of both houses—can produce substantial savings of legislative time and effort. These committees have been used extensively in a few States for several years, notably in Massachusetts, Maine, and Connecticut. In fact, the legislatures in Maine and Connecticut use *only* joint committees. Nearly half the State legislatures now have one or more joint committees.

The use of **interim committees**, which function *between* legislative sessions, is also growing. These groups study particular problems and then report their findings and recommendations to the next session.

FOR REVIEW

1. **Identify:** joint committees, interim committees.
2. Who presides over the lower house in your State? The upper house?
3. Why does the legislature rely so heavily on its committees?

6. The Legislative Process

As You Read, Think About:

- What the sources of bills are that are introduced into State legislatures.
- What role pressure groups have.
- How State legislators cast their votes.
- What veto power a governor has.
- What recommendations have been made to improve State legislatures.

The basic function of the legislature is to make law. You can follow the major steps in the legislative process in a typical State in the diagram on page 572. Because that diagram is fairly descriptive, and the lawmaking machinery in each State is much like that in Congress (pages 324–337), we shall comment only briefly here.

Sources of Bills

Legally, only a member may introduce a bill in either house in any of the State legislatures. So, in the strictest sense, legislators themselves are *the* source of all measures introduced. In broader terms, however, the lawmakers are the real source, the authors, of only a relative handful of bills.

A large number of bills come from *public* sources, from officers and agencies of State and local government. The governor's office is always a major source. Every governor has a legislative program of some sort, and often, an extensive and ambitious one. Much of what the lawmakers do is shaped by proposals from the governor's office.

Many bills are born in other public places too. Take, for example, a measure to raise the maximum interest rate the State can pay on the money it borrows. That bill would very likely be prepared in the State treasurer's office. Similarly, an increase in the maximum penalty for some crime might be proposed by the attorney general. A bill to give cities a larger share of the money raised by the State's gasoline tax might have come from a city council or from a city manager's office.

Bills also come from a wide range of *private* sources. In fact, the largest single source for proposed legislation in the States appears to be pressure groups. Remember, those groups and their lobbyists have one overriding purpose: to influence public policy to benefit their own special interests. Of course, some bills do originate with private individuals—lawyers, physicians, business people, farmers, and other citizens—who, for one reason or another, think that "there ought to be a law . . ."

Voting

In most States votes on the floor may be taken in a number of ways, and for a number of purposes.

The most important vote on a measure usually comes when the bill is finally to be approved or rejected by the chamber. In most of the States this point is at third reading. Votes are taken at several other steps in the legislative process, however. Among them are votes on amendments, on motions to limit or to close debate, and on motions to re-refer, or to send a measure back to committee.[12]

[12]One of these other votes may in fact be the critical vote that decides the fate of a measure. The real test of a bill may come with the vote on a key amendment to it. Once that vote is taken, the question of final passage or defeat may be just a formality.

Viva Voce Most votes taken on the floor are voice votes called *viva voce*. The presiding officer puts the question and then judges the outcome from the shouts of "aye" versus the shouts of "no." The major advantage of voice votes is the speed with which they can be taken. The method allows the presiding officer some very useful latitude in judging the result, however.

Division of the House Some votes are taken by a process known as a *division of the house,* also called a "standing vote." Those for and then those against a motion rise and are counted by the presiding officer. A standing vote is usually taken when the chair's reading of a voice vote has been challenged from the floor.

Teller Vote In this process members' votes are cast and counted as they file past "tellers." Usually, two members (the tellers, one for and one against the question) stand in front of the chamber, while the other members pass between them telling their votes. A teller vote usually produces a more reliable tally than either a voice or a standing vote. Like those two other methods, the teller vote does not report how each member has cast his or her vote.

Record Vote Commonly called a "roll-call vote," a record vote is one in which each member's vote is recorded—put in the permanent record. Roll calls are time consuming, and they are often used as a delaying tactic. *

The time a legislature spends in the voting process can be substantial over the course of a session. As a result, many States now use electronic devices ("scoreboards") to speed voting.

The Governor's Veto

Once the legislature has approved a measure, it must go to the governor, who, in every State except North Carolina, has the **veto** power.

We shall look at the veto and the governor's other legislative powers in the next chapter. For now, these quick points: Unlike

*REINFORCEMENT Ask the class: Which one of the voting procedures discussed records how each member voted?

FOCUS ON:

How Do Representatives "Represent"?

State legislators must cast hundreds of votes in each legislative session. Many votes involve only relatively routine matters—questions of organization or procedure, minor bills, and so on. But a large number of them, including some organizational and procedural votes, are of far-reaching importance.

So, very few questions relating to the lawmaking process can be more vital than this: How do legislators see their role in the governing process? Or, put it another way: On what basis should a legislator vote?

In broad terms, each lawmaker has four options here: He or she can behave (vote) as a *trustee,* as a *delegate,* as a *partisan,* or as a *politico.*

Those who see their role as that of trustee believe that each question is to be decided on its own merits. For them, conscience and independent judgment are—must be—their guides. Trustees try to vote questions as they see them, no matter what views may be held by a majority of their constituents or by any of the other groups that seek to influence their decisions.

The delegates often see themselves as the agents of those who elected them. They believe that they should—must—follow the wishes of their constituents. Delegates are, therefore, willing to suppress their own views, ignore those of the party's leaders, turn deaf ears to the arguments of their legislative colleagues and of special interests from outside their districts, and so on—all "for the sake of the folks back home."

The partisans are those legislators who owe their first allegiance to their political party. They feel duty-bound to support the party's platform and to vote in line with the positions that are taken by its leaders. Most studies of legislative voting behavior indicate that partisanship is the leading factor in influencing legislators' votes on most important measures.

The politicos attempt to combine the basic elements of the other three roles. They try, as best they can, to balance these often conflicting factors: their own views of what is best for their constituents and/or the State as a whole, the political facts of life, and the peculiar pressures of the moment.

1. If you were in the State legislature, which of these roles would you choose for yourself? Why would you reject each of the others? Could you play different roles on different issues? How?
2. Into which of these four categories—trustee, delegate, partisan, politico—would you place each of the legislators who now represent your locale (and you) at the State capital?

the President, the governors of 43 States have the **item veto**. That is, those governors can veto parts of a bill without rejecting the whole measure.[13] Remember, the governor, like the President, can use the *threat* of a veto as a lever to influence the actions of the legislature.

[13]In all States except Indiana, Maine, Nevada, New Hampshire, Rhode Island, Vermont and, of course, North Carolina. The power is usually, but not everywhere, restricted to items in appropriations bills.

Improving the State Legislatures

The State legislatures are human creations; like their creators, none is perfect.

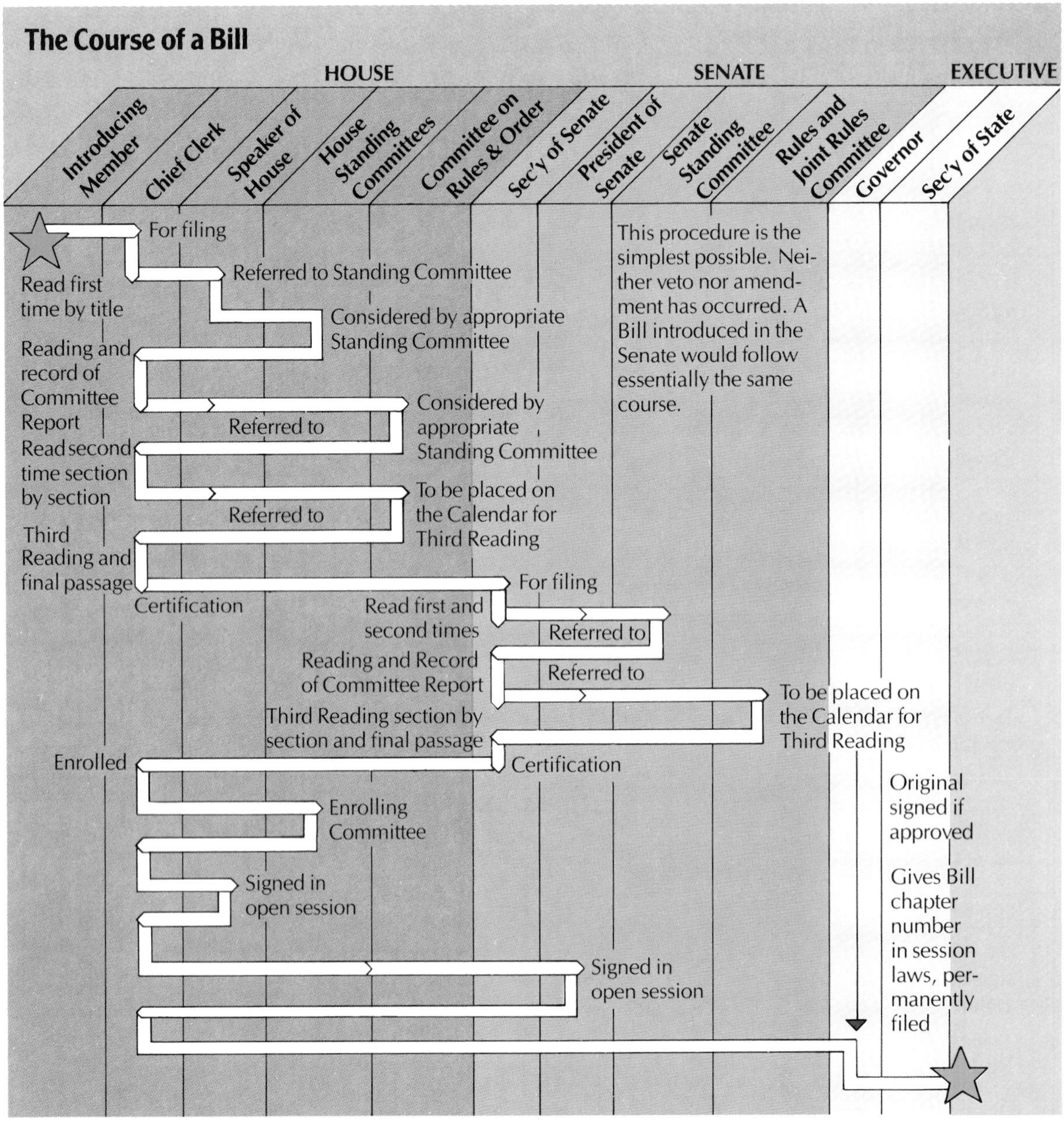

Steps in the lawmaking process of each State are much like those of Congress.

Fortunately, however, we are now seeing some real improvements among them. Among the more important changes: the move to annual sessions, significant pay increases, the growing use of electronic data processing, and greatly expanded staff and research support for legislators.

Much remains to be done. Several authorities—and especially the Council of State Governments and the National Conference of State Legislatures—have long urged certain steps to upgrade the 50 State lawmaking bodies. They recommend that:

1. Restrictions on the length of regular sessions be removed. The legislature should be able to meet as often and for as long as needed.

REINFORCEMENT Ask the class to study the above diagram, and discuss its similarities to the course of a bill in the U.S. Congress (diagram on p. 333).

2. Adequate salaries and allowances be provided—enough to permit competent persons to serve as legislators.
3. Legislative terms of office be lengthened and staggered to provide for continuity in membership.
4. The lieutenant governor be eliminated as a legislative figure.
5. More effective regulation of lobbyists and of legislators' conflicts of interest be enacted.
6. Legislators and committees be given adequate professional research, secretarial, and other staff aides and facilities.
7. Legislative rules be revised as needed to speed up procedures, but with due regard for deliberation and for minority viewpoints.
8. Committees be reduced in number where possible, and be organized in terms of subject matter, equalization of workload, and cooperation between the two houses.
9. Committees operate "in the sunshine" —that is, hold open meetings; public hearings should be held on all major bills, and permanent and public records of all committee actions should be kept.
10. The legislature control the auditing function to make sure that public funds are spent in the manner and purposes for which the legislature appropriated them; see page 591.

FOR REVIEW

1. **Identify:** voice vote, division of the house, teller vote, record vote, roll call.
2. What appears to be the largest single source for bills in the several State legislatures?
3. Does the governor of your State have the item-veto power? Why is the governor's ability to threaten use of the veto an important part of the legislative process?
4. Summarize the 10 recommendations for the improvement of State legislatures.

7. Direct Legislation

As You Read, Think About:

- What the forms of the initiative are.
- What the forms of the referendum are.

Beginning with South Dakota in 1898, several States now allow voters to take a direct part in the lawmaking process, through the *initiative* and the *referendum*.

The Initiative

On page 548 we noted that the voters may propose—initiate by petition—constitutional amendments in 17 States. In 21 States voters may initiate ordinary statutes, as well.[14]

Among these 21 States, the initiative takes two quite different forms: the more common *direct initiative* and the little-used *indirect initiative*.[15]

In both the direct and indirect initiative, a certain number of qualified voters must sign initiative petitions to propose a law. The key difference between them lies in what happens to the proposed measure once enough valid signatures have been collected.

Where the direct initiative is used, the measure goes directly to the ballot, usually at the next general election. If the voters approve it, it becomes law. If not, it dies.

In the indirect initiative, the proposal goes *first* to the legislature. That body may pass it, making it a law. If it does not, the measure *then* goes to the voters.

The number of voters who must sign petitions to initiate a statute varies. In North Dakota, for example, that number must be at least 2 percent of the population of the State. In Arkansas, Michigan, and Washington, it is 8 percent of the votes cast for governor in the

[14]Alaska, Arkansas, Arizona, California, Colorado, Idaho, Maine, Massachusetts, Michigan, Missouri, Montana, Nebraska, Nevada, North Dakota, Ohio, Oklahoma, Oregon, South Dakota, Utah, Washington, Wyoming. These 21 States also provide for the initiative at the local level. It can be found in at least some cities and counties in about half the other States, as well.

[15]Maine and Massachusetts provide only for the indirect form. Michigan, Nevada, Ohio, South Dakota, Utah, and Washington have both.

BUILDING GOVERNMENT SKILLS

Writing a Letter to the Editor

Has a newspaper or magazine article ever made you want to respond in some way? One way to express your thoughts and concerns is to write a letter to the editor.

Letters to the editor are letters of opinion written by readers. In newspapers, these letters are often included in the Op-Ed (opinion and editorial) page. Magazines usually publish these letters on the pages immediately following the table of contents.

People write letters to the editor to express their opinions about a particular public policy, about an editorial viewpoint, or about the way a particular policy or event was reported. For example, a recent issue of a major daily newspaper contained letters to the editor concerning lay-offs by a major employer, equal pay for women, and distribution of emergency food aid in famine areas.

Newspapers and newsmagazines usually try to print the letters that best represent many peoples' opinions. They also tend to favor letters that are clearly written, interesting, and entertaining. When writing a letter to the editor, follow these guidelines:

- If you are commenting on a specific article or column, refer to the name of the reporter or columnist, the main idea of the article or editorial column, and the date it appeared in the newspaper or magazine.
- Be concise. Most letters to the editor consist of two to four paragraphs.
- Be direct. State your position clearly and offer two or three reasons for it.
- Offer a fresh perspective. For example, you may notice that in a column or article about school closings, the reporter neglected to include viewpoints of students. You can provide this viewpoint in your letter to the editor.

Letters to the editor are written like normal business letters except that the salutation is: "To the Editor."

1. Read the letters to the editor in a newspaper for several days. Make a copy of one letter. In a brief paragraph, explain what makes it effective.
2. Read the news section of a newspaper. Write a letter to the editor on one article you have read. For an example, note the "sample" letter below.

416 Main St.
Santa Anna, TX 00001
April 20, 1986

Editor
Santa Anna *News*
Santa Anna, TX 00001

To the Editor:

In the *News'* October 16 article about funding for Route 14, reporter Hope neglected to mention its controversy.

As a community member, I am concerned about the increase in noise, air pollution, traffic, and accidents that will result from the extension. My neighbors and I feel that it threatens to divide a community.

Perhaps the State legislature would consider allocating more funds for Route 14 so that it can be built around our community.

Sincerely,

Susan James

last election, and in Arizona, 10 percent of all registered voters in the State.

As fairly typical examples of the process, Montana's voters dealt with two initiative measures at the 1984 general election. They approved one of them—a law to permit the sale of dentures by licensed dental technicians, as well as by licensed dentists. The measure they defeated would have eliminated the State's milk price control program.

* The Referendum

The **referendum** involves the submission, or referral, of legislative acts to the voters. Three different forms of the referendum are now used among the States: the *mandatory,* the *optional,* and the *popular.*

The mandatory referendum is involved whenever the legislature *must* refer a measure to the voters. Thus, in every State except Delaware, the legislature must submit proposed amendments to the constitution to the electorate. Several States require voter approval on bond measures.

An optional referendum measure is one that the legislature refers to the voters voluntarily. Such measures are rare. When one does appear on a State's ballot, it involves a "hot potato" question, one the lawmakers would rather not decide themselves.

The popular referendum is the form most often connected with the idea of "direct legislation." It is now found in 24 States, the 21 States with the statutory initiative and three others: Maryland and New Mexico, and Kentucky, where it may be used *only* for measures relating to property taxes.

Under the popular referendum, the people may demand that a measure passed by the legislature be referred to them for final action. In short, they may insist on the right to veto an act of the legislature.[16]

Their demand must be made by petitions signed by a certain number of qualified voters. That number varies—for example, 5 percent of the votes cast for governor at the last election in California and Nebraska, and 6 percent of all qualified voters in Ohio.

Most attempts to use the popular referendum in fact fail—usually because the opponents of a measure cannot find enough public support (cannot gather enough signatures) for their petitions. There is another important point: A State legislature, considering a measure that might be the target of a referral effort, sometimes short-circuits the process by exercising its optional referendum power.

As one of very few recent examples of the successful use of the device: In 1977 Oregon's legislature passed a measure to raise, in fact, double, the State's automobile and other motor vehicle registration and license fees. The bill's opponents, having lost their fight in the legislature, mounted a referendum campaign and soon gathered more than enough signatures. The new law, referred to the voters at the general election in November 1978, was voted down.

In each two-year span, the voters now face some 300 initiative and referendum measures among the States. Most of those measures appear on the general election ballots every other November.

FOR REVIEW

1. **Identify:** direct legislation.
2. What is the initiative? Compare the two basic forms of this device.
3. What is the referendum? Compare the three forms of this device.
4. Are these devices available in your State?

[16]In most States, a measure passed by the legislature does not become effective at the time it is enacted. Rather, it becomes a law at some later time, as fixed by the State constitution, usually 60 or 90 days after the legislature has adjourned. In most States with the popular referendum, then, this delay permits time to circulate petitions against a measure before it goes into effect. Thus, if the petition campaign is successful, the measure does not become effective unless and until it is finally approved by the voters.

There are some measures that must become effective at once. To these, the legislature may attach an *emergency clause*—a provision in the bill making it immediately effective upon enactment. To prevent the legislature from abusing its use of the emergency clause, several States allow the governor to veto such provisions. Oregon forbids an emergency clause in *any* tax measure.

*ENRICHMENT Have the class discuss: Both the initiative and the referendum offer the citizens of each State a direct role in the legislative process. Which involves a higher degree of participation?

SUMMARY

The legislature is the lawmaking branch of State government. It is a *bicameral*—two-chambered—body in all but one of the States. Only Nebraska has a *unicameral*—single-chambered—legislature today.

The size of the legislature and of each house varies considerably among the 50 States. In each of them, however, the seats in both houses are now apportioned on the basis of population equality. The long-standing pattern of rural over-representation in most States was swept away by the "reapportionment revolution" of the 1960s and early 1970s. That dramatic change was set off by the United States Supreme Court in *Baker* v. *Carr,* 1962. In a series of cases, beginning with *Reynolds* v. *Sims,* 1964, the Court has repeatedly applied the "one-man, one-vote" rule. It has consistently held that the 14th Amendment's Equal Protection Clause requires that legislative districts in each State contain substantially equal numbers of persons.

Each State's constitution sets out formal qualifications for membership in the legislature. The informal qualifications, those imposed by practical politics, are far more important, however. Legislators are elected by popular vote in every State. Senators are chosen for four-year terms in 38 States and for two-year terms in the other 12. Representatives serve two-year terms in 45 States and four-year terms in only 4. Legislative pay is relatively low in most States and, because of this, many qualified men and women refuse to run for legislative office.

The steadily increasing volume of legislative business has led most of the States to provide for annual legislative sessions. Only 12 States now schedule regular sessions on a biennial basis. Special sessions may be called by the governor in every State and by the legislature itself in just over half of them.

In each State the legislature possesses all of those governmental powers that (1) the State constitution does not give exclusively to the executive or judicial branches of the State's government or to its local units and (2) neither the State nor the National Constitution denies to the legislature. Its powers include the broad police power and other nonlegislative powers.

The organization and the lawmaking procedures of the typical State legislature are much like those of Congress. The presiding officers are powerful figures within the legislature and elsewhere in the politics of the State. As in Congress, a major share of the legislature's work is done in committees. Bills originate with public and private sources. The governor holds the veto power in every State except North Carolina. In 43 States that power includes the item veto.

Through devices of direct legislation—the initiative and the referendum—voters in some States may take a direct part in the lawmaking process.

CHAPTER REVIEW

Key Terms/Concepts*

bicameral (557)
unicameral (557)
apportionment (559)
reapportionment (560)
standing committee (568)
joint committee (569)
interim committee (569)
veto (570)
item veto (571)
initiative (573)
referendum (575)

*These terms are included in the Glossary.

Keynote Questions

• **1.** What is the main purpose of each State legislature?

• **2.** What two factors have influenced bicameralism among the State's legislatures?

• **3.** What are the advantages and disadvantages of bicameralism?

• **4.** Why is unicameralism often recommended as one of the major steps that could raise the

The dots represent skill levels required to answer each question or complete each activity: • requires recall and comprehension • • requires application and analysis • • • requires synthesis and evaluation

quality of State legislatures? Which State has a unicameral legislature?

- **5.** What two practices accounted for the imbalance between rural and urban representation in State legislatures?
- **6.** How was this imbalance—urban underrepresentation and rural overrepresentation—corrected?
- **7.** What is a veto session?
- **8.** In general, what powers does each of the State legislatures have? Why is it impossible to list all the powers?
- **9.** What are the chief duties of the presiding officers of the State legislatures? In what ways do these duties serve as a major source of power?
- **10.** What are the two most important contributions committees make to the State lawmaking process?
- **11.** How does an interim committee contribute to the State lawmaking process?
- **12.** How does the item-veto power differ from veto power?
- **13.** What is the difference between direct initiative and indirect initiative?
- •• **14.** Briefly describe in a paragraph each of the three forms of referenda.

Skill Application

Testing a Hypothesis: All hypotheses, unproven generalizations based on limited data, must be tested to determine whether or not they are valid. A valid hypothesis is based on fact and cannot be disproven by additional information.

To test a hypothesis, you gather factual data and determine whether the data supports or refutes your hypothesis. For example, if you hypothesize that an increase in wheat prices causes the price of bread to rise, you could check an almanac or *Statistical Abstract* to find out the price of wheat for the last 10 years. Then, check the price of bread for the last 10 years. If an increase in wheat prices is accompanied by an increase in bread prices for those 10 years, your hypothesis is valid for those 10 years.

In the course of checking a hypothesis, you might have to refine it. Based on new information, your original hypothesis would be more accurate if you stated that a shortage of wheat caused the price of bread to rise *over the last 10 years*. In refining your hypothesis, you should ask yourself certain questions. In this case, is an increase in wheat prices the only reason for the increase in the price of bread?

The following three sentences are hypotheses about State legislatures. Test each hypothesis, using information in this chapter. Then indicate whether or not the hypothesis is valid. If it seems to be valid, list other sources of information that might help prove or disprove the hypothesis.

1. The committee system in State legislatures is set up much like the committee system in the United States Congress.
2. The rural areas of most States remain more powerful than the urban areas.
3. The vote-getting characteristics of candidates for State legislator vary from State to State and district to district.

For Thought and Discussion

- ••• **1.** Do you support or oppose the direct participation of voters in lawmaking through the use of referenda or initiatives? Why?
- ••• **2.** The first recommendation for improving the State legislatures (page 572) states:

  > Restrictions on the length of regular sessions be removed. The legislature should be able to meet as often and for as long as needed.

  Do you agree or disagree with this recommendation? Why?
- ••• **3.** In his classic study, *The American Commonwealth* (1888), Lord Bryce wrote: "The legislature is so much the strongest force in the several States that they may almost call it government and ignore all other authorities." Does this observation still apply to your State? Why or why not?

Suggested Activities

- •• **1.** Draw a flow chart to show how a bill becomes law in your State's legislature.
- •• **2.** Interview one of your representatives in the State legislature or a member of a representative's staff. Some questions to ask might be: How do you view your job—as a trustee, a delegate, a partisan, or a politico? What are some of the challenges of the job? What are some of the important issues to be considered by the legislature?

Energy in the Executive is a leading character in the definition of good government.
—Alexander Hamilton

21 The Governor and State Administration

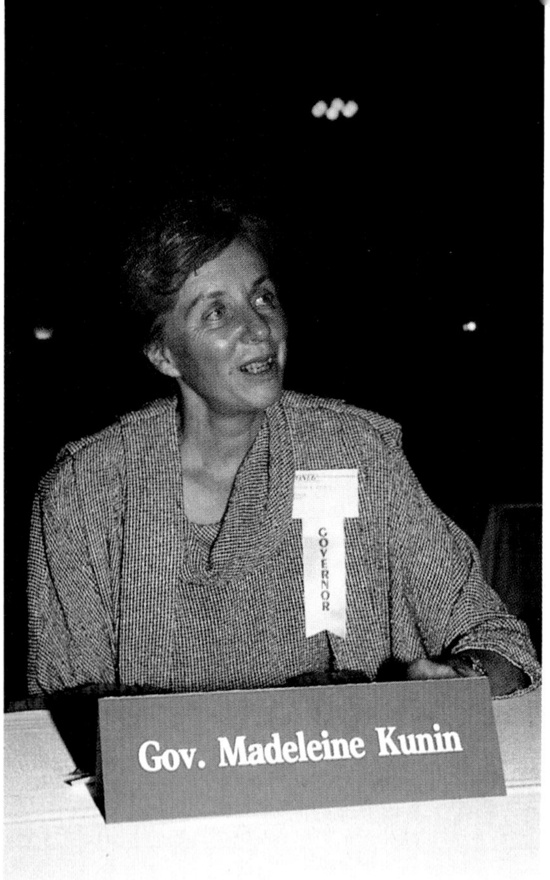

CHAPTER OBJECTIVES

To help you to

Learn · Know · Understand

The origins and development of the office of governor.

The shape of the office today, in terms of formal and informal qualifications, selection, tenure, compensation, and duties.

The other executive offices and their principal functions.

The governor is the principal executive officer in each of the 50 States. The governor is always a central figure in State politics and is often a well-known national personality, as well. Governors today hold an office that is the direct descendant of the earliest public office in American politics: the colonial governorship, established in Virginia in 1607.

1. The Governorship

As You Read, Think About:

- How the office of governor developed historically.
- What the qualifications, selection, term, succession, and compensation are for State governors.
- Why the informal qualifications for the office are so important.

Much of the colonial resentment that finally exploded into revolution was directed at the royal governors. That attitude was carried over into the first State constitutions. The new State governors were given,

Franklin D. Roosevelt is sworn into office for a second term as Governor of New York in 1930. Facing Page: Born in Switzerland, Madeleine Kunin of Vermont became that State's first woman governor in 1985.

for the most part, little real authority. Most of the powers the first State governments did have were given to the legislature. In every State except Massachusetts and New York, the governor was chosen by the legislature, and in most of them only for a one-year term. Only in Massachusetts and South Carolina did the governor have the power to veto acts of the legislature. To quote James Madison at the Philadelphia Convention in 1787: "The executives of the States are little more than ciphers; the legislatures are omnipotent."

That original separation of powers soon proved unsatisfactory, however. Many of the State legislatures abused their powers. Several fell prey to special interests, and the weak governors were unable to respond. So, as new constitutions were written, and the older ones revised, the powers of the legislatures were curbed and the powers of the governors generally increased.

Through the early years of the 1800s, the power to choose the governor was taken from the legislature and given to the people. The veto power was vested in the governor, and the gubernatorial powers of appointment and removal were increased, as well.

At the same time, however, new popularly elected officers, boards, and commissions were also created in several States. These executive officers were, supposedly, a part of the governor's administration. In fact, they were largely independent of the governor's control, because they, too, were elected by the voters. As we shall see, many States still suffer from that development.

The most dramatic changes in the governorship have come in the past 60 years or so. Beginning with Illinois in 1917, most States have reorganized and strengthened the executive branch to make the governor the State's chief executive in something more than name. Of course, some States have gone further than others in this direction. In all of them, however, the governor is a much more powerful figure than was the case even a few years ago. The move to a stronger governorship continues among the States. *

*ENRICHMENT Discuss: Is the governor of your State more than the State's chief executive in name?

In 1982, Governor Tony Anaya of New Mexico became the nation's first Mexican-American to be elected governor.

Qualifications

To become the governor of any of the States, a person must meet two quite different sets of requirements. He or she[1] must satisfy both the *formal* qualifications set by the State's constitution and those *informal* qualifications set by the State's politics.

Formal Qualifications With some variations, the State constitutions require that the governor (1) be an American citizen, (2) be of at least a certain age, usually 25 or 30, (3) have lived in the State for some period of time, most often for at least five years, and (4) be a qualified voter.[2]

Clearly, these requirements are not very difficult ones. In fact, they are met by hundreds of thousands of persons in every State. It is those other qualifications—the political ones—that have the real meaning and importance here.

Informal Qualifications Any person who wants to be governor—or hold any other elected office, for that matter—must first satisfy certain political requirements. He or she must be "available," that is, must have those characteristics that will attract the party's nomination and then attract the voters in the general election.[3] Exactly what, in particular, those characteristics are varies from State to State, and even from election to election. Race, sex, religion, personality, name familiarity, party membership, experience, stands on the issues, the ability to use television effectively—these and several other factors are all a part of the mix.

Selection

In every State the governor is chosen by popular vote. In all but four States, only a plurality is needed for election. But if no candidate wins a clear majority in Georgia or Louisiana, the two top vote-getters meet in a second, or runoff, election. If no one wins a clear majority in Mississippi, the winner is chosen by the lower house of the legislature. In Vermont, both houses choose.

The major parties' gubernatorial candidates are usually picked in primaries. In a few States, however, conventions pick the candidates; see page 234-235. Nearly half the States now provide for the joint election of the governor and lieutenant governor. In those States, each party's candidates for those offices run as a team, and the voter casts one vote to fill both posts.

Term

The one-year gubernatorial term has disappeared. Nearly everywhere the governor is now chosen for a four-year term. Only three States provide for a two-year term.[4]

Half the States still place some limit on the number of terms governors may serve. In

[1]Only eight women have ever been elected to the office of governor, and three of them are now (1987) serving; Martha Layne Collins of Kentucky, elected in 1983; Madeleine Kunin of Vermont, elected in 1984 and reelected in 1986; and Kay Orr of Nebraska, elected in 1986. Governor Orr is the first Republican woman to become a governor. The other five women (like governors Collins and Kunin, Democrats): Nellie T. Ross (Wyoming, 1925–1927); Miriam A. Ferguson (Texas, 1925–27, 1933–35); Lurleen Wallace (Alabama, 1967–1968); Ella T. Grasso (Connecticut, 1975–1980); and Dixy Lee Ray (Washington, 1977–1981).

[2]In Kansas and Ohio the constitution sets no formal qualifications for the office. Only one State sets the minimum age above 30—Oklahoma, where the governor must be at least 31. In a few States, California, Massachusetts, Ohio, and Wisconsin, for example, it is legally, but almost certainly not politically, possible for one to become governor at 18.

[3]See our discussion of availability on pp. 389, 561.

[4]New Hampshire, Rhode Island, Vermont.

*REINFORCEMENT Discuss in class: The informal qualifications to become governor are possibly more important than the formal qualifications. What informal qualifications are needed to win?

four States, they cannot serve more than one term.[5] In 24 others, they cannot serve more than two consecutive terms.[6]

Those governors who do run for another term most often win. Over time, about two-thirds of them have been successful. James Rhodes, the governor of Ohio from 1963 to 1971 and again from 1975 to 1983, holds the modern record for gubernatorial service—16 years. The most successful of all modern gubernatorial candidates was Orval Faubus, governor of Arkansas from 1955 to 1967. He won six consecutive two-year terms.[7]

Succession

Every State constitution provides for a successor should the governorship become vacant. In 43 States the lieutenant governor is first in the line of succession; see page 590. In Maine, New Hampshire, New Jersey, and West Virginia, the president of the senate succeeds. In Arizona, Oregon, and Wyoming the office passes to the secretary of state.

Occasionally a governor dies in office. Many are also politically ambitious. For example, every so often, one resigns in mid-term to become a United States Senator or to accept a presidential appointment. When a vacancy occurs, it usually sets off a game of political musical chairs in the State.[8]

Removal The governor may be removed from office by the **impeachment** process in all States except Oregon. Only four governors have been removed since Reconstruction, and none in over 50 years.[9]

The governor may be *recalled* by the voters in 15 States.[10] This has happened only once, however, to Governor Lynn J. Frazier of North Dakota in 1921—but he was elected to the United States Senate the next year.

Party Control of Governorships

Following Elections of	Republicans	Democrats
1946	25	23
1948	18	30
1950	25	23
1952	30	18
1954	21	27
1956	20	28
1958	14	34
1960	16	34
1962	16	34
1964	17	33
1966	25	25
1968	31	19
1970	21	29
1972	19	31
1974[a]	13	36
1976	12	37
1978	18	32
1980	23	27
1982	16	34
1984	16	34
1986	24	26

[a]James B. Longley, an independent, was elected to a four-year term as governor of Maine in 1974.

[5]Kentucky, Mississippi, New Mexico, Virginia.

[6]Alabama, Alaska, Delaware, Florida, Georgia, Hawaii, Indiana, Kansas, Louisiana, Maine, Maryland, Missouri, Nebraska, Nevada, New Jersey, North Carolina, Ohio, Oklahoma, Oregon, Pennsylvania, South Carolina, South Dakota, Tennessee, West Virginia. In three of these States (Delaware, Missouri, North Carolina), the ban is an absolute two-term limit. In the others it is a limit of two *consecutive* terms.

[7]The all-time record for both gubernatorial service and electoral success belongs to George Clinton of New York. He sought and won seven three-year terms as governor and held the office from 1777 to 1795 and again from 1801 to 1804. Clinton was later Vice President of the United States, from 1805 to 1812.

[8]Over time, most newly elected Presidents have appointed one or more governors of their own party to high federal posts. (Ronald Reagan did not follow this historical pattern, however.) With a vacancy in the governorship, the political plans and timetables of ambitious public figures are affected.

[9]William Salzer of New York in 1913; James E. Ferguson of Texas in 1917; J.C. Walton of Oklahoma in 1923; and Henry S. Johnston of Oklahoma in 1929. "Pa" Ferguson was later pardoned by the Texas legislature and announced at once his candidacy for the governorship. But the State Supreme Court held the legislature's pardon unconstitutional in 1920. His wife, Miriam A. ("Ma") Ferguson, then ran for and won the office in 1924 and again in 1932, as we noted on page 580.

[10]Alaska, Arizona, California, Colorado, Georgia, Idaho, Kansas, Louisiana, Michigan, Montana, Nevada, North Dakota, Oregon, Washington, Wisconsin. The **recall** is a petition procedure by which voters may remove an elected official from office before the completion of his or her regular term. The process generally works this way: If a certain number of qualified voters, usually 25 percent of the number who voted in the last general election, sign recall petitions, a special election must be held at which the voters decide whether to recall, or remove, the officeholder.

State Governors: Terms and Salaries

State	Term in Years	Annual Salary
Alabama	4	$70,223 and residence
Alaska	4	$69,401 and residence
Arizona	4	$75,000
Arkansas	4	$35,000 and residence
California	4	$85,000 and residence
Colorado	4	$70,000 and residence
Connecticut	4	$65,000 and residence
Delaware	4	$70,000 and residence
Florida	4	$90,570 and residence
Georgia	4	$82,530 and residence
Hawaii	4	$80,000 and residence
Idaho	4	$55,000 and residence
Illinois	4	$93,266 and residence
Indiana	4	$66,000 and residence
Iowa	4	$65,000 and residence
Kansas	4	$65,000 and residence
Kentucky	4	$63,036 and residence
Louisiana	4	$73,400 and residence
Maine	4	$70,000 and residence
Maryland	4	$75,000 and residence
Massachusetts	4	$75,000
Michigan	4	$85,800 and residence
Minnesota	4	$87,942 and residence
Mississippi	4	$63,000 and residence
Missouri	4	$81,000 and residence
Montana	4	$50,452 and residence
Nebraska	4	$40,000 and residence
Nevada	4	$77,500 and residence
New Hampshire	2	$68,665 and residence
New Jersey	4	$85,000 and residence
New Mexico	4	$60,000 and residence
New York	4	$100,000 and residence
North Carolina	4	$100,000 and residence
North Dakota	4	$60,862 and residence
Ohio	4	$65,000 and residence
Oklahoma	4	$70,000 and residence
Oregon	4	$72,000 and residence
Pennsylvania	4	$85,000 and residence
Rhode Island	2	$49,500
South Carolina	4	$80,000 and residence
South Dakota	4	$55,120 and residence
Tennessee	4	$85,000 and residence
Texas	4	$94,348 and residence
Utah	4	$60,000 and residence
Vermont	2	$63,600
Virginia	4	$85,000 and residence
Washington	4	$63,000 and residence
West Virginia	4	$72,000 and residence
Wisconsin	4	$86,149 and residence
Wyoming	4	$70,000 and residence

Sources: State constitutions and statutes and information furnished by appropriate State officials.

Compensation

The table on this page shows that gubernatorial salaries now average about $80,000 a year. The spread is fairly wide among the States, however, from the few where the pay is quite low to as much as $100,000 in New York and North Carolina. Most States also provide the governor with an official residence, generally called "the governor's mansion," and a more or less generous expense account.

To a governor's salary and other material compensation must be added the intangibles of honor and prestige that go along with the office. Indeed, it is this factor, along with a sense of public duty, that often brings many of our better citizens to seek the office. About a fourth of United States Senators are former governors, and a number of Senators later served as governors. Former Chief Justice Earl Warren went to the High Court from the governor's chair in California. Several Presidents were governors before entering the White House including, since 1900: Theodore Roosevelt, Woodrow Wilson, Calvin Coolidge, Franklin Roosevelt, Jimmy Carter, and Ronald Reagan. *

FOR REVIEW

1. **Identify:** succession.
2. Describe in a brief summary the development of the office of governor from 1776 to the present.
3. What are the formal and the informal qualifications one must meet in order to become governor?
4. How is the governor chosen in every State?
5. For what term is the governor elected in your State? Is that tenure limited?
6. How may the governor be removed from office in your State?
7. Who succeeds to the office in case of a vacancy?
8. What salary does your governor receive? Is your governor provided an official residence?

*ENRICHMENT Have the class discuss why the intangible compensations of honor and prestige might prompt a citizen to seek public office.

2. The Governor at Work

As You Read, Think About

- What the many roles are that the governor plays.
- What executive, legislative, and judicial powers the governor exercises.
- What additional powers the governor has.

The powers and duties of the governor of each State may be grouped under three major headings and one lesser one: (1) executive, (2) legislative, (3) judicial, and (4) miscellaneous and ceremonial. A useful understanding of the nature of the office can be gained by examining each of these individual categories.

The Many Roles of the Governor

Notice first that the governor, like the President, plays many roles. He or she is, at the same time, an executive, an administrator, a legislator, a party leader, an opinion leader, and a ceremonial figure. What the office in fact amounts to depends very largely on how the governor plays each, and all, of those roles. How he or she does so depends, in turn, on the strength of the governor's personality, "political muscle," and overall abilities.

Some, often most, of the governor's formal powers are hedged with constitutional and other legal restrictions. But the powers the office of the governor does have, together with its prestige, make it quite possible for a capable, persuasive, dynamic incumbent to be a "strong" governor, one who can accomplish much for the State and the public good.

One noted authority on State politics insists that the powers of any and all governors rest very largely on their talents of persuasion:

> Their power depends on their ability to persuade administrators over whom they have little authority, legislators who are jealous of their own powers, party leaders who are selected by local constituents, federal officials over whom governors have little authority, and a public that thinks governors have more authority than they really have. Thus, the role of governors is, above all, that of a persuader—

Governor Mario Cuomo of New York extended a warm welcome to President Corazon Aquino of the Phillippines when she visited New York City in September of 1986.

*REINFORCEMENT Have the class discuss the many functions of the governor and the influence he or she has on the course of State politics and national politics.

of their own administrators, State legislators, federal officials, party leaders, the press, and the public.[11]

Executive Powers

The Presidency and the governorship can be likened in several ways, but the comparison can be pushed too far. Recall, the Constitution of the United States makes the President *the* executive in the National Government. State constitutions, on the other hand, regularly describe the governor as the *chief* executive in State government.

This difference between the words *the* and *chief* is a critical one. Most State constitutions divide the executive power among several "executive officers," and so really make the governor only "first among equals." As we shall see, these other executive officers are almost always popularly elected. Because they are, they are very largely beyond the governor's direct control.

In most States, then, the executive authority is fragmented. It is held by several separate, and independently chosen, officers. Only a part of that authority is in fact held by the governor. Yet, whatever the realities of power may be, it is the governor to whom the people look for leadership in State affairs and hold responsible for their conduct and condition.

The basic legal responsibility of the governor is regularly found in a constitutional provision directing the chief executive to "take care that the laws be faithfully executed." Though the executive authority may be divided, the governor is given a number of specific powers with which to accomplish that job effectively.

Appointment and Removal The governor can best carry out the duty to execute —enforce and administer—the law with subordinates of his or her own choosing. Hence, the powers of appointment and removal are, or should be, among the most important in the chief executive's arsenal.

[11]Thomas R. Dye, *Politics in States and Communities*, 4th ed., (Englewood Cliffs, N.J.: Prentice-Hall, 1981), p. 162.

A leading test of any administrator is his or her ability to select loyal and able assistants. Two major factors work against the governor's effectiveness here, however. First, of course, is the existence of those other elected executives. The people choose them and the governor cannot remove them.

Second, the State's constitution and statutes place restrictions on the governor's power to hire and fire. In most States the constitution requires that most of the governor's major appointees be confirmed by the State senate.* Moreover, the legislature often sets qualifications and other conditions that must be met by those appointed to the offices it has created by statute. In a vigorous two-party State, for example, the law often requires that not more than a certain number of the members of each board or commission be from the same political party. This means, of course, that the governor must appoint some members of the opposing party to posts in his or her administration.

There are many other legal limits of this kind. Consider one more example: The law often requires that those persons the governor appoints to any of the State's professional licensing boards must themselves be licensed to practice in the particular field that that board regulates. Thus, only licensed realtors can be appointed to the real estate board; only licensed MDs can serve on the board of medical examiners; and so on.

Still, the governor has the authority to fill many important posts. To help accomplish that task more effectively, recent reorganization efforts have stressed this recommendation: Place governmental functions in the hands of a small number of agencies, each headed by a single administrator chosen by and answering directly to the governor.

Supervision of Administration The governor is the State's chief administrator—again, not *the* and not the *only*, but the *chief* administrator.

Alone, the governor cannot possibly "take care that the laws be faithfully executed." Unaided, he or she cannot enforce all of the State's laws, perform all of its many functions, and provide all of its many services.

*REINFORCEMENT Have the class discuss: Senate confirmation of major appointees is required by most States. How does this serve to limit the executive powers of the governor?

BUILDING GOVERNMENT SKILLS

Recognizing Leadership Styles

Of all the skills in government, none is more important than leadership. Leaders make things happen. Leaders are powerful, but their power depends on other people. A person can lead only if others follow.

Leaders can do both good and evil. Sometimes people can be led astray by particularly powerful leaders. An extreme example was Hitler's leadership of Nazi Germany.

In the United States we make it difficult for leaders to exert too much power. That is why our government has so many checks and balances: to prevent the concentration of power in any one person's hands.

Leadership is more than being in a position of power. Even the President does not always get his way simply by demanding it. In order to get bills he favors through Congress, for example, he often has to persuade, argue, threaten, or negotiate.

Leadership is hard to define because it takes many forms and leaders come in many shapes and sizes. Think of some leaders. Probably you will think of current political leaders such as President Reagan or historic figures such as Abraham Lincoln.

Leaders are not only elected political figures, of course. Many leaders are religious figures, business people, teachers, and other professionals. Other leaders are ordinary citizens who organize school and community events, set an example in sports or art, or simply take the initiative in their home or workplace. The point is that anyone can be a leader in some situation.

Here are some of the most common types of leadership.

Leading by Example—One way to lead is to simply set an example that others want to follow. A governor who is honest and works hard may lead others to follow his or her example. Sometimes people lead without recognizing that they are doing it, such as sports or music stars who are admired and copied.

Leading by Convincing—A second common way to lead is to convince people that some action is in their interests. Sometimes convincing is only a matter of showing people what their interests really are; for example, in a business deal the initiator of the deal shows the other parties how the deal will make them money. At other times, convincing may be more difficult, for example, when the President tries to convince Americans to spend more money on defense.

Leading by Converting—Perhaps the most difficult form of leadership is changing the way people feel about an issue and converting them to the leader's point of view. One familiar form of this leadership type is religious conversion. Sometimes politicians can also convert followers to some new belief, for example, a belief that socialism is good or that segregation is wrong. These conversions are not based on calculations of interest, but rather on fundamental moral values.

Leaders do not have to use only one leadership style, of course. Many leaders use some of each approach.

1. Think of a leader you have heard or read about. What leadership style does he or she use?
2. Think of someone you know personally who shows leadership? How does he or she lead?
3. Think of some time when you have been a leader? How would you describe your leadership style?

That work is done, day to day, by the thousands of men and women who staff the agencies that make up the State's executive branch. The governor must supervise that work by managing and overseeing the administration.

That is, the governor must do these things, as far as he or she *can*. Many of the State's agencies are subject to the governor's direct control. But, remember, many are not. They are headed by other elected officials. For instance, an elected attorney general regularly heads the department of justice and an elected secretary of state administers the election laws.

At base, the governor's ability to supervise State administration depends, first, on the extent to which the constitution and statutes make that possible. Second, that ability depends on the governor's ability to operate through such informal channels as party leadership, appeals to the public, or the governor's talents of persuasion.

The Budget We shall take a close look at the budget-making process in Chapter 24, but we must look into that subject for a moment here.

As we suggested earlier, a budget is much more than a balance sheet, much more than a dull recitation of dollars from here and dollars for that. A budget is a *political* document, a highly important policy statement. Its numbers reflect the struggle over "who gets what," and who does not.

Public agencies, no less than private businesses, can do little without money. Clearly, those who hold the purse strings have a large measure of control over the activities, and even the very lives, of public agencies.

In most States the governor now has the power to make the State's budget. That is, the governor prepares the annual or biennial budget that goes to the legislature. The legislature may make changes in the governor's financial plan, of course. It may appropriate this or that amount, or nothing, for this agency and that program, as it chooses. *But*, and this is the vital point, the governor's budget recommendations carry a great deal of weight.

The governor's budget-making power can be, and often is, a powerful tool with which he or she can control State administration. Although unable to appoint or remove the head of a certain agency, for example, the governor can use the budget-making power to affect that agency's programs. So the governor can have a real impact on the attitudes and behavior of that official. *

Military Powers Every State constitution makes the governor the commander in chief of the State militia—in effect, the State's units of the National Guard.

The National Guard is the *organized* part of the State militia. In a national emergency, the National Guard may be "called up" —ordered into federal service by the President.[12]

When the State's Guard units are not in federal service, which is most of the time, they are commanded by the governor. The governor's chief military aide, the adjutant general, serves as the highest ranking officer of the State's National Guard.

On various occasions, governors find it necessary to call out the Guard. Among the reasons: to deal with such emergencies as prison riots, to aid in relief and evacuation and prevent looting during and after a flood or some other natural disaster, to help State police reduce holiday traffic accidents, and so on.

Legislative Powers

The State's principal *executive* officer has three quite important formal *legislative* powers: (1) to send messages to the legislature, (2) to call the legislature into special session, and (3) to veto measures passed by the legislature. These powers, together with the governor's own political clout, often make the governor, in fact, the State's chief legislator.

[12]All of the States' National Guard units were federalized in 1940 and served as part of the nation's armed forces in World War II. Many units also saw combat duty in both Korea and Vietnam. National Guard units are not often called into federal service in domestic crisis situations, however; see pages 80, 422.

*REINFORCEMENT As the chief administrator of the State, the governor has budget-making power. How can he or she use this power to ensure that agency officials "toe the line"?

Governor Bill Clements of Texas responds to a question at a press conference.

The Message Power The message power is really the power to recommend legislation. A strong governor can do much with it.

As we noted earlier, much of what the legislature does centers on the governor's program for legislative action. That program is given to the lawmakers in a yearly State of the State address, in the budget, and in several special messages. The most effective governors regularly push their programs by using the formal message power together with a number of informal tactics. These include appeals to the people, close contacts with key legislators, a shrewd use of the appointive power, and so on.

Special Sessions The governor in every State has the power to call the legislature into special sessions.[13]

Special sessions have become fairly common among the States, as both the volume and the complexity of State business have grown. This is most true in those States that still schedule regular biennial sessions, and even more so where the length of the biennial session is limited.

The basic purpose of the governor's power to call a special session is to permit the State to meet extraordinary situations. That power can also be an important part of the governor's legislative arsenal. On occasion, a governor has used the threat of a special session to persuade reluctant legislators to pass a particular bill before adjourning the regular session.

The Veto Power Except for North Carolina, the governor in every State has the power to **veto** measures passed by the legislature. This power, as well as the *threat* to use it, is often the most potent power the governor has in influencing the work of the legislature.

In most States the governor has only a few days, most often five,[14] in which to sign or veto a measure. If no action is taken within the period set—and the legislature remains in session—the measure then becomes a law.[15]

THE POCKET VETO. Unlike the President, the governor does not have the **pocket veto** in most States. That is, those bills the governor neither signs nor vetoes *after* the legislature adjourns become law without his or her signature.

The governor does have the pocket veto in 13 States, however.[16] Take Oklahoma, for example. There the governor has five days, not counting Sunday, to act on a measure while the legislature remains in session. If

[13]See page 564. In several States the constitution forbids the legislature to consider any matters except those for which the special session is called. In most, however, the lawmakers may deal with any matters they choose. That fact sometimes makes a governor reluctant to call a special session. Recall, too, that the legislature may call itself into special session in just over half of the States. When it does, its agenda is usually unlimited.

[14]Three days in Iowa, Minnesota, New Mexico, North Dakota, Wyoming; 6 days in Alabama, Georgia, Maryland, Rhode Island, Wisconsin; 7 days in Florida, Indiana, Virginia; 10 days in Colorado, Delaware, Hawaii, Kansas, Kentucky, Louisiana, Maine, Massachusetts, New Jersey, New York, Ohio, Pennsylvania, Tennessee, Texas, Utah; 12 days in California; 14 days in Michigan; 15 days in Alaska, Missouri; 60 days in Illinois; and 5 days in the other 16 States. In most States, Sundays are excluded from the count.

[15]The period *after* adjournment is somewhat longer in several States—*e.g.* 20 days in Arkansas and Texas; 30 days in Georgia and Iowa; 45 days in Alaska and New Jersey. On "veto sessions" in some States, see page 564.

[16]Alabama, Delaware, Hawaii, Massachusetts, Michigan, Minnesota, New Hampshire, New Mexico, New York, Oklahoma, Vermont, Virginia, Wisconsin.

FOCUS ON:

The "Typical" Governor

As we said at the very beginning of this chapter, the governor is everywhere a central figure in State politics and is very often a well-known personality in national politics, as well.

Governors (and gubernatorial candidates) come in a wide range of shapes and sizes among the 50 States. That is, they do with one large exception: They are very seldom female. Of the more than 2000 persons who have served as State governors over the past two centuries, only eight have been women—and only three women hold that office today; see page 581. (Thirty-six of the 50 governorships were up for election in 1986, and seven women—more than ever before—were among the 72 major party gubernatorial candidates. Only two of them were elected: Kay Orr as Nebraska's governor and Madeleine Kunin as Vermont's governor.)

The "typical" State governor today can be described in these terms: He is a native of the State, in his mid-to-late 40s, married, a college graduate, a veteran of the armed forces, and an attorney by profession.

In most cases, the governor began his political life in the State legislature or as a local prosecuting attorney. Some moved from a seat in the legislature directly to the governor's chair. More often, however, the State's chief executive served as the lieutenant governor or held some other Statewide elective office before winning the governorship.

1. Compare a short biography of the governor of your State to this profile of the "typical" governor. How does your governor differ from and how is he or she similar to the "typical" governor?
2. What appeal does the "typical" governor have for voters? Why are the particular characteristics discussed in this profile important to voters?
3. In what ways would holding State-wide elective office benefit a gubernatorial candidate?
4. Why do you think so few women have sought the governorship?

the session ends during the five-day period, the governor then has another 15 days in which to act. If the bill is neither signed nor vetoed within that 15-day period, it dies and the pocket veto has been applied.

THE ITEM VETO. In 43 States[17] the governor's veto power includes the **item veto.** That is, the governor may veto one or more provisions—items—in a bill without rejecting the entire measure.

The power is most often, but not always, restricted to items in appropriations bills. It allows the governor to delete those money items that he or she thinks are excessive or finds undesirable for some other reason.

The item veto is regularly used to check extravagant legislative appropriations. Sometimes, though, legislators will vote for certain spending proposals and "pass the buck" for balancing the State's budget on to the governor. Often, the governor finds the item veto a useful weapon with which to persuade or punish lawmakers who oppose his or her program.

THE LEGISLATURE'S POWER TO OVERRIDE. In no State does the governor have an absolute veto power, except where the pocket veto is involved. That is, the governor's veto is subject to a vote to override it in the legislature.

[17]The exceptions are Indiana, Maine, Nevada, New Hampshire, Rhode Island, Vermont, North Carolina.

The vote needed to override varies by State, but two-thirds of the full membership in each house is most common.

In actual practice, not many bills are vetoed. Less than 5 percent of all measures passed by the State legislatures are rejected * by governors. When the veto power is used, it is quite effective. Less than 10 percent of all vetoes are overridden.

Judicial Powers

In every State the governor has several powers of a judicial nature. Most of them are usually referred to as the powers of executive clemency—powers of mercy that may be shown toward those convicted of crime.

By the power to **pardon** a governor may release a person from the legal consequences of a crime. In most States, a pardon may be either full or conditional and cannot be granted until *after* conviction. In most States, too, a pardon cannot be granted in cases involving treason or impeachment.

The power to commute reduces the sentence imposed by a court. Thus, a death sentence may be commuted to life imprisonment, or the commutation may be to "time served," which means that the prisoner is then released.

The power to **reprieve** postpones the execution of a sentence. Reprieves are usually granted for a few hours or a few days, to allow more time for an appeal or because new evidence in a case has been found.

The power to remit eliminates or reduces a fine imposed upon conviction.

The power to **parole** allows the release of a prisoner short of the completion of the term of a sentence. Paroles are usually conditional and supervised. They are also a regular, and often controversial, part of the criminal corrections process.[18]

The governor may have some or all of these powers, but they are often shared with one or more boards, such as with a board of pardons and/or a parole board. Governors have not often used their clemency powers too freely, but it can happen. In her first term (1925–27), Governor "Ma" Ferguson of Texas pardoned 3,737 convicted felons—an average of more than five a day. The pardons came so thick and fast that several Texas newspapers ran daily "pardon columns" rather than separate news stories.[19]

Miscellaneous Duties

Every governor must perform many other, often time-consuming duties. To list only a few is to suggest their scope. The governor receives official visitors and welcomes other distinguished persons to the State, dedicates new buildings and parks, opens the State fair and attends countless local celebrations, addresses many organizations and public gatherings, and crowns beauty contest, spelling bee, and soap-box derby winners. The governor is an *ex officio* (by virtue of office) member of several boards and commissions and therefore must attend at least several of their meetings. Then, too, the governor is often called on to help settle labor disputes, to travel elsewhere in the country and sometimes abroad to promote the State and its trade interests, and to endorse worthy causes. The list is endless.

FOR REVIEW

1. **Identify:** chief executive, appointment/removal powers, budget-making power, military powers, message power, commute, remit.
2. What is meant by the observation that "the governor wears many different hats"?
3. In what major way is the executive power fragmented in most States?
4. Why are the governor's powers of appointment and removal important?
5. What are the governor's legislative powers? Judicial powers?

[18]An extradition request from another State also puts the governor in a judicial role; see page 87.

[19]"Ma" first sought and won the governorship after the State Supreme Court struck down her husband's legislative pardon; see note 9, page 581.

*ENRICHMENT Have the class discuss: Which of the legislative powers is most important to the governor's role as chief legislator? Or are they equally important?

3. Other Executive Officers

As You Read, Think About:

- What the titles and functions are of the officers who share executive authority with the governor.
- Why there is need for an administrative reorganization in the executive branch of the States.
- What the basic guidelines are that are often advocated for such reorganization.

As we have noted several times, in nearly every State the governor must share the control of his or her administration with a number of other elected officials.

Only three States—Maine, New Jersey, and Tennessee—make the governor the only popularly elected executive officer. Among those three States, only New Jersey now allows the governor to appoint all of the other principal officers in the executive branch of the State's government.[20]

The other executive officers most often found among the States include the lieutenant governor, secretary of state, treasurer, auditor or comptroller, attorney general, and superintendent of public instruction, or commissioner of education. No useful treatment of the executive function can afford to overlook them.

The Lieutenant Governor

The office of lieutenant governor now exists in 43 States and is filled by the voters in 42 of them.[21]

The formal duties of the lieutenant governor are much like those of the Vice President, that is, there is little to do. He or she succeeds to the governorship if there is a vacancy in the office and presides over the senate in most, but a declining number, of States; see page 567.

The office is often regarded as a steppingstone to the governorship, sometimes by succession, of course, but often by means of future elections. Seven States seem to get along quite well without a lieutenant governor. Many people have urged that the office be abolished everywhere. In 1981, David O'Neal, then the lieutenant governor of Illinois, made that proposal in a forthright way. He resigned because, he said, the office gave him "nothing to do."

The Secretary of State

The office of secretary of state exists everywhere but in Alaska, Hawaii, and Utah. The post is filled by the voters in 36 States, by the governor in eight,[22] and by the legislature in Maine, New Hampshire, and Tennessee.

The secretary of state is the State's chief clerk and record-keeper. He or she has charge of a great variety of public documents, records the official acts of the governor and the legislature, usually administers the election laws, and is "the keeper of the Great Seal of the State." As with most of these other elected executives, little real power or authority to act or to make decisions is given the secretary of state. Most of his or her duties are closely detailed by law.

The Treasurer

The voters in 38 States elect a treasurer. The governor appoints the treasurer in Alaska, Michigan, New Jersey, New York, and Virginia, and the legislature does so in Maine, Maryland, New Hampshire, and Tennessee.[23]

[20]In Maine the secretary of state, treasurer, and attorney general are elected by the legislature. In Tennessee the secretary of state and treasurer are also chosen by the legislature, and the attorney general is selected by the State Supreme Court.

[21]In Tennessee the presiding officer of the senate (the speaker) is also, by statute, the lieutenant governor. The office does not exist in seven States: Arizona, Maine, New Hampshire, New Jersey, Oregon, West Virginia, and Wyoming.

[22]Delaware, Maryland, New Jersey, New York, Oklahoma, Pennsylvania, Texas, Virginia. In Alaska, Hawaii, and Utah, the usual duties of the office are assigned to the lieutenant governor.

[23]Elsewhere, the duties of the treasurer are handled by the Director of Fiscal Services in the Department of Administrative Services in Georgia, the Director of the Department of Budget and Finance in Hawaii, and the Director of the Department of Administration in Montana. Each of these officials is appointed by the governor.

*ENRICHMENT Have the class research the duties of the State's lieutenant governor. Use an adjoining State if yours does not have one. Are these duties sufficient to justify the position?

State comptrollers are responsible for overseeing the spending of all State agencies.

The treasurer is the custodian of State funds, often the State's chief tax collector, and regularly the State's paymaster. The treasurer's major job is to make payments out of the State treasury. Most of those payments go to meet the many agency payrolls and to pay bills for goods or services supplied to the State. Here, the treasurer must work closely with the auditor, as we shall see in a moment.

The State often has surplus monies, dollars not currently at work. These monies are funds not yet appropriated by the legislature, contributions to the public employees retirement system, and the like. In most States the treasurer manages these surplus monies. The treasurer deposits them in banks and in such other places as the short-term notes of the Federal Government, bonds issued by local governments, and even the private stock and bond markets. The interest on those investments usually brings a nice profit to the State's treasury. In short, the treasurer is the State's banker.

* The Auditor or Comptroller

Every State's constitution forbids the spending of any State money unless the legislature has authorized that spending. Thus, money cannot be spent unless the legislature has first passed a law appropriating the funds for it.

The Preaudit and the Postaudit *Before* a particular expenditure is made, some public official must carry out the *preaudit* function. That is, that officer must issue a warrant, or check, certifying that the outlay is legal and that the money for it is in the State treasury.

Some public official must also carry out the *postaudit* function. That is, *after* expenditures are made, that officer must review and verify the accounts of all officers and agencies handling public funds. That officer must make periodic checks to see that the spending was in fact made in accord with the law.

Most experts in public finance agree that these two safeguarding functions should be carried out by two separate officers. They recommend that someone, named by and responsible to the governor, do all of the preaudit work. Experts urge that someone else, named by and responsible to the legislature, conduct all postaudits. They recommend that the governor's preaudit agent, a comptroller, keep public officers and agencies on the straight and narrow path as they spend the public's money. They urge that the legislature's postaudit agent, an auditor, police the books and weed out misdeeds and unauthorized practices.

Only 15 States presently give the preaudit job to a gubernatorial appointee and the postaudit task to a legislative appointee.[24] In most other States, some elected official, either the auditor or the comptroller, is involved in one or both of these functions.

Only 21 States now give the all-important postaudit task to an officer chosen by and answerable to the legislature.[25] Putting the postaudit function in the hands of an officer in the executive branch runs the same sort of risk as that involved in asking the fox to guard the chicken coop.

---

[24]Alabama, Alaska, Arizona, Arkansas, Colorado, Connecticut, Florida, Kansas, Maine, Nevada, New Hampshire, New Jersey, North Dakota, Texas, and Wisconsin.

[25]The 15 States in note 24 and Georgia, Idaho, Illinois, Michigan, Montana, and South Dakota.

*ENRICHMENT Discuss: Some recommend that the governor appoint a comptroller, and the legislature an auditor, to guard spending. Will this maintain the system of checks and balances?

The Attorney General

The attorney general (AG) is the State's lawyer. The voters fill the post in 43 States. The governor names the AG in five States: Alaska, Hawaii, New Hampshire, New Jersey, and Wyoming; in Maine the legislature chooses the AG, and in Tennessee the Supreme Court does so.

The AG acts as the legal adviser to the governor and other State officers and agencies, and often to the legislature. He or she represents the State in court and oversees the work of local prosecutors.

Much of the power and importance of the office centers on the attorney general's opinions. These are formal written interpretations of constitutional and statutory law. These opinions answer questions raised by the governor, other executive officers, legislators, and local officials regarding the lawfulness of their actions or proposed actions. In most States these opinions have the force of law unless the courts rule otherwise.

The Superintendent of Public Instruction

The chief school administrator is the overall supervisor of the public school system in every State. Most often this officer is known as the superintendent of public instruction or the commissioner of education. He or she usually shares authority with a State board of education.

The voters still choose the chief school officer in 16 States, in most cases on a nonpartisan basis.[26] The post is filled by the governor in 6 States,[27] and by the board in the other 28.[28]

[26]Arizona, California, Florida, Georgia, Idaho, Indiana, Kentucky, Montana, North Carolina, North Dakota, Oklahoma, Oregon, South Carolina, Washington, Wisconsin, and Wyoming.

[27]Maine, New Jersey, Pennsylvania, Tennessee, Texas, and Virginia.

[28]The members of the board are themselves chosen by the voters in 13 States: Alabama, Colorado, Hawaii, Idaho, Kansas, Louisiana, Massachusetts, Michigan, Nebraska, Nevada, New Mexico, Ohio, Utah. Generally members are picked by the governor elsewhere in the country. There is no State board of education in Wisconsin.

Other Officers and Agencies

The offices we have just reviewed are the major ones to be found in all or most of the 50 States. There are, of course, many other agencies. They vary in number, name, and function from State to State. Some offices were created by constitutional provision, others by statute. Some are elected by the voters, others are appointed by the governor or, in some cases, by someone else.[29]

In many States several public functions are handled by boards or commissions, rather than by an agency headed by a single administrator. Thus, the management of correctional, mental, or educational institutions is often in the hands of a several-member board. Examples include the State Board of Prisons and Parole or the State Board of Education. Laws relating to agriculture, public health, or highways are the responsibility of a State Board of Agriculture, a State Board of Health, or a State Highway Commission. Public utilities and other corporations are regulated by a Public Service Commission. There are also a number of licensing and examining bodies in every State, as the Board of Medical Examiners, the Board of Barber Examiners, the Department of Motor Vehicles, and so on.

Administrative Reorganization

As one function after another was added to the work of State government, boards and commissions were established to handle them. Often these new agencies were set up to meet a current need, but had little concern for their place in an orderly, structured executive branch. Usually, they were made independent of one another, and often even of the governor. The certain result was confusion and, at times, chaos.

Overlapping and duplication of effort, waste and inefficiency, a lack of coordination

[29]These officers and various boards and commissions are so numerous and vary so much from State to State that it would be pointless to try to treat them here. Nearly every State puts out a *Blue Book* or other directory, which at least lists, and often describes the organization and functions of, all State agencies.

*ENRICHMENT Have the class discuss the fact that elected public officials have an ethical responsibility to work toward administrative reorganization.

Dr. A. Craig Phillips, Superintendent of Public Instruction in North Carolina, was the voters' choice in 1984 to supervise the State's public schools.

—sometimes mixed with graft and often touched with favoritism—came to characterize most State administrations. Today, some States are plagued by the haphazard way in which the executive branch developed.

Every State has made at least some progress in executive branch reorganization in the past few decades. Those reform efforts have been stepped up in most States in recent years. Among the most effective administrations today are those in Alaska, California, Hawaii, Michigan, Missouri, New Jersey, New York, and North Carolina. Still, much remains to be done in most States.

Experts in public administration have put together a number of guidelines for State executive branch reorganization. Their recommendations have been summarized by the Council of State Governments:[30]

(1) Consolidate all administrative agencies into a relatively small number of departments, usually 10 to 20, on the basis of function or general purpose. The number of these departments should be small enough to fit within the governor's effective "span of control."
(2) Establish clear lines of authority and responsibility running from the governor at the top of the hierarchy down through the entire organization.
(3) Establish appropriate staff (advisory, planning, budget) agencies immediately responsible to the governor.
(4) To the greatest extent possible, eliminate multi-headed agencies (boards and commissions) for administrative work.
(5) Establish an independent auditor, with authority for postaudit only.

There is a trend among the States to reorganize along departmental lines—that is, to place all similar and related activities under a single overall agency, or a department. In the most thorough reorganizations, each department is headed by one administrator, appointed by and answering to the governor. The departments most common today are administration, agriculture, corrections, education, environmental protection, finance, health, insurance, justice, labor, military, natural resources, public works, transportation, and welfare.

FOR REVIEW

1. **Identify:** preaudit, postaudit, opinions.
2. List and identify the major executive officers besides the governor found in most States and their functions. Which of them are found in your State? What are the responsibilities of each?
3. Describe the duties of the secretary of state on the State level.
4. What essential authorization must a State have in order to spend State money?
5. How are these other officers chosen in most States? In your State?
6. What are the basic guidelines for State administrative reorganization identified by the Council of State Governments?

[30]The Council, founded in 1935, is a research and reporting agency supported by each of the 50 States. It maintains a central headquarters at Lexington, Kentucky, and other offices in New York, Chicago, Atlanta, San Francisco, and Washington, D.C. It publishes a monthly newsletter, *State Government News;* a biennial volume of current statistical information and commentary, *The Book of the States;* as well as many specialized reports.

SUMMARY

The present-day office of governor is the direct descendant of the colonial governorships and is the oldest of all elective offices in American politics. Most of the limited powers of the first State governments were given to the legislature. The early State governors had little authority. Gradually that original separation of powers was revised, especially as the legislatures tended to abuse their powers. The governorship has been strengthened in greater or lesser degree everywhere, especially in the past few decades.

The governor is elected by popular vote in every State. In most the State constitution sets out formal qualifications for the office, but in all of them the informal, or political, qualifications are more meaningful. Governors are now chosen for two-year terms in three States and for four-year terms in the rest. Half of the States still place some constitutional limitation on gubernatorial tenure.

The governor's salary ranges from $35,000 a year in some States to $100,000 in New York and North Carolina. Most governors also receive an expense allowance and live in a home provided by the State. The governor may be removed by impeachment in every State except Oregon and by recall in Oregon and 14 other States. Succession falls first to the lieutenant governor in 43 States, to the president of the senate in 4, and to the secretary of state in the other 3.

In nearly every State the executive power is fragmented. It is shared by the governor and several other elected executive officers over whom the governor has little or no control. The executive powers are hedged by a number of constitutional and statutory restrictions. The powers include appointment and removal, supervision of administration, command of the National Guard, and budget-making. The governor's legislative powers include sending messages to the legislature, calling special sessions of that body, and, except in North Carolina, vetoing measures it enacts, including the item veto in 43 States. The governor's judicial powers are those of executive clemency. The governor must also carry out a number of miscellaneous chores, many ceremonial. In every State, the governor's real power depends on his or her personality, political clout, and talents of persuasion.

There are several other major executive offices, usually elective, in every State. The major ones are lieutenant governor, secretary of state, treasurer, auditor, attorney general, and superintendent of public instruction. Recent years have seen an interest among the States in reorganizing the executive branch.

CHAPTER REVIEW

Key Terms/Concepts*

impeachment (581)
recall (581)
special session (587)
veto power (587)
pocket veto (587)
item veto (588)
pardon (589)
reprieve (589)
parole (589)

*These terms are included in the Glossary.

Keynote Questions

• **1.** How has the office of governor changed since the first State governors?

• **2.** What are the formal and informal qualifications for governor?

• **3.** How are governors selected in all of the States?

•• **4.** Explain the two methods by which a governor can be removed from office.

The dots represent skill levels required to answer each question or complete each activity: •requires recall and comprehension • •requires application and analysis • • •requires synthesis and evaluation

5. How does the governor's executive authority in the States differ from the President's executive authority?
6. Why are the appointment and removal powers and the budget-making powers so important to the governor?
7. What are the three formal legislative powers of a governor? How can a governor use these powers to promote his or her own legislative proposals?
8. What are the judicial powers of a governor?
9. List three examples of the miscellaneous duties performed by a governor.
10. What is the role of the secretary of state in State government?
11. Why are the opinions of the attorney general important?
12. What problems with State government have prompted States to reorganize their executive branches in the last few decades? How did these problems arise?

Skill Application

Recognizing Cause and Effect: In thinking about government and public policy, recognizing cause and effect is an important skill. This skill enables you to evaluate past policies and to predict better the results of future policies.

A cause is an action or event that makes change occur. The change itself is the effect. In this chapter, you have read that the haphazard way in which State executive agencies were set up resulted in confusion and chaos in the executive branch. In other words, the haphazard addition of agencies *caused* an *effect*—confusion.

In trying to recognize cause and effect, you have to be careful. Often the causes and effects are more complicated than they first appear. When you think you have identified a cause for a specific change, always check yourself by asking, "Could anything else account for (or explain) these changes?"

In each of the sentences below, identify the cause and the effect. Then answer this question: Are there any other actions or events that could account for these effects? Write your answers on a separate piece of paper.

1. The original States delegated most of the power to the legislature because the former colonists resented the authority of the royal governors.
2. The governor can use the threat of a veto to influence the State legislature's position on a bill.
3. In 1981, David O'Neal resigned as lieutenant governor of Illinois because, he said, the office gave him "nothing to do."
4. The governor called upon the National Guard to quell the prison riot.

For Thought and Discussion

1. What informal qualifications do you think are necessary to be elected governor in your State?
2. In recent years, almost half of the States have required candidates for governor and lieutenant governor to run as a team. Why have so many States adopted this requirement?
3. Why would experts in the financial field recommend that someone responsible to the governor should perform the preaudit function, while a person responsible to the legislature should perform the postaudit function? What is this plan designed to prevent?
4. In New Jersey the governor is the only executive officer elected by the voters, and he or she appoints all principal officers in the executive branch. No other State so completely concentrates executive authority and responsibility in the governorship. Do you think your State should have such an arrangement? Why or why not?

Suggested Activities

1. Prepare a chart showing the political career of the current governor of your State. To which political party does he or she belong? What were the major issues in the last election?
2. Use local newspapers or call the governor's office to find out what major legislation has been proposed by the governor of your State in the last legislative session. Summarize three pieces of legislation using the following questions: Why was the legislation proposed by the governor? How has the State legislature responded? Do you agree or disagree with the governor's proposals?

Where law ends, Tyranny begins.
–John Locke

22

The State Court Systems

CHAPTER OBJECTIVES

To help you to:

Learn · Know · Understand

The overall organization of the several State court systems (with especial reference to your State's judiciary).

The various methods by which judges are selected among the States.

The distinctions between and the duties of the grand jury and the petit jury.

The different kinds of law applied by State courts.

Courts are tribunals established by law for the administration of justice according to law. All the courts of a State make up its court system, the State *judiciary*.

Remember, there are two separate and distinct sets of courts in the United States: the federal courts, which we looked at in Chapter 18, and those of each of the 50 States. The federal courts have jurisdiction over certain classes of cases, as we noted on pages 514–518. All other cases heard in courts in the United States—the overwhelming number, by far—are heard in State courts. Only a very small proportion of cases are heard in the federal courts.

The principal function of the State courts is to decide disputes between private persons and between private persons and government. State courts protect the rights of individuals, as guaranteed in both the federal and the State constitutions. They determine the innocence or guilt of persons accused of committing a crime. Moreover, they also act as a check on the conduct of both the executive and the legislative branches of government.

Judge Roy Bean (seated at table, at left) tries a horse thief in Langtry, Texas, in 1900. Law officers were scarce then in parts of the West, and JPs often decided cases that carried severe penalties, even the death penalty. *Facing page:* The County Courthouse of Travis County, Texas

1. Organization of State Court Systems

As You Read, Think About:

- How State court systems are organized.
- What the functions are that justices of the peace and magistrates' courts fulfill.
- What kinds of cases the general trial courts, intermediate appellate courts, and State supreme courts hear.
- What the advantages are of the unified court system.

Each State constitution creates a court system, but most of these documents leave the many details of organization to the legislature. Over the next few pages we shall look at the structure of the 50 State judiciaries, working our way up the judicial hierarchy.

Justices of the Peace

Justices of the peace—JP's—stand on the lowest rung of the State judicial ladder. They preside over what are commonly called justice courts.

JP's were once found nearly everywhere in the country. They are gradually disappearing, and have been for several decades. Until well into this century, however, they served a useful purpose. Travel was difficult, and much of the nation's population was rural. The existence of JP's allowed people to obtain a hearing for minor offenses quickly and cheaply. But time has largely passed JP's by. They, and their justice courts, have been done away with in about half of the States, and their number has been greatly reduced in most of the rest. JP's can still be found in many smaller towns and rural areas in a number of States, however. *

JP's are almost always popularly elected. Most often, they are chosen on a partisan

*REINFORCEMENT Have the class discuss: Why are justices of the peace being phased out? Point out that we are living in an increasingly urban society.

ballot, by the voters of a township or some other district within a county, and for a short term, most often two or four years.

In area their jurisdiction[1] usually covers an entire county, but it is also limited, in that JP's hear only lesser legal matters. Most JP's can hear only minor civil cases[2] and misdemeanors.[3]

Mostly, JP's try misdemeanors—cases involving such petty offenses as traffic violations, disturbing the peace, public drunkenness, and the like. They can almost never settle civil disputes involving more than a few hundred dollars. They do issue certain kinds of warrants, hold preliminary hearings, and often perform marriages.[4]

In some places, JP's are still paid out of the fines they take in. The more and the heavier the fines they impose, the higher their incomes. This "fee system" raises serious questions about the fairness of the treatment a defendant can expect.[5]

Magistrates' Courts

Magistrates are the city cousins of JP's. For the most part, magistrates handle those minor civil complaints and misdemeanor cases that arise in an urban setting. They preside over what are generally called magistrates' courts or, in some places, police courts. Those courts are much like the justice courts, with just about the same jurisdiction. Magistrates, like JP's, are usually popularly elected and for short terms.

Both the justice courts and the magistrates' courts are sometimes criticized because, very often, their judges are not trained in the law. Some years ago, a California study found that the State's nonlawyer local judges included several ministers, schoolteachers, real estate agents, druggists, and grocers, including one whose wife held court when he went fishing. Most States, including California, now require that *all* judges be licensed attorneys. *

Municipal Courts

Unhappy experiences with magistrates' courts have led to the creation of municipal courts in many cities. First established in Chicago in 1906, municipal courts are now found in most of the nation's larger cities and many of its middle-sized and small ones.

The jurisdiction of municipal courts is citywide. They can often hear civil cases involving several thousands of dollars as well as the usual run of misdemeanors. Many municipal courts are organized into divisions, which hear cases of a given kind, for example, civil, criminal, juvenile, small claims, traffic, and probate divisions.

Consider the small claims division, often called the small claims court, to illustrate this arrangement. Many people cannot afford the costs of suing for the collection of a small debt. A paper carrier, for example, can hardly afford a lawyer to collect a month's subscription from a customer. An elderly widow may have the same problem with a tenant's back rent, and many merchants are forced to forget an overdue bill or sell it to a collection agency.

---

[1]Jurisdiction is the power of a court to hear—to try and to decide—a case; literally, the power to "say the law"; see page 514.

[2]A **civil case** is a suit brought by one party against another for the enforcement or protection of some private right or for the prevention or redress of a tort (a private wrong). A **criminal case** is one brought by the State against a person accused of committing a crime —a public wrong. The State is at times a party in a civil suit. It is always a party in a criminal trial, as the prosecution. In the strictest sense, the terms *suit* and *trial* may be and are used interchangeably in the law. In general usage, however, suit is most often used to refer to civil actions and trial to criminal proceedings. A judicial proceeding that is neither a suit nor a trial is usually called a **hearing.**

[3]Crimes are of two kinds: felonies and misdemeanors. A **felony** is the greater crime and may be punished by a heavy fine and/or imprisonment or even death. A **misdemeanor** is the lesser offense, punishable by a small fine and/or a short jail term.

[4]A **warrant** is a court order authorizing, or making legal, some official action, for example, a search warrant or an arrest warrant. A preliminary hearing is generally the first step in a major criminal prosecution. There the judge decides if the evidence is in fact enough to hold that person—bind that person over—for action by the grand jury or the prosecutor.

[5]Many insist that the fee system means that "JP" really stands for "judgment for the plaintiff." The practice also encourages "fee splitting"—an arrangement in which judges can increase the number of misdemeanors they hear by agreeing to share their fees with those arresting officers who bring such cases to them. The "speed trap" is probably the best known and most common result of a fee-splitting situation.

*REINFORCEMENT Discuss in class: Why do most States require that all judges be licensed attorneys? Stress that over the years the law has become so complex that legal training must be a prerequisite.

Small claims courts have been set up for just such situations. In them, a person can bring a claim for little or no cost. The proceedings are usually informal, and the judge often handles the matter without attorneys for either side.

General Trial Courts

Most of the more important civil and criminal cases heard in U.S. courts are heard in the State's general trial courts.

Each State is divided into a number of judicial districts, or circuits, each generally covering one or more counties. For each district there is a general trial court, known variously as district, circuit, county, or superior courts or courts of common pleas. Most legal actions brought under State law are begun in these courts.

The judges of these trial courts are popularly elected in two-thirds of the States, usually for four-year, six-year, or eight-year terms. The governor appoints them in most of the other States, as we shall see. In those districts where the caseload is heavier, each of these courts frequently has several judges.

These general trial courts are courts of "first instance." That is, they exercise original jurisdiction over most of the cases they hear. When cases do come to them on appeal from such lower courts as a municipal court, a trial *de novo* is usually held, that is, a new trial, as though the case had not been heard before.

The cases heard in trial courts are tried before a single judge. Most often, a petit jury, or the trial jury, hears and decides the facts at issue in a case, and the judge interprets and applies the law involved in the case. Criminal cases are presented for trial either by a grand jury or on motion of the prosecuting attorney.

The trial court is seldom limited as to the kinds of cases it may hear. Although its decision on the *facts* in a case is usually final, disputes over questions of *law* may be carried to a higher court.

In the more heavily populated districts of some States, cases involving such matters as the settlement of estates or the affairs of minors are heard in separate trial courts, often called surrogate, probate, or orphans' courts. In most States and districts, however, these matters are part of the regular case load of the general trial courts.

At small claims court hearings, the judge often handles claims in a single, brief session with no involvement of attorneys for either side.

Intermediate Appellate Courts

All but a few States now have one or more intermediate appellate courts. They are courts of appeal that stand between the trial courts and the State's supreme court. These appellate courts serve to ease the burden of the high court.

Like the trial courts, the appellate courts have different names among the States, but they are most often called the court of appeals.[6] Their judges are chosen by the governor in a few States, for example, in New York and New Jersey. Most often, the judges are picked by the voters, usually for terms of six or eight years, but for as long as 12 years in both California and Missouri.

Most work of these courts involves the review of cases decided in the trial courts. That is, these appeals courts exercise mostly

[6]In New York the general trial court is called the Supreme Court; the intermediate appellate court is the Appellate Division of the Supreme Court; the State's highest court is known as the Court of Appeals.

*ENRICHMENT Assign to the students a report on your local general trial court: What is it called, how does the judge obtain his or her seat on the bench, etc.

The prosecuting attorney's role in a typical criminal trial is to present the State's case to the judge and jury. How is the jury selected?

appellate jurisdiction. Their original jurisdiction, where it exists, is limited to a few specific kinds of cases, election disputes, for example. In exercising their appellate jurisdiction, these courts do not hold trials. Rather, they hear oral arguments from attorneys, study the briefs—written arguments—that attorneys submit, and review the record of the case in the lower court.

Ordinarily, an appellate court does not concern itself with the *facts* in a case. Rather, its decision turns on whether the *law* was correctly interpreted and applied in the court below. Its decision *may* be reviewed by the State's high court, but, in practice, its disposition of a case is usually final.

The State Supreme Court

The State's supreme court is the highest court in its judicial system.[7] Its major function is to review the lower court decisions that are appealed to it.

The size of the supreme court is fixed by the State constitution. In most States five or seven justices sit on the high bench. There are nine justices of the supreme court in seven States, however: Alabama, Iowa, Minnesota, Mississippi, Oklahoma, Texas, and Washington.

The justices, including a chief justice, are appointed by the governor in 22 States.[8] They are selected by the legislature in four States,[9] and by the voters in the other 24.

The State supreme court is the court of last resort in the State's judicial system. It has the final say in all matters of State law. But, remember, many cases also raise questions of *federal* law. So, some State supreme court decisions *may* be reviewed by the United States Supreme Court. In fact not very

[7]The State's highest court is known by that title in 45 States. But in Maine and Massachusetts it is called the Supreme Judicial Court; in Maryland and New York, the Court of Appeals; and in West Virginia, the Supreme Court of Appeals. Two States actually have *two* high courts. In Oklahoma and in Texas, the Supreme Court is the highest court in *civil* cases, and a separate Court of Criminal Appeals is the court of last resort in criminal cases.

[8]By the governor directly in Delaware, Maine, New Hampshire, New Jersey, and New York; and by the governor through some version of the Missouri Plan, page 604, in Alaska, Arizona, California, Colorado, Florida, Hawaii, Indiana, Iowa, Kansas, Maryland, Massachusetts, Missouri, Nebraska, Oklahoma, South Dakota, Vermont, and Wyoming.

[9]Connecticut, Rhode Island, South Carolina, and Virginia.

many of them are.[10] Recall, an appeal from a State's high court will be heard in the federal Supreme Court *only* if (1) a "federal question"—some matter of federal law—is involved in the case *and* (2) the Supreme Court agrees to hear that appeal. Otherwise, review is not available.

In short, most State supreme court decisions are final. The oft-heard claim "I'll fight this case all the way to the United States Supreme Court" is almost always just so much hot air.[11]

Unified Court Systems

The typical State court system is organized geographically rather than by types of cases. Thus, the general trial courts are most often organized so that each hears those cases arising within its own district, circuit, or county, no matter what the subject matter may be.

In these map-based systems, a judge must hear cases in nearly all areas of the law. A backlog of cases may and often does build up in some courts while judges sit with little to do in others. Moreover, uneven interpretations and applications of the law may and sometimes do occur from one part of the State to another.

To overcome these difficulties, a number of States have begun to abandon geographical organization in recent years. They have turned, instead, to a **unified court system,** one that is organized on a functional, or * case-type, basis.

In a completely unified court system, there is technically only one court for the entire State. It is presided over, or administered by, a chief judge or judicial council. There are a number of levels within the single court, such as supreme, intermediate appellate, and general trial sections. At each level within each section, divisions are established to hear cases in certain specialized or heavy caseload areas of the law—criminal, juvenile, family relations, and other areas that need special attention.

In such an arrangement, a judge can be assigned to that section or division to which his or her talents and interests seem best suited. To relieve overcrowded dockets, judges may be moved from one section or division to another. In short, the unified court system is a modern response to the old common law adage: "Justice delayed is justice denied."

The move to a unified arrangement was pioneered by New Jersey in the late 1940s. Today at least half the States have taken some steps in that direction.

FOR REVIEW

1. **Identify:** judiciary, magistrate, preliminary hearing, small claims court, petit jury, intermediate appellate court
2. What is a court? What functions do courts perform?
3. What is a court's jurisdiction?
4. What is the difference between a civil case and a criminal case? A felony and a misdemeanor?
5. What are the differences and similarities between justice courts and municipal courts?
6. What is the function of general trial courts?
7. Why do nearly all States now have intermediate appellate courts?
8. What is the primary function of each State's supreme court?
9. Under what circumstances will a decision of a State's highest court be reviewed by the United States Supreme Court?
10. What is a unified court system? Why is it widely recommended?

[10] However, we did look at several such cases in Chapters 5 and 6, most especially cases involving the 14th Amendment's Due Process and Equal Protection Clauses.

[11] State law regularly gives its lower courts final jurisdiction over many types of minor cases. That is, review cannot be sought in a higher State court. In those cases, the lower court is the State's court of last resort. If any review is to be had, it can be only in the United States Supreme Court. Such reviews are extremely rare.

*ENRICHMENT Discuss: Although a unified court system may alleviate the problems that arise in map-based systems, the number of court cases does not change. How, then, can this system work?

2. The Selection of Judges

As You Read, Think About:

- What the methods are by which judges are chosen in the various States.
- What the advantages and disadvantages are of each method.
- Why the Missouri Plan for the selection of judges is so widely recommended.

More than 15,000 judges sit in the State and local courts today. They are most often chosen in one of three ways: by (1) popular election, (2) appointment by the governor, or (3) appointment by the legislature.[12]

In the colonies, judges were regularly appointed by the colonial governor. With independence, selection by the State legislature became the practice. The influence of Jacksonian democracy, which colored much of American political thought in the 19th century, persuaded most States to move to popular election of judges, however.

Selection Today

Most States use only one or another of the major methods of selection for all or at least most judgeships. There are many variations, however.

Popular election is by far the most widely used method by which judges are picked around the country. About three-fourths of all judges sitting in American courts today are chosen by the voters.

In fact, in 13 States popular election is the *only* method by which judges are chosen.[13] In most of the other States, most or at least some judges are also chosen at the polls. About half of all judicial elections are nonpartisan contests today.

Selection by the legislature is the least commonly used of the three major methods. The legislature now chooses all or at least most judges in only four States: Connecticut, Rhode Island, South Carolina, and Virginia.

The governor appoints nearly a fourth of all State judges today. In three States—Delaware, Massachusetts, and New Hampshire—all judges are named by the governor. In several other States, the governor has the power to appoint all or many judges, but under a Missouri Plan arrangement, as we shall see in just a moment.

How Should Judges Be Selected? Most of us believe that judges should be independent, that they should "stay out of politics." Whatever method of selection is used, then, should be designed with that goal in mind.

Nearly all authorities agree that selection by the legislature is the most political of all the methods of choice—and few favor it. So, the question is really: Which is better, popular election of judges or appointment by the governor?

Three of every four judges that preside over the nation's courts are chosen by popular vote.

[12]Some judges are selected by other means in some States. In Ohio, for example, all judges, except those of the Court of Claims, are elected by the voters; the judges of the Court of Claims are appointed by the Chief Justice of the State Supreme Court. In Alabama, Michigan, Mississippi, Oregon, Texas, Washington, and Wisconsin, all judges are popularly elected except for municipal court judges, who are chosen in accord with city charter provisions, usually by the city council.

[13]The exceptions are vacancies caused by deaths or by midterm resignations, which are usually filled by appointments made by the governor. The 13 States are Arkansas, Illinois, Kentucky, Louisiana, Minnesota, Montana, Nevada, New Mexico, North Carolina, North Dakota, Pennsylvania, West Virginia, and Wisconsin.

*REINFORCEMENT Discuss in class: What are the advantages and disadvantages of each of the three methods used to select judges?

FOCUS ON:

Judging the Judges

Unlike federal court judges, nearly all State judges are either elected or appointed to fixed terms of office. Still, the rate of judicial turnover is low in every State. Once a person becomes a judge, he or she tends to remain in office over time. Most elected judges seek reelection, most often successfully, and most appointed judges are regularly reappointed.

Most State judges are quite able. Unfortunately, some few are not. The problem of an unfit judge is sometimes solved by death, resignation, retirement, or by failure to win reelection or reappointment. But if an unfit judge does stay in office, what then?

Every State except Oregon provides for the impeachment process. Two other methods of removal have been available in some States for several decades: (1) the legislative address, a process by which the legislature may direct the governor to remove a judge and (2) the recall, a process we looked at on page 581.

Those methods are cumbersome and are very seldom used, however. Thus, only one judge—a trial judge in Madison, Wisconsin, in 1977—has been recalled in the past 40 years. He was recalled for having made highly sexist remarks during a rape trial in his court.

Three-fourths of the States have now adopted another method for the judging of judges. Beginning with California in 1960, they have created boards or commissions for that purpose.

California's Commission on Judicial Performance is fairly typical. It has nine members: five sitting judges named by the State supreme court, two lawyers chosen by the State bar, and two citizens appointed by the governor.

The Commission investigates any charge that a judge is unfit for office. If it finds merit in a complaint, it may try to settle matters in confidential discussions with the judge involved. If the facts seem to justify removal, and the judge will not leave office voluntarily, the Commission may take the case to the supreme court. With that step, the State's high court may take whatever disciplinary action it finds necessary, ranging from public censure to removal from office.

1. How are judges chosen in your State? For what terms? How may they be removed from office?
2. Does your State have some kind of judicial qualifications commission? How does it function?

Those who agree on popular election generally make the democratic argument. Because judges "say the law," interpret and apply it, they should be chosen by and answer directly to the people. Some also argue that the concept of separation of powers is undercut if the executive (the governor) has the power to name the members of the judicial branch.

Those who favor appointment by the governor argue that the judicial function should be carried out only by those who are well qualified. The fact that a person has the support of a political party or is a good vote-getter does not mean that person has the capacity to be a good judge. Proponents of executive appointment insist it is the best way to ensure that those who preside in courts will have the qualities most needed in that role: absolute honesty and integrity, fairness, and the necessary training and ability in the law.

At best, deciding between these two positions is difficult. The people have often made excellent choices, and governors have not always made wise and nonpolitical ones. Still, most authorities come down on the side of gubernatorial appointment, largely because those characteristics that make a good judge and those that make a good candidate are not often found in the same person.

Popular election is both widely used and widely supported. Moves to abandon it have been strongly opposed by party organizations. So, most moves to revise the method of judicial selection have kept at least some element of voter choice.

The Missouri Plan For some 60 years now, the American Bar Association (ABA) has sponsored an approach that combines the election and appointment processes. A version of the ABA's plan was first adopted in California in 1934 and then in Missouri in 1940. Because its adoption in Missouri involved much political drama, and so attracted wide attention, the method is often called * The Missouri Plan.

Missouri's version of the plan is more or less typical of its shape in those other States where it is now used. The governor appoints the seven justices of the State's supreme court, the 31 judges of the court of appeals, and all judges who sit in certain of the State's trial courts.[14] The governor must make those appointments from a panel, or list, of three names recommended by a judicial nominating commission. The commission is made up of a sitting judge, several members of the bar, and private citizens.

Each judge named by the governor then serves until the first general election after he or she has been in office for at least a year. The judge's name then appears on the ballot, without opposition. The voters decide whether or not that judge should be kept in office.

If the vote is favorable, the judge then serves a regular term—six years for a trial court judge and 12 years for one who sits on a higher court in Missouri. Thereafter, the judge may seek further terms in future retain-reject elections.

Should the voters reject a sitting judge, the process begins again. The governor makes a new appointment from the commission's list, and so on.

In nearly half the States, some form of the Missouri Plan is now used for selecting at least some judges. California and Missouri pioneered the device, and then stood alone for several years. But the number of States that use the plan has been growing steadily over the past decade or so.

FOR REVIEW

1. **Identify:** popular election.
2. What three major methods are used to select State judges? Which is the most widely used?
3. What is the Missouri Plan? Why is some version of it favored by nearly all students of judicial administration?

3. The Jury System

As You Read, Think About:

- What a grand jury is and how it functions.
- What a petit jury is and how it functions.

A jury is a body of persons selected according to law who hear evidence and decide questions of fact in a court case. There are two basic types of juries in the American legal system: (1) the grand jury and (2) the petit jury.

The major function of the **grand jury** is to determine whether the evidence against a

[14]Presently, the judges of the circuit and probate courts in St. Louis City and County and in the three counties (Jackson, Platte, and Clay) in the Kansas City metropolitan area. All other judges are elected on a partisan ballot, but the plan may be adopted by the voters in any of the State's judicial districts.

*ENRICHMENT The Missouri Plan offers a solution to the debate of how judges should be elected. Ask the class how voter choice is incorporated into the plan, and if they think the plan is, indeed, an answer.

BUILDING GOVERNMENT SKILLS

Serving on a Jury

The trial of all crimes, except in cases of impeachment, shall be by jury; and such trial shall be held in the State where the said crimes shall have been committed; but when not committed within any State the trial shall be at such place or places as the Congress may be by law have directed.

—*United States Constitution, Article III, Section 2, Clause 3*

Everyone charged with a crime in the United States has the right to a trial by jury. You have probably seen or read about juries on television, in newspapers, or in books.

The procedure may vary a little from place to place, but this is the basic framework. Imagine you are a potential juror. You will receive a letter, called a summons, that will tell you the time and place to which you should report for jury duty. By law, your employer cannot fire or penalize you for time lost while serving as a juror, but you should let your employer know you have been summoned as soon as possible.

Once you enter the courthouse, you will probably have to wait with other citizens who have been called for jury duty. After a while, you will go to a courtroom where the defense attorney, the prosecuting attorney (or the plaintiff's attorney if the case is a civil case), and a judge will ask you questions. You may be asked questions first in the large group, and then individually.

By asking questions, the lawyers hope to uncover any potential biases that you may hold against his or her client. In addition, they want to determine if you have any prior knowledge of the defendant or of the case.

If, for any number of reasons, you are disqualified, or struck, from a case, you will either be asked to return on another day or to wait for another case that day.

If you are chosen to serve on the jury for the case, you will take an oath with the other jurors and receive instructions from the judge. The judge will tell you about court proceedings and remind you that as a juror you can only decide the case based on the testimony presented during the trial. You may not use anything learned about the case outside of the courtroom, and you cannot speak to anyone.

As the case begins, the prosecutor or the plaintiff presents its side first. The defense goes next. Listen carefully to the testimony because you are not allowed to take notes.

When the case is finished and both sides have presented all their arguments, the jurors will be asked to reach a verdict. In a civil case, this means deciding if the defendant is at fault and liable for damages.

If the case is a criminal case, the jury is asked to decide whether the defendant is guilty or not guilty. In most cases, the judge will give the jury instructions about the law.

In most States a unanimous vote is required to reach a verdict. In some, however, only an extraordinary majority is required.

When the jury has reached a verdict, you will be led back into the courtroom. The foreman of the jury will deliver the verdict.

1. Why do you think that defense lawyers are very careful about choosing juries? Prosecuting attorneys? Give examples.
2. Most States restrict the number of "strikes" both the defense attorney and the prosecuting attorney have. Why? What are the regulations on this process in your State?
3. Interview a person who has served on a jury. What did he or she think of the process in general?

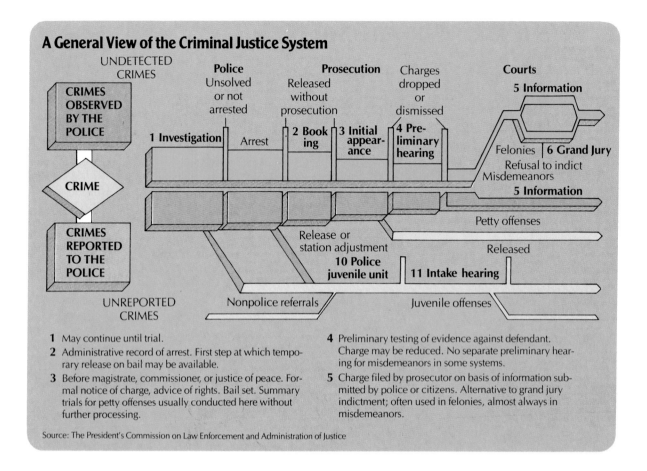

A General View of the Criminal Justice System

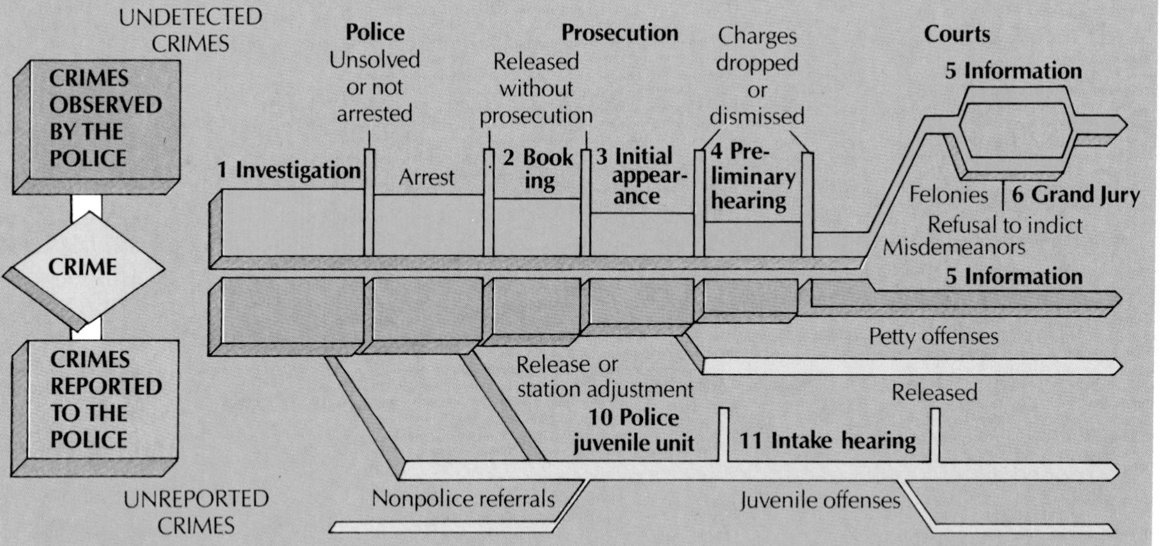

1 May continue until trial.

2 Administrative record of arrest. First step at which temporary release on bail may be available.

3 Before magistrate, commissioner, or justice of peace. Formal notice of charge, advice of rights. Bail set. Summary trials for petty offenses usually conducted here without further processing.

4 Preliminary testing of evidence against defendant. Charge may be reduced. No separate preliminary hearing for misdemeanors in some systems.

5 Charge filed by prosecutor on basis of information submitted by police or citizens. Alternative to grand jury indictment; often used in felonies, almost always in misdemeanors.

Source: The President's Commission on Law Enforcement and Administration of Justice

person charged with crime is sufficient to justify a trial. The grand jury is used only in criminal proceedings. The petit jury is the trial jury, and it is used in both civil and criminal cases.

The Grand Jury

The grand jury has from 6 to 23 persons, depending on the State. Where larger juries are used, generally at least 12 jurors must agree that an accused person is probably guilty before a formal accusation is made. Similarly, with smaller juries, an extraordinary majority is needed to indict, or bring the formal charge.

When a grand jury is impaneled, or selected, the judge instructs the jurors to find a true **bill of indictment** against any and all persons whom the prosecuting attorney brings to their attention and who they think are probably guilty. The judge also instructs them to bring a presentment, or accusation, against any persons who they, of their own knowledge, believe have violated the State's criminal laws in that judicial district.

The grand jury meets in secret. To preside over its sessions, either the judge appoints or the jurors select one of their number to serve as the foreman. The prosecuting attorney presents witnesses and evidence against persons suspected of crime. The jurors may question those witnesses and summon others to testify against a suspect. No one is allowed in the jury room except the grand jurors, the prosecutor, witnesses, and, in some States, a stenographer. All are sworn to secrecy.

After receiving the evidence and hearing witnesses, the grand jury deliberates, with only the jurors themselves present. With the completion of their review, they move to the

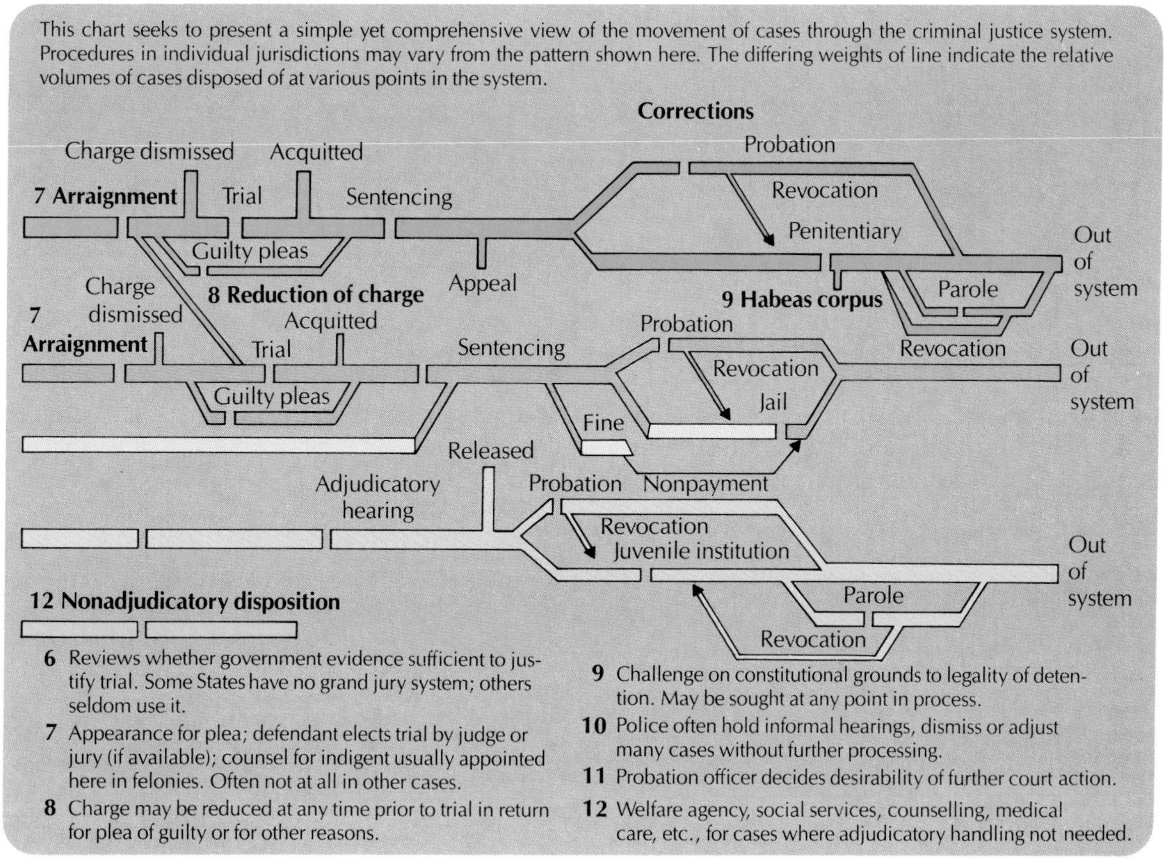

courtroom. There their report, including any indictments they may have returned, is read in their presence.

Accusation by Information The grand jury is cumbersome and time consuming. It adds to the already considerable delay and the expense of the criminal process. Hence, most of the States today depend more heavily on a much simpler process of accusation: the information.

An **information** is a formal charge filed by the prosecutor, without the action of a grand jury. The information is now used for most minor offenses. More than half the States now use it in most of the more serious cases, as well.

The use of the information has much to recommend it. It is far less costly and time consuming. Then, too, since grand juries most often follow the prosecutor's recommendations, many argue that a grand jury is really unnecessary.

The chief objection to abandoning the grand jury appears to be the fear that some prosecutors may abuse their powers—that they will be overzealous and overly energetic and forceful at the expense of both defendants and justice.

The Petit Jury

As we have seen, the **petit jury** is the trial jury. It hears the evidence in a case and decides the disputed facts. In some very few instances, it may also have the power to interpret and apply the law, but that is almost always the function of the judge.

The number of trial jurors may vary. As it developed in England, the jury consisted of "12 men good and true." Although 12 is still the usual number, a lesser number, often 6,

*ENRICHMENT Discuss in class: An accusation by information is often used in place of the grand jury. Do you agree that it is an adequate replacement or does it abuse the system? Be sure students support their opinions.

By permission of Johnny Hart and News America Syndicate

now fill jury boxes in several States. As we read in Chapter 6, women are now allowed everywhere to serve on juries.

In over a third of the States, jury verdicts need not be unanimous in civil and minor criminal cases. Rather, some extraordinary majority is needed. In most States, however, verdicts must be unanimous in all cases. If a jury cannot agree on a verdict (a "hung jury"), either another trial with a new jury is held or the matter is dropped.

Misdemeanor cases and civil proceedings in which only minor sums are involved are often heard without a jury. That is, they are heard in a **bench trial,** by the judge alone. In several States even the most serious of crimes may be heard without a jury—*if* the accused, fully informed of his or her rights, waives the right to trial by jury.

Selection of Jurors

Jurors are picked in more or less the same way in most States. Periodically, some county official[15] or special jury commissioners prepare a list of persons eligible for jury service. The lists are generally quite long. Depending on the State, the lists are drawn from the poll books or the tax assessor's rolls. When jurors are needed, names are picked from these lists at random.

The sheriff serves each person with a court order, a writ of *venire facias,* meaning you must come. After eliminating those who, for good reason, cannot serve, the judge prepares a list of those who can: the panel of *veniremen.* Persons under 18 and those over 70 years of age, illiterates, the ill, and criminals are commonly excluded. In many States those in occupations vital to the public interest—physicians, druggists, teachers, firefighters, and the like—are also excused. Those for whom jury service would mean real hardship are often excused, too.

As with the grand jury, the States are moving away from the use of the trial jury. The greater time and cost of jury trials are leading reasons. The competence of the average jury and the impulses that may lead it to a verdict are often questioned, as well.

Much criticism of the jury system is directed not so much at the system itself as at its *operation.* Several things should be said for the jury system. It has both a long and an honorable place in the development of Anglo-American law. Its high purpose is to promote a fair trial, by providing an impartial body to hear the charges brought in either civil or criminal cases. It tends to bring the common sense of the community to bear on the law and its application. It gives the citizen a chance to take part in the administration of justice, and it fosters a greater confidence in the judicial system.

FOR REVIEW

1. **Identify:** impaneled, writ of *venire facias,* panel of *veniremen.*
2. What is the primary duty of a grand jury? What process is now often used as an alternative to it?
3. What is an indictment? A presentment? An information?
4. What does the petit jury do?

[15]Most often it is the clerk of the court, the sheriff, or the county governing body, and sometimes the presiding judge, and in New England, officers of the town.

4. Kinds of Law Applied by State Courts

As You Read, Think About:

- What kinds of law are applied by State courts.
- What the difference is between common law and equity.
- Who may hand down advisory opinions and declaratory opinions.

The **law**—the code of conduct by which society is governed—is made up of several different forms of law.[16] In dealing with cases that come before them, State courts apply *these various forms of law:

Constitutional law—the highest form of law—is based on the provisions of the United States Constitution and the State constitution, and judicial interpretations of them.

Statutory law—the law, or, statutes enacted by legislative bodies, including the United States Congress, the State legislature, the people through the initiative or referendum, and city councils and other local legislative bodies.

Administrative law—the rules, orders, and regulations that are issued by federal, State, or local executive officers, acting under proper constitutional and/or statutory authority.

Criminal law—that portion of the law that defines public wrongs (offenses against the public order) and provides for their punishment.

Civil law—that portion of the law relating to human conduct, to disputes between private parties, and to disputes between private parties and government not covered by criminal law.

Minor violations of criminal law (misdemeanors)—such as traffic or parking violations—are handled by traffic courts in most cities and suburbs.

We have dealt with each of these forms of law at many places in this book to this point. The State courts also apply two other forms of law: common law and equity.

Common Law

The **common law** makes up a large part of the law of each of the States except Louisiana.[17] It is *unwritten, judge-made* law. It has developed, over centuries, from those generally accepted ideas of right and wrong that have gained judicial recognition. It covers

[16]In its overall sense, the term *law* may be defined as the whole body of "rules and principles of conduct which the governing power in a community recognizes as those which it will enforce or sanction, and according to which it will regulate, limit, or protect the conduct of its members"; *Bouvier's Law Dictionary*, 3rd revision, vol. II, pp. 1875–76. For us, the term *community* refers to the United States, any of the States, and/or any unit of local government.

[17]Because of the early French influence, Louisiana's legal system is very largely based on French legal concepts, derived from Roman law. The common law has worked its way into Louisiana law, however.

*ENRICHMENT Ask the class to list several laws that affect their lives and then decide which of the above forms these laws take.

Joseph Mirachi, 1984. The New Yorker Magazine, Inc.

"As it turned out, my battery of lawyers was no match for their battery of eyewitnesses."

nearly all aspects of human conduct. Common law is applied by State courts, *except* when in conflict with written law.

The common law originated in England. It grew out of the decisions made by the king's judges on the basis of local customs. It developed as judges, coming upon situations similar to those found in earlier cases, applied and reapplied the rulings from those earlier cases. Thus, little by little, the law of those cases became *common* throughout the land—and, in time, throughout the English-speaking world. That is, the common law developed as judges followed the **precedent** of earlier decisions—as they applied the rule of **stare decisis,** "let the decision stand."[18]

The common law is *not* a rigidly fixed body of rules controlled in every case by a clear line of precedents that can be easily found and applied. Judges are regularly called on to interpret and reinterpret the existing rules in the light of changing times and circumstances. Or, common law may be described this way: Most legal disputes in American courts are fought out very largely over the application of precedents. The opposing lawyers try to persuade the court that the precedents support their side of the case or that the general line of precedents should not, for some reason, be followed. The judge must weigh the precedents, and their applicability, in reaching a decision.

The importance of the common law in the American legal system cannot be overstated. Statutory law does override common law, but many statutes are based on the common law. Statutes are, in effect, common law translated into written law. They are interpreted and applied by the courts according to common law tradition and meaning.

Equity

Equity is a branch of the law that supplements the common law. It developed in England to provide equity—"fairness, justice, and right"—when remedies under the common law fell short of that goal.

Over the years common law became somewhat rigid. Remedies were available only through various writs, or orders, issued by the courts. If no writ was suited to the relief sought in a case, no action could be taken by the courts.

Those who were thus barred from the courts—for whom there was no adequate remedy at common law—appealed to the king for justice. These appeals became so numerous that they were usually referred to the chancellor, a member of the king's council. By the middle of the 14th century, a special court of chancery, or equity, was set up. Over time, a system of rules developed, and equity assumed a permanent place in the English legal system.

Perhaps the most important difference between common law and equity today is this: The common law is mostly *remedial* while equity is *preventive.* That is, the common law applies to or provides a remedy for matters *after* they have happened; equity seeks to stop wrongs *before* they occur.

To illustrate this point, suppose your neighbors plan to add a room to their house.

[18]American courts generally follow the rule. A decision, once made, becomes a precedent—a guide to be followed in all later, similar cases, unless compelling reasons call for its abandonment and the setting of a new precedent.

They intend to build, even though you protest. You think that a part of the planned addition will in fact be on your land, and you know that it will destroy your rose garden. You can prevent the construction by getting an **injunction**—a court order prohibiting, or enjoining, a specified action by the party named in the order. A court is likely to grant the injunction for two reasons: (1) the immediacy of the threat to your property and (2) the fact that the law can offer no fully satisfactory remedy once your garden has been destroyed. It is true that money damages might be assessed under common law, but no amount of money can give back the pride or the pleasure your plants now give you.

The English colonists brought both equity and the common law to America. At first, the two forms of law were administered by different courts. In time, though, most States provided for the administration of both forms by the same courts; procedural differences between the two are disappearing.

Advisory Opinions

Ordinarily, a court will not act on a question unless it is presented in a case actually before it. Even then, it will do so only when the issue is "ripe for decision." Among other things, this means that, as a general rule, courts will not issue advisory opinions.[19]

In 11 States, however, the supreme court can render advisory opinions. That is, in those States the high court may indicate its views on the constitutionality or legal effects of a law or a proposed change in the law. In each of these States, these opinions are available to the governor and, in all except three, to the legislature, as well.[20]

These advisory opinions have a number of advantages. They can be useful guides to the legislature, for example, as a measure that it considers breaks new ground or about which serious constitutional questions have been raised. Advisory opinions can be of similar help to the governor in deciding whether to sign or veto a bill or whether a law already on the books is in fact enforceable.

As the term suggests, these opinions are *advisory* only. They are not binding on the decision of later cases, except in Colorado. Most legal authorities do not favor giving this power to the State supreme court. Instead, they believe that it should belong to the attorney general; see page 592. *

Declaratory Judgments

In nearly all States, the principal courts may render declaratory judgments. These judgments are available *before* an actual case is instituted. The judgments are declarations of the legal rights and obligations of the parties to a controversy before a lawsuit is filed. They may be sought by any person involved in a controversy over his or her rights under any legal instrument, such as a statute, a will, or a contract.

Declaratory judgments are legally binding on the parties involved. They serve to prevent the doing of a wrong, to avoid loss or injury, or to forestall long and costly legal battles.

FOR REVIEW

1. **Identify:** equity, writs, chancery, declaratory judgments, advisory opinions.
2. What are the five kinds of law that State courts apply?
3. What is the common law? How did it originate?
4. How are precedents used in common law?
5. How did equity originate?
6. What is the chief difference between common law and equity?

---

[19]Court opinions do sometimes contain comments *(dicta)* on some points other than the precise issue involved in deciding a particular case. The *dicta* in court opinions, especially in those of higher courts, can be quite important, as indications of a court's views on related matters and as indications of future decisions.

[20]To both the governor and the legislature in Alabama, Colorado, Maine, Massachusetts, Michigan, North Carolina, New Hampshire, and Rhode Island; to the governor only in Delaware, Florida, and South Dakota. Neither the United States Supreme Court nor any other federal court will render advisory opinions.

*ENRICHMENT Advisory opinions are just that—advisory. Ask the class to discuss whether the power of these opinions should be given to the State supreme court or the attorney general.

SUMMARY

A court is a tribunal established by law to administer justice according to law. The State courts—not the federal courts—hear most of the cases heard in American courts.

The details of the structure of the 50 separate State court systems are quite complicated, and there are many differences from State to State. Justice courts, magistrates' or police courts, and/or municipal courts in all or most of the States hear minor civil and misdemeanor cases.

The general trial courts, known by a variety of names among the States, are the principal courts of first instance. They are the courts in which most of the major civil and criminal cases begin and generally end in the United States.

The intermediate appellate courts, found in most States, stand between the trial courts and the State supreme court. They hear appeals from the lower courts and serve to relieve the highest court of much of its appellate burden.

The supreme court stands at the top of the State's judicial system. Except for cases that might be appealed to the United States Supreme Court, it is generally the court of last resort—the final interpreter of the State's constitution and laws.

Most State judges are selected in one of three ways: (1) popular election, (2) appointment by the governor, or (3) appointment by the legislature. About three-fourths of them are chosen by the voters—about as often as not on a partisan ballot. The Missouri Plan is a selection process that combines the processes of executive appointment and popular election.

There are two major types of juries in the judicial process: (1) the grand jury, which decides if the evidence is sufficient to warrant trial in a criminal case; and (2) the petit (trial) jury, which hears and decides the facts at issue in both civil and criminal cases. In most States an information may be filed by the prosecutor as an alternative to accusation by the grand jury.

The State courts apply several kinds of law: constitutional, statutory, and administrative law; civil and criminal law; and common law and equity. Eleven of the State supreme courts may give advisory opinions and, in most States, they may render declaratory judgments.

CHAPTER REVIEW

Key Terms/Concepts*

justices of the peace (597)
misdemeanor (598)
felony (598)
warrant (598)
appellate jurisdiction (600)
grand jury (604)
indictment (606)
information (607)
petit jury (607)
bench trial (608)
constitutional law (609)
statutory law (609)
administrative law (609)
criminal law (609)
civil law (609)
common law (609)
precedent (610)
stare decisis (610)
equity (610)
injunction (611)

*These terms are included in the Glossary.

Keynote Questions

• **1.** How many separate court systems are there in this country today?

• **2.** What word is regularly used to identify a court's power to hear (*i.e.*, to try and to decide) a case?

• **3.** What distinguishes a civil from a criminal case? A felony from a misdemeanor?

• **4.** What courts are often found at the lowest trial level in a State's court system?

• **5.** Most of the more important civil and criminal cases are first heard in what courts in your State?

• **6.** Why have most of the States now established intermediate appellate courts?

*The dots represent skill levels required to answer each question or complete each activity:
• requires recall and comprehension • • requires application and analysis • • • requires synthesis and evaluation

• **7.** What is the primary function of each State's supreme court?

• **8.** Under what circumstances will a decision of a State's highest court be reviewed by the United States Supreme Court?

•• **9.** How are judges selected in your State? What is the Missouri Plan?

•• **10.** What process is often used as an alternative to the grand jury? Why?

• **11.** What is the basic function of a trial (petit) jury?

• **12.** What several different forms of law are applied by State courts?

•• **13.** What is the common law? Equity? What is probably the chief distinction between them?

• **14.** What is the rule of *stare decisis*?

Skill Application

Using a Flow Chart: The chart on pages 606-607, "A General View of the Criminal Justice System," presents a comprehensive view of the movement of cases through the criminal justice system. An important component of this chart is its key, which explains what is involved in certain procedures at various points in the system. Study the chart and its key and answer the following questions:

1. At what point is an official record made of an arrest?
2. What is the purpose of a preliminary hearing?
3. At what point may a defendant make a choice between being tried by a judge or being tried by a jury?
4. At what point(s) may a defendant challenge the legality of his or her detention on constitutional grounds?
5. What often happens when a juvenile is detained and referred to a police juvenile unit?
6. What is meant by "nonadjudicatory disposition"?

For Thought and Discussion

• **1.** What did John Locke mean when he wrote the thought we quoted on page 596: "Where law ends, Tyranny begins"? Who was Locke?

••• **2.** How are judges selected in your State? What changes, if any, do you think should be made in that process? Why? Who might be expected to be against such changes? Why?

•• **3.** If you had the power to name the judges of the courts of your State, what qualifications would you seek in those you selected? Would those qualifications vary depending upon the court involved?

•• **4.** Are *justice* and *law* synonymous terms? Explain your response.

••• **5.** Over the years, the office of justice of the peace and justice courts have been abolished in about half of the States and their number greatly reduced in most of the others. They have been replaced with local courts presided over by judges trained in the law. Do you think this trend should be maintained? Why (or why not)? In many States, justices of the peace are still paid out of the fines they collect; the more fines they impose, the higher their income. Why is this "fee system" vigorously opposed by most students of judicial administration?

••• **6.** Are crimes more likely to be prevented by the *severity* of the punishments imposed or by the *certainty* of punishment? Give reasons for your response.

Suggested Activities

•• **1.** Attend sessions of a local court and write a report describing the proceedings and your impressions of them.

• **2.** Invite a judge, a prosecutor, or a practicing attorney to speak to the class on the courts, their organization, procedures, and functions.

• **3.** Construct a diagram of the courts of your State. Show the jurisdiction of the several courts and by whom and for what term their judges are chosen.

• **4.** Prepare a report to the class on some case currently being tried in a court in your locale. Describe the facts in the dispute and the procedures involved in the trial process.

••• **5.** Hold a moot court session—that is, a mock trial—in which the steps of a trial are reenacted.

••• **6.** Stage a debate or class forum on the following topic: *Resolved,* That felony cases should be decided by a two-thirds majority verdict rather than by the present unanimous verdict requirement.

How can a people unaccustomed to freedom in small affairs learn to use it temperately in great affairs?
–Alexis de Tocqueville

23 Governing the Communities

CHAPTER OBJECTIVES

To help you to

Learn · Know · Understand

How the nation's 3,041 counties vary in terms of geographic size, population, governmental framework, and basic functions.

Reform efforts in the organization of county governments.

Towns and townships as units of government and how they differ.

The roles of special districts in the governmental process.

The differences between the legal status of cities and that of other units of local government.

Types of city charters and the three major forms of city government in this country.

The problems of urban and suburban sprawl.

Government in the United States is very often discussed in terms of three basic layers: National, State, and local. The basic components of the federal system, however, are the National Government and the 50 States.

All local governments in the United States are creatures of the States. Each of the 50 States, either through its constitution or its laws, establishes, and may abolish, any or all of these units. To whatever extent local governments can provide services, regulate activities, collect taxes, or do anything else, they can do so *only* because the State has established them and permits them to. As they exercise the powers they have, then, local governments are exercising *State* powers, powers that have been delegated to them by the State.

Another way of describing this is to remind you that each of the 50 States has a *unitary* form of government (see page 7).

As we have noted several times, it is the States and especially their local governments that most directly and continuously affect the daily business of living in this country.

ENRICHMENT Have the class discuss: What is the relationship between State and local governments? Have the students cite examples from their own community.

The range and variety of services provided to residents of rural towns, as those who live in the village of East Corinth, Vermont (shown at left), are very different from the kind of services provided to residents of a large municipality such as Los Angeles, California, part of the largest metropolitan area in the United States.

As only one measure of their everpresent importance, consider the *sheer number* of local governments in the United States. In its latest tabulation, the Census Bureau reported 82,341 separate units of government across the nation. As the following table below shows, 82,290 of these units—nearly all of them—are at the *local* level.

Type of Government	Units
National Government	1
State Governments	50
Local Governments	82,290
Counties	3,041
Municipalities	19,076
Townships	16,734
School Districts	14,851
Special Districts	28,588

In this chapter we turn to these local units of government, so often described as those "closest to the people."

1. The Counties

As You Read, Think About:

- What the relationship is between local governmental units and the States.
- What the major elements are of county governments.
- What officials run county governments.

The 3,041 **counties** cover nearly all of the United States. Organized county governments are found in all States except Connecticut and Rhode Island. In Louisiana what are known elsewhere as counties are called **parishes,** and in Alaska they are known as **boroughs.** There are several places across the country where no organized county government exists—as you can see in the table on page 619. About 10 percent of the nation's population lives in those areas today.

Counties serve almost solely as judicial districts in the New England States. In these States, towns carry out most of the functions undertaken by counties elsewhere. The functions of rural local government are shared by counties and townships in those States from New York and New Jersey west to the Dakotas, Nebraska, and Kansas. In the South and the West, counties are the major units of government in rural areas.

Number, Size, and Population

The number of counties runs from none in Connecticut and Rhode Island and three in Delaware and Hawaii to as many as 254 in Texas. There is no close relationship between the size of a State and the number of counties it has.

In terms of area, San Bernardino County in southern California is the largest. It covers 52,064 square kilometers (20,102 square miles). Arlington County in Virginia is the smallest, covering only 67.6 square kilometers (26 square miles). Within most States, there is also a marked difference in the area covered by each county.

Counties also vary widely in terms of population. More than 7.4 million persons now live in Los Angeles County in California. At the other end of the scale, only 91 residents were counted in Loving County, in western Texas, in the 1980 census. Most counties, in fact, 75 percent of them, serve populations of fewer than 50,000.

County Government Structures: Ones of Organized (?) Chaos

Most people know, or care to know, little about the government of their county.

If county governments have any one principle of organization in common, it is that of *confusion. In the typical county, no one official can be called the chief administrator. Rather, authority is divided among a number of elected officials and boards, each largely independent of the others. As a result, it is often impossible to fix the responsibility for laxity, inefficiency, or inaction, or worse, in the conduct of county affairs.

The structures of county government differ, often considerably. But, as you can see from the chart on this page, it typically has four major elements: a governing body, elected officials, a number of boards, and appointed bureaucrats.

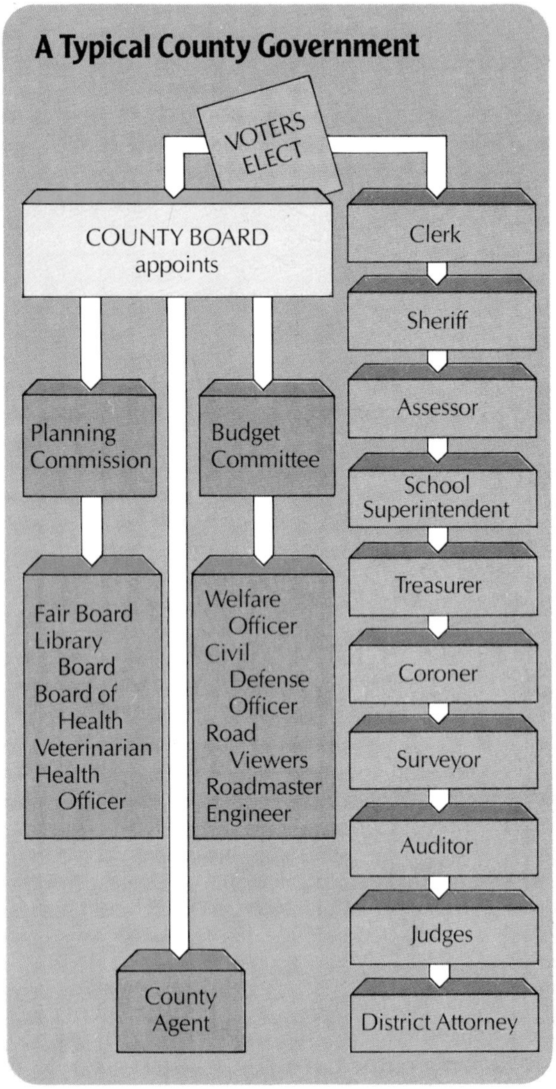

In many counties, the county board has both executive and legislative powers. However, the board's executive power is usually shared with other elected officials, each with responsibility for a department. Why might such an arrangement make for confusion?

A Governing Body The governing body of the county is often called the "county board." It is known by at least 20 other names among the States, for example: the board of commissioners, board of supervisors, police jury, fiscal court, county court, and board of chosen freeholders.

The members of the board, whatever its title, are almost always popularly elected.

*REINFORCEMENT Have the class discuss the real and potential problems of county governments. Ask for specific examples.

Shown in session here is a meeting of a county board in Texas, known in that State as the Commissioners Court. As in many States, its members serve four-year, overlapping terms.

They are usually chosen from districts in the county rather than on an at-large basis.[1] Terms of office run from one to eight years, but four-year terms are the most common.

Generally, county boards may be grouped into two types: boards of commissioners and boards of supervisors. The board of commissioners is the smaller and more common type. Found everywhere in the South and West, the board is also well–known elsewhere. It most often has three or five, but some have seven or more, members. The members, usually called commissioners, are elected only to these bodies. As a rule, they hold no other public office.

The board of supervisors is typically a much larger body, having an average of about 15 members but sometimes running to as many as 80 or more. The supervisors are elected from each of the several townships in the county, as in New York, Nebraska, and Wisconsin. Each supervisor is usually an officer of his or her township as well as a member of the countywide governing body.

The powers held by the county governing bodies are prescribed, and often very narrowly defined, in the State constitution and acts of the State legislature. However restricted they may be, the powers of these boards are generally both executive *and* legislative, despite the American tradition of separation of powers.

Their most important legislative powers are those dealing with finance. County boards levy taxes, appropriate funds, and incur limited debts. They also have a number of lesser legislative powers, many in the

[1]In *Avery* v. *Midland County*, 1968, a case from Texas, the U.S. Supreme Court held that the 14th Amendment's Equal Protection Clause "forbids the election of local officials from districts of disparate size." The Court there extended the "one-man, one-vote" rule to the local level and has followed that holding in several later cases; see pages 301, 560.

Local Governments in the United States

State	All Local Governments	Counties	Local Governments, By Type			
			Munici-palities	Town-ships*	School Districts	Special Districts
US TOTAL	82,290	3,041	19,076	16,734	14,851	28,588
Alabama	1,018	67	434	—	127	390
Alaska	156	8	142	—	—	6
Arizona	452	14	76	—	232	130
Arkansas	1,424	75	472	—	372	505
California	4,102	57	428	—	1,111	2,506
Colorado	1,544	62	267	—	185	1,030
Connecticut	479	—	33	149	16	281
Delaware	217	3	56	—	19	139
District of Columbia	2	—	1	—	—	1
Florida	969	67	391	—	95	417
Georgia	1,268	158	533	—	187	390
Hawaii	18	3	1	—	—	14
Idaho	1,018	44	198	—	117	659
Illinois	6,467	102	1,280	1,434	1,049	2,602
Indiana	2,865	91	564	1,008	305	897
Iowa	1,871	99	955	—	456	361
Kansas	3,795	105	627	1,367	326	1,370
Kentucky	1,241	119	425	—	180	517
Louisiana	468	62	301	—	66	39
Maine	806	16	22	475	98	195
Maryland	439	23	152	—	—	264
Massachusetts	798	12	39	312	81	354
Michigan	2,643	83	532	1,245	599	184
Minnesota	3,529	87	855	1,795	436	356
Mississippi	858	82	292	—	169	315
Missouri	3,117	114	926	325	557	1,195
Montana	1,029	54	126	—	399	450
Nebraska	3,324	93	535	470	1,069	1,157
Nevada	184	16	17	—	17	134
New Hampshire	517	10	13	221	160	113
New Jersey	1,591	21	323	245	548	454
New Mexico	319	33	96	—	89	101
New York	3,249	57	615	928	726	923
North Carolina	905	100	484	—	—	321
North Dakota	2,795	53	365	1,360	325	692
Ohio	3,393	88	941	1,318	669	377
Oklahoma	2,212	77	581	—	638	916
Oregon	1,454	36	241	—	352	825
Pennsylvania	5,198	66	1,019	1,549	514	2,050
Rhode Island	122	—	8	31	3	80
South Carolina	645	46	265	—	92	242
South Dakota	1,767	64	312	996	196	199
Tennessee	913	94	335	—	15	469
Texas	4,180	254	1,121	—	1,124	1,681
Utah	504	29	224	—	40	211
Vermont	664	14	57	237	273	83
Virginia	407	95	229	—	—	83
Washington	1,734	39	265	—	300	1,130
W. Virginia	633	55	231	—	55	292
Wisconsin	2,592	72	580	1,269	408	263
Wyoming	395	23	91	—	56	225

*Includes "towns" in the six New England States, Minnesota, New York, and Wisconsin.

Source: Census Bureau, *Census of Governments, 1982.*

regulatory field. For example, county boards pass health and zoning ordinances and control amusement places found outside incorporated communities, especially those where liquor is sold.

Most county boards carry out a number of administrative functions. They supervise the road program and manage county property, such as the courthouse, jails, hospitals, parks, and the like. County boards are often responsible for the administration of welfare programs and the conduct of elections. They also appoint certain county officers, deputies, and assistants of many kinds, as well as most other county employees. They also fix the salaries of most of those who work for the county.

Recall that most boards share their executive powers with other elected officials. Efficiency, economy, and accountability, therefore, are often almost impossible to achieve.

Elected Officials A number of officials with countywide jurisdiction are separately elected. These other officers, and their principal duties, are most likely to include:

- The sheriff—who keeps the jail, furnishes police protection in rural areas, carries out the orders of the local courts, and is often the tax collector.
- The clerk—who registers and records such documents as deeds, mortgages, birth and marriage certificates, and divorce decrees. The county clerk often administers elections within the county, and acts as secretary to the county board and as clerk of the local courts.[2]
- The assessor—who appraises, or sets the value of, all of the taxable property in the county.
- The treasurer—who keeps county funds and makes authorized payments from these funds.
- The auditor—who keeps financial records and authorizes payments to meet county obligations.

[2]In several States a separate officer known as the recorder or the register of deeds has custody of those documents dealing with property transactions.

The Areas Within the United States Lacking Independently Organized County Government

1. Areas with governments legally designated as city-counties, operating primarily as cities:
   Alaska: City and Borough of Anchorage, City and Borough of Juneau, City and Borough of Sitka
   California: City and County of San Francisco
   Colorado: City and County of Denver
   Hawaii: City and County of Honolulu
   Montana: Anaconda-Deer Lodge County, Butte-Silver Bow County
2. Areas with certain county offices, but as part of another government (city or town):
   Florida: Duval County (Jacksonville)
   Georgia: Muscogee County (Columbus)
   Indiana: Marion County (Indianapolis)
   Kentucky: Lexington-Fayette Urban County
   Louisiana: Orleans Parish (New Orleans), East Baton Rouge Parish (Baton Rouge)
   Massachusetts: Nantucket County (town of Nantucket), Suffolk County (Boston)
   New York: Bronx, Kings, New York, Queens, and Richmond Counties (all New York City)
   Pennsylvania: Philadelphia County (Philadelphia)
3. Areas designated as metropolitan government, operating primarily as a city:
   Tennessee: Metropolitan Government of Nashville and Davidson County
4. Cities completely independent of any county:
   District of Columbia: Washington
   Maryland: Baltimore[a]
   Missouri: St. Louis[b]
   Nevada: Carson City
   Virginia: 41 "independent cities"
5. Unorganized areas with county designations:
   Connecticut: Fairfield, Hartford, Litchfield, Middlesex, New Haven, New London, Tolland, Windham Counties
   Rhode Island: Bristol, Kent, Newport, Providence, Washington Counties
   South Dakota: Shannon, Todd Counties (attached to other counties for governmental purposes)
6. Other unorganized county-type areas:
   Alaska: 12 census areas
   Montana: Area within Yellowstone National Park[c]

[a]Baltimore is distinct from Baltimore County.
[b]St. Louis is distinct from St. Louis County.
[c]Areas of the Park within Idaho and Wyoming are included in county areas in those States.

*REINFORCEMENT Have the class discuss: What are the functions of county boards? Have the students cite specific examples in their community.

- The district attorney—who is the prosecuting attorney, carries out criminal investigations, and prosecutes those who break the law.
- The superintendent of schools—who is responsible for the administration of all or many of the public elementary and secondary schools in the county.
- The coroner—who investigates violent deaths and certifies the causes of deaths unattended by a physician.

Many other county officers are often elected. They include a surveyor, who surveys land and sets boundary lines; an engineer, who supervises the building of county roads, bridges, drains, and other improvements; and one or more judges of local courts.

A Number of Boards or Commissions
These bodies, whose members are also sometimes elected, have authority over a number of county functions. They commonly include a fair board, a library board, a planning commission, a hospital board, a board of road viewers, a board of health, and, sometimes, a civil service commission. Members of the county board often serve *ex officio* in various capacities on one or more of these other agencies.

An Appointed County Bureaucracy
Counties now employ more than 1.8 million men and women. They do the day-to-day work of each of the nation's 3,041 counties.

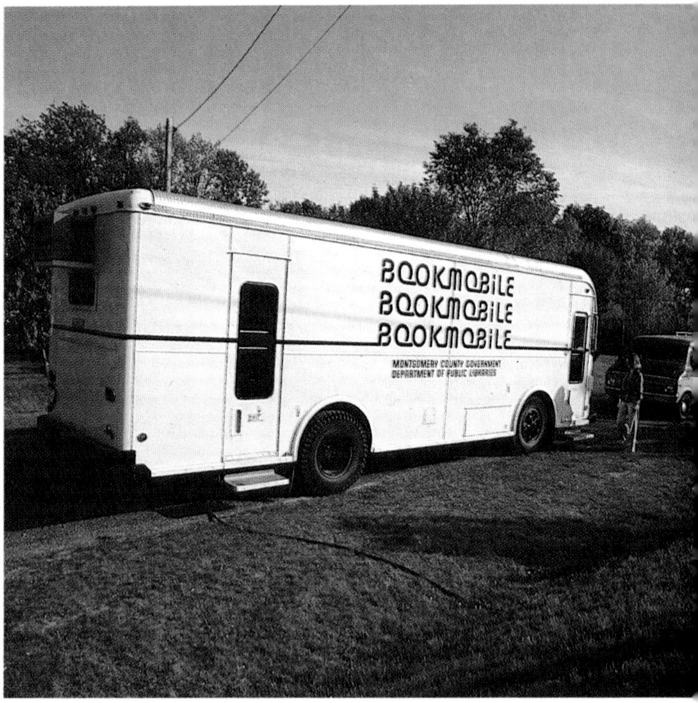

A service popular with many residents of Montgomery County, Maryland, is that provided by its Department of Public Libraries.

Functions of Counties

Because counties are creatures of the State, they are responsible for the administration of State laws and such county laws as the State's constitution and legislature allow them to make.

Historically, counties have been institutions of *rural* government. Most counties remain rurally oriented today. Though there is some difference from State to State, their major functions reflect their rural character. The most common ones are to keep the peace and maintain jails and other correctional facilities; assess property for tax purposes; collect taxes and expend county funds; build and repair roads, bridges, drains and other such public works; and maintain schools. Counties record deeds, mortgages, marriage licenses, and other documents; issue licenses for such things as hunting, fishing, and marriage; administer elections; care for the poor; and protect the health of the people who live in the county.

Many counties have taken on other functions as they have become more urbanized. Two-thirds of the people in the United States today live within the boundaries of 375 of the nation's 3,041 counties. Several of these more heavily populated counties, such as Los Angeles County, now offer many of the public services and facilities that are usually found in cities. They do such things as provide water and sewer service; have professionally trained police, fire, and medical units; and operate airports and mass transit systems. Some also enforce zoning and other land-use regulations, and many have built and operate auditoriums, sports stadiums, golf courses, and other recreational facilities.

*REINFORCEMENT Counties began as institutions of rural government, yet the United States is becoming an urban-based society. Ask the class how counties can keep up with this trend.

FOR REVIEW

1. **Identify:** county government, boards of commissioners, boards of supervisors.
2. How many units of local government are there in the United States? How many of each type?
3. What is the basic relationship between each State and its local governments?
4. What are the major weaknesses in most county governments?
5. As creatures of the State, what are the basic responsibilities of counties?

2. Reform of County Government

As You Read, Think About:

- What the principal weaknesses are of county government.
- What the several plans are that have been advocated to correct these weaknesses.

We have already said that county organization can be described as chaotic and that public apathy is a leading justification for that description. Three major weaknesses of county government also justify it.

First is its chaotic and headless structure. It is all but impossible to locate responsibility in the jungle of independently elected officers, boards, and commissions that is generally found. Lax, inefficient, and wasteful government, unresponsive government, government by the "courthouse gang," favoritism in awarding public contracts, instances of outright corruption—the list of indictments goes on and on.

Second, the large number of popularly elected offices adds to the chaos. Faced with the long ballots that typify county elections, voters are hard pressed to cast the informed votes on which good government must depend. Further, many elected county officials hold jobs that have nothing to do with the making of basic public policy, but that do demand professional qualifications. Popular election is not the best way to fill those offices with the talented persons who should hold them.

The size and the number of counties in most States is a third weakness. Nearly every one of the counties now in existence was laid out in the days of the horse and the stagecoach. At that time, it made good sense to draw county lines so that no one lived more than a dozen miles or so from the county seat. But most counties are geographically ill-suited to the realities of today.

Steps Toward Reform

The need for thoroughgoing reform of county government has long been recognized. In some places, steps have been taken in that direction.

County Home Rule One of the barriers to real change in the structure of county government lies in the legal status of counties. Recall that they are creations of the State. Their structure and functions are usually closely defined by State constitutions and statutes.

Over half the States have now lowered that barrier by providing for county **home rule.** That is, these States allow some or all of their counties—subject to approval by the local voters—to decide the details of their own governmental structures.

This major step to reform is now available to some 1,500 of the nation's counties. Yet, only about 100 of them have adopted home rule charters.[3]

In some States without home rule, the legislature has offered counties an optional arrangement that would allow them to choose from different patterns of organization. Each pattern is set out in more or less detail in statutes. In Virginia, for example, a county may select from two or three options, depending on its population.

In a few places striking reforms have come by direct action of the State legislature. Tennessee offers a very notable example.

[3]On the encouraging side, the list does include eight of the most populous counties: Los Angeles, San Diego, and Alameda counties in California; Erie, Nassau, Suffolk, and Westchester counties in New York; and Dade County in Florida.

There, the legislature set up a unique unit of government by combining a county and a major city: the Metropolitan Government of Nashville and Davidson County.

Trend to a Stronger Executive The major efforts to restructure county government have focused on its most prominent weakness: fragmented executive authority. Three newer patterns of organization have emerged, especially in urban counties: (1) the city manager, (2) the chief administrative officer, and (3) the elected chief executive.

The **county manager plan** is modeled along the lines of the council-manager form of city government now in wide use in middle-sized and smaller cities (see pages 636–637). Under this arrangement, the elected county board remains the legislative, policymaking arm of county government. The executive function—the administration of county affairs—is in the hands of a manager who is hired by and answers to the board. Ideally, the manager is a trained career administrator who appoints all of the other administrative officers of the county and directs their work.

The county manager plan separates the policymaking and policy-administering functions, placing administrative responsibility in a single and visible officer. It adds professional competence to county management and shortens the ballot. The plan has the hearty support of most students of local government.

The plan has not spread among counties as it has at the city level, however. Only some 50 counties use it. Among them, however, are several urban counties, including Sacramento, San Mateo, and Santa Clara counties in California; Dade County in Florida; Anne Arundel and Montgomery counties in Maryland; Durham County in North Carolina; and McMinn County in Tennessee.

The plan has not been more widely adopted for one main reason: Elective county officers are deeply entrenched, both constitutionally and politically, in so many places around the country.

The chief administrative officer model is a limited version of the manager plan. A chief administrative officer, often called the CAO, is chosen by the board and answers to that body. Unlike a manager, the CAO often has only very limited or no power in several important areas, such as appointments and budgets.

The CAO plan is a compromise of sorts between the traditional multiple executive arrangement and the stronger manager system. Los Angeles County was one of the first to provide for a chief executive officer, in 1944. The number of counties with CAO's has grown rapidly in the past decade or so, to more than 500 today.

The elected chief executive plan is patterned after the strong mayor-council form of city government (see pages 634–635). The plan features the county board and an elected chief executive, most often known as the county president, mayor, or supervisor.

The plan has several advantages. It separates the legislative and executive functions, places administrative responsibility in the chief executive, and cuts the length of the ballot. Although certainly an improvement on the traditional county structure, the plan does have the shortcomings found in the mayor-council form of city government. In short, its success depends on the extent of the powers given to the county president *and* that officer's personality and political clout.

Cook County in Illinois (Chicago) has had an elected president since the 1890s. He or she is popularly chosen as a member of the county board, chairs its meetings, and has broad powers of appointment, budget-making, and veto.

Thirty years ago only three counties had an elected chief executive; today there are some 60 of them.

County Consolidation As we noted earlier, the boundaries of most counties were horse-drawn. Clearly combining two or more adjacent counties would make them much more effective units of government. Yet, despite the many serious studies and proposals in several States, little has ever come of that idea. Local pride, politics, and economics stand as major impediments to any such effort.

*REINFORCEMENT Have the class discuss: Which of these three patterns of organization would you choose if you were restructuring your county government? Why?

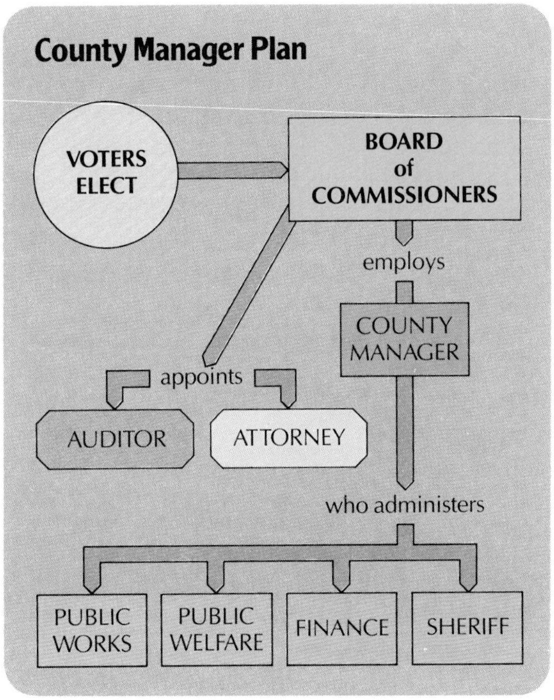

Compare this plan with the one shown on page 616. Which requires fewer elected officials? Which plan more clearly separates the policy-making and policy-administration functions?

County-City Consolidation Consolidation of another sort has met with a bit more success, as you can see from the table on page 619. In several places, a major city and the county around it have been joined into a single unit of government. San Francisco, Denver, and the Metropolitan Government of Nashville and Davidson County are major examples of mergers.

County-City Separation The table on page 619 also lists those situations where a quite different path has been taken. Several cities and the counties surrounding them have been separated from each other. Baltimore and St. Louis are two examples of these "independent cities."[4]

[4]A special situation exists in Virginia. There, whenever a city's population reaches 10,000, it automatically becomes an "independent city," that is, a separate governmental unit no longer a part of the surrounding county.

FOR REVIEW

1. **Identify:** county manager plan, chief administrative officer model, elected chief executive plan.
2. What are the three major weaknesses of county government?
3. List and explain one reform effort being tried for each weakness.

3. Towns and Townships

As You Read, Think About:

- What towns and townships are and why they are found in certain areas.
- How towns and townships are governed.

The town or **township** is found as a separate unit of local government in nearly half the States. Generally, as you can see in the table on page 618, it is found in States stretching from New England through the Middle West. It is little known in the South or the West.[5]

The New England Town

The town is a major unit of local government in New England. Except for just a few cities, each of the six States in the region is divided into towns. Each town generally includes all of the rural *and* the urban areas within its boundaries. The town is the unit that delivers most of those services that come from cities and counties elsewhere in the country.

The roots of the New England town reach back to colonial beginnings. The Pilgrims landed at Plymouth Rock in 1620 as an organized congregation. They quickly set up

[5]The term *town* is used in some States as the legal designation for smaller urban places; it is also sometimes used as another word for township. *Township* is also a federal public lands survey term, used to identify geographic units (often called *congressional townships)*, each having exactly 36 square miles (36 *sections)*.

a close-knit community in which their church and their government were almost one. Other Puritan congregations followed the Pilgrims' pattern. The desire to be near the church, the real or imagined Indian threat, the severe climate, and the fact that the land was not suited to large farms or plantations led the settlers to form tight little communities. Their settlements were soon known as "towns," as in England.[6]

At least in form, much of town government today is little changed from colonial times. The main feature is the *town meeting*, long praised as the ideal vehicle of direct democracy. The town meeting is an assembly open to all the town's eligible voters. It meets yearly, and sometimes oftener, to levy taxes, make spending and other policy decisions, and elect officers for the next year.

Between town meetings the board of selectmen, chosen at the annual meeting, manages the town's business. Typically, the board is a three-member body and has responsibilities for such things as roads, schools, care of the poor, sanitation, and so on. Other officers regularly selected at the annual meeting include the town clerk, a tax assessor, a tax collector, a constable, road commissioners, and school board members.

The ideal of direct democracy is still alive in many smaller New England towns. It has given way, however, to the pressures of time, population, and the complexities of public problems in many of the larger towns. There, representative government has largely replaced it. The officers of the town are often elected before the yearly gathering. Many of the decisions once made by the assembled voters are now made by the selectmen. In recent years several towns have gone to a town manager system for the day-to-day administration of local affairs.

Townships

Outside of New England, townships are found as units of local government in those States bounded by New York and New Jersey on the east and the Dakotas, Nebraska, and Kansas on the west. In none of those States do the townships blanket the State, however. Where they are found, they are mostly county subdivisions.

In New York, New Jersey, and Pennsylvania, townships were formed as areas were settled and the people needed the services of local government. As a result, the township maps of those States often resemble crazy-quilts. But from Ohio westward, township lines are more regular. They mostly follow the lines drawn in federal public land surveys, and many are perfect squares.

About half of these States provide for annual township meetings, like those held in New England towns. Otherwise, most townships have much the same governmental mechanisms. The governing body is a three-member or five-member board, generally called the board of trustees or board of supervisors. Often, its members are popularly elected for two-year or four-year terms. In many places, however, the board's members serve because they hold other elected township offices, such as supervisor, clerk, and treasurer. There is often an assessor, a constable, a justice of the peace, and a body of road commissioners.

Unlike in New England, a municipality *within* a township, especially one of large size, usually exists as a separate governmental entity. Thus, township functions tend to be rural, involving such matters as roads, cemeteries, noxious weed control, drainage, and minor law enforcement. In some States, however, the township is also the basic unit of public school administration.

Many believe that townships have outlived their usefulness. More than half the States get along without them, suggesting that they are not indispensable. Many rural townships have been abolished in the past few decades, the victims of declining populations, improvements in transportation, and a host of other factors.

[6]When a clan in England or in Northern Europe settled in a particular place, it usually built a wall around it. In Old English, the wall was a *tun*. In time the space within the wall became known as the tun, and then the town. As the New England towns grew in number and in population, it became necessary to survey their boundaries. The small and irregular shapes that resulted were called "townships" (town shapes). The suffix *ship* comes from the Old English word *scip*, meaning "shape."

*ENRICHMENT Discuss in class: Why is the town meeting considered the "ideal vehicle of direct democracy"? Point out that in a democracy the supreme authority rests with the people.

The township hall of Model, North Dakota. In that State, townships serve as units of county government, and their functions tend to be rural rather than urban in nature.

Some of the more densely populated townships appear to have brighter futures than their county cousins, however. This seems especially true in the suburban areas around some larger cities. Some States, like Pennsylvania, now allow townships to exercise many of the powers and furnish many of the services once reserved to cities.

FOR REVIEW

1. **Identify:** town, board of selectmen.
2. What is the major unit of local government in New England?
3. Why has the town meeting been praised by political theorists?
4. What is the general condition of township government elsewhere in the country?

4. Special Districts

As You Read, Think About:

- Why special districts are created.
- How special districts are governed.

As we first noted on page 618, there are now thousands of **special districts** across the country. These are independent local units created to perform a single and occasionally a few related governmental functions at the local level. These districts are found in almost mind-boggling variety and in every State.

The school districts are by far the most widely found examples. Including them, there are more than 43,000 special districts today. The first of these districts was created by New York in 1812 for school purposes. By the 1950s, there were more than 50,000

Many sanitation districts have facilities for purifying water, as this water filtration plant.

In some locales, rescue teams have been trained to deal with emergencies unique to an area.

school districts. Reorganizations have cut that number to less than 15,000 today.

Most of the other special districts, which serve a wide range of purposes, have been created since the Depression of the 1930s, and their numbers are still growing. They are found most often, but by no means always, in rural and suburban areas. Many special districts have been created to provide water, sewage, or electrical service; to furnish fire, police, or sanitation protection; and to build and maintain bridges, airports, swimming pools, libraries, or parks. Others have been created for such purposes as soil conservation, housing, slum clearance, public transportation, irrigation, or reforestation. There are even, in many places, special districts for dog control or mosquito or other insect pest control purposes.

The reasons for the creation of these units are many. A leading one has been the felt need to provide some service in a wider or a smaller area than that covered by a county or a city. For example, stream pollution may very well be a problem in each of several counties through which a river flows. Or there might be a desire to build recreational facilities at several places along the river's course. In many cases, special districts have been formed because other local governments could not, or would not, provide the services desired. For example, fire protection might be provided in some out-of-the-way locale by setting up a special district.

Special districts have been set up for a host of other reasons, as well: for example, to sidestep constitutional limits on the size of a city's or a county's debt, to finance some public service out of users' fees instead of general tax revenues, to insulate some public function from "politics," and to take advantage of some federal grant program.

An elected board is generally the governing body for a special district. It has the power to lay taxes (usually on property), or charge fees. Of course, it has the power to spend and to carry out its function(s).

FOR REVIEW

1. What are special districts?
2. What is the most common example of this type of governmental unit?

*ENRICHMENT Contact your local government for a list of the special districts serving your area. Ask students how the functions these districts carry out are in their interests.

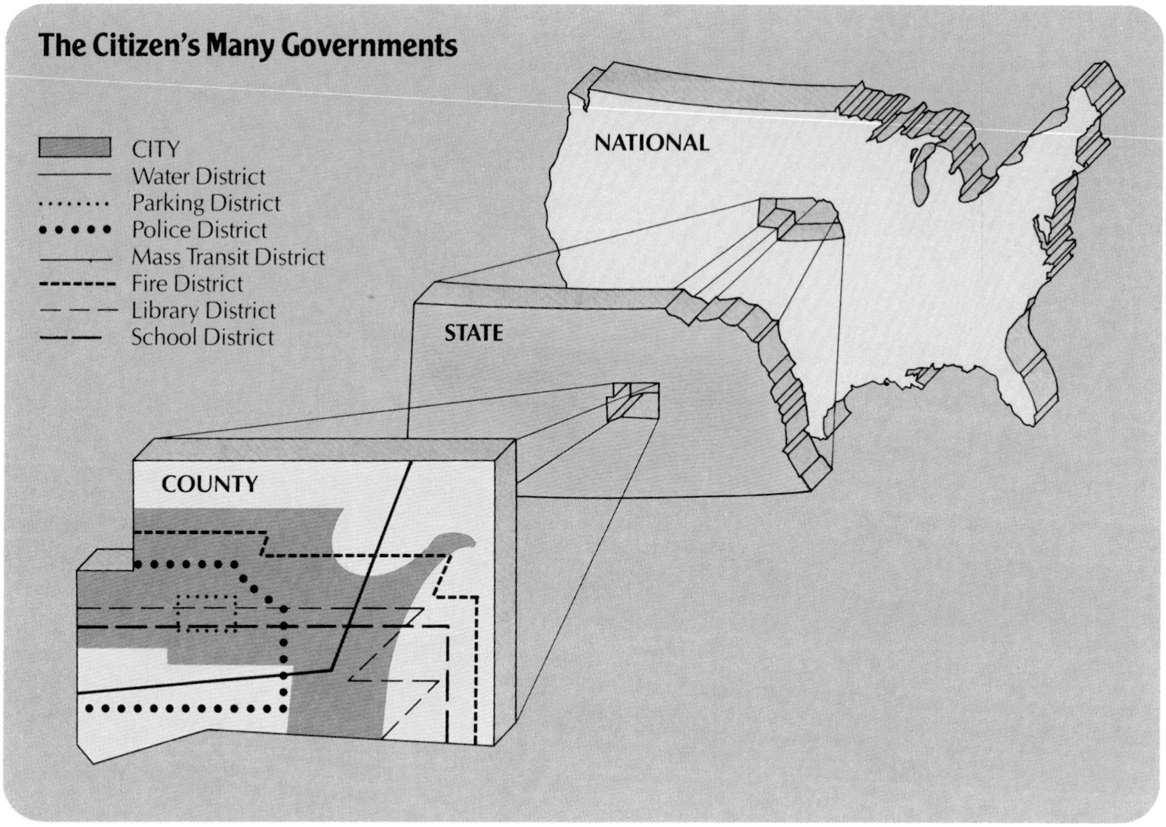

Why do you think so many governmental units exist at the county (or local) level, in contrast to those at the State or the national level?

5. The Cities: Growth, Legal Status, Charters

As You Read, Think About:

- What the side effects are of urban growth.
- What the legal status of cities is.
- What the different kinds of city charters are.

To this point we have dealt with those local governments that are, for the most part, rural—in their functions and, very often, in their outlook. Now we turn to *the* principal unit of local government in this country: the city.

Urban Growth

We are fast becoming a nation of city dwellers. Where once our population was small, largely rural, and agricultural, it is now huge, largely urban, and industrial.

The nation's cities have grown spectacularly, especially in the past 100 years. When the first census was taken in 1790, only 3,929,214 persons were living in the United States. Of these, only 201,655 people, or 5.1 percent, lived in the few cities. Philadelphia was then the largest city, with 42,000; 33,000 lived in New York and 18,000 in Boston.

Nine years before the first census, James Watt had patented his double-acting steam engine, making large-scale manufacturing possible. Robert Fulton patented his steamboat in 1809 and George Stephenson, his locomotive in 1829. These inventions made the transportation of raw materials to factories and, in turn, the wide distribution of manufactured goods readily possible. Almost overnight, home manufacturing gave way to industrial factories and populations

Urban Population Growth

Census	Total Population	Urban Population	Percent Urban
1790	3,929,214	201,655	5.1
1800	5,308,483	322,371	6.1
1810	7,239,881	525,459	7.3
1820	9,638,453	693,255	7.2
1830	12,866,020	1,127,247	8.8
1840	17,069,453	1,845,055	10.8
1850	23,191,876	3,543,716	15.3
1860	31,443,321	6,216,518	19.8
1870	28,558,371	9,902,361	25.7
1880	50,155,783	14,129,735	28.2
1890	62,047,714	22,106,265	35.1
1900	75,994,575	30,159,921	39.7
1910	91,972,266	41,998,932	45.7
1920	105,710,620	54,157,973	51.2
1930	122,775,046	68,954,823	56.2
1940	131,669,275	74,423,702	56.5
1950	150,697,361	96,467,686	64.0
1960	179,323,175	125,268,750	69.9
1970	203,235,298	149,377,944	73.6
1980	226,504,825	166,934,056	73.7

began to concentrate in the new industrial and transportation centers. Cities began to grow rapidly.

The invention of several mechanical farm implements reduced the labor needed on farms. More was grown by fewer people, and the surplus farm population began to move to the cities. By 1860 the nation's population had increased more than sevenfold. The *urban* population had multiplied *thirty* times. By 1900 two-fifths and by 1920 about half our people lived in urban areas.

According to the 1980 census, 166.7 million Americans, 73.7 percent, nearly three-fourths of our population, live in the nation's cities and their surrounding suburbs.

The shift from a predominantly rural to a largely urban society in the United States is a matter of tremendous significance. That change has had dramatic consequences. * When large numbers of people live close to one another, the relationships among them are far more complex than those among people who live in less densely settled areas. The rules governing their behavior become more numerous and detailed. Their local governments must furnish them with a wide range of services. Water, police and fire protection, streets, sewers, traffic regulation, public health facilities, schools, and recreation are needed. As population increases, so do the number and cost of services.

The Legal Status of Cities

Depending on local custom and State law, municipalities may be known as cities, towns, boroughs, or villages. The use and meaning of these terms vary among the States.[7] The larger municipalities are known

[7]Do not confuse the town (village) in the South and West with the New England town (township); or boroughs in Connecticut, New Jersey, and Pennsylvania with the boroughs in Alaska where they are substitutes for counties; see pages 615-616. In the New England States, villages have been created in only a very few instances. This is because the town is sufficiently organized to collect the necessary taxes and furnish the necessary services that villages provide elsewhere.

*REINFORCEMENT Have the class discuss: What is the relationship between the population and the role of local governments?

FOCUS ON:

Video-Game Arcades

Video games—and more particularly, video-game arcades—have caused cries of outrage in many communities across the country. Several cities have passed ordinances to discourage them. Some of those local laws limit the attendance of young people at arcades to certain hours, usually nonschool hours, and/or require that those under a certain age (usually 17) be accompanied by an adult. The laws of other cities and towns flatly prohibit such places.

Many who favor those ordinances fear that young people are wasting valuable time and too much money on video games, and some critics claim that they encourage gambling. In some places, local officials say that teenagers have broken into vending machines, parking meters, and other coin caches to feed the games and their habit.

For their part, most arcade owners argue that their games provide a "healthy outlet" for young people, and that they help them to develop both physical coordination and mental skills.

There are now many cases, in many courts, raising a number of questions about the games, the arcades, and their regulation. To this point, only a very few of those cases have reached the United States Supreme Court. The High Court has rendered a meaningful judgment in only one of them.

In *Marshfield Family Skateland* v. *Town of Marshfield,* 1983, the Court dismissed a constitutional challenge to an ordinance that bans video arcades in Marshfield, Massachusetts. It rejected, as "trivial," the contention that the playing of games like "Pac-Man" and "Donkey Kong" is a form of expression protected by the 1st and 14th Amendments. The Supreme Court's action amounted to a significant setback to the efforts of the video-game industry to fend off such local restrictions.

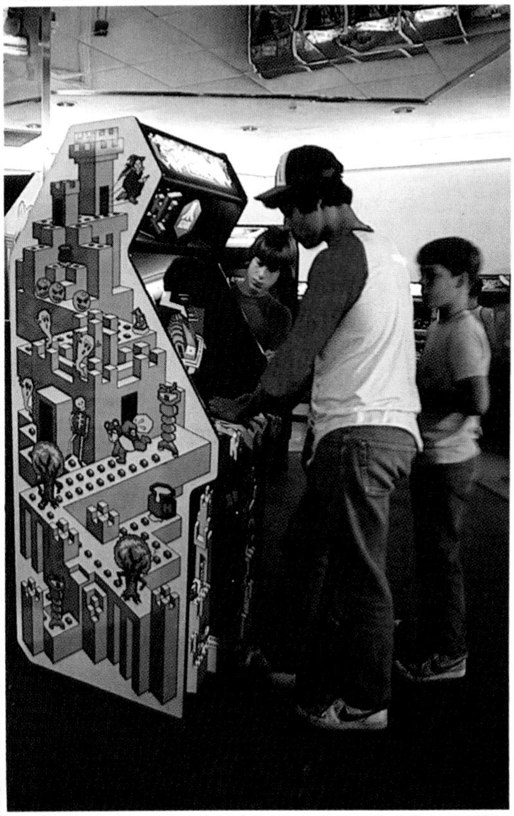

The Supreme Court will likely face a number of similar cases over the next few years.

1. Have you been to one of these arcades? What do you think of them? Are they "passing fads," or do you think they are here to stay?
2. What is your view of the various attempts to regulate them? Why have many of those attempts come in the form of licensing ordinances?

The skyline of San Francisco has changed dramatically since the Gold Rush days of 1849, when crews abandoned their ships to flock to the gold fields, leaving many vessels idle in San Francisco Bay. In 1850, San Francisco's population numbered some 35,000. By 1980, the year of the most recent census, San Francisco's population had grown to about 679,000.

everywhere as cities, and the *usual* practice is to use that title only for those communities with a fair-sized population.

* ***Cities Subordinate to the State*** Remember that each of the 50 State governments is unitary in form. Consequently, each State has complete authority and control over *all* units of local government within its borders. Remember, too, that all of these units including cities are "creatures of the State." Each was created by the State, received its powers from the State, and is subject to a variety of limitations imposed by the State.

The State's authority over cities is reflected in provisions in the State constitution and in laws passed by the legislature. In our early history, State constitutions had few provisions relating to cities. State authority was largely exercised through the legislature.

As cities grew in size and number, this legislative domination produced many difficult situations. State legislatures, largely dominated by members from the rural areas, were often unfamiliar with the needs and problems of cities. Many of the laws they passed were either very unfair or impractical. Many rural legislators were suspicious or jealous of cities and their residents. These legislators then sought to restrict the growth of those cities.

Today, because of that legislative abuse of power, most of the State constitutions contain a large number of provisions relating to municipal government and its problems. Generally, these provisions deal with incorporation, city charters, offices, elections, council meetings and procedures, and financial matters.

Incorporation Cities are **incorporated**[8] —made into a legal body—by the State. Each State sets out in its constitution or by statute the conditions and the procedures under which a community may become an incorporated municipality. Generally, a State requires that at least a certain number of persons must live in a given area before incorporation can take place.

[8]The term comes from Latin *in* (into) *corpus* (body). To say that cities are incorporated is another, and legal, way of saying that they are creatures of the State.

*REINFORCEMENT Discuss in class: In what ways are the cities subordinate to the State? How has this relationship evolved?

In a few States, an incorporated community may come into being only by a special act of the legislature. In fact, this is the historic means by which most cities were established. Today a petition generally has to be signed by a certain number of the residents of a locale and then submitted to some public officer. When that officer, usually a judge, finds that the requirements have been met, the area is declared to be incorporated, that is, to be a municipal corporation. In most States that declaration cannot become effective until the qualified voters in the area approve that action at a special election.

The fact that cities are incorporated highlights a very important difference between city and county government. Cities are called into being largely because of concentrations of population, at the request of their residents, and to provide them with certain public services. Remember that counties, on the other hand, exist largely in order to serve the administrative needs of the State. Cities do act as agents of the State, of course, for example, in law enforcement and public health. But the *principal* reason for the existence of a city is the convenience of those who live within it.

The City Charter

The **charter** is the city's basic law, its constitution. Its contents may vary from city to city, but commonly the charter names the city, describes its boundaries, and declares it to be a **municipal corporation.** As a municipal corporation, the city is a legal (artificial) person. As such, it has the right to sue and be sued in the courts, to have a corporate seal, to make contracts, and to acquire, own, manage, and dispose of property.

Regularly, the charter also sets out the other powers vested in the city and outlines its form of government. It provides how and for what terms its officers are to be chosen, outlines their duties, and deals with finances and other matters.

There are five distinct types of city charters that have been used or are presently found among the 50 States: special, general, classified, optional, and home rule.

The Special Charter In colonial days each city received its charter from the governor. With Independence, the State legislatures took on this duty, providing a charter for each city in the State by passing a special act. That practice is still followed in a few States—Delaware, Maine, New Hampshire, and Vermont among them.

The special-act arrangement allows for flexibility. It also means that each city is subject to continuing and detailed supervision by the legislature. Any real change in its organization, powers, or functions can come only if the legislature acts. In those States that still follow this practice, the legislature spends much of its session considering a great many bills of purely local concern.

The General Charter Many State legislatures abused the special charter system. Often those cities whose voters proved loyal to the majority party received better treatment than that given to others. In several States many city charters became hopeless reflections of the ignorance, jealousies, and suspicions of rural legislators.

Reactions to the special charter process grew to the point where, by the mid-1800s, some States went to the other extreme. They adopted a general charter—one for *all* cities in the State.

This eliminated the practice of singling out one or a few cities for special treatment. It failed, however, to take account of the many differences between and among cities, for example, between a busy industrial center and a small farm community.

No State today provides a single charter for all its cities. But many cities still operate under a charter dating from the days when the State did.

The Classified Charter The weaknesses of both the special and the general charter approaches led to the development of the classified charter system. Under this arrangement, all municipalities in the State are classified by population, and a uniform charter is granted to those in the same class.

The classified method minimizes discriminations among cities and, at the same time, allows flexibility in meeting the needs of cities of different sizes. Still, it leaves much to be desired. There may be, and often are, very real differences between cities with approximately the same number of inhabitants. Take, for example, a coastal city where the population is growing and the economy is brisk. Its needs are very different from those of a mining community where the population is static or declining and business is poor.

Where classification is used, the legislature can play games with the population ranges—and in some States it has. For example, a State may have only one city with a population greater than 500,000 or only one city with a population between 200,000 and 300,000. Classification then really amounts to the old special charter system in disguise. Several States provide for the classified charter arrangement, but most often in combination with the optional approach.

The Optional Charter Several States have turned to the optional charter system.[9] Under this arrangement, the State offers all cities—or, often those in each population group—a choice from among a number of charters. Usually each city's choice is made subject to the approval of its voters.

The optional charter process has much to recommend it, especially where the legislature offers a fairly broad menu of charters. Still, it does not allow for the fullest possible consideration of peculiar local circumstances or local preferences. In effect, it is really a compromise between near domination of cities through special charters and home rule for them.

****The Home Rule Charter*** More than three-fourths of the States now provide for municipal home rule. That is, they provide, in the constitution or by statute, that some or all cities may draft, adopt, and amend their own charters.

[9]Cities operating under optional charters are most frequently found in Illinois, Iowa, Kansas, Massachusetts, Minnesota, New Jersey, and Pennsylvania.

Like many Atlantic seaport cities, Baltimore's new Inner Harbor area, home of the U.S. Navy's first ship, the U.S.S. *Constellation,* is the result of major renewal and revitalization projects.

In 36 of these States, municipal home rule has been established in the constitution.[10] In eight States, however, the grant rests on the basis of legislative enactment alone.[11] The difference between *constitutional* and *legislative* home rule can be a vital one. Legislative home rule is less secure because any later legislature can retract the grant if it chooses to do so.

In some of these States—in Hawaii, Michigan, Minnesota, Ohio, and Oregon, for example—*any* municipality may write and adopt its own charter. In many other States, only *certain* cities may do so, for example, only those with a population of more than 5,000 in Missouri, Nebraska, and Texas.

[10]Alaska (1959), Arizona (1912), California (1879), Colorado (1902), Connecticut (1965), Georgia (1950), Hawaii (1959), Illinois (1970), Iowa (1968), Kansas (1960), Louisiana (1946), Maine (1969), Maryland (1915), Massachusetts (1960), Michigan (1908), Minnesota (1896), Missouri (1875), Montana (1972), Nebraska (1912), Nevada (1924), New Mexico (1949), New York (1923), North Dakota (1966), Ohio (1912), Oklahoma (1908), Oregon (1906), Pennsylvania (1922), Rhode Island (1951), South Dakota (1962), Tennessee (1953), Texas (1912), Utah (1932), Washington (1889), West Virginia (1936), Wisconsin (1924), Wyoming (1972).

[11]Delaware, Florida, Indiana, Mississippi, New Hampshire, North Carolina, South Carolina, Vermont.

*REINFORCEMENT The home rule charter has become the most common form of city charter. Ask the class to discuss why the other forms listed have not been as widely used.

Typically, home rule provisions give to cities "the powers of local self-government" or all powers relating to "municipal affairs." Home rule is never complete and absolute, however. It never creates a "free city." The State always keeps at least some, and often considerable, control over its home rule cities. There is always difficulty in separating those matters of purely *local* concern from those of general, State-wide import. As routine examples: setting speed limits on city streets that are also State highways, or the regulation of a city sewage system that empties into a river flowing through the State. The questions, and vexations, of city versus State authority in such cases must often be settled in the courts.

A home rule charter may be written and proposed by the city council or by an elected charter commission. To become effective, it must be approved by the city's voters and, in some States, by the legislature, as well. Once adopted, amendments may be made by council proposal and voter ratification. In many home rule cities amendments can also be proposed by initiative petition.

Changing Municipal Boundaries

As a city grows, the areas around it are likely to grow, too. These areas often cause rather serious problems for the city itself. Shacks may present fire hazards, septic tanks may threaten the city's water, and taverns may make law enforcement difficult.

Methods for the **annexation,** or adding, of territory to the city are usually provided by the State constitution or by an act of the legislature. Annexation generally must be voted on by the residents of the area that is to be annexed. In some cities, its voters must also act on the question. Compulsory annexation, that is, forcing an area into the city, is rare.

Suburbs often resist annexation. So, most States give their cities some *extra-territorial powers*. That is, those cities can regulate certain matters such as roadhouses, sanitation, and fire hazards in the settled areas around them.

Cities sometimes encourage suburbs to be annexed by dangling a carrot. For example, a city may agree not to raise taxes in the area for a certain number of years.

FOR REVIEW

1. **Identify:** city, urban growth, municipal home rule.
2. What proportion of our population was urban in 1790? By 1980?
3. What is a city charter? What five distinct types have been or are being used?

6. The City: Forms of Government, Functions, City Planning

As You Read, Think About:

- What the forms of city government are.
- Why city planning and zoning are vital.

Which is the more important: a particular form of city government or those who operate it? That question has been argued for centuries. In 1733 Alexander Pope penned this couplet:

> For forms of government let fools contest;
> Whate'er is best administer'd is best.

Certainly, good people are essential to good government. They can make at least something of even the worst of forms. Still, the form is also important. The better the form of government, the more chance there is that capable people will be attracted to public service. Also, the better the form the greater is the likelihood that the public will get the kind of government it needs.

Forms of City Government

Every city charter, however adopted, provides for one of three general forms of city government. Although cities vary from one

Henry C. Cisneros, Mayor of San Antonio, Texas, takes a message during a meeting of the city council. San Antonio has a council-manager form of government.

to another, each has (1) a mayor-council, (2) a commission, or (3) a council-manager form of government.

The Mayor-Council Form The **mayor-council** form is the oldest and still the most widely used type of city government. It features an elected mayor as the chief executive and an elected council as its legislative body.

The council is almost always unicameral. In fact, Everett, Massachusetts, is the only city that has a two-chambered council today. The typical council has five, seven, or nine members, but some larger cities have more. Chicago now has the largest council, with 50 members.

The members of the council are popularly elected everywhere. Terms of office run from one to as many as six years, but four-year terms are the most common. Council members are now most often elected from the city at-large, and that is the trend. Many cities, including several larger ones, however, choose council members from *wards,* or that is, districts within the city.

A move to nonpartisan city government began in the early 1900s. Its champions believed that (1) political parties were a major source for corruption in city government and (2) partisan contests at the State-wide and national levels have little to do with municipal problems and local issues. Today, less than a third of our cities still run their elections on a partisan basis.

Generally the mayor is also elected by the voters. In some places, however, the office is filled by appointment by the council from among its own members. The mayor presides at council meetings, usually may vote only to break a tie, and may recommend and usually veto ordinances. In most cities the veto can be overridden by the council.

Mayor-council governments are often described as either of the *strong-mayor* type, or the *weak-mayor* type, depending on the powers given to the mayor. This classification is useful for purposes of description. Notice, however, that the description tends to overlook or blur the importance of *informal power* in city politics.

In the **strong-mayor** type, the mayor heads the city's administration, usually has the power to hire and fire employees, and prepares the budget. Typically, the mayor is otherwise able to exercise strong leadership in the making of city policy and the running of its affairs.

In the **weak-mayor** type, the mayor has much less formal power. Executive duties are often shared with such other elected officials as the clerk, treasurer, city engineer, police chief, and council members. Powers of appointment, removal, and budget are shared with the council or exercised by that body alone; the mayor seldom has a veto power.

Most mayor-council cities operate under the weak-mayor rather than the strong-mayor plan. But the latter form is generally found in larger cities.

EVALUATION. The success of the mayor-council form depends in very large measure on the power, ability, and influence of the mayor. In weak-mayor cities, responsibility for action or inaction is hard to fix.

The strong-mayor plan helps to solve the problems of leadership and responsibility.

*REINFORCEMENT Discuss in class: Compare the three forms of city government. What type does your city follow?

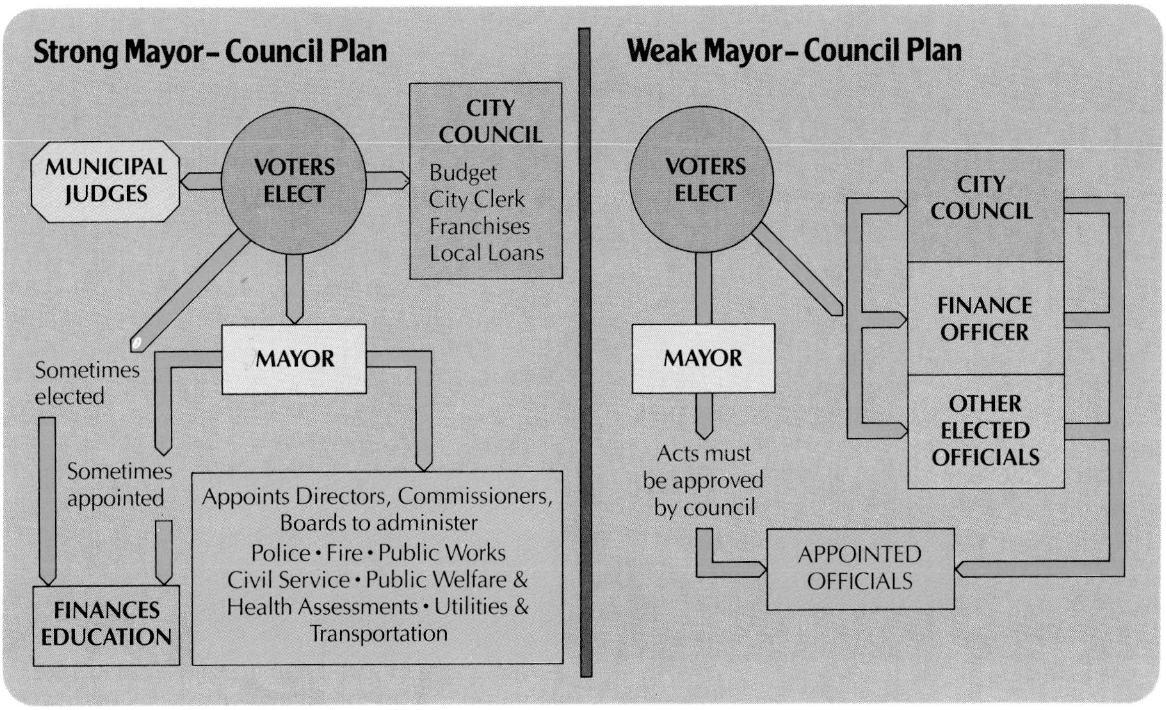

Compare and contrast the mayor-council plans above. What prevents a mayor of a city governed under a weak mayor-council plan from having greater power?

Still, it has three large weaknesses. First, it depends very heavily on the capacities of the mayor. Recall, political *and* administrative talents are not often combined in the same person.

Second, a major dispute between the mayor and the council can stall the workings of city government. But, notice, this is another way of saying that the mayor-council form incorporates the principles of separation of powers and checks and balances. Third, the form is quite complicated and so is often little understood by the average citizen.

The Commission Form Only a few of our cities now have a commission form of government. Some of the larger cities include Portland (Oregon), St. Paul, Tulsa, Mobile, Lexington (Kentucky), and Jackson (Mississippi).

The **commission form** is rather simple and uncomplicated. Three to nine, but usually five, commissioners are popularly elected. *Together,* they form the city council, pass ordinances, and control the purse strings. *Individually,* they head the different departments of city government—police, fire, public works, finance, parks, and so on. Thus, both legislative and executive powers are centered in one body.[12]

Depending on the city, either the voters or the commissioners themselves choose one of the commissioners to serve as the mayor. Like the other commissioners, the mayor heads one of the city's departments. He or she also presides at council meetings and represents the city on ceremonial occasions. The mayor generally has no more authority than the other commissioners and rarely has the veto power.

---

[12]The commission form was born in Galveston, Texas, in 1901. A tidal wave had swept the island city the year before, killing 7,000 persons and laying much of it to waste. The old mayor-council regime was too incompetent and corrupt to cope with the emergency. The Texas legislature gave Galveston a new charter, providing for five commissioners to make and enforce the law in the stricken city. Intended to be temporary, the arrangement proved so effective that it soon spread to other Texas cities and then elsewhere in the country. Its popularity has waned, however. In 1960 Galveston's voters approved a new city charter providing for council-manager government.

The commissioners are usually elected for two-year or four-year terms, and almost always from the city at-large and on nonpartisan ballots. Unlike their counterparts in mayor-council and council-manager cities, they regularly serve as full-time officers.

EVALUATION. The simplicity of the commission form, and especially its short ballot, won the support of municipal reformers in the first 20 years or so of this century. However, experience with it pointed up serious defects. Its popularity fell off rapidly from a peak use in some 500 cities in 1920 to little more than 100 today.

The commission form has three chief defects. First, the lack of a single chief executive (or, the presence of several chiefs among equals) makes it difficult to fix responsibility. This also means that the city generally has no effective political leadership. Second, there is a built-in tendency toward "empire-building"—or, several separate empires, as each commissioner tries to draw as much of the city's money and power as he or she can to his or her own department. Finally, there is a lack of coordination at the topmost levels of policymaking and administration. Each commissioner is likely to equate the public good with the peculiar interests and functions of his or her department.

The Council-Manager Form The **council-manager plan** is a modification of the mayor-council form. It features (1) a strong council, of usually five or seven members, elected at-large on a nonpartisan ballot, (2) a weak mayor, chosen by the voters, and (3) a manager, the city's chief administrative officer, named by the council.[13]

The council is the city's policymaking body. The manager carries out the policies the council makes and is directly responsible to that body for the efficient administration of the city. The manager serves at the council's pleasure and may be dismissed at *any* time and for *any* reason that the city council chooses.

Today, most city managers are professionally trained career administrators. As chief administrator, the manager directs the work of all city departments and has the power to hire and fire all city employees. The manager also prepares the budget for council consideration, and then controls the spending of the funds the council appropriates.

EVALUATION. The council-manager plan has the backing of nearly every student of municipal affairs, and its use has spread widely. It is now found in more than 5,000 communities, including about half of those with populations of 250,000 or more.

The council-manager plan has three major advantages over either the mayor-council or the commission forms of city government. First, it is simple in form. Second, it is clear who has the responsibility for policy, on the one hand, and for its application, on the other. Third, it relies on experts

Harold Washington, Mayor of Chicago—the nation's second-largest city—holds an informal, on-the-street interview with young students.

[13]The form was born in Staunton, Virginia, in 1908, when that city hired a general manager to direct the city's work. That step attracted the support of municipal reformers and was soon pushed throughout the country. The first charter to provide for a council-manager form was granted by the South Carolina legislature to the city of Sumter in 1912.

City councilors of Austin, Texas, are televised during a work session.

who can use modern techniques of budgeting, planning, computerization, and other administrative tools.

According to the theory behind the council-manager form, the nonpolitical manager carries out the policies enacted by the council; and the council will not bypass the manager to interfere in the details and routine of city administration. In fact, the sharp distinction between policymaking and policy-application seldom exists in practice. The manager is very often the chief source for new ideas and fresh approaches to the city's problems. In addition, a city council often finds it politically useful to share the responsibility for controversial decisions with the "expendable" city manager.

Some critics of the plan hold that it is undemocratic because the chief executive is not elected. Others say that it does not offer strong political leadership. This is a particular shortcoming, they argue, in larger cities, where the population is often quite diverse and its interests are competitive. Support for this view can be seen in the fact that only four cities with over half a million residents now have manager government: Dallas, San Diego, San Antonio, and Phoenix.[14]

[14]Several other major but smaller cities also use the manager form, including Cincinnati, Toledo, Oklahoma City, Austin, Fort Worth, Tucson, Oakland, Sacramento, and San Jose.

Municipal Functions

A city exists primarily to provide services to those who live in it. Those services, which cities provide day in and year out, are so extensive that it is almost impossible to catalog them. Nearly all larger, and many smaller, cities issue annual reports on the city's condition. These are often book-length publications. *

Consider *some* of the many things that most or all cities do: provide police and fire protection; build and maintain streets, sidewalks, bridges, street lighting systems, parks and playgrounds, swimming pools, golf courses, libraries, hospitals, schools, correctional institutions, day-care centers, airports, public markets, parking facilities, auditoriums, and sports arenas. They furnish such public health and sanitation services as sewers and waste water treatment, rubbish and garbage collection and disposal, and disease prevention and eradication programs. Cities operate water, gas, light, and transportation systems. They regulate traffic, building practices, noise pollution, and public utilities.

Then, too, many cities build and manage public housing projects, clear slums, provide summer youth camps, build and operate docks and other harbor facilities, and maintain tourist attractions. Several cities have built their own hydroelectric power dams.

*ENRICHMENT Divide the class into three groups. Assign to each group a form of city government to research for a panel discussion on how each operates on a day-to-day basis.

As are many sports arenas and stadiums, Arlington Stadium, home of the Texas Rangers, is a municipally-owned sports facility—in this case, by the city of Arlington, Texas.

Many cities operate farms in connection with their sewage disposal plants and have set up other recycling programs. The list is endless.

City Planning

With few exceptions, most American cities developed haphazardly, without plan, and with no eye to the future. The results of this shortsightedness can be seen almost everywhere. The most obvious, and damaging, examples can be seen in what is often called the "core area" or the "inner city," the older and usually overcrowded central sections of larger cities.

Industrial plants were placed anywhere their owners chose to build them. Rail lines were run through the heart of the community. Towering buildings shut out the sunlight from the too-narrow streets below. Main roads were laid out too close together and sometimes too far apart. Schools, police and fire stations, and other public buildings were squeezed onto cheap land or put where the political organization could make a profit. Examples are endless.

Fortunately, many cities have seen the need to create order out of their random growth. Most have established some sort of planning agency, usually a planning commission, supported by a trained professional staff.[15] A number of factors have prompted this step. The need to correct past mistakes has often been an absolutely compelling one, of course. Then, too, many cities have recognized the values that can come, and the pitfalls that might be avoided, through well-planned and orderly development. Importantly, cities have been spurred on by the Federal Government. Most federal grant and loan programs require that cities that seek aid must first have a master plan as a guide to future growth.

Washington, D.C., is one of the few cities in the nation that began as, and has remained, a planned city. Its basic plan was drawn before a single building was erected. In 1790 Congress decided to locate the nation's capital along the Potomac River. President Washington gave the task of laying out the new city to an engineer, Major Pierre-Charles L'Enfant.

L'Enfant designed the city on a grand scale, with adequate parks and beautiful circles. Parallel streets, running in an east-west direction, were named according to the alphabet, and those running at right angles were numbered. Twenty-one avenues shortened distances by cutting diagonally through the city, and trees and shrubs were planted at the intersections. Wide streets were provided, and large areas reserved for public buildings.

The original plan has been followed fairly closely through the years. The National Capitol Planning Commission guides the city's development today.

City Zoning **Zoning** is the practice of dividing a city into a number of districts, or zones, and regulating the uses to which property in each of them may be put. Gener-

[15] The first city planning commission was created in Hartford, Connecticut, in 1907. Only a handful of cities with populations of 10,000 or more do not have some kind of planning agency today.

*REINFORCEMENT Discuss in class: How has the urbanization of the United States contributed to a growth in the demand for professional city planners?

Zoning ordinances and how they are applied can be key factors in controlling city growth. Left: A single-family dwelling has escaped destruction as a new building is constructed around it in Atlantic City, New Jersey. Right: An applicant submits a request for a zoning permit.

ally, a zoning ordinance places each parcel of land in the city into one of three zones: residential, commercial, or industrial. Each of these is then divided into subzones. For example, each or several residential zones may be broken down into several areas. One may be just for single-family residences. Another may allow both one-family and two-family dwellings. In still another, apartment houses and other multifamily units may be allowed.[16]

Zoning is really a phase of city planning—and an important means for assuring orderly growth. It began to come into general use only as recently as the 1920s. Zoning still meets opposition from many who object to this interference with their right to use their property as they choose. Even so, nearly every city of any size in the United States is zoned today. The only major exception is Houston, where zoning was turned down by popular vote.

Zoning ordinances must be *reasonable*. Remember that the 14th Amendment prohibits any State, and its cities, the power to deprive any person of life, liberty, or property without due process of law. Each of the 50 State constitutions contains a similar provision.

Clearly, zoning *does* deprive a person of the right to use his or her property for certain purposes. Thus, if an area is zoned only for single-family dwellings, one cannot build an apartment house or a service station on his or her property in that zone. Zoning can also reduce the value of a particular piece of property, for example, a choice corner lot may be much more valuable with a drive-in restaurant on the property than a house.[17]

While zoning may at times deprive a person of liberty or property, the key question

[16]Most zoning ordinances also prescribe limits on the height and area of buildings, determine how much of a lot may be occupied by a structure, and set out several other such restrictions on land use. They often have "set-back" requirements, which state that structures must be placed at least a certain distance from the street and from other property lines.

[17]However, nonconforming uses in existence *before* a zoning ordinance is passed are almost always allowed to continue. Most ordinances give the city council the right to grant exceptions, called variances, in cases where property owners might suffer undue hardships.

Chicago Tribune-New York News Syndicate, Inc.

"The zoning commission would like to point out an irregularity!"

always is: Does it do so *without due process?* That is, does it do so *unreasonably?*

The question of reasonableness is one for the courts to decide. The Supreme Court first upheld zoning as a proper use of the police power in 1926, in a case involving an ordinance enacted by the city council of Euclid, Ohio.[18]

FOR REVIEW

1. What are the three major forms of city government?
2. Why did city planning become so generally and vitally necessary?
3. What is meant by due process?

[18]*Euclid* v. *Amber Realty Co.*, 1926; on the police power, see pages 131–133.

7. Suburbanitis and Metropolitan Areas

As You Read, Think About:

- Why population has shifted so dramatically from cities to suburbs.
- How the shift from the cities has affected the makeup of urban populations.
- What metropolitan areas as governmental units consist of.

The growth and sprawl of the suburbs have raised many problems for cities, as well as for suburban residents.

Suburbanitis

Most larger cities, and many smaller ones, suffer from what has been called "suburbanitis." Today over a third of our total population, and half of our urban population, live in suburbs.

From 1950 to 1980, the nation's population grew by 53 percent, by more than 75 million persons. Most of that spectacular increase came in the suburban population. It jumped some 42 million, about 85 percent, over those years. Many of the nation's larger cities *lost* population in the 1950s and 1960s while their fringe areas grew by leaps and bounds. The move to suburbia continues in the 1980s.

This dramatic shift in population can be explained on several grounds. Many quite understandable desires have helped to bring it about, including desires for more room; cheaper land; less smoke, dirt, noise, and congestion; and greater privacy. At the same time, people wished for more neighborliness, less crime, newer and better schools, safer streets and playing conditions, lower taxes, and higher social status. The car and the freeway have turned millions of once rooted city dwellers into mobile suburbanites.

Businesses have followed customers to the suburbs, often clustering in modern and convenient shopping centers. Many industries have moved from the central city in search of cheaper land, lower taxes, and a more stable

*ENRICHMENT "Suburbanitis" afflicts many of our major cities. Ask the class to discuss what they feel are the reasons for this condition, and how it might be alleviated.

BUILDING GOVERNMENT SKILLS

Volunteering

From the beginning of the history of the United States, Americans have formed voluntary organizations. Some of these organizations were formed to promote causes—the temperance societies, the abolitionists, and the civil rights groups. Others were formed to build hospitals, schools, and libraries. Still others advanced religious ideas and ideals.

Observers of American society, such as Alexis de Toqueville, have commented with astonishment at the great number of associations in the United States. Many authors have written about the role of volunteerism and of charitable giving in American democratic society; Ralph Waldo Emerson, Booker T. Washington, and Henry David Thoreau are just a few.

This tradition of volunteerism continues in the United States today. According to a Gallup survey, over one-half (53 percent) of all American teenagers and adults did volunteer work for some organization in 1983.

Volunteers today help to raise funds and to build schools, churches, temples, clinics, hospitals, and libraries in the United States and throughout the world. One volunteer program—the Peace Corps—is sponsored by the Federal Government and provides technical assistance to nations throughout the world.

At home, Americans do volunteer work for churches, temples, and other religious organizations on a regular basis. Many organizations depend on volunteers. Consider the Boy Scouts and Girl Scouts, the Red Cross, and the Boys and Girls Clubs.

Volunteers are always needed—to read to the blind, to tutor, to visit shut-ins, to work in hospitals, to serve meals to the poor, and to provide support to local governments. The list of volunteer activities goes on and on.

Why do people volunteer? Most people volunteer because they are interested in the work and because they enjoy helping others. Volunteering can also provide valuable job experience.

Since the possibilities for volunteer experiences are many, you may find it overwhelming to figure out what you might want to do. When considering volunteering, consider these questions first:

- — What am I interested in doing now? In the future?
- — What talents and/or skills could I contribute to an organization?
- — What kind of training will I receive?
- — How much time can I spend on volunteer activity per week (month)?
- — What kind of transportation can I arrange?
- — Which organizations/institutions might benefit from my time and skills? From which organizations will I learn?

If you have problems identifying organizations, check with your local government. Many local governments publish or keep copies of directories of local voluntary organizations. Also talk with parents, teachers, guidance counselors, neighbors, and friends.

If you have a definite idea of the organization you want to work with but you do not know what you can offer, make an appointment with the volunteer coordinator to discuss it.

1. Answer the questions about volunteering listed above.
2. Based on the answers, identify which organizations you would most like to volunteer for, if any. How would you contact and present yourself to your first choice?

labor supply. Industries have also been looking for an escape from city building codes, health inspectors, and other regulations. These developments have themselves stimulated growth.

Suburban growth has sharpened a great many problems for core cities. As many of the better-educated, high-income families have moved out, they have taken their civic, financial, and social resources with them. They have left behind a central city, which in contrast to its suburbs has much higher percentages of older persons, low-income families, blacks, and other minorities. The cities also have more older buildings and substandard housing, more unemployment, and higher crime rates. Inevitably, both the need for and the stress on city services have multiplied.

Providing for fire protection services is a major consideration of suburban communities that have undergone rapid growth.

Metropolitan Areas

Suburbanites face their share of problems too. Water supply, sewage disposal, police and fire protection, transportation, and traffic control are only some of them. Duplication of functions by cities or by city and county can be wasteful and dangerous. More than one fire has burned on while neighboring fire departments quibbled over which of them was responsible for fighting it.

Attempts to meet the needs of **metropolitan areas,** that is, of the cities *and* the areas around them, have taken several forms. Over the years, annexation has been the standard means. Outlying areas have simply been brought within a city's boundaries. As we have noted, many suburbanites resist annexation. Cities, too, have often been slow to take on the burdens involved.

Another approach involves the creation of *special districts,* to which we referred on page 625. The best known and most common are school districts, but there are now more than 28,000 sanitary, water, fire protection, and other special districts across the country. Many of them have been created especially to meet the problems of heavily populated urban areas. Their boundaries frequently cut across county and city lines, and they are often called *metropolitan districts.*

These metropolitan districts are generally set up for a single purpose, for example, for park development in the Cleveland Metropolitan Park Development District. There is no reason why a district's authority cannot be expanded to cover other functions, however. The Metropolitan District Commission (MDC), created by Massachusetts, controls sewage, water supply, and park development for the city of Boston and several neighboring communities. The MDC also has a number of planning functions in the District as a whole. Boston has only about a third of the District's population; the balance lives within 40 other municipalities.

City-county consolidation and, on the other hand, city-county separation have also been tried in some places, including St.

*REINFORCEMENT Metropolitan areas are often more accurately termed "urban sprawl." Discuss in class the problems arising from rapid growth, and how metropolitan areas can cope with them.

Dade County's new "Metrorail," an above-ground rapid transit system, carries passengers between downtown Miami and South Miami. In a few years, the line is scheduled to reach cities north and west of Miami.

Louis, Denver, San Francisco, Baltimore, and Philadelphia, as we noted on page 619.

Yet another approach is increasing the authority of counties. Among local governments around the country, counties are generally the largest in area and are most likely to include those places demanding new and increased services.

The functions of many urban counties have been increased in recent years, as we noted earlier. Dade County (Miami), Florida, has undertaken the nation's most ambitious approach to metropolitan problems. In 1957 its voters approved the first home rule charter to be designed "to create a metropolitan government." Under it, a countywide metropolitan government (Metro) is responsible for areawide functions. These include fire and police protection; an integrated water, sewer, and drainage system; zoning; expressway construction; and the like. Miami and the other 26 cities within the county continue to perform the strictly local functions and services.

FOR REVIEW

1. What factors have been especially responsible for the spectacular growth of the nation's suburban population?
2. What sorts of problems has "suburbanitis" caused for cities? For the suburban areas themselves?
3. What is a metropolitan district? What newer approach has been tried in Dade County? What are the other major approaches attempted elsewhere?

SUMMARY

There are 82,000 units of local government in the United States. Among them are 3,041 counties, 16,000 townships, some 44,000 special districts, and 19,000 municipalities.

Counties serve as judicial districts in New England, share responsibility for rural government with townships in the Northeast and the Midwest, and are the predominant rural units in the South and West. Only a few places do not lie in the boundaries of some county.

Counties vary in size, population, and number. Legally, they are creatures of the State and administer State law and ordinances that the State's constitution and legislature allow them to pass.

Most county government is in urgent need of reform. Its weaknesses are its headlessness, too many elective offices, and the failure to separate executive and legislative functions. The geographic size and number of counties in most States pose real problems.

Townships are also predominantly rural units, found from the New England States westward to the Dakotas. In New England the *town* is regularly the major vehicle of local government. Elsewhere, townships have been largely outmoded by modernization and by urbanization.

Special districts are units of local government created to carry out one or occasionally a few functions. They are found in every State. School districts are by far the most common example.

Cities have grown spectacularly in the past century. A once agricultural population is now largely industrial and urban. Three-fourths of all our people live in urban areas today.

Municipalities—known as cities, towns, villages, and boroughs—are creatures of the State. But, importantly, they also exist for the convenience of their residents. They have a huge range and variety of functions and services.

A city's *charter* is its fundamental law and may be *special, general, classified, optional,* or *home rule* in form.

Three major forms of city government are found in the United States: the *mayor-council* form (the most widely used), the *commission* form, and the *council-manager* form.

Cities have grown haphazardly and with no eye to the future. Most have now recognized the need for effective planning. *Zoning* is a principal tool with which orderly growth can be obtained.

"Suburbanitis" has caused many serious problems in and for central cities, and for the suburbs, as well. A number of *metropolitan districts* have been formed and the functions of some urban counties have been increased to meet the problems raised by suburbanization.

CHAPTER REVIEW

Key Terms/Concepts*

- counties (615)
- parishes (615)
- boroughs (615)
- home rule (621)
- county manager plan (622)
- township (623)
- special districts (625)
- incorporated (630)
- charter (631)
- municipal corporation (631)
- annexation (633)
- mayor-council government (634)
- strong-mayor (634)
- weak-mayor (634)
- commission form (635)
- council-manager plan (636)
- zoning (638)
- metropolitan areas (642)

*These terms are included in the Glossary.

Keynote Questions

• 1. Why are the powers of local governments really State powers?

• 2. What are the four major elements of a typical county government?

• 3. List five functions of counties.

• 4. For each of the following county reform plans, briefly describe the plan and indicate which current weakness it addresses: (a) county home rule; (b) county manager plan; (c) county-city consolidation.

• 5. How do the towns of New England differ from the townships to be found elsewhere in the country?

The dots represent skill levels required to answer each question or complete each activity:
• requires recall and comprehension • • requires application and analysis • • • requires synthesis and evaluation

• **6.** What is one of the reasons for the creation of special districts? Give an example.
• **7.** What is the difference between the reason that cities exist and the reason that counties exist?
• **8.** What is municipal home rule?
• **9.** Why do most States give their cities some extraterritorial powers?
• **10.** List the strengths and weaknesses of each of the three forms of city government.
• **11.** What are two of the factors that have prompted cities to establish planning commissions?
• **12.** Why did so many people move to the suburbs between 1950 and 1980?

Skill Application

Reading a Government Organization Chart: Charts showing the organization of a form of government differ somewhat from other organization charts. In the United States, governments include both elected and appointed officials. The elected officials are usually responsible for the appointment of other officials. Government organization charts not only show which official is in charge, but also which officials are appointed and which are elected. Look at the chart on page 616, "A Typical County Government." The chart shows that the voters elect the county board and all the positions listed in the column on the right. The county board then appoints all of the officials listed below it. You can tell this because these positions are represented by a different color. The arrows indicate levels of authority. The county board, for example, oversees the planning commission and the budget committee. It also supervises the work of the welfare officer and the engineer among others. By reading this chart, you have an overview of a typical county government.

By comparing government organization charts, you can gain a quick overview and comparison of two forms of government. Look at the charts on page 635, "Strong Mayor-Council Plan" and "Weak Mayor-Council Plan." Answer each of the following questions for both forms of government.

1. Which officials are elected by the voters?
2. Which elected officials are permitted to appoint other officials?
3. Does the city council have to approve acts by the mayor?
4. Which services, if any, is the mayor responsible for administering?
5. With which other officials, if any, does the mayor share the power to appoint?

For Thought and Discussion

••• **1.** Do you think that every city should be allowed to draft its own charter? Why or why not? Every county? Why or why not?
••• **2.** On page 633, the author posed this question: "Which is more important: the form of government or those who run it?" Which do you think is more important? Why?
•• **3.** What are the advantages and disadvantages of electing city (or county) council members from: (1) wards or districts; (b) the city (or county) at large; (c) a combination (one member elected from each ward, and several members elected at large).
••• **4.** In what ways might annexation by a city benefit a suburban area? Be a disadvantage for a suburban area? Why do you think that many areas resist annexation?

Suggested Activities

•• **1.** Prepare an organization chart showing the major features of your city or county government. Indicate whether or not each position is filled by appointment or by election. Also include the names of the current office holders.
•• **2.** Draw a map of your county or city that shows its division into wards and/or districts. In which ward or district is your school? Your home?
••• **3.** Obtain a copy of your city or county zoning ordinance(s) and the accompanying map(s). You can obtain these documents from local zoning boards. Do you recommend any changes in the zoning laws? Why or why not? Are any changes in zoning currently being considered in your area? Do you approve or disapprove? Why?
••• **4.** Stage a debate or class forum on one of the following topics: (a) *Resolved,* that this city's chief of police be hereafter selected by popular vote; (b) *Resolved,* that all counties in this State be abolished.

Finance is not mere arithmetic; finance is great policy.
–Woodrow Wilson

24

Financing State and Local Governments

CHAPTER OBJECTIVES

To help you to

Learn · Know · Understand

The huge amounts of money involved in State and local government finance today.

The major sources of State and local government income.

The political as well as the financial shape of public budgets and the budget-making process.

Government is an expensive proposition, and it is becoming more so from year to year. Just as the costs of government at the national level have risen to astronomical heights in recent decades, so have its costs at the State and local levels. Altogether, the 50 States and their thousands of local governments now take in and spend some $750 billion a year.

State and local spending amounted to less than $1 billion a year for *all* purposes at the turn of the century. Just 20 years ago, in 1967, that spending came to less than $100 billion a year. Today, it is running at a rate of more than seven times that amount.

This dramatic and continuing rise can be traced to two major causes. One is inflation, of course. It affects the price of government in the same way it affects the price of everything else we buy. The other cause is that over time we, the people, have demanded that more and still more services be provided by our many governments.

Government can do little without money. Where does it come from? Where does it go? It is to these *vital* questions we now turn.*

*ENRICHMENT Discuss in class: Taxes are always "hot" political issues. Why is this so? Ask students to identify those things that they think government should do and how they think those functions should be paid for.

The total revenue of State and local governments, estimated at some $750 billion in 1987, is only about 9 percent less than the total projected receipts of the Federal Government for 1987.

1. State and Local Taxing Powers

As You Read, Think About:

- What limitations exist on State and local taxing powers.
- What the principles of sound taxation are.

The huge amounts of money consumed by State and local government come from both tax and nontax sources. This year the States will take in more than $220 billion in taxes, and all their local units will collect as much as $170 billion. In addition, the 50 states and their local governments will also receive another $350 billion or so from a number of nontax sources.

Taxes are charges made by governments, compulsory levying of a fee to raise money for public purposes.

Limitations on State and Local Taxing Powers

The power to tax is one of the major powers reserved to each of the States. In the strictly legal sense, then, it is limited only by those restrictions imposed by the Federal Constitution and by its own fundamental law.[1]

Every local unit acquires its taxing power from its parent State. Thus, its power to tax is limited by State constitutional *and* statutory provisions as well as by the restrictions set out in the Constitution of the United States.

Federal Limitations The Federal Constitution places only a few restrictions on State and local taxing powers.

INTERSTATE AND FOREIGN COMMERCE. As we have already seen, the Constitution forbids the States the power to "lay any imposts or

[1]The power to tax is also limited by any number of *practical* considerations, that is, by a variety of quite important economic and political factors in each State.

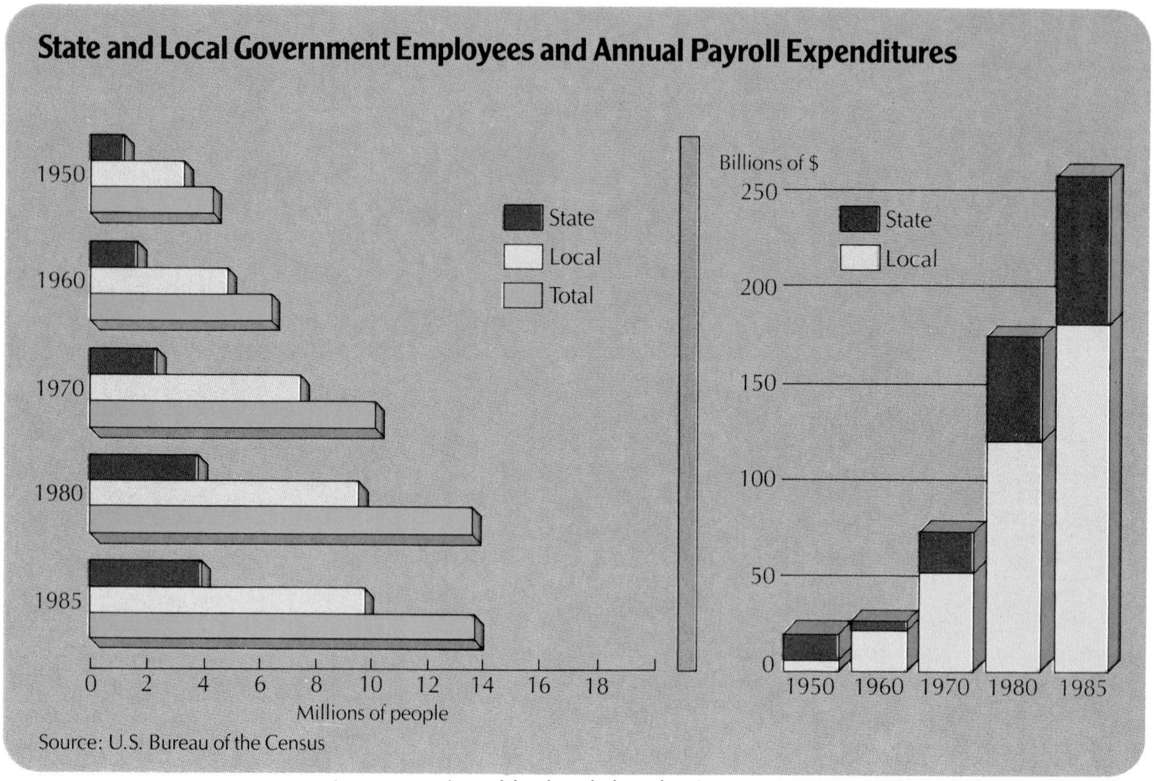

Why do you think more people are employed by local than by State governments?

duties on imports or exports" and "any duty of tonnage."[2]

In effect, the States are prohibited from taxing interstate and foreign commerce. The Supreme Court has often held that because the Constitution gives to Congress the power to regulate that trade, the States are generally forbidden to do so. But, recall (page 75), a State may *incidentally affect* it. So, States may, and do, tax many kinds of property used in that commerce, for example, land, buildings, trucks, aircraft, and many other related things.

THE NATIONAL GOVERNMENT AND ITS AGENCIES. Since the Supreme Court's decision in *McCulloch* v. *Maryland,* 1819, the States have been forbidden to tax the Federal Government including any of its agencies or functions; see pages 355-357. They are so forbidden because, as Chief Justice Marshall summarized the situation: "The power to tax involves the power to destroy."

[2]Article I, Section 10, Clauses 2 and 3.

THE 14TH AMENDMENT. The Due Process and Equal Protection Clauses place limits on the power to tax at the State and local levels.

Essentially, the Due Process Clause requires that taxes be (1) imposed and administered *fairly,* (2) *not* so heavy as to actually *confiscate* (seize) property, and (3) imposed only for *public* purposes.

The Equal Protection Clause forbids the making of *unreasonable* classifications for taxing purposes. Notice that most tax laws involve some form of classification. For example, an income tax classifies, for it is applied only to that class of persons who have income. Likewise, a cigarette tax is collected only from those who buy cigarettes and a property tax, only from those who own property. Of course, the Clause does not prevent these and similar classifications, because they are *reasonable* ones. It does forbid tax classifications made on such bases as race, religion, nationality, political party membership, or similarly *unreasonable* factors, however.

State Constitutional Limitations Each State's own constitution limits the taxing powers of that State and also those of its local governments, and often in great detail.

Most State constitutions provide that taxes shall be levied only for public purposes and that they be applied uniformly. Most also provide that taxes be collected only within the geographic limits of the governmental units that levy them and that no arbitrary or unreasonable classifications be made for tax purposes.

Most State constitutions also exempt the properties of churches, private schools, museums, cemeteries, and the like from taxation. Many set maximum tax rates. For example, many fix the State's sales tax at a certain percentage and/or the local property tax at no more than so many mills[3] per dollar of assessed valuation. The use of certain kinds of taxes, such as a sales or an income tax, is prohibited by some States.

As local units have no independent powers, the only taxes they may impose are those the State allows them to levy. The States have been notoriously reluctant in the matter. Even those units with home rule charters are closely restricted in terms of what and how they can tax.

The Principles of Sound Taxation

Any tax, taken by itself, can be shown to be unfair. If a government's total revenues were to come from one tax—say, a sales, an income, or a property tax—its tax system would be very unfair. Some people would bear a much greater burden than others, and some would bear little or none. Yet, each tax should be defensible as *part* of a tax system.

More than 200 years ago, in his classic *The Wealth of Nations,* published in 1776, the English economist Adam Smith laid out four principles of a sound tax system. Most tax experts today cite the same four. Smith stated the four principles:

[3]A *mill* is one-thousandth of a dollar, or one-tenth of a cent. Thus, if the local property tax rate is 20 mills, one who owns property assessed at $50,000 would pay a property tax of $1,000.

1. The subjects of every state ought to contribute towards the support of the government, as nearly as possible, in proportion to their respective abilities; that is, in proportion to the revenue which they respectively enjoy under the protection of the state.
2. The tax each individual is bound to pay ought to be certain and not arbitrary.
3. Every tax ought to be levied at the time, or in the manner, in which it is most likely to be convenient for the contributor to pay it.
4. Every tax ought to be so contrived as to take out and to keep out of the pockets of the people as little as possible over and above what it brings into the public treasury. . . .

Shaping a tax system, let alone any single tax, to meet these standards of equality, certainty, convenience, and economy is just about impossible. Still, that goal should be pursued. *

FOR REVIEW

1. **Identify:** interstate and foreign commerce, Due Process Clause, Equal Protection Clause.
2. The 50 States now collect about how much in taxes each year? Their local governments? From nontax sources?
3. What four major restrictions does the Federal Constitution place upon the taxing powers of the individual States and their local units?
4. What is the other source of legal restriction upon each State's power to tax?
5. Summarize Adam Smith's four principles of a sound tax system.

2. Types of State and Local Revenue

As You Read, Think About:

- What kinds of taxes State and local governments levy.
- What kinds of nontax receipts State and local governments receive.

*REINFORCEMENT Have students discuss the kinds of taxes they pay. Do they meet the four principles set out by Adam Smith in his *The Wealth of Nations?*

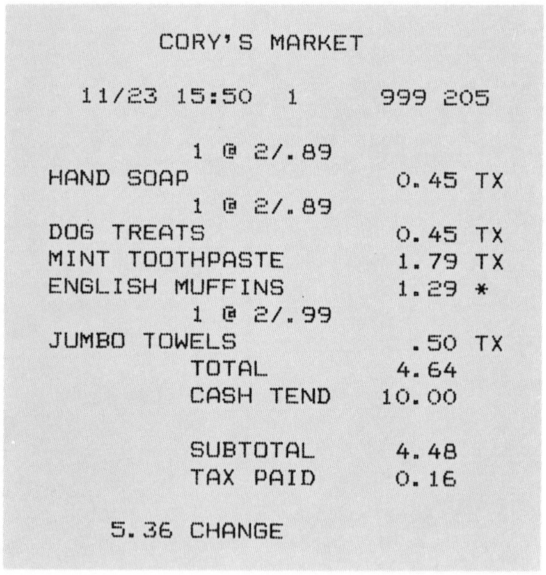

CORY'S MARKET

11/23 15:50 1 999 205

1 @ 2/.89		
HAND SOAP	0.45	TX
1 @ 2/.89		
DOG TREATS	0.45	TX
MINT TOOTHPASTE	1.79	TX
ENGLISH MUFFINS	1.29	*
1 @ 2/.99		
JUMBO TOWELS	.50	TX
TOTAL	4.64	
CASH TEND	10.00	
SUBTOTAL	4.48	
TAX PAID	0.16	

5.36 CHANGE

A sales receipt shows items that are taxed at a 5 percent rate in Massachusetts.

Beyond the limits we have noted, a State may levy taxes as it chooses. The legislature decides what taxes the State will levy, and at what rates. It also decides what taxes the local units—counties, cities, school districts, and so on—may levy.[4]

The Sales Tax

The sales tax is the single most important source of income among the 50 States today. It now accounts for about half of all tax monies collected by the States.

A **sales tax** is a tax placed on the sale of various commodities and is paid by the purchaser. It may be either general or selective in form. A general sales tax is one applied to the sale of most commodities. A selective sales tax is one placed only on the sale of certain commodities, such as cigarettes, liquor, or gasoline.

Today, 45 States levy a general sales tax.[5] The rate is often 4 or 5 percent, but the rate runs from a low of 2 percent in Oklahoma to 7.5 percent in Connecticut. In most States certain items are exempted from the tax. Among them are foods, or certain food items such as milk or bread, drugs, newspapers, or sales under a certain amount.

In most States the tax is collected by the retailer as each sale is made. That is, the tax is paid by customers as they buy taxable items. In a few States, however, the tax is not levied on each separate sale but, instead, on a retailer's total sales. Where this is the practice, the sales tax is often called a gross receipts tax. In either case, it is the customer who pays the tax. The retailer acts as the tax collector and turns the receipts over to the State at regular intervals.

Every State now levies a selective sales tax on gasoline and other motor fuels, alcoholic beverages, insurance policies, and cigarettes. Most States also have a selective sales tax on such other things as hotel and motel accommodations, theater and other amusement admissions, restaurant meals, automobiles, and parimutuel betting.

There are two major reasons why the sales tax is so widely used. First, it is relatively easy to collect. Second, it is a fairly dependable revenue producer. Notice that it is a **regressive tax**—one not geared to the ability to pay. It falls most heavily on those with lower incomes.

Several larger and many smaller cities, and some counties, also levy a sales tax—a "piggy-back" tax, added on to and collected with the State tax.

The Income Tax

The **income tax,** levied on individuals and/or corporations, yields more than 35 percent of State tax revenues today. Forty-three States levy an individual income tax; 46 have some form of corporate income tax.[6]

The individual income tax rates are usually **progressive**—that is, the higher the income, the higher the tax rate. The rates vary

[4]A State constitution sometimes grants certain taxing powers directly to local governments, but this is not common.

[5]All except Alaska, Delaware, Montana, New Hampshire, and Oregon. Each of these States does impose various selective sales taxes, however.

[6]Nevada, Texas, Washington, and Wyoming levy neither type of income tax. Alaska, Florida, and South Dakota impose only the corporate tax. Oil-rich Alaska abolished its tax on personal incomes in 1980.

*REINFORCEMENT Have the class discuss the differences between regressive and progressive taxes. Why is the progressive income tax considered to be the fairest?

"The Small Society," by Brickman.
Washington Star Syndicate, Inc.

among the States, from 1 or 2 percent on lower incomes in most States to 15 percent or more on the highest incomes in some States. Various exemptions and deductions are allowed in the figuring of one's taxable income. Over half the States now tie the details of their own tax return very closely to those of the returns that taxpayers must file with the Federal Government each year.

The corporate income tax rates are most often uniform, a certain fixed percentage of income. Only a few States fix the rates on a graduated, or progressive, basis.

The progressive income tax is held by many to be the fairest, or the least unfair, form of taxation, especially because it may be closely geared to the ability to pay. If the rates are too high, however, the tax can discourage incentive. The high federal income tax rates tend to force the States to keep theirs relatively low.

Some cities also levy a small income tax. Local income taxes will never become important revenue producers unless and until both federal and State rates are cut substantially. The chances of that happening are dim, however.

The Property Tax

The **property tax** is the chief source of income for local governments today. It accounts for approximately 80 percent of their tax receipts. Once the principal source of State income, it now brings in only about 1 percent of all State revenues.

The property tax may be levied on (1) real property—land, buildings, and improvements that go with the property if sold, or (2) personal property—either tangible or intangible. Tangible personal property includes all movable wealth that is visible and the value of which can be easily assessed. Examples include farm implements, livestock, pianos, television sets, automobiles, and air conditioners. Examples of intangible personal property include such things as stocks, bonds, mortgages, promissory notes, and bank accounts. Because intangibles can often be hidden from the tax assessor, they are not taxed in many States. In others, they are taxed at a lower rate than tangible personal property.

The process of determining the value of the property to be taxed is known as **assessment.** The task is usually carried out by an elected county, township, or city assessor. Only in a handful of States must he or she be a trained specialist, and in those States the assessor is usually appointed rather than elected. Most tax authorities believe that election is not likely to produce competent assessors. Further, the possibility exists that elected assessors will underassess to avoid antagonizing the voters, on whom they depend for their office.

Where personal property is taxed, the assessment is regularly made each year. Real property is usually assessed less often, commonly every second or fourth year. The assessor is expected to visit the property and examine it in order to determine its value. In fact, the assessment is often made simply on the basis of the last year's figures, which were arrived at in the same way.

Property is usually assessed at less than its true market value. Most property owners seem better satisfied if the assessment is set at, say, one-half of its real value. Thus, a house assessed at $30,000 may actually be worth $60,000. If the tax rate is set at 20 mills, or 2 percent, the tax will be $600. In reality, this result is the same as a 10 mill, or a 1 percent, tax on the $60,000 house.[7]

[7]Several reasons are given for assessing property at a fraction of its market value—none of them valid. Among them are: the belief that full assessment means higher taxes; the wish to lessen the share of State or county taxes paid by an assessed area; political considerations, especially the desire of an assessor to be reelected; and the difficulty of making a fair full-value assessment.

Home builders must first obtain building permits. Here one is displayed with a zoning permit at a neighborhood construction site.

* Three major arguments are commonly made in favor of the property tax. First, because property is protected—and its value is often enhanced—by government, it may properly be required to contribute to the support of government. Second, the rate at which the tax is levied may be readily adjusted to meet governmental needs. Finally, it is a dependable source of revenue.

Similarly, there are three major criticisms of the property tax. First, the tax is not geared to the ability to pay. Although the amount of real property one owns may have been a fair measure of one's wealth in our earlier history, it is not today. Second, it is all but impossible, even with the most competent of assessors, to assess all taxable property on a fair and equal basis. Third, personal property, especially intangible property, is often, and readily, concealed.

Inheritance or Estate Taxes

Every State except Nevada levies inheritance or estate taxes, so-called "death taxes." An **inheritance tax** is one levied on the beneficiary's share of an estate, and an **estate tax** is one levied directly on the full estate itself.

Business Taxes

A wide variety of business taxes, in addition to the corporate income tax, are also an important source of revenue in most States.

Over half the States impose severance taxes. These are taxes placed on the removal of such natural resources as timber, oil, gas, minerals, and fish from the land or water.

Every State has several different license taxes. These are fees that permit persons to engage in a business, occupation, or activity which is otherwise unlawful. All States require that corporations be licensed to do business in the State. Certain kinds of businesses—chain stores, amusement parks, bars and taverns, and transportation lines—must also have an additional license to operate.

Then, too, persons who wish to engage in certain businesses or occupations must themselves be licensed. Most or all States require the licensing of doctors, lawyers, dentists, morticians, barbers, hairdressers, plumbers, engineers, electricians, and many others. Many local governments impose their own business license taxes, as well.

License taxes other than for business purposes are levied in all States, too, and are an important revenue source. The most important are those for motor vehicles and motor vehicle operators. Others include such permits as hunting, fishing, and marriage licenses.

Nearly half the States have levies known as documentary and stock transfer taxes. These are charges made on the recording, registering, and transfer of such documents as mortgages, deeds, and securities. Some States also impose capital stock taxes, which are levied on the total assessed value of the shares of stock issued by a business concern.

*REINFORCEMENT Have the class discuss the arguments for and against the property tax. Is it a fair tax?

BUILDING GOVERNMENT SKILLS

Comparing Costs and Benefits

Every day you choose among different courses of action—deciding whether to take one class or another, deciding whether or not to apply to college, and so on. Like you, government officials often have to choose among several options. One way to decide is to compare the costs and benefits of each.

Imagine you are the mayor of a small town. You have to decide what to do with a vacant lot near the center of town. You can either build a new parking garage or you can use the land for a park.

Both options seem like good ideas. The parking garage would ease the shortage of parking spaces in the downtown area. Also the city government would get money from the sale of the lot and from taxes. On the other hand, your town has few green spaces and using the land as a park would make the downtown area more pleasant. These are the benefits of the options.

Neither option is free, however. Both involve some costs. The parking garage would require the city to widen the street in front of the lot and to install sidewalks. The park would require paying a landscaping company to clear the land and plant trees.

How should you decide what to do? One way is to measure the benefits you expect from each project, subtract the costs of each, and then choose the project with the highest "net benefit." Obviously, if the costs of an option are greater than the benefits you would not choose it. If both options have higher costs than benefits, you might be better off doing nothing at all.

To use this approach, you first need to list all the costs and benefits of each option. Then you need to figure out how to value each cost and benefit.

Determining the value of some benefits and costs may be more difficult. You may not be sure how much it is worth to ease the parking shortage or how much having a park is worth. For these benefits you will have to rely on value judgments of others.

For the purpose of this example, assume that you have collected all the information you need. Use that information to make a table like the one below.

PARKING GARAGE (thousands of $)

Benefits		**Costs**	
Sale of Lot	$500	Widen street	$200
Tax revenue	$50	New sidewalk	$150
Eased parking Shortage	$100	Total	$350
Total	$650		

Benefits − Costs = $300

PARK (thousands of $)

Benefits		**Costs**	
Improved Downtown	$300	Landscaping	$300
Recreation	$500	Trees and bushes	$250
Total	$800	Total	$550

Benefits − Costs = $250

1. If you believe these numbers, which project would you choose?
2. Suppose you think the benefits of the park have been underestimated. The real benefits are closer to $1,000,000. Now what is the net benefit of the park project? Which option would you choose now?
3. Can you think of other costs and benefits for either project? Do they change your decision?
4. What advantages can you see of using this cost-benefit approach? What do you think might be some problems with this approach?

Drawing by Ed Arno © New Yorker Magazine, Inc.

Poll Taxes

Only New Hampshire now levies a poll tax—a head or capitation tax. In effect, it is a tax on the privilege of living and breathing. Recall that the poll tax was once widely used as a suffrage qualification in the South.

Other Taxes

A number of other taxes are imposed at the State and/or local levels. More than half the States levy amusement taxes—usually on the tickets of admission to theaters, sports events, circuses, and the like. Payroll taxes produce huge sums, over $70 billion among the States today. But money produced by these taxes is held in trust funds for such social welfare programs as unemployment, accident insurance, and retirement programs.

State-Local Tax Sharing

Because the States tax so many different sources of revenue, their local governments often find it impractical to tax. So, increasingly, the States now share with their local units portions of certain taxes, either as they are collected or by appropriations made by the legislature.

For example, most States give a portion of the income from gasoline taxes and motor vehicle licenses to cities and counties. The State can use this redistribution to try to equalize the financial resources of local units—and also attach some strings to the use of the money.

Nontax Receipts

State and local governments now take in some $350 billion a year from a wide range of nontax sources.

An aerial view of Miami's Orange Bowl. Many States levy an amusement tax on tickets of admission to sports events.

Federal Funds A large portion of that huge amount comes from the federal government each year, much of it in the form of grants-in-aid, as we noted on page 82. The many different federal grants totaled almost $95 billion in 1981. But, acting on President Reagan's budget recommendations, Congress made substantial cuts in most of the grant programs for 1982 and beyond. The overall total will likely come to less than $80 billion this year.

Government-Operated Businesses Each of the States and many of their local governments make money from a number of different publicly operated business enterprises. Toll bridges and toll roads are found in many parts of the country. Several States, most notably Washington, are in the ferry business. North Dakota markets a flour sold under the brand-name "Dakota-Maid" and is also in the commercial banking business. The city of Milwaukee, Wisconsin, makes and sells a plant fertilizer, "Milorganite." California operates a short railway line in San Francisco.

Eighteen States are in the liquor-dispensing business, selling it through State-operated stores.[8] For years, Washington and Oregon jointly owned a distillery in Kentucky and sold its product in their outlets.

Many cities own and operate their water, electric power, and bus transportation systems. Some cities operate farmers' markets; rent out space in their office buildings, warehouses, and housing projects; own and operate dams and wharves, and so on. The receipts from these businesses, often including profits, go toward the support of the governments that own them.

Other nontax sources include such things as court fines, the sale or leasing of public lands, interest earned from investments, and the like. Twenty–two States today—Arizona, California, Colorado, Connecticut, Delaware, Illinois, Iowa, Maine, Maryland, Massachusetts, Michigan, Missouri, New Hampshire, New Jersey, New York, Ohio, Oregon, Pennsylvania, Rhode Island, Vermont, Washington, and West Virginia—conduct lotteries.

A licensed street vendor sells flowers along a street in Hartford, Connecticut. The fee levied for his license was collected by the city.

Borrowing

Borrowing may be classified as a source of nontax revenue. But, since they must be repaid, loans are hardly in the same class as other nontax receipts.

States and their local governments often must borrow money for unusually large undertakings, such as public buildings or bridges and highways, that cannot be paid for out of current income. That borrowing is most often done by issuing bonds, much as the Federal Government does. Generally, State and local bonds are fairly easy to market because the interest from them is not taxed by any level of government.

[8]Alabama, Idaho, Iowa, Maine, Michigan, Mississippi, Montana, New Hampshire, North Carolina, Ohio, Oregon, Pennsylvania, Utah, Vermont, Virginia, Washington, West Virginia, Wyoming. North Carolina's stores are operated by the counties; Wyoming's liquor monopoly operates only at the wholesale level.

FOCUS ON:

State Lotteries

Twenty-two States and the District of Columbia run public lotteries. A lottery is a kind of raffle that the government runs. The prize is various amounts of money ranging from a few dollars to millions of dollars.

Why do some States run public lotteries and why are several other States considering setting up lotteries? For the same reason that each of the 13 colonies, the Second Continental Congress, and many of the early States ran lotteries: To raise money for the public treasury.

Until a century ago, State lotteries were common in the United States. Scandals over the use and abuse of lottery revenue, however, led to their elimination. In recent years, States faced with financial problems have looked for ways, other than increasing taxes, to raise money. Some of these States have set up lotteries, with safeguards against abuse, to raise needed funds.

In most of the 22 States, lottery revenue either is added to the general fund so that it can be used for any purpose or is used specifically to support public education. However, two States earmark lottery revenue for different purposes. In Pennsylvania, the revenue supports programs for the elderly. In Massachusetts, lottery income is distributed to local governments.

Although present-day State lotteries have not been plagued by major scandals, they are still controversial. Supporters of lotteries describe them as forms of "voluntary taxation." Many supporters also argue that people will gamble no matter what the law says, so the State may as well get its "piece of the action." The money raised from this "gambling" can then be used for good purposes.

Some opponents of State lotteries regard any and all forms of gambling as morally reprehensible. Other opponents view lotteries as regressive forms of taxation. That is, lotteries take money from a great many people and pay benefits to only a few. Still others argue that because lottery tickets are most attractive to those who can least afford them, the lotteries really work to make poor people that much poorer.

1. Does your State run a lottery, or is your State considering setting up a lottery? What is the revenue used for? (What will the revenue be used for?)
2. Do you support or oppose State lotteries? Develop further arguments beyond the few mentioned above to support your position.

A United States lottery ticket of 1776

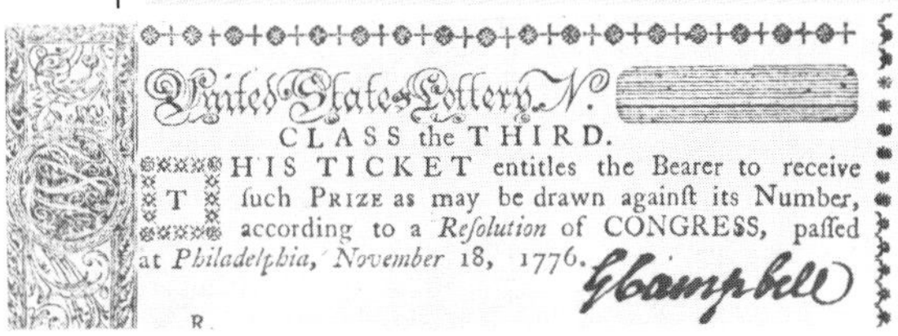

United States Lottery. No.

CLASS the THIRD.

THIS TICKET entitles the Bearer to receive ſuch PRIZE as may be drawn againſt its Number, according to a *Reſolution* of CONGRESS, paſſed at *Philadelphia*, *November* 18, 1776.

G Campbell

R

Many State and local governments have, in times past, had to default on their debts. Thus, most State constitutions now place detailed limits on the power to borrow.

The States' debts now exceed $180 billion, and all local governments owe not quite twice that much today.

FOR REVIEW

1. **Identify:** general sales tax, selective sales tax, real property, personal property, severance taxes, documentary and stock transfer taxes, capital stock taxes, poll tax.
2. What tax produces the largest amount of revenue among the 50 States today?
3. What two forms of the income tax are levied by most States today?
4. What tax produces the largest amount of revenue for local governments today?
5. Local governments commonly tax what two kinds of property?
6. What are the major arguments usually made for and against the sales tax? The income tax? The property tax?
7. What other taxes are often laid by a State and/or its local units?
8. From what principal nontax sources do State and local governments draw income?

3. The State Budget

As You Read, Think About:

- Why a budget is both a financial and a political document.
- What the term *executive budget* means.
- What the steps are in the State budget-making process.
- What the major functions are for which State and local monies are spent.

We have already suggested that a budget is much more than bookkeeping entries and dollar signs. It is a financial plan, a plan for the control and use of public money, public personnel, and public property. It is also a political document, a highly significant statement of public policy. Here, in its budget, the State sets its priorities and decides who gets what and how much, and who does not.

Until at least the 1920s, few State budgets could be dignified as a "plan." No officer or agency reviewed the needs of State government and its agencies and measured them against the available resources. No officer or agency cut those needs where necessary and then presented a carefully constructed, cohesive financial program to the legislature.

Instead, State budgets were jerry-built, the results of haphazard and uncoordinated steps centering in the legislature. Regularly, the various State agencies appeared before legislative appropriations committees, each seeking its own funding and often in bitter competition with one another. Their chances of success depended far less on either need or merit than on the political influence they could exert. When the legislature adjourned, no one had any real idea of how much it had appropriated or for what. Extravagance and waste, problems unmet, debt, favoritism, and graft were all parts of the process.

State budgets are very different today. They remain highly charged and vitally important political documents, but they are the products of what is, by and large, an orderly, planned process.

Forty-seven States have now adopted the executive budget. That is, they have given the governor two vital powers: (1) the power to prepare the State budget, and (2) once the legislature has acted on it, the power to execute the budget, that is, the authority to administer the different funds the legislature has appropriated. In most States the governor has the help of the director and the professional staff of a budget agency, appointed by and answering to the governor.[9]

The governor's key role in the budget process has been important in strengthening that office among the States, as we noted on

[9]Responsibility for the preparation of the budget is shared by the governor and the legislature in the other three States: Mississippi, South Carolina, and Texas.

*REINFORCEMENT The budget of any governmental unit, at the State, or local level, is inevitably a political document. Ask students why this is (must) be so.

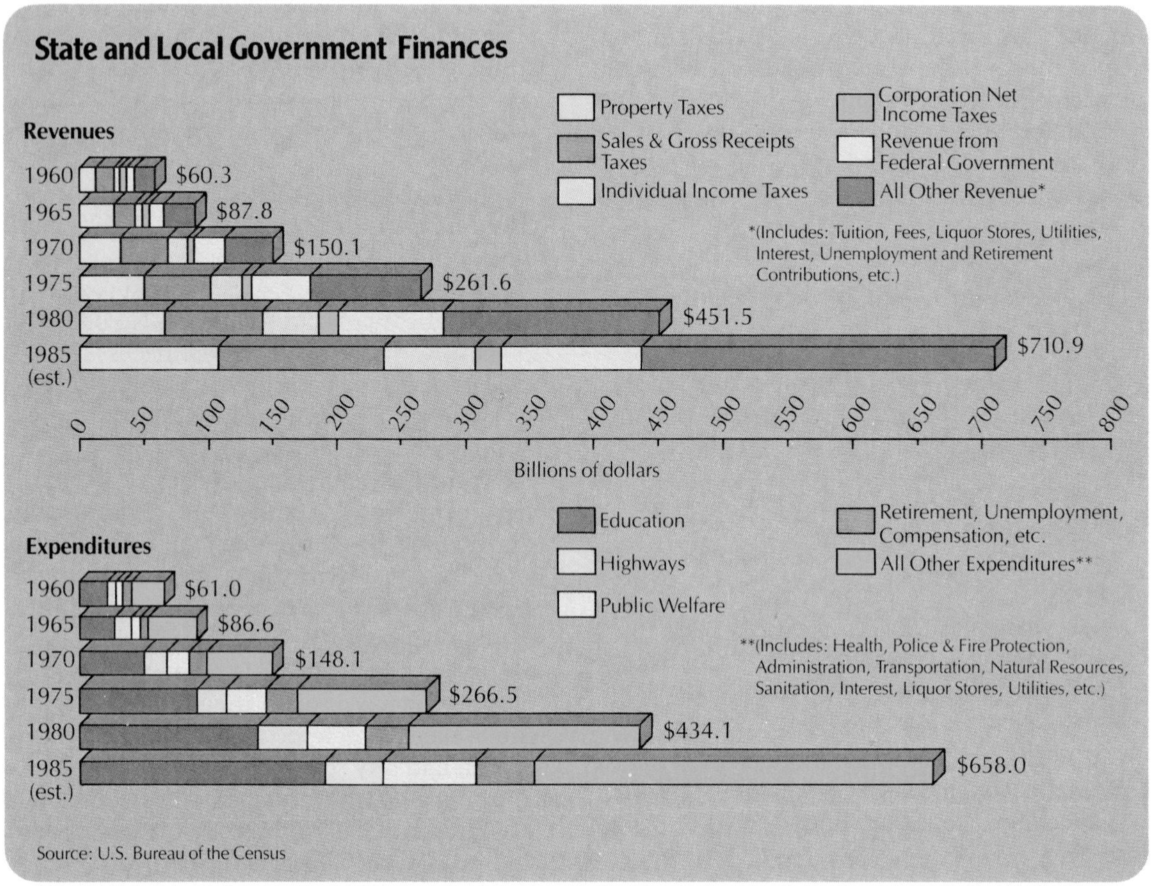

Have expenditures of State and local governments exceeded revenues in any of the years shown? Is more spent on education or public welfare?

page 586. Recall, the executive budget is a key feature of council-manager government. It has also been put into place in most strong mayor-council cities.

Steps in the Budget Process

The basic steps in the budget process are much the same at the State and local levels as they are at the federal level:

1. Each agency prepares estimates of its needs and expenditures in the upcoming fiscal period.
2. Those estimates are reviewed by an executive budget agency.
3. The revised estimates and all supporting information are brought together in a single financial program, the budget, for the governor to present to the legislature.
4. The budget is considered, part by part, the necessary funds are appropriated, and the necessary revenue measures, if any, are passed by the legislature.
5. The execution of the budget—the actual spending—approved by the legislature is supervised by the governor.
6. The execution of the budget is given an independent check, the postaudit.

Pattern of Expenditures

On page 646, we noted the high rate of State and local government spending, which is now some $750 billion a year.

Each of the 50 states, and their tens of thousands of local governments, spend for so many different purposes that it would be next to impossible to list them all. Another

*ENRICHMENT Ask the class to discuss the additional sources of revenue listed above. Which do they think are more lucrative to the State: these sources or taxes?

look at the graphs on page 658 will show that four major functions stand out as the most costly: education, highways, public welfare, and retirement and unemployment compensation. They account for nearly three-fifths of all State and local spending—some $350 billion in 1985.

Of these four items, education is by far the most expensive entry in most State and local budgets. School spending has climbed tenfold since the 1950s, and continues to increase year to year. Highways usually rank next each year, followed by welfare and then by retirement and jobless programs, although not always in that order.

The patterns of spending for other functions are often quite different among the States. The differences depend largely on the degree to which a given State is urbanized. All the States and their local units now spend well over $200 billion each year for such items as the protection of persons and property, debt payments and interest, developing and conserving natural resources, recreational facilities, correctional institutions, and general government.

FOR REVIEW

1. What is a budget? What is an executive budget? Why is it a highly important political document?
2. Why have nearly all of the States given the budget-making power to the governor?
3. Summarize the six basic steps in the budget process.
4. What are the four most costly functions of the States and their local governments today?

The budgets of virtually all local governments—from small townships to large cities—provide for fire protection; some counties and large municipalities also provide for health and hospital care.

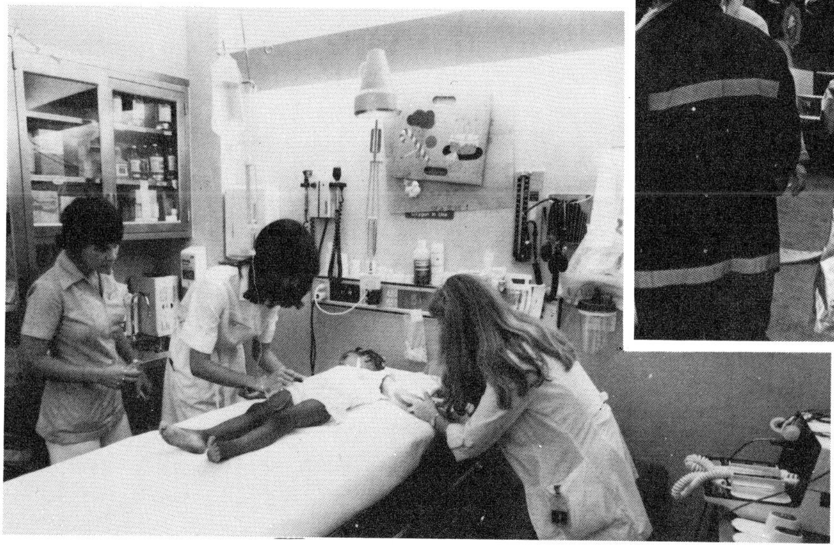

SUMMARY

Money is just as essential to the existence of government at the State and local levels as it is to the Federal Government. Just as the cost of government at the national level has increased sharply in the past few decades, so have the costs at the State and local levels.

Taxes are charges imposed by a legislative body upon persons or property to raise money for public purposes. The principles of sound taxation center on the four concepts of equality, certainty, convenience, and economy.

The Federal Constitution, each State constitution, State laws, and city and county charters place many limits on taxing powers.

The principal State and local tax sources include the property tax, the general and selective sales taxes, the individual and corporation income taxes, the inheritance or estate tax, and various business and license taxes.

Nontax receipts come chiefly from federal grants, government-operated businesses, and such other sources as court fines and the sale or leasing of public lands.

Borrowing, which is subject to strict limitations in most States, is only in a sense a nontax source of revenue.

Each State now has a budget system for the planned and more or less effective control of State finances. The budget-making process involves six steps: preparation of estimates, review of estimates, consolidation and presentation of the budget, consideration and adoption of the budget, execution of the budget, and a postaudit.

About three-fifths of all State and local spending today goes for: education, highways, public welfare, and public retirement and unemployment compensation programs. Of these, education is by far the most costly.

CHAPTER REVIEW

Key Terms/Concepts*

taxes (647)
sales tax (650)
regressive tax (650)
income tax (650)
progressive tax (650)
property tax (651)
assessment (651)
inheritance tax (652)
estate tax (652)

*These terms are included in the Glossary.

Keynote Questions

• **1.** What two major factors have contributed to the dramatic and continuing rise in the cost of State and local government?

• **2.** What federal restrictions limit a local government's power to tax? State restrictions?

• **3.** What are the four standards generally accepted as the basic principles for a sound tax system?

• **4.** Why is a sales tax a regressive tax? Why are sales taxes so important to the States?

• **5.** What is an individual income tax? Corporate income tax? Does your State levy either tax?

• **6.** What three major arguments are usually made for the property tax? Against it?

• **7.** Why do the States now usually share some of the proceeds from certain taxes with their local governments?

• **8.** From which nontax source do State and local governments usually draw the most income? Why?

• **9.** Why are State budgets such important documents?

• **10.** How do State and local governments usually finance large undertakings, such as a major building program?

The dots represent skill levels required to answer each question or complete each activity:
• requires recall and comprehension • • requires application and analysis • • • requires synthesis and evaluation

- **11.** What powers does the governor have in States that have adopted executive budgets?
- **12.** What four major items are most costly for State and local governments today?

Skill Application

The Use of Percentages to Identify Trends: Budget-makers are not all-wise seers. Still, they must try to read the future. For example, they must anticipate (estimate) governmental income in the next fiscal year.

To estimate governmental income for the next fiscal year, they rely on an examination of the past and trends, or patterns of increase or decrease of revenues over time. Those trends are often expressed in percentage terms.

Look at the bar graph on page 658, "State and Local Government Finances." In 1960, State and local revenues were $60.3 billion. In 1965, these revenues increased to $87.8 billion. To figure out the percentage increase, subtract the earlier year dollar amount from the more current year dollar amount. Then divide the result by the earlier year amount and multiply by 100. In this case, for the years 1960 and 1965, you would do this:

1. $87.8 - 60.3 = 27.5$

2. $\frac{27.5}{60.3} = .456$

3. $.456 \times 100 = 45.6\%$

By doing this, you find that State and local revenues increased by 45.6 percent from 1960–1965. If you know the percentage increase for 1965–1970, 1970–1975, 1975–1980, and 1980–1985, you might be able to detect a trend—a guide that may be of some help in planning for the future. Use the graphs on page 658 to answer the following questions:

1. What was the percentage increase in State and local revenues from: 1965–1970, 1970–1975, 1975–1980, 1980–1985?

2. What general trend does this data show for State and local revenue?

3. What was the percentage increase in State and local expenditures from: 1960–1965, 1965–1970, 1970–1975, 1975–1980, 1980–1985?

4. What general trends do these data show for State and local expenditures?

5. Given the trends you found, what advice would you give State and local budget planners for the time period 1986–1990?

For Thought and Discussion

- •• **1.** Given that both taxes are so regressive, why do you think that States continue to rely on sales taxes, and local governments on property taxes? Do you think these types of taxation should continue? Why or why not?
- ••• **2.** Should States, cities, and/or counties engage in business-like enterprises? Why or why not?
- ••• **3.** Do you think that the State individual income tax violates any of Adam Smith's four principles of a sound tax system? If so, is the deviation justified? Why or why not? If not, why not?
- ••• **4.** The author stated on page 649: "Shaping a tax system—let alone any single tax—to meet these standards of equality, certainty, convenience, and economy is just about impossible." Do you agree or disagree? Why?
- ••• **5.** State and local governments spend nearly three-fifths of their budgets on four items: education, highways, public welfare, and retirement and unemployment compensation. Do you agree with these spending priorities? If so, why? If not, how would you change the pattern of spending and why?

Suggested Activities

- • **1.** Obtain copies of the current budgets of your State and your city or county. Compare and contrast the budgets. On which five items does the State spend the most money? The city or county? Identify three items, if any, on which both the State and the city or county spend funds. Identify several items that are different.
- •• **2.** Compare and contrast your State's income tax system to that of a neighboring State. You can obtain this information from the revenue offices of the States. How might the differences affect the economies of the States? The services provided by the States?
- •• **3.** Interview an official in your county or city to find out the basic steps in the budget process. What political influences affect the budget process?

Unit 8

Politics and Economics: A World Perspective

THIS IS A book about government—in particular, a book about government in the United States. But the United States does not stand alone in the world. It is a nation with globe-spanning interests and far-flung obligations. Political, economic, and military developments in the rest of the world directly affect our nation's well-being.

Over the past several decades, the United States has knitted a global network of alliances that now link this nation with a broad array of countries in Europe, Asia, Latin America, and elsewhere. U.S. companies and individuals engage in trade across an even wider span of the globe, blending the U.S. economy into the world economy. Hundreds of thousands of Americans, in and out of uniform, live, work, and travel in foreign lands. In short, the world we live in is one world.

This unit discusses political and economic systems from an international perspective. It will help you to compare our own institutions, processes, ideas, and values with those to be found elsewhere. It will help you to understand how various systems are different—and how they are similar. Chapter 25 takes a look at governments abroad. Chapter 26 looks at the world's principal economic systems.

A view of Moscow's Red Square. Within the Kremlin Wall, which bounds Red Square, lies the seat of the Soviet Union's government.

Government, even in its best state, is but a necessary evil; in its worst state, an intolerable one.
–THOMAS PAINE,
COMMON SENSE

25 Comparative Politics: Major Foreign Governments

CHAPTER OBJECTIVES

To help you to

Learn · Know · Understand

The nature of the democratic government in Great Britain.

The nature of the French system of government.

The political traditions and present-day governmental system of Japan.

The elements of the totalitarian dictatorship in the Soviet Union.

WE MAKE THIS point early in Chapter 1: No two governments are, or ever have been, exactly alike. But governments can be grouped, or classified, into several distinct types. In Chapter 1 we looked at unitary, federal, and confederate governments. We distinguished between parliamentary and presidential systems. We noted the differences between dictatorial and democratic rule. In this chapter we turn to a more specific examination of other governments in the world. We will focus on four nations: Great Britain, France, Japan, and the Soviet Union.

1. Great Britain

As You Read, Think About:

- How the government of the United States resembles that of Great Britain.
- How the British government is based on tradition and on an unwritten constitution.

British government is democratic government. So, too, is American government; and,

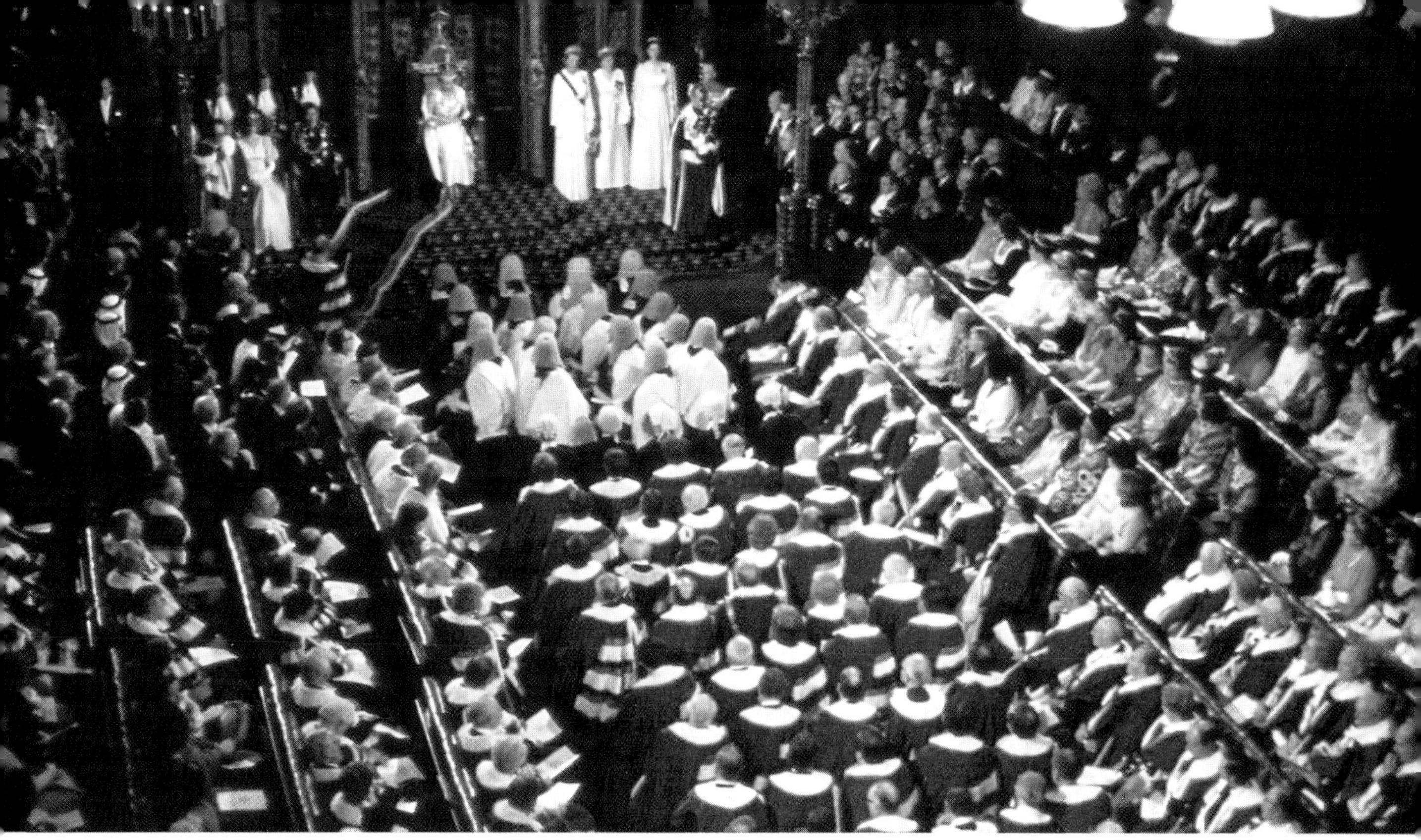

Facing page: Dominating this view of London, England, is the majestic Parliament Building, with its "Big Ben" on the Clock Tower. *Above:* Queen Elizabeth II presides over the ceremony for the opening of Parliament, held in the House of Commons.

as we have seen, the roots of the American political system are buried deep in English political and social history. Yet there are large and important differences between the two systems of government. Most of those differences grow out of this fundamentally important point: Unlike government in the United States, government in Great Britain[1] is unitary and parliamentary in form and rests upon an *unwritten constitution.*

[1]Great Britain is, officially, the United Kingdom of Great Britain and Northern Ireland. Its 56 million people live on two major and several minor islands northwest of Europe. Great Britain contains four principal parts: England, with 80 percent of the population and more than half of the land area; Wales, conquered by England in the 13th century; Scotland, joined to England and Wales by the Act of Union that created Great Britain in 1707; and Northern Ireland, which became part of the United Kingdom in 1800.

The Unwritten Constitution

It is not strictly true to say that the British constitution is unwritten. Parts of the constitution can, indeed, be found in books and charters. But there is no single document that constitutes the British constitution—as there is, say, a Constitution of the United States.

The British constitution has both a written and an unwritten part. The written part includes historic charters, significant laws (or *acts of Parliament*), and innumerable court decisions. The unwritten part derives from customs and usages—practices that have gained acceptance over time. We call the written parts the *law of the constitution* and the unwritten parts the *conventions of the constitution.* *

The Law of the Constitution Many historic documents figure in Britain's written constitution. Perhaps the best known is the Magna Carta of 1215 (see page 29). Others, of which you read in Chapter 2, include the Petition of Right of 1628 and the Bill of

*REINFORCEMENT Ask the class to think about the differences in being governed under a written vs. an unwritten constitution.

Rights of 1689. Each of those documents was a landmark in the centuries-long struggle to limit the powers of the English monarch and advance the concept of due process of law.

Certain acts of Parliament also form a basic part of the British constitution. One example of these is the Representation of Peoples Act of 1969. That act lowered the voting age in all British elections from 21 to 18. In the United States, you will recall, such a change required a formal amendment to the Constitution.[2]

Finally, court decisions are another part of the law of the constitution. Centuries of court decisions have created a body of legal rules covering nearly every aspect of human conduct. Such decisions, as you have read (page 609), make up the *common law.*

The Conventions of the Constitution The truly unwritten part of the British constitution consists of the customs and practices of British politics. For example, no document says that Parliament must hold a new session each year. It just does. There are no written rules giving the lower house of Parliament the power to choose and dismiss a Prime Minister. That central feature of Britain's government is the product of hundreds of years of custom.

Continuity and Change With its open-ended constitution, Britain has a flexible set of rules that is always evolving and open to change. A majority vote in Parliament can easily remove an old provision of the constitution or add a new one. The flexibility of this system can be very useful. But there is always the danger of ill-considered and hasty action that might fundamentally alter the people's rights, without the delays and safeguards that a system such as our own would impose.

The Monarchy

The United States, France, and other countries that have no hereditary rulers are called *republics*. Britain, in contrast, is a *monarchy*. Its hereditary ruler, or monarch, bears the title of Queen (as at present) or King. While English monarchs once ruled with absolute power, their role has dwindled and they are now little more than figureheads.[3] Because her powers and duties are controlled by Britain's unwritten constitution, Elizabeth II (Britain's Queen since 1952) is known as a constitutional monarch.

In formal terms, all acts of the British government are performed in the name of the Queen. However, the real power of government is exercised by the Prime Minister and other high officials.[4] The Queen does appoint the Prime Minister, but her choice must be accepted by a majority in the House of Commons. Traditionally, therefore, the Queen chooses the leader of the majority party in that house to be Prime Minister. She has no power to dismiss the Prime Minister and no veto over acts of Parliament.

Today's British monarch reigns but does not rule. Nonetheless, the institution of monarchy serves an important function. The Queen stands as a living symbol of the British state, as a focus of loyalty and pride. Periodic proposals to do away with the monarchy inevitably bring an outpouring of support for "our dear Queen."

Parliament

Parliament—and in particular the House of Commons—is the central institution of British government. It holds both the legislative and the executive powers of the nation —powers that in the United States are divided between separate and independent branches of government. By its legislative power, Parliament passes Britain's laws. By its executive power, it chooses some of its

[2]The 26th Amendment, effective in 1971.

[3]Most other present-day monarchs, especially in industrial democracies like Sweden, Norway, and Japan, are also figureheads. In the developing world, however, the monarchs of such nations as Saudi Arabia and Morocco still wield considerable power.

[4]It is common to distinguish between the individual who symbolizes a nation's sovereignty (the head of state) and the individual who directs the government (the head of government). In the United States, the President is both head of state and head of government. In Britain, the Queen is head of state, and the Prime Minister is head of government.

ENRICHMENT Have students contrast the present-day role of Britain's constitutional monarch with that of former ruling monarchs.

Prime Minister Margaret Thatcher campaigns for a fellow party member.

members (the Prime Minister and the Cabinet) to administer the departments of government and run the nation's affairs. In the British system, therefore, as in all parliamentary systems, government is built on the fusion of powers. That is, the legislative and executive powers of government are fused (merged, combined) in Parliament and a Cabinet. (The judicial power is lodged partly in Parliament and partly in the courts.)

Britain's Parliament is bicameral, its two parts being the House of Lords and the House of Commons. Most power resides in the lower body, the House of Commons.

The House of Lords The upper chamber, the House of Lords, is an aristocratic body of more than 1,100 members. More than 800 of those members have inherited their positions. They hold noble titles—as dukes, marquesses, earls, viscounts, and barons—and are known as hereditary peers. Other members are appointed for life by the monarch. Among them are archbishops and bishops of the Church of England, law lords (eminent judges), and so-called life peers. Life peers are individuals who have been honored for careers in science, literature, the arts, politics, or business. Attendance at sessions of the Lords rarely exceeds 200.

The House of Lords holds no real power over legislation. If it rejects a bill passed by the House of Commons, the Commons has only to approve the bill a second time and it becomes law. The Lords can merely delay but not block a bill's passage.[5] The upper house can also amend a bill and return it to the lower house. The lower house can—and usually does—remove the amendment by a simple majority vote.

Clearly, the House of Lords does not fit the pattern of representative democracy. Various critics have urged that it be abolished —a deed that the House of Commons could readily accomplish by passing a law. Defenders of the upper house argue that it plays a useful role, however. By delaying passage of a controversial bill, they say, it may allow tempers to cool and give the lower house time to weigh the full effects of its bill.

Besides its legislative role, the House of Lords performs a judicial function. Its nine law lords serve as the final court of appeals in both civil and criminal cases in the British court system. It is important to note that the British courts and judges, including the law lords, do not possess the power of judicial review. They cannot overrule a law or an act of government, even if they believe that it violates the constitution.

The House of Commons The lower house, known familiarly as "the Commons," is a representative body. Its 650 members are called MPs (for "Members of Parliament"). All are popularly elected from single-member *constituencies*, or districts,

[5]The upper house has 30 days to act on a money bill and one year to act on other bills.

which are roughly equal in population. Currently, there are 523 constituencies in England, 38 in Wales, 72 in Scotland, and 17 in Northern Ireland.

A general election (one in which all seats in the Commons are at stake) takes place at least once every five years. (Election dates, as we shall see, are not firmly fixed.) If an MP dies or resigns, a special election (called a "**by-election**") is held in that MP's constituency to choose a replacement.

The Commons meets in Westminster, a borough of London, in a small, rectangular chamber within the majestic building of Parliament. The high-ceilinged House chamber was originally designed for just 350 members. It is, quite literally, a political arena. The members of rival parties sit on facing rows of benches talking and sometimes hooting at one another.[6] An open space occupies much of the center of the chamber, with a raised chair at one end for the presiding officer, known as the Speaker.[7] Leading members of the major parties sit on the front rows of benches. Those who occupy the remaining rows are known as "backbenchers."

The majority party largely controls the work of the Commons. While any MP can introduce a bill, most measures are in fact offered by *the government* (as the Prime Minister and the Cabinet are collectively called). Eight standing committees consider bills and prepare them for final consideration by the full chamber. Committees in the Commons are generalists, not highly specialized subject-matter groups (as are, for example, the Agriculture, Foreign Affairs, and Budget Committees of the U.S. House of Representatives). Any committee may consider any bill. Their main task is to put measures in proper form for final floor consideration. All bills sent to committee must be reported to the floor, where a party-line vote generally follows the will of the government.

[6]It is not uncommon for MPs to loudly heckle a rival.

[7]The Speaker—an MP chosen by the Commons—acts as a neutral referee. The Speaker runs unopposed for reelection in a local constituency and is regularly returned to the speakership. These customs are part of the conventions of the British constitution.

The Government

The Prime Minister and the Cabinet represent the executive arm of the British government. In U.S. terms, they would be called "the administration." In a parliamentary system, such officials are called "the government."

The Prime Minister The Prime Minister, although formally appointed by the Queen, is in fact responsible to the House of Commons. When a single party holds a majority in the Commons, as usually happens, that party's leader becomes Prime Minister. If no single party holds a majority, a **coalition** must be formed. In this sense, a coalition is a temporary alliance of parties for the purpose of forming a government. Two or more parties must agree on a common choice for Prime Minister and on a joint slate of Cabinet members.[8]

The Cabinet The Prime Minister selects the members of the Cabinet. Most Cabinet members, or **ministers,** are members of the House of Commons. A few may sit in the House of Lords.

Collectively, the Prime Minister and the Cabinet provide political leadership, both in the making and the carrying out of public policy. Individually, Cabinet ministers head the various executive departments. One minister serves as Foreign Secretary (responsible for foreign affairs). Another serves as Chancellor of the Exchequer (responsible for finance). All told there are about 20 ministers, each with his or her own "portfolio" (department and functions). The size of the Cabinet may vary, depending on the desires of the Prime Minister.

The Prime Minister and the Cabinet are accountable to the House of Commons. An almost daily feature of parliamentary sessions is "question hour," when the Cabinet

[8]Britain's last coalition government served during World War II, from 1940 to 1945. It was headed by Prime Minister Winston Churchill, a Conservative. The Cabinet included members of the Conservative, Labor, and Liberal parties. Britain is the only parliamentary democracy in Europe that has not had a coalition government since World War II.

In Great Britain, all persons over 18 years old who are British subjects or citizens of Northern Ireland are entitled to vote in general elections if they are properly registered. *Inset:* A Conservative campaigns for a seat in the House of Commons.

ministers appear in the Commons to answer questions about their area of responsibility. Any MP may ask a question about any relevant subject.

Major opposition parties appoint their own teams of potential Cabinet members. Each of these opposition MPs "shadows" (watches) one particular member of the Cabinet. If an opposition party should gain a majority, its so-called **shadow cabinet** would be ready to run the government.

* ***Calling Elections*** There is no fixed timetable for elections in the British parliamentary system. The key restraint is that general elections must be no more than five years apart. Normally, it is the Prime Minister who decides when an election will take place. This may be at any time during the five-year term. As a rule, Prime Ministers call an election when they calculate that their own party's chances are favorable. If they guess right, they may be returned to office with an enlarged majority. If they guess wrong, the opposition may take over the government.

Occasionally, quite a different set of circumstances triggers an election. These circumstances occur when a government "falls" as a result of losing the confidence (or support) of Parliament. Normally, a government with a clear majority has no trouble keeping Parliament's support. But an opposition party may whittle down the majority

*ENRICHMENT Ask the class to debate the advantages and disadvantages of the British system of having no fixed timetable for elections.

by winning a series of by-elections. Or, rarely, some members of the majority may become disgruntled and vote against the government. Parliament is judged to have withdrawn its support if the House of Commons votes against the government on a critical issue—that is, loses a vote of confidence. When that happens, the government falls, and the Prime Minister must ask the Queen to dissolve Parliament (end its session) and call a new general election.

Clearly, this basic feature of British parliamentary government avoids a problem sometimes found in the American system of presidential government—continuing controversy, even deadlock, between the executive and legislative branches. But just as clearly, it does not allow for any system of checks and balances between them.

The Party System

Two major parties have dominated British politics in recent decades. Smaller parties add spice to the system by providing competition—and sometimes giving the bigger parties a scare.

The "Big Two" are the Conservative Party and the Labor Party. The Conservative Party draws its main support from middle- and upper-class Britons. It tends to favor private economic initiatives over governmental involvement in economic life. The Labor Party appeals largely to working-class voters. It tends to favor socialism. (For a discussion of British socialism, see Chapter 26.)

Among the smaller parties, two have a fairly broad base of support. One is the Liberal Party, which was one of the Big Two before being displaced by Labor in the 1920s. The other is the Social Democratic Party, a moderate splinter group that broke away from the Labor Party in 1981.[9] Several other small parties promote the interests of the various nationalist groups in Wales, Scotland, and Northern Ireland.

British parties are more highly organized and centrally directed that the major parties in American politics. High levels of party loyalty and party discipline characterize the British system. One result is that voters tend to choose MPs almost solely by party label rather than on the basis of individual qualifications.

Local Government

You will recall that Britain has a *unitary* form of government. The powers of government are centralized—held at the national level. There is no U.S.–style division of powers between a federal and a State level. In Britain, all governments below the national level are legally "creatures" of Parliament, and Parliament can theoretically take away their powers or abolish them as it chooses.

The responsibilities of local government include providing local residents with such services as police and fire protection, education, public health and housing, and road and street maintenance. Local officials are popularly elected. But their field of action is limited by a dependence on the National Government for most public funds.

FOR REVIEW

1. **Identify:** parliamentary government, unitary government, monarchy, Parliament, fusion of powers, Prime Minister, Cabinet.
2. In what sense does Britain have an "unwritten" constitution? Describe the law of the constitution and the conventions of the constitution.
3. What is the essential role of the Queen in British government today?
4. Cite three major differences between (a) the British Parliament and the U.S. Congress, (b) the Prime Minister and the President.
5. Describe the difference between the British and the American two-party systems.

[9]Liberals and Social Democrats formed a loose alliance in the 1983 general election and won one-fourth of the votes (but a far smaller proportion of seats in Parliament). The 1983 election returned the Conservative government of Prime Minister Margaret Thatcher, in power since 1979. Conservatives won 397 of the 650 seats in the Commons, and Labor won 209.

*ENRICHMENT Discuss: Do there seem to be any similarities of political thought between Britain's Conservative and Labor Parties and the Republican and Democratic Parties in the United States?

Shown in session is the lower house of France's Parliament, the National Assembly.

2. France

As You Read, Think About:

- How the French system of government has developed since Napoleon II.
- What the role and powers of the French President are.

The French system of government shares many features with Britain's parliamentary system, while differing in significant ways. Like Britain, France[10] is a democracy whose head of government bears the title Prime Minister. But France is not a monarchy. Its head of state is an elected President, and this President is the dominant political figure in the nation.

Among the oldest nations in Europe, France emerged, in very nearly its present geographic form, during the Middle Ages. For the better part of a thousand years a succession of absolute monarchs held sway. The French Revolution of 1789 put a sharp end to that long period of relative stability. Since 1789, France has known a bewildering succession of rulers—kings, emperors,[11] premiers, presidents. The present political system, known as the Fifth Republic, was established in 1958.

The Constitution

Like the United States, France has a written constitution—one basic document. The constitution of 1958 is the *sixteenth* such document that France has had since 1789. To understand the nation's chaotic constitutional history, let us examine a slice of its recent past.

Fall of the Third Republic When the armies of Nazi Germany swept across France in the early years of World War II, the Third Republic and its democratic system collapsed. Germans occupied Paris, the French capital, and much of the nation's territory in 1940. A French government led by a military officer moved to the small city of Vichy, from which it ruled the unoccupied (southern) part of France. Finally this too came under German occupation. General Charles de Gaulle, meanwhile, formed a government in exile in London and led "Free French" forces that fought with the Allies against Germany. Upon the liberation of France in 1944, De Gaulle formed a provisional government in Paris and organized a return to democratic rule.

The Fourth Republic In 1946 the French people approved a new constitution, setting up the Fourth Republic. Crippled from the start by two main factors, the Fourth Republic lasted for just 12 years. First, there was a (purposely) weak executive. It consisted of a ceremonial President and a *Premier* (the equivalent of a prime minister) with little real power. Second, so many political parties held seats in Parliament that it was almost impossible to create a stable coalition to operate the government. With 20

---

[10]About four-fifths as large as Texas in area, France has a population of 55 million.

[11]The last French monarch was Emperor Napoleon III, who reigned over the Second Empire from 1852 to 1870. A series of democratic systems began with the founding of the Third Republic in 1870.

The French Presidential System

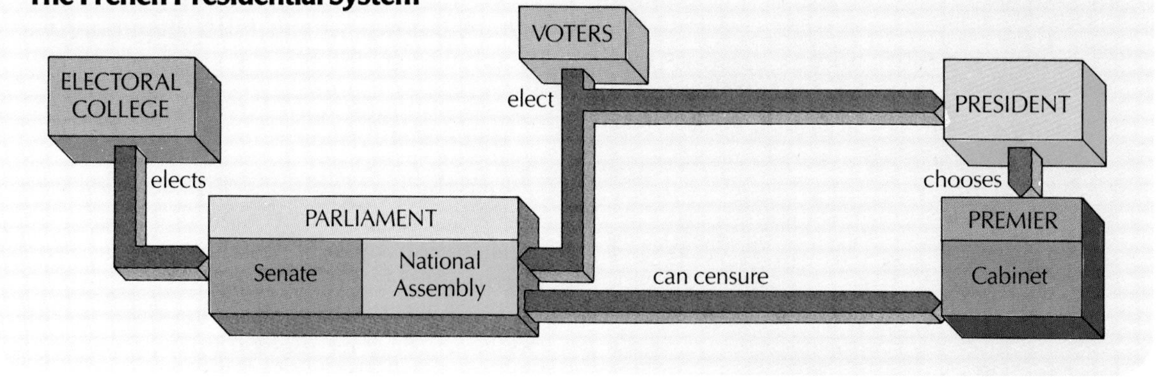

The President of France has the power to dissolve the National Assembly, except during a time of national emergency. Does the President of the United States have this equivalent power?

governments and 17 different Premiers in 12 years, France was often in a state of paralysis or crisis.

Matters came to a head in 1958, during a war of independence in French-ruled Algeria. The parties in Parliament could not agree on how to deal with the war. Finally, Parliament summoned General de Gaulle out of retirement to lead a coalition government as Premier. Calling for the creation of a strong executive, De Gaulle supervised the rapid preparation of a new constitution. Within a matter of weeks, the document had been drawn up, and French voters had approved it in a referendum. The Fifth Republic took the place of the Fourth.

The Fifth Republic France's present constitution seeks to remedy the instability of the past by placing power in the hands of a strong executive. The constitution retains France's traditional parliamentary system, but in a new form. The President now overshadows Parliament. The arrangement of powers can best be described as a mixed parliamentary-presidential system, with presidential dominance.

Amending the Constitution Under the 1958 constitution, constitutional amendments may be proposed by a majority vote in both houses of Parliament. The President chooses from two possible methods of ratification. The proposal may be submitted to a joint session of Parliament, with a three-fifths vote required for adoption. Or it may be submitted to a popular referendum, with a majority vote required.

The President

French voters choose the President in a nationwide election, to serve a term of seven years. If no candidate wins a clear majority, a second election takes place two weeks after the first. To date, each presidential election has required such a runoff.[12] The President may serve an unlimited number of terms.

The French President wields considerable power. Like the chief executive in other systems, the President runs foreign affairs and commands the military. But some powers are unique to the French system. For example, the President may call a referendum on an important national issue. Also, the President may use dictatorial authority in an emergency.[13] *

[12]Originally, the 1958 constitution called for the indirect election of the President. Voting was by an electoral college composed of members of both houses of Parliament and principal local officials. An amendment approved in a 1962 referendum provided for direct election. De Gaulle, the first President under the Fifth Republic, won reelection in 1965 but resigned in 1969.

[13]The emergency power has been used only once. De Gaulle invoked it in 1961 when a group of army generals rebelled over Algerian policy.

*REINFORCEMENT What is an example of an executive power that is unique to the French system?

The President appoints the Premier and may preside over meetings of the Cabinet. The President also helps to shape the bills that are submitted to Parliament. The President may even dissolve Parliament and call a general election. Thus, the President exerts influence on both the executive and legislative branches of government. All Presidents under the Fifth Republic have used their influence effectively to control the direction of national affairs.

The Premier and Cabinet

The Premier appoints the members of the Cabinet, and together they form the government. In the British system, you will recall, the government holds all of the executive power. In the French system, the government must share that power with the President, who is truly the *chief* executive.

As in Britain, the Cabinet members direct specific departments of government. In contrast to the British system, however, the French Premier and Cabinet may not hold seats in Parliament. Cabinet ministers tend to be administrators and specialists rather than prominent political figures.

In the French system, even more than in the British, control over legislation rests in the government's hands. Members of Parliament have only limited power to propose bills and amendments or to bring down the government. If the government wants to rush through an important bill, it may declare the bill to be a "matter of confidence." In that case, the bill automatically becomes law without a vote unless the lower house adopts a motion of censure, by an absolute majority of all members. Passage of a motion of censure causes the government to fall.[14] Even if the government does not declare a "matter of confidence," the opposition may submit a motion of censure. But the opposition may initiate only one censure vote per session.

The Parliament

In France, as in Britain, there are two houses of Parliament.[15] The upper house is known as the Senate. The lower and more important house is the National Assembly.

The Senate The 316-member Senate has only limited powers. Members serve nine-year terms, with one-third being elected every three years. An electoral college chooses the senators in indirect elections; the college consists of local officials and members of the National Assembly. The Senate cannot be dissolved.

The National Assembly The National Assembly has 577 members, called **deputies.** The deputies serve five-year terms, unless parliament is dissolved and new general elections are called before the end of their term.

The French do not seem to be able to make up their minds about how to elect the National Assembly. They have used variations of two main election methods. One method, in effect from 1958 to 1985, uses single-member districts with election by majority vote in two stages. This is similar to the method of choosing the French President. The alternative system (used during the 4th Republic and again in 1985) is called *proportional representation*, or PR. It uses multi-member districts. Under PR, each party receives seats in proportion to its vote in an election district. If a party receives two-fifths of the vote in a district having 5 seats, it gets two of the seats. Voters cast their ballots for a list of candidates, rather than for individuals. The two systems tend to have different outcomes, the first favoring larger and fewer parties, the second giving representation to a greater number of small parties.

Powers of Parliament The powers of Parliament are strictly limited. On the budget, for example, the two houses have a limited

---

[14]You should note that the fall of the government does not affect the President's position. Presidents remain in office for a full seven-year term, unless they resign or die.

[15]"Parliament" *(parlement* in French) is the official title of a majority of the world's national legislative bodies. It comes from the French verb *parler,* meaning "to speak, to confer, to parley."

Socialists cheer Mitterrand's victory in 1981.

say. Some matters—including defense—are outside Parliament's jurisdiction altogether, and on those matters the government may issue ordinances that have the force of law.

In order to become a law, a bill must be passed by both houses and signed by the President. Both houses do not have to pass the same version of a bill, however. When the two houses disagree, the National Assembly may pass its version without Senate approval and send it to the President for signature. In most cases of disagreement, however, joint committees of the two houses are able to work out a compromise.

Political Parties

Under the Fifth Republic, many of France's old political parties have vanished or merged into new and larger parties. Many features of the constitution have contributed to this consolidation. Among those features: direct election of the President, two-round elections, and the concentration of powers in the hands of the executive.

Four major parties have dominated the recent French scene. On the right are the Gaullists (officially the Rally for the Republic) and in the center the Union for French Democracy. On the left are the Socialists and the Communists.[16] In the run-up to the 1986 general election, a far-right party called the National Front also became significant. All of the French parties tend to be much more ideological—more readily distinguished on a spectrum of right to left—than the major American parties.

[16]The parties of the right and center held power from 1958 until 1981. In May 1981, François Mitterrand, a Socialist, was elected President. A month later, the Socialists won a general election and became the majority party in the National Assembly.

Local Government

France, a unitary state, has one of the most highly centralized governments among all of the world's democracies. Nearly all aspects of local government are directed and controlled by the Cabinet ministries in Paris.

The current structure of local government dates to the Revolution of 1789. The country is divided into 96 départements—small units drawn largely along geographic rather than political, social, or economic lines. The central government appoints an official called a préfet to run each department. Each département is subdivided into communes, of which some 36,000 exist. Elected mayors and councils at the commune level are responsible for the delivery of local services.

Until 1982, préfets exercised close supervision of the locally elected governments, tightly controlling their purse strings. Now the powers of the local units have been enlarged, although few practical effects have become evident.

FOR REVIEW

1. **Identify:** premier, Fifth Republic, motion of censure, National Assembly, coalition government, runoff election.
2. How does France's present constitution remedy the instability of the past?
3. Describe three major differences between the presidency in France and in the United States.
4. How does Parliament's control over legislation in France differ from Parliament's control in Britain?
5. What four major parties have dominated French politics?
6. What is the basic role of the Premier and the Cabinet today?

3. Japan

As You Read, Think About:

- What the characteristics are of a parliamentary monarchy.
- How Japan has a highly centralized government.

Japan, like Great Britain, is an island nation;[17] and, like both Britain and France, it is a parliamentary democracy. The history of democratic government in Japan is quite brief, however; it spans only the past 40 years.

According to legend, the Japanese state was founded by the Emperor Jimmu in 660 B.C.; but the earliest written records indicate that it began to emerge about 1,000 years later, in the 4th century A.D. The country evolved in almost complete isolation, untouched by forces and events in the outside world, over the next 1,500 years.

Through that long period of seclusion, a political system developed that was not unlike that of medieval Europe. It was built around the person of the mikado—an emperor who governed by divine right and was, at least in theory, an absolute ruler. Real authority was exercised in his name by the shogun (a military dictator) and a number of noble families (the daimios), supported by their warrior servants (the samurais).

Japan was finally opened to Western influences in the middle years of the last century,[18] and the nation was soon committed, even driven, to becoming a modern state. That drive eventually led to the Japanese attempt to conquer all of East Asia and then to its crushing defeat in World War II.

Japan was occupied by the United States for nearly seven years following the war, from 1945 to 1952. Far-reaching social, political, and economic reforms were put in place at the direction of the American occupation forces, commanded by Douglas MacArthur. The nation's remarkable postwar economic recovery was begun during that period and so, too, was the development of its present political system. Today, Japan is the only democracy in the largely underdeveloped and largely undemocratic non-Western world.

The Constitution

Japan's constitution explicitly rejects the old ways, under which the Emperor was considered to hold "sovereign power." Now such power rests with the Japanese people. They can express their will by secret ballot in elections that are held under universal adult suffrage.

The constitution contains quite an extensive listing of basic freedoms—in effect, a bill of rights. Important rights include freedom of speech, freedom of the press, freedom of religion, equality of the sexes, the right to work, and the right "to maintain minimum standards of wholesome and cultured living."

Also part of the constitution is a unique anti-military clause. The clause says that the Japanese people "forever renounce war as a sovereign right of the nation." It adds: "Land, sea, and air forces, as well as other war potential, will never be maintained."

United States officials insisted on the clause because they feared a revival of Japanese militarism. Later, they began to see Japan as an ally in the Cold War. With encouragement from the United States, Japanese leaders since 1954 have given the clause a narrow interpretation. They say that it rules out an army, a navy, and an air force, but not a "self-defense force." Japan has rebuilt its three military arms, calling them "Ground, Maritime, and Air Self-Defense Forces." The anti-military clause of the Japanese constitution remains technically in force.

[17] In its four main islands off the east coast of Asia, Japan fits 120 million people into an area slightly smaller than California.

[18] Dutch and Portuguese traders had limited contacts with the Japanese in the 16th and 17th centuries. The country was not opened to any meaningful Western contacts until 1853, however, when a United States naval squadron, commanded by Commodore Matthew C. Perry, made a polite but firm visit. Japan and the United States concluded a commercial treaty the following year, and the Japanese then proceeded to negotiate similar agreements with other Western powers.

*REINFORCEMENT Ask the class how the interpretation and practice of the anti-military clause of the Japanese constitution has changed over time. Discuss reasons for this.

FOCUS ON:

Japan's "Bill of Rights"

Japan's new constitution, replacing the Meiji Constitution of 1889, went into effect on May 1, 1947. The new document swept away prewar traditions of militarism and authoritarianism and entrusted the reins of power to the people. Its "Bill of Rights," which consists of 31 articles that are concerned with the rights and duties of the people of Japan, form the real foundation for Japan's democracy. Listed here are 11 of these articles (some extracted)*, and the rights they guarantee:

Article 13. All of the people shall be respected as individuals. Their right to life, liberty, and the pursuit of happiness shall, to the extent that it does not interfere with the public welfare, be the supreme consideration in legislation and in other governmental affairs.

Article 14. All of the people are equal under the law and there shall be no discrimination in political, economic or social relations because of race, creed, sex, social status, or family origin.

Peers and peerage shall not be recognized.

No privilege shall accompany any award of honor . . . beyond the lifetime of the individual who now holds or hereafter may receive it.

Article 15. The people have the inalienable right to choose their public officials and to dismiss them. . . .

Universal adult suffrage is guaranteed with regard to the election of public officials.

In all elections, secrecy of the ballot shall not be violated. . . .

Article 16. Every person shall have the right of peaceful petition for redress of damage, for the removal of public officials, for the enactment, repeal, or amendment of laws, ordinances, or regulations and for other matters; nor shall any other person be in any way discriminated against for sponsoring such a petition.

Article 18. No person shall be held in bondage of any kind. Involuntary servitude, except as punishment for crime, is prohibited.

Article 19. Freedom of thought and conscience shall not be violated.

Article 20. Freedom of religion is guaranteed to all. No religious organization shall receive any privileges from the state, nor exercise any political authority.

No person shall be compelled to take part in any religious act, celebration, rite, or practice.

The state and its organs shall refrain from religious education or any other religious activity.

Article 21. Freedom of assembly and association as well as speech, press, and all other forms of expression are guaranteed. . . .

Article 31. No person shall be deprived of life or liberty, nor shall any other criminal penalty be imposed, except according to procedure established by law.

Article 34. No person shall be arrested or detained without being at once informed of the charges against him or without the immediate privilege of counsel; nor shall he be detained without adequate cause; and upon demand of any person such cause must be immediately shown in open court. . . .

Article 37. In all criminal cases the accused shall enjoy the right to a speedy and public trial by an impartial tribunal. . . .

At all times the accused shall have the assistance of competent counsel who shall, if the accused is unable to secure the same by his own efforts, be assigned to his use by the state.

1. In noting the nature of the guarantees defined in the articles here, why is it important to keep this fact in mind: Japan's new constitution was drawn up mainly by American Occupation authorities.
2. Which of the articles listed here remind you of provisions in the 1st Amendment to the U.S. Constitution?

*From *The Constitution of Japan* (Washington, D.C.: United States Department of State Publication 2836, Far Eastern Series 22)

A view of Japan's National Diet Building, which was built in 1936.

Local Government

Like Britain and France, Japan has a highly centralized government. The country is divided into 47 subdivisions called prefectures. The prefectures get much of their money from the national government and often carry out policies made at the national level. Local voters elect a governor and a one-house parliament in each prefecture.

The National Diet

Under the constitution, Japan's parliament—the National Diet—is considered the highest organ of state power. The Diet contains an upper house, called the House of Councilors, and a lower house, called the House of Representatives. As in Britain and France, the lower house wields the greater power.

The Prime Minister and at least half of all Cabinet ministers must be members of the Diet. Usually the Prime Minister comes from the lower house.

House of Councilors The House of Councilors has prestige but little power. Its 252 members sit for six years, in staggered terms. Three-fifths of the members are elected from districts that are based on prefectures. The remaining two-fifths are elected by the nation as a whole. Because it has fewer responsibilities than the lower house, the House of Councilors tends to serve an essentially deliberative, advisory role.

House of Representatives The House of Representatives has many important powers. It "makes" and can also "break" the Prime Minister. By a vote of no confidence, the house can force the Prime Minister either to resign or to dissolve the House of Representatives and call an early election. In addition, the lower house has full power to make treaties, raise funds, and make appropriations. On other matters, bills must be passed by both the lower and upper houses. But the lower house can override a negative vote in the upper house by passing a bill for a second time, by a two-thirds majority.

The 511 members of the House of Representatives are elected from 123 election districts. The Japanese system uses multi-seat districts, with voters choosing more than one representative. Representatives serve for four years—or less, if the house is dissolved and new elections take place sooner.

Consensus Politics The atmosphere in both houses of the National Diet is sedate compared to that in the legislative bodies in Britain and the United States. Japanese society places great stress on avoiding confrontation. Therefore, politicians seek to reach **consensus,** or broad agreement, on issues. A political majority tries to avoid pushing through a bill against strong opposition from a minority. The two sides can usually work out some sort of compromise.

Most of the bills that are introduced in the National Diet are drawn up by the government or by the bureaucracy. As in other

ENRICHMENT Discuss how the Japanese aversion to confrontation is reflected in their politics.

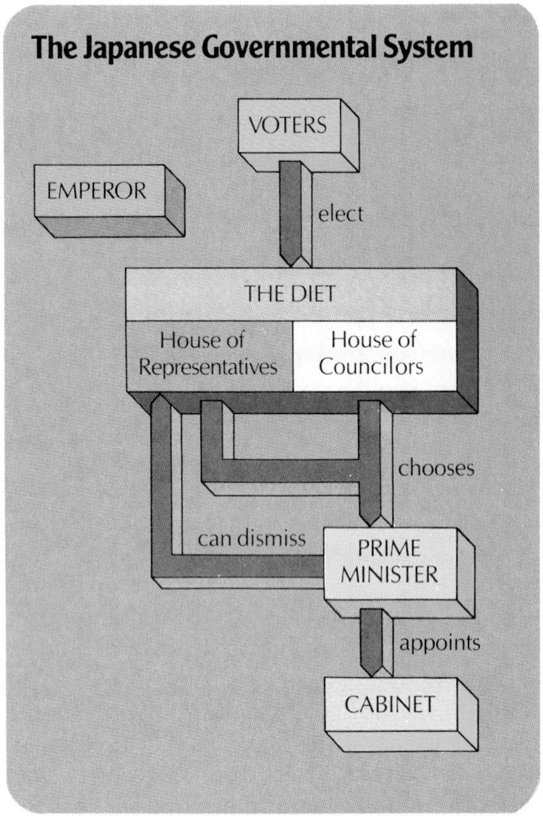

In what way does this chart indicate that the Emperor of Japan has no real power?

parliamentary democracies, government proposals usually become law. Members of the opposition do not just stay in the background, however. They pose sharp questions to Cabinet members in debate. They also take an active part in the deliberations of parliamentary committees.

Prime Minister and Cabinet

The Prime Minister and the Cabinet perform the executive functions of government. The Cabinet members serve as heads of major departments. Those members of the Cabinet who are not members of Parliament are usually borrowed from the bureaucracy.

Voting to choose a Prime Minister usually takes place along party or factional lines. (Some parties are divided into factions.) The Prime Minister thus represents the majority party or a majority coalition within the House of Representatives.

The Prime Minister appoints the members of the Cabinet. Membership in the Cabinet is considered a great honor, and appointment may be a reward for faithful service to the Prime Minister. Under a system known as collective responsibility, Cabinet members are considered to act as a group. A member who feels unable to support a Cabinet decision usually resigns.

The Prime Minister has the power to dissolve the House of Representatives (but not the House of Councilors). This step, called **dissolution,** leads to immediate elections for a new house.

The Bureaucracy

The large Japanese bureaucracy, or civil service, enjoys unusual respect within Japanese society. It also wields great power. Top members of the bureaucracy are technocrats, or experts in technical and administrative affairs. They include many of the leading graduates of Japan's top universities, who compete to win civil service positions. Jobs in the bureaucracy do not pay as well as many business jobs, and they demand long hours. Nonetheless, such jobs are highly prized by Japanese who wish to serve the public or who seek the prestige of civil service rank.

Japan's vast bureaucracy developed under the old imperial system, before World War II, when emperors sought to modernize the nation as rapidly as possible. The bureaucracy undertook many tasks—in economic as well as administrative matters. Today, Japan's bureaucracy plays a key role in Japan's economy. The Ministry of Trade and Industry helps to coordinate the plans and strategies of dozens of large Japanese firms, both private and public. Such an activist policy has been widely credited with helping Japan to build one of the world's most dynamic capitalist economies.

The Party System

Japan has a multi-party political system dominated by one very powerful force. This strong force is the Liberal Democratic

Speaking into a microphone is Japan's Prime Minister Yasuhiro Nakasone, leader of the Liberal Democratic Party since 1982.

Party (LDP).[19] Despite the "liberal" in its name, the LDP is a party of the right that follows a moderate–to–conservative policy. Its supporters include major business leaders, farmers, office workers, and people of the middle class. Since 1955, when it was formed, the LDP has provided all of Japan's Prime Ministers, although it has sometimes had to rule in coalition with another party.

The LDP itself is a coalition, for it contains a number of powerful interest groups or factions that disagree on many issues. However, all of the factions support free enterprise. They also unite behind the basically pro-U.S. foreign policy that Japan has followed since World War II. Leaders of the factions bargain with one another to win support for various goals. By custom, the faction leaders band together to support one of their number for Prime Minister.

Several other parties hold seats in the National Diet. The largest opposition group is the leftist Japan Socialist Party, or JSP. The JSP criticizes Japan's pro-U.S. foreign policy and has spoken against the concept of "self-defense forces." Many of the JSP's supporters belong to the nation's large trade unions. Leftist and centrist factions jockey for power within the party.

Other important political groups include the Japan Communist Party (JCP) and the Komeito, or Clean Government Party. The Communists' supporters are concentrated in major cities. The Komeito has close ties to a Japanese religious group. It supports conservative policies and calls for the "purification" of Japanese life.

The Courts

Japan has an independent judicial system that helps to protect basic freedoms guaranteed by the constitution's bill of rights. The courts have the power to review laws passed by the National Diet and to declare them unconstitutional. Japan's Supreme Court has done this only rarely.

On three of those rare occasions in the 1970s and 1980s, the Court ruled that the method of apportioning seats in the Diet is unconstitutional. By the court's reckoning, votes in rural districts often count four or

[19]The LDP's Yasuhiro Nakasone became Prime Minister in 1982. The party lost its majority in a general election in December 1983, but Nakasone was able to form a new government with the support of independents. The LDP won 250 seats out of 511, or six short of a majority.

*REINFORCEMENT Discuss the basic philosophy of the political party which dominates in Japan.

five times as much as votes in urban districts. This is because a lightly populated rural district may be able to elect as many members of the National Diet as a large city district.[20] Parliament has talked about making changes but has been slow to act.

Japan's court system is based on Roman law and uses no juries.

FOR REVIEW

1. **Identify:** Emperor, oligarchy, National Diet, technocrats.
2. Cite one similarity and one difference between the Japanese constitution and the United States Constitution.
3. What exclusive powers does the Japanese House of Representatives hold?
4. What is consensus politics? What is its effect?
5. What is collective responsibility?
6. What role does the bureaucracy play in the Japanese economy?
7. What power is possessed by the judicial system in Japan?

4. The Soviet Union

As You Read, Think About:

- How the government of the Soviet Union is so radically different from the government of the United States.
- What the relationship is between the Soviet government and the Communist Party.

Unlike Great Britain, France, or Japan, the Soviet Union is not a democracy. It is a totalitarian dictatorship.

Recall, a *dictatorship* is a country ruled by one person or a small group of people. In the Soviet Union, the rulers are the leaders of the Communist Party—a group of perhaps a dozen powerful individuals. The Communist Party holds absolute power, with no checks and balances to help protect individual rights.

A government that is *totalitarian* exercises* control over almost every aspect of a nation's life. In the Soviet Union, the Communist Party and the government keep a tight grip on political and economic affairs. They control such means of communication as newspapers, books, radio, and television. In this way, the nation's leaders restrict people's access to opinions that go against party policies. They make it hard for opponents of the ruling group to organize effectively and win public support.

Regular elections take place in the Soviet Union, but they offer no mechanism for ousting the ruling group. Most of the candidates represent the Communist Party. The voters cannot choose among competing parties and programs.

A Union of Republics

The official name of the Soviet Union is the Union of Soviet Socialist Republics (or U.S.S.R.).[21] The country is a successor to the czarist Russian Empire, which came to an end after the two Russian revolutions of 1917. The first revolution ousted Czar Nicholas II and replaced him with a provisional democratic government. The second revolution, eight months later, overthrew the provisional government and put the Communist Party in power.[22]

The U.S.S.R. officially came into being in 1922. It is a federation of separate units, called republics, organized along ethnic lines. Today the U.S.S.R. contains 15 republics. By far the biggest and most important is the Russian Soviet Federal Socialist Republic (or simply "Russia"), which occupies

[20] In the United States, such imbalances were largely eliminated after a "one-man, one-vote" ruling by the United States Supreme Court in 1964. (See page 301.)

[21] The U.S.S.R. is larger than any other country in area. Stretching across much of Europe and Asia, it contains some 272 million people and ranks third in population behind China and India.

[22] The group of Communists who seized power were called *Bolsheviks*. The second Russian revolution is sometimes called the "Bolshevik Revolution."

*ENRICHMENT Ask the students to consider the drastic changes in their lives which would result if they lived under a totalitarian government.

The world's largest country in land area, the Soviet Union has, since the end of World War II, devoted a large share of its resources to developing a military force that is foremost in the world.

three fourths of the U.S.S.R.'s land area and contains about half of the nation's people. Moscow, the capital of the Soviet Union, is also the capital of Russia.

Ethnic Russians, who live mainly in the Russian Republic, dominate the political and cultural life of the Soviet Union. But the nation also contains many non-Russian people. Among them are Ukrainians, Latvians, Lithuanians, Estonians, Tadzhiks, and Uzbeks. All told, the Soviet Union contains more than 100 ethnic groups, speaking at least 60 different languages.

Historical Development

Lenin The first Soviet ruler was Vladimir Ilyich Lenin, the leader of the Bolshevik Revolution. Lenin began the process of transforming an ancient, tradition-bound society into the world's first communist nation. He created a new system of government that contained several layers of elected bodies called soviets, or councils. There were soviets at the factory level, soviets at the city level, and soviets at the regional and national levels. Despite this elaborate system of representation, decisions were made at the top, by Communist Party leaders, and passed down to lower levels.

Stalin After Lenin died in 1924, power gradually passed to a new leader named Josef Stalin. Stalin consolidated his power during the 1930s by ruthlessly eliminating all rivals in a series of purges.[23]

Under Stalin, the Soviet government took firm control of industry and agriculture.

[23]Technically, a purge is a "purification." Stalin "purified" the party and government by having his rivals jailed or executed.

Farmers and others who resisted were shot or sent to forced labor camps in Siberia (the northern part of the Russian Republic that lies mostly in Asia). At a heavy cost in human suffering, Stalin managed to mold the Soviet Union into a major industrial and military power. (You will read about the Soviet economic system in more detail in Chapter 26.)

World War II proved a severe test for Stalin's leadership. Nazi Germany invaded the Soviet Union in 1941, smashing much of the country's industry and flattening entire cities. After bitter fighting, Soviet forces drove the Germans back across eastern Europe. Some 20 million Soviet citizens had been killed by the time the war ended in 1945.

The Soviet Union emerged from the war holding political control over eastern Europe. It became one of the world's two superpowers, rivaling the United States in military strength. After the war, Stalin helped to guide the rapid rebuilding of Soviet industry and agriculture. He maintained a tight grip on power until his death in 1953.

****Since Stalin*** Stalin's successors have not held absolute power in their own hands, as Stalin did. They have had to share power with their colleagues in the Communist Party leadership. Under men like Nikita Khrushchev, Leonid Brezhnev, and Mikhail Gorbachev, the harsh repressiveness that marked Stalin's years has now eased. Political debate is somewhat freer. Also, fewer people are being sent to Siberian labor camps. However, Stalin's successors have not changed the basic character of communist rule. The Soviet Union remains a totalitarian dictatorship.

The Soviet Constitution

The Soviet system of government is spelled out in a detailed constitution. In form, this constitution is similar to those of western democracies. In concept and operation, however, it is strikingly different.

Like western constitutions, the Soviet document lists a number of civil rights, such as freedom of speech and religion. It also lists economic rights—for example, the right to free medical care. The rights of Soviet citizens are closely linked to a series of duties. Among these are the duty to perform military service and the duty to work in a "socially useful occupation."

The Soviet constitution has a number of qualifications that apply to basic rights. Such terms as "in accordance with the aims of building communism" and "in order to strengthen and develop the socialist system" serve to limit the scope of those rights. Free speech cannot be used to oppose the aims of building and supporting communism. Freedom of assembly does not extend to holding meetings that might weaken or threaten the socialist system.

Moreover, the constitution sets up no independent institutions that could limit the power of the ruling party. The Communist Party commands the courts, as it commands other institutions of Soviet society.

The Dominant Role of the Communist Party

The Soviet constitution gives the Communist Party a unique and powerful role. The party serves, says the document, as "the leading and guiding force of Soviet society." It "determines general prospects for the development of society and the lines of the U.S.S.R.'s domestic and foreign policy." It "directs the creative activity of the Soviet people." It does this in order to promote the "struggle for the victory of communism" in a planned and scientific way.

The Chosen Ones The Soviet Communist Party is an elite party, made up of specially chosen people. Fewer than 10 percent of adult citizens are party members. Each member belongs to a local unit called a *primary party organization.*[24] Primary party organizations are found in apartment buildings and factories, on farms and ships, in offices and shops. A unit may have as few as a

[24]Formerly such units of the Communist Party were called *cells.*

*ENRICHMENT Stalin's harsh strategies molded the Soviet Union into a major industrial and military power. Discuss Stalin's successors in comparison.

BUILDING GOVERNMENT SKILLS

Analyzing National Interest

Each nation in the world acts to promote its own interest. *National interest* is defined as the sum of the security, political, economic, and ideological and/or ethical concerns of a nation.

Each nation in the world is unique. Each has its own history, geography, mix of resources, and people; therefore, the national interests of countries differ from one another.

Because a nation's circumstances change from year to year, and because we all have different perceptions of a nation's concerns, ideas about national interest also vary from year to year and from person to person.

Security Interests

The most important aspect of any nation's interest is its concern for survival. Interests that concern the survival of the nation's people, institutions, and ways of life are security interests. Nations maintain military forces because they must have security.

Political Interests

The political interests of a nation refer to the nation's concern for influencing other nations—both in a one-on-one relationship, and in international forums such as the United Nations. For example, the Group of 77 is a loose political alliance of the developing nations that belong to the United Nations. (When this group organized about 20 years ago, 77 nations joined together. Today, the Group of 77 includes about 120 nations.) They organized because they believed that if they voted and voiced opinions together, rather than separately, they would have more influence in the United Nations.

Economic Interests

All nations are concerned with the well-being of their economies. The different resources available to a nation, the amount of money it has, and the amount and kind of goods and services it produces all affect its economic interests. A nation, for example, will trade with another nation to obtain resources that are scarce. To maintain the trade relationship, the nations may have to negotiate trade agreements.

Ideological and Ethical Interests

Ideologies affect nations' perceptions of which actions by other nations are right and wrong and which are acceptable and unacceptable. For example, because the U.S. values free speech and expression highly, it sometimes condemns governments that jail people for criticizing the government.

Mix of Interests

As you may have seen by now, all these interests—security, political, economic, and ideological—are interrelated. To give one general example of how they relate, consider the importance of maintaining a military. Nation A builds a military for security reasons, because it fears an attack from Nation B. In order to pay for the military, it needs money, so it trades with Nations C and D. It also needs minerals and other resources, so it trades with Nation E. To strengthen its support, both militarily and politically, Nation A joins an alliance with several other nations.

1. Use the four components of national interest described above to analyze the national interests of the countries you read about in this chapter.
2. Read a newspaper article about a foreign policy action or statement by the United States. Identify the component(s) of national interest that may justify the action or statement.

dozen members or as many as several hundred members.

Party Watchdogs Primary units serve as watchdogs to make sure the other institutions of society are meeting their responsibilities. They monitor factory production. They check to make sure that daycare is available for parents who work. They investigate complaints by workers against their bosses. They hold meetings to whip up support for party goals. In performing these and many other tasks, primary units help to keep higher officials informed about what the Soviet people are thinking and saying.

Parallel Organizations The Communist Party is organized in a way that parallels the organization of government. Each level of government—local, regional, republican, national—has its corresponding level of party officials. In this way, party officials can make sure that government officials are carrying out the party's wishes.

Officially, the highest organ of the party is the All-Union Party Congress. With some 5,000 members, the party congress meets in the nation's capital every few years. Its main function is to elect a smaller body called the Central Committee.

Top Party Bodies The Central Committee has about 500 members and is in charge of party affairs between sessions of the party congress. It is too big to wield power effectively. Therefore, the Central Committee delegates its power to two smaller bodies that it chooses. One is the Political Bureau, or **Politburo,** which makes party policy. The other is the **Secretariat,** which is the party's executive arm.

The Politburo contains from 15 to 25 members. Among those members are the key officials of the Soviet government—although the government is formally separate from the party structure.

The Secretariat normally has 10 to 12 members. Its head is the most powerful of all Soviet officials, the General Secretary. The General Secretary presides over meetings of the Politburo and has wide powers to place political allies in key party positions. For years, it was common for the General Secretary to lead the government as well as the party, taking the title of Premier. Mikhail Gorbachev, who gained power in 1985, assumed only the title of General Secretary and arranged for another man to become Premier.

"Democratic Centralism" The Communist Party and other Soviet institutions operate on a principle that Communists call **democratic centralism.** In theory, party members at each level debate an idea fully and make decisions that they then pass up through the party hierarchy. Finally, the top levels of the party ratify the decision. In practice, however, major decisions are made at the top. In short, "democratic centralism" means rule from the top down.

The Governmental Structure

Like the Communist Party, the Soviet government has a many-layered structure. At * each layer there is an elected legislative body called a soviet. Each layer has various administrative bodies as well.

The Supreme Soviet The national legislature, called the **Supreme Soviet,** has two houses of equal rank. One is called the *Soviet of the Union.* Voters elect its members from districts of roughly equal population. The other is called the *Soviet of Nationalities.* Voters of each republic and of other ethnic subdivisions[25] elect the members of this body.

The Supreme Soviet has little real power. Its members serve for five-year terms. They meet for only a few days twice a year. Their main job is to applaud the speeches of party leaders and to approve laws that have been drawn up in advance. In theory, the Supreme Soviet elects the members of two higher government bodies, the Presidium and the Council of Ministers. But top party leaders make the actual choices.

[25]For example, autonomous regions and national areas within republics.

*REINFORCEMENT Ask the students to identify the four main layers in the structure of the Soviet government and their functions.

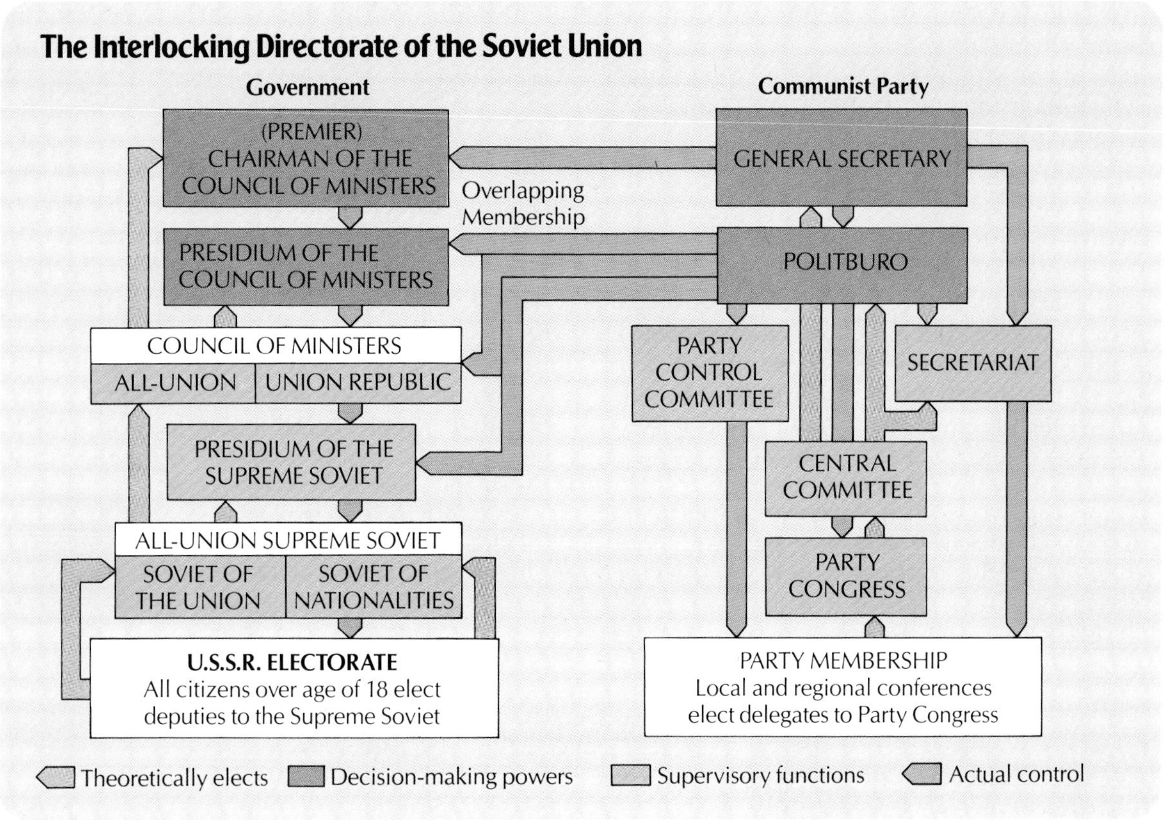

How does this chart show that actual control of the government in the Soviet Union stems from groups within the Communist Party, rather than from governmental units?

The Presidium The members of the *Presidium* (whose number varies from two to three dozen) also serve for five-year terms. They have the power to issue decrees that have the force of law. They may also draw up legislation for the Supreme Soviet to approve. The Presidium elects one of its members to serve as head of state, or President. The Soviet President is traditionally a figurehead with only ceremonial duties.

The Council of Ministers The *Council of Ministers* is roughly equivalent to the cabinet in a parliamentary democracy. It has the power to issue decrees. Its members —typically numbering many dozens —include the heads of government departments. Because it is so large, the Council of Ministers leaves the making of important decisions to a committee called the *Presidium of the Council of Ministers.* The head of the Council of Ministers is commonly called the *Premier,* or head of government.

The Judiciary The Soviet Union has a court system that is technically independent but in reality under control of the Communist Party. Several layers of courts exist, at local and higher levels. At the top is the Supreme Court of the U.S.S.R. Members of the various soviets elect the judges at each level, generally for five-year terms. Like courts in Britain, Soviet courts have no power to rule laws unconstitutional. However, Soviet courts are charged with making sure that government officials obey the law.

Power in the Soviet Union

Soviet voters have only limited opportunity to influence the political life of their country. The Soviet constitution makes no provision for a transfer of power from one set of officials to another set. When changes take place either in the party or in the government, they generally result from decisions that are made by small groups of high party officials.

Coalition Building Under Stalin, one man controlled the course of the entire nation. The situation today is more complex. Soviet rule is collegial (shared by several people) rather than *personal.* As a result, top party officials must win the support of their colleagues for major decisions. In effect, members of the Politburo and other important bodies must build coalitions, or temporary alliances, in order to get their plans approved.

The Role of Elections Soviet elections are highly-publicized events. Most of the candidates belong to the Communist Party. They give speeches setting forth the party's views and explaining party policies. In this way, party leaders can get Soviet citizens to focus on issues that the leaders consider important.

About one candidate in four is not a party member. Such candidates do not attack communism, for that would violate the Sovi-

Mikhail S. Gorbachev, General Secretary of the Soviet Union, addresses the opening session of the Russian Federation of the Supreme Soviet in Moscow's Grand Kremlin Palace.

et constitution. They do not belong to competing parties, for no such parties are allowed.

As a rule, only one candidate runs for each position on the ballot. Most voters merely deposit the ballot in the ballot box, thus casting a vote for each official candidate. Voters who wish to cross off a name must take the ballot to a booth. Thus, observers can see who is voting against an official candidate.

Most candidates in Soviet elections receive huge majorities. Voting is considered a solemn duty, and election turnout is usually high. To outside observers, the Soviet voting *process seems an empty ritual. To Soviet authorities, however, it is a way of validating the rule of the Communist Party and ensuring loyalty to the regime.

FOR REVIEW

1. **Identify:** Russian revolutions of 1917, republics, Lenin, Stalin, purges.
2. In what ways is the Soviet government totalitarian?
3. How have Soviet politics differed since Stalin?
4. What is the role of the Communist Party in the Soviet Union?
5. What is the Central Committee? What two smaller bodies does it choose?
6. From which body is the Premier chosen?
7. What role do elections play in the Soviet Union?
8. Identify the four main "layers" in the structure of the Soviet government.

Under which form of government is a system of checks and balances available to check against abuses of power by legislative or executive branches?

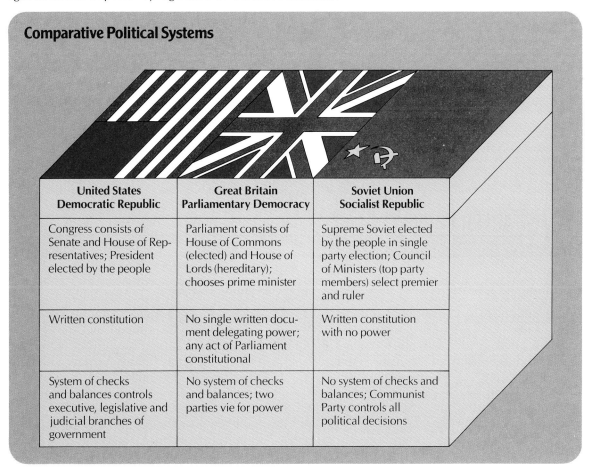

Comparative Political Systems

United States Democratic Republic	Great Britain Parliamentary Democracy	Soviet Union Socialist Republic
Congress consists of Senate and House of Representatives; President elected by the people	Parliament consists of House of Commons (elected) and House of Lords (hereditary); chooses prime minister	Supreme Soviet elected by the people in single party election; Council of Ministers (top party members) select premier and ruler
Written constitution	No single written document delegating power; any act of Parliament constitutional	Written constitution with no power
System of checks and balances controls executive, legislative and judicial branches of government	No system of checks and balances; two parties vie for power	No system of checks and balances; Communist Party controls all political decisions

*ENRICHMENT Contrast the "empty ritual" of voting in the Soviet Union with the totally threat-free voting privilege we enjoy in the United States.

SUMMARY

In this chapter we compared the governments of Great Britain, France, Japan, and the Soviet Union.

The British government is democratic, unitary, and parliamentary. British law is based on an unwritten constitution. That is, the constitution is not contained in one document. The head of state of Britain is a monarch who reigns but does not rule. Parliament holds both legislative and executive powers; it passes laws and chooses some of its members to run the nation's affairs and the executive departments. Parliament is bicameral. It is composed of the House of Lords and the House of Commons; the House of Commons holds most of the governmental powers. Elections must be held at least every five years.

French government is unitary and democratic. It is headed by an elected President who serves for seven years. The French constitution, written in 1958, established a mixed parliamentary-presidential system, with presidential dominance. Many of the President's duties are similar to the duties of the President of the United States; however, the French President may use dictatorial powers during an emergency and dissolve Parliament. The upper house is the Senate; the lower house is the National Assembly.

Japan is a parliamentary monarchy. The head of government is the Prime Minister and the head of state is called Emperor. The Japanese Constitution contains a listing of basic rights and a unique anti-military clause. Local governments, prefectures, carry out policies made at the national level. The legislature, the National Diet, is bicameral. The House of Councilors, the upper house, has little power. The House of Representatives, the lower house, can "make or break" the Prime Minister, make treaties, raise funds, and make appropriations.

The Soviet Union is a totalitarian dictatorship. Although elections are held, voters cannot choose among competing parties and programs —most candidates represent the Communist Party. Although the Soviet Constitution lists civil rights, these rights cannot be used to oppose communism. The Communist Party is dominant in order to promote the "struggle for the victory of communism." Both the Communist Party and the Soviet government are many-layered. Primary party units serve as watchdogs to ensure that other institutions of society are meeting their responsibilities. The Central Committee is in charge of party affairs between sessions of the Party Congress.

CHAPTER REVIEW

Key Terms/Concepts*

by-elections (668)
coalition (668)
ministers (668)
shadow cabinet (669)
deputies (673)
consensus (677)
dissolution (678)
Politburo (684)
Secretariat (684)
democratic centralism (684)
Supreme Soviet (684)

*These terms are included in the Glossary.

Keynote Questions

• **1.** What is the difference in form between the United States Constitution and the British constitution?

• **2.** How is the British Prime Minister chosen? What are the PM's duties?

• **3.** What does it mean when a government "falls" in Britain?

• **4.** For the three countries listed, make a chart to show how the parliament is organized (for

The dots represent skill levels required to answer each question or complete each activity: • requires recall and comprehension • • requires application and analysis • • • requires synthesis and evaluation

example, the House of Representatives and the Senate in the United States); how many members serve in each house; and how they are chosen: Britain, France, Japan.

• **5.** Which leader chooses the Cabinet in Britain? France? Japan?

• **6.** How do political parties in Britain differ from parties in the United States?

• **7.** How is the President chosen in France? What unique powers does he or she wield?

•• **8.** What is the basic similarity among local governments in Britain, France, and Japan?

• **9.** Why did United States officials insist on the anti-military clause in Japan's constitution? How has this clause been interpreted since the Cold War?

• **10.** How is the Japanese Prime Minister chosen? What powers does the Prime Minister wield?

• **11.** What is the role of the Japanese judiciary in the government?

• **12.** How are the 15 Soviet republics organized?

•• **13.** Compare and contrast the Soviet constitution to western constitutions.

• **14.** What is the role of the primary party organizations in the Soviet Union?

• **15.** What is the difference between the Politburo and the Secretariat? What is the General Secretary's role?

• **16.** What are the powers of the Presidium and the Council of Ministers?

Skill Application

Classifying Governments: In Chapter 1, you examined the general classifications of government (pp. 6–12). In this chapter, you looked at four specific nations and their governments. By putting the information from these two chapters together, you can classify the governments and then compare them on a more general level.

Read pp. 6–12 in Chapter 1 to refresh your memory.

1. Make a list of the characteristics of the following classifications of government: unitary and federal; parliamentary and presidential; dictatorship and democracy.

2. For each of the nations listed here, write the classifications that best describe the government of that nation. For example, the United States government is federal, presidential, and a democracy.

a. Soviet Union
b. France
c. Japan
d. Britain

For Thought and Discussion

••• **1.** The Japanese bureaucracy, especially the Ministry of Trade and Industry, has played an active role in the Japanese economy. Would such a relationship between business and government be possible in the United States? Why or why not? What are the advantages and disadvantages of the Japanese bureaucracy's involvement in business?

•• **2.** How does control of the means of communication help the Soviet government keep a firm grip on political and economic affairs? What justification does the Soviet state offer for this type of control?

•• **3.** Compared to the presidential systems of the United States and France, what are the advantages of the parliamentary systems of government of both Britain and Japan? What are the disadvantages?

••• **4.** Do you think it is possible for a government to be both totalitarian and decentralized? Why or why not?

Suggested Activities

•• **1.** Choose one of the nations covered in this chapter, and follow newspaper articles and newsmagazine stories about that nation for a period of one week. Keep a journal of the nation's activities and its relations with the United States. At the end of the week, carefully review your journal. What suggestions can you offer for managing relations between that nation and the United States (or another nation)?

• **2.** Write to the embassy of one of the nations covered in this chapter. (Embassy addresses are listed in the *Congressional Directory.*) Obtain information and an organization chart of the nation's government. Prepare a bulletin board display or a poster which illustrates the government's structures.

[In a free enterprise system, the individual] intends only his own gain, and he is . . . led by an invisible hand to promote an end which was no part of his intention. . . . By pursuing his own interest he frequently promotes that of the society more effectually than when he really intends to promote it.
—ADAM SMITH

26 Comparing Economic Systems

CHAPTER OBJECTIVES

To help you to

Learn · Know · Understand

The characteristics and structures of a capitalist economy.

The nature of socialist political and economic thought.

The varying forms of communism in thought and practice.

PEOPLE'S ECONOMIC NEEDS are the same all over the world. People need food, clothing, and a place to live. Economic needs such as these are met by the production of goods and services.

The basic production processes are much the same in all countries. Farmers set out each morning to plow fields, milk cows or camels, and sow and harvest crops. Factory workers tend machines that clatter and turn out streams of products. Office workers busy themselves at their desks and computer consoles and conference tables.

But the ways in which economic life is organized vary greatly from one country to another. Who owns the tractors and cows and machines? Who decides whether a factory will produce tin cans or trumpets? What choices does a consumer have when shopping for groceries or for a home? Which decisions are made by the government and which decisions are made by individuals and groups? The answers to such questions depend to a large extent on what type of economic system a country uses.

Recall, the modern world has three basic types of economic systems—capitalism,

In some nations, as the USSR and China, agricultural and industrial resources are owned and controlled by the state; in the United States, they are mostly privately owned. *Above:* An offshore oil rig. *Facing page:* A harvest scene in the USSR.

socialism, and communism. The economic system in the United States is based on capitalism. A number of European democracies and many developing countries base their economies on socialism, usually blended with capitalism in one way or another. Totalitarian nations such as the Soviet Union and China base their economies—like their political systems—on communism.

1. Capitalism

As You Read, Think About:

- What the types of resources are that are important to a nation's economy.
- What the main characteristics are of a free enterprise system.
- What the basic types of business organizations are.

Capitalism, the American system, is based on private ownership of property. We can divide property into two basic kinds. One kind is personal property, such as your toothbrush and your bed. Personal property may be privately owned under all the major economic systems. The other kind of property is productive property, such as a worker's tools or a farmer's fields or a factory's machines. What is distinctive about capitalism is that private individuals and companies control most of the productive property. As we shall see, under both socialism and communism the basic means of production are owned by the public or the government.

Factors of Production

Four types of resources are especially important for a nation's economy. These basic resources are known as *factors of production.*

Land Fields, forests, mountains, and bodies of water are considered part of a nation's land. Land can be put to a variety of economic uses. If the fields have suitable soil and if water is available, the fields can be

*REINFORCEMENT Discuss in class the importance of who controls the productive property in a country. How is the individual affected when the productive property is controlled privately? By the government?

farmed. Forests provide wood and other products. Mountainous regions, and flatter areas as well, often contain valuable mineral resources like iron, coal, and petroleum. Many of the products of the land are used as raw materials for industries.

Labor A second factor of production is a human resource—labor. Men and women who work in mines, factories, offices, hospitals, and other places all provide labor that is an essential part of a nation's economy.

Capital The money, factories, and machinery that are used to produce goods and services are called *capital.* Unlike land and labor, which are called *primary* factors of production, capital has to be made before it can be used. In other words, capital is a product of the economy that is then put back into the economy to make more products.

Say you own a bicycle on which you deliver groceries after school. You paid for the bicycle; it is your capital, which you have put to use to earn an income. If you used the bicycle solely for pleasure, it would not be capital. Then it would be personal property, not productive property.

Someone who owns capital and puts it to productive use is called a **capitalist.** The term is most often applied to people who own large businesses or factories. We call our economy *capitalistic* because it depends on the energy and drive of thousands of individual capitalists, from the student delivering groceries to the shareholder in a company to the owner of banks and industries.

Management A special type of skilled labor is of particular importance in the modern economy. This is the labor involved in organizing the other factors of production and making businesses run efficiently. Those who perform such labor are engaged in the process of management, which is the fourth major factor of production.

The Free Enterprise System

A capitalist economy is often called a *free enterprise system.* In such a system, individuals are free to start and run their own businesses—their own enterprises. They are also free to dissolve, or end, those businesses. Free enterprise systems have five noteworthy characteristics.

Private Ownership In a free enterprise system, as we have seen, most of the means of production are privately rather than publicly owned. The owners are sometimes individuals. Often, however, they are groups of people who share ownership of a company.

Respect for Private Property A free enterprise system can work only when property rights are guaranteed. In the United States, the Constitution provides such protection. The Fifth Amendment states that no person may "be deprived of life, liberty, or property without due process of law." It also requires that "just compensation" be paid to owners when private property is taken for public use.

Individual Initiative Under capitalism, basic decisions about what to produce and how to produce it are left to private decision-makers. Let us take an example. If supplies of antifreeze run low, public officials do not order factories to produce more antifreeze. That is the job of private businesses. If antifreeze companies do not or cannot step up production by themselves, an enterprising capitalist may see a chance to make some money by starting up a new antifreeze company. Or perhaps someone can invent and sell a new product to take the place of antifreeze. A person who takes the initiative of starting or expanding a business is called an **entrepreneur.**

Competition Because people are free to enter a new business at any time, there are usually several companies making the same product. Companies must compete against one another to win customers. Competition among multiple sellers helps to hold down prices, since customers are likely to buy from the company with the lowest price. Competition thus promotes efficiency. It may also boost quality, as each firm strives to produce a better product and thus win more customers.

Capitalism emphasizes the private ownership of businesses, from small shops with a single owner to giant corporations with thousands of owners.

Under competitive conditions, the **laws of supply and demand** determine prices. Supply is the quantity of goods or services for sale. Demand is the desire of potential buyers for those goods and services. As supplies become more plentiful, prices tend to drop. As supplies become limited, prices tend to rise. By the same token, if demand drops —that is, if there are few buyers—sellers will probably lower their prices in order to make a sale. If demand rises, sellers can raise prices.

Competition does not always work smoothly. Sometimes a single business becomes so successful that its rivals go out of business. A firm that is the only source of a product or service is called a **monopoly.** Monopolies can be very powerful in the marketplace. Practically speaking, they can charge as much as they want for a product. Since there is no other supplier, the consumer must pay up or do without. Political leaders in the United States decided late in the 19th century that monopolies were dangerous because they concentrated immense economic power in a few hands. American leaders were especially concerned about a type of monopoly called a trust.[1] Most types of monopolies are now illegal in the United States under **antitrust laws.**

Freedom of Choice A fifth characteristic of free enterprise is that consumers, entrepreneurs, and workers enjoy freedom of choice. Consumers can choose from a variety of products and services. Entrepreneurs can switch from one business to another. Workers can quit their jobs and take new ones. However, federal and State governments do place certain restrictions on freedom of choice. There are rules, for example, against the sale of products deemed dangerous or undesirable. Entrance into some businesses or professions is restricted by licensing and other requirements, and so on.

Profit and Loss

Why do entrepreneurs invest in businesses? What drives the capitalist economy forward? The best answer is: profit.

To understand what profit is, we must first understand the idea of investment. An investment is a sum of money or capital that is put into a business enterprise. If you buy a bicycle to start a business delivering groceries, what you pay for the bicycle is an investment. You may also have to invest in other items—a carrier rack, for example. Your *profit* will be the amount of money you earn from your business, after you have subtracted all of your investments. Profit is the difference between investment and earnings. If your earnings are less than your investment, you have not made a profit; instead, you have taken a loss.

Risk-taking, therefore, is an essential part of the free enterprise system. Entrepreneurs

[1]A device by which several corporations in the same line of business combine to eliminate competition and regulate prices. The Sherman Antitrust Act of 1890 remains the basic law against monopolies today. It prohibits "every contract, combination in the form of a trust or otherwise, or conspiracy in restraint of trade or commerce among the several States, or with foreign nations."

*REINFORCEMENT Have the class discuss the role of profit in a capitalist economy. How does it affect each of the above characteristics of a free enterprise system?

take risks. Will they make a profit or take a loss? Only time will tell. Every year, many businesses fail for lack of profit. Businesses that survive tend to be those that have learned to make the most efficient use of the factors of production.

Government Regulation

In theory, free enterprise works automatically. People can enter or leave a business at will. Prices rise and fall according to supply and demand. Adam Smith, a Scottish philosopher of the 18th century, said it was as if an "invisible hand" were guiding people to do what was best for society. No guidance from government is necessary, said Smith. If all individuals pursue their own private interests, the good of all will be assured.

The system that Smith advocated is called *laissez-faire* ("leave alone"). It calls for the government to keep its hands off the economy. In practice, however, governments have tended to step in, either to give a helping hand to certain parts of the economy or to stop what people saw as abuses.

One of the earliest steps taken by the United States was the setting up of institutions to control the money supply. Another early step was the establishment of a *tariff*—a tax on imports. On many occasions, the Federal Government has set a high, "protective" tariff to protect United States industries by raising the prices of imported goods. In the 19th century the Federal and State governments gave land and money to investor-owned railroads as a means of promoting economic growth. Government aid to business takes many forms today. Examples include low-cost loans to help United States firms make sales abroad, and tax breaks for businesses that invest in rundown city centers.

Government efforts to curb abuses have also been many and varied. You have already read of **antitrust laws.** The Interstate Commerce Commission, established in 1887, works to regulate interstate freight rates. Government bodies on the federal and State level regulate such utilities as telephone rates and the price of electricity.[2]

The government's role in our economy takes many other forms, as well. Social welfare measures range from Social Security payments for retired workers to "welfare" payments for people without other incomes.[3] *

Culver Pictures, Inc.

In the 1870s, railroads came under severe public criticism for their monopolistic, abusive practices—as, for example, rate gouging and corrupting public officials. Acting to prevent such unfair practices, Congress created the Interstate Commerce Commission in 1887 and empowered it to regulate interstate freight rates.

A Mixed Economy

The United States cannot be said to have a purely capitalist economy. Today, economists usually describe the United States system as a "mixed economy." Free enterprise is still the controlling principle. But laissez-faire has been modified by a variety of government controls.

[2]In recent years, however, a number of government regulations have been phased out, or less vigorously enforced.

[3]See Chapter 16, page 467.

*ENRICHMENT Ask the class for examples of the government's regulatory role in our economy. Have the class cite specific examples in their community.

None of the world's economies, including our own, works smoothly all of the time. A key characteristic of capitalist economies has always been their tendency to be subject to "up" and "down" swings, from "boom" to "bust," in what are known as business cycles. Many of the government's economic activities today are aimed at cushioning the effects of those cycles. By fiscal policy (controlling taxes and spending) and monetary policy (controlling the money supply), the government tries to keep the economy perking along.

Despite persistent and often serious problems, our economy generally works well. It provides a large segment of the population of the United States with one of the world's highest standards of living.

Consumers in Charge? People from other countries who visit the United States are often surprised at the great variety of choices available to the consumer. Mouthwash comes in pink, yellow, green, blue, and other colors. Sweaters can be zip-up or pullover, V-necked or round-necked, long-sleeve or short-sleeve. Businesses spend great amounts of money determining exactly what types of products consumers will buy. Behind it all is the profit motive, of course, for the company that meets or creates a consumer "need" stands to gain more sales, and presumably more profits.[4]

There are two ways of looking at the role of consumers in our society. By one light, consumers reign. They "call the shots." If businesses produce breakfast cereals that contain raisins and chocolate-covered flakes, it is because consumers want such a product. Some people, however, say that consumers do not really reign at all—that businesses "call the shots." They say that businesses turn out not necessarily the products that consumers want, but the products that can be sold for a profit. Either way, however, the result is a great variety of products for consumers to choose from.

[4]If a company guesses wrong, however, and produces a car like the Edsel that few people will buy, it may suffer a loss.

Business Organization

While the United States economy contains gigantic companies with thousands of employees and with plants all over the world, most businesses in the United States are relatively small. Some 80 percent of businesses employ fewer than 20 people.

There are three basic types of business organizations—sole proprietorships, partnerships, and corporations. Each has its advantages and disadvantages.

Sole Proprietorships Businesses owned by a single individual are **sole proprietorships.** Typical of businesses in this category might be a beauty shop, a garage, or a doctor's practice. A major advantage of sole proprietorships is that decisions may be made quickly, by the single owner. A major disadvantage is that the owner is personally liable for debts the business may build up.

Partnerships **Partnerships** are businesses owned by two or more individuals, called partners. An advantage is that a partnership can draw on the resources of more than one person for capital to start or expand the business. A disadvantage is that each partner is legally responsible for the business. If one partner should "take the money and run," the other is stuck with any debts that may result. Another disadvantage is that partnerships end if a partner leaves or dies. Then a new partnership must be formed.

Corporations **Corporations** have many owners, called shareholders.[5] Unlike partnerships, corporations may continue indefinitely. A shareholder's death does not affect the legal status of the corporation.

Corporations also have other advantages. They can draw their capital from hundreds and even thousands of investors, thus enabling them to finance such costly projects as putting an earth satellite in orbit or building an oil pipeline. At regular intervals, the corporation distributes profits to its owners.

[5]A share is a fraction of ownership in the corporation.

BUILDING GOVERNMENT SKILLS

Exchanging Foreign Currency

If you ever travel to a foreign country, you will have to exchange your dollars for the currency of that country. Every country has its own kind of money. The British use pounds, the French use francs, and the Mexicans use pesos. Exchange rates determine how much of each of these currencies you can get for your dollars.

Exchange rates not only affect you when you leave the country, they also affect the price of imports we buy here. The fewer dollars it takes to buy French francs, for example, the cheaper French clothes are in the United States. This is good for people who buy French clothes, but it may be bad for American clothesmakers who cannot make clothes as cheaply.

Now let us look at how exchange rates work. You are arriving in London and want to change your dollars into pounds. You see that the exchange rate is \$1.40 per pound. In other words, to buy a pound will cost you \$1.40. Each of your dollars will buy less than one pound, actually about .7 of a pound. If you want to exchange \$100, you will get .7 × \$100 = 70 pounds.

Now it is a week later and you are leaving Great Britain. You have been very frugal, so you have 10 pounds left that you want to change back to dollars. Since each pound is worth \$1.40, you will get 10 × \$1.40 = \$14.00.

1. A month later and you are traveling to Mexico. You get off the plane in Mexico City with \$100 to change into pesos. You see that the exchange rate is .0026 dollars to the peso, less than a penny for each peso. This is the equivalent of 380 pesos for each dollar. How many pesos can you get for your \$100? If you have 1000 pesos left when you leave Mexico, how many dollars should you expect to get?
2. You cannot afford to go to France, but you want to buy a jacket imported from France. In France, it would cost 100 francs. If the exchange rate is .12 dollars to the franc, how many dollars should the clothes cost here?
3. Suppose the dollar strengthens relative to the franc. A dollar will now buy more francs, that is, it takes even less of a dollar to buy a franc. The new rate is .10 dollars to the franc. How much would that jacket cost in dollars? What does this suggest about the effect of a strong dollar on the amount of goods the U.S. imports?

Tourists browse in a Mexico City market.

The payment that shareholders receive is called a *dividend.* Unlike sole proprietors or partners, shareholders are responsible only for the amount of money they have invested in a business. If the business fails, they may lose that amount, but no more. The shareholders have *limited liability,* and are not held responsible for any debts the business might have.

One disadvantage of corporations is that their income is taxed twice. First, the corporation pays a tax on its profits. Then, shareholders must pay a tax on their dividends.[6]

FOR REVIEW

1. **Identify:** factors of production; capital; free enterprise; investment; profit.
2. On what fundamental principle is capitalism based?
3. What are the four basic resources of a nation's economy?
4. What are the five characteristics of a free enterprise system?
5. How does competition promote efficiency?
6. What are the three basic business types in the United States?

2. Socialism

As You Read, Think About:

- How socialism is both an economic and a political philosophy.
- How socialism developed in the 1800s and the basic features of how socialism is practiced today.
- What the economic reforms were that Britain's Labor Party carried out in the 1940s.
- What "nationalization" is and government's role in a "command economy."
- What the major arguments are for and against socialism.

[6]The federal tax on dividends, however, is lower than the tax on most other incomes.

Socialism is based on public ownership of the basic means of production. In socialist countries as in capitalist ones, personal property is privately owned. What is distinctive about socialism, however, is that important industries are owned or at least controlled by the government. The government uses its control to attempt to guide the economy by setting targets for both production and distribution.

Socialism varies greatly from one country to another. In some countries, like the African nation of Tanzania, almost all industries are publicly owned. In others, like Sweden and Britain, some large industries are publicly owned and some are privately owned. Socialism and capitalism may, and often do, exist side-by-side in the same country.

Socialism is both an economic and a political philosophy. Supporters of socialism see it as the way to true democracy. Political equality is not enough, they say. Full equality requires that the public, through its elected representatives, should have control of the centers of economic power.

In practice, socialism may be either democratic or undemocratic. Socialism is strong in both Great Britain and Sweden, which are among the world's leading democracies. However, socialism also exists in countries that have authoritarian governments. Critics of socialism argue that it leads to a dangerous concentration of economic power that an unjust government can easily abuse.

Socialism and the Industrial Revolution

Socialist ideas are very old. In many eras of history, groups of people have owned property in common and tried to divide incomes equally. Modern socialism, however, developed as a reaction against the poverty and misery that accompanied the early Industrial Revolution.

The Industrial Revolution was characterized by the shift from small-scale to large-scale production that began in Great Britain during the late 18th century. Work that once had been done at home was now done in factories. The skills of trained artisans were less in demand, for unskilled workers could tend the machines that now did much of the

REINFORCEMENT Have the class discuss the nature of a socialist government. In what ways is socialism both an economic and political philosophy?

work. As a rule, wages for unskilled workers were very low. This was to be expected under the laws of supply and demand, for the supply of unskilled workers was large.

Many observers of 19th-century British factory towns were appalled by the conditions they found there. Women and men worked as long as 14 or 16 hours a day under noisy, dusty, and often unsafe conditions. Small children performed many tasks, receiving even lower wages than adults. Most workers and their families lived in dank, unhealthful slums, earning barely enough to stay alive.

Robert Owen Among the many observers who expressed moral outrage at such conditions was a Welsh capitalist named Robert Owen. Owen sought to improve the conditions of workers at cotton mills of which he was a part owner. He started schools for the children and built better housing for workers' families. Owen concluded that the answer to the evils of the Industrial Revolution was a system that provided a more equal distribution of wealth. Owen's followers in the 1820s were the first people to be called "socialists."

Karl Marx Another critic of capitalism —one whose influence spread to many countries—was a German thinker named Karl Marx. In his best-known work, *Das Kapital* (1867), Marx traced the development of economic life over the vast sweep of history. According to him, capitalism was but one stage in human development. Capitalism was better than feudalism, which it replaced. But it was deeply flawed, because it allowed rich capitalists to exploit the *proletariat,* or working class. Capitalists did this, said Marx, by skimming off the cream of the workers' labor in the form of profits.

Marx painted history as a continuing struggle among economic classes. Each class, he contended, used violence to pursue its goals. By controlling economic power, capitalists and their allies controlled the police power of the state and used it to hold workers down. But such efforts, Marx argued, were doomed to failure in the end. According to Marx, history would move on to its inevitable next stage—the coming to power of a "dictatorship of the proletariat." That, in turn, would lead to an ultimate stage, which Marx called communism. Under communism, as Marx saw it, economic classes would cease to exist. The class struggle—and the need for dictatorship —would finally end.

Socialists and Communists A powerful socialist movement took shape among European workers and thinkers during the middle and late 19th century. Almost all socialists accepted Marx's criticism of capitalism. But the socialist movement divided sharply over how to fight capitalism. Some, claiming Marx as their guide, argued that only a violent revolution could bring socialism about. People who took this position came to be called "communists." Others argued that socialism could be attained by peaceful means, through the democratic process. Today, the terms "socialist" or "social democrats" are usually reserved for people who adopt democratic methods.

The British Labor Party

One of the best-known socialist parties is Britain's Labor Party. Founded in 1900, it supported a variety of programs that eventually transformed British life. Among the party's successes were the adoption of old-age pensions, health insurance, and unemployment insurance between 1908 and 1911.

The biggest changes, however, followed a Labor victory in the elections of 1945. Holding a majority of the seats in the House of Commons, the Labor Party controlled the British government from 1945 to 1951. It introduced a sweeping program of socialist changes. The Bank of England, major industries such as coal and steel, the railroads, the airlines, and the electric system came under public ownership. Social welfare legislation was expanded to provide free health care and other benefits.[7]

[7]Britain's system of state-financed health care is sometimes called *socialized medicine.*

ENRICHMENT Ask the class to compare the practices and attitudes of socialist and communist countries. What countries of the world are communist? Which are socialist?

Under Margaret Thatcher, a Prime Minister from the Conservative Party, Britain restored some of its public industries to private owners in the 1980s. But many socialist measures remain in effect today.

Nationalization

The taking of private industry for public use is called nationalization. In democratic countries such as Britain, the government usually pays the former owners for their loss. The government pays what it calculates to be a "fair" price. (The former owners do not always agree, however, that what they are receiving is enough. They may file a court suit demanding a higher price.)

Sometimes, especially in developing countries, governments nationalize industries without paying any compensation at all. Or a government may say it will pay —but only after a period of years.

In some countries, all important businesses are nationalized, from the giant steel mill to the corner grocery store. More often, nationalization is selective. Socialist governments usually want to control the most important industries, but they may allow many types of businesses to remain in private hands. Sometimes a government will buy a company's shares on the stock market, just as a private investor might do. By buying 51 percent of the shares—and sometimes even less—a government can gain the right to name the management of the company. As a result, the government can then control the policies of the company.

A goal of many socialist governments is to give each company's workers a say in deciding how the company is run. Sweden's Social Democratic Party, for example, has a plan for gradually transferring ownership of private companies to their workers. Elected worker representatives sit on companies' boards of directors and help to make decisions.

Companies that have been nationalized or that are otherwise controlled by the public are said to belong to the **public sector.** The part of the economy that is in private hands is said to belong to the **private sector.**

Nationalized since 1946, the Bank of England—on Threadneedle Street, London—serves as the Government's banker and the "banker's bank."

The Command Economy

Economies can be divided into two broad categories, depending on how basic decisions are made. Under capitalism, as we have seen, the government's role is a limited one. Key decisions are made by thousands of private individuals and companies through the give and take of the marketplace. For that reason, capitalist economies are called **market economies.**

Under socialism—and also communism—decision-making is much more centralized. Public bodies can plan how an economy will develop over a period of years. Governments set targets for production. They guide investment into specific industries. In theory,

In Great Britain, many types of small business enterprises are permitted to remain in private hands, as this grocery store in England.

therefore, governments can direct the economy along desired paths. Thus, socialist and communist economies are called **command economies.**

A document called the *five-year plan* plays a key role in many command economies. The plan is a blueprint showing how leaders want the economy to develop over the next five years. Making a five-year plan is an intricate process, drawing on experts from many areas of national life. The purpose is to set economic goals for the future and to plan how to achieve those goals most efficiently.

Public Services and Taxes

Socialists stress the goal of assuring that everyone in a society is decently fed and housed. Stated another way, socialists aim to guarantee the public welfare by providing for the equal distribution of basic goods and services. Socialists argue that the fairest way to do this is through taxes that place most of the burden on the upper and middle classes.

The Welfare State Countries that provide extensive social services at little or no cost to the users are called **welfare states.** In such countries, medical and dental services may be provided free or for a small charge. People who lose their jobs or who are physically unable to work receive government payments that are nearly as high as their former wages. All people above retirement age receive government pensions. Parents may receive government payments for each child until the child reaches the age of 18. Through such means, welfare states provide "cradle-to-grave" benefits.

Under socialism, many other public services are also considered to be government's responsibility. Such services may range from free university educations to free housing for the poor.

High Taxes Because social services such as the above are quite expensive, taxes in socialist countries tend to be high. It is not uncommon for taxes to take 50 or 60 percent of an individual's total income. (This compares to around 30 percent in the United States.) Tax rates are usually graduated —that is, set at different levels for people of different incomes. The highest rates fall on the upper classes and may amount to 90 percent of a wealthy person's income.

Socialism in Developing Countries

Socialism has won a large following in developing countries. There, public ownership and central planning are widespread.

One reason for socialism's appeal is that most developing countries are "starting from scratch" at building industry. Such countries have no tradition of locally controlled, large-scale industry. Large industries that do exist often are owned by foreign interests such as multinational companies. (A multinational company is a firm that is based in one country and has holdings in many other countries.) By nationalizing a

REINFORCEMENT Have the class discuss the appeal of socialism in developing countries. Why has socialism won such a large following in these areas?

foreign-owned company and placing local people in charge, a political leader may win broad public support.

Socialism also appeals to leaders who want to mobilize an entire nation behind a program of industrial growth. Through central planning, leaders can channel investment into the parts of the economy they think are most essential.

Often, however, guided growth of this sort requires painful sacrifices by a nation's people. High taxes skim off a large part of people's income. The government may devote so much attention to one or two basic industries that the production of consumer goods or food may be neglected. Then public unrest may develop and spread.

Political instability is a persistent problem in developing nations. It is one reason for the tendency of socialist and other governments in such nations to turn to authoritarian methods. Few developing nations have succeeded in establishing the democratic versions of socialism that are found in parts of the industrial world.

Major Criticisms

Both capitalist and socialist economies have their strengths and their weaknesses. For supporters of capitalism, it is easy to see weaknesses in the theory and practice of socialism. For supporters of socialism, on the other hand, it is capitalism that is riddled with faults.

Critics say socialist countries have a tendency to develop too many layers of bureaucracy. They say this complicates decision-making and has a deadening effect on individual initiative. As a result, critics say, socialist economies are slower to take advantage of new technologies. They tend to fall behind capitalist economies.

In the eyes of socialism's critics, the smooth running of an economy is too complex to be directed by central planners. Too many unpredictable events are involved, critics claim. Too many clashing interests are at stake. For all its faults, the "invisible hand" of the market economy works more efficiently than the visible hand of the command economy, say socialism's critics.

Another criticism is that socialism deprives people of the freedom to decide for themselves how to use their income. Most of a person's income goes to taxes. The government decides how the money will be spent. Since earners get to keep only a fraction of their earnings, they have little incentive to work harder and earn more. Why work hard when your basic needs will be taken care of anyway? So ask socialism's critics.

In response, socialists point to the inequalities of wealth and power that exist under capitalism. Socialists argue that socialism evens out inequalities and thus is morally superior to capitalism. In their view, socialism makes political democracy work more smoothly by supplementing it with economic democracy.

Defenders of socialism also argue that it gives workers and ordinary citizens more control over their daily lives. Under capitalism, they say, a company's management can abruptly decide to close a factory that is no longer making money. The company has no obligation to ask its workers' opinions, even though such a decision can throw thousands out of work and disrupt an entire community. This could not happen under socialism, the argument goes. Workers and community leaders would sit on the company's board. They would help decide what was best for the entire work force and community—not just for the company's shareholders.

FOR REVIEW

1. **Identify:** public ownership; proletariat; labor party; five-year plans.
2. How does socialism differ from capitalism?
3. What roles did Robert Owen and Karl Marx play in the development of socialism? What social and economic conditions were they responding to?
4. To which group of people does the term "socialist" refer today?
5. Why do socialist governments nationalize important industries?
6. State two criticisms of socialism and two criticisms of capitalism.

3. Communism

As You Read, Think About:

- What the main distinction is between socialism and communism.
- How the means of production are owned and controlled by the state in the Soviet Union.
- How all areas of economic activity are subject to five-year plans in the Soviet Union.
- The extent to which agricultural production is managed and controlled by the state in the USSR.
- Why an underground economy exists in the USSR.
- How the economies of Yugoslavia and China are different from the Soviet Union's.

Communism blends public ownership of the means of production with totalitarian political controls. Many economic practices are similar to those of socialism. Politically, however, communism is quite different from socialism. It depends on firm control over society by a single, all-encompassing political party, the Communist Party.

The Soviet Union was the first communist state and for many years provided the sole example of a communist economy in operation. Soviet communism came to be rigid and harsh, with almost no room for private entrepreneurship or response to market forces. Since the 1940s, communist governments have come to power in other nations, and most have followed the rigid practices of the Soviet Union. A few exceptions now exist, however. One is Yugoslavia, which blends communist political controls with what has been called "market communism." Another is the People's Republic of China, which began in the 1980s to encourage small private business ventures to operate in the shadow of large state-owned enterprises.

The Soviet Economy

Officially, the Soviet Union describes itself as a socialist state on the road to communism. The communist stage of society will not be reached until class differences are totally abolished. Then, say Soviet leaders, the "dictatorship of the proletariat" will end and true communism will exist. As you can see, Soviet theory borrows heavily from the ideas of Karl Marx. Marx is one of two

An embroidery factory in the Soviet Union. Why do you think a portrait of Lenin is displayed so prominently in this place of work?

A truck factory in the Soviet Union's Volga Region. Hours of work, wages, and production targets are all mandated by the government in this and all other factories—large and small—in the Soviet Union.

historical figures claimed as founders of Soviet-style communism. The second is Lenin. Soviet leaders make frequent references to "Marxist–Leninism" as the official ideology of the state.

Private and Public Property While private property does exist in the Soviet Union, its role in the economy is small. Personal property, as in other economic systems, may be privately owned and inherited. People own their own furniture, for example. Some people own cars or even houses. (It is more common, however, for Soviet citizens to live in apartments that they rent from the state.)

All land and most other productive property is owned by the state. Factories, restaurants, and other businesses are among those under public ownership. People may go into business for themselves—as plumbers, for example—but they may not hire anyone to work for them. To hire an employee would be to exploit that person's labor, according to communist theory.

The Soviet government exercises firm control over wages, prices, and production. It also controls all labor unions and forbids workers to go on strike. *

Social Welfare In the Soviet Union, as under democratic socialism, the government seeks to meet the basic needs of all people. Public benefits include free education, free medical service, organized vacation trips for

*REINFORCEMENT Discuss in class the communist economy of the Soviet Union. In what respects does it resemble a socialist economy?

groups of workers, pensions, and daycare centers for small children of working parents. The Soviet constitution gives great emphasis to social welfare as part of a person's basic rights.

One basic right under the Soviet constitution is the right to hold a job. Indeed, holding a job is considered a duty for both women and men in the Soviet Union. The nation has suffered from a labor shortage since the 1940s, when World War II killed off 20 million Soviet citizens. Soviet women hold many of the same jobs that men do, in factories, in offices, in hospitals, and on farms.

Central Planning

The Soviet Union has a command economy, to a much greater extent than do European nations that practice democratic socialism. Communist Party officials keep a tight grip on the Soviet economy. The blueprints for the economy are five-year plans drawn up by a state agency known as Gosplan. (The name comes from the Russian words in the agency's formal name, the State Planning Committee.)

Five-Year Plans The planning process is quite intricate and drawn out. Each factory, farm, or other enterprise carefully calculates what its needs will be for the next five-year period. For example, a factory estimates how many raw materials it will need and what goods it will be able turn out. Plans from thousands of enterprises move up through the bureaucracy. They pass through the suitable government ministries and are modified along the way.

Finally, at the very top, Gosplan officials assemble one overall plan. The plan sets aside a certain amount of money for each separate industry—clothing, truck-making, and so on. Then the departments of government that run each industry divide up the money. They allot a certain amount to each business enterprise. They also inform each factory or farm or office what particular raw materials it will receive and how much it will be expected to produce in the five-year period. Each enterprise must meet a target, known as a quota—a share of the overall production target. The chief goal of business managers, therefore, is meeting quotas and not making profits.

Nearly all areas of economic activity in the Soviet Union are subject to five-year plans. In theory, the plans allow government officials to funnel economic resources into the particular industries or geographical regions where they are needed most. They also allow the government to mold the economy in desired directions, rather than letting it grow in a helter-skelter way. Moreover, the plans allow Communist Party leaders to maintain strict control over the nation's economic direction.

Problems in Practice While Soviet-style central planning works smoothly in theory, in practice it runs into problems. Over the years party officials have tried various schemes to eliminate those problems. So far they have had little success. *

Plant managers may sometimes take short cuts in trying either to meet or to exceed quotas. For instance, they may skimp on materials, or they may hurry the work along too fast. The resulting products may be of low quality—but, at least, the plant has met its quota.

Both Soviet leaders and consumers recognize that Soviet industry has "quality problems." Leaders often exhort workers to pay greater attention to quality. Consumers have learned to avoid goods made toward the end of the week, when workers may be rushing to meet the week's quota. To find when an item was made, consumers look for the date of production, which is often stamped on the package.

Another problem with rigid Soviet-style planning is that there has traditionally been little room for change or innovation. It has been less risky for a manager or worker to follow customary procedures than to try something new that might or might not work out. In recent years, Soviet leaders have tried to overcome this problem. They have offered money and other incentives to those who come up with better ways of doing their jobs.

*REINFORCEMENT Ask the class: What are the problems of the command economy in the Soviet Union?

FOCUS ON:

A Soviet Consumer's Complaints

Newspapers and magazines published in the Soviet Union sometimes carry letters to the editor in which complaints are registered about the quality and quantity of goods available to the Russian consumer. An anonymous letter appeared in a Moscow youth newspaper, *Komsomolskaya Pravda*, shortly after successful launchings of Soviet rockets in 1959. The letter contained these revealing comments:

> Dear Editors:
>
> I have never written you about good or bad, nor have I written you about making excuses for myself or with praise for the way landscaping is carried on. But, [I'm writing] not for the sake, as they say, of "trying my hand," but in order to express my opinion (and not only my own!) about what I've been reading and hearing since the rocket launchings.
>
> So our scientists have launched a rocket to the moon. I'm not going to dispute the fact that it actually "landed on the moon." If it's on the moon, so it's on the moon. Of course it's an important event, and it stirred up a big fuss. But, let's have a look, as they say, at the other side of the coin, and ask this kind of question: What have these Sputniks and rockets given the simple mortal, including me. I, for example, on the eve of the rocket's launching was in debt for 300 rubles, and I'm still in debt 300 rubles, in spite of the successful launching.
>
> Doesn't it seem to you that the craze for these Sputniks and the cosmos is untimely, or, more precisely, premature. What I mean to say by this is that we're still up to our necks in earthly matters: there isn't enough living space, nursery schools, goods are expensive. And that rocket, I don't doubt, eats up so much money that everybody would probably groan if they knew the cost of it.
>
> Tell any worker: Now you look here, Ivan, if we don't launch this rocket your little Volodya would start going to a kindergarten, that a yard of cloth would cost not 4 rubles, but half that, that you could buy an electric iron in a store—and I'm certain that he'd say: "For God's sake, don't launch those rockets."
>
> Rockets, rockets, rockets!—who needs them now! . . . give me something better for the table. . . .
>
> Those Sputniks and rockets leave me cold. It's too early for them. They're useless.

1. Which aspect of Soviet planning seems to be of greater concern to the letter writer: the production of capital goods or the production of consumer goods? Explain your reasoning.
2. What do you think the writer means by the phrase "earthly matters"?

Shopping in the Soviet Union often means a long wait in line with other shoppers.

Comparative Economic Systems

	COMMUNISM (planned economy)	DEMOCRATIC SOCIALISM (mixed market economy)	CAPITALISM (market economy)
ECONOMIC CONDITIONS	□ Government owns nearly all means of production □ State plans and directs all economic activities □ Government decides what and how much to produce	□ Government owns major means of production and decides the items and the quantity to be produced □ Private investments are allowed, though they are regulated closely	□ Nearly all means of production are owned by individuals, not by the State □ Consumer expenditures determine what goods and quantity of these goods is to be produced
ECONOMIC EFFICIENCY	□ Production varies from efficient to poor (depending on government priorities)	□ Limited government regulation has saved many ailing enterprises □ Without competition, however, efficiency tends to go down	□ Free competition can mean greater efficiency and lower prices □ Freedom to make profit also means investors risk loss
EMPLOYMENT AND STANDARD OF LIVING	□ Full employment (including conscript labor) utilized to achieve the economic goals of the government □ People work for the good of the nation □ Government decides how people are to be rewarded □ High prices, few luxuries	□ High standard of living with full employment and economic security as future goals □ Free health, medical and hospital care, and education □ Great part of wages go to taxes □ People buy consumer goods freely	□ High standard of living with full employment and economic security as goals □ Incomes are based on individual's contribution to production □ Belief in minimum standard of living

Under which type of economic system is the individual granted the most freedom to make his or her own economic decisions? Which system permits the least freedom to someone who wants to start a small business?

Soviet Agriculture

Despite the large area devoted to farmland and the massive investments provided by planners, agriculture has been a persistent weak point in the Soviet economy. Soviet farms often fall far short of their quotas. As a result, the government of the Soviet Union has been forced to resort to frequent purchases of grains and other products from abroad.

Geography is partly to blame for Soviet agriculture's problems. While the Soviet Union has large areas of rich soil, its climate tends to be drier and colder than that of the United States. Droughts—prolonged dry spells—are frequent.

Soviet agriculture is far less mechanized than American agriculture, so more farm workers are necessary. In the United States, farmers make up about 4 percent of the work force. In the Soviet Union, 25 percent of workers are farmers. All told, Soviet farms employ eight times as many workers as do farms in the United States and produce four-fifths as much.

Quite a large portion of Soviet agriculture has been **collectivized**—that is, it has been put under public or group (as opposed to private) ownership. There are two basic types of farms in the public sector. These are known as state farms and collective farms.

State Farms Farms that are owned directly by the government are known as state farms. They occupy about two-thirds of Soviet farmland. They tend to be very large —sometimes covering tens of thousands of acres. Workers receive wages, just as if they held factory jobs. Orders about what the farm will produce are handed down by central planners. Those who work hardest and produce the most may receive bonuses at the end of the year. But the workers on state farms have no share in the ownership of their farms.

Collective Farms The remaining one-third of Soviet land is mainly in collective farms. These are farms on land that is owned by the government but which is rented to groups, or collectives, of farmers. The workers on a collective farm share in the farm's ownership and receive a portion of any profits at the end of the year. They also receive a wage, and they elect their own board of managers.

Private Farms and Plots A small proportion of Soviet land is worked by private farmers and their families. In addition, many of the workers on collective farms and state farms also tend private plots in their spare time. While private plots make up less than 5 percent of total farmland, they account for about 25 percent of the value of farm production. Private plots tend to be devoted to high-value crops such as fruits and vegetables, rather than to the grains that are commonly grown on large farms. Farmers also raise chickens, pigs, and other animals on their small, private plots. A typical farm family may receive a fourth or more of its income from the crops and the animals it raises.

Problems of Soviet Agriculture A number of problems have held down the output of Soviet farms. In addition to the harsh climate already mentioned, Soviet agriculture has been hampered by bureaucratic red tape and a lack of incentives. Despite central planners' efforts, fertilizer is not always available on time and spare parts for machinery are often lacking. Since farmers must "make hay while the sun shines," any delay can have serious consequences.*

In recent years, Communist Party leaders have focused attention on the deficiencies of Soviet agriculture. They have invested in more and better machinery. They have promoted research aimed at finding better ways of raising crops and animals. In the early 1980s, Soviet leaders also introduced reforms in farm management. To give workers an incentive to try harder, managers invited workers to form teams and bid on specific farm jobs. Each team received a set amount of money for doing its job—say, fattening pigs. The faster the team worked and the less money it spent on raw materials, the more it could keep as its "profit."

The Underground Economy

Because the official Soviet economy often fails to provide goods and services that meet Soviet consumers' needs, many people run their own businesses on the side (or "on the left," as Russians say). For example, people repair cars in their backyards. They run beauty shops in the kitchens of their apartments. They find ways to buy extra butter and sell it to people who don't want to stand in line at the grocery store. Such unofficial enterprises make up what is called the **underground economy.**

The underground economy supplements people's incomes and helps to ease shortages of goods and services. The government tolerates much of the activity, since it meets a real need. By one estimate, up to 18 percent of all consumer spending goes into the underground economy, helping to produce 12 percent of the Soviet people's personal income.

*ENRICHMENT Have the class discuss the problems of Soviet agriculture. In what respects are its problems due to its own organization?

Above: A farm scene in Yugoslavia, where, unlike in the U.S.S.R., about 85 percent of the arable land is privately owned. *Right:* A tourist booth on the grounds of an ancient castle in Yugoslavia. Tourism is privately operated in Yugoslavia, but controlled by the state in the Soviet Union.

In China today, small businesses are permitted to operate under private ownership, as is the shop (at left) that produces ceramic wares. *Right:* A food market in China, where farmers today have greater leeway in deciding what and how much to produce for the market.

Yugoslavia's "Market Socialism"

Yugoslavia, in Eastern Europe, has a communist government and public ownership of the means of production. But Yugoslavia does not have a command economy. Factories and other businesses are generally owned and managed by committees elected by workers. Prices are set not by central planners but by market forces—by the law of supply and demand. As a result, Yugoslavia's economic system has been dubbed "market socialism."

Yugoslavia's way of communism developed for a variety of historical reasons. For one thing, Yugoslavia resisted Soviet political domination and pulled away from the Soviet bloc in 1948. Because it contains many separate language groups, Yugoslavia did not establish a rigidly centralized government. The six republics and two autonomous regions making up Yugoslavia retain a measure of self-rule. Each region has its own Communist Party that is jealous of its rights. Regional leaders do not want the central government to become too powerful.

The central government does draw up a five-year plan, but the plan serves as a guide rather than a rigid blueprint. Each business enterprise sets its own prices. It buys its own raw materials and makes its own marketing arrangements. Yugoslav agriculture is largely under private control.

China's Middle Way

China has been under Communist Party rule since 1949. At first, the communist government tried to erase all traces of capitalism. It created a rigid command economy in the Soviet style. Except for a brief period in the 1960s, there was little room for private enterprise. This situation lasted until after the death of communist leader Mao Zedong in 1976.

A new communist leader, Deng Xiaoping, gained control in 1978. Under Deng, China thoroughly revamped its economy. The government reversed the collectivization of agriculture, allowing a return to private farming. It took steps to decentralize Chinese industry and to allow a role for market forces in the setting of prices. China even invited foreign private companies to invest in projects within China.

Today China has a unique blend of capitalism, socialism, and communism. Capitalist elements include small private business such as restaurants and farms. Medium- and large-sized enterprises are under state or collective ownership. China has moved away from rigid quotas, giving the managers of each business greater leeway in deciding how to operate. At the top, however, the Communist Party remains in tight control.

Deng's reforms have contributed to a rapid rise in Chinese living standards. Per capita income rose from $300 in 1980 to $450 in 1985. While this is still very low by the standards of the industrial world, it is high by comparison to China's past. While most Chinese seemed to welcome Deng's reforms, some elements of the communist leadership found them disturbing. They warned of such possibilities as soaring prices, corruption, and the rise of a new capitalist class. It remains to be seen whether China will keep its new economic system once the aging Deng is gone.

FOR REVIEW

1. **Identify:** Marxist–Leninism; Gosplan; market socialism.
2. How does communism mainly differ from socialism?
3. What is the role of private property in the Soviet economy? Public property?
4. How are the Soviet five-year plans formulated? For what purpose?
5. What are the state farms? Collective farms?
6. Why has an underground economy developed in the Soviet Union?
7. Explain how the People's Republic of China today has a unique blend of capitalism, socialism, and communism.

*ENRICHMENT Have the class compare the economies of Yugoslavia and China. In what ways are they different from the Soviet Union?

SUMMARY

Although people's economic needs and the basic production processes are much the same, the organization of economic life varies greatly from one country to another. The modern world has three basic types of economic systems—capitalism, socialism, and communism.

Under all three systems, personal property may be privately owned. Under capitalism, however, productive property, such as a factory's machines or a farmer's fields, is controlled by private individuals and companies. The free enterprise system, a term often used for capitalism, has five characteristics: private ownership of the means of production, respect for private property, individual initiative, competition, and freedom of choice. The hope for profit drives the capitalist economy forward. Economists usually describe the United States economy as a mixed economy since the government plays some roles.

Socialism is based on public ownership of the basic means of production. Important industries are owned or controlled by the government. Socialism varies greatly from one country to another, and can be democratic or undemocratic. Modern socialism developed as a reaction against the poverty and misery of the Industrial Revolution. Karl Marx was the leading socialist thinker. Many socialist governments nationalize, or take private property for public use.

Socialist nations are often characterized by the welfare state and high taxes. Socialism appeals to developing nations because central planning enables leaders to channel investment into essential parts of the economy. Few developing nations have succeeded in establishing democratic versions of socialism.

Critics of socialism view it as too bureaucratic, claim that central planners cannot respond to the complexities of the economy, and assert that socialism deprives people of freedom to decide how to use their income. Critics of capitalism point to the inequalities of wealth and power that exist under capitalism, and argue that capitalism denies workers control over their daily lives.

Communism blends public ownership of the means of production with totalitarian political controls. It depends on firm control over society by the Communist Party. The Soviet government exercises firm control over wages, prices, and production. It seeks to meet the basic needs of all people. A state agency known as Gosplan draws up five-year plans for the economy.

CHAPTER REVIEW

Key Terms/Concepts*

capitalist (692)
entrepreneur (692)
laws of supply and demand (693)
monopoly (693)
antitrust laws (693)
sole proprietorships (695)
partnerships (695)
corporations (695)
public sector (699)
private sector (699)
market economies (699)
command economies (700)
welfare states (700)
collectivized (707)
underground economy (707)

*These terms are included in the Glossary.

Keynote Questions

• 1. How do capitalism, socialism, and communism differ concerning the means of production?

• 2. What are the four basic resources referred to as factors of production? Briefly describe the importance of each.

• 3. How do the laws of supply and demand determine prices under competitive conditions?

• 4. What is the role of investment and profit in a capitalist economy?

The dots represent skill levels required to answer each question or complete each activity:
• requires recall and comprehension • • requires application and analysis • • • requires synthesis and evaluation

- **5.** Why do economists refer to the United States economy as a mixed economy?
- **6.** Outline the major ideas that Marx contributed to the development of socialism.
- **7.** What sweeping changes were introduced in Britain by the Labor Party from 1945 to 1951?
- **8.** What is the difference between a command economy and a market economy?
- **9.** State three reasons for socialism's appeal to developing nations.
- **10.** How are five-year plans developed in the Soviet Union? What is their purpose?
- **11.** Briefly describe some of the problems that have occurred as the result of central planning in the Soviet Union.
- **12.** Describe the two basic types of farms in the Soviet public sector.
- **13.** Why has the underground economy developed in the Soviet Union?
- **14.** How do the economies of Yugoslavia and China differ from the economy of the Soviet Union?

Skill Application

Classifying Economies: In this chapter you learned that economies can be divided into two broad categories—command economies and market economies—depending on how basic decisions are made. In understanding the world today, you will find it helpful to be able to recognize these two forms of economies. You will be able to understand some of the problems in negotiating trade agreements, some of the disputes among nations, and some of the reasons for other nation's decisions.

1. Make a list of the characteristics of a market economy and a list of the characteristics of a command economy.

2. Read each of the following sentences. Use your list to decide which type of economy would most likely act in the way described by the sentence. Write the type of economy on your paper.

- **a.** The new government moved to nationalize the banking industry.
- **b.** Too few consumers were buying the new cereal, so the manufacturer stopped making it.
- **c.** The Ministry of Trade worked with the car manufacturer to develop a production schedule for the next three years.
- **d.** Because too many people were out of work in one region, the government decided that the new chemical plant should be located there.
- **e.** The company invested in research and development of a new treatment for a fatal disease.
- **f.** The worker's committee decided that the company should produce several new kinds of tools.

For Thought and Discussion

- **1.** What faults do capitalists find with communism? What faults do communists find with capitalism? Why?
- •• **2.** "There are two ways of looking at the role of consumers in our society." (p. 695) Do consumers "call the shots" or do businesses? Explain.
- **3.** Why can socialism exist in both democratic nations and in authoritarian nations?
- ••• **4.** Yugoslavia and China are both communist nations. However, they each pursue economic policies that are different from the Soviet Union's. What can the Soviet Union learn from Yugoslavia and China? What can Yugoslavia and China learn from the Soviet Union?

Suggested Activities

- **1.** Obtain information from the embassy of a nation that has a market economy and a nation that has a command economy. Ask for information on the economy, including major industries, agriculture, and participation in international organizations. Prepare a poster that compares and contrasts the two economies.
- •• **2.** Choose a nation, other than the United States, and follow the economic affairs of that nation. How is it similar to or different from the United States? Does the nation trade with the United States? Use newspapers and news magazines as sources, and keep a record of the nation's economic activity over a period of one or two weeks.

Stop the Presses

On this and the following pages you will find a number of last-minute additions, changes, and corrections which, for reasons of timing, could not be included in the main body of the text itself.

■ The landmark Immigration Reform and Control Act of 1986 made a number of important changes in the way this country treats aliens. In its most significant provisions, the new law makes it unlawful for employees to hire illegal aliens and offers legal status (amnesty) to many illegal aliens now in the United States. As he signed the measure, President Reagan declared: "Future generations of Americans will be thankful for our efforts to humanely regain control of our borders and thereby preserve the value of one of the most sacred possessions of our people, American citizenship."

Employers who knowingly hire illegal aliens will be subject to fines of as much as $10,000 for each offense and, in repeat cases, jail terms.

The law's amnesty program will be in effect for a one-year period, from mid-1987 to mid-1988. During that time, aliens who can show that they entered the United States before January 1, 1982, and have lived here continuously "in an unlawful status" since then, can apply for legal status. Those who do so, and are accepted, will become temporary legal residents of this country. If they keep that status for 18 months, they can then apply for permanent residence and, eventually, for American citizenship. Pages 166-173.

■ The Democrats won control of the United States Senate in the 1986 elections. As a result, John C. Stennis (D., Mississippi), is now President *pro tem* of the Senate. Senator Stennis has been a member of the Senate since 1947.

The Senate's Majority Leader is expected to be Robert C. Byrd (D., West Virginia), and the 16 standing committees in the upper house to be chaired by these Senators, all Democrats:

Agriculture	Patrick J. Leahy (Vermont)
Armed Services	Sam Nunn (Georgia)
Banking	William Proxmire (Wisconsin)
Budget	Lawton Childs, Jr. (Florida)
Commerce	Ernest F. Hollings (South Carolina)
Energy	J. Bennett Johnston (Louisiana)
Environment	Quentin Burdick (North Dakota)
Finance	Lloyd Bentsen (Texas)
Foreign Relations	Clairborne Pell (Rhode Island)
Governmental Affairs	John Glenn (Ohio)
Judiciary	Joseph R. Biden, Jr. (Delaware)
Labor	Edward M. Kennedy (Massachusetts)
Rules	Wendell H. Ford (Kentucky)
Small Business	Dale Bumpers (Arkansas)
Veterans' Affairs	Alan Cranston (California)

James C. Wright, Jr. (D., Texas) is the Speaker of the House in the 100th Congress. Mr. Wright has been a member of the House since 1957. Thomas P. ("Tip") O'Neill (D., Massachusetts), who had served as Speaker since 1977, did not seek reelection to the House in 1986. The new Majority Leader in the lower house is Representative Thomas S. Foley (D., Washington). Pages 58, 314-317, 319-324.

■ Among the many civil rights cases to be decided by the Supreme Court in 1987 two loom especially large. One of them is an Establishment Clause case and the other involves affirmative action.

In *Edwards* v. *Aguillard* the Court is called upon to decide the constitutionality of a 1981 Louisiana law. That statute requires that "creation science" be taught in the public schools of that State whenever the theory of evolution is taught. *Johnson* v. *Santa Clara County*, a case from California, raises the claim of "reverse discrimination" based on sex, rather than race. Pages 78, 103-107, 163-166, 519-526.

■ The more than 900-page Tax Reform Act of 1986 marked the most sweeping revision of the federal tax code since the adoption of the 17th Amendment in 1913. The new law provides for a dramatic reduction in income tax rates and for the elimination or reduction of dozens of tax breaks for both individuals and corporations. Most of the measures provisions took effect in January 1, 1987, and so apply to income to be reported in 1988.

The existing individual tax rate structure (with 14 brackets and rates ranging from 11 to 50 percent) is replaced with a temporary 5-bracket system for 1987, and a two-bracket system thereafter. When the two-bracket system becomes fully effective (in 1988), income up to $29,750 will be taxed at 15 percent and all income above that level will be subject to a 28 percent tax.

The existing corporate tax structure (with a top rate of 46 percent) is to be replaced with a simplified system with a top rate of 34 percent. The new corporate rates are to be phased in over the next few years.

Even with those dramatic rate cuts, the law is designed to be "revenue neutral" —neither increasing nor decreasing total federal revenues. At base, that goal is accomplished through the elimination of a very large number of tax breaks (exemptions and deductions) formerly available to corporations in figuring their taxable income. In short, a significant part of the income tax burden is shifted from individuals to business. The Treasury Department estimates that the new law will reduce the taxes paid by individuals by about $122 billion over the next six years and increase the taxes of corporations by more than $120 billion in that same period. Page 345-346, 465-469.

■ A majority of the states (27) now provide for lotteries to help pay for such public services as education. Lottery measures were approved by the voters in five states in 1986: Florida, Idaho, Kansas, Montana, and South Dakota. Pages 653, 654.

■ Clearly, the off-year elections of 1986 produced no indisputable answer to this intriguing question: Did the elections of 1980 and 1984 signal the start of yet another era in our politics, an era to be dominated by the Republican Party?

The table on the following page provides a very instructive profile of the American electorate. It is based on *New York Times*/CBS News "exit polls"—interviews with 8,997 voters as they left their polling places in 188 randomly selected precincts around the country on election day, November 4, 1986. Pages 182-184, 192, 220-227, 266-267, 269-274, 295.

Profile of the Electorate: The Vote for House of Representatives, 1986

% of Total Vote	Voters	Democrats	Republicans
	Total	**52%**	**48%**
48	Men	51	49
52	Women	54	46
87	Whites	49	51
8	Blacks	86	14
3	Hispanics	75	25
16	18-29 years old	51	49
32	30-44 years old	52	48
34	45-49 years old	54	46
28	60 and older	52	48
8	Not a high school graduate	57	43
32	High school graduate	55	45
29	Some college	50	50
31	College graduate	51	49
26	From the East	52	48
37	From the Midwest	53	47
12	From the South	56	44
25	From the West	51	49
46	White Protestant	43	57
32	Catholic	55	45
4	Jewish	70	30
8	White Fundamentalist or Evangelical Christian	31	69
15	Under $12,500 income	56	44
26	$12,500 to $24,999	53	47
21	$25,000 to $34,999	52	48
21	$35,000 to $50,000	53	47
17	Over $50,000	47	53
39	Democrat	81	19
34	Republican	20	80
25	Independent	52	48
16	Liberal	71	29
46	Moderate	58	42
34	Conservative	35	65
29	Professional or manager	50	50
14	Other white collar worker	54	46
34	Blue collar worker	55	45
2	Agricultural worker	56	44
13	Homemaker	50	50
2	Fulltime student	57	43
11	Government employee	62	38
2	Unemployed	63	37
19	Retired	52	48
27	Union Household	63	37
25	Women employed outside home	56	44
58	Voted for Reagan	35	65
30	Voted for Carter or Mondale	83	17
2	First-time voter	49	51

REFERENCE SECTION

The United States: A Statistical Profile*

State	Capital	Population (in thousands) 1970	1980	Percent Change	Area in square miles	Percent Land Federally Owned[1]	Population per sq. mi.
United States	**Washington, D.C.**	**203,302**	**226,546**	**+11.4%**	**3,618,770**	**32.1%**	**63.9**
Alabama	Montgomery	3,444	3,890	+12.9%	51,705	3.5%	76.7
Alaska	Juneau	303	402	+32.8%	591,004	89.5%	0.7
Arizona	Phoenix	1,775	2,718	+53.1%	114,000	40.2%	23.9
Arkansas	Little Rock	1,923	2,286	+18.9%	53,187	10.1%	43.9
California	Sacramento	19,971	23,668	+18.5%	158,706	47.4%	151.4
Colorado	Denver	2,210	2,890	+30.8%	104,091	36.0%	27.9
Connecticut	Hartford	3,032	3,108	+ 2.5%	5,018	0.3%	637.8
Delaware	Dover	548	594	+ 8.4%	2,044	3.2%	307.6
Florida	Tallahassee	6,791	9,746	+43.5%	58,664	10.5%	180.0
Georgia	Atlanta	4,588	5,463	+19.1%	58,910	6.1%	94.1
Hawaii	Honolulu	770	965	+25.3%	6,471	19.2%	150.1
Idaho	Boise	713	944	+32.4%	83,564	64.8%	11.5
Illinois	Springfield	11,110	11,427	+ 2.8%	56,345	1.8%	205.3
Indiana	Indianapolis	5,195	5,490	+ 5.7%	36,185	2.3%	152.8
Iowa	Des Moines	2,825	2,914	+ 3.1%	56,275	0.6%	52.1
Kansas	Topeka	2,249	2,364	+ 5.1%	82,277	1.4%	28.9
Kentucky	Frankfort	3,221	3,661	+13.7%	40,409	5.6%	92.3
Louisiana	Baton Rouge	3,645	4,206	+15.4%	47,752	4.0%	94.5
Maine	Augusta	994	1,125	+13.2%	33,265	0.7%	36.3
Maryland	Annapolis	3,924	4,217	+ 7.5%	2,044	3.3%	428.7
Massachusetts	Boston	5,689	5,737	+ 0.8%	8,284	1.7%	733.3
Michigan	Lansing	8,882	9,262	+ 4.3%	58,527	9.7%	162.6
Minnesota	St. Paul	3,806	4,076	+ 7.1%	84,402	6.7%	51.2
Mississippi	Jackson	2,217	2,521	+13.7%	47,689	5.8%	53.4
Missouri	Jefferson City	4,678	4,917	+ 5.1%	69,697	5.1%	71.3
Montana	Helena	694	787	+13.3%	147,046	29.5%	5.4
Nebraska	Lincoln	1,485	1,570	+ 3.7%	77,355	1.4%	20.5
Nevada	Carson City	489	800	+63.8%	110,561	81.7%	7.3
New Hampshire	Concord	738	921	+24.8%	9,279	12.8%	102.4
New Jersey	Trenton	7,171	7,365	+ 2.7%	7,787	3.0%	986.2
New Mexico	Santa Fe	1,775	2,718	+28.1%	121,593	33.3%	10.7
New York	Albany	37,213	36,787	− 3.7%	49,108	0.8%	370.6
North Carolina	Raleigh	5,084	5,882	+15.7%	52,669	6.9%	120.4
North Dakota	Bismark	618	653	+ 5.7%	70,702	6.4%	9.4
Ohio	Columbus	10,657	10,798	+ 1.3%	41,330	1.3%	263.3
Oklahoma	Oklahoma City	2,559	3,025	+18.2%	69,956	4.0%	44.1
Oregon	Salem	2,092	2,633	+25.9%	97,073	48.9%	27.4
Pennsylvania	Harrisburg	11,801	11,864	+ 0.5%	45,308	2.4%	264.3
Rhode Island	Providence	950	947	−0.3%	1,212	0.9%	897.8
South Carolina	Columbia	2,591	3,122	+20.5%	31,113	6.2%	103.4
South Dakota	Pierre	666	691	+ 3.7%	77,116	6.4%	9.1
Tennessee	Nashville	3,926	4,591	+16.9%	42,144	7.8%	111.6
Texas	Austin	11,199	14,229	+27.1%	266,807	2.1%	54.3
Utah	Salt Lake City	1,059	1,461	+37.9%	84,899	61.0%	17.8
Vermont	Montpelier	445	511	+15.0%	9,614	5.4%	55.2
Virginia	Richmond	4,651	5,347	+14.9%	40,767	9.3%	134.7
Washington	Olympia	3,413	4,132	+21.1%	68,139	28.4%	62.1
West Virginia	Charleston	1,744	1,950	+11.8%	24,231	7.1%	80.8
Wisconsin	Madison	4,418	4,706	+ 6.5%	56,153	5.4%	86.5
Wyoming	Cheyenne	332	470	+41.3%	97,809	49.1%	4.8
Washington, D.C.		757	638	−15.6%	69	31.5%	10,132

***All data based on 1980 census results, except where otherwise indicated. [1]Data for 1982**

Sources: *Statistical Abstract of the United States*, Bureau of the Census

State	Population			% Foreign born	% High School Graduates	Per Capita			Value of	
	% Urban	Black (in thousands)	Of Spanish Origin[2] (in thousands)			Annual Income	Federal Income Tax[3]	State/Local Taxes[4]	Factory Shipments (in $ billions)	Farm Marketings (in $ billions)
United States	**73.7%**	**26,495**	**14,609**	**6.2%**	**63.3%**	**$ 9,503**	**$1,116**	**$ 987**	**$1,850.9**	**$139.5**
Alabama	60.0%	996	33	1.0%	56.7%	$ 7,477	$ 769	$ 650	$ 28.6	$ 1.9
Alaska	64.3%	14	10	3.9%	82.8%	$12,916	$1,925	$4,189	$ 1.8	$ .01
Arizona	83.8%	75	441	6.0%	72.3%	$ 8,832	$ 955	$1,007	$ 11.2	$ 1.7
Arkansas	51.6%	374	18	0.9%	54.9%	$ 7,166	$ 663	$ 654	$ 16.5	$ 3.1
California	91.3%	1,819	4,544	14.8%	73.6%	$10,920	$1,212	$1,172	$ 176.8	$ 13.7
Colorado	80.6%	102	340	3.8%	78.1%	$10,042	$1,227	$ 990	$ 15.4	$ 3.2
Connecticut	78.8%	217	124	8.5%	70.5%	$11,536	$1,610	$1,070	$ 28.0	$ .3
Delaware	70.6%	96	10	3.4%	67.8%	$10,066	$1,250	$1,059	$ 8.0	$ .3
Florida	84.3%	1,343	858	10.9%	67.2%	$ 9,201	$1,114	$ 758	$ 33.3	$ 3.9
Georgia	62.4%	1,465	61	1.7%	73.4%	$ 8,061	$ 862	$ 770	$ 43.2	$ 2.7
Hawaii	86.5%	17	71	14.0%	72.8%	$10,222	$1,044	$1,278	$ 3.5	$ .4
Idaho	54.0%	3	37	2.3%	75.4%	$ 8,044	$ 747	$ 754	$ 5.0	$ 2.0
Illinois	83.3%	1,675	636	7.3%	65.0%	$10,471	$1,333	$1,084	$ 121.3	$ 8.0
Indiana	64.2%	415	87	1.9%	65.9%	$ 8,896	$1,068	$ 744	$ 63.4	$ 4.7
Iowa	58.6%	42	26	1.7%	71.2%	$ 9,336	$1,685	$ 967	$ 30.7	$ 10.5
Kansas	66.7%	126	63	2.0%	72.3%	$ 9,942	$1,123	$ 926	$ 24.1	$ 5.7
Kentucky	50.9%	259	27	0.9%	51.9%	$ 7,648	$ 781	$ 740	$ 28.8	$ 2.8
Louisiana	68.6%	1,238	99	2.1%	58.0%	$ 8,525	$1,036	$ 841	$ 50.3	$ 1.6
Maine	47.5%	3	5	3.8%	68.5%	$ 7,672	$ 745	$ 858	$ 7.7	$ .4
Maryland	80.3%	958	65	4.6%	66.7%	$10,385	$1,278	$1,104	$ 20.3	$ .9
Massachusetts	83.8%	221	141	8.4%	72.7%	$10,089	$1,171	$1,243	$ 43.5	$ .3
Michigan	70.7%	1,199	162	4.4%	68.2%	$ 9,872	$1,125	$1,075	$ 92.9	$ 2.8
Minnesota	66.9%	53	32	2.7%	72.4%	$ 9,688	$1,073	$1,125	$ 33.0	$ 6.6
Mississippi	47.3%	887	25	0.9%	55.1%	$ 6,680	$ 638	$ 648	$ 17.4	$ 2.2
Missouri	68.1%	3	52	1.8%	63.7%	$ 8,720	$ 998	$ 759	$ 38.7	$ 4.2
Montana	52.9%	2	10	2.3%	75.4%	$ 8,361	$ 886	$1,000	$ 5.0	$ 1.4
Nebraska	62.9%	48	28	1.9%	73.8%	$ 9,137	$ 995	$ 963	$ 13.6	$ 6.5
Nevada	85.3%	51	54	6.7%	75.5%	$10,761	$1,380	$ 972	$ 8.8	$ .2
New Hampshire	52.2%	4	6	4.2%	72.0%	$ 7,672	$ 745	$ 740	$ 6.6	$ .1
New Jersey	89.0%	925	492	10.3%	67.8%	$10,976	$1,411	$1,137	$ 68.5	$ .4
New Mexico	72.1%	24	477	4.2%	68.2%	$ 7,891	$ 841	$ 879	$ 3.1	$ 1.2
New York	84.6%	2,402	1,659	13.4%	66.2%	$10,283	$1,147	$1,494	$ 112.2	$ 2.6
North Carolina	48.0%	1,319	57	1.5%	55.3%	$ 7,753	$ 804	$ 748	$ 56.0	$ 3.6
North Dakota	48.8%	3	4	2.3%	66.5%	$ 8,759	$ 859	$ 847	$ 2.1	$ 2.5
Ohio	73.3%	1,077	120	2.7%	67.4%	$ 9,430	$1,116	$ 810	$ 114.0	$ 4.2
Oklahoma	67.3%	205	57	1.8%	66.7%	$ 9,187	$1,038	$ 827	$ 21.8	$ 3.2
Oregon	67.9%	37	66	4.2%	74.7%	$ 9,356	$1,011	$ 979	$ 18.9	$ 1.6
Pennsylvania	69.3%	1,047	154	3.6%	64.5%	$ 9,389	$1,066	$ 978	$ 107.9	$ 2.7
Rhode Island	87.0%	28	20	8.8%	60.7%	$ 9,174	$1,013	$ 992	$ 1.4	$ .03
South Carolina	54.1%	949	33	1.4%	54.0%	$ 7,298	$ 726	$ 708	$ 25.4	$ 1.1
South Dakota	46.4%	2	4	1.4%	68.5%	$ 8,028	$ 735	$ 789	$ 2.7	$ 2.7
Tennessee	60.4%	726	34	1.0%	55.4%	$ 7,662	$ 848	$ 656	$ 36.4	$ 1.8
Texas	79.6%	1,710	2,986	6.0%	61.4%	$ 9,538	$1,259	$ 806	$ 159.0	$ 9.2
Utah	84.4%	9	60	3.5%	80.3%	$ 7,656	$ 759	$ 840	$ 8.8	$ .6
Vermont	33.8%	1	3	4.2%	70.5%	$ 7,832	$ 803	$ 900	$ 3.2	$ .4
Virginia	66.0%	1,009	80	3.2%	62.5%	$ 9,357	$1,111	$ 856	$ 33.1	$ 1.5
Washington	73.5%	106	120	5.8%	77.0%	$10,198	$1,310	$ 989	$ 35.4	$ 2.6
West Virginia	36.6%	65	13	1.1%	56.6%	$ 7,665	$ 855	$ 796	$ 11.2	$ .2
Wisconsin	64.2%	183	63	2.7%	70.0%	$ 9,347	$ 987	$1,061	$ 50.2	$ 4.7
Wyoming	62.7%	3	24	1.9%	78.1%	$11,042	$1,442	$1,399	$ 2.8	$ .7
Washington, D.C.	100.0%	449	18		68.0%	$12,296	$1,516	$1,475	$ 12.2	--

[2]Persons of Spanish origin may be of any race. [3]Individual (personal) income [4]Includes property, sales, and income taxes

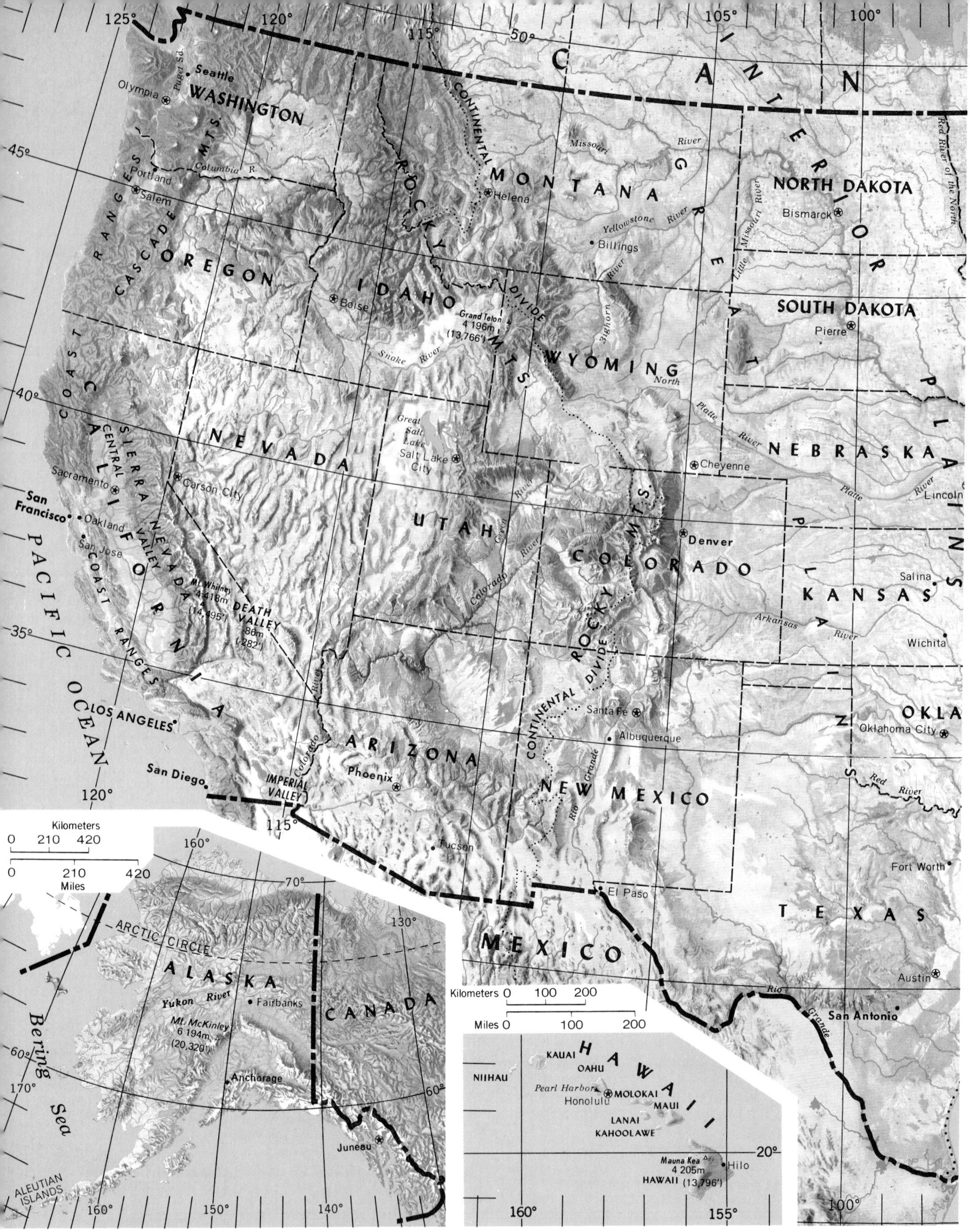

Note that this map is drawn to a different scale than the 48 states and Hawaii.

TUNDRA | EVERGREEN FORESTS | FORESTS | FARMLAND

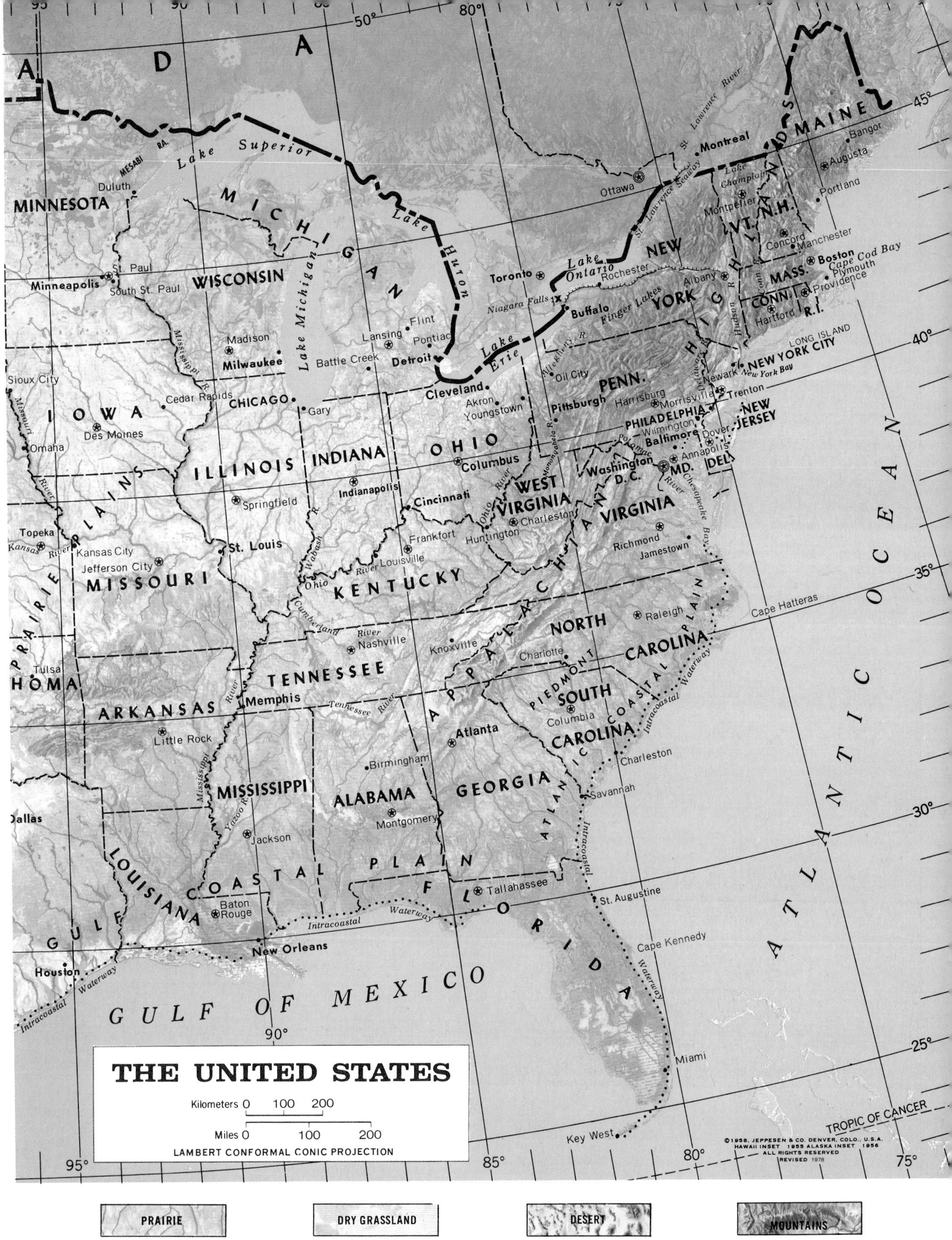

THE UNITED STATES
Kilometers 0 100 200
Miles 0 100 200
LAMBERT CONFORMAL CONIC PROJECTION
©1958, JEPPESEN & CO. DENVER, COLO., U.S.A.
HAWAII INSET 1955 ALASKA INSET 1956
ALL RIGHTS RESERVED
REVISED 1978
PRAIRIE
DRY GRASSLAND
DESERT
MOUNTAINS
CANADA
MINNESOTA
WISCONSIN
MICHIGAN
IOWA
ILLINOIS
INDIANA
OHIO
MISSOURI
KENTUCKY
TENNESSEE
ARKANSAS
MISSISSIPPI
ALABAMA
GEORGIA
FLORIDA
LOUISIANA
NORTH CAROLINA
SOUTH CAROLINA
VIRGINIA
WEST VIRGINIA
PENN.
NEW YORK
NEW JERSEY
MD.
DEL.
Washington D.C.
CONN.
R.I.
MASS.
VT.
N.H.
MAINE
NEW ENGLAND HIGHLANDS
PRAIRIE PLAINS
APPALACHIAN
PIEDMONT
ATLANTIC COASTAL PLAIN
GULF COASTAL PLAIN
ATLANTIC OCEAN
GULF OF MEXICO
TROPIC OF CANCER
Lake Superior
Lake Michigan
Lake Huron
Lake Erie
Lake Ontario
Lake Champlain
Finger Lakes
Niagara Falls
St. Lawrence River
St. Lawrence Seaway
MESABI RA.
Mississippi R.
Missouri River
Kansas River
Ohio River
Wabash R.
Cumberland River
Tennessee River
Yazoo R.
Allegheny R.
Monongahela R.
Potomac
Hudson R.
Conn. R.
Delaware R.
Chesapeake Bay
Cape Cod Bay
New York Bay
LONG ISLAND
Cape Hatteras
Cape Kennedy
Intracoastal Waterway
Duluth
St. Paul
Minneapolis
South St. Paul
Madison
Milwaukee
Chicago
Gary
Sioux City
Cedar Rapids
Des Moines
Omaha
Topeka
Kansas City
Jefferson City
St. Louis
Springfield
Indianapolis
Lansing
Flint
Pontiac
Detroit
Battle Creek
Cleveland
Akron
Youngstown
Columbus
Cincinnati
Frankfort
Louisville
Nashville
Knoxville
Memphis
Little Rock
Tulsa
Dallas
Houston
Jackson
Baton Rouge
New Orleans
Birmingham
Montgomery
Atlanta
Tallahassee
Savannah
Charleston
Columbia
Charlotte
Raleigh
Richmond
Jamestown
Huntington
Charleston
Pittsburgh
Oil City
Harrisburg
Morrisville
Philadelphia
Trenton
Newark
New York City
Wilmington
Baltimore
Annapolis
Dover
Buffalo
Rochester
Albany
Toronto
Ottawa
Montreal
Montpelier
Concord
Manchester
Boston
Plymouth
Providence
Hartford
Portland
Augusta
Bangor
St. Augustine
Miami
Key West

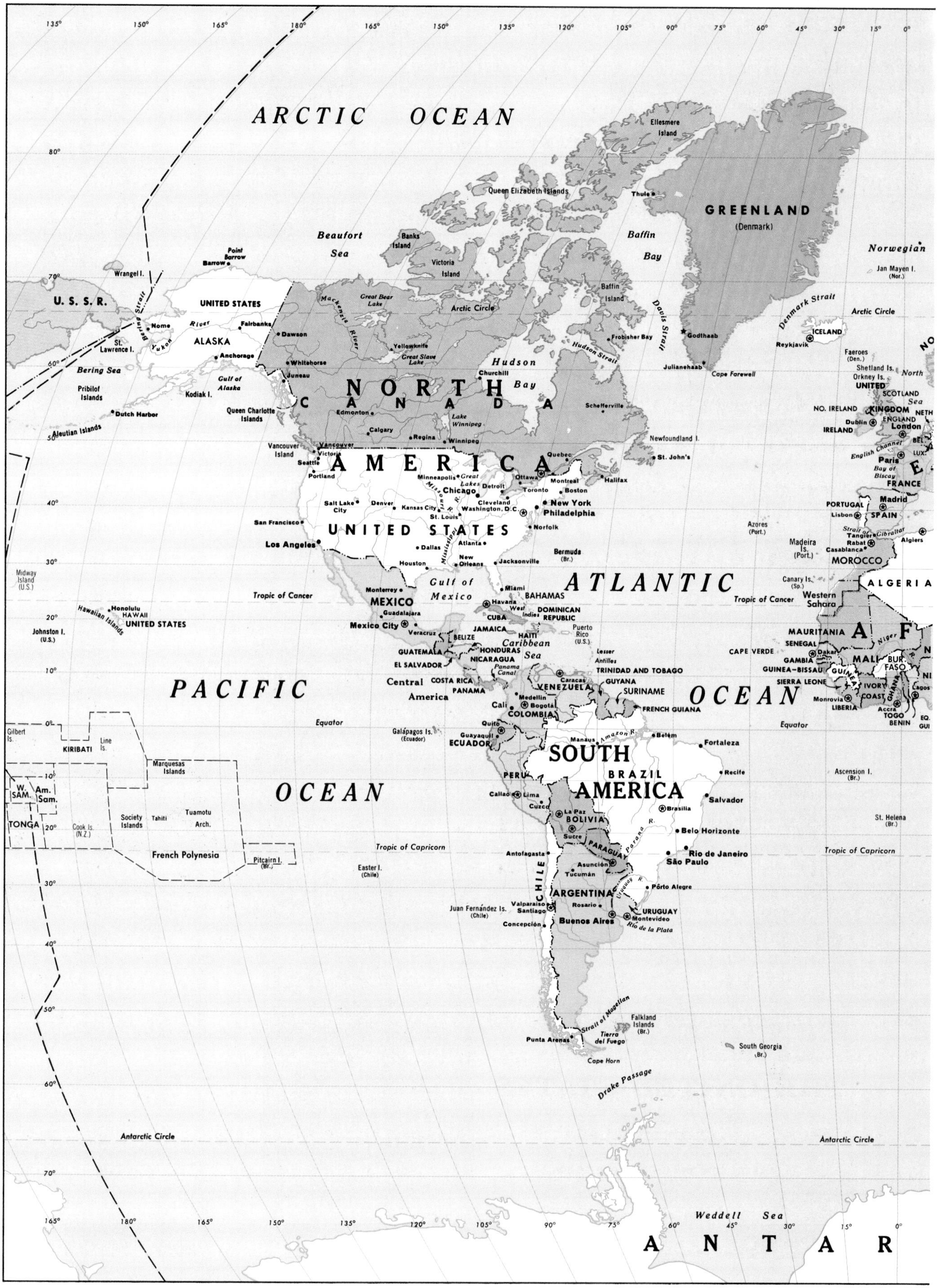

ARCTIC OCEAN
Ellesmere Island
Queen Elizabeth Islands
Thule
GREENLAND
(Denmark)
Beaufort Sea
Banks Island
Baffin Bay
Norwegian
Jan Mayen I. (Nor.)
Wrangel I.
Point Barrow
Barrow
Victoria Island
Baffin Island
U. S. S. R.
UNITED STATES
Great Bear Lake
Arctic Circle
Davis Strait
Denmark Strait
Arctic Circle
Bering Strait
Nome
River
Fairbanks
Dawson
Mackenzie River
ALASKA
Yukon
St. Lawrence I.
Yellowknife
Great Slave Lake
Frobisher Bay
Godthaab
ICELAND
Reykjavik
Hudson Strait
Anchorage
Whitehorse
Hudson
Faeroes (Den.)
Bering Sea
Juneau
Gulf of Alaska
Churchill
Bay
Julianehaab
Cape Farewell
Shetland Is.
North
Orkney Is.
Pribilof Islands
Kodiak I.
NORTH
CANADA
UNITED
SCOTLAND
Sea
Dutch Harbor
Queen Charlotte Islands
Edmonton
Schefferville
NO. IRELAND
KINGDOM
Dublin
ENGLAND
London
IRELAND
Aleutian Islands
Calgary
Lake Winnipeg
Regina
Winnipeg
Newfoundland I.
Vancouver Island
Vancouver
Victoria
Seattle
AMERICA
Quebec
St. John's
English Channel
Paris
Bay of Biscay
Portland
Minneapolis
Great Lakes
Ottawa
Montreal
Halifax
FRANCE
Missouri R.
Chicago
Detroit
Toronto
Boston
Salt Lake City
Denver
Kansas City
Cleveland
New York
Philadelphia
PORTUGAL
Madrid
Washington, D.C.
St. Louis
Lisbon
SPAIN
San Francisco
UNITED STATES
Norfolk
Azores (Port.)
Strait of Gibraltar
Tangier
Los Angeles
Dallas
Atlanta
Madeira Is. (Port.)
Rabat
Algiers
Casablanca
Mississippi R.
Bermuda (Br.)
MOROCCO
Houston
New Orleans
Jacksonville
Midway Island (U.S.)
Gulf of Mexico
ATLANTIC
Canary Is. (Sp.)
ALGERIA
Tropic of Cancer
Monterrey
Miami
BAHAMAS
Tropic of Cancer
Western Sahara
Havana
West Indies
DOMINICAN REPUBLIC
Honolulu
HAWAII
Hawaiian Islands
UNITED STATES
MEXICO
Guadalajara
CUBA
Mexico City
JAMAICA
Puerto Rico (U.S.)
MAURITANIA
AFRICA
Johnston I. (U.S.)
Veracruz
BELIZE
HAITI
Caribbean
Niger R.
SENEGAL
GUATEMALA
HONDURAS
Sea
Lesser Antilles
CAPE VERDE
Dakar
MALI
EL SALVADOR
NICARAGUA
Panama Canal
GAMBIA
GUINEA-BISSAU
BUR. FASO
TRINIDAD AND TOBAGO
Central America
COSTA RICA
Caracas
GUYANA
SIERRA LEONE
GUINEA
PACIFIC
PANAMA
VENEZUELA
SURINAME
OCEAN
Monrovia
IVORY COAST
GHANA
Lagos
Medellín
Bogotá
LIBERIA
Accra
Cali
COLOMBIA
FRENCH GUIANA
TOGO
BENIN
Gilbert Is.
Equator
Quito
Equator
Line Is.
KIRIBATI
Galápagos Is. (Ecuador)
Guayaquil
ECUADOR
Manaus
Amazon R.
Belém
Fortaleza
Marquesas Islands
SOUTH
AMERICA
BRAZIL
PERU
Recife
Ascension I. (Br.)
W. SAM.
Am. Sam.
OCEAN
Callao
Lima
Salvador
Cuzco
La Paz
Brasília
St. Helena (Br.)
Society Islands
Tahiti
Tuamotu Arch.
BOLIVIA
TONGA
Cook Is. (N.Z.)
Sucre
Belo Horizonte
Paraná R.
PARAGUAY
French Polynesia
Tropic of Capricorn
Antofagasta
Rio de Janeiro
Tropic of Capricorn
Pitcairn I. (Br.)
Asunción
São Paulo
Easter I. (Chile)
Tucumán
CHILE
Uruguay R.
Pôrto Alegre
ARGENTINA
Juan Fernández Is. (Chile)
Valparaíso
Santiago
Rosario
URUGUAY
Buenos Aires
Montevideo
Río de la Plata
Concepción
Strait of Magellan
Falkland Islands (Br.)
Tierra del Fuego
Punta Arenas
South Georgia (Br.)
Cape Horn
Drake Passage
Antarctic Circle
Antarctic Circle
Weddell Sea
ANTAR

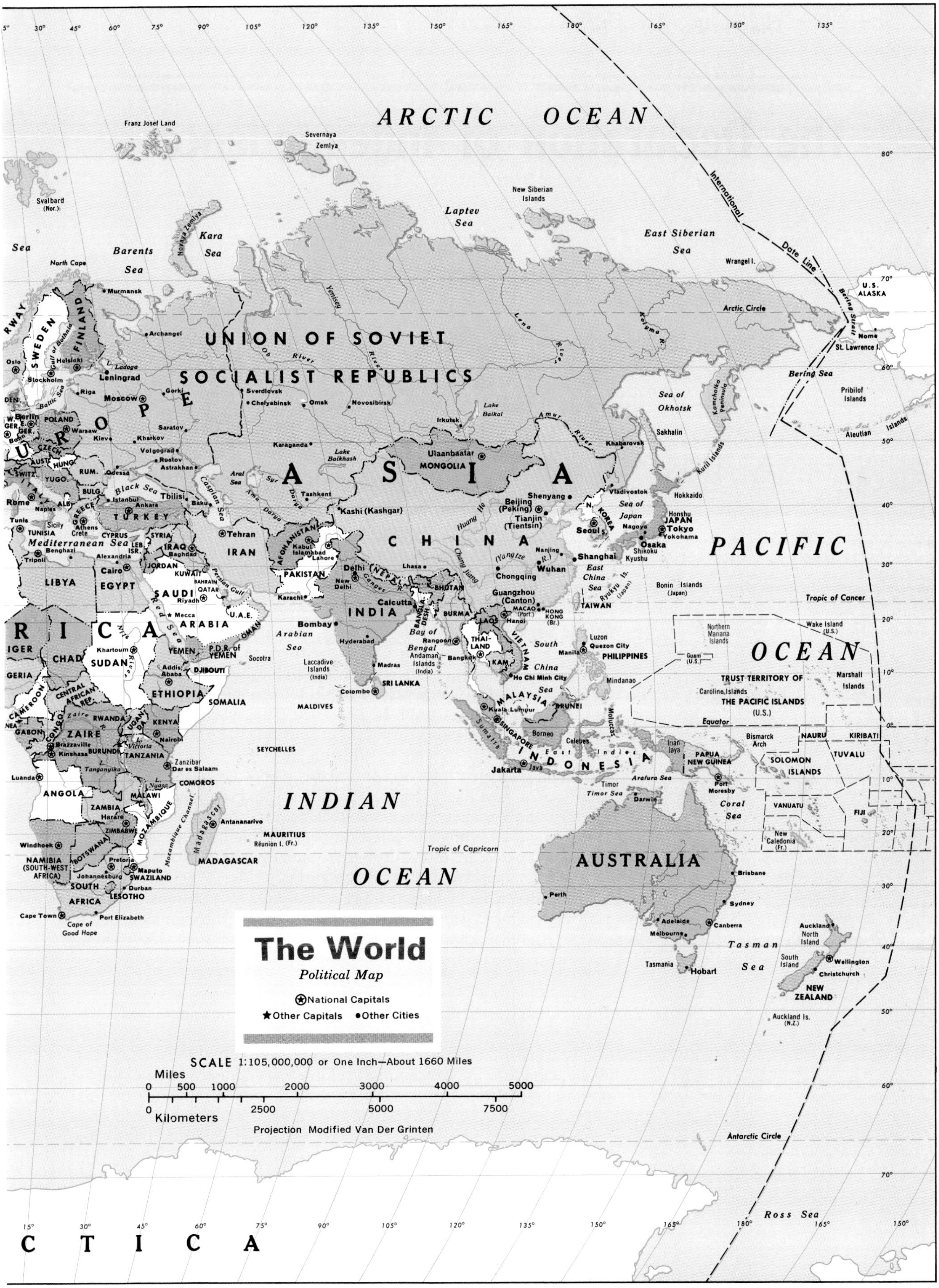

The World
Political Map
National Capitals
Other Capitals
Other Cities
SCALE 1:105,000,000 or One Inch—About 1660 Miles
Miles
0 500 1000 2000 3000 4000 5000
0 2500 5000 7500
Kilometers
Projection Modified Van Der Grinten
ARCTIC OCEAN
PACIFIC OCEAN
INDIAN OCEAN
UNION OF SOVIET SOCIALIST REPUBLICS
ASIA
EUROPE
CHINA
INDIA
MONGOLIA
JAPAN
AUSTRALIA
NEW ZEALAND
INDONESIA
PHILIPPINES
MALAYSIA
Franz Josef Land
Severnaya Zemlya
Svalbard (Nor.)
Barents Sea
Kara Sea
Laptev Sea
East Siberian Sea
New Siberian Islands
Wrangel I.
International Date Line
Arctic Circle
Bering Strait
Bering Sea
Sea of Okhotsk
U.S. ALASKA
Nome
St. Lawrence I.
Pribilof Islands
Aleutian Islands
Kamchatka Peninsula
Sakhalin
Kuril Islands
Hokkaido
Honshu
Shikoku
Kyushu
Sea of Japan
Tokyo
Yokohama
Nagoya
Osaka
Seoul
N. KOREA
S. KOREA
Vladivostok
Khabarovsk
Shenyang
Beijing (Peking)
Tianjin (Tientsin)
Shanghai
Nanjing
Wuhan
Chongqing
Guangzhou (Canton)
MACAO (Port.)
HONG KONG (Br.)
TAIWAN
East China Sea
Ryukyu Is. (Japan)
Bonin Islands (Japan)
Tropic of Cancer
Wake Island (U.S.)
Northern Mariana Islands
Guam (U.S.)
TRUST TERRITORY OF THE PACIFIC ISLANDS (U.S.)
Marshall Islands
Caroline Islands
Equator
NAURU
KIRIBATI
TUVALU
SOLOMON ISLANDS
Bismarck Arch
PAPUA NEW GUINEA
Port Moresby
VANUATU
FIJI
New Caledonia (Fr.)
Coral Sea
Arafura Sea
Timor Sea
Timor
Darwin
Brisbane
Sydney
Canberra
Adelaide
Melbourne
Perth
Tasmania
Hobart
Tasman Sea
Auckland
North Island
South Island
Wellington
Christchurch
Auckland Is. (N.Z.)
Antarctic Circle
Ross Sea
Luzon
Quezon City
Manila
Mindanao
South China Sea
Moluccas
Celebes
Borneo
BRUNEI
Kuala Lumpur
SINGAPORE
Sumatra
Java
Jakarta
East Indies
Irian Jaya
Ho Chi Minh City
KAM.
VIETNAM
LAOS
Hanoi
THAILAND
Bangkok
BURMA
Rangoon
Andaman Islands (India)
Bay of Bengal
BANGLADESH
Calcutta
BHUTAN
NEPAL
Lhasa
Delhi
New Delhi
Ganges
Bombay
Hyderabad
Madras
SRI LANKA
Colombo
Laccadive Islands (India)
MALDIVES
Arabian Sea
PAKISTAN
Karachi
Lahore
Kabul
Islamabad
AFGHANISTAN
Kashi (Kashgar)
Tashkent
Huang He
Chang Jiang (Yangtze R.)
Irkutsk
Lake Baikal
Ulaanbaatar
Amur River
Lena River
Kolyma R.
Yenisey
Ob River
Irtysh River
Novosibirsk
Omsk
Karaganda
Lake Balkhash
Aral Sea
Syr Darya
Amu Darya
Sverdlovsk
Chelyabinsk
Gorki
Moscow
Leningrad
L. Ladoga
Archangel
Murmansk
North Cape
Saratov
Volgograd
Rostov
Astrakhan
Kharkov
Kiev
Odessa
Caspian Sea
Black Sea
Tbilisi
Baku
Tehran
IRAN
IRAQ
Baghdad
SYRIA
LEB.
ISR.
JORDAN
KUWAIT
BAHRAIN
QATAR
Persian Gulf
SAUDI ARABIA
Riyadh
Mecca
U.A.E.
OMAN
YEMEN
P.D.R. of YEMEN
Socotra
Red Sea
TURKEY
Ankara
Istanbul
CYPRUS
GREECE
Athens
Crete
Mediterranean Sea
FINLAND
SWEDEN
NORWAY
Helsinki
Stockholm
Oslo
Gulf of Bothnia
Baltic Sea
DEN.
POLAND
Warsaw
Berlin
Bonn
W. GER.
E. GER.
CZECH.
AUST.
HUNG.
SWITZ.
RUM.
YUGO.
BULG.
ALB.
Rome
Naples
Sicily
Tunis
TUNISIA
Tripoli
Benghazi
LIBYA
EGYPT
Cairo
Alexandria
Nile
SUDAN
Khartoum
CHAD
NIGER
NIGERIA
CAMEROON
CENTRAL AFRICAN REP.
GABON
CONGO
Brazzaville
Kinshasa
ZAIRE
Zaire R.
RWANDA
BURUNDI
UGANDA
KENYA
Nairobi
L. Victoria
L. Tanganyika
TANZANIA
Zanzibar
Dar es Salaam
ETHIOPIA
Addis Ababa
DJIBOUTI
SOMALIA
SEYCHELLES
COMOROS
ANGOLA
Luanda
ZAMBIA
MALAWI
L. Nyasa
MOZAMBIQUE
Mozambique Channel
ZIMBABWE
Harare
BOTSWANA
Windhoek
NAMIBIA (SOUTH-WEST AFRICA)
Pretoria
Johannesburg
Maputo
SWAZILAND
Durban
LESOTHO
SOUTH AFRICA
Cape Town
Cape of Good Hope
Port Elizabeth
Madagascar
MADAGASCAR
Antananarivo
MAURITIUS
Réunion I. (Fr.)
Tropic of Capricorn
ANTARCTICA

The Declaration of Independence

In Congress, July 4, 1776

THE UNANIMOUS DECLARATION OF THE THIRTEEN UNITED STATES OF AMERICA

When in the Course of human events, it becomes necessary for one people to dissolve the political bands which have connected them with another, and to assume among the powers of the earth, the separate and equal station to which the Laws of nature and of Nature's God entitle them, a decent respect to the opinions of mankind requires that they should declare the causes which impel them to the separation.

The opening paragraph of the Declaration describes the basic purpose of the document: to set out the reasons why the former colonists have declared their independence.

The Political Theory of the Declaration

endowed: provided

transient: fleeting

usurpation: unlawful seizure of power

absolute despotism: government by a ruler with unlimited powers

We hold these truths to be self-evident, that all men are created equal, that they are endowed by their Creator with certain unalienable Rights, that among these are Life, Liberty and the pursuit of Happiness. That to secure these rights, Governments are instituted among Men, deriving their just powers from the consent of the governed; That whenever any Form of Government becomes destructive of these ends it is the Right of the People to alter or to abolish it, and to institute new Government, laying its foundation on such principles and organizing its powers in such form, as to them shall seem most likely to effect their Safety and Happiness. Prudence, indeed, will dictate that Governments long established should not be changed for light and transient causes; and accordingly all experience hath shown, that mankind are more disposed to suffer, while evils are sufferable, than to right themselves by abolishing the forms to which they are accustomed. But when a long train of abuses and usurpations, pursuing invariably the same Objects evinces a design to reduce them under absolute Despotism, it is their right, it is their duty, to throw off such Government, and to provide new Guards for their future security.

The Declaration was written by a five-member committee appointed by the Second Continental Congress on June 11, 1776. The document was very largely the work of Thomas Jefferson, who chaired the committee. Its other members (John Adams, Benjamin Franklin, Roger Sherman, and Robert Livingston) made minor changes in Jefferson's original draft before the final version was reported to Congress. Jefferson drew heavily from the ideas of English philosopher John Locke to declare these "self-evident" truths: the equality of all men; the natural rights of men, granted to them by God; the principle of limited government; government only by the consent of the governed; and the right to rebel against tyrannical government.

The "Injuries and Usurpations"

Such has been the patient sufferance of these Colonies; and such is now the necessity which constrains them to alter their former Systems of Government. The history of the Present King of Great Britain is a history of repeated injuries and usurpations, all having in direct object the establishment of an absolute Tyranny over these States. To prove this, let Facts be submitted to a candid world.

tyranny: unfair, oppressive rule by an absolute authority

He has refused his Assent to Laws, the most wholesome and necessary for the public good.

He has forbidden his Governors to pass Laws of immediate and pressing importance, unless suspended in their operation till his Assent should be obtained; and when so suspended, he has utterly neglected to attend to them.

He has refused to pass other Laws for the accommodation of large districts of people, unless those people would relinquish the right of Representation in the Legislature, a right inestimable to them and formidable to tyrants only.

inestimable: unmeasurable

He has called together legislative bodies at places unusual, uncomfortable, and distant from the depository of their public records, for the sole purpose of fatiguing them into compliance with his measures.

depository: storage for the safe-keeping of valuable items

He has dissolved Representative Houses repeatedly, for opposing with manly firmness his invasions on the rights of the people.

He has refused for a long time, after such dissolutions, to cause others to be elected; whereby the Legislative powers, incapable of Annihilation, have returned to the People at large for their exercise; the State remaining in the mean time exposed to all the dangers of invasions from without, and convulsions within.

annihilation: total destruction

convulsions: violent upheavals

He has endeavored to prevent the population of these States; for that purpose obstructing the Laws for Naturalization of Foreigners; refusing to pass others to encourage their migration hither, and raising the conditions of new Appropriations of Lands.

He has obstructed the Administration of Justice, by refusing his Assent to Laws for establishing Judiciary powers.

He has made Judges dependent on his Will alone for the tenure of their offices, and the amount and payment of their salaries.

tenure: term; length of service

He has erected a multitude of New Offices, and sent hither swarms of Officers to harass our people and eat out their substance.

He has kept among us in time of peace, Standing Armies, without the Consent of our legislatures.

He has affected to render the Military independent of, and superior to, the Civil Power.

He has combined with others to subject us to a jurisdiction foreign to our constitutions, and unacknowledged by our laws; giving his Assent to their Acts of pretended Legislation:

For quartering large bodies of armed troops among us;

quartering: the providing of room and board for soldiers

For protecting them, by a mock Trial, from punishment for any Murders which they should commit on the Inhabitants of these States;

For cutting off our Trade with all parts of the world;

For imposing taxes on us without our Consent;

For depriving us, in many cases, of the benefits of Trial by Jury;

For transporting us beyond Seas, to be tried for pretended offenses;

For abolishing the free System of English Laws in a neighboring Province, establishing therein an Arbitrary government, and enlarging its Boundaries, so as to render it at once an example and fit instrument for introducing the same absolute rule into these Colonies;

arbitrary: according to whim, with no reason

For taking away our Charters, abolishing our most valuable Laws, and altering, fundamentally, the Forms of our Governments;

For suspending our own Legislatures, and declaring themselves invested with Power to legislate for us in all cases whatsoever.

abdicated: renounced, given up

He has abdicated Government here, by declaring us out of his Protection, and waging War against us.

He has plundered our seas, ravaged our Coasts, burned our towns, and destroyed the lives of our people.

perfidy: treachery

He is at this time transporting large Armies of foreign Mercenaries to complete the works of death, desolation and tyranny, already begun with circumstances of Cruelty and perfidy scarcely paralleled in the most barbarous ages, and totally unworthy the Head of a civilized nation.

He has constrained our fellow Citizens taken Captive on the high Seas to bear Arms against their Country, to become the executioners of their friends and Brethren, or to fall themselves by their Hands.

insurrections: rebellions

He has excited domestic insurrections amongst us, and has endeavored to bring on the inhabitants of our frontiers the merciless Indian Savages whose known rule of warfare is an undistinguished destruction of all ages, sexes, and conditions.

redress: compensation for past wrongs

In every stage of these Oppressions We have Petitioned for Redress in the most humble terms. Our repeated Petitions have been answered only by repeated injury. A Prince whose character is thus marked by every act which may define a Tyrant, is unfit to be the ruler of a free people.

consanguinity: relationship by blood or place of origin

Nor have We been wanting in attentions to our British brethren. We have warned them from time to time of attempts by their legislature to extend an unwarrantable jurisdiction over us. We have reminded them of the circumstances of our emigration and settlement here. We have appealed to their native justice and magnanimity, and we have conjured them by the ties of our common kindred to disavow these usurpations, which, would inevitably interrupt our connections and correspondence. They too have been deaf to the voice of justice and of consanguinity. We must, therefore, acquiesce in the necessity, which denounces our Separation, and hold them, as we hold the rest of mankind, Enemies in War, in Peace Friends.—

The body of the Declaration sets out the long list of grievances and cites the repeated but unsuccessful attempts to redress them by peaceful means.

The Formal Proclamation of Independence

rectitude: highly principled moral conduct

We, therefore, the Representatives of the United States of America, in General Congress, Assembled, appealing to the Supreme Judge of the world for the rectitude of our intentions, do, in the Name, and by the Authority of the good People of these Colonies, solemnly publish and declare, That these United Colonies are, and of right ought to be Free and Independent States; that they are Absolved from all Allegiance to the British Crown, and that all political connection between them and the State of Great Britain, is and ought to be totally dissolved, and that as Free and Independent States, they have full Power to levy War, conclude Peace, contract Alliances, establish Commerce, and to do all other Acts and Things which Independent States may of right do. And for the support of this Declaration, with a firm reliance on the protection of Divine Providence, we mutually pledge to each other our Lives, our Fortunes and our sacred Honor.

The final paragraph of the Declaration makes the formal pronouncement of independence from Great Britain, and claims for the United States all of the rights to which an independent nation is entitled.

JOHN HANCOCK

NEW HAMPSHIRE
Josiah Bartlett
William Whipple
Matthew Thornton

MASSACHUSETTS BAY
Samuel Adams
John Adams
Robert Treat Paine
Elbridge Gerry

RHODE ISLAND
Stephan Hopkins
William Ellery

CONNECTICUT
Roger Sherman
Samuel Huntington
William Williams
Oliver Wolcott

NEW YORK
William Floyd
Philip Livingston
Francis Lewis
Lewis Morris

NEW JERSEY
Richard Stockton
John Witherspoon
Francis Hopkinson
John Hart
Abraham Clark

DELAWARE
Caesar Rodney
George Read
Thomas M'Kean

MARYLAND
Samuel Chase
William Paca
Thomas Stone
Charles Carroll
of Carrollton

VIRGINIA
George Wythe
Richard Henry Lee
Thomas Jefferson
Benjamin Harrison
Thomas Nelson, Jr.
Francis Lightfoot Lee
Carter Braxton

PENNYSLVANIA
Robert Morris
Benjamin Rush
Benjamin Franklin
John Morton
George Clymer
James Smith
George Taylor
James Wilson
George Ross

NORTH CAROLINA
William Hooper
Joseph Hewes
John Penn

SOUTH CAROLINA
Edward Rutledge
Thomas Heyward, Jr.
Thomas Lynch, Jr.
Arthur Middleton

GEORGIA
Button Gwinnett
Lyman Hall
George Walton

An Outline of the Constitution of the United States

The American Constitution is the most wonderful work ever struck off at a given time by the brain and purpose of man.
—William E. Gladstone

Preamble

Article I. Legislative Department
- Section 1. *Legislative Power; the Congress*
- Section 2. *House of Representatives*
- Section 3. *Senate*
- Section 4. *Elections and Meetings*
- Section 5. *Legislative Proceedings*
- Section 6. *Compensation, Immunities, and Disabilities of Members*
- Section 7. *Revenue Bills; President's Veto*
- Section 8. *Powers of Congress*
- Section 9. *Powers Denied to Congress*
- Section 10. *Powers Denied to the States*

Article II. Executive Department
- Section 1. *Executive Power; the President; Term; Election; Qualifications; Compensation; Oath of Office*
- Section 2. *President's Powers and Duties*
- Section 3. *President's Powers and Duties*
- Section 4. *Impeachment*

Article III. Judicial Department
- Section 1. *Judicial Power; Courts; Terms of Office*
- Section 2. *Jurisdiction*
- Section 3. *Treason*

Article IV. Relations of States
- Section 1. *Full Faith and Credit*
- Section 2. *Privileges and Immunities of Citizens*
- Section 3. *Protection Afforded to States by the Nation*

Article V. Provisions for Amendment

Article VI. Public Debts; Supremacy of National Law; Oath
- Section 1. *Validity of Debts*
- Section 2. *Supremacy of National Law*
- Section 3. *Oaths of Office*

Article VII. Ratification of Constitution

1st Amendment. Freedom of Religion, Speech, Press, Assembly, and Petition

2nd Amendment. Bearing Arms

3rd Amendment. Quartering of Troops

4th Amendment. Searches and Seizures

5th Amendment. Criminal Proceedings; Due Process; Eminent Domain

6th Amendment. Criminal Proceedings

7th Amendment. Civil Trials

8th Amendment. Punishment for Crimes

9th Amendment. Unenumerated Rights

10th Amendment. **Powers Reserved to the States**

11th Amendment. **Suits Against States**

12th Amendment. **Election of President and Vice President**

13th Amendment. **Slavery and Involuntary Servitude**

Section 1. *Slavery and Involuntary Servitude Prohibited*
Section 2. *Power of Congress*

14th Amendment. **Rights of Citizens**

Section 1. *Citizenship; Privileges and Immunities; Due Process; Equal Protection*
Section 2. *Apportionment of Representation*
Section 3. *Disqualification of Officers*
Section 4. *Public Debt*
Section 5. *Power of Congress*

15th Amendment. **Right to Vote—Race, Color, Servitude**

Section 1. *Suffrage Not to Be Abridged*
Section 2. *Power of Congress*

16th Amendment. **Income Tax**

17th Amendment. **Popular Election of Senators**

Section 1. *Popular Election of Senators*
Section 2. *Senate Vacancies*
Section 3. *Inapplicable to Senators Previously Chosen*

18th Amendment. **Prohibition of Intoxicating Liquors**

Section 1. *Intoxicating Liquors Prohibited*
Section 2. *Concurrent Power to Enforce*
Section 3. *Time Limit on Ratification*

19th Amendment. **Equal Suffrage—Sex**

Section 1. *Suffrage Not to Be Abridged*
Section 2. *Power of Congress*

20th Amendment. **Commencement of Terms; Sessions of Congress; Death or Disqualification of President-Elect**

Section 1. *Terms of President, Vice President, Members of Congress*
Section 2. *Sessions of Congress*
Section 3. *Death or Disqualification of President-Elect*
Section 4. *Congress to Provide for Certain Successors*
Section 5. *Effective Date*
Section 6. *Time Limit on Ratification*

21th Amendment. **Repeal of 18th Amendment**

Section 1. *Repeal of Prohibition*
Section 2. *Transportation, Importation of Intoxicating Liquors*
Section 3. *Time Limit on Ratification*

22nd Amendment. **Presidential Tenure**

Section 1. *Restriction on Number of Terms*
Section 2. *Time Limit on Ratification*

23rd Amendment. **Inclusion of District of Columbia in Presidential Election System**

Section 1. *Presidential Electors for District of Columbia*
Section 2. *Power of Congress*

24th Amendment. **Right to Vote in Federal Elections—Tax Payment**

Section 1. *Suffrage Not to Be Abridged*
Section 2. *Power of Congress*

25th Amendment. **Presidential Succession; Vice Presidential Vacancy; Presidential Inability**

Section 1. *Presidential Succession*
Section 2. *Vice Presidential Vacancy*
Section 3. *Presidential Determination of Inability*

26th Amendment. **Right to Vote—Age**

Section 1. *Suffrage Not to Be Abridged*
Section 2. *Power of Congress*

The Constitution of the United States of America

PREAMBLE

We the People of the United States, in Order to form a more perfect Union, establish Justice, insure domestic Tranquility, provide for the common defence, promote the general Welfare, and secure the Blessings of Liberty to ourselves and our Posterity, do ordain and establish this Constitution for the United States of America.

The Preamble states the broad purposes the Constitution is intended to serve—to establish a government that: provides for greater cooperation among the States, ensures justice and peace, provides for defense against foreign enemies, promotes the general well-being of the people, and secures liberty now and in the future. The phrase *We the People* emphasizes the fact of representative government.

Article I

LEGISLATIVE DEPARTMENT

SECTION 1. *Legislative Power; The Congress*

All legislative powers herein granted shall be vested in a Congress of the United States, which shall consist of a Senate and House of Representatives.

Section 1 Legislative power, Congress Congress, the nation's lawmaking body, is bicameral in form; that is, it is composed of two houses: the Senate and the House of Representatives. The Framers of the Constitution purposely separated the lawmaking power from the power to enforce the laws (Article II, the Executive Branch) and the power to interpret them (Article III, the Judicial Branch). This system of separation of powers is supplemented by a system of checks and balances; that is, in several provisions the Constitution gives to each of the three branches various powers with which it may check, restrain, the actions of the other two branches.

SECTION 2. *House of Representatives*

1. The House of Representatives shall be composed of members chosen every second year by the people of the several States, and the electors in each State shall have the qualifications requisite for electors of the most numerous branch of the State legislature.

Clause 1 Election Electors means voters. Members of the House of Representatives are elected every two years. Each State must permit the same persons to vote for United States Representatives as it permits to vote for the members of the larger house of its own legislature. The 17th Amendment (1913) extends this requirement to the qualification of voters for United States Senators.

2. No person shall be a Representative who shall not have attained to the age of twenty-five years, and been seven years a citizen of the United States, and who shall not, when elected, be an inhabitant of that State in which he shall be chosen.

Clause 2 Qualifications A member of the House of Representatives must be at least 25 years old, an American citizen for seven years, and a resident of the State he or she represents. In addition, political custom requires that a Representative also reside in the district from which he or she is elected.

3. Representatives ~~and direct taxes*~~ shall be apportioned among the several States which may be included within this Union, according to their respective numbers, ~~which shall be determined by adding to the whole number of free persons, including those bound to service for a term of years and excluding Indians not taxed, three-fifths of all other persons~~. The actual enumeration shall be made within three years after the first meeting of the Congress of the United States, and within every subsequent term of ten years, in such manner as they shall by law direct. The number of Representatives shall not exceed one for every thirty thousand, but each State shall have at least one Representative; and, until such enumeration shall be made, the State of New Hampshire shall be entitled to choose three, Massachusetts eight, Rhode Island and Providence Plantations one, Connecticut five, New York six, New Jersey four, Pennsylvania eight, Delaware one, Maryland six, Virginia ten, North Carolina five, South Carolina five, and Georgia three.

Clause 3 Apportionment The number of Representatives each State is entitled to is based on its population, which is counted every 10 years in the census. Congress reapportions the seats among the States after each census. In the Reapportionment Act of 1929, Congress fixed the permanent size of the House at 435 members with each State having at least one Representative. Today there is one House seat for approximately every 550,000 persons in the population.

The words "three-fifths of all other persons" referred to slaves and reflected the Three-Fifths Compromise reached by the Framers at Philadelphia in 1787; the phrase was made obsolete, was in effect repealed, by the 13th Amendment in 1865.

apportionment: distribution of seats in a legislative body among electoral districts according to population

4. When vacancies happen in the representation from any State, the executive authority thereof shall issue writs of election to fill such vacancies.

Clause 4 Vacancies The executive authority refers to the governor of a State. If a member leaves office or dies before the expiration of his or her term, the governor must call a special election to fill the vacancy.

5. The House of Representatives shall choose their Speaker and other officers; and shall have the sole power of impeachment.

Clause 5 Officers; impeachment The House elects a Speaker, customarily chosen from the majority party in the House. Impeachment means accusation. The House has the exclusive power to impeach, or accuse, civil officers; the Senate (Article I, Section 3, Clause 6) has the exclusive power to try those impeached by the House.

SECTION 3. *Senate*

1. The Senate of the United States shall be composed of two Senators from each State ~~chosen by the legislature thereof~~ for six years; and each Senator shall have one vote.

*The blue lines indicate portions of the Constitution altered by subsequent amendments to the document.

Clause 1 Composition, Election, Term Each State has two Senators. Each serves for six years and has one vote. Orginally, Senators were not elected directly by the people, but by each State's legislature. The 17th Amendment now provides for the popular election of Senators.

2. Immediately after they shall be assembled in consequences of the first election, they shall be divided, as equally as may be, into three classes. The seats of the Senators of the first class shall be vacated at the expiration of the second year; of the second class, at the expiration of the fourth year; and of the third class, at the expiration of the sixth year; so that one-third may be chosen every second year; ~~and if vacancies happen by resignation, or otherwise, during the recess of the legislature of any State, the executive thereof may make temporary appointments until the next meeting of the legislature, which shall then fill such vacancies~~.

Clause 2 Classification The Senators elected in 1788 were divided into three groups so that the Senate could become a "continuing body." Only one-third of the Senate's seats are up for election every two years.

The 17th Amendment provides that a Senate vacancy is to be filled at a special election called by the governor; State law may also permit the governor to appoint a successor to serve until that election is held.

3. No person shall be a Senator who shall not have attained to the age of thirty years, and been nine years a citizen of the United States, who shall not, when elected, be an inhabitant of that State for which he shall be chosen.

Clause 3 Qualifications A Senator must be at least 30 years old, a citizen for at least nine years, and a resident of the State from which elected.

4. The Vice President of the United States shall be President of the Senate, but shall have no vote, unless they be equally divided.

Clause 4 Presiding officer The Vice President presides over the Senate, but may vote only to break a tie.

pro tempore: Latin for "temporarily"

5. The Senate shall choose their other officers, and also a President pro tempore, in the absence of the Vice President, or when he shall exercise the office of President of the United States.

Clause 5 Other officers The Senate chooses its own officers, including someone to preside when the Vice President is not there. That Senator is called the president pro tempore.

6. The Senate shall have the sole power to try all impeachments. When sitting for that purpose, they shall be on oath or affirmation. When the President of the United States is tried, the Chief Justice shall preside; and no person shall be convicted without the concurrence of two-thirds of the members present.

Clause 6 Impeachment trials The Senate conducts the trials of those officials impeached by the House. The Vice President presides unless the President is on trial, in which case the Chief Justice of the United States takes charge of the proceedings. To convict an official two-thirds of the members present must vote a guilty verdict.

No President has ever been convicted. In 1868 the House impeached President Andrew Johnson but the Senate acquitted him of the charges by one vote. In 1974 the Judiciary Committee of the House of Representatives recommended to the House that President Richard M. Nixon be impeached, but he resigned from office before further action could be taken.

7. Judgment in cases of impeachment shall not extend further than to removal from office, and disqualification to hold and enjoy any office of

honor, trust, or profit under the United States; but the party convicted shall, nevertheless, be liable and subject to indictment, trial, judgment, and punishment, according to law.

Clause 7 Penalty on conviction The only punishment allowed for an official who is convicted in an impeachment case is removal from office and disqualification from holding any other federal office. However, the convicted official may still be tried in a regular court of law for the same offense.

indictment: accusation by a grand jury; a finding that there is sufficient evidence to warrant a criminal trial

SECTION 4. *Elections and Meetings*

1. The times, places, and manner of holding elections for Senators and Representatives, shall be prescribed in each State by the legislature thereof: but the Congress may at any time, by law, make or alter such regulations, except as to the places of choosing Senators.

prescribe: order

Clause 1 Election In 1842 Congress required that Representatives be elected from districts within each State with more than one seat in the House. The districts in each State are drawn by that State's legislature. Six States now have only one seat in the House: Alaska, Delaware, North Dakota, South Dakota, Vermont, and Wyoming. The 1842 law also directed that Representatives be elected in each State on the same day: the Tuesday after the first Monday in November of every even-numbered year. In 1914 Congress also set that same date for the election of members of the Senate.

2. The Congress shall assemble at least once in every year, and such meeting shall be on the first Monday in December, unless they shall by law appoint a different day.

Clause 2 Sessions Congress must meet at least once a year. The 20th Amendment changed the opening date to January 3.

SECTION 5. *Legislative Proceedings*

1. Each House shall be the judge of the elections, returns, and qualifications of its own members, and a majority of each shall constitute a quorum to do business; but a smaller number may adjourn from day to day, and may be authorized to compel the attendance of absent members, in such manner, and under such penalties, as each House may provide.

Clause 1 Admission of members; quorum In 1969 the Supreme Court held that the House cannot exclude any member-elect who satisfies the qualifications set out in Article I, Section 2, Clause 2.

A quorum is the minimum number of persons required to be present to conduct business. A majority of the House or Senate constitutes a quorum. However, in practice, much business is transacted in each house with less than a quorum present. A member who wishes to stop such activity need only to "call for a quorum." If the roll call count reveals less than a majority present, business will be terminated for lack of a quorum.

2. Each House may determine the rules of its proceedings, punish its members for disorderly behavior, and, with the concurrence of two-thirds, expel a member.

Clause 2 Rules Each house has adopted detailed rules to guide its proceedings. Each house may discipline members for unacceptable conduct; expulsion requires a two-thirds vote.

3. Each House shall keep a journal of its proceedings, and, from time to time, publish the same, excepting such parts as may, in their judgment, require secrecy; and the yeas and nays of the members of either House, on any question, shall, at the desire of one-fifth of those present, be entered on the journal.

Clause 3 Record Each house must keep and publish a record of its meetings. The *Congressional Record* is published for every day that either house of Congress is in session, and provides a written record of all that is said and done at such a session.

4. Neither House, during the session of Congress, shall, without the consent of the other, adjourn for more than three days, nor to any other place than that in which the two Houses shall be sitting.

Clause 4 Adjournment Once in session, neither house may suspend (recess) its work for more than three days without the approval of the other house. Both houses must always meet in the same location.

SECTION 6. *Compensation, Immunities, and Disabilities of Members*

1. The Senators and Representatives shall receive a compensation for their services, to be ascertained by law, and paid out of the treasury of the United States. They shall, in all cases, except treason, felony, and breach of the peace, be privileged from arrest during their attendance at the session of their respective Houses, and in going to, and returning from, the same; and for any speech or debate in either House, they shall not be questioned in any other place.

Clause 1 Salaries; immunities Senate and House members set their own salaries and are paid by the United States Government. This provision establishes "legislative immunity." The purpose of this immunity is to allow members to speak and debate freely in Congress itself. Treason is strictly defined in Article III, Section 3. A felony is any serious crime. A breach of the peace is any indictable offense less than treason or a felony; this exemption from arrest is of little real importance today.

emolument: salary, fee

2. No Senator or Representative shall, during the time for which he was elected, be appointed to any civil office under the authority of the United States, which shall have been created, or the emoluments whereof shall have been increased during such time; and no person, holding any office under the United States, shall be a member of either House during his continuance in office.

Clause 2 Restrictions on office holding No sitting member of either house may be appointed to an office in the executive or in the judicial branch if that position was created or its salary was increased during that member's current elected term. The second part of this clause—forbidding any person serving in either the executive or the judicial branch from also serving in Congress—reinforces the principle of separation of powers.

SECTION 7. *Revenue Bills, President's Veto*

1. All bills for raising revenue shall originate in the House of Representatives, but the Senate may propose or concur with amendments as on other bills.

Clause 1 Revenue bills All bills that raise money must originate in the House. However, the Senate has the power to amend a revenue bill, sent to it from the lower house.

2. Every bill which shall have passed the House of Representatives and the Senate, shall, before it become a law, be presented to the President of the United States; if he approve, he shall sign it, but if not, he shall return it, with his objections, to that House in which it shall have originated, who shall enter the objections at large on their journal, and proceed to reconsider it. If, after such reconsideration, two-thirds of the House shall agree to pass the bill, it shall be sent, together with the objections, to the

other House, by which it shall likewise be reconsidered, and, if approved by two-thirds of that House, it shall become a law: But in all such cases the votes of both Houses shall be determined by yeas and nays, and the names of the persons voting for and against the bill shall be entered on the journal of each House respectively. If any bill shall not be returned by the President within ten days (Sunday excepted) after it shall have been presented to him, the same shall be a law, in like manner as if he had signed it, unless the Congress, by their adjournment, prevent its return, in which case it shall not be a law.

Clause 2 Enactment of laws; veto Once both houses have passed a bill, it must be sent to the President. The President may: (1) sign the bill, thus making it law; (2) veto (reject) the bill, whereupon it must be returned to the house in which it originated; or (3) allow the bill to become law without signature, by not acting upon it within 10 days of its receipt from Congress, not counting Sundays. The President has a fourth option at the end of a congressional session: If he does not act on a measure within 10 days, and Congress adjourns during that period, the bill dies; the "pocket veto" has been applied to it. A presidential veto may be overridden by a two-thirds vote in each house.

3. Every order, resolution, or vote, to which the concurrence of the Senate and House of Representatives may be necessary (except on a question of adjournment), shall be presented to the President of the United States; and before the same shall take effect, shall be approved by him, or, being disapproved by him, shall be repassed by two-thirds of the Senate and House of Representatives, according to the rules and limitations prescribed in the case of a bill.

Clause 3 Other measures This clause refers to joint resolutions, measures Congress often passes to deal with unusual, temporary, or ceremonial matters. A joint resolution passed by Congress and signed by the President has the force of law, just as a bill does. As a matter of custom, a joint resolution proposing an amendment to the Constitution is not submitted to the President for signature or veto. Concurrent and simple resolutions do not have the force of law and, therefore, are not submitted to the President.

SECTION 8. *Powers of Congress*

The Congress shall have power

1. To lay and collect taxes, duties, imposts, and excises, to pay the debts, and provide for the common defence and general welfare of the United States; but all duties, imposts, and excises, shall be uniform throughout the United States;

excise: tax on goods made or sold within the country

Clause 1 The 18 separate clauses in this section set out 27 of the many expressed powers the Constitution grants to Congress. In this clause Congress is given the power to levy and provide for the collection of various kinds of taxes, in order to finance the operations of the Government. All federal taxes must be levied at the same rates throughout the country.

2. To borrow money on the credit of the United States;

Clause 2 Congress has power to borrow money to help finance the Government. Federal borrowing is most often done through the sale of bonds on which interest is paid. The Constitution does not limit the amount the Government may borrow.

3. To regulate commerce with foreign nations, and among the several States, and with the Indian tribes;

Clause 3 This clause, the Commerce Clause, gives Congress the power to regulate both foreign and interstate trade. Much of what Congress does, it does on the basis of its commerce power.

4. To establish a uniform rule of naturalization, and uniform laws on the subject of bankruptcies, throughout the United States;

Clause 4 Congress has the power to determine how aliens may become citizens of the United States. Congress may also pass laws relating to bankruptcy.

5. To coin money, regulate the value thereof, and of foreign coin, and fix the standard of weights and measures;

Clause 5 Congress has the power to establish and require the use of uniform gauges of time, distance, weight, volume, area, and the like.

6. To provide for the punishment of counterfeiting the securities and current coin of the United States;

Clause 6 Congress has the power to make it a federal crime to falsify the coins, paper money, bonds, stamps, and the like of the United States.

7. To establish post offices and post roads;

Clause 7 Congress has the postal power, the power to provide for and regulate the transportation and delivery of mail; "post offices" are those buildings and other places where mail is deposited for dispatch; "post roads" include all routes over or upon which mail is carried.

8. To promote the progress of science and useful arts, by securing, for limited times, to authors and inventors, the exclusive right to their respective writings and discoveries;

Clause 8 Congress has the power to provide for copyrights and patents. A copyright gives an author or composer the exclusive right to control the reproduction, publication, and sale of literary, musical, or other creative work. A patent gives a person the exclusive right to control the manufacture or sale of his or her invention.

inferior: lower in rank

9. To constitute tribunals inferior to the Supreme Court;

Clause 9 Congress has the power to create the lower federal courts, all of the several federal courts that function beneath the Supreme Court.

10. To define and punish piracies and felonies, committed on the high seas, and offences against the law of nations;

Clause 10 Congress has the power to prohibit, as a federal crime: (1) certain acts committed outside the territorial jurisdiction of the United States, and (2) the commission within the United States of any wrong against any nation with which we are at peace.

11. To declare war, grant letters of marque and reprisal, and make rules concerning captures on land and water;

Clause 11 Only Congress can declare war. However, the President, as Commander in Chief of the armed forces (Article II, Section 2, Clause 1), can make war without such a formal declaration. Letters of marque and reprisal are (were) commissions authorizing private persons to outfit vessels (privateers) to capture and destroy enemy ships in time of war; they are forbidden in international law by the Declaration of Paris of 1856, and the United States has honored the ban since the Civil War.

12. To raise and support armies; but no appropriation of money to that use shall be for a longer term than two years;

13. To provide and maintain a navy;

Clauses 12 and 13 Congress has the power to provide for and maintain the nation's armed forces. It established the Air Force as an independent element of the armed forces in 1947, an exercise of its inherent powers in foreign relations and national defense. The two-year limit on spending for the Army insures civilian control of the military.

appropriation: measure passed by a legislative body granting permission to spend specified amounts of money for specified purposes

14. To make rules for the government and regulation of the land and naval forces;

Clause 14 Today these rules are set out in a lengthy, oft-amended law, the Uniform Code of Military Justice, passed by Congress in 1950.

15. To provide for calling forth the militia to execute the laws of the Union, suppress insurrections, and repel invasions;

16. To provide for organizing, arming, and disciplining the militia, and for governing such part of them as may be employed in the service of the United States, reserving to the States respectively the appointment of the officers, and the authority of training the militia, according to the discipline prescribed by Congress;

Clauses 15 and 16 In the National Defense Act of 1916, Congress made each State's militia (volunteer army) a part of the National Guard. Today, Congress and the States cooperate in its maintenance. Ordinarily, each State's National Guard is under the command of that State's governor; but Congress has given the President the power to call any or all of those units into federal service when necessary.

17. To exercise exclusive legislation in all cases whatsoever, over such district (not exceeding ten miles square) as may, by cession of particular States, and the acceptance of Congress, become the seat of the Government of the United States, and to exercise like authority over all places, purchased by the consent of the legislature of the State in which the same shall be, for the erection of forts, magazines, arsenals, dockyards, and other needful buildings; and

cession: transfer; grant

Clause 17 In 1791 Congress accepted land grants from Maryland and Virginia and established the District of Columbia for the nation's capital. Assuming Virginia's grant would never be needed, Congress returned it in 1846. Today, the elected government of the District's 69 square miles operates under the authority of Congress. Congress also has the power to acquire other lands from the States for various federal purposes.

18. To make all laws which shall be necessary and proper for carrying into execution the foregoing powers, and all other powers vested by this Constitution in the Government of the United States, or in any department or officer thereof.

vested: given the control of

Clause 18 This is the Necessary and Proper Clause, also often called the Elastic Clause. It is the constitutional basis for the many and far-reaching implied powers of the Federal Government.

SECTION 9. *Powers Denied to Congress*

1. The migration or importation of such persons as any of the States now existing shall think proper to admit, shall not be prohibited by the Congress prior to the year one thousand eight hundred and eight; but a tax or duty may be imposed on such importation, not exceeding ten dollars for each person.

Clause 1 "Such persons" referred to slaves. This provision was part of the Commerce Compromise, one of the bargains struck in the writing of the Constitution. Congress outlawed the slave trade in 1808.

2. The privilege of the writ of habeas corpus shall not be suspended, unless when, in cases of rebellion or invasion, the public safety may require it.

Clause 2 A writ of habeas corpus, the "great writ of liberty," is a court order directing a sheriff, warden, or other public officer, or a private person, who is detaining another to "produce the body" of the one being held in order that the legality of the detention may be determined by the court.

3. No bill of attainder or *ex post facto* law shall be passed.

Clause 3. A bill of attainder is a legislative act that inflicts punishment without a judicial trial. See Article I, Section 10, and Article III, Section 3, Clause 2. An *ex post facto* law is any criminal law that operates retroactively to the disadvantage of the accused. See Article I, Section 10.

4. No capitation, or other direct tax, shall be laid, unless in proportion to the census or enumeration hereinbefore directed to be taken.

Clause 4 A capitation tax is literally a "head tax," a tax levied on each person in the population. A direct tax is one paid directly to the government by the taxpayer—for example, an income or a property tax; an indirect tax is one paid to another private party who then pays it to the government—for example, a sales tax. This provision was modified by the 16th Amendment, giving Congress the power to levy "taxes on incomes, from whatever source derived."

duty: tariff; tax on imported goods

5. No tax or duty shall be laid on articles exported from any State.

Clause 5 This provision was a part of the Commerce Compromise made by the Framers in 1787. Congress has the power to tax imported goods, however.

6. No preference shall be given by any regulation of commerce or revenue to the ports of one State over those of another, nor shall vessels bound to, or from, one State, be obliged to enter, clear, or pay duties, in another.

Clause 6 All ports within the United States must be treated alike by Congress as it exercises its taxing and commerce powers. Congress cannot tax goods sent by water from one State to another, nor may it give the ports of one State any legal advantage over those of another.

7. No money shall be drawn from the treasury, but in consequence of appropriations made by law; and a regular statement and account of the receipts and expenditures of all public money shall be published from time to time.

Clause 7 This clause gives Congress its vastly important "power of the purse," a major check on presidential power. Federal money can be spent only in those amounts and for those purposes expressly authorized by an act of Congress. All federal income and spending must be accounted for, regularly and publicly.

8. No title of nobility shall be granted by the United States; and no person holding any office of profit or trust under them shall, without the consent of the Congress, accept of any present, emolument, office, or title, of any kind whatever, from any king, prince, or foreign state.

Clause 8 This provision, preventing the establishment of a nobility, reflects the principle that "all men are created equal." It was also intended to discourage foreign attempts to bribe or otherwise corrupt officers of the government.

SECTION **10** ***Powers Denied to the States***

1. No State shall enter into any treaty, alliance, or confederation; grant letters of marque and reprisal; coin money; emit bills of credit; make anything but gold and silver coin a tender in payment of debts; pass any bill of attainder, *ex post facto* law, or law impairing the obligations of contracts, or grant any title of nobility.

emit: issue

Clause 1 The States are not sovereign governments and so cannot make agreements or otherwise negotiate with foreign states; the power to conduct foreign relations is an exclusive power of the National Government. The power to coin money is also an exclusive power of the National Government. Several powers forbidden to the National Government are here also forbidden to the States.

2. No State shall, without the consent of the Congress, lay any imposts or duties on imports or exports, except what may be absolutely necessary for executing its inspection laws; and the net produce of all duties and imposts, laid by any State on imports or exports, shall be for the use of the treasury of the United States; and all such laws shall be subject to the revision and control of the Congress.

Clause 2 This provision relates to foreign, not interstate, commerce. Only Congress, not the States, can tax imports; and the States are, like Congress, forbidden the power to tax exports.

3. No State shall, without the consent of Congress, lay any duty of tonnage, keep troops, or ships of war, in time of peace, enter into any agreement or compact with another State, or with a foreign power, or engage in war, unless actually invaded, or in such imminent danger as will not admit of delay.

Clause 3 A duty of tonnage is a tax laid on ships according to their cargo capacity. Each State has a constitutional right to provide for and maintain a militia; but no State may keep a standing army or navy. The several restrictions here prevent the States from assuming powers that the Constitution elsewhere grants to the National Government.

Article II

EXECUTIVE DEPARTMENT

SECTION **1.** ***President and Vice President***

1. The executive power shall be vested in a President of the United States of America. He shall hold his office during the term of four years, and together with the Vice President, chosen for the same term, be elected as follows:

Clause 1 Executive power, term This clause gives to the President the very broad "executive power," the power to enforce the laws and otherwise administer the public policies of the United States. It also sets the length of the presidential (and vice-presidential) term of office; see the 22nd Amendment, which places a limit on presidential (but not vice-presidential) tenure.

2. Each State shall appoint, in such manner as the legislature thereof may direct, a number of Electors, equal to the whole number of Senators and Representatives, to which the State may be entitled in the Congress; but no Senator or Representative, or person holding an office of trust or profit, under the United States, shall be appointed an Elector.

Clause 2 Electoral college This clause establishes the "electoral college," although the Constitution does not use that term. It is a body of presidential electors chosen in each State, and it selects the President and Vice President every four years. The number of electors chosen in each State equals the number of Senators and Representatives that State has in Congress.

~~3. The Electors shall meet in their respective States, and vote by ballot for two persons, of whom one, at least, shall not be an inhabitant of the same State with themselves. And they shall make a list of all the persons voted for, and of the number of votes for each; which list they shall sign and certify, and transmit, sealed, to the seat of the Government of the United States, directed to the President of the Senate. The President of the Senate shall, in the presence of the Senate and House of Representatives, open all the certificates, and the votes shall then be counted. The person having the greatest number of votes shall be the President, if such number be a majority of the whole number of Electors appointed; and if there be more than one, who have such majority, and have an equal number of votes, then, the House of Representatives shall immediately choose, by ballot, one of them for President; and if no person have a majority, then, from the five highest on the list, the said House shall, in like manner, choose the President. But in choosing the President, the votes shall be taken by States, the representation from each State having one vote; a quorum for this purpose shall consist of a member or members from two-thirds of the States, and a majority of all the States shall be necessary to a choice. In every case, after the choice of the President, the person having the greatest number of votes of the Electors shall be the Vice President. But if there should remain two or more who have equal votes, the Senate shall choose from them, by ballot, the Vice President.~~

Clause 3 Election of President and Vice President This clause was replaced by the 12th Amendment in 1804.

4. The Congress may determine the time of choosing the Electors, and the day on which they shall give their votes; which day shall be the same throughout the United States.

Clause 4 Date Congress has set the date for the choosing of electors as the Tuesday after the first Monday in November every fourth year, and for the casting of electoral votes as the Monday after the second Wednesday in December of that year.

5. No person, except a natural-born citizen, or a citizen of the United States at the time of the adoption of this Constitution, shall be eligible to the office of President; neither shall any person be eligible to that office, who shall not have attained to the age of thirty-five years, and been fourteen years a resident within the United States.

Clause 5 Qualifications The President must be a native-born citizen of the United States, at least 35 years old, and have been a resident of the United States for at least 14 years.

~~6. In case of the removal of the President from office, or of his death, resignation, or inability to discharge the powers and duties of the said office, the same shall devolve on the Vice President,~~ and the Congress may by law provide for the ease of removal, death, resignation or inability, both of the President and Vice President, declaring what officer shall then act as President, and such officer shall act accordingly, until the disability be removed, or a President shall be elected.

Clause 6 Vacancy This clause was modified by the 25th Amendment (1967), which provides expressly for the succession of the Vice President, for the filling of a vacancy in the Vice Presidency, and for the determination of presidential inability.

7. The President shall, at stated times, receive for his services a compensation, which shall neither be increased nor diminished during the period for which he shall have been elected, and he shall not receive, within that period, any other emolument from the United States, or any of them.

Clause 7 Compensation The President now receives a salary of $200,000 and a taxable expense account of $50,000 a year. Those amounts cannot be changed during a presidential term; thus, Congress cannot use the President's compensation as a bargaining tool to influence executive decisions. The phrase "any other emolument" means, in effect, any valuable gift; it does not mean that the President cannot be provided with such benefits of office as the White House, extensive staff assistance, and much else.

8. Before he enter on the execution of his office, he shall take the following oath or affirmation:

"I do solemnly swear (or affirm), that I will faithfully execute the office of President of the United States, and will, to the best of my ability, preserve, protect, and defend the Constitution of the United States."

Clause 8 Oath of office The Chief Justice of the United States regularly administers this oath or affirmation, but any judicial officer may do so. Thus, Calvin Coolidge was sworn into office in 1923 by his father, a justice of the peace in Vermont.

SECTION 2. *President's Powers and Duties*

1. The President shall be Commander in Chief of the army and navy of the United States, and of the militia of the several States, when called into the actual service of the United States; he may require the opinion, in writing, of the principal officer in each of the executive departments upon any subject relating to the duties of their respective offices, and he shall have power to grant reprieves and pardons for offences against the United States, except in cases of impeachment.

reprieve: official warrant granting postponement of a sentence, especially of death

Clause 1 Military, civil powers The President, a civilian, heads the nation's armed forces, a key element in the Constitution's insistence on civilian control of the military. The President's power to "require the opinion, in writing . . . " provides the constitutional basis for the Cabinet. The President's power to grant reprieves and pardons, the power of clemency, extends *only* to federal cases.

pardon: release from the punishment or other legal consequences of a crime

concur: agree

2. He shall have power, by and with the advice and consent of the Senate, to make treaties, provided two-thirds of the Senators present concur; and he shall, nominate, and, by and with the advice and consent of the Senate, shall appoint ambassadors, other public ministers, and consuls, judges of the Supreme Court, and all other officers of the United States whose appointments are not herein otherwise provided for, and which shall be established by law; but the Congress may by law vest the appointment of such inferior officers, as they think proper, in the President alone, in the courts of law, or in the heads of departments.

Clause 2 Treaties, appointments The President has the sole power to make treaties; to become effective, a treaty must be approved by a two-thirds vote in the Senate. In practice, the President can also make executive agreements with foreign governments; these pacts, which are frequently made and usually deal with routine matters, do not require Senate consent. The President appoints the principal officers of the executive branch and all federal judges; the "inferior officers" are those who hold lesser posts.

3. The President shall have power to fill up all vacancies that may happen during the recess of the Senate, by granting commissions which shall expire at the end of their next session.

Clause 3 Recess appointments When the Senate is not in session, appointments that require Senate consent can be made by the President on a temporary basis, as "recess appointments."

SECTION **3.** ***President's Powers and Duties***

He shall, from time to time, give to the Congress information of the state of the Union, and recommend to their consideration such measures as he shall judge necessary and expedient; he may, on extraordinary occasions, convene both Houses, or either of them, and in case of disagreement between them, with respect to the time of adjournment, he may adjourn them to such time as he shall think proper; he shall receive ambassadors and other public ministers; he shall take care that the laws be faithfully executed, and shall commission all the officers of the United States.

expedient: suitable; proper; reasonable

The President delivers a State of the Union Message to Congress soon after that body convenes each year. That message is delivered to the nation's lawmakers and, importantly, to the American people, as well. It is shortly followed by the proposed federal budget and an economic report; and the President may send special messages to Congress at any time. In all of these communications, Congress is urged to take those actions the Chief Executive finds to be in the national interest. The President also has the power: to call special sessions of Congress; to adjourn Congress if its two houses cannot agree for that purpose; to receive the diplomatic representatives of other governments; to insure the proper execution of all federal laws; and to empower federal officers to hold their posts and perform their duties.

SECTION **4.** ***Impeachment***

The President, Vice President, and all civil officers of the United States, shall be removed from office on impeachment for, and conviction of, treason, bribery, or other high crimes and misdemeanors.

misdemeanor: a crime less serious than a felony, punishable by a small fine and/or a short jail term

The Constitution outlines the impeachment process in Article I, Section 2, Clause 5 and in Section 3, Clauses 6 and 7.

Article III

JUDICIAL DEPARTMENT

SECTION **1.** ***Courts, Terms of Office***

The judicial power of the United States shall be vested in one Supreme Court, and in such inferior courts as the Congress may from time to time ordain and establish. The judges, both of the Supreme and inferior courts, shall hold their offices during good behavior, and shall, at stated time, receive for their services a compensation which shall not be diminished during their continuance in office.

ordain: decree; establish

The judicial power conferred here is the power of federal courts to hear and decide cases, disputes between the government and individuals and between private persons (parties). The Constitution creates only the Supreme Court of the United States; it gives to Congress the power to establish other, lower federal courts (Article I, Section 8, Clause 9) and to fix the size of the Supreme Court. The words "during good behavior" mean, in effect, for life.

SECTION **2.** ***Jurisdiction***

1. The judicial power shall extend to all cases, in law and equity, arising under this Constitution, the laws of the United States, and treaties made, or which shall be made, under their authority; to all cases affecting ambassadors, other public ministers, and consuls; to all cases of admiralty and maritime jurisdiction; to controversies to which the United States shall be a party; to controversies between two or more States, ~~between a State and citizens of another State,~~ between citizens of different States, between citizens of the same State claiming lands under grants of different States, ~~and between a State, or the citizens thereof, and foreign states, citizens, or subjects~~.

equity: body of law developed to supplement the common law, to provide justice where the common law fails to do so

Clause 1 Cases to be heard This clause sets out the jurisdiction of the federal courts; that is, it identifies those cases that may be tried in those courts. The federal courts can hear and decide—have jurisdiction over—a case depending on either the subject matter or the parties involved in that case. The jurisdiction of the federal courts in cases involving States was substantially restricted by the 11th Amendment in 1795.

2. In all cases affecting ambassadors, other public ministers and consuls, and those in which a State shall be a party, the Supreme Court shall have original jurisdiction. In all the other cases before mentioned, the Supreme Court shall have appellate jurisdiction, both as to law and fact, with such exceptions and under such regulations as the Congress shall make.

Clause 2 Supreme Court jurisdication Original jurisdiction refers to the power of a court to hear a case in the first instance, not on appeal from a lower court. Appellate jurisdiction refers to a court's power to hear a case on appeal from a lower court, from the court in which the case was originally tried. This clause gives the Supreme Court both original and appellate jurisdiction. However, nearly all of the cases the high court hears are brought to it on appeal from the lower federal courts and the highest State courts.

3. The trial of all crimes, except in cases of impeachment, shall be by jury; and such trial shall be held in the State where the said crimes shall have been committed; but when not committed within any State the trial shall be at such place or places as the Congress may by law have directed.

Clause 3 Jury trial in criminal cases A person accused of a federal crime is guaranteed the right to trial by jury in a federal court in the State where the crime was committed; see the 5th and 6th Amendments. The right to trial by jury in *serious* criminal cases in the State courts is guaranteed by the 6th and 14th Amendments.

SECTION **3.** ***Treason***

1. Treason against the United States shall consist only in levying war against them, or in adhering to their enemies, giving them aid and comfort. No person shall be convicted of treason unless on the testimony of two witnesses to the same overt act, or on confession in open court.

Clause 1 Definition Treason is the only crime defined in the Constitution. The Framers intended the very specific definition here to prevent the loose use of the charge of treason—for example, against persons who criticize the government. Treason can be committed only in time of war and only by a citizen or a resident alien.

2. The Congress shall have power to declare the punishment of treason, but no attainder of treason shall work corruption of blood, or forfeiture except during the life of the person attained.

Clause 2 Punishment Congress has provided that the punishment that a federal court may impose on a convicted traitor may range from a minimum of five years in prison and/or a $10,000 fine to a maximum of death; no person convicted of treason has ever been executed by the United States. No legal punishment can be imposed on the family or descendants of a convicted traitor. Congress has also made it a crime for any person (in either peace or wartime) to commit espionage or sabotage, to attempt to overthrow the government by force, or to conspire to do any of these things.

Article IV

RELATIONS AMONG STATES

SECTION 1. *Full Faith and Credit*

Full faith and credit shall be given in each State to the public acts, records, and judicial proceedings of every other State. And the Congress may, by general laws, prescribe the manner in which such acts, records, and proceedings shall be proved, and the effect thereof.

Each State must respect—recognize the validity of—the laws, public records, and court decisions of every other State.

SECTION 2. *Privileges and Immunities of Citizens*

1. The citizens of each State shall be entitled to all privileges and immunities of citizens in the several States.

Clause 1 Residents of other States In effect, this clause means that no State may discriminate against the residents of other States; that is, a State's laws cannot draw unreasonable distinctions between its residents and those of any of the other States. See Section 1 of the 14th Amendment.

2. A person charged in any State with treason, felony, or other crime, who shall flee from justice, and be found in another State, shall, on demand of the executive authority of the State from which he fled, be delivered up, to be removed to the State having jurisdiction of the crime.

Clause 2 Extradition The process of retaining a fugitive to another State is known as "interstate rendition" or, more commonly, "extradition." Usually, that process works routinely, but the word "shall" here must be read as "may," because the Supreme Court has several times held that a governor cannot be forced to return a fugitive, no matter the reason for refusing to do so.

3. No person held to service or labor in one State, under the laws thereof, escaping into another, shall, in consequence of any law or regulation therein, be discharged from such service or labor, but shall be delivered up on claim of the party to whom such service or labor may be due.

Clause 3 Fugitive slaves This clause was nullified by the 13th Amendment, which abolished slavery in 1865.

SECTION 3. *New States; Territories*

1. New States may be admitted by the Congress into this Union; but no new State shall be formed or erected within the jurisdiction of any other State, nor any State be formed by the junction of two or more States, or parts of States, without the consent of the legislatures of the States concerned as well as of the Congress.

Clause 1 New States Only Congress can admit new States to the Union. A new State may not be created by taking territory from an existing

State without the consent of that State's legislature. Congress has admitted 37 States since the original 13 formed the Union. Five States—Vermont, Kentucky, Tennessee, Maine, and West Virginia—were created from parts of existing States. Texas was an independent republic before admission. California was admitted after being ceded to the United States by Mexico. Each of the other 30 States entered the Union only after a period of time as an organized territory of the United States.

2. The Congress shall have power to dispose of and make all needful rules and regulations respecting the territory or other property belonging to the United States; and nothing in this Constitution shall be so construed as to prejudice any claims of the United States, or of any particular State.

construed: interpreted

Clause 2 Territory, property Congress has the power to make laws concerning the territories, other public lands, and all other property of the United States.

SECTION 4. ***Protection Afforded to States by the Nation***

The United States shall guarantee to every State in this Union a republican form of government, and shall protect each of them against invasion; and on application of the legislature, or of the executive (when the legislature cannot be convened), against domestic violence.

The Constitution does not define "a republican form of government," but the phrase is generally understood to mean a representative government. The Federal Government must also defend each State against attacks from outside its border and, at the request of a State's legislature or its governor, aid its efforts to put down internal disorders.

Article V

PROVISIONS FOR AMENDMENT

The Congress, whenever two-thirds of both Houses shall deem it necessary, shall propose amendments to this Constitution, or, on the application of the legislatures of two-thirds of the several States, shall call a convention for proposing amendments, which, in either case, shall be valid, to all intents and purposes, as part of this Constitution, when ratified by the legislatures of three-fourths of the several States, or by conventions in three-fourths thereof, as the one or the other mode of ratification may be proposed by the Congress; provided ~~that no amendment which may be made prior to the year one thousand eight hundred and eight shall in any manner affect the first and fourth clauses in the ninth section of the first Article; and~~ that no State, without its consent, shall be deprived of its equal suffrage in the Senate.

This section provides for the methods by which formal changes can be made in the Constitution. An amendment may be proposed in one of two ways: by a two-thirds vote in each house of Congress, or by a national convention called by Congress at the request of two-thirds of the State legislatures. A proposed amendment may be ratified in one of two ways: by three-fourths of the State legislatures, or by three-fourths of the States in convention called for that purpose. Congress has the power to determine the method by which a proposed amendment may be ratified. The amendment process cannot be used to deny any State its equal representation in the United States Senate. To this point, 26 amendments have been adopted. To date, all of the amendments except the 21st Amendment were proposed by Congress and ratified by the State legislatures. Only the 21st Amendment was ratified by the convention method.

Article VI

NATIONAL DEBTS, SUPREMACY OF NATIONAL LAW, OATH

SECTION 1. *Validity of Debts*

All debts contracted and engagements entered into, before the adoption of this Constitution, shall be as valid against the United States under this Constitution, as under the Confederation.

Congress had borrowed large sums of money during the Revolution and later during the Critical Period of the 1780s. This provision, a pledge that the new government would honor those debts, did much to create confidence in that government.

SECTION 2. *Supremacy of National Law*

This Constitution, and the laws of the United States which shall be made in pursuance thereof, and all treaties made, or which shall be made, under the authority of the United States, shall be the supreme law of the land; and the judges in every State shall be bound thereby, anything in the constitution or laws of any State to the contrary notwithstanding.

This section sets out the Supremacy Clause, a specific declaration of the supremacy of federal law over any and all forms of State law. No State, including its local governments, may make or enforce any law that conflicts with any provision in the Constitution, an act of Congress, a treaty, or an order, rule, or regulation properly issued by the President or his subordinates in the executive branch.

SECTION 3. *Oaths of Office*

The Senators and Representatives before mentioned, and the members of the several State legislatures, and all executive and judicial officers, both of the United States and of the several States, shall be bound, by oath or affirmation, to support this Constitution; but no religious test shall ever be required as a qualification to any office or public trust under the United States.

This provision reinforces the Supremacy Clause; all public officers, at every level in the United States, owe their first allegiance to the Constitution of the United States. No religious qualification can be imposed as condition for holding any public office. The oath taken by members of Congress is as follows:

> I do solemnly swear (or affirm) that I will support and defend the Constitution of the United States against all enemies, foreign and domestic; that I will bear true faith and allegiance to the same; that I take this obligation freely, without any mental reservation or purpose of evasion, and that I will well and faithfully discharge the duties of the office on which I am about to enter. So help me God.

Article VII

RATIFICATION OF CONSTITUTION

The ratification of the conventions of nine States shall be sufficient for the establishment of this Constitution between the States so ratifying the same.

Done in Convention, by the unanimous consent of the States present, the seventeenth day of September, in the year of our Lord one thousand seven hundred and eighty-seven, and of the Independence of the United States of America the twelfth. *In Witness* whereof, we have hereunto subscribed our names.

Attest: *William Jackson,*
Secretary

George Washington
President and Deputy from Virginia

NEW HAMPSHIRE
John Langdon
Nicholas Gilman

MASSACHUSETTS
Nathaniel Gorham
Rufus King

CONNECTICUT
William Samuel Johnson
Roger Sherman

NEW YORK
Alexander Hamilton

NEW JERSEY
William Livingston
David Brearley
William Paterson
Jonathan Dayton

PENNSYLVANIA
Benjamin Franklin
Thomas Mifflin
Robert Morris
George Clymer
Thomas Fitzsimons
Jared Ingersoll
James Wilson
Gouverneur Morris

DELAWARE
George Read
Gunning Bedford, Jr.
John Dickinson
Richard Bassett
Jacob Broom

MARYLAND
James McHenry
Dan of St. Thomas Jennifer
Daniel Carroll

VIRGINIA
John Blair
James Madison, Jr.

NORTH CAROLINA
William Blount
Richard Dobbs Spaight
Hugh Williamson

SOUTH CAROLINA
John Rutledge
Charles Cotesworth Pinckney
Charles Pinckney
Pierce Butler

GEORGIA
William Few
Abraham Baldwin

The Constitution became the law of the land with the convening of the first session of Congress on March 4, and the inauguration of President George Washington on April 30, 1789.

AMENDMENTS

The first 10 amendments, the Bill of Rights, were each proposed by Congress on September 25, 1789, and ratified by the necessary three-fourths of the States on December 15, 1791. These amendments were originally intended to restrict the National Government—not the States. However, the Supreme Court has several times held that most of their provisions also apply to the States, through the 14th Amendment's Due Process Clause.

1ST AMENDMENT. *Freedom of Religion, Speech, Press, Assembly, and Petition*

Congress shall make no law respecting an establishment of religion, or prohibiting the free exercise thereof, or abridging the freedom of speech, or of the press; or the right of the people peaceably to assemble, and to petition the government for a redress of grievances.

abridging: curtailing

The 1st Amendment sets out five basic liberties: The guarantee of freedom of religion is both a protection of religious thought and practice and a command of separation of church and state. The guarantees of freedom of speech and press assure to all persons a right to speak, publish, and otherwise express their views. The guarantees of the rights of assembly and petition protect the right to join with others in public meetings, political parties, pressure groups, and other associations to discuss public affairs and influence public policy. None of these rights is guaranteed in absolute terms, however; like all other civil rights guarantees, each of them may be exercised only with regard to the rights of all other persons.

2nd Amendment. *Bearing Arms*

infringed: violated

A well-regulated milita being necessary to the security of a free state, the right of the people to keep and bear arms shall not be infringed.

Each State has the right to maintain a militia, a volunteer armed force for its own protection; however, both the National Government and the States can and do regulate the possession and use of firearms by private persons.

3rd Amendment. *Quartering of Troops*

No soldier shall, in time of peace, be quartered in any house, without the consent of the owner; nor, in time of war, but in a manner to be prescribed by law.

This amendment was intended to prevent what had been common British practice in the colonial period; see the Declaration of Independence. This provision is of virtually no importance today.

4th Amendment. *Searches and Seizures*

The right of the people to be secure in their persons, houses, papers, and effects, against unreasonable searches and seizures, shall not be violated; and no warrants shall issue, but upon probable cause, supported by oath or affirmation, and particularly describing the place to be searched and the persons or things to be seized.

The basic rule laid down by the 4th Amendment is this: Police officers have no general right to search for or seize evidence or seize (arrest) persons. Except in particular circumstances, they must have a proper warrant (a court order) obtained with probable cause (on reasonable grounds). This guarantee is reinforced by the exclusionary rule, developed by the Supreme Court: Evidence gained as the result of an unlawful search or seizure cannot be used at the court trial of the person from whom it was seized.

5th Amendment. *Criminal Proceedings; Due Process; Eminent Domain*

No person shall be held to answer for a capital, or otherwise infamous, crime, unless on a presentment or indictment of a grand jury, except in cases arising in the land or naval forces, or in the militia, when in actual service, in time of war, or public danger; nor shall any person be subject, for the same offence, to be twice put in jeopardy of life or limb; nor shall be compelled, in any criminal case, to be a witness against himself; nor be deprived of life, liberty, or property, without due process of law; nor shall private property be taken for public use, without just compensation.

A person can be tried for a serious federal crime only if he or she has been indicted (charged, accused of that crime) by a grand jury. No one may be subjected to double jeopardy—that is, tried twice for the same crime. All persons are protected against self-incrimination; no person can be legally compelled to answer any question in any governmental proceeding if that answer could lead to that person's prosecution. The 5th Amendment's Due Process Clause prohibits unfair, arbitrary actions by the Federal Government; a like prohibition is set out against the States in the 14th Amendment. Government may take private property for a legitimate public purpose; but when it exercises that power of eminent domain, it must pay a fair price for the property seized.

eminent domain: power of a government to take private property for public use

6th Amendment. *Criminal Proceedings*

In all criminal prosecutions, the accused shall enjoy the right to a speedy and public trial, by an impartial jury of the state and district wherein the crime shall have been committed, which district shall have been previously ascertained by law; and to be informed of the nature and cause of the accusation; to be confronted with the witnesses against him; to have compulsory process for obtaining witnesses in his favor; and to have the assistance of counsel for his defence.

compulsory: required

A person accused of crime has the right to be tried in court without undue delay and by an impartial jury; see Article III, Section 2, Clause 3. The defendant must be informed of the charge upon which he or she is to be tried, has the right to cross-examine hostile witnesses, and has the right to require the testimony of favorable witnesses. The defendant also has the right to be represented by an attorney at every stage in the criminal process.

7th Amendment. *Civil Trials*

In suits at common law, where the value in controversy shall exceed twenty dollars, the right of trial by jury shall be preserved; and no fact, tried by a jury, shall be otherwise re-examined in any court of the United States than according to the rules of the common law.

This amendment applies only to civil cases heard in federal courts. A civil case does not involve criminal matters; it is a dispute between private parties or between the government and a private party. The right to trial by jury is guaranteed in any civil case in a federal court if the amount of money involved in that case exceeds $20 (most cases today involve a much larger sum); that right may be waived (relinquished, put aside) if both parties agree to a bench trial (a trial by a judge, without a jury).

8th Amendment. *Punishment for Crimes*

Excessive bail shall not be required, nor excessive fines imposed, nor cruel and unusual punishment inflicted.

Bail is the sum of money that a person accused of crime may be required to post (deposit with the court) as a guarantee that he or she will appear in court at the proper time. The amount of bail required and/or a fine imposed as punishment must bear a reasonable relationship to the seriousness of the crime involved in the case. The prohibition of cruel and unusual punishment forbids any punishment judged to be too harsh, too severe for the crime for which it is imposed.

9th Amendment. *Unenumerated Rights*

The enumeration in the Constitution of certain rights shall not be construed to deny or disparage others retained by the people.

disparage: discredit; show disrespect for

The fact that the Constitution sets out many civil rights guarantees, expressly provides for many protections against government, does not mean that there are not other rights also held by the people.

10th Amendment. *Powers Reserved to the States*

The powers not delegated to the United States by the Constitution, nor prohibited by it to the States, are reserved to the States respectively, or to the people.

This amendment identifies the area of power that may be exercised by the States. All of those powers the Constitution does not grant to the National Government, and at the same time does not forbid to the States, belong to each of the States, or to the people of each State.

11th Amendment. *Suits against States*

The judicial power of the United States shall not be construed to extend to any suit in law or equity, commenced or prosecuted against one of the United States by citizens of another State or by citizens or subjects of any foreign state.

Proposed by Congress March 4, 1794; ratified February 7, 1795, but official announcement of the ratification was delayed until January 8, 1798. This amendment repealed part of Article III, Section 2, Clause 1. No State may be sued in a federal court by a resident of another State or of a foreign country; the Supreme Court has long held that this provision also means that a State cannot be sued in a federal court by a foreign country or, more importantly, even by one of its residents.

12th Amendment. *Election of President and Vice President*

The Electors shall meet in their respective States, and vote by ballot for President and Vice President, one of whom, at least, shall not be an inhabitant of the same State with themselves; they shall name in their ballots the person voted for as President, and in distinct ballots the person voted for as Vice President; and they shall make distinct lists of all persons voted for as President, and of all persons voted for as Vice President, and of the number of votes for each, which lists they shall sign, and certify, and transmit, sealed, to the seat of the Government of the United States, directed to the President of the Senate; the President of the Senate shall, in the presence of the Senate and the House of Representatives, open all the certificates, and the votes shall then be counted; the person having the greatest number of votes for President shall be the President, if such number be a majority of the whole number of Electors appointed; and if no person have such a majority, then, from the persons having the highest numbers, not exceeding three, on the list of those voted for as President, the House of Representatives shall choose immediately, by ballot, the President. But in choosing the President, the votes shall be taken by States, the representation from each State having one vote; a quorum for this purpose shall consist of a member or members from two-thirds of the States, and a majority of all the States shall be necessary to a choice. And if the House of Representatives shall not choose a President, whenever the right of choice shall devolve upon them, before the fourth day of March next following, then the Vice President shall act as President, as in case of death, or other constitutional disability, of the President. The person having the greatest number of votes as Vice President, shall be the Vice President, if such number be a majority of the whole number of Electors appointed; and if no person have a majority, then, from the two highest numbers on the list, the Senate shall choose the Vice President; a quorum for the purpose shall consist of two-thirds of the whole number of Senators; a majority of the whole number shall be necessary to a choice. But no person constitutionally ineligible to the office of President shall be eligible to that of Vice-President of the United States.

Proposed by Congress December 9, 1803; ratified June 15, 1804. This amendment replaced Article II, Section 1, Clause 3. Originally, each elector cast two ballots, each for a different person for President. The person with the largest number of electoral votes, provided that number was a majority of the electors, was to become President; the person with the second highest number was to become Vice President. This arrangement produced an electoral vote tie between Thomas Jefferson and Aaron Burr in 1800; the House finally chose Jefferson as President in 1801. The 12th Amendment separated the balloting for President and Vice President; each elector now casts one ballot for someone as President and a second ballot for another person as Vice President. This amendment was modified by Section 1 of the 23rd Amendment, providing electors for the District of Columbia. The 12th Amendment also provides that the Vice President must meet the same qualifications as those that are set for the Presidency in Article II, Section 1, Clause 5.

13th Amendment. *Slavery and Involuntary Servitude*

Section 1. Neither slavery nor involuntary servitude, except as a punishment for crime, whereof the party shall have been duly convicted, shall exist within the United States, or any place subject to their jurisdiction.

Section 2. Congress shall have power to enforce this article by appropriate legislation.

Proposed by Congress January 31, 1865; ratified December 6, 1865. This amendment forbids slavery in the United States and in any area under its control. It also forbids other forms of forced labor, except punishments for crime; but some forms of compulsory service are not prohibited—for example, service on juries or in the armed forces. Section 2 gives to Congress the power to carry out the provisions of Section 1 of this amendment.

14th Amendment. *Rights of Citizens*

Section 1. All persons born or naturalized in the United States, and subject to the jurisdiction thereof, are citizens of the United States and of the State wherein they reside. No State shall make or enforce any law which shall abridge the privileges or immunities of citizens of the United States; nor shall any State deprive any person of life, liberty, or property, without due process of law, nor deny to any person within its jurisdiction the equal protection of the laws.

immunities: protections

Proposed by Congress June 13, 1866; ratified July 9, 1868. Section 1 defines citizenship. It provides for the acquisition of United States citizenship by birth or by naturalization. Citizenship at birth is deemed according to the principle of *jus soli*—"the law of the soil,"where born; naturalization is the legal process by which one acquires a new citizenship at some time after birth. Under certain circumstances, citizenship can also be gained at birth abroad, according to the principle of *jus sanguinus*—"the law of the blood," to whom born. This section also contains two major civil rights provisions: the Due Process Clause forbids a State (and its local governments) to act in any unfair or arbitrary way; the Equal Protection Clause forbids a State (and its local governments) to discriminate against, draw unreasonable distinctions between, persons.

Most of the rights set out against the National Government in the first eight amendments have been extended against the States (and their local governments) through Supreme Court decisions involving the 14th Amendment's Due Process Clause.

SECTION 2. Representatives shall be apportioned among the several States according to their respective numbers, counting the whole number of persons in each State, excluding Indians not taxed. But when the right to vote at any election for the choice of electors for President and Vice President of the United States, Representatives in Congress, the executive and judicial officers of a State, or the members of the legislature thereof, is denied to any of the male inhabitants of such State, being twenty-one years of age and citizens of the United States, or in any way abridged, except for participation in rebellion or other crime, the basis of representation therein shall be reduced in the proportion which the number of such male citizens shall bear to the whole number of male citizens twenty-one years of age in such State.

The first sentence here replaced Article I, Section 2, Clause 3, the Three-Fifths Compromise provision. Essentially, all persons in the United States are counted in each decennial census, the basis for the distribution of House seats. The balance of this section has never been enforced and is generally thought to be obsolete.

SECTION 3. No person shall be a Senator or Representative in Congress, or elector of President and Vice President, or hold any office, civil or military, under the United States, or under any State, who, having previously taken an oath, as a member of Congress, or as an officer of the United States, or as a member of any State legislature, or as an executive or judicial officer of any State, to support the Constitution of the United States, shall have engaged in insurrection or rebellion against the same, or given aid or comfort to the enemies thereof. But Congress may, by a vote of two-thirds of each House, remove such disability.

This section limited the President's power to pardon those persons who had led the Confederacy during the Civil War. Congress finally removed this disability in 1898.

incurred: assumed; contracted
void: without legal effect

SECTION 4. The validity of the public debt of the United States, authorized by law, including debts incurred for payment of pensions and bounties for services in suppressing insurrection or rebellion, shall not be questioned. But neither the United States nor any State shall assume or pay any debt or obligation incurred in aid of insurrection or rebellion against the United States, or any claim for the loss or emancipation of any slave, but all such debts, obligations, and claims shall be held illegal and void.

SECTION 5. The Congress shall have power to enforce, by appropriate legislation, the provisions of this article.

Section 4 also dealt with matters directly related to the Civil War. It reaffirmed the public debt of the United States; but it invalidated, prohibited payment of, any debt contracted by the Confederate States and also prohibited any compensation of former slave owners.

15TH AMENDMENT. ***Right to Vote—Race, Color, Servitude***

SECTION 1. The right of citizens of the United States to vote shall not be denied or abridged by the United States or by any State on account of race, color, or previous condition of servitude.

SECTION 2. The Congress shall have power to enforce this article by appropriate legislation.

Proposed by Congress February 26, 1869; ratified February 3, 1870. The immediate purpose of this amendment was to guarantee to newly-freed slaves their right to vote. It has a much broader application today.

16TH AMENDMENT. *Income Tax*

The Congress shall have power to lay and collect taxes on incomes, from whatever source derived, without apportionment among the several States, and without regard to any census or enumeration.

derived: obtained

Proposed by Congress July 12, 1909; ratified February 3, 1913. This amendment modified two provisions in Article I: Section 2, Clause 3, and Section 9, Clause 4. It gives to Congress the power to levy an income tax, a direct tax, without regard to the populations of any of the States.

17TH AMENDMENT. *Popular Election of Senators*

The Senate of the United States shall be composed of two Senators from each State, elected by the people thereof, for six years; and each Senator shall have one vote. The electors in each State shall have the qualifications requisite for electors of the most numerous branch of the State legislatures.

When vacancies happen in the representation of any State in the Senate, the executive authority of such State shall issue writs of election to fill such vacancies: Provided, That the legislature of any State may empower the executive thereof to make temporary appointment until the people fill the vacancies by election as the legislature may direct.

This amendment shall not be so construed as to affect the election or term of any Senator chosen before it becomes valid as part of the Constitution.

Proposed by Congress May 13, 1912; ratified April 8, 1913. This amendment repealed those portions of Article I, Section 3, Clauses 1 and 2 relating to the election of Senators. Senators are now elected by the voters in each State. If a vacancy occurs, the governor of the State involved must call an election to fill the seat; the governor may appoint a Senator to serve until the next election, if the legislature has authorized that step.

18TH AMENDMENT. *Prohibition of Intoxicating Liquors*

~~SECTION 1. After one year from the ratification of this article the manufacture, sale or transportation of intoxicating liquors within, the importation thereof into, or the exportation thereof from the United States and all territory subject to the jurisdiction thereof for beverage purposes is hereby prohibited.~~

~~SECTION 2. The Congress and the several States shall have concurrent power to enforce this article by appropriate legislation.~~

~~SECTION 3. This article shall be inoperative unless it shall have been ratified as an amendment to the Constitution by the legislatures of the several States, as provided in the Constitution, within seven years of the date of the submission hereof to the States by Congress.~~

Proposed by Congress December 18, 1917; ratified January 16, 1919. This amendment outlawed the making, selling, transporting, importing, or exporting of alcoholic beverages in the United States. It was repealed in its entirety by the 21st Amendment in 1933.

19TH AMENDMENT. *Equal Suffrage—Sex*

The right of citizens of the United States to vote shall not be denied or abridged by the United States or by any State on account of sex.

Congress shall have power to enforce this article by appropriate legislation.

Proposed by Congress June 4, 1919; ratified August 18, 1920. No person can be denied the right to vote in any election in the United States on account of his or her sex.

20th Amendment. ***Commencement of Terms; Sessions of Congress; Death or Disqualification of President-Elect***

Section 1. The terms of the President and Vice President shall end at noon on the 20th day of January, and the terms of Senators and Representatives at noon on the 3d day of January, of the years in which such terms would have ended if this article had not been ratified; and the terms of their successors shall then begin.

Section 2. The Congress shall assemble at least once in every year, and such meeting shall begin at noon on the 3d day of January, unless they shall by law appoint a different day.

Proposed by Congress March 2, 1932; ratified January 23, 1933. The provisions of Sections 1 and 2 relating to Congress modified Article I, Section 4, Clause 2, and those provisions relating to the President, the 12th Amendment. The date on which the President and Vice President now take office was moved from March 4 to January 20. Similarly, the members of Congress now begin their terms on January 3. The 20th Amendment is sometimes called the "Lame Duck Amendment" because it shortened the period of time a member of Congress who was defeated for reelection (a "lame duck") remains in office.

Section 3. If, at the time fixed for the beginning of the term of the President, the President-elect shall have died, the Vice President-elect shall become President. If a President shall not have been chosen before the time fixed for the beginning of his term, or if the President-elect shall have failed to qualify, then the Vice President-elect shall act as President until a President shall have qualified; and the Congress may by law provide for the case wherein neither a President-elect nor a Vice President-elect shall have qualified, declaring who shall then act as President, or the manner in which one who is to act shall be selected, and such person shall act accordingly until a President or Vice President shall have qualified.

This section deals with certain possibilities that were not covered by the presidential selection provisions of either Article II or the 12th Amendment. To this point, none of these situations has occurred. Note that there is neither a President-elect nor a Vice President-elect until the electoral votes have been counted by Congress, or, if the electoral college cannot decide the matter, the House has chosen a President or the Senate has chosen a Vice President.

Section 4. The Congress may by law provide for the case of the death of any of the persons from whom the House of Representatives may choose a President whenever the right of choice shall have devolved upon them, and for the case of the death of any of the persons from whom the Senate may choose a Vice President whenever the right of choice shall have devolved upon them.

Congress has not in fact ever passed such a law. See Section 2 of the 25th Amendment, regarding a vacancy in the Vice Presidency; that provision could some day have an impact here.

Section 5. Sections 1 and 2 shall take effect on the 15th day of October following the ratification of this article.

SECTION 6. This article shall be inoperative unless it shall have been ratified as an amendment to the Constitution by the legislatures of three fourths of the several States within seven years from the date of its submission.

Section 5 set the date on which this amendment came into force. Section 6 placed a time limit on the ratification process; note that a similar provision was written into the 18th, 21st, and 22nd Amendments.

21ST AMENDMENT. *Repeal of 18th Amendment*

SECTION 1. The eighteenth article of amendment to the Constitution of the United States is hereby repealed.

SECTION 2. The transportation or importation into any State, Territory, or possession of the United States for delivery or use therein of intoxicating liquors, in violation of the laws thereof, is hereby prohibited.

SECTION 3. This article shall be inoperative unless it shall have been ratified as an amendment to the Constitution by conventions in the several States, as provided in the Constitution, within seven years from the date of the submission hereof to the States by the Congress.

Proposed by Congress February 20, 1933; ratified December 5, 1933. This amendment repealed all of the 18th Amendment. Section 2 modifies the scope of the Federal Government's commerce power set out in Article I, Section 8, Clause 3; it gives to each State the power to regulate the transportation or importation and the distribution or use of intoxicating liquors in ways that would be unconstitutional in the case of any other commodity. The 21st Amendment is the only amendment Congress has thus far submitted to the States for ratification by conventions.

22ND AMENDMENT. *Presidential Tenure*

SECTION 1. No person shall be elected to the office of the President more than twice, and no person who has held the office of President, or acted as President, for more than two years of a term to which some other person was elected President shall be elected to the office of the President more than once. But this Article shall not apply to any person holding the office of President when this Article was proposed by the Congress, and shall not prevent any person who may be holding the office of President, or acting as President, during the term within which this Article becomes operative from holding the office of President or acting as President during the remainder of such term.

SECTION 2. This article shall be inoperative unless it shall have been ratified as an amendment to the Constitution by the legislatures of three fourths of the several states within seven years from the date of its submission to the States by the Congress.

Proposed by Congress March 24, 1947; ratified February 27, 1951. This amendment modified Article II, Section I, Clause 1. It stipulates that no President may serve more than two elected terms. But a President who has succeeded to the office beyond the midpoint in a term to which another President was originally elected may serve for more than eight years. In any case, however, a President may not serve more than 10 years. Prior to Franklin Roosevelt, who was elected to four terms, no President had served more than two full terms in office.

23RD AMENDMENT. *Presidential Electors for the District of Columbia*

SECTION 1. The District constituting the seat of Government of the United States shall appoint in such manner as the Congress may direct:

A number of electors of President and Vice President equal to the whole number of Senators and Representatives in Congress to which the District would be entitled if it were a State, but in no event more than the least populous State; they shall be considered, for the purposes of the election of President and Vice President, to be electors appointed by a State; and they shall meet in the District and perform such duties as provided by the twelfth article of amendment.

Section 2. The Congress shall have power to enforce this article by appropriate legislation.

Proposed by Congress June 16, 1960; ratified March 29, 1961. This amendment modified Article II, Section I, Clause 2 and the 12th Amendment. It included the voters of the District of Columbia in the presidential electorate; and provides that the District is to have the same number of electors as the least populous State—three electors—but no more that that number.

24th Amendment. ***Right to Vote in Federal Elections—Tax Payment***

Section 1. The right of citizens of the United States to vote in any primary or other election for President or Vice President, for electors for President or Vice President, or for Senator or Representative in Congress, shall not be denied or abridged by the United States or any State by reason of failure to pay any poll tax or other tax.

Section 2. The Congress shall have power to enforce this article by appropriate legislation.

Proposed by Congress September 14, 1962; ratified January 23, 1964. This amendment outlawed the poll tax, or any other tax, as a condition for taking part in the nomination or election of any federal officeholder—that is, in any process connected with selecting the President, Vice President, or members of Congress. From 1966 on, the Supreme Court has several times held that the 14th Amendment's Equal Protection Clause forbids any tax-paying qualification for voting in any State or local election.

25th Amendment. ***Presidential Succession, Vice Presidential Vacancy, Presidential Inability***

Section 1. In case of the removal of the President from office or of his death or resignation, the Vice President shall become President.

Proposed by Congress July 6, 1965; ratified February 10, 1967. Section 1 revised the inexact wording of the provision relating to presidential succession in Article II, Section 1, Clause 6. In effect, it wrote into the Constitution the precedent set by Vice President John Tyler, who succeeded to the Presidency on the death of William Henry Harrison in 1841.

Section 2. Whenever there is a vacancy in the office of the Vice President, the President shall nominate a Vice President who shall take office upon confirmation by a majority vote of both Houses of Congress.

This section provides for the filling of a vacancy in the office of Vice President. Prior to its adoption, the office had been vacant on 16 occasions and had remained unfilled for the remainder of each term involved. When Spiro Agnew resigned the office in 1973, President Richard Nixon selected Gerald Ford in accord with this provision; and, when President Nixon resigned in 1974, Gerald Ford became President and then chose Nelson Rockefeller as Vice President.

Section 3. Whenever the President transmits to the President *pro tempore* of the Senate and the Speaker of the House of Representatives his written declaration that he is unable to discharge the powers and duties of his office, and until he transmits to them a written declaration to the contrary, such powers and duties shall be discharged by the Vice President as Acting President.

Until the adoption of the 25th Amendment, no procedure had been adopted to determine when or whether the President is so incapacitated as to be unable to perform the powers and duties of the Presidency.

SECTION 4. Whenever the Vice President and a majority of either the principal officers of the executive departments or of such other body as Congress may by law provide, transmit to the President *pro tempore* of the Senate and the Speaker of the House of Representatives their written declaration that the President is unable to discharge the powers and duties of his office, the Vice President shall immediately assume the powers and duties of the office as Acting President.

Thereafter, when the President transmits to the President *pro tempore* of the Senate and the Speaker of the House of Representatives his written declaration that no inability exists, he shall resume the powers and duties of his office unless the Vice President and a majority of either the principal officers of the executive department or of such other body as Congress may by law provide, transmit within four days to the President *pro tempore* of the Senate and the Speaker of the House of Representatives their written declaration that the President is unable to discharge the powers and duties of his office. Thereupon Congress shall decide the issue, assembling within forty-eight hours for that purpose if not in session. If the Congress, within twenty-one days after receipt of the latter written declaration, or, if Congress is not in session, within twenty-one days after Congress is required to assemble, determines by two-thirds vote of both Houses that the President is unable to discharge the powers and duties of his office, the Vice President shall continue to discharge the same as Acting President; otherwise, the President shall resume the powers and duties of his office.

This section deals with the possibility of a circumstance in which a President will not be able to detemine the fact of incapacity. To this point, Congress has not established the "such other body" referred to here. This section contains the only typographical error to be found in the Constitution; in its second paragraph, the word "department" should in fact read "departments."

26TH AMENDMENT. ***Right to Vote—Age***

SECTION 1. The right of citizens of the United States, who are eighteen years of age or older, to vote shall not be denied or abridged by the United States or by any State on account of age.

SECTION 2. The Congress shall have the power to enforce this article by appropriate legislation.

Proposed by Congress March 23, 1971; ratified July 1, 1971. This amendment sets age 18 as the minimum age for voting in all elections in the United States.

Historical Documents

THE CODE OF HAMMURABI

The Code of Hammurabi, believed to date just before 1750 B.C., is a series of laws decreed by Hammurabi, the ruler of the city of Babylon when that ancient city was at the peak of its power. Inscribed on stone columns over seven feet high, these laws were intended to inform the people of what they could and could not do. They were written down and codified so that judges and administrators would have a uniform set of rules to follow in deciding disputes and imposing penalties for crimes. The Code consists of 280 sections that deal with such matters as: land tenure, property rights, trade and commerce, family relations, and the administration of justice. Selected sections of the Code are excerpted below.

■ If a man practice [robbery] and be captured, that man shall be put to death. . . .

■ If a man has come forward in a lawsuit for the witnessing of false things, and has not proved the thing that he said, if that lawsuit is a capital case, that man shall be put to death. If he came forward for witnessing about corn or silver, he shall bear the penalty (which applies to) that case.

■ If a man has concealed in his house a lost slave or slave-girl belonging to the Palace or to a subject, and has not brought him (or her) out at the proclamation of the Crier, the owner of the house shall be put to death.

■ If a fire has broken out in a man's house, and a man who has gone to extinguish it has cast his eye on the property of the owner of the house and has taken the property of the owner of the house, that man shall be thrown into the fire.

■ If a man is subject to a debt bearing interest, and Adad (the Weather-god) has saturated his field or a high flood has carried (its crop) away, or because of lack of water he has not produced corn in that field, in that year he shall not return any corn to (his) creditor. He shall . . . not pay interest for that year.

■ If a man has donated field, orchard or house to his favourite heir and has written a sealed document for him (confirming this), after the father has gone to his doom, when the brothers share he (the favorite heir) shall take the gift that his father gave him, and apart from that they shall share equally in the property of the paternal estate.

■ If an artisan has taken a child for bringing up, and has taught him his manual skill, (the child) shall not be (re)claimed. If he has not taught him his manual skill, that pupil may return to his father's house.

■ If a man aid a male or female slave . . . to escape from the city gates, he shall be put to death. . . .

■ If a man be in debt and sell his wife, son, or daughter, or bind them over to service, for three years they shall work in the house of the purchaser or master; in the fourth year they shall be given their freedom. . . .

■ If a builder has made a house for a man but has not made his work strong, so that the house he made falls down and causes the death of the owner of the house, that builder shall be put to death. If it causes the death of the son of the owner of the house, they shall kill the son of that builder.

■ If a man would put away [divorce] his wife who has not borne him children, he shall give her money to the amount of her marriage settlement and he shall make good to her the dowry which she brought from her father's house and then he may put her away.

■ If a son has struck his father, they shall cut off his hand.

■ If a man has destroyed the eye of a man of the 'gentleman' class, they shall destroy his eye. If he has broken a gentleman's bone, they shall break his bone. If he has destroyed the eye of a commoner or broken a bone of a commoner, he shall pay one mina (about $300) of silver. If he has destroyed the eye of a gentleman's slave, or broken a bone of a gentleman's slave, he shall pay half (the slave's) price.

■ If a gentleman's slave strikes the cheek of a man of the 'gentleman' class, they shall cut off (the slave's) ear.

■ If a gentleman strikes a gentleman in a free fight and inflicts an injury on him, that man shall swear 'I did not strike him deliberately', and he shall pay the surgeon.

THE MAGNA CARTA

One of the great documents of liberty, the Magna Carta (Great Charter) rested on the fuedal principle that the king and nobles had mutual contractual obligations. Its provisions limited the power of the crown and firmly planted the principle that the king, like other Englishmen, is subject to law. It became a symbol of political liberty and the foundation of constitutional government. Listed here are excerpts from 13 of its 63 articles:

1\. That the English church shall be free, and shall have her rights entire, and her liberties inviolate; and we will that it be thus observed; and our will is that it be observed in good faith by our heirs forever.

2\. We also have granted to all the freemen of our kingdom, for us and for our heirs forever, all the underwritten liberties, to be had and holden by them and their heirs, of us and our heirs forever. . . .

12\. No scutage or aid shall be imposed in our kingdom, unless by the general council of our kingdom; except for ransoming our person, making our eldest son a knight and once for marrying our eldest daughter; and for these there shall be paid no more than a reasonable aid.

14\. And for holding the general council of the kingdom concerning the assessment of aids, except in the three cases aforesaid, and for the assessing of scutage, we shall cause to be summoned the archbishops, bishops, abbots, earls, and greater barons of the realm, singly by our letters. And furthermore, we shall cause to be summoned generally, by our sheriffs and bailiffs, all others who hold of us in chief, for a certain day, that is to say, forty days before their meeting at least, and to a certain place. And in all letters of such summons we will declare the cause of such summons. And summons being thus made, the business shall proceed on the day appointed, according to the advice of such as shall be present, although all that were summoned come not.

15\. We will not in the future grant to any one that he may take aid of his own free tenants, except to ransom his body, and to make his eldest son a knight, and once to marry his eldest daughter; and for this there shall be paid only a reasonable aid. . . .

36\. Nothing from henceforth shall be given or taken for a writ of inquisition of life or limb, but it shall be granted freely, and not denied. . . .

39\. No freeman shall be taken or imprisoned, or diseised, or outlawed, or banished, or in any way destroyed, nor will we pass upon him, nor will we send upon him, unless by the lawful judgment of his peers, or by the law of the land.

40\. We will sell to no man, we will not deny to any man, either justice or right.

41\. All merchants shall have safe and secure conduct to go out of, and to come into, England, and to stay there and to pass as well by land as by water, for buying and selling by the ancient and allowed customs, without any unjust tolls, except in time of war, or when they are of any nation at war with us. . . .

42\. It shall be lawful, for the time to come, for any one to go out of our kingdom and return safely and securely by land or by water, saving his allegiance to us (unless in time of war, by some short space, for the common benefit of the realm).

60\. All the aforesaid customs and liberties, which we have granted to be holden in our kingdom, as much as it belongs to us, all people of our kingdom, as well clergy as laity, shall observe, as far as they are concerned, towards their dependents.

61\. And whereas, for the honor of God and the amendment of our kingdom, and for the better quieting the discord that has arisen between us and our barons, we have granted all these things aforesaid. Willing to render them firm and lasting, we do give and grant our subjects the underwritten security, namely, that the barons may choose five and twenty barons of the kingdom, whom they think convenient, who shall take care, with all their might, to hold and observe, and cause to be observed, the peace and liberties we have granted them, and by this our present Charter confirmed. . . .

63\. . . . It is also sworn, as well on our part as on the part of the barons, that all the things aforesaid shall be observed in good faith, and without evil duplicity. Given under our hand, in the presence of the witnesses above named, and many others, in the meadow called Runnymede, between Windsor and Staines, the 15th day of June, in the 17th year of our reign.

MADISON'S *NOTES*: DEBATE OF JUNE 6 ON THE VIRGINIA PLAN

James Madison's Notes *enable readers today to gain a glimpse of the debates that took place behind closed doors at the Constitutional Convention held in Philadelphia in the summer of 1787. Excerpted here are portions of Madison's* Notes *on the debate of June 6 on the Virginia Plan's call for a bicameral (two house) legislature.*

MR. PINCKNEY [S.C.], according to previous notice and rule obtained, moved "that the first branch of the national legislature be elected by the state legislatures, and not by the people," contending that the people were less fit judges in such a case, and that the legislatures would be less likely to promote the adoption of the new government if they were to be excluded from all share in it.

MR. RUTLEDGE [S.C.] seconded the motion.

MR. GERRY [Mass.]: Much depends on the mode of election. In England the people will probably lose their liberty from the smallness of the proportion having a right of suffrage. Our danger arises from the opposite extreme; hence in Massachusetts the worst men get into the legislature. Several members of that body had lately been convicted of infamous crimes. Men of indigence, ignorance, and baseness spare no pains, however dirty, to carry their point against men who are superior to the artifices practised. He was not disposed to run into extremes. He was as much principled as ever against aristocracy and monarchy. It was necessary, on the one hand, that the people should appoint one branch of the government in order to inspire them with the necessary confidence. . . . His idea was that the people should nominate certain persons in certain districts, out of whom the state legislatures should make the appointment.

MR. WILSON [Pa.]: He wished for vigor in the government, but he wished that vigorous authority to flow immediately from the legitimate source of all authority. The government ought to possess not only, first, the *force* but, second, the *mind or sense* of the people at large. The legislature ought to be the most exact transcript of the whole society. Representation is made necessary only because it is impossible for the people to act collectively. . . .

MR. SHERMAN [Conn.]: If it were in view to abolish the state governments, the elections ought to be by the people. If the state governments are to be continued, it is necessary, in order to preserve harmony between the national and state governments, that the elections to the former should be made by the latter. The right of participating in the national government would be sufficiently secured to the people by their election of the state legislatures. The objects of the Union, he thought, were few: (1) defense against foreign danger; (2) against internal disputes and a resort to force; (3) treaties with foreign nations; (4) regulating foreign commerce and drawing revenue from it. These, and perhaps a few lesser objects, alone rendered a confederation of the states necessary. All other matters, civil and criminal, would be much better in the hands of the states. . . .

COLONEL MASON [Va.]: Under the existing Confederacy, Congress represent the *states,* not the *people* of the states; their acts operate on the *states,* not on the individuals. The case will be changed in the new plan of government. The people will be represented; they ought therefore to choose the representatives. The requisites in actual representation are that the representatives should sympathize with their constituents, should think as they think and feel as they feel, and that, for these purposes, [they] should even be residents among them. Much, he said, had been alleged against democratic elections. He admitted that much might be said; but it was to be considered that no government was free from imperfections and evils and that improper elections, in many instances, were inseparable from republican governments. . . .

MR. MADISON [Va.] considered an election of one branch, at least, of the legislature by the people immediately as a clear principle of free government, and that this mode, under proper regulations, had the additional advantage of securing better representatives as well as of avoiding too great an agency of the state governments in the general one. He differed from the member from Connecticut (Mr. Sherman) in thinking the objects mentioned to be all the principal ones that required a national government. Those were certainly important and necessary objects; but he combined with them the necessity of providing more effectually for the security of private rights and the steady dispensation of justice.

Interferences with these were evils which had more, perhaps, than anything else produced this Convention. Was it to be supposed that republican liberty could long exist under the abuses of it practised in some of the states? . . .

All civilized societies would be divided into

different sects, factions, and interests, as they happened to consist of rich and poor, debtors and creditors, the landed, the manufacturing, the commercial interests, the inhabitants of this district or that district, the followers of this political leader or that political leader, the disciples of this religious sect or that religious sect. In all cases where a majority are united by a common interest or passion, the rights of the minority are in danger. What motives are to restrain them? . . .

Conscience, the only remaining tie, is known to be inadequate in individuals; in large numbers, little is to be expected from it. . . .

What has been the source of those unjust laws complained of among ourselves? Has it not been the real or supposed interest of the major number? Debtors have defrauded their creditors. The landed interest has borne hard on the mercantile interest. The holders of one species of property have thrown a disproportion of taxes on the holders of another species.

The lesson we are to draw from the whole is that where a majority are united by a common sentiment, and have an opportunity, the rights of the minor party become insecure. In a republican government the majority, if united, have always an opportunity. . . .

MR. DICKINSON [Del.] considered it as essential that one branch of the legislature should be drawn immediately from the people and as expedient that the other should be chosen by the legislatures of the states. This combination of the state governments with the national government was as politic as it was unavoidable. In the formation of the Senate, we ought to carry it through such a refining process as will assimilate it as near as may be to the House of Lords in England. He repeated his warm eulogiums on the British constitution. He was for a strong national government but for leaving the states a considerable agency in the system. The objection against making the former dependent on the latter might be obviated by giving to the Senate an authority permanent and irrevocable for three, five, or seven years. Being thus independent, they will speak and decide with becoming freedom.

MR. READ [Del.]: Too much attachment is betrayed to the state governments. We must look beyond their continuance. A national government must soon of necessity swallow all of them up. They will soon be reduced to the mere office of electing the national Senate. He was against patching up the old federal system; he hoped the idea would be dismissed. It would be like putting new cloth on an old garment. The Confederation was founded on temporary principles. It cannot last; it cannot be amended. If we do not establish a good government on new principles, we must either go to ruin or have the work to do over again. . . .

MR. PIERCE [Ga.] was for an election by the people as to the first branch and by the states as to the second branch, by which means the citizens of the states would be represented both *individually* and *collectively*.

GENERAL PINCKNEY wished to have a good national government and at the same time to leave a considerable share of power in the states. An election of either branch by the people, scattered as they are in many states, particularly in South Carolina, was totally impracticable. He differed from gentlemen who thought that a choice by the people would be a better guard against bad measures than by the legislatures. . . .

The state legislatures also, he said, would be more jealous and more ready to thwart the national government if excluded from a participation in it. The idea of abolishing these legislatures would never go down.

MR. WILSON would not have spoken again but for what had fallen from Mr. Read; namely, that the idea of preserving the state governments ought to be abandoned. He saw no incompatibility between the national and state governments, provided the latter were restrained to certain local purposes; nor any probability of their being devoured by the former. . . .

On the question for electing the first branch by the state legislatures as moved by Mr. Pinckney, it was negatived.

THE FEDERALIST No. 10 (James Madison)

One of the 26 essays believed to have been written by James Madison, the tenth of the Federalist *papers presents Madison's observations on dealing with the "mischiefs of factions" and the advantages of a republican (representative) form of government over that of a pure democracy.*

AMONG THE NUMEROUS ADVANTAGES promised by a well-constructed Union, none deserves to be more accurately developed than its tendency to break and control the violence of faction. The friend of popular governments never finds himself so much alarmed for their character and fate as when he contemplates their propensity to this dangerous vice. He will not fail, therefore, to set a due value on any plan which, without violating the principles to which he is attached, provides a proper cure for it. The instability, injustice, and confusion introduced into the public councils have, in truth, been the mortal diseases under which popular governments have everywhere perished; as they continue to be the favorite and fruitful topics from which the adversaries to liberty derive their most specious declamations.

The valuable improvements made by the American constitutions on the popular models, both ancient and modern, cannot certainly be too much admired; but it would be an unwarrantable partiality to contend that they have as effectually obviated the danger on this side, as was wished and expected. Complaints are everywhere heard from our most considerate and virtuous citizens, equally the friends of public and private faith, and of public and personal liberty, that our governments are too unstable, that the public good is disregarded in the conflicts of rival parties, and that measures are too often decided, not according to the rules of justice and the rights of the minor party, but by the superior force of an interested and overbearing majority. However anxiously we may wish that these complaints had no foundation, the evidence of known facts will not permit us to deny that they are in some degree true.

It will be found, indeed, on a candid review of our situation, that some of the distresses under which we labor have been erroneously charged on the operation of our governments; but it will be found, at the same time, that other causes will not alone account for many of our heaviest misfortunes; and, particularly, for that prevailing and increasing distrust of public engagements, and alarm for private rights, which are echoed from one end of the continent to the other. These must be chiefly, if not wholly, effects of the unsteadiness and injustice with which a factious spirit has tainted our public administrations.

By a faction, I understand a number of citizens, whether amounting to a majority or minority of the whole, who are united and actuated by some common impulse of passion, or of interest, adverse to the rights of other citizens, or to the permanent and aggregate interests of the community.

There are two methods of curing the mischiefs of faction: the one, by removing its causes; the other, by controlling its effects.

There are again two methods of removing the causes of faction: the one, by destroying the liberty which is essential to its existence; the other, by giving to every citizen the same opinions, the same passions, and the same interests.

It could never be more truly said than of the first remedy that it was worse than the disease. Liberty is to faction what air is to fire, an ailment without which it instantly expires. But it could not be less folly to abolish liberty, which is essential to political life, because it nourishes faction, than it would be to wish the annihilation of air, which is essential to animal life, because it imparts to fire its destructive agency.

The second expedient is as impracticable as the first would be unwise. As long as the reason of man continues fallible, and he is at liberty to exercise it, different opinions will be formed. As long as the connection subsists between his reason and his self-love, his opinions and his passions will have a reciprocal influence on each other; and the former will be objects to which the latter will attach themselves. The diversity in the faculties of men, from which the rights of property originate, is not less an insuperable obstacle to a uniformity of interests. The protection of these faculties is the first object of government. From the protection of different and unequal faculties of acquiring property, the possession of different degrees and kinds of property immediately results; and from the influence of these on the sentiments and views of the respective proprietors ensues a division of the society into different interests and parties.

The latent causes of faction are thus sown in the nature of man; and we see them everywhere brought into different degrees of activity, according to the different circumstances of civil society. A zeal for different opinions concerning religion, concerning government, and many other points, as well of speculation as of practice; an attachment of different leaders ambitiously contending for preeminence and power; or to persons of other descriptions whose fortunes have been interesting to the human passions, have, in turn, divided mankind into parties, inflamed them with mutual animosity, and rendered them much more disposed to vex and oppress each other than to cooperate for their common good. So strong is this propensity of mankind to fall into mutual animosities that, where no substantial occasion presents itself, the most frivolous and fanciful distinctions have been sufficient to kindle their unfriendly passions and excite their most violent conflicts. But the most common and durable source of factions has been the various and unequal distribution of property.

Those who hold and those who are without property have ever formed distinct interests in society. Those who are creditors and those who are debtors fall under a like discrimination. A landed interest, a manufacturing interest, a mercantile interest, a moneyed interest, with many lesser interests, grow up of necessity in civilized nations and divide them into different classes, actuated by different sentiments and views. The regulation of these various and interfering interests forms the principal task of modern legislation and involves the spirit of party and faction in the necessary and ordinary operations of the government.

No man is allowed to be a judge in his own cause, because his interest would certainly bias his judgment and, not improbably, corrupt his integrity. With equal, nay, with greater reason, a body of men are unfit to be both judges and parties at the same time; yet what are many of the most important acts of legislation but so many judicial determinations, not indeed concerning the rights of single persons, but concerning the rights of large bodies of citizens? And what are the different classes of legislators but advocates and parties to the causes which they determine? Is a law proposed concerning private debts? It is a question to which the creditors are parties on one side and the debtors on the other. Justice ought to hold the balance between them. Yet the parties are, and must be, themselves the judges; and the most numerous party or, in other words, the most powerful faction must be expected to prevail.

Shall domestic manufactures be encouraged, and in what degree, by restrictions on foreign manufactures? [These] are questions which would be differently decided by the landed and the manufacturing classes, and probably by neither with a sole regard to justice and the public good. The apportionment of taxes on the various descriptions of property is an act which seems to require the most exact impartiality; yet there is, perhaps, no legislative act in which greater opportunity and temptation are given to a predominant party to trample on the rules of justice. Every shilling with which they overburden the inferior number is a shilling saved to their own pockets.

It is in vain to say that enlightened statesmen will be able to adjust these clashing interests and render them all subservient to the public good. Enlightened statesmen will not always be at the helm. Nor, in many cases, can such an adjustment be made at all without taking into view indirect and remote considerations, which will rarely prevail over the immediate interest which one party may find in disregarding the rights of another or the good of the whole.

The inference to which we are brought is that the *causes* of faction cannot be removed and that relief is only to be sought in the means of controlling its *effects*.

If a faction consists of less than a majority, relief is supplied by the republican principle, which enables the majority to defeat its sinister views by regular vote. It may clog the administration, it may convulse the society; but it will be unable to execute and mask its violence under the forms of the Constitution. When a majority is included in a faction, the form of popular government, on the other hand, enables it to sacrifice to its ruling passion or interest both the public good and the rights of other citizens. To secure the public good and private rights against the danger of such a faction, and at the same time to preserve the spirit and the form of popular government, is then the great object to which our inquiries are directed. Let me add that it is the great desideratum by which this form of government can be rescued from the opprobrium under which it has so long labored and be recommended to the esteem and adoption of mankind.

By what means is this object attainable? Evidently by one of two only. Either the existence of the same passion or interest in a majority at the same time must be prevented, or the majority, having such coexistent passion or interest, must be rendered, by their number and local situation, unable to concert and carry into effect schemes of oppression. If the impulse and the opportunity be suffered to coincide, we well know that neither moral nor religious motives can be relied on as an adequate control. They are not found to be such on the injustice and violence of individuals and lose their efficacy in proportion to the number combined together, that is, in proportion as their efficacy becomes needful.

From this view of the subject it may be concluded that a pure democracy, by which I mean a society consisting of a small number of citizens who assemble and administer the government in person, can admit of no cure for the mischiefs of faction. A common passion or interest will, in almost every case, be felt by a majority of the whole; a communication and concert result from the form of government itself; and there is nothing to check the inducements to sacrifice the weaker party or an obnoxious individual. Hence it is that such democracies have ever been spectacles of turbulence and contention; have ever been found incompatible with personal security or the rights of property; and have in general been as short in their lives as they have been violent in their deaths. Theoretic politicians, who have patronized this species of government, have erroneously supposed that by reducing mankind to a perfect equality in their political rights, they would, at the same time, be perfectly equalized and assimilated in their possessions, their opinions, and their passions.

A republic, by which I mean a government in which the scheme of representation takes place, opens a different prospect and promises the cure for which we are seeking. Let us examine the points in which it varies from pure democracy, and we shall comprehend both the nature of the cure and the efficacy which it must derive from the Union.

The two great points of difference between a democracy and a republic are: first, the delegation of the government, in the latter, to a small number of citizens elected by the rest; secondly, the greater number of citizens, and greater sphere of country, over which the latter may be extended.

The effect of the first difference is, on the one hand, to refine and enlarge the public views by passing them through the medium of a chosen body of citizens, whose wisdom may best discern the true interest of their country, and whose patriotism and love of justice will be least likely to sacrifice it to temporary or partial considerations. Under such a regulation, it may well happen that the public voice, pronounced by the representatives of the people, will be more consonant to the public good than if pronounced by the people themselves, convened for the purpose. On the other hand, the effect may be inverted. Men of factious tempers, of local prejudices, or of sinister designs may, by intrigue, by corruption, or by other means, first obtain the suffrages, and then betray the interests of the people. The question resulting is, whether small or extensive republics are more favorable to the election of proper guardians of the public weal; and it is clearly decided in favor of the latter by two obvious considerations:

In the first place, it is to be remarked that, however small the republic may be, the representatives must be raised to a certain number, in order to guard against the cabals of a few; and that, however large it may be, they must be limited to a certain number, in order to guard against the confusion of a multitude. Hence, the number of representatives in the two cases not being in proportion to that of the two constituents, and being proportionally greater in the small republic, it follows that, if the proportion of fit characters be not less in the large than in the small republic, the former will present a greater option, and consequently a greater probability of a fit choice.

In the next place, as each representative will be chosen by a greater number of citizens in the large than in the small republic, it will be more difficult for unworthy candidates to practice with success the vicious arts by which elections are too often carried; and the suffrages of the people being more free, will be more likely to center in men who possess the most attractive merit and the most diffusive and established character.

It must be confessed that in this, as in most other cases, there is a mean, on both sides of which inconveniences will be found to lie. By enlarging too much the number of electors, you render the representative too little acquainted with all their local circumstances and lesser interests; as by reducing it too much, you render him unduly attached to these and too little fit to comprehend and pursue great and national objects. The federal Constitution forms a happy combination in this respect: the great and aggregate interests being referred to the national, the local and particular to the state legislatures.

The other point of difference is the greater number of citizens and extent of territory which may be brought within the compass of republican than of democratic government; and it is this circumstance principally which renders factious combinations less to be dreaded in the former than in the latter. The smaller the society, the fewer probably will be the distinct parties and interests composing it; the fewer the distinct parties and interests, the more frequently will a majority be found of the same party; and the smaller the number of individuals composing a majority, and the smaller the compass within which they are placed, the more easily will they concert and execute their plans of oppression. Extend the sphere and you take in a greater variety of parties and interests; you make it less probable that a majority of the whole will have a common motive to invade the rights of other citizens; or if such a common motive exists, it will be more difficult for all who feel it to discover their own strength and to act in unison with each other. Besides other impediments, it may be remarked that, where there is a consciousness of unjust or dishonorable purposes, communication is always checked by distrust in proportion to the number whose concurrence is necessary.

Hence, it clearly appears that the same advantage which a republic has over a democracy, in controlling the effects of factions, is enjoyed by a large over a small republic—is enjoyed by the Union over the states composing it. Does the advantage consist in the substitution of representatives whose enlightened views and virtuous sentiments render them superior to local prejudices and to schemes of injustice? It will not be denied that the representation of the Union will be most likely to possess these requisite endowments. Does it consist in the greater security afforded by a greater variety of parties, against the event of any one party being able to outnumber and oppress the rest? In an equal degree does the increased variety of parties comprised within the Union increase this security? Does it, in fine, consist in the greater obstacles opposed to the concert and accomplishment of the secret wishes of an unjust and interested majority? Here, again, the extent of the Union gives it the most palpable advantage.

The influence of factious leaders may kindle a flame within their particular states but will be unable to spread a general conflagration through the other states. A religious sect may degenerate into a political faction in a part of the Confederacy; but the variety of sects dispersed over the entire face of it must secure the national councils against any danger from that source. A rage for paper money, for an abolition of debts, for an equal division of property, or for any other improper or wicked project will be less apt to pervade the whole body of the Union than a particular member of it; in the same proportion as such a malady is more likely to taint a particular county or district than an entire state.

In the extent, and proper structure of the Union, therefore, we behold a republican remedy for the diseases most incident to republican government. And according to the degree of pleasure and pride we feel in being republicans, ought to be our zeal in cherishing the spirit and supporting the character of Federalists.

ARTICLES OF CONFEDERATION

To all to whom these Presents shall come, we the undersigned Delegates of the States affixed to our Names send greeting. Whereas the Delegates of the United States of America in Congress assembled did on the fifteenth day of November in the Year of our Lord One Thousand Seven Hundred and Seventy seven, and in the Second Year of the Independence of America agree to certain articles of Confederation an perpetual Union between the States of Newhampshire, Massachusetts-bay, Rhode-island and Providence Plantations, Connecticut, New York, New Jersey, Pennsylvania, Delaware, Maryland, Virginia, North-Carolina, South-Carolina and Georgia in the Words following, viz. "Articles of Confederation and perpetual Union between the states of Newhampshire, Massachusetts-bay, Rhode-island and Providence Plantations, Connecticut, New-York, New-Jersey, Pennsylvania, Delaware, Maryland, Virginia, North-Carolina, South-Carolina and Georgia.

[Art. I.] The Stile of this confederacy shall be "The United States of America."

[Art. II.] Each state retains its sovereignty, freedom and independence, and every Power, Jurisdiction and right, which is not by this confederation expressly delegated to the United States, in Congress assembled.

[Art. III.] The said states hereby severally enter into a firm league of friendship with each other, for their common defence, the security of their Liberties, and their mutual and general welfare, binding themselves to assist each other, against all force offered to, or attacks made upon them, or any of them, on account of religion, sovereignty, trade, or any other pretence whatever.

[Art. IV.] The better to secure and perpetuate mutual friendship and intercourse among the people of the different states in this union, the free inhabitants of each of these states, paupers, vagabonds and fugitives from Justice excepted, shall be entitled to all privileges and immunities of free citizens in the several states; and the people of each state shall have free ingress and regress to and from any other state, and shall enjoy therein all the privileges of trade and commerce, subject to the same duties, impositions and restrictions as the inhabitants thereof respectively, provided that such restriction shall not extend so far as to prevent the removal of property imported into any state, to any other state of which the Owner is an inhabitant; provided also that no imposition, duties or restriction shall be laid by any state, on the property of the united states, or either of them.

If any Person guilty of, or charged with treason, felony, or other high misdemeanor in any state, shall flee from Justice, and be found in any of the united states, he shall upon demand of the Governor or executive power, of the state from which he fled, be delivered up and removed to the state having jurisdiction of his offence.

Full faith and credit shall be given in each of these states to the records, acts and judicial proceedings of the courts and magistrates of every other state.

[ART. V.] For the more convenient management of the general interests of the united states, delegates shall be annually appointed in such manner as the legislature of each state shall direct, to meet in Congress on the first Monday in November, in every year, with a power reserved to each state, to recall its delegates, or any of them, at any time within the year, and to send others in their stead, for the remainder of the Year.

No state shall be represented in Congress by less than two, nor by more than seven Members; and no person shall be capable of being a delegate for more than three years in any term of six years; nor shall any person, being a delegate, be capable of holding any office under the united states, for which he, or another for his benefit receives any salary, fees or emolument of any kind.

Each state shall maintain its own delegates in a meeting of the states, and while they act as members of the committee of the states.

In determining questions in the united states, in Congress assembled, each state shall have one vote.

Freedom of speech and debate in Congress shall not be impeached or questioned in any Court, or place out of Congress, and the members of congress shall be protected in their persons from arrests and imprisonments, during the time of their going to and from, and attendance on congress, except for treason, felony, or breach of the peace.

[ART. VI.] No state without the Consent of the united states in congress assembled, shall send any embassy to, or recieve any embassy from, or enter into any confer rence, agreement, or alliance or treaty with any King, prince or state; nor shall any person holding any office of profit or trust under the united states, or any of them, accept of any present, emolument, office or title of any kind whatever from any king, prince or foreign state; nor shall the united states in congress assembled, or any of them, grant any title of nobility.

No two or more states shall enter into any treaty, confederation or alliance whatever between them, without the consent of the united states in congress assembled, specifying accurately the purposes for which the same is to be entered into, and how long it shall continue.

No state shall lay any imposts or duties, which may interfere with any stipulations in treaties, entered into by the united states in congress assembled, with any king, prince or state, in pursuance of any treaties already proposed by congress, to the courts of France and Spain.

No vessels of war shall be kept up in time of peace by any state, except such number only, as shall be deemed necessary by the united states in congress assembled, for the defence of such state, or its trade; nor shall any body of forces be kept up by any state, in time of peace, except such number only, as in the judgment of the united states, in congress assembled, shall be deemed requisite to garrison the forts necessary for the defence of such state; but every state shall always keep up a well regulated and disciplined militia, sufficiently armed and accounted, and shall provide and constantly have ready for use, in public stores, a due number of field pieces and tents, and a proper quantity of arms, ammunition and camp equipage.

No state shall engage in any war without the consent of the united states in congress assembled, unless such state be actually invaded by enemies, or shall have received certain advice of a resolution being formed by some nation of Indians to invade such state and the danger is so imminent as not to admit of a delay, till the united states in congress assembled can be consulted: nor shall any state grant commissions to any ships or vessels of war, nor letters of marque or reprisal, except it be after a declaration of war by the united states in congress assembled, and then only against the kingdom or state and the subjects thereof, against which war has been so declared, and under such regulations as shall be established by the united states in congress assembled, unless such state be infested by pirates, in which case vessels of war may be fitted out for that occasion, and kept so long as the danger shall continue, or until the united states in congress assembled shall determine otherwise.

[ART. VII.] When land-forces are raised by any

state for the common defence, all officers of or under the rank of colonel, shall be appointed by the legislature of each state respectively by whom such forces shall be raised, or in such manner as such state shall direct, and all vacancies shall be filled up by the state which first made the appointment.

[ART. VIII.] All charges of war, and all other expences that shall be incurred for the common defence or general welfare, and allowed by the united states in congress assembled, shall be defrayed out of a common treasury, which shall be supplied by the several states, in proportion to the value of all land within each state, granted to or surveyed for any Person, as such land and the buildings and improvements thereon shall be estimated according to such mode as the united states in congress assembled, shall from time to time direct and appoint. The taxes for paying that proportion shall be laid and levied by the authority and direction of the legislatures of the several states within the time agreed upon by the united states in congress assembled.

[ART. IX.] The united states in congress assembled, shall have the sole and exclusive right and power of determining on peace and war, except in the cases mentioned in the sixth article—of sending and receiving ambassadors—entering into treaties and alliances, provided that no treaty of commerce shall be made whereby the legislative power of the respective states shall be restrained from imposing such imposts and duties on foreigners, as their own people are subjected to, or from prohibiting the exportation or importation of any species of goods or commodities whatsoever—of establishing rules for deciding in all cases, what captures on land or water shall be legal, and in what manner prizes taken by land or naval forces in the service of the united states shall be divided or appropriated.—of granting letters of marque and reprisal in times of peace—appointing courts for the trial of piracies and felonies committed on the high seas and establishing courts for receiving and determining finally appeals in all cases of captures, provided that no member of congress shall be appointed a judge of any of the said courts.

The united states in congress assembled shall also be the last resort on appeal in all disputes and differences now subsisting or that hereafter may arise between two or more states concerning boundary, jurisdiction or any other cause whatever; which authority shall always be exercised in the manner following. Whenever the legislative or executive authority or lawful agent of any state in controversy with another shall present a petition to congress stating the matter in question and praying for a hearing, notice thereof shall be given by order of congress to the legislative or executive authority of the other state in controversy, and a day assigned for the appearance of the parties by their lawful agents, who shall then be directed to appoint by joint consent, commissioners or judges to constitute a court for hearing and determining the matter in question: but if they cannot agree, congress shall name three persons out of each of the united states, and from the list of such persons each party shall alternately strike out one, the petitioners beginning, until the number shall be reduced to thirteen; and from that number not less than seven, nor more than nine names as congress shall direct, shall in the presence of congress be drawn out by lot, and the persons whose names shall be so drawn or any five of them, shall be commissioners or judges, to hear and finally determine the controversy, so always as a major part of the judges who shall hear the cause shall agree in the determination: and if either party shall neglect to attend at the day appointed, without shewing reasons, which congress shall judge sufficient, or being present shall refuse to strike, the congress shall proceed to nominate three persons out of each state, and the secretary of congress shall strike in behalf of such party absent or refusing; and the judgment and sentence of the court to be appointed, in the manner before prescribed, shall be final and conclusive; and if any of the parties shall refuse to submit to the authority of such court, or to appear to defend their claim or cause, the court shall nevertheless proceed to pronounce sentence, or judgment, which shall in like manner be final and decisive, the judgment or sentence and other proceedings being in either case transmitted to congress, and lodged among the acts of congress for the security of the parties concerned: provided that every commissioner, before he sits in judgment, shall take an oath to be administered by one of the judges of the supreme or superior court of the state, where the cause shall be tried, "well and truly to hear and determine the matter in question, according to the best of his judgment, without favour, affection or hope of reward:" provided also that no state shall be deprived of territory for the benefit of the united states.

All controversies concerning the private right of soil claimed under different grants of two or more states, whose jurisdictions as they may respect such lands, and the states which passed such grants are adjusted, the said grants or either of them being at the same time claimed to have originated antecedent to such settlement of jurisdiction, shall on the petition of either party to the congress of the united states, be finally determined as near as may be in the same manner as is before prescribed for deciding disputes respecting territorial jurisdiction between different states.

The united states in congress assembled shall also have the sole and exclusive right and power of regulating the alloy and value of coin struck by their own authority, or by that of the respective states—fixing the standard of weights and measures throughout the united states.—regulating the trade and managing all affairs with the Indians, not members of any of the states, provided that the legislative right of any state within its own limits be not infringed or violated—establishing and regulating post-offices from one state to another, throughout all the united states, and exacting such postage on the papers passing thro' the same as may be requisite to defray the expences of the said office—appointing all officers of the land forces, in the service of the united states, excepting regimental officers.—appointing all the officers of the naval forces, and commissioning all officers whatever in the service of the united states—making rules for the government and regulation of the said land and naval forces, and directing their operations.

The united states in congress assembled shall have authority to appoint a committee, to sit in the recess of congress, to be denominated "A Committee of the States," and to consist of one delgate from each state; and to appoint such other committees and civil officers as may be necessary for managing the general affairs of the united states under their direction—to appoint one of their number to preside, provided that no person be allowed to serve in the office of president more than one year in any term of three years; to ascertain the necessary sums of Money to be raised for the service of the united states, and to appropriate and apply the same for defraying the public expences —to borrow money, or emit bills on the credit of the united states, transmitting every half year to the respective states an account of the sums of money so borrowed or emitted,—to build and equip a navy—to agree upon the number of land forces, and to make requisitions from each state for its quota, in proportion to the number of white inhabitants in such state; which requisition shall be binding, and thereupon the legislature of each state shall appoint the regimental officers, raise the men and cloath, arm and equip them in a soldier like manner, at the expence of the united states, and the officers and men so cloathed, armed and equipped shall march to the place appointed, and within the time agreed on by the united states in congress assembled: But if the united states in congress assembled shall, on consideration of circumstances judge proper that any state should not raise men, or should raise a smaller number than its quota, and that any other state should raise a greater number of men than the quota thereof, such extra number shall be raised, officered, cloathed, armed and equipped in the same manner as the quota of such state, unless the legislature of such state shall judge that such extra number cannot be safely spared out of the same, in which case they shall raise officer, cloath, arm and equip as many of such extra number as they judge can be safely spared. And the officers and men so cloathed, armed and equipped, shall march to the place appointed, and within the time agreed on by the united states in congress assembled.

The united states in congress assembled shall never engage in a war, nor grant letters of marque and reprisal in time of peace, nor enter into any treaties or alliances, nor coin money, nor regulate the value thereof, nor ascertain the sums and expences necessary for the defence and welfare of the united states, or any of them, nor emit bills, nor borrow money on the credit of the united states, nor appropriate money, nor agree upon the number of vessels of war, to be built or purchased, or the number of land or sea forces to be raised, nor appoint a commander in chief of the army or navy, unless nine states assent to the same: nor shall a question on any other point, except for adjourning from day to day be determined, unless by the votes of a majority of the united states in congress assembled.

The congress of the united states shall have power to adjourn to any time within the year, and to any place within the united states, so that no period of adjournment be for a longer duration than the space of six Months, and shall publish the Journal of their proceedings monthly, except such parts thereof relating to treaties, alliances or military operations as in their judgment require secresy; and the yeas and nays of the delegates of each state on any question shall be entered on the Journal, when it is desired by any delegate; and the delegates of a state, or any of them, at his or their request shall be furnished with a transcript of the said Journal, except such parts as are above excepted, to lay before the legislatures of the several states.

[Art. X.] The committee of the states, or any nine of them, shall be authorised to execute, in the recess of congress, such of the powers of congress as the united states in congress assembled, by the consent of nine states, shall from time to time think expedient to vest them with; provided that no power be delegated to the said committee, for the exercise of which, by the articles of confederation, the voice of nine states in the congress of the united states assembled is requisite.

[Art. XI.] Canada acceding to this confederation, and joining in the measures of the united states, shall be admitted into, and entitled to all the advantages of this union: but no other colony shall be admitted into the same, unless such admission be agreed to by nine states.

[Art. XII.] All bills of credit emitted, monies borrowed and debts contracted by, or under the authority of congress, before the assembling of the united states, in pursuance of the present confederation, shall be deemed and considered as a charge against the united states, for payment and satisfaction whereof the said united states, and the public faith are hereby solemnly pledged.

[Art. XIII.] Every state shall abide by the determinations of the united states in congress assembled, on all questions which by this confederation are submitted to them. And the Articles of this confederation shall be inviolably observed by every state, and the union shall be perpetual; nor shall any alteration at any time hereafter be made in any of them; unless such alteration be agreed to in a congress of the united states, and be afterwards confirmed by the legislatures of every state.

And whereas it hath pleased the Great Governor of the World to incline the hearts of the legislatures we respectively represent in congress, to approve of, and to authorize us to ratify the said articles of confederation and perpetual union. Know ye that we the undersigned delegates, by virtue of the power and authority to us given for that purpose, do by these presents, in the name and in behalf of our respective constituents, fully and entirely ratify and confirm each and every of the said articles of confederation and perpetual union, and all and singular the matters and things therein contained: And we do further solemnly plight and engage the faith of our respective constituents, that they shall abide by the determinations of the united states in congress assembled, on all questions, which by the said confederation are submitted to them. And that the articles thereof shall be inviolably observed by the states we respectively represent, and that the union shall be perpetual. In Witness whereof we have hereunto set our hands in Congress. Done at Philadelphia in the state of Pennsylvania the ninth Day of July in the Year of our Lord one Thousand seven Hundred and Seventy-eight, and in the third year of the independence of America.

Josiah Bartlett
John Wentworth
Junr August 8th 1778
On the part & behalf of the State of New Hampshire

John Hancock
Samuel Adams
Elbridge Gerry
Francis Dana
James Lovell
Samuel Holten
On the part and behalf of The State of Massachusetts Bay

William Ellery
Henry Marchant
John Collins
On the part and behalf of the State of Rhode-Island and Providence Plantations

Roger Sherman
Samuel Huntington
Oliver Wolcott
Titus Hosmer
Andrew Adams
On the part and behalf of the State of Connecticut

Jas Duane
Fras Lewis
Wm Duer.
Gouv Morris
On the Part and Behalf of the State of New York

Jno Witherspoon
Nathl Scudder
On the Part and in Behalf of the State of New Jersey. Novr 26, 1778.—

Robt morris
Daniel Roberdeau
Jona bayard Smith.
William Clingan
Joseph Reed
22d July 1778
On the part and behalf of the State of Pennsylvania

Tho M:Kean
Feby 12 1779
John Dickinson
May 5th 1779
Nicholas Van Dyke,
On the part & behalf of the State of Delaware

John Hanson
March 1 1781
Daniel Carroll do
On the part and behalf of the State of Maryland

Richard Henry Lee
John Banister
Thomas Adams
Jno Harvie
Francis Lightfoot Lee
On the Part and Behalf of the State of Virginia

John Penn
July 21st 1778
Corns Harnett
Jno Williams
On the part and Behalf of the State of No Carolina

Henry Laurens
William Henry Drayton
Jno Mathews
Richd Hutson.
Thos Heyward Junr
On the part & behalf of the State of South-Carolina

Jno Walton
24th July 1778
Edwd Telfair.
Edwd Langworthy
On the part & behalf of the State of Georgia

GEORGE WASHINGTON'S FAREWELL ADDRESS

In his Farewell Address (September 19, 1796), Washington presented his reasons for retiring from the presidency, his views on the necessity for a strong union of states, and his warnings against the "baneful effect" of political parties and of "foreign entanglements." The excerpts that follow focus on his comments on the "true policy" that the United States should follow in the conduct of its relations with foreign nations.

Observe good faith and justice toward all nations. Cultivate peace and harmony with all. Religion and morality enjoin this conduct. And can it be that good policy does not equally enjoin it? It will be worthy of a free, enlightened, and, at no distant period, a great nation to give to mankind the magnanimous and too novel example of a people always guided by an exalted justice and benevolence. . . .

In the execution of such a plan nothing is more essential than that permanent, inveterate antipathies against particular nations and passionate attachments for others should be excluded, and that, in place of them, just and amicable feelings toward all should be cultivated. The nation which indulges toward another an habitual hatred or an habitual fondness is in some degree a slave. It is a slave to its animosity or to its affection, either of which is sufficient to lead it astray from its duty and its interest. . . .

The nation prompted by ill will and resentment sometimes impels to war the government, contrary to the best calculations of policy. The government sometimes participates in the national propensity, and adopts through passion what reason would reject. . . .

So, likewise, a passionate attachment of one nation for another produces a variety of evils. Sympathy for the favorite nation, facilitating the illusion of an imaginary common interest in cases where no real common interest exists, and infusing into one the enmities of the other, betrays the former into a participation in the quarrels and wars of the latter without adequate inducement or justification. . . .

As avenues to foreign influence in innumerable ways, such attachments are particularly alarming to the truly enlightened and independent patriot. How many opportunities do they afford to tamper with domestic factions, to practice the arts of seduction, to mislead public opinion, to influence or awe the public councils! Such an attachment of a small or weak toward a great and powerful nation dooms the former to be the satellite of the latter.

Against the insidious wiles of foreign influence (I conjure you to believe me, fellow citizens) the jealousy of a free people ought to be *constantly* awake, since history and experience prove that foreign influence is one of the most baneful foes of republican government. . . .

The great rule of conduct for us in regard to foreign nations is, in extending our commercial relations, to have with them as little *political* connection as possible. So far as we have already formed engagements [French treaty], let them be fulfilled with perfect good faith. Here let us stop.

Europe has a set of primary interests which to us have none, or a very remote, relation. Hence she must be engaged in frequent controversies, the causes of which are essentially foreign to our concerns. Hence, therefore, it must be unwise in us to implicate ourselves by artificial ties in the ordinary vicissitudes of her politics, or the ordinary combinations and collisions of her friendships or enmities.

Our detached and distant situation invites and enables us to pursue a different course. If we remain one people, under an efficient government, the period is not far off when we may defy material injury from external annoyance; when we may take such an attitude as will cause the neutrality we may at any time resolve upon to be scrupulously respected; when, belligerent nations, under the impossibility of making acquisitions upon us, will not lightly hazard the giving us provocation; when we may choose peace or war, as our interest, guided by justice, shall counsel.

Why forgo the advantages of so peculiar a situation? Why quit our own to stand upon foreign ground? Why, by interweaving our destiny with that of any part of Europe, entangle our peace and prosperity in the toils of European ambition, rivalship, interest, humor, or caprice?

It is our true policy to steer clear of permanent alliances with any portion of the foreign world, so far, I mean, as we are now at liberty to do it. For let me not be understood as capable of patronizing infidelity to existing engagements. I hold the maxim no less applicable to public than to private affairs that honesty is always the best policy. I repeat, therefore, let those engagements be observed in their genuine sense. But in my opinion it is unnecessary and would be unwise to extend them.

Taking care always to keep ourselves by suitable establishments on a respectable defensive posture, we may safely trust to temporary alliances for extraordinary emergencies.

Harmony, liberal intercourse with all nations, are recommended by policy, humanity, and interest. But even our commercial policy should hold an equal and impartial hand, neither seeking nor granting exclusive favors or preference; . . . constantly keeping in view that it is folly in one nation to look for disinterested favors from another; that it must pay with a portion of its independence for whatever it may accept under that character; that by such acceptance it may place itself in the condition of having given equivalents for nominal favors, and yet of being reproached with ingratitude for not giving more. There can be no greater error than to expect or calculate upon real favors from nation to nation. It is an illusion which experience must cure, which a just pride ought to discard.

AMERICAN'S CREED

I believe in the United States of America as a government of the people, by the people, for the people; whose just powers are derived from the consent of the governed; a democracy in a Republic; a sovereign Nation of many sovereign States; a perfect Union, one and inseparable; established upon those principles of freedom, equality, justice, and humanity for which American patriots sacrificed their lives and fortunes.

"I therefore believe it is my duty to my country to love it; to support its Constitution; to obey its laws; to respect its flag; and to defend it against all enemies."

PLEDGE OF ALLEGIANCE

I pledge allegiance
to the Flag
of the United States of America,
and to the Republic
for which it stands,
one Nation under God,
indivisible,
with liberty
and justice for all.

THE EMANCIPATION PROCLAMATION

Whereas on the 22d day of September, A.D. 1862, a proclamation was issued by the President of the United States, containing, among other things, the following, to wit:

"That on the 1st day of January, A.D. 1863, all persons held as slaves within any State or designated part of a State the people whereof shall then be in rebellion against the United States shall be then, thenceforward, and forever free; and the executive government of the United States, including the military and naval authority thereof, will recognize and maintain the freedom of such persons and will do no act or acts to repress such persons, or any of them, in any efforts they may make for their actual freedom.

"That the executive will on the 1st day of January aforesaid, by proclamation, designate the States and parts of States, if any, in which the people thereof, respectively, shall then be in rebellion against the United States; and the fact that any State or the people thereof shall on that day be in good faith represented in the Congress of the United States by members chosen thereto at elections wherein a majority of the qualified voters of such States shall have participated shall, in the absence of strong countervailing testimony, be deemed conclusive evidence that such State and the people thereof are not then in rebellion against the United States."

Now, therefore, I, Abraham Lincoln, President of the United States, by virtue of the power in me vested as Commander-in-Chief of the Army and Navy of the United States in time of actual armed rebellion against the authority and government of the United States, and as a fit and necessary war measure for suppressing said rebellion, do, on this 1st day of January, A.D. 1863, and in accordance with my purpose so to do, publicly proclaimed for the full period of one hundred days from the first day above mentioned, order and designate as the States and parts of States wherein the people thereof, respectively, are this day in rebellion against the United States the following, to wit:

Arkansas, Texas, Louisiana (except the parishes of St. Bernard, Plaquemines, Jefferson, St. John, St. Charles, St. James, Ascension, Assumption, Terrebonne, Lafourche, St. Mary, St. Martin, and Orleans, including the city of New Orleans), Mississippi, Alabama, Florida, Georgia, South Carolina, North Carolina, and Virginia (except the forty-eight counties designated as West Virginia, and also the counties of Berkeley, Accomac, Northhampton, Elizabeth City, York, Princess Anne, and Norfolk, including the cities of Norfolk and Portsmouth), and which excepted parts are for the present left precisely as if this proclamation were not issued.

And by virtue of the power and for the purpose aforesaid, I do order and declare that all persons held as slaves within said designated States and parts of States are, and henceforward shall be, free; and that the Executive Government of the United States, including the military and naval authorities thereof, will recognize and maintain the freedom of said persons.

And I hereby enjoin upon the people so declared to be free to abstain from all violence, unless in necessary self-defense; and I recommend to them that, in all cases when allowed, they labor faithfully for reasonable wages.

And I further declare and make known that such persons of suitable condition will be received into the armed service of the United States to garrison forts, positions, stations, and other places, and to man vessels of all sorts in said service.

And upon this act, sincerely believed to be an act of justice, warranted by the Constitution upon military necessity, I invoke the considerate judgment of mankind and the gracious favor of Almighty God.

THE MAYFLOWER COMPACT

In ye name of God Amen. We whose names are underwritten, the loyall subjects of our dread soveraigne Lord King James, by ye grace of God, of Great Britaine, Franc, & Ireland king, defender of ye faith, & c. Haveing undertaken, for ye glorie of God, and advancemente of ye Christian faith and honour of our king & countrie, a voyage to plant ye first colonie in ye Northerne parts of Virginia, doe by these presents solemnly & mutualy in ye presence of God, and one of another, covenant, & combine ourselves togeather into a Civill body politick; for our better ordering, & preservation & furtherance of ye ends aforesaid; and by vertue hereof to enacte, constitute, and frame such just & equall Lawes, ordinances, Acts, constitutions, & offices, from time to time, as shall be thought most meete & convenient for ye generall good of ye colonie: unto which we promise all due submission and obedience. In witnes whereof we have hereunder subscribed our names at Cap-Codd ye -11- of November, in ye year of ye raigne of our soveraigne Lord King James of England, France, & Ireland ye eighteenth, and of Scotland ye fiftie fourth. Ano Dom. 1620.

Glossary

Number(s) after each definition refer to page(s) where the term is discussed.

Act of admission A Congressional act admitting a United States territory into the Union as a State. 89

Administration The officials and agencies of the executive branch which carry out the public policies established by the legislative branch of the government. 429

Administrative law Law made up of the rules, orders, regulations issued (under proper constitutional and/or statutory authority) by officers and agencies in the executive branch. 609

Affirmative action Policy that requires that both public and private organizations take positive steps to overcome the effects of past discrimination against blacks, women, and other minority groups, especially in employment and education. 164

Alien One who is not a citizen (or national) of the state in which he/she lives; usually, an alien owes allegiance to a foreign power but may gain citizenship by naturalization. 99

Ambassador A personal representative appointed by the head of a nation to represent that nation in matters of diplomacy. 476

Amendment A change in, or addition to, a constitution. 60, 544

Amnesty A general pardon offered to a group of law violators. 425

Anarchy The total absence of government. 16

Annexation An addition to the territory of a city as provided by the State constitution or by an act of the legislature. 633

Anti-Federalists Those persons who opposed the adoption of the Constitution in 1787–1788. 49

Antitrust laws Legislation designed to prevent the formation or continuation of monopolies or other organizations which act in restraint of trade. 693

Appeal Legal proceeding in which a case is carried from a lower court to a higher court for review. 523

Appellate jurisdiction Exercise of judicial authority in courts of appeal that stand between the trial courts and the States' highest courts to ease the burden of the higher court in deciding whether a law was correctly interpreted by the lower court; limited to a few specific cases presented by attorneys in oral argument and briefs (written arguments). 600

Apportionment Distribution of seats in a legislative body among electoral districts; *e.g.*, the allocation of the 435 seats in the House of Representatives among the 50 States according to their respective populations. 296, 559

Appropriations Legislative grants of money for a specific purpose. 465

Assessment The process of determining the value of property for purposes of taxation. 651

At-large An election in which an official is selected by the voters of a major district rather than those of a subdivision thereof. 299

Authoritarian Form of government in which individual liberty is completely subordinate to the authority of the state, which is itself controlled by one person or a small group; see *dictatorship.* 9

Bail Money the accused may be required to post (deposit with the court) as a guarantee that he/she will appear in court at the proper time. 152

Bankruptcy Court action to release a person or corporation from unpaid debts. 350

Bench trial A misdemeanor or civil proceeding (often heard without a jury) in which only minor sums are involved. 608

Bicameral Having two houses in the legislative body. 31, 293, 557

Bill A proposal presented to a legislative body for possible enactment as a law. 325

Bill of attainder Legislative act which inflicts punishment upon a particular person or group without a court trial. 142

Bill of Rights First 10 amendments to the Constitution, dealing mostly with civil rights. 63, 98, 542

Blanket primary An election in which candidates for the same office are grouped on the ballot without regard to party affiliation. 236

Block grant One type of federal grants-in-aid to the States and/or their local governments; block-grant monies are to be used in some particular but broadly defined area of public policy *(e.g.,* education or highways). 83

Borough The Alaskan term for county; see *counties,* 615

Boycott Refusal to buy or sell an opponent's goods in order to influence his/her behavior. 34

Brief Document prepared by an attorney and submitted to a court, setting forth arguments and citing evidence in a client's behalf. 525

Budget Both a financial plan and a political document; a detailed statement of estimated receipts (revenue, income) and planned expenditures (spending, outgo) during a specified period (usually a fiscal year). 404

Bureaucracy Any large, complex administrative structure; the hierarchical organization of positions and agencies in the executive branch of a government. 429

By-elections Special elections held in the constituency of a member of parliament who either resigned or died. 668

Cabinet Presidential advisory body, traditionally composed of the heads of the executive departments and those other officers *(e.g.,* the Vice President) the President may choose to appoint to it. 406

Capitalism Economic system based on private (individual and corporate) ownership of the means of producing goods and services and upon private initiative, competition, and profit, often referred to as the free enterprise or private enterprise system; see *free enterprise, laissez-faire, mixed economy, private enterprise.* 17

Capitalist One who embraces the economic system of capitalism (in which goods and services are produced under a free enterprise system); see *capital-*

ism, free enterprise, laissez-faire, mixed economy, private enterprise. 692

Caucus A meeting of a group of like-minded persons to select the candidates they will support in an upcoming election; see *legislative caucus, party caucus.* 232

Censure Empowerment by members of each chamber of a legislative body to discipline members for improper conduct. 301

Certificate A method of putting a case before the Supreme Court; a process used when a lower court is not clear about the procedure or the rule of law that should apply in a case, and asks the Supreme Court to certify the answer to a specific question in the matter. 523

Certiorari, writ of Order issued by a higher court directing a lower court to send up the record of a case for its review. 523

Charter City's basic law, granted by the State, which defines its boundaries, sets out its powers, and outlines its form of government. 30, 631

Checks and balances System of overlapping the powers of the separate legislative, executive, and judicial branches of a government, to permit each branch to check (restrain, balance) the actions of the others; see *separation of powers.* 56, 541

Citizen One who owes allegiance to a state and is entitled to its protection; American citizenship may be acquired by birth (1) in the United States or (2) to American citizen-parents abroad, and (3) by naturalization. 167

Civil law That body of law relating to human conduct, including disputes between private persons and between private persons and government, not covered by criminal law. 609

Civil rights Constitutionally guaranteed rights to freedom of expression, freedom and security of the person, fair trial, and fair and equal treatment by the law. 38, 98

Civil service Collective term for most civilian employees of a government, especially those hired through a merit system, (elected officials, top-ranking policy-makers appointed by them, and judges are not considered part of the civil service). 459

Closed primary Form of the direct primary in which only party members may vote; see *open primary.* 236

Cloture Procedure that may be used to limit or end floor debate in a legislative body (especially to cut off a filibuster). 336

Coalition An alliance of political groups. 668

Coattail effect Influence a popular candidate for a top office *(e.g.,* President or governor) can have on the voters' support of other candidates of his/her party on the same ballot. 242

Cold War Period of political and ideological conflict, tensions between the United States and the Soviet Union since World War II. 495

Collective security Basic purpose of the U.N. and a major goal of American foreign policy, to create a worldwide system in which all or most nations agree to take joint action to meet any threat to or breach of international peace. 493

Collectivized Under public or group ownership. 707

Command economies Economic systems in which the government directs the economy along a government-determined path. 700

Commerce power Exclusive power of Congress to regulate interstate and foreign trade. 348

Commission form Form of city government in which elected commissioners serve collectively as the city council and separately as heads of the city's administrative department. 635

Committee chairman Member who heads a standing committee in either chamber of Congress; see *standing committee.* 317

Committee of the Whole The House of Representatives viewed as one large committee rather than as the House. 331

Common law That body of law made up of generally accepted standards of rights and wrongs developed over centuries by judicial decisions rather than in written statutes, a major basis of the American legal system, often called "judge-made law"; see *equity.* 609

Communism Economic and political system built on the theories of Karl Marx, based on the collective (centralized state) ownership and control of property and the means of production, with all individuals expected to contribute to society according to ability and receive from it according to need; an extreme form of socialism. 21

Commutation The power to reduce the length of a sentence for a crime. 425

Compromise The resolution of conflict in which concessions are made by all parties to achieve a common goal. 14

Concurrent powers Powers held by both the National Government and the States in the federal system *(e.g.,* powers to tax and to define and punish crimes). 76

Concurrent resolution Measure passed by both houses of a legislature that does not have the force of law nor require the chief executive's approval; often used to express the legislature's opinion on an issue or for internal rules or housekeeping purposes; see *joint resolution.* 326

Concurring opinion Written explanation of the views of one or more judges who support a decision reached by a majority of the court but disagree with the grounds for that decision. 525

Confederation Form of government in which an alliance of independent states (regional governments) creates a degree of national unity through a central government of very limited power; the member states have supreme authority (sovereignty) over all matters except in those few areas in which they have expressly delegated power to the central government. 7

Conference committee Temporary joint committee of both houses of a legislature, created to reconcile (compromise) any differences between the two houses' versions of a bill. 323

Consensus General agreement or accord. 677

Constituent All of the residents represented by a legislator or other elected officeholder. 305

Constitution Body of fundamental (supreme) law, setting out the basic principles, structures, processes, and functions of a government and placing limits upon its actions; may be written (as in the United States) or unwritten (as in Great Britain). 54

Constitutionalism Basic principle that government and those who govern are bound by (must obey) the fundamental law (the constitution); the rule of law; see *limited government.* 56

Constitutional law The highest form of law, that based upon the provisions of the Constitution of the United

States and the State constitution, and judicial interpretations of them. 609

Containment Basic feature of American foreign policy since World War II, resistance to the expansion of Soviet power and influence in world politics. 495

Copyright The exclusive, legal right of a person to reproduce, publish, or sell his own literary, musical, or artistic creations. 351

Corporations Businesses that are owned by shareholders and which are authorized to act as single individuals under the law. 695

Council-manager plan Form of city government with an elected council as the policy-making body and an appointed, professional administrator (city manager) responsible to the council for the running of the city's government. 636

Counties The major units of local government in most States; existing as agencies of the State and empowered in law enforcement, welfare agencies, and maintenance of highways, schools, and courts. 615

County-manager plan Legislative policymaking body, the elected county board, whose executive function is carried out by a manager hired by and answering to the board. 622

Criminal law That body of law which defines crimes (public wrongs, offenses against public order) and provides for their punishment. 609

Customs duties Taxes (tariffs) on goods brought into the United States; see *tariff*. 469

De facto segregation Racial or other segregation *(e.g.,* in schools or housing) that exists "in fact," because of private rather than governmental actions; see *de jure segregation*. 160

Defendant In a civil suit, the person (party) against whom a court action is brought by the plaintiff; in a criminal case, the person charged with (accused of) the crime. 516

De jure segregation Racial or other segregation that exists "by law," as a result of some governmental action *(e.g.,* a statute or an administrative decision); see *segregation*. 158

Delegated powers Those powers (expressed, implied, inherent) granted to the National Government by the Constitution. 73

Democracy System of government in which supreme authority rests with the people (popular sovereignty, the people rule); may be direct, where the people make public policies by their votes, or representative, where the people choose public officeholders to act in their behalf. 3

Democratic centralism Method by which lower echelons of the Communist Party debate and pass on decisions to the higher party organization; in practice decision-making is made by the higher officials. 684

Denaturalization Court revocation of naturalized citizenship through due process of law; often used for subversives or those who misrepresented themselves in the naturalization process. 170

Deputies Members of the French National Assembly chosen for a five-year term by popular election. 673

Deterrence Basic feature of American foreign policy, to maintain such massive military strength that that very fact will tend to prevent (deter) any attack upon this country or its allies. 494

Dictatorship Form of government in which the power to govern is held by one person or a small group; see *totalitarian*. 9

Diplomatic immunity An exception to the laws of sovereignty whereby ambassadors of foreign governments are not subject to all the laws of the state to which they are accredited. 477

Direct democracy A system of government in which the people participate directly in decision making through the voting process. 11

Direct primary See *open primary*. 235

Direct tax A tax levied by and paid directly to the government. 345

Discharge petition A petition to bring a bill back into consideration after it has been tabled (put aside) by Congress. 328

Dissenting opinion Written explanation of the views of one or more judges who disagree with (dissent from) a decision reached by a majority of the court; see *majority opinion*. 525

Dissolution Disintegration into fragments or parts. 678

Division of powers Basic principle of federalism; the constitutional provisions by which governmental powers are divided between units of government on a geographic basis (in the United States, between the National Government and the States); see *federalism*. 73

Double jeopardy Trial a second time for a crime of which the accused was acquitted in the first trial; prohibited by the 5th and 14th Amendments. 144

Draft Compulsory service in the military. 487

Due process The constitutional guarantee to apply fair and consistent legal procedures in courts of law to protect citizens against arbitrary actions by the government. 129

Due Process Clause Constitutional guarantee (in the 5th and 14th Amendments) that government will not deprive a person of life, liberty, or property unfairly, arbitrarily, unreasonably; see *due process*. 101

Electoral college Group of persons (presidential electors) chosen in each State and the District of Columbia every four years who make a formal selection of the President and Vice President. 377

Electorate All of the persons entitled to vote in a given election. 205

Eminent domain Power of a government to take private property for a public use. 352

Enabling act A congressional act that allows the people of a United States territory to prepare a constitution and thus become eligible for admission into the Union. 89

Entrepreneur A person who organizes, operates, and assumes the risk for a business enterprise. 692

Equal time doctrine A rule in the Communications Act of 1934 providing that if a radio, television station, or network makes air time available to one candidate for a public office, it must offer time to all other candidates for that office on the same terms. 117

Equity That body of law developed to supplement the common law, to provide justice in cases where the common law falls short of that goal; see *injunction*. 610

Espionage Spying for a foreign power. 120

Estate tax A tax levied directly on the estate of a deceased person; see *inheritance tax.* 467, 652

Excessive entanglement standard A three-pronged test to ensure that only nonreligious activities in a parochial school may benefit from a State's school aid laws. 108

Excise taxes Taxes levied on the production, transportation, sale, or consumption of goods or services; see *sales tax.* 467

Exclusionary rule A guarantee adopted by the Supreme Court stating that evidence gained as the result of an illegal act by police officers cannot be used against the person from whom it was seized. 138

Exclusive powers Most of the delegated powers; those held by the National Government alone (exclusively) in the federal system. 76

Executive agreement Pact made by the President with the head of a foreign state; a binding international agreement with the force of law but which (unlike a treaty) does not require Senate approval. 65, 420

Executive branch The section of a presidential style of government responsible for executing the laws enacted by the legislature. 7, 56

Executive orders Rules, regulations issued by a chief executive *(e.g.,* the President or a governor) or his/her subordinates, based upon either constitutional or statutory authority and having the force of law. 415

Expatriation Act by which one renounces (forfeits, gives up) his or her citizenship. 168

Ex post facto law Criminal law applied retroactively (before the fact) to the disadvantage of the accused; prohibited by the Constitution. 143

Expressed powers Those delegated powers of the National Government which are given to it in so many words (expressly, literally) by the Constitution. 73

Extradition Legal process by which a fugitive from justice in one State is returned (extradited) to it from another State. 87

Fairness doctrine An FCC rule that says that radio and television broadcasters must present all sides of important public issues. 117

Federal government A system of government characterized by a division of powers between a central government and several geographically determined regional governments. 7

Federalism Form of government based on a constitutional division of powers on a geographic basis *(e.g.,* in the United States between the National Government and the States). 58, 72

Federalists Those persons who supported the adoption of the Constitution in 1787–1788; most of them became members of the Federalist Party after the Constitution became effective in 1789. 49

Felony Serious criminal offense *(e.g.,* murder, robbery) punishable by correspondingly severe penalties; see *misdemeanor.* 598

Filibuster Various tactics (usually prolonged floor debate) aimed at defeating a bill in a legislative body by preventing a final vote on it; this practice of "talking a bill to death" is most often associated with the U.S. Senate; see *cloture.* 334

Fiscal year Twelve-month period used by a government for its record-keeping, budgeting, revenue-collecting, and other financial management purposes; the National Government's fiscal year now runs from October 1 through the following September 30. 405

Foreign policy The actions and stands that every nation takes in every aspect of its relationships with other countries—diplomatic, military, commercial, and all others; everything a nation's government says and does in world affairs. 474

Formal amendment A modification in the Constitution brought about through one of four methods set forth in the Constitution. 60

Franchise Suffrage, the right to vote. 204

Free enterprise An economic system based on private ownership, individual initiative, profit, and competition; see *capitalism, private enterprise.* 17

Full Faith and Credit Clause Constitution's requirement (Article IV, Section 1) that each State accept (honor the validity of, give full faith and credit to) the public acts, records, and judicial proceedings of every other State. 87

General election Regularly scheduled election at which the voters choose (make the final selection of) public officeholders. 230

Gerrymandering Select legislative boundaries for the purpose of achieving a partisan advantage. 213, 299

Government That complex of offices, personnel, and processes by which a state is ruled, by which its public policies are made and enforced. 5

Grand jury Body of 12 to 23 persons convened by a court to decide whether or not there is enough evidence against a particular person to justify bringing that person to trial for a particular crime; see *indictment, petit jury.* 145, 604

Grants-in-aid programs Financial aid given (granted) by one government to another *(e.g.,* by the National Government to the States and/or their local governments), with the funds available subject to certain conditions ("strings") and to be used for certain purposes; see *block grants.* 82

Habeas corpus, writ of Court order that a prisoner be brought before the court and that the detaining officer *(e.g.,* sheriff, warden) show cause (explain, with good reason) why the prisoner should not be released; designed to prevent illegal arrests and unlawful imprisonments. 142

Home rule Powers of local self-government granted, in varying degree, by a State's constitution or statutes to cities and/or counties. 621

Impeachment Formal charge (accusation of misconduct) brought against a public official by the lower house in a legislative body; trial, and removal upon conviction, occurs in the upper house. 359, 581

Implied powers Those delegated powers of the National Government implied by (inferred from) the expressed powers; those "necessary and proper" to carry out the expressed powers; see *delegated powers, expressed powers.* 73, 354

Income tax A tax levied on individual and corporate income; the two together providing approximately 70 percent of total national tax receipts. 650

Incorporated The official status of a municipality as a legal body acknowledged by the State; from the Latin *in corpus* (into body). 630

Independent Regulatory Commission Agency semi-independent of the executive branch, with administrative and also quasi-legislative and quasi-judicial functions, designed to regulate some important aspect of the economy *(e.g.,* the Federal Trade Commission, the National Labor Relations Board). 453

Independents Voters who do not identify with or regularly support the candidates of any particular party. 227

Indictment (bill of) Accusation by a grand jury; a formal finding by that body that there is sufficient evidence against a named person to warrant his/her criminal trial. 145, 606

Indirect tax A tax, usually collected by a business, which the business passes on to the government. 346

Informal amendment A change made in the Constitution not by actual written amendment, but by the cumulative experience of government under the Constitution; the methods include: (1) legislation passed by Congress; (2) actions taken by the President; (3) decisions of the Supreme Court; (4) the activities of political parties; and (5) customs. 65

Information Formal charge of crime brought against a named person by the prosecutor (directly, rather than by a grand jury); see *indictment.* 607

Inherent powers Those delegated powers of the National Government which, although not expressly granted by the Constitution, belong to it because it is the national government of a sovereign state. 73

Inheritance tax A "death tax" levied on the beneficiary's share of an estate; see *estate tax.* 652

Initiative Petition process by which a certain percentage of voters can put a proposed constitutional amendment or statute on the ballot for popular approval or rejection; available in nearly half of the States, in either the direct or indirect form. 548

Injunction Court order which requires or forbids some specific action; may be either temporary or permanent. 213, 611

Institutions Established customs, laws, and practices of a society. 26

Interest group See *pressure group.* 275

Interim committee Committee in a legislative body which functions between legislative sessions; this group studies particular problems and then reports its findings and recommendations to the next session. 569

Interstate compact Formal agreement between or among States, authorized by the Constitution (Article I, Section 10), subject to approval by Congress. 86

Isolationism Basic part of American foreign policy until World War II; a policy of refusing to become generally involved in world affairs, of avoiding "entangling alliances." 473

Item veto Power held by 43 State governors (but not the President) to eliminate (veto) one or more provisions (items) in a bill without rejecting the entire measure; see *veto.* 571, 588

Joint committee Legislative committee composed of members of both houses. 323, 569

Joint resolution Legislative measure which must be passed by both houses and approved by the chief executive to become effective; similar to a bill, with the force of law, and often used for unusual or temporary purposes. 325

Judicial branch A nation's court system. 56

Judicial review Power of the courts to determine the constitutionality of the actions of the legislative and executive branches of government; a basic feature of the American system of government. 58, 520, 541

Judiciary Judicial branch of a government, its system of courts. 512

Jurisdiction Power of a court to hear (to try and decide) a case; literally, its power "to say the law." 514

Jus sanguinis Acquisition of American citizenship at birth, because of the citizenship of one or both parents; the "law of the blood," to whom born. 167

Jus soli Acquisition of American citizenship at birth, because of birth in the United States; the "law of the soil," where born. 167

Justices of the peace Elected officials who preside over minor civil cases and misdemeanors; jurisdiction is generally very limited; see *civil law, misdemeanor.* 597

Laissez-faire Economic doctrine advocating little or no government intervention in the economy; based on Adam Smith's view that if everyone pursues his/her own self-interest all will benefit; literally (French) "to let alone"; see *capitalism.* 18

Legislative branch The section of a presidential style of government responsible for enacting laws. 7, 56

Legislative caucus Meeting of all members of one party in a particular house of a legislature, to select floor leaders, fill committee posts, and plan strategy in the legislative session; see *caucus.* 233, 313

Libel Publication of statements that wrongfully damage another's reputation; see *slander.* 113

Liberal constructionist One who believes that the provisions of the Constitution, and in particular those granting power to government, are to be construed in broad terms. 342

Limited government Basic principle of the American system of government; that government is not all-powerful, that it may do only those things the people have given it the power to do; see *constitutionalism, popular sovereignty.* 28, 55, 97, 541

Literacy Test of a potential voter's ability to read and write; once used in several States to prevent voting by blacks (and/or other minorities) but now outlawed. 210

Lobbying Activities of an agent (lobbyist) for a pressure group, usually to influence the passage or defeat of legislation or the shape of administrative actions. 285

Majority At least one more than half *(e.g.,* over 50 percent of the votes in an election). 183

Majority floor leader Party leader and spokesman, selected by caucus, who directs party forces in legislative battles; see *majority whip.* 316

Majority opinion Written statement by a majority of the judges of a court in support of a decision made by that court. 525

Majority whip The assistant to the leader of the majority party in the legislature. 316

Major parties The dominant parties in a governmental system *(e.g.,* the Republicans or Democrats in American politics); see *minor party.* 179

Mandate Support for and/or commands relating to policy stands that a constituency gives to its elected officials. 266

Market economies Economic systems in which free enterprise cooperates with and is supported by government regulation. 699

Mass media Those means of communication which reach (inform, influence the opinions of) large audiences, especially television, radio, and newspapers. 263

Mayor-council (government) A unicameral form of city government featuring an elected mayor as chief executive and an elected council as the legislative body. 634

Merit system Hiring and promotion of government employees on the basis of qualifications and performance (demonstrated merit) rather than political or other considerations; see *civil service*. 464

Metropolitan areas Term for the large cities and the surrounding separate (but economically and socially integrated) communities. 642

Ministers British cabinet members. 668

Minority floor leader Party leader and spokesman, selected by caucus, who directs party forces in legislative battles; see *minority whip*. 316

Minority whip The assistant to the leader of a minority party in the legislature. 316

Minor/third party One of the less widely supported political parties in a governmental system *(e.g.,* the Libertarians and Socialists in American politics); see *major party*. 182

Miranda Rule A listing of the Constitutional rights which suspects must be advised of before police questioning; (1) that they have a right to remain silent; (2) that anything they say may be used against them in court; (3) that they have a right to an attorney before questioning begins; (4) that an attorney will be appointed for them by the court if they cannot afford one; (5) that they may bring the questioning to an end at any time. 151

Misdemeanor Crime less serious than a felony *(e.g.,* a traffic violation), punishable by a small fine and/or short jail term; see *felony*. 598

Mixed economy Economic system in which both private enterprise and government regulation play important roles. 18

Monopoly The control of an industry by one or a few companies, effectively strangling competition. 693

Multiparty system Political system in which three or more major parties compete for public offices; see *one-party, two-party system*. 185

Municipal corporation The status of a city as a legal (artificial) person, as set forth in the charter; this status gives the city the right to sue and be sued in court, to have a corporate seal, to make contracts, and to acquire, own, manage, and dispose of property. 631

Nationalize To transfer to the national government the management and ownership of private companies. 20

Naturalization Legal process by which a person born a citizen of one country becomes a citizen of another. 167

Nomination Process of selecting (naming) candidates for office. 197

Nonpartisan election Election held to fill nonpartisan offices (most often judicial, city, and school district offices), in which candidates do not represent or run as the nominees of political parties. 237

Off-year election Congressional or other general election held in the years between presidential elections; mid-term election. 303

One-party system Political system in which only one party exists, or in which only one party has a reasonable chance of winning elections. 185

Open primary Form of the direct primary in which any qualified voter may participate, without regard to his/her party allegiance. 236

Oversight function Review by legislative committees of the policies and programs of the executive branch. 322

Pardon Grant of a release from the punishment or legal consequences of a crime, by the President (in a federal case) or a governor (in a State case). 425, 589

Parishes The Louisiana term for counties; see *counties*. 615

Parliamentary government Form of government in which the executive leadership (usually, a prime minister and cabinet) is chosen by and responsible to the legislature (parliament), as in Great Britain. 8

Parole Release of a prisoner short of the completion of the term of a sentence. 589

Partnership Ownership of a business by two or more individuals. 695

Party caucus A meeting of party leaders to select candidates to run for political office; see *caucus*. 232

Party identification Person's sense of attachment, loyalty to a political party. 226

Passport A certificate issued by a government to its citizens who travel or live abroad; they entitle their holders to the privileges accorded to them by international custom and treaties. 478

Patent A license issued to an inventor granting the exclusive right to manufacture and sell his or her invention for a limited period of time. 351

Petit jury Body of (usually) 12 persons who hear the evidence and decide questions of fact in a court case; see *trial jury, grand jury*. 607

Picketing An activity involving patrolling of a business site by workers who are on strike; an attempt by the workers to inform the public of the controversy and to persuade customers and others not to deal with the employer involved. 117

Plaintiff In civil law, the party who brings a suit or some other legal action against another (the defendant) in court. 516

Platform Written declaration of the principles and policy positions of a political party (and its candidates for office), usually drafted at that party's convention. 387

Plurality In an election, at least one more vote than that received by any other candidate; a plurality may or may not be a majority of the total vote; see *majority*. 183

Pocket veto Type of veto a chief executive may use after a legislature has adjourned; it is applied when the President (or the governor in 15 States) does not formally sign or reject a bill within the time period allowed to do so; see *veto*. 337, 587

Police power Power of a State (and its local governments) to act to protect and promote the public health, safety, morals, and welfare. 131

Policy committee Committees in the Senate that formulate party goals and strategy. 317

Politburo The highest policy-making committee of the Communist Party in the Soviet Union. 684

Political Action Committee (PAC) Political arm of a special interest group that seeks to influence elections and public policy decisions. 285, 249

Political efficacy Belief a person has that his/her participation in politics *(e.g.,* voting) can affect the workings of government. 218

Political party Organized group that seeks to control government through the winning of elections and the holding of public office. 179

Political socialization Complex process by which individuals acquire their political attitudes and opinions. 220, 261

Polling place Particular location where those voters who live in a particular area vote in an election. 242

Poll tax Tax (now unconstitutional) that had to be paid in some States before a person was allowed to vote. 211

Popular sovereignty Basic principle of the American system of government; that the people are the only source of any and all governmental power, that government must be conducted with the consent of the governed; see *constitutionalism, limited government.* 37, 55, 541

Precedent Previous court decisions which influence (usually are the basis for) the deciding of later and similar cases; see *stare decisis.* 610

Precinct A local voting district. 208, 242

Presentment Formal accusation of crime brought by a grand jury of its own motion (not, as in an indictment, on the motion of the prosecutor). 145

Presidential electors The persons elected by the voters to represent them in making a formal selection of the President and Vice President; see *electoral college.* 378

Presidential government Form of government characterized by a separation of powers between independent and coequal executive and legislative branches, as in the United States. 8

Presidential primary Election at which a party's voters (1) choose some or all of a State party organization's delegates to that party's National Convention, and/or (2) express a preference among various contenders for the party's Presidential nomination. 382

President of the Senate The Vice President of the United States. 316

President *pro tempore* The temporary presiding official of the Senate in the absence of the Vice President. 316

Pressure group Private organization which tries to persuade government to respond to the shared attitudes (public policy positions) of its members. 267

Private bill Legislative measure that applies only to certain persons or places, rather than to the country (or the State) as a whole; see *public bill.* 325

Private enterprise An economic system based on private ownership, individual initiative, profit, and competition; see *capitalism, free enterprise.* 17

Private sector The portion of a country's economy that is comprised of companies that are privately owned. 699

Probable cause A 4th Amendment guarantee that people, their houses, papers, and personal possessions are protected from search and seizure unless the court is shown valid reasons for issuing a warrant for such a search and seizure. 137

Progressive tax Any tax in which the rate at which it is levied increases as the tax base (the amount subject to the tax) increases; a tax levied at varying (progressively higher) rates, with each step in the rate schedule geared to the taxpayer's ability (resources with which) to pay *(e.g.,* the federal income tax); see *regressive tax.* 650

Propaganda A technique of persuasion, aimed at influencing public opinion to create a particular popular belief. 283

Property tax A tax levied on (1) real property (land and buildings), or (2) personal property (tangible and intangible personal wealth); property taxes provide 85 percent of revenues for local government units; see *assessment.* 651

Public bill Legislative measure which applies to the nation (or the State) as a whole; see *private bill.* 325

Public-interest group An organization which seeks actively to influence public officials to implement certain public policies of benefit to all, regardless of membership in or support for the group. 282

Public opinion Those attitudes held (shared) by a significant number of persons on matters of government and politics; expressed group attitudes. 260

Public opinion poll A formal survey of public attitudes. 268

Public policies Course(s) of action taken by government in response to the problem(s) it faces; the end product of governmental decision-making. 5

Public sector The portion of a country's economy that is comprised of companies that are privately owned. 699

Quasi-legislative, quasi-judicial Ability of government bodies with certain executive (administrative) functions to exercise certain legislative-like (rule-making) and judicial-like (decision-making) powers *(e.g.,* the several federal independent regulatory commissions). 454

Quorum Least number of members who must be present for a legislative body to conduct business. 331

Quota sample In scientific polling, a group chosen to be interviewed in which the members of each of several groups *(e.g.,* blacks, women) are included in proportion to their percentage in the total population; see *random sample, sample.* 271

Random sample In scientific polling, a sample to be interviewed drawn such that each member of the population has an equal chance to be included in it; see *quota sample, sample.* 271

Ratification Formal approval, final consent to the effectiveness of a constitution, constitutional amendment, or treaty. 38

Reapportionment Redistribution of political representation on the basis of population shift following the 10-year census. 296, 560

Recall Petition process by which voters can remove an elected State or local official from office in mid-term. 581

Recognition The exclusive power of a President to establish formal diplomatic relations with foreign states. 420

Referendum Process in which a measure passed by a legislature is submitted (referred) to the voters for final approval or rejection; may be mandatory, optional, or popular in form. 575

Regional security alliances Defensive alliances formed by negotiating mutual defense treaties with countries which agree to take collective action to meet aggression in various parts of the world. 500

Registers Lists of viable job candidates maintained by the Office of Personnel Management in the federal recruiting, examining, and hiring process. 463

Registration Process by which voters establish their eligibility to vote in elections; also known as enrollment. 210

Regressive tax Any tax levied at a flat rate—*i.e.,* falls most heavily on those least able to pay it *(e.g.,* a sales tax), see *progressive tax.* 650

Representative democracy A system of government in which the people elect officials to represent them indirectly in making laws and running the government; see *representative government.* 11

Representative government System of government in which public policies are made by officials who are selected by the voters and held accountable to them in periodic elections; see *democracy, representative democracy.* 28

Reprieve An official postponement of execution of a sentence, either for humanitarian purposes, or to await evidence; see *pardon.* 425, 589

Republic See *representative government.* 11

Reserved powers Those powers held by the States in the American federal system. 74

Resolution Measure relating to the internal business of one house in a legislature, or expressing that chamber's opinion on some matter, without the force of law; see *concurrent resolution, joint resolution.* 326

Reverse discrimination A description of affirmative action by critics of that policy, that giving preference to females and/or non-whites is unfair to (discriminates against) members of the majority group; see *affirmative action.* 164

Rider Provision, unlikely to pass on its own merit, added to an important bill certain to pass so that it will "ride" through the legislative process. 326

Right of legation The right of a nation to send and receive diplomatic representatives. 476

Rule of law See *constitutionalism.* 56

Runoff primary An election in which the two candidates (in the same party) with the most votes run against each other to determine who will be on the ballot for the general election. 237

Sabotage Destructive act intended to hinder a nation's defense effort. 120

Sales tax A tax paid by the purchaser on the sale of commodities; the single most important source of income among the States. 650

Sample In scientific polling, a small number of people chosen as a representative cross-section of the total population (universe) to be measured (surveyed); see *quota sample, random sample.* 271

Secretariat Executive arm of the Central Committee of the Soviet government; headed by the General Secretary. 684

Sedition Spoken, written, or other action promoting resistance to lawful authority; especially advocating the violent overthrow of a government. 120

Segregation Separation or isolation of a racial or other group from the rest of the population in education, housing, or other areas of public or private activity; see *de jure segregation, de facto segregation.* 158

Select committee Legislative committee created for a limited time and for some specific purpose; also known as special committee; see *standing committee.* 321

Senatorial courtesy Unwritten rule that the Senate will not approve the appointment of an officer to serve within a State *(e.g.,* a federal district judge) if a Senator of the President's party from that State objects to the appointment. 416

Seniority rule Unwritten rule in both houses of Congress, that the top posts in the formal and the party organization in each chamber will (with rare exception) be held by "ranking members"—*i.e.,* those with the longest records of service; applied most strictly to committee chairmanships. 319

Separate-but-equal doctrine Racial segregation laws (aimed at blacks and minorities) which argued a constitutional basis for offering separate facilities to blacks and minorities on the basis that they were equal to white facilities (as the Constitution required); in practice they were often inferior. 157

Separation of powers Basic principle of the American system of government, that the executive, legislative, and judicial powers are (must be) divided among three independent and coequal branches of government; see *checks and balances.* 56, 541

Session The regular period of time during which a legislative body assembles and conducts business. 294

Shadow cabinet Potential cabinet members who shadow (watch) elected cabinet members in preparation for taking over the positions should their party win a majority in an election. 669

Shield laws State laws designed to protect reporters against being forced to disclose confidential news sources. 116

Single-issue parties Political parties that concentrate on a single public policy issue. 193

Single-member district Electoral district from which a single officeholder is chosen by the voters (rather than several, as in a multi-member district); see *at-large.* 183, 298

Slander Speech that wrongfully damages a person's reputation; see *libel.* 113

Socialism Economic and political system based on the public (collective, social) ownership of the means by which goods and services are produced, distributed, and exchanged. 19

Sole proprietorship Ownership of a business by one individual. 695

Sovereignty Supreme, absolute power of a state within its own territory. 4

Speaker of the House The presiding officer of the House of Representatives, usually chosen from the majority party. 315

Special district Local unit of government, created to perform (usually) a single public function in a locale *(e.g.,* a school or library district). 625

Special-interest group An organization of individuals who share a common objective or viewpoint and seek actively to influence public officials; see *interest group, pressure group, political action committee.* 275

Special session An extraordinary session of a legislative body called by the president of the country or the governor of a State for legislative action in times of crisis. 294, 587

Split-ticket voting Voting for candidates of more than one party in the same election; see *straight-ticket voting.* 201, 226

Spoils system Practice of awarding government jobs, contracts, and other favors on the basis of party loyalty, political support, rather than on the basis of merit. 460

Standing committee Regular (permanent) committee in a legislative body to which bills in a specified subject-matter area are referred; see *select committee.* 320, 568

Stare decisis Rule of precedent; a policy generally followed by courts, that the precedents set by earlier decisions should be followed in deciding later and similar cases, literally (Latin) "let the decision stand"; see *precedent.* 610

State In international affairs, a sovereign member of the world community (often called a country or nation); in the United States, one of the 50 members (States) in the Union. 4

Statutory law Law (statutes) enacted by a legislative body. 553, 609

Straight-ticket voting Voting for the candidates of but one party in an election; see *split-ticket voting.* 226

Straw vote Unscientific measurement of public opinion; usually, asking the same question of a large number of people (who may, but probably do not, represent an accurate cross-section of the population). 268

Strict constructionist One who advocates a narrow interpretation of the Constitution's provisions, in particular those granting power to government. 342

Strong Mayor System in which mayor has power to hire and fire employees and prepare the budget. 634

Subcommittees Divisions of existing committees which are formed to address specific issues. 328

Suffrage Right to vote. 204

Supply and demand, laws of The belief that prices depend upon the demand for goods (the greater the supply, the lower the price will be; the greater the demand, the higher the price will be). 693

Supreme Soviet National legislature of the Soviet Union; composed of two houses of equal rank—The Soviet of the Union, and The Soviet of Nationalities. 684

Symbolic speech Expression of beliefs, ideas by conduct rather than in speech or print *(e.g.,* by wearing an armband or flying a flag). 117

Tariff Tax (customs duty) levied on imports, to raise revenue and/or protect the domestic economy. 469

Taxes Charges (money demands) made by government on persons or property to raise funds for public purposes and/or to regulate conduct; see specific category. 647

Term The specified length of time served by elected officials in their elected offices. 294

Totalitarian Form of government in which the power to rule embraces all (the totality of) matters of human concern; see *authoritarian, dictatorship.* 9

Township A term used for a subdivision of a county in States in the Midwest and the Northeast; see *county.* 615, 623

Trial jury See *petit jury.* 607

Treason Crime of disloyalty which, says the Constitution (Article III, Section 3), "shall consist only in levying war against (the United States), or in adhering to their enemies, giving them aid and comfort"; can be committed only by a citizen and only in wartime. 120

Treaty Formal agreement made between or among sovereign states. 418

Two-party system Political system in which the candidates of only two (major) parties have a reasonable chance of winning elections; see *multiparty, one-party system.* 182

Unconstitutional Contrary to constitutional principles. 58

Underground economy Individuals' unofficial businesses which supplement government-regulated incomes. 707

Unicameral Having one house in the legislative body. 31, 557

Unitary government Form of government in which all of the powers of the government are held by (centralized in) a single agency, as in Great Britain; local governments are completely subordinate to and have only those powers given to them by the central government; see *federalism.* 7

Veto Chief executive's power to reject a bill passed by a legislature; literally (Latin) "I forbid"; see *item veto, pocket veto.* 337

Veto power A Constitutional power that enables the President to return legislation to the Congress unsigned with reasons for his objection; see *pocket veto.* 424, 505, 587

Visa A permit to enter another state, obtained from the country one wishes to enter. 478

Ward Local unit of party organization; also, a district within a city for city council elections. 208

Warrant Court order authorizing a public official to proceed in a manner specified by that order *(e.g.,* a search warrant); also, an order to pay out public funds (as in a check) issued by an officer with the legal authority to do so. 137, 598

Weak Mayor System in which mayor shares power with other elected officials. 634

Welfare states Governments that assume the role of promoter of citizen welfare through programs sponsored by the government; opponents charge that such a system destroys individual initiative. 700

Winner-take-all system An almost obsolete system whereby the presidential aspirant who won the preference vote in a primary automatically won the support of all the delegates chosen in the primary. 383

Writ of certoriari See *certoriari, writ of.* 523

Writ of habeas corpus See *habeas corpus, writ of.* 142

Zoning Practice of dividing a city or other unit of government into districts (zones) and regulating by law (a zoning ordinance) the uses of land in each of them. 638

Index

Note: Entries with a page number followed by an (*n*) denote reference to a footnote on that page; those followed by a (*p*) denote a photo.

Acknowledgments

Unit One
0–1-Library of Congress. **2**-Harper's Weekly, July 22, 1876. **3**-Sal DiMarco, Jr. **4**-Scala/Art Resource. **7**-Cynthia Johnson/Gamma Liaison. **9**-UPI/Bettmann Newsphotos. **11**-Library of Congress. **13**-Talbot Lovering/ Allyn and Bacon. **14**-Kerr/Uniphoto. **17**-Craig Aurness/ Woodfin Camp and Associates. **19**-(left) Pozarik/Gamma Liaison; (right) Breton Littlehales/Folio, Inc. **20**-Doherty/Gamma Liaison. **23**-Sovfoto. **26**-Library of Congress. **27**-The New York Public Library. **30**-The Granger Collection, New York. **34**-Library of Congress. **36**-Courtesy, The Henry Francis du Pont Winterthur Museum. **37**-Library of Congress. **41**-The Granger Collection, New York. **43**-Library of Congress. **49**-Independence National Historical Park Collection. **50**-(left) Bowdoin College Museum of Art; (center) Library Company of Philadelphia; (right) National Portrait Gallery/Smithsonian Institution, Washington, D.C. **54**-National Park Service. **55**-Jim Pickerell/Black Star. **63**-Library of Congress. **70**-Farrell Grehan/Photo Researchers. **71**-Bill Fitz-Patrick/The White House **75**-Murray Greenberg/Monkmeyer Press. **76**-Baron Wolman/Woodfin Camp and Associates. **78**-Supreme Court Historical Society. **81**-Leif Skoogfors/Woodfin Camp and Associates. **83**-Drew Harmon/Folio, Inc. **85**-Billy E. Barnes/Uniphoto. **86**-Michael Petty pool/Uniphoto. **91**-Camera Hawaii.

Unit Two
94–95-Robert Llewellyn. **96**-William B. Folsom/Uniphoto. **97**-Paul Conklin. **98**-Bettmann Archive. **100**-Russell Lee/Library of Congress. **103**-D. Doopy/Uniphoto. **107**-Mimi Forsyth/Monkmeyer Press. **109**-John Riley/Folio, Inc. **110**-Maxim Engel/Woodfin Camp and Associates. **112**-(top) Ethan Hoffman/Archive Pictures, Inc.; (bottom) Owen Franken/Sygma. **116**-Ira Wexler/ Folio, Inc. **118**-Herman Kokojan/Black Star. **119**-Chris Cross/Uniphoto. **121**-UPI/Bettmann Newsphotos. **123**-LePelley in the Christian Science Monitor 1984. **125**-© Taylor/TexaStock. **128**-Library of Congress. **129**-Bruce Davidson/Magnum Photos. **133**-(left) William B. Folsom/Uniphoto; (right) Boston Globe Photo. **135**-Courtesy; The Washington Post. **136**-Gerald Davis/Woodfin Camp and Associates. **139**-Paul Conklin. **144**-Michal Heron/Woodfin Camp and Associates. **147**-Paul Conklin. **148**-Montgomery County Court, Maryland. **150**-(left) Jeff Dunn; (right) Paul Conklin. **154**-Paul Conklin. **157**-Library of Congress. **161**-Robert Kelley/Life Magazine; (inset) Gordon Parks/Life Magazine. **162**-Freda Leinwand/Monkmeyer Press. **165**-NASA. **166**-Chip Henderson/Woodfin Camp and Associates. **172**-Greenwood/ Gamma Liaison.

Unit Three
176–177-John Martucci, Talbot Lovering/McClenaghan Collection/and the Dewitt Collection; University of Hartford. **178**-NBC Photo by Alan Singer. **179**-The Boatmen's National Bank of St. Louis. **180**-Talbot Lovering/Dewitt Collection/University of Hartford, and the McClenaghan Collection. **183**-The Granger Collection, New York. **184**-Talbot Lovering/McClenaghan Collection. **186**-(left) Michael J. Pettypool/Uniphoto; (right) Les Moore/Uniphoto. **189**-Edmund Sullivan/ Dewitt Collection/University of Hartford. **191**-Dewitt Collection/University of Hartford/Edmund Sullivan. **193**-Edmund Sullivan/Dewitt Collection/University of Hartford. **194**-Talbot Lovering/McClenaghan Collection. **198**-(left) Paul Conklin; (right) Sloan/Gamma/Liaison. **199**-National Republican Congressional Committee. **204**-Daniel Brody/Stock Boston. **205**-Max Winter/Picture Group, Inc. **207**-Library of Congress. **211**-Ed Kashi/Gamma Liaison. **212**-UPI/Bettmann Newsphotos. **214**-Tim Ribar/Uniphoto. **220**-Brad Bower/Picture Group, Inc. **225**-New York Historical Society. **227**-Larry Downing/Woodfin Camp and Associates. **230**-Library of Congress. **231**-Gamma Liaison. **233**-Library of Congress. **234**-Edmund Sullivan/Dewitt Collection. **235**-Edmund Sullivan Collection. **236**-Paul Conklin/Monkmeyer Press. **238**-William J. Ranney. **241**-Mark Pokempner/Click Chicago. **243**-Daemmrich/ TexaStock. **244**-Indiana State Election Board. **245**-Massachusetts Election Commission. **246**-© Sullivan/ TexaStock. **247**-Les Moore/Uniphoto. **249**-© Sullivan/ TexaStock. **252**-Chick Harrity/U.S. News and World Report. **253**-Roddey Mims/Uniphoto. **254**-Wide World Photos. **255**-Paul Conklin. **258**-Owen Franken/Stock Boston. **259**-John Ficara/Woodfin Camp and Associates. **260**-(left) Ken Heinen; (right) Ray Fairall/Photoreporters. **264**-Wally McNamee/Woodfin Camp and Associates. **267**-© Sullivan/TexaStock. **270**-Literary Digest. **271**-Marc Pokempner, Click/Chicago. **273**-UPI Bettmann Newsphotos. **276**-Doug Menuez/Picture Group, Inc. **277**-Wally McNamee/Woodfin Camp and Associates. **279**-Al Stephenson/Picture Group, Inc. **281**-Drew Harmon/Folio, Inc. **282**-(left) Courtesy, League of Women Voters; (right) Paul Conklin. **286**-Ken Heinen.

Unit Four
290–291-Robert Llewellyn. **292**-Terry Ashe/Uniphoto. **293**-Corcoran Gallery of Art. **302**-Paul Conklin. **307, 308**-Library of Congress. **312**-The Granger Collection, New York **313**-Mark S. Reinstein/Uniphoto. **314**-Terry Ashe. **316**-Wide World Photos. **317**-Wally McNamee/ Woodfin Camp and Associates. **321**-Paul Conklin. **323**-Jim Pickerell. **325**-United States House of Representatives. **329**-Shepard Sherbell/Picture Group, Inc. **330**-Terry Ashe. **333**-(top) Talbot Lovering, Allyn & Bacon; (bottom left) United States House of Representatives; (bottom center) Paul Conklin; (bottom right) Library of Congress. **335**-Wide World Photos. **337**-Okamoto/ National Archives, LBJ Library. **340**-John Bowden/Folio, Inc. **341**-UPI/Bettman Archives. **348**-Ray F. Hillstrom/ Gartman Agency. **351**-U.S. Patent Office. **352**-Kenneth Garrett/Woodfin Camp, Inc. **354**-Roger Tully/Black Star. **357**-U.S. Coast Guard. **359**-J.P. Laffont/Sygma. **360**-Dennis Brack/Black Star. **361**-Claude Urraca/ Sygma.

Unit Five

364–365-Ken Heinen. **366**-Roloc Color Slides. **367**-John Ficara/Woodfin Camp and Associates. **368**-J.L. Atlan/Sygma. **373**-Library of Congress. **374**-Régis Bossu/Sygma. **377**-Edmund Sullivan/Dewitt Collection. **380**-Paul Meredith, Click/Chicago. **382**-David Marie/Folio, Inc. **384**-Paul Conklin. **386**-(left) Linda Palmer for the Representatives; (right) Paul Conklin. **387**-Dennis Brack/Black Star. **388**-Terry Ashe. **389**-Paul Conklin. **392**-UPI Bettmann Newsphotos. **402**-Library of Congress. **403**-Fred Ward/Black Star. **405**-Ken Heinen. **407**-Library of Congress. **409**-Paul Conklin. **410**-Edmund Sullivan/Dewitt Collection, University of Hartford. **415**-Ken Heinen. **416**-Dennis Brack/Black Star. **421**-James Natchwey/Black Star. **423**-Bill Fitzpatrick/The White House. **428**-Ellis Herwig/Stock Boston. **429**-Library of Congress. **435**-Tim Murphy/U.S. News and World Report. **436**-(left) Drew Harmon/Folio, Inc., (right) Tannenbaum/Sygma. **438**-(top) Ted Charles/Uniphoto; (bottom) Dan McCoy/Rainbow; (right) Paul Conklin. **439**-U.S. Department of Agriculture. **440**-© Sullivan/TexaStock. **441**-(bottom left) USDA Soil Conservation Service; (top) Paul Conklin; (bottom right) Dan McCoy/Rainbow. **442**-Dan McCoy/Black Star. **443**-Ira Wexler/Folio Inc. **444**-Paul Conklin. **445**-J. Bernot/Stock Boston. **446**-Jim Pickerell/Click Chicago. **447**-(top) Hank Morgan/Rainbow; (bottom) U.S. Coast Guard. **449**-(left) Dan McCoy/Rainbow; (right) John Ficara/Woodfin Camp, Inc. **453**-Dan McCoy/Rainbow. **455**-Peter Frank/Click Chicago. **456**-U.S. Postal Service. **459, 460, 461**-Library of Congress. **463**-Paul Conklin. **467**-Dewitt Collection, University of Hartford. **472**-ACME. **473**-Owen Franken/Sygma. **474**-George C. Marshall Research Library. **476**-UPI Bettmann Newsphotos. **477**-Jim Pozarik/Gamma Liaison. **481**-(left) Korith/Gamma Liaison; (right) David Hume Kennerly/Liaison. **482**-U.S. Navy. **485**-NASA. **487**-M. Philippot/Sygma. **489**-Library of Congress. **491**-Panama Canal Official Photo. **492**-Life Collection of Art from W.W.II/U.S. Army photograph. **494**-Stern/Black Star. **496**-U.S. Army Photograph. **497**-(left) UPI/Bettman Newsphotos; (right) Vernon Merritt/Black Star. **499**-Cynthia Johnson/Gamma Liaison. **502**-National Archives. **504**-George Holton/Photo Researchers.

Unit Six

510–511-Robert Lleywellyn. **512**-Paul Conklin. **513**-Wesley Bocxe/Photo Researchers. **517**-Mimi Forsyth/Monkmeyer Press. **522**-Wide World Photos. **525**-Yoichi R. Okamoto/Photo Researchers. **528**-B. Seitz/ Photo Researchers. **530**-Paul Conklin. **533**-(top) Alan Reininger/Woodfin Camp and Associates; (center) T. Moore/Woodfin Camp and Associates; (bottom) Frankmuller May/Woodfin Camp and Associates.

Unit Seven

536–537-© Berrera/TexaStock. **538**-Talbot Lovering/Allyn and Bacon. **539**-George Catlin/Virginia Historical Society. **544**-Gene Stevens. **546**-Courtesy; New Hampshire Election Committee. **552**-(left) Jeff Lowenthal/Woodfin Camp and Associates; (right) Billy E. Barnes/Uniphoto. **556**-Al Cook/Uniphoto. **557**-© Folda/TexaStock. **561**-© Sullivan/TexaStock. **565**-William Hubbell/ Woodfin Camp and Associates. **568**-State of Minnesota House of Representatives. **569**-© Daemmrich/TexaStock. **578**-Cooper & Coughlin. **579**-F.D.R. Library. **580**-Stacy Pick/Uniphoto. **583**-Wide World Photos. **587**-© Michael Sullivan/TexaStock. **591**-MD State Comptroller's Office. **593**-Bruce Clark, N.C. Department of Public Instruction. **596**-© Daemmrich/TexaStock. **597**-National Archives. **599**-Sidney/Monkmeyer Press. **600**-Roger Clark/Photo Researchers. **602**-Sam Pierson, Jr./Photo Researchers. **609**-(center) Les Moore/Uniphoto; (right) Ann McQueen/Stock Boston. **614**-Robert Frerck/Click Chicago. **615**-Chuck O'Rear/Woodfin Camp and Associates. **617**-© Daemmrich/TexaStock. **620**-Kennith Garrett/Woodfin Camp and Associates. **625**-© Sullivan/TexaStock. **626**-(left) Michael Heron/Woodfin Camp and Associates; (right) © Sullivan/TexaStock. **629**-Chuck O'Rear/Woodfin Camp and Associates. **630**-(left) Library of Congress; (right) Christopher Springmann. **632**-Greg Pease/Folio Inc. **634**-© Daemmrich/Texa Stock. **636**-Steve Leonard/Click Chicago. **637, 638**-© Daemmrich/TexaStock. **639**-(left) Mike Yamashita/Woodfin Camp and Associates; (right) John V.A.F. Neal/Photo Researchers. **642**-Ric Ferro/Florida Fotobanc. **643**-Ric Ferro/Florida Fotobanc. **646**-Bill Gallery/Stock Boston. **647**-Jim Pickerell. **652**-Daniel Brody/Stock Boston. **654**-Allyn and Bacon. **655**-Jim Pickerell. **656**-(left) American Antiquarian Society, Worchester; (right) Dan Miller/Woodfin Camp and Associates. **659**-(left) R. Johnson/Pedier; (right) John Carroll, Metro/Five Rescue.

Unit Eight

662–663-Sovfoto. **664**-Anthony Howarth/International Stock Photo. **665**-Peter Abbey/Camera Press. **667**-Stuart Franklin/Sygma. **669**-Frank Spooner/Gamma Liaison. **669**-Stuart Franklin/Sygma. **671**-Shostal. **674**-William Karel/Sygma. **677**-Paolo Koch/Photo Researchers. **679**-Matsumoto/Sygma. **681**-G. Henoch/Gamma Liaison. **686**-Sovfoto. **690**-Sygma. **691**-Randy G. Taylor/Sygma. **693**-M. Parv./Archive Pictures Inc. **696**-Talbot Lovering/Allyn and Bacon. **699**-Audrey Stirling/International Stock Photo. **700**-S. Doherty/Gamma Liaison. **702**-Mimi Cotter/International Stock Photo. **703**-Sygma. **705**-Apesteguy/Gamma Liaison. **708**-All, Burton C. Rush/Briarcliff Manor.